A HANDBOOK
on
PSALMS

The Handbooks in the **UBS Handbook Series** are detailed commentaries providing valuable exegetical, historical, cultural, and linguistic information on the books of the Bible. They are prepared primarily to assist practicing Bible translators as they carry out the important task of putting God's Word into the many languages spoken in the world today. The text is discussed verse by verse and is accompanied by running text in at least one modern English translation.

Over the years church leaders and Bible readers have found the UBS Handbooks to be useful for their own study of the Scriptures. Many of the issues Bible translators must address when trying to communicate the Bible's message to modern readers are the ones Bible students must address when approaching the Bible text as part of their own private study and devotions.

The Handbooks will continue to be prepared primarily for translators, but we are confident that they will be useful to a wider audience, helping all who use them to gain a better understanding of the Bible message.

Helps for Translators

UBS Handbook Series:

A Handbook on . . .

Leviticus

The Book of Joshua

The Book of Ruth

The Book of Job

The Book of Psalms

Lamentations

The Book of Amos

The Books of Obadiah, Jonah, and Micah

The Books of Nahum, Habakkuk, and Zephaniah

The Gospel of Matthew

The Gospel of Mark

The Gospel of Luke

The Gospel of John

The Acts of the Apostles

Paul's Letter to the Romans

Paul's First Letter to the Corinthians

Paul's Second Letter to the Corinthians

Paul's Letter to the Galatians

Paul's Letter to the Ephesians

Paul's Letter to the Philippians

Paul's Letters to the Colossians and to Philemon

Paul's Letters to the Thessalonians

The Letter to the Hebrews

The First Letter from Peter

The Letter from Jude and the Second Letter from Peter

The Letters of John

The Revelation to John

Guides:

A Translator's Guide to . . .

Selections from the First Five Books of the Old Testament

Selected Psalms

the Gospel of Mark

the Gospel of Luke

Paul's Second Letter to the Corinthians

the Letters from James, Peter, and Jude

Technical Helps:

Old Testament Quotations in the New Testament

Short Bible Reference System

New Testament Index

The Theory and Practice of Translation

Bible Index

Fauna and Flora of the Bible

Marginal Notes for the Old Testament

Marginal Notes for the New Testament

The Practice of Translating

A HANDBOOK ON

Psalms

by Robert G. Bratcher
and William D. Reyburn

UBS Handbook Series

United Bible Societies
New York

Books in the series of Helps for Translators may be ordered from a national Bible Society or from either of the following centers:

United Bible Societies
European Production Fund
D-70520 Stuttgart 80
Postfach 81 03 40
Germany

United Bible Societies
1865 Broadway
New York, New York 10023
U.S.A.

L.C. Cataloging-in-Publication Data:

Bratcher, Robert G.
    [Translator's handbook on the book of Psalms]
    A handbook on Psalms / by Robert G. Bratcher and William D. Reyburn.
        p. cm. — (UBS handbook series) (Helps for translators)
    Originally published under title: A translator's handbook on the book of Psalms.
    Includes bibliographical references and index.
    ISBN 0-8267-0119-1
    1. Bible. O.T. Psalms—Translating. 2. Bible. O.T. Psalms—Criticism, interpretation, etc. I. Reyburn, William David. II. Title. III. Series. IV. Series: Helps for translators.
BS1430.2.B74 1993
223'.2077—dc20
92-40983
CIP

ABS-2/94-200-1,650-CM-3-104640

iv

Contents

CONTENTS

Preface

Translators frequently find that the churches waiting for their new Bibles are eager to have the Book of Psalms available. In many cases this is because psalms play an important role in the worship life of the Christian community. However, the Book of Psalms is one of the most difficult to translate because of the poetic form of the original. Of equal difficulty is the problem of rendering the psalms as either prose or poetry in the receptor language, and translators must first determine how good poetry is prepared in their language, and whether poetry is limited to certain subjects only, excluding or including the subjects covered in the Book of Psalms. It may therefore be wise for translators to gain experience in the Old Testament by working first with books that have less complex problems; this, however, is not always possible. Therefore many translators have indicated that there is a special need for a Handbook on this book of the Bible.

A Translator's Handbook on the Book of Psalms has been in preparation for more than ten years. During that time workers in the field discovered that the Revised Standard Version (RSV) makes a better base for discussion than does Today's English Version (TEV), especially for explaining the form and function of the ancient Hebrew text to translators who have not been taught Hebrew; the authors therefore had to revise their work, which had been based on TEV, and use RSV instead. TEV is now one of many models demonstrating problems in translation as well as possible ways to generate a good translation. Toward the end of the project the Revised English Bible and the New Revised Standard Version became available, but it is to be regretted that it was already too late to use them in any systematic fashion. Translators may wish to have these new versions available as they deal with the Book of Psalms.

The RSV and TEV texts are presented verse by verse in parallel columns. Quotations from RSV in the verse under discussion are printed in <u>**underlined boldface**</u>, while those from TEV are printed in "**boldface within quotation marks.**" Quotations from other portions of RSV or of TEV are displayed in the same way as quotations from other versions of the Scriptures, namely, in ordinary print and within quotation marks.

This Handbook, like others in the series, concentrates on exegetical information important for translators, and it attempts to indicate possible solutions for translational problems related to language or culture. The authors do not consciously attempt to provide help that other theologians and scholars may seek but which is not directly related to the translation task. Such information is normally sought elsewhere. One source of information that will prove useful to scholars and translators is *Theology of the Psalms,* by H.-J. Kraus. Many theological terms are discussed with a thoroughness not possible within the scope of this Handbook.

A limited Bibliography is included for the benefit of those interested in further study. The Glossary explains technical terms according to their usage in this volume. The translator may find it useful to read through the Glossary in order to become aware of the specialized way in which certain terms are used. An Index gives the location by page number of some of the important words and subjects discussed in the Handbook, especially where the Handbook provides the translator with help in rendering these concepts into the receptor language.

The editor of Helps for Translators continues to seek comments from translators and others who use these books, so that future volumes may benefit and may better serve the needs of the readers.

Abbreviations Used In This Handbook

General Abbreviations, Bible Texts, Versions, and Other Works Cited
(For details see Bibliography.)

A.D.	*Anno Domini* (in the year of our Lord)	KJV	King James Version
		Mft	Moffatt
ASV	American Standard Version	NAB	New American Bible
AT	American Translation	NEB	New English Bible
B.C.	Before Christ	NIV	New International Version
BDB	Brown-Driver-Briggs (lexicon)	NJB	New Jerusalem Bible
		NJV	New Jewish Version
BJ	*Bible de Jérusalem*	POCL	Portuguese common language version
FRCL	French common language version		
		RSV	Revised Standard Version
GECL	German common language version	RV	Revised Version
		SPCL	Spanish common language version
HOTTP	Hebrew Old Testament Text Project		
		TEV	Today's English Version
JB	Jerusalem Bible	TOB	*Traduction œcuménique de la Bible*
JPS	Jewish Publication Society		
K-B	Koehler-Baumgartner (lexicon)	ZÜR	Zürcher Bibel

Books of the Bible

Gen	Genesis	Jer	Jeremiah
Exo	Exodus	Lam	Lamentations
Lev	Leviticus	Ezek	Ezekiel
Num	Numbers	Dan	Daniel
Deut	Deuteronomy	Hos	Hosea
Josh	Joshua	Nah	Nahum
1,2 Sam	1,2 Samuel	Hab	Habakkuk
1,2 Kgs	1,2 Kings	Zech	Zecharaiah
1,2 Chr	1,2 Chronicles	Mal	Malachi
Neh	Nehemiah	Matt	Matthew
Psa	Psalms	Eph	Ephesians
Pro	Proverbs	Col	Colossians
Eccl	Ecclesiastes	Heb	Hebrews
Song	Song of Songs	Rev	Revelation
Isa	Isaiah		

Translating the Psalms

The English word "Psalms" is a transliteration of the Greek *psalmoi,* which is the title of the book in the Greek translation of the Old Testament, the Septuagint (see also Luke 20.42; Acts 1.20). "Psalter" is a collective term, meaning all 150 psalms. The Latin title *Psalmi* is found in some printed editions of the Hebrew text. The Hebrew name of the biblical book is *sefer tehillim* ("book of praises") or simply *tehillim.* By extension the Hebrew noun "praise" means also "song of praise," as in the Hebrew title of Psalm 145, "A Song of Praise by David" (see also its use in 22.25a, "my praise").

Most translators will have translated the word "psalms" in Luke and Acts. Now, however, the translator must think in terms of a meaningful title for the complete collection of the psalms, since these are bound to play an important role in the church, which until now may have known them, if at all, through a second language. In some languages "The Book of Psalms" is translated "Songs of worship," "Chanting for praising God," "Songs about God."

1. The Canonical Collection

The complete collection of 150 psalms is divided into five books, each one of which ends with an appropriate doxology: Psalms 1–41 (41.13); 42–72 (72.18-19); 73–89 (89.52); 90–106 (106.48); 107–150 (Psa 150 is the concluding doxology for the whole collection). It is quite clear that the final collection was reached only after a lengthy process in which several smaller collections were brought together (Toombs, "The compilation of the Psalter," detects six stages). Two early collections were the psalms of Asaph (Psalms 73–83) and the psalms of the group of Korah (Psalms 42; 44–49). Another group was the "Songs of Ascents" (Psalms 120–124). Additional evidence of the process of compilation is furnished by the psalm which appears in two editions: as Psalm 14 it uses the proper name Yahweh (the Yahwistic version); as Psalm 53 it uses the generic name *'elohim* "God" (the Elohistic version). Psalm 18 is to be found also in 2 Samuel 22.1-51; Psalm 70 is the same as Psalm 40.13-17; and Psalm 108 consists of Psalms 57.7-11 and 60.5-12.

Another example of editorial arrangement is to be found in the conclusion of Book Two, Psalm 72.20: "This is the end of the prayers of David, son of Jesse"; yet an additional 18 psalms are attributed to David.

Some manuscripts of the Septuagint and some ancient versions include Psalm 151, attributed to David, which narrates his fight with the giant Goliath.

Some translators may translate only selected psalms, while others will translate all 150. To assist the people and help them to become familiar with the traditional order of the entire Psalter, it is recommended that the translation keep the psalms in the order they occur in the Hebrew text and are presented in this Handbook.

1

Differences in the numbering of the psalms are explained in section 7, below, and in the Appendix.

2. The Psalms: Literary Types

To discover how best to restructure a particular psalm so as to evoke an attitude or emotion in today's readers equivalent to that experienced by the original readers, the translator must try to discover the psalmist's intention in writing the particular psalm being translated. On the one hand the translator must convey to the reader all the information contained in the text. On the other hand the translator must succeed, to some degree, in finding the appropriate forms in the receptor language which will create in the readers of the language the same response that was created in the original listeners and readers. An attempt to determine the psalmist's intent and how he designed his psalm to accomplish his goal makes it possible to assign most of the psalms to one or more literary types. Of course some psalms do not easily fit into any one classification, and some cannot be classified. Commentators do not always agree on the precise system of names to apply in classifying the psalms, but on the whole most of them would agree with the following classification (as set forth by Toombs):

a. **Laments**: in these psalms the individual or the community cries out to God, complaining about some painful situation, asking God to help, and promising to offer a sacrifice to God in thanksgiving for the help received. More psalms are classified as laments than as any other type. See Psalm 13 as an example of individual lament, and Psalm 44 as a community lament.

b. **Hymns**: these may also be called songs of praise. They generally contain three elements: (1) a call to praise God; (2) the reason why praise should be offered to God; (3) another call to praise God. Sometimes the praise is offered by an individual (Psalm 8), and at other times it is offered by the community (Psalm 115).

c. **Thanksgiving**: these psalms generally include praise to God for having saved the individual or the people, a statement of the situation from which God has saved them, a confession that it was God who saved, and a concluding expression of thanksgiving and praise. Psalm 34 is an example of individual thanksgiving, and Psalm 67 of community thanksgiving.

d. **Songs of Confidence**: these are expressions of assurance that God will save the psalmist; while total deliverance has not been experienced, still the psalmist knows that God will answer his prayer. In Psalm 11 we hear an individual; in Psalm 125 the whole community is at prayer.

e. **Hymns of Zion**: in these hymns Zion, that is, Jerusalem, is addressed as God's dwelling place, and is praised. Psalms 46, 48, 76, and 87 fall into this category.

f. **Enthronement Psalms**: these psalms are often associated with the New Year festival, in which, according to some scholars, a service acclaimed God's sovereignty over Israel and the world by means of a ritual in which God was once again installed as King. Psalms 29, 47, 93, and 95–99 are classified as enthronement psalms.

g. **Royal Psalms**: these psalms praise the king of Israel as God's representative ("son") on earth, the one through whom God brings victories to God's people and the defeat of their enemies. Psalms 2, 18, 20, 21, 45, 72, 89, 101, 110, 132, and 144 are listed as royal psalms.

h. **Pilgrim Psalms**: these were sung by pilgrims as they came to Jerusalem for one of the great annual festivals. Most of these hymns are included in psalms that fall under other categories, but Psalms 84 and 122 qualify as pure pilgrim songs.

i. **Wisdom Psalms**: these are psalms whose major purpose is to instruct the people about Torah, the Law of God. They consist mostly of praise of right conduct and condemnation of evil conduct, and assure the worshiper that obedience to God's Law will bring prosperity and well-being. Some of the Wisdom Psalms are Psalms 1, 37, 49, and 73; and great parts of Psalm 119 qualify as wisdom poems.

j. **Liturgies**: psalms such as 15, 24, 50, 75, and 85 are classified as liturgies, since they are so closely related to the Temple service. The specific setting of a given psalm may usually be determined by its content.

Some psalms cannot be definitely classified under any one heading. Toombs lists the following as psalms of mixed types: 9–10, 14, 27, 36, 40, 77, 94, and 107.

3. The Poetry of the Psalms

This Handbook is only the second in a series which will deal with books of the Bible written in poetic style. The first was *A Translator's Handbook on the Book of Amos*, and translators are advised to read its introduction, whether or not they have translated Amos. The present introduction represents a shift in focus and emphasis, mainly in the area of Hebrew parallelism. Since the publication of *A Translator's Handbook on the Book of Amos*, a number of studies have appeared which throw light on Hebrew poetics, and particularly on parallelism. (See the Bibliography, especially the books by Kugel, Alter, Watson, and Berlin.)

The line between prose and poetry is difficult to draw and, according to Kugel, represents a split view inherited from Greek writers and is inappropriate for the Hebrew Old Testament. He views what others have called verse or poetry in the Bible as heightened rhetorical style. It is Alter, however, who demonstrates the dynamics of parallelism and illustrates the poetic nature of parallel lines. In spite of Kugel's reluctance to accept the term poetry (outside of his title), throughout this Handbook the authors use the term without apology, since we believe it describes the kind of discourse in which the psalms are written.

Many of the difficulties that arise in understanding biblical poetry would be cleared up if we could turn to a native reader and have him read the psalm just as it was read when it was composed. This, unfortunately, is not possible for several reasons. The accent marks and vowels we have in our Hebrew editions of the Bible were fixed at least a thousand years after most of the poems were composed. In that long interval many sounds were changed, distinctions between consonants had shifted, accents, vowels, and syllables were modified. There is no record of how poetry sounded to the ear, and in some cases words have changed meanings. Because these ancient poems were not written down in poetic lines, it is not always possible to know where one line ends and the next begins. Furthermore, modern interpreters are often at a loss because they do not know the communicative situation—who wrote the psalm, for whom, under what circumstances.

Our ignorance should not lead us to despair. However, it is sometimes the case in this Handbook that clear solutions are not possible.

3

Before taking up the subject of Hebrew parallelism, it should be pointed out that the translator of the psalms, like any translator of poetry, is involved in a complex undertaking. On the one hand he must seek to translate what the psalm says, its informational content, but he must also take into consideration that the psalm is loaded with poetic devices which the original author built into his psalm for a purpose, or better, for many purposes. The writer selects one form rather than another in order to get our attention, to focus our attention, and to lead the reader to discover new perceptions of biblical truths. In so doing he is constantly calling upon the expressive function of his language, realized in the use of acrostics, chiasmus, metaphors, clusters of images, repetitions, alliterations, similes, ellipsis, wordplay, sound imitation, refrains, personification of abstracts, word pairs, gender matching, inversions, and particularly parallel lines. The first two of these devices may be described as follows:

Acrostic Psalms: there are eight of these, in which a successive letter of the Hebrew alphabet is used at the start of each verse, or line, or stanza (Psa 119), beginning with *alef,* the first letter, and ending with *taw,* the last letter. They are: 9–10, 25, 34, 37, 111, 112, 119, and 145. Only someone with the rare literary skills of a Monsignor Ronald Knox would dare attempt represent this feature in translation. (And see Psalm 25 in the *New Jerusalem Bible*.)

Chiasmus: this is a literary device in which the various semantic elements in line b appear in reverse order of that followed in line a.

> O LORD God of hosts, hear my prayer;
>   give ear, O God of Jacob!(Psa 84.8)

> Let my prayer come before thee,
>   incline thy ear to my cry!(Psa 88.2)

> With long life I will satisfy him,
>   and show him my salvation.(Psa 91.16)

In the following example (Psa 37.21-22) the two verses are chiastic: "the wicked . . . the righteous . . . those blessed by the LORD . . . those cursed by him"; and the second line contrasts in some way with the preceding one, traditionally called "antithetic":

> The wicked borrows, and cannot pay back,
>   but the righteous is generous and gives;
> for those blessed by the LORD shall possess the land,
>   but those cursed by him shall be cut off.

Parallelism

Many poetic devices such as word-play, sound imitation, or gender matching are seldom translatable, because they are closely tied to the structures of the source language. Parallel lines, on the other hand, are carriers of the informational content and are normally translatable into other languages. Parallel lines are the very ground upon which Hebrew poetic style is built. It is necessary, therefore, for the translator to have a clear picture of what parallelism is and how it functions.

4

Most translators will be familiar with the traditional classification of parallelism: synonymous, antithetical, and synthetic. In synonymous parallelism the second line was said to be a restatement of the first, and so the two lines were viewed as a way of saying the same thing twice:

> I will praise the LORD as long as I live;
> I will sing praises to my God while I have being. (Psa 146.2)

In antithetical parallelism the second line contrasts with something asserted in the first line.

> All the horns of the wicked he will cut off,
> but the horns of the righteous shall be exalted. (Psa 75.10)

Synthetic parallelism was the term reserved for everything that did not seem to fit the first two categories. However, a close look at Psalm 146.2 shows that the two lines do not say the same thing and so are not really synonymous. In the same way the second line of Psalm 75.10 is not really antithetical because it agrees with the first line. An objective look at parallel lines in Hebrew poetry leads one to the conclusion that the possible relations between parallel lines are nearly limitless.

There are two major linguistic features that characterize poetic discourse. The first is the way in which the poet says something in an unexpected way. He plays on the letters, sounds of words, grammar, and sentences so that these deviations are made to stand out. In doing this he has a purpose in mind. On the other hand he may focus on certain regularities in the language and cause these features to be prominent. Parallelism is the result of focusing on the regularity of repetition. However, it would be wrong to assume that, because repetition is made prominent, linguistic irregularities are lacking. Quite the opposite is the case. Even where lines are parallel and much is repeated, the poet usually builds into them a great deal of irregularity. He creates patterns of sound through acrostics and chiasmus or by carefully selecting words for their sounds rather than for their meanings, he may drop a word or add a phrase to obtain a balance of stresses, or invert the normal word order to call attention. Most of these deviations take place at the sound or grammatical level, and therefore it is difficult if not impossible, or even unwise, to try to imitate them in the receptor language. In contrast, however, parallel lines operate largely on the semantic level, and it is because of this that we find there the meaning content which we must translate.

While parallelism of meaning is the most obvious characteristic of parallelism, it is not the only one. Two lines may be parallel syntactically without having much parallelism of meaning. Or they may be parallel in alliteration of consonants or vowels, or of stresses. Here again, the fact that two lines are syntactically alike or different, that each word begins with the same consonant, or that the same number of stresses are found in each line, are functions of the Hebrew language and may or may not have any relevance for translation. What the translator needs to know is what poetic purpose was served by this or that poetic device and how that purpose is expressed in the receptor language.

When two or three lines are semantically parallel, they will either be dynamic or static, or at least partially dynamic or partially static. In dynamic semantic parallelism line b picks up the thought of line a and shifts it to a heightened level of intensification. The poetic device employed to accomplish this is the use in line b of a term or image that is more specific or concrete than its matching member in line a. Likewise line b may match some common term in line a by a figure of speech. Occasionally line a will have a standard term, and a literary term will be used in line b. The net effect is to produce a sharpening of the image as the reader moves from the term or image in line a to line b. Translators should be prepared to find exceptions to these rules. Before taking up static semantic parallelism, some examples and brief discussion will be given.

> Then he will speak to them in his wrath,
> and terrify them in his fury . . . (Psa 2.5)

The step-up of poetic feeling is not between "wrath" and "fury," but between "speak" and "terrify." In line b "terrify" does not merely illumine "speak to them," but rather shifts "speak to them" to a different kind of encounter in which the Lord deals with his enemies. The shift is to a more specific activity with a specific result implied. If line b heightens the intensity to a new level, then the meaning has been affected. The two parallel lines become an inseparable unit, and their translation is not accomplished in English by simply setting the two lines down side by side on the model "a is so and b is so." What is required in translation is quite a different model, one which says in English, for example, "not only a but also b," "a but more still b," "a and furthermore b," "a and in fact b," "a even b." The differentiation between the two semantically similar lines might be translated by saying, for example, "He not only warns them in anger, but even more he terrifies them with his fury." In some languages a translation model may be "He will be angry and speak to them; in fact, he will be so angry at them their strength will melt."

> . . . at thy rebuke, O LORD,
> at the blast of the breath of thy nostrils. (Psa 18.15b)

The semantically parallel elements are "rebuke" in line a and "blast of the breath of thy nostrils" in line b. Line b shifts to a forceful metaphor, suggesting perhaps the picture of the hot breath blown from the nostrils of an angry bull. The effect is that of stepping up the poetic intensity and bringing the reader's first impression of "rebuke" to a more intense level of perception and feeling. The first line looks ahead to the second and the second looks back to the first, and so the two are interlocked into a unit. To telescope, that is, to combine and shorten the two lines into one, would be to set aside the poetic intensification, the sharpening of the image which the psalmist uses to change our perception.

> The heavens are telling the glory of God;
> and the firmament proclaims his handiwork. (Psa 19.1)

In this verse the psalmist is again saying something similar in each line. Therefore the two lines are semantically parallel, but the writer has chosen to reverse the syntactic order in the second line so that the two lines read in Hebrew: subject, verb, object / object, verb, subject. In spite of the difference in word order, the dynamic of the two lines is that of shifting to a new height of intensity in line b. The step-up is from a common term in line a to a more specific one in line b. The translator may use the same term for heavens in both lines. However, to reflect the intensification of the image, it will be necessary to do more than simply set down the two lines as two separate statements. For example, "The sky shows us how wonderful God is; even more, it makes clear to us the great things he has made" or "The heavens not only show us how great God is, they go even further by making it clear what wonderful things he has made." These model translations make adjustments for the problem of inanimate objects performing human events, that is, "heavens tell" and "firmament proclaims."

> For my life is spent with sorrow,
>   and my years with sighing;
> my strength fails because of my misery,
>   and my bones waste away. (Psa 31.10)

In this verse there are two pairs of semantically parallel lines. In both pairs line b can be seen employing different devices to heighten the poetic intensification. In 10a it is the whole expanse of "my life" which is matched in b by the more specific "my years." The general term "sorrow" in line a is matched by the picturable and dramatic expression "sighing" in line b. In line c the straightforward "strength fails" is transformed in b by the dramatic use of a metaphor, "bones waste away." The repeated movement toward the specific and dramatic serves in both cases to sharpen the image. The differentiation in focus between the matching lines should find its expression in translation. For example, in English we might say "My life is not only exhausted by sorrow, I have even spent it all in tears; I am so run down from my troubles, that I am even worn to the bone."

> For you hate discipline,
>   and you cast my words behind you. (Psa 50.17)

In this verse line b uses a figure, "cast my words behind you," to match "hate discipline" in line a. The result is a step-up of intensity, or b going beyond a. TEV's rendering dismisses the figure in line b, as is frequently the case. Furthermore, it makes no attempt to reflect the "more than that" contained in line b. However, we can adapt it easily as one kind of model. For example, "You refuse to let me correct you, you even reject my commands" or "You refuse to let me teach you, you even go so far as to reject what I command you to do." Many languages will be able to keep a metaphor in line b; for example, ". . . you even wipe away my words."

> Behold, I was brought forth in iniquity,
>   and in sin did my mother conceive me. (Psa 51.5)

"I was brought forth" in line a is matched in line b by reaching back to the earlier act of conception. It is not a case of b being more concrete, dramatic, or figurative, but rather a further specification of time. The psalmist is saying "I have been sinful from the day I was born, in fact even since the day my mother became pregnant with me."

7

Static semantic parallelism, in contrast to dynamic semantic parallelism, brings together two lines in which <u>b</u> repeats essentially what <u>a</u> has said without intensification, sharpening of the image, or providing dramatic effect. Line <u>b</u> mirrors line <u>a</u>, or at least part of <u>a</u>, or <u>b</u> repeats <u>a</u> and adds something similar. Line <u>b</u> does not go beyond <u>a</u> and provide a new insight into the meaning of <u>a</u>. Static parallel lines then say the same thing twice or nearly the same thing twice, and so may be referred to as synonymous parallelism.

> O LORD, rebuke me not in thy anger,
>   nor chasten me in thy wrath! (Psa 38.1)

Here line <u>b</u> mirrors line <u>a</u>. At most the repetition serves to make the request emphatic. Line <u>b</u> introduces nothing by way of a more specific, figurative, dramatic image. The translator must decide how to treat such parallelism. TEV, for example, does not translate all such lines in the same way. Sometimes it prefers to keep both lines, and other times it will telescope the two lines into one: "O LORD, don't punish me in your anger!" TEV has tried to retain the emphasis of the repetition through the use of the exclamation mark.

> For the LORD will not forsake his people;
>   he will not abandon his heritage. (Psa 94.14)

These lines are semantically but not syntactically parallel. The Hebrew word order in the second line has been changed to provide variety. There is no attempt by the psalmist to intensify or raise the poetic heightening of "forsake his people" through "abandon his heritage." The repetition merely lends emphasis to the whole. In this example TEV has kept both lines, "The LORD will not abandon his people; he will not desert those who belong to him." There is no exclamation mark, which in the context is probably not needed. The translator's decision to retain both lines will depend upon the function of line repetition in the receptor language.

> O offspring of Abraham his servant,
>   sons of Jacob, his chosen ones! (Psa 105.5)

These parallel lines refer to the same people and are two ways of speaking of the people of Israel. The function of the repetition is to make the address form emphatic. For the psalmist's readers who expected to get everything in pairs, these pairs were readily available. Before the first line was completed, the listener had already anticipated the second line. Dropping one of the lines in translation of static parallelism is not the same as dropping a line in dynamic semantic parallelism.

Since this is an address form, the translator may wish to make it clear by introducing "you," as in TEV. If the reader is still likely to understand each line as referring to different people, a further adjustment will be required, and in some cases the two lines can be telescoped into one.

Although semantically parallel lines are found throughout the psalms, the translator is faced more often by parallel lines which are not like those described above. Probably most common are those in which there is a logical relation between the lines:

In peace I will both lie down and sleep;
for thou alone, O LORD, makest me dwell in safety. (Psa 4.8)

Line a is a consequence of line b, and in some languages the order will have to be changed; for example, "Because you alone keep me perfectly safe, I lie down and sleep in peace," or as in TEV, "When I lie down, I go to sleep in peace."

Just as parallel lines are used to intensify, repeat with emphasis, or show logical relations, they often tell a story. In Psalm 105 each line carries the narrative forward, sometimes with repetition and sometimes without.

When they were few in number,
of little account, and sojourners in it,
wandering from nation to nation,
from one kingdom to another people,
he allowed no one to oppress them;
he rebuked kings on their account . . . . (Psa 105.12-14)

In summary, parallel lines form the very groundwork for Hebrew poetry. The translator must ask the following questions when translating parallel lines: 1. Are the lines semantically parallel or not? 2. If they are semantically parallel, are they dynamic or static? If they are dynamic, there will probably be a general term in the first line and poetic intensification in the second line through the use of a more specific, figurative, or dramatic term or image. In static parallelism the second line merely mirrors the first without sharpening the focus and stepping up the intensification. 3. If the two (or three) lines are not semantically parallel, is there a logical or other relation between them? Having decided on the nature of the parallelism, the translator must then find the most meaningful and stylistically acceptable way to render the lines.

4. The English Headings of the Psalms

The TEV provides headings for all the psalms, and in some instances has two or more in a given psalm; in Psalm 119 there are headings for all twenty-two stanzas. RSV does not have headings. In this Handbook other headings are cited, all of them from translations currently in use, in English or some other language. Translational comments on the headings are based on the TEV heading, which appears at the head of the TEV psalm.

5. The Hebrew Titles of the Psalms

Nearly all the Hebrew psalms have a title which gives the name of the person to whom it is attributed or to whom it is dedicated, either "by" or "for" (the Hebrew *le* may mean either. Often there is information about the type of composition and also a musical direction, and sometimes there is a brief statement of the circumstances under which the psalm was composed. There are thirty-four so-called "orphan psalms," which have no title; in the Septuagint only seventeen psalms lack a title.

a. **Authorship.** David appears as the author of seventy-three psalms. Others who are cited as writers of the psalms are: Moses (Psa 90); Solomon (Psa 72; 127); Asaph

(Psa 50; 73–83); the group of Korah (Psa 42–49; 84; 85; 87; 88); Heman the Ezrahite (Psa 88); and Ethan the Ezrahite (Psa 89). It is to be noticed that Psalm 88 is attributed to the group of Korah and to Heman. There is no certainty about the precise meaning of "Jeduthun," which appears in RSV as a proper name in the titles of Psalms 39, 62, and 77.

There is much difference of opinion about how certain we can be that the people to whom the psalms are attributed actually did compose them. The translator, however, is bound to include this information, since it is part of the final form in which the psalms were accorded canonical status (see section 6, below).

b. **Type of Composition.** Some psalms indicate what kind of composition they are; several different Hebrew terms are used, and the meaning of some of them is in dispute. The RSV rendering of these terms follows: (1) "Psalm" translates the Hebrew *mizmor*, which means a song accompanied by musical instruments. It appears in the title of fifty-seven psalms (see Psa 3) and appears nowhere else in the Hebrew Old Testament. It is translated *psalmos* in the Septuagint. (2) "Song" occurs thirty times and often appears together with the word for "psalm" (see Psa 30; 48). The word is a general term for song (see its use in 28.7). (3) "Song of Ascents" appears in the title of Psalms 120–134. There are several explanations of this phrase; the most common one is that it indicates a song to be sung by pilgrims as they made their way up to Jerusalem, to worship in the Temple at one of the annual festivals. (4) "Maskil" is found in the title of thirteen psalms (32; 42; 44; 45; 52–55; 74; 78; 88; 89; 142). Its precise meaning is unknown; most incline to the meaning "an artistic composition" (see its use in 47.7b). (5) "Miktam" occurs six times (Psa 16; 56–60), always in association with David. There is no certainty about its meaning. (6) "Shiggaion" appears in the title of Psalm 7; some translate it "lament." (7) "Prayer" is used in the title of five psalms (17; 86; 90; 102; 142); it appears also in 72.20, at the conclusion of Book Two (see also the title of Habakkuk 3). (8) "Praise," which translates the word that in its plural form is the title of the whole collection, appears in the title of Psalm 145.

c. **Musical Notations.** Again, the RSV rendering of these notations is used. (1) "To the choirmaster" appears in the title of fifty-five psalms; most of them bear the name of David, and only two of them (66; 67) are anonymous. This seems to refer to the conductor of the Temple choir, and means that the composition was to be handed over to him for use in the Temple. Others, however, take the phrase to mean "Of the choirmaster," meaning that the psalm belonged to an earlier collection of psalms known as "The choirmaster's collection." (2) "With stringed instruments": Psalms 4; 6; 54; 55; 67; 76. (3) "For the flute": Psalm 5. (4) "According to Alamoth": Psalm 46. (5) "According to the Sheminith": Psalms 6; 12. (6) "According to the Gittith": Psalms 8; 81; 84. (7) "According to Jeduthun": Psalms 62; 77; Psalm 39 has "to Jeduthun." "Jeduthun" may be a person's name, but this is not certain.

Selah is a musical notation which does not appear in the heading but in the body of the psalms. It is used seventy-one times (in thirty-nine psalms); elsewhere in the Old Testament it is used three times in Habakkuk 3. There are different opinions about its precise meaning (see the discussion at its first occurrence, in 3.2). The word **Higgaion**, which appears in the text of Psalm 19.14 ("meditation") and of Psalm 92.4b ("melody"), is used as a musical notation at 9.16.

d. **Names of Melodies.** These refer to the melody to which a particular psalm was to be sung. There are nine of these, four of which RSV transliterates: "according to Muth-labben" (Psa 9); "according to Shushan Eduth" (Psa 60); "according to Mahalath" (Psa 53); and "according to Mahalath Leannoth" (Psa 88). The other five are translated, as follows: "according to The Hind of the Dawn" (Psa 22); "according to Lilies" (Psa 45; 69); "according to Lilies. A Testimony" (Psa 80); "according to the Dove on Far-off Terebinths" (Psa 56); "according to Do Not Destroy" (Psa 57–59; 75).

e. **Liturgical Use.** It should be obvious by now that the final collection of the 150 psalms was influenced by the use of these prayers, songs, and hymns in the worship at the Temple. The Psalter was the hymnbook used in worship in the Temple after the Babylonian exile, and some of the psalms have indications as to when they were to be used. "For the Sabbath" (Psa 92); "for the memorial offering" (Psa 38; 70); "for the thank offering" (Psa 100); "at the dedication of the Temple" (Psa 30); and "for instruction" (Psa 60).

f. **Historical References.** Thirteen psalms, all of which are associated with David, have information about the historical setting of the psalm: Psalms 3; 7; 18; 34; 51; 52; 54; 57; 59; 60; 63; and 142. It should be noticed that there is a wide difference of opinion among scholars about the historical accuracy of these notes.

6. The Translation of the Titles

There are different ways in which these titles (and *Selah*) are handled by translators. Current modern English translations vary. (1) Some include all the material as the title of the psalms: RSV, NIV, NAB, NJB. NJV also includes them as titles, but it differs from the others in that it follows the Hebrew verse numbering, in which the title appears as verse 1, and the text of the psalm usually begins as verse 2. (2) TEV includes as a footnote, under the heading "Hebrew title," the name of the author, the type of composition, the liturgical use, and the historical setting; TEV does not include the musical notations, the instruments, or the names of the melodies. (3) Spanish common language version (SPCL) places in the margin the titles that contain historical material, and omits all other titles. (4) NEB omits everything. In its "Introduction to the Old Testament" (page xxi) the reason is given: "they are almost certainly not original." It is recommended that *all* the material be translated; in most cases, if not all, this material can be placed in a footnote.

The transliterations *Selah* and *Higgaion* are used by RSV, NIV, and NJV; NJB translates "Pause" and "Muted music"; NEB, NAB, and TEV omit them altogether. It may be best to disregard these altogether, inasmuch as there is no certainty as to their meaning. If a translator does decide to translate them, the best procedure may be to translate them as NJB has done.

7. The Numbering of the Psalms

The numbering of the psalms in the Septuagint (and the Vulgate) differs from the numbering used in the Hebrew text. Consequently Roman Catholic translations that still follow the Vulgate numbering will differ from translations that follow the Hebrew text. The relation between the two systems is as follows:

11

Hebrew text		Septuagint/Vulgate	
Psa	1–8	Psa	1–8
	9		9.1-21
	10		9.22-39
	11–113		10–112
	114–115		113
	116.1-9		114
	116.10-19		115
	117–146		116–145
	147.1-11		146
	147.12-20		147
	148–150		148–150

It is also important to note that the Hebrew title for a psalm may be a part of verse one, all of verse one, or may even consist of the first two verses. Some modern translations follow the Hebrew verse numbers, while others, such as RSV and TEV, regularly begin the verse numbering after the title. A complete tabulation of the four differing number systems is provided in the Appendix of this Handbook.

8. A Note on the Divine Name "Yahweh."

Although it is not used either by RSV or TEV, "Yahweh" appears frequently in the body of this Handbook. "Yahweh" represents the Hebrew proper name for God, *YHWH* (four consonants without vowels), whose precise derivation and meaning are disputed (see Exo 3.14-15; 6.2-3). RSV and TEV "LORD," as a representation of the Hebrew name, conforms to a long tradition that goes back to the Septuagint *Kurios* and the Vulgate *Dominus*, both of which mean "Lord." Like "LORD," they are titles, not proper names. Nearly all standard translations in English and in other languages do the same. One exception was the American Standard Version (1901), which departed from "LORD" of the King James Version (1611) and the English Revised Version (1881) and used instead "Jehovah."

The written practice of using the title "Lord" conforms to the oral tradition followed in the public reading of the Hebrew Scriptures in the synagogue. In the past, as in the present, whenever the divine name *YHWH* appeared in the text, the reader said *Adonai*, a Hebrew title meaning "(my) Lord," since it was held that the holy name of God should not be uttered.

In the body of the commentary, the writers of this Handbook have felt that the translator should be aware of the fact that the English title "LORD" is not a translation of the Hebrew proper name *YHWH*, since, by definition, a title is not a proper name, not even a title spelled with small capital letters. Perhaps the time will come when standard translations of the Hebrew Scriptures, both Jewish and Christian, will provide a transliteration of the Hebrew, following the lead of *La Bible de Jérusalem*, which has *Yahvé* (English version "Yahweh," Portuguese version *Iahweh*) as the proper name of the God of Israel.

9. A Note on Jerome and the Vulgate.

The user of this Handbook will notice that sometimes reference is made to the **Vulgate** (Vg), that is, the Latin translation of the Bible that was done by Jerome in the late fourth century and early fifth century and which was officially adopted by the Roman Catholic Church. Sometimes, however, reference is made to **Jerome** (Jer). The two are not the same.

There are three Latin translations of the Book of Psalms that are related to Jerome: (1) the earliest revision of the Old Latin Version, made around 383, at the bidding of Bishop Damasus, of Rome. Some contend that Jerome really did not revise the Old Latin, and that what is called the "Roman" Psalter is actually the Old Latin. It is still used in St. Peter's Basilica in Rome, in St. Mark's Cathedral in Venice, and in Milan. (2) Around 390 Jerome did a translation of the Psalms from the Septuagint; it is believed that he also used the Hexapla, Origen's edition of the Old Testament in six versions (the Hebrew text; a Greek transliteration of the Hebrew text; and four Greek versions: Septuagint, Aquila, Symmachus, and Theodotion). Due to its popularity in Gaul, it became known as the "Gallican" Psalter. It is this Latin version that was included in the Vulgate Bible, and is the one referred to as "Vulgate." (3) After moving to Bethlehem, Jerome made a translation of the Old Testament from the Hebrew text. The Psalter of this translation, known as "according to the Hebrew," is the one referred to as "Jerome." It has never been included in any Bible nor used in the public worship of the Church.

10. A Note on "HOTTP"

This Handbook refers frequently to "HOTTP," which stands for *Preliminary and Interim Report on the Hebrew Old Testament Text Project,* Volume 3: *Poetical Books.*

The HOTTP committee identified four phases in the development of the Hebrew text: (1) The "oral or written literary products in forms as close as possible to those originally produced"; (2) the "earliest attested text," defined as "the earliest form or forms of the text which can be determined by the application of techniques of textual analysis to existing textual evidence"; (3) the "Proto-Masoretic text," the consonantal text as authorized by Jewish scholars shortly after A.D. 70; (4) the Masoretic text, "as determined by the Masoretes in the 9th and 10th centuries A.D."

The committee's goal was to ascertain the form or forms of the second phase of the text. Once it determined this phase of the text in Hebrew, it supplied a translation of it into English and French. A translator will not always find in the committee's decision an answer to a *translation* problem, inasmuch as the overriding concern of the HOTTP committee was to deal with *textual* problems. The committee was at pains to explain this matter, and its statement on page xviii should be read carefully. Not every HOTTP textual proposal will commend itself to the translator, especially in decisions that are classified "C" (meaning there is "considerable doubt" about the form of the text) and "D" (meaning the form of the text is "highly doubtful").

Translators and translation consultants are urged to familiarize themselves with the principles employed by the committee and to be well acquainted with the "Factors Involved in Textual Decisions" (pages ix-xv) in order to gain maximum profit from this valuable textual help.

Title

The Psalms: the Hebrew name of this book is "Book of Praises." The word translated "praises" is used in the normal sense of the noun "praise" (see 22.3; 34.1; 48.10 in the Revised Standard Version [RSV], which uses the English noun). It is also used in the sense of "a song of praise" (see 40.3b; 106.12b), which is what it means in the title of the book. It is used as a title of a psalm only for Psalm 145, "A song of praise of David."

In the ancient Greek translation of the Hebrew Bible, the Septuagint, the title is *PSALMOI,* the plural of a Greek word meaning "song of praise" (see the plural in Luke 20.41; 24.44; Acts 1.20; and the singular in Acts 13.33). The English word "psalm" comes from the Greek word.

Translators often transliterate some form of the word "Psalms," usually from Greek or from a major language in the area. Some languages use expressions such as "Songs of praise," "Songs of worship," or "Chants to praise God." In some languages it is necessary to say, for example, "The book of the songs to praise the LORD." In Muslim areas where the Arabic term *zabur* (plural *mazmur*) is widely known, it may be best to transliterate this title and, if appropriate, to add a descriptive subtitle.

Book One

(Psalms 1–41)

Psalm 1

This psalm serves as an introduction, or prologue, to the collection of the Psalms in its final form. It is a teaching, or wisdom, psalm advising the readers to dedicate themselves to the study of the Law of God, the Torah, and warning them of the consequences if they don't.

The psalm consists of two strophes. The first one (verses 1-3) describes the truly pious person, stating what he refuses to do (verse 1), what he does (verse 2), and then describing him as like a healthy tree (verse 3). The second strophe (verses 4-6) compares the evil person to chaff, which is blown away by the wind. Such a person will not share the future happiness of the righteous but will instead be destined to destruction.

As suggested in the introduction, "Translating the Psalms," it will help the translator to see how certain psalms are built up so that the parallelism within verses contributes to the larger structure of the psalm and thus gives shape and meaning to the whole. Unlike some psalms, Psalm 1 is both brief and tightly knit, based as it is on oppositions. These oppositions or contrasts are sharpened forcefully and logically by the use of well-placed markers at the beginning of verses 2a, 4a, 4b, and 5a. Verse 1 has three parallel lines, an exception to the usual two. The first two lines consist of a metaphor ("walk," "stand") used in relation to the general category of "the wicked" and "sinners." The third line (usually the second) narrows down to the more specific "scoffers." The happy person is defined as one who does not do as these persons do. The second verse has two positive parallel lines, establishing the first contrast and marked as such. "Delights in the law of the LORD" in line a provides the ground or basis, which is typically followed in line b by the consequence "on his law he meditates." Having established the contrast, the psalmist turns in verse 3 to a comparison (which will provide the basis for a further contrast). In verse 3 parallelism is not emphasized. The image used is the tree. It is planted in a productive place, fruitful, and dependable. Verse 3 summarizes: "he is prosperous," which again anticipates the opposite fate of the wicked, to be summarized at the end of verse 6.

In Hebrew verse 4a says "Not so the wicked." Line b then makes concrete what the suggested opposition is: "but merely chaff which the wind drives away." Thus the psalmist, using the contrasts of the solidly planted tree and the instability of chaff, poetically heightens the difference between the two kinds of persons. Verse 5 opens as a conclusion to the psalm and returns to the wicked and sinners mentioned in verse 1. Here the parallelism is complete in that in line a "stand [a different verb than in verse 1] in the judgment" is a common expression, whereas in line b "the congregation of the righteous" represents a shifting to a heightened level of vocabulary. It is at this point that the word "righteous" is introduced as a way of speaking about the kind of person who has all along been the focus of attention but until now has never been named. Verse 6 completes the conclusion, in which line a repeats "the righteous" from line b of the previous verse and contrasts "the way of the righteous" with the "way of the wicked" in line b.

It is instructive to note that a chiastic pattern is developed in verses 5 and 6: wicked, sinners, righteous, righteous, wicked. Furthermore, the psalmist contrasts the syntactic order of the two clauses in verse 6 so that line a has the verb before the object, while in line b the verb is placed at the end. Thus, having established the contrasts, the psalm closes by picking up again "the way" from verse 1b and "the wicked" from verse 1a, and tying the end to the beginning like a loop.

HEADING: "**True Happiness**" (Today's English Version [TEV]); "The prosperity of the pious"; "The person whom God approves"; "The two ways." In many languages it is not possible to combine abstracts such as "true" and "happiness." Furthermore, "happiness" must often be represented by a verb. It is therefore often more natural to express the idea of the TEV title in some such form as "The perfect way for people to be happy." "True" as a qualifier must often be rendered by means of a figurative expression; for example, "The straight road that leads to happiness" or "The good path on which to walk in order to be happy."

1.1   RSV   TEV

Blessed is the man	Happy are those
who walks not in the counsel of the wicked,	who reject the advice of evil men,
nor stands in the way of sinners,	who do not follow the example of sinners
nor sits in the seat of scoffers;	or join those who have no use for God.

Blessed is the term regularly used in the Old Testament to describe a person who is in a good situation and deserves to be congratulated. The Hebrew word does not mean precisely that God blesses, or rewards, such a person; rather it means that such a person is happy, or fortunate, deserving congratulations. It is translated in the Septuagint by the same Greek adjective used in the Beatitudes (Matt 5.3-11), and the same word or phrase should be used here that is used to translate the Greek word in Matthew. A word such as "Lucky," which implies chance, should not be used.

In some languages the congratulation expressed here is lost when the third person is retained, and therefore requires a shift to the second person; for example, "How fortunate you are" or "What great happiness is yours." In some languages the congratulation may be expressed more naturally at the end of the verse rather than at the beginning.

The man: "the person." TEV and others use the plural form "**Happy are those who . . .**" in order to avoid making the psalm apply only to males. Or else, "The person who . . . is happy (or, fortunate)."

Such a person is described by three expressions which are more or less synonymous, that is, the three describe the same kind of behavior in different ways, using the Hebrew verbs "walk . . . stand . . . sit" in a figurative way. Some scholars see a progression of thought from casual acquaintance to permanent association, but this seems unlikely.

Walks not in the counsel of the wicked: "does not behave as wicked people say he should," "whose conduct does not follow the advice of evil men." The Hebrew verb "to walk" is often used in a figurative sense: "to live one's life," "to act," "to behave." **Counsel** means "advice," "instruction," or "teaching" given by one person to another.

Nor stands in the way of sinners: "does not follow the path taken (or, indicated) by sinners," "does not imitate the example of sinful people." The English expression "to stand in someone's way" means to block a person's progress and is not the correct meaning here.

In some languages "advice" is closely related to opinion, and therefore it is necessary to say, for example, "who say 'No' to the evil words of bad people," "who keep away from bad people's evil words," "or who avoid what evil people say they should do." In some languages there are expressions such as "to follow in the footprints," meaning to imitate the behavior of someone. In such cases the metaphor can appropriately be retained at least in part as "who do not follow in the footprints of evil men."

The two nouns **wicked** and **sinners** are quite general and describe those who do not obey God, as God's will is made explicit in the Torah. The third noun, scoffers, refers to people who openly scorn religion or God, people who are practicing atheists, as it were. The term is used quite often in Proverbs (see 1.22; 14.6; 24.9; 29.8).

Nor sits in the seat of scoffers: "does not join (or, associate with) people who make fun of religion (or, of God)." In many languages the verb "sit" has also the meanings of "to be" or "to exist," and by extension "to accompany someone." The characteristic movement in parallel lines is seen here, where the general terms **wicked** and **sinners** are replaced by the more specific **scoffers**.

In translation it is important to keep the thrust of the poetic imagery if at all possible. Therefore before translating **walk . . . stand . . . sit** as nonmetaphors, the translator should see if these expressions will fit his language naturally. If they do not, then he may find other figurative expressions which may be used. Failing this, the translator is advised to use nonfigurative expressions.

Most languages have abundant terms expressing ridicule, often accompanied by derogatory gestures. Frequently figurative language expresses ridicule; for example, "shake the finger," "wag the head," or "make faces." Hence the full expression **sits in the seat of scoffers** is sometimes rendered "sit with people who wag their heads at God."

1.2   RSV   TEV

> but his delight is in the law of the   Instead, they find joy in obeying
>   LORD,   the Law of the LORD,
> and on his law he meditates day   and they study it day and night.
>   and night.

In this verse the psalmist gives the positive qualities of "the righteous" (see verses 5,6). It may be better to begin a new sentence here, as in TEV.

But: the contrast between what precedes and what follows should be clear and emphatic. TEV "**Instead**" is stronger than **but**; New Jewish Version (NJV) has "rather." Even stronger would be "On the contrary."

His delight is in the law of the LORD: "he takes pleasure (or, finds joy) in reading (or, obeying) the Law of the LORD." It may not be normal to speak simply of **in the law**, as RSV does, and so a verb such as "obey," or "read," or "think about," or "learn" may be necessary. Or "but he loves the Law of the LORD."

The law of the LORD: here this term refers to the Torah, which is the most important part of the Hebrew Scriptures, that is, the first five books (traditionally known as the Books of Moses). The word "Torah" means teaching, instruction, guidance. It stands generally for the Hebrew faith, Yahweh's revelation of himself as the God of the Hebrew people, and particularly for the written record of that revelation in the Hebrew scriptures, especially the first five books. NJV translates "the teaching of the LORD." It is obedience to the Law that makes for a righteous person's joy, not the book as such.

In translation it is important to make clear the relation between **delight** and **the law of the LORD**. This may often be done by using two verb forms, as in TEV's "**find joy**" and "**obeying**." The first can often be the cause and the second the result; for example, "Because they obey the Law of the LORD, they are happy." In some languages **law** merely refers to regulations sent out from local officials. In order to avoid a restricted meaning of the term **law**, it is better to shift to "teaching" or "instruction." Furthermore, it may be necessary to indicate that the "teaching" comes from God, in contrast to a "teaching" which is about God.

The LORD translates the distinctive Hebrew name for God; see Exodus 3.13-15, and see the TEV footnote at Exodus 3.15. The name is transliterated "Jehovah" or "Yahweh." The majority of English translations represent the name by the title "the Lord," following the tradition begun by the Septuagint, which instead of transliterating the Hebrew name translated it by *ho Kurios*, "the Lord" (which is what the New Testament writers also did); and see Vulgate *Dominus*. Most English translations write the word in small capital letters, LORD; the American Standard Version (ASV) has "Jehovah," Moffatt (Mft) has "the Eternal," and the New Jerusalem Bible (NJB) has "Yahweh."

There are many problems related to the translation of LORD. Most readers will be familiar with the term that has been used in the translation of the New Testament, where "Lord" applies to both God and Jesus Christ. Now in the Psalms it will apply to God alone. Readers of the New Testament bring to the reading of the Psalms their feeling for the meaning of "Lord" as they have acquired it in the New Testament, and this is not always satisfactory in the Old Testament. The same applies to such terms as God, angel, spirit, and many others. In some cases the term used to translate "Lord" in the New Testament has never found complete acceptance, and translators are sometimes faced with the task of revising the term. Essentially there are four approaches which are followed: (1) LORD may be expressed by a term or phrase often designating a religious deity in the local culture; for example, "holy high one who guides us" or "sacred person who rules over us." (2) The term may be borrowed from Hebrew and adapted to the phonology of the receptor language. In that case "Yahweh" serves as a base for the adaptation. The borrowing may be from Arabic "Rabb" or some other widely known language in the area. (3) If a borrowed term is used it may be desirable to add a word or phrase to make clear that this is a term designating God. (4) Finally, the translator may use only a descriptive phrase such as "the one who is eternal" or "the one who commands us." Sometimes a descriptive term such as "the one who commands us" refers mainly to a military commander or a government officer. In such cases it will be preferable to follow one of the other solutions. Translators should consider each of these approaches in the search for a satisfactory rendering of this important term.

Meditates: "reads carefully," "studies," "pores over." The Hebrew verb is defined as "read in an undertone" (see Josh 1.8), meaning intensive, careful reading and study. However, many languages make no distinction between reading and studying, and attempts to describe a mumbling kind of reading may distract from the essential force of reading diligently. Hence, **meditates** may often be rendered as "reading and thinking about." In cases where it is desirable to express the intensive aspect of reading, one may say "they read it carefully day and night," or "they read and think about its teachings all the time," or "they are always reading and thinking about its teachings."

RSV   TEV

He is like a tree
  planted by streams of water,
that yields its fruit in its season,
and its leaf does not wither.
In all that he does, he prospers.
	They are like trees that grow be-
	  side a stream,
	that bear fruit at the right time,
	and whose leaves do not dry up.
	They succeed in everything they
	do.

This verse is remarkably like Jeremiah 17.8; see also Psalm 92.12-14.

The righteous are compared to healthy trees, provided with abundant water, which "**bear fruit at the right time**" (TEV), that is, at the proper season of the year.

The verb **planted** is taken by some commentators to mean "transplanted" (see Ezek 17.8,10,22; 19.10,13); most translations have simply "planted," since the important thing is not whether the tree is planted or transplanted, but that it grows where there is plenty of water.

Streams of water: a literal translation of the Hebrew phrase, which means either a natural course of water or an artificial canal. In either case it supplies fresh running water to the tree. However, the picture of fruit trees growing beside a water course in the dry Middle East is quite different from that of trees growing along low-lying or swampy stream beds in the tropics. In the tropics fruit trees are often grown away from streams, since they require better drainage. Accordingly they depend on the rains for their water, and a desirable rendering may be "They are like trees that grow where there is plenty of water" or "They are like trees that grow well because they are well watered."

Season may often be rendered as in TEV, "**at the right time**," or "always," or in some languages "without ever failing."

Its leaf does not wither: "its leaves don't wither." The withering of leaves is an indication that the tree is dying, or dead, and so in some languages it may be more effective to say "it does not die" or "it stays strong and healthy."

In all that he does, he prospers: see Joshua 1.8b. Some think that **a tree** is the subject of this last line (see American Translation [AT] "and whatever it bears comes to maturity"; see also NJV). But most commentaries and translations take the righteous person to be the subject; so TEV "**they succeed**." The verb "to prosper" includes all areas of life, not only spiritual but also financial and physical.

If translators keep the plural subject, as in TEV, they must make certain that the pronoun refers to the persons compared to the trees, and not to the trees themselves. In some cases it will be best to introduce a new subject; for example, "People who follow God's way." **Prospers** is translated in some languages by means of idiomatic expressions; positively it may sometimes be said "People who follow God's way will see goodness" or ". . . will touch good things," or negatively, ". . . will not fail to see good things."

1.4 RSV	TEV

The wicked are not so,
    but are like chaff which the
        wind drives away.
	But evil men are not like this at
	    all;
	they are like straw that the
	    wind blows away.

This verse presents a strong contrast to the preceding one; in the Septuagint the contrast is even stronger: "The evil are not like this, not at all like this" (this is followed by NJB).[1]

So refers to the whole description of the righteous in verses 1-3. The translation of "this" as in TEV may cause a problem, since the reader may not realize that it points to the entire preceding clause. The contrast may be rendered more clearly as "But bad people do not succeed at all," or "But evil people do not do well," or "But evil people fail in all they do."

The wicked (same as verse 1) are compared to the worthless **chaff**, which in the process of winnowing grain was blown away by the wind. After the cut grain stalks were tramped and crushed on the threshing floor, they were pitched into the air by use of a winnowing shovel. The grain fell to the ground and the chaff (or, straw) was blown away. The main point of the comparison is the worthlessness of **chaff**, which is allowed to be blown away because it is of no value whatever.

The translation of **chaff** presents no problem in cultures where grains are grown. Elsewhere it is often necessary to use a descriptive phrase which indicates something light and of little value that can be blown by the wind; for example, "dry grass" or "dry leaves."

1.5 RSV	TEV

Therefore the wicked will not
    stand in the judgment,
    nor sinners in the congregation
        of the righteous;
	Sinners will be condemned by God
	    and kept apart from God's own
	        people.

Therefore: this introduces the consequence of the worthless nature of the wicked. Unlike TEV, it should be formally represented in translation; for example, "And so," "For this reason," or "On account of this."

In line a the Hebrew text repeats **the wicked** from verse 4, and in line b it has the synonymous term **sinners**. TEV has combined the two, using "sinners" as the subject of both lines, since the same people are meant, and not two different groups. These two lines are typically parallel, in that line a uses the common term **judgment**, whereas line b shifts to the rarer and more literary expression **congregation of the righteous**. The second line carries the condemnation of the wicked even further by saying "what's more, they [the 'wicked,' now called 'sinners'] will not be part of God's

---

[1]The Hebrew Old Testament Text Project (HOTTP) prefers the Masoretic text ("C" decision).

own people." Translators will often use one term for **wicked** and **sinners** here, as well as in verse 1. In any case, they should be certain that the text does not imply that the two lines speak of two different groups.

Will not stand in the judgment: "will be condemned by God when they are judged." This line is obviously a close parallel to the next line; **the wicked** are the same as **sinners**, and what is said of them in this line must parallel or complement what is said of them in the next line. The verb "to stand" is understood by some scholars to mean "to be resurrected," but most believe that it is a figure of acquittal in a court of judgment; that is, **not stand** means not to be acquitted, and so, "be condemned." NJV translates "will not survive (judgment)," and New English Bible (NEB) "shall not stand firm." In the second line the same verb (which is not repeated in Hebrew) means "will not be together with the righteous people." The main question to be answered is whether the psalmist is talking about the final Day of Judgment or thinking about the judgment of God which falls upon everyone in this life and particularly, in Hebrew thought, in the common life of the people of God. The next verse, which speaks of Yahweh's knowing "the way of the righteous" while "the way of the wicked" disappears, seems to support the former interpretation, that is, "there on the Day of Judgment sinners will be condemned; they will not be with God's own people." However, should the translator prefer the other interpretation, something like the following can be said: "Therefore sinners will be punished by God; they cannot be a part of God's people."

Stand in the judgment will often remain unclear to the reader unless God is named as the one who judges the wicked. In some languages it is necessary to avoid a passive construction and say "God will condemn evil people," or if it is desirable to make more explicit the failure of the wicked at the judgment, then one may render it "God will not find evil people innocent when he judges them."

Nor sinners: in Hebrew the one verb "to stand" is used for both lines; it may be necessary, as TEV does, to have another verb for line **b**, since **not stand . . . in the congregation of the righteous** means that the wicked will not be included among the righteous people. The translation of line **b** can be "they (or, the sinners) will not be included among the righteous," "there will be no place for sinners in the gathering (or, assembly) of the righteous."

Most translations of verse 5 appear as a pair of coordinate statements concerning the wicked (RSV, TEV). However, if the translator is to make clear the relation of the second line to the first, it is necessary to show that the second line goes beyond the first; for example, "what is more, they will be kept apart . . ." or "they will even be kept apart . . . ." In languages in which the passive is not used, it may be necessary to say, for example, "not only that, but God will not accept them as part of his own people," or as direct address, ". . . God will say 'You are not part of my people.' "

The phrase **the congregation of the righteous** means all God-fearing Israelites (see 111.1). Here it stands for those whom God rewards in this life or will reward on Judgment Day. Something like "the faithful," or "those who obey God," or "those whom God will declare innocent" may be used. Or else, "**God's own people.**" TEV "**kept apart**" supplies the implied verb in line **b**. Line **b** may be handled as the consequence of line **a**, that is, "God will judge evil people, and therefore they will not be among his people."

1.5

The word **congregation** should not be translated by a word or phrase that indicates an organized religious group, especially a Christian group. Here it means simply "all the righteous," "all of God's people," "all the people who worship God."

1.6   RSV   TEV

> for the LORD knows the way of   The righteous are guided and
>   the righteous,   protected by the LORD,
> but the way of the wicked will   but the evil are on the way to
>   perish.   their doom.

For: verse 6 gives the reason why the destinies of **the righteous** and **the wicked** are different. The outcomes of the two separate groups are pictured as "ways," that is, roads, one of which is safe and secure, while the other leads to destruction.

The force of the verb "to know" in line a is that of care and concern. "It involves approval, care, guidance" (Kirkpatrick); "it is under his protection" (Toombs). NJV "cherishes"; NJB "watches over"; Spanish common language version (SPCL) "takes care of." If the TEV language is followed, it may be better to use an active construction: "The LORD guides and protects the righteous."

In contrast, the way followed by the wicked **will perish**, that is, will lead to destruction and death. NEB and JB have "the way (or, path) of the wicked is doomed"; another way of saying it would be "the way followed (or, chosen) by the wicked leads to destruction (or, death)." See Psalms 68.2; 73.27; 92.9. The translator will recognize the difficulty of keeping the parallelism of line a, **way of the righteous**, and line b, **way of the wicked**. This is due to the metaphorical use of the word **know** in line a and to the combination of **way** and **perish** in line b. Because of the necessity of restructuring for the sake of meaning, the elements which are parallel in Hebrew are lost in many languages, but the translator must maintain the contrast between the righteous and the wicked.

Psalm 2

This is one of the psalms known as "Royal Psalms," written to celebrate the coronation of the king of Israel. Since the king has been chosen by God, who is the ruler of all the world, he will have universal dominion.

The psalm is composed of four strophes. In the first one (verses 1-3) the psalmist describes the rebellion of nations and their rulers against God and the king; in the second one (verses 4-6) he describes God's reaction to the plots of the rebels; in the third strophe (verses 7-9) the king relates how the Lord promised to give him worldwide dominion; and in the last one (verses 10-12c) the psalmist warns the rebels to submit to God or face certain destruction. The psalm closes (verse 12d) with a pronouncement of blessing on those who go to God for protection.

HEADING: "**God's Chosen King**" (TEV); "Universal God and universal king"; "A warning to the nations"; "The king as God's son." As in most of the headings of the psalms, it will be necessary in many translations to recast nouns as verbs and supply a subject and often an object. Here it may be possible to say, for example, "God says to the king 'You are my son,' " or in indirect speech, "God says that the king is his son."

2.1	RSV	TEV

	Why do the nations conspire,
	    and the peoples plot in vain?
		Why do the nations plan rebel-
		    lion?
		Why do people make their
		    useless plots?

The two lines of this verse are parallel and are in the form of a question, to show how foolish and useless are the rebellion and the plots being planned against Yahweh and his chosen king. The second line repeats the first one, adding the affirmation that the plots will not succeed. The question is not a request for information but is a way of expressing contempt and astonishment at the attempt of Israel's enemies to defeat Israel's king. "How dare the nations plan rebellion?" Or, as a statement, "It is completely useless for the nations to plan rebellion." The French common language version (FRCL) uses a question and a statement: "The nations are in an uproar—but why? The peoples plot, but it is useless!"

It is not necessary to have two different words in translation to represent <u>the nations</u> and <u>the peoples</u>, since the two refer to the same group. In the context of this psalm, these are Gentile nations, who were considered pagans (SPCL translates "Why are the pagan peoples in turmoil? Why do they . . . ?").

In some languages there is no term for "nation" as a large, independent political unit. The largest political group may be called a "tribe." It is sometimes unnatural to say that tribes are planning rebellions, and so one must speak of the leaders of the tribes rebelling. It may also be necessary to indicate against whom the people are conspiring. Hence, "Why do the chiefs of the foreign tribes conspire against God and his people?"

Conspire translates a verb found only here in the Old Testament; it is variously defined: "rage" (AT, New American Bible [NAB]), "uproar" (NJB, FRCL), "assemble," and Briggs has "consult together." It would seem that a meaning such as **conspire** (or TEV "**plan rebellion**") more readily fits the context, as a closer parallel to the verb in line b.

The verb translated **plot** is the same that in 1.2 is translated "meditates"; here it is a whispering, a murmuring, of conspirators. And the phrase **in vain** means "without success," "**useless**" (TEV). NJB has "impotent muttering."

In these two parallel lines only the second contains **in vain**. Although it is true that conspiring in line a is equally useless, the addition of **in vain** in the second line serves to heighten the element of failure in relation to the verbs of both lines. It is not implied that the **nations** conspire with some degree of success, and that only the **peoples** fail in their plotting. If the translation gives this impression, the translator is advised to make clear that what is done in both lines is without success.

It may not be possible in some languages to maintain the parallelism of the two clauses; and in these cases they may have to be reduced to one; for example, "Why do the leaders of the foreign tribes plot against God and his chosen king? Their plotting will fail," or as a statement, "The chiefs of the pagan tribes conspire against God and his chosen leader, but they will not succeed."

2.2

RSV	TEV
The kings of the earth set themselves, and the rulers take counsel together, against the LORD and his anointed, saying,	Their kings revolt, their rulers plot together against the LORD and against the king he chose.

Lines a and b appear to repeat verse 1. However, there is a movement taking place between them. In verse 1 those who conspire are a general category, "nations, people." In verse 2 the movement is toward the more specific, **kings of the earth** and **rulers**. The same sort of movement from the general to the more specific can be seen in the verbs of the two verses. Verse 2 ends by saying whom the conspiracies are against. The translator should determine to what extent he is able to represent this narrowing-down process. It may not be possible at all, due to the need to use more specific descriptive terms in verse 1, and the need to state in verse 1 that it is the Lord and his anointed who are the object of the plotting. However, the translator should make it clear that the **kings** and **rulers** of verse 2 are the same persons as in verse 1. TEV has done this with "**Their kings . . . their rulers.**"

This verse describes the rulers of the pagan nations of verse 1. There is no difference in meaning here between **the kings of the earth** and **the rulers**; both refer to the leaders of the pagan nations of verse 1. The phrase **of the earth** may indicate a certain contempt for those rulers; they are no more than earthly kings, compared with the king of Israel, whose authority comes from God (see the contrast between them in 89.27).

The two verbs translated **set themselves** and **take counsel together** describe how the pagan rulers plot to cooperate in their rebellion against Yahweh and the king of Israel. The English phrase **set themselves** is not very clear, and the meaning is more clearly expressed by "take their stand" or "stand ready." FRCL takes the Hebrew verb to mean "prepare themselves for combat," which fits in nicely in the context.

Anointed translates the verbal noun *mashiah*, "anointed one," from which comes the word "Messiah." The word reflects the custom of setting apart a person chosen for high office by pouring olive oil on him (see Judges 9.8 and 1 Sam 9.16 for the anointing of kings; and see Lev 8.12 and Num 3.3 for the anointing of priests). Here it means the king, whose anointing indicated that he was the one chosen by God to be the king of Israel. Rebellion against the chosen king of Israel was rebellion against the God of Israel.

His anointed may best be expressed in translation as "The king whom God has chosen" or "The king whom God has appointed." Because of its Christian connotation the word "Messiah" should not be used here.

Verses 1-2 are quoted in Acts 4.25-26.

2.3	RSV	TEV
	"Let us burst their bonds asunder, and cast their cords from us."	"Let us free ourselves from their rule," they say; "let us throw off their control."

The rebellious kings and rulers propose to set themselves free from the dominion of Yahweh and the king of Israel. The **bonds** and **cords** are figures for "rule" and "control." They are close synonyms and may be translated in various ways: "fetters . . . bonds" (NJB, NAB); "fetters . . . chains" (NEB); "cords . . . ropes" (NJV). Such nonfigurative words as "rule," "dominion," "authority," "control," or "sovereignty" are equally suitable, but in some languages verbs or verbal phrases will be better than abstract nouns.

If the RSV language is imitated, it should be clear that **their bonds** and **their cords** are the bonds and cords that Yahweh and the king of Israel have used to imprison and subdue the pagan rulers.

The parallelism of verse 3 is not to be taken as simply line b repeating line a. Line b carries a thought beyond line a, the idea being "what is more, let us get rid of their control." **Burst their bonds** and **cast their cords** are used figuratively here, but switching to nonfigurative language may reduce the poetic impact. In many languages quoted material requires special introductory or closing forms to identify the material as a quotation. **Let us burst their bonds** may require recasting as direct imperatives; for example, "Break the bonds," or with deliberate force, "We shall break the bonds." It may be necessary to make explicit that **their bonds** and **their**

<u>cords</u> refer to "the cords the LORD and his king have put on us." The same applies in the nonfigurative form, where **"their rule"** and **"their control"** may require rendering "The rule of the LORD and his king over us" or "We shall free ourselves from the LORD and the king who rule and control us."

<u>**2.4**</u>	RSV	TEV

He who sits in the heavens laughs;	**From his throne in heaven the**
the LORD has them in derision.	**Lord laughs**
	and mocks their feeble plans.

The second strophe (verses 4-6) begins with a description of how God reacts to the plots of the pagan rulers. God is spoken of as **He who sits in the heavens**, that is, the one who sits on his throne in heaven (line <u>a</u>), and he is named **the LORD** (line <u>b</u>). TEV has combined the two, to make clear that they refer to the same subject; NEB also, "The Lord, who sits enthroned in heaven."

It should be made clear that <u>sits</u> means to reign, or rule, as king; it should not just indicate that the Lord is sitting in heaven rather than standing. That is why TEV has "**From his throne in heaven.**" The plural form **the heavens** reflects the concept of a series of heavenly levels, three or seven in number, at the highest of which Yahweh lives.

In translation it is sometimes necessary to add the object on which one sits; for example, "stool," "chair," "mound," or "log." In languages where the particular term lacks the primary meaning of "authority," it is better to say "place of authority."

It should be noticed that RSV **the LORD** translates the name Yahweh, which is found in many Hebrew manuscripts; TEV has translated the traditional Hebrew text, the Masoretic text, which has the title "*Adonai*," meaning "the Lord."

The Lord **laughs** and makes fun of the pagan rulers. The two verbs are close in meaning, and a translation may use one verb, as SPCL does: "The Lord, who reigns in heaven, makes fun of them." TEV has "**their feeble plans**" as the object of the verb "mocks," but it may be better to say "them," that is, the rulers themselves.

In 1.1 "scoffers" are people who make fun of God; here it is God who mocks the pagan rulers. Nevertheless, in many languages the idiomatic expressions used for a person making fun of another person can equally be used of God ridiculing the rulers; for suggestions see 1.1.

<u>**2.5**</u>	RSV	TEV

Then he will speak to them in his	**Then he warns them in anger**
wrath,	**and terrifies them with his fury.**
and terrify them in his fury,	
saying,	

From amusement Yahweh's emotion turns to anger. It seems better to maintain the descriptive present tense, as TEV does: "**he warns . . . and terrifies**" (also Mft, FRCL, NJB, NEB, NAB). Verses 5-6 still deal with the Lord's reaction to the rebels.

The two nouns **wrath** and **fury** describe his attitude. Such human traits are ascribed quite naturally by Old Testament writers to God, in their conviction that he "was actively, vigorously, and personally involved in man's history" (Toombs). The noun translated **fury** is used in the Old Testament only with God as subject. It means literally "burning," that is, an anger that consumes and destroys the enemy (see Exo 15.7).

He will speak to them (or "he warns them," "he rebukes them," or "he threatens them") and **terrify them**: for this last verb see also 83.15. Mft translates "he . . . scares them." Many languages will follow more closely the Hebrew form of speaking to them **in his wrath**. However, in many cases "speaking" does not carry the negative injunction implied. Furthermore, anger involves a strong emotional element which is often stated in physiological terms such as "hot heart" or "hot stomach." It may be best then to render the warning as a negative command in direct address; for instance, "God is angry and says, 'Do not act this way.'" In some languages the full line will be: "With a hot stomach God says, 'Do not act like this.'"

The parallelism of verse 5 is a typical case of line _b_ representing a dramatic intensification of line _a_, from the ordinary **speak** to the intense **terrify**. It may be possible to represent this movement in the parallelism; for example, "He will be angry and speak to them; he will be so angry their strength will fail," or "He will warn them because he is angry; so angry is he that their hearts run away," or "Being angry at them he will speak out; he will scare them to death."

In many languages the idea **terrify**, used in both TEV and RSV, implies some kind of physical loss and is sometimes expressed figuratively as "the breath departed," "the heart ran away," "the strength ran out," or "the strength melted."

2.6	RSV	TEV
	"I have set my king 　on Zion, my holy hill."	"On Zion,_a_ my sacred hill," he 　says, "I have installed my king."

_a_ ZION: _The term "Zion" (originally a designation for "David's City," the Jebusite stronghold captured by King David's forces) was later extended in meaning to refer to the hill on which the Temple stood._

The Hebrew verb translated **have set** means literally "to pour out," and some scholars see here the meaning of "anoint" (so NJB, AT); but most take it to mean establish firmly, that is, to install (NJV); NEB has "I have enthroned."[1]

My king is the king that God chose to rule his people (verse 2).

---

[1]Here the Septuagint has the king as the speaker: "I have been installed (as king) by him on Zion, his holy hill."

The name **Zion** was applied to the hill (Mount Moriah) on which Solomon built the Temple; by extension the name was applied to the Temple, to the city of Jerusalem, and sometimes to the whole land of Israel. The hill is called **holy** because it belongs exclusively to God.

Since Zion and Jerusalem are both used in the psalms with reference to the city of Jerusalem, there is some advantage in translating both terms as "Jerusalem," particularly as most readers today know of the existence of a city by that name. However, since Zion and Jerusalem occur in a variety of contexts, it is advisable to keep both terms and provide a supplementary note in the glossary. It is also necessary to make sure in most contexts that Zion and Jerusalem are not two separate places. The expression **my holy hill** should not be translated so that it means "my tabooed mountain," but rather that it is dedicated to God; for example, "the hill which is given to God" or, in languages which do not have a passive voice, ". . . which people have dedicated (or, set apart as sacred) to me." In this passage it is possible to indicate the relation of God to the hill as one of "belonging"; for example, "On Zion, my own hill." The expression **my king** may present a problem in that in ordinary usage it is spoken by one of the king's subjects with the meaning "the king who rules me." In the present context the meaning is "the king God has chosen." The full expression may then be rendered " 'On Zion, my hill,' says God, 'I have placed the king I have chosen.' "

2.7　　　　　RSV　　　　　　　　　　　　　　　　TEV

I will tell of the decree of the LORD: He said to me, "You are my son, today I have begotten you.	"I will announce," says the king, "what the LORD has declared. He said to me: 'You are my son; today I have become your father.

In this verse the king himself speaks. TEV makes this explicit, and translators should make certain that the change of speakers is clear to the readers of the psalm. The king announces **the decree of the LORD**. The Hebrew noun translated **decree** means an authoritative statement, a pronouncement of some kind.[2] In this instance it is the declaration **You are my son, today I have begotten you**. This figurative language reflects the message from Yahweh which Nathan gave to David about David's successor as king of Israel (2 Sam 7.14; see also Psa 89.26-27). It may be easier to say in translation "**I have become your father**" (TEV) or "I become your father" (NEB); NJB has "have I fathered you." God adopts the king as his son and confers his own authority on him. The king of Israel is God's representative, or deputy, on earth.

---

[2]Crim (*Royal Psalms*, page 42) alludes to "the testimonies" in 2 Kings 11.12 and takes "the decree" here to refer "to the verbal evidence of divine sonship—most probably the oracle of the Davidic Covenant as recorded in 2 Samuel 7."

It is important in translation to make clear the change of speaker in 2.7. **Decree of the LORD** may be rendered in some languages as "the order spoken by the LORD," "the words spoken by the LORD," or "the words the LORD spoke."

Today is the day the king was enthroned.

The words of this verse are applied to Jesus in the New Testament; see Mark 1.11; 9.7 and parallels; Acts 13.33; Hebrews 1.5; 5.5.

Care should be taken not to leave the reader thinking that the Hebrew psalmist was writing about Jesus Christ. In English, by the use of capital letters at the beginning of words and titles, it is possible to imply that Jesus Christ is being referred to. So the New International Version (NIV) in verse 2 has "his Anointed One," in verse 6 "my King," in verse 7 "You are my Son," and in verse 12 (see below) "Kiss the Son." This goes beyond the limits of a faithful translation and introduces meanings and concepts that were not in the mind of the original biblical author.

The major problem in translating verse 7b is making clear to whom the pronouns refer. This may often be done by using direct speech; for instance, "God said to me, 'You, king, are now my son' " or indirectly "God told me that I the king am his son."

The expression **today I have begotten you** may create confusion, as a king is not normally **begotten** on the day he is made king. It may be necessary to relate this explicitly to the day of enthronement; for example, "On this the day of your becoming king I have become your father."

2.8	RSV	TEV
	Ask of me, and I will make the nations your heritage, and the ends of the earth your possession.	Ask, and I will give you all the nations; the whole earth will be yours.

Ask of me means "Ask me to give you." In some languages it may be better to translate "Ask me to give you all the lands of the earth and I will do so." Or else, as a conditional, "If you ask me, I will give you . . . ."

Here God promises the king universal dominion, authority over all **the nations** (same word as in verse 1). The phrase **the ends of the earth** means "all the earth," "from one end of the earth to the other" (see 22.27; 48.10; 59.13). Line b, **ends of the earth**, represents the use of a metaphor following a nonmetaphor in line a. The meaning is essentially the same, but in the rhetorical use of parallelism, the more vivid expression is kept for the second line.

Heritage is a term often used in the Old Testament of what God gives his people; it involves the idea of permanent possession. Many times it refers to the land of Canaan as Israel's gift from God (see Deut 4.21); the word **possession** is similarly used (see Gen 17.8; Deut 32.49). The noun "heritage" and the verb "to inherit" do not, in a context like this, carry the meaning ordinarily associated with these terms, that is, of a gift or a right that is given someone at the death of the one who previously owned the gift or held the right. So TEV translates "**I will give you.**"

Because it is unnatural in many languages to "give" or "inherit" a social entity such as a tribe, it will often prove more satisfactory to say "to cause to rule the nations." Likewise, asking for a favor often requires a response word. For example, "Ask me and I will say yes by making you rule over all tribes in the world. Indeed, you will own the whole world" or ". . . the whole world will be yours."

2.9   RSV   TEV

> You shall break them with a rod   You will break them with an iron
>   of iron,   rod;
>   and dash them in pieces like a   you will shatter them in pieces
>   potter's vessel."   like a clay pot.' "

You shall break them . . . and dash them in pieces: both statements describe how the king of Israel will defeat and destroy the Gentile nations. The second verb implies a more thorough destruction than the first one; so TEV **"break"** and **"shatter . . . in pieces."** One of the most common techniques to achieve intensification in biblical parallelism is the use of the simile in the second clause. The intensification of poetic effect is made here also by the contrast of breaking with an iron rod and the shattering of a fragile clay pot. The translator's ability to maintain the degree of contrast will depend on the verbs used and the existence of clay pots, well known for their tendency to be easily smashed. It may not be natural to use this figurative language, and so the following may be better: "You will defeat (or, subdue) them . . . you will destroy them completely."[3]

A rod of iron is a figure of the ruthless power the king will use to defeat the pagan nations (NJV "with an iron mace"). In some languages it is unnatural to speak of "breaking" nations with an instrument. Other figures of speech which are natural in the language may be found which will symbolize despotic rule; for example, "to trample with the feet" or "to strike with the fist."

A potter's vessel: "pottery" (NIV); **"a clay pot"** (TEV, NEB); "pots" (NJB). This was easily broken and could not be put back together. Here it is a figure of complete and permanent destruction.

In most areas of the world, **potter's vessel** can be translated as a "clay pot." However, where clay pots are not made and known, a substitute, breakable article of local manufacture may be used.

---

[3]The verb in line a of the Masoretic text is "break"; but the same consonants of the Masoretic text, with different vowels, which are given in the margin of the text, mean "to rule," and this is how the Septuagint, Syriac, and Vulgate translate it (also NAB, NIV, and FRCL). And this is the form also in which the text is used in Revelation 2.27; 12.5; 19.15.

2.10   RSV   TEV

> Now therefore, O kings, be wise;   Now listen to this warning, you
>   be warned, O rulers of the   kings;
>   earth.   learn this lesson, you rulers of
>   the world:

In this strophe (verses 10-12) the speaker is either the psalmist or the king; it is impossible to determine which one is intended. TEV takes the psalmist to be the speaker; RSV could be understood to have the psalmist or God as the speaker.

Be wise in line a is general, while line b focuses more specifically with **be warned**. TEV reverses the order: "**listen to this warning . . . learn this lesson.**" NAB has "give heed . . . take warning"; AT "be cautious . . . take warning"; NJB "come to your senses . . . learn your lesson."

This warning is given because of Yahweh's promise to his chosen king that he would rule over the whole world. So the **kings** and the **rulers of the earth** are to obey the order that is given in the following verses.

The command **be wise** is difficult in many languages to express as an order. The expression may be recast; for example, "act in a wise way," or "act like a wise person." **Be wise** may also be rendered "show that you understand." Verse 10 may be rendered, for example, "You kings, show you understand these words; you rulers, pay attention to this warning"; or "You kings, act like wise men; you rulers, listen to this warning."

2.11-12   RSV   TEV

> 11 Serve the LORD with fear,   11 Serve the LORD with fear;
>   with trembling 12 kiss his feet,[a]   tremble 12 and bow down to
>   lest he be angry, and you perish in   him;[b]
>   the way;   or else his anger will be quickly
>   for his wrath is quickly kindled.   aroused,
>   and you will suddenly die.
>   Blessed are all who take refuge in   Happy are all who go to him for
>   him.   protection.

[a] Cn: The Hebrew of 11b and 12a is uncertain.

[b] *Probable text* tremble . . . him; *some other possible texts* with trembling kiss his feet *and* with trembling kiss the son *and* tremble and kiss the mighty one; *Hebrew unclear.*

The first line of verse 11 has the idea not only of political submission to Yahweh, but may also include the idea of worship; so NEB has "worship the LORD with reverence"; Mft "worship the Eternal reverently" (see also SPCL). The word **fear** in the Old Testament, especially when God is the object, often has the meaning of awe, respect, reverence.

Line b is difficult if not impossible to understand. It appears to shift to the more concrete form, here expressed as a metaphor, whatever its form and meaning may be. The complete line in the Masoretic text seems to mean "and rejoice with trembling. 12 Kiss the son" (so ASV). The first verb in Hebrew means "rejoice" elsewhere, and commentators like Briggs strongly defend that meaning here; but the command "rejoice in trembling" is very strange (so *Traduction œcuménique de la Bible* [TOB]; also NIV "rejoice with trembling"). Jerusalem Bible (JB) translates "tremble"; NJV has "tremble with fright."[4]

The expression **with trembling** refers in many languages to a person who is cold and shivering. Therefore it is often best to avoid a term referring to the physical event and say, for example, "make yourself humble" or "make yourself low."

For the beginning of verse 12, ASV has "kiss the son" (so Hebrew Old Testament Text Project [HOTTP]); NIV "Kiss the Son" turns the Hebrew text into a Christian text. The difficulty is that such a translation assumes that in the Masoretic text the word *bar* is Aramaic (and so means "son"), and not Hebrew; but the psalm is in Hebrew, and the Hebrew word for "son" is *ben* (see verse 7). The ancient versions are of no help: Septuagint (followed by Vulgate) has "take hold of discipline (or, instruction), so that the Lord will not be angry." The Hebrew word *bar* means (among other things) "pure"; so Jerome translated "worship in purity." Most modern commentators and translators agree that it is most unlikely that "Kiss the son" is what the Masoretic text means. As Kirkpatrick put it in his commentary of over eighty years ago, "This rendering must certainly be abandoned," and he gave the reasons why. So modern translations, like RSV and TEV, change the Hebrew text, either by emending it or punctuating it differently. (To emend the Hebrew text means to change it, either by a change of one or two letters in a word, or by a more extensive change, which at times may be based on the text of an ancient version such as the Greek Septuagint. Sometimes a distinction must be made between emending the Hebrew text and emending the Masoretic text, since in some passages some of the ancient Hebrew manuscripts, such as the Qumran manuscripts, will be different from the Masoretic text.) SPCL has "Worship the Lord with joy and reverence; bow down before him with fear"; NEB "tremble, and kiss the king"; NAB "with trembling pay homage to him"; NJB "with trembling kiss his feet" (also Zürcher Bibel [ZÜR]); NJV "pay homage in good faith"—with a footnote saying that the meaning of the Hebrew is uncertain.

Until more light is shed on the subject, the translator's best course is to follow one of the standard translations. However, a literal translation of **kiss his feet** in many languages will be misleading. It is therefore preferable in such cases to use a nonfigurative expression such as "bow down to him," or the appropriate physical gesture for doing obeisance before a high-ranking person, such as "stoop before him," "lower the head before him," or "crouch in front of him."

TEV **"his anger will be quickly aroused"** combines two separate statements in the Hebrew text, "he will be angry . . . for his anger is quickly aroused" (see RSV).

---

[4]HOTTP says the Hebrew means "and exult with trembling." The Septuagint has "be joyful in him with trembling." In this context "in him" means "because of what he has done."

The Hebrew verb "be angry" used here appears thirteen times in the Old Testament and is used only of God.

Anger as a possessed state is not natural in some languages and must accordingly be expressed as an event word, often in physical terms; for instance "to be hot in the stomach," "to have a burning heart," or "to have red eyes." If the translator follows the combining of the parallel statements as in TEV, then both may be rendered as one line; for example, "God's heart will quickly become hot." If the statements are not combined, amplification indicating the suddenness of the anger must be handled as a separate clause; for example, "God will be angry at you; because he becomes angry at people quickly."

You perish in the way is a literal translation of the Hebrew; the meaning is "you will die suddenly (or, unexpectedly)," that is, before the normal time, as a result of God's anger.

The last line of verse 12 is a closing benediction. The translation of the benediction often requires an appropriate connector or a double space in printing to mark the break with the preceding lines.

For **Blessed** see 1.1.

Take refuge in him translates a verb which appears some twenty-four times in Psalms and is always used with God as the protector. The expression **take refuge in him** must often be recast as a verbal phrase with the meaning of "covering," "caring for," or "helping." The last line may sometimes be rendered, for example, "But how happy are the people God takes care of" or "But how fortunate are the people God helps."

Psalm 3

This psalm is a lament by an individual, as are Psalms 4–7 and thirty-four others. There are more psalms of this kind than of any other.

The psalm divides into four strophes: (1) the psalmist's complaint (verses 1-2); (2) an expression of confidence in the Lord's help (verses 3-4); (3) assurance of the Lord's protection (verses 5-6); (4) a closing prayer (verses 7-8). The speaker seems to be the king (verses 3,6-7), but no certain inference can be drawn from the text of the psalm itself.

The psalmist's concern for his personal safety is emphasized through the recurrence of the first person pronoun in every verse except verse 8, where it shifts to the collective, "thy people." Reference is made to the Lord in every verse except verse 6; even here it is the sustaining effect of the Lord in verse 5 that enables the psalmist to face his enemies. The image of the enemy is found in verses 1, 2, 6, and 7. Thus, in the center of this psalm (verses 3, 4, 5) and in the conclusion, the focus is shifted away from the enemy but returns to the enemy in verse 6 in a mood of confidence, and in verse 7 the enemy, now identified with the wicked, is destroyed. In terms of poetic balance the psalm consists of the enemy and I (verses 1, 2); the Lord and I (verses 3, 4, 5); the enemy and I (verse 6); the enemy and the Lord (verse 7); and the victorious Lord and the blessed people (verse 8).

HEADING: "**Morning Prayer for Help**" (TEV); "Morning prayer of the virtuous man under persecution"; "Trust in God in time of danger"; "A God of deliverance."

Hebrew Title: **A Psalm of David, when he fled from Absalom his son**.

The title of this psalm refers to David's flight from Absalom, narrated in 2 Samuel 15–16.

The translation of the Hebrew title depends on the term used for psalms in the New Testament. The term employed should normally be "songs," meaning poems which are sung or chanted. Usually such a term requires a qualifier such as "praise," "religious," or "worship"; for example, "songs for worship" or "songs for praising God." The initial words, translated **A Psalm of David**, are translated by FRCL "A psalm belonging to the collection of David." In many languages it will be clearer to make explicit the writing of the psalm as taking place after the "fleeing"; for example, "This is a religious song David wrote after he ran away from his son named Absalom."

RSV   TEV

1   O LORD, how many are my foes!   1   I have so many enemies, LORD,
        Many are rising against me;   so many who turn against me!
2   many are saying of me,   2   They talk about me and say,
        there is no help for him in   "God will not help him."
        God.   *Selah*

The psalmist complains to Yahweh about his enemies, who not only threaten
him with harm (verse 1b) but also claim that God will not help him (verse 2).
Nothing is said about why they are against him or the kind of danger they pose.
Verses 1 and 2 show in their line arrangement a progression, in that in verse 1a the
psalmist states his case. In verse 1b his enemies are **rising against me**. In verse 2a
they go so far as to speak against him, and verse 2b gives the content of their talk,
no help for him.

How many are my foes!: this word order is normally employed in a question;
in English it is better to say "My foes are so many!"

Are rising against me: the verb "to rise" may mean "to rebel"; if correct, this
implies that the psalmist is the king. See the use of the verb in 2 Samuel 18.31-32.

Are saying of me: literally "are talking about my soul." The Hebrew noun for
"soul," *nefesh,* is often used to refer to the whole person, and in such instances it
should not be translated by "soul" or "spirit."[1]

There is no help for him in God: the noun translated **help** may also be
translated "salvation," "deliverance," "rescue"; in some instances it may mean
"victory" (NEB). It is better to use a verb to translate it here: "God will not save
him!" or "God is not going to help him!"

Selah: the meaning of the Hebrew *selah,* which occurs 71 times in Psalms,
continues to be unknown. The Septuagint translates "musical pause"; most modern
translations that represent the word have simply "*Selah*" (ASV, AT, RSV, NJV, NIV),
which means nothing. TOB, NJB, and FRCL have "pause"; Mft, ZÜR, NEB, German
common language translation (GECL), and TEV omit. SPCL has a long footnote, giving
the probable meaning of the word, and justifying its exclusion from the text. Unless
a translator feels sufficiently assured of the meaning of the word so as to be able to
translate it, it seems best to omit it. Most probably the word was not part of the
original text of the individual psalms.

3.3   RSV   TEV

But thou, O LORD, art a shield   But you, O LORD, are always my
    about me,   shield from danger;
my glory, and the lifter of my   you give me victory
    head.   and restore my courage.

---

[1]See note on *nefesh* at the end of this psalm (page 40).

<u>Shield</u> is a common metaphor for protection, often used of God (see 7.10; 18.2). The phrase **about me** completes the idea of protection. The large shield was big enough to protect the whole body from the enemy's sword or arrows. The translation here can be "you are my protecting shield," "you are a shield to protect me." If the metaphor does not make sense, a simile may be used: "you are like a shield that protects me," "you protect me like a shield." In languages which lack a term for <u>shield</u> or any other protective device used in battle, the translator may employ a descriptive phrase; for example, "the thing that protects." On the other hand a nonfigurative expression may be better; for example, "You, LORD, are the one who protects me from danger."

It is more common in parallel lines for the first line to be nonfigurative and the second to contain the figure. Verse 3 is an exception with figures in both lines. If one takes both lines as a unit, the meaning may be expressed "LORD, you are not only a shield for me, but you also make me victorious and give me courage" or "LORD, you are like a shield, you even give me the victory and renew my strength."

Yahweh is also called **my glory**. The Hebrew word for <u>glory</u> has a variety of meanings, one of which is "honor, reputation," which fits well in this context. Since the king's honor was dependent upon his being victorious over his enemies, it is possible that here this specific meaning is intended; so TEV "**you give me victory.**" NIV has "you bestow glory on me." Simply to translate "my glory," as NJV, NEB, and NJB do, carries no meaning in English. Briggs proposes "the one in whom I glory"; Mft "thou whom I do glorify"; Knox "my champion." Toombs takes it to mean the psalmist's "worth as a man," for which he is indebted to the Lord. It is more likely, however, that the meaning is "**victory**" (TEV) or "honor," which can be expressed by "you give me great honor."

The lifter up of my head: "you hold my head high." This phrase is a metaphor for restoring confidence, courage, and hope to one who is discouraged. Delitzsch comments: "He comforts and helps him." Briggs takes it to mean victory, while Kirkpatrick thinks it means that the Lord saves him and restores him to his throne. SPCL translates "You are the one who encourages me." FRCL says "you supply me with dignity and pride." Another possibility is "you maintain my honor and hold my head high."

The translator is encouraged always to use meaningful figures of speech, provided they translate correctly the meaning of the text. Sometimes metaphors which are newly made or have become obsolete are of little communicative value and may give the reader an entirely wrong understanding. Many languages use metaphors to express "to comfort" or "to encourage"; for example, "to make the heart cool" or "to strengthen the insides." In such cases it will be necessary to add a causative element; for example, "You cause my insides to rest" or "You make my heart sit coolly."

3.4   RSV   TEV

I cry aloud to the LORD,   I call to the LORD for help,
   and he answers me from his   and from his sacred hill^d he
    holy hill.   *Selah*   answers me.

^{d} SACRED HILL: *See 2.6.*

I cry aloud: the Hebrew is literally "I call (with) my voice," which probably means "I cry aloud" (as most translations in English have it). TEV makes explicit what is implicit, that is, that the psalmist is calling for help. **Cry aloud** can easily be misunderstood, as it is difficult to imagine crying or weeping which is not done aloud. Therefore the TEV rendering is more natural, as it expresses both means and purpose.

He answers me: that is, by sending help. Many languages distinguish between answering a question and responding to a request. Here the expression required is the latter. However, a verbal response may mean nothing more than acknowledging that one has heard, and consequently it may be necessary to say "he replied and helped me."

Yahweh's **holy hill** is Mount Zion, where the Temple stood (see 2.6). In some instances it may be well to make this explicit, "He answers me from the Temple on Mount Zion, his holy hill."

3.5-6   RSV   TEV

5 I lie down and sleep;   5 I lie down and sleep,
   I wake again, for the LORD   and all night long the LORD
    sustains me.   protects me.
6 I am not afraid of ten thousands 6 I am not afraid of the thousands
    of people   of enemies
   who have set themselves against   who surround me on every side.
    me round about.

The psalmist expresses his confidence in God to protect him. At night he sleeps soundly and peacefully. The statement **I wake again** indicates that he sleeps securely the whole night long, because the Lord **sustains** him. When he wakes up the next morning, he discovers that nothing has bothered or threatened him during the night. The verb translated **sustains** means to provide security and safety; to protect, support, uphold (see 37.17,24; 145.14). In translation it may be necessary to recast the phrase **I lie down and sleep** as a temporal clause; for example, "When I lie down and sleep." The verb **wake** should express the idea of awaking in the morning following a night of sleep. If there is no distinction made between awaking from sleep and awaking after the night's sleep is completed, then it is advisable to follow TEV's "**all night long.**"

In some languages it may be clearer to give first the reason why the psalmist can lie down and sleep all night when he has so many enemies. Therefore it may be necessary to shift the reason clause of verse 5 forward; for example, "Because the LORD protects me, I lie down and sleep, and in the morning I awaken."

In verse 6 the psalmist picks up "many are my foes" from verse 1 and gives them a number. As in verse 1b he again says they are **against me**.

The psalmist does not even fear **ten thousands of people**. The Hebrew word is a plural form, meaning simply very many; no precise number is intended. The singular form may mean 10,000 (see 2 Sam 18.7). In some languages the idea of very large numbers is rendered "more than a man can count." These were probably foreign enemies, and their position, **"who surround me on every side"** (TEV), indicates war and may sometimes be rendered, for example, "who make war against me" or "who come like soldiers to kill me."

3.7	RSV	TEV
	Arise, O LORD! Deliver me, O my God! For thou dost smite all my ene- mies on the cheek, thou dost break the teeth of the wicked.	Come, LORD! Save me, my God! You punish all my enemies and leave them powerless to harm me.

In verse 1a it was the enemies who were "rising against me." Now the psalmist, whose courage has been restored, calls out **Arise, O LORD!** using the same verb as in verse 1a.

Arise: a cry for help, asking Yahweh to bestir himself, to take action. So FRCL has "Intervene, Lord." The idea may be implicit that God is to rise from his heavenly throne in order to go into action; see the word as used in the marching song of the Israelites in their wilderness wanderings (Num 10.35; see also Psa 68.1). But the general idea of "act," "take action," is probably what the Hebrew verb means.

Deliver me: the verb is related to the noun translated "help" in verse 2. In this context the translation "Save me" (TEV and others) seems the best in English.

Deliver me, O my God requires two adjustments in some languages: First, it may be necessary to state the condition from which deliverance is sought. Here it is from enemies. Secondly, the expression **my God** may have to be recast as "the God whom I worship," since God may not be thought of as one's possession.

The psalmist reminds God of his readiness to act, as an incentive for him to act now. **For** introduces the ground or basis on which the psalmist calls for God to help him. The psalmist knows that God can and will defeat his enemies.

The two figures of God "smiting the enemies on the cheek" and "breaking the teeth of the wicked" represent his attacking them and defeating them. To **smite . . . the cheek** was an insulting gesture of humiliation and shame (see 1 Kgs 22.24; Job 16.10; Micah 5.1). To **break the teeth** was a figure for making the enemy powerless to harm (see 58.6).

These two parallel lines are to be considered as a whole. There is no intention of the psalmist to make one statement about his enemies and another about wicked people. The parallelism is that of process followed by consequence. The structure is two noun phrases bracketed by verbs. Literally in Hebrew "For you strike my enemies on the cheek, the teeth of the wicked you break." The focusing is done by placing the consequence in the second clause. In order to maintain the unity of the two lines in translation, it may be clearer to say, for example, "When you hit my enemies in the face, you break their teeth to pieces." If the translator wishes to replace these forceful figures with nonfigurative expressions (see TEV), the process-consequence relation should be reflected in the translation.

In translation it may be necessary to employ a different set of metaphors; for example, **smite . . . enemies** is sometimes rendered "to bend the enemy's head down," "to take away the enemy's name," or "to cause the enemy's eyes to lower." The translation of **break the teeth** will again require in most languages a different figure of speech or an expression meaning "to render those wicked enemies harmless" or "take away their power so that they cannot harm me."

Instead of the descriptive present tense, **"You punish . . . and leave"** (TEV; also RSV and others), the Hebrew perfect tense may be translated as a future (AT) or as a way of referring to action in the past (Briggs, Kirkpatrick). NIV translates as though the Hebrew were imperative. Dahood interprets the initial Hebrew conjunction as an emphatic particle introducing a wish: "O that you yourself would smite all my foes on the jaw!" It seems best to follow RSV and TEV.

3.8 RSV	TEV
Deliverance belongs to the LORD; thy blessing be upon thy people! *Selah*	Victory comes from the LORD— may he bless his people.

Deliverance or "Victory" translates the Hebrew word for "salvation" or "help" (see verse 2); the precise meaning of the word is determined by the context. So the translations vary here: "salvation" (AT, NJB), "help" (Mft), "victory" (NEB), "deliverance" (NIV, NJV).

Belongs to the LORD: the literal Hebrew expression "to (or, of) the LORD the salvation" will require some restructuring in many languages. Often a causative relation must be expressed to show that it is the Lord who gives the victory; for example, "The LORD makes his people triumph" or "The LORD causes his people to be safe from danger."

In line b Yahweh is addressed directly in the second person (RSV **thy blessing**); to avoid a switch of persons, TEV retains the third person referent of line a. **Blessing** is the broadest term possible that includes all the benefits that God bestows on his people, the people of Israel.

NEB has an alternative rendering in a footnote: "O Lord of salvation, May thy blessing rest upon thy people."

In some languages the term used for **blessing** tends to be a verbal act only; for example, "God speaks well of them." However, it would seem that a more positive beneficial result is expected in such contexts as this. Other more satisfactory expressions may be "You, God, give good gifts" or "You give kindness and good things."

A Note on the Hebrew Term *nefesh*

The noun *nefesh* appears in the Book of Psalms 144 times, of which 105 are "my *nefesh*." The essential component of the word seems to be "breath" as that which characterizes a living being, so that "a living being" or "life" is the prevalent meaning of the word (see in Gen 1.20 "the waters are to produce swarms of living *nefesh*," that is, living creatures; and Gen 2.7 "and the man became a living *nefesh*," that is, a living being).

In the vast majority of instances in the Psalms *nefesh* means the (whole) person as such, and not a particular component of a human being. "My *nefesh*" means "I," "me," or "myself"; "his *nefesh*" means "he," "him," or "himself"; and so forth. So in 6.4a "save my *nefesh*" is to be translated "save me" or "save my life" (see also 17.13b; 33.19a; 34.22a; 35.17b; 55.18a; 56.13a). In 31.13d "to try to kill my *nefesh*" means "to try to kill me" (see also 35.4b; 56.6c; 59.3a; 63.9a; 70.2b). Passages which speak of taking the psalmist's *nefesh* to, or saving it from, (the power of) Sheol mean "take to death" or "save from death" (see 16.10a; 30.3a; 49.15a; 86.13b; 88.3b; 84.48b).

The word can refer to human life as such; 49.8a speaks of "the ransom for his *nefesh*," that is, the ransom for a person's life; in 119.109a the psalmist says he is ready to risk his *nefesh*, that is, to risk his life.

The *nefesh* is also spoken of as the seat or center of emotions and feelings, such as desire (35.25b), hunger, longing (78.18b; 119.20a,81a; 143.6b); courage, hope, or determination (107.5b,26b; 138.3b), despair (42.5a,6a,11a; 44.25a); joy (19.8b; 86.4a; 94.19b); serenity (131.2a).

The word can be applied to God. In 11.5b it is said that Yahweh's *nefesh* "hates those who love violence," meaning that Yahweh hates them passionately.

In two passages *nefesh* is paired with the body (31.9c) and the flesh (63.1b,c) as a way of emphasizing the psalmist's total involvement in the feelings being expressed.

In 69.1b and 105.18b *nefesh* means "neck."

In every instance the translator must take into account the specific context in which the word is used in order to determine the best way to represent its meaning faithfully and naturally in that passage.

(For further guidance, see H. F. Peacock, *The Bible Translator* 27:2 (April 1976), pages 216-219.)

Psalm 4

This psalm is another lament by an individual who finds himself persecuted by his enemies. It consists of a prayer for help (verse 1), a denunciation of the psalmist's enemies (verses 2-3), a warning to them (verses 4-5), and a statement of confidence in God's help (verses 6-8).

Parallelism is not highly developed in this psalm. The psalm is divided into two parts. Verses 1-3 are based on the themes of supplication with God's response, and verses 4-8 upon trust in God. Verse 1 opens with "answer me when I call" and closes with "hear my prayer." Verse 3 closes by repeating the theme and reversing the order, "the LORD hears when I call." Verses 4-8 center on trust in God. There is again a balancing of the theme, in that the image in verse 4b is that of meditating silently on one's bed, and verse 8 closes with the image of sleeping in safety.

There is not enough information in the psalm to allow us to know who the author was. If in verse 2 the Hebrew phrase means "important men" (see comments below), it is possible that he was a poor man being oppressed by wealthy men (see verse 7). The reference to a night's sleep (verse 8; see also 3.5) may reflect the ritual in which the person asking for God's help spent the night in the Temple, expecting to receive on the following morning a favorable reply to his prayer of complaint.

HEADING: TEV's "Evening Prayer for Help" is based on verse 8 and makes this psalm a companion to Psalm 7. Other headings are "The only security"; "Confidence in God"; "A hymn of faith"; "Complete trust in the LORD." As in Psalm 3, the TEV heading will often require adjusting; for example, "The psalmist asks God to help him in the evening" or "Before he goes to sleep the psalmist prays to God."

Hebrew Title: **To the choirmaster: with stringed instruments. A Psalm of David.**

Besides stating that David wrote this psalm, the Hebrew title has a musical direction, for the conductor of the Temple choir, that the psalm is to be sung accompanied by stringed instruments. A note addressed **To the choirmaster** appears with fifty-five psalms; the direction **with stringed instruments** appears also with psalms 6; 54; 55; 67; 76. TEV does not include the musical instructions.

4.1   RSV   TEV

RSV	TEV
Answer me when I call, O God of my right! Thou hast given me room when I was in distress. Be gracious to me, and hear my prayer.	Answer me when I pray, O God, my defender! When I was in trouble, you helped me. Be kind to me now and hear my prayer.

Answer me: see 3.4. This must be rendered by a term which invites an attentive response, and should not be translated by a term which only means "reply to my question." Where ambiguity would result it is better to use an expression meaning "listen and help" or "pay attention."

I call: "I pray for help." FRCL "I call to you for help."

In his prayer the psalmist addresses God as **God of my right**. The Hebrew word translated **right** (*tsedeq*)is a legal term and means defense or vindication against the charges brought by one's accuser. Briggs defines the phrase as "the God who vindicates his cause against his adversaries and establishes his right." NEB translates "maintainer of my rights"; NJV "my vindicator"; NJB "upholder of my right." A different interpretation is given by NAB, "O my just God." The Hebrew word takes on various meanings, according to the context. When applied to people it usually means obedience to God's will as expressed in the Law; when applied to God it describes him as one who always does what is right. In particular it means his activity on behalf of his people. Thus the word sometimes means "saving deed," "salvation." In some languages one may reverse the order of the two clauses and say "O God, you are my defender. So please listen to me and help me when I pray."

Thou hast given me room: TEV "You helped me" takes the Hebrew expression "you gave me room" to mean freedom of movement as opposed to the restrictive circumstances of the **distress** that kept him a prisoner. The Hebrew word for **distress** implies confinement in a limited space. SPCL has "in my distress you gave me relief." NJV translates the whole line "You freed me from distress." Another possibility is "you have set me free."

TEV makes the first clause a temporal dependent clause indicating condition, "**When I was in trouble**"; the second clause is the result: "**you helped me**." For many languages this is a more natural arrangement. TEV's "**trouble**" and "**helped**" are generic terms. The translator should attempt wherever possible to use specific and picturable renderings; for example, "When I was snared you set me free" or "when I was tied up you untied me."

Be gracious translates a verb which means to show favor, kindness, compassion, mercy. NJB has "take pity on me"; NAB "have pity on me"; NJV "have mercy on me." TEV has "now" in order to make the petition even stronger; since God has helped him in the past, he should do the same now.

Be gracious to me is rendered in many languages by idiomatic terms having to do with physical and emotional responses; for example, "Have a white heart for me," "Be pained for me," or "Cry in your heart for me."

Hear my prayer: "answer my prayer," "give me what I ask for."

4.2	RSV	TEV
	O men, how long shall my honor suffer shame?	How long will you people insult me?
	How long will you love vain words, and seek after lies?	How long will you love what is worthless
	Selah	and go after what is false?

O men translates the Hebrew phrase "sons of man." Some scholars (see Kirkpatrick, Cohen, Weiser) believe that this means men of rank, wealth, importance (see 49.2; 62.9). So NAB translates "Men of rank"; Knox "Great men of the world"; GECL "You rich men have power"; SPCL "You who think you are great men." Mft, somewhat differently, "Proud men." Other scholars see here an emphasis upon their mortality: NEB "Mortal men." There is no way of knowing who these men were except that they were the psalmist's enemies.

The questions are not requests for information; they are protests and denunciations aimed at the psalmist's enemies.

Shall my honor suffer shame: "insult me" (TEV) represents what is literally "my glory into shame." Here the word "glory" seems to mean reputation, fame, **honor** (RSV). The idea appears to be that the psalmist's enemies, by means of slanders and lies, are deliberately defaming him. Dahood takes "my glory" here to refer to God, "my Glorious One." The Septuagint has a different text: "How long will you men be stupid?" (literally "heavy of heart"); this text is preferred by NJB "be heavy of heart"; *Bible de Jérusalem* (BJ) has "shut your hearts"; NAB "be dull of heart"; Mft "how long will you be so misguided." It is recommended that the Hebrew text be followed, as represented by RSV and TEV.

In translation it is important to make clear the shift of person addressed in 4.2; for example, "And now you people . . . ." The question beginning with **how long** may in some languages require shifting to a negative question; for example, "Will you people never stop insulting me?" Or an emphatic statement may be better, such as "You people will never stop insulting me!"

It is impossible to be sure what **vain words** and **lies** refer to. The two expressions in Hebrew are synonymous, and the word for **vain words** means what is of no value, useless, worthless (see the same word in 2.1). It may be, as some scholars suggest, that this language reflects a trial in court in which the accused man denies the charges brought against him and affirms his innocence, at the same time accusing his adversaries of being liars (verses 1-5). With less probability, a few see here a reference to idols, so that the accusation is that of idolatry. TEV has used two general expressions, **"what is worthless"** and **"what is false."** NJV "illusions" and "frauds" suggests dishonest conduct, and this may be the best way to translate these two expressions.

Love . . . seek after: the two verbs represent the attitude and the activity of the psalmist's enemies. It may be more effective to represent these two phrases by more specific actions, as FRCL has done: "you who love to accuse without cause and who try to dishonor me."

Selah: see 3.2.

4.3 RSV	TEV
But know that the LORD has set apart the godly for himself; the LORD hears when I call to him.	Remember that the LORD has chosen the righteous for his own, and he hears me when I call to him.

Still addressing his accusers, the psalmist reminds them that **the godly** are Yahweh's special people, and so are helped and protected by him. In this certainty he knows that Yahweh will answer his prayer.

But know serves to remind the psalmist's enemies of his certainty and may be rendered, for example, "Don't forget that" or "You can be sure that." In some languages an equivalent expression is "Hold this word in your heart."

The verb translated **set apart** means literally to treat in a special way, differently (in a good sense). This is the verb that appears in the Masoretic text; but a slightly different verb appears in some Hebrew manuscripts (also reflected in some ancient versions), which means "act wonderfully." So NJB has "Yahweh performs wonders"; NAB "the LORD does wonders"; FRCL "The Lord has done me a great favor." Most translations, like RSV and TEV, follow the Masoretic text; SPCL translates "the Lord prefers." Either meaning makes sense, but it seems best here to follow the Masoretic text (which HOTTP prefers).

The idea of choosing often involves putting aside those which are preferred. Other terms also have the meaning of choosing, but may highlight the idea of selecting the undesirable people in order to dispose of them. **For himself** may require a rendering which expresses more of a purposive act; for example, "to be his own people" or "to belong to himself."

The godly translates a Hebrew word which means "loyal, devoted, pious." The Hebrew singular is probably generic, meaning all who are godly or righteous. But it may refer to the psalmist himself (see FRCL above); it may therefore be rendered "his loyal servant".

NEB emends the text to get "Know that the Lord has shown me his marvelous love"; in the same way Weiser, "But know that the Lord did wondrously show his mercy to me." The Masoretic text (**godly** or "**righteous**") makes sense, however, and should be followed.

The godly or "**righteous**" is expressed differently in many languages. In some it is related to the quality of "straightness," in others to "truth" and to "loyalty" or "obligation." In other languages it is expressed as "right" versus "left," where "right" indicates everything that is masculine, strong, true, and good, as contrasted with "left," which is associated with the opposites of "right," including female qualities. Some languages prefer to express righteous by figurative expressions; for example, "People who have white hearts" or "people with straight livers."

4.4   RSV   TEV

> Be angry, but sin not;
>   commune with your own hearts
>   on your beds, and be silent.
>   *Selah*

> Tremble with fear and stop sin-
>   ning;
>   think deeply about this,
>   when you lie in silence on your
>   beds.

The sense of the first Hebrew verb is disputed; the root meaning seems to be "be excited, perturbed," whether with fear, anger, or joy. The Septuagint takes it in the sense of anger, and it is in this sense that the passage is quoted in Ephesians 4.26; and that is how RSV, NEB, ZÜR, and FRCL have translated it here. But most modern translators and commentators take it in the sense of fear: Briggs, Kirkpatrick, Weiser; NAB, NJV, and others. Certainly this seems more appropriate as a warning to the psalmist's enemies. If a translator chooses the meaning of anger, the sense of the line must be something like "If you are angry, do not sin" (FRCL) or "Don't let your anger lead you into sin."

In many languages it is unnatural to command someone to experience an emotional state such as fear or anger. For this reason the relation between the emotion and the following command is not readily apparent without recasting the anger part as a dependent clause. Many languages express fear in terms of such figures as "trembling heart" or "breath departed." Here also the rendering may be more meaningful with a subordinate clause expressing the fear; for example, "even when your heart trembles from fear of God's punishment, do not sin" or "although you are afraid of what might happen to you, do not let this make you sin."

The next line is literally "talk in your hearts on your beds and be silent," which is an advice to the psalmist's enemies to meditate quietly and in private on what the psalmist is saying. NIV "when you are on your beds, search your hearts and be silent." The word **beds** (or, "couches") may imply nighttime, or else simply privacy (so Weiser); and the verb translated "be silent" may mean "be inactive," that is, don't do anything. NJV has "sigh."

Some languages express meditation and reflection in ways very close to the Hebrew form. But the same expression in other languages would imply that such a person is mentally unstable. It is therefore sometimes necessary to say "think about these words" or "remember these words." In many cultures practically the only privacy a person has is at night on his bed. The entire sentence can often be rendered "When you lie down on your bed at night, think about these words and be silent."

4.5   RSV   TEV

    Offer right sacrifices,   Offer the right sacrifices to the
      and put your trust in the LORD.   LORD,
                         and put your trust in him.

It is impossible to tell who is being addressed, whether the psalmist's accusers (addressed in verses 2-4) or people in general. It may be that the *Selah* at the end of verse 4 indicates a shift in address, but this is not certain. Commentators are divided on the subject. RSV and TEV division of strophes implies that the same people are still being addressed (also NEB, NAB, SPCL, FRCL).

Right sacrifices are those required by the Law, those that Yahweh commanded (see TOB). Some understand the Hebrew phrase "sacrifices of righteousness" to mean sacrifices offered in the right spirit (so Delitzsch, Kirkpatrick); NJB has "Loyally offer sacrifice"; another possible rendering is "Offer sacrifice in the right way."

For an understanding of the sacrificial system in the Old Testament, translators should consult a Bible dictionary; see also the chart of types of sacrifices in *A Translator's Handbook on Leviticus*, page 5. There were different kinds of sacrifice, and animal sacrifices included the killing of cattle, sheep, goats, doves, and pigeons. A sacrificial bird or animal was brought to the altar, where it was killed by a priest, burned, and thereby offered to God as a gift. The Hebrew term used in verse 5 will occur in 27.6; 50.8; 51.19; 106.28; and 107.22.

Sacrifices presents few problems in translation where sacrificial rituals are practiced or at least known. Where a descriptive expression must be used, "gifts killed for God" or "gifts that are burned and given to God" offer reasonable alternatives. The translation **put your trust in the LORD** frequently requires a "heart" idiom such as "having a thick heart for someone" or "placed one's heart upon another." The two lines may be rendered "Give to the LORD the burned gifts which he requires, and rest your heart upon him."

4.6

RSV	TEV
There are many who say, "O that we might see some good! Lift up the light of thy countenance upon us, O LORD!"	There are many who pray: "Give us more blessings, O LORD. Look on us with kindness!"

Here the psalmist seems to be directing his words not to his enemies but to people who were dissatisfied with their condition, and who piously repeated the standard phrases of prayer and devotion (so Toombs). The first part of the quoted material may be understood as a prayer, a wish (TEV, RSV, and others), or as a question, "Who will give us . . . ?" (see Delitzsch, Weiser, Dahood; TOB, NJB).

The wish **we might see some good** expresses in a very general way the desire for better things: "O for good days!" (NJV); "If only we might be prosperous again!" (NEB); FRCL "O, how we would love to see prosperity!" TEV makes it a direct request to God, connecting this line with the following one.

The second request, **Lift up the light of thy countenance upon us**, is either still part of what the **many** are praying for (so RSV, TEV, NEB, Mft), or is the psalmist's own prayer (so Kirkpatrick, Weiser; see AT, NJV, TOB, SPCL, NAB).

The language resembles that of the priestly blessing in Numbers 6.24-26. The figure "lift up the light of your face" means to be kind, to show a friendly disposition, to bestow favor.[1] The translator must decide whether a suitable figure is available in the language to render the plea for God's favor, and then whether or not to include it with the prayer of the preceding line, as with TEV and RSV, or to make it the prayer of the psalmist, both being possible. If **Lift up the light . . .** is taken as the prayer of the psalmist, it may be necessary to indicate the shift of speaker, perhaps by placing the closing quotes after **O LORD!** For example, "I ask you to be kind to me, LORD."

---

[1] NEB has changed the vowels of the Masoretic text's imperative form "lift up" and made it a perfect, "has lifted up," and has interpreted this as lifting away, removing: "But the light of thy presence has fled from us." This is possible but does not seem very probable.

　　　　RSV　　　　　　　　　　　　　　　　TEV

Thou hast put more joy in my heart 　than they have when their grain and wine abound.	But the joy that you have given me 　is more than they will ever have with all their grain and wine.

The psalmist assures himself of God's goodness, and declares that even in his present difficulties God has given him more happiness than that experienced by his wealthy accusers, whose grainfields and vineyards have produced abundant harvests. The implied idea is that the spiritual benefits resulting from his loyalty and devotion to Yahweh are far better than the material wealth of his opponents.[2]

It may be necessary in some languages to make explicit those to whom **they** refers: "those people" or "the people who say those things."

The psalmist says **Thou hast put . . . joy in my heart** (TEV "the joy that you have given me"), a way of saying "You have filled me with joy," "You have given me joy," "You have made me happy." It is not necessary in English always to use the word "heart" to represent the thought of the Hebrew expression. In general, "heart" in Hebrew thought represented the thinking function, "mind" (see 10.6,11, "he thinks in his heart"); it could also represent the center of emotion (see 5.9b, "their heart is destruction," TEV "they only want to destroy"); and often it represents the inner self, the whole person (see 7.10b, "the upright in heart," TEV "those who obey him"; 13.5 "my heart shall rejoice," TEV "I will be glad"). The translator must decide in each passage whether or not "heart" in the target language carries the same meaning as "heart" does in the context of the passage being translated.

In translation it is often necessary to restructure comparatives and superlatives. For instance, "You have given me joy. That joy surpasses the joy they have from their grain and wine." In some cases it will be essential to make explicit the connection between joy and the grain and wine; for example, "The joy people have from harvesting their grain and drinking their wine." In areas where grain and wine are not found, the major crop will normally substitute for grain, or one may simply say "the harvest." And if wine is unknown, it may in this context be possible to allow the local crop to represent both grain and wine as a single symbol of wealth; otherwise, one may translate **wine** as "favorite drink."

4.8　　　　RSV　　　　　　　　　　　　　　　　TEV

In peace I will both lie down and sleep; 　for thou alone, O LORD, makest me dwell in safety.	When I lie down, I go to sleep in peace; 　you alone, O LORD, keep me perfectly safe.

---

[2]The Qumran Hebrew manuscript, and the Septuagint, Syriac, and Vulgate, add "and olive oil" after "grain and wine." Most commentators and translators reject this as a scribal addition.

The psalmist concludes with a prayer of confidence in the Lord's power to protect him from all attacks: "As soon as I lie down, I go to sleep in peace (or, I fall asleep peacefully)," that is, with no fear of possible dangers during the night. Or **peace** may mean safety, security; so NJV "Safe and sound I lie down . . . ."

Alone may refer to the psalmist himself, as the Septuagint translates: "you have made me dwell alone . . . ." The idea then is that God keeps him far from his enemies, and they cannot hurt him (so Delitzsch, Briggs, Kirkpatrick). NJV translates "for You alone, O LORD, keep me secure" but provides an alternative in the footnote: "for You, O LORD, keep me alone and secure." A translator should feel free to follow either interpretation of the Hebrew text; the meaning represented by RSV and TEV seems preferable.

Psalm 5

This psalm is a lament by an individual who feels oppressed and persecuted by his enemies. He begins with a prayer to the Lord for help (verses 1-3), followed by a statement of God's displeasure with wrongdoers (verses 4-6), by which the psalmist implies that he is not proud, wicked, violent, and deceitful, as his enemies are. He then expresses his confidence in God's great love and prays for his guidance (verses 7-8); he prays for the destruction of his enemies (verses 9-10) and ends the psalm with a prayer for God's protection and his blessings on all who love him (verses 11-12).

HEADING: "**A Prayer for Protection.**" Other headings are: "Morning prayer"; "Beginning the day with God"; "Prayer for divine help." The TEV heading must often be changed to a full clause; for example, "The psalmist asks God to protect him" or "The psalmist prays that God will take care of him."

<u>Hebrew title</u>: **To the choirmaster: for the flutes. A Psalm of David** (TEV "**A psalm by David**").

The musical direction given **To the choirmaster** (see comments on the Hebrew title of Psalm 4) tells him to use **flutes** in the accompaniment of this psalm. Only here does this Hebrew word appear in the Old Testament, and it may mean "wind instruments" in general or "flutes" in particular. NJV, which transliterates the Hebrew term, says that the meaning of the word is uncertain.

In many languages the term **choirmaster** must be rendered by means of a descriptive phrase; for example, "The one who leads when people sing" or "The leader of the singers."

<u>**5.1**</u>

RSV	TEV

Give ear to my words, O LORD;
   give heed to my groaning.
	Listen to my words, O LORD,
	   and hear my sighs.

Lines <u>a</u> and <u>b</u> of verse 1 express essentially the same meaning. However, **my groaning** is a characteristic intensification of **my words** in line <u>a</u>. Furthermore, in Hebrew the syntactic order of the two lines is reversed and therefore chiastic—a device the psalmist uses to heighten the impact of the verse as a unit. Line <u>a</u> of verse 2 continues with the same word order as line <u>b</u> of verse 1, providing a transition through syntactic repetition. Translators must find the devices in their own languages which signal this kind of intensification. Simply following the English or Hebrew will not necessarily result in a good and accurate translation. In English we may try to represent this effect of the parallelism by saying, for example, "Listen to what I am saying, O LORD; don't you hear how I am crying out each word?" or "LORD, hear what I am saying to you; I am even calling out in tears."

Give ear is a somewhat literal translation of a Hebrew request, **"Listen"** (TEV).

The psalmist's **words** refer to his prayers to Yahweh, and **groaning** in line b indicates that he prays because he is suffering and in distress. The noun translated **groaning** appears only here and in 39.3 (RSV "mused"). It is related to the verb translated "meditate" in 1.2, and some take the noun here to mean "meditation" (so NEB "inmost thoughts"), which does not fit the context as well.

5.2-3	RSV		TEV
2	Hearken to the sound of my cry, my King and my God, for to thee do I pray.	2	Listen to my cry for help, my God and king!
3	O LORD, in the morning thou dost hear my voice; in the morning I prepare a sacrifice for thee, and watch.	3	I pray to you, O LORD; you hear my voice in the morning; at sunrise I offer my prayer*g* and wait for your answer.

g prayer; *or* sacrifice.

Hearken translates another Hebrew verb meaning "listen, pay attention."

In this psalm God is addressed as **my King**, a common designation for God in prayer (see 84.3). TEV has reversed the order, **"my God and king,"** so as to avoid the possibility that the person who hears the text being read may misunderstand that a human being is being addressed, **my King**, as well as **my God**. If the translator follows either RSV, **my King and my God**, or TEV, **"my God and king,"** the phrase may be misunderstood to mean two different persons. In such a case the expression may be recast in the form of a relative clause; for example, "my God, who is my king."

There is a difference of opinion about the third line of verse 2: some connect it with what precedes (RSV, AT, NAB, SPCL); others connect it with what follows (TEV, NEB, NJB, FRCL). The meaning is not greatly affected by the difference, and a translator should feel free to choose either one. In the Masoretic text division of verses, **O LORD** is at the beginning of verse 3. For better balance of lines, TEV places the verse number 3 at the beginning of the following line (see NJB and NAB, which do not).

In verse 3 the Hebrew word for **morning** is used twice; TEV uses the synonyms "morning" and "sunrise" for greater poetic effect.

Languages divide time in very different ways, and it is often necessary to decide if the time referred to is before sunrise, during sunrise, or immediately following sunrise. The essential feature here is early morning daylight and corresponds in time to what is known to Muslims as *salat al fajar*, which is the first and earliest of the five daily prayers.

The choice between TEV **"offer my prayer"** and RSV **prepare a sacrifice** (see TEV footnote) depends on the exegesis of the Hebrew verb, which means "to put in order, to arrange" (see TOB "I get everything ready for you"). It is disputed whether it refers to prayer (Delitzsch, Briggs, Kirkpatrick; AT, Mft, NAB, NIV, NJV) or to a sacrifice (Weiser, Oesterley, Taylor, Toombs; RSV, NEB, ZÜR). NJB and SPCL have "I lay my case before you," and FRCL "I prepare myself to be received by you, and I wait."

Some languages render "**prayer**" as "speaking to God." Since the exegetical opinion is quite divided between "prayer" and "sacrifice," it is recommended that there be a note for the meaning not employed in the text.

And watch is a literal translation of the Hebrew; in the context of prayer it means "and wait for your answer" (Kirkpatrick); Knox has "await thy pleasure."

5.4	RSV	TEV
	For thou art not a God who delights in wickedness; evil may not sojourn with thee.	You are not a God who is pleased with wrongdoing; you allow no evil in your presence.

Thou art not a God: instead of the negative form, it may be better to use a positive expression such as "you are a God who does not like (or, who hates) wickedness." The verb translated **delights** is from the same root as the noun "(his) delight" in 1.2. The translation can be "is happy with, takes pleasure in."

In describing God's holy nature, the psalmist contrasts God's nature with the abstract qualities **wickedness** and **evil**, meaning wicked and evil people. In some languages it may be better to make this explicit and say ". . . who is not happy with wicked people."

Sojourn is a translation of the verb meaning "to dwell, stay, live." Briggs translates "evil cannot be Thy guest"; NEB "evil can be no guest of thine" (and in the footnote "an evil man cannot be thy guest"). FRCL has "an evildoer is not welcome in your house," and NJB "no sinner can be your guest."

Many languages have special terms expressing temporary hospitality offered to a guest. Such an expression will render the Hebrew verb used here. However if an abstract such as **evil** can not be personified, it may be necessary to say, for example, "evil people can never receive hospitality from you" or "you do not give hospitality to evil men."

5.5-6	RSV	TEV
5	The boastful may not stand before thy eyes; thou hatest all evildoers.	5 You cannot stand the sight of proud men; you hate all wicked people.
6	Thou destroyest those who speak lies; the LORD abhors bloodthirsty and deceitful men.	6 You destroy all liars and despise violent, deceitful men.

Yahweh's judgment on sinners is described in four different ways: (1) they **may not stand**, or "cannot remain," in his presence (literally "cannot stand before your eyes"). Care should be taken in translating this expression, so as not to give the impression that the psalmist is talking about not going to heaven. The expression fits well with the idea of God as king (verse 2), who does not allow criminals and lawbreakers to come into his presence (see 101.7). So the translation can be "You do not allow proud people to come into your presence." The main idea here is that God will not listen to their prayers as they come into the Temple to worship him; see the next verse and 15.1-5. The expression **stand before thy eyes** refers to entering God's holy presence and is rendered in some languages as "enter where you are" or "come near to you."

(2) The Lord "hates" them, (3) "destroys" them, and (4) **abhors** them. This is not simply descriptive; it is the psalmist's way of calling down God's anger and punishment on his enemies. All these verbs denote strong dislike, revulsion, and hatred, and are part of the very human vocabulary that the Old Testament writers use of God's attitude toward sin.

In line **b** of verse 6, **the LORD** is referred to in the third person; TEV keeps the second person, which is used in verses 4-6a.

The sinners are described as **boastful**, **evildoers**, **those who speak lies**, **bloodthirsty**, and **deceitful**. **Bloodthirsty** translates what is literally "man of bloods," which may be translated as "the violent" (NJB) or "murderous" (NJV). In translation **bloodthirsty** or "murderous" must sometimes be rendered, for example, "people who want in their hearts to kill others" or "people who go about killing others." The word translated **deceitful** may mean "traitors" (NEB); SPCL translates "traitors and assassins," and another possible version is "murderous and treacherous men."

5.7	RSV	TEV

But I through the abundance of thy steadfast love will enter thy house, I will worship toward thy holy temple in the fear of thee.	But because of your great love I can come into your house; I can worship in your holy Temple and bow down to you in reverence.

The Hebrew of verse 7 has two lines arranged in chiastic order, reflected in the clause order of both RSV and TEV. Line **b** reverses the order of line **a**, and in this way worship in the Temple is bracketed by **steadfast love** in line **a** and **fear of thee** in line **b**. Translators may not be able to retain this clause order. If chiastic arrangement of lines is not good poetic style, it should not be kept.

The psalmist is confident of God's great love; the word RSV translates **steadfast love** is the Hebrew word *chesed*, which includes the idea of love and devotion, and faithfulness to a promise or a covenant. When used to describe God its emphasis is on God's faithfulness to his covenant with his people, his promise to be their God always, and to protect them and take care of them. It describes his special feeling for his people. When the word is used of God, RSV nearly always translates **steadfast love**; one notable exception in the Psalms is in 23.6a, where RSV has "mercy" (and see footnote). NJV, NEB, and SPCL here are like TEV, "love"; others use "faithfulness," "faithful love" (NJB), or "loyalty." When the Hebrew word is used of people, RSV prefers "kindness" (see 101.1).

In most languages it is difficult to find a single term to express the various components contained in the Hebrew term translated **steadfast love**. Moreover, phrases which attempt to express these elements fully become awkward and grammatically or stylistically unwieldy. Therefore it may be best to seek an expression which combines the care or love of a superior for an inferior, and which includes faithfulness or loyalty; for example, "because you love me like a father loves a child," "because you are always faithful in your love," "because you love me faithfully," or "because you love me always."

God's **house** is the same as his **holy temple** in the next line; both refer to the Temple in Jerusalem. The Hebrew preposition translated by RSV **toward** (also NEB) seems to place the worshiper outside the Temple; yet in the previous line he affirms he can enter it. Consequently some translate "before" (NJB, Mft); others "at" (NAB, NJV); FRCL has "facing," and Oesterley translates "in." The word translated **temple** can be taken in the larger sense of the whole complex of the Temple area, with all its buildings and courtyards, or in the more restricted sense of the main sanctuary, the Holy Place. The FRCL footnote says that "**your house**" means the whole Temple area, with all its courts and buildings, while "**your holy Temple**" means the sanctuary proper, where only priests could enter. This may well be correct, and a translator may prefer to express this meaning: "I will enter your Temple and bow toward the (or, your) sanctuary."

In many languages the combination of **thy house** and **thy holy temple** will be understood as two distinct places. In such cases it may be necessary therefore to translate "I can come to you; and I can worship in your holy Temple." In languages which translate temple as "place of worship," one may say "I will come to your place of worship; and I can worship you there." **Holy** is often rendered by words meaning "pure," "clear," or "unblemished." Since the central meaning of an object which is "holy" is "dedicated to God," it is sometimes possible to express this quality as simply "God's Temple," or in the present context, "in the Temple which belongs to you" or "in the Temple where you are worshiped."

In order to balance the lines, TEV supplies in line d the verb **"bow down"** as a parallel to **"worship"** in line c.

Will enter . . . will worship: RSV translates these verbs as a declaration of (future) fact; TEV, NEB, and NJB translate as a possibility, that is, the psalmist's situation is such that he is able at any time to enter Yahweh's presence.

"In reverence" (TEV) translates what is literally **fear** (see 2.11). Here the worshiper is a devout Hebrew, and so "reverence" (also NJB) or "awe" (NEB) seems more appropriate. Weiser defines "the fear of God" thus: "that clear-sighted awareness of the essential difference between the majesty of God and human inadequacy, which in the Old Testament excludes any kind of gross familiarity and self-assurance in man's intercourse with God."

5.8   RSV   TEV

Lead me, O LORD, in thy righteousness
because of my enemies;
make thy way straight before
me.

LORD, I have so many enemies!
Lead me to do your will;
make your way plain for me to
follow.

The psalmist prays for Yahweh's leadership, especially needed because of his **enemies**; the Hebrew word used here occurs also in 27.11; 54.7; 56.2; 59.10.

In order to make the verse flow more smoothly, TEV places the psalmist's statement about his enemies first, and then the double petition. So SPCL, "O Lord, because of my enemies, lead me . . . take me . . . ."

"**To do your will**" (TEV) translates what is literally **in thy righteousness**. The Hebrew word *tsedaqah* stands for the expression of God's will for his people as found in the Torah, the Law of Moses. It is God's will that they obey his laws and follow his ways; consequently **thy righteousness** is synonymous with **thy way** in line **c**. If **thy righteousness** is taken as describing the character of God, then verse 8 can sometimes be rendered "Lord, you who are straight, lead me because I have many enemies."

Make . . . straight translates a verb meaning "to be straight, smooth, right"; here it is a metaphor for making it possible for the psalmist easily to follow Yahweh's guidance, obey Yahweh's will for him, which is what **thy way** means. So FRCL translates "smooth out in front of me the way that you call me to follow." If the metaphor of **way** needs to be abandoned, the translation can be "make it easy for me to do what you want."

5.9   RSV   TEV

For there is no truth in their
mouth;
their heart is destruction,
their throat is an open sepulchre,
they flatter with their tongue.

What my enemies say can never
be trusted;
they only want to destroy.
Their words are flattering and
smooth,
but full of deadly deceit.

In verses 9-10 the psalmist describes his enemies and asks God to punish them. This section picks the subject up from verse 6, so it is necessary to make explicit the subject of the verbs, as TEV, "my enemies," has done. They are liars (line **a**); literally "there is no firmness (or, straightness) in their mouth." The idea is more that of not being trustworthy or dependable than that of not being truthful. NEB "there is no trusting what they say"; NJB "not a word from their lips can be trusted." Line **b** is literally "their inward parts (are) destruction," meaning that their desires, thoughts, and wishes are to destroy.[1] The implied object of their **destruction** is not things but people. They are cruel and vindictive.

Continuing his use of concrete language, the psalmist speaks of **their throat** (line c) and **their tongue** (line d). TEV has taken the two to refer to the same thing, that is, speech, and for greater effect has reversed lines c and d. **"Their words are flattering and smooth"** translates "they make smooth their tongues," which is a picture of insincere, pious, unctuous flattery.

Before giving up the poetic images of **mouth**, **heart**, **throat**, and **tongue**, the translator should make certain that these are unsatisfactory, for whatever reason. In some languages it will be more natural to say, for example, "my enemies' tongues do not speak the truth, in their livers they want to destroy people, their stomachs are full of deadly deceit, and they flatter people with their lips."

The translator may follow the lead of TEV and reverse lines c and d, in which case "flattering words" is instrumental and **"deadly deceit"** is a final consequence.

"Full of deadly deceit" translates the figure **an open sepulchre**, which means the constant threat of violence and death. Most English translations retain the metaphor "their throat is an open grave" (NJV), but it is doubtful that this means anything to most readers. **"Deadly deceit"** may be recast in some languages as "to lead people to the grave by speaking deceitful words" or "they deceive people and cause them to die."

This verse is cited in Romans 3.13.

<u>5.10</u> RSV	TEV

Make them bear their guilt, O God;
   let them fall by their own counsels;
because of their many transgressions cast them out,
   for they have rebelled against thee.
	Condemn and punish them, O God;
	   may their own plots cause their ruin.
	Drive them out of your presence because of their many sins
	   and their rebellion against you.

The prayer is that God will demonstrate the guilt of the psalmist's enemies by punishing them. The Hebrew verb in line a means "hold guilty, declare guilty." Dahood has "Punish them," NEB "Bring ruin on them," AT and NJV "Condemn them." TEV expresses the idea of their guilt and punishment by **"Condemn and punish them."** In some languages where the implied legal procedure is lacking, it may be necessary to say, for example, "God, declare my enemies guilty and punish them," or one may use a statement of cause and result, "because my enemies are guilty, punish them."

The next request is that they be brought to ruin by their own evil plans (see 2 Sam 15.31). NJB has "make their intrigues their own downfall"; NEB and NJV "let

---

[1]Instead of "destruction" the Septuagint has "emptiness, vanity"; this seems to be the basis of NEB "they are nothing but wind."

them fall by their own devices." Requests in English expressed with "may" or "let" must often be recast in translation; for example, "God, cause their own plots to ruin them." In some languages such commands or requests may also be restructured as intensive future statements: "Their own plots will certainly cause their ruin."

The psalmist speaks further of their **"many sins"** (TEV) or **many transgressions**, and of their **"rebellion"** (TEV), and prays to God, **cast them out**, which may refer to punishment in this life or else to the final condemnation and punishment on Judgment Day (see 1.5).

Counsels refers here to evil plans aimed at the destruction of someone. In translation it is often possible to say "plans made to harm others" or "decisions which aim to deceive people."

5.11

RSV	TEV
But let all who take refuge in thee rejoice, let them ever sing for joy; and do thou defend them, that those who love thy name may exult in thee.	But all who find safety in you will rejoice; they can always sing for joy. Protect those who love you; because of you they are truly happy.

In the closing strophe (verses 11-12) the psalmist turns his thoughts to the happiness and security enjoyed by those who love and obey Yahweh. The first two lines of verse 11 may be understood either as a petition for God's people (RSV) or as a description of them (TEV). It seems better to take these two lines as a prayer on behalf of God's people: "may all who find safety in you rejoice."

Three verbs are used to describe their joy: **rejoice** (line a), **sing for joy** (line b), and **exult** (line d). These all refer to happiness, or joy, which is expressed openly by means of words, gestures, and song.

The expression **take refuge** in this context is said to be "in you" and therefore sometimes requires recasting. In many languages it is more common to speak of God as the one who protects and the people as the ones he protects; for example, "Rejoice, you people whom God protects." **Let them ever sing for joy** can be rendered in many languages as a direct imperative, "Always sing for joy," "Sing joyfully at all times," or as in some languages, "Sing always with cool hearts."

Defend may be understood as a request (TEV, RSV, and most other translations) or as a declaration, "you defend" (so NJB "You shelter them, they rejoice in you"). The verb means literally to cover, to screen, in the sense of protecting.

As is evident, line d may relate to line c as a result (RSV) or as a cause (TEV). If in line c **defend** is understood as an imperative, it seems better to take line d as result, as do most translations (RSV, NEB, NAB, AT); if **defend** is taken as an indicative ("you defend"), it seems preferable to understand line d as a statement (NJB).

"Those who love you" (TEV) is literally **those who love thy name**. As often in the Old Testament, **name** stands for the person as revealed by his character and actions; it is his reputation. To "love the name of God" may be misunderstood, and it seems better in a dynamic equivalence to use the personal pronoun, or the name "God" itself. In some languages the term for love used as love for one's family is often not usable in referring to love for another person or for God. Some languages express such love idiomatically; for example, "their hearts are warm for God" or "they hold God in their hearts."

The prepositional phrase **in thee** (in **exult in thee**) means "because of you," that is, "because of what you have done on their behalf."

5.12	RSV	TEV

RSV	TEV
For thou dost bless the righteous, O LORD; thou dost cover him with favor as with a shield.	You bless those who obey you, LORD; your love protects them like a shield.

For **bless** see "blessing" in 3.8.

Here **the righteous** (one, singular) is a collective term for all who obey Yahweh's commandments. For this reason TEV translates with a plural phrase, **"those who obey you."**

The parallelism of verse 12 suggests a movement from the general statement of blessing in line a to the more picturable covering of someone with a shield in line b. The idea may be rendered in English as "You bless those who obey you, LORD; you go so far as to shield them from their enemies" or ". . . what is more, you protect them from those who would hurt them."

The Lord's **"love"** (TEV) or **favor** translates a word meaning "kindness."

In languages where it is unnatural to speak of love protecting someone, it is necessary to recast this to make God the actor, and express love or kindness as the manner in which God protects; for example, "you lovingly protect them like a shield" or "you love them, and so you protect them like a shield." **As with a shield** is elliptical and in some languages requires completing; for example, "you protect them like a shield protects a warrior."

The word for **shield** here is different from the one used in 3.3; here it is a large shield used to protect the whole body.

Psalm 6

This psalm is a lament by an individual who is sick and near death (verses 4-5); he also has enemies who add to his troubles (verses 8-10). The psalm is divided into four strophes: (1) a complaint to the Lord (verses 1-3) followed by (2) a plea to God to save the psalmist from death (verses 4-5); (3) after describing his complete misery (verses 6-7), (4) the writer affirms his faith in God's help, and at the same time denounces his enemies (verses 8-10).

HEADING: "**A Prayer for Help in Time of Trouble**" (TEV); "A prayer for relief from foes"; "Prayer in time of distress"; "The cry of a sick man." In translation it may be necessary to recast the TEV heading to say, for example, "The psalmist asks God to help him" or "The psalmist prays that God will rescue him from evil people."

Hebrew Title: **To the choirmaster: with stringed instruments; according to The Sheminith. A Psalm of David.**

The instruction given **To the choirmaster** is the same as in Psalm 5, with the additional phrase **according to The Sheminith** (also in Psa 12). The Hebrew word means "eighth," and it has been understood by some scholars to mean an eight-stringed instrument (so TOB) or else a deep tone (vocal or instrumental), that is, an octave lower. So FRCL translates "accompaniment at a (lower) octave." But Oesterley points out that the Hebrews had no eight-toned scale, and confesses ignorance of the meaning of the word. The same Hebrew word is used in 1 Chronicles 15.21, where six Levites are directed to **lead with lyres according to the Sheminith**; TEV translates "to play the low-pitched harps." If the translator follows the Hebrew title, it may be necessary to recast it slightly to use a verbal phrase; for instance, "A religious song which David wrote."

6.1

RSV	TEV
O LORD, rebuke me not in thy anger, nor chasten me in thy wrath.	LORD, don't be angry and rebuke me! Don't punish me in your anger!

In two parallel lines the psalmist prays to the Lord not to **rebuke** him and not to **chasten** him—two common verbs, which in this context mean practically the same thing. The psalmist repeats his request; line b is not an additional request, as RSV **nor** implies. Also synonymous are the two phrases **in thy anger** and **in thy wrath**, as in 2.5 (see also 38.1). The psalmist prays like this because he believes that his sickness is the result of God's anger with him for his sins.

Psalm 6

his psalm is a lament by an individual who is sick and near death (verses 4-5);
has enemies who add to his troubles (verses 8-10). The psalm is divided into
·ophes: (1) a complaint to the Lord (verses 1-3) followed by (2) a plea to God
the psalmist from death (verses 4-5); (3) after describing his complete misery
6-7), (4) the writer affirms his faith in God's help, and at the same time
·ces his enemies (verses 8-10).

IEADING: "A Prayer for Help in Time of Trouble" (TEV); "A prayer for relief
·es"; "Prayer in time of distress"; "The cry of a sick man." In translation it
necessary to recast the TEV heading to say, for example, "The psalmist asks
help him" or "The psalmist prays that God will rescue him from evil people."

v Title: **To the choirmaster: with stringed instruments; according to The
·ith. A Psalm of David.**

·he instruction given **To the choirmaster** is the same as in Psalm 5, with the
·nal phrase **according to The Sheminith** (also in Psa 12). The Hebrew word
"eighth," and it has been understood by some scholars to mean an eight--
·d instrument (so TOB) or else a deep tone (vocal or instrumental), that is, an
·lower. So FRCL translates "accompaniment at a (lower) octave." But Oesterley
·out that the Hebrews had no eight-toned scale, and confesses ignorance of the
·g of the word. The same Hebrew word is used in 1 Chronicles 15.21, where
·ites are directed to **lead with lyres according to the Sheminith**; TEV translates
·y the low-pitched harps." If the translator follows the Hebrew title, it may be
·ry to recast it slightly to use a verbal phrase; for instance, "A religious song
·David wrote."

RSV	TEV
· LORD, rebuke me not in thy anger, nor chasten me in thy wrath.	LORD, don't be angry and rebuke me! Don't punish me in your anger!

· two parallel lines the psalmist prays to the Lord not to **rebuke** him and not
·**ten** him—two common verbs, which in this context mean practically the same
·he psalmist repeats his request; line **b** is not an additional request, as RSV **nor**
·. Also synonymous are the two phrases **in thy anger** and **in thy wrath**, as in
·e also 38.1). The psalmist prays like this because he believes that his sickness
·esult of God's anger with him for his sins.

58

and wishes are to destroy.[1] The implied object of their **destruction** is not things but people. They are cruel and vindictive.

Continuing his use of concrete language, the psalmist speaks of **their throat** (line c) and **their tongue** (line d). TEV has taken the two to refer to the same thing, that is, speech, and for greater effect has reversed lines c and d. **"Their words are flattering and smooth"** translates "they make smooth their tongues," which is a picture of insincere, pious, unctuous flattery.

Before giving up the poetic images of **mouth**, **heart**, **throat**, and **tongue**, the translator should make certain that these are unsatisfactory, for whatever reason. In some languages it will be more natural to say, for example, "my enemies' tongues do not speak the truth, in their livers they want to destroy people, their stomachs are full of deadly deceit, and they flatter people with their lips."

The translator may follow the lead of TEV and reverse lines c and d, in which case "flattering words" is instrumental and **"deadly deceit"** is a final consequence.

"Full of deadly deceit" translates the figure **an open sepulchre**, which means the constant threat of violence and death. Most English translations retain the metaphor "their throat is an open grave" (NJV), but it is doubtful that this means anything to most readers. **"Deadly deceit"** may be recast in some languages as "to lead people to the grave by speaking deceitful words" or "they deceive people and cause them to die."

This verse is cited in Romans 3.13.

5.10 RSV	TEV
Make them bear their guilt, O God; let them fall by their own counsels; because of their many transgressions cast them out, for they have rebelled against thee.	Condemn and punish them, O God; may their own plots cause their ruin. Drive them out of your presence because of their many sins and their rebellion against you.

The prayer is that God will demonstrate the guilt of the psalmist's enemies by punishing them. The Hebrew verb in line a means "hold guilty, declare guilty." Dahood has "Punish them," NEB "Bring ruin on them," AT and NJV "Condemn them." TEV expresses the idea of their guilt and punishment by "**Condemn and punish them.**" In some languages where the implied legal procedure is lacking, it may be necessary to say, for example, "God, declare my enemies guilty and punish them," or one may use a statement of cause and result, "because my enemies are guilty, punish them."

The next request is that they be brought to ruin by their own evil plans (see 2 Sam 15.31). NJB has "make their intrigues their own downfall"; NEB and NJV "let

---

[1]Instead of "destruction" the Septuagint has "emptiness, vanity"; this seems to be the basis of NEB "they are nothing but wind."

55

them fall by their own devices." Requests in English expressed with "may" or "let" must often be recast in translation; for example, "God, cause their own plots to ruin them." In some languages such commands or requests may also be restructured as intensive future statements: "Their own plots will certainly cause their ruin."

The psalmist speaks further of their **"many sins"** (TEV) or **many transgressions**, and of their **"rebellion"** (TEV), and prays to God, **cast them out**, which may refer to punishment in this life or else to the final condemnation and punishment on Judgment Day (see 1.5).

Counsels refers here to evil plans aimed at the destruction of someone. In translation it is often possible to say "plans made to harm others" or "decisions which aim to deceive people."

5.11   RSV   TEV

> But let all who take refuge in thee
>   rejoice,
>   let them ever sing for joy;
> and do thou defend them,
>   that those who love thy name
>   may exult in thee.

> But all who find safety in you will
>   rejoice;
>   they can always sing for joy.
> Protect those who love you;
>   because of you they are truly
>   happy.

In the closing strophe (verses 11-12) the psalmist turns his thoughts to the happiness and security enjoyed by those who love and obey Yahweh. The first two lines of verse 11 may be understood either as a petition for God's people (RSV) or as a description of them (TEV). It seems better to take these two lines as a prayer on behalf of God's people: "may all who find safety in you rejoice."

Three verbs are used to describe their joy: **rejoice** (line a), **sing for joy** (line b), and **exult** (line d). These all refer to happiness, or joy, which is expressed openly by means of words, gestures, and song.

The expression **take refuge** in this context is said to be "in you" and therefore sometimes requires recasting. In many languages it is more common to speak of God as the one who protects and the people as the ones he protects; for example, "Rejoice, you people whom God protects." **Let them ever sing for joy** can be rendered in many languages as a direct imperative, "Always sing for joy," "Sing joyfully at all times," or as in some languages, "Sing always with cool hearts."

Defend may be understood as a request (TEV, RSV, and most other translations) or as a declaration, "you defend" (so NJB "You shelter them, they rejoice in you"). The verb means literally to cover, to screen, in the sense of protecting.

As is evident, line d may relate to line c as a result (RSV) or as a cause (TEV). If in line c **defend** is understood as an imperative, it seems better to take line d as result, as do most translations (RSV, NEB, NAB, AT); if **defend** is taken as an indicative ("you defend"), it seems preferable to understand line d as a statement (NJB).

"Those who love you" (TEV) is literally **those who love thy name**. As often in the Old Testament, **name** stands for the person as revealed by his character and actions; it is his reputation. To "love the name of God" may be misunderstood, and it seems better in a dynamic equivalence to use the personal pronoun, or the name "God" itself. In some languages the term for love used as love for one's family is

often not usable in referring to love for another person o
express such love idiomatically; for example, "their hea
"they hold God in their hearts."

The prepositional phrase **in thee** (in **exult in thee**
that is, "because of what you have done on their behalf

5.12   RSV

> For thou dost bless the righteous,
>   O LORD;
>   thou dost cover him with favor
>   as with a shield.

> You bl
>   Lo
> your
>   sh

For **bless** see "blessing" in 3.8.

Here **the righteous** (one, singular) is a collective
weh's commandments. For this reason TEV translates w
who obey you."

The parallelism of verse 12 suggests a movement
of blessing in line a to the more picturable covering of so
b. The idea may be rendered in English as "You bless t
you go so far as to shield them from their enemies"
protect them from those who would hurt them."

The Lord's **"love"** (TEV) or **favor** translates a wor

In languages where it is unnatural to speak of lov
necessary to recast this to make God the actor, and exp
manner in which God protects; for example, "you lovingl
or "you love them, and so you protect them like a s
elliptical and in some languages requires completing; for
like a shield protects a warrior."

The word for **shield** here is different from the one
shield used to protect the whole body.

he als
four s
to sav
(verse
denou

from
may b
God t

Hebre
Shem

additi
mean
string
octave
points
mean
six Le
"to pl
neces
which

6.1

to cha
thing.
impli
2.5 (s
is the

In this verse line <u>b</u> follows line <u>a</u> syntactically and semantically. Line <u>b</u> functions only to emphasize, and introduces nothing more concrete or picturable than line <u>a</u>. Therefore in translation, in some languages the closeness of the meaning of the two lines may appear as unwarranted repetition. In such cases the language may offer more effective means of emphasis than repetition, and the translator may be best advised to use the devices of the language rather than merely copy the two lines, particularly in languages in which there may not be synonyms such as **rebuke** and **chasten**, **anger** and **wrath**.

Rebuke: the Hebrew verb in this context means more than a verbal rebuke or censure; it is better to translate "condemn" (NEB, FRCL) or, as a closer parallel to the next line, "chastise." And in line <u>b</u> the verb for **chasten** has the sense of "discipline, correct"; here "punish" is the best translation.

In line <u>a</u> TEV has two commands: "**be angry**" and "**rebuke**." RSV on the other hand has one command: **rebuke**, and **in thy anger** is a phrase of manner. In order to represent the psalmist as assuming the anger of God as background for the pleas, it may be better to say "LORD, in spite of your anger, do not rebuke me" or "Although you are angry, LORD, do not rebuke me" (see FRCL).

6.2-3	RSV	TEV
2	Be gracious to me, O LORD, for I am languishing; O LORD, heal me, for my bones are troubled.	2 I am worn out, O LORD; have pity on me! Give me strength; I am completely exhausted
3	My soul also is sorely troubled. But thou, O LORD—how long?	3 and my whole being is deeply troubled. How long, O LORD, will you wait to help me?

In these two verses the psalmist describes the terrible effects of his illness: (1) he is **languishing** (NEB "I am weak"; NJB "I am fading away"); (2) he is also "**completely exhausted**" (TEV), which translates what is literally "my bones are disturbed" (or "terrified," which is what the word means in 2.5, "he terrifies them"). Some translations have the idea of fright: NJV "my bones shake with terror." The idea of fear, though possible, does not fit the context as well as that of exhaustion brought on by a wasting illness (see Mft "my health is broken"; FRCL "I have no more resistance").

Line <u>b</u> of this verse moves the image of exhaustion to the figurative level, <u>bones</u> <u>are troubled</u>. The translator must ask if the heightening effect is maintained in the language by this kind of movement. The opposite may be true, and if that is the case, the translator should experiment by reversing the order of the lines.

The translator will note that in RSV the plea precedes the reason in lines <u>a</u> and <u>b</u>, whereas in TEV the reason comes before the plea in line <u>a</u> and follows it in line <u>b</u>. However, whether or not the translator will maintain the parallelism or modify it depends upon the total effect of the message on the reader. In some languages the idea of being "**worn out**" is expressed as "my blood is like water" or "my strength does not hold me." The relation of reason to request may need to be explicit; for example, "Because I am weak, LORD, have pity on me." Many languages prefer figurative expressions in speaking of physical states, just as Hebrew does in "my bones are troubled." In English one may say "I am bone tired."

Bones (verse 2b) and **soul** (verse 3a) are the psalmist's way of referring to himself in terms of his physical and his emotional condition. It is possible in some languages to speak of the combined physical and emotional state in figurative terms—for example, "blood and spirit"—while in others it is necessary to say "my body and I," or, for example, "my body has become loose" or "I swallow trouble."

So the psalmist pleads with God: (1) **be gracious to me** (see 4.1), and (2) **heal me**. The Hebrew verb for **heal** in verse 2b is better translated as "restore (me) to health," "cure (me)." In some languages there are several verbs meaning "heal," depending on the part of the body which is affected. In such cases one must try to employ a generic term or say, as in TEV, "make me strong" or, since the meaning is to restore one to health, "make me healthy again."

Since verse 3a goes so closely with the last part of verse 2b, TEV, NEB, NJB, and others join it directly to verse 2 instead of making it a separate sentence, as RSV does. That is, line a of verse 3 should be translated as if it were line c of verse 2. Here the image of being exhausted is extended from the **bones** to the *nefesh*, the **soul**, but the psalmist has reversed the word order in the Hebrew to provide still greater extension of the image of exhaustion.

In a burst of anguish the psalmist cries **how long**, that is, how long will Yahweh wait before answering his prayer for healing? This indicates that often he had asked God to heal him, but his prayers had not been answered. **How long** should not be translated as a demand for a specific time reply, for the intent of the statement is to complain that the delay has been too long. In some languages this expression is best stated as a negative command, "Do not delay long, LORD" or "Do not wait too long, LORD."

TEV makes a complete sentence of verse 3b by supplying a verb; but instead of "to help," it may be better to use the specific verb "to heal."

6.4	RSV		TEV
	Turn, O LORD, save my life; deliver me for the sake of thy steadfast love.		Come and save me, LORD; in your mercy rescue me from death.

In this strophe (verses 4-5) the psalmist renews his pleas, asking God to save him from imminent death. **Turn** in the Hebrew text can mean either to turn toward the psalmist (TEV; see NEB "Turn back") or else to change one's attitude, which seems to be what RSV means. The verb is often used to denote a change of mind, repentance. NJB translates "relent," and GECL "quit being angry." The idea of requesting someone to come and help may in some languages be expressed as "give ear to me" or "have eye for me." In the sense of a change of mind or attitude, one may sometimes say "walk on a different road" or "follow a new path."

Save and **deliver** are synonyms. **My life** translates "my *nefesh*" (see 3.2), and the plea **save my life** means "save me from dying," "don't let me die"; so TEV in line b has **"rescue me from death,"** which prepares the way for the reference to "the world of the dead" in verse 5.

Deliver me in line b̲, which is parallel to **save my life** in line a̲, is more specific due to its context, **for the sake of thy steadfast love**. In this sense line b̲ shows intensification. It may be rendered, for example, "even more, deliver me . . ." or "more than that, deliver me . . . ."

Some languages have terms for **save** which combine the ideas of "save" and "restore." Others are more limited in their area of meaning. Some languages express **save** as "to cause to see life" or "to make live."

For **steadfast love** see 5.7. The sense of **for the sake of** is better expressed by "on account of" or "because." Yahweh's **steadfast love** is the ground, or basis, for the psalmist's prayer. In some translations it may be better to place it first, as follows: "Because you love me, LORD, save me!" or "You love me, LORD, so save me!"

6.5 RSV	TEV
For in death there is no remembrance of thee; in Sheol who can give thee praise?	In the world of the dead you are not remembered; no one can praise you there.

The parallelism in verse 5 is based on the general image of death in the first clause, which becomes the concrete and specific image of death, called **Sheol**, in the second clause. As will be seen in other verses, line a̲ is a statement and line b̲ is a rhetorical question, the equivalent of a strong negative statement, as in TEV **"no one can praise you there."**

This verse reflects the belief that in Sheol, the world of the dead, a person was cut off from God. This was a common belief at that time and held the greatest terror for the devout Israelite. Sheol was the destiny of all who died, the good and bad alike, Israelites and Gentiles as well. It was a dark, dusty, silent abyss in the depths of the earth, where there was no vitality, no joy, no life, but only a pale, shadowy, unreal existence, apart from God. For statements about Sheol see Numbers 16.30-32; Job 3.17-19; Psalms 30.9; 88.10-12; Isaiah 14.9-11; 38.18.

There is no remembrance: in Sheol God is **"not remembered"** (TEV) nor is he praised; that is, there is no mention of him in prayer or praise. To "remember" Yahweh is to recount what he has done for his people.

Sheol or **"the world of the dead"** is sometimes rendered "the place where dead people go" or "where the dead people are put." The translator must be careful that this is not identified with the local cemetery. In many languages it is best to avoid the passive form "you are not remembered" and say "after people have died they cannot think of you, God." FRCL translates: "After a person has died he does not think about you anymore; among the dead no one can praise you any longer." TEV has avoided the parallel use of **Sheol** in line b̲ by using **"there."** This may sometimes be translated "in that place no one will say you are great."

Sheol in line b̲ makes specific the more general **death** in line a̲ and thus calls the reader's attention more forcefully to death. The translator may be able to reflect the movement from death to Sheol more clearly than in TEV by saying, for example,

"When people are dead they no longer think of you [God]. In that dark place of the dead, will anyone say a good word about you? Certainly not." If the rhetorical question is not used, it may be possible to translate, for example, "when people die, they forget you [God]; when they go to the place of the dead, they will no longer praise you."

TEV transforms the rhetorical question in the second line into a statement. If a rhetorical question is used, it must clearly imply a negative answer: "Who can praise you in Sheol? No one!" or "Can anyone praise you in Sheol? No!"

6.6	RSV	TEV

RSV	TEV

I am weary with my moaning;
  every night I flood my bed with
    tears;
  I drench my couch with my
    weeping.
	I am worn out with grief;
	  every night my bed is damp
	    from my weeping;
	  my pillow is soaked with tears.

The parallelism is that of a statement in the first clause, followed by over-statement in the two following clauses. In this way the psalmist calls attention to the seriousness of his pain, which grows from **moanings** to a flood of tears and weeping. TEV has managed to reflect something of this intensification, with "**damp**" in line b followed by "**soaked**" in line c.

The psalmist describes his intense grief with an exaggerated description of the deep sorrow which makes him flood his bed with tears every night; TEV (line b) has used more restrained language, "**my bed is damp**." In line c **my couch** is synonymous with **my bed** in line b; TEV (also NJB, NEB) uses "bed" and "pillow" as more natural contemporary equivalents.

I am weary with my moaning must often be recast so that "**grief**" or **moaning** is the cause of being tired; for instance, "my moaning has made me tired." The Hebrew noun translated **moaning** carries the idea of actual groans, sighs, or moans that accompany suffering and pain, so that a more vivid word than TEV's "**grief**" is required. In languages where one's physical condition cannot be said to cause another such condition, this may be rendered as two coordinate statements, "I am very sad and so I am tired." The literary exaggeration of **I flood my bed . . .** may sometimes require reduction as in TEV or, for example, "every night I cry in my bed." "**Soaked**" and **drench** are likewise strong hyperboles which in some languages are better rendered "and my tears cause my pillow to be wet." The translator should recognize the nature of the movement of intensification within the successive parallel lines and seek to represent it in the translation. This may not always be done by translating TEV or RSV literally. In this verse the psalmist has used hyperbole to accomplish this goal, but other languages have available different means for reaching the same objective.

For similar descriptions of intense grief, see 31.9-10; 69.3.

6.7   RSV   TEV

> My eye wastes away because of   I can hardly see;
>   grief,   my eyes are so swollen
>   it grows weak because of all my   from the weeping caused by my
>   foes.   enemies.

The psalmist's intense weeping has affected his eyesight; his eyes "waste away" and "grow weak." (RSV **My eye . . . it** is not a natural way in English of speaking about one's eyes.) It is rather strange that **my foes** in line b is parallel with **grief** in line a. Some scholars therefore emend the Hebrew for **my foes** in line b to the noun meaning "my distress," which has a similar sound. NEB (without footnote) has "woes" instead of **foes**; ZÜR has "distress." It is better, however, to stay with the Hebrew text as it is, since there is no textual evidence to support the change.

In some languages it may not be apparent that **grief** is the cause of **my eye wastes away**. TEV has placed the reason, "**from the weeping**," in the third line, thus giving a clearer rendering. This can also be translated "Because my enemies have made me cry very much, my eyes hurt and have grown weak."

His enemies no doubt taunt him (as in 3.2) with the accusation that God has abandoned him, and this makes him weep.

6.8-9   RSV   TEV

> 8   Depart from me, all you workers   8   Keep away from me, you evil men!
>   of evil;   The LORD hears my weeping;
>   for the LORD has heard the   9   he listens to my cry for help
>   sound of my weeping.   and will answer my prayer.
> 9   The LORD has heard my supplica-
>   tion;
>   the LORD accepts my prayer.

In this last strophe (verses 8-10) the psalmist assures himself of God's help and denounces his enemies, predicting their punishment.

Depart from me: either "Go away" or "Stay away."

Workers of evil, like "evildoers" in 5.5, is a very general term for people who are sinful, wicked, bad.

My weeping must often be rendered by a clause such as "the LORD hears me when I cry" or ". . . when I cry to him for help."

Line a of verse 9 states the fact, and line b, which parallels it with each word, gives the consequence. TEV expresses the consequence in line b through the use of "**and will**" in the second line.

Supplication (or "**cry for help**") translates a word meaning "request for favor or help" and must often be rendered "ask for help" or "beg for help," since crying is often restricted to "weeping" and "shouting."

Accepts translates a verb meaning "receive," used here in the sense of a favorable response to the psalmist's pleas. So TEV translates "**will answer**."

It is to be noticed that in these two verses RSV has translated the verbs in 8b and 9a with the past tense, and in 9b with the present tense; TEV, however, has the present tense in 8b and 9a, and the future tense in 9b. Some use the past tense for all three (SPCL, FRCL), and NJV uses the present tense for all three. A translator should feel free to use the tense appropriate for an expression of complete confidence; the psalmist knows that Yahweh listens to his prayer and will answer it.

6.10	RSV	TEV

All my enemies shall be ashamed and sorely troubled; they shall turn back, and be put to shame in a moment.	My enemies will know the bitter shame of defeat; in sudden confusion they will be driven away.

The Lord's punishment of the psalmist's enemies is expressed with the verb "to be ashamed," which describes the result of defeat and humiliation. TEV has tried to make explicit why the enemies will be ashamed, by translating "**will know the bitter shame of defeat**." In many languages "shame" is described idiomatically; for example, "will lose face completely" or "lose face lose eye."

Troubled translates a verb meaning to terrify, dismay (as in 2.5). NEB translates the two verbs in line a "shall be confounded and dismayed"; NJV "will be frustrated and stricken with terror."

In some languages it is necessary to introduce God as the agent who causes shame to the psalmist's enemies; for example, "God will give burning faces to my enemies" or "God will cause my enemies to hide their faces."

Sorely troubled may often be rendered "and he will fill their hearts with fear" or "he will give them double hearts," indicating confusion.

Turn back translates the verb that in verse 4 is translated "turn"; here the enemies are "turned back," that is, are "**driven away**" (TEV) by Yahweh, or else "they will retreat" (see NJB). In many cases it may be essential to make explicit the causative agent; for example, "God will drive them away" or "God will make them leave."

RSV **be put to shame in a moment** and TEV "**in sudden confusion**" (also NJB, NEB) translate "be ashamed in a moment"—a picture of confusion and humiliation. SPCL uses vivid language, "As quickly as the blinking of eyes they will run away, ashamed."

Psalm 7

This psalm is a lament by an individual who, having been accused of all sorts of wrongdoing, swears that he is innocent and asks God to punish his enemies. Confident of a favorable answer to his prayer, he thanks God.

The psalmist begins by asking God to save him from his enemies, who threaten him with death (verses 1-2); this is followed by a strong protestation of his innocence (verses 3-5). He calls upon God to judge him and pronounce him innocent (verses 6-9), after which he declares that God is ready to punish evildoers (verses 10-13). Following a description of how the wicked bring disaster on themselves (verses 14-16), the psalmist closes with a prayer of thanks, certain that God will answer him (verse 17).

Again there is not enough specific information in the psalm itself to allow us to know who the writer was. It appears that he had been accused of the sins listed in verses 3-4, and he is defending himself against those charges.

HEADING: "**A Prayer for Justice**" (TEV); "An appeal to the Divine Judge"; "Prayer of the virtuous under persecution"; "The LORD is a just judge." The TEV title contains two nouns connected by a preposition. In many languages it will be necessary to express both of these as verbs, and consequently one must introduce the two agents: the psalmist and God. "**Justice**" may sometimes be rendered "to decide matters in a right way" or "to cut affairs fairly," where "cut" is used figuratively, meaning to judge. The TEV title may be rendered "The psalmist prays asking God to judge matters in the right way."

Hebrew Title: **A Shiggaion of David, which he sang to the LORD concerning Cush a Benjaminite.**

The Hebrew word *shiggaion* occurs here and in Habakkuk 3.1, where the plural form is used in the title of Habakkuk's prayer, "according to the Shigionoth" (RSV). The Septuagint and the Vulgate translate "psalm." Some scholars explain the word as derived from a verb meaning "to wander," meaning that the psalm is described as having an uneven character; so AT "A dithyramb," which is a poem in a wild, irregular strain. But this hardly fits the nature of the psalm itself. Or else the music was "a fast-paced melody" (Toombs). No one knows exactly what the Hebrew term means.

No person by the name of **Cush** is mentioned in the Old Testament; the Septuagint and the Vulgate translate "Cushite," that is, an Ethiopian (TEV "Sudanese"). An Ethiopian appears in 2 Samuel 18.21-23 as the man who took to David the news of Absalom's death; of course he was not a Benjaminite. The Talmud identifies Cush as Saul (Saul's father, a Benjaminite, was named Kish, 1 Sam 9.1). Another identification is Shimei (2 Sam 16.11-13); others identify the person as

Sheba (2 Sam 20.1-11), a Benjaminite who rebelled against David. But all these are only speculations.

7.1-2	RSV		TEV
1	O LORD my God, in thee do I take refuge; save me from all my pursuers, and deliver me.	1	O LORD, my God, I come to you for protection; rescue me and save me from all who pursue me,
2	lest like a lion they rend me, dragging me away, with none to rescue.	2	or else like a lion they will carry me off where no one else can save me, and there they will tear me to pieces.

I take refuge translates the verb used in 2.12. It may be that the phrase which TEV translates "**I come to you**" refers specifically to the Temple, where the psalmist would have gone for the ritual in which he would declare his innocence and wait for God to acquit him. **I take refuge** may have to be recast with two verbs and two different subjects; for example, "I come to you and you take care of me."

The two verbs **save** and **deliver** are used synonymously (see comments on 6.4). It is not always possible to find synonyms for **save** and **deliver**. In some languages to preserve the parallelism a single expression may have to be used twice. Some languages express **save** as "to cause one to see life" or "to snatch someone away from death."

My pursuers is the way the psalmist describes his enemies (see also verse 5). This may be better rendered "those who persecute me."

In some languages it will be necessary to express the purpose of being pursued. In other cases **my pursuers** must be recast as a verbal phrase, and therefore it may be necessary to say, for example, "save me from my enemies who hunt me like an animal" or ". . . who chase me in order to harm me."

TEV has restructured verse 2 in order to get the various items in their proper order, "**carry me off . . . and . . . tear me to pieces.**" **Rend me** translates the Hebrew expression "tear my *nefesh* to pieces" (see comments on 3.2). The language is vivid: the psalmist's enemies will physically tear him limb from limb and kill him (see verse 5).

Enemies are often compared to **a lion** in the Book of Psalms, indicating their ferocious, destructive nature (see 10.9; 17.12; 22.13). In languages where the lion and its hunting habits are not known, it is often necessary to introduce a classifier such as "wild animal"; for example, "wild animal called lion." Or it is necessary to replace it by a known animal of the same kind, such as a leopard. If neither is available, **lion** can be replaced by "wild animal." If the substitution of "wild animal" results in weakening the feeling aroused by the simile, then it is better to restructure in nonfigurative language; for example, "or else they will drag me off" or "If you don't save me, my enemies will tear me to pieces."

RSV   TEV

3   O LORD my God, if I have done   3-4   O LORD, my God, if I have
        this,   wronged anyone,
     if there is wrong in my hands,   if I have betrayed a friend
4   if I have requited my friend with   or without cause done violence
        evil   to my enemy[j]—
     or plundered my enemy without   if I have done any of these
        cause,   things—

[j] without cause done violence to my enemy; or shown mercy to someone who wronged me unjustly.

Verses 3-5 show how parallel images may interact semantically and syntactically over several verses. Verses 3-4 have four "If" clauses, and verse 5 has four corresponding consequential clauses, stated as "Let" commands. The dynamics of the progression from the general to the concrete is seen in comparing the vivid clauses of verse 5 with the more general ones of verses 3-4.

For **my God** in verse 3a, see discussion in 3.7.

In these two verses the psalmist denies the accusations that have been brought against him. He denies three charges:

(1) "**I have wronged anyone**" (TEV) translates **there is wrong in my hands**. The word for **wrong** means "injustice, unrighteousness"; Briggs thinks it specifically means accepting bribes, but no translation takes it in this narrower sense. In translation this expression may often be rendered as "I have done evil to someone" or "I have not been straight with someone."

(2) "**I have betrayed a friend**" (TEV) or, as NEB translates, "repaid a friend evil for good"; NJB "repaid my ally with treachery." Another rendering can be "repaid a friend with evil." "**Betrayed**" must sometimes be rendered "I have given a friend to his enemy" or "I have sold someone to his enemy." Here the Hebrew for **my friend** is "the one who is at peace with me" (see also 55.20, where the same Hebrew expression is used for "his friends").[1]

(3) **I have . . . plundered my enemy without cause**: the meaning of the Hebrew text is uncertain. Literally it says "or have rescued my enemy for nothing." Possible explanations are as follows:

(a) Some scholars believe that a scribe transposed two Hebrew consonants, so that a verb meaning "to do violence to" or "to oppress" was changed to one which means "to rescue, deliver." The meaning is then "or if I have without cause done violence to (or, plundered) my enemy" (so SPCL, NIV; also possible is "robbed without provocation one who was hostile to me"), or else "or if I have done violence to someone who without cause was my enemy" (so FRCL "I have plundered the one who for no reason robbed me"). The idea of "plunder" in some languages is phrased "take someone's possessions by force." RSV and TEV accept this interpretation, which

_____

[1] Another possible translation of the Masoretic text is "If I have repaid evil with evil" (FRCL); this is what the Septuagint has.

follows the ancient versions (see footnote in *Biblia Hebraica Stuttgartensia*. See also AT; Delitzsch, Weiser. However, apart from the evidence of the ancient versions, there is no manuscript evidence to support this interpretation.

(b) Some take the Hebrew text as an affirmation: "I have shown mercy to someone who wronged me unjustly"; so KJV, ASV, NAB; NJV has "I who rescued my foe without reward"; this interpretation can also be "I who rescued one who without cause was hostile to me." This transforms what is meant to be an accusation of wrongdoing into a statement of the psalmist's virtue. However, it seems impossible to understand the Hebrew text in this way, since the "if" at the beginning of line a modifies line b as well.

(c) The meaning which the Hebrew text seems to require is that given in the TEV footnote, "If I have shown mercy to someone who wronged me unjustly." NJB has "or spared someone who attacked me unprovoked" and states in a footnote that this is the law that requires payment of evil for evil as well as good for good (see Exo 21.23-25). To take revenge upon one's enemy would therefore not be thought of as evil or sinful; an enemy was rightly to be condemned and punished. This is the meaning defended by Briggs and Oesterley and expressed by BJ, NJB, and NEB. TOB combines this with the preceding: "if I have wronged my ally by allowing my adversary to escape."[2]

Both RSV and TEV keep the conditional form of the Hebrew text in verses 3-4, which requires the sentence to go without a pause to the end of verse 5. So it may be better to do as SPCL has done, and use a series of rhetorical questions (which clearly imply the answer "No"): "Have I by any chance committed a crime? Have I by any chance paid back my friend evil for good? Have I by any chance without reason oppressed my enemy?" And then verse 5 can begin, "If that is so, then . . ." or "If I have done any of these things, then . . . ."

It should be noted that TEV places at the end of verses 3-4 "**if I have done any of these things,**" which in the Hebrew comes at the beginning of verse 3, **if I have done this**. The translator must decide which of the two seems more natural in the receptor language.

7.5	RSV	TEV
	let the enemy pursue me and overtake me,	then let my enemies pursue me and catch me,
	and let him trample my life to the ground,	let them cut me down and kill me
	and lay my soul in the dust.	and leave me lifeless on the ground!
	Selah	

The dynamics of the parallelism in verse 5 is that each successive line goes beyond the previous line in intensity. In this verse the psalmist declares himself ready to be attacked and even to be killed by his enemies if he is guilty of any of the

---

[2]For a more detailed discussion of the matter, see *The Bible Translator* 23:2 (April 1972), pages 241-242.

charges brought against him. The psalmist says "Let my enemies pursue me and catch me; in fact, let them beat me to death, and even leave my dead body in the dust."

Pursue is the verb used also in verse 1; the Hebrew text is "pursue my *nefesh*" (see comments on 3.2).

To the ground and **in the dust** are parallel. This is a vivid description of being beaten or trampled to death.

The verb **lay** translates the causative form of the verb "to live (somewhere), to dwell," meaning "to place." It may be that what is literally "cause to live in the dust" means "cause to live in Sheol"; so Dahood, who takes "dust" (or "mud," as he prefers) as one of the names for Sheol (as it clearly is in 22.15, "dust of death"). NIV "and make me sleep in the dust" can be misunderstood.

My soul translates the Hebrew "my glory" (see comments on 3.3). It is parallel to "my *nefesh*" (line a) and **my life** (line b); all three are ways of speaking of the individual. For the last line NJV has "and lay my body in the dust."

In some languages it will not be possible to translate verses 3-4 as a series of conditional clauses to be followed by the consequential clauses of verse 5 without badly distorting the meaning. However, the translator should seek to reformulate the three verses so that the relations between them as well as the buildup of intensity in verse 5 is evident to the readers. Therefore in some languages it is necessary to relate the commands of verse 5 to each of the "if" clauses in verse 3. Also, in languages where the "if" clause must follow the command, a further step in restructuring is required; for example, "let my enemies pursue me and catch me if I have wronged anyone; let them cut me down and kill me if I have betrayed a friend; let them leave me lifeless on the ground if I have shown mercy to someone who wronged me unjustly." Alternatively, some languages express apparent conditions in the following manner: "I may have betrayed a friend; in that case let my enemies pursue me" or "It is possible that I betrayed a friend; if I did that, then let my enemies pursue me . . . ."

Selah: see comments on 3.2.

7.6	RSV	TEV
	Arise, O LORD, in thy anger, lift thyself up against the fury of my enemies; awake, O my God;*b* thou hast appointed a judgment.	Rise in your anger, O LORD! Stand up against the fury of my enemies; rouse yourself and help me! Justice is what you demand,

b Or *for me*

With this verse the psalmist begins a strophe (verses 6-9) in which he calls upon God, the Judge of all humankind, to judge him and declare him innocent of the charges against him.

With three verbs the psalmist calls upon Yahweh to act: **Arise . . . lift thyself up . . . awake**. These are ways of asking him to take action against the psalmist's enemies and defeat them. The first two are quite close in meaning; see "Arise, O

LORD" in 3.7. The third one, **awake**, does not necessarily imply that Yahweh is asleep, but only that he is inactive; so TEV **"rouse yourself,"** NJV "bestir Yourself."

In line **b** the noun **fury** may be parallel to **anger** in line **a**, so that the line may mean "Stand up in fury against my enemies"; so AT, NEB, NJV footnote. Although the Hebrew word for **fury** is not the same as other words already used in Psalms, it is not significantly different. It appears in four other passages, referring always to God's anger (78.49b; 85.3a; 90.9a,11b); RSV consistently translates "wrath."

Fury of my enemies must often be recast, since **fury** will in some cases not function as the object of **lift thyself up against**, but only as a description of the enemies. In such cases it may be rendered "stand up against my furious enemies," or figuratively, "protect me from my hot-hearted enemies." The word for **enemies** is the same as in 6.7.

In line **c** TEV **"and help me"** (SPCL "and be on my side") translates the Masoretic text "for me" (as in the RSV footnote). But if different vowels are used, the two consonants of the Hebrew word mean "my God"; so RSV, NEB, NIV, NJB (Septuagint has "O Lord my God").[3]

The last words of the verse in Hebrew have no obvious connection with what precedes; literally "you have decreed justice (or, judgment)." Both NEB and NJB (which have "my God") take it as a description of God, "you who demand that justice shall be done" (see also SPCL, FRCL); NJV and BJ are like RSV; NAB is different, "wake to the judgment you have decreed" (which is none too clear). Mft has "Awake to aid us, to maintain the right"; Weiser, "Appoint a judgment."[4]

The word for **"justice"** (or, **judgment**) is *mishpat* (used in 1.5), a word which covers the widest area possible of conformity to rule, custom, command, right; it may be used in the abstract sense of justice, of what is right, fitting, proper, or in the concrete sense of an act of judgment, including the concept of the final Day of Judgment.

Since it is difficult or impossible in many languages to speak of "decreeing judgment," it is often necessary recast this expression. Taking **"justice"** in the sense of conforming to rules, it is possible to say "God requires that people live right," or in the sense of God's judgment, "God will judge people" or "God has fixed a time to judge everyone."

TEV has joined the last words of this verse to the next verse; that this is the way the Hebrew text is to be understood is by no means certain.

7.7   RSV   TEV

Let the assembly of the peoples be gathered about thee; and over it take thy seat[c] on high.	so bring together all the peoples around you, and rule over them from above.[k]

---

[3]HOTTP ("B" decision) prefers "unto me," meaning "in my favor."

[4]HOTTP says the Hebrew may mean "you have (in fact) ordained judgment," or "you who have ordained judgment" or ". . . ordain judgment."

^c Cn: Heb *return*   ^k *Probable text* rule over them from above; *Hebrew* return above over them.

The first line describes the gathering of all humankind around God; literally, "the gathering of the peoples." It is the psalmist's prayer that God will gather all peoples around him in order to judge them.

In the second line the Hebrew text has the verb "to turn, return" (as in 6.4); so the Septuagint has "return to the height." It is possible to make sense of it, as does Kirkpatrick: "Once more occupy the throne of judgment above the assembly" (so BJ and NJB "return above it on high"; also AT). This would imply that the psalmist felt that God had abandoned his place of judgment, and he is asking God to resume his role as Judge of all humankind. While possible this does not seem very probable, and most commentators and translators change the text from the verb "return" to the imperative of the verb meaning "to sit," either as judge (which is more probable in the context) or as ruler: so RSV, TEV, NEB, NAB, NJV, ZÜR, FRCL. HOTTP says that either interpretation is possible: "and on high take your seat" or "and return to the heights."

A literal rendering of **take thy seat on high** will often mean to sit down on a high object. If it is natural to use figurative language to indicate the place of authority, it may be possible to say in some cases "sit on your stool in heaven." If such idiomatic language is not natural, the "seat of authority" should be replaced with "govern" or "rule," as in TEV. **On high** is most often expressed by the place referred to as God's abode; for example, "in the sky," "up," or "in heaven."

7.8	RSV	TEV
	The LORD judges the peoples; judge me, O LORD, according to my righteousness and according to the integrity that is in me.	You are the judge of all mankind. Judge in my favor, O LORD; you know that I am innocent.

The Hebrew text has two different verbs for "to judge" in lines a and b. The first one is less used than the second one, which is related to the noun "judgment" in verse 6.

In line a TEV translates **The LORD** by "**You**" and thus continues the form of address begun in 7.6. **Judge**, whether verb or noun, is not be to understood in the sense of condemning but in the sense of deciding the guilt or innocence of the one being judged. Most languages have terms for neutral or impartial judging, and some are used idiomatically; for example, "you are the one who cuts the affairs of people." Where no expression for judging is ready at hand, it is sometimes possible to say "you are the one who decides if people are right or wrong."

On the basis of his own **righteousness** and **integrity**, the psalmist appeals to God to judge in his favor, to acquit him of the charge brought against him (NJV "vindicate me"). The first noun (line b) is the one translated "right" in 4.1; the second one (line c) means "perfection, faultlessness, integrity." TEV has combined the two and rendered the clause as a claim which the Lord readily acknowledges:

"**You know that I am innocent.**" SPCL has "judge me according to my honor; judge me according to my innocence."

According to my righteousness may sometimes be rendered as a clause of cause, "because I am right," and **according to the integrity that is in me** as "because I am without fault." Accordingly lines b and c would be "judge me as innocent because I am right and because I am without fault" or "decide my case in my favor because I am right and I have done no wrong."

7.9	RSV	TEV

RSV	TEV
O let the evil of the wicked come to an end, but establish thou the righteous, thou who triest the minds and hearts, thou righteous God.	You are a righteous God and judge our thoughts and desires. Stop the wickedness of evil men and reward those who are good.

TEV has restructured this verse, placing first the statement about God and then the request for him to act. In the first half of the verse in Hebrew (see RSV), there is a particle which expresses a strong wish; so RSV **O let . . . but establish**. TEV has expressed the meaning by using the imperative of the two verbs, "**stop**" and "**reward.**" NEB follows Jerome, who understands the Hebrew noun to say "righteousness," and therefore NEB has in the text "establish the reign of righteousness"; in the margin it has "the cause of the righteous" (following the Hebrew text).

Let . . . come to an end (TEV "**Stop**") is not a request to permit evil to end but a command in the third person that this evil must stop. TEV's "**Stop the wickedness of evil men**" makes this clear, but even this may need to be recast in translation, since it may not be natural to speak of stopping an abstract quality. One must often say, therefore, "Stop bad people from doing evil acts."

Establish thou (TEV "**reward**") is literally "make firm, cause to prosper, establish." "**Reward**" must sometimes be translated by "give good things" or "give gifts"; for example, "give gifts to people who do good things."

God, who is **righteous**, judges people's **minds and hearts**. The verb translated **triest** means to put to the test, to examine, to prove. **Minds and hearts** (TEV "**thoughts and desires**") translates what is literally "hearts and kidneys" (so KJV "hearts and reins"). The heart is often spoken of as the place in the human body where thinking is done, and the kidneys were regarded as the center of feelings and desires. NJV has "conscience" as a translation of "kidneys"; in some cultures this may not be an appropriate concept, so something like "feelings," or "emotions," or "desires" will be better. **Minds and hearts** is often expressed idiomatically, "what the heart thinks and what the insides wish."

There is an advantage gained by placing **thou righteous God** as an identifying statement, "**You are a righteous God,**" at the beginning of verse 9, since verses 8, 10, and 11 (see RSV) also begin with similar expressions. **Righteous** refers here to the nature of God and is rendered idiomatically in some languages as "straight," "clean," or "white heart"; for example, "You are a God who has a white heart."

7.10-11	RSV		TEV

	RSV		TEV
10	My shield is with God, who saves the upright in heart.	10	God is my protector; he saves those who obey him.
11	God is a righteous judge, and a God who has indignation every day.	11	God is a righteous judge and always condemns the wicked.

God's protection is described by the metaphor **My shield is with God**, which means that God is the one who provides him with protection (see comments on "shield" in 3.3). Normally **shield** may be retained in translation if it is commonly used in a figurative sense; for example, as a comparison, "God is my shield" or "God is like a shield to me"; or if the shield is known but not used in these kinds of expressions, it may be sometimes used as an explained figure, "God defends me like a shield protects a warrior."

The Hebrew word translated **with** by RSV may be understood to mean "upon" (see NJV footnote) or "near" (TOB). NEB, SPCL, and NIV supply other vowels to the Hebrew consonants to get "Most High." Most translations take the line to mean "God is my shield."

The upright in heart are those who follow God's commands, who do what he requires; so TEV "those who obey him."

The phrase **righteous judge**, used of God, means that he judges people fairly and honestly.

Who has indignation every day (TEV "**Always condemns the wicked**") translates what is literally "who is indignant every day." The idea of indignation is contained in the verb, which means "to scold, to curse"; here the meaning is not simply that of his attitude as an angry God, but as one who passes sentence, who condemns. So NJV "pronounces doom." TEV has supplied "**the wicked**" as clearly implicit in the text. SPCL "condemns evil at all times." Also possible is "indignation against wrong."

7.12-13	RSV		TEV

	RSV		TEV
12	If a man^d does not repent, God^d will whet his sword; he has bent and strung his bow;	12	If they do not change their ways, God will sharpen his sword. He bends his bow and makes it ready;
13	he has prepared his deadly weapons, making his arrows fiery shafts.	13	he takes up his deadly weapons and aims his burning arrows.

^{d} Heb *he*

As the RSV footnote shows, the subject of the verbs in these verses is not specified; the Hebrew text says simply "If he does not turn, he will sharpen his sword"—and so to the end of verse 13. Weiser, NJB, FRCL, and NJV take the subject of verses 12-13 to be the wicked man himself, the enemy; so in these translations, in verse 12 the man gets ready to destroy, and in verse 13 his weapons turn against him and kill him. (NEB is not altogether clear, but seems to make God the subject of all the verbs in verses 13-14). NIV (with alternative in the footnote) takes God as the subject of all the verbs in verses 12-13, translating the initial verb, "If he does not relent."

It seems best to do as most modern translations have done and take the first verb to refer to the wicked, "If they do not change their ways" (literally, "turn"; see comments on 6.4), and the other verbs to refer to God. In translation it will often be necessary to avoid the use of an indefinite subject such as **a man** (TEV "**they**") and to say instead "wicked people." Whether the "if" clause precedes or follows the result clause depends on the usage in the receptor language. **Repent** is frequently expressed in idiomatic terms; for example, "to change the heart," "to have a new heart," or "to walk a new path."

Vivid figures are used of God getting ready to destroy the wicked: he **will whet his sword; he has bent and strung his bow,** that is, he is taking aim and is preparing to shoot his arrows (see similar language in 11.2). These expressions depicting offensive action imply a further action, that is, using the sharpened sword and the bent bow to fight the wicked enemy. In many languages such indirect and figurative statements are quite natural, but where there is no apparent connection in meaning, one may make the meaning clear by a purpose clause; for example, "God will sharpen his sword to attack evil people, if they do not repent; he will bend and string his bow to shoot the wicked people, if they do not change their evil ways." RSV has taken the Hebrew verb for "prepare" at the end of verse 12 in the sense of "stringing (the bow)"; NJV has "he . . . aims it." The same verb is used in verse 13a, where TEV has "**he takes up,**" and RSV **he has prepared.**

Deadly weapons refers to weapons which can cause death, and must sometimes be translated "weapons which kill people."

The last line of verse 13 is literally "making his arrows into burning (darts)." Most understand this to reflect the practice in ancient warfare of wrapping inflammable material around the tip of the arrow, setting it on fire, and then discharging the arrow. Some, however, take the Hebrew verb to mean "sharpen" (instead of "make ablaze"); so NJV "makes his arrows sharp." In languages where bows and arrows are unknown, a more generic term such as "weapons" may be used. In those cases where weapons are unknown in the language, a descriptive phrase must be used; for example, "things people use to hurt other people."

SPCL reverses the order of the two lines of verse 13 so as to have the line "he aims his flaming arrows" follow immediately after "he bends his bow" in verse 12b.

7.14	RSV	TEV

Behold, the wicked man conceives evil,	See how wicked people think up evil;
and is pregnant with mischief, and brings forth lies.	they plan trouble and practice deception.

Behold calls attention to the entire line and is often rendered as "Look," "Listen," or in idiomatic ways such as "Eye" or "Ear to this." It is not necessary to understand from the introductory expression **Behold** that the psalmist is addressing someone in particular; verses 14-16 are a brief meditation on how the wicked are punished by their own evil.

In the Hebrew text the subject of the verbs is still unexpressed, but since it is obviously not God (as in the preceding verses), both TEV and RSV refer it explicitly to the wicked: **the wicked man** (generic singular) and **"wicked people"** (plural).

In vivid terms the psalmist describes the beginning, development, and appearance of evil in terms of procreation: conception, gestation, birth (RSV **conceives . . . is pregnant . . . brings forth**); see Job 15.35. NIV has "is pregnant . . . conceives . . . gives birth to." (NJV mixes the metaphors with "he hatches . . . conceives . . . gives birth.")

The three nouns, **evil**, **mischief** (as in verse 16b), and **lies**, are variously translated. NAB takes **lies** (TEV **"deception"**) in the sense of "failure"; NIV has "disillusionment." Many languages are not able to maintain effectively the procreation figure in all three lines, and many in none. It is particularly strange and unnatural in many languages to speak of a man being **pregnant with mischief**. One may sometimes say, for example, "He is the father of evil plans" or, as a simile, "He fathers evil plans as a man has sons." **Conceives** must often be recast as "to think of ways to do evil deeds." **"Plan trouble"** (TEV) must often be recast as "to think of ways to cause people to have trouble." **Brings forth lies** may sometimes be rendered "to tell lies to people."

7.15-16

	RSV		TEV
15	He makes a pit, digging it out, and falls into the hole which he had made.	15	But in the traps they set for others, they themselves get caught.
16	His mischief returns upon his own head, and on his own pate his violence descends.	16	So they are punished for their own evil and are hurt by their own violence.

Here the psalmist describes how the evil that people plan to do to others recoils on its authors (see 5.10). A man digs a pit for someone else to fall into, and then he falls in it himself; see 9.15; 35.7-8; 57.6; Ecclesiastes 10.8. TEV has used the more general figure of being caught in a trap that has been set to catch others, since that is more readily understood.

Pit and **hole** are synonyms.

In cultures where animals are caught by causing them to fall into holes dug in the ground, the Hebrew figure will serve very well. However, it will often be necessary to indicate the sequence, that is, first digging the pit and then the digger falling in it. It is also necessary in some languages to indicate the purpose; for example, "wicked people first dig a hole to catch other people, and later they themselves fall into that hole."

The idea is repeated for emphasis in different terms in verse 16; literally **His mischief** (same word in verse 14b) and **his violence** act like a boomerang and return to hurt him. TEV has avoided **head** and **pate** (the latter is today almost obsolete), preferring to use the pronoun **"they."** Another possibility is to have "on himself" in line a and "on his head" in line b (see NEB, NJV). It is often unnatural to have an abstract expression such as **His mischief** as the instrument or means of "punishment." This idea must often be recast to say "they do evil things, and these very things cause them to suffer" or "because they do evil deeds their own deeds make them suffer."

Some languages can keep the form of the Hebrew metaphor **mischief returns upon his own head**. The following parallel line, however, is even more difficult. **On his own pate his violence descends** must often be recast if it is to make sense. **Violence** must often be expressed as a verb or handled as an attributive to an event; for example, "because they use great strength to injure people, they will be injured in the same way themselves" or because they are people who force others . . . ."

It is quite clear that the two lines of verse 16 are nearly identical in meaning. However, in Hebrew the word order is different, in that the verb **returns** occurs as the first word in line a and **descends** as the last word in line b. Thus line b, which repeats and emphasizes line a, does so by reversing the word order. The translator should seek equivalent poetic devices in the receptor language which will be stylistically pleasing and emphatic in their intention.

7.17

<table>
<tr><td></td><td>TEV</td></tr>
<tr><td>I will give to the LORD the thanks due to his righteousness, and I will sing praise to the name of the LORD, the Most High.</td><td>I thank the LORD for his justice; I sing praises to the LORD, the Most High.</td></tr>
</table>

The psalmist concludes with a vow of gratitude, confident that the Lord has answered his prayer and proven his innocence. Some prefer the descriptive present "I thank" (TEV, NJB); others the future **I will give . . . thanks** (RSV, AT, NEB, NAB). The Hebrew verb for "to thank" is the one translated "praise" in 6.5 (RSV) and appears many times in Psalms.

Righteousness: instead of the abstract quality (TEV "**justice**") it may be better to use a verbal phrase of action; for example, "I give thanks to the LORD because he does what is right."

The verb for **sing praise** (to praise with musical accompaniment) is the verb from which the noun translated "psalm" in the Hebrew titles is formed. In some languages **I will sing praise** must be rendered as two coordinate events; for example, "I will sing and I will praise the LORD," where the latter is "I will say the LORD is great."

For **name** see comments on 5.11.

The divine title 'elyon, **the Most High**, is used 21 times in Psalms. It describes Yahweh as the greatest, the most powerful, of all the gods. The translation of this title may sometimes be "God who is above all gods" or "God who is greater than all others."

Psalm 8

This psalm is a hymn which celebrates the glory of God and the worth of humankind. It opens with praise of God's majesty (verses 1-2), followed by a reflection on the human being: though insignificant when compared with God's creation (verses 3-4), the true worth of human beings is revealed in their having been appointed by the Creator as rulers over all other created beings (verses 5-8). The psalm closes with the same praise of God's majesty with which it begins (verse 9).

As suggested in the introduction to this Handbook, "Translating the Psalms," the translator of the Book of Psalms must learn to read the form of each psalm before undertaking to translate it. In many cases the themes and the weaving together of the various themes will be brought into perspective only when the translator is conscious of those themes and how they are interconnected. Psalm 8 begins and ends by praising God "in all the earth." The "all" of the earth is shown in stages of downward movement from the heavens to the creatures of the seas. The order of creation in Genesis 1 is followed (but not every example of it). The second parallel line is often used to make a reference specific. At the very thematic center the poet has placed the question about man in two lines that are the same in meaning and in word order. No other lines are treated in this way. Therefore the poem balances at this midpoint of the contrast of man with the rest of creation. As Alter points out, "the only verb in the poem attached to a human action is 'see' at the beginning of line 4." He goes on to remark that the only active verb associated with a created object is in line 8b, "whatever passes along the paths of the sea." Thus by this restriction the poet depicts God as acting upon all realms of creation and permitting man to observe.

HEADING: **"God's Glory and Man's Dignity"** (TEV); "The majesty of God and the dignity of human beings"; "The power of the divine name"; "The paradox of man." Translators wishing to use the TEV heading will often have to recast it to say something like "The psalmist compares the greatness of God and people," or "People are great, but God is greater," or from the text itself, "People can see the greatness of God everywhere."

Hebrew Title: **To the choirmaster: according to The Gittith. A Psalm of David.**

The direction given **to the choirmaster** (see Psa 4) is **according to The Gittith** (also in the Hebrew title of Psa 81; 84). The meaning of the Hebrew word is unknown. It seems to be an adjective derived from "Gath," and it has been conjectured that it refers either to a musical instrument (so FRCL "accompaniment on the harp of Gath") or to a tune from Gath (see NJB "on the . . . of Gath"). The FRCL footnote suggests "to be sung in the style of the people of Gath." Another explanation associates it with the pressing of grapes, as a song to be sung during the grape harvest (this is supported by the Septuagint, "for the wine presses"; see also the Vulgate).

8.1-2	RSV	TEV

	RSV	TEV

1	O LORD, our Lord,
	    how majestic is thy name in all
	      the earth!
	
	    Thou whose glory above the heav-
	      ens is chanted
		O LORD, our Lord,
		    your greatness is seen in all the
		      world!
		Your praise reaches up to the
		      heavens;

2	by the mouth of babes and
	    infants,
	thou hast founded a bulwark be-
	    cause of thy foes,
	    to still the enemy and the
	      avenger.
		2 it is sung by children and ba-
		    bies.
		You are safe and secure from all
		    your enemies;
		    you stop anyone who opposes
		    you.

The opening words are "Yahweh, our Lord," the first being the personal name of God, followed by his title. Mft maintains the distinction with "O thou Eternal One, our Lord"; see NEB and SPCL "O Lord our sovereign"; FRCL "Lord, our master." (Coverdale, in 1535, translated "O Lorde oure Governoure.") Most English translations, since they follow the tradition begun by the Septuagint, obscure the distinction between the two (see comments on "LORD" in 1.2).

The vocative form requires some adjustments in many languages, such as "God, you who are our Lord" or "God, you who rule over us."

The psalmist praises Yahweh's majesty, which is known **in all the earth**. In translation it will often be necessary to recast this expression in an active sense; for example, "People everywhere see how great you are."

For **name** see comments at 5.11. God's greatness is apparent everywhere; his fame is acknowledged by all peoples. The adjective translated **majestic** (RSV, NJV, NJB) is also translated "glorious" (AT, NEB), "powerful" (BJ). The idea of power is made explicit in SPCL, "your name rules (or, has dominion) in all the world." This, however, is not a very good model to follow.

It is difficult to decide how to translate the last part of verse 1 and connect it to the first part of verse 2. The end of verse 1 in the Hebrew is "whose glory you are to place above the heavens." "You are to place" represents the imperative of the verb for "to give" (so Briggs, who omits "whose" as a scribal addition, and translates "O set Thy splendour above the heavens!"). HOTTP takes the Masoretic text form to be the infinitive of the same verb "to give," meaning here "you have set"; so NIV. But the Koehler-Baumgartner lexicon (K-B) takes the Masoretic text form to be the imperative of another verb, "to recount, tell."

Most commentators and translators regard the Masoretic text as deficient, and several solutions are proposed: (1) to place different vowels with the consonants of the Masoretic text so as to get the passive form of the verb "to tell," namely, "whose glory is told (or, praised)"; so AT, RSV, NEB, TEV; (2) to place other vowels with the same consonants to get the perfect form of the same verb: "your name which tells (or, proclaims)"; (3) another solution, proposed by Dahood, is to maintain the consonants of the Masoretic text but to divide them in such a way as to arrive at a form of the Hebrew verb meaning "to serve, worship, adore"; so ZÜR "I will adore your majesty."

There are other proposals which involve a change in the consonants of the Masoretic text: (1) change to the perfect of the verb for "to give," yielding "(which) you placed" (Oesterley; NAB); (2) change to the verb meaning "to spread, stretch out"; so NJV "You who have covered the heavens with Your splendor"; SPCL "your glory extends beyond heaven!"

In the face of so many choices, perhaps the best one is to go with the majority of modern translations, that is, "whose glory is told (or, praised)."

TEV **"Your praise"** means "the praise that people offer you." In many languages this expression must be recast or it will mean "the praise which you make." To avoid this wrong interpretation it is often better to say "we praise you" or "people say you are great."

Above the heavens: the translation of what is literally "over the heavens" (TEV **"up to the heavens"**) depends on whether this phrase modifies **glory** (so RSV) or the verb (so NEB "Thy majesty is praised high as the heavens"). **"Up to the heavens"** can be translated as the degree of the praise, as in TEV; for example, "People praise you so greatly it reaches the heavens." One should avoid giving the impression of merely making such a loud noise that it fills the sky, although this is also part of the idea. If, on the other hand, **above the heavens** describes the glory of God, this line can be "your greatness which is higher than heaven."

The first line of verse 2 is also variously understood; the Masoretic text has "from the mouth of infants and children you have founded (or, established) strength," which some interpreters take to mean that God has built his defenses out of the praise offered him by children and infants (Kirkpatrick, Oesterley, Weiser; so KJV, SPCL, NJV, TOB). The interpretation followed by most modern translations, however, is to connect "from the mouths of infants and children" with what precedes in verse 1, and begin a new sentence with "You have built a stronghold . . . ." This is the best way to handle the text.

Some scholars take **bulwark**, that is, "stronghold," to be a reference to the firmament, built to keep out the forces of chaos (Gen 1.6), or else a reference to the highest level of heaven, where God lives. **Chanted by the mouth of babes and infants** must often be recast in translation to an active expression, and **"Your praise"** (**glory**) may be required as the complement of **chanted**; for example, "children and babies sing about your greatness" or "children and babies sing words telling how great you are."

The word translated **bulwark** (literally, "strength, might, power") is translated "praise" by the Septuagint and Vulgate, and in modern times by NAB and NIV. Instead of the verb for "establish (or, build)" in the Hebrew text, NEB emends the verb to one which produces the translation "thou hast rebuked the mighty."

God's opponents are described with three terms: **foes**, **the enemy**, and **the avenger** (from the verb meaning "to take vengeance"); the last two appear also in 44.16. **Avenger** refers to one who takes action to pay someone back for real or presumed wrongs. **"Opposes you"** in TEV makes God the object of the "avenger." However, **the enemy and the avenger** may be taken as acting against the psalmist. In this case the rendering may be "you stop my enemies and those who take vengeance against me." If one interprets **enemy** and **avenger** in a generalized sense, then this line may be rendered "you stop the enemies and anyone who tries to harm another in return." TEV's "**stop**" in verse 2 may wrongly be taken to mean "preventing enemies and avengers from moving about." The meaning is, however, "to put an end to them" and may be rendered "you destroy enemies and avengers." It seems best to take all three terms to refer to God's enemies.

As translated by the Septuagint, the first line of verse 2 of the Hebrew text is quoted in Matthew 21.16.

8.3-4	RSV		TEV
3	When I look at thy heavens, the work of thy fingers, the moon and the stars which thou hast established;	3	When I look at the sky, which you have made, at the moon and the stars, which you set in their places—
4	what is man that thou art mindful of him, and the son of man that thou dost care for him?	4	what is man, that you think of him; mere man, that you care for him?

The reflection on God's sovereign greatness leads the psalmist to wonderment at God's concern for human beings, who are so insignificant in comparison with God's awesome works of creation. The translation of **look at thy heavens** should not imply the mere act of seeing but rather should suggest contemplation. It is therefore sometimes necessary to say "when I look at and think about . . . ." God made the **heavens** with his own hands (**the work of thy fingers**; see also 102.25). The plural **heavens** may reflect the idea of several levels of heaven (three or seven) in the Hebrew concept of the universe, or else it is a way of saying "the vast heaven."

Languages indicate space above the earth in very different ways. Some simply refer to everything as "up," while others make such distinctions as (1) the area of clouds and (2) the area where the moon and stars are. In addition, many languages use figurative expressions to indicate the realm where God is said to be; for example, "God's town," "God's house," or "the high home." Here the term for sky should be the area where the moon and stars are thought to exist.

As commentators point out, the psalmist is looking up at the sky at night, since he mentions **the moon and the stars** but not the sun. Of them he says "**you set** [them] **in their places**" (TEV). The verb **established** means here to put firmly in place, reflecting the thought of that time that the moon and the stars were set in the solid vault of heaven. It should be noted that TEV "**you set**" is to be understood as a past tense; it would be better to have "you have set."

Verse 3 contains four dependent clauses, and all four serve as an introduction to the double rhetorical question of verse 4. Moreover, this arrangement is made complex by the fact that there is an implied cause in verse 3 relating it to verse 4. By observing creation the psalmist is led to ask the question in verse 4. Furthermore, the psalmist is contrasting the smallness of man with the greatness of the heavens. The translator must determine:

(1) whether it is possible or natural for the clauses in verse 3 to give rise to the question in verse 4;

(2) whether or not verse 3 can remain as four dependent clauses or must be restructured;

(3) whether or not a rhetorical question requires an explicit reply; and

(4) whether or not the contrastive picture between **man** in verse 4 and the heavenly bodies in verse 3 is sufficiently clear.

In some languages it will be necessary in (1) to introduce the question; for example, "When I look at the sky which you have made, at the moon and the stars which you have set in their places, I ask this question: . . . ." Regarding (2), for languages which will not permit series of dependent clauses to precede a question, these clauses may be recast as statements; for example, "I look at the sky you have made; I look at the moon and the stars which you set in their places. Therefore I ask, what are people . . . ?" In respect to (3), if the receptor language requires a reply, one may say "What are people, that you think of them? They are nothing." Concerning (4), in some languages it may be necessary to make the contrast between the smallness of people and the greatness of heavenly bodies more explicit; for example, "What are mere people that you think of them?" Alternatively, one may speak of the "vast heavens" and the "great moon and stars" in order to highlight the contrast with man; for example, "What are people—so small as they are—that you care for them?"

The rhetorical question in verse 4 eloquently expresses the psalmist's wonder at God's care for humankind. The two lines are exactly parallel, both making the same point in different ways. Both **man** and **the son of man** mean "humankind" or "a human being." It should be emphasized that the Hebrew phrase translated **son of man** means "human being," with emphasis on the creature's frailty and mortality, as one made of the dust of the earth. In languages where the use of male-oriented language is considered undesirable, it is important to avoid saying **man**, if at all possible. So FRCL "The human being . . . a mere individual." In some languages **man** in the generic sense is rendered by the use of the plural. **The son of man** may need to be rendered with a qualifier to indicate "mere humanity"; for example, "a plain human being," "simply people," or "nothing more than people." The line is repeated in 144.3; in Job 7.17 it is used ironically.

The verb **art mindful** is literally "remember" in the sense of being concerned about, and in some languages is rendered idiomatically as "to have a warm heart for" or "to feel in one's insides for."

The Hebrew verb for **care for** is used in a great variety of ways; the basic idea is to look for what is missing, to worry about, and to do something for it. One translation can be "show concern." The verb is often used of God taking care of his people by going to them and acting on their behalf (see its use in 65.9a; 80.14c; 106.4b, where it is translated by a number of English verbs).

8.5	RSV	TEV

8.5

RSV

Yet thou hast made him little less
    than God,
  and dost crown him with glory
    and honor.

TEV

Yet you made him inferior only to
    yourself;^m
  you crowned him with glory and
    honor.

^m yourself; *or* the gods, *or* the angels.

The greatness of the human being is seen in the fact that God made him inferior only to *elohim*, a word whose precise meaning here is disputed. Translations and their supporters are as follows:

(1) **God**: the ancient Greek versions by Aquila, Symmachus, and Theodotion; Jerome; ASV, RSV, TEV.
(2) "Angels": Septuagint (quoted in Heb 2.7), Syriac, Targum, Vulgate; KJV, NAB, ZÜR, FRCL, NJV footnote.
(3) "The gods": Dahood. NIV has "the heavenly beings."
(4) "A god": NEB, BJ, NJB, TOB, SPCL. Mft and NJV have "little less than divine"; "almost divine" also represents this meaning.

The word *elohim* (the plural of *el*, "god") can mean different things, depending on the context; its broadest sense is that of divine beings as distinct from human beings, and it is most likely that it is used in this sense in this passage. So the preferred translation is "God" or, perhaps, "the divine beings."

The verbal phrase translated **made him little less** is the causative of the verb "to lack," followed by the adjective "little": "you have caused him to be little less than . . . ." **Little less than God** is not to be taken as rough equality with God, but viewed as higher than the rest of creation. In order to make clear the relation of **less than** and "inferior to," it is sometimes necessary to indicate a complement of **made**; for example, "you made people to have a place only a little beneath you" or "you created people and gave them a place which is below only you."

Glory and honor are, so to speak, the crown which marks the human creature's exalted position as ruler of all other created beings. This figurative language may have to be recast in translation. **Crown** refers here to man's authority over created life and can be rendered "you made him to be like a king and gave him glory and greatness" or "you gave him power to rule and gave him splendor and honor."

The Septuagint translation of 8.5-7 is quoted in Hebrews 2.6-8.[1]

8.6-8	RSV	TEV
6	Thou hast given him dominion over the works of thy hands; thou hast put all things under his feet,	6 You appointed him ruler over everything you made; you placed him over all creation:
7	all sheep and oxen, and also the beasts of the field,	7 sheep and cattle, and the wild animals too;
8	the birds of the air, and the fish of the sea, whatever passes along the paths of the sea.	8 the birds and the fish and the creatures in the seas.

---

[1]It should be noted that in verse 5 the Septuagint translation of the Hebrew "a little" is taken by the author of Hebrews to mean "a little while" (Heb 2.7,9).

In these three verses the psalmist lists "**all creation**" (TEV) over which God has placed humankind as ruler. <u>**The work of thy hands**</u> is a way of saying "the things that you made" (see "the work of thy fingers" in verse 3). "To put under the feet of" means "to make (someone) a ruler, to place under his dominion." <u>**Thou hast given him dominion over the works of thy hands**</u> must often be recast as two verb phrases; for example, "You have put him in charge and made him to rule over all you created."

Verse 6b is cited in 1 Corinthians 15.27.

The psalmist is thinking primarily of the animals, and so by the usual classification he lists them all: (1) domestic animals, **sheep and oxen** (or "**cattle**," TEV); (2) wild animals, literally **the beasts of the field**; (3) wild birds; (4) marine life, <u>**the fish of the sea,**</u> including (5) the sea monsters (verse 8b; see Gen 1.21), which were classified separately from ordinary fish (see GECL "the fish and monsters in the sea"). Many translations, however, take <u>**whatever passes along the paths of the sea**</u> to be only a more inclusive statement about all marine creatures.

Some languages do not have general terms for certain classes of animals. As there is no symbolic value attached to sheep or cattle here, an expression for any or all domestic animals may be used. **Beasts of the field** are sometimes referred to as "forest animals" or "bush animals" in contrast to "village animals." <u>**Of the seas**</u> as attributive to the <u>**fish**</u> may have to be recast in many languages where the seas are unknown. Hence one must often say "the big fish from the big rivers" or "big animals that live in the big waters."

<u>**8.9**</u>	RSV	TEV

O LORD, our Lord,
   how majestic is thy name in all
     the earth!

O LORD, our Lord,
   your greatness is seen in all the
     world!

The psalm closes with the same eloquent words with which it begins.

Psalm 9

Originally Psalms 9 and 10 were one composition, each strophe beginning with a successive letter of the Hebrew alphabet, beginning with *alef* (the first letter) and ending with *taw* (the last letter), a total of 22 strophes. But the poem was altered, and some of the strophes are now missing. For the details on the acrostic device used throughout the two psalms, see the commentaries. The majority of translations do not indicate the strophes by the Hebrew letters; AT, however, prints the Hebrew letters over the strophe, and NJB, BJ, and FRCL give the names of the letters in the margin.

Four Hebrew manuscripts, the Septuagint, and the Vulgate have the two psalms as one (that is, Psalm 9). This explains why in Psalms 10–146 the numbering of the psalms in the Septuagint is one number behind the numeration in the Hebrew text and, similarly, why the numbering in the translations based on the Vulgate lags one number behind the numbering in the translations based on the Hebrew text. (See the introduction, "Translating the Psalms," and the Appendix for the exact equivalence between the two systems.)

The mechanical device used in the composition of this psalm accounts for the lack of order and the frequent change from one subject to another. There is a mixture of forms in this psalm: a hymn, in which an individual praises God for delivering him from death (9.1-4, 9-12); a song, celebrating God's judgment on the heathen (9.5-8, 15-20); and a lament by an individual who is suffering persecution at the hand of his enemies (9.13-14; 10.1-18).

Psalm 9 begins with thanksgiving to God for having rescued the psalmist from his enemies (verses 1-4), followed by an affirmation of the destruction of the wicked by God, who is the righteous and just king of all the world (verses 5-8). After affirming God's protective care of those who trust him, and thanking him for it (verses 9-12), the psalmist prays the Lord to rescue him from death (verses 13-14). The psalm closes with a denunciation of the wicked and a prayer to God to condemn them (verses 15-20).

HEADING: "**Thanksgiving to God for His Justice**" (TEV); "Thanksgiving for the overthrow of hostile nations"; "The wicked shall be overthrown"; "God crushes the wicked and saves the humble." If the translator follows the TEV title, the nominal forms may have to be recast as verbs; for example, "I will thank God because he judges in the right way."

Hebrew Title: **To the choirmaster: according to Muth-labben. A Psalm of David.**

The meaning of the Hebrew musical direction **according to Muth-labben** is unknown. It appears nowhere else; it may be the name of a tune (so Knox, "To the mood of the song, Mut Labben"). The Hebrew words might mean "Death to the son" or "Die for the son" (NIV "To the tune of 'The death of the son' "), or they could be a corruption of *al-alamoth* (as in the title of Psa 46; so FRCL "accompaniment at a high pitch"). The ancient versions are of no help.

9.1-2	RSV		TEV
1	I will give thanks to the LORD with my whole heart; I will tell of all thy wonderful deeds.	1	I will praise you, LORD, with all my heart; I will tell of all the wonderful things you have done.
2	I will be glad and exult in thee, I will sing praise to thy name, O Most High.	2	I will sing with joy because of you. I will sing praise to you, Almighty God.

TEV has used the second person of address in verse 1a in order to maintain consistency with verses 1b-2. In Hebrew it is the third person.

In verse 1a the verb for **give thanks** is the same as in 7.17a, and in verse 2b the verb for **sing praise** is the same as in 7.17b. If the translator follows TEV "I will praise you," this expression may often be rendered as "I will make you great" or "I will speak highly of your name." Sometimes such expressions may be handled as direct address, "I will say, 'Your name, Lord, is truly great,' " "You, Lord, are great" or "Your reputation, Lord, is truly good." The sincerity and intensity of the psalmist's gratitude is stressed with the phrase **with my whole heart**.

Wonderful deeds translates the participle of a verb used in 4.3 and which occurs quite often in Psalms to refer to the extraordinary acts of Yahweh on behalf of the people of Israel. Such deeds are described figuratively in some languages as ones which "take the breath away," "take away the heart," or "open the mouth."

Translators should always be alert to unsuitable meanings which may result from transferring expressions from one language to another. TEV very frequently uses the verbal clause "things you have done" or "what you (or, he) have (or, has) done." In some languages this expression is used as a euphemism or indirect way of speaking about sexual relations. Translators who are faced with this particular problem would be well advised to check under "do" in the *Concordance to the Good News Bible,* edited by David Robinson.

In verse 2a the two verbs **be glad and exult** are synonymous, the first of which appears many times in Psalms; the second one is used only here and in 5.11; 25.2; 68.3. **In thee**: "because of what you have done" (see also comments on 5.11).

For **name** see comments on 5.11. **I will sing praise to thy name** (TEV "you") in verse 2b may require recasting in order to show the relation between the two events of "singing" and "praising," and their relation to "you" or **thy name**. For example, "I will sing, and in this way I will praise you," or "I will speak of your great name when I sing about you," or "When I sing I will say this: 'Your name is great.' "

For the title **Most High** see comments on 7.17.

| **When my enemies turned back, they stumbled and perished before thee.** | **My enemies turn back when you appear; they fall down and die.** |

It seems better, with TEV (also NEB, NJV, NIV, SPCL), to use the descriptive present, **"turn back . . . fall down and die,"** instead of the historic past, **turned back . . . stumbled and perished** (RSV; also FRCL).

For **turned back**, compare the use of the same verb, "turn," in 6.4. Here the emphasis is on the idea of turning back in defeat, a retreat.

Stumbled translates a verb meaning "to stagger, totter, stumble." The statement in this verse seems to suggest soldiers fleeing from their enemies in battle, but no certain inference can be drawn from the text itself.

Before thee ("**when you appear**" TEV) translates the Hebrew "before your face," that is, "in your presence." Here it indicates not simply the place where the psalmist's enemies fall down and die but the reason for their destruction, that is, in their being faced by Yahweh in his anger (see 21.9; 34.16). NJB "at your presence"; NEB "at thy appearing." Also possible is "when you confront them."

The Hebrew text, as reflected in RSV, makes line a a dependent clause and line b the main clause. TEV on the other hand takes "before your face" from line b and makes this a subordinate clause of line a (similarly SPCL), and thus relates the two parts of line a as result followed by reason. In some languages it may be necessary to put "before your face" or "**when you appear**" as the opening clause, followed then by three coordinate clauses of result. **Before thee** (TEV "**you appear**") must be expressed in some languages as "to show oneself" or "to be seen"; for example, "when my enemies see you, they turn back, they fall to the ground and die" or "when you show yourself to my enemies, they run away, fall down and die."

| **For thou hast maintained my just cause; thou hast sat on the throne giving righteous judgment.** | **You are fair and honest in your judgments, and you have judged in my favor.** |

For: it is better, with RSV, to indicate that verse 4 gives the ground, or reason, for the psalmist's affirmation in verse 3.

Thou hast maintained my just cause translates "you accomplished my right and my cause"; for "my right" see comments on "judgment" in 7.6; the word for **cause** is a legal term, meaning a claim in court, a legal case. The line may be rendered "you upheld my right and my cause" (NAB, NIV) or "you have given fair judgement in my favour" (NJB). FRCL is better: "You have done the right thing for me, you have given me justice." In some languages it is necessary to recast the process of judging in terms of two events in which the second is a consequence of the first; for example, "you have judged me and found me innocent" or "you have judged my case and found that I was right."

For greater ease of understanding, TEV has reversed the two lines. The psalmist sees the Lord as an "honest" (or, "righteous") judge, or, as RSV has it, **righteous judgment**. For **righteous** see comments on "right" in 4.1; for **judgment** see comments on "to judge" in 7.8. Yahweh sits on the throne to judge, as both ruler and judge of all humanity.

TEV gives first the general statement and then the specific application. RSV, following the Hebrew order, gives the specific event before the general statement. In all such cases the translator must determine for his or her language which order is more natural. In some languages the logical relation of reason to result may be clearer; for example, "because you are fair and honest in your judging, you have judged in my favor."

9.5	RSV	TEV
	Thou hast rebuked the nations, thou hast destroyed the wicked; thou hast blotted out their name for ever and ever.	You have condemned the heathen and destroyed the wicked; they will be remembered no more.

In verses 5-6 the psalmist turns his thoughts to Israel's enemies, the heathen. He is so confident that God will do it that he speaks of their total annihilation and the destruction of their cities as an accomplished fact. God has "**condemned**" (TEV) them, literally **rebuked** them (also 68.30; 119.21). The context requires more than the rather mild idea of chiding or admonishing. Kirkpatrick defines Yahweh's rebuke as "the effectual sentence of His wrath which carries its own execution with it." FRCL translates "threaten"; NJV "You blast the nations." See in 76.6 what God's "rebuke" does.

In Hebrew verse 5 has two verbs in the first line and one verb in the second. God's judgment of the heathen moves in each successive verb to greater intensification, from rebuke to destruction to total extermination, even down to the very name. The translator should represent this progressive intensification in his translation, in so far as the language enables him.

Rebuked the nations with the meaning of "**condemned**" is sometimes rendered "judged against." As direct address it can be rendered "You have said to the heathen, 'You are truly guilty.' "

The nations: see comments on 2.1. In English **nations** does not carry the distinctive connotation of the word used by the biblical writer, so something like TEV "**the heathen**" is better; FRCL has "these barbarians"; SPCL "the pagans."

Since the Hebrew word for **nations** meant not only all the people and nations who were not Jews, but also carried connotations of worshiping false gods, it is often difficult in other languages to find an equivalent expression. In some versions translators have used "other nations with their false gods" or "nations serving false gods." They are characterized as **wicked** and deserve punishment.

Their complete and permanent destruction is pictured vividly: **thou hast blotted out their name for ever and ever**. The verb **blotted out** (to wipe out, blot out, exterminate) means that in the future no one will even remember that these people had ever existed (see Deut 9.14; 29.20). It is better, with RSV, to keep God as the actor in line b: "you have caused them to be forgotten for ever." In order to retain the force of the original poetic expression, the translator is encouraged to use figurative language, provided that such expressions are natural in the receptor language. Some languages speak of "washing away the name," "wiping away the name," or "causing the name to melt away."

9.6   RSV   TEV

The enemy have vanished in ever-   Our enemies are finished forever;
   lasting ruins;   you have destroyed their cities,
  their cities thou hast rooted   and they are completely forgot-
   out;   ten.
  the very memory of them has
   perished.

Verse 6 is an extension of verse 5, with a shift of focus to **ruins** and destroyed cities in lines a and b, while line c returns to the image of oblivion, or no more remembrance of them. In translation the extending of verse 6 beyond verse 5 and building on it should be reflected. For example, verse 6 may begin "What is more, our enemies are for ever in ruins . . ." or "Furthermore our enemies . . . ."

The text of this verse is not easy to figure out; the general sense is clear enough, but the specific relations among the words is in doubt. The Hebrew seems to say "The enemy (a collective term interpreted as plural) are finished, ruins forever; their cities you have pulled up; disappeared is the very memory of them." Most translations render these words as RSV and TEV have done; AT, however, connects "ruins forever" with "cities," as follows: "Perpetual ruins are the cities which thou hast rooted up"—which gives more sense but which does not conform to the Hebrew division of the lines. If the translator follows the TEV expression "**our enemies are finished**," there may be some problems, since in many languages only processes can be said to "finish." In some cases one may say "our enemies are lost forever to our eyes," or in an active construction, "never again can we look upon our enemies, because they are gone forever."

Have vanished in everlasting ruins: "have been completely destroyed and have disappeared forever."

The same fate that fell on the wicked came also upon **their cities**: God has "rooted them out." The verb is used more naturally of plants or trees; only here is it applied to a city, but it refers to nations in Deuteronomy 29.28; Jeremiah 12.14. Here FRCL uses a modern equivalent: "you have emptied their cities of people."

The very memory of them has perished: TEV seems to give the meaning of the Hebrew line, "**they are completely forgotten**," which is literally "perished their memory, they," with the pronoun at the end providing emphasis. However, that pronoun is placed at the beginning of the following line (in order to provide a line beginning with the Hebrew letter *he*), but it is not separated from the preceding line, so that it is taken as emphatic by RSV, **the very memory**; this is also the judgment of HOTTP. NEB and FRCL take the Hebrew consonants of that word to represent the verb "to thunder, to roar," and NEB translates "The Lord thunders," placing this clause at the beginning of verse 7. The TEV rendering, if taken literally, can mean that people will try to recall them and be unable to do so. Since the idea here is that the remembrance of these persons will disappear, it is sometimes necessary to say "no one will ever think of them again" or "their names will disappear from people's thoughts."

9.7-8	RSV	TEV

RSV	TEV
7 But the LORD sits enthroned for ever, he has established his throne for judgment; 8 and he judges the world with righteousness, he judges the peoples with equity.	7 But the LORD is king forever; he has set up his throne for judgment. 8 He rules the world with righteousness; he judges the nations with justice.

The beginning of verse 7 should be marked by a contrast: the enemies and the cities perish, but the Lord remains forever.

The Lord is again pictured in his role as ruler and judge of all people. **Sits enthroned** translates the verb "to sit"; see comments on "thy seat" in 7.7. Here the Lord's throne is thought of as being in heaven (contrast with verse 11, below). The verb "to sit" may have the more general sense of "dwell, abide, remain," and that is how the Septuagint has translated it here; so NJV "But the Lord abides forever."

The verb translated **he has established** means "make firm, set up"—see 7.9; 8.3.

For judgment means "in order to judge (humankind)."

Verses 7-8 are a semantic unit in which the images of throne and judgment in verse 7 are carried forward into verse 8. In the latter, as in verse 6, there is a focusing taking place. This focusing is upon the manner of God's judgment, **with righteousness**. In order to make clear the relation of verse 8 to verse 7, a connective is needed in English; for example, verse 8 can begin with "In fact, God rules the world with righteousness" or "Furthermore, God judges . . . ." Another way is to begin verse 7 "But not only is the LORD on his throne" and begin verse 8 "he even judges the world . . ." or "he also rules the world . . . ."

The two lines in verse 8 are parallel and synonymous; the two verbs for "to judge" are those used in 7.8; **the world** is expanded with **the peoples**; and **righteousness** and **equity** are identical in meaning. A common English idiom for saying the two is "fairly and squarely." **Righteousness** and **equity** are expressed idiomatically in some languages in a negative manner; for example, "he does not judge with two mouths" or "he does not judge with money." Rendered positively, "he judges with a true word" or "he judges with one mouth."

Some translations (NEB, SPCL, NIV, NJB) have the two verbs in verse 8 in the future tense, "He will rule . . . he will judge." This may be followed by the translator, but the present tense seems preferable.

	RSV		TEV
9	The LORD is a stronghold for the oppressed, a stronghold in times of trouble.	9	The LORD is a refuge for the oppressed, a place of safety in times of trouble.
10	And those who know thy name put their trust in thee, for thou, O LORD, hast not forgotten those who seek thee.	10	Those who know you, LORD, will trust you; you do not abandon anyone who comes to you.

Is translates the imperfect of the verb "to be"; some take it as a wish, "May the LORD be" (NJB, NEB, TOB); some commentators, following the Septuagint, change the Hebrew vowels to get "The LORD has become."

The psalmist's thought now turns to how Yahweh protects those who trust him. The word translated **stronghold** means a secure height or a high wall or fortress, and occurs often in Psalms as a metaphor for God's protection (NJV "haven"); it is repeated in line b. For poetic effect TEV uses two terms, "**a refuge . . . a place of safety.**" **Stronghold** or "fortress" as structures are often unknown in many cultures, and attempts to invent descriptive terms such as "big house for defense" do not always yield satisfactory results. Consequently, in such cases it is usually best to transfer to a nonmetaphor, as TEV has done; for example, "The LORD protects the oppressed."

The oppressed (also 10.18; 74.21) are powerless people who are crushed, exploited, discriminated against, whose only hope is the Lord. **Oppressed** is in a sense elliptical and is expressed in some languages as "people who are pushed down" or "people whose necks are held down by others."

The word translated **trouble** means more narrowly "drought" (used only here, in 10.1, and in Jer 14.1).

Verse 10 reaches back to verse 5 and contrasts **those who know thy name** with the wicked, whose name God has blotted out. Therefore it is important in translation to reflect the contrast by using related expressions in the two verses.

To "know the name of Yahweh" is to have a personal relationship with him of trust and dependence; for **name** see comments on 5.11. **Who know thy name** most often means nothing more than being acquainted with the name of someone. In many languages it will be necessary to fill out the missing components; for example, "those who know you in their hearts" or "people who truly know you."

Forgotten here has the sense of "forsake, neglect, abandon"; negatively expressed, "not help." It is well to begin line b of verse 10 with **for**, giving the ground, or reason, for the psalmist's statement in line a.

Seek translates a verb meaning "to look for." It has a broad range of meaning: "to search, inquire about, go to for information." With God as object it may mean "to pray to, worship, or serve him." Sometimes it shades over into the meaning "to care for," that is, to like, to be concerned about (as in 142.4 "no man cares for me"). So Dahood translates here "those who care for you"; NJV "those who turn to you." In the translation of **those who seek thee**, it is necessary to avoid giving the impression that God is a lost object to be found. TEV avoids this problem with "**who comes to you.**" However, in many languages it is necessary to add the purpose of coming; for example, "you do not abandon anyone who comes to you for help" or ". . . anyone who comes to worship you."

9.11   RSV   TEV

> Sing praises to the LORD, who   Sing praise to the LORD, who
>   dwells in Zion!   rules in Zion!
> Tell among the peoples his   Tell every nation what he has
>   deeds!   done!

In verses 11-12 the psalmist exhorts the people to **sing praises** to Yahweh (see the verb in 7.17b), who **dwells in Zion**.

Sing praises to the LORD often requires recasting as "Sing and praise the LORD" or "Sing and say that the LORD is truly great."

The verb "to dwell" translates the verb which means "to sit" (see comments on "thy seat" in 7.7) and may mean here "to live" (RSV, NEB, NJB), or "to rule" (TEV); NJV, SPCL have "who reigns in Zion"; FRCL "who has his throne in Zion"; Dahood "the King of Zion." If a verb meaning "sit" is used idiomatically in the sense of "to dwell" (a rather common usage), it may be necessary to say "sits and rules"; otherwise "rules" will be sufficient.

Zion is the poetic name for Jerusalem and, in a more restricted sense, the Temple, where Yahweh rules over his people (see comments on 2.6).

The peoples are here, as elsewhere, foreign nations. In many languages it is more natural to tell something to people than to nations, but in some cases it may be necessary to express both, "the people of the different nations."

His deeds translates a word often used in Psalms of God's actions on behalf of his people, freeing them from bondage in Egypt and taking them to the Promised Land; it is synonymous with "wonderful deeds" in 9.1 (some have "his mighty acts").

9.12   RSV   TEV

> For he who avenges blood is   God remembers those who suffer;
>   mindful of them;   he does not forget their cry,
> he does not forget the cry of the   and he punishes those who
>   afflicted.   wrong them.

Verse 12 has a chiastic arrangement in Hebrew in which line a ends with "he remembers" and line b begins with "he does not forget." The second line emphasizes God's remembering, and remembering who is to be avenged is the task of the "seeker of bloods" (see next paragraph). Therefore line b, **he does not forget**, emphasizes the content of both verb and subject in line a. TEV has kept all the elements of the parallelism but has switched their order.

Yahweh is referred to in the Hebrew as "the seeker of bloods" (RSV and NIV literal rendition **he who avenges blood** is not normal English; see also NEB and NJB). The expression defines the person whose duty it was to seek out a murderer and kill him; usually this person was a close relative of the dead person. So TEV "**he punishes** those who wrong them," and SPCL "he punishes those who treat them violently." This better brings out the meaning of "blood"; or else, "those who brutally mistreat them" or even "who kill them." Yahweh, as the God of his people, wreaks vengeance on their enemies (Gen 9.5-6; Ezek 33.6; see in 2 Chr 24.22 the dying prayer of the murdered Zechariah).

Is mindful of and **does not forget** express God's constant concern and care. **Forget the cry of the afflicted** is somewhat ambiguous in RSV and in the TEV form, as it may imply merely forgetting what their cry sounds like. In order to avoid this kind of wrong meaning, it is sometimes necessary to render the meaning as a positive expression, "he always pays attention to their cry," "he knows when the afflicted cry out," or "he listens to the cry of the afflicted."

The afflicted translates a term often used in Psalms for those who are poor, persecuted, exploited, and in particular the pious Israelites who, oppressed by their fellow human beings, had only Yahweh as their source of hope and security. In some instances the word will be translated "the humble," with emphasis on their submissive reliance on God. It is often necessary to specify who or what causes people to be **afflicted**, or to **"suffer"**; for example, "those who suffer from evil people" or "those whom evil people oppress."

For greater ease of understanding, TEV has restructured the material in this verse; in RSV **them** in line a does not refer to something previously mentioned, but refers forward to **the afflicted** in line b. The advantage of the reordering in TEV is evident. **"Remembers"** in line a is parallel to **"not forget"** in line b, and **"those who suffer"** is parallel to **"their cry,"** while the resulting strong action of punishing is kept for the final line.

9.13-14	RSV	TEV

13	Be gracious to me, O LORD!
	Behold what I suffer from those
	   who hate me,
	O thou who liftest me up from
	   the gates of death,
		13 Be merciful to me, O LORD!
		   See the sufferings my enemies
		     cause me!
		Rescue me from death, O LORD,

14	that I may recount all thy praises,
	   that in the gates of the daugh-
	   ter of Zion
	I may rejoice in thy deliverance.
		14 that I may stand before the
		     people of Jerusalem
		   and tell them all the things for
		     which I praise you.
		I will rejoice because you saved
		   me.

In these two verses the psalmist prays to God to deliver him from death; there is no obvious connection between this petition and the glad cry of praise for God's help in verses 11-12. From here to the end of Psalm 10 the composition has the form of a lament by an individual.

Be gracious: see comments on 4.1.

What I suffer translates a word that is used also in verse 12, there translated "the afflicted."

"My enemies" (TEV) is literally **those who hate me** (RSV); the same verb is used in 5.5. Instead of the verb meaning "to hate," one Hebrew manuscript has the verb

for "to lift up"; so NEB ". . . look upon my affliction, thou who hast lifted me up
. . . ."

TEV has translated verse 13c as a plea, "**Rescue me**" (so Dahood, who comments that the participle "apparently has the force of an imperative"; also SPCL, NJB, NIV). Such interpretation fits better with the following verse, "in order that . . . ," as a consequence of the action requested. Most translations, however, take it as a participial phrase descriptive of Yahweh as "you who rescue me from death." BJ translates as a statement, "You rescue me."

The gates of death is a figurative phrase for the world of the dead, Sheol, as a city with gates (see Job 38.17; Psa 107.18; Isa 38.10; Matt 16.18); for "Sheol" see comments on 6.5. **The gates of death** must usually be replaced by a nonmetaphor meaning simply "**death**," as in TEV. "To lift up from the gates of death" means to save from death, to prevent the person from dying. As elsewhere, this refers to premature death, to sudden, unexpected death caused by disease or enemies.

In verse 14 the psalmist expresses his desire to **recount all thy praises . . . in the gates of the daughter of Zion** ("stand before the people of Jerusalem and tell them," TEV).

Recount or "tell" translates the verb used also in 9.1.

Thy praises translates a word meaning praise offered to God, thanksgiving, gratitude, which is often used in Psalms (in Hebrew the Book of Psalms has the title "Praises").

In the gates represents the open place near the gates, inside the city, where people gathered for social, legal, and commercial purposes; so TEV's rendering, "**before the people of Jerusalem**."

The Hebrew expression **the daughter of Zion** is a poetic name for Jerusalem and its people; it is more correctly translated "Daughter Zion." NJV attempts to catch the poetic quality with "Fair Zion."

TEV "**that I may stand before the people**" would imply in some languages that the psalmist is simply reclining and wants to stand upright, rather than to appear in their presence. Therefore this clause may be recast as "in order that I may go to the people of Jerusalem."

Rejoice: the Hebrew verb means to express joy by means of glad cries.

For **deliverance** see comments on 3.8; this salvation is from imminent death.

9.15-16   RSV   TEV

15   The nations have sunk in the pit   15   The heathen have dug a pit and
     which they made;   fallen in;
     in the net which they hid has   they have been caught in their
     their own foot been caught.   own trap.
16   The LORD has made himself   16   The LORD has revealed himself by
     known, he has executed judg-   his righteous judgments,
     ment;   and the wicked are trapped by
     the wicked are snared in the   their own deeds.
     work of their own hands.
                    Higgaion. Selah

93

In these two verses the psalmist speaks of the punishment of the heathen in vivid terms of their being victims of their own evil plans (see 7.15-16).

For **nations** see comments on 2.1.

Two figures are used: that of a **pit**, such as was dug in order to catch wild animals, and that of a **net**, used for catching birds, fish, or small animals. For **pit** see comments on 7.15. Instead of **net**, which is not used widely in English as a specific term for an instrument to catch animals, TEV uses the more generic term "**trap**." The verb translated **have sunk in** appears in Psalms only here and in 69.2,14. The verb "to hide" is often used with "traps" and "nets" (see 31.4; 35.7-8; 64.5; 140.5; 142.3).

In cultures where trapping animals in pits is unknown, it will be necessary to make explicit the purpose of such a pit; for example, "It is just as though the heathen have dug a pit to make their enemies fall in and have fallen in themselves."

In allowing the wicked to be "**trapped by their own deeds**" (TEV), Yahweh reveals himself as a just judge. The expression **the LORD has made himself known** must often be recast as "the LORD has shown who he is."

The words "**by his righteous judgments**" (TEV) translate "he has done justice" (so SPCL; AT and RSV **he has executed judgment**); NEB "Justice is done." "**His righteous judgments**" is a nominal phrase which must often be recast as a clause, and the object of the event of judging must often be made explicit; for example, "he judges people in the right way." This entire clause can then be related to the previous one as a clause of means: "The Lord has shown who he is by the fact that he judges people in the right way."

In the last statement (verse 16b), "by the work of his hands the wicked (person) is snared," "his hands" is usually taken to mean the hands of the wicked person himself; but Briggs and Mft take it to mean the hands of Yahweh: "as his hands have trapped the ungodly."[1] **In the work of their own hands** and TEV's "**by their own deeds**" are used to express the means by which they are caught. In this context **the work of their own hands** refers specifically to **the pit** and **the net** that they had prepared in order to trap their enemies; it is therefore better to translate "are trapped by the devices they themselves built." In languages which require an active verb, line b of verse 16 must be recast; for example, "the evil deeds which bad people do trap them." If the term "net" is used, one must be careful to indicate specifically the type of nets used to catch wild animals, and not one of the various nets used only for fishing.

Higgaion appears also in 19.14, where it means "meditation," and in 92.3b, where it is translated "melody." If it is related to the verb for "to meditate" (1.2), it may mean a quiet melody. NJB translates "Muted music" (so TOB); FRCL "interlude."

Selah: see comments on 3.2.

---

[1]Instead of understanding the verb in the Masoretic text in line b as the passive of the verb "to snare" (RSV **are snared**, TEV "**are trapped**"), HOTTP ("C" decision) takes the Masoretic text pointing (so Briggs) as the participle of the verb "to push" or "to stumble," meaning either "Yahweh pushes" or "the wicked stumble." It seems better to take the text as RSV, TEV, and others have done.

9.17   RSV   TEV

> The wicked shall depart to Sheol,
> all the nations that forget God.

> Death is the destiny of all the
> wicked,
> of all those who reject God.

For **Sheol** see comments on 6.5.

Depart translates the verb "to turn" (see comments on 6.4). Some commentators stress the notion of "returning" here, along the lines of the biblical idea of a person at death returning to the dust from which he was made (104.29). Instead of translating the verb as an indicative **shall depart**, it may be translated as a wish, "May the wicked depart" (see NJV, NJB, FRCL).

The wicked in line a is parallel with **the nations** (or, "the heathen" in line b. See comments on **the nations** in 2.1. Line b of verse 17 depends for its meaning on the verb in line a. That is, what happens to the **wicked** also happens to the **nations that forget God**. The second line carries the first one further and may be translated, for example, "Wicked people are on their way to death; in fact, everyone who forgets God is headed for death."

To **forget God** means to ignore him (NJV), reject him, not worship him (see also 44.20; 50.22). NEB has "are heedless of God." Cohen defines it thus: "Deliberately ignore His precepts and rebel against His rule." **Forget God** tends to mean that people fail to remember God's name or fail to recognize him. "**Reject God**" (TEV) is sometimes rendered "they say God is worthless," or "they say 'No' to God," or "they refuse to obey God."

9.18   RSV   TEV

> For the needy shall not always be
> forgotten,
> and the hope of the poor shall
> not perish for ever.

> The needy will not always be ne-
> glected;
> the hope of the poor will not be
> crushed forever.

The psalmist affirms the concern of Yahweh for the oppressed, as contrasted with the fate of the wicked in verse 17. The passive verb **shall not . . . be forgotten** has God as the implied actor: "God will not forget them." Here "forget" means "not care for, neglect." In translation a positive expression may be better: "God will help (or, rescue) the needy," " God will answer the prayers of the needy."

In two parallel lines the oppressed are described as **the needy** and **the poor** (same word as in verse 12). In many languages, particularly among marginal peoples, terms for **the poor** are often lacking. Consequently it is necessary to use a descriptive phrase such as "those who are weak and pitiful," "people who have nothing," "people who live far from the chief's compound," or "people who own only one small pig."

Typical of parallel lines is the absence of a connector in Hebrew, particularly when the first clause expresses a negative. Here the second clause in TEV can be improved by beginning it "nor shall the hope."

The hope of the poor is their hope that God will rescue them from their troubles. **Hope** may sometimes be rendered "to look forward with confidence." In many languages it is not possible to speak of an emotional event such as hope perishing, as in RSV, or "**crushed**," as in TEV, but one can destroy or crush the poor who hope. Consequently this statement may be recast as "the poor who look forward with confidence in God will not be crushed forever." In an active sense this may be rendered "God will not forever destroy the poor people who look to God with confidence that he will help them," or **hope** can be kept in focus by translating "the poor will always continue to hope that God will save them."

For ever appears to suggest that, although the poor seem to be forgotten by God, they will not always remain that way. In time their **hope** for God's help will be rewarded.

9.19-20	RSV	TEV
19	Arise, O LORD! Let not man prevail; let the nations be judged before thee!	Come, LORD! Do not let men defy you! Bring the heathen before you and pronounce judgment on them.
20	Put them in fear, O LORD! Let the nations know that they are but men! *Selah*	Make them afraid, O LORD; make them know that they are only mortal beings.

The psalm ends with a prayer to Yahweh to take action against **the nations**.

Arise: see comments on 3.7. **Prevail** or "**defy**" (TEV) translates a verb meaning "to be strong, overcome, prevail." So FRCL "don't allow man to be stronger than you," and NJB "human strength shall not prevail."

In the context of God judging the heathen, it would seem that **prevail** focuses mainly on being successful in court. Therefore **Let not man prevail** can be translated "Men must not win their case," or "Men must not defend themselves successfully when you judge them," or ". . . not be able to escape condemnation."

The first line of verse 20 is literally "put terror to them, LORD"; but the Hebrew word translated "terror" by ancient versions and modern translations is not spelled as usual (see the commentaries; NJV footnote). The Septuagint translated the consonants with different vowels, resulting in the word for "lawgiver," as follows: "O Lord, appoint a lawgiver over them!" It is best to follow RSV and TEV here.

Men ("**Mortal beings**," TEV) translates the same word translated **man** in verse 19; the emphasis is on human beings as frail mortals, in comparison with the eternal God (see 10.18). The phrase may be rendered "all people are doomed to die"; for example, "that they are nothing more than people who are doomed to die."

Selah: see 3.2.

Psalm 10

In its present form as a separate psalm (see introduction to Psa 9), this psalm is a lament by an individual who is persecuted and oppressed by wicked men, and who calls to the Lord for help. The psalmist complains to the Lord about the Lord's apparent lack of concern for his plight (verse 1), and then denounces at length the vicious character and violent actions of his enemies (verses 2-11). He calls on the Lord to punish the wicked (verse 12-15), praises the Lord's greatness (verse 16), and closes the psalm with a confident statement about the Lord's willingness to rescue the helpless (verses 17-18).

HEADING: "**A Prayer for Justice**" (TEV); "Prayer for help against oppressors"; "Prayer of the oppressed"; "Prayer asking for God's help." In many languages the TEV wording must be recast as two clauses; for example, "The psalmist prays that God will judge matters rightly"; see Heading of Psalm 7.

10.1	RSV	TEV
	Why dost thou stand afar off, O LORD? Why dost thou hide thyself in times of trouble?	Why are you so far away, O LORD? Why do you hide yourself when we are in trouble?

The psalmist complains that Yahweh seems **afar off** (see similar sentiment in 22.1), and that he has "hidden himself" (see the plea in 55.1). It is the protest of a person who sees no evidence of God's concern or care. God seems totally indifferent to human suffering or needs.

Since this is not a request for information, the meaning may be expressed by means of statements: "Lord, you are so far away! We are in trouble, but you hide yourself from us!" In some languages, to be "far away" must be said in relation to something else. In the present case it may be understood to be the psalmist, identified with the poor in contrast to the wicked: "Why are you so far from us, LORD?"

For **times of trouble** see comment on "trouble" in 9.9.

10.2	RSV	TEV
	In arrogance the wicked hotly pursue the poor; let them be caught in the	The wicked are proud and persecute the poor; catch them in the traps they

schemes which they have de- vised.	have made.

The **arrogance** of the wicked is their proud assumption that they can with impunity persecute and harass **the poor**. **Arrogance** as a description of **the wicked** may in some languages be expressed as "evil men who think big of themselves" or "evil men with swollen hearts."

The verb translated **hotly pursue** (TEV "**persecute**") is the same one that in 7.13 means "set ablaze." NAB has "harass"; FRCL "exploits"; NJV "hounds." "**Persecute**" must often be rendered as "cause someone to suffer." Line a may then be "Evil men think big of themselves and cause those to suffer who have nothing."

Line b of the verse is translated as a plea by RSV, NEB, NJV; however, NAB, NIV, SPCL, and FRCL take it as a statement: "they (the poor) are caught in the traps that they (the wicked) have made." As a request, the thought is similar to that in 9.15. As a direct command it is often necessary to make clear that God is the one who causes this to happen.

The word for **schemes** is general, meaning plan, device, plot (also in verse 4; 21.11; 139.20); TEV uses the concrete expression "**traps**" (also SPCL).

10.3

RSV	TEV
For the wicked boasts of the de- sires of his heart, and the man greedy for gain curses and renounces the LORD.	The wicked man is proud of his evil desires; the greedy man curses and rejects the LORD.

Boasts of (TEV "**is proud**") translates a verb meaning "to praise," which is used many times in Psalms; here, however, it has a bad sense, as in 5.5, "the boastful."

Desires translates a word which means wish, appetite, craving (see 78.29-30); **of his heart** represents what is literally "of his *nefesh*" (see comments on 3.2). TOB translates "The wicked boasts of having achieved his purpose"; FRCL "brags about his ambitions." TEV has "**evil desires**," but it would be better simply to say "desires" or "ambitions." **Boasts** refers to a verbal activity, as does **curses** in line b. In many languages it will be more natural to recast verse 3a into direct address; for example, "Evil men boast and say, 'The things my heart wishes for are great.' " **Greedy** translates a Hebrew word that focuses upon taking what does not belong to one, and may be rendered as "people who take advantage of others" or "People who make profit from others."

Curses: this translates a Hebrew verb whose normal meaning is "to bless, praise." Here, however, it is used as a euphemism for "to curse." For other instances of the verb used with this meaning, with God as object, see 1 Kings 21.10,13; Job 1.5,11. HOTTP, however, regards the word as a scribal correction, made in order to soften the language,[1] and takes the meaning to be "he blesses." NEB "in his greed

---

[1]Such a scribal correction is technically known by its Hebrew name *tiqqun soferim*. Such changes by the copyists were made usually when they thought the text spoke improperly of God.

gives wickedness his blessing" and NIV "he blesses the greedy" are both possible (see ASV footnote) but are not very probable (see Kirkpatrick). It seems best to follow RSV, TEV, and the great majority of translations.

Curses should not be understood in this context as bringing down evil upon God in the sense of invoking an injurious curse, but rather in speaking evil of him; for example, "greedy people use evil words to speak against God."

Renounces translates a verb that means to belittle, despise, treat without respect (also in verse 13; 74.10,18).[2] Line b of verse 3 may be rendered in direct address: "men who take advantage of others speak evil words and say, 'You, LORD, are nothing.' "

10.4	RSV	TEV
	In the pride of his countenance the wicked does not seek him; all his thoughts are, "There is no God."	A wicked man does not care about the LORD; in his pride he thinks that God doesn't matter.

This verse in Hebrew is not altogether clear; the sense seems to be "The wicked man in his pride never seeks, there is not God (are) all his thoughts." But the division of phrases and lines in the Hebrew text makes this rendering debatable.

TEV has restructured the various elements, placing at the beginning of line b "**in his pride**," which modifies the "**wicked man**" of line a.

Pride (only here is the noun used in Psalms) comes from a verb meaning "to be haughty, arrogant"; see Proverbs 16.18 "a haughty spirit." Some commentators take the phrase "in the pride of his face" to refer to God, meaning God's anger; so Briggs, who translates verse 4 as what the wicked man thinks about God.

Does not seek him: for the verb "to seek" see 9.10. It is to be noted that there is no object expressed in the Hebrew text (RSV supplies **him**). Some take the statement "he does not seek" as being part of the wicked man's thoughts about God, meaning that he thinks "He (God) does not call to account" (NAB, NJV). FRCL has "he does not demand anything." Applied to the wicked man himself, **seek** here means "to be concerned about, think about, care about."

If the translator follows the rearrangement of TEV, the expression "**does not care about the LORD**" may often be rendered as "the LORD is not important to him" or "pays no attention to the LORD." If on the other hand the form of RSV is preferred, **seek him** will need to be recast in order to avoid giving the impression that God has been lost. It is the relationship to God that man seeks; for example, "because they are proud, evil people do not want to have anything to do with God."

Thoughts translates the word rendered "schemes" in verse 2.

There is no God translates the Hebrew words; but as commentators point out, this is not philosophical atheism, a denial of God's existence, but practical atheism,

---

[2]The Septuagint represents a different text: "The sinner is acclaimed for the desires of his heart, and the wicked man is praised" (the two verbs of the Hebrew text were taken to be passive forms).

a way of life which does not take God and his demands into account; so TEV **"God doesn't matter."** NJB footnote comments "Denying the action of Providence, he speaks and acts as if there were no God at all." NJV translates "God does not care"; NIV "in all his thoughts there is no room for God." See also 14.1.

10.5	RSV	TEV

His ways prosper at all times; thy judgments are on high, out of his sight; as for all his foes, he puffs at them.	**A wicked man succeeds in everything. He cannot understand God's judgments; he sneers at his enemies.**

This verse continues the long and bitter meditation on the wicked.

His ways means the way of life, plans, and actions, as in 1.6. **Prosper** translates a verb found only here and in Job 20.21, "to endure, be strong." **Prosper** may be rendered as "to get all one wants." In some languages one may say, for example, "evil people always get what they desire." The psalmist is not stating an absolute truth; in his despair he is saying that this is what seems to happen.

In line <u>b</u> the psalmist speaks of God's **judgments** as being beyond the wicked man's understanding, using the striking statement "Your judgments are high, far away from him!" FRCL translates "The judgments of God don't affect him."[3] **On high** refers to the purpose and nature of God's judging and can be rendered, for example, "he cannot understand how God judges people" or "he cannot understand God's way of judging people."

NEB, instead of taking the word for **foes** in the sense of the verb "to be hostile," takes it as "restraint": "he scoffs at all restraint." While possible, this does not seem very probable, and RSV and TEV should be followed.

Puffs translates a verb meaning "to hiss, breathe hard." NJV has "snorts," NJB "scoffs," TOB "spits." The Hebrew term means to hold in contempt. In many languages such expressions are rendered in idiomatic language; for example, "to wag the head at" or "to shake the fingers at." In nonfigurative language one may say "they consider their enemies to be worthless" or "they treat their enemies as if they were nothing."

10.6	RSV	TEV

He thinks in his heart, "I shall not be moved; throughout all generations I shall not meet adversity."	**He says to himself, "I will never fail; I will never be in trouble."**

---

[3]HOTTP says that the Hebrew word for **on high** may be interpreted in two ways: (1) "your judgments are on high, far from his eyes" (as RSV); or (2) "O Most High, your judgments are far from his eyes."

The expression "He says in his heart" is a biblical way of saying "he thinks, he says to himself," which may be rendered in some languages by the same figurative expression or by a similar idiom.

I shall not be moved translates the causative of the verb meaning to totter, stagger, fall (see 13.4; 15.5; 16.8).

In line b some scholars take the Hebrew phrase "to generation and generation" to refer to the descendants of the wicked man, who believes that they will always be free from trouble. Most, however, take the expression to mean "at all times, forever," or combined with the negative, "never." But it should be noticed that line b, **"I will never be in trouble"** (TEV), may be considered as part of what the psalmist is saying about the wicked man, as follows: "(the man) who is never in trouble"; so NJB and HOTTP. However, the interpretation followed by the majority seems to be preferable.

The second line of this verse is an example of shifting to a heightened expression for the purpose of emphasizing the impossibility of the wicked person being in trouble. TEV's **"I will never"** follows the same wording as in line a and fails to give the emphasis required by the parallelism. In English this may be better done, for example, by "I will never fail; as long as time lasts I will be free of trouble," or by a combination of positive and negative clauses, as "I will always be successful; in fact, I shall never in all the world fail."

10.7	RSV	TEV

His mouth is filled with cursing and deceit and oppression; under his tongue are mischief and iniquity.	His speech is filled with curses, lies, and threats; he is quick to speak hateful, evil words.

The wicked man's **mouth is filled with curses, deceit** (as in 5.6), and **oppression** (that is, "threats"; the Hebrew word is found also in 55.11; 72.14; and Pro 29.13). In some languages it is not natural to speak of the **"speech"** or the **mouth** being filled with curses, and therefore it is sometimes necessary to recast line a as a temporal clause; for example, "Whenever he speaks, he curses people, lies to people, and threatens people." Cursing here does not refer to the use of profanity but rather to the invocation of a source of power through a word formula to cause someone harm.

It should be noted that in the Hebrew the first word of verse 7, "curse," is placed at the end of the preceding line; some commentators and translators connect it with that line, taking it as a verb. So NJB "Free of trouble himself, he wishes it on others." The majority, however, take it as RSV and TEV do.

"Is quick to speak" (TEV) translates **under his tongue**. Some scholars see here the idea of such words being to the liking of the evil man; they are like tasty morsels which he savors (Kirkpatrick); see Job 20.12. TOB translates "He is always ready for"; NJV and NIV have "His mouth is full of"; SPCL has "his words hide (oppression and evil)." The idea expressed by TEV and TOB seems to be the most natural way to understand the phrase, but the meaning represented by NJV and NIV is also possible.

Mischief translates a word meaning trouble, misfortune, evil (it occurs in 7.14,16, and also in verse 14, below). The word **iniquity** translates a word appearing many times in Psalms; in some instances it may have the specific meaning of a magic spell by means of which the speaker brings trouble on his victim. If **iniquity** is taken as a magic spell, it may be thought of as the result of a curse pronounced in line a, and in most cases will require a repetition of the curse term or its synonym as used in line a; for example, "His mouth is full of evil curses which cause people harm" or "With his mouth he curses people and binds them with his evil words."

As translated in the Septuagint, verse 7a (in part) is quoted in Romans 3.14.

10.8-9 RSV	TEV
8 He sits in ambush in the villages; in hiding places he murders the innocent.	8 He hides himself in the villages, waiting to murder innocent people. He spies on his helpless victims;
His eyes stealthily watch for the hapless,	9 he waits in his hiding place like a lion.
9 he lurks in secret like a lion in his covert;	He lies in wait for the poor;
he lurks that he may seize the poor,	he catches them in his trap and drags them away.
he seizes the poor when he draws him into his net.	

In these two verses the psalmist describes how the wicked oppress the poor. In vivid figures he pictures the whole process in terms of a criminal hiding in order to rob and kill; of a lion waiting to pounce on the helpless prey; and of a hunter catching an animal in a trap.

Ambush translates a word found only here and in Judges 9.35; Joshua 8.9; and 2 Chronicles 13.13. **Sits in ambush** must be clarified in some languages along the line taken by TEV, **"hides"** in line a and **"waiting"** in line b. **Villages** were communities unprotected by walls, and so easily attacked. (Instead of the word in the traditional Hebrew text, K-B and NJB prefer a similar Hebrew word meaning "reeds.") **The innocent** are usually those who are not guilty, but in the present context, where they are helpless victims, they are simply good people and may be rendered "helpless people" or "people who have no one to protect them."

His eyes stealthily watch ("He spies," TEV) translates the literal "his eyes shelter" (the Hebrew verb means "to hide" or "to treasure"). Although most translations assume this verb can be translated "to spy," some follow the Septuagint and change the Hebrew text to a form of a Hebrew verb which means "to watch"—so NEB. The meaning is not greatly affected by the change.[4]

The hapless translates a term whose precise meaning is unknown (it also appears in verses 10, 14, and nowhere else). Most commentators and translators take

---

[4]HOTTP says that the Masoretic text may be interpreted in two ways: (1) "his eyes are hidden (to observe) the poor," meaning "in secret he spies on the poor"; or (2) "his eyes watch out for the poor," that is "he keeps his eyes on the poor."

it to mean "unfortunate, helpless, out of luck." The English word **hapless** means "unlucky."

He lurks in secret like a lion in his covert: "he hides and waits like a lion in its lair." This portrays the evil man crouching in some hiding place, waiting to spring out like a lion on his victim. If **lion** is unknown, the translator may have to replace it by a local animal that stalks its prey as a lion does.

For **the poor** see comment on "the afflicted" in 9.12; NJV has here "the lowly." For **net** see comment on 9.15b.

10.10	RSV	TEV

The hapless is crushed, sinks down, and falls by his might.

The helpless victims lie crushed; brute strength has defeated them.

This verse, especially line a, is difficult to understand; commentaries and translations offer a variety of explanations. The general sense of the text seems clear enough: it describes how **the hapless** are defeated; NJB, however, following in part the Septuagint, takes line a to refer to the wicked oppressor, and translates "He keeps watch, crouching down low" (also Weiser; AT, SPCL); likewise TOB, which continues in the next line, "and with all his weight he falls on the weak." HOTTP also takes the verb in line a to refer to the wicked oppressor.[5]

Line b is literally "and he (the victim) falls by his (the oppressor's) *atsum*," a word that elsewhere usually means "a great number," which does not fit the context here. AT has "mighty men." Some think that the figure of a lion is intended, and that this word refers to the lion's claws; so SPCL "the helpless fall into his claws," and NJB "falls into his clutches." NEB has "fall into his toils"; Dahood supposes "his pit." In view of the uncertainty, it seems best to use a general word, such as "power" or **might** (RSV); notice, however, that RSV **by his might** is meant to refer to the might of the wicked, of verses 3-9. In some languages it will be more satisfactory to reverse lines a and b and thus give the general cause **"brute strength"** first and then the specific consequence; for example, "Because he is so strong he has defeated them; he crushes the helpless victim down."

If the translator chooses to follow the interpretation of TOB and others, the translation can be "He bends down over them, and falls on them with all his weight."

10.11	RSV	TEV

He thinks in his heart, "God has forgotten,

The wicked man says to himself, "God doesn't care!

---

[5]The Masoretic text has two forms here: the *ketiv* (the written text) is "and being crushed"; the *qere* (the text to be read) is "he crouches," which is preferred by HOTTP.

<table>
<tr>
<td>he has hidden his face, he will
never see it."</td>
<td>He has closed his eyes and will
never see me!"</td>
</tr>
</table>

This verse is similar in thought to verse 4b. The subject (unexpressed in Hebrew) is assumed still to be "the wicked man" of verses 3-9 (see 94.7-9); however, it could be the victim of verse 10 (see the similar feeling in verse 1), but no translation takes it this way (unless this is what RSV means). It is possible to render this passage as direct address, as in TEV and RSV, or as indirect address, as follows: "The evil person thinks in his heart that God has forgotten about what he has done, that God has closed his eyes and that he will never see him." However, if the translator prefers to understand that the victim is the subject, then the translation may be (following the TEV model of verse 11) "They say to themselves, 'God doesn't care! . . .' "

Thinks in his heart: see comments on verse 6a.

Has forgotten, that is, God is not concerned, he "**doesn't care**" (TEV); NJV "is not mindful." The figure **he has hidden his face** means that God has turned his face away so as not to see; TEV uses an equivalent figure "**has closed his eyes**." SPCL has "he covers his face," which means he deliberately avoids looking at the evil deed (so NIV).

There is no expressed object for the verb "to see" in line b; it could be the wicked man (TEV "**me**") or the crime (RSV **it**); or else, as NJV has it, "he never looks," NEB "(he) has seen nothing," FRCL "he never sees anything."

<table>
<tr>
<td>**10.12-13**</td>
<td>RSV</td>
<td>TEV</td>
</tr>
</table>

<table>
<tr>
<td>12</td>
<td>Arise, O LORD; O God, lift up thy
hand;
forget not the afflicted.</td>
<td>12</td>
<td>O LORD, punish those wicked
men!
Remember those who are suf-
fering!</td>
</tr>
<tr>
<td>13</td>
<td>Why does the wicked renounce
God,
and say in his heart, "Thou wilt
not call to account"?</td>
<td>13</td>
<td>How can a wicked man despise
God
and say to himself, "He will not
punish me"?</td>
</tr>
</table>

The psalmist calls on Yahweh to take action: **Arise . . . lift up thy hand**. For **Arise** see comments on 3.7. The figure "to lift up the hand" may mean either to save (the helpless) or to punish (the oppressor); here the latter is meant. NJV "Strike at him"; or else "prepare to strike." **Lift up thy hand** may sometimes be translated by another metaphor or by a nonmetaphor; for example, "O God, cause them to suffer" or "O God, make them feel pain."

Forget not: this can be represented by a positive statement, "Take care of," "Be concerned with."

The afflicted ("**Those who are suffering**," TEV) translates "the oppressed" (see comments on "afflicted" in 9.12). Languages which use the expression "to make the wicked suffer" (line a) must avoid giving the impression that the psalmist is asking God in line b to remember these wicked ones. In order to avoid this possible confusion, it may be necessary to say in line b "remember the innocent people who suffer."

Renounce translates the same verb used in verse 3a and may sometimes be rendered as "to leave behind," "to turn away from," or "to let go."

Call to account translates the verb "to seek." Here, used of God, it means that God will not require the wicked man to pay for his evil deeds. The structure of verse 13 requires in many languages certain modifications, if it is not to be misleading and difficult to follow. The potential confusion is due to the fact that the statement "**He will not punish me**" is attached to the double question. In some languages it will be clearer to make each question independent; for example, "Why does the wicked person reject God? Why does he say in his heart that God will not punish him?" Or, using direct discourse, ". . . say in his heart, 'God will not punish me.' " Another way may be to shift the questions to statements; for example, "The wicked person despises God; he says in his heart that God will not punish him." A more forceful expression can be "How dare the wicked person despise God and say to himself that God will not punish him!"

10.14	RSV	TEV
	Thou dost see; yea, thou dost note trouble and vexation, that thou mayst take it into thy hands; the hapless commits himself to thee; thou hast been the helper of the fatherless.	But you do see; you take notice of trouble and suffering and are always ready to help. The helpless man commits himself to you; you have always helped the needy.

The psalmist strongly denies the claim of the wicked in verse 13 that God is not concerned; on the contrary, God does see, he does take note of people's **trouble** and **vexation** (the second noun appears in 6.7a, meaning there "grief"). SPCL, however, refers these two words to the evildoers, translating "You yourself have noticed their irritating evil." NJV seems to do the same: "You take note of mischief and vexation!" **See** often requires an indication of what is seen. Here the object is general, and one may say "but you see everything that happens." **Note** is sometimes rendered "pay attention to." **Trouble and vexation** must often be rendered as clauses; for example, "people who are in trouble and who suffer."

The meaning of line b in Hebrew is disputed; literally it says "to take in your hand." Some interpret this in a good sense, to help, to save (so NAB "taking them in your hands"; FRCL "you keep watch to take his cause in hand"; also NJB). Others, however (see Briggs), take it to have the unfavorable meaning of avenging, taking revenge (see 28.3); so KJV "to requite it with thy hand"; NJV "to requite is in Your power"; and SPCL "you will give them what they deserve." The Septuagint translates "to deliver them into your hands"—so AT. If the translator takes this expression as referring to God's favorable activity, then it will often be necessary to make explicit the goal of God's help. This can refer to the **hapless** in the next line or the troubled and suffering in the preceding line; for example, "you are always ready to help them." If, on the other hand, one takes the expression **take it into thy hands** to refer to an unfavorable act, one may have to say "in order that you can avenge them" or "so that you punish their enemies."

For **the hapless** see comments on verse 8.

Commits translates a verb meaning to leave, let go, abandon; here it has the sense of abandoning oneself, that is, trusting oneself completely to God. This idea is expressed in some languages by idioms such as "to lean upon God," "to rest one's heart on God," or "to put oneself in God's hands."

The fatherless, or "the orphan," is used here as a representative of all those who have no one to support them and protect them from exploitation and oppression (also verse 18). TEV uses a term which includes them all, **"the needy."** The standard biblical phrase for the helpless and oppressed people is "widows, orphans, and resident aliens." Normally the term "orphan" is too restrictive in meaning to be used here, and so the expression used for "the poor" in 9.18 can serve.

10.15   RSV   TEV

> Break thou the arm of the wicked   Break the power of wicked and
>   and evildoer;   evil men;
> seek out his wickedness till thou   punish them for the wrong they
>   find none.   have done
>   until they do it no more.

Arm is here, as often, a figure for power, strength, might. In expressive terms the psalmist asks God to break the power of the wicked and eliminate completely the evil they do. **Break**, as used in both RSV and TEV, is a figurative expression which in some languages will have to be replaced by another figure such as "wipe away," "undo" or "cut away." In other languages a nonmetaphor will be required, such as "Take away the power" or "Don't let wicked and evil men be powerful."

Seek out his wickedness means deal with it, eliminate it so completely that "you will not find any left at all." Or else, "make them pay for all their evil until there is no more to pay for." NJV has "so that when You look for his wickedness You will find it no more." Some take the object of the verb **find** to be the wicked man, not his wickedness: Knox "let him be seen no more"; NAB "let them not survive." If the translator follows the TEV model, it may be necessary to recast lines <u>b</u> and <u>c</u>; for example, "punish them until they do no more wrong."

10.16   RSV   TEV

> The LORD is king for ever and   The LORD is king forever and
>   ever;   ever.
> the nations shall perish from   Those who worship other gods
>   his land.   will vanish from his land.

In some languages both LORD and **king** will have to be possessed; for example, "Our LORD is our King." Sometimes **for ever and ever** may have to be recast as "he never ceases to rule" or "he will always rule."

After acclaiming Yahweh as the universal and everlasting **king**, the psalmist announces the doom of the heathen (**the nations**: see comments on 2.1 and 9.5): they will **perish from his land**. The meaning is not that of natural death, but of their being removed from the land of Israel. **His land** is the Lord's land. Some commentators and translators take it as past tense, "they have perished" (Kirkpatrick; NEB, NAB, NJB, BJ); others as future (AT, RSV, SPCL, FRCL, TEV); the Septuagint translates as imperative, addressed to the heathen, "Vanish!"; Briggs takes it as an imperative addressed to God, "Destroy the nations." The context seems to favor the future tense.

10.17-18

	RSV	TEV

RSV	TEV
17 O LORD, thou wilt hear the desire of the meek; thou wilt strengthen their heart, thou wilt incline thy ear	17 You will listen, O LORD, to the prayers of the lowly; you will give them courage.
18 to do justice to the fatherless and the oppressed, so that man who is of the earth may strike terror no more.	18 You will hear the cries of the oppressed and the orphans; you will judge in their favor, so that mortal men may cause terror no more.

In these last two verses the psalmist expresses his confidence that God will answer the prayer of those who cry to him for justice against their enemies; they are **the meek**, **the fatherless** (see verse 14), and **the oppressed** (see 9.9). **The meek** may sometimes be rendered "those who have a low place" or "people whom others look down on" (see comments on "afflicted" in 9.12).

Thou wilt hear means more than just hear the prayers of the people; it means to pay attention to and to answer.

Desire (same Hebrew word as in verse 3) means here the requests or prayers of the oppressed.

Strengthen translates the verb meaning to make strong or firm (see comments on "establish" in 7.9), here in the sense of giving confidence, courage. "**Give them courage**" is rendered idiomatically in some languages as "to make their hearts strong" or "to make firm their insides."

At the end of verse 17, "your ear will pay attention" can be taken as a complete statement, "You will listen," or it may go with the next verse, as RSV and TEV have done. TEV starts verse 18 with this verbal phrase and supplies the implicit object, "**the cries of the oppressed and the orphans**." It is important that "**You will hear**" not be rendered in such a way as to imply hearing without concern. It will often be necessary to say "you will listen to the pleas of the poor and the orphans and help them."

Do justice to ("**Judge in their favor**" TEV) translates the same verb as the second one for "judge" used in 7.8. It expresses the confidence that God is on the side of the oppressed and will give them their rights.

The phrase **man who is of the earth** is a way of speaking of human beings as frail mortal creatures (see similar thought in 9.19-20; see also comments on "man" in 8.4). Mft has "mortal man"; NJB "earthborn humans"; another possibility is "mere earthborn man."

Strike terror is the way most translations represent the Hebrew verb; NEB, however, translates the last line of the verse "that fear may never drive men from their homes again"; this is not very probable. FRCL is better: "so that no one on earth may ever again be a tyrant."

Psalm 11

This psalm is a song of confidence by an individual who is sure that God answers prayer, rewards good people, and punishes evil ones. The text gives no clue of the author's situation other than that, in verses 1 and 4, he has gone to the Temple, where he addresses friends who had advised him to flee. He rebukes them for suggesting that he run away (verses 1-3), and expresses his confidence in Yahweh's readiness to punish and to reward (verses 4-7).

This short psalm is not characterized by repetitive images. However, it is worthwhile to note how the contrasting themes of safety–destruction, punishment–reward, are laid out by the poet. The psalm opens on the theme of safety: "In the LORD I take refuge." Immediately in verse 1b the movement swings toward the opposite pole. The image is that of a bird fleeing for its life, and is followed in verse 2 by that of the hunter readying his arrow. The destructive arrow is for the upright in heart and is shot in the darkness. In verse 3 the destruction is completed and the righteous is left helpless and insecure. At this point of defeat the poet reaches back again where he began, and now the Lord is supremely in charge, in the Temple where the righteous will encounter him, on his throne in heaven where all forces are subject to his rule. In contrast with the wicked who destroy the righteous in the dark, his eyes are watching both the good and the wicked. In verse 5 he has tested them both, and he hates the wicked, who love to destroy. Out of his hate for the destroyers, who had to bend bows and fix their arrows to shoot, he sends down a rain of burning punishment. With verse 7 destruction and punishment are gone. As in the beginning, the theme is quiet safety. Unlike God's hating the destroyers, he loves those who do good. They will no longer be shot at in the darkness but will be rewarded by seeing God's face.

HEADING: "**Confidence in the LORD**" (TEV); "The confidence of the virtuous"; "Unshaken confidence in God"; "Confidence in God's concern for justice." Following TEV, the title of this psalm must often make explicit the one who has "**Confidence in the LORD**." This may be expressed as "The psalmist" or, as in verse 1, "I." "**Confidence**" may be rendered "I trust" or idiomatically in various ways; for example, "I rest my heart on the LORD" or "I recline on my LORD."

Hebrew Title: <u>**To the choirmaster. Of David**</u> (TEV "**By David**").

No specific direction is given <u>**to the choirmaster**</u> (see Hebrew title of Psa 4). The Masoretic text has only "By David"; two Hebrew manuscripts and the Septuagint have "A psalm by David."

11.1-2	RSV	TEV

	RSV	TEV
1	In the LORD I take refuge; how can you say to me, "Flee like a bird to the mountains;*e*	I trust in the LORD for safety. How foolish of you to say to me, "Fly away like a bird to the mountains,*p*
2	for lo, the wicked bend the bow, they have fitted their arrow to the string, to shoot in the dark at the upright in heart;	because the wicked have drawn their bows and aimed their arrows to shoot from the shadows at good men.

e Gk Syr Jerome Tg: Heb *flee to your mountain, O bird*

p Some ancient translations like a bird to the mountains; *Hebrew* bird, to your *(plural)* mountains.

For the verb translated **take refuge**, see comments at 2.12; most translations in English are like RSV (see also 31.1; 71.1). The interrogative **how?** is a rebuke: "How dare you . . . ?" or, as TEV, "**How foolish of you!**" The psalmist knew that his safety lay in trusting Yahweh, not in running away, as his friends (**you**) had suggested. Line **b** in verse 1 may be taken as an exclamation, as in TEV, or as a question, as in RSV. In some languages the exclamatory force will require a strong statement; for example, "You are very wrong when you say to me." In some languages **you** of line **b** is inappropriate, since no antecedent has been introduced as a referent. One may then say "How foolish my friends are to advise me and say . . . ."

To me is in Hebrew "to my *nefesh*" (see discussion at 3.2).

The last part of verse 1 in the Masoretic text is "fly (imperative, second person singular) to your (plural) mountain, bird."[1] Most translations, like RSV and TEV, follow the ancient versions, making a slight change in the Hebrew text.

In some languages the simile **flee like a bird** may not suggest the elements of silence and speed. In such cases it will be better to say "Escape silently to the mountains as a bird flies."

For lo in verse 2a, RSV, is an obsolete English phrase. The Hebrew phrase introduces the reason for the preceding command: "You must do this *because* . . . ." Some, like NIV and NJB, try to retain the Hebrew by translating "For look," but this is not a natural expression in English.

The threats of **the wicked** are likened to the actions of hunters, who prepare to shoot their arrows at animals (see 7.12). The figure here is quite elaborate: they **bend** their bows, they **have fitted** the arrows to the bowstring, in order **to shoot** at **the**

---

[1]The second person singular form is the *qere*, supported by ancient versions and many Hebrew manuscripts; the *ketiv* is the second person plural. HOTTP prefers the *qere*, "you (singular) flee," and takes the singular "bird" to be collective, meaning "birds." The possessive pronominal suffix "your" with "mountain" is plural: "your (plural) mountain." So HOTTP recommends the following translation: "flee (imperative plural) to your mountains, birds." But in the context this doesn't make much sense, since this command is directed to the psalmist.

upright in heart. The bending of the bow in RSV refers to stringing the bow, readying it for shooting. In order to fit the string onto the bow, the string was first attached to one end of the bow. Then, with that end of the bow on the ground, the hunter pressed his foot against the lower part of the bow, to bend it so that he could slip the other end of the string over the upper notched end of the bow. When the bent bow was released, the string was pulled tight. In order to avoid giving the impression that **bend the bow** meant drawing or pulling back the string with fitted arrow, it may be necessary to say, for example, "the wicked string their bows" or "wicked people bend their bows to string them." TEV does not speak of bending the bow but says "**have drawn their bows**," which refers to tensing the bow with fitted arrow. The psalmist is using here a three-clause parallelism which is somewhat of a narrative, in that it depicts a process; they first string the bow, fit the arrow to it, and then shoot. In languages in which this process is commonly known, no problem should arise. However, in cases where the translator must use long, descriptive phrases to describe the process, the images run the risk of being obscure and so emphasized that the reader may lose track of their relation to the rest of the poem. In languages in which bow and arrow are unknown, the translator may have to supply an equivalent weapon. If no such figure is available, the translator will have to say something like "wicked people are always ready to secretly harm good people" or "evil people are always waiting in hiding to injure good people."

In the dark: the wicked, hiding in a dark place (Dahood "ambush"), shoot their arrows at "**good men**" (literally **upright in heart**, as in 7.10). The word translated **upright** is used often in Psalms of pious, godly, law-abiding people.

11.3	RSV	TEV
	if the foundations are destroyed, what can the righteous do?"	There is nothing a good man can do when everything falls apart."

This verse (together with verse 2) is taken as part of the advice given by the psalmist's friends; it is possible, however, to take verses 2-3 as the psalmist's own words in explaining to his friends why their advice is impractical (Anderson).

If the foundations are destroyed is a figure for the complete breakdown of law and order in the community (see 82.5). FRCL translates "The standards of the society are in ruins."

The question **What can the righteous do?** is a way of saying that there is nothing they can do; but the text may be translated "What have the righteous accomplished?" that is, all their efforts to maintain law and order have been useless (Kirkpatrick; see NJV footnote). Some (Dahood; see also NIV and NJV footnote) take the singular "the righteous" as a title for God, "the Righteous One." It seems better to take the word to refer to people, not to God.

The sudden introduction of **the foundations** with no apparent connection to verse 2 creates confusion. Therefore TEV has bridged this gap by switching the two lines. If the translator follows TEV, it may still be necessary to make clear that the **foundations destroyed** are the results of the acts of the wicked in verse 2. Consequently it may be clearer to say, for example, "and there is nothing good people can do when the wicked destroy the laws" or ". . . the people's customs."

Some languages prefer the order of statement of condition followed by result, as in RSV. TEV uses a result clause followed by a temporal clause, which is also a condition. It is also possible to use a temporal clause followed by a rhetorical question, which may require an answer; for example, "When everything falls apart, what can a good man do? He can do nothing."

11.4

RSV	TEV
The LORD is in his holy temple, the LORD's throne is in heaven; his eyes behold, his eyelids test, the children of men.	The LORD is in his holy temple; he has his throne in heaven. He watches people everywhere and knows what they are doing.

In this strophe (verses 4-7) the psalmist expresses his complete confidence in Yahweh, who **is in his holy temple**, whose **throne is in heaven**. It is probable that here **temple** refers to Yahweh's heavenly dwelling, as the next line defines it (see also 18.6); it is possible, but not probable, that the psalmist is speaking of the Temple in Jerusalem and is affirming that Yahweh, who rules in heaven, is present with his people in the Temple. In the expression **his holy temple, holy** refers to being dedicated to God or being set apart for God's use (see 5.7). In the present context it is also possible to say, for example, "in God's own Temple," since the Temple is holy by belonging to him. One may also say "in the Temple belonging to God." **The LORD's throne is in heaven** may be expressed in nonfigurative terms; for example, "The LORD rules from heaven."

Yahweh is described as watching and judging the actions of all humankind. Two parallel statements portray this in picturesque language: **his eyes behold** and **his eyelids test** (same verb as in 7.9, "triest"). He sees and evaluates everything that everybody does. Very rarely will a translation want to follow the Hebrew and say, as RSV does, **his eyelids test**. Most translations will use the verbs "watch" or "see," and "judge" or "evaluate." SPCL translates "with his eyes open the Lord watches all men carefully"; FRCL "He doesn't lose sight of human beings, he judges them at a glance." Aside from the similar word order and phonetic features in Hebrew, the semantic parallelism in verse 4 shows two double lines, in which **throne** in line b is a part of **temple** in line a, and **eyelids** in line d is a part of **eyes** in line c. TEV has retained this "part" feature of the parallelism in the first two lines but has switched to the nonmetaphors **"watches"** and **"knows"** in the last two lines. Translators may be able to come closer to the Hebrew pair in a natural manner, as in SPCL and FRCL.

The Hebrew expression "sons of man" (RSV **children of men**) in this context means all people, all humanity.

11.5

RSV	TEV
The LORD tests the righteous and the wicked,	He examines the good and the wicked alike;

> and his soul hates him that
> loves violence.

> the lawless he hates with all his
> heart.

The actions of all people, **the righteous and the wicked**, are examined, tested (the same verb as in verse 4) by Yahweh; his attitude toward "**the lawless**" (literally "the one who loves violence"; same word as in 7.16b) is expressed by "his *nefesh* hates" (see the verb in 5.5). **The LORD tests** must often be expressed as "The LORD decides the case of the good and the wicked people," "The LORD judges both the good and the wicked," or "The LORD looks at the deeds of the good and the wicked to know how they are."

By joining **and the wicked** to line b, the verse in Hebrew may be interpreted differently: "He examines the good; but the wicked and the lawless his soul hates" (Kirkpatrick; ASV, Mft, TOB, NJV, NIV, FRCL); RSV and TEV are like NJB, NEB, NAB, ZÜR, SPCL. One cannot be dogmatic, but it seems that the interpretation followed by RSV and TEV is preferable.

In verse 5 line b raises the intensity of God's testing the wicked (and the righteous) by saying that he hates the wicked, who are now called "lovers of violence." The translation should not give the impression that two different groups are implied.

Him that loves violence: This generic singular phrase is plural in meaning, "all who love violence," that is, all who break the law, who attack and injure others.

11.6　　　　　RSV　　　　　　　　　　　　TEV

> On the wicked he will rain coals of
> fire and brimstone;
> a scorching wind shall be the
> portion of their cup.

> He sends down flaming coals[q] and
> burning sulfur on the wicked;
> he punishes them with scorch-
> ing winds.

> [q] *One ancient translation* coals; *Hebrew* traps.

The punishment that Yahweh sends (or, better, "will send," with RSV and others) is described as consisting of **coals of fire** (that is, live coals), **brimstone** ("burning sulfur"), and **a scorching wind**.

He will rain: "he will cause to come down (like rain)" (see also 78.24,27). This expression may also be rendered "he will cause to fall like rain" or "he will cause the sky to send down."

The first punishment in the Masoretic text is the plural of the word for "trap" (so Septuagint, Vulgate), which seems to be a scribal error for the plural of the word for "coal" (so Briggs), which is nearly the same in Hebrew. Therefore Briggs, Anderson, and others (BJ, NJB, NAB, NEB) correct the Hebrew text, following the Greek translation by Symmachus. But some translations like RSV take the Masoretic text as though it meant "coals" (NJV, NIV). HOTTP says that the Masoretic text means "snares" and has there the wider sense of "misfortunes." It seems best to stay with RSV and TEV, "burning coals" or "**flaming coals**." It should be remembered that **coals** refers to charcoal, not mineral coal.

Brimstone (or "**burning sulfur**") is associated with the destruction of Sodom and Gomorrah (Gen 19.24-25). Sulfur is a yellow substance which burns with a great heat and produces an unpleasant smell; it is found in volcanic regions, either as a solid or as a gas. Fire and burning sulfur are used in the biblical descriptions of the destruction which God sends or will send on various nations and peoples (see Isa 30.33; 34.9; Ezek 38.22; Rev 14.10; 19.20; 20.10; 21.8). "**Burning sulfur**" may sometimes be rendered "flames which smell bad" or "yellow flames with bad odor."

Scorching wind is a reference to the hot desert wind that kills plants (see 90.5-6; 103.15-16; Isa 40.6-7). People who live near major deserts usually have specific terms to describe hot winds which blow from the desert. Such winds may also be rendered "winds that scorch things," "winds that dry things up," or "winds that burn the plants." The Hebrew word translated **wind** also means breath, spirit, or (God's) Spirit, depending on the context. Here **wind** is meant. **Scorching** translates a word that is found only here, in 119.53, and in Lamentations 5.10.

The figure **the portion of their cup** means that which is allotted to a person by God, what that person receives as his or her destiny, or lot, in this life (see 16.5; 23.5; 75.8; Rev 14.10). It is never an impersonal destiny or fate, but God's doing. It usually, but not always, refers to something unpleasant or painful. **The portion of their cup** must often be recast as a clause; for example, "that which God gives to them," or idiomatically in some languages, "the way God cuts their affairs," meaning God's evaluation or judgment of their lives. Since the reference is to the destruction which God determines for their wickedness, the notion may sometimes be rendered, for example, "God cuts the affairs of the wicked with a scorching wind" or, in nonfigurative terms, "in the end God gives the wicked a burning wind."

11.7	RSV	TEV

For the LORD is righteous, he loves righteous deeds; the upright shall behold his face.	The LORD is righteous and loves good deeds; those who do them will live in his presence.

The psalm closes with a statement of confident assurance in Yahweh's justice and love. As in other places, the abstract quality **righteous**, applied to Yahweh, may be better translated by a phrase describing actions; for example, "The LORD always does what is right." The **righteous deeds** are those which people perform and which earn for them the Lord's approval. **The upright** is the same expression used in verse 2.

The expression **shall behold his face** (same verb as in verse 4) reflects the practice of admitting to the presence of the king only those who were qualified by reason of their proven devotion and loyalty to him. The thought in the psalm may be of the blessings which come from the presence and favor of the Lord in this life, or else of being in his presence after death.

"**His presence**" may not be expressed in some languages in nominal form since "**presence**" is not an object in which a person may live. Therefore, the translator must often say "they will live where God is," "they will be in the place where God is," or "they will live with God."

Psalm 12

This psalm expresses the distress of a group of people, that is, the people of Israel. It is usually classified as a "community lament."

The specific cause of the people's grief is not clearly stated, but verses 1-3 seem to describe a time when order and justice in the community had broken down. The psalmist voices the general complaint against the anarchy which has fallen upon the nation (verses 1-4), and the Lord responds (verse 5), perhaps through the voice of a prophet or of a priest in the Temple. The psalm closes with a note of assurance, perhaps a response from the congregation, that the Lord will protect those who obey him (verses 6-8).

The translator who reads Psalm 12 carefully will notice that the main theme is the contrast between men who deceive each other, and God whose promises are pure, like "silver refined in a furnace, purified seven times." A bit of analytical reading will enable the translator to see some of the major structural features upon which the theme is built. Viewing structural features often requires reading the poem at the stanza level rather than just verse by verse. Such a reading will show that this psalm is laid out in a chiastic pattern of the type A-B-C-C'-B'-A':

> A (verse 1): Help us, LORD, for there are no faithful among the sons of men.
> B (verse 2): Everyone speaks lies and flattery.
> C (verses 3-4): The LORD should cut off the lying boasters.
> C' (verse 5): The LORD responds, "I will now arise and protect the despoiled."
> B' (verse 6): The LORD speaks the truth, pure and refined.
> A' (verses 7-8): Protect us, LORD, for evil is everywhere among the sons of men.

The images in verses 3-4 are a complete chiasmus: lips–tongue; tongue–lips. The chiastic pattern, which is merely an orderly repetition, serves to give cohesion to the parts by linking one stanza with another in a regular manner. This linkage finally ties the end back to the beginning, "among the sons of men."

By comparing RSV and TEV the translator will see that RSV, being a more formal type of translation, has retained the words which repeat, and thus RSV makes it easier for the reader to see the repetition. However, without adjusting the stanzas according to the above outline, the pattern still remains somewhat obscure. TEV, by shifting to nonfigures, often obscures such structures in order to communicate the nonpoetic meaning of the psalm. For example, in TEV "the sons of men" is considered redundant in verse 1 and is represented by "everyone" in verse 8. This does not mean that verse 8 in TEV does not link back up with verse 1. It does, but not in the specific manner of the Hebrew or RSV. In other words, the cohesion at word level in Hebrew is replaced by a looser form of cohesion and linkage at the phrase, clause, or semantic level in TEV. It is for this reason that English speakers usually prefer to memorize a more literal text; the repetition of words serves as a prompt, just as when many of the psalms were recited from memory in classical Hebrew. Before translating TEV or some other dynamic equivalent translation, the translator should take into consideration first of all the poetic possibilities in the receptor language and the needs of the readers.

HEADING: "**A Prayer for Help**" (TEV); "Against a deceitful world"; "The word of the LORD in a corrupted world." The TEV title requires recasting into two clauses in some languages; for example, "The psalmist prays that God will help Israel" or "The psalmist asks God to help his people."

Hebrew Title: **To the choirmaster: according to The Sheminith. A Psalm of David** (TEV "**A psalm by David**").

The direction given to the choirmaster, **according to The Sheminith**, is the one found also in the title of Psalm 6.

12.1	RSV	TEV

Help, LORD; for there is no longer any that is godly; for the faithful have vanished from among the sons of men.	Help us, LORD! There is not a good man left; honest men can no longer be found.

Help translates the Hebrew verb "to save," which is used some forty-seven times in Psalms; it means to rescue, save, deliver from illness, physical peril, enemies, or death—anything that threatens the well-being or life of the one who prays. It is the verb from which the noun "savior" is formed, as is the proper name Joshua (which in its Greek form becomes Jesus). In translation it is frequently necessary to make explicit the condition from which one is being saved or rescued. In the present context "evil" or "evil people" is implied.

Since the psalm expresses the feeling of a group, TEV, SPCL, and GECL have added "us" (the Septuagint has "me").

In exaggerated language the psalmist says that "the godly have come to an end (same verb as in 7.9), and the faithful have vanished." For **godly** see comments at 4.3.

The faithful translates an adjective formed from a verb meaning to be firm, true, constant; here the word may be taken either as "faithful people" (so RSV, TEV, BJ, NJB, NJV) or as an abstract, "faithfulness, loyalty" (so NEB, NAB). The personal form seems more likely, since it is parallel with the **godly** in line a. NJV translates the two "the faithful . . . the loyal"; FRCL "the loyal . . . the trustworthy people." It is often unnatural to speak elliptically of people by a quality which characterizes them, as in **the faithful**. One may say, however, "people who remain loyal to you" or "people who follow you faithfully."

The verb in the Hebrew text translated **have vanished** is a form that is otherwise unknown; most scholars correct it to a verb found elsewhere (see 77.8, where the other verb "come to an end" is also used as a parallel).[1]

For **the sons of men** see comment at 11.4, where RSV translates the same Hebrew expression as "the children of men." The expression **among the sons of men** is not explicitly rendered in TEV. In other languages it may be necessary to complete the idea of disappearing; for example, "they are no longer seen by men's eyes," or actively, "people no longer see them."

12.2	RSV	TEV
	Every one utters lies to his neighbor; with flattering lips and a double heart they speak.	All of them lie to one another; they deceive each other with flattery.

Lies translates a word which means something worthless, fraudulent, fictitious, untrue.

To his neighbor is a way of saying "to one another," "to everyone." It is important in translation to avoid the term for **neighbor** which simply means the person who lives nearby. It is necessary to express the idea of reciprocity in lying, "**lie to one another**," as in TEV.

Verse 2 is characteristic of parallel lines in that the second line repeats the idea of the first, but does so in idiomatic language. If the receptor language uses or accommodates naturally this type of "going beyond" in the second line, the translator should use it. The Hebrew metaphor may be inappropriate, and hence different ones will have to be used. When switching to nonfigures or to different figures, the translator must consider the implication for the whole of the psalm, because the same words may occur again, as **lips** will be repeated in verses 3-4. For translation suggestions on "flatter" see 5.4. Deceit is sometimes rendered "with two mouths," "with two livers," or "with the heart going on two paths."

With flattering lips is literally "lips of smoothness"; the noun "smoothness" is related to the verb for "flatter" found in 5.9 (which is similar in thought to this verse). The Hebrew expression translated **a double heart** is literally "a heart and a heart"; it portrays the idea of deceit, double-dealing, "a forked tongue." NJV has "duplicity"; or it may be "dishonest motives."

In line **b** **lips** and **heart** may be contrasted, as FRCL does: "their lips flatter, but their heart deceives."

---

[1]HOTTP is of the opinion that the verb may be translated either "they are diminished" (that is, there are fewer of them; so the Septuagint) or "they have disappeared" (that is, there are no more left).

12.3-4   RSV   TEV

3   May the LORD cut off all flatter-
      ing lips,
      the tongue that makes great
      boasts,
4   those who say, "With our tongue
      we will prevail,
      our lips are with us; who is our
      master?"

3   Silence those flattering tongues, O
      LORD!
      Close those boastful mouths
      that say,
4   "With our words we get what we
      want.
      We will say what we wish,
      and no one can stop us."

TEV sacrifices the chiastic pattern of **lips–tongue**, **tongue–lips** and produces "tongue–mouths," "words–say." The translator should in no case attempt to retain a poetic device, such as chiasmus, at the expense of a clear rendering of the meaning.

With vivid language the psalmist asks Yahweh to stop all lying and boasting. **Cut off** is not meant literally but means to put a stop to, perhaps by banishment or by death. The term used for "Silence" or **cut off** depends on the nature of the expression used for "flatter." In some languages this will be "close the mouths of those who speak flattering words" or "stop those who flatter others."

All . . . lips and **the tongue** stand for people who flatter (same word as in verse 2) and who boast (literally "saying great things") that with their words they are able to get their way. In some languages it is not possible to speak of a part of the person as representing the whole person, and one must say, for example, "silence people who . . ." or "stop people who . . . ."

The first line in verse 4 is "we will win with our tongue"; the verb means to prevail, succeed. See NAB "We are heroes with our tongues"; NJB "In our tongue lies our strength"; FRCL "We know what to say in order to succeed." **With our tongue** refers to clever talk used to obtain evil ends, and may be expressed "by speaking clever words we get what we want."

The second statement is **our lips are with us**, meaning that their words are at their command, to help them get what they want; SPCL "our tongue defends us."

The third statement, **who is our master?** is a rhetorical question which in the context means that no one can prevail against them; they can do whatever they want, so powerful are their words. This question may be better represented by a strong affirmation, "No one can tell us what to do" or "We do not have to obey anyone."

NJV joins the last two statements: "with lips such as ours, who can be our master?" In some languages it will be advisable to abandon the literal **tongue . . . lips**, and to use "words, speech, talking," or the equivalent, in order to avoid what may appear to be incongruous or slightly ridiculous.

12.5   RSV   TEV

"Because the poor are despoiled,
      because the needy groan,
   I will now arise," says the
      LORD;
"I will place him in the safety

"But now I will come," says the
      LORD,
"because the needy are op-
      pressed
   and the persecuted groan in

for which he longs."

pain.
I will give them the security they
long for."

Yahweh's reply comes to reassure the psalmist (or the people). Those he comes to help are called **the poor** (see comments on 9.12) and **the needy** (a noun used some thirty-three times in Psalms to refer to those who suffer discrimination, injustice, oppression). They are said to be **despoiled** (TEV "oppressed"), which translates a word found only here in Psalms—literally, "they suffer violence." They also **groan** (the noun "groan" is found also in 79.11; 102.20). **The poor are despoiled** may be expressed as a passive as in RSV or may be recast in an active construction; for example, "because evil people cause those who are in need to suffer."

For **I will now arise** see comment at 3.7.

In line c RSV **him** and **he** contrast oddly with the plural forms **the poor** and **the needy** in line a. It is better to use the plural forms in line c, as does TEV, "**them**" and "**they**."

The word for **safety** is a noun formed from the verb "to save" (see verse 1). This must sometimes be rendered as a verb; for example, "I will defend them," or "I will protect them," or "I will keep them safe."

The additional phrase in Hebrew, translated **for which he longs**, is difficult to understand. The Masoretic text is "he puffs at him" (same verb as in 10.5), which is rather odd in the context; but most commentaries and translations take it as RSV and TEV have done (Dahood; ASV, BJ, NJB, NEB, NAB, SPCL). NJV takes it as a reference to Yahweh, "He affirms to him." TOB is different: "I will put in a safe place the one on whom they spit." If **safety** has been translated as a clause, it will be necessary to make **for which he longs** another clause; for example, "I will defend them as they desire" or "I will protect them because they desire it."

12.6   RSV   TEV

The promises of the LORD are
   promises that are pure,
silver refined in a furnace on
   the ground,
purified seven times.

The promises of the LORD can be
   trusted;
they are as genuine as silver
refined seven times in the furnace.

In the final strophe (verses 6-8) the psalmist reassures himself and his readers that Yahweh will keep his promise and will save those who trust in him. In liturgical usage perhaps this was the response of the congregation or of the choir to the assurance given in verse 5.

Using the figure of refined, pure silver, completely freed from all impurities, the psalmist calls the Lord's promises **pure**: "the words of Yahweh (are) pure words." The meaning is that they are completely true and reliable, they can be trusted.

For the verb **refined** see also 17.3; 18.30; 26.2; 66.10; 105.19; 119.140.

Purified translates a verb which means to wash, to clean, to filter out the dirt.

The two Hebrew words translated by RSV as **a furnace on the ground** are problematic. The Hebrew text separates the two, so that the first part is "silver refined in a furnace," and the second is "on the ground (or, earth) purified seven times." The word translated **furnace** occurs only here in the Old Testament, and its meaning is uncertain (K-B and Holladay define it "entrance"). Dahood translates the two lines "silver purged in a crucible, of clay refined seven times"; Briggs proposes "he shall be purified seven times"; NJV has "in an earthen crucible." Toombs suggests that it is "probably a metal worker's technical term, perhaps referring to the pouring of the melted silver into an earthen mold" (so, essentially, HOTTP). NJB has "natural silver which comes from the earth seven times refined," which is explained in a footnote as "already refined when found, God's word is pure of any deceit."

In view of such uncertainty, it seems best to translate this obscure phrase in a general sense, such as TEV has done, or else, like NIV, "like silver refined in a furnace of clay, purified seven times." It should be noted that **seven times** means many times in general, that is, as many times as needed to get rid of all the impurity.

Verse 6 presents the translator with several problems arising from the figurative analogy employed. In some languages it is quite natural to speak of words being **pure**, "clear," or even "shining" and "white." It is not so common, however, for **promises** to be described in such terms. Therefore the translator may have to say "The promises which the LORD spoke are pure words" or "The LORD spoke clean words when he promised . . . ." Where the refining of silver is known, it is possible to translate lines b and c as a simile; for example, "they are like silver" or "they are pure like silver that has been refined over and over." As an apposition: "they are pure silver refined many times." Where silver is little known or unknown, but refining is well known, it may be possible to substitute another metal. If the refining of precious metals is not known in the receptor culture, the translator may have to drop the analogy. However, one should attempt to keep a reflection of the poetic imagery if possible; for example, "When the LORD promises, you can trust his words, you can depend upon them, they have been tested and proven over and over."

12.7-8	RSV	TEV

	RSV	TEV
7	Do thou, O LORD, protect us, guard us ever from this genera- tion.	7-8 Wicked men are everywhere, and everyone praises what is evil.
8	On every side the wicked prowl, as vileness is exalted among the sons of men.	Keep us always safe, O LORD, and preserve us from such people.

TEV has reversed the two verses so as to place the request last, as a logical consequence of the universal corruption depicted in verse 8. RSV and TEV have taken verse 7 as a petition, and this is the preferred interpretation; some, however (Dahood; NAB, NIV, FRCL, SPCL), take it as a statement: "You protect us . . . ."

The two verbs **protect** and **guard** are synonymous, both used quite often in Psalms.

This generation refers to the evil people described in verse 8 (TEV "**such people**"); as Kirkpatrick remarks, it carries an ethical sense, classifying people as either good or bad, as the case may be.

Prowl translates the common word for "go, walk"; the noun translated **vileness** is found only here in the Old Testament and comes from the verb meaning to be worthless, intemperate.

Exalted translates the verb meaning to be high: "evil is highly spoken of, is highly thought of" is the idea; SPCL "everybody praises wickedness."

Vileness is exalted ("**everyone praises what is evil**") may require recasting as "speak well of the evil which people do" or "say good words about the evil deeds which people do."

For **the sons of men** see verse 1 and comments at 11.4.

Psalm 13

This psalm is a lament by an individual, which conforms perfectly to the model for such compositions: (1) a complaint to the Lord (verses 1-2); (2) a prayer for help (verses 3-4); and (3) an expression of confidence (verses 5-6).

This psalm, unlike the preceding one, has no chiastic structure. It is described by Alter as a "structure of intensification" in which each repeated element, "How long," introduces additional material which has the effect of heightening or intensifying the theme of supplication. The poem has three stanzas: Verses 1-2 develop the moment of desperation in which the psalmist finds himself. In verses 3-4, when desperation reaches its climax, the psalmist calls out to God with the verbs "look," "answer," and "give light," lest his enemies defeat him. In the third stanza, verses 5-6, the psalmist affirms his faith by a strong contrastive, "But I have trusted . . . ." This short poem, which begins with a cry of distress, soars to a song of praise to God. In six short verses the transformation has swiftly moved from suffering disaster to confident trust and thanksgiving.

There is nothing in the psalm to indicate for certain the occasion which prompted it (Weiser thinks it was illness) or who wrote it. Verses 2 and 4 speak of the psalmist's enemies, but nothing specific is said about them.

HEADING: **"A Prayer for Help"** (TEV); "A confident appeal"; "Prayer of one in sorrow"; "A prayer in faith." If translating the TEV heading, one will often find it necessary to make explicit the one who prays and for whom the help is intended; for example, "The psalmist asks God to help him" or "The writer prays asking God to help him."

Hebrew Title: **To the choirmaster. A Psalm of David** (TEV "A psalm by David").

The title is practically the same as that of Psalm 11; for **choirmaster** see title of Psalm 4.

13.1

RSV	TEV
How long, O LORD? Wilt thou forget me for ever? How long wilt thou hide thy face from me?	How much longer will you forget me, LORD? Forever? How much longer will you hide yourself from me?

The psalmist's lament (verses 1-2) is reinforced by the repetition of **How long?** at the beginning of each of the four lines of the two verses, thereby emphasizing his feeling of having been completely abandoned by Yahweh. For **How long** see comments at 6.3. **How long** is not so much a question regarding the precise time the state of God's silence will end, but rather a plea that Yahweh break the long silence and reveal his power. In some languages, when this clause is translated as a question, a reply regarding the time will be expected. In such cases it is better to recast the question in some such form as "Will you go on always forgetting me; will you forget me forever, LORD?" or negatively, "Will you never remember me, LORD; will you forget me forever?" In some languages a negative request will be more natural; for example, "LORD, do not forget me forever."

Forget and **hide thy face** are both found in 10.11. **Forget** is a deliberate act, to neglect, ignore, overlook. In translation **forget me** must not imply that God is absentminded and forgets who the psalmist is or what his name is. It is often possible to shift to the idea of being abandoned. If the expression "Don't delay" is used in the first part of line a, the entire command may be expressed "Don't delay too long to hear me" or "Don't wait long to look at me."

Some take the word translated **for ever** to mean "completely" (see NEB).

Hide thy face (or, "hide yourself") indicates either anger or indifference (Kirkpatrick). Here the idea of anger seems implied. **Hide thy face** is a figure that may not be used in some languages. In such cases, therefore, it may be necessary to switch to another figure; for example, "turn your back to me," "close your eyes to me," or "look at me as if I were nothing."

13.2	RSV	TEV
	How long must I bear pain*f* in my soul, and have sorrow in my heart all the day? How long shall my enemy be exalted over me?	How long must I endure trouble? How long will sorrow fill my heart day and night? How long will my enemies triumph over me?

f Syr: Heb *hold counsels*

Bear pain: according to the RSV footnote this translates the Syriac (see also NAB); the Hebrew text means "hold counsels."[1] But according to some scholars the Hebrew text can be translated "How long shall I continue devising plans (in my mind)?" That is, the psalmist in vain tries to think of ways to improve the situation. So NJB "How long must I nurse rebellion in my soul?" taking the word to have the same meaning here that it has in 106.43b (so K-B, Holladay). Some scholars hold that the Hebrew word itself can mean pain, anguish (see references in Anderson); so TEV, NEB, SPCL; NJV "cares"; BJ "grief"; TOB "worry"; Dahood "doubts."

---

[1]The Masoretic text is *etsot,* which normally means "plans"; Syriac (see the margin of *Biblia Hebraica Stuttgartensia*) is *atsabot* "pains." The verb means "to place, put"; and "to put pain," as Briggs points out, is a unique expression, so that the scribes (according to him), by deleting one letter from the Hebrew noun, changed the original "pains" into "plans" of the Masoretic text.

In translation it is often necessary to distinguish between physical pain and emotional distress, distress being appropriate in this passage. <u>Sorrow</u> is frequently spoken of by figures of speech such as "a heavy heart" or "a spoiled heart."

<u>Soul</u> translates *nefesh* (see 3.2), which is parallel to **heart** in the next line. For an earlier use of **heart**, see 4.7.

<u>All the day</u> (TEV "day and night") translates a word meaning "by day, in the daytime," which seems to represent the intensity and extensiveness of the psalmist's sorrow, since grief is ordinarily associated with the nighttime.[2] What TEV has done on a translational basis is done on a textual basis by NEB and NJB, following the Septuagint, which adds "and by night." NJV, SPCL, FRCL translate "all day"; NAB "every day." <u>All the day</u> must often be expressed as "all the time," "without sleeping," or "without closing the eyes."

<u>Be exalted</u> translates the verb "to be high" (see also 12.8). <u>My enemy</u> is taken by TEV to be a collective noun, **"my enemies"** (as it clearly is in verse 4a, parallel with "my adversaries" in verse 4b). Dahood understands it to mean death and translates "my Foe" (as in verse 4). **"Enemies"** must sometimes be rendered as "people who hate me" or "people who fight me." The entire expression in line <u>c</u> may sometimes be expressed in translation as "How long will the people who hate me win their battle?" or as a negative request, "Don't let those who hate me cause me to fall."

13.3-4	RSV		TEV
3	Consider and answer me, O LORD my God; lighten my eyes, lest I sleep the sleep of death;	3	Look at me, O LORD my God, and answer me. Restore my strength; don't let me die.
4	lest my enemy say, "I have prevailed over him"; lest my foes rejoice because I am shaken.	4	Don't let my enemies say, "We have defeated him." Don't let them gloat over my downfall.

In this strophe (verses 3-4) the psalmist pleads with Yahweh for help.

<u>Consider</u> translates the verb used in 10.14, which means take notice, pay attention, listen, look.

<u>Answer me</u>: "help me," "do as I ask."

The phrase **lighten my eyes** (literally "give light to my eyes") means to restore one's strength, health, vigor (see 38.10; 1 Sam 14.27,29; Ezra 9.8), since bright eyes were considered the sign of good health. NJV has "Restore the luster to my eyes." In many languages it is possible to use a different figure to express **lighten my eyes**, with the sense of giving strength to someone; for example, "make me strong like a young man," "give me fresh breath," or "make my hands strong."

---

[2]HOTTP says the Hebrew may be interpreted in two ways: (1) "all the day," "for length of days," meaning every day; (2) "(even) by day," that is, in daytime as well as at night.

The psalmist reinforces his plea by listing the consequences if Yahweh does not answer him: (1) he will die (literally "sleep in death"); (2) his enemies will claim that they have defeated him (literally "be able over him," that is, win, prevail, overcome); (3) they will **"gloat"** (same verb as that translated "rejoice" in 9.14) over his downfall.

The sleep of death: whenever possible it is advisable to use meaningful figures of speech in the translation of poetry. Many languages use figures to express death; for example, "to fall into the place of the dead," "to go away" or "to be carried away."

Translators should pay particular attention to the switching of pronouns in verse 4a. In some languages it will not be natural to switch from first to third person, and even in direct discourse it will often be clearer to use the second person in the final phrase: "we have defeated you."

I am shaken translates the same verb as in 10.6, to shake, totter. We can only speculate about the of defeat or downfall this was; it could be the psalmist's death, as Anderson suggests, or else his misfortune in general.

In some languages syntactic adjustments will be required in order to make clear that the psalmist is speaking of his future condition, if God does not intervene. This may often be done by making the consequence a conditional clause; for example, "don't let me be defeated, because my enemies will be proud" or "don't let me fail so that my enemies can rejoice."

<u>13.5-6</u>	RSV		TEV
5	But I have trusted in thy steadfast love; my heart shall rejoice in thy salvation.	5	I rely on your constant love; I will be glad, because you will rescue me.
6	I will sing to the LORD, because he has dealt bountifully with me.	6	I will sing to you, O LORD, because you have been good to me.

In contrast with his enemies' wickedness, the psalmist, in this closing strophe (verses 5-6), expresses reliance on Yahweh and his trust in him. The personal pronoun at the beginning of verse 5 in Hebrew may be emphatic: "But I, on my part"; so NEB, NJB, FRCL.

I have trusted translates a verb meaning to rely on, depend on, place confidence in (see the related noun in 4.8). The continuative aspect may be better represented in English by "I am trusting" or "I always trust." **Trusted** must be translated idiomatically in many languages; for example, "have a thick heart" or "place your heart upon."

Steadfast love translates a complex set of relations and emotions. It is frequently necessary to render these in a clause containing a verb with both actor and object made explicit. Line <u>a</u> may thus be rendered "I will place my heart upon you because you love me faithfully" or ". . . because you love me all the time." See comment on **steadfast love** in 5.7.

Rejoice is the same verb as in verse 4b.

125

Thy salvation (TEV **"you will rescue me"**) must often be recast as a verbal clause and expressed idiomatically; for example, "cause me to live" or "make me see life." See also comments at 3.8.

I will sing translates a verb that is used many times in Psalms. TEV **"to you, O LORD"** is a change from the third person, **to the LORD**, to the second person of direct address, a change made to maintain uniformity with the preceding verse. In translation it is often necessary to make explicit the object of the singing; for example, "I will sing songs to you."

Has dealt bountifully means "has treated generously" (TEV **"you have been good"**). This translates a verb which means to deal with, either in a good or a bad sense, depending on the context; see 7.4 "if I have requited . . . evil." Here it obviously means to benefit, bless, be good to.

NAB takes the last line of verse 6 to be the words that in the first line the psalmist vows to sing: "Let me sing of the LORD, 'He has been good to me.' "

By a slight change of the Masoretic text, which has "to me" at the end of verse 6, Dahood gets a divine title, "because the Most High has done (good)."[3] This is possible but is not very probable; the Masoretic text is to be preferred.

---

[3]At the end of verse 6, the Septuagint adds "and I will sing praise to the name of the Lord, the Most High," which BJ and NJB follow.

Psalm 14

This psalm does not conform to any one type into which the psalms are normally classified. It resembles a lament by the community, but there are elements which reflect wisdom and prophetic themes (verses 1,2,5-6). It is almost completely identical with Psalm 53; one of the main differences is that Psalm 14 uses the personal name of God, "Yahweh," while Psalm 53 uses the generic term, "God."

The psalm opens with a vivid description of the total corruption which characterizes the time (verses 1-3), followed by a prediction of the punishment that will fall on the wicked (verses 4-6); it closes with a prayer of hope for the future (verse 7). There is no way of determining whether the psalm reflects a particularly dark period in the nation's existence when it was being oppressed by pagan powers, or a period in which corruption ran high in Israel itself (so Weiser). Much depends on understanding who are "the evildoers" and "my people" in verse 4. The accusation of not worshiping God (verses 3-4) makes more sense if directed against Israelites than against Gentiles, who were by definition pagans.

HEADING: "**The Wickedness of Men**" (TEV); "A lament over widespread corruption"; "The reign of folly"; "The faithful and their God in a corrupt world." The TEV heading, if used, may have to be recast, because the noun "**wickedness**" must often be expressed as verb; for example, "The evil deeds which people do." Or, if it is desired to emphasize the quality of evil in people, one may say "People are the doers of evil deeds."

Hebrew Title: **To the choirmaster. Of David** (TEV "**By David**").
    The title is the same as that of Psalm 11.

14.1   RSV   TEV

The fool says in his heart, "There is no God." They are corrupt, they do abominable deeds, there is none that does good.	Fools say to themselves, "There is no God!" They are all corrupt, and they have done terrible things; there is no one who does what is right.

In the Old Testament **the fool** is not always or only a person with no sense; he is one who stubbornly rejects the highest wisdom of all, the fear of God, which is how wisdom begins (see Pro 1.7; 9.10; Job 28.28; Psa 11.10). He is the person who disregards God, who convinces himself or herself that God does not matter (see

10.4,6,11,13). Translations vary in their attempt to bring out the spiritual dimension of the word: NEB "The impious fool"; FRCL "those who say that God is powerless"; NJV "The benighted man"; another possibility is "The arrogant man."

Fool is expressed in some languages by means of abnormal body parts; for example, "black liver" or "gourd head." In other languages a **fool** is said to be lacking something in the mind or brains; for example, "no-think kind of person" or "mind-gone-away kind of person."

Says in his heart in some languages implies the babbling of an idiot rather than the thoughts of a person who is consciously rejecting God's wisdom. Therefore it is sometimes clearer to say "the foolish kind of person thinks to himself . . . ."

There is no God is not a philosophical denial of God's existence; it is to reject the belief that God matters, that God's will is of any importance in human affairs (see 10.4).

They are corrupt translates a verb that means to be worthless, vile, completely immoral. **They are corrupt** is difficult to translate in this form, since it is not immediately clear who the referent is. Therefore it may be advisable to render **they** as "evil people." **Corrupt** in the sense of worthless or vile may often be expressed in translation by means of figures such as "having small hearts," "being with a cold heart," or "having eyes that see only bad things."

The adjective **abominable** represents another form of the verb which in 5.6 is translated "abhors" (TEV "despise"); another possibility is "detestable."

Some translations join the two verbs as parallel: NJB "their deeds are corrupt and vile"; NJV "man's deeds are corrupt and loathsome."

Good translates a word meaning morally good, legally sanctioned, religiously approved, with as wide a range of application as possible. FRCL translates the line "No one acts as he should." The last line is repeated in verse 3, with the intensifying expression "no, not one" giving a poetic unity to this first part of the psalm. Many languages make a distinction between good as a quality of an object and good as a right kind of behavior. In such cases it is best to translate the Hebrew in the sense of behavior. The expression which results is often figurative; for example, "there is no person who walks the straight road" or "no one is entirely straight."

The style of verses 1 and 3 is that of hyperbole, that is, it contains exaggerated statements. The purpose of such a style is to make the statements as vivid as possible, particularly at the beginning, in order to catch the attention of the reader. The translator should be sure the style used will retain an equivalent exaggerated vividness.

14.2

RSV	TEV
The LORD looks down from heaven upon the children of men, to see if there are any that act wisely, that seek after God.	The LORD looks down from heaven at mankind to see if there are any who are wise, any who worship him.

The psalmist pictures Yahweh looking down from heaven at humankind to see if there is any person who acts wisely. For comments on the Hebrew expression **children of men**, see 11.4. **Act wisely** translates the same word used in 2.10. Such persons are defined in the next line as **that seek after God**. For the expression **seek after God**, see comments on 9.10. This verse describes the wise person as the opposite of the fool: the wise person worships and serves God; the fool disregards God completely.

14.3 RSV TEV

They have all gone astray, they are all alike corrupt; there is none that does good, no, not one.

But they have all gone wrong; they are all equally bad. Not one of them does what is right, not a single one.

The verb translated **gone astray** means to depart, leave—in a moral sense, to leave the right path, to go wrong, to sin. **Gone astray** will often require adjustments in translation, otherwise the reader may understand nothing more than being physically lost. Some languages express the idea as "evil people are those who have left the straight path" or "evil people are those whose heads were turned."

The verb translated **are . . . corrupt** is found only here, in 53.3, and Job 15.16. (The Arabic cognate is used of milk that turns sour.) The extreme language is like that used in Genesis 6.5 of humankind before the Flood.

The text of verses 1b,2b-c,3 is quoted from the Septuagint, in modified form, in Romans 3.10-12.

14.4 RSV TEV

Have they no knowledge, all the evildoers who eat up my people as they eat bread, and do not call upon the LORD?

"Don't they know?" asks the LORD. "Are all these evildoers ignorant? They live by robbing my people, and they never pray to me."

It seems that **my people** in this verse indicates that Yahweh is the speaker; TEV, FRCL, and GECL make this explicit. However, commentators are not agreed. The third person reference to **the LORD** in the last line may indicate that the psalmist is the speaker.

The questions are rhetorical, implying amazement that people who know better do not act properly. Yahweh condemns **the evildoers** as deliberately disregarding the divine punishment which they will receive for their sins. Of course they know what they are doing and what are the consequences of their evil deeds. SPCL translates as a statement of fact.

The TEV question without an object may require some recasting in translation; for example, "Don't evil people know anything?" In languages where the rhetorical question demands a reply, one may say "Don't evil people know anything? Of course, they know." In some languages it will be preferable to translate line a as a negative statement: "Evil people seem to know nothing at all, but they really know what they are doing."

The second line of the Hebrew text is difficult to understand; it is literally "eating my people they eat bread." There are various explanations: some change the text to get "they eat my (that is, Yahweh's) bread," which implies that these evildoers are corrupt priests. Most, however, take the line in a general sense, as do RSV, TEV, NEB, NAB, and others. Mft has "who devour my people with extortion"; FRCL "who nourish themselves by exploiting my people"; another possibility is "who live in plenty by exploiting my people." NEB has "who devour my people as they eat bread" (that is, who think no more of "devouring" God's people than they do of eating food); NJB has two lines: "they are devouring my people, this is the bread they eat."

Many languages use the word **eat** with the meaning of destroy or exploit, and therefore in these languages it will be quite natural to say "evil people eat my people." In order to avoid the repetition of "people," **my people** may be translated by an expression showing relationship to God; for example, "evil people eat those who follow me" or "evil men eat those who obey me."

Bread is not a universal food, and translators should not force its use and give the impression that eating bread is a common act. In some areas bread is nearly unknown. In others it is known but eaten only on ceremonial or festival occasions, or by people who live in cities. The most commonly consumed daily food should be used. In some areas it will be appropriate to say "Evil people eat my followers as commonly as they eat their cassava" or ". . . just as they eat corn," or more generally ". . . as they eat their food."

Call upon the LORD: the Hebrew expression "to call upon Yahweh" means to pray to him, to invoke his name in worship.

14.5	RSV	TEV

There they shall be in great terror, for God is with the generation of the righteous.	But then they will be terrified, for God is with those who obey him.

The psalmist calls down divine punishment on these evildoers. It is not clear what **There** refers to, other than the general sense of the place at which the divine punishment comes (Cohen). TEV, AT, NAB **"then."** NIV has "there they are" (see also FRCL). NJB footnote explains **There** as a reference to Zion, where Yahweh will manifest his power (also Weiser).

They shall be in great terror translates an emphatic statement, "they will tremble with fear," recalling passages which speak of Yahweh filling the enemies of the Israelites with dread (see Exo 23.27; Deut 11.25). Mft has "Ha! There they are in panic."

In some languages it will be necessary to recast line <u>a</u> in the active voice, indicating God as the actor; for example, "God will terrify those evil people." "Terrify" will sometimes be expressed idiomatically, frequently expressing some physical loss to the person; for example, "the strength melted" or "the heart shrank." Line <u>a</u> may then sometimes be rendered "God will cause the hearts of evil people to shrink" or "their strength will melt away because of God."

God is with: in this context **with** means more than merely being present; it means "be on the side of," "be in favor of," in the active sense of helping and protecting.

For **generation** see comments at 12.7. Here **the generation of the righteous** refers to the godly Israelites, the devout, who do what God requires. Some take the word translated **generation** to mean here "assembly" (so Dahood, Anderson) and translate as NEB has done, "God was in the brotherhood of the godly"; NIV "God is present in the company of the righteous"; NJV "God is present in the circle of the righteous" (see the similar phrase, but not the same word, in 1.5b). Line <u>b</u> may sometimes be rendered "God helps his people who obey him" or "God protects his loyal people."

<u>14.6</u> RSV	TEV
You would confound the plans of the poor, but the LORD is his refuge.	Evildoers frustrate the plans of the humble man, but the LORD is his protection.

In **You would confound** the pronoun is plural, and the phrase refers to the evildoers described in the previous verses. The verb is a causative of the verb "be ashamed" (see 6.10), meaning here to put to shame, that is, to defeat, humiliate, "frustrate" (TEV); NJV "set at nought"; SPCL "mock." The Hebrew term translated **confound** is expressed in some languages as "to make fun of" or "laugh at."

RSV **would confound** translates the verb as a planned, potential act, not as an actual act. It seems better to translate as a fact, as do TEV and others.

The word translated **plans** is taken by some to mean "anguish" (see 13.2); SPCL translates "hopes." **Plans** may also be understood in terms of desires or wishes.

The poor is either one who is materially poor (so RSV) or else one who has nothing to sustain him except humble trust in God (see 9.12, where RSV translates "the afflicted"). The term **poor** is sometimes rendered as "a man who has nothing," "the one who lives far from the chief's compound" or "a person having only one pig."

The noun translated **refuge** is formed from the verb "to be safe" (see comments at 2.12). **The LORD is his refuge** must often be rendered "The LORD is the one who takes care of him" or "The LORD is the one who protects him from danger."

RSV   TEV

O that deliverance for Israel	How I pray that victory
would come out of Zion!	will come to Israel from Zion.
When the LORD restores the	How happy the people of Israel
fortunes of his people,	will be
Jacob shall rejoice, Israel shall	when the LORD makes them
be glad.	prosperous again!

The first line of the concluding verse is interpreted as a wish, a prayer, by most translations. Some, however, follow the Septuagint and translate it as a question: "Who will bring Israel salvation (or, victory) from Zion?" (BJ, NJB, TOB). It is recommended that the line be translated as a fervent wish or as a prayer.

The wish expressed in RSV **O that** is represented in FRCL by "Oh, how I wish I could see . . . ," which is effective.

For comments on **deliverance** see 3.8.

Out of Zion is an elliptical expression for "from Yahweh, who lives on Zion," that is, in the Temple (see comments on 2.6).

A major difficulty arising from this verse is related to the reference to delivery for Israel coming from Zion without an explicit agent of deliverance. Some languages require that the agent causing the victory be explicit. The intensive expressed by "How" and **O** must sometimes be rendered by terms indicating strength; for example, "I pray strongly that God who lives in Zion will save Israel" or "I ask with all my heart . . . ."

The Hebrew expression translated **restores the fortunes** sometimes has the more limited meaning of bringing back the people from exile (so BJ, NJB, TOB); here, however, it seems to be used in a more general sense (so most commentaries and translations). It is found also in 53.6; 85.1; 126.1,4.

The two exactly parallel statements, **Jacob shall rejoice,** and **Israel shall be glad,** refer not to the patriarch Jacob, also called Israel, but to the people of Israel. The verbal parallelism can be retained, as SPCL does: "the descendants of Jacob will rejoice, all the people of Israel."

In the second half of this verse the translator may follow TEV: "**people of Israel.**" However, some may find that readers acquainted with traditional translations will object to this kind of reduction of form. In such cases it will be helpful to make explicit that these refer to the descendants of Jacob, who are the people of Israel; for example, "The descendants of Jacob, who are the people of Israel, will be glad when God gives them their wealth again."

Some take the last line as an exhortation: "Let them be happy" (Dahood). This is possible, but the meaning represented by RSV and TEV is to be preferred.

Psalm 15

This psalm appears to be a liturgical composition to be used by pilgrims as they went to the Temple to attend one of the great religious festivals (also Psa 24). In verse 1 the pilgrims ask the question about who is allowed to enter the Temple, and the answer, given probably by priests, lists the necessary moral qualifications (which seem to be ten in all) in verses 2-5b. The psalm closes with a promise to those who meet these conditions (verse 5c).

The theme of Psalm 15 is given in the opening questions of verse 1, which consist of two lines that are nearly equivalent in meaning and identical in syntax, except for the "going beyond" element in the second clause. There "holy" is added. The structure of the poem is a neatly balanced arrangement of plusses and minuses. Verse 2 has three positive verbs. Verse 3 follows with three negatives. Verse 4 switches back again to three positive statements until the end of verse 4c, where again the negative reappears (and does not change), making with verse 5a and 5b three negatives. The poem closes then with a positive and a negative. In diagram form we have:

$$
\begin{array}{rccc}
1. & \text{Question} & & \\
2. & + & + & + \\
3. & - & - & - \\
4. & + & + & + \\
\text{4c-5ab.} & - & - & - \\
5c. & + & - & \\
\end{array}
$$

In terms of the alternation of plusses and minuses, it is possible to think of the poem as chiastic, or perhaps simply as alternating lines ABABab. The contrast of plusses and minuses set down in alternating lines serves the purpose of focusing the attention upon the exemplary conduct of those who would enter the Temple for worship.

HEADING: "**What God Requires**" (TEV); "The guest of God"; "The friend of God"; "Who can be Yahweh's guest?" The TEV title may be adapted to some languages by filling in the meanings; for example, "God requires those who worship him to do these things" or "These are the things God wants people to do when they worship him."

Hebrew Title: **A Psalm of David** (TEV "A psalm by David").

15.1   RSV   TEV

> O LORD, who shall sojourn in thy tent?
>   Who shall dwell on thy holy hill?

> LORD, who may enter your Temple?
>   Who may worship on Zion, your sacred hill?[v]

> [v] SACRED HILL: See 2.6.

The question is asked by pilgrims as they stand in front of the gates of the Temple in Jerusalem, as though they were visitors asking for lodging. The Temple is called "your tent" (see 27.4-5; 61.4), which recalls the Tent (or, Tabernacle) which was Yahweh's dwelling place during the wanderings in the wilderness, and the tent which David built on Mount Zion to shelter the Covenant Box (2 Sam 6.12,16-17). SPCL and NIV translate "your sanctuary." Yahweh's **holy hill** also refers to the Temple; it is Mount Zion, on which the Temple was built (see comments on 2.6). TEV adds "**Zion**" to make this clear.

The two verbs **sojourn** and **dwell** are nearly synonymous, although some see **sojourn** as referring to temporary residence and **dwell** as referring to permanent residence. (But see 61.4, where the Hebrew for **sojourn** is used with the addition "for ever.") NEB has "lodge . . . dwell"; Dahood "be a guest . . . dwell." TEV has abandoned the figure and uses the words that would actually apply to the situation: "**enter**" and "**worship**." FRCL has "who can be received . . . and find lodging."

Translators may be able to stay closer to the Hebrew parallelism than TEV has done, provided **sojourn** and **dwell** are to be contrasted in terms of permanence. This contrast is somewhat strengthened by the final line, "never be moved." The question should not be asked as simply a future tense but should be expressed as permission to be granted, as in TEV "**may**." In some languages this may be rendered "Who is able?" or "Who is empowered to?" It may also be "Whom do you allow?"

Tent will normally not serve as a basis for the meaning of "**Temple**," which in many languages must be rendered by an expression indicating "prayer house," "worship house," "singing house," or "sacrifice house." Translators should avoid using the New Testament term used to translate "synagogue." If TEV's "**enter**" is followed, in some cases "**enter your Temple**" must be completed by a phrase of purpose; for example, "who are the people who may enter your temple to worship you?"

TEV has named **thy holy hill** as "Zion," which has some advantage, since it is a place name which recurs frequently in the Psalms. **Holy hill** should not be rendered by a phrase meaning "tabooed mountain" but be expressed by a term or terms indicating that the hill is dedicated to the service of God.

15.2   RSV   TEV

> He who walks blamelessly, and does what is right,
>   and speaks truth from his heart;

> A person who obeys God in everything
>   and always does what is right,
> whose words are true and sincere,

The conditions for entering the Temple and worshiping there are given by the priests (verses 2-5b). These conditions are all moral and spiritual, not ritual and ceremonial; they have to do with character and conduct.

In translation it will often be necessary to indicate that verses 2-5 are the responses to the question asked in verse 1. This may be done by making the question element more explicit in verse 1; for example, "LORD, I inquire from you, who are the persons who can enter your temple to worship you?" Verse 2 may then contain an explicit response marker; for example, "The LORD answers . . ." or "The answer is . . . ."

(1) A worshiper must "walk perfectly" and "do justice." Both phrases describe conduct. For **walks** as way of life, see comments on 1.1. In languages where **walks** indicates behavior, the translator is encouraged to keep the idiom if possible. However, in some languages another idiom can be used; for example, "The person who follows a straight path" or "The person who poles his canoe in clear waters."

The word translated **blamelessly** is related to the word "perfection" in 9.6. NJB has "whoever lives blamelessly." To be "blameless" is to obey the commands of God in everything (see Anderson).

For comments on **right** see 4.1.

(2) The next qualification has to do with speech: **speaks truth from his heart**. The word translated **truth** (*'emeth*) comes from a root meaning "to be firm, reliable, trustworthy." The phrase **from his heart** may be taken to indicate sincerity (so TEV; see SPCL "speak the truth with all his heart"); but see NJV "in his heart acknowledges the truth." "**Whose words are true**" is said in some languages as "he who speaks with one mouth," and in others, "he whose words are straight." Many languages use expressions based on the heart; for example, "he who speaks from a white heart." TEV "**true and sincere**" is an attempt to include the element **from his heart**. Another way is "with his whole heart he speaks the truth" (SPCL). GECL has "he insists on thinking and speaking only the truth" (see also FRCL).

<u>15.3</u>	RSV	TEV
	who does not slander with his tongue,	and who does not slander others.
	and does no evil to his friend,	He does no wrong to his friends
	nor takes up a reproach against his neighbor;	and does not spread rumors about his neighbors.

(3) The next qualification for entering the Temple has to do with **slander**, spreading malicious gossip or speaking ill of others. **Tongue** represents the organ of speech, and it is not necessary to say literally in English (as does RSV) **slander with his tongue**. In some languages, however, the literal phrase may be quite effective. The verb translated "to slander" occurs rarely; some think it has here the meaning "to spy on" (so Briggs). **Slander** is sometimes expressed idiomatically as "taking away people's names," "saying bad words about people" or "putting dirt on people's backs."

(4-5) The next two qualifications use two synonymous terms, **friend** and **neighbor**, both referring to fellow Israelites in general.

Does no evil has the broadest sense possible of "does no harm to," "does nothing bad to."

The term **friend** presents certain problems for the translator in some languages. In many face-to-face societies a person forms few if any associations on an entirely voluntary basis. One's friends are nearly always kinsmen and are designated by the appropriate kinship term. Therefore it is sometimes necessary to say "he does no harm to the people he goes about with" or "he does not injure people who work beside him."

Reproach (TEV "**rumors**") translates a word meaning taunt, scorn, contempt. Dahood has "slur"; NEB "tells no tales against"; FRCL "does not insult"; NJB "casts no discredit on." From the meaning of the verb **take up** in line c, NJV gets a different sense altogether: "or borne a reproach for [his acts toward] his neighbor," that is, he has never so acted against his neighbor as to have been reproached for it. This does not seem very likely.

Neighbor is expressed idiomatically in some languages as "younger-brother-older-brother," referring to everyone in the community.

In translation it is important that it be clear that each passage after verse 1 is a reply to the original question. In some languages a string of replies to a single question will require markers to show that the replies are the response unit of the discourse. In some cases this may be done by using two section headings; for example, the first, "Who may worship God?" and the second inserted before verse 2, "This is the person who may worship God." In some languages careful use of connectives will be required between the responses, to give more cohesion to the response unit; for example, "He must be a person who obeys God . . . and in addition does what is right, moreover what he says must be true and sincere, furthermore he is a person who does not slander other people . . . ." In some languages the tying together of the response unit may be done by inserting at several points something equivalent to "and this also . . . ."

<u>15.4</u> RSV	TEV

in whose eyes a reprobate is despised,
  but who honors those who fear the LORD;
who swears to his own hurt and does not change;
	He despises those whom God rejects,
	  but honors those who obey the LORD.
	He always does what he promises, no matter how much it may cost.

(6) The next qualification is literally "despised in his eyes (is) the reprobate." A **reprobate** is a person who has been reproved or rejected by God because of his or her evil way of life. The verb is used in the active voice with God as subject in 53.5; 78.59,67; 89.38; with a person as subject in 36.4; 118.22. FRCL translates "he does not respect those of whom God disapproves." SPCL takes **reprobate** to reflect human judgment and translates "he looks with contempt on those who deserve contempt." NEB has "who shows his scorn for the worthless."

The verb "to despise" in Psalms usually has God as the subject: 22.24; 51.17; 69.33; 73.20; 102.17 (see also 22.6b; 119.141). **Despised** is sometimes expressed as "to consider as nothing," "to look down upon." Line a is rendered in some languages "he looks down on the person God has considered evil" or "he considers as nothing the evil person whom God says 'No' to."

(7) "To honor" someone is to applaud his actions, to think highly of him, to speak of him with praise and admiration. **Honors** may be rendered by such expressions as "to say he is great" or "to speak well of his name." This line is rendered in some languages as "he says that the man is great who follows God's way." To **fear the LORD** means to reverence, obey, worship, serve him (see comments on 2.11). **Those who fear the LORD** are the exact opposites of the **reprobate**.

(8) The meaning of the next qualification is disputed. (a) The Septuagint (followed by Syriac, Vulgate) combines the consonants of the Hebrew text (after the verb **who swears**) with vowels that make it mean "to his neighbor" ("he makes a promise to his neighbor and does not break it"). Briggs favors this. (b) The Hebrew text seems to mean "who swears to (do) evil," which is obviously wrong. Dahood understands the Hebrew preposition here to indicate separation, and translates "to do no wrong." (c) The majority of commentaries and translations take it in the sense that RSV and TEV take it: a person who keeps his promise even though it hurts him, financially or otherwise.

Swears to his own hurt implies that the person invokes the supernatural as a witness or sanction for his statements. **Swear** is rendered in some languages as "I say this before God" or "I say this and God cuts it," meaning that God decides if it is true and applies the appropriate sanction if it is not true. This line may be rendered "he swears before God that what he says he will do, and does not change his words" or "he tells God he will do something, and he really does it."

15.5	RSV	TEV
	who does not put out his money at interest, and does not take a bribe against the innocent.	He makes loans without charging interest and cannot be bribed to testify against the innocent.
	He who does these things shall never be moved.	Whoever does these things will always be secure.

The last two qualifications have to do with financial and legal situations. (9) **Interest** in financial transactions with a fellow Israelite was forbidden (Lev 25.36-37), but permitted in dealing with non-Israelites (Deut 23.19-20). The situation in this passage is that of helping someone in time of distress, not a business loan in commercial affairs (see Dentan, Dahood). It is pointed out that in some commercial loans transacted in other societies at that time, interest ran as high as fifty percent a year. **Interest**, although extremely common in most areas, is not always known. In such cases one may say "he gives money to the one who borrows and does not take back more than he gave" or "he lends things to someone who needs them and gets back only what he lent."

(10) To **take a bribe against the innocent** means to accept money or some other kind of favor as payment for testifying falsely against an innocent person at a trial (see Exo 23.8; Deut 16.19; 27.25). **Bribe** is often expressed idiomatically; for example, "to bite with money" or "to close the eyes with gifts." **Innocent** may be rendered "who has done no bad deed." Line b may be translated "People cannot close his eyes with money to make him speak against those who have done no wrong" or "he does not accept gifts so that he will say things against . . . ."

The psalm closes with a promise for those who comply with these require-ments: they will **never be moved** (for comments on the verb see 10.6). The security here spoken of is no doubt spiritual, but it also includes the material aspect, since in the thought of that time the two were obviously related (see 30.6). **Never be moved** (TEV **"secure"**) is rendered idiomatically in some languages as "not falling" or "sitting firmly." The concluding line may sometimes be translated "People who live like this will always sit firmly" or "People who act in this way will not be carried off."

Psalm 16

This psalm, like Psalm 11, is a song of confidence which opens with a statement of faith in Yahweh's ability to protect and bless (verses 1-2). This is followed by praise for faithful Israelites and condemnation of idol worshipers (verses 3-4), but there is much uncertainty concerning the meaning of these two verses (see below). Then the psalmist describes the Lord's goodness to him (verses 5-6) and thanks him for his guidance and his protecting presence (verses 7-8). In the last part of the psalm (verses 9-11), he praises Yahweh's power to protect him from death and to keep him happy in his presence.

There is no way of knowing who the psalmist is. From the statement about idol worship (verse 4), Dahood infers that he was a converted Canaanite; others have suggested he was a priest, or the king. Verses 9-10 imply that he had been delivered from untimely death, and that this is the reason why he praises Yahweh.

HEADING: "**A Prayer of Confidence**" (TEV); "Faith and hope"; "God the supreme good"; "The decisive choice." TEV's title must often be recast to indicate who is praying. The confidence is the attitude of the psalmist toward God, and the title may be rendered, for example, "The psalmist prays and trusts in God."

Hebrew Title: **A Miktam of David** (TEV "**A psalm by David**").

The meaning of the Hebrew word **Miktam** (also in the titles of Psalms 56-60) is uncertain. Some scholars relate the word to a verb meaning "to cover," and so define it as "expiation, atonement." Dahood, following the Septuagint, suggests it means "an inscription on a stone slab." Other explanations are offered (see Kirkpatrick, page xx). In view of such uncertainty TEV uses the general word "**A psalm.**"

16.1-2	RSV		TEV
1	Preserve me, O God, for in thee I take refuge.	1	Protect me, O God; I trust in you for safety.
2	I say to the LORD, "Thou art my Lord; I have no good apart from thee."*g*	2	I say to the LORD, "You are my Lord; all good things I have come from you."

g Jerome Tg: The meaning of the Hebrew is uncertain

In verse 1 the psalmist prays for continued protection and expresses his trust in God to keep him safe.

139

<u>Preserve</u>: the Hebrew verb "to keep" means to keep safe, protect, take care of.

<u>In thee I take refuge</u>: "I go to you for safety," "I trust you to protect me." For further comments on the verb <u>take refuge</u>, see 2.11; see also 7.1; 11.1; 12.7. <u>In thee I take refuge</u> must often be recast in translation, because it is sometimes unnatural to take refuge in a person rather than a place. For this reason it may be best to follow TEV here. "<u>I trust in you for safety</u>" must often be expressed as two coordinate concepts, "I trust you" and "you keep me safe." Since "I trust you" expresses a psychological attitude, it is sometimes expressed idiomatically; for example, "I lay my heart on you" or "I put my heart where you are." Verse 1 may then sometimes be rendered "I put my heart where you are, and you keep me safe" or "Protect me, God, because I lay my heart on you."

The first line of verse 2 in the Hebrew text starts with the verb "to say" in the second person feminine singular form, "You say." Most commentaries and translations follow many Hebrew manuscripts (and the Septuagint, Syriac, Jerome) which have the first person singular <u>I say</u>; this is also the preference of HOTTP.

The real significance of <u>say</u> in this context is not merely to introduce the words that are spoken but to introduce a confession of faith; for example, "I declare" or "I confess," or perhaps "I say truly."

The double reference to <u>the LORD</u> and to <u>my Lord</u> may present some difficulty. LORD refers to the divine name, "Yahweh" (see discussion of <u>LORD</u> at 1.2), while <u>my Lord</u> translates the Hebrew title 'adon (see comments on 8.1). In some languages <u>Lord</u> must be possessed, while in others it is expressed as "the one who rules me." Therefore it will often be necessary to render this line as "I say truly (or, declare) to Yahweh (or, the LORD), 'You are really the one who rules me.' "

The second line of verse 2 is difficult to understand. The Hebrew text seems to say "my good is not upon (or, above) you," which does not make much sense in the context. Most translations give the sense "all my good comes only from you" or "I have no good (or, happiness) apart from you" (so TEV, RSV, FRCL, GECL, following in general the sense given by Jerome), or else "I have no greater good than you" (TOB). There are other explanations (see the commentaries). Dahood proposes "you are my Lord, my Good, there is none above you," and SPCL translates "You are my Lord, my good; nothing can be compared to you."

It is recommended that the meaning of either RSV or TEV be followed, or else something like "all my happiness comes from you."

<u>16.3</u> RSV	TEV
As for the saints in the land, they are the noble, in whom is all my delight.	How excellent are the LORD's faithful people! My greatest pleasure is to be with them.

There is a great difference of opinion among commentators and translators on the meaning of this verse. Literally the Hebrew says "concerning (or, to) the holy ones which (are) in (or, of) the earth (or, land) they and the mighty ones, all my delight (is) in them." RSV renders this <u>As for the saints in the land, they are the noble</u>. TEV has taken "the holy ones in the land" and "the mighty ones" (in the sense of "excellent") as a double reference to faithful Israelites: "**How excellent are the LORD's faithful people**"; similarly FRCL.

However, the Hebrew expression for "the holy ones" may mean Canaanite gods or foreign gods in general (see Anderson). Dahood, who believes the author is a Canaanite who converted to Yahwism, takes this as a reference to the past: "As for the holy ones who were in the land, and the mighty ones in whom was all my delight" (so TOB). NEB rearranges the text and changes some words to get "The gods whom earth holds sacred are all worthless, and cursed are all who make them their delight"; there are two alternatives in the margin. NJV takes the word to refer to divine beings and translates "As to the holy and mighty ones that are in the land, my whole desire concerning them is that . . . ." Briggs prefers to follow the Septuagint, translating "To the saints who are in the land, Yahweh makes wonderful all His good pleasure in them" (similarly Weiser). Another possible version is "As for the gods in the land, the mighty ones in whom I take no pleasure" (with note and alternative renderings in the margin). SPCL translates verses 3-4a "The idols of the land are powerful, according to those who delight in them, who increase the number of their images and follow them with great devotion." FRCL translates verse 3: "As for the faithful ones who are in the land, they are the ones who have the true greatness that I respect"; a footnote indicates that the translation involves two minor conjectures. In the face of such diversity of opinion, a translator must be content with providing a rendering about which he or she cannot be certain. The best thing to do is follow RSV or FRCL. Unlike RSV and TEV, there should be a footnote indicating that the Hebrew text is very uncertain.

In this verse the translator must decide which of various interpretations to follow. If the Hebrew term is rendered **saints**, as in RSV, it may be necessary to avoid the idea of church images or pictures. Likewise to be avoided is a description of the moral character of a certain class of saintly people. **Saints** used in the Old Testament as well as in the New Testament refers to "God's people" or "people belonging to God."

<u>**16.4**</u>   RSV   TEV

Those who choose another god multiply their sorrows;[h] their libations of blood I will not pour out or take their names upon my lips.	Those who rush to other gods bring many troubles on them-selves.[x] I will not take part in their sacri-fices; I will not worship their gods.

[h] Cn: The meaning of the Hebrew is uncertain

[x] *Probable text* Those . . . themselves; *Hebrew unclear.*

Again there is much uncertainty over the meaning of the first line of this verse. The text seems to say, "They increase their troubles (or, sorrow), another (one) they hasten to." RSV translates the last Hebrew word as <u>**choose**</u> (translated "**rush to**" in TEV). This verb has two meanings: (1) to obtain something by paying for it; (2) to go quickly or do something quickly. Anderson prefers to derive the form from a verb meaning "to lust for," and understands the text to mean "those who lust after other gods." It is also possible to take the verb to mean "to turn to" (as an extension of "to exchange"); NJV has "espouse"; Weiser understands "flatter." It is recommended that the meaning expressed by RSV and TEV (and FRCL) be followed.[1]

In some languages both "**rush to**" and **choose** will be more ambiguous than in English. It will sometimes be advisable to select an event term which also is relational, such as "follow" or "serve"; for example, "People who serve other gods will have trouble."

The psalmist declares he will have no part in idol worship: (1) He will not "pour out blood offerings" (**libations of blood**) as part of the ritual sacrifices, probably the blood of the sacrificed animals. Some, however, take the word to refer to persons offering wine to their gods to pay for the blood they had spilled, that is, the murder of innocent victims. In languages where the pouring of libations is well known, a local expression can no doubt be used. However, if the practice is unknown an adjustment to a more generic level is possible, as in TEV. In many languages where sacrifice is unknown, a descriptive phrase may be used; for example, "I will not kill animals and give them as gifts to them" or "I will not give them burned gifts in the form of animals."

(2) The psalmist will not "mention their names" (**take their names upon my lips**), which may refer to the people who worship idols, and the psalmist vows not to have anything to do with them; he will not even speak of them. It seems more likely, however, that **their names** are the names of the gods being worshiped, and that the vow is not to worship them (see Anderson). To "mention their names" is to invoke them in worship. In some languages it will be possible to keep something of the form of the final line; for example, "I will not speak their names in prayer" or "when I pray I will not call out their names."

16.5	RSV	TEV
	The LORD is my chosen portion and my cup; thou holdest my lot.	You, LORD, are all I have, and you give me all I need; my future is in your hands.

Using metaphors which were familiar to his readers, the psalmist in verses 5-6 shows how good Yahweh has been to him. (1) Yahweh, he says, is **my chosen portion** (literally "the portion of my share"; see discussion in 11.6 on "the portion of their cup"). This is language which reflects the division of the land of Canaan among the various tribes, each tribe being allotted its share of the land, except the tribe of Levi; the Lord himself was its share (Deut 10.8-9). Here, in a striking reversal of the figure, the psalmist says that Yahweh has been allotted to him. This may be difficult to express in translation. TEV has made the rendering of verse 5 more personal by

---

[1]HOTTP offers the following translation of verses 3-4a: "(and I said) concerning the holy ones who are on the earth, and the mighty ones in whom all my desire (was placed): 'May their pains be multiplied, (those) who hasten (towards) a foreign (god).' "

employing direct address. This model can be followed in many languages. Because of the historical reference in the term **portion**, referring to the division of the land, it may be necessary to say, for example, "LORD, you are what I inherit." It may be necessary to explain "inherit" in this context in a footnote.

(2) Yahweh is **my cup**, which stands for the destiny that God assigns him (see 11.6). SPCL translates somewhat differently, "you fill me with blessings." **Cup**, meaning destiny, may require shifting to nonfigurative speech and will often require the use of a clause, as in TEV; for example, "you decide how I will live" or, figuratively, "you make the path where I will go." GECL abandons figurative language altogether and translates the line "Lord, you provide me with what I need."

(3) Yahweh "maintains my lot" (RSV **holdest my lot**). This again reflects the custom of reaching decisions about God's will, including the division of the land among the tribes, by casting lots (see Num 26.55-56). What the psalmist has comes from Yahweh, who protects and guides him. So the figure means that Yahweh guarantees his future, his destiny. NJV translates "You control my fate"; FRCL and GECL "you hold my destiny in your hands"; SPCL "my life is in your hands."

<u>16.6</u>   RSV   TEV

> The lines have fallen for me in pleasant places;
> yea, I have a goodly heritage.

> How wonderful are your gifts to me;
> how good they are!

The metaphors in this verse are also taken from the division of the land of Canaan among the Hebrew tribes. The word translated **lines** is "cord, rope" (see "cords" in 18.4-5), which was used in measuring off a plot of ground; it came also to mean, by extension, the plot of ground, the field, thus measured off. See NJB "the measuring-line marks out for me a delightful place"; NJV "Delightful country has fallen to my lot"; also possible is "A pleasant territory has been marked out as mine." The psalmist is not speaking of a plot of land, or field; he is using the word figuratively, meaning everything that Yahweh has done for him, everything that Yahweh has given him.

The word translated **pleasant** appears also in verse 11c. In order to avoid misunderstanding the reference as being a plot of ground, the translator should follow TEV. Other renderings may be "I have inherited good things from you" or "the things you gave me are pleasant." If the receptor language has a measuring term that can be used figuratively, it may be possible to say "what you have measured off to give me is pleasant" or "the things you have counted out for me are good."

Yea translates a strong affirmative particle. NEB, NAB, NJV, NJB have "Indeed"; NIV "Surely." **Goodly** translates a word meaning delightful, fine, excellent.

The Hebrew word for **heritage** normally refers to the inheritance received at the death of one's father, and the word was applied to the land of Canaan as that which the Israelites had received from Yahweh, emphasizing the fact that their possession of it was a gift from God. By transfer the word was applied to all of God's gifts to his people (see also its use in 28.9). However, the term used in translation should not imply that God had to die before they could receive it. FRCL translates the verse, "This is a destiny that pleases me, a privilege that delights me."

143

16.7	RSV	TEV

I bless the LORD who gives me counsel; in the night also my heart instructs me.	I praise the LORD, because he guides me, and in the night my conscience warns me.

In verses 7-8 the psalmist praises Yahweh for all his goodness to him. To **bless the LORD** is to praise him, to thank him for his blessings. Here the psalmist praises Yahweh because he instructs him, **gives me counsel**. This instruction is moral and spiritual. GECL translates "who tells me what I should do"; TEV "he guides me."

The expression **bless the LORD** must normally be recast to express praise, as in TEV. "**Praise**" is sometimes rendered "I speak well of the LORD" or "I say the LORD is great." Where the cause clause must precede the consequence of the action, the full expression may be rendered "Because the LORD teaches me, I will speak well of him."

In the night translates a plural in Hebrew which can mean "during the watches of the night" or "every night." Briggs takes it as an intensive plural, "in the dark night." **Heart** translates the word for "kidneys" (see comments on 7.9); in English "conscience" (TEV, NJV, TOB) seems the best translation.

The verb for **instructs me**, translated "**warns**" in TEV, means to correct, discipline, chasten, instruct (see "chasten" in 6.1b; 2.10 "take warning"). Dahood understands this to be a reference to Yahweh himself and translates "(his) heart instructs me." SPCL also takes Yahweh to be the subject of the verb, and translates "in my inmost being he corrects me night after night." It seems better, however, to take it as a first person singular pronoun, the psalmist's own conscience. Anderson comments: "the poet's own conscience . . . bears witness to the divine word."

The expression **my heart instructs me** may have to be recast in some languages if it is to be taken as in the TEV sense of "**conscience**." For example, "what I know in my heart tells me," "the thoughts I have in my innermost teach me," or "my thoughts show me the way to go."

Note how the parallel expressions **counsel** and **instructs** cover similar areas of meaning. In some languages it is not possible to render **instructs** with two different words. In such cases the translator must often translate both lines a and b with the same word. However, if the Hebrew term in line b is taken in the wider sense of "to correct" or "to discipline," it may be possible to render line b "in the night my heart shows me the good road to follow" or "in the night I think about the right way to live."

16.8	RSV	TEV

I keep the LORD always before me; because he is at my right hand, I shall not be moved.	I am always aware of the LORD's presence; he is near, and nothing can shake me.

Verses 8-11b are quoted, exactly as they appear in the Septuagint, in Acts 2.25-28; verse 10b is also quoted in Acts 13.35.

The idea expressed in **I keep the LORD always before me** means to keep him in mind; NJV "I am ever mindful of the LORD's presence"; FRCL "I never lose sight of the Lord." Also possible is "I constantly fix my mind on the Lord." In translation TEV language can be used, "I always remember that the LORD is present with me," or it may be rendered "I know the LORD is always near me."

He is at my right hand means he is present, near to help, available. The place at the right of a person was where his defender in a trial would stand (see 109.31). SPCL translates "with him at my right, nothing can make me fail." Being at the right hand means in some languages that one is in an honored position or is available to help. For the verb **be moved** see comments on 10.6. Yahweh's presence provides security to the psalmist, and he cannot be defeated.

The relation between the two parts of the last line (**because**) should be formally stated or clearly implied. For TEV this can be made clearer by having "he is near, and so nothing . . . ."

16.9	RSV	TEV
	Therefore my heart is glad, and my soul rejoices; my body also dwells secure.	And so I am thankful and glad, and I feel completely secure,

Therefore: the psalmist's happiness and sense of security is a result of Yahweh's nearness to him (verse 8b).

The psalmist praises Yahweh for saving him from death. The three words **heart**, **soul** (literally "glory"; see comments on 7.5), and **body** (or, "flesh") are not meant as different parts of the psalmist's being, nor do they distinguish between his physical nature and the emotional or spiritual aspects of his being, but are ways of speaking about himself as a whole.[2]

The emotions expressed in **heart is glad** and **soul rejoices** must often be recast in translation to speak of other body organs (stomach, liver, kidneys, throat). Accordingly one may sometimes say, for example, "my stomach is warm and my kidneys happy" or "my liver is bright and my innermost sings." If body parts are not used in this way, it is always possible, with a certain poetic loss, to say, for example, "I am glad, very glad."

Dwells, with **my body** as the subject, describes the condition or state of the psalmist; he "is" or "remains" **secure** (see comments on "in safety" in 4.8).

My body also dwells secure is again a part representing the whole, and in many languages it will be more natural to replace **body** with the pronoun "I"; for example, "I live in safety" or "I am safe."

---

[2]It should be noticed that a number of scholars, including Dahood, instead of *kavod* "glory" of the Masoretic text, use the vowels for *kaved* "liver" as the seat of inner life, like "heart" and "kidneys"; the Septuagint has "my tongue."

16.10   RSV   TEV

For thou dost not give me up to Sheol, or let thy godly one see the Pit.	because you protect me from the power of death. I have served you faithfully, and you will not abandon me to the world of the dead.

Give me up translates "abandon my *nefesh*" (see comments at 3.2); and for **Sheol** see comments at 6.5. The psalmist is confident that Yahweh will keep him from dying prematurely.

Sheol may often be rendered "The place where dead people go." However, the translator must be able to distinguish between this place and the local cemetery which may be in the mind of the reader.

The term **godly one** refers to the psalmist himself (see comments on "godly" in 4.3). It is also possible to translate "your loyal servant"; SPCL "your faithful friend." TEV uses a verbal phrase, "**I have served you faithfully.**" Some, however, take the term to be generic, a way of speaking of all of Yahweh's faithful people. It seems best to take it as a reference to the psalmist. (NIV "your Holy One" takes the Hebrew text to refer to Jesus Christ.)

The verb **see** means here, as often in the Bible, "to experience."

The term **Pit** (see comments at 7.15; 9.15) is used synonymously with **Sheol** and is elsewhere also used of the world of the dead (see 30.9; 49.9; 103.4). The Septuagint translators mistakenly derived the word for **Pit** from the Hebrew verb meaning "to corrupt," and this is why the passage means something quite different in the quotation in Acts 2.27. It should be noticed that both here and in verse 9a ("my tongue rejoices"), NIV has forced the Hebrew text to conform to the meaning of the Septuagint, as quoted in Acts 2.25-26.

TEV has restructured line <u>b</u> of this verse quite radically, due mainly to "**I have served you faithfully**" as a meaningful equivalent of what RSV represents as **thy godly one**.

It is disputed whether or not the passage speaks of resurrection (as it is applied to Christ in Acts 2.25-28,31; 13.35). Some scholars believe that it does; Dahood understands it to mean that the psalmist believes that, like Enoch and Elijah, he will go directly into the presence of God without having died. Others believe the text means that the psalmist has been kept from untimely, unexpected death. H. H. Rowley takes a mediating position, speaking of it as "a glimpse, rather than . . . a firm faith" (in the resurrection). Briggs believes that it means that the psalmist hopes that in Sheol itself he will still have Yahweh with him. Whatever the interpretation, the translation should be faithful to the text as it is: "You do not abandon me to Sheol, you do not allow your devoted (or, faithful) servant to go down to the grave (or, the world of the dead)."

16.11   RSV   TEV

Thou dost show me the path of life;	You will show me the path that leads to life;

| in thy presence there is fulness of joy, in thy right hand are pleasures for evermore. | your presence fills me with joy and brings me pleasure forever. |

The verb in line <u>a</u> is the causative form of "to know," literally "you will cause me to know" (NJV "You will teach me"); most English translations have <u>show</u> or "reveal." **The path of life** is "the path that leads to life" (TEV); Dahood sees this as eternal life. TEV has translated the verb in the future tense, "**You will show me.**" It may be better to follow RSV and translate in the present tense, expressing repeated or continuous action: "You always show me . . . ."

Presence (Hebrew "face") and **right hand** are used synonymously, meaning close presence, companionship, care, protection. RSV **in thy right hand** means that God holds in his right hand gifts or blessings that will bring eternal pleasure to the psalmist. It seems better, however, to understand the Hebrew to mean "at your right hand," that is, "close to you," parallel with "in your presence" in the preceding line. In many passages "the right hand" is specifically the place of privilege and honor (see 45.9; 110.1). In some instances the two metaphors may be clear and effective in representing the meaning; in other cases nonfigurative language may be better. GECL translates "from your right hand comes eternal happiness."

The two words <u>joy</u> and **pleasures** (see verse 6) are also used synonymously; **fulness of joy** is complete joy, "perfect joy" (NJV).

In thy presence . . . may have to be recast into a temporal clause; for example, "When you are near me I am joyful" or "When you are near my heart is cool." The parallel line **in thy right hand . . .** is rendered in some languages "because you are near to me, my heart is always cool" or "because you are with me . . . ."

The word translated **for evermore** does not necessarily mean "eternally"; as Anderson points out, it can mean "for life," as in Exodus 21.6, "the slave shall serve his owner for life."

147

Psalm 17

This psalm is a lament by a person who feels persecuted and oppressed by his enemies and has no one to protect him except God. It thus belongs to the general category of individual laments. Some scholars, however, have concluded that there is a category of "psalms of innocence," and include this psalm in that classification, along with such other psalms as 7, 16, 35, and 139.

The psalmist begins with a fervent plea to God (verses 1-2), followed by a strong protest of his innocence, his complete obedience to God (verses 3-5). Again he prays for protection (verses 6-9a), and then he describes his enemies as merciless and cruel, waiting to destroy him (verses 9b-12). Once more he asks the Lord to save him (verses 13-14), and ends the psalm with a calm statement of his confidence in God (verse 15).

Psalm 17 can be analyzed as an alternating series of pleas or commands and statements, in which there is a degree of balance in the number and order. Based on the occurrence of Hebrew verbs, there is a predominance of three verb commands and three verb statements, which reflect in some cases the three-line structure of the parallelism. Verse 1 begins with three commands addressed to God: "hear," "listen," "give ear." Verse 2 follows with two more: "judge" and "see." With verse 3 the pattern shifts to three statements or if-clauses (with a pair of consequences). To this point, if one wants more symmetry, it is possible to say that verses 1-2 have five commands and verse 3 five statements. Verses 4-5 continue the line of statements with three more, while verse 6 has two statements and two commands. At the very center of the poem (verses 7-8) the command line again has three. With verse 9 the focus shifts to the wicked, with five descriptive statements made in verses 9-11. Verse 13 alternates again to the command domain with four, followed in verse 14 with three commands, and verse 15 concludes the poem, returning to three verbs of statement.

It will be noticed that verse 12 has been omitted from the list. There are two sets of similes in this psalm. The first, "as the apple of thy eye/in the shadow of thy wings," closes the stanza of verses 7-8, which begins with "show thy steadfast love" and closes with the introduction of the enemies. The second simile (verse 12), "like a lion/as a young lion," again marks a juncture, standing as it does between the final statement about the enemies and the call to God to arise and confront the enemy. Translators should watch for the way in which similes are used for opening and closing parts of a psalm or the entire psalm.

Finally, the conclusion of Psalm 17 does not link up with the beginning but with the center of the poem. In verse 7 the psalmist calls upon God to "show thy steadfast love," and in the end he is able to say in confidence "I will see your face."

Nothing in the psalm allows us to say who the writer was nor what were the specific circumstances which prompted this prayer.

HEADING: "**The Prayer of an Innocent Man**" (TEV); "A prayer for justice"; "A prayer for vindication." If the translator follows the TEV heading, the word "**Innocent**" will most likely carry the meaning of one who has been acquitted of charges. "**Innocent**" here refers to the correctness of the psalmist's life before God. Therefore the heading may often be rendered as "A good person prays to God." Where "pray" must take an object, one may say "A good man asks God to help him" or "An honest man asks God to do what is right."

Hebrew Title: **A Prayer of David** (TEV "**A prayer by David**").
The word translated **Prayer** occurs quite often in Psalms, including verse 1b of this psalm. Besides this psalm, it is also found in the titles of Psalms 86; 90; 102; 142.

17.1 RSV	TEV
Hear a just cause, O LORD; attend to my cry! Give ear to my prayer from lips free of deceit!	Listen, O LORD, to my plea for justice; pay attention to my cry for help! Listen to my honest prayer.

The opening words in Hebrew are literally "Listen LORD (to) justice," but there is no preposition governing the noun translated "justice." Most translations take the word here to mean "a plea for justice." GECL translates "Lord, I want justice." The Greek translation by Aquila, and Jerome, both translate as though the Hebrew text were "(to) a righteous man," which Briggs prefers. This expression must in some languages be restructured as a temporal clause, and **just cause** must often be rendered as an event which God does; for example, "Hear me, LORD, when I beg you to do the right thing" or, idiomatically, "Hear me, LORD, when I ask you to set me on the right path."

The three parallel verbs, **Hear**, **attend**, **Give ear**, are varieties of ways of saying the same thing: "listen . . . pay attention . . . hear."

The word translated **my cry** means a loud cry, either of joy or despair, according to the context.

My prayer from lips free of deceit is a literal translation of the Hebrew text, which TEV renders more simply as "**My honest prayer**." See also comment on "deceitful" in 5.6. It is a sincere, truthful prayer that he addresses to God. FRCL translates "(my prayer) comes from a sincere heart." If the translator follows TEV's "**honest prayer**," it may be necessary to recast this expression, since in many languages "**honest**" may be used in reference to people but not to prayers. Two examples are "Listen, LORD, to the prayer of an honest man" or "Listen, LORD, to the words an honest man prays." This may be expressed idiomatically as "Listen, LORD, to the prayer of a man with a white heart."

Some translations make the last line a reason clause explaining why the Lord should hear his prayer; for example, "because my words do not come from lips that tell lies."

17.2	RSV	TEV

From thee let my vindication
come!
Let thy eyes see the right!

You will judge in my favor,
because you know what is right.

Some translations take this verse to be a plea (RSV, NIV, NEB, FRCL, TOB); others take it to be a statement (TEV, NJV, NJB). Either is possible, but a plea seems to fit the context better.

The first plea, **From thee let my vindication come**, means "Judge in my favor," "Declare me innocent." The Hebrew noun translated **vindication** is used in 7.6 (where RSV translates "judgment"); see comment on the word there.

The second petition, **Let thy eyes see the right**, means "Pay attention to (or, Take note of) what is right." The psalmist is asking Yahweh to fix attention on, that is, be determined to do, what is fair and right (see comments on "equity" in 9.8b).

"**Judge**" is expressed in some languages idiomatically as "to cut the words." If the translator takes this verse as a plea or command, it will often be necessary to complete the thought with a full clause; for example, "cut the words and show that I have done no wrong," or positively, "cut the words and show that I am right."

17.3-4	RSV	TEV

3 If thou triest my heart, if thou
visitest me by night,
if thou testest me, thou wilt find
no wickedness in me;
my mouth does not transgress.
4 With regard to the works of men,
by the word of thy lips
I have avoided the ways of the
violent.

3 You know my heart.
You have come to me at night;
you have examined me com-
pletely
and found no evil desire in me.
I speak no evil, 4 as others do;
I have obeyed your command
and have not followed paths of
violence.

Some translations (RSV, NAB) take the first three clauses in a conditional sense ("If you try . . ." or "Should you try . . ."); others, like TEV, FRCL, SPCL, NJV, take them as statements of fact. Either is possible, but it seems better to follow TEV and others and translate as a statement. In some languages it is not natural to express a series of conditional clauses followed by a single consequence, as in RSV. In such cases it will be best to follow TEV. In some cases line a will appear misplaced, because it will seem more natural to occur after line c, as a consequence of lines b and c. This is not necessarily the case where these lines are rendered as conditional clauses.

The psalmist protests that he is completely innocent. (1) **If thou triest** (or, If you examine) **my heart** ("triest" is the same verb used in 7.9). (2) **If thou visitest me by night** (the verb is translated "care for" in 8.4). This visitation **by night** may imply a night spent in the Temple, where the psalmist would, perhaps by means of dreams or visions, be aware of the presence of Yahweh. (3) **If thou testest me** is literally "refine" (see use of "refined" and comments in 12.6). This is a picture of one undergoing "fiery" tests in order to have all impurities removed. In some languages it is possible to maintain the imagery of refining; for example, "You have tried me by putting me in fire." Or it is sometimes possible to restructure this line as a simile; for example, "You have tried me as gold is refined in fire."

As a result of all this examining and testing, **thou wilt find no wickedness in me**. This rendering (same meaning as in TEV, NEB, NAB) involves a slight change in the Hebrew text, which says "you will find nothing, I have purposed"; with a change of vowels the word for "I have purposed" becomes "my evil conduct" (see 26.10a; 119.150a). HOTTP, however, prefers to keep the Hebrew text form, for which there are two possible interpretations in the context of the line that follows: (1) "my plans (thoughts) do not go beyond my mouth," which means, my thoughts and my words agree; (2) "if I devise something wicked, this should not cross my mouth," that is, I must not reveal any wicked thoughts I have had.

The next statement, **my mouth does not transgress** (TEV "I speak no evil"), may be taken as an independent statement (RSV and others), or else it may be connected to the following two Hebrew words, which are the beginning of verse 4, "according to the deeds of man." TEV has followed the latter alternative, translating **"as others do"**; see NJB "I have not sinned with my mouth [4] as most people do" (also NAB, SPCL). It is also possible to have "I utter no evil plan. [4] However other men act . . . ." NEB and NJV represent other ways of handling the text. **My mouth does not transgress** is sometimes rendered idiomatically; for example, "I speak with one mouth" or "The words I speak are straight."

RSV takes the first two words of the Hebrew text of verse 4 as a clause that is connected to what follows: **With regard to the works of men . . .** . This makes for a complex structure, not easy to understand.

"I have obeyed your command" (TEV) translates what appears in RSV as **by the word of thy lips**. RSV connects this phrase with what follows: **by the word of thy lips I have avoided the ways of the violent** (also SPCL). But there is difficulty with the Hebrew passage which RSV translates **I have avoided the ways of the violent**. The RSV and TEV renderings seem to involve taking the verb meaning "keep, obey, observe" (see NAB "I have kept the ways of the law") in the sense "I have kept from," thus rendering **I have avoided**. But this normally requires the Hebrew preposition "from" (as in 121.7), which is not here, or else it requires the passive form of the verb, "I have been kept from." The Syriac (according to Briggs) supplies the preposition "from": "I have kept from." Delitzsch and others say that here the statement "I have kept the paths of the violent" has the implication "I have kept from going along them," and point to the use of the same verb in 1 Samuel 25.21; but in this passage the verb may mean "to guard, protect." K-B classifies the verb here in the same category in which it is used in 1 Samuel 1.12, "Eli observed her mouth" (see also Zech 11.11 "watching me"). So here the Hebrew text may mean "I have observed the paths of violent people." So NJV "I have kept in view of the fate of the lawless." RSV **have avoided** and TEV **"have not followed"** have the same meaning.

Ways translates the same word used in 16.11, "path." NJV translates "fate," and in the margin it refers to this meaning for "paths" in Proverbs 1.19; TOB has "I have followed the prescribed paths." The word translated **the violent** is literally a burglar, a robber (the word appears only here in Psa); see Jeremiah 7.11 "a den of robbers." **The ways of the violent** must often be restructured in translation, because the reference is to people who behave in a violent manner; for example, "I have not acted with anger" or "I have not followed the path of men who use strong force against others."

One possible way to translate the three lines is:

> I speak no evil,
> 4 nor have I followed men's evil deeds and violent ways,
>   for I have obeyed your command.

FRCL translates as follows:

> I have made no comments
> 4 on the actions of others,
>   but I have applied myself
>   to do what you have commanded.
> On the difficult path
> 5   I firmly keep my feet.

There are almost as many different renditions of these lines as there are commentaries and translations.[1]

17.5   RSV   TEV

My steps have held fast to thy   I have always walked in your way
** paths,**   and have never strayed from it.
my feet have not slipped.

The psalmist uses the familiar figure of walking down a road to refer to his complete submission to Yahweh's commands. The word translated **paths** is literally "track (of a wagon), course"; see its use in 65.11, "the tracks of your chariot." "**In your way**" or **thy paths** must indicate the way the Lord has directed people to go, and not merely indicate a path which belongs to the Lord. One may recast this as "I have always followed the way you have gone" or "I have always walked where you have shown me."

For the verb translated **slipped** (literally "totter, stagger") see its use in 10.6, "be moved." The parallelism in this verse expresses the movement from the general **steps** in line <u>a</u> to the specific **feet** in line <u>b</u>. The meaning is to be understood as "Not only have my steps stayed on your paths, but my feet have never even slipped." TEV, which replaces **steps** and **feet** with "**walked**" and "**strayed**," does not bring out the intensification.

---

[1]The Septuagint translates the second part of verse 4 "because of the words of your lips I have kept to difficult paths."

17.6   RSV   TEV

I call upon thee, for thou wilt   I pray to you, O God, because you
   answer me, O God;   answer me;
incline thy ear to me, hear my   so turn to me and listen to my
   words.   words.

With this strophe (verses 6-9a) the psalmist renews his pleas for God's help.

Incline thy ear (TEV "**Turn to me**") translates the phrase "to bend the ear" (used of God also in 31.2; 71.2; 86.1; 102.2; 116.2), that is, to pay attention to, to listen. Some languages use expressions for "listen" which mean mere hearing. Others use terms whose focus is on obeying. Neither of these is appropriate in this passage, in which the writer is asking for close attention. This is rendered in some cases "put your ear on this" or "have two ears for my words."

The psalmist now reaches back to verse 1 to repeat his call to God to **hear**. In doing so he takes the Hebrew verb for **hear** from the beginning of verse 1a and repeats it at the end of verse 6b, thus creating a chiasmus with the opening verse. This device has as its purpose to call attention by repeating in reverse order. TEV has accomplished the same arrangement with "**listen**" in both verses.

The two petitions in line b may be taken as synonymous and be reduced to one request: "listen to my petition (or, prayer)." However, in typical parallelism something is added in the second clause to carry the idea forward and heighten its effect. Here two verbs are used to increase the intensification. In fact, line b may be considered a consequence of line a, or as specification of the verb **call** in line a. As consequence it may then be rendered "therefore give me your ear and hear what I have to say," or as in TEV, "**so turn to me and listen . . . .**" In some languages it may not be possible to have two similar verbs for "listen" in line b; for example, "listen to me carefully and pay attention to my words (or, prayer)."

17.7   RSV   TEV

Wondrously show thy steadfast   Reveal your wonderful love and
   love,   save me;
O savior of those who seek   at your side I am safe from my
   refuge   enemies.
from their adversaries at thy
   right hand.

The verb translated **wondrously show** is the same one used in 4.3a, "set apart," where it means "treat in a special way." For comments on **steadfast love** see 5.7.

RSV translates the second line as the vocative phrase **O savior of those who seek refuge**. TEV has joined **those who seek refuge** to **their adversaries**: "I am safe from my enemies." All other English translations consulted keep the vocative phrase, as RSV does; in some of them it becomes very long (see NIV). The translator will have to determine whether such a form in the target language is natural and fairly easy to understand.

In most languages it will be necessary to indicate the receivers of **thy steadfast love** and the one who provides refuge in **those who seek refuge**. **Steadfast love** refers to the love that God has for his people, and may be rendered "Show your people the great love you always have for them." It will often be necessary to recast the vocative **O savior of** . . . as a second-person address form; for example, "You are the one who saves your people who come to you for protection from their enemies."

The last word in Hebrew, **at thy right hand**, is taken by most as the place where the oppressed, the persecuted, find protection: "at your side" or "near you" (see also comments at 16.8). Others (see NJV, NEB, NIV) take it to mean the way in which God saves: "with your right hand." Some, however, take it to apply to the enemies, "the enemies at your side," that is, "those who oppose you" (so Weiser, Anderson; also possible is "those who defy you"). **Adversaries** is literally "those who rise up against."

17.8-10   RSV   TEV

8   Keep me as the apple of the eye;   8   Protect me as you would your very
        hide me in the shadow of thy   eyes;
        wings,   hide me in the shadow of your
9   from the wicked who despoil me,   wings
        my deadly enemies who sur-   9   from the attacks of the wicked.
        round me.

                                                         Deadly enemies surround me;
10   They close their hearts to pity;   10   they have no pity and speak
        with their mouths they speak   proudly.
        arrogantly.

TEV and RSV differ on the division of the strophes; most translations agree with RSV, but NAB divides as does TEV. It may be better to follow RSV.

The first line of verse 8 is literally "Guard me as the pupil, the daughter of the eye"; "pupil" in Hebrew is literally "little man" (as reflected in one's eye) and **apple** is an English figure for the Hebrew figure "daughter" (see the same figure in Deut 32.10; Pro 7.2). In Hebrew, as in English and many other languages, **the apple of the eye** is especially precious and must be carefully protected. **Apple of the eye** is frequently expressed as "the child of the eye," "the daughter of the eye," or "the fruit of the eye."

The next figure, **the shadow of thy wings**, is a vivid way of speaking about security (also in 36.7; 57.1; 61.4; 63.7; 91.4). The figure may come from the animal world or from the winged creatures called "cherubim" whose wings stretched over the Covenant Box, symbolizing Yahweh's presence with his people (Exo 25.18-20).

In some languages it may be necessary to switch from **hide me** to "protect me"; for example, "Protect me in the shade of your wings." Where it is necessary to give a fuller expression to make the figurative meaning clear, one can often combine the figure with a simile; for example, "Protect me like a bird protects its young under its wings."

From the wicked is literally "from the face of the wicked," which may mean "from the fury of the wicked" (see Anderson). The verb translated **despoil** is a strong one; it means to completely destroy, devastate (in 91.6a it is used for "plague, pestilence").

Deadly enemies (AT, RSV, TEV, NEB, FRCL, SPCL) translates a phrase "my enemies in *nefesh*." Some take *nefesh* here in the sense of greed (Briggs, Anderson), "my enemies, who in their greed" (NAB "my ravenous enemies"). Others take it to refer to the psalmist himself, as in "my enemies . . . try to kill me" (see comments on "of me" in 3.2). **My deadly enemies** may require recasting, particularly in languages where "my enemies" is expressed as "people who fight against me" or "people who hate me." Here one may say, for example, "people who fight me and want to kill me."

The verb translated **surround** has the sense of "close in on" (see also 22.16; 48.12).

In verse 10 **They close their hearts to pity** (TEV "they have no pity") translates the Hebrew "They have shut tight their fat." It is generally agreed that this means lack of compassion (see NJB "engrossed in themselves"); some, however, see it as a figure of rebellion against God (see Isa 6.10, where "a fat heart" stands for stubbornness, unwillingness to obey God). Any reference to obesity should be avoided in translation (see TOB "they are stuffed with fat"; Dahood "clogged with their blubber").

Arrogantly translates a word meaning pride (also in 10.2) and is sometimes expressed figuratively as "having a swollen heart."

17.11	RSV	TEV
	They track me down; now they surround me; they set their eyes to cast me to the ground.	They are around me now, wherever I turn, watching for a chance to pull me down.

They track me down; now they surround me: in the Hebrew text the verse begins with a noun phrase, "our steps"; with a change of vowels the text becomes a verbal phrase, "they advance on me"; so RSV and other translations.[2] NJV, however, follows the Hebrew text and translates "Now they hem in our feet on every side"; there is no great difference in meaning. TEV has recast the first line, combining the force of the two verbs "they advance" and "they surround."

They set their eyes means "they watch," with the implication "watch for an opportunity," "wait for a chance."

There is some difficulty with the form of the verb in line b which means "to turn, bend" (see its use in verse 6, "incline"), which is here translated **to cast**. Most scholars agree that this is the sense intended. NAB, however, takes it to refer to the enemies, "crouching to the ground, they fix their gaze . . . ." And NJV translates the

---

[2]There is one Hebrew manuscript that has "they advance on me." The next verb **they surround** has in the Masoretic text (the *qere*) the first plural suffix "us"; the singular "me" is *ketiv*. HOTTP ("C" decision) prefers the text "they advance (against me), now they surround me."

line "they set their eyes roaming over the land," which is not a natural English sentence.

Ground: Dahood combines the last word in the Hebreew text of verse 11 with the first word of verse 12 to get "land of Perdition," that is Sheol, and which some other scholars consider likely. If the translator adopts this interpretation, the translation can be "they are waiting for a chance to send me to my grave (or, to put me to death)."

17.12	RSV	TEV

They are like a lion eager to tear,
    as a young lion lurking in am-
    bush.

They are like lions, waiting for me,
    wanting to tear me to pieces.

Again the enemies are compared to ferocious, cruel lions (see comments at 7.2; 10.9). In the first line the Hebrew is "his likeness (is) like lion" (the word for "likeness" is found only here in the Old Testament). The word translated **eager** means "to be pale (with longing, emotion)" (see 84.2; Gen 31.30).

The parallelism of **lion** and **young lion** is not an attempt to talk about two different lions or kinds of lions, as TEV shows. Rather the structure of parallel lines often moves from a noun in the first line to a noun phrase in the second line. In terms of line **b** saying something more than line **a**, the second line goes beyond the emotion of **eager to tear** to moving into position for the kill. Although TEV has reversed the two lines, the intensification has been preserved.

For comments on **tear** see "rend" in 7.2.

The verb translated **lurking** is the common verb "to live, dwell"; and **ambush** translates the word for "hiding place," already seen in 10.8,9. **Lurking in ambush** may sometimes be rendered "waiting in its hiding place to attack" or "waiting to attack someone who will not see them."

17.13	RSV	TEV

Arise, O LORD! confront them,
    overthrow them!
Deliver my life from the wicked
    by thy sword,

Come, LORD! Oppose my enemies
    and defeat them!
Save me from the wicked by your
    sword;

The psalmist begins his plea to Yahweh to save him (verses 13-14) with the familiar request **Arise, O LORD!** (see 3.7; 7.6; 9.19; 10.12). **Arise** does not mean to stand up; rather, it is a plea to begin the action mentioned in the context, **confront**. TEV therefore has "Come." If the translator follows **Arise** as in RSV, it will be important to consider the implication of the expression, since in many languages the term varies according to the various positions involved, such as from lying or sitting.

Confront translates the phrase "meet his face," that is, to challenge, oppose. TEV "**Oppose my enemies**" must often be rendered as "fight against my enemies."

<u>Overthrow</u> translates the causative form of the verb "bow down": "cause to bow down," that is, "throw them down."

<u>Deliver</u> translates a Hebrew verb different from the one used in 12.1 ("Help"). It means "rescue, save, protect."

<u>My life</u> in Hebrew is "my *nefesh*" (see comments at 3.2). <u>Sword</u>, as in 7.12, is used as a figure of God's power to destroy. <u>Thy sword</u> presents a problem where swords are unknown. In some languages a term has been introduced through another language, but with little meaning; for example, "police knives." In such cases it will be clearer to translate what the sword symbolizes; for example, "Save me through your power from the hands of wicked people" or "Because you are strong, save me from evil people."

17.14 RSV	TEV
from men by thy hand, O LORD, from men whose portion in life is of the world. May their belly be filled with what thou hast stored up for them; may their children have more than enough; may they leave something over to their babes.	save me from those who in this life have all they want. Punish them with the sufferings you have stored up for them; may there be enough for their children and some left over for their children's children!

On this verse Anderson comments: "This verse is in some disorder and/or corrupt." And *Old Testament Translation Problems* says "Translation here involves guesswork, for the text is corrupt."

RSV's <u>from men by thy hand, O LORD</u> is a literal translation of the Hebrew, "from men by your hand, Yahweh," which repeats in essence verse 13b, "Deliver . . . from the wicked by thy sword."

<u>From men whose portion in life is of the world</u>: in the Hebrew this is "from men (who) from life (or, world) (is) their share in life." For further comments on the word "share," see "chosen portion" in 16.5. The word translated <u>life</u> can mean either "lifetime," as in 39.5, or "world," as in 49.1. There is little agreement on the meaning of this second line. Dahood's translation of the first two lines (which involves a change in the Hebrew text) fits the context:

> Slay them with your hand, O Yahweh,
> slay them from the earth,
> Make them perish from among the living!

Other translations are: NEB "thrust them out of this world in the prime of their life"; TOB "With your hand, O Lord, thrust them out of mankind, out of mankind and the world"; NJV "from men, O Lord, with Your hand, from men whose share in life is fleeting"; SPCL "with your power, Lord, save me from them; cast them out of this world, which is their heritage in this life!"; also possible is "deliver me by your power, O Lord, from men who enjoy life-long prosperity." The translation of TEV and RSV is reflected also in NJB ("from mortals whose part in life is in this world") and NAB ("from mortal men whose portion of life is in this world"); those men are characterized as people whose only concern and interest is limited to this material world and what it offers.[3]

Following TEV and some other translations, "**have all they want**" may have to be rendered more concretely; for example, "people who have food to waste" or "people who own all the things they can want."

The rest of the verse is also difficult, since it is impossible to decide whether it has a good or a bad sense. The Hebrew text says "and (may) your treasure fill their belly, be filled their sons, and (may) they leave something to their children." It is a plea that Yahweh's "treasure" (a noun appearing only here in the Old Testament) be allotted to those people, and to their children and grandchildren. (1) This is taken in a bad sense by Briggs, Taylor, Toombs, Weiser, Anderson, Oesterley (RSV, Mft, TEV, FRCL). It is a request, as Toombs puts it: "Let the family of the wicked suffer to the third generation." And Taylor comments that "a formula of blessing is grimly employed for a curse." (2) It is taken in a good sense, either as a statement of fact or as a plea, by Delitzsch, Kirkpatrick, Cohen (NEB, NAB, NJB, TOB, SPCL). If taken in a good sense, it is easier to understand it as a statement of fact; so NEB "gorged as they are with thy good things, blest with many sons, and leaving their children wealth in plenty." If taken as a request, then it must be understood that the psalmist is asking Yahweh to bless the wicked with the good things of this life, while he himself prefers the divine fellowship (verse 15). Though possible (see SPCL), this does not seem very likely. Some languages may render these lines as "stuff the parents' stomachs until they hurt, make their children eat until they vomit, and may there still be some left for the grandchildren."

Both NJV and Dahood take a different approach: the first word, "your treasure," is taken to mean "your treasured ones," that is, the godly, and so the blessings of plenty are requested for them, their children, and their grandchildren. So NJV "But as for Your treasured ones, fill their bellies . . . ." This is possible, and some translators may prefer it. Everything consdered, the first possibility is preferable.

17.15	RSV	TEV

As for me, I shall behold thy face in righteousness; when I awake, I shall be satisfied with beholding thy form.	But I will see you, because I have done no wrong; and when I awake, your presence will fill me with joy.

The psalm closes, typically, with a statement of serene confidence.

---

[3]HOTTP says there are two ways verse 13b-14a may be interpreted: (1) "rescue my life from the wicked (by) your sword, from wretched people (by) your hand, LORD, from wretched people of the world whose lot (is) in life . . ."; (2) "rescue my life from the wicked (by) your sword, from wretched people (by) your hand, LORD, from wretched people (who have) their lot in life without duration."

As for me: RSV takes the Hebrew first person pronoun to be emphatic, establishing a sharp difference between the wicked and their fate, and the psalmist's own future. If the translator follows this interpretation, a possible translation is "But I, on my part" or "But my own situation is this."

I shall behold thy face (TEV "**I will see you**") may be rendered in some languages more effectively as "I will be in your presence" or "I will be where you are," but the choice of translation may depend on the translator's interpretation of **when I awake**.

It is difficult to decide what is meant by **in righteousness**, which modifies **I shall behold thy face**. NEB has "my plea is just"; NJV "Then I, justified (will behold your face)"; SPCL "But I, in truth, will be satisfied (to see you face to face)"; also possible is "when I am acquitted." TEV has taken the word to mean the basis for the psalmist's confidence that he will see Yahweh, "**because I have done no wrong.**" Similarly GECL "I have no fault," and NJB "But I in my uprightness will see your face."

It is also difficult to determine what **when I awake** refers to. Some scholars believe that this psalm and those like it were used by an individual in a ritual in the Temple; he would spend the night there, waiting for Yahweh's answer (see Weiser, Anderson). The following morning, therefore, when he awoke, he would expect to receive Yahweh's favorable response. Others, however, take it to refer to awaking from death, that is, resurrection (so Dahood). In translation it is best, if possible, to use a word meaning literally "to wake up" which does not exclude either possibility (that is, of waking up from sleep or "waking up" from death).

I shall be satisfied can be taken in the sense of "I will be sated," that is, "filled" (so NJV). It seems better to take it in the sense of "be pleased," "be content."

Thy form recalls Num 12.8, where Yahweh states that Moses has spoken to him face to face and has seen his "form." It is doubtful the psalmist thought of Yahweh as having a material body; so TEV "**your presence**"; NEB "a vision of thee"; NJV "the vision of You." The Septuagint translated "and I shall be filled at the appearance of your glory." TEV's "**your presence**" may need to be rendered "where you are." In some languages line 15b may be rendered idiomatically as "When I awake, my heart will sit cool because I am in the place where you are" or, nonfiguratively, "When I awake, I will be happy because I am near you."

Psalm 18

This psalm is generally classified as a royal song of thanksgiving to God for victory. But the difference between the situation in the first part of the psalm (personal deliverance from death and enemies, verses 4-6, 16-19) and the situation in the second part (defeat of enemies in battle, verses 37-42) has led some to conclude that they were originally two separate psalms which were eventually joined as one. Others, however, believe it was originally one composition, with perhaps some later additions. The psalm, with a few differences, appears also in 2 Samuel 22.1-51.

Psalm 18 is considered an individual praise psalm, in contrast with the communal praise psalms. It begins with a hymn praising Yahweh for his help (verses 1-3), followed by a description of the psalmist's desperate situation, from which Yahweh saved him (verses 4-6). Then there is a long account of how Yahweh came with power and might (verses 7-15) and rescued him from his enemies (verses 16-19). The next section (verses 20-27) is a statement about the psalmist's character and conduct as the reason why Yahweh answers his plea and saves him, followed by an eloquent description of the Lord's goodness to him (verses 28-34).

The psalmist then portrays how Yahweh enabled him to defeat his enemies in battle (verses 35-42) and subdue his rebellious subjects, both national and foreign (verses 43-45). The psalmist praises the Lord for giving him victory (verses 46-49), and the psalm closes with a statement about God's constant love for King David and his descendants (verse 50).

An alternate way of analyzing the psalm is as follows: It opens with a proclamation: "I love thee, O LORD" (verses 1-2). There follows a summary of purpose (verse 3) which tells what the psalmist intends to do, namely, "call upon the LORD." Then comes a long flashback (verses 4-24) in which the psalmist recounts the marvelous ways in which God has delivered him from his enemies and made him victorious. Beginning with verse 25 he reports or testifies to God's dealings with the good and the wicked and with himself. At verse 49 the direction of narrative ends and he makes a vow: "I will extol thee . . . sing praises to thy name." Verse 50 concludes with a summary reason for the vow. The advantage of viewing these literary blocks is that their boundaries suggest transition points where translators may wish to insert section headings to assist the reader, or make explicit in the body of the text that a change of development is taking place. Leaving spaces between blocks of printed text does not necessarily help the reader to follow the changes of direction in the poem.

Alter suggests that such psalms as this one illustrate how parallelism is used not only to generate movement between the two lines of a verse, but also to carry the narrative-like development forward from one couplet to the next. His analysis, based on the form of the psalm as found in 2 Samuel 22, proposes that 68% of the parallel lines contain "a clear element of dynamic movement from the first verse to the second." 53% of these cases involve intensification or specification, and 47% are characterized as "consequential," in which the first line is in some way the cause, and the second line the effect or consequence. 22% of the lines have a relatively static relation, and the remaining 10% are divided between those which are antithetical pairs, highly questionable as to being static or dynamic, and a few unresolved textual obscurities. (An introduction to most of these terms and concepts is found at the beginning of this Handbook, under "Translating the Psalms," section 3, "The Poetry of the Psalms.")

The psalmist has used static parallelism to open and close the psalm. All the parallel lines which show consequentiality are to be found in the flashback narrative-like section. Intensification is found everywhere except at the opening and closing.

HEADING: **"David's Song of Victory"** (TEV); "A royal song of thanksgiving"; "Song of triumph for the king"; "A song of victory"; "Thanksgiving for help and victory." If the translator follows the TEV heading, it will often be necessary to render the two nouns as verbs; for example, "David sings a song that tells how God helped him in battle" or "David sings to God because he has defeated his enemies."

Hebrew Title: **To the choirmaster. A Psalm of David the servant of the LORD, who addressed the words of this song to the LORD on the day when the LORD delivered him from the hand of all his enemies, and from the hand of Saul. He said:** (TEV **"The words that David, the LORD's servant, sang to the LORD on the day the LORD saved him from Saul and all his other enemies."**).

The first part of the title, **To the choirmaster** and **A Psalm of David**, are standard (see title to Psa 13). The rest of it relates the psalm to David's victories over his enemies and his escape from King Saul (see 1 Sam 23.7-14). Beginning with **addressed the words of this song** to the end of the title, the text is exactly like that of 2 Samuel 22.1 (with the exception of the word for **the hand**, which is a different word in 2 Sam). Here David is called **the servant of the LORD**, and the composition is called "a song" (literally, "the words of this song which David spoke"). For comments on the verb **delivered**, see 7.1. The two words for **hand** mean power.

18.1	RSV	TEV
	I love thee, O LORD, my strength.	How I love you, LORD! You are my defender.

Verse 1 is a single line without parallelism. However, Yahweh is called **my strength**, and the parallel lines which follow in verse 2 go on to make concrete images of **my strength**.

The verb translated **love** occurs rarely in Psalms (and infrequently elsewhere); it has more the idea of being compassionate, merciful. But in this context the meaning is as ancient versions and modern translations have rendered it, **love**. When one translates **I love thee**, special caution must be taken to avoid a meaning such as "I want to possess you." In some languages the term for **love** has little to do with feelings of mercy or compassion. The latter emotions are frequently expressed in idiomatic phrases; for example, "my stomach moves for you," "my heart is warm for you," "my kidneys are for you," and many other similar expressions.

Yahweh is the psalmist's **strength**, either as the source of the psalmist's power, or as his "defender." **My strength** as a description of the Lord must often be recast, because a possessed quality can sometimes only be thought of as belonging to the one speaking to God. Therefore it is often necessary to make **my strength** into a verb phrase; for example, "you are the one who strengthens me" or "you are the one who protects me."

18.2 RSV	TEV
The LORD is my rock, and my fortress, and my deliverer, my God, my rock, in whom I take refuge, my shield, and the horn of my salvation, my stronghold.	The LORD is my protector; he is my strong fortress. My God is my protection, and with him I am safe. He protects me like a shield; he defends me and keeps me safe.

By means of six metaphors the verse describes Yahweh's protection: (1) **rock**, that is, a boulder or large rock, a place where one can defend oneself (see also 31.2; 42.9; 71.3); (2) **fortress** (also 31.2,3; 71.3; 91.2; 144.2), a place that cannot be conquered; it may be a natural formation such as a circle of large rocks, or it may be one built as a defense against enemy forces; (3) **rock** (another word, which occurs very frequently in Psalms; Dahood prefers the meaning "my mountain"); here it is probably a synonym of the first word; (4) **shield**: see description at 3.3; (5) **the horn of my salvation**: a metaphor for strength and power (see 72.4,5), used of God only here and in 2 Samuel 22.3 (see also Luke 1.69), probably owing its meaning to the horns of a bull (NJV translates "my mighty champion"); **of my salvation** can be rendered "that saves me"; (6) **stronghold**: see comments at 9.9; a place of safety, either natural (like a cave) or man-made.

It is possible to consider **and my deliverer** as the second line and **The LORD is my rock, and my fortress** as the first line. In this case **my deliverer** makes specific what is called **my rock** and **my fortress** in the first line. The second set of parallel lines in verse 2 is completely static, in that there is only a piling up of "strength" images, and, as suggested above, the psalmist has reserved this device for the opening and closing of the psalm. TEV has not managed to keep **my deliverer** and has therefore lost part of the parallelism. The static nature of the parallelism is reflected in TEV, which uses two images, **"fortress"** and **"shield,"** and reduces the others to **"protector," "protection," "safe," "protects,"** and **"defends."**

There are two nonmetaphors: **my deliverer** (see comments on the verb in 7.1; 17.13) and **I take refuge** (see comments in 2.12).

TEV uses figurative and nonfigurative language: metaphor (**"strong fortress"**), simile (**"like a shield"**), abstract noun (**"my protection"**), descriptive title (**"my protector"**), and verbal phrases (**"defends me and keeps me safe"**). Variety of expression and clarity of meaning, in poetic form, should be the aim.

In this verse there are five choices the translator must face: (a) to keep the literal translation of the Hebrew, if and only if the meanings are clear and the figures natural; (b) to substitute other known figures from the receptor language; (c) to keep the figure, but modified to a simile, explaining its meaning through the introduction of a verb; (d) to replace the figures with nonfigurative expressions; or finally (e) to combine two or more of the foregoing. Some examples are "The LORD protects me like a rock and a fortress," or "The LORD guards me as a rock or fortress protects people," or "My God, you are like a rock which defends me," or "You defend me like a shield."

Horn of my salvation denoted the place a person could obtain asylum or protection from enemies. This expression can almost never be translated literally without providing the reader with detailed explanations. It is best to follow solution (d) above, using a nonfigurative expression as in TEV; for example, "he saves me from my enemies" or "he keeps my enemies from harming me."

<u>18.3</u>   RSV   TEV

I call upon the LORD, who is wor-   I call to the LORD,
  thy to be praised,   and he saves me from my ene-
and I am saved from my ene-   mies.
  mies.   Praise the LORD!

This verse marks the summary intention of the psalm. The relation between the two parallel lines is that of consequence. The psalmist calls upon Yahweh, and as a result he is **saved from my enemies**. If the translator wishes to help the reader understand the function of the verse in the entire poem, it will be necessary to consider carefully how this can be done in terms of the receptor language. This may be done by putting the final line first; for example, "Praise the LORD! I call out, and so he saves me from my enemies."

I call upon the LORD should not be rendered by a term which means to shout at someone. Also in many languages it is necessary to indicate the purpose in the calling; for example, "I call to the LORD for help" or "I call to the LORD, 'Help me!'"

Who is worthy to be praised in the Hebrew is the first word in the verse, a passive participle of the verb "to praise" (as in 48.1; 96.4). TEV translates it as "**Praise the LORD!**" and places it at the end of the verse. Its relation to what follows in the Hebrew is not quite clear, and emendations have been proposed. But NEB, NJB, and others take it as RSV has, **who is worthy to be praised** or "who should be praised," which may be rendered "people (or, everybody) should praise him." NAB has "Praised be the Lord, I exclaim." Dahood and others connect it with the preceding word (the last word in verse 2), "my stronghold, worthy of praise."

Worthy to be praised must often be recast as an active construction, and in the present context it may be necessary to shift to the first person as the one who praises; for example, "I praise the LORD" or "I say the LORD is good."

For **I am saved** see comments on "help" in 12.1.

	RSV		TEV
4	The cords of death encompassed me, the torrents of perdition assailed me;	4	The danger of death was all around me; the waves of destruction rolled over me.
5	the cords of Sheol entangled me, the snares of death confronted me.	5	The danger of death was around me, and the grave set its trap for me.

With verse 4 begins the long body of the psalm in the form of a review of the past, or a flashback recalling God's great acts in rescuing the psalmist from his enemies. Although there is the occasional verse with static parallelism, the text is made up of parallel lines which enable a movement between lines and between verses so that the great moments of a story unfold. In this sense poetic lines are somewhat narrative without becoming an epic. The translator's perception of the dynamics of the parallelism will help him to select those devices in his own language which will contribute to the heightening effect or the consequence in the second of two parallel lines.

The parallelism in verses 4 and 5 is not typical. Both the a and b lines of each verse have a metaphor. The more typical structure is for the metaphor to occur in the second line, which is more vivid and intensive. However, 18.4 is a clear case of intensification; in line a the **cords of death** merely **encompass**, but in line b they turn into violent action. TEV's rendering, which substitutes "**danger of death**" in line a, intensifies line b with the figure "**waves of destruction**" and the active verb "**rolled over me.**" Verse 5 and the first two lines of verse 6, on the other hand, have parallel lines in which the second merely restates the first. There is no heightening of effect, no specification, and no consequence. The poet has simply chosen to introduce the flashback section by piling up images for the sake of emphasizing his threatened existence at some time in the past. With the second couplet in verse 6 begins the predominant structure of movement between parallel lines and between verses.

The phrase **the cords of death** in verse 4a is not quite synonymous with **the torrents of perdition** in line b, and some prefer to adopt for line a the text in 2 Samuel 22.5a, "the waves of death" (see NAB, NJB, BJ, Dahood). **Cords of death** portrays death as a hunter with a net trying to trap people, or with ropes trying to tie them up.

In the four lines of these two verses, **death . . . perdition . . . Sheol . . . death** are all parallel, all indicating the danger of sudden death, either through sickness, or at the hands of enemies, or in battle. The psalmist thought that death was imminent; he was as good as dead.

It is generally assumed that the word translated **perdition** is another name for Sheol (for which see comments on 6.5). The dangers that threatened the psalmist with death are likened to **cords, torrents,** and **snares,** all of which are metaphors for instruments of capture and destruction.

The four verbs are matched to the metaphors: (1) verse 4a, **cords** with **encompassed**, meaning "tie up, bind" (also 2 Sam 22.5; Psa 40.12; 116.3; "closed in" in Jonah 2.5); (2) verse 4b, **torrents** with **assailed**, meaning "fall upon, roll over, overwhelm"; some take the verb to mean "terrify"; (3) verse 5a, **cords** with **entangled**, meaning "be around," that is, tie up (see the verb in 17.11); (4) verse 5b, **snares** with **confronted**, meaning "to face, to meet" (as in 17.13).

In many languages it is not natural to refer to death as **the cords of death**; however, other metaphors are often available: trap, snare, pit, and fire. One may sometimes say "the snares of death were around me" or "traps that kill were around me."

Torrents of perdition may sometimes be substituted by "floods that destroy."

Cords of Sheol may sometimes be replaced by such figures as "the traps of death catch me" or "the traps which kill take hold of me."

18.6	RSV	TEV

In my distress I called upon the
    LORD;
  to my God I cried for help.
From his temple he heard my
    voice,
  and my cry to him reached his
    ears.

In my trouble I called to the
    LORD;
  I called to my God for help.
In his temple he heard my voice;
  he listened to my cry for help.

In my distress must sometimes be rendered as a clause; for example, "When I saw trouble," or idiomatically, "When trouble took hold of me." **Distress** is the same word used in 4.1.

I cried in line <u>b</u> translates a verb which is related to the noun **my cry** in line <u>d</u> (see the noun in 5.2; it also occurs in verse 41 of this psalm).

His temple is probably heaven (see 11.4), from where God comes to the psalmist's rescue (verses 9-10); but some see here a reference to the Temple in Jerusalem.

My voice is a substitute for speaking, and in some languages there is no noun for voice as such, but only a verb for speaking. Therefore this line may often be rendered "he heard me when I spoke to him."

Line <u>d</u>, **cry reached his ears**, makes specific the more general form in line <u>e</u> **heard my voice**. Note that TEV adds "**for help**," which also moves in the direction of greater specificity. Translators may find that this kind of movement may be made in the noun or in the verb.

The last line in Hebrew is "and my cry for help to his face entered his ears" (the parallel in 2 Sam 22.7 is only "and my cry for help in his ears"). Some see "to his face" (that is, **to him**) as redundant here and favor omitting it, but the majority keep it.

18.7	RSV	TEV

Then the earth reeled and rocked;
  the foundations also of the
    mountains trembled

Then the earth trembled and
  shook;
  the foundations of the moun-

and quaked, because he was angry.	tains rocked and quivered, because God was angry.

Verse 7 in Hebrew has a bracketing structure in which **earth** and **foundations of the mountains** are enclosed at the beginning by **reeled and rocked** and at the end by **trembled and quaked**. The four verbs are similar in meaning, and the relation between the lines is relatively static, except for the earth being replaced by the more literary **foundations . . . of the mountains.**

This verse begins with a connective showing that the action is in response to a previous one, **Then**. It is important in translation to mark this connective, since it signals the start of a process which will continue probably until the end of verse 24.

The long description of Yahweh's coming (verses 7-15) employs the kind of language associated with Yahweh's appearance to his people on Mount Sinai (Exo 19.16-19; see also Judges 5.4-5; Psa 29.4-9; 144.5-6). The first picture is that of an earthquake, and there is a good alliterative effect in Hebrew, "the earth *tig'ash* and *tir'ash*," which some translations try to reproduce: RSV, Dahood **reeled and rocked**; Knox "shivered and shook"; TOB "*se trouble et trembla*"; GECL "*wankte und schwankte.*" In some languages an earth tremor is expressed idiomatically as "the mountain roared" or "the volcano snored."

The foundations . . . of the mountains: it was thought that the mountains reached down to and rested upon the depths of the earth, the world of the dead. So Dahood takes **earth** in line a to refer to Sheol. **The foundations also of the mountains** may sometimes be rendered as "where the mountains sit" or "the legs of the mountains."

The verb translated **trembled** occurs also in 4.4a (see comments there on "Be angry"); and **quaked** translates the same verb translated **reeled** in line a.

18.8	RSV	TEV

Smoke went up from his nostrils, and devouring fire from his mouth; glowing coals flamed forth from him.	Smoke poured out of his nostrils, a consuming flame and burning coals from his mouth.

This verse portrays vividly the angry God. The order in which **smoke**, **fire** and **coals** occur suggests a progression. There is also the reflection of intensification in the order given. Translators may have to modify the imagery somewhat, but it is best to maintain the order, as progression is essential to the preparation and coming down of Yahweh to rescue the psalmist from his enemies.

The picture is that of a volcano in eruption: **smoke . . . fire . . . coals**. **Devouring fire** may be rendered as "fire that burns things up" or "flame that destroys things." It seems that both **devouring fire** and **glowing coals** issued out of Yahweh's mouth (literally the coals "flamed forth from him"). Some understand **from him** in line c to be "from it" and translate "and coals were kindled at it" (NJB); see also NAB "that kindled coals into flames." Some languages make no distinction between nose and nostrils.

The nouns **smoke**, **fire**, and **coals** do not perform the events themselves. Rather, Yahweh causes them to be acted upon. Accordingly in some languages it is necessary to say, for example, "God made smoke go out of his nostrils and sent devouring fire and burning coals out of his mouth" or "God breathed out smoke and spat out hot fire and burning coals."

18.9	RSV	TEV
	He bowed the heavens, and came down; thick darkness was under his feet.	He tore the sky open and came down with a dark cloud under his feet.

In terms of the dynamics of the poem, it is best to consider verse 9 as consisting of three lines, like verse 8: **He bowed down the heavens/came down/thick darkness was under his feet**. Here the second parallel line is used to carry the action forward. In some cases it may be necessary to make the sequence of events more explicit by saying, for example, "Then he came down toward earth," or "After that he came down," or "Having bent the heavens like a hunter bends a bow, he came down."

The picture in verses 9-12 is that of a thunderstorm. The verb of the action exerted on **the heavens** may mean "to stretch" (see 104.2 "stretched out the heavens like a tent"); here the idea is that of bending down, or else "spread apart" (like curtains; so Cross and Freedman). NJB has "parted"; NJV "bent." **Bowed the heavens** is a figure which may require some adjustment in the direction of a simile; for example, "he opened the sky like a person opens a curtain" or "he tore the sky apart like a person tears a cloth."

Came down: God is portrayed as making an opening in the firmament and descending to earth in order to save the psalmist.

The **thick darkness . . . under his feet** refers to dark clouds (see Neh 1.3, where the clouds are the carpet on which God rests his feet). The **darkness** associated with it is to hide him from sight (see 97.2; 1 Kgs 8.12; Exo 19.16; 20.21).

18.10	RSV	TEV
	He rode on a cherub, and flew; he came swiftly upon the wings of the wind.	He flew swiftly on his winged creature;[x] he traveled on the wings of the wind.

[x] WINGED CREATURE: *See Word List.*

Psalm 104.3 has a parallel to this verse: "You use the clouds as your chariot and ride on the wings of the wind."

The **cherub** (plural "cherubim") in the Old Testament is a winged creature, guarding the heavenly throne of Yahweh; see the description in Ezekiel 1.5-14; 10.21. There were gold figures of cherubim above the Covenant Box (Exo 25.17-11), which were thought of as Yahweh's throne (see 1 Sam 4.4; 2 Sam 6.2; 2 Kgs 19.15); and 1

Chronicles 28.18 speaks of "the golden chariot of the cherubim." Here the cherub serves as a chariot on which Yahweh rides. **The wings of the wind** in line <u>b</u> is parallel with the <u>cherub</u> in line <u>a</u>.

The verb translated <u>rode</u> is related to the noun "chariot" in Hebrew. And <u>came swiftly</u> in line <u>b</u> translates a verb used of birds of prey that "swoop" down (see Deut 28.49; Jer 48.40); some translations have "gliding" (NJV, SPCL).

<u>He rode on a cherub</u> presents several problems for translators. Since <u>cherub</u> is largely unknown or misunderstood, a descriptive phrase will be required in many cases. However, one must not give the impression that it is a variant of some locally known large bird. Translators should normally avoid transliterating the term unless it is accompanied by a descriptive phrase, and even then the transliterated form may not be helpful. In most translations a descriptive note such as is found in TEV will be helpful. If the descriptive phrase is confusing for the reader, it may be better to borrow the term from a major language in the area. Phrases like "winged animal" or "flying being" may be meaningless, and "a flying thing" may be equated with anything from an insect to an airplane.

<u>Wings of the wind</u> may require adjustment in languages where wind is not spoken of as having wings. In some cases this expression must be rendered as "the wind blew him there swiftly like a bird flies."

18.11	RSV	TEV

	He made darkness his covering around him,
	    his canopy thick clouds dark with water.
		He covered himself with darkness;
		    thick clouds, full of water, surrounded him.

Continuing the use of images that accompany a storm, the psalmist speaks of Yahweh's "hiding place," that is, <u>his covering</u> (see the verb in 13.1), and of his "shelter" (<u>canopy</u>), which is probably a temporary structure, a "booth" made of branches (as in the Festival of Shelters). <u>Canopy</u> here is parallel with <u>covering</u> in line <u>a</u> and in this context means something that covered and hid Yahweh as he rode down on the cherub. So it is better to imitate TEV, or FRCL "He hid himself in the heart of a cloud, he covered himself with thick clouds, dark as deep water" (see also GECL). NEB has "hiding place . . . canopy"; also possible is "hiding place . . . tent." However, it is important to note that line <u>b</u> carries the thought of line <u>a</u> forward by making it more vivid. The verse may be translated in such a way as to reflect this "going beyond" in the second line by saying, for example, "He covered himself with darkness; even more, he hid himself in dark, rainy storm clouds."

<u>He made darkness his covering</u> may be preserved as a figure by rendering it "he dressed himself with darkness" or "the dark night was his clothing," or nonfiguratively "he hid in the darkness."

The figure in the second line, <u>his canopy thick clouds dark with water</u>, may sometimes be expressed by terms often used by farming and pastoral people alike who erect temporary shelters in fields and pastures; or, stated more generally, "The thing which covered him was made of dark rain clouds."

RSV   TEV

Out of the brightness before him
    there broke through his clouds
    hailstones and coals of fire.
	Hailstones and flashes of fire
	    came from the lightning before
	    him
	    and broke through the dark
	    clouds.

After pausing in verse 11 to build again the picture through intensification, the poet resumes the progression of events. Whatever difficulties we may have with the mixture of hailstones and coals of fire, there is clearly a sequence, in that these elements are displayed subsequent to the brightness. TEV's rendering makes the sequence clear.

There is some uncertainty about the meaning of this verse, which is literally "from the brightness before him his clouds passed through, hailstones and coals of fire." TEV has tried to draw a consistent picture by keeping **"the dark clouds"** as Yahweh's "covering" through which come **"hailstones and flashes of fire."** The second item is particularly puzzling, since <u>coals of fire</u> are not associated with a thunderstorm; FRCL and TEV **"flashes of fire"** takes it to refer to darts of lightning (so Dahood), and takes **the brightness** to mean **"lightning."** Briggs takes the Hebrew "from brightness" to mean "without brightness," that is, darkness, and connects this with the last two words of the preceding verse: "thick clouds of the skies without brightness." Another possible translation is "At the brightness before him the clouds rolled away; there were hailstones and blazing coals." SPCL has "A dazzling light issued from his presence; hailstones and blazing coals erupted from the clouds." The picture is not consistent, and there may be a mixture of images of a thunderstorm and of a volcano in eruption. It may be best to follow TEV.

If the translator follows the imagery found in TEV, it may be necessary to recast the sentence so that the lightning is the agent; for example, "The lightning before him threw out hailstones and flashes of fire, which came down through the dark clouds."

RSV   TEV

The LORD also thundered in the
    heavens,
and the Most High uttered his
    voice,
hailstones and coals of fire.
	Then the LORD thundered from
	    the sky;
	and the voice of the Most High
	    was heard.[a]

[a] *One ancient translation (and see 2 S 22.14)* was heard; *Hebrew* was heard hailstones and flashes of fire.

Verse 13 is instructive in that it reverses completely the normal order of general to specific parallelism. Perhaps by now the translator is prepared to see the figurative language, the specific term, the consequence, the effect in the second of two parallel lines. That the biblical poets were not slaves of their poetic devices should encourage translators to experiment also. If in the receptor language intensification is sacrificed by the reversal, the translator may switch the lines. He should determine first what the difference in poetic meaning would be, if any.

For the verb "to thunder" used of Yahweh, see 29.3; TEV **"from the sky"** and RSV **in the heavens** reflect a difference in the Hebrew manuscripts. **The LORD also thundered** may be unnatural in many languages, since only the sky is said to thunder. Therefore this expression may have to be recast as "The LORD spoke like thunder from the sky" or "When the LORD spoke it sounded like thunder."

The Most High is sometimes rendered "God who is above all others" or "God who is the greatest god." For similar comments on **the Most High**, see 7.17. For comments on **voice** see verse 6.

The Hebrew text has the words **hailstones and coals of fire** at the end of this verse (as at the end of verse 12); this seems an obvious repetition here and does not fit the context as the object of the verbal phrase **uttered his voice**. It is omitted by the Septuagint and is not in the parallel 2 Samuel 22.14; NJB, BJ, FRCL, NAB, NEB also omit.[1] It seems best to omit this phrase.

18.14	RSV	TEV

<table>
<tr><td>And he sent out his arrows, and
    scattered them;
he flashed forth lightning, and
    routed them.</td><td>He shot his arrows and scattered
    his enemies;
with flashes of lightning he sent
    them running.</td></tr>
</table>

The parallelism of verse 14 carries two functions. If **them** is taken to refer to the enemies, the action of destroying the enemies is brought forward. At the same time line b, **flashed forth lightning,** is an intensification of **sent out his arrows**. The "more than that" of the second line should be represented in translation; for example, "He shot his arrows . . . ; he even flashed them with lightning . . . ."

In this verse the parallel form indicates that the **"flashes of lightning"** are Yahweh's **arrows** that he shoots. In areas where the shooting of **arrows** is not known, it may be necessary to substitute another weapon.

The Hebrew text does not say what (or who) is referred to by **them** in both lines. Some take it to be the arrows themselves; others, like TEV, SPCL, take it to be a reference to **"his enemies."** The two verbs **scattered** and **routed** ("to confuse, bring into commotion") seem to apply more naturally to people than to weapons, and so it is recommended that **"his enemies"** be given as the object of the two verbs.

18.15	RSV	TEV

<table>
<tr><td>Then the channels of the sea were
    seen,</td><td>The floor of the ocean was laid
    bare,</td></tr>
</table>

---

[1]HOTTP ("C" decision) retains the phrase, citing factors 5 (assimilation to parallel passages) and 1 (narrow basis for a variant form of the text).

and the foundations of the world were laid bare, at thy rebuke, O LORD, at the blast of the breath of thy nostrils.	and the foundations of the earth were uncovered, when you rebuked your enemies, LORD, and roared at them in anger.

In verse 15 the psalmist uses some degree of heightening in line b with **foundations of the world**. However, the degree is slight in the first pair. By contrast, in the second pair the movement from **thy rebuke** to **the blast of the breath of thy nostrils** is a vivid rhetorical leap, which TEV attempts with "**roared at them in anger.**"

The language used in this verse recalls the parting of the waters of the Red Sea (that is, the Sea of Reeds; see comments at 106.7) when the Israelites fled from Egypt (see Exo 15.8; Psa 106.9). The ocean bed is spoken of in terms of the streams under the ocean (**channels of the sea**), which were believed to supply the ocean with water. The furious rage of Yahweh is pictured as **the blast of the breath of thy nostrils**. But this can be an explicit reference to the strong wind which parted the waters of the sea, and some translations interpret it this way (SPCL "the strong breath that he blew").

In languages which cannot use the passive voice, **channels of the sea were seen** and **foundations . . . were laid bare**, it may be necessary to say, for example, "He made the waters of the sea dry up" and "He made the bottom of the earth bare." **Foundations of the world** may be expressed as "the ground on which the earth stands," or in some languages "the legs of the earth." See also "founded it" (the world) in 24.2.

TEV has made the rebuke and the raging breath to be directed against the enemies; but they can be understood as directed at the ocean bed and the earth's foundations. Toombs sees in verse 15 the picture of Yahweh cleaving his way through the sea and the foundations of the earth down into Sheol, from where he draws forth the psalmist (verse 16).

Line c **at thy rebuke . . .** stands as a temporal clause and chronologically precedes the actions in lines a and b. For this reason it may be more meaningful in some languages to place the final two lines at the beginning. As in 9.5 the English word **rebuke** is too mild for the action described. Something like "roaring" (NJB) or "mighty roaring" (NJV) is better.

18.16-17 RSV TEV

16 He reached from on high, he took me,
    he drew me out of many waters.
17 He delivered me from my strong enemy,
    and from those who hated me;
    for they were too mighty for me.

16 The LORD reached down from above and took hold of me;
    he pulled me out of the deep waters.
17 He rescued me from my powerful enemies
    and from all those who hate me—
    they were too strong for me.

In verses 16-19 the psalmist describes how God rescued him from his enemies. In some languages translators will need to indicate the instrument of **reached**; for example, "the LORD reached his hand down from above and took hold of me," as in TEV.

Draw . . . out: the verb is used only here, 2 Samuel 22.17, and Exodus 2.10 (where it is given as the source of the name Moses).

Many waters refers to the primordial watery mass, that is, the "deep" that was "without form and void" (see 93.3-4; Gen 1.2), which described the chaos and disorder that existed before the creative word of God was uttered (see Gen 1.6-7). Here it is used in a figurative sense of death, the deadly peril from which Yahweh saved the psalmist.

The verb translated **delivered** is used in 7.1, and the verb translated **hated** appears in 5.5. It is very probable that the singular **strong enemy** in line a of verse 17 is the same as its parallel, the plural **those who hated me**, in line b; Dahood, however, takes both as singular ("Foe . . . Enemy"), referring to death. This does not seem very likely.

In some languages translators will need to examine the position of the reason clause, **for they were too mighty for me**, to determine if it should be shifted ahead of the first two lines, such as, "My enemies were too strong for me to defeat them, and so the LORD . . . ."

18.18-19   RSV   TEV

18   They came upon me in the day of   18   When I was in trouble, they at-
        my calamity;   tacked me,
     but the LORD was my stay.   but the LORD protected me.
19   He brought me forth into a broad   19   He helped me out of danger;
        place;   he saved me because he was
     he delivered me, because he   pleased with me.
        delighted in me.

The psalmist continues talking about his enemies.

The word translated **calamity** is found only here in Psalms; it means "disaster" or, in a more abstract sense, "danger," "peril" (NEB). In Deuteronomy 32.35 TEV translates it "doom." **In the day of my calamity** is generic, and some languages do not express the circumstances resulting from trouble in a nonspecific manner. Therefore it is sometimes necessary to say "when I was trapped" or "when they tied me up."

The word translated **my stay** is a noun meaning "support," used only here, 2 Samuel 22.19, and in Isaiah 3.1 (the noun comes from the verb "to lean on, to rely on"; see Isa 50.10).

The line **He brought me forth into a broad place** (Hebrew, literally "he caused me to forth into a roomy place"; see 31.8; 118.5) means to rescue from danger, which is thought of as a place in which the person is confined or hemmed in by trouble and distress (see comments on "distress" in 4.1).

Delivered means "saved"; see also comments on 6.4; for **he delighted in** see comments on 1.2.

18.20-21 RSV TEV

18.20-21	RSV		TEV
20	The LORD rewarded me according to my righteousness; according to the cleanness of my hands he recompensed me.	20	The LORD rewards me because I do what is right; he blesses me because I am innocent.
21	For I have kept the ways of the LORD, and have not wickedly departed from my God.	21	I have obeyed the law of the LORD; I have not turned away from my God.

In verses 20-24 the psalmist declares his complete innocence, the integrity and uprightness of his character and conduct. It is to be noticed that in verses 20-24 and 35-38, TEV uses the present tense of the verbs to indicate habitual, or continuous, action, while RSV has the past tense, indicating specific, isolated events. Most translations in English are like RSV, but there is no certain way to determine which is correct. TEV (also NJB) is preferred, but the translator should feel free to follow RSV.

Verse 20 again has the metaphor in the second line (**cleanness of my hands**) as a means of stepping up the vividness of the parallelism. This heightening is lost in TEV, which has "**because I am innocent.**"

For the verb "to reward" see in 13.6 the verb that RSV translates "dealt bountifully" (TEV "been good"). Here it has the same general meaning of "do good to" or "be good to." **The LORD rewarded me** may be rendered idiomatically in some languages; for example, "The LORD looks at me for good" or "The LORD puts good on my head."

For **righteousness** see comments on "of my right" in 4.1. Here the word describes the psalmist as a person who is careful always to act and speak in conformance to the Law of Moses, the Torah. A "righteous" person, in this context, is above everything else one who obeys God in all things, as verse 21 makes abundantly clear. **According to my righteousness** may be rendered, for example, "because I do what God requires," "because I obey God," or idiomatically "because I follow carefully on God's road."

Cleanness of my hands: clean hands are a sign of innocence (see 24.4; 26.6), as TEV explicitly states.

The verb translated **recompensed** is "to turn" (see 6.4) in the causative form, "he causes to turn," meaning to requite, to repay (here in a good sense).

The ways of the LORD: the ways in which Yahweh wants his people to walk, their behavior, conduct as required by the Law. So TEV "**the Law of the LORD**"; FRCL "the precepts of the Lord."

The verbal phrase **(I) have not wickedly departed from** translates "I have not been wrong from," meaning to do wrong by turning away from God. So the translation can be "I have not committed the sin of turning away from God." NIV "I have not done evil by turning from my God" could be understood to mean that in turning away from God the psalmist had not done evil. **Departed from my God** is sometimes rendered "I have not left God's road" or "I have not shown my back to

18.20-21

God." **My God** may have to be recast as "the God whom I worship" or "the God whom I obey."

18.22-24   RSV   TEV

22 For all his ordinances were before me, and his statutes I did not put away from me. 23 I was blameless before him, and I kept myself from guilt. 24 Therefore the LORD has recompensed me according to my righteousness, according to the cleanness of my hands in his sight.	22 I have observed all his laws; I have not disobeyed his commands. 23 He knows that I am faultless, that I have kept myself from doing wrong. 24 And so he rewards me because I do what is right, because he knows that I am innocent.

In verse 22 **ordinances** and **statutes** are both synonyms of "the ways of the LORD" in verse 21; and the verbs in verse 22 **were before me** and **not put away** are also synonyms of "kept" and "not wickedly departed from" in verse 21.

The word translated **ordinances** is the word translated "judgment" in 7.6 (see comments); and **statutes** stands for a word which means a legal prescription, regulation, decree (see comments in 2.7 on "decree of Yahweh"). If the translator follows TEV's "**observed all his laws**," one must avoid the idea of merely looking at the laws without actually obeying them. In languages where it is not possible to render the synonyms **ordinances** and **statutes** as nouns, it is often possible to do so by verbs; for example, "I have obeyed everything he showed me to do" or "I have not refused anything he taught me to do."

In verse 23 **blameless** translates the word meaning perfect (see "integrity" in 7.8); and the phrase **before him** may mean either in his presence or in his sight (that is, from his point of view); "in his sight" seems more probable. TEV represents this meaning by "**He knows that . . . .**" **Blameless** may often be rendered "no one can accuse me of doing wrong" or "I have done no evil things."

Guilt is generally understood to refer to a person's awareness of having done wrong and feeling bad about it. The Hebrew word is better represented by "evil" (NJB), "sinning" (NJV), "sin" (NIV), or "**doing wrong**" (TEV).

Verse 24 is practically a repetition of verse 20; **recompensed** translates the verb which appears also in verse 20b. As in verse 20, TEV translates the verb as a continuous present ("**rewards me**"), while RSV takes the verb to refer to past action (**has recompensed me**). Either is possible, but it seems advisable to follow TEV here. **The cleanness of my hands** may sometimes be rendered idiomatically; for example, "because my heart is white" or "because my stomach is hollow." As in verse 20, the translator should see if the intensification of line b is accomplished by placing the figure in the second line. If so, it may still be necessary to employ a different figure.

RSV   TEV

	RSV		TEV
25	With the loyal thou dost show thyself loyal; with the blameless man thou dost show thyself blameless;	25	O LORD, you are faithful to those who are faithful to you; completely good to those who are perfect.
26	with the pure thou dost show thyself pure; and with the crooked thou doest show thyself perverse.	26	You are pure to those who are pure, but hostile to those who are wicked.

The translator should note that there is a shift in pronominal use starting with verse 25. Until this point all references to God have been in the third person; now, however, the second person will be used in the following five verses (25-29), except in the second line of verses 28-29. Furthermore, there is at the same time a clear shift in the type of parallelism starting with verse 25, a discourse marker made of static parallelism. That is, the two lines of verses 25-26 say very much the same thing, with no "going beyond" in the second line. The poet will again revert to third-person reference to God in another five verses (30-34).

In verses 25-27 the psalmist no longer speaks in personal terms, as in verses 20-24, but speaks in general terms of the Lord's attitude toward the good and the wicked.

In verses 25-26 the psalmist attributes the same qualities to God as are found in people. The thought is that God matches the good qualities (verses 25a,b,26a) and the bad quality (verse 26b) he finds in people.

The first quality (verse 25a) is loyalty, faithfulness (see 5.7). On the part of God it means that he keeps his promises; on the part of human beings it means they faithfully obey God. **Loyal** and "**faithful**," being terms which contain a reciprocal relationship, must often be recast to make explicit the relationship involved; for example, "With people who trust in you, you are a one-heart LORD," "With people who follow you, you are a LORD of one way," "You can be counted on to help those who always obey you," or "You sustain people who rest on you." In many languages the same word cannot be used naturally of God and of human beings, so the translation must carefully distinguish between God's "faithfulness," that is, his constant love, and a person's "faithfulness," that is, obedience to God.

The second quality (verse 25b) is perfection, lack of fault, or **blameless** (see also verse 23). It is difficult to find one word which can be used in the same sense of God and of a person; that is why TEV has "**completely good . . . perfect.**"

The third quality (verse 26a) is purity, which is practically synonymous with **blameless** in the preceding line (NEB, however, takes the Hebrew verb here to means "be savage," and not "be pure"). **Thou dost show thyself pure** in reference to God and people is often difficult to express by the same term. In reference to people the focus is upon their blameless condition, but when speaking of God the meaning is more related to the goodness, that is, the kindness, of God. This may sometimes be rendered, for example, "you are good to those whose hearts are white" or "you are kind in regard to those who have shining hearts."

The last quality (verse 26b) is expressed in two different words: for people it is the word **crooked**; for God it is a verb meaning "to be wise, astute, cunning" (see

Job 5.13b "cunning men"). This half-verse is translated in different ways: one possibility is "you outwit the cheat"; NJV "with the perverse, you are wily"; NAB "toward the crooked you are astute"; NJB "cunning to the crafty." Perhaps "you are cunning (or, shrewd) with those who are crooked" is the best way to represent the meaning.

18.27   RSV   TEV

> For thou dost deliver a humble   You save those who are humble,
>   people;   but you humble those who are
>   but the haughty eyes thou dost   proud.
>   bring down.

It does not seem necessary to make the transition to verse 27 as RSV **For** does, since no cause and effect relation between verses 26 and 27 seems indicated.

Deliver translates the verb translated "help" in 12.1.

For **a humble people** see comments on "the afflicted" in 9.12, and on "the meek" in 10.17, where the same Hebrew term occurs.

Haughty eyes is a figure for pride, arrogance; see Proverbs 6.17, where "haughty eyes" is one of the seven things that God hates.

The verb **bring down** translates the causative form of a verb meaning "to be low." It means to humiliate, shame, defeat (in contrast with **deliver** in line a). **Haughty eyes** in Hebrew are "high eyes," and so the act of "bringing down" or "lowering" is a play on the idea of downward movement. In some languages this same wordplay can be maintained; for example, "but you lower the heads of those who carry them high" or "but you bend people down who put their noses up."

18.28   RSV   TEV

> Yea, thou dost light my lamp;   O LORD, you give me light;
>   the LORD my God lightens my   you dispel my darkness.
>   darkness.

In this section (verses 28-34) the psalmist praises God for his goodness to him.

Yea is not commonly used and is not required in translation by the Hebrew text.

The statement **thou dost light my lamp** (in the parallel 2 Sam 22.29 "thou art my lamp") is a figure meaning that Yahweh gives life, vitality, prosperity, health. **Lamp** here is not a metaphor for wisdom or knowledge. The idea is not that God dispels the darkness of ignorance, but rather the darkness of sin, destruction, and death, and continuously gives the psalmist life and strength (as the next verse makes clear). For the same figure for the Law of Yahweh, see 119.105a. The **lamp** in those days was a small clay bowl, filled with olive oil, with a wick floating in it, one end protruding through a spout on the side of the bowl.

In some languages it is necessary to state a reason for the statement **light my lamp**; for example, "LORD, you put a light in my path so I can see." The second line is difficult to translate whether one follows TEV or RSV, since in many languages one does not perform an action on darkness in order to produce light. It is possible, however, to say "you make a light and the darkness is gone" or "when you make light there is no more darkness."

It is to be noticed that the Hebrew (see RSV) addresses God in the second person in line a and refers to him in the third person in line b. As is often done, TEV maintains the second person of address in both lines.

18.29

RSV	TEV
Yea, by thee I can crush a troop; and by my God I can leap over a wall.	You give me strength to attack my enemies and power to overcome their defenses.

The phrase **by thee** means "with your help" or "you enable"; so TEV "**You give me strength**." The verb in line a is translated **crush** by RSV; it seems more likely that it means "run to," that is, "**attack**" (TEV, SPCL). See NIV "advance against"; FRCL "launch an assault."[2]

A troop means a band or group of warriors; however, the parallel in the next line ("a wall") and one Greek translation of the parallel in 2 Samuel 22.30 lead some scholars to conjecture here in line a a word meaning a wall of stones instead of **a troop**. So NEB, NJB, FRCL; NJV "rush a barrier"; BJ "break through the ramparts." A **troop** or a "band of warriors" may be rendered as a "line of soldiers." In some languages it will be necessary to make explicit, as does TEV, how God enables the writer to perform these feats; for example, "when you make me strong," or "because you are with me . . . ," or "because you help me . . . ."

Leap over a wall in line b means to break through (literally "climb up") a wall around a city, which defends it against enemy attacks. Therefore many English translations have "scale a wall," which means to climb over it. In translation it may be necessary to say, for example, "a wall around a city" or "a wall which protects a city," in order not to give the idea of the wall of a house.

18.30-31

	RSV		TEV
30	This God—his way is perfect; the promise of the LORD proves true; he is a shield for all those who take refuge in him.	30	This God—how perfect are his deeds! How dependable his words! He is like a shield for all who seek his protection.
31	For who is God, but the LORD?	31	The LORD alone is God; God alone is our defense.

---

[2]HOTTP says the Hebrew verb may be translated in various ways: "I will run (against) a band (of raiders)"; "I will dislodge a band (of raiders)"; "I will crush a band (of raiders)."

> And who is a rock, except our
> God?—

In some languages the expression **This God** will only serve to distinguish a near God from a less-near one. In order to avoid such ambiguity of reference, it will often be necessary to render **This God** as "The God whom I worship," or shift to the possessive, "My God." Some translations (see SPCL, FRCL, NEB) disregard the unusual Hebrew construction (literally "The God") and have simply "The way of God is perfect" or something like it. This may be preferred by the translator.

God's **way** is either his own conduct or else the way he sets forth for his people. Here it seems to refer to God's conduct. For comments on **perfect** see verse 23. **His way is perfect** will sometimes require recasting in the form "he does everything just right."

Proves true translates the verb "to refine" (see comments in 12.6); the idea is that of being completely free of flaw or impurity, and therefore trustworthy, dependable. **The promise of the LORD proves true** must often be rendered "you can always depend on the LORD's words" or "you can always believe what the LORD says."

For a discussion of **shield** see 3.3; for **take refuge in him** see comments on 2.12. If the shield or equivalent protective device is unknown, it is often necessary to employ a descriptive phrase; for example, "he is like a covering that protects people," or simply avoid the analogy and say "he is the place people go to for protection."

The rhetorical question in verse 31 is a way of making a strong affirmation: "No one else but Yahweh is God; no one except our God is a rock." For **rock** see comment in verse 2b. In many instances **our God** will have to be translated "the God we worship" or "God, whom we worship."

18.32-33	RSV	TEV
	32 the God who girded me with strength, and made my way safe.	32 He is the God who makes me strong, who makes my pathway safe.
	33 He made my feet like hinds' feet, and set me secure on the heights.	33 He makes me sure-footed as a deer; he keeps me safe on the mountains.

RSV has verse 32 as an added comment on God, following the rhetorical question of verse 31. It is probably better to follow TEV and start a new sentence in verse 32.

RSV uses the past tense of the verbs in verses 32-33, thereby referring to a specific event in the past. TEV and many other translations use the present tense, indicating habitual action on the part of God. This seems preferable.

The phrase **girded me with strength** means to make strong (see also verse 39). In some languages it will be necessary to restructure **the God who** to say "God is the one who makes me strong," otherwise the meaning may be taken as "he is one of the gods." In languages where strength is more apt to be taken as sexual virility, it is possible to say "who makes me able to do great things."

The verbal phrase **made . . . safe** in verse 32b is in Hebrew "gave perfection" (see the word "blameless" in verse 23). In this context some take this to mean faultless conduct; SPCL "makes my behavior faultless"; NEB "makes my way blameless"; also possible is "kept my actions faultless." This, however, does not fit the context as well as the meaning of providing security. If the translator takes the Hebrew for "my way" in line <u>b</u> to refer to conduct, this line may sometimes be rendered "he makes my life straight." If this line is taken as in TEV and RSV, referring to safe travel, it may be necessary to make explicit the purpose; for example, "he makes my road safe for me to walk on."

In verse 33 the idea of **feet like hinds' feet** (that is, those of a deer) may mean swiftness (SPCL, NAB) or sure-footedness (Kirkpatrick: "agility, swiftness, and sure-footedness").

Secure on the heights can mean victorious in battle (so Briggs) or, continuing the previous idea, to be secure even when on high, dangerous places (so Anderson); or else, to be in high places where one is safe from one's enemies. Where it is possible to maintain the simile, this should be done. However, the translator must make certain that the animal is associated with speed and sure-footedness. If no such animal is known for these characteristics, then it will be best to avoid the simile; for example, "he makes my legs able to run fast." Where **heights** are unknown one must use the term for hill and qualify it by "the highest."

18.34   RSV   TEV

He trains my hands for war,   He trains me for battle,
   so that my arms can bend a   so that I can use the strongest
   bow of bronze.   bow.

Many translators will find, like TEV, that the substitution of **hands** and **arms** for the whole person is not satisfactory. The purpose of the instruction must often be expressed as a verb; for example, "He teaches me how to fight" or "He shows me the way to make war."

A bow of bronze would be very heavy, and only a strong man would be able to use it. But since a bronze bow would be a rather unusual weapon, Anderson thinks that the language means a bow that shoots arrows tipped with bronze (see Job 20.24b, where the words may mean either a bronze bow or a bronze arrow). It seems best here to say "a bronze bow," "a bow made of bronze." If the bow is known but bronze is not, it may be best to say "so that I can bend a metal bow" or perhaps ". . . an iron bow." The heightening effect may best be expressed as "He not only trains me to fight; he even enables me to bend a metal bow."

179

18.35 RSV	TEV
Thou hast given me the shield of thy salvation, and thy right hand supported me, and thy help*ⁱ* made me great.	O LORD, you protect me and save me; your care has made me great, and your power has kept me safe.

ⁱ Or *gentleness*

Verse 35 has both a textual and a structural problem. From the latter point of view, lines a and b both contain a figure, but line b does not appear to heighten the effect. Line c even reduces the power of the images of **shield** and **right hand** with the colorless **thy help**. None of the alternative wordings suggested for **help** causes line c to fit the usual pattern. It may, however, be possible to take line c as a consequence of the first two lines, in which case the meaning is "and so your help has made me great." In terms of the discourse structure, there is support for this interpretation. Verse 35 initiates a new flurry of parallel lines which are narrative (verses 35-42), in that they describe how God enabled the psalmist to defeat his enemies.

The shield of thy salvation is a figure of protection and safety in battle. The phrase **thy salvation** refers to God's saving the psalmist, not to God's being saved. In languages where the shield is unknown or only partially known through a loan word, it will often be best to transfer to a nonfigurative expression as in TEV. Even if **shield** is maintained, it will often be misleading to express **salvation** as a noun, as in RSV. A verb phrase may be better; for example, "you give me your shield which saves me" or, more fully, "you give me your shield which saves my life."

Right hand means power or help; and the verb translated **supported** means to keep safe, hold up, sustain. In some languages it will be appropriate to keep the expression **right hand**, as this is the hand that is associated with strength.

In line c the word translated **help** (TEV "**care**," or RSV footnote "gentleness") elsewhere means humility (Pro 15.33; 18.12; 22.4; Zech 2.3). NJV has "care" (or, in a footnote, "condescension"); SPCL "kindness"; NEB "providence"; another possibility is "loving care" (with footnote). Some have related the word to the verb "to answer" (as it is in 2 Sam 22.36) and translate "by your answering (you have made me great)"; FRCL "you answer my cries for help and make me strong."*³*

TEV has reversed lines b and c, as a more natural progression of thought.

18.36 RSV	TEV
Thou didst give a wide place for my steps under me, and my feet did not slip.	You have kept me from being captured, and I have never fallen.

---

*³*HOTTP says either translation is possible: "your response has made me great" or "your subjugation (of my enemies) has made me great."

The verbal phrase **give a wide place for** (see "given me room" in 4.1) means to provide space for military maneuvers, or else to provide freedom, so that one will not be captured. See how the related noun "a broad place" is used in verse 19.

If one is to follow the TEV, **"from being captured,"** it may be necessary to avoid the passive construction; for example, "you have not let anyone capture me" or "you have not allowed my enemies to catch me." On the other hand the translator may wish to keep the parallelism between steps and feet.

The relation between lines <u>a</u> and <u>b</u> is that of consequence, which RSV and TEV translate with the conjunction **and** at the beginning of line <u>b</u>. It is possible to make the consequence even more clear by sacrificing the imagery and saying, for example, "Because you kept me from being captured, I . . ." or "You have kept my enemies from taking me; therefore, they have never defeated me." Translators should, however, attempt to keep the images or supply other images.

The word for **feet** (or, ankles) occurs only here and in 2 Samuel 22.37. The idea expressed by **my feet did not slip** is that the psalmist was always able to keep standing and to keep fighting his enemies.

18.37-38	RSV	TEV

	RSV	TEV
37	I pursued my enemies and over-took them; and did not turn back till they were consumed.	I pursue my enemies and catch them; I do not stop until I destroy them.
38	I thrust them through, so that they were not able to rise; they fell under my feet.	I strike them down, and they cannot rise; they lie defeated before me.

For verses 37-42 RSV uses the past tense of specific events; TEV has the present tense of habitual or continuing actions. The translator must decide which seems better. In line with similar cases, it is recommended that TEV be followed.

The verbs **pursued** and **overtook** both occur in 7.5. **They were consumed** translates a verb meaning to cease, to be finished, be wiped out. The use of the passive form, as RSV has done, might imply that someone else "consumed" them; it seems better to use the active voice, with the psalmist as the subject.

In verse 38 **I thrust . . . through** translates a verb meaning to break in pieces (TEV "I strike . . . down"); here, of course, it refers to defeat in battle. The English phrase "thrust through" means specifically to drive a sword or a lance through someone's body; the Hebrew verb does not have that specific sense. The phrase **they fell under my feet** is a picture of destruction and death, not that of the defeated enemy meekly submitting to the victor. In some languages expressions for killing people depend upon the manner of action; for example, intentional or unintentional, by witchcraft, ambush, secretly planned, and the like. In this context the psalmist refers to battles with enemy troops where intentional killing of enemy soldiers is understood. Since the parallelism of verse 38 is one of consequences, the verse may be rendered, for example, "When I beat my enemies down (knock them down), they cannot get up again; so they die at my feet defeated" or ". . . they are finished."

      RSV   TEV

	RSV		TEV
39	For thou didst gird me with strength for the battle; thou didst make my assailants sink under me.	39	You give me strength for the battle and victory over my enemies.
40	Thou didst make my enemies turn their backs to me, and those who hated me I destroyed.	40	You make my enemies run from me; I destroy those who hate me.

For **gird me with strength** see comments on verse 32. **Assailants** translates "those who rise up against" (see comments on "Arise" in 3.7).

In verse 39b the verb translated **sink** means to bow down, to bend, in defeat and death. In some languages it is possible to keep the figure of subjection; for example, "you have put my enemies under my feet" or "you have thrown my enemies behind me." **My assailants** is parallel with **my enemies** in verse 39b, and with **those who hated me** in verse 40b. These are not three different groups but three ways of talking about the same people.

In verse 40a the Hebrew is "my enemies you gave me (their) back"; this is generally taken to mean flight in battle. But the noun may mean "the back of the neck," and so Dahood takes it to be a picture of the victor placing his foot on the neck of his defeated enemy, as in Joshua 10.24 (so NEB).

The verb **destroyed** is a translation of "to silence," that is, by killing.

18.41-42   RSV   TEV

	RSV		TEV
41	They cried for help, but there was none to save, they cried to the LORD, but he did not answer them.	41	They cry for help, but no one saves them; they call to the LORD, but he does not answer.
42	I beat them fine as dust before the wind; I cast them out like the mire of the streets.	42	I crush them, so that they become like dust which the wind blows away. I trample on them like mud in the streets.

For **They cried for help** see "I cried for help" in verse 6b. In some languages **They cried for help** will have to be recast as direct address: "They cried and said 'Help us!'"

In line b of verse 41 there is no verb in Hebrew for **they cried**; the verb in line a carries over into line b. The parallelism of verses 41-42 is that of intensification of images in the second line. Line b of 41 may be heightened by translating "they even cried to the LORD . . ." or "they went so far as to cry to the LORD . . . ."

I beat them fine as dust before the wind is literally "I make dust of them like the dust on the face of the wind," a picture of complete defeat. Both RSV and TEV have adjusted the Hebrew "I make dust of them" through the use of more specific verbs, **beat** and "**crush**," which attempt to express both the act of defeating the enemy and reducing something to dust. Many languages will be able to use other specific verbs and retain the simile; for example, "I will stamp on them and grind them like dust blown by the wind." In some languages the simile may require explanation; for example, "I defeat them and make them as weak as dust blown by the wind" or ". . . dust which the wind blows away."

RSV translates the Masoretic text, **I cast them out**; TEV and many others (NEB, NAB, NJV, NJB, FRCL, SPCL) translate a different verb, "**I trample on them**," which is found in many Hebrew manuscripts and also in the parallel 2 Samuel 22.43. This seems to fit the context better than the traditional Masoretic text.[4]

In some languages it will be necessary to repeat "my enemies" as the subject in verse 41 and as the object of crush and trample in verse 42.

The figure of **mire of the streets** must in some languages be rendered "mud in the footpaths" or "dirt where people walk."

Intensification in line b of verse 42 may be brought out more forcefully by saying, for example, "Not only did I turn them to dust, but I threw them out like mud in the streets" or "I smashed them to dust like the wind blows away; more than that, I trampled on them like dirt on the path."

18.43	RSV	TEV

Thou didst deliver me from strife
with the peoples;[j]
thou didst make me the head of
the nations;
people whom I had not known
served me.

You saved me from a rebellious
people
and made me ruler over the
nations;
people I did not know have now
become my subjects.

[j] Gk Tg: Heb *people*

In verses 43-45 the psalmist describes how God made him ruler and kept him secure from rebellious subjects, both national and foreign.

For **didst deliver** see the same verb in 17.13. The Hebrew phrase "the strivings of a people" in line a is taken by TEV to mean rebellious subjects, that is, a civil uprising (so Weiser, Briggs); thus also possible is "people who rebel against me." It may be advisable to make the meaning clear by translating "my people," as NJB does. RSV has chosen to follow the Septuagint **peoples**, thus making line a parallel with lines b and c; it seems better, however, to stay with the singular form of the Hebrew text and take it to mean the people of Israel.[5] "**A rebellious people**" must sometimes be expressed as "people who refuse to obey their rulers" or "people who say 'No' to their chief." **Head of the nations** means ruler of Gentile nations, as the following

---

[4]HOTTP prefers the Masoretic text, which it translates "I will sweep them out."

[5]HOTTP ("B"decision) prefers the singular form of the Masoretic text.

lines show. The king of Israel rules over a great empire (see the account of David's conquests in 2 Sam 8.1-14).

Nations must often be rendered "tribe" when this is the largest political unit known.

People whom I had not known is a way of referring to foreigners; and the Hebrew verb "to serve" here means to come under his rule, to become his subjects.

18.44-45	RSV	TEV

RSV	TEV
44 As soon as they heard of me they obeyed me; foreigners came cringing to me.	44 Foreigners bow before me; when they hear me, they obey.
45 Foreigners lost heart, and came trembling out of their fastnesses.	45 They lose their courage and come trembling from their fortresses.

For the verb tenses, see comment at verse 37.

In verse 44 TEV has reversed the lines in order to make the subject **foreigners** come first (see 2 Sam 22.45). **As soon as they heard of me they obeyed me** translates "At the hearing of the ear they obey me." Some see this as a reference to an incident like the one related in 2 Samuel 8.9-12, where King Toi of Hamath surrendered to King David. The meaning of **they heard of me** (RSV) is that they heard he was a great and powerful king; this may be the meaning intended by the Hebrew, but TEV **"hear me"** is also possible (see FRCL, NJB).

Came cringing (TEV **"bow"**) translates a verb which has the idea of forced, unwilling submission. NJV has "cower"; also possible is "cringe." **Came cringing to me** must be expressed in some languages as "they squat on the ground in front of me" or "they bent their heads down in my presence."

In verse 45 the verbal phrase **lost heart** (TEV **"lose their courage"**) translates a Hebrew verb which means to fade away, to wither (see 1.3 of leaves that do not wither). **Lost heart** is expressed idiomatically sometimes as "the heart grows small" or "the stomach becomes white."

The verb translated **came trembling** occurs only here in the Old Testament; this is the meaning given the word by Holladay and followed by NAB, BJ, NJB, NJV, SPCL. Others define the verb simply "to come out, to emerge"; the Septuagint translates "they came out limping."

The word translated **fastnesses** means a fortified, strongly held position, perhaps a rocky refuge; it is not an elaborate "fortress" in the modern sense. This term is sometimes rendered "the place where people hide from their enemies" or "the place where people go to for protection from their enemies."

18.46	RSV	TEV

RSV	TEV
The LORD lives; and blessed be my rock,	The LORD lives! Praise my defender!

and exalted be the God of my salvation,	Proclaim the greatness of the God who saves me.

In this final section (verses 46-49) the psalmist praises Yahweh for giving him victory over his enemies. Here again the psalmist brings the series of events to a close and opens a new stage in the discourse through the use of static parallelism. The two lines say approximately the same thing. Typical of the praise section in many psalms, verses 46-49 pile on image after image, with little or no heightening effect in the second line.

The LORD lives is a cry of confidence in Yahweh as a living god who constantly acts on behalf of his people; it is not the same as saying "Long live the Lord!" **The LORD lives** may be rendered in some languages as "I know God is alive" or "I know God really lives."

Blessed be: this passive has the force of an imperative: "Bless." Used of God, "to bless" means to praise (see comments in 16.7).

For **rock** see the use of the term in verses 2b,31.

The passive verbal phrase **exalted be** is a way of exhorting the people to "exalt" God, that is, announce or proclaim his great power and might. So it is better to translate, as TEV has done, as an exhortation for others to proclaim God's greatness, or else, as GECL has done, "I will extol God."

The noun phrase **the God of my salvation** means "the God who saves me" (TEV). The word for **salvation** here perhaps means victory (as in 3.8, "deliverance").

18.47-48   RSV   TEV

	RSV			TEV
47	the God who gave me vengeance and subdued peoples under me;		47	He gives me victory over my enemies;
48	who delivered me from my enemies;			he subdues the nations under me
	yea, thou didst exalt me above my adversaries;		48	and saves me from my foes.
	thou didst deliver me from men of violence.			O LORD, you give me victory over my enemies and protect me from violent men.

The verbal phrase **gave me vengeance** (here plural, "acts of vengeance") means retribution. The related verb is often used of God as one who punishes the enemies of Israel because of their evil actions. The idea of "getting even" is not entirely absent from the word but need not necessarily be stressed in translation. NJV has here "vindicated me," SPCL "avenged me," FRCL "gives my revenge." The thought here is that the defeat of the enemies in battle (as the next line makes clear) is the way in which the psalmist "got even" with them. So TEV translates "He gives me victory over my enemies," the same meaning expressed in the next line, **subdued peoples under me**. **Gave me vengeance** must sometimes be rendered "helps me defeat my enemies."

Delivered is the same verb used in verse 43.

185

In verse 48 the word translated by RSV **yea** is omitted by some manuscripts and also in the parallel in 2 Samuel 22.49 (and is omitted by TEV). It is a way of emphasizing what follows; in current English "indeed" would be the proper way to represent it.

Adversaries in verse 48b is "those who rise up against," as in verse 39b, "assailants."

For **deliver** see 7.1.

Men of violence: the Hebrew is singular, "man of violence," usually interpreted as a collective term; some, however, take it to be a reference to Saul (who is mentioned in the Hebrew title of the psalm). It is better to represent it as a plural. For **violence** see comments on 7.16. **Men of violence** may often be rendered as "men who kill others" or "men who injure others."

18.49   RSV   TEV

> For this I will extol thee, O LORD,   And so I praise you among the
>   among the nations,   nations;
>   and sing praises to thy name.   I sing praises to you.

Verse 49 refers back to the events in verses 47-48 as the reason why the psalmist praises God.

The two verbs **extol** and **sing praises** are also used in 7.17 (see comments there on "give . . . thanks" and "sing praises").

Nations may be specifically "the heathen" (see comments at 2.1).

I will extol thee . . . among the nations may be rendered "I will speak well of you to the tribes."

For **name** see comments on 5.11. The expression **sing praises to thy name** may sometimes require adjusting; for example, "I will sing and say that your name is (or, you are) great."

This verse is quoted in Romans 15.9.

18.50   RSV   TEV

> Great triumphs he gives to his   God gives great victories to his
>   king,   king;
>   and shows steadfast love to his   he shows constant love to the
>   anointed,   one he has chosen,
>   to David and his descendants   to David and his descendants
>   for ever.   forever.

The psalm closes with a triumphant note, a statement of God's constant love for King David and his descendants forever (see 2 Sam 7.16).

Triumphs is the plural of the Hebrew word for "salvation" (see 3.8). Here it means the king's victories over his enemies, which he achieves because God himself is with him and enables him to win.

To his king should not be rendered in such a manner as to be understood as "the king who is over God," but rather as "the king whom God has appointed."

For **steadfast love** see comments on 5.7; for **his anointed** see comments on 2.2.

The word **descendants** translates a collective noun, "seed"; here it refers to David's male descendants, his successors as kings of Israel (see NJB "his heirs").

Psalm 19

This psalm consists of two different compositions: one, a hymn celebrating God's glory as revealed by the sky and the sun (verses 1-6), and the other, a poem in praise of the Law, in which Yahweh's will is revealed (verses 7-14). The two differ in content, style, and poetic meter. Most scholars think that the first poem is considerably older, since it reflects themes similar to those of Near Eastern mythologies, while the second one reflects a time in which the written Law (the Torah) was already the basis of the faith of Israel.

HEADING: TEV has two headings: for verses 1-6, **"God's Glory in Creation"** and for verses 7-14, **"The Law of the LORD"** (similarly Weiser). Others combine the two ideas in one heading, or else have only one of them: "God's glory in the heavens and in the law"; "Yahweh, the sun of righteousness"; "God's praise in the physical and moral universe." In translation it will often be necessary to use a verb phrase to relate **"God's Glory"** to the act of creating; for example, "God shows his glory by creating the world" or "When God creates the world people see how great he is."

Hebrew Title: **To the choirmaster. A Psalm of David** (TEV "A psalm by David").
The title is the same as the one to Psalm 4.

19.1   RSV   TEV

> The heavens are telling the glory
>   of God;
>   and the firmament proclaims
>   his handiwork.

> How clearly the sky reveals God's
>   glory!
>   How plainly it shows what he
>   has done!

Verse 1 in Hebrew is a complete chiasmus. The Hebrew word order in line a is a-b-c, and in line b the parallel equivalent words follow the order c-b-a. Chiasmus is used structurally sometimes as an opener and sometimes to relieve monotony. None of the translations consulted reverse the word order in the second line, as a grammatically awkward sentence would result. The translator should be aware that the psalmist is here using this device as the opener of the psalm, and should examine the use of chiasmus for similar or other reasons in the receptor language.

The heavens in line a is synonymous with **the firmament** in line b. No difference between the two is intended, since both of them are visible to humankind, revealing **the glory of God**, that is, his power, greatness, and majesty, which are manifest in the created universe (**his handiwork**). Most translations maintain the poetic force of the lines by using two terms. Of the translations consulted FRCL is best: "The sky . . . the starry vault."

188

The verb "to tell" (**are telling**) and its parallel **proclaims** poetically attribute human functions to the created universe, which makes known to all humankind God's greatness.

The firmament was thought of as a solid plate (the Hebrew word derives from a verb meaning "to stamp, beat out"; see Job 37.18); this plate kept the waters above separated from the waters below (see Gen 1.6). Genesis 1.14-15, 17,20 have the phrase "the firmament of the heavens." NJV and Dahood translate here "the heavens . . . the sky." Whether the translator uses different terms for **heavens** and **firmament** or the same term for both, the intensification of line **b** may be kept by saying, for example, "more than this, the heavens speak out about God's great works," or both lines, "The sky shows us how wonderful God is; even more, it makes very clear to us the great things he has made." If the translator follows TEV, which uses exclamation marks, then in some languages the exclamatory force will have to be made by intensifying the verb phrase; for example, "The sky truly shows the glory of God" or, through the use of an imperative, "See how the sky shows that God is great!" In some languages it will be necessary to shift from inanimate subjects to people; for example, "When people look at the sky, they can clearly see how great God is; they can plainly see in the sky the great things he has made," or by shifting to second person, "If you look up you can see how great God is; there you can see God's great work."

His handiwork (Hebrew "the work of his hands") refers to God's activity in creating the universe. Where it is possible to keep the imagery of God's hands, it should be done. However, where such pictures are not possible, one may follow the direction taken by TEV. Many languages distinguish between work done to form some object such as a pot or an arrow, and work which has a more general goal. In such languages the former usage would be appropriate here.

19.2	RSV	TEV
	Day to day pours forth speech, and night to night declares knowledge.	Each day announces it to the following day; each night repeats it to the next.

Here **day** and **night** are pictured as passing on the proclamation of God's glory. The verb in line **a**, **pours forth**, means to pour out, like a spring, and indicates a continuous, uninterrupted proclamation. **Speech** in line **a** and **knowledge** in line **b** have to do with the proclamation of God's glory; line **a** means "Each day talks about God's glory to the next day," and line **b** means "Every night shares its knowledge of God with the following night."

In some languages it will be unnatural to speak of **day** and **night** in a personified manner, as if they can speak. In those cases these expressions may be recast to say something like "Day after day people can see the glory of God, night after night they can see how great God is." However, since verses 3-4 refer to speech, words, and voice, it may be better to shift to a simile and say, for example, "Each day announces it like a person speaking; each night repeats it to the following night like a person repeats words."

19.3-4b RSV	TEV

3   There is no speech, nor are there words;
     their voice is not heard;
4   yet their voice[k] goes out through all the earth,
     and their words to the end of the world.
	3 No speech or words are used, no sound is heard;
	4 yet their message[c] goes out to all the world
	     and is heard to the ends of the earth.

[k] Gk Jerome Compare Syr: Heb *line*	[c] *Some ancient translations* message; *Hebrew* line.

The statement in verse 3 is emphatic: without any **speech** or **words** or audible **voice**, the report about God's glory continues to be made. **Their** in verses 3b and 4a,b refers to "the heavens" and "the firmament" of verse 1. In verse 3b the meaning can be that they did speak but were not heard, as RSV's literal translation implies. It seems preferable, however, to understand the line to mean "they uttered no audible voice." Weiser translates the verse differently: "There is no language nor are there words in which their voice is not heard." This is possible but does not seem very likely.

Speech should not be rendered as a speech given in the form of a public address but as the generic event, the act of speaking. In some languages it will be necessary to shift to a clause saying, for example, "they do not talk using words," or using a simile, "they do not make words like people who talk with their mouths."

In line a of verse 4 the Hebrew text has "their line"; following ancient versions, many commentaries and translations understand the text to say "their voice." Dahood and HOTTP, however, maintain that the Hebrew word means "their call." NEB interprets "line" as the string of a musical instrument and translates "their music" (so TOB). Since the report is soundless, something like "message, report" is better than **voice** (some may have "their testimony").

Yet their voice goes out must often be rendered "yet what they say can be heard everywhere." If one keeps the parallelism, **all the earth** may be rendered as "everywhere," and **the end of the world** as "wherever people live on the earth."

As translated by the Septuagint, verse 4a,b is quoted by Paul in Romans 10.18 and applied to the spread of the Christian message.

19.4c-5 RSV	TEV

4c   In them he has set a tent for the sun,
5   which comes forth like a bridegroom leaving his chamber,
     and like a strong man runs its course with joy.
	4c God made a home in the sky for the sun;
	5 it comes out in the morning like a happy bridegroom,
	     like an athlete eager to run a race.

The psalmist concentrates on the sun (verses 4c-6) as the greatest of all created things. In contrast with the tendency of many ancient peoples to worship the sun as a god, Hebrew faith held firmly to the unique position that Yahweh alone was the sole ruler of the universe. It is God who "pitched a tent" in the sky for the sun, where it spends the night before coming out in the morning. <u>Tent</u> in modern English is a temporary dwelling place, which is not necessarily implied by the Hebrew word; so TEV has "**home.**"

In them means "In the heavens"; so TEV "**in the sky.**" TOB, however, takes it to refer to the ends of the earth.[1] It will sometimes be necessary to indicate that the house in the sky is "for the sun to live in."

The sun is pictured as **a bridegroom** and as **a strong man**, figures which are intended to convey a sense of vitality, strength, joy, endurance. <u>Like a bridegroom</u> is sometimes expressed "like a happy man who leads his bride to his village" or "like a man who has married a woman."

The word translated **chamber** is found only here and in Isaiah 4.5 ("canopy") and Joel 2.16. In connection with **bridegroom**, this **chamber** refers to a temporary pavilion, or canopy, provided for newlyweds and set up in the groom's home. To avoid unnecessary cultural difficulties, the translation can be "it leaves its room in the morning . . . ."

In this context the **strong man** is most probably an athlete rather than a warrior or a fighter (see NAB footnote). TEV "**athlete**" must sometimes be rendered "runner," or simply "like a man who runs a race."

19.6	RSV	TEV
	Its rising is from the end of the heavens, and its circuit to the end of them; and there is nothing hid from its heat.	It starts at one end of the sky and goes across to the other. Nothing can hide from its heat.

The route that the sun follows is pictured as a half circle which takes it from **one end of the heavens** to the other. Some may convey the thought with the word "horizon": "it rises on one horizon and completes its course on the other." It will sometimes be necessary to make clear where the movement starts; for example, "the sun starts its trip at one end of the sky."

The word translated **heat** always means "sun" elsewhere in the Old Testament (Job 30.28; Song 6.10; Isa 24.23; 30.26); so Briggs takes it here to mean "nothing can hide from his (that is, God's) sun."

---

[1]Instead of "in them" of the Masoretic text, some prefer to follow a text meaning "in the sea" (see Weiser).

19.7-9 RSV	TEV
	The Law of the LORD

7 The law of the LORD is perfect,
    reviving the soul;
  the testimony of the LORD is sure,
    making wise the simple;
8 the precepts of the LORD are
    right,
    rejoicing the heart;
  the commandment of the LORD is
    pure,
    enlightening the eyes;
9 the fear of the LORD is clean,
    enduring for ever;
  the ordinances of the LORD are
    true,
    and righteous altogether.
	7 The law of the LORD is perfect;
	    it gives new strength.
	  The commands of the LORD are
	    trustworthy,
	    giving wisdom to those who lack
	    it.
	8 The laws of the LORD are right,
	    and those who obey them are
	    happy.
	  The commands of the LORD are
	    just
	    and give understanding to the
	    mind.
	9 Reverence for the LORD is good;
	    it will continue forever.
	  The judgments of the LORD are
	    just;
	    they are always fair.

In this poem (verses 7-14) the psalmist first describes the Law of Yahweh in six different ways (verses 7-9), praises its attractiveness and worth (verses 10-11), and prays for help from the Lord in obeying it (verses 12-14).

In verses 7-9 six words are used for the Law, the sacred record of Yahweh's instructions to his people (see Psa 119, where eight words are used). The first one, *torah* (**law**), is used in 1.2 (see comments); the sixth one, **ordinances** (the plural of *mishpat*), was seen as "judgment" in 7.6. The other words are: verse 7c **testimony**, a word meaning reminder, instruction; verse 8a **precepts**, a word always used in the plural, meaning orders, legal directives; verse 8c **commandment**, meaning law, command. All five of these words are nearly synonymous in this context, since the psalmist was searching for words that emphasize different aspects of the same thing, God's Law. The translator will have to determine whether to use a single term for all, or a similar set of terms.

In many languages **law** means only orders and regulations sent out from local bureaucrats. In order to avoid such a restricted meaning, it will often be necessary to render **law** as "the teaching given by God" or "the instructions God gave the people." Although the Hebrew term *torah* is used in verse 8, translators working in languages strongly influenced by Islamic terminology should not use *towarat,* because this term is applied to the Hebrew Scriptures generally.

The testimony of the LORD may often be rendered as "what the LORD tells you to do" or "all that the LORD says."

The only difficulty arises with **the fear of the LORD** in verse 9a. As Dahood points out, all other possessive phrases **of the LORD** have the Lord as subject, not object; here, however, the traditional understanding of "fear" as reverence or awe makes the Lord the object. FRCL, however, translates "The respect that the LORD inspires is pure." Several commentators prefer to emend the Hebrew to say "the word of Yahweh" (as in 119.38), and GECL translates "His word." Some with to translate the Hebrew text as "religion," explaining in a footnote that this represents what the Lord requires of his people. Although it does not sound very natural, the translation "**Reverence** (or, Respect) **for the LORD**" is probably the best one. **Fear of the LORD** must often be recast as a verbal phrase; for example, "it is good for people to worship the Lord." Line **b** of verse 9 may then be rendered "they will worship him forever."

The ordinances of the LORD (TEV "**judgments**") must be expressed in some languages as "what the LORD decides is fair and true," or idiomatically, "when the LORD cuts the words he cuts them fairly."

The six adjectives used are not all entirely synonymous, but there is overlapping in meaning: **perfect** (see "blameless" in 18.23); **sure** (see in 12.1 the verb "to be sure, reliable, faithful"); **right** (with much the same meaning; see "upright" in 11.2); **pure** (see 18.26; a "pure commandment" is one that is right, fair, just); **clean** (synonym of **pure**; see 12.6); and **righteous** (fair, just). Translations of these six adjectives vary: NJV "perfect, enduring, just, lucid, pure, true"; NJB "perfect, trustworthy, honest, pure, pure, true." In translation the most important thing is to use adjectives that will naturally apply to the subject. In some languages **perfect** is rendered as "the best," "without any fault," "could not be better." TEV's "**trustworthy**" is sometimes rendered "you can depend on it," or idiomatically, "you can put your heart on it."

The four effects of the Law on those who obey it are described in verses 7-8: verse 7b **reviving the soul** ("turning the *nefesh*"; see 3.2), that is, giving renewed vitality and strength to one's whole being; verse 7d **making wise the simple**, in which **simple** means an inexperienced, uninstructed, naïve person; verse 8b **rejoicing the heart**, that is, bringing joy to the person; and verse 8d **enlightening the eyes**, which probably means bringing understanding, wisdom (see 119.105,130), or else, as in 13.3b, restoring strength (as NJV renders it).

In verse 9 the secondary lines **b** and **d**, instead of stating the effects of the Law and commandments on those who obey them, further describe them: **enduring forever** (see verb in 18.3) and **righteous altogether**, or "are always right" (TEV "always fair"; see the adjective "right" in 4.1).

19.10-11	RSV	TEV

10	More to be desired are they than gold,
	  even much fine gold;
	sweeter also than honey
	  and drippings of the honey-comb.
		10	They are more desirable than the finest gold;
			  they are sweeter than the purest honey.

11	Moreover by them is thy servant warned;
	  in keeping them there is great reward.
		11	They give knowledge to me, your servant;
			  I am rewarded for obeying them.

They (verse 10) and **them** (twice in verse 11) refer back to "the ordinances" (TEV "The judgments") of verse 9b. In translation it is often necessary to reintroduce the subject of line a; for example, "The judgments of the LORD are worth more than gold."

In verse 10 **gold** and **fine gold** refer to the same kind of substance, as do **honey** and **drippings of the honeycomb**. TEV has combined the terms and used superlative forms: **"finest gold . . . purest honey."** **Fine gold** in line b is a more specific instance of the general category of **gold** in line a. In the same way **drippings of the honeycomb** in line d is the more visual sense of **honey** in line c. In this verse TEV makes no attempt to keep the double parallelism. The translator, however, should consider how the psalmist is creating a focusing movement between the lines through the use of increasingly picturable images. The translator's task is to use the devices available in the receptor language to accomplish the same effect. The **honeycomb** is the structure built out of beeswax by bees, to hold their eggs and the honey. The same comparisons are used in 119.72,103. **Finest gold** must often be expressed as "gold without any sand." **"The purest honey"** must sometimes be said "honey without anything added."

Moreover translates a Hebrew word often used to associate two items, or else to emphasize an additional item, as here. It appears also at the beginning of verse 13 (where RSV and TEV translate it "also"). Here something like "In addition" or "They also . . ." will express the idea.

In verse 11a the verb is usually translated **is . . . warned** or ". . . instructed." Dahood and TOB, however, take the verb in another sense (as in Dan 12.3): "to be enlightened." NJV has "your servant pays them heed." Verse 11a must sometimes be rendered "Your judgments instruct me."

It is debated whether **thy servant** is generic, meaning anyone who obeys Yahweh, or specific, referring to the psalmist (so TEV, FRCL, SPCL), as it clearly does in verse 13. It seems better to understand it as specific. The expression **thy servant** should not refer to a domestic employee, or a slave, or one of the many kinds of workers who are bound to an owner through indebtedness. In this verse the psalmist calls himself a servant because of his obedience and faithful devotion to God. If the receptor-language term for **servant** has unwanted connotations, it will be best to recast this verse. The sense is made even more difficult for some languages by the psalmist referring to himself in the third person. For example, one may translate "I follow you faithfully, and your judgments teach me" or "Your way of judging people teaches me, and I obey what you say."

The **reward** is primarily spiritual, but it includes the material. Verse 11b may often be expressed "I receive good things when I obey them."

19.12	RSV	TEV
	But who can discern his errors? Clear thou me from hidden faults.	No one can see his own errors; deliver me, LORD, from hidden faults!

The rhetorical question of line a is a way of making a strong statement of fact (as in 18.31): "No one can discern his errors!" The translator must decide either to make a statement, as in TEV, or to ask a question, as in RSV. In many languages it is not natural to "see" such abstract things as errors. Therefore it is often necessary to recast this kind of expression; for example, "When a person makes his own mistakes he does not know it" or "When a person acts in the wrong way he does not know that he is doing so."

The verb translated **Clear** may mean either forgiveness (as the various translations that use "cleanse" or something similar mean: NEB, NAB, BJ, NJB, SPCL), or else freedom from such sins (as the parallel thought in verse 13a suggests). The meaning "forgive" or "do not punish" seems the best.

Hidden faults are not to be taken as faults which the psalmist purposely conceals, but ones which are unknown to the psalmist. Therefore it is sometimes necessary to translate "Save me, LORD, from faults which I am ignorant of" or "Save me, LORD, from the faults I do not know I do."

19.13   RSV   TEV

    Keep back thy servant also from   Keep me safe, also, from willful
       presumptuous sins;   sins;
      let them not have dominion   don't let them rule over me.
       over me!   Then I shall be perfect
    Then I shall be blameless,   and free from the evil of sin.
      and innocent of great transgres-
      sion.

The initial plea, **Keep back**, means "Restrain," "Do not allow," "Don't let."

Presumptuous sins (in contrast with "hidden faults" in verse 12b) are those that are committed knowingly and deliberately (TEV "**willful sins**"). The Hebrew says only "from arrogant (ones)," which some take to refer to people (TOB, FRCL, GECL, NJV footnote); but it seems more likely that it refers to sins. SPCL has "pride." The idea of "**willful sins**" may sometimes be rendered as "bad things which I do and know I do" or "evil things I know I do."

Let them not have dominion over me in line **b** portrays sins as living beings, or powers, that can rule a person.

The verb **be blameless** means "faultless, complete, lacking nothing"; in 9.6 it is used in a bad sense, "vanished, finished." **I shall be blameless** may be expressed negatively in some languages as "I will not have done anything evil," or idiomatically, "I will be a person without any bad marks on me."

Shall be . . . innocent translates the same verb used in verse 12b, "clear."

Transgression translates a word meaning "rebellion, disobedience" (see 5.10, where the term occurs also in a context of rebellion). Dahood translates "the great crime," which he defines as idolatry, and this is quite possible. The difficulty in translating it simply "grave, serious sin" is that this implicitly allows the possibility of the psalmist's committing little sins; so TEV has "**the evil of sin**." "Evil of sin" as two nouns that are rather synonymous in meaning is difficult to express in translation. However, since the component of "**sin**" is here rebellion against God, it is possible to say, for example, "I will not be guilty of disobeying God" or "I will not be guilty of turning away from God."

Let the words of my mouth and the meditation of my heart be acceptable in thy sight, O LORD, my rock and my redeemer.	May my words and my thoughts be acceptable to you, O LORD, my refuge and my redeemer!

The third-person command expressed in English by **Let the words . . .** must often be restructured in translation as a wish or request; for example, "I ask that the words . . ." or "I pray that the words . . . ."

The psalmist asks that Yahweh accept his **words** and thoughts (**meditation**). The **mouth** represents the source of words, and the **heart** the source of thoughts. TEV has taken the mouth and heart to be redundant in this context. Hence the figures symbolizing the speaking and thinking activities have been dropped. In some languages **words of my mouth** must be replaced by "words of my tongue."

Meditation translates the word that is used as a musical term in 9.16.

Acceptable translates the noun "favor" (see 5.12), that is, good will, pleasure (of Yahweh). **Be acceptable** in this context must often be recast in the active voice; for example, "I ask that you accept all that I say and think" or "I pray that you will receive gladly the words my tongue speaks and the thoughts my insides think." In some languages "accept" does not carry the implied meaning of positive regard, and one must therefore translate "I ask that you accept as good the words . . ." or "May you find that my words and thoughts are good to receive."

For **rock** see comments on the second Hebrew word for "rock" in 18.2. **Redeemer** translates the title of the individual, the *go'el* usually the nearest of kin, who had the duty of providing for a relative who needed help—in particular, in the case of murder, of seeking out and killing the murderer (see the similar expression in 9.12). Here Yahweh is proclaimed the protector and savior of the psalmist. One may say "my Protector"; FRCL "my Defender"; SPCL "my liberator."

Psalm 20

This psalm, a prayer for victory in battle, appears to have been composed for use at the time a sacrifice was offered before battle. Oesterley calls it unique in the Psalter. It is classified as a royal psalm (see Psa 2; 18), since it is clear that the one going into battle is the king. In the first part (verses 1-5) the psalmist (or else the congregation) in the Temple asks the Lord to give the king victory in battle; in the second part (verses 6-8) the king (or a prophet, or a priest) affirms his confident belief that the Lord will be with the king and give him victory; the psalm closes (verse 9) with a repetition of the request, by the priests.

HEADING: **"A Prayer for Victory"** (TEV); "Prayer for the king in time of war"; "Prayer for the king"; "Prayer before a battle." It will often be necessary, when translating the heading of the TEV, to indicate the person who prays. **"Victory"** must often be expressed as a verb phrase; for example, "The psalmist prays that God will help him defeat his enemies."

Hebrew Title: **To the choirmaster. A Psalm of David** (TEV "A psalm by David").
The title is the same as the one for Psalm 13.

<u>**20.1**</u>

RSV	TEV
The LORD answer you in the day of trouble! The name of the God of Jacob protect you!	May the LORD answer you when you are in trouble! May the God of Jacob protect you!

This psalm has an envelope structure in the sense that it is enclosed between **The LORD answer you** in verse 1 and **answer us when we call** in the final verse. Verses 1 through 5 contain a series of requests addressed to God in the third person. In some languages these must be in the form of commands.

A literal translation of **answer you in the day of trouble** may mean that the Lord is merely being asked to reply to a question from the troubled king. In order to avoid such a misunderstanding, it will be necessary in some languages to say, for example, "May the LORD help you" or "May the LORD rescue you."

The pronoun **you** in the singular form may be misleading and cause readers to imagine that it is the reader who is referred to. Since the reference is to the king (see verse 9), it will be necessary in some languages to substitute "king" for **you**, and if king must be possessed, then "our king" will be most appropriate. In some languages the appropriate honorific form of the pronoun **you** plus "our king" may

197

be combined; for example, "May the LORD help you, our king, when you are in trouble."

According to the usual interpretation, **the day of trouble** refers to battle (this can be "in time of danger"); Dahood takes the word here to have the specific meaning of "siege." (But Weiser doubts that the psalm has to do with military conflict, and understands it to refer to the festival in which Yahweh was proclaimed King of Israel.)

For comments on **name** see 5.11. The title **the God of Jacob** occurs some 11 times in Psalms and recalls Yahweh as the God of the ancestor of the Israelites, the founder of the nation. **The God of Jacob** must sometimes be rendered "the God of our ancestor Jacob" or "the God whom our ancestor Jacob worshiped." Care must be taken in translation not to imply that **the God of Jacob** in line b is another God, different from **the LORD** in line a. Following TEV terminology, the translation can be "May he, who is the God of Jacob, protect you!"

Protect is a translation of the causative form of a verb meaning "to be high"; therefore "put you out of reach (of your enemies)" is the idea. Briggs, however, takes it to mean victory.

20.2   RSV   TEV

> May he send you help from the
>   sanctuary,
>   and give you support from Zion!

> May he send you help from his
>   Temple
>   and give you aid from Mount
>   Zion.

Send you help in both RSV and TEV is somewhat redundant because it is God who sends and God who helps. Therefore in order to avoid giving the impression that God sends someone else to do the helping, it may often be clearer to translate, for example, "May he (the LORD) help you," or if the element of "send" is to be retained, "From his sanctuary may he reach out and help you" or "May he come to you and help you."

Sanctuary translates the word "holy (place)," that is, the Temple, which is holy because it is the dwelling place of Yahweh, the holy God. **Sanctuary**, which translates the Hebrew word meaning "holy place," is more concretely focused in line b with **Zion**. **Zion** refers to the hill on which the Temple was built (see also comments on 2.6) and is used here synonymously with **the sanctuary**. **Sanctuary** is sometimes rendered "God's great prayer house" or "the worship house of God in Jerusalem." Because of the close parallelism of lines a and b, it will sometimes be best to reduce these to one line; for example, "May he send you help from his great prayer house on mount Zion," otherwise such close parallelism may strike the reader as unnecessary repetition.

It should be noticed that the **and** at the beginning of line b may lead the reader to infer that two separate and distinct requests are being made. Of course line b is a poetic restatement of line a, with a more specific form of reference. It may therefore be better to make the two lines two complete sentences, not formally connected.

20.3

RSV	TEV
May he remember all your offerings, and regard with favor your burnt sacrifices! *Selah*	May he accept all your offerings and be pleased with all your sacrifices.

From this verse it is inferred that the psalm was used after the king had offered his sacrifices to God. **Remember** means to keep in mind, in a favorable sense, and so "**accept**," and **regard with favor** is literally "to make fat," that is, to consider them as extra fine offerings. The two verbs are nearly synonymous in their parallel use here.

The word for **offerings** is a general word for all kinds of ritual offerings. Later it came to be used only of grain and olive oil offerings. **Burnt sacrifices** were the animal sacrifices in which the animal was burned completely on the altar. In languages where sacrifices are not known, it will be necessary to use descriptive phrases; for example, "animals that are killed and burned and offered to God," or "gifts that are burned for God," or "animals killed and offered to God by burning." See comment on sacrifices in 4.5.

Lines a and b are quite synonymous. However, the general category of **offerings** in line a is made specific with **burnt sacrifices** in line b, thus heightening the poetic effect in the movement of the two lines. In languages where a general term for **offerings** is available, it will often be possible to say, for example, "May he remember your offerings, and even more, may he look with favor on your burnt sacrifices" or "May God never forget the things you have offered to him, and even more, may he be pleased with the burnt offerings you have given him."

The comments made on the **and** in verse 2 apply to the **and** in this verse.

For *Selah* see comments on 3.2.

20.4-5

	RSV		TEV
4	May he grant you your heart's desire, and fulfil all your plans!	4	May he give you what you desire and make all your plans succeed.
5	May we shout for joy over your victory, and in the name of our God set up our banners! May the LORD fulfil all your petitions!	5	Then we will shout for joy over your victory and celebrate your triumph by praising our God. May the LORD answer all your requests.

In parallel lines (verse 4) the wish is expressed that Yahweh give the king his **heart's desires** (literally "according to your heart") and **fulfil all** his **plans**, a reference to victory in the coming battle. **May he . . . fulfill all your plans** may often be rendered as "may God enable you to do all the things you have been thinking about" or "may God make it possible for you to succeed in your plans."

If Yahweh does so, then the people worshiping in the Temple, where this psalm is being used, will **shout for joy** (see also comments on "my cry" in 17.1) and celebrate the **victory** of the king in battle (see comments on 3.8 for the noun for "salvation, deliverance, victory"). RSV takes the first part of verse 5 as a prayer, **May we . . .** , while TEV takes it as a statement, "**Then we . . . .**" It seems better to take it as a statement (see FRCL, SPCL, NIV, TOB). **Shout for joy over your victory** must often be transformed into two clauses, the second being the cause of the first; for example, "may we shout for joy because you have defeated our enemies." In some languages it will be more natural to express this line as direct address, "may we shout for joy and say, 'You, king, have defeated our enemies.' "

Set up our banners: to "hold high the banner" was a sign of victory (this verb is used only here and in Song 6.4,10); to do so **in the name of our God** is to praise him for giving victory. Since the practice of setting up banners, or flags, as a sign of victory is unknown to many modern readers, TEV has discarded the figure and uses the general statement "**celebrate your triumph**." The TEV expression may sometimes be rendered "we will sing songs because you have won the battle" or "we will be happy because you have defeated our enemies." Or else the line may be rendered "we will praise our God by singing songs because you have won the battle." In some languages it will be more appropriate to speak of celebration as dance; for example, "we will dance and say our God is great because he has made you win the battle."

In verse 5c the verb **fulfil** is the same as the one in verse 4b. Here, with **your petitions** as the object, **fulfil** is not a natural way of saying this in English. Something like "give you all you ask for" is better.

20.6	RSV	TEV

RSV	TEV
Now I know that the LORD will help his anointed; he will answer him from his holy heaven with mighty victories by his right hand.	Now I know that the LORD gives victory to his chosen king; he answers him from his holy heaven and by his power gives him great victories.

In the second part of the psalm (verses 6-9) the king (or a priest) responds in the confidence that the prayer has been answered. Something takes place between verse 5 and verse 6, assuring the king of a favorable answer from Yahweh.

In verses 6 to the end there is no further use of "you" in reference to the king; the king is now referred to in the third person. In cases where this change of address form will result in confusion, the following adjustments are possible: (a) change "you" in verses 1-5 to "he;" (b) substitute "you" for "he" in verses 6-9; or (c) leave the pronouns as they are and insert a subtitle before verse 1; for example, "The writer speaks to the king," and a subtitle before verse 6, "The writer speaks to the people."

Now I know means that the psalmist, who has been in an attitude of expectation and prayerful hope, reaches a turning point in his liturgical experience. **Now** marks both a time and a transition. It signals a change from one state of knowing to another. In some languages this expression must be recast to say, for example, "Now

I have learned" or "I have found out now," or as a contrast, "But now I am aware that . . . ."

Will help translates the verb "to save" (corresponding to the noun "victory" of verse 5a).

For **anointed** see comments on 2.2. TEV's equivalent "**to his chosen king**" must sometimes be rendered "to the king God has chosen." In many languages attempts to represent the Hebrew translated **anointed** will result in misunderstanding and require a footnote for clarification. Therefore it is normally best to speak of "the chosen king."

He will answer him may create unnecessary ambiguity of reference, particularly since line 6a ended by mentioning the king. Therefore it will be clearer in translation to say "God answers the king." **Answer** again must mean to listen and to act, not merely to give a reply.

His holy heaven: Yahweh is at the same time in the Temple (verse 2) and in heaven. **His holy heaven** in a literal translation may mean nothing more than "the high taboo place." In order to avoid such a possible misunderstanding, **holy** must often be rendered as "belonging to God" or "set apart for God." The full line may then be rendered, for example, "He responds to him from heaven, which is his," "he says 'Yes' to his chosen king from his place in heaven," or "From heaven, which belongs to him, he answers his chosen king."

By his right hand is a figure for God's power (see comments on 18.35). Line c may be translated "Because the LORD is powerful, he enables the king to defeat his enemies" or "So the king will be able to win his battles, because the LORD is strong and helps him."

20.7-8	RSV	TEV
7	Some boast of chariots, and some of horses; but we boast of the name of the LORD our God.	Some trust in their war chariots and others in their horses, but we trust in the power of the LORD our God.
8	They will collapse and fall; but we shall rise and stand upright.	Such people will stumble and fall, but we will rise and stand firm.

In verse 7 in Hebrew the verb for **boast** appears only once, after **we**, but it applies to all three: **some . . . some . . . we**; it is the causative of the verb "to remember," meaning to make mention of something as the cause for victory, and to do so in terms of boasting or trusting. (Dahood derives the verb from a form meaning "to be male," that is, to be strong.) Instead of accepting the Hebrew text "we will be made to remember," some prefer a conjecture supported by the Septuagint and Syriac, "we are strong" (Briggs, NAB). Some may prefer to use two verbs: "rely" in line a and "invoke" in line b; FRCL does so: "depend on" and "make our appeal to." TOB, NJV, and NJB translate "call on," which indicates "rely on"; this may be the best translation of the verb.

Chariots must in most languages be adjusted by means of a descriptive phrase; for example, "war carts." The translator may choose to use **boast** as in RSV rather than TEV's **"trust."** **Boast** is often expressed idiomatically as "to make oneself chief" or "to speak with a swollen heart." Line **a** would then be rendered "some people speak with swollen hearts about their war carts" or "some people act like chiefs when they talk about . . . ."

In some languages it will be necessary to avoid the ellipsis **and some of horses** and either express the verb **boast** again or use a close synonym; for example, "and other people put their hearts on their horses."

For **name** see comments on 5.11.

The expression **the LORD our God** must often be translated as "the LORD who is our God," otherwise readers may be mistakenly led to think that the Lord and God are two persons.

Collapse and fall pictures military defeat, while **rise and stand upright** portrays victory in battle. **They** of line **a** refers back to those mentioned in line 7a and not to those in 7b (TEV's **"Such people"** is not clear, and the reader may mistakenly assume it refers to the second part of verse 7, not to the first part). So it will sometimes be clearer to say "people who trust in chariots and horses will stumble and fall." **Rise and stand upright** reverses the action of the preceding line. Many languages distinguish between rising from a lying position and rising from a sitting position. The former will serve in such languages to mark the contrast with falling.

20.9   RSV   TEV

> Give victory to the king, O LORD;   Give victory to the king, O LORD;
>   answer us when we call.*[l]*   answer*[e]* us when we call.

[l] Gk: Heb *give victory, O LORD, let the*   *[e]* *Some ancient translations* answer; *He-*
King answer us when we call   *brew* he will answer.

The Hebrew text may be taken to mean what the RSV footnote has, in which "the King" refers to Yahweh; or else it may mean, as the TEV footnote has it, "Give victory to the king, O LORD; he will answer us when we call," in which "he" should refer to Yahweh but appears to refer to the king (since the third person is used, not the second); see TOB "The king will answer us on the day we call to him." Consequently TEV, RSV, and others (SPCL, NEB, NAB, BJ, NJB) follow the Septuagint, Targum, and Jerome, and express the imperative **answer us**, addressed to Yahweh.*[l]*

Give victory to the king, O LORD must often be restructured as "O LORD, help the king defeat his enemies."

Answer us must not be translated by a term meaning to give a verbal reply, but rather by a term for responding to a request. Some languages distinguish between

---

*[l]*HOTTP ("C" decision) offers four possible interpretations of the Masoretic text without suggesting a preference: (1) "O LORD, save; may the king answer us the day we call (to him)"; (2) "O LORD, save; may the king (that is, God) answer us the day we call (to him)." And with a different division of the Hebrew phrases: (3) "O LORD, save the king; may he (the king) answer us the day we call (to him)"; (4) "O LORD, save the king; He (that is, God) will answer us the day we call (to him)."

answers that are direct or indirect, polite or impolite, evasive or frank. In the present context one can sometimes say "hear us and help us." If the translator wishes to preserve the formal feature of "answer you" in verse 1 corresponding to **answer us** in this final verse, the same term should be used in both places.

Psalm 21

This psalm seems to have been intentionally placed next to Psalm 20, since it praises God for victory in battle, and is thus an appropriate complement to Psalm 20 (so Dahood, Dentan). Notice how verse 2 matches the request in 20.4. But there are difficulties in restricting the use of this psalm to one such specific occasion; as Toombs points out, it could fit a number of situations. Many see it as a coronation psalm.

There is some uncertainty whether it is Yahweh or the king who is spoken of in verses 8-12; however, the structure of the psalm makes it more likely that these verses refer to Yahweh. In verses 1-6 the speaker (or speakers) praises Yahweh (who is addressed in the second person) for the blessings he has poured out on the king (who is spoken of in the third person). In verse 7, however, both Yahweh and the king are spoken of in the third person. Verses 8-12 have the second person of address, except in the second half of verse 9. Commentators disagree on who is addressed (see comments in the paragraph below). The psalm closes (verse 13) with praise to Yahweh, who is addressed in the second person.

This psalm is based upon the contrast in the way God uses his power to reward the king, and how he uses his power to destroy his enemies. The poem is framed by the recurring words "in thy strength" found in verses 1 and 13. The theme of power runs throughout the poem in the nouns of "help," "blessing," "life," "hand," "right hand," "glory," "splendor," "majesty," "fire," "bows," and "power." In verses 1-7 Yahweh "gives," "does not withhold," "bestows," "makes glad," and "makes blessed." In contrast the enemies are dealt with by "find out," "make them a blazing oven," "swallow," "consume," "destroy," "put to flight," and "aim at their faces." Most of the parallel lines exhibit intensification as the dominant movement. However, verse 10 is mainly static, each line saying approximately the same thing, and verse 12 has effect followed by cause, normally in the opposite order. Verse 7, which is at the approximate center of the psalm, shifts to the third person in reference to God. Verses 8-12 have "you," which many translators and commentators take to refer to the king. However, two factors favor God as the referent: (a) the central theme of God's power is praised, not the king's power; and (b) verse 9, the only three-line parallelism, would not follow the movement of intensification if line 9a referred to the king while 9b and 9c clearly refer to Yahweh.

Briggs outlines the psalm as follows: (1) verses 1-6: praise for victory; (2) verse 7: chorus affirms the king's trust in Yahweh; (3) verses 8-12: assurance of future victories of Yahweh; (4) verse 13: chorus of praise.

HEADING: **"Praise for Victory"** (TEV); "King by the grace of God"; "A coronation liturgy"; "The coronation of the king"; "Thanksgiving and prayers for the king." In many languages the TEV heading will require expanding "praise" and "victory" into two clauses; for example, "The psalmist praises God because he has defeated his enemies."

Hebrew Title: <u>**To the choirmaster. A Psalm of David.**</u>
The title is the same as the one for Psalm 13.

21.1-2	RSV		TEV
1	In thy strength the king rejoices, O LORD; and in thy help how greatly he exults!	1	The king is glad, O LORD, because you gave him strength; he rejoices because you made him victorious.
2	Thou hast given him his heart's desire, and hast not withheld the request of his lips. *Selah*	2	You have given him his heart's desire; you have answered his request.

The two lines of verse 1 are parallel: <u>rejoices</u> (as in 9.2) and <u>exults</u> (as in 9.14). <u>**In thy strength**</u> is synonymous with <u>**in thy help**</u> (that is, "victory"; see comment on 3.8), both referring to the fact that Yahweh has given the king the power to defeat his enemies in battle. It was by means of the <u>**strength**</u> and the <u>**help**</u> that Yahweh gave him that the king was able to defeat the enemy. <u>**The king rejoices**</u> must often be expressed idiomatically; for example, "the chief's heart is white" or "the chief's heart rests coolly." Here <u>**thy help**</u> means "the victory you gave him"; this translates the same Hebrew word ("salvation") which is translated "deliverance" in 3.8. TEV's <u>**"you made him victorious"**</u> must often be recast to say "you helped him conquer his enemies" or "you enabled him to defeat his enemies."

In some translations it may be useful to have the vocative <u>**O LORD**</u> at the beginning of line <u>a</u>, not at the end. And in some languages <u>**the king**</u> will have to be identified as "our king" or "the king of our country."

Verse 2 is also composed of two parallel lines: <u>**Thou hast given**</u> and <u>**(thou) hast not withheld**</u>. This last verb is used in the Psalms only here and in 84.11. <u>**His heart's desire**</u> (see comment at 10.3 for "desire") is paralleled by <u>**the request of his lips**</u> (a phrase in which the word for <u>**request**</u> appears only here in the Old Testament). The <u>**request**</u> was for victory in battle (see 20.4).

If the translator follows TEV <u>**"answered his request,"**</u> care should be taken to avoid a rendering which means "gave a verbal rely to what he asked." Here the meaning may be translated, for example, "you, God, have given him the things he asked you for" or "you have let him have everything he asked for." Translators should avoid the use of a positive statement in <u>a</u> and a negative in <u>b</u>, if that form is not stylistically acceptable.

21.3-4 RSV	TEV
3 For thou dost meet him with goodly blessings; thou dost set a crown of fine gold upon his head.	3 You came to him with great blessings and set a crown of gold on his head.
4 He asked life of thee; thou gavest it to him, length of days for ever and ever.	4 He asked for life, and you gave it, a long and lasting life.

It is not certain precisely what **thou dost meet him** refers to; some take it to mean at the time of the king's return from battle. More than likely it is a way of saying that, in answer to the king's prayer, Yahweh gave him **goodly blessings**, that is, fine or special blessings, not only for him personally but for his people as well. In the sense that God gives blessings to the king, line a may be rendered "You, God, received the king and gave him good gifts" or "You, God, welcomed the king and gave him good things."

Line b of verse 3 refers clearly to the day the king was crowned; some, however, take the words to mean a new proclamation of the king's sovereignty (see 1 Sam 11.13-15). RSV (also TOB, NJB) translates verse 3 with the English present tense of the verbs, and TEV (also NIV, NJV) with the past tense. The past tense in English seems better here, referring to a specific event. The present tense implies continuous or repeated action.

In verse 4 **life** means not just longevity as such, but a long and prosperous reign; and what the Lord gave the king was not immortality, but "**a long and lasting life**" (see also SPCL). Some, however, like Dahood, think this means eternal life, or else it means children, through whom the king would continue to live. Anderson refers to the language of the royal court, in which petition was made that the king live "forever" (see 1 Kgs 1.31; Neh 2.3; Dan 2.4); see also Psalm 23.6. **Life** must often be recast as a verb phrase. Furthermore the expression **He asked life of thee** must often be rendered as a causative; for example, "He asked that you make him to live," or idiomatically, "He asked that you make his eyes see well for many many years."

The heightening which is evident in verse 4 can be rendered, for example, "He asked you for life, and you gave it to him, indeed, you gave him a very long and lasting life" or "He asked for life . . . , you gave him even more than that, you gave him . . . ."

21.5-6 RSV	TEV
5 His glory is great through thy help; splendor and majesty thou dost bestow upon him.	5 His glory is great because of your help; you have given him fame and majesty.
6 Yea, thou dost make him most blessed for ever;	6 Your blessings are with him forever,

thou dost make him glad with the joy of thy presence.	and your presence fills him with joy.

Yahweh has given the king **glory** (honor, fame; see 3.3; 7.5), **splendor** (fame, majesty; see 8.1 the "majesty" of Yahweh's name), and **majesty** (dignity, splendor; see 8.5), three attributes of a powerful and prosperous king. The king of Israel has these qualities because Yahweh has given him victory over the enemy (see NIV "the victories you gave"). **Thy help** in line a means the same as it does in verse 1a.

In languages which show a strong preference for placing the reason clause before the consequence, it will be necessary in verse 5a to reverse the TEV and RSV clause order; for example, "because you have helped him his glory is great." In many languages it is not natural to possess an abstract such as **glory**, since this is something others attribute to a person or recognize in a ruler. Therefore it is sometimes necessary to say, for example, "Because you help him the people say that he is great" or "Because of your help they say he is a big chief."

It should be noticed that in line b RSV has the present tense; the TEV past tense is preferred. **Majesty** is not used in some languages as an object to be given to someone. It is more common for it to be treated as a quality of an object; for example, "you have made him a great king" or "you have given him great power to rule the people."

Yea in verse 6a is RSV's way of representing a Hebrew particle that shows emphasis, but which here may not have that much force. NIV has "Surely," and NEB "for"; most translations do not represent it formally.

Thou dost make him most blessed for ever (that is, "You are always blessing him") means that God blesses the king. Some (see NAB, TOB) take the words to mean "You make him a blessing," that is, for his people (see Weiser, Anderson). It seems better to follow the interpretation of RSV and TEV.

Make him most blessed cannot in some languages be expressed as a possessed object, as in TEV **"Your blessings are with him."** One must often speak of "good things" or "good gifts." Therefore **"your blessings"** must often be rendered, for example, "you give him good gifts forever" or "you give him good things forever." If the alternative interpretation is followed, it may be necessary to say, for example, "you cause him to give good things to his people."

The thought in verse 6b is the same as found in 16.11b. As God's "son" (see 2.7) the king enjoyed the presence of God with him, and this brought him great **joy**. The Hebrew is emphatic and somewhat redundant; this emphasis may be expressed by "make him extremely glad." In some languages a noun such as **presence** cannot perform an event such as **make him glad**. Therefore it is often necessary to recast this type of expression to say "because you are with him he is joyful" or "he is happy because you are near him."

21.7   RSV   TEV

For the king trusts in the LORD; and through the steadfast love	The king trusts in the LORD Almighty;

<table>
<tr><td>of the Most High he shall not
be moved.</td><td>and because of the LORD's constant love
he will always be secure.</td></tr>
</table>

of the Most High he shall not
be moved.

and because of the LORD's constant love
he will always be secure.

All the words in this verse have already been noted: **trusts** (13.5); **steadfast love** (5.7); **the Most High** (7.17); and the verb "shake, fall," of the statement (**shall not**) **be moved** (10.6). The name Yahweh in line a and the title **the Most High** in line b are represented in TEV by "LORD Almighty" and "the LORD."

The king trusts in the LORD must in some languages be rendered idiomatically as "the king puts his heart on the LORD" or "the king gives his heart to the LORD."

Steadfast love of the Most High must often be restructured further than in TEV. If not, there is the possibility of misunderstanding this expression to mean that the love is a possession of the Lord rather than the act which the Lord does to someone. This expression may sometimes be rendered "because the LORD loves him greatly."

Shall not be moved is a promise that the king will not be removed by force from his throne. The meaning of this statement must in some languages be expressed idiomatically as "he shall sit a long time" or "he shall sit firmly."

21.8   RSV   TEV

| Your hand will find out all your enemies; your right hand will find out those who hate you. | The king will capture all his enemies; he will capture everyone who hates him. |

Who is the subject (addressed in the second person) in verses 8-12? No one is named; in the second part of verse 9 "the LORD" is named, in the third person, and then the second person is resumed. TEV has taken the second person to refer to the king, and so has "**The king**" in verse 8a (so Kirkpatrick, Briggs, Toombs, Taylor, and others; also TOB, SPCL, NAB, BJ, NJB). RSV's use of **you** and **your** makes it clear that it takes the king to be the subject. Another way of making the king the subject is to change in verse 7 from the third person to the second person vocative, "You, O king," and keep the second person in verses 8-12 (as SPCL has done). NJV takes the second person to refer to Yahweh (so Anderson, Weiser, Dahood, Crim). The language in places seems more appropriate of Yahweh (especially the first part of verse 9, "when you appear"); but the switch to the third person in the second part of the verse ("The LORD will swallow them up") has been taken by some to mean that "you" in the first part of verse 9 refers to the king. FRCL takes the subject in verses 8-12 to be God, who is addressed, in verse 8, "O King, you . . . ."

Hand and **right hand** seem to be used synonymously; but Dahood understands them to mean "left hand" and "right hand." **Your hand** in reference to the power of the king is the expression of a part for the whole. In some languages it will be possible to maintain this imagery, either as "your hand" or "his hand," while in other languages it will be preferable and less ambiguous to follow the lead of TEV. The verb **find out** in both lines does not mean simply to discover, but to grab, to "**capture**" (NIV has "lay hold on . . . seize").

	RSV		TEV
9	You will make them as a blazing oven when you appear. The LORD will swallow them up in his wrath; and fire will consume them.	9	He will destroy them like a blazing fire when he appears. The LORD will devour them in his anger, and fire will consume them.
10	You will destroy their offspring from the earth, and their children from among the sons of men.	10	None of their descendants will survive; the king will kill them all.

In verse 9a **You will make them as a blazing oven** means that the king (or Yahweh) will destroy the enemies with fire; they will burn up like the fire in an **oven**. Should a translator retain the word **oven**, it should be remembered that this was one made of hardened clay or of brick; it would not be made of metal.

When you appear translates "at the time of your face," in which "face" stands for presence, here an angry presence (see 34.16).

In the second half of verse 9, **swallow** and **consume** are used synonymously, appropriate to **wrath** and **fire**. The fire is to be thought of as an expression of Yahweh's fury; and Dahood translates "his fire," carrying over the "his" of "his anger" to "fire." In some languages it will be necessary to indicate an object of the destroying fire; for example, "he will destroy them as a blazing fire destroys things," or idiomatically sometimes, "he will eat them as fire eats things up."

Swallow them up in his wrath may require more recasting than was done in TEV. One way is to expand the expression into two clauses, one the cause and the other the consequence; for example, "because he is angry he will swallow them up." **Swallow** as an idiomatic expression of destruction may need to be replaced by other figures such as "eat," "wipe away," or "blow into dust."

The parallel lines of this verse display intensification. In line a God (according to some, the king) **makes them as . . .** ; in line b he **swallows them up**; and in line c **the fire will consume them**, which is literally "eat them." If the heightening in the succeeding lines is to be preserved with God as the subject of the first two lines, it may be translated, for example, "When the LORD appears he will turn them into a fiery oven; more than that, he will angrily swallow them up, and fire will devour them."

Translators should be aware that the structure of intensification is often changed when recast as cause and effect clauses. However, in some cases there will be little or no choice. The main task of the translator is to determine the devices in the receptor language which most clearly reveal the heightening effect found in much of biblical parallelism.

In verse 10 the two Hebrew phrases used for "descendants" are "their fruit" and "their seed," both used metaphorically of offspring.

Their offspring is commonly rendered as "their children" or "their grandchildren." It is possible sometimes to say "those who follow after him" or "Those who came down from him."

From the earth serves to express the totality of the action of destruction, and is rendered in TEV through the use of **none . . . will survive**. In some languages it will be more natural to say "he will kill every one of their children" or "he will not stop killing until he has killed the last child."

In order to avoid needless repetition the translator will note that TEV has employed the pronoun "**them**" in line **b** instead of using another synonym for descendants.

For the phrase **the sons of men**, see 11.4.

21.11-12	RSV	TEV

	RSV		TEV
11	If they plan evil against you, if they devise mischief, they will not succeed.	11	They make their plans, and plot against him, but they will not succeed.
12	For you will put them to flight; you will aim at their faces with your bows.	12	He will shoot his arrows at them and make them turn and run.

The evil plans and plots of the enemies of the king will not succeed (verse 11). It will be better in most translations to say specifically "Your enemies" or "The king's enemies" instead of **they**, which could be taken by the reader to refer to "their offspring . . . their children" of verse 10.

The first verb in verse 11 in Hebrew (RSV **plan**) means "to stretch out, extend, direct toward," in the sense of directing a plot against someone; the second verbal phrase (**devise mischief**) is the same as the one used in 10.2b ("schemes . . . devised"). **Plan evil** in line **a** is matched by the synonymous **devise mischief** in line **b**. In modern English **mischief** rarely carries the implication of something evil or destructive; it is normally synonymous with "trick" or "prank," whereas here the meaning is more serious, "wicked plan." RSV makes the two lines in verse 11 conditional; the translator may prefer to follow the TEV, which presents the actions as facts, things actually done (so NJV, NEB).

They plan evil is difficult to render clearly in that form because it is not indicated what the evil refers to. Therefore in many languages it will be necessary to say "they think of evil things to do against him," or idiomatically, "their minds give birth to bad things they can do to him."

Devise mischief must sometimes be rendered as "they think up ways to injure him."

Succeed is sometimes rendered idiomatically as "seeing goodness" or "touching happiness."

In verse 12 TEV has reversed the two lines for easier understanding. **Put them to flight** translates what is literally "you will place their back," that is, in flight. NEB translates differently: "you will catch them round the shoulders."

Bows translates the word "bow strings," a meaning the Hebrew word has here only; elsewhere it means tent ropes. TEV has chosen to say "**shoot his arrows**" as being more natural and clearer than **aim . . . your bows**. It may be that the psalmist means the enemies turn and run when they see the king aiming his arrows at them (so NIV); but it seems more natural to take the phrase to mean that they run when he actually shoots his arrows. (Of course it is implied that the king's warriors are all shooting arrows, not the king alone; but it seems better to stay with the literal form of the text here.)

It is not necessary to represent the literal **aim at their faces**; NJB is somewhat ludicrous with its rendering: "you will make them turn tail, by shooting your arrows in their faces."

21.13 RSV	TEV
Be exalted, O LORD, in thy strength! We will sing and praise thy power.	We praise you, LORD, for your great strength! We will sing and praise your power.

The speakers in this verse are the people of Israel, at worship in the Temple.

Line a is difficult to understand: **Be exalted . . . in thy strength** means either "Show your greatness by using your power" or else "Because of your strength you are exalted" (that is, praised, as TEV has it). FRCL has "Lord, show your great power." Dahood takes the verb here to mean "Rejoice, O Yahweh, in your triumph"; Anderson takes it as an emphatic statement, "You shall be exalted"; SPCL "Rise with your power" (so JB); others "Rise, Lord, show your power." The translation of this verse will depend upon which interpretation the translator follows.

Be exalted as an impersonal command is difficult in many languages, since it is far more common to command someone to act. If one follows the TEV rendering, it will often be necessary to change from a noun phrase to a verb phrase; for example, "Because you do great deeds, we say you are a great LORD."

Unless syntactic reasons make it impossible, the translator should preserve the envelope structure of the psalm by employing in verse 13 the same expression used in verse 1 for **in thy strength**.

In line b the two verbs may be understood as indicating two distinct actions: **sing** and **praise**. It may be, however, that the meaning is "By means of songs (or, singing) we will praise your powers."

Instead of the abstract quality **power** at the end of the verse, NJV translates "Your mighty deeds," and SPCL "your victories"; either one of these two is recommended as a good dynamic equivalence translation.

Psalm 22

This psalm begins as a cry of despair by an individual who is sick and near death, the object of people's scorn, not of their pity; it then becomes a song of praise to God for hearing and answering the psalmist's cry. The first section (verses 1-21) may be divided into three parts, each of which contains a desperate plea for help, joined to an affirmation of faith and praise (verses 1-5, 6-11, 12-21). In the second section (verses 23-31) the psalmist promises to praise the Lord in public worship (verses 22-24), and to offer the Lord the sacrifices he had promised (verses 25-26); he ends by affirming the future universal dominion of the Lord (verses 27-31).

This psalm is characterized by two types of poetic movement: a series of alternating shifts downward and upward (negative and positive feelings), and a sustained shift from exclusion to inclusion in the final upward swing. Transitions between the movements are well marked. The opening double question (RSV) and verse 2 express the negative feelings, the downwardness of the psalmist in relation to God; for example, "forsaken," "far from helping," "not answer," and "no rest." In verses 3-5 the feeling goes suddenly upward as it shifts away from the psalmist to Israel and to God. But in verses 6-8 the direction turns downward again, with the psalmist and Israel in focus. In the following two verses the movement turns upward again as the psalmist reflects upon God's care for him at birth, and in verse 11 his feelings level out as he thinks of the dangers about him. This represents a transition to the steep plunge he takes as he complains of dangers and of his physical torments in verses 12-18, the longest sustained negative section in the poem. Again this sharp movement glides to a halt as he asks God to "help," "deliver," and "save" him. From this point the only direction is upward and outward. In verse 22 the psalmist promises to praise God. In verse 23 the subject expands to Israel, in verse 27 it is "all the ends of the earth," "the family of nations," and in verse 31 it is "people not yet born" who will know God's salvation. So the psalmist's depression and hope, which struggled in lonely, uncertain contest, are finally resolved in an all-embracing proclamation. The movement may be diagrammed as follows:

Actors (Passive and Active)	Psalmist and God	Israel and God	Psalmist and Israel	Psalmist and God	Psalmist and God	Psalmist and Wicked	Psalmist and God and Enemies	Psalmist and God and Israel	Everyone and God
Verse	1-2	3-5	6-8	9-10	11	12-18	19-21	22-26	27-31
Movement					Transition		Transition		

This psalm is widely used and quoted in the New Testament; its vivid description of suffering and despair was felt to be highly appropriate for the passion of Christ. Verse 1a is cited in Matthew 27.46; Mark 15.34; verses 7 and 8 are alluded to in Matthew 27.39,43; Mark 15.29; verse 18 is quoted in John 19.24 and alluded to in Matthew 27.35; Mark 15.24; Luke 23.34; and verse 22 is quoted in Hebrews 2.12.

HEADING: **"A Cry of Anguish and a Song of Praise"** (TEV); "The sufferings and hope of the virtuous man"; "The cry of a desolate spirit"; "Dereliction and deliverance." If the translator follows the TEV heading, it will often be necessary to recast the two noun phrases; for example, "The psalmist cries because he is pained, and then sings a song to praise God."

Hebrew Title: **To the choirmaster: according to The Hind of the Dawn. A Psalm of David.**
The direction to the choirmaster is "According to the deer of the dawn." Most take this to have been the name of the tune to which the psalm was to be sung.

22.1-2	RSV		TEV
1	My God, my God, why hast thou forsaken me? Why art thou so far from helping me, from the words of my groaning?	1	My God, my God, why have you abandoned me? I have cried desperately for help, but still it does not come.
2	O my God, I cry by day, but thou dost not answer; and by night, but find no rest.	2	During the day I call to you, my God, but you do not answer; I call at night, but get no rest.

As an opener the question form is common in the psalms. (See also Psa 2; 10; 13; 52; 74.) Its purpose is to arouse interest in the listener or reader, who will want to find out how the question will be answered or dealt with by the end of the poem. This does not mean that the question form cannot be modified in the receptor language, but the translator should have a valid reason before doing so.

In these two verses the psalmist cries to God in despair because God does not answer him. The two anguished questions in verse 1 dramatically express the psalmist's desolation and hopelessness. He cannot understand why God has abandoned him. But even in his suffering he still addresses God as **My God, my God**, thereby affirming his own faith in and dependence on God, who seems so distant and silent. He feels that God has **forsaken** him (see similar expression in 10.1), that he doesn't pay any attention to his loud groans, to his cries of pain. **Why hast thou forsaken me?** is often expressed as "why have you left me?" or "why have you gone away from me?"

In verse 1b RSV's literal rendering of the Hebrew makes for unnatural English, since the prepositional phrase **from the words of my groaning** is governed by the verb phrase **Why art thou so far**. The line has been reordered in a more natural manner in TEV, which provides a clear model for the translator. In some languages it may be necessary to make more explicit than does TEV that it is God whom the writer is calling to for help; for example, "I have cried for you to help me, but you do not come to me." Should the translator wish to stay closer to the Hebrew form, however, something like the following may be said: "Why do you remain so far away from me, and refuse to help me or even to listen to my anguished cries?"

The two parallel references to time in verse 2, **by day . . . by night**, indicate that the psalmist never stops praying for help; but it is all useless, since God does not answer his plea.

The word for **rest** in verse 2 occurs only here and in 39.2 ("I was silent") and 62.1 ("waits in silence"); and perhaps in 65.1. It seems to mean "silence," and the Hebrew phrase "no silence for me" indicates that his pain is not alleviated, he gets no relief, which would come if God were to listen to him and answer his pleas.

22.3	RSV	TEV

Yet thou art holy, enthroned on the praises of Israel.	But you are enthroned as the Holy One, the one whom Israel praises.

The initial word **Yet** serves to remind Yahweh, so to speak, that his silence, his failure to help the psalmist, is not consistent with his past actions on behalf of his people; or it may be the psalmist's way of reassuring himself: since Yahweh had helped in the past, he will do so now.

Even in his deepest despair the psalmist still trusts in God, the one who in the past has saved the people of Israel. Verse 3 is literally "But you are the Holy One sitting upon the praises of Israel," which is variously understood. As "the Holy One" God is the transcendent God, above and beyond his people, yet not indifferent to them, for he calls them to be his own people, completely dedicated to him; and so they also become holy in his sight. **Thou art holy** is often difficult in translation, since there are a number of things in the Scriptures which are called holy, and often the reference to God's holiness must be rendered in a different way. Places and objects which are said to be holy normally have reference to their quality of being set aside for special religious use. However, it is not possible to speak of God's holiness in a similar manner. It is possible to speak of God's holiness in reference to worship, and therefore to say, for example, "you are worthy of our worship," "you are the one people pray to," or "you are God and we bow in prayer to you."

Yahweh's throne in the Temple was thought of as the winged creatures, above the Covenant Box (see 80.1), and the prayers and praise of the people were directed toward it. In a figurative sense, therefore, Yahweh was **enthroned on the praises of Israel**. Thus "the praises of Israel are your throne"; SPCL "You reign, praised by Israel." NAB, following some manuscripts of the Septuagint, translates "You are enthroned in the holy place." Dahood has "While you sit upon the holy throne, the Glory of Israel."

Enthroned on the praises of Israel is highly lyrical but will be meaningless if translated literally in many languages. The restructuring of TEV is suggestive; however, in many languages it will be necessary to be more explicit than TEV and to say, for example, "you sit on your throne as king, and are the one whom the people of Israel pray to" or "you rule from the king's chair, and you are [the] God whom your people worship."

<u>22.4-5</u>   RSV   TEV

| 4 | In thee our fathers trusted; they trusted, and thou didst deliver them. | 4 | Our ancestors put their trust in you; they trusted you, and you saved them. |
| 5 | To thee they cried, and were saved; in thee they trusted, and were not disappointed. | 5 | They called to you and escaped from danger; they trusted you and were not disappointed. |

By using the verb "to trust" three times, the psalmist emphasizes the close relationship in the past between the ancient Israelites' trust in Yahweh and Yahweh's actions on their behalf. For **trusted** see comment at 13.5; for **deliver** see comment at 17.13. **Trusted** must often be translated by an idiomatic expression such as "they put their hearts on" or "they have a thick heart with him."

Were saved must often be shifted to an active construction; for example, "you saved them." TEV's **"escaped from danger"** may give the wrong impression that by running away they saved themselves from harm; the meaning is that Yahweh saved them.

Were not disappointed: see the same verb ("be put to shame") in 6.10. The meaning is that God kept his promises and saved them. In some languages this will be rendered idiomatically; for example, "their hearts did not heat with shame," or nonfiguratively, "God did what he said" or "God saved them as he said he would."

<u>22.6-7</u>   RSV   TEV

| 6 | But I am a worm, and no man; scorned by men, and despised by the people. | 6 | But I am no longer a man; I am a worm, despised and scorned by every- |

215

7 All who see me mock at me,
    they make mouths at me, they
    wag their heads;
	one!
	7 All who see me make fun of me;
	    they stick out their tongues and
	    shake their heads.

Again the psalmist expresses his despair, and sees himself as **a worm** (perhaps a maggot; see Exo 16.20). The figurative language of verse 6a must be clear to the readers; the psalmist is not stating a fact when he says he is not **a man** but only **a worm**. The psalmist is giving the view of others concerning himself. Therefore it may be better to translate "People say that I am like a worm, not like a man" or "People don't call me a man; they call me a worm." If the comparison with a worm gives the wrong idea, it may be necessary to add an attributive; for example, "worthless as a worm" or "miserable as a worm."

In verse 6b **men** and **the people** are parallel and synonymous; they are not two different groups, but two ways of referring to the same people. He is the object of everyone's scorn, for he claims to be a faithful servant of Yahweh, yet Yahweh does not answer his prayers.

Mock at me in verse 7a is the general term for deride, make fun of; and line **b** uses two verbal phrases that specify how people make fun of him.

In verse 7b the Hebrew is literally "they shoot out the lips" (see similar language in 35.21; Job 16.10), an expression of derision. As Anderson says, it is "obviously a gesture of scorn, although its exact nature is unknown." Dahood has "they gape at me"; NEB is like RSV; Weiser translates "open wide their mouths in derision"; NJV "they curl their lips." SPCL "they make faces at me" and TEV "**they stick out their tongues**" are cultural equivalents.

Wag their heads is another gesture of derision (the verb used here in the Septuagint is the same one used in Mark 15.29). Languages do not appear to lack for terms for derision; for example, "to talk about someone with laughter" or "to pile words on someone's head." Some languages prefer expressions referring to facial or other body gestures; for example, "they shook their heads at them" or "they flapped their lips at them."

22.8

RSV	TEV

"He committed his cause to the
  LORD; let him deliver him,
  let him rescue him, for he de-
  lights in him!"
	"You relied on the LORD," they
	  say.
	  "Why doesn't he save you?
	  If the LORD likes you,
	    why doesn't he help you?"

Verse 5 is a direct quotation of what the psalmist's enemies say about him; this should be made explicit, as TEV does by having "**they say.**"

In the Masoretic text the verb in line **a** is in the imperative mood, "rely"; with the Septuagint, Syriac, Vulgate, and Jerome the Hebrew consonants are given other vowels, and the verb becomes "he relied." Most translators follow this text; TOB and NJV, however, translate the Masoretic text's imperative. The verb means "to roll" and is taken to mean "He rolled (his cause, his suffering) on the LORD." Dahood has another derivation: "he lived for Yahweh." TEV uses direct address, "**You relied on the LORD**," instead of the third person of the Hebrew text (see RSV). In some languages this shift may be helpful, but care should be taken to make clear that in verse 9 "you" is God, to whom the psalmist speaks. **He committed his cause** means that the psalmist (referred to in the third person by his enemies) depended on Yahweh to take care of him. Translations vary: "trusts in" (NIV), "trusted himself to" (NJB). In some cases this must be expressed in an idiomatic manner; for example, "he hung his heart on the LORD" or "he rested on the LORD."

Let him deliver him: this is the way in English of expressing the third person imperative (so most English translations), which translators may prefer to follow. TEV use of the second person of direct address, "**You**," makes it easier to use a question form, which emphasizes the elements of scorn and derision.

The two verbs **deliver** and **rescue** are synonymous, two different ways of saying the same thing. TEV has also restructured the second half of the verse, making it a scornful question.

He delights in him can be understood as "Yahweh delights in the psalmist" or "the psalmist delights in Yahweh"; the former seems more likely. The meaning can be expressed by "the LORD is his friend," or "the LORD coves (or, likes) him."

The taunts are all the more devastating because they imply that the psalmist was lying when he claimed that he had depended on the Lord and that the Lord loved him. To the psalmist's enemies it is clear, from the fact that the Lord has done nothing to help him, that the Lord really does not care for him. See the use of the language in Matthew 27.39,43; Mark 15.29; Luke 23.35.

22.9-10	RSV	TEV
9	Yet thou art he who took me from the womb; thou didst keep me safe upon my mother's breasts.	9 It was you who brought me safely through birth, and when I was a baby, you kept me safe.
10	Upon thee was I cast from my birth, and since my mother bore me thou hast been my God.	10 I have relied on you since the day I was born, and you have always been my God.

Yet: turning once more from his distress, the psalmist now bases his hopeful plea for help (verses 9-11) on his own past experience of the Lord's faithful care (verses 9-10).

With expressive figures the psalmist speaks of Yahweh's care of him ever since he was born. In verse 9a the verb "draw out" (**took . . . from**) is used only here in the Old Testament; the psalmist does not actually mean that the Lord pulled him out of the womb, but, as TEV expresses it, he brought him safely through birth. **Took me from the womb** may normally be kept closer to the pictorial language of the Hebrew than TEV has chosen; for example, "you are the one who brought me out of my mother's womb." If the figurative language of the Hebrew is inappropriate, the translator can follow the model of TEV. If the figurative language is retained in 9a, then it will be appropriate to do so in 9b.

My mother's breasts in line **b** is a way of referring to the time when he was a baby, while he was still being nursed. Some translations take the two lines as descriptive of what happens at the birth of a child. So NEB "But thou art he who drew me from the womb, who laid me at my mother's breast" (see also FRCL). This may be used if the translator is certain the readers will not understand that in a literal fashion God did the work of a midwife.

In verse 10a the language, as Dahood points out, implies that the Lord had adopted him: "I was placed in your custody." NJV has "I became Your charge at birth." SPCL, somewhat differently, "Even before I was born I was entrusted to your care." RSV **Upon thee was I cast** is not a natural English expression.

In verse 10b the language is literally "from the womb of my mother my God (are) you." This does not mean that as a newborn baby the psalmist had acknowledged Yahweh as his God, but that from his birth God had cared for, protected, him. NJB has "from the womb I have belonged to you." **Hast been my God** must often be recast, since God may not be thought of as being possessed; for example, "you have been the God who watches over me" or ". . . the God who takes care of me."

22.11   RSV   TEV

Be not far from me,   Do not stay away from me!
   for trouble is near   Trouble is near,
   and there is none to help.   and there is no one to help.

The psalmist uses the two spacial terms **not far** and **near** to emphasize the danger he is in. In some languages it may be more natural to phrase the request in positive terms, "Stay close to me." In this case the second line can be "for trouble is not far away."

The **trouble** refers to the enemies around him (verses 12-13). The expression **trouble is near** presents a problem for some languages, since such abstracts are not naturally associated with space, that is, in being in a position. However, one may often say "my enemies who trouble me are near."

22.12-13   RSV   TEV

12 Many bulls encompass me,   12 Many enemies surround me like
       strong bulls of Bashan sur-   bulls;
       round me;   they are all around me,
13 they open wide their mouths at   like fierce bulls from the land of
       me,   Bashan.
       like a ravening and roaring lion.   13 They open their mouths like lions,
                                               roaring and tearing at me.

In Hebrew verse 12 is chiastic, a syntactic device frequently used to give variety to the poetic form. Translators need not follow this form but should be aware that the poet has deliberately shifted word order in the two lines. Chiasmus is one of the syntactic techniques in Hebrew poetry for marking stanza boundaries. (See also verse 16.)

The psalmist compares his enemies to fierce bulls and ferocious lions. TEV has turned into a simile ("**like . . . bulls**") what is in Hebrew a metaphor (**bulls**). Why his enemies attack him is not made clear, but the picture of the psalmist's complete helplessness before them is dramatically drawn.

In verse 12 line a emphasizes the number of his enemies (**Many**), and line b their power (**strong**).

Bashan was a territory on the east side of the Jordan River, with good grazing fields, famous for its cattle (see also Amos 4.1 "cows of Bashan"). In those areas where neither the cow nor the bull is known, a local substitute may be used. Since the bulls represent the psalmist's enemies, it will be more meaningful to make this explicit, as in TEV. It will normally be necessary to add a note indicating the location and the significance of Bashan. But, like GECL, a translation may choose to omit the place name **Bashan**, since its function here is simply that of an adjective meaning "fierce" or "wild."

In verse 13 **they open** refers back to the "many enemies" spoken of as **bulls** in verse 12a; it is unlikely that the figure of **bulls** is still in the psalmist's mind, as RSV implies. The reader should not be led to think that bulls open their mouths like lions. Since the reference is to the way the enemies behave, it may be best to make this explicit. In languages where the lion is not sufficiently known it may be necessary to introduce a classifier; for example, "wild animal called lion" or replace lion by a local animal of similar traits. If neither of these possibilities is open, one may simply say "wild animal."

The figure of **a ravening and roaring lion** is similar to the ones used in 7.2; 17.12.

22.14	RSV	TEV
	I am poured out like water, and all my bones are out of joint; my heart is like wax, it is melted within my breast;	My strength is gone, gone like water spilled on the ground. All my bones are out of joint; my heart is like melted wax.

The psalmist describes his condition in vivid terms, which are not necessarily descriptive of physical ailments, but rather of his utter distress and misery (so Weiser). Some scholars, however, particularly in verse 15, see these as symptoms of fever or the like (see Kirkpatrick).

The figure **poured out like water** in line a seems to describe complete exhaustion, utter weakness. TEV uses similes instead of metaphors, and expands line a into two lines in order to bring out more clearly the force of **poured out**. The expression **poured out like water** can have a variety of meanings in different languages. TEV restructures the expression to make the meaning of "weakness" clear.

All my bones are out of joint: the psalmist says his bones are separating from one another; it is as though the process of total decay were already far advanced.

22.14

The figure **my heart is like wax . . . melted** means the psalmist has lost all courage and hope (see a similar figure in Josh 7.5). Lines 14cd of RSV have been reduced to one line in TEV, omitting **within my breast** (Hebrew "bowels") as being redundant. The term used in many translations for **wax** refers specifically to beeswax. Any substance which is readily melted and known for that characteristic will serve.

22.15	RSV	TEV

RSV	TEV
my strength is dried up like a potsherd, and my tongue cleaves to my jaws; thou dost lay me in the dust of death.	My throat*h* is as dry as dust, and my tongue sticks to the roof of my mouth. You have left me for dead in the dust.

h Probable text throat; *Hebrew* strength.

In line <u>a</u> TEV (as well as NEB, NAB, NJB, BJ, FRCL, GECL, SPCL, ZÜR) follows a conjecture, "**My throat**," for the Masoretic text **my strength**, which RSV prefers. HOTTP says that it is possible that "**My throat**" was the original text, but stays with the Masoretic text, since there is no ancient witness in support of "**My throat**."

A **potsherd** is a piece of broken clay jar, completely dry and brittle. TEV substitutes "dust" for **potsherd**. While potsherds are found in many parts of the world, they are not always associated with expressions for "dryness." If translators follow the wording of "**throat**," they should find an idiomatic expression which will render the idea of dryness in the throat. Simply saying "my throat is dry like a broken pot" will in most cases communicate nothing of the extreme degree of a parched throat.

The word which RSV translates **jaws** occurs only here in the Old Testament. It is more natural in English to speak of the tongue sticking to the roof of the mouth (TEV) than of it sticking to the jaws. What has been said about **potsherd** also applies to **jaws** in 15b.

In the last line the psalmist attributes his desperate condition to Yahweh himself. Dahood, however, takes the verb form as being third feminine (not second masculine), in a collective sense, "they put me" (so AT), and NEB changes to passive, "I am laid low." The majority, however, take the Masoretic text to mean that the psalmist is saying that it is Yahweh who has brought him to the brink of death. **The dust of the earth** is a poetic phrase for the grave, recalling also Sheol as a place of dust (see Job 7.21; Psa 7.5, 90.3).

22.16	RSV	TEV

RSV	TEV
Yea, dogs are round about me; a company of evildoers encircle me; they have pierced*m* my hands and feet—	A gang of evil men is around me; like a pack of dogs they close in on me; they tear at*i* my hands and feet.

m Gk Syr Jerome: Heb *like a lion*   *i Some ancient translations* they tear at; *others* they tie; *Hebrew* like a lion.

In verses 16-18 the psalmist pictures himself as practically dead, as his enemies close in and tear at him like a band of wild dogs. Afterward, as though he were already dead, they proceed to gamble for his clothes.

In this verse the psalmist calls his enemies **dogs**; TEV has turned the metaphor into a simile, "**like a pack of dogs**," placing "A gang of evil men" in line <u>a</u> (for RSV **a company of evildoers** in line <u>b</u>).

In line <u>c</u> the Masoretic text begins "like a lion"; the Septuagint took the Hebrew to be a form of the verb "to dig" (as in 7.15); Aquila, Symmachus, and Jerome took the Hebrew to be a form of the verb "to tie" (and two Hebrew manuscripts have "they tie"); there are other explanations as well.[1] No one solution can be dogmatically proposed as the correct one; the majority of translations use a word appropriate to the action of "a pack of dogs." FRCL and TOB, however, have "they tie." NJV attempts to stay with the Masoretic text by translating "like lions [they maul] my hands and feet."

	22.17-18 RSV		TEV
17	I can count all my bones— they stare and gloat over me;	17	All my bones can be seen. My enemies look at me and stare.
18	they divide my garments among them, and for my raiment they cast lots.	18	They gamble for my clothes and divide them among themselves.

I can count all my bones (verse 17a) pictures the psalmist as dead, his flesh stripped off (as by dogs) and his bare skeleton lying in public view; or else, with no logical connection with verse 16, the psalmist sees himself as so weak and thin that he is nothing more than skin and bones, and this is a much more likely interpretation. (RSV's line <u>a</u> in verse 17 is actually a parenthetic expression, marked by a dash before and after; this means that **they stare** refers to the same people as "they have pierced" in verse 16, but most readers will not recognize this fact.) In some languages it may be unnatural to speak of counting one's bones, even in a poetic discourse, and the passive construction of TEV may not be available. In such cases it may be necessary to say, for example, "I can see all my bones." TEV has provided a subject, "**my enemies**," which is necessary because the antecedent of the pronoun **they** is quite distant.

RSV translates the second verb in verse 17b by **gloat over**, while TEV has "stare." The Hebrew verb is the same one used in 10.14 (where it is parallel with "see") and 13.3 and means, quite generally, "regard, notice," in parallel with the first

---

[1]See BJ; K-B *Lexicon* under *'arah* II; Dahood; Weiser. HOTTP says that the Masoretic text appears to be a plural participle, "(they are) mangling" ("B" decision).

verb "look"; so FRCL has "they look at me fixedly." It may be that the context allows for the meaning **gloat over**, and the translator should feel free to use a word that means that.

In verse 18 **my garments** in line a and **my raiment** in line b are synonyms, both referring to the psalmist's clothes; the **raiment** is not a piece of clothing different from the **garments**. (In John 19.23-24 the quotation from the Septuagint of this passage is taken to mean separate items of clothing.)

The psalmist's enemies **cast lots** (probably small marked stones) to determine who will get his clothes. The parallelism in verse 18 focuses upon the general word **divide** in line a and the specific word **cast lots** in line b. Again, the word order in the second line is the reverse of the first line. The Hebrew text does not mean that two different actions were performed, that is, the division of some items of clothing and then the casting of lots for another item. The meaning is that by means of casting lots they divided the psalmist's clothes among themselves. **Cast lots** in RSV is replaced by the more generic "gamble" in TEV. By using "gamble" before "**divide,**" TEV succeeds in giving the impression that these lines describe the whole procedure for apportioning the clothing. Games of chance are not universal. Therefore it will be necessary in some languages to avoid both the specific expression and the generic one. One may, however, speak of getting something by playing a game against someone; for example, "they played a game to see who would get my clothes" or "they held a contest to see who would win my clothes."

22.19-21	RSV	TEV

	RSV	TEV
19	But thou, O LORD, be not far off! O thou my help, hasten to my aid!	19 O LORD, don't stay away from me! Come quickly to my rescue!
20	Deliver my soul from the sword, my life[n] from the power of the dog!	20 Save me from the sword; save my life from these dogs.
21	Save me from the mouth of the lion, my afflicted soul[o] from the horns of the wild oxen!	21 Rescue me from these lions; I am helpless[j] before these wild bulls.

[j] *Some ancient translations* I am helpless; *Hebrew* you answered me.

[n] Heb *my only one*
[o] Gk Syr: Heb *thou hast answered me*

In these verses the psalmist once more pleads desperately with the Lord to save him from his enemies, whom he calls **dog**, **lion**, and **wild oxen**.

Verse 19a is practically the same as verse 11a. In verse 19b RSV **my help** translates a word meaning "strength, power," found nowhere else in the Old Testament. TEV has failed to represent this phrase, which can be translated "My helper, come quickly to my rescue!" or "My helper, come quickly and rescue me!"

In verse 20a **Deliver my soul** (TEV "Save me") translates "save my *nefesh*" (see 3.2). The parallel in line b is the adjective used as a noun, "my only one," which in parallel with "my *nefesh*" always refers to something like "the only life I will ever have"; so RSV **my life**, as in 35.17. There is no need to imitate RSV and provide the literal Hebrew phrase in a footnote. Some may have "the life that is precious to me." NAB translates "my loneliness," which it explains as "his desolate soul," but this is not a good model to follow.

From the sword in verse 20a means "from violent death"; and verse 20b is literally "from the hand of the dog," where "hand" means **power**. Dahood and NEB take the Masoretic text to mean "from (the blade of) the ax," but this interpretation is not certain. TEV has **"these dogs,"** and in verse 21 **"these lions"** and **"these wild bulls,"** to indicate that these are metaphors for cruel enemies, not animals.

Deliver my soul from the sword presents a particularly difficult set of problems for a translator. In many languages it is not possible to be saved from an inanimate object such as a sword. In these cases it may be possible to say, for example, "Don't let my enemies kill me with their swords" or "Protect me from the swords of my enemies." If the term **sword** is not familiar, it is better to say, for example, "Don't let my enemies kill me."

In verse 21 there is a parallel between **the mouth of the lion** and **the horns of the wild oxen**, both of them metaphors for the psalmist's enemies.

In line b of verse 21 the Masoretic text is "and from the horns of the wild oxen you answered me." Instead of the Masoretic text "you answered me," the Septuagint, Syriac, and Jerome have translated as though the Hebrew text were "my oppressed (self)," without a verb in this line; so TEV, RSV, AT, NAB, BJ, NJB; NEB has "my poor body." But some stay with the Masoretic text, in the sense of "you defended me"—so Kirkpatrick.[2] TOB separates it from the preceding words and makes it independent, as the beginning of the next section: "You have answered me!" Weiser and NJV translate it as though it were an imperative, "Answer (or, Rescue) me!" Dahood has another way of handling the Masoretic text: "make me triumph." It seems better to follow the Versions, as RSV and TEV have done, and it is preferable to join line b with line a as RSV has done, as part of the psalmist's plea, with the verb of line a carrying over into line b. In line with the HOTTP recommendation, however, a translator may choose to follow the Masoretic text, taking the verb "to answer" in the sense of "to defend" or "to rescue," as follows: "You have rescued (or, protected) me from the horns of the wild oxen."

For **wild oxen** see *Fauna and Flora of the Bible,* page 63.

22.22 RSV	TEV
I will tell of thy name to my brethren; in the midst of the congregation I will praise thee:	I will tell my people what you have done; I will praise you in their assembly:

[2] HOTTP stays with the verb "to answer" ("B" decision) and says it can be translated "you will answer me" (an expression of confidence), or "answer me" (a prayer), or "you have answered me" (an expression of gratitude).

In the second section of the psalm (verses 22-31), the psalmist turns to praise and thanksgiving, promising to give thanks in public (in the Temple) for what Yahweh has done (verses 22-24).

In line a of verse 22, **thy name** stands for the things that Yahweh has done and which have brought him fame: "I will tell my people the things for which you are famous."

My brethren are the psalmist's fellow Israelites, and the **congregation** is the people gathered for public worship in the Temple. One must be careful in translation not to give the idea that the psalmist is speaking of his male siblings. In many languages "**my people**" will refer to one's relatives, which in a sense is in line with the reference to his fellow Israelites. If the meaning is too restricted to the family group, it is possible to employ an expression such as "the people of my tribe."

In some languages it will be best to render **in the midst of the congregation I will praise thee** as "where the people meet to worship you, I will praise you."

22.23-24　　　　　RSV　　　　　　　　　　　　　　　TEV

23	You who fear the LORD, praise him! all you sons of Jacob, glorify him, and stand in awe of him, all you sons of Israel!	23	"Praise him, you servants of the LORD! Honor him, you descendants of Jacob! Worship him, you people of Israel!
24	For he has not despised or abhorred the affliction of the afflicted; and he has not hid his face from him, but has heard, when he cried to him.	24	He does not neglect the poor or ignore their suffering; he does not turn away from them, but answers when they call for help."

TEV takes verses 23-24 as the content of the psalmist's praise, and so places them within quotation marks (see also FRCL). NJV does the same but restricts the direct quote to verse 23.

The people are called **You who fear the LORD** (that is, who worship, serve, obey him), and in Hebrew "seed of Jacob" and "seed of Israel" for **sons of Jacob . . . of Israel**, synonymous phrases meaning Israelites in general (for "seed" meaning descendants, see comments at 18.50).

Fear the LORD should not be translated by a term which merely implies fright. More significant than the reaction of fright is that of awesome respect. In some languages it will be necessary to combine both reverence and worship or obedience; for example, "You who respect and worship the LORD."

In verse 23 there are three parallel verbs: **praise**, **glorify**, and **stand in awe**, literally "be afraid of" (see 33.8, where it is parallel to another verb meaning "to fear").

Glorify him in the sense of showing honor to God may be expressed in terms of the way one uses words; for example, "say that God is great" or "speak well of

God." It is sometimes possible to render the idea of honor in terms of attitude; for example, "show great respect for him" or "have good thoughts about him." Finally, one may refer to the position of the body; for example, "bow down before him" or "kneel in front of him."

Sons of Jacob in TEV is "descendants of Jacob." In some languages descendants are spoken of as "ones who came down from Jacob" or "those who followed grandfather Jacob." And RSV sons of Israel is represented in TEV by "people of Israel."

RSV takes verse 24 as referring to Yahweh's past actions, while TEV, by use of the present tense of the verbs, represents the continuous or repeated actions of Yahweh in response to people's needs.

RSV represents the Hebrew form, with the two verbs followed by the one compound object, the affliction of the afflicted. TEV has realigned the various semantic elements, using two verbs and two direct objects, which makes for a more natural and clear statement in English (so NEB).

For hid his face see discussion of 13.1; it means disregard, not notice, not answer. And heard means to respond to cries for help and to act. For English style it is better, with TEV, to make the object plural, "them," not singular him of RSV.

In line a, for the afflicted see comment at 9.12. Instead of the noun the affliction (as RSV translates) Dahood derives the word from a verb meaning "to sing," and translates "the song of the afflicted," a proposal that Anderson endorses. NJV, somewhat differently, has "the plea of the lowly."

22.25-26	RSV	TEV
25	From thee comes my praise in the great congregation; my vows I will pay before those who fear him.	25 In the full assembly I will praise you for what you have done; in the presence of those who worship you I will offer the sacrifices I promised.
26	The afflicted[p] shall eat and be satisfied; those who seek him shall praise the LORD! May your hearts live for ever!	26 The poor will eat as much as they want; those who come to the LORD will praise him. May they prosper forever!

[p] Or poor

In these two verses the psalmist states that he will keep his promise, and that in return for the Lord's blessings he will offer to the Lord his thanksgiving offering in the Temple.

Line a of verse 25 is literally "From you my praise in the large assembly" (RSV From thee comes my praise in the great congregation). As Anderson remarks, "God is both the source and the object of the writer's praise." TEV has taken "from you" to mean "you are the reason why," and represents this by "(I will praise you) for what you have done." Thus one may translate "you are the theme of my praise." SPCL follows a slightly different text (see Taylor): "I will praise your faithfulness."

The expression **great congregation** is found also in 35.18; 40.9,10; it means the same as "congregation" in verse 22.

In line <u>b</u> the verb **pay** translates a Hebrew verb meaning to be whole or complete; so here it means "I will offer (all) the sacrifices I promised (to make)." It is better in English to speak of offering sacrifices that the psalmist had promised, rather than RSV **my vows I will pay**. The expression "**offer the sacrifices**" requires in some languages a descriptive phrase such as "to give God the gifts of burned animals."

Notice that RSV follows the Hebrew in switching from the second person of address in line <u>a</u> (**thee**) to the third person in line <u>b</u> (**him**). TEV has the second person in both lines, which is easier to understand.

In this kind of thank offering there was a fellowship meal (see Lev 3.1-5) in which the worshipers ate part of the sacrificed animals. In verse 26 the psalmist declares that **the afflicted** (see comments on 9.12), whom he has invited to the meal, **shall eat and be satisfied**. FRCL makes this explicit: "I will invite the humble; may they eat as long as they are hungry!"

In verse 26b **those who seek him** (see comment at 9.10) is parallel with **those who fear him** in verse 25b; these are the worshipers, who come into the presence of Yahweh (**seek him**) in the Temple.

In the last line the psalmist wishes health, prosperity, happiness, for all his guests. TOB translates "A long and happy life to you!"; NJV "Always be of good cheer"; SPCL "may you (plural) live many years"; or one can say "Long life to you all!" BJ, NJB, and NAB take this line as the praise offered by those who are sharing in the meal. RSV **your** may not be readily understood as referring to the people mentioned in the two previous lines. It may be better to follow TEV and use here the third person plural, in agreement with lines <u>a</u> and <u>b</u>.

Many languages have set expressions to wish someone special health and long life, particularly in connection with feasting and drinking. In some cases such phrases are too limited in their context and may be objectionable for use in the Scriptures. It may be necessary when using such expressions to employ a more complete clause construction; for example, "May God give you happiness forever" or "God give you good things all your life."

22.27-28	RSV	TEV
27	All the ends of the earth shall remember and turn to the LORD; and all the families of the nations, shall worship before him.^q	27 All nations will remember the LORD. From every part of the world they will turn to him; all races will worship him.
28	For dominion belongs to the LORD, and he rules over the nations.	28 The LORD is king, and he rules the nations.

^q Gk Syr Jerome: Heb *thee*

The psalm closes (verses 27-31) with a proclamation of the universal reign of Yahweh in the future.

NEB, FRCL, and SPCL translate verse 27 as a command (or a prayer): "Let all nations . . . ."

The two phrases **the ends of the earth** and **all the families of the nations** are used synonymously, meaning "all nations, all races"; **families** is used here in the broad sense of tribe or race. In some languages **all the ends of the earth** may be rendered "all the tribes of the world."

The verbs **remember**, **turn to**, and **worship** express the actions of repentance and adoration, in which "to remember" means to call Yahweh to mind, to acknowledge him, in acts of confession and praise (see 6.5). If one uses TEV, to **"remember the LORD"** may have little meaning in some languages, or may merely mean that those who have forgotten him will recall him. For this reason it will sometimes be preferable to translate this expression "remember to praise the Lord." The expression **families of the nations**, if translated literally, will have little meaning in some languages, and the TEV term **"races"** must often be translated "tribes" or "clans."

At the end of verse 27, the Masoretic text has "before you"; RSV justifies the change to the third person **him** on the basis of ancient versions; but the change of pronouns in Hebrew is quite frequent, and no textual variant need be sought to justify translating **him** (see Anderson; and notice verse 25, where "from you" in line a is followed by "him" in line b—both referring to Yahweh).

It is well to follow RSV at the beginning of verse 28 and say **For** or "Because" as the reason why in the future all people will worship Yahweh. **Dominion belongs to the LORD** is better translated "The LORD is ruler" or, as some translations have it, "Kingly power belongs to the LORD." FRCL and SPCL are like TEV.

22.29	RSV	TEV
	Yea, to him*r* shall all the proud of the earth bow down; before him shall bow all who go down to the dust, and he who cannot keep himself alive.	All proud men will bow down to him;*k* all mortal men will bow down before him. *k* *Probable text* will bow down to him; *Hebrew* will eat and bow down.

r Cn: Heb *they have eaten and*

This verse presents difficulties in text and exegesis, and translations vary considerably. The Hebrew text has three lines; the first one is "they have eaten and they will bow down, all the fat ones of the earth." The solution proposed by Briggs and others (followed by RSV, NAB, TEV, BJ, NJB, SPCL) is that in place of the Masoretic text "they have eaten" the text should be "indeed to him," and the "and" before the next word should be removed. But TOB, NJV, and HOTTP all follow the Masoretic text.

The phrase in the Masoretic text, "All those in full vigor shall eat and prostrate themselves" (NJV), is understood differently by Dahood and others (NAB, NEB;

Toombs, Weiser). Others change the Masoretic text "fat ones" to "those who sleep," meaning the dead in Sheol; so FRCL "even those who sleep in the underworld." This certainly offers a more fitting parallel to line b, which has "before his face will bow all who go down to the dust"—that is, all mortal beings—or perhaps, "all who are about to die" (TOB).

The translator may wish to follow the Masoretic text, in which "shall eat" does not make much sense in the context. NIV probably comes as close to making sense as any: "All the rich of the earth will feast and worship," this line contrasting with the following "all who go down to the dust." Or else the translator may choose to follow the emended text represented by RSV and TEV. **All the proud of the earth**, depending on which wording the translator follows, may be rendered in some languages by idiomatic expressions; for example, "those who walk with their noses high," "those who have big thoughts of themselves," "those who speak great words of themselves."

All who go down to the dust will have no reference to death in many languages. "Mortal men" may be rendered "people who die." The translator must make certain that they are not said to die as the result of bowing down to the Lord.

Line c (which Weiser omits as a later doctrinal addition) is literally "and his *nefesh* he cannot keep alive" (so RSV; TEV has combined it with **"mortal men"** in line b as another way of speaking of **who go down to the dust**; SPCL has "for they have no life in themselves"). But others translate this differently: NEB (and similarly NAB, JB) "But I shall live for his sake" (in which the Masoretic text *lo'* "not" is changed, with ancient versions, to *lo* "for him"). TOB has "he [Yahweh] has not let them live."

22.30-31 RSV TEV

	RSV		TEV
30	Posterity shall serve him; men shall tell of the Lord to the coming generation,	30	Future generations will serve him; men will speak of the Lord to the coming generation.
31	and proclaim his deliverance to a people yet unborn, that he has wrought it.	31	People not yet born will be told: "The LORD saved his people."

In verse 30a the Hebrew for **Posterity** is simply "seed, generation"; but one Hebrew manuscript and the Septuagint have "my seed"; so NEB, NAB, JB, SPCL. In some languages **Posterity** or **"future generations"** may be rendered "people who are not yet born."

In this verse **Lord** is the title (see comment at 8.1), not the proper name Yahweh.

The coming generation (verse 30b) involves a slight change in the text. The Masoretic text has "to the generation 31 they will come"; instead of the Masoretic text "they will come," TEV follows the Septuagint, which indicates "coming" as part of verse 30.

In verse 31 the word which RSV has translated **deliverance** and TEV **"saved"** is taken here by BJ, NJB, NAB to mean "justice, righteousness"; the interpretation of RSV seems preferable in this context. Care should be taken in line a not to appear to say that some people, before they are born, will be told of how Yahweh saved his people. Something like the following may be said: "In the future, people who at this time have not even been born will be told . . . ." In languages where passive constructions are rare or not used, one may say, for example, "people will tell others who have not yet come into the world, 'The LORD saved his people.' "

That he has wrought it: the psalm ends with the declaration "that (or, because) he acted" (that is, he intervened and saved his people). TEV puts this into direct discourse, "**The LORD saved his people**." SPCL has "they will tell of his justice and of his deeds."

Psalm 23

This psalm—probably the most widely known in all the Psalter—is a song of confidence by one who has experienced Yahweh's love and care. The most common interpretation is that which sees two word pictures: Yahweh as shepherd (verses 1-4) and as host (verses 5-6). Some, however, try to make the whole psalm fit the category of the shepherd metaphor; others see an additional metaphor, that of guide (verses 3-4). Nothing in the text indicates who the author was; he has known danger (verse 4) and persecution from enemies (verse 5), but Yahweh has protected him and led him.

The reader of this psalm will search in vain for the typical type of parallelism in which the second line repeats and emphasizes similar words found in the first line. In fact, aside from verse 2, the line halves are very different in meaning and length. Furthermore there is a lack of symmetry, an absence of word pairing, of chiastic patterns, of envelope figure—all of those features which tend to give a poem its particular shape. There is, on the other hand, an economy of words, a terseness of style. However, as Kugel points out, the basic structure of a first line plus short pause, followed by a second related line with longer pause, is just as much present in this psalm as elsewhere where this high rhetorical style is found in the Hebrew Scriptures. In Kugel's view the essence of paralleling is not two lines which say more or less the same thing in slightly different words, but rather what he calls "first part—pause—next part—bigger pause." This is diagrammed as:

In this view the rough limits on the length of the clauses and the equivalences of words in the two clauses is secondary. "B, being connected to A—carrying it further, echoing it, defining it, restating it, contrasting with it, *it does not matter which*—has an emphatic 'seconding' character, and it is this, more than any aesthetic of symmetry or paralleling, which is the heart of biblical parallelism."[1]

In view of this the translator is faced in this psalm with the same basic structure of parallelism as in the preceding psalms.

Another feature of the psalm which gives close unity to verses 1-4 is lexical cohesion. That is, the following words are drawn from the central theme of shepherding: shepherd, lie down, green pastures, lead, still waters, restore, paths, walk, valley, rod, and staff. In verses 5-6 the imagery shifts, but the wider theme of care and protection carries on to the end.

---

[1]Kugel, *The Idea of Biblical Poetry*, page 51.

HEADING: "**The LORD Our Shepherd**" (TEV); "Shepherd and host"; "The good shepherd"; "You, LORD, are with me"; "The LORD, shepherd and host." In languages which have a term for shepherding animals, the TEV heading may sometimes be adjusted to say, for example, "The LORD is the one who shepherds us." In other languages it may be necessary to say "The LORD is the one who takes care of us." Some translators have added a simile, "as a man takes care of sheep." However, in some areas where animals are not cared for, this added expression will only distract from the central meaning. Even where the term for shepherd can be used, the translator must avoid an ambiguous meaning which may imply that the Lord is caring for the psalmist's sheep. This ambiguity can be avoided by saying "The LORD is the one who shepherds me," or by using two verb phrases, "The LORD is my shepherd and takes care of me."

<u>Hebrew Title</u>: **A Psalm of David**.

23.1	RSV	TEV
	The LORD is my shepherd, I shall not want;	**The LORD is my shepherd; I have everything I need.**

Parallelism may not appear evident in this verse. However, it is the dependence of line <u>b</u> on line <u>a</u> to complete its sense that makes the second line parallel to the first. In some languages this dependence will have to be more explicitly stated.

Yahweh is often spoken of as the **shepherd** of Israel (see 28.9; 77.20; 78.52; and especially Ezek 34.11-16). In many languages where domestic animals such as sheep, camels, or llamas are cared for, the translation of **shepherd** normally presents no difficulty. However, in those parts of the world where domestic animals such as sheep and goats wander freely as scavengers, there may be no term for shepherd, and the practice of tending such animals is largely unknown. Even in some parts of the world where sheep are raised, a shepherd is a person sent out to look after the sheep because such a person is either too young or too incompetent to do more serious tasks. Therefore it is essential in any situation to consider the connotations attached to the local practice of shepherding. In this verse the shepherd is **the LORD**, and the best translations may be the ones suggested in the comments on the title.

I shall not want: the verb means to lack, to be without, not to have (see 8.5, where the verb means "be less"). NJB and NJV have "I lack nothing"; NIV "I shall not be in want." Knox's rhetorical question is effective: "how can I lack anything?" The use in English of the verb **want** (RSV, NAB, NEB) can be misunderstood, since the usual meaning of "to want" is "to desire."

In some languages it will be necessary to make clear the relation between Yahweh being one's shepherd and the consequence of not lacking anything; for example, "Because the LORD is my shepherd, I shall not lack anything" or "The LORD is the one who watches over me; therefore I shall have need of nothing."

	23.2	RSV	TEV

<table>
<tr><td>

he makes me lie down in green
    pastures.
He leads me beside still waters;[s]

</td><td>

He lets me rest in fields of green
    grass
and leads me to quiet pools of
    fresh water.

</td></tr>
</table>

[s] Heb *the waters of rest*

The sameness of word order, semantic similarities and line length of the two clauses make the parallelism in this verse quite obvious. In line **a** "he causes me to lie down" is paralleled in line **b** by "he leads me," and the same is true of the paired expressions at the end of the two lines. The movement between the two lines is nearly static. They simply say that **a** is so, and **b** is so.

He makes me lie down: the causative form of the verb "to lie down" does not have the sense of "he forces me to lie down," as RSV **he makes me lie down** seems to say (also NEB, NJV, NIV). The idea is that the shepherd finds a place (**green pastures**) where the sheep can lie down and rest. So NJB "he lets me lie."

Green pastures: places in fields or meadows where the grass is abundant, a good place for the sheep to graze and rest. This may need to be rendered "fields where there is much grass to eat" or "good fields to graze in."

Still waters translates "waters of quietness." NJV has "water in places of repose"; SPCL "brooks of quiet waters." Also possible is "refreshing streams." This is not a stagnant pool, but a place where the fresh water flows gently, making it easy for the sheep to drink it. In some languages this is "streams of fresh water" or "rivers with good water."

	23.3	RSV	TEV

<table>
<tr><td>

he restores my soul.[t]
He leads me in paths of righteous-
    ness[u]
    for his name's sake.

</td><td>

He gives me new strength.
He guides me in the right paths,
    as he has promised.

</td></tr>
</table>

[t] Or *life*
[u] Or *right paths*

He restores my soul: this line is literally "He causes my *nefesh* to return" (for *nefesh* see comment at 3.2). The meaning is to restore vitality, vigor, strength; to renew, invigorate. This statement seems to express the result of Yahweh's care, as described in verse 2. GECL, in fact, makes this line a continuation of the sentence in the previous verse, ". . . and [you] give me new strength."

He restores my soul must sometimes be rendered in idiomatic terms; for example, "he puts a new heart in me" or "he makes my liver like new."

The phrase **paths of righteousness** has been variously understood. Anderson proposes "paths which lead to happiness"; NJV (like TEV) has "right paths"; SPCL "straight paths"; FRCL "the good (or, pleasant) way." If the figure of a shepherd leading his sheep is still uppermost in the psalmist's mind, the meaning must be that the paths are those which avoid dangerous places and which lead to abundant pastures, where the sheep may graze in safety and tranquillity.

For his name's sake: the phrase "on account of his name" occurs also in 25.11; 31.3; 79.9; 106.8; 109.21; 143.11. It means in the first instance "for the sake of his reputation" (see Anderson); NJV, NJB, and Dahood translate "as befits his name"; SPCL, somewhat differently, "bringing honor to his name." TEV has taken "name" here to stand for Yahweh's reputation as one who keeps his promises (see discussion of "name" at 5.11); see Toombs: "because that is the kind of God he is"; FRCL "because he is the shepherd of Israel." And Taylor comments: "the good shepherd will not be false to himself."

The expression **for his name's sake**, if it is to have any meaning, requires some recasting, as in TEV. In the first place there must often be some connection between being led in "the good paths" and "his name's sake." This may be a relation of reason and result. One may sometimes say "he leads me along straight paths because he is that kind of Lord." In terms of reputation it is possible to render lines b and c as "he leads me on straight paths because that is what he is known for" or "because he is the shepherd of his people, he leads me along straight paths."

23.4 RSV TEV

Even though I walk through the valley of the shadow of death,ᵛ I fear no evil; for thou art with me; thy rod and thy staff, they comfort me.	Even if I go through the deepest darkness, I will not be afraid, LORD, for you are with me. Your shepherd's rod and staff protect me.

ᵛ Or *the valley of deep darkness*

In this verse the psalmist switches from the third person (**The LORD is**) to the second person of direct address (**thou art with me**). Translations may follow the Hebrew, as RSV and TEV have done; or else, like GECL, they may cast all the psalm in the second person, beginning with verse 1, "You, LORD, are my shepherd . . . ."

The valley of the shadow of death: the Hebrew word translated **valley** is translated in the Septuagint by "the midst" (so Dahood, "in the midst of total darkness"). And the word traditionally translated **the shadow of death** elsewhere means simply darkness (see 44.19; 107.10; Job 3.5; 10.22; 12.22; 16.16; Isa 9.2). As it appears here in the Masoretic text, however, the word may be taken as a compound, meaning "darkness of death" (so the Septuagint). Most modern translations avoid the word "death": GECL "dark valley"; Weiser "the valley of deep darkness"; FRCL "the dark valley"; SPCL "the darkest of all valleys." "A dark ravine" (with footnote) is another suggestion. But NEB has "a valley dark as death," NJB "a ravine as dark as death," and TOB "a ravine of shadow and death." The word itself does not necessarily mean death; but by definition a dark ravine is a dangerous place. For a discussion of this and other matters in this psalm, see John Eaton, *The Bible Translator* 16.171-176.

If the translator follows the exegetical suggestion "darkness of death," it will sometimes be necessary to say, for example, "if I go through the darkness that is like death" or "if I go through darkness where there is no life."

The word translated **evil** means here danger, harm, injury.

The **rod** was a club used to drive away wild animals; the **staff** was a long stick used for support in walking. Kirkpatrick takes the two words to be a poetic description of the shepherd's crook, using two names for the one instrument. So FRCL "your shepherd's rod, that is what reassures me." Most translations, however, have two different words. TEV has used the traditional "**rod and staff**"; but since there will be many readers who will not know what these are, TEV qualifies them with "**Your shepherd's rod and staff.**"

They comfort me: the verb "to comfort" means here to provide assurance, security, safety. NAB has "give me courage"; TOB, FRCL "reassure me"; SPCL "fill me with confidence."

The expression **thy rod and thy staff they comfort me** may require in some languages more adjustments than have been made in TEV. In some areas there is nothing known as a special instrument for herding animals. In some cases it will be necessary to indicate that these instruments are not simply possessed but are carried by the shepherd; for example, "the rod and staff which you carry." In some areas these will simply be known as "the club and the cane" or "the stick." In some languages it may be better to express the meaning in nonfigurative language: "You protect me and keep me safe," "You protect me from all harm and danger."

23.5	RSV	TEV

	Thou preparest a table before me
	  in the presence of my enemies;
	thou anointest my head with oil,
	  my cup overflows.
		You prepare a banquet for me,
		  where all my enemies can see
		    me;
		you welcome me as an honored
		    guest
		  and fill my cup to the brim.

In this verse the figure changes from Yahweh as shepherd to Yahweh as host. The background may be that of the fellowship meal which followed the thanksgiving sacrifice in the Temple (see 22.26; see Anderson).

Thou preparest a table refers to the preparation of a meal or a feast.

Since Yahweh is the host, the presence of the psalmist's **enemies** is no threat to him; he is under Yahweh's protection and care. There may be a tone of derision, as the psalmist taunts his enemies by reminding them that they cannot harm him.

Thou anointest my head with oil: to rub a guest's head with olive oil was part of the prescribed etiquette followed by a solicitous host as he welcomed his guests; it was neglected by the Pharisee Simon, as he received Jesus (Luke 7.46). Since the custom and its meaning are unknown to the average English-speaking reader, TEV has abandoned the figure and expressed the meaning with "**you welcome me as an honored guest.**" FRCL keeps the figure and explains it: "You receive me by pouring a bit of perfumed oil on my head."

In languages where there are terms which symbolize the receiving of guests, **thou anointest my head with oil** may be substituted by the equivalent expression in the receptor language. Where there are no such equivalent expressions or practices, the translator normally has two choices: (a) to explain the anointing with oil without reference to the custom, as in TEV; or (b) to explain it and retain the reference to the custom. In the latter case one may say, for example, "you welcome me as an honored guest by rubbing my head with oil."

The **cup** which the host offers his guest is filled to the brim with wine, a gesture of generosity. Some take the Hebrew word translated **overflows** (which occurs only here in the Old Testament) to mean intoxicating, that is, the wine is strong and fully satisfies the guest's desires. This does not seem very likely.

The expression **my cup overflows** lacks an agent who causes this to happen, and one is supplied in TEV, **"you ... fill my cup to the brim."** However, in some languages it will be necessary to make clear that the cup refers to the one which the guest is drinking from; for example, "you fill the cup I drink from to the very top" or, if it is not advisable to use "cup," "you give me all I can drink."

23.6 RSV	TEV
Surely[w] goodness and mercy[x] shall follow me all the days of my life; and I shall dwell in the house of the LORD for ever.[y]	I know that your goodness and love will be with me all my life; and your house will be my home as long as I live.

[w] Or *Only*
[x] Or *kindness*
[y] Or *as long as I live*

Surely translates a conjunction that gives emphasis to what follows; it can be rendered "I am certain (or, sure) that." Or else the word can mean "Only," so that the translation can be "Nothing but your goodness and love."

Mercy translates the word which in 5.7 is translated "steadfast love." Yahweh's "goodness and love" are pictured as his messengers, which accompany the psalmist (see similar language in 43.3; 85.10-11).

TEV has recast **goodness and mercy** into **"your goodness and love."** In some languages it is not possible to speak of abstract qualities as following or accompanying someone. It is more often natural for someone to do or be characterized by these qualities. Therefore it is sometimes necessary to say, for example, "because you are good and because you love me, you will be with me all my life."

The verb translated **follow** means "to accompany," "to go with"; it should not be given the meaning of "to pursue, to run after."

I shall dwell: the verb appears in the Masoretic text as a form which means "I shall return" (so FRCL); but the Hebrew consonants can be read with other vowels (following the Septuagint) to mean **I shall dwell**, which is done by most commentators and translations.[2]

The house of the LORD is most probably a reference to the Temple. The meaning of the psalmist's declaration is that he wants to worship Yahweh in the Temple all his life or, in an extended sense, always to experience Yahweh's presence and power with him. Dahood, however, takes **the house of the LORD** to be Yahweh's heavenly abode, in which the psalmist wants to live forever. The expression **the house of the LORD** may be the local designation of a church building. If that is the case, it will be better to speak of the Temple in Jerusalem.

For ever: the Hebrew phrase "length of days" at the end of the verse is taken by most to mean "a very long time," "**as long as I live**" (TEV, FRCL, GECL; see 21.4; 91.16). NJV has "for many long years," NJB "for all time to come," and SPCL "and in your house, O LORD, I will live always."

---

[2]HOTTP says that all ancient versions and ancient Jewish grammarians took the verb to mean "to sit down, to dwell." There are two possible interpretations: (1) "and I shall dwell" or (2) "and I shall return."

Psalm 24

Like Psalm 15, this psalm is a liturgy that was to be used by pilgrims as they came to the Temple in Jerusalem for a religious festival. The psalm begins with a hymn of praise to Yahweh as creator and lord of the universe (verses 1-2). This is followed by a liturgy used by the pilgrims as they request permission to enter the Temple: the question is asked as to who may enter (verse 3), followed by the answer (verses 4-6). The last part of the psalm (verses 7-10) demands entrance for Yahweh, who is probably represented by the Covenant Box, which is being taken into the Temple.

This brief psalm is based upon the refrain or chorus in which a "who" question is followed by audience response. The refrain not only provides for audience participation but also serves to give structure to the psalm. Verses 1-2 are statements, each verse consisting of two parallel lines. There are three refrains in verses 3, 8, 10, followed in each case by responses. The key word "raise" with its variants is found in verse 3 "ascend," "stand"; verse 4 "not lift up"; verse 7 "lift up," "be lifted up"; and verse 9 "lift up," "be lifted up." These words, along with the repeated refrain form, provide cohesion between the two halves of the psalm, verses 1-6 and verses 7-10.

HEADING: "**The Great King**" (TEV); "The king of glory"; "At the gate of the Temple"; "Yahweh is the king of glory." In adapting the TEV heading, it may be necessary to make clear that it is God who is king, "God is the great king."

Hebrew Title: **A Psalm of David**.

24.1-2	RSV		TEV
1	The earth is the LORD's and the fulness thereof, the world and those who dwell therein;	1	The world and all that is in it belong to the LORD; the earth and all who live on it are his.
2	for he has founded it upon the seas, and established it upon the rivers.	2	He built it on the deep waters beneath the earth and laid its foundations in the ocean depths.

In the opening hymn of praise (verses 1-2), the two lines of verse 1 are parallel, both of them stating that the earth and all things and beings on it belong to Yahweh; literally "To Yahweh (belong) the earth and its fulness, the world and those who dwell in it." This includes all created things, animate and inanimate, human and animal.

Earth and **world** are not distinguished here in their meanings. The Hebrew word translated **earth** is simply the general term and is far more common than the Hebrew term translated **world**. In many translations it will not be possible to find synonyms. Consequently one must sometimes say "The world and everything on it belong to the LORD; all the people on it are his too" or "Everything in the world belongs to the LORD; even all the people belong to him."

Fulness thereof means everything that is in the world, all the objects and beings that fill it.

For: as translated by RSV and others, this gives the justification for the statement in line a about Yahweh's complete dominion over the world.

In verse 2 RSV uses the past perfect of the verbs (**has founded . . . established**); TEV's simple past ("**built . . . laid**") seems more appropriate, since the verbs refer to the act of creation.

Verse 2 is also made up of two parallel lines, both of them saying the same thing about how Yahweh created the world. The two verbs, "to found, establish" and "to make firm" (see 7.9), are nearly synonymous, as are the two nouns **the seas** and **the rivers**, both of them referring to the vast subterranean ocean, "**the deep waters beneath the earth**" (TEV; see Gen 7.11; Exo 20.4; Psa 136.6), upon which the earth rested. **The earth** was thought to be supported by pillars (the "foundations"), which were also the bases of the mountains (see 18.7,15; 1 Sam 2.8; Pro 8.29; Jonah 2.6), which reached down to the underworld. For a more complete description of the Hebrew view of the world, see the discussion and illustration at 104.5-6. Simply to translate the two words literally by **the seas** and **the rivers**, as RSV has done, fails to convey the meaning of the original. NJV "the ocean . . . the nether-streams" is hardly an improvement. SPCL has combined and shortened the lines as follows: "For the Lord laid the foundations of the earth, and placed it firm on the seas and the rivers." Here "the seas and the rivers" is also misleading. **The seas** and **the rivers** were probably used quite commonly as a pair of terms with poetic effect in Hebrew, but this effect will usually be lost in translation.

He has founded it upon the seas is difficult to translate, where the largest body of water is a local river. However, the switch from **seas** to "**deep waters**," as in TEV, provides a model. Furthermore, it will often be necessary to provide a footnote which will clarify this Hebrew view of the universe.

24.3	RSV	TEV

Who shall ascend the hill of the LORD? And who shall stand in his holy place?	Who has the right to go up the LORD's hill?[n] Who may enter his holy Temple?
	[n] THE LORD'S HILL: The hill in Jerusalem on which the Temple was built.

Verses 3-6 are an "entrance liturgy" in which the pilgrims ask about require-ments for entering the Temple (verse 3) and are answered, probably by priests (verses 4-6), in a fashion similar to that in Psalm 15.

The hill of the LORD is Mount Zion (see comment at 2.6), and **his holy place** is the Temple. The pilgrims want to know what Yahweh requires of those who want to worship in his Temple (see TEV "**has the right . . . may**"). RSV **shall ascend . . . shall stand** may convey merely the idea of simple future tense, as if the psalmist simply wants to know who will go up Mount Zion and go into the Temple. But the question is about what kind of person will be allowed to worship in the Temple. So NEB "Who may go up . . . who may stand," FRCL "Who will be allowed," and GECL "Who has access to the Lord's hill? Who dares walk on the holy ground?" are much better. The two verbs **ascend** and **stand** picture the pilgrims chanting as they go up the Temple mount and stop before the entrance to the Temple.

The translator may wish to make explicit that the purpose of climbing Mount Zion and entering the Temple is to worship Yahweh. **His holy place** or "his holy Temple" may sometimes be translated as "the Temple that has been dedicated for worshiping the LORD" or "the worship house which the people have set apart for worshiping God."

24.4	RSV	TEV

He who has clean hands and a
   pure heart,
who does not lift up his soul to
   what is false,
and does not swear deceitfully.

Those who are pure in act and in
   thought,
who do not worship idols
or make false promises.

Verses 4-6 are the answer to the question in verse 2.

Hands and **heart** stand for deeds and thoughts, external actions and internal motivations. **Clean hands** in some languages will have no reference to proper behavior, and in most languages will require recasting, as in TEV "**pure in act**," which may be expressed as "those who do right" or "those who have good thoughts." However, if a figure is available, it should be used.

Line **b** in the Hebrew text followed by RSV and TEV is "who does not lift up his *nefesh* to a lie" (for *nefesh* see comment at 3.2, and for "lie" see comment at 12.2). Here (as in 31.6; Jonah 2.8) the word "lie" probably refers to "**idols**" (TEV, NIV, SPCL; so Dahood and others). Some, however, take the line to mean "who does not love (or, practice) lies" (see AT, NEB); Weiser has "who does not direct his thoughts to wrongdoing."

It should be noted that most translators follow the text of many Hebrew manuscripts and ancient versions, "his *nefesh*"; but the Masoretic text has "my *nefesh*," which is explained as a synonym for "my (that is, Yahweh's) name," and the sense of the line is "who does not use the LORD's name for false purposes" (see Exo

24.4

20.7).[1] So NJV translates "who has not taken a false oath by My life"; similarly TOB "who does not use God for an evil purpose."

If the translator follows the idea of worshiping idols, it may be possible to say, for example, "who do not worship images of God" or "who do not pray to likenesses of God." **Idols** may sometimes be called "gods made of wood" or "stone gods."

In the third line **swear deceitfully** is generally taken to mean "to make false promises" or "to bear false testimony under oath"; it can, however, as a parallel to the preceding line, mean "or use the name of an idol in making a promise" (see Dahood).

24.5   RSV   TEV

He will receive blessing from the   The LORD will bless them and
   LORD,   save them;
and vindication from the God of   God will declare them innocent.
   his salvation.

In line a the verb **will receive** is literally "he [that is, the person] will carry [a **blessing from the LORD**]."

TEV has expressed the three nouns **blessing**, **vindication**, and **salvation** by three verbal phrases: "bless . . . save . . . declare innocent." **Blessing from the LORD** is often rendered "good things from the LORD."

The Hebrew word translated **vindication** (TEV "declare . . . innocent") is a noun which may mean "righteousness, deliverance, salvation," and sometimes "prosperity." Dahood translates "generous treatment"; FRCL "approval"; NEB, TOB, BJ "justice"; NAB "a reward." NJB has "saving justice," and NJV "a just reward." TEV's **declare them innocent** may require some restructuring; for example, "God will say they have no fault." If it is preferable to transform this into direct discourse, one may say "God will say, 'You are without fault.'"

The phrase **the God of his salvation** (see 18.46) means "God, his savior" (NIV) or "the God who saves him." FRCL "his God, the Savior," is better than TEV's **and save them.**

As seen in RSV, **LORD** in line a is parallel to **God of his salvation** in line b. TEV has broken the latter title into components and shifted "save them" to line a. This requires restructuring the parallelism. The result is a shifting of focus from the one (or persons) being described in verses 3-6, to focus on the Lord, who is not highlighted until verses 7-10. The translator should make every effort to keep the focus upon the person who is allowed to "stand in his holy place." This may have to be done by saying, for example, "He is the one whom the LORD blesses; the very one whom the saving God declares innocent" or "They are the people whom . . . ."

---

[1]In the Masoretic text the *ketiv* is "his *nefesh*"; the *qere* is "my *nefesh*." HOTTP does not consider this passage.

	RSV	TEV

24.6

Such is the generation of those
who seek him,
who seek the face of the God of
Jacob.^z   *Selah*

Such are the people who come to
God,
who come into the presence of
the God of Jacob.

^z Gk Syr: Heb *thy face, O Jacob*

The word **generation**, as in 12.7, refers to people who have certain moral qualities. **Such is the generation** may be rendered sometimes as "The people are like this" or "The people who come to God are like this."

The two synonymous Hebrew verbs for **seek** are used in the sense of going to the Temple to worship Yahweh. If a rendering like TEV **"come into the presence"** is used, care should be taken that the readers not understand that the psalmist was talking about going to heaven.

In line **b** the Masoretic text has "those who seek your face, Jacob"; two Hebrew manuscripts and Syriac have "your face, God of Jacob" (the Septuagint has "those who seek the face of the God of Jacob"), which is the meaning preferred by TEV, RSV, NEB, NAB, NJB, BJ, SPCL.[2]

For *Selah* see comments on 3.2.

24.7

	RSV	TEV

Lift up your heads, O gates!
and be lifted up, O ancient doors!
that the King of glory may come
in.

Fling wide the gates,
open the ancient doors,
and the great king will come in.

In verse 7 the pilgrims demand that the Temple gates be opened to admit entrance to the Lord, who is probably represented by the Covenant Box, which is being carried in by Levites. (In 2 Sam 6.2 the Covenant Box bears the name of the Lord Almighty; and in 1 Sam 4.21, when the Covenant Box is captured by the Philistines, God's glory departs from Israel.) From inside the Temple the priests (verse 8a) ask who demands entry, to which the procession replies (verse 8b,c).

The poetic language, **your heads, O gates . . . O ancient doors**, refers to the Temple gates. It is not certain what the word **heads** means, if indeed it refers poetically to some part of the gates; NAB takes it to mean "the lintels," the horizontal pieces above the gates; JB "arches." **Gates** in line **a** and **doors** in line **b** are two different ways of speaking of the same thing, that is, the Temple gates. Some translations therefore combine the two and have only "Open wide, eternal gates!" or something similar (see GECL, SPCL). Commentators suggest that the meaning is

---

[2]HOTTP prefers "your face, Jacob" ("B" decision) but does not explain what this means. A translator should only prefer the vocative "Jacob" if he or she makes clear to the reader what it means.

hat the gates are too small for such a great king, the Lord, to enter, and so they are commanded to raise their lintels in order to make room for the king to enter. Most translations have the idea of "raising" or "lifting up," but TEV has used the more natural expressions "**Fling wide . . . open**," which are directed not to the gates themselves but to the Levites in the Temple who were responsible for opening them. It should be noted that the Hebrew expression "lift up the head" can mean "rejoice." The translator must decide if the gates are to be opened or if they are to rejoice. In many languages the decision will be made in favor of the former, since inanimate objects such as gates do not rejoice.

The **ancient doors** points to the fact that Jerusalem was already an ancient city when David captured it. Some, however, take the word to mean "eternal," reflecting the idea that the gates of the sanctuary were the earthly counterpart of the heavenly dwelling of God, and that when the earthly gates were opened the heavenly gates also opened.

The **King of glory** (verses 7c, 8a) is the majestic, mighty, victorious king. For **glory** as an attribute of kings, see comments on 21.5. In languages where "glory" means life in heaven, the genitive phrase **King of glory** may suggest that the title means "King of heaven." But **of glory** has the force of an adjective, "glorious." GECL has "mightiest king . . . mighty king."

24.8	RSV	TEV
	Who is the King of glory?	Who is this great king?
	The LORD, strong and mighty,	He is the LORD, strong and
	the LORD, mighty in battle!	mighty,
		the LORD, victorious in battle.

In answer to the priests' question in line a, the pilgrims reply in lines b, c.

Verse 8a is a question asked perhaps by the priests, the same as in the reply given in verse 4. But there is likely to be some misunderstanding of the reading unless the change of speakers is clearly marked. This may be done outside the text or within the text.

The great king is described as **strong and mighty**, **mighty in battle**. This should be represented quite literally of strength and might in fighting battles.

24.9-10	RSV		TEV
9	Lift up your heads, O gates!	9	Fling wide the gates,
	and be lifted up,*a* O ancient		open the ancient doors,
	doors!		and the great king will come in.
	that the King of glory may come	10	Who is this great king?
	in.		The triumphant LORD—he is the
10	Who is this King of glory?		great king!
	The LORD of hosts,		
	he is the King of glory!		
	Selah		

a Gk Syr Jerome Tg Compare verse 7:
Heb *lift up*

    The same ritual is followed in verses 9-10 as in verses 7-8: the demand for entry (verse 9), the request for identification (verse 10a), and the final statement (verse 10b,c).

    In verse 9b the Masoretic text has the active "lift up," but a few Hebrew manuscripts, as well as the ancient versions, have the passive "be lifted up," as in verse 7.[3]

    The final answer (verse 10b) identifies the great king as "Yahweh of hosts." The word translated **hosts** means "army" (see 44.9; 60.10; 68.12; 108.11); in 1 Samuel 17.45 Yahweh is identified as the leader of the Israelite armies (see Psa 89.8). In some places in the Old Testament, **hosts** is used of the angels, and the idea in the title may well mean that Yahweh is sovereign over all powers, heavenly as well as earthly. The Hebrew word has been transliterated into English and other languages ("Sabaoth"; see KJV James 5.4); it is variously translated as "almighty, all-powerful, supreme" (see TOB, SPCL). Most English translations have used the word "hosts," which does not mean much to the average Bible reader. **LORD of hosts** is sometimes rendered "LORD of the armies." Since the focus is upon the powerfulness of the Lord, the expression may often be rendered, for example, "the LORD who is the strongest of all" or "the LORD who has more power than anyone."

---

[3]Most translations see no need to have a textual footnote as RSV does. The meaning in verse 9b is exactly the same as in verse 7b, regardless of the form of the Hebrew verb followed.

Psalm 25

This psalm is a lament by an individual who prays to God for help in his troubles (verses 2,3,16-18a,19-20), for forgiveness (verses 7,11,18b), and for guidance (verses 4-5). The psalm is one of the nine acrostic psalms (see Psa 9–10): each verse begins with a different letter of the Hebrew alphabet, going in order from *alef*, the first letter (verse 1), to *taw*, the last letter (verse 21). There are, however, some places where the device is not maintained: the letter *waw* (which should come as the last line of verse 5) is not represented in the Masoretic text (a few manuscripts include it), nor the letter *qof* (which should be verse 18); and the last verse is outside the scheme altogether. NJB follows an acrostic sequence, from "Adoration" in verse 1 to "Virtue" in verse 21, improving on the original by providing the right letter ("s" in English) at the beginning of verse 16.

Some scholars feel this psalm does not maintain a regular progression of thought, but switches abruptly from one subject to another, and from personal plea to impersonal statement. The difficulty of composing an acrostic poem may account for this. Anderson suggests a general division into three parts: (1) verses 1-7, prayers for help, guidance, forgiveness; (2) verses 8-14, God's character and attributes; (3) verses 15-21, another series of petitions for help. The last verse (verse 22) is a general prayer on behalf of Israel.

However, the structure of Psalm 25 may also be seen as a balanced set of petitions interlaced with praise and assurance. Following the opening address of praise and trust, there are two sets of petitions. These are followed in verses 8-10 by praise to God. Verse 11 is again a single petition followed in verses 12-15 by a statement of assurance of security for the one who obeys the Lord. Then in verses 16-18 the psalmist petitions the Lord to deliver and forgive him, and in verses 19-22 there is a final set of petitions, culminating in a request for the redemption of Israel. This alternation of themes may be listed as follows:

Address of praise and trust	1-2a
1st Petition	2b-3
2nd Petition	4-7
Praise	8-10
3rd (Central) Petition	11
Assurance	12-15
4th Petition	16-18
5th Petition	19-22

In spite of the limitations imposed by the acrostic feature, the poet has constructed a highly regular and symmetrical pattern in which a single petition for forgiveness stands at the center of the psalm, with two sets of petitions on either side. The theme of forgiveness is repeated in the inner petitions, 2 and 4. And "enemies" is repeated in the outer petitions, 1 and 5. The transformation from individual concern to that of the entire people takes place only in the closure, "Redeem Israel." In this way the psalmist closes abruptly through a sudden switch from exclusion to inclusion.

HEADING: "**A Prayer for Guidance and Protection**" (TEV); "Prayer in danger"; "Prayer for guidance and help"; "Prayer asking for God's guidance." The TEV heading may require shifting from noun phrases to complete clauses; for example, "The psalmist prays for God to guide him and to protect him."

Hebrew Title: **A Psalm of David**.

The Masoretic text has simply "by David"; the word "psalm" is probably implied. RSV supplies it everywhere the word is not used in the Hebrew text.

25.1-2	RSV	TEV
1	To thee, O LORD, I lift up my soul.	1 To you, O LORD, I offer my prayer;
2	O my God, in thee I trust, let me not be put to shame; let not my enemies exult over me.	2 in you, my God, I trust. Save me from the shame of defeat; don't let my enemies gloat over me!

To "lift up the *nefesh*" (verse 1) means to pray to God, to worship him (see 86.4; 143.8). NJB has "Adoration . . . I offer to you." NJV, however, translates "I set my hope on You." The idea of prayer or adoration seems quite suitable here.

The expression **I lift up my soul** requires considerable recasting to express its meaning. TEV's "**I offer my prayer**" suggests a model for many languages. However, since it is often necessary to speak of prayer as talking to God, one must include both elements of worship and of speaking with God; for example, "LORD, I speak with you and I worship you" or "LORD, I talk to you when I worship you."

The phrase **my God**, with which verse 2 begins, is placed in the Masoretic text at the end of the previous line in verse 1 in order to make the second line begin with the letter *bet* (the first letter of "**in you**"), which is the second letter of the Hebrew alphabet. The expression **my God, in thee I trust** presents two problems for many languages, since God cannot be possessed like other objects. Therefore one must sometimes say, for example, "God, you whom I worship" or "God, you are the one I worship." The second problem is that for some languages the idea of trusting is expressed in metaphorical language; for example, "to put one's heart on" or "to lie down on." The full line may then be rendered sometimes "O God, whom I worship, I place my heart upon you."

For **shame** see comments on 6.10; either the shame of defeat, or of misfortune and disgrace. TOB translates the line "Do not disappoint me"; FRCL "Do not leave me disillusioned." One of the worst things about the psalmist's defeat, or disgrace, would be that his enemies would make fun of him (see 22.7-8). The expression **let me not be put to shame** may be handled as in TEV, where "defeat" is the cause of the shame the psalmist would suffer. Following the suggestion of making a request, one may say, for example, "do not let me be sorry that I trusted in you."

The verb translated **exult** is used in 5.11 and 9.2, where RSV translates "exult [in thee]." This line requests the same thing as the preceding line, that is, that Yahweh keep the psalmist's enemies from defeating him. The relation between the two lines should be clear in translation. The expression **exult over me** may sometimes be rendered as "do not let them make fun of me," "do not let them laugh at me," and "do not let them say that I am nothing."

25.3	RSV	TEV

RSV	TEV
Yea, let none that wait for thee be put to shame; let them be ashamed who are wantonly treacherous.	Defeat does not come to those who trust in you, but to those who are quick to rebel against you.

Yea translates the initial word of the verse; here, however, its main function is to fit the acrostic scheme. TEV therefore omits it for reasons of style.

The psalmist asks that the **shame** of disgrace or defeat should not come to those who **wait for** Yahweh. This verse is understood as a statement by TEV, NEB, NJB, FRCL; but RSV, NJV, NAB, GECL, SPCL understand it as a request, which seems to fit the context better. The Hebrew verb **wait for** expresses an attitude of hope, expectation, confidence.

TEV "**Defeat does not come**" must in many languages be recast to say, for example, "Those who trust in you will not be defeated" or, stated positively, "Those who trust in you will defeat their enemies."

In line b **are . . . treacherous** (TEV "**to rebel**") translates a verb meaning to deal treacherously with, in the sense of being a traitor or a rebel. The adverb means "without cause" or "in vain"; so NJB "groundlessly" (see 7.4). It can mean "unsuccessfully"; so NJV "empty-handed." NEB, BJ, SPCL have "without cause"; NAB "heedlessly." TEV has taken it in the sense of "without motive," and so translates "quick to rebel"; RSV **wantonly** means needlessly, without justification.

25.4-5	RSV		TEV

	RSV		TEV
4	Make me to know thy ways, O LORD; teach me thy paths.	4	Teach me your ways, O LORD; make them known to me.
5	Lead me in thy truth, and teach me, for thou art the God of my salvation; for thee I wait all the day long.	5	Teach me to live according to your truth, for you are my God, who saves me. I always trust in you.

The two lines of verse 4 are parallel and synonymous: **thy ways** and **thy paths** refer to the conduct, the way of life that Yahweh requires of those who worship him; and the verbs **make me know** and **teach me** mean the same in this context. FRCL translates line b "teach me to live as you want me to." It is often necessary to supply a verb in such expressions which will bring into focus the participation of the one speaking; verse 4a, for example, "Teach me to follow your ways, O LORD." Also in verse 4b of RSV, "Teach me to walk on the paths which you show me."

In verse 5 Yahweh's **truth** is his will for his people; some take it to mean here faithfulness, either the psalmist's faithfulness to Yahweh or Yahweh's faithfulness in keeping his promises (for example, "Guide me by your faithfulness"; Dahood "to walk faithful to you"; see also 26.3). The expression **Lead me in thy truth**, if understood to mean the will of God, can sometimes be rendered "Teach me to obey what you want your people to do" or "Show me the way you want your people to go." If **thy truth** is understood as God's faithfulness, then it is possible to speak of the psalmist's response to that faithfulness; for example, "Make me know that I can trust you completely" or "Teach me that I can rely on you."

Line a of verse 5 has two verbs, **Lead** and **teach**. TEV has combined them, "Teach me to live," and SPCL has made them closely parallel, "Guide me, lead me in your truth," which may be the best model to follow.

For **the God of my salvation**, see comment on 24.5; for **wait** see verse 3. TEV "always" translates the Hebrew phrase "the whole day."

It should be noted that NEB, BJ, JB (also NAB footnote) transfer the words of verse 7c, "on account of your goodness, O LORD," to the end of verse 5. It is not necessary to do this.

25.6	RSV	TEV

Be mindful of thy mercy, O LORD,	Remember, O LORD, your kind-
and of thy steadfast love,	ness and constant love
for they have been from of old.	which you have shown from
	long ago.

The psalmist pleads with Yahweh to remember how he, Yahweh, has always manifested **mercy** (or "kindness") and **steadfast love** (or "faithfulness"; see 5.7) for his people, ever since the beginning of their history. If Yahweh calls to mind what he did in the past, he will do the same in the present time.

The major problem in the translation of verse 6 is that the two noun phrases, **thy mercy** and **thy steadfast love**, which the psalmist asks God to remember, are events which God has done. Therefore it will often be more natural to express these as clauses; for example, "Remember, O LORD, how you have been kind to your people and how you have showed them your great love" or "Do not forget, O LORD, how you have always been kind and loved your people."

They have been from of old: see SPCL, "which you have always manifested to us"; NJV has "they are old as time"; NEB "shown from ages past." Something like "which you have always done for us in the past" or ". . . always done ever since you have been our God" seems to be the best way to translate this phrase.

RSV   TEV

> Remember not the sins of my
> youth, or my transgressions;
> according to thy steadfast love
> remember me,
> for thy goodness' sake, O LORD!

> Forgive the sins and errors of my
> youth.
> In your constant love and good-
> ness,
> remember me, LORD!

On the basis of Yahweh's attitude toward his people, the psalmist prays for himself. **Remember not [my sins]** is equivalent to "Forgive [my sins]"; the psalmist prays that God will not keep a record of the **sins** and **transgressions** (or, wrongs; see 19.13) he committed when he was young. So "Do not recall . . ."; see FRCL "Don't think any longer about . . . ." **The sins of my youth** must often be recast as two clauses; for example, "the sins I did when I was a young person."

On the contrary, the psalmist wants the Lord to remember him on the basis of his—the Lord's—**steadfast love** and **goodness**. The two noun phrases may be translated as clauses, "Because you love (your people)," and "because you are good (to your people)."

The last two lines (as in RSV) are not precisely parallel: "according to your constant love, remember me, on account of your goodness, Yahweh." But the thought is parallel, and TEV has combined the two elements (also SPCL); NJV translates the third line "as befits Your goodness, O LORD." The semantic parallelism is contained in the two contrasting petitions, **remember not** in line a and **remember me** in line b. However, in translation it may not be possible to retain the parallelism in this manner. If "remember me" simply means to recall who I am, it will be better shift to "think about me," "be good to me," or "take care of me."

In some languages it will be necessary to restructure the last two lines of this verse as reason and request; for example, "because you always love your people and are good to them, remember me, LORD."

RSV   TEV

8   Good and upright is the LORD;   8   Because the LORD is righteous
    therefore he instructs sinners in   and good,
    the way.   he teaches sinners the path they
9   He leads the humble in what is   should follow.
    right,   9   He leads the humble in the right
    and teaches the humble his way.   way
                                             and teaches them his will.

Good and upright: these are the two qualities which characterize Yahweh's dealings with his people; he is kind, good, generous, and he is also fair and just, always doing what is right.

In verse 8 **the way** is Yahweh's will for sinners; and the Hebrew verb for **instruct** is the one from which the Hebrew word for "Law" (*torah*) is formed. TOB's footnote comments that **sinners** here are those who miss the right path they should take. TEV makes verse 8 two propositions, the first the reason and the second the result.

It will sometimes be necessary in translation to shift from the two modifiers **good and upright** by saying, for example, "the LORD is good and always does what is right." It may be necessary in some languages to speak of the Lord judging fairly, since judging is closely related to God's righteousness; for example, "God is good and judges people fairly."

In verse 9 the two lines are parallel. **The humble** are those who trust in God, not in themselves (see 9.12, where RSV has "the afflicted"). The two verbs **he leads** and **teaches** are parallel verbs; and **what is right** in line a (see 7.6) is defined in line b by **his way**, that is, the way he wants his people to follow, to live.

Verse 8 ends in **way**, and the same Hebrew root is used in the verb in verse 9, **leads**, with the noun repeated again at the end of verse 9, **way**. In this manner the psalmist has given cohesion to the two verses. In line b of verse 9, **teaches** is the more specific development of **leads** in line a.

He leads the humble may have to be expressed in some languages in a negative manner; for example, "he leads people who do not feel proud," or stated idiomatically, "he leads people who do not have swollen hearts."

25.10	RSV	TEV
	All the paths of the LORD are steadfast love and faithfulness, for those who keep his covenant and his testimonies.	With faithfulness and love he leads all who keep his covenant and obey his commands.

Verse 10, although printed in the Hebrew Bible as a two-part line, is lacking in any of the characteristics of parallel lines. It is a single statement with no seconding and related second part attached.

The first line, **All the paths of the LORD are steadfast love** (see 5.7) **and faithfulness** (see comments on "truth" in 15.2), means that Yahweh's faithfulness and love are manifested as he leads his people (see SPCL "He always acts with love and truth with those . . .").

In line b **his covenant and his testimonies** may be a literary figure known as hendiadys, that is, the two express one subject, "the commands of his covenant." For the word translated **testimonies** (TEV "commands") see comments at 19.7b (where it is parallel with "law" in verse 7a). The **covenant** is the agreement, the pact, between Yahweh and the people of Israel, which Yahweh gave them at Mount Sinai and which the people promised to obey (see Exo 24.3-8); it was the fundamental charter for the nation.

The difficulty in expressing the phrase **his covenant** arises from the fact that God's covenant results not from bargaining with his people, but rather from God's initiative. Furthermore, the keeping of the covenant depends upon God's faithfulness in spite of his people's failings in the relationship. Most languages can only supply terms in which it is people who reach agreements, pacts, alliances. While these terms must be used, it will almost always be necessary to give a more detailed note in the footnotes or glossary to explain the unique features of the covenant with God.

<u>25.11-12</u>   RSV   TEV

11   For thy name's sake, O LORD,   11   Keep your promise, LORD, and
        pardon my guilt, for it is great.   forgive my sins,
12   Who is the man that fears the   for they are many.
        LORD?   12   Those who obey the LORD
     Him will he instruct in the way   will learn from him the path they
        that he should choose.   should follow.

For the phrase **For thy name's sake** in verse 11a, see comment at 23.3.

The verb translated **pardon** (TEV **"forgive"**) in verse 11 is used in the Psalms only here and at 103.3; the related adjective "forgiving" appears in 86.5 and nowhere else in the Old Testament.

<u>Guilt</u> is the (painful) awareness of having sinned, the sense of being culpable of wrongdoing. But the Hebrew word in this context is better represented by the wrong or evil actions performed, that is, wickedness (NEB), iniquity (NJV, NIV), sin (NJB), evil (SPCL), wrongdoings (FRCL). See its use in 18.23a, where the same comment applies.

The question in verse 12a (RSV) is not a request for information but is a forceful way of identifying the person whom Yahweh instructs in line <u>b</u>. Such a literary device is not very common in English and may be misunderstood by the reader. Consequently TEV has used a descriptive statement (using the plural form), "**Those who obey the LORD.**" Another way of handling this is "Whoever obeys the LORD . . . ." Or else, "If anyone wants to obey the LORD, the LORD will teach that person the way (or, path) to follow." For the phrase "fear the LORD," see comments at 5.7.

If in verse 12b the translator chooses to keep the focus on Yahweh as the main actor, the translation can be "will be taught by him" (instead of "**will learn from him**"). If the verb "to teach," with its possible implications of a classroom, is not naturally applied to God in this context, the more general verb "to show" or "to tell" can be used.

<u>25.13-14</u>   RSV   TEV

13   He himself shall abide in prosperi-   13   They will always be prosperous,
        ty,   and their children will possess
     and his children shall possess   the land.
        the land,   14   The LORD is the friend of those
14   The friendship of the LORD is for   who obey him
        those who fear him,   and he affirms his covenant
     and he makes known to them   with them.
        his covenant.

In verse 13 **He himself** translates the Hebrew "his *nefesh*."

The verb translated **abide** means in other passages "to spend the night." Here it means "to continue, to stay." **Abide in prosperity** should not be translated in such a manner as "to have wealth," for this is too limiting. Furthermore, in many languages it will be necessary to state the source of the prosperity, that is, God. One may say, for example, "The LORD will always give them good things" or "The LORD will always bless them with a good life."

Children translates the word "seed," meaning descendants, offspring (see comment on 18.50). In this context the affirmation in verse 13b is that the descendants of those who obey Yahweh will continue to live in the land of Israel (see especially 37.9,11,22,29), that is, they will not be driven out of the land by their enemies. So it may be preferable to translate "their descendants will possess (or, continue to live in) the land." In some languages **possess the land** may be rendered "own the land" or "be owners of the land."

In verse 14 the noun translated **friendship** has in some contexts the specific meaning of "secret," either in a good sense of advice and counsel, or in a bad sense of a plot (see 64.2). Anderson suggests that here, in parallel with **his covenant** in line b, the word may mean "counsel" (so NJV); NEB has "confides his purposes," FRCL "confides his secret," and NJB "possess his secret," with a footnote stating that this means "intimacy with God." The main point is the intimate relationship which Yahweh's followers have with him. Here, as elsewhere, to **fear** Yahweh means to honor, respect, obey him.

In verse 14b **makes known** seems to have the sense of affirming, not that of disclosing for the first time. Or else, like FRCL, "he teaches them the duties of the covenant," or "he teaches them what his covenant requires of them." The verb is an infinitive, "to make known to them," and so some take "covenant" as the subject, not the object ("his covenant will impart knowledge to them"); this is not very likely. **Make known to them his covenant** should not be translated in such a way as to imply that they did not know what the covenant was. If the translator follows the lead of TEV, it may be possible to say, for example, "he reminds the people that his covenant is true" or "he tells the people, 'My covenant with you is real.' "

25.15-16	RSV	TEV

15	My eyes are ever toward the LORD, for he will pluck my feet out of the net.	15	I look to the LORD for help at all times, and he rescues me from danger.
16	Turn thou to me, and be gracious to me; for I am lonely and afflicted.	16	Turn to me, LORD, and be merciful to me, because I am lonely and weak.

From verse 15 to verse 21 the psalmist again pleads with Yahweh for help against his enemies, whose precise nature and the threat they pose are not specifically stated.

In verse 15a the expression **My eyes are ever toward** means "I always look to (Yahweh)" as a source of help; that is, "I depend on Yahweh to help me at all times."

The net in verse 15b is the hunter's net with which he catches animals; here it is a figure of danger (see 9.15). RSV begins the line with **for**, which is to be preferred over TEV's "**and**." In many languages it will be possible to keep some type of figurative language where RSV has **pluck my feet out of the net**. In some languages it is possible to say, for example, "he will set me free from the trap" or "he will free me from the snare."

The danger in line **b** may be actual (so FRCL "for he will free me from the net in which I'm caught"), or potential (as RSV implies); or it may be a general statement (complementing line **a**), "for he always rescues me from danger." This last interpretation seems to be the best.

The plea in verse 16 emphasizes the psalmist's distress and weakness; Yahweh alone can help him. **Turn thou to me** translates the Hebrew "face me." In some languages this expression can be rendered "Pay attention to me," "Look at me," or "Look and listen to me." The request **be gracious** is not simply that Yahweh will have compassion on him, feel sorry for him, but that Yahweh will, because of his mercy, do something in answer to the psalmist's plea. See similar language in 4.1c.

Lonely: that is, alone, without anyone to help him or protect him.

Afflicted: "persecuted, oppressed, mistreated"; see discussion at 9.12.

25.17-18 RSV TEV

	RSV		TEV
17	Relieve the troubles of my heart, and bring me[b] out of my dis- tresses.	17	Relieve me of my worries and save me from all my trou- bles.
18	Consider my affliction and my trouble, and forgive all my sins.	18	Consider my distress and suffer- ing and forgive all my sins.

[b] Or *The troubles of my heart are en-larged; bring me*

In verse 17 **Relieve** translates a verb meaning to enlarge, make room for (see 4.1b and comments). The Masoretic text is the perfect tense third plural form of the verb, "they are enlarged" (see RSV footnote; SPCL and NJV translate this form, "My deep distress increases"); TEV, RSV, and most others read the Hebrew text as the imperative second singular "**Relieve**" and join the final letter of the word, the *waw*, to the following verb (where it becomes "and"), with no change in the Hebrew consonantal text.[1] The Masoretic text makes sense, and translators may prefer to follow it.

---

[1]HOTTP stays with the Masoretic text ("A" decision) and suggests two possible translations: (1) "the troubles have widened my heart; from my distresses bring me out"; (2) "the troubles of my heart have widened too much; from my distresses . . . ."

The psalmist uses four nouns to describe his sad situation: **troubles, distresses, affliction**, and **trouble**. For **troubles** see 20.1 and comments. The word translated **distresses** seems to emphasize the element of physical and emotional stress which a person experiences when subjected to danger or deprivation. In Deuteronomy 28.53,55,57 and Jeremiah 19.9, for example, it is used of the terrible distress brought on by a siege; in 1 Samuel 22.2 it appears to refer primarily to financial distress. In Psalm 107.6,13,19,28 it appears in a refrain which sums up the toil and trouble people experienced; in these verses it is parallel to another noun commonly translated "trouble"; in Psalm 119.143 it is joined to the word "trouble." And in Job 15.24 and Zephaniah 1.15 it is also parallel with the word "trouble" (or "anguish").

Consider in verse 18a translates the verb "to see," meaning here "to take notice of," "to become aware of," "to pay attention to."

The world **affliction** in verse 18a is related to the word translated "afflicted" (see its use in 9.12), a word often used of the poor, the oppressed, the disadvantaged among the people.

The word translated **trouble** in verse 18a is a general word descriptive of almost any kind of unpleasant situation brought on deliberately by evil people or arising out of difficult circumstances; see its use in 55.10b; 73.5b; 90.10. In this last passage RSV uses the expressive English phrase "toil and trouble," where "toil" is the English word for the Hebrew word translated **trouble** in this verse.

In verse 18b **forgive** translates the verb meaning "lift up" in the sense of removing, taking away (sins). This petition is made because it is the psalmist's **sins** that have caused all his suffering. **Forgive** is expressed in various manners in different languages; for example, "to wipe away sins," "throw sins away," "hand back sins to someone" (as in the remitting of a debt), and "forget someone's sins."

25.19-20	RSV	TEV

19   Consider how many are my foes,
      and with what violent hatred
      they hate me.

20   Oh guard my life, and deliver me;
      let me not be put to shame, for
      I take refuge in thee.

19   See how many enemies I have;
      see how much they hate me.

20   Protect me and save me;
      keep me from defeat.
      I come to you for safety.

Consider: see verse 18a.

In describing his enemies' hatred, the psalmist calls it a **violent hatred**, which can mean a hatred that leads to violence, or else a very strong hatred. **Violent hatred** will often have to be recast as an idiomatic clause; for example, "they hate me with hearts that can kill." In some languages one may translate "they hate with black hearts" or "in their hatred their stomachs do evil."

Guard my life (verse 20) translates "protect my *nefesh*" (see discussion at 3.2); **deliver** is here the same verb as in 7.2.

For **shame** see verses 2-3; the negative **not be put to shame** (TEV "**keep me from defeat**") can be stated in a positive way, "make me victorious," "give me victory over my enemies." For **refuge** see comment at 2.12. It is best to follow RSV, **for I take refuge in thee**, as the ground, or reason, for the psalmist's request for safety.

25.21   RSV   TEV

> May integrity and uprightness
>   preserve me,
>   for I wait for thee.

> May my goodness and honesty
>   preserve me,
>   because I trust in you.

The **integrity** (literally "perfection"; see 7.8) and **uprightness** of which the psalmist speaks may be attributes of God (so Anderson); others, like TEV, take them to refer to the psalmist's character (Kirkpatrick; SPCL). The second interpretation seems preferable. Some commentators see the two qualities personified as messengers sent by God to protect the psalmist. Most translations leave the matter ambiguous; the choice in RSV of the words **integrity and uprightness**, however, seems to refer them to the psalmist. FRCL translates differently: "I depend on you to keep me in innocence and in honesty."

The indirect command expressed with **May** plus a noun must often be recast in the form of an explicit wish; for example, "I ask that goodness and honesty preserve me." In many languages it will not be possible for the qualities of goodness and honesty to perform an action on their own. Hence it will in those cases be necessary to say, for example, if one is following the TEV model, "O LORD, because I am good and honest, keep me safe." On the other hand, if the translator takes these attributes as belonging to God, this may be rendered "because you are good and honest, I ask you to keep me safe."

For **I wait for thee** see verse 3.

It should be noted that some translations (NEB, NAB, BJ, NJB) follow the Septuagint in adding to the end of verse 21 "O LORD."

25.22   RSV   TEV

> Redeem Israel, O God,
>   out of all his troubles.

> From all their troubles, O God,
>   save your people Israel!

This verse falls outside the acrostic scheme (verse 21 begins with *taw,* the last letter of the Hebrew alphabet); it is a general petition, probably added later (see the same in verse 22 of Psa 34).

Redeem: save, set free, deliver. The verb chosen to translate this must go naturally with **troubles**.

Israel is a way of speaking of God's people, the Israelites. It is for this reason that TEV has "**your people Israel**"; this can be translated "save us, who are your people called Israel!"

Psalm 26

This psalm appears to be the claim made by a man that he is innocent of unspecified charges of wrongdoing which have been brought against him. There is nothing in the text that enables us to know what he was accused of doing, nor the circumstances in which he refutes the charges; verses 6-8, however, seem to show that a ritual in the Temple was the occasion of the psalm. The psalm opens with a plea to the Lord for vindication, supported by the psalmist's claim of innocence of any wrongdoing (verses 1-5). This is followed by a description of the ritual in the Temple (verses 6-7), after which there is a new plea for vindication (verses 8-11). The psalm ends with a statement of confidence in the Lord (verse 12).

The form of this psalm consists of four petitions accompanied by claims or reasons why God should respond, and ends with a vow or promise to praise God. The structure is rather symmetrical, as can be seen in the following listing:

Petition–Claim	Verse 1
Petition	2
Claim	3
Claim	4
Claim	5
Claim	6
Claim	7
Claim	8
Petition	9-10
Petition–Claim	11
Vow–Claim	12

HEADING: "**The Prayer of a Good Man**" (TEV); "The prayer of an innocent man"; "The claims of the righteous"; "The safety of a pure life." The TEV heading may have to be recast in some languages to say, for example, "A man who has done no wrong prays to God."

Hebrew Title: **A Psalm of David**.
See title of Psalm 25.

26.1-2	RSV		TEV

1	Vindicate me, O LORD,
	    for I have walked in my integri-
	        ty,
		1	Declare me innocent, O LORD,
			    because I do what is right
			    and trust you completely.

> and I have trusted in the LORD
> without wavering.
>
> 2   Prove me, O LORD, and try me;
> test my heart and my mind.
>
> 2   Examine me and test me, LORD;
> judge my desires and thoughts.

<u>Vindicate</u>: the Hebrew verb is "to judge" (see 7.8b and discussion), meaning here to declare innocent, to show to be guiltless. **Vindicate me** or "**declare me innocent**" requires in some languages that the opposing party be mentioned; for example, "Make me true before my accuser." Some languages say "make a just decision for me," "cut the words in my favor," or "judge my case favorably."

The verb "to walk" in line <u>b</u> is used in a figurative sense, meaning to live, to conduct oneself. The declaration **I have walked in my integrity** means "my conduct is beyond reproach," "my behavior is free of wrongdoing." NIV translates "I have led a blameless life."

In line <u>c</u> the verb translated **waver** means to shake, to totter (see 18.36, of feet that "slip"). In this same line Yahweh is referred to in the third person (see RSV); for consistency, TEV maintains the second person of line <u>a</u>.

The two verbs in verse 2a are synonymous, meaning to try, test, prove, examine. The first verb, **Prove**, has already appeared in 7.9, "who triest the minds"; the second verb, **try**, only here in the Psalms is used of God "trying" a person; elsewhere in the Psalms it is used of people putting God to the test (see 78.18).

In verse 2b **test** translates the Hebrew verb "refine," meaning to take out all impurities (see comments on 12.6; 17.3).

My heart and my mind translates the Hebrew "my kidneys and my heart" (see 7.9). Most translations have "my heart and my mind"; SPCL, however, has "my thoughts and my innermost feelings," and FRCL has "my thoughts and my feelings."

<u>**26.3**</u>   RSV   TEV

> For thy steadfast love is before my
> eyes,
> and I walk in faithfulness to
> thee.*c*
>
> *c* Or *in thy faithfulness*
>
> Your constant love is my guide;
> your faithfulness always leads
> me.*q*
>
> *q* your faithfulness always leads me; *or* I
> live in loyalty to you.

<u>For</u>: this introduces the basis for the psalmist's plea in the preceding verse, "Vindicate me." It should be made explicit in translation, as RSV has done.

For **steadfast love** see comment at 5.7, and for **faithfulness** see comment at 15.2.

The phrase **before my eyes** in line <u>a</u> may mean "I am always aware of" (see SPCL) or "I keep in mind." NJV has "my eyes are on Your steadfast love."

The major problem in translating verse 3 is that **steadfast love** is an event rather than a quality, and therefore it must in many languages be expressed as a clause such as "you love me faithfully." One may follow TEV with some further shifting to say "you love me faithfully and you guide me." Or, following the alternative interpretation of **before my eyes**, one may say "I always remember that you love me faithfully" or "I never forget your constant love for me."

In line <u>b</u> the meaning of **I walk in faithfulness to thee** may be "I live in loyalty to you" (TEV footnote; RSV, SPCL). But the phrase **"your faithfulness"** speaks of **faithfulness** as an attribute of God (TEV), that is, his faithfulness in doing what he promises (see how the term is used in 25.10); consequently TEV's rendering is to be preferred. Some, however, translate the Hebrew word as "truth" (NEB, NAB, NIV, TOB, NJB). So NJB has "I live my life by your truth." It seems better to translate the word as **faithfulness** rather than as "truth."

26.4-5	RSV	TEV
4	I do not sit with false men, nor do I consort with dissemblers;	4 I do not keep company with worthless people; I have nothing to do with hypocrites.
5	I hate the company of evildoers, and I will not sit with the wicked.	5 I hate the company of evil men and avoid the wicked.

Continuing to protest his innocence, the psalmist makes clear that he avoids altogether associating with evil, worthless people. In these four lines (verses 4-5) the same thought is expressed in four different ways.

For <u>sit with</u> in verses 4a and 5b, see comments on 1.1. The expression may be rendered as in TEV or idiomatically as in some languages: "I do not tie myself up with" or "I don't eat my food with."

In verse 4a **false men** translates "men of fraud." NEB and NAB have "worthless"; NJV "scoundrels"; TOB "impostors," and NIV "deceitful men." Dahood takes the phrase to mean idol-worshipers. **"Worthless people"** (TEV) is sometimes expressed as "people who cheat others."

Consort translates a verb which is very frequently used in the Old Testament. It means, generally, "to enter"; here the idea is of entering someone's house, and so "associate with," "keep company with."

Dissemblers in verse 4b is literally "those who hide themselves," that is, who conceal their real thoughts or motives; so TEV, NJV, NJB, NEB, and NIV have **"hypocrites."** (For a detailed treatment of "hypocrites," see *A Translator's Handbook on the Gospel of Mark*, pages 224-225.) Most languages have an abundance of terms or expressions for hypocrites. Many languages base the expression on the basis of a double image; for example, "two tongues," "two hearts, "two throats," "two livers." Others focus on a false manner of speaking: "to have a sweet mouth" or "to have a straight mouth and a crooked heart." Others base the expression upon some cultural aspect such as "spreading a clean carpet."

In verse 5 the two words translated <u>evildoers</u> and <u>the wicked</u> are synonymous and indicate in the broadest terms possible people who aren't good. <u>Evildoers</u> is used in 22.16a; the word translated <u>the wicked</u> appears eighty-one times in the Psalms.

26.6-7 RSV	TEV

6   I wash my hands in innocence,
    and go about thy altar, O LORD,
7   singing aloud a song of thanksgiving,
    and telling all thy wondrous deeds.
	6 LORD, I wash my hands to show
	    that I am innocent
	    and march in worship around
	    your altar.
	7 I sing a hymn of thanksgiving
	    and tell of all your wonderful deeds.

In a ritual in the Temple, after claiming his innocence, the psalmist confirms his claim by ritually washing his hands (see Deut 21.6-9; Matt 27.24) and marching around the altar (see 42.4; 118.27).

The word translated **innocence** is literally "empty, bare"—that is, there is no wrongdoing in him. **In innocence** will require saying in some languages "I have done no wrong."

To bring out the ritual aspect of the march, NJB translates "join the procession around your altar"; TEV tries to do the same with "**march in worship around your altar.**" The idea of marching around the altar may require a footnote in order to make its meaning clear. **Thy altar** must often be rendered "the place where people worship you."

Singing translates the infinitive of the causal form of the verb "to hear," meaning "cause to be heard."

Song of thanksgiving must often be translated "a song in which people give thanks to God."

For **telling** and **wondrous deeds** see comments at 9.1. **Wondrous deeds** may sometimes be translated "the great things you have done."

Verse 7b gives the content of the thanksgiving song of verse 7a, and so the translation can be "I sing a hymn of thanks to you, in which I tell of all the wonderful things you have done."

26.8 RSV	TEV

O LORD, I love the habitation of
    thy house,
    and the place where thy glory
    dwells.
	I love the house where you live, O
	    LORD,
	    the place where your glory
	    dwells.

The phrase in line a, **the habitation of thy house** (that is, "**the house where you live**") can be understood to mean "(I love) to live in your house" (so Dahood). But most translations understand the Hebrew text as do RSV and TEV. In place of the Masoretic text "habitation," NEB, BJ, and NJB prefer "beauty," agreeing with the Septuagint.

The habitation of thy house, that is, the Temple, is further defined in line b as **the place where thy glory dwells**. Yahweh's glory is the manifestation of his presence and power, usually described in terms of a dazzling light (see Exo 33.18,22; 40.34; 1 Kgs 8.10-11). **The place where thy glory dwells** is sometimes difficult to translate, because **glory** is normally an attributive of God and not an animate being which can be said to perform the act of dwelling. However, by recasting this expression it is possible to say something like "the place where you are gloriously present," or "the place where your power and light are seen," or "the place where people can see how great you are."

26.9-10   RSV   TEV

9   Sweep me not away with sinners,   9   Do not destroy me with the sin-
        nor my life with bloodthirsty   ners;
        men,   spare me from the fate of mur-
10   men in whose hands are evil de-   derers—
        vices,   10   men who do evil all the time
        and whose right hands are full   and are always ready to take
        of bribes.   bribes.

Sweep . . . away in verse 9 translates a verb meaning to gather, to take away. So SPCL "Do not take away my life." Or the translation can be "Don't treat me as you treat sinners."

The expression **Sweep me not away with sinners** will be a problem in languages in which it will not be natural to speak of sweeping away people as though they were dirt. However, the figurative expression may be kept by adding a simile; for example, "do not sweep me away with sinners like a woman sweeps her house." **With sinners** implies "together with sinners," and this component may have to be added to avoid unnecessary ambiguity.

In line a the Hebrew for **me** is "my *nefesh*," which is parallel to **my life** in line b.

Bloodthirsty men may mean "people who are ready to murder," that is, violent people (NJB); or, as TEV has it, "**murderers**" (also FRCL, NJV). TEV has introduced a verb, "**spare**," in line 9b, otherwise the ellipsis may cause difficulty in understanding. One may also say "do not let me die like men who kill others will die" or "do not take away my life like you will take away the lives of murderers."

In whose hands are evil devices: "people who are ready to commit crimes," or perhaps "people who are skilled at committing crimes."

In verse 10b **whose right hands are full of bribes** does not make clear whether this refers to those who offer bribes or those who take them; perhaps the taking of bribes is what is in focus here (see 15.5b). NJV translates the verse "who have schemes at their fingertips, and hands full of bribes." **Bribes** are often spoken of as "secret money," "hidden money," or "money for closing the eyes."

26.11-12   RSV   TEV

11   But as for me, I walk in my integ-   11   As for me, I do what is right;
        rity;   be merciful to me and save me!
        redeem me, and be gracious to
        me.   12   I am safe from all dangers;

259

12 My foot stands on level ground;   in the assembly of his people I
      in the great congregation I will   praise the LORD.
        bless the LORD.

As for me: this is an emphatic phrase, stressing the differences between evil people and the psalmist.

Line <u>a</u> of verse 11 means the same as line <u>b</u> of verse 1.

For **be gracious** see comment at 25.16; and for **redeem** see comment at 25.22.

TEV, GECL, and NIV separate verse 12 from verse 11, thereby indicating that this last verse expresses the psalmist's assurance that Yahweh has answered his prayer. It may indicate that the psalmist has had some sort of response to his prayer.

In verse 12 the phrase **level ground** may be meant literally, of the level place in the Temple court (so Briggs; see Mft "on the temple floor"), or figuratively, either of right conduct (see TOB footnote; NJB has "I take my stand on the right path") or of a place of safety, where there is no danger of stumbling or of a sudden attack (TEV; see "solid ground" in TOB, SPCL, FRCL, GECL; see Weiser, Oesterley, Kirkpatrick).

The great congregation translates the plural of a word meaning "**assembly**"; this plural form occurs only here and in 68.26. It refers to the people of Israel gathered for worship in the Temple (see 22.22,25).

In verse 12b "to bless Yahweh" means to praise him (see comment at 16.7). **I will bless the LORD** must often be rendered "I will say the LORD is great" or "I will say 'LORD, you are great.' " Notice that TEV alone uses the present tense; all other translations consulted have the future tense, which may be preferable.

Psalm 27

This psalm includes both a song of confidence (verses 1-6) and a lament by an individual who feels beset by troubles (verses 7-14). The majority of commentators believe that originally they were two separate compositions; some, however, see it as a unity (Toombs). Anderson's reasons why he sees two separate psalms are convincing. Of the standard translations, only NAB indicates that this is a composite work.

In the first part (verses 1-6) the psalmist expresses his confidence in the Lord (verse 1), followed by a description of how God will protect him from his enemies (verses 2-3). As a devout worshiper of Yahweh, in the Temple he will be safe from all troubles (verses 4-6).

In the second part (verses 7-14) the psalmist calls on the Lord to help him (verses 7-10), to guide him (verse 11), and to protect him (verse 12), ending his petition with a statement of confidence (verses 13-14).

HEADING: "**A Prayer of Praise**" (TEV); "Confidence in Yahweh and a prayer for help"; "A song of assurance"; "In God's company there is no fear." The TEV heading consists of two nouns which must in many languages be recast as verb phrases; for example, "The psalmist prays to God and praises him."

Hebrew Title: **A Psalm by David.**

See title of Psalm 24. The title in the Septuagint is "By David, before he was anointed."

27.1	RSV	TEV
	The LORD is my light and my salvation; whom shall I fear? The LORD is the stronghold*d* of my life; of whom shall I be afraid?	The LORD is my light and my salvation; I will fear no one. The LORD protects me from all danger; I will never be afraid.

d Or *refuge*

Only here in the Old Testament is Yahweh called **my light**; this means he is the source of life and vitality (see 18.28). He is also called **my salvation**, that is, the one who saves me; **the stronghold of my life** is a figure of protection and security. FRCL has "the protector of my life," and SPCL "The Lord defends my life." Both declarations (lines a and c) are followed by rhetorical questions, which use two

261

synonymous verbs: "Of whom shall I be afraid/be terrified?" These questions are emphatic ways of stating that the psalmist, because of his confidence in Yahweh's power to protect him, is not afraid of anyone.

The LORD is my light and my salvation requires restructuring in many languages, because light and salvation can not be expressed as possessed objects of the psalmist, as they appear in many translations. Recast as verb phrases it is possible to say, for instance, "The LORD is the one who gives me life and who saves me." If it is preferable to retain the idea of **light** in the first clause, it is possible in many languages to say "The LORD is the one who brightens my way and who saves me."

The expression **stronghold of my life** may require recasting as a clause, as in TEV or SPCL. However, it may sometimes be retained as a noun, if the meaning is fully clear. This may require shifting to a simile; for example, "The LORD is like a fortress for me," or with an associated verb, "The LORD protects me like a fortress."

Many translators will prefer to follow the RSV model, making lines b and d rhetorical questions. However, if this is done, one must reply to those questions where such replies are the natural style in the language. The reply here will be "No one." If instead of rhetorical questions the translator chooses to use declarative statements, as TEV does, it may be advisable to make the connection between the statement and the consequence quite clear by means of "and so" or "therefore," as follows: "The LORD . . . salvation, and so I will fear no one. The LORD . . . from danger; therefore I will never be afraid."

27.2-3   RSV   TEV

2   When evildoers assail me,   2   When evil men attack me and try
          uttering slanders against me,*e*   to kill me,
      my adversaries and foes,   they stumble and fall.
          they shall stumble and fall.   3   Even if a whole army surrounds
                                                         me,
3   Though a host encamp against   I will not be afraid;
          me,   even if enemies attack me,
      my heart shall not fear;   I will still trust God.*s*
      though war arise against me,
          yet I will be confident.   *s* still trust God; *or* not lose courage.

e Heb *to eat up my flesh*

The parallelism in verses 2-3 is not based on semantic repetition in the lines, but rather on the seconding line indicating consequence. The idea is that if a happens then b happens.

The psalmist's enemies are called **evildoers** who **assail** him and try "to devour his flesh" (see RSV footnote and NIV). Since most languages will not be able to use the Hebrew metaphor "eat up my flesh," the second verbal phrase is understood by some to mean slander (Mft, RSV); others, however, take it in the sense of tear to pieces, destroy (Weiser; NEB, TOB, NAB, SPCL), which seems more reasonable here.

In line c the psalmist's enemies are called **my adversaries and foes**, two synonymous words which have very little difference in meaning. Care should be taken not to make it appear that these are different from the **evildoers** in line <u>a</u>, as a careless reading of RSV might indicate. Something like NJV would be better: "it is they, my foes and my enemies, who stumble and fall."

TEV has not attempted to retain the first line of the second pair of parallel lines in RSV, **my adversaries and foes**, as this line only serves to repeat **evildoers** from line <u>a</u>. Translators must decide to what extent they will retain the formal aspect of such parallelism before deciding to follow TEV.

They shall stumble and fall is not necessarily meant in a literal fashion; it is a vivid way of saying that they will be defeated and therefore unable to carry out their evil plans.

In verse 3a <u>host</u>, and <u>war</u> in verse 3c, indicate that the psalmist is a king facing a foreign army (so Eaton). Where <u>host</u> is taken to mean army, some languages have terms for soldiers, but not for such a large grouping of soldiers as an army. Here it may be possible to say, for example, "a line of men who fight" or "a large company of soldiers," where "company" does not refer to a specific military unit, but rather to a group of unspecified size.

Encamp against me: this is language appropriate for a military maneuver; "besiege me" or "get ready to attack me" can also be used.

In some languages it may be clearer to begin line <u>c</u> with "and even if a war . . . ."

In verse 3d, if the verb is intransitive, it means **I will be confident** (RSV; also TEV footnote, TOB, NIV, NJB, SPCL); if taken as transitive, with the object "God" implied, it will mean "**I will still trust God**" (TEV; so Briggs).

27.4

RSV	TEV
One thing have I asked of the LORD, that will I seek after; that I may dwell in the house of the LORD all the days of my life, to behold the beauty of the LORD, and to inquire in his temple.	I have asked the LORD for one thing; one thing only do I want: to live in the LORD's house all my life, to marvel there at his goodness, and to ask for his guidance.

The psalmist says his one and only desire is to **dwell in the house of the LORD**, the Temple, **all the days of my life** (see 23.6). **Seek after** in line <u>b</u> is parallel with **have asked** in line <u>a</u>, indicating that this is the thing he desires most.

In the Temple the psalmist will **behold the beauty of the LORD**. **Behold** may sometimes be expressed in translation as "to look at with awe" or "to look at and say 'That is marvelous.'" Line 4d can sometimes be expressed "to look at God's beauty and say 'Isn't it wonderful!'"

The noun translated **beauty** occurs only here and in 90.17, in Psalms; elsewhere it is found in Pro 3.17; 15.26; 16.14; Zech 11.7,10. The word means grace, favor, kindness, goodness. Translations of this passage vary: RSV **beauty** is also in AT, NEB, NJV, TOB, SPCL; NAB and Dahood have "loveliness"; Mft "goodness"; ZÜR "friendliness." NJB translates "to enjoy the sweetness of Yahweh," and FRCL "to rejoice in his friendship." It seems clear that the word is being used in a spiritual sense (so Anderson); some think it is possible that a specific object—the Covenant Box—is meant; Briggs thinks it is the beauty of the worship in the Temple.

The second purpose, **to inquire [in his temple]** translates a verb which elsewhere means "attend to, bestow care on." K-B defines its meaning here as "take pleasure (in)." It is not certain what it specifically means in this passage; most take it in a general sense, "to worship," "to pray," "to ask for divine guidance," "to seek God's will." Taylor defines it: "to inquire of God guidance in all the situations of existence."

Dahood believes that verses 4-5 express the psalmist's desire to spend eternity in heaven with God. Although Christians today may have that idea in mind when they use this psalm, it was probably not what the writer was thinking.

27.5-6   RSV   TEV

5   For he will hide me in his shelter   5   In times of trouble he will shelter
        in the day of trouble;   me;
    he will conceal me under the cover   he will keep me safe in his Tem-
        of his tent,   ple
    he will set me high upon a rock.   and make me secure on a high
                                                     rock.

6   And now my head shall be lifted   6   So I will triumph over my enemies
        up   around me.
    above my enemies round about   With shouts of joy I will offer
        me;   sacrifices in his Temple;
    and I will offer in his tent   I will sing, I will praise the
        sacrifices with shouts of joy;   LORD.
    I will sing and make melody to the
        LORD.

The psalmist expresses his confidence in Yahweh's ability to protect him in the Temple from danger; **his shelter** in verse 5a and **his tent** in verse 5c refer to the Temple as a refuge.

In verse 5d **set me high upon a rock** is a figure also of safety, a high place above and beyond the attacks of the enemy. If the literal "high rock" is misunderstood, the meaning may be represented by "and make me secure in a safe place." There are some areas of the world where it will be difficult for people to imagine being secure on a high rock, particularly where such rocks do not exist. In such cases it is recommended that the translator shift to "safe place," or else use a figure for safety that all will recognize.

In verse 6a "to have the head lifted up above the enemies" is a figure of triumph. **My head shall be lifted up**, if used in this form, may create serious ambiguities. However, "**triumph**" is sometimes spoken of as "standing on the heads of one's enemies."

In gratitude for Yahweh's protection the psalmist promises to offer sacrifices in his Temple and to **make melody to the LORD** in public worship. See 4.5 for a discussion of **sacrifices**. **Offer sacrifices** is sometimes translated "I will burn gifts and worship God." Line 6c may sometimes be rendered "I will sing songs and say the LORD is great."

The vow or promise of the psalmist, **I will sing . . . to the LORD**, is characteristic of the closure pattern and may suggest for translators that a second heading is appropriate before verse 7. For example, "The psalmist asks the LORD to take care of him."

27.7-9a	RSV	TEV

7	Hear, O LORD, when I cry aloud, be gracious to me and answer me!	7 Hear me, LORD, when I call to you! Be merciful and answer me!
8	Thou hast said, "Seek ye my face." My heart says to thee, "Thy face, LORD, do I seek."	8 When you said, "Come worship me," I answered, "I will come, LORD."
9	Hide not thy face from me.	9 Don't hide yourself from me!

In this separate composition (verses 7-14) the psalmist begins by pleading for the Lord's help.

In verse 7a **when I cry aloud** translates the Hebrew "(hear) my voice I call." The meaning need not be to call loudly, to shout, as RSV interprets it. It means to call, plead insistently.

For verse 7b see the almost identical request in 4.1c. **Be gracious** translates a verb that means "be kind," "be compassionate." The expression **be gracious** is often rendered in idiomatic language; for example, "have a warm heart" or "feel sorrow in your liver." Sometimes the same psychological state is expressed with terms dealing with pain; for instance, "feel pain for me" or "see misery for me."

Verse 8 in the Masoretic text is "To you (singular) my heart said, Seek (plural) my face. Your face, Yahweh, I will seek." RSV, without changing the Masoretic text, has taken **Seek ye my face** as the Lord's command, to which the psalmist responds, **My heart says . . . .**" TEV is like RSV. The trouble with this way of translating the text is that in the Masoretic text "To you my heart said" comes before "Seek ye my face," and not before "Your face, LORD, I will seek."

There are other ways of dealing with the text. NEB has changed the Hebrew to get " 'Come,' my heart says, 'Seek his face.' " BJ, NJB, and NIV have "of you my heart has said, 'Seek his face.' " Another version is " 'For you,' says my heart, 'is God's command: "Seek my face." ' " FRCL has "I reflect on what you have said, 'Turn (plural) to me.' And so, O Lord, I turn to you." It hardly seems possible to take the Masoretic text to mean what RSV and TEV say it does; some change in the Hebrew text seems required.[1]

---

[1]HOTTP proposes two different ways of translating the Masoretic text: the first one is unintelligible; the second one can be rendered "My heart tells me that you have commanded, 'Seek (plural) my face'; and so, O LORD, I seek your face."

27.7-9a

The verb "to seek [the face of Yahweh]" means to worship him, to offer him sacrifice (see 24.6b).

The strophe ends with line a of verse 9, with the petition **Hide not thy face from me** (see 13.1 and comments).

27.9b-10	RSV		TEV
9b	Turn not thy servant away in anger,	9b	Don't be angry with me;
	thou who hast been my help.		don't turn your servant away.
	Cast me not off, forsake me not,		You have been my help;
	O God of my salvation!		don't leave me, don't abandon me,
10	For my father and my mother have forsaken me,		O God, my savior.
	but the LORD will take me up.	10	My father and mother may abandon me,
			but the LORD will take care of me.

The psalmist pleads strongly with Yahweh not to **turn** him **away**, not to **cast** him **off** or **forsake** him. The two verbs in verse 9d are quite synonymous; both mean "abandon, leave behind, forsake" (see 94.14, where both are used together again). As if to make his case stronger he refers to himself as **thy servant**, that is, one who has been obedient and devoted to Yahweh. In some languages **thy servant** may appear as if it refers not to the psalmist but to another servant whom the Lord uses. In order to avoid this ambiguity, it may be necessary to say "Don't turn me, your servant, away." For translation comments on **servant** see 19.11.

Lines b and d are descriptions of Yahweh, each one following the psalmist's strong plea. The first one, **thou who hast been my help**, should not be translated in such a way as to imply that Yahweh is no longer the psalmist's help. For comments on **O God of my salvation**, see 18.46. The translator must decide the best way to handle these appositive phrases. Perhaps the best way is to place them first, as declarative sentences, and then have the pleas that are based on them: "You have always helped me, so don't be angry and reject me. You have been my savior, so don't leave me now, don't abandon me."

It seems better, with TEV, AT, NEB, JB, NAB, NJV, to take verse 10a as a possibility—"**My father and mother may abandon me**"—and not as a fact (RSV, TOB). It may be necessary in many languages to express the possibility of being abandoned by parents by recasting this as an "if" clause; for example, "even if my father and my mother abandon me, the LORD will take care of me."

Take me up translates a verb that means "to gather" (see its use in a much different context in "sweep . . . away" in 26.9), here in the sense of to welcome, to receive (as an orphan), almost "to adopt."

RSV   TEV

11   Teach me thy way, O LORD;   11   Teach me, LORD, what you want
     and lead me on a level path   me to do,
     because of my enemies.   and lead me along a safe path,
12   Give me not up to the will of my   because I have many enemies.
     adversaries;   12   Don't abandon me to my enemies,
     for false witnesses have risen   who attack me with lies and
     against me,   threats.
     and they breathe out violence.

For **teach** see comments on "instructs" in 25.8; for **lead** see its use in 23.3; and
for **path** see its use in 16.11.

Thy way is the way that Yahweh wants the psalmist to take, that is, how he, the
psalmist, should live as a worshiper of Yahweh. In verse 11b the word **level** (see
"level ground" in 26.12) may mean "**safe**" (as TEV has it) or "without obstacles"
(FRCL); however, as Anderson says, it may be "a way of life that is right in the sight
of God" (also Weiser).

The two different words, **my enemies** and **my adversaries** in verses 11c, 12a, are
synonymous.

In verse 12a the Hebrew text is "Don't give me to the *nefesh* of my enemies."
The word *nefesh* here (see 3.2) is taken to mean **will** by RSV and others; NEB and
Weiser have "greed"; TOB "desire." FRCL is vivid: "Don't let me fall into their claws
(or, clutches)."

The enemies are described as **false witnesses** who **breathe out violence**. The
verbal phrase **breathe out violence** is a vivid portrayal of hostility and hatred. The
language suggests a trial in which lying and hostile witnesses accuse the psalmist of
having committed a crime. Whether this is conventional language or whether it
reflects an actual situation is impossible to decide. If the translator follows the
suggestion of **false witnesses**, it is possible sometimes to say "men who tell lies about
what I have done have stood up" or "people sit down to decide my affair and tell lies
about me."

RSV   TEV

13   I believe that I shall see the good- 13   I know that I will live to see
     ness of the LORD   the LORD's goodness in this
     in the land of the living!   present life.
14   Wait for the LORD;   14   Trust in the LORD.
     be strong, and let your heart   Have faith, do not despair.
     take courage;   Trust in the LORD.
     yea, wait for the LORD!

The first word in the Masoretic text of verse 13 usually means "unless." That
it was difficult to understand is shown by the dots which mark it in the Masoretic
text, indicating doubts as to its genuineness; it is omitted by five Hebrew manuscripts
and by the Septuagint. It is probably best understood as a way of saying "I would give

up hope *unless* (I believed)"; so FRCL; and NJV similarly, "Had I not had the assurance that I would enjoy the goodness of the Lord in the land of the living . . . ." RSV, TEV, TOB, and NEB omit the word.

The expression **see the goodness of the LORD** requires some adjustment in many languages, since it is often not possible to speak of seeing abstract qualities such as goodness. One may say, for example, "I will know how very good the LORD is" or "I will understand that the LORD does good things."

The statement **I shall see . . . in the land of the living** is taken by the majority of commentators to mean "I will live to see the Lord's goodness"; if the word for **land** is taken to mean the land of Israel, then "to his people" (or, "in Israel") may be implied. FRCL translates "to see the goodness of the Lord in this land where we live." But, as TEV indicates, the phrase is a way of talking about the present life in contrast with the existence after death. Dahood translates "in the land of life eternal," that is, heaven; while modern Christians may wish to use the psalm in that sense in worship, this was quite likely not the intended meaning of the psalmist.

The words of verse 14 are addressed either by the psalmist to himself or to the congregation, or by the priest (or prophet) in the Temple to the psalmist, in response to the psalmist's statement.

For **Wait** meaning "trust" see comments on 25.3. The command **be strong** means to be courageous, confident.

Let your heart take courage: see comments on **heart** in 4.7. A natural equivalent in English of this command may be "be courageous" or, in a negative form, "don't lose hope."

Just as the final letter of the alphabet can mark the end of a poem, so sometimes does a three-line parallelism or tricolon. The form of the closure in verse 14 is A-B-A, in which **be strong and let your heart take courage** is framed between the two occurrences of **Wait for the LORD**. If this particular order creates difficulties in a language, it should be adjusted to one of the natural orders for closure of poems in the receptor language.

Psalm 28

Like Psalms 7 and 17 this psalm is an individual lament by one who feels the threat of enemies and has no one to help him but Yahweh. The psalmist begins with a plea to the Lord to hear his cry for help (verses 1-2); then he begs the Lord not to punish him (verse 3), but to punish his enemies (verses 4-5). Evidently in response to the Lord's favorable answer to his plea, the psalmist praises him for answering him (verses 6-7), and the psalm closes with what seems to be a later liturgical addition (verses 8-9), to make the psalm suitable for congregational worship (see Anderson).

Much like Psalm 26, this one is a series of petitions, praises, and assurances. Following the opening address to the Lord in 1a, there are four petitions in verses 1b, 2, 3, and 4. Verse 5 inserts a statement of assurance, followed by praise in verse 6. Two further statements of assurance come in verses 7-8, and in verse 9 the psalm closes with a final petition.

Nothing in the psalm allows us to know who the psalmist was or the specific danger he was in.

HEADING: **"A Prayer for Help"** (TEV); other headings are "If God be silent"; "The silence of God means death"; "Petition and thanksgiving." The TEV heading will often require adjusting in the direction of two verb phrases; for example, "The psalmist prays and asks God to help him."

Hebrew Title: **A Psalm of David**.

28.1-2

RSV

1 To thee, O LORD, I call;
      my rock, be not deaf to me,
   lest, if thou be silent to me,
      I become like those who go
         down to the Pit.
2 Hear the voice of my supplication,
      as I cry to thee for help,
   as I lift up my hands
      toward thy most holy sanctu-
         ary.*f*

f Heb *thy innermost sanctuary*

TEV

1 O LORD, my defender, I call to
      you.
   Listen to my cry!
   If you do not answer me,
      I will be among those who go
         down to the world of the
         dead.
2 Hear me when I cry to you for
      help,
   when I lift my hands toward
      your holy Temple.

269

In his opening plea to the Lord (verses 1-2) the psalmist addresses him as **my rock** (see 18.2 and comments), which is a figure for "my defender" or "my refuge." The expression **my rock** should only be kept if the symbolism intended is sufficiently meaningful. However, in no case does the rock belong to the psalmist; rather, he is the goal of the activity of the Lord's defense. Therefore it will often be necessary to say "O LORD, you who defend me" or "O LORD, you who protect me from my enemies."

In lines <u>b</u> and <u>c</u> of verse 1, two different verbs are used, **be . . . deaf** and **be silent**. In this context they mean not to listen to the psalmist and not to answer his cry for help.

Lest with the subjunctive (**I become**) is not a common expression in English. The meaning is more naturally expressed by "For, if you remain silent, I will be like . . ." (NIV).

In verse 1 the word **Pit** is used as a synonym for Sheol, the world of the dead (also in 30.3; 88.4,6; 143.7). The psalmist is saying that if the Lord does not answer him, he will be like those who are dying or are already dead, for he will go down to Sheol—he will die. **The Pit** may be meaningless as a place for the dead in some languages, and "**the world of the dead**" may be too vague to carry the meaning of dying. Therefore it will sometimes be necessary to say simply "I will die."

In verse 2 line <u>b</u> is attached to line <u>a</u> and is incomplete without reference to line <u>a</u>. The same is true of the following two lines in RSV. There is no heightening or other movement between the lines, nor is there static parallelism. Since lines <u>b</u>, <u>c</u>, and <u>d</u> merely stand in a dependency relation to line <u>a</u>, it is possible to show this dependency in other ways. TEV has created two lines from the four in RSV by equating **voice of my supplication** with **I cry . . . for help**, and expressed the other two dependent lines as "**when I lift my hands . . . .**" The result is a clearer two-line parallelism. Translators may follow this model or keep the longer lines as attached lines.

For **supplication** see comments on 6.9; the expression **voice of my supplication** means "loud plea, cry for help" (also in verse 6a). NIV has "cry for mercy."

The figure **I lift up my hands** in verse 2 is the attitude of prayer and petition; **thy most holy sanctuary** translates the word for the Most Holy Place, the innermost sanctuary of the Temple (see RSV footnote), where the Covenant Box was kept.

The expression **I lift up my hands toward thy most holy sanctuary** presents the translator with several problems. Since the lifting up of hands may not carry the meaning of praying, it will often be necessary to make the meaning explicit; for example, "I lift up my hands in prayer."

The second problem concerns the word **toward**. The focus of **toward** is to indicate that the one praying is facing the Temple. In some languages it may be difficult to understand how lifting the hands up will also point them in the direction of the Temple. To make this matter of two directions clearer, it will often be necessary to say, for example, "I face your holy Temple and lift up my hands to pray" or "I turn looking at your holy Temple and raise my hands to pray."

Holy sanctuary may be looked at as two related but separate translation problems. **Holy** is associated in the Scriptures with the Spirit of God, with certain kinds of people such as holy prophets, and with various material objects such as priestly clothing, ark, and Temple. In connection with people the term "holy" indicates their relationship to God. Holy objects on the other hand normally involve some ceremonial aspect of relationship to God which can be designated as "dedicated." In many languages "holy" may be spoken of as "dedicated to worship" or "belonging to God for worship."

The term **sanctuary** or **"Temple"** is translated in some languages as "God's big prayer house" or "God's big singing house." The full expression may then sometimes be rendered "the great prayer house which is dedicated to you" or "the big God-house where people worship you."

28.3   RSV   TEV

Take me not off with the wicked,   Do not condemn me with the
    with those who are workers of   wicked,
    evil,   with those who do evil—
who speak peace with their   men whose words are friendly,
    neighbors,   but who have hatred in their
while mischief is in their hearts.   hearts.

Take . . . **off** in line a translates the verb "drag away," used with punishment, exile, or death as the destination. Here it can mean "Do not take me off to die with the wicked." Some take the verb to mean "to count," that is, to rank, classify (Dahood; see NJV). It may be necessary to render this as "Do not condemn me when you condemn the wicked."

The wicked in line a are further described as **workers of evil** in line b. And in line c they are described as men who "speak *shalom*," that is, who greet others in a friendly fashion, but this only serves to conceal the hatred that is **in their hearts**. The English word **mischief** is not strong enough for the Hebrew word; NJV, NEB have "malice"; NAB "evil"; NJV "treachery."

28.4   RSV   TEV

Requite them according to their   Punish them for what they have
    work,   done,
    and according to the evil of   for the evil they have com-
    their deeds;   mitted.
requite them according to the   Punish them for all their deeds;
    work of their hands;   give them what they deserve!
render them their due reward.

The petition for Yahweh to punish the wicked because of their evil deeds is stated in three different ways. **Requite** translates the Hebrew verb "give," used twice (lines a and c); it means here "give back" or "reward" in a bad sense, and so "punish." The verb translated **render** in line d is the causative of the verb "turn," meaning "to cause to turn," that is, "to pay back" (see SPCL) or "to give" (TEV, NJV, NEB). In lines a to c three different nouns are used for what these evildoers have done: **their work** . . . **their deeds** . . . **the work of their hands**, which are three different ways of referring to the same thing. The psalmist's plea comes to a climax in line <u>d</u>; of the translations consulted in English, TEV **"give them what they deserve!"** is the most natural expression. The psalmist is convinced of the evil nature of his enemies and that they rightly deserve the punishment he prays for them.

Line <u>a</u> contains no specific reference to the evil acts they have done. However, in some languages it will be necessary to be more specific. In such languages it is possible to say, for example, "Punish them for the bad deeds they have done to people." Line <u>b</u> may then be rendered "and for the evil way they have lived."

<u>**28.5**</u>　　　　RSV　　　　　　　　　　　　　　　　TEV

Because they do not regard the works of the LORD, or the work of his hands, he will break them down and build them up no more.	They take no notice of what the LORD has done or of what he has made; so he will punish them and destroy them forever.

Because: RSV places this first; but since it introduces a fairly long statement, it is better to use the TEV construction, with the statement first and the consequence following, both standing as independent clauses.

Regard: the verb means "to perceive, notice, be aware of." Here the negative **do not regard** means do not think important, think to be of no value, despise. **Do not regard** may sometimes be rendered "they do not say what God has done is great" or "they say that God has done nothing."

In this verse the psalmist uses the same words for Yahweh's "works" that he used for the enemies' deeds in verse 4: **the works [of the LORD]** uses the word in verse 4a, and **the work [of his hands]** corresponds to verse 4c. **The work of his hands** may be rendered "the great things he has made" or "the things he has created."

In line <u>c</u> the verbs are "tear down" and "[not] rebuild," which describe a permanent destruction. This line is taken as a statement by RSV, TEV, and NIV (also Briggs, Anderson, Weiser, Dahood); most translations, however, take it as a wish: "May he tear them down . . . !"

This kind of language seems to identify the psalmist's enemies as pagan Gentiles.

<u>**28.6-7**</u>　　　　RSV　　　　　　　　　　　　　　　　TEV

6　Blessed be the LORD! for he has heard the voice of my supplications.	6　Give praise to the LORD; he has heard my cry for help.
7　The LORD is my strength and my shield; in him my heart trusts; so I am helped, and my heart exults, and with my song I give thanks to him.	7　The LORD protects and defends me; I trust in him. He gives me help and makes me glad; I praise him with joyful songs.

The sudden change to praise and thanksgiving seems to indicate that the Lord has answered the psalmist's prayer to punish his enemies, and so the psalmist calls on the people to praise the Lord; literally, "Blessed be Yahweh" (see comments on 18.46). Some languages require that the content of the praise or blessing be explicit; for example, "I say that God is wonderful," or in direct address, "My God, you are wonderful."

The voice of my supplications: see verse 2.

In verse 7a the word **strength** is used not only by RSV but by most other translations; the Hebrew word may mean "fortress," and so TEV has **"protects."** For **shield** see comment at 3.3. Some take the two nouns **strength** and **shield** as a hendiadys: Dahood "my strong shield"; SPCL "my mighty protector." In languages where the shield is well known and can serve as a figurative manner of speaking of the Lord's protection, it should be used. Otherwise one can follow the lead of TEV.

My heart trusts: for the verb see its use in 13.5, and for **heart** see comments on 4.7. Here the translation can be "I trust him with all my heart," "I rely on him completely."

I am helped: it may be better to use the active voice of the verb, with Yahweh as subject. SPCL has "I trusted in him completely, and he helped me."

My heart exults: "I am happy," "I am filled with joy."

In line **d** the Masoretic text has "with my song"; the Septuagint has "with my will (or, desire)." NEB changes the vowels of the Hebrew text to give the wording "with my whole body."[1] It is best to follow the Masoretic text.

28.8   RSV   TEV

The LORD is the strength of his   The LORD protects his people;
    people,   he defends and saves his chosen
  he is the saving refuge of his   king.
    anointed.

TOB takes verses 8-9 as the song which the psalmist speaks of in verse 7d.

Strength of his people: see verse 7 "my strength." At the end of the line, instead of **people** the Masoretic text has "to them"; some Hebrew manuscripts, and the Septuagint and Syriac, have "to his people," which is followed by TEV, RSV, and others, and is preferred by HOTTP.

Refuge translates a word meaning mountain fort, stronghold (as in 27.1); **saving refuge** means a refuge that saves. "Safe refuge" (NEB, NJB) is more in keeping with normal English. SPCL translates "a help and a refuge," and GECL has "is saved by him as in a fortress." For **his anointed** see comments on 2.2.

Some scholars feel that the parallelism between **his people** in line **a** and **his anointed** in line **b** suggests that the latter refers to the people as a whole, not just the

---

[1]HOTTP was divided in its judgment of the relation between the Masoretic text, "song," and the Septuagint (which it renders "heart"). It recommends that the Masoretic text be translated, and suggests that in a note translators may wish to indicate the Septuagint wording.

king (so NJB, in footnote); while possible, this does not seem too probable. **His anointed** or "**his chosen king**" requires some adjustment in many languages; for example, "the king God has chosen."

28.9	RSV	TEV

<table>
<tr><td>O save thy people, and bless thy
    heritage;
be thou their shepherd, and
    carry them for ever.</td><td>Save your people, LORD,
    and bless those who are yours.
Be their shepherd,
    and take care of them forever.</td></tr>
</table>

This closing prayer is addressed to Yahweh in the second person; so TEV introduces the vocative "LORD" at the end of the first line.

Here **thy heritage** is parallel with **thy people**; the people of Israel were considered to be Yahweh's special possession, who belonged to him alone (see 1 Kgs 8.53). See the king's "heritage" in 2.8 and the people's "heritage" in 16.6.

The Lord, as **shepherd** (see 23.1), is asked to **carry them for ever**; the verb **carry** brings to mind the picture of a shepherd carrying his sheep (see Isa 40.11); TEV "**take care of them**" broadens the concept to describe the shepherd's role as a whole, of which one particular aspect was to carry the sheep whenever necessary. In languages in which the term for **shepherd** has the proper meaning to be used in this context, it should be used. Where it does not, or there is no such term, the translator will have to speak of the function of the shepherd, that is, "caring and protecting"; for example, "take care of your people, LORD" or "watch over your people, LORD."

Psalm 29

This psalm is a hymn in praise of God's power manifested in a storm. The psalm draws much of its imagery from Canaanite poems in honor of the Canaanite storm god Baal (see the commentaries). It opens with a call to the gods to assemble and worship Yahweh (verses 1-2), after which comes the main body of the hymn (verses 3-9), in which the awesome power of Yahweh in the storm is described. Seven times the phrase "the voice of Yahweh" is used to describe the effects of the storm. The psalm closes with a prayer to the almighty Lord to bless his people (verses 10-11).

One of the outstanding structural features of Psalm 29 is its chiastic shape. The translator may perceive this more readily by reading each verse, and then its corresponding verse containing the same idea or corresponding lexical item. It should be noticed that the center of the chiasmus in verse 7 is the only verse consisting of a single line.

									Verse	
A	-	-	-	-	-	-			1-2	LORD (four times)
	B	-	-	-	-	-			1	strength
		C	-	-	-	-			3	waters
			D	-	-	-			4	majesty
				E	-	-			5	cedars
					F	-			6	Lebanon
						G			7	flashes
					F'	-			8	Kadesh
				E'	-	-			9	oaks
			D'	-	-	-			10	enthroned
		C'	-	-	-	-			10	flood
	B'	-	-	-	-	-			10	strength
A'	-	-	-	-	-	-			10-11	LORD (four times)

HEADING: "The Voice of the LORD in the Storm"; other headings are "The powerful voice of God"; "Hymn to the Lord of the storm"; "God's majesty in the storm." The TEV heading can be adjusted in some languages by saying "The LORD speaks in the storm" or "When the LORD speaks it is like a storm."

Hebrew Title: **A Psalm of David**.

The Septuagint adds "For the last day of the Festival of Shelters," one of the main Hebrew festivals, which was held 15-22 Tishri (around the first part of October).

29.1 RSV	TEV
Ascribe to the LORD, O heavenly beings,*ᵍ* ascribe to the LORD glory and strength.	Praise the LORD, you heavenly beings; praise his glory and power.

ᵍ Heb *sons of gods*

The parallel arrangement in this verse is the so-called "staircase" form, in which the statement in line <u>a</u> is incomplete (the verb **Ascribe** requires a direct object), and the statement is made complete in line <u>b</u>, where the direct object **glory and strength** is supplied.

The petition in this verse is literally "Give . . . glory and power to Yahweh," which means to offer him praise or honor for the glory and power he possesses. So TEV and SPCL **"Praise"**; FRCL has "Come honor the Lord." RSV's **Ascribe** is no longer common English and makes for a difficult text. The verb "to ascribe" means to assign a quality or attribute to someone, that is, to affirm that that person possesses such a quality or attribute. It does not mean to confer such an attribute on someone, but to acknowledge it. In terms of God it means to proclaim that God possesses these qualities, and to praise him for having them.

Heavenly beings translates the Hebrew phrase "sons of gods," which may be understood either as the gods of the other nations or as angels (Briggs; NJB footnote), or even as the stars (see Anderson). The Septuagint has "Sons of god," and so do BJ, NJB, NAB; Weiser "sons of gods"; FRCL "heavenly powers"; NJV, ZÜR, SPCL "divine beings"; Dahood, NEB, TOB "gods." In the translation of **heavenly beings** translators normally have two areas of choice: either they can follow one of the suggested interpretations such as angels or stars, or they can seek to use a generic term. In some languages the term "spirits" will provide the only reasonable alternative. However, spirits are thought of as dwelling in nature and not being heavenly. In some languages the term for "powers" may be used.

Ascribe to the LORD glory and strength often requires recasting beyond that which TEV uses, for one must often translate **glory** as being the content of the praise; for example, "say that God is powerful and glorious" or "say that God is wonderful and has great power."

29.2 RSV	TEV
2 Ascribe to the LORD the glory of his name; worship the LORD in holy array.	2 Praise the LORD's glorious name; bow down before the Holy One when he appears.*ʸ*

276

^v when he appears; *or* in garments of worship; *or* in his beautiful Temple.

The glory of his name is a very difficult phrase to understand as the direct object of the verb **Ascribe**. Something like "Proclaim (or, Tell) how glorious (or, majestic) is the name of the LORD" is more meaningful (compare the discussion of 96.7-8a). And if **name** is taken to stand for "Yahweh" (see 5.11 and comments), then it is possible to translate as FRCL has done: "Come proclaim the glory of the Lord." **The glory of his name** must often be recast in such a form as "that his name is great" or "that he is great."

The last phrase, translated **in holy array**, is variously understood. The Hebrew phrase appears here and in 96.9, and 1 Chronicles 16.29; the word translated **array** appears also in 2 Chronicles 20.21; Proverbs 14.28 ("glory"), and nowhere else in the Old Testament, and seems to mean "adornment." Weiser has "when he appears in his sanctuary," and SPCL "in his beautiful sanctuary." NEB and NJB have "the splendour of holiness"; Toombs "when he appears in his holiness"; NJV "majestic in holiness"; TOB "when his holiness shines forth"; NAB "in holy attire"; FRCL "when he reveals his holiness"; and Dahood "when the Holy One appears." The diversity of translations shows there is no agreement on the exact meaning of the phrase, and a translator should feel free to use the rendering that seems to best fit the context. If the translator follows TEV's **"Holy One,"** meaning God, it is usually impossible to use the terms for "holy" which are associated with objects or with persons (see comment at 28.2). Some languages use such terms as bright, shining, pure, and brilliant. It is important to avoid using a term which has the central meaning of clean or cleansed.

29.3-4	RSV		TEV
3	The voice of the LORD is upon the waters; the God of glory thunders, the LORD, upon many waters.	3	The voice of the LORD is heard on the seas; the glorious God thunders, and his voice echoes over the ocean.
4	The voice of the LORD is powerful, the voice of the LORD is full of majesty.	4	The voice of the LORD is heard in all its might and majesty.

Is upon the waters: this is not a natural English expression, and the sense of the Hebrew must be "is heard on" or "goes across" **the waters**. SPCL has "resounds over the waters," and NEB "echoes over the waters." TOB takes the Hebrew to mean "rules the waters"; the Hebrew can be taken to mean "against the waters." **The waters** in line a and **many waters** in line c may refer to the Mediterranean Sea; some take them to refer to the primeval waters, present at creation (Gen 1.6-7). A general descriptive phrase such as "the seas . . . all the seas" is to be preferred.

In poetic language the thunder is called "the voice of Yahweh" (see also 18.13). **The voice of the LORD**, which is used in verses 3 to 9, requires being changed to a verb in some languages where there is no term for voice apart from speaking. Hence it may be necessary to restructure the nominal phrase into a "when" clause; for example, "when the LORD speaks, he is heard on the seas." In languages in which it is not natural to say that **God thunders**, it may be necessary to say "The glorious God speaks like thunder" or "When the glorious God speaks, it is like the thunder of a storm."

The God of glory: "the majestic, glorious, powerful God" (see "glory" in 26.8). For **thunders** see the similar passage in 18.13.

TEV has taken **the voice** of line a as carrying over as the subject of line c (which lacks a verb and which appears to make **the LORD** the subject); many translations take line c to mean "the LORD is upon the many waters" (see NEB, SPCL); others "the LORD rules the mighty ocean." It seems better to take **The voice (of the LORD)** as the subject of line c.

In languages where "speak" instead of "voice" must be used in verse 4, it will often be necessary to say, for example, "When the LORD speaks he shows his power, when he speaks he shows how great he is," or the second line may sometimes be expressed "when the LORD speaks he shows the people what a great chief he is."

29.5-6	RSV	TEV
5	The voice of the LORD breaks the cedars, the LORD breaks the cedars of Lebanon.	5 The voice of the LORD breaks the cedars, even the cedars of Lebanon.
6	He makes Lebanon to skip like a calf, and Sirion like a young wild ox.	6 He makes the mountains of Lebanon jump like calves and makes Mount Hermon leap like a young bull.

The furious storm, still described as **The voice of the LORD**, breaks down even **the cedars of Lebanon**, trees that were famous for their massive size and strength (see Fauna and Flora, page 108). In languages where large cedars, particularly those that grow in Lebanon, are unknown, an illustration may be required. **The voice . . . breaks the cedars** may sometimes be rendered "when the LORD speaks he breaks the strongest trees, he even breaks the strong trees of Lebanon." Alternatively, if there is a tree well known for its size and strength, a term for such a tree may be substituted.

In verse 6 the Hebrew **Lebanon** is not the country but "the mountains of Lebanon"; and **Sirion** is the Phoenician name for Mount Hermon, the highest mountain in Syria (9150 feet, or 2789 meters), some 42 miles (67 kilometers) northeast of Lake Galilee. Since many readers are acquainted with Lebanon as a country, it may be advisable to indicate in the text "mountains of Lebanon."

In poetic language the psalmist describes how the mountains shake in the storm; some suggest that the storm is accompanied by an earthquake, but poetic license must be allowed for. In languages where the **calf** and **ox** are unknown, other domestic animals may be substituted.

The picture of a range of mountains jumping may be beyond even the poetic expression of some people. In some cases it may be necessary to say "he shakes the mountains called Lebanon and they jump like a calf jumps" or "when the LORD causes an earthquake, the mountains of Lebanon go up and down like a jumping animal."

29.7-8	RSV		TEV
7	The voice of the LORD flashes forth flames of fire.	7	The voice of the LORD makes the lightning flash.
8	The voice of the LORD shakes the wilderness, the LORD shakes the wilderness of Kadesh.	8	His voice makes the desert shake; he shakes the desert of Kadesh.

The **flames of fire** are lightning (see similar description in 18.13-14). **Kadesh** is usually identified as the place 50 miles (80 kilometers) south of Beersheba, through which the Israelites passed on their way to Canaan (Num 20; 33.36-37). Some, however, think it much more likely that here it is to be identified as Kadesh on the Orontes River, in Syria (see Dahood and NAB footnote).

The word translated **wilderness** or "**desert**" (TEV) refers to a desolate area that is not cultivated nor inhabited by farming people. Because it is out beyond the limits of where people settle, a **wilderness** is looked upon as dangerous. It may be inhabited by nomads and their herds, and by wild animals. In the Middle East such areas are treeless but often have grassy patches where herds can graze. In areas where such wildernesses are unknown, translators must often use a descriptive phrase; for example, "rocky region," "place where no house is," or "place where people don't settle."

29.9	RSV	TEV
	The voice of the LORD makes the oaks to whirl,^{h} and strips the forests bare; and in his temple all cry, "Glory!"	The LORD's voice shakes the oaks^w and strips the leaves from the trees while everyone in his Temple shouts, "Glory to God!"

^{h} Or *makes the hinds to calve*

^{w} *Probable text* shakes the oaks; *Hebrew* makes the deer give birth.

There is much dispute over the meaning of lines a and b. The Masoretic text in line a has the plural noun "deers," which would make the verb mean "writhe," that is, to go into labor, to give birth (so Weiser, Dahood; NEB, NJV, TOB). But many commentators and translators prefer to read the noun as the Hebrew word for "oaks" (or, terebinths), which would make the verb mean "shake" or the like (AT, RSV, TEV, NAB, BJ, NJB, SPCL, ZÜR, Mft). The same translational procedure applies for **oak** as for "cedars" in verse 5.

Line <u>b</u> is also variously understood; the Masoretic text seems to mean "and it strips the forests." But some assign another meaning to the verb (see K-B and Holladay, following Driver), "bring to premature birth," and conjecture that the noun that follows means "young goat" (while others emend to the Hebrew word for "mountain goat," as in 104.18). Most favor keeping the two lines parallel, with <u>oaks</u> and <u>forests</u>, or else "deer" and "goats" (see NEB "The voice of the Lord makes the hinds calve and brings kids early to birth"; so FRCL). NJV, however, has "makes hinds to calve" and "strips forests bare" (also AT and Dahood).[1]

The final line seems to refer to public worship in the Temple at Jerusalem. Some take this to be a poetic description of all living beings in all the earth proclaiming Yahweh's greatness; this, however, seems improbable.

29.10-11 RSV	TEV
10 The LORD sits enthroned over the flood; the LORD sits enthroned as king for ever. 11 May the LORD give strength to his people! May the LORD bless his people with peace!	10 The LORD rules over the deep waters; he rules as king forever. 11 The LORD gives strength to his people and blesses them with peace.

Above the furious storm Yahweh <u>sits enthroned over the flood . . . as king for ever</u>. It seems probable (Toombs; GECL, FRCL) that the word "flood" here refers to the waters above the sky (Gen 1.6-7; Psa 104.3; 148.4). Some, however, see here a reference to the flood of Genesis 7–8, for which the same Hebrew word is used (and the Septuagint translation here seems to support that interpretation). So NJV "The LORD sat enthroned at the Flood"; Dahood "Yahweh has sat enthroned from the flood"; also Weiser, Briggs, Kirkpatrick, BJ, and NJB). If the translator follows the RSV and the more literal rendering of the Hebrew, he may say, for example, "The LORD sits like a chief on his stool commanding the seas." If such a picture strains the poetic imagination, one may follow TEV. However in some languages it is not possible to rule over water. Hence in such cases one may say "The LORD commands everything, even the seas." If the translator follows the reference to the flood, it may be possible to say "The LORD sat on his throne at the flood."

<u>The LORD sits enthroned as king forever</u> may require some recasting as in TEV, or in some cases the symbolic language may be retained; for example, "The LORD sits on his royal stool, and he is chief of all peoples forever."

Verse 11 may be taken as a petition (Weiser; RSV, NAB, NJV, FRCL) or as a statement (Briggs; TEV, NEB, NIV, BJ, NJB, AT, TOB, SPCL).

---

[1]HOTTP takes line <u>a</u> to mean "the voice of the LORD makes the hinds calve" (as in RSV footnote; "B" decision), and says line <u>b</u> may mean either "it strips the forests bare" or "it brings kids (early) to birth."

Strength is not bodily strength but the strength of the nation, prosperous and able to defend itself from its enemies. **Strength** must often be recast as a verb; for example, "The LORD strengthens his people," or as a causative, "The Lord makes his people powerful."

Peace stands not just for cessation of hostilities, but for well-being, prosperity, happiness, success.

Bless his people with peace may sometimes be translated "May the LORD give good things to his people and make them joyful."

Psalm 30

This thanksgiving song was composed by a man who had been seriously ill and had almost died (verse 1), and whose prayer to the Lord had been answered (verses 2-3). Perhaps it was sung in the Temple, at the presentation of an offering of thanksgiving to God.

The psalm opens with a prayer of thanks to Yahweh (verses 1-3), followed by an invitation to all the people to join the psalmist in praising God (verses 4-5). The psalmist then describes his past experience, when he felt confident of the Lord's care; but the Lord withdrew his protection, and the psalmist cries to him for help (verses 6-10). The psalm closes with a burst of praise to Yahweh for his goodness (verses 11-12).

Psalm 30, like Psalm 29, exhibits the characteristics of a poem-length chiasmus. Using the words of RSV, the corresponding repeated words or ideas may be laid out as follows:

A	-	-	-	-	-	Verse 1	extol
	B	-	-	-	-	-	2	healed me
		C	-	-	-	-	3	Sheol
			D	-	-	-	4	praise
				E	-	-	5	weeping
					F	-	6	not be moved
					F'	-	7	established
				E'	-	-	8	cried
			D'	-	-	-	9	praise
		C'	-	-	-	-	9	Pit
	B'	-	-	-	-	-	10-11	mourning into dancing
A'	-	-	-	-	-	-	12	praise

The translator should note how the theme of praise recurs in a somewhat evenly-spaced pattern, that is, in the opening verse and then in verses 4, 9, and 12. The psalm draws attention to the use of language as the means of praising God. This is done by the repeated use of terms belonging to the domain of communication and expression: extol, rejoice, cry, sing praises, give thanks, weeping, joy, supplication, tell, hear, mourning, dancing, gladness, not be silent.

HEADING: **"A Prayer of Thanksgiving"** (TEV); "Thanksgiving after mortal danger"; "Joy in the morning"; "Thanks be to God"; "His anger is but for a moment." In some languages the TEV heading will have to be recast as "The psalmist gives God thanks" or "The psalmist prays to God and thanks him."

Hebrew Title: **A Psalm of David. A Song at the dedication of the Temple.**
The title indicates that at some time the psalm was adapted for use in the Festival of Dedication of the Temple, which celebrated the restoration and rededication of the altar in the Temple by the Jewish patriot Judas Maccabeus in 165 B.C. The festival, which lasted eight days, began on the 25th day of Chislev (around December 10). There is no doubt that the Hebrew title is late and does not reflect the original life-setting of this psalm (see Anderson).

30.1-3	RSV		TEV
1	I will extol thee, O LORD, for thou hast drawn me up, and hast not let my foes rejoice over me.	1	I praise you, LORD, because you have saved me and kept my enemies from gloating over me.
2	O LORD my God, I cried to thee for help, and thou hast healed me.	2	I cried to you for help, O LORD my God, and you healed me;
3	O LORD, thou hast brought up my soul from Sheol, restored me to life from among those gone down to the Pit.*i*	3	you kept me from the grave. I was on my way to the depths below,*y* but you restored my life.

i Or that I should not go down to the Pit

y THE DEPTHS BELOW: The world of the dead (see 6.5).

The opening verb **I will extol** means not only to praise but to speak highly of (see its use in 12.8b). So the translation can be "I will proclaim your greatness" (FRCL); TOB, NEB, NIV have "exalt." RSV uses the future tense, TEV the present tense; either is possible, but the present tense seems to be more fitting. The expression **for thou hast drawn me up** (from Sheol, or the Pit, in verse 3) may be translated "because you have rescued, delivered, saved me." It expresses the reason why **I will extol thee**. In some languages the reason will occur before the result clause.

In these words of thanksgiving (verses 1-3) the psalmist praises God for "drawing him up" (verse 1a), a verb used of drawing water out of a well (see Exo 2.16,19); in this instance Yahweh drew the psalmist out of Sheol, the pit in the depths of the earth (verse 3; see 28.1). This is poetic language and must not be understood literally that Yahweh had pulled the psalmist bodily from Sheol; it means that Yahweh did not allow the psalmist to die (as seen in verses 2-3).

The gloating of enemies at the psalmist's distress (RSV **rejoice over me**) is a frequent theme in Psalms (see 25.2). The expression **rejoice over me**, with the meaning of gloating or ridiculing, is translated in some languages in idiomatic terms such as "to turn the nose up at someone," "to wag the head at," or in nonfigurative language, "to say that he is no one at all."

In verse 2 the psalmist recounts the event which prompted this prayer: he was sick and prayed for Yahweh to heal him, and Yahweh did heal him.

In verse 3a the psalmist describes his escape from death: "you brought up my *nefesh* (see 3.2) from Sheol" (see comment at 6.5); the thought is repeated in verse 3b, "you kept me alive from going down to the Pit." In the graphic description of his narrow escape from death, the psalmist says that he was already in the company of the dead on their way down to Sheol (see similar language in 28.1), but Yahweh **restored** his **life**. The language could be read as though it referred to resurrection; it is, however, a vivid expression about being kept alive, about not being allowed to die (see similar language in 16.10; 56.13).

A literal translation of TEV **"you kept me from the grave"** could mean that the psalmist was prevented from approaching a grave. **Brought up my soul from Sheol** can be rendered "you kept me from dying," or stated positively, "you caused me to go on living." **Restored me to life** must sometimes be said "you caused me to see life" or "you put new life into me." **Those gone down to the Pit** will require considerable adjustment in many languages; for example, "I was already nearly dead" or "I had already given up living."

RSV's footnote in verse 3 translates the same Hebrew text as the TEV text. The RSV text represents a different Hebrew text, but the difference between the two is only in the Hebrew vowels. It seems better to translate the text followed by TEV.

30.4	RSV	TEV

RSV	TEV
Sing praises to the LORD, O you his saints, and give thanks to his holy name.	Sing praise to the LORD, all his faithful people! Remember what the Holy One has done, and give him thanks!

The psalmist now invites the people to join him in praising God; the setting is probably the Temple, where the psalmist is offering a thanksgiving sacrifice.

In line a **his saints** means God's own people (see comments on "the godly" in 4.3, where the same Hebrew term appears). The Hebrew word is related to the noun usually translated "steadfast love" (see 5.7), and its principal component of meaning is that of faithfulness to God. The word **saints** or "holy people" in many translations has meanings which are not biblical. **Saints** are called such because of their special relationship with God. Therefore in translation they may be called by a term which represents that relationship, such as **"faithful"** in TEV. Also they are often referred to as "God's people," or in the present context, "his own people."

The second part of the verse is literally "and give praise to the remembrance of his holiness"; the Hebrew for **name** does not occur; the word "remembrance" (see 6.5) here means the mention of God in worship and adoration (see 135.13, where "name" and "remembrance" are used synonymously). Many translations take the Hebrew phrase "the remembrance of his holiness" to mean **his holy name**; this may be "at the remembrance of his holiness"; FRCL "praise him by proclaiming his holiness"; TOB "highly praise him by recalling his holiness"; NJB "remember his unforgettable holiness." GECL is perhaps the best translation: "Thank him and reflect on this, that he is holy!" TEV takes the phrase to mean **"Remember what the Holy One has done,"** with the idea of giving thanks mentioned separately in the last line. It is unnatural in some languages to speak of remembering a possessed quality such as holiness. Therefore it is often necessary to say "remember that he is holy," or negatively, "do not forget that he is holy." See the discussion of **holy** in 28.2.

30.5

RSV	TEV
For his anger is but for a moment, and his favor is for a lifetime. Weeping may tarry for the night, but joy comes with the morning.	His anger lasts only a moment, his goodness for a lifetime. Tears may flow in the night, but joy comes in the morning.

The psalmist's reference to Yahweh's **anger** is caused by the fact that sickness was considered to be punishment for sin, and so was considered proof that Yahweh was angry with him. But the psalmist contrasts the Lord's short-lived anger (**for a moment**) with his permanent favor (**for a lifetime**).

In some languages **anger** is expressed metaphorically as "heat," "blood," or "redness of the eyes." One may sometimes say "the redness of God's eyes lasts only for a little while" or "God's heat against people goes away after a moment."

The word **favor** means an attitude of goodwill, of approval, of readiness to bless.

Dahood takes the Hebrew word for **lifetime** to mean "eternal life." NEB, however, takes the words to mean "In his anger is disquiet, in his favour there is life." And NJV translates line b "and where He is pleased there is life."

His favor is for a lifetime may sometimes be translated, for example, "God's good heart shows itself to a person for a whole lifetime" or "God will make a person see his clean liver for as long as that person lives."

In the second part of the verse the psalmist contrasts spending a night crying and the happiness that comes in the morning.

In some languages it will be necessary to indicate the person who is **weeping**, since **"tears"** and **"joy"** are the results of someone's feelings. It appears from the context, particularly verses 2 and 8, that it is the psalmist who cries in the night. Therefore one may say, for example, "although I cry in the night, I will be glad in the morning." SPCL uses the plural, "If we cry throughout the night, in the morning we shall have joy."

In line c the verb translated **tarry** means literally "to spend the night."

30.6-7

	RSV		TEV
6	As for me, I said in my prosperity, "I shall never be moved."	6	I felt secure and said to myself, "I will never be defeated."
7	By thy favor, O LORD,	7	You were good to me, LORD;

thou hadst established me as a strong mountain;	you protected me like a mountain fortress.
thou didst hide thy face, I was dismayed.	But then you hid yourself from me, and I was afraid.

The psalmist recalls his past, when in his ease he boasted of his success; but when Yahweh withdrew his presence, he felt afraid.

The word translated **prosperity** is found only here; it means quietness, ease. One may translate "when things went well"; NJV "when I was untroubled"; NEB and NJB have "Carefree"; both TEV and SPCL translate "I felt secure."

For verse 6b see the same statement in 10.6.

In verse 7a **thy favor** translates the same word that appears in verse 5b.

The exact meaning of the Hebrew in verse 7b is disputed, though the general sense of security is clear enough. NJB has "Your favour, Yahweh, set me on unassailable heights"; NAB, following the Septuagint, "You had endowed me with majesty and strength"; another possible version is "you established strength for my mountain"; similarly AT and TOB.[1] Dahood has "by your favor you made me more stable than the mighty mountains"; NJV "You . . . made [me] firm as a mighty mountain." NEB, however, translates "it was thy will to shake my mountain refuge"; this, however, is quite improbable. **Established me as a strong mountain** will have little meaning where the highest hill is a barely-noticeable elevation of ground. In such areas it will be necessary to employ a different figure of strength or to avoid the use of the figure altogether; for example, "you protect me like a strong fortress" or "you are like a fortress and you protect me."

For **thou didst hide thy face**, see comment at 13.1. It was the psalmist's illness that caused him to conclude that Yahweh had forsaken him, and for this reason he **was dismayed**, that is, afraid (see the same verb, translated "terrify," in 2.5).

30.8-10   RSV   TEV

8	To thee, O LORD, I cried; and to the LORD I made supplication:	8	I called to you, LORD; I begged for your help:
9	"What profit is there in my death, if I go down to the Pit? Will the dust praise thee? Will it tell of thy faithfulness?	9	"What will you gain from my death? What profit from my going to the grave? Are dead people able to praise you?
10	Hear, O LORD, and be gracious to me! O LORD, be thou my helper!"		Can they proclaim your unfailing goodness?

---

[1]HOTTP also takes the Masoretic text to mean "by your favor you had established strength for my mountain" ("B" decision). It is unclear what "my mountain" means in this context, and HOTTP does not explain.

> 10 Hear me, LORD, and be merciful!
>   Help me, LORD!"

The psalmist pleads with Yahweh, arguing that his death will be of no value to Yahweh, since in Sheol the dead do not praise him (see 6.5 for the same idea).

In verse 8 the Hebrew text changes from the second person of address in line a to the third person in line b; TEV maintains the second person in both lines.

I made supplication: the verb in line b means to ask for mercy, favor, help. NIV has "I made my appeal," NJB "I cry for mercy," and NEB "I plead for mercy."

Verses 9-10 are the psalmist's prayer for help. It may be helpful to introduce them with the words "I said" or "I prayed."

The rhetorical questions in verse 9 all call for a negative answer. It should be noted that the Hebrew text in verse 9 says "What gain is there in my death [literally 'in my blood'], in my going down to the Pit?" which TEV has interpreted as profit to Yahweh (also Kirkpatrick, Weiser, Taylor, Cohen; FRCL, GECL, TOB). Some, however, see it as a question of the psalmist's own gain; he is saying he would profit nothing by dying, for in Sheol he cannot praise God and proclaim his faithfulness (see Anderson). But this would be a strange argument, and the former view is more probable. Death is Yahweh's doing, and the psalmist argues that his death would bring no profit to Yahweh.

TEV's **"from my death"** will in some languages be translated "if I die." **The Pit** is Sheol (as in 16.10).

In verse 9c dead people are spoken of as **the dust**. Sheol, the world of the dead, was pictured as a place of darkness and dust (see 22.15,29; 88.10-12; 115.17 for descriptions of Sheol). The question the psalmist asks God, **will the dust praise thee?** is most appropriate as a rhetorical question and in many languages will require a reply, "No!" In some languages it will be necessary to make clear that it is the dead in the dust who are referred to, or simply **"dead people"** as in TEV.

The Hebrew word translated **faithfulness** in some contexts means "truth" (see 15.2); so NEB has "proclaim thy truth." Most, however, take it here to mean "faithfulness, steadfastness, loyalty" (TEV **"unfailing goodness"**). **Thy faithfulness** is often expressed by a verb phrase; for example, "people can always trust in you."

The plea in verse 10 uses the same verb **be gracious** used in 4.1c; here SPCL translates "have compassion on me"; NIV "be merciful to me," NJB "take pity on me."

As in 10.14d, **helper** in line b is equivalent to "savior." It means not simply to assist, to lend a hand, but to rescue, to save, from a desperate situation.

30.11-12 RSV	TEV
11 Thou hast turned for me my mourning into dancing; thou hast loosed my sackcloth and girded me with gladness,	11 You have changed my sadness into a joyful dance; you have taken away my sorrow and surrounded me with joy.
12 that my soul^j may praise thee and not be silent.	12 So I will not be silent; I will sing praise to you.

> O LORD my God, I will give
> thanks to thee for ever.

> LORD, you are my God;
> I will give you thanks forever.

j Heb that glory

The psalm concludes on a joyful note, as the psalmist describes the joy that is his after Yahweh has restored him to health. In vivid terms he portrays the change from sorrow to happiness: "You changed my mourning into a dance; you took off my sackcloth garment and clothed me with joy." (It was customary to wear a garment made of rough sackcloth in times of mourning or distress.)

The expression **turned . . . my mourning into dancing** is a translation problem in some languages, because dancing in some areas is related to mourning and not to happiness. In such cases the translator must use the symbolism of joy to express the transformation from sorrow to happiness; for example, "you turned my sadness into singing" or "I cried in sadness for the dead, but you caused me to beat the drum for joy."

In some language areas there is special clothing that is worn when in mourning, or special articles such as bags or paints are put on the body of the mourner. The expression **thou hast loosed my sackcloth** may be adapted to fit the local mourning customs; for example, "you have taken off my bag of mourning" or "you have removed my death paints." In languages where the expression **girded me with gladness** will be unnatural, it is possible to make some adjustments such as "you have dressed me in clothing that shows I am glad" or "you have put on me clothing that brings me joy."

RSV makes verse 12 the purpose of the action described in verse 11: **that my soul may . . . .** TEV takes verse 12 as the result, **"So I will not . . . ."** It seems better to treat the verse as result, or consequence, and not as purpose.

In verse 12a **my soul** (TEV "I") translates the Hebrew "glory," to which the Septuagint adds the first singular pronoun, giving the wording "my glory"; for this meaning of "glory" see comments on 7.5; 16.9. NJV translates "[my] whole being."[2] NEB has "my spirit," NIV and NJB "my heart," and FRCL "with all my heart." TOB is the only translation consulted that reflects the absence of the possessive pronoun in the Hebrew text: "the soul sings to you without pause."

---

[2]HOTTP prefers the Masoretic text, "glory," and says it can be understood in two ways: (1) "I praise you"; (2) "people praise you, O Glory" (a title for God).

Psalm 31

This psalm cannot easily be identified with any one type, since it combines elements of sorrow (verses 9-13), statements of confidence (verses 3,4,14-15), thanksgiving (verses 7-8,19-20), and pleas for punishment of enemies (verses 4,17-18). Some see it as a composite work. Its principal note seems to be that of thanksgiving for deliverance from danger and distress, perhaps from a siege.

This psalm consists of an alternating series of statements of trust and petitions for deliverance, and concludes with a command to trust, "love the LORD" and "be strong." Although the lengths of the respective units are quite uneven, the pattern of alternation is unbroken from beginning to end. Reasons accompany three petitions as well as two statements of trust. The full scheme may be tabulated as follows:

1a	T		
1b-2d	P		
3a	T		
3b-4b	P	+	R
5a-8b	T	+	R
9a-13	P	+	R
14	T		
15b-17a	P	+	R
17b	T	+	R
17c-18	P		
19-22	T	+	R
23-24	Command to T		

P = Petition
R = Reason
T = Trust

The translator should note while reading the psalm that each of the reasons, excepting that accompanying 9a-13, is related to the notion of trusting; for example, 4b "refuge"; 5b "redeemed me . . . faithful God"; 7b "seen my affliction"; 8a "not delivered me . . . to my enemies"; 8b "set my feet in a broad place"; 17b "I call on you"; 21b "shown his steadfast love." In verses 9a-13 the reason element takes on the form of a lament. The repeated and intertwining theme of trust throughout this psalm makes it imperative that "trust in God" appear in the heading.

HEADING: "**A Prayer of Trust in God**" (TEV); "Prayer in distress, and thanksgiving for escape"; "Prayer in time of ordeal"; "Complete confidence in the LORD." The TEV heading can be adapted for some languages by saying, for example, "The psalmist prays and puts his trust in God."

Hebrew Title: **To the choirmaster. A Psalm of David.**
For a similar title see Psalm 13.

31.1-2

RSV	TEV

1 In thee, O LORD, do I seek refuge;
    let me never be put to shame;
        in thy righteousness deliver me!
2 Incline thy ear to me,
    rescue me speedily!
    Be thou a rock of refuge for me,
    a strong fortress to save me!
	1 I come to you, LORD, for protection;
	        never let me be defeated.
	    You are a righteous God;
	        save me, I pray!
	2 Hear me! Save me now!
	    Be my refuge to protect me;
	    my defense to save me.

The translator will notice that in these two verses three different words are used for "to save"; and further notice should be taken of the fact that RSV and other translations do not try to be completely consistent in the translation of these synonymous verbs as they appear in different psalms. The translator should feel free to use the most appropriate word in the context, without trying to be always consistent.

Petitions in prayer in English use the imperative mood, so that God is commanded to be or do something. In some languages it may be necessary to use a different style, more in keeping with prayer. One doesn't command, but asks, petitions, or requests God to do something.

The psalmist's plea for help and protection (verses 1-2) is phrased in familiar terms. For **I seek refuge** see comments on 2.12; **be put to shame**, see 6.10 and comments; **righteousness**, see comments on 5.8; **deliver**, see 17.13 and comments.

Anderson points out that **righteousness** here has the sense of keeping one's pledged word; the psalmist appeals to God's promise to protect him. **Righteousness** is expressed in some languages as "straight" or "just." In some cases it will be necessary to recast **in thy righteousness** (TEV "**You are a righteous God**"); for example, "you are a God who always does what is right," "you are a God who acts fairly" or, because "fair" and "just judgment" is an important aspect of God's dealing with his people, in some languages one may say "you are a God who judges fairly."

In verse 2, for **incline thy ear** see comments on 10.17 and 17.6; **rescue** is the verb that in 7.1 is translated "deliver"; **refuge** translates the word that in 27.1 is translated "stronghold"; and for **strong fortress** see comments on 18.2.

Incline thy ear to me may often be rendered by other figures of speech; for example, "put your ear on my words" or "have two ears for what I say."

In many languages it is not natural to command someone to be an inanimate object such as a **rock**. However, it is normally possible to supplement an imperative with a simile; for example, "protect me as a rock protects a person" or "give me protection and shelter like a rock that shelters a person."

Strong fortress may be expressed in a nonfigurative manner as in TEV, or the translator may substitute another known figure such as a shield, or combine the nonfigure with a simile; for example, "defend me the way a strong fortress defends people."

The translator should note that in 2c and 2d the common pattern used in parallelism, in which the literal item appears in the first line and the metaphor in the second, is set aside, since both **rock** and **strong fortress** (literally "house of fortress") are both metaphors.

It should be noted that verses 1-3a of this psalm are almost exactly like Psalm 71.1-3.

31.3-4	RSV	TEV

3	Yea, thou art my rock and my fortress; for thy name's sake lead me and guide me,	3 You are my refuge and defense; guide me and lead me as you have promised.
4	take me out of the net which is hidden for me, for thou art my refuge.	4 Keep me safe from the trap that has been set for me; shelter me from danger.

In verse 3 the word for **fortress** is the same as in verse 2; **rock** is here a different one from the one in verse 2, but it has the same meaning (it is also used in 18.2).

For thy name's sake: see discussion at 23.3.

The two verbs **lead me and guide me** are used in 23.2,3; here the two forms in Hebrew make for a pleasant alliteration: *taneheni* and *tenahaleni*.

For the phrase in verse 4 "to hide a net," see the comments at 9.15. The expression **take me out of the net** gives the impression that the psalmist is already caught. However, see TEV. The intention is that the writer asks to be spared from being caught in the trap. In some languages this can best be expressed, for example, "Don't let me pass where my enemies have laid their traps" or "Guide me away from the hidden traps of my enemies."

Refuge is the same word used in verse 2 "[a rock] of refuge." The translator should follow RSV in the last line, translating it as a statement, and not as a petition as in TEV.

31.5	RSV	TEV

Into thy hand I commit my spirit; thou hast redeemed me, O LORD, faithful God.	I place myself in your care. You will save me, LORD; you are a faithful God.

The first part of this verse is quoted in Luke 23.46 as it is translated in the Septuagint, except that the Septuagint has the future tense of the verb, and in Luke 23.46 the present tense is used. The Hebrew verb translated **commit** means to entrust, leave in the care of, leave in custody. **My spirit** here means "myself"; the words are not being said by a dying man, and so they do not mean precisely what they mean in Luke 23.46. The psalmist is committing himself to Yahweh's care and protection (as in verse 15a), to keep him safe from his enemies.

For **redeemed** see comment at 25.22. **"You will save me"** is how TEV translates **thou hast redeemed me** (also AT, NAB); NJV, BJ, Mft translate in the present tense; SPCL, NIV, and Dahood translate as a plea, in the imperative mood; RSV, NJV, NEB, and FRCL translate it as a statement of a past fact. In the context a petition is appropriate; a strong affirmation of trust, however, seems the best choice.

For **faithful God** see discussion of "faithfulness" at 30.9; some here translate "God of truth" (KJV, NIV, NEB, NJB, SPCL) in contrast with "vain idols" in verse 6. The expression **faithful God** must be rendered in some languages as "you are a God in whom people can trust."

31.6-7   RSV   TEV

6   Thou hatest[k] those who pay re-   6   You hate those who worship false
        gard to vain idols;   gods,
    but I trust in the LORD.   but I trust in you.
7   I will rejoice and be glad for thy   7   I will be glad and rejoice
        steadfast love,   because of your constant love.
    because thou hast seen my   You see my suffering;
        affliction,   you know my trouble.
    thou hast taken heed of my
        adversities,

[k] With one Heb Ms Gk Syr Jerome:
Heb *I hate*

As the RSV footnote shows, **Thou hatest** is the wording of one Hebrew manuscript and of the ancient versions (also Anderson; TEV, NEB, NAB, BJ, NJB); Weiser, Dahood, NJV, TOB, FRCL, SPCL have "I hate."[1] Either wording can be defended; in favor of "You hate" is that fact that **but I trust the LORD** in line b contrasts the psalmist with **those who pay regard to vain idols**. If "I hate" is chosen, it may be better to begin line b with "and" and not **but**: "and I trust in you" (the psalmist's hatred for idolaters complementing his trust in Yahweh).

The second verb in verse 6a (RSV **pay regard to**) usually means protect, guard (see "protect" in 12.7); here it has the sense of "revere" (K-B); SPCL, NEB, NAB translate **"worship,"** like TEV; NJB has "worshippers"; NJV translates "rely on."

The phrase translated **vain idols** (NEB "useless idols"; NIV "worthless idols") is "deceptive illusions"; the noun means a transitory vapor, or mist, which is

---

[1]HOTTP prefers the Masoretic text, "I hate" ("C" decision).

insubstantial and soon vanishes. In Jonah 2.8 the phrase has the same meaning as here (so Briggs, Anderson, Weiser). Some, however, take it in the sense of "empty folly" (NJV) or "false vanities" (AT). The translation of **vain idols** will depend upon the way in which this Hebrew expression is to be interpreted. If it is taken in the sense of "empty vanities," it may be rendered in some languages as "things that have no worth" or "worthless things in which people cannot put their trust." If it is taken in the more traditional sense of idols, one may say, for example, "idols that have no value," "idols that can do nothing," or "wooden gods that are really nothing."

In verse 7 the statement of the psalmist's coming joy results from his consciousness of Yahweh's care, expressed in the following two lines, which are nearly synonymous: **thou hast seen . . . thou hast taken heed**, and **my affliction . . . my adversities**. The verb translated **taken heed of** may have the more effective sense of "care for" (Anderson; NEB) or "watch over" (NAB), or else "take care of." The parallelism with **hast seen** in the preceding line, however, seems to favor "**know**" here (TEV).

My adversities translates the Hebrew "the troubles of my *nefesh*" (see 3.2).

31.8 RSV TEV

| and hast not delivered me into the hand of the enemy; thou hast set my feet in a broad place. | You have not let my enemies capture me; you have given me freedom to go where I wish. |

The translator should feel free to begin verse 8 as a new sentence, as TEV and others do. The language is that of a hunt, in which the psalmist's enemies are trying to capture him. The language here is conventional for this kind of psalm, and nothing may be inferred with any certainty concerning the specific nature of the danger the psalmist was in.

The verb phrase **hast not delivered me** is a strong negative affirmation of Yahweh's protection and care. However Yahweh did it, he kept the psalmist safe from his enemies.

For the figure **thou hast set my feet in a broad place**, see comments on 18.19. This expression may be translated in some languages by idiomatic terms; for example, "you have untied my ropes" or "you have removed my wall."

31.9-10 RSV TEV

| 9 | Be gracious to me, O LORD, for I am in distress; my eye is wasted from grief, my soul and my body also. | 9 | Be merciful to me, LORD, for I am in trouble; my eyes are tired from so much crying; I am completely worn out. |
| 10 | For my life is spent with sorrow, and my years with sighing; my strength fails because of my misery,*l* | 10 | I am exhausted by sorrow, and weeping has shortened my life. |

and my bones waste away.

^{l} Gk Syr: Heb *iniquity*

I am weak from all my troubles;^{a}
even my bones are wasting
away.

^{a} *Some ancient translations* troubles;
Hebrew iniquity.

Verses 9-13 continue to provide reasons why the psalmist petitions the Lord. Unlike the other reasons given, all of which have to do with trust in God, this section is a personal lament, and since it stands out from the overall pattern of the psalm, it may be best to provide it with a separate title; for example, "The psalmist fears his enemies" or "The psalmist suffers from sickness and enemies."

From a statement of serene confidence and trust (verses 7-8), the psalmist now turns to a description of his pitiable condition and an urgent plea for Yahweh to save him. For **Be gracious to me** see 4.1c and comments.

It is impossible to know whether the language in these two verses is to be taken literally or is conventional language portraying spiritual and emotional upheaval. The psalmist is in distress and is so completely **wasted** from weeping that he feels his life has been shortened. For **my eye is wasted from grief** in verse 9b, see 6.7a and comments, where the same statement is made. The wording of verse 9b-c may suggest that the psalmist's **eye** was something separate from his **body**. This is poetic language, of course, and is a vivid way of portraying how worn out he is. In many languages the passive usage in verses 9 and 10 will require shifting to active constructions. In some languages trouble and sorrow as well as many other emotional and physical states of the body are said to possess or hold the person; for example, "trouble has taken hold of me."

In verse 10a **spent** means "**exhausted**," worn out. In line **b** the verb "are spent" is to be understood; TEV has supplied "**has shortened**."

In verse 10c the Masoretic text has "in iniquity," which is preferred by Weiser and HOTTP ("C" decision), TOB, FRCL, NJV; the ancient versions translate "in trouble," which is the text followed by RSV, TEV, NEB, NAB, BJ, NJB, GECL, SPCL.

Line **d my bones waste away** represents a heightening of line **a** through the use of a metaphor, since the wasting away of bones would only happen to a corpse that is decaying. Although TEV has retained the metaphor, it will probably be better to use a metaphor having to do with bodily weakness. The heightening effect can be translated, as in TEV, with "**even**." However, in English it will be more idiomatic to say something like "I am weak from all my troubles; I am even worn to the bone" or "more than that, I am totally exhausted."

<u>31.11-12</u>   RSV   TEV

11 I am the scorn of all my adversar-
    ies,
    a horror^m to my neighbors,
    an object of dread to my acquain-
    tances;
    those who see me in the street

11 All my enemies, and especially my
    neighbors,
    treat me with contempt;
    Those who know me are afraid of
    me;
    when they see me in the street,

flee from me.		they run away.
12 I have passed out of mind like one who is dead;	12	Everyone has forgotten me, as though I were dead;
I have become like a broken vessel.		I am like something thrown away.

ᵐ Cn. Heb exceedingly

The psalmist's suffering is further increased by his enemies; he feels that everyone has abandoned him, and he is left without any friends.

Everyone avoids the psalmist, either because of his loathsome disease or else because they fear that he is the object of God's anger.

Scorn of my adversaries must be translated in some languages as "My enemies say that I am no one at all," or in direct discourse, "My enemies say to me, 'You are nothing!' "

In verse 11b the Masoretic text "exceedingly" is difficult to understand (see RSV footnote). Several ways of dealing with the text have been proposed: RSV understands the text to say **a horror**; NAB understands "scorn"; NEB places different vowels with the same Hebrew consonants of the Masoretic text to get "burden"; BJ understands "trash, garbage," and NJB "loathsome." TOB translates lines a and b of the Masoretic text "I am insulted by all my adversaries, even more by my neighbors," and this is the way TEV and FRCL have understood the text.[2] NIV has "Because of all my enemies, I am the utter contempt of my neighbors" (similarly NJV). This does not seem as probable as the way TOB has translated the passage.

Street, which implies a pedestrian thoroughfare, must be rendered sometimes as "trail" or "path."

In line a of verse 12, the psalmist compares himself to someone who has died and has been forgotten by all. **Dead** in line a is paralleled by **a broken vessel** in line b, which translates a participle meaning "perished" and a noun meaning "utensil, article, thing." The Hebrew phrase is variously translated: NEB and NJB "something lost"; NJV "an object given up for lost"; SPCL "a smashed jar"; or else "a broken vessel." The translator should choose the word that goes best with "object, article, thing." The same simile is used in Jeremiah 22.28.

---

[2]HOTTP says the first part of the verse may be interpreted as follows: "for all my adversaries I have become a laughing-stock, above all, even for my neighbors" ("A" decision).

31.13   RSV   TEV

> Yea, I hear the whispering of
>   many—
>   terror on every side!—
> as they scheme together against
>   me,
>   as they plot to take my life.

> I hear many enemies whispering;
>   terror is all around me.
> They are making plans against
>   me,
>   plotting to kill me.

In line a the psalmist says only that he hears many people **whispering**; in the context it is clear that he is referring to enemies who are plotting against him. So NEB "whispering threats." NIV and NJV have "slander," which is possible but does not seem probable here.

In line b **terror on every side!** may be taken as what the **many** of line a are **whispering**; so, in different ways, NEB, TOB, SPCL. This seems to fit the context of a siege. Or else it may be the psalmist's own perception of his situation: he is surrounded by frightful enemies, who fill him with dread. The expression occurs frequently in Jeremiah (as in Jer 20.3,10).

Lines c and d are parallel and nearly synonymous; line d makes clear what his enemies are planning to do, that is, to kill him.

31.14-15   RSV   TEV

> 14 But I trust in thee, O LORD,
>   I say, "Thou art my God."
> 15 My times are in thy hand;
>   deliver me from the hand of my
>   enemies and persecutors!

> 14 But my trust is in you, O LORD;
>   you are my God.
> 15 I am always in your care;
>   save me from my enemies,
>   from those who persecute me.

Now the psalmist expresses his trust in God, confident that God will rescue him from his enemies. In verse 14 it is not necessary to have the psalmist quoting himself, particularly if that will appear to be somewhat strange and unusual, and so TEV may be a good model. But if it is effective, the translator should follow the Hebrew form as RSV has it.

In verse 15a **My times** is taken to mean "my fate" (NJV), "destiny" (NAB; see GECL), "fortunes" (NEB), "life" (SPCL, FRCL). Dahood takes **times** as being the seven stages of life; so it means "my whole life" (see Anderson; see NJB "every moment of my life").

My enemies and persecutors are not two different groups; the meaning is "my enemies, those who persecute me."

Persecutors is sometimes rendered "people who cause me to suffer." TEV, which has recast the noun **persecutors** as a clause, has created an additional line. Translators may find it desirable to do likewise.

RSV TEV

	RSV		TEV
16	Let thy face shine on thy servant; save me in thy steadfast love!	16	Look on your servant with kindness; save me in your constant love.
17	Let me not be put to shame, O LORD, for I call on thee; let the wicked be put to shame, let them go dumbfounded to Sheol.	17	I call to you, LORD; don't let me be disgraced. May the wicked be disgraced; may they go silently down to the world of the dead.
18	Let the lying lips be dumb, which speak insolently against the righteous in pride and contempt.	18	Silence those liars— all the proud and arrogant who speak with contempt about righteous men.

The psalmist prays for Yahweh to help him, the Lord's **servant** (verses 16-17b), and to punish his enemies and put them to death (verses 17c-18).

The plea in verse 16a, **let thy face shine**, is similar to the expression in 4.6, which is used also in 67.1; 80.3,7,19; 119.135; it means to look on someone with favor, mercy, kindness. In many languages **let thy face shine on thy servant** must be recast to say, for example, "be kind to me who serves you," or idiomatically, "have a warm heart for me your servant."

It should be clear in translation that **thy servant** is the psalmist himself.

In verse 16b **in thy steadfast love** indicates the reason, or motivation, which will lead Yahweh to **save** the psalmist. So a translation can say "because of your great love for me" or "since you love me."

For the plea in verse 17 that the psalmist's enemies, and not he himself, **be put to shame**, see verse 1 and 25.2-3. **Put to shame** must be rendered in some languages idiomatically; for example, "Do not give me a burning face" or "Do not make me hide my face." TEV reverses lines a and b of verse 17, and the translator should feel free to do the same if it is effective in the target language.

The language the psalmist uses in describing his enemies is standard, and it is impossible to know the exact nature of the lies about the psalmist that they were spreading. Whatever they were, he wanted his enemies to die.

In verse 17d the word translated **dumbfounded** may be taken to mean "lifeless," although it usually means that one is so surprised as to be silent. NJV translates "be silenced in Sheol," and NJB "go down to Sheol in silence." Dahood derives the verbal form from "to hurl," translating "be hurled into Sheol." SPCL is quite good: "hurl them into the silence of the grave." **Go dumbfounded to Sheol** may be translated in some languages as "let them die and go silently to the grave" or "let them die and be put in the silent grave." In some translations it may be more effective to make the prayer a direct plea to God: "Defeat and humiliate the wicked; send them down to the silent world of the dead."

In verse 18a the Hebrew is "May those lying lips be bound" (the verb that is used of binding sheaves or grain). In some languages it is possible to use figures which approximate closely the Hebrew usage; for example, "Tie shut the mouths of those who speak lies."

In verse 18b **insolently** translates a word found only here and in 1 Samuel 2.3; Psalms 75.5; 94.4. The basic meaning is that of arrogance, pride; those liars "**speak with contempt**" (TEV) against righteous people.

<table>
<tr><td>31.19</td><td>RSV</td><td>TEV</td></tr>
</table>

RSV	TEV
O how abundant is thy goodness, which thou hast laid up for those who fear thee, and wrought for those who take refuge in thee, in the sight of the sons of men!	How wonderful are the good things you keep for those who honor you! Everyone knows how good you are, how securely you protect those who trust you.

In verses 19-22 the psalmist praises Yahweh for his goodness to him and to other devout Israelites.

In line a the Hebrew word "great" may indicate quantity (RSV **abundant**) or quality (TEV "**wonderful**"). The verb translated **thou hast laid up** portrays Yahweh's **goodness** as a treasure which he accumulates and guards, and from which, at the appropriate time, he gives out to those who honor him. **Those who fear thee** refers to people who reverence God and worship him. In some translations one must say "people who worship you" or "people who bow down before you" (see comments on "fear" in 5.7).

In the second part of the verse TEV has specified the act of **goodness** which Yahweh bestows on those who seek protection with him. A translation may imitate more closely the form of the Hebrew, as follows: "In full view of everyone, you give good things to those who go to you for protection."

For the verb translated **take refuge**, see comment at 2.12. **In the sight of the sons of men** indicates that Yahweh's goodness is evident and manifest, seen by everyone (for **sons of men** see 11.4 and comment).

RSV	TEV
In the covert of thy presence thou hidest them from the plots of men; thou holdest them safe under thy shelter from the strife of tongues.	You hide them in the safety of your presence from the plots of men; in a safe shelter you hide them from the insults of their enemies.

31.20

In line a the Hebrew is "you hide them in the hiding place of your face"—the word "face" here meaning, as often, "presence." For the same sentiment, expressed in similar language, see 27.5. **In the covert of thy presence** is translated in TEV by two noun phrases, "**in the safety of your presence.**" However, in many languages this expression will have to be recast; for example, "You hide them in a safe place where you are present." When combining lines a and b, one may say "You hide them where you are present, and keep them safe from people's plots."

In line b the word translated **plots** occurs only here in the Old Testament; it seems to mean "roughness" and is variously interpreted: NEB "men in league together"; NJB "human plotting"; BJ "intrigues"; NJV "scheming men"; ZÜR "ravings"; Dahood "slanderings." AT, NAB translate as do RSV and TEV.

The **shelter** here may be, as in 27.5, the Temple (so Taylor), or it may be God's general care and protection.

The **strife of tongues** in line d may be taken either as "**insults**" (TEV, SPCL) or as "accusations, attacks" (see NIV).

31.21-22   RSV   TEV

21 Blessed be the LORD,   21 Praise the LORD!
      for he has wondrously shown   How wonderfully he showed his
        his steadfast love to me   love for me
      when I was beset as in a be-   when I was surrounded and
        sieged city.   attacked!
22 I had said in my alarm,   22 I was afraid and thought
      "I am driven far^{n} from thy   that he had driven me out of
        sight."   his presence.
      But thou didst hear my supplica-   But he heard my cry,
        tions,   when I called to him for help.
      when I cried to thee for help.

^{n} Another reading is *cut off*

Blessed be: see comments at 18.46 and 16.7.

He has wondrously shown his steadfast love requires more adjustments in some languages than in TEV. This is so since in some languages it is not possible to "show love." Hence it is often necessary to say, for example, "he has loved me in a wonderful way" or "he has loved me very much. How wonderfully he has done it!"

In verse 21c the Masoretic text is "in a besieged city" (which RSV translates as a simile). Some take the adjective here to mean "stress" (see K-B) and change the Hebrew for "in a city" to Hebrew for "in a time," which results in "in time of stress" (SPCL); others make other changes to get "in time of trouble." NJV takes the Masoretic text to refer to the Lord, "a veritable bastion." TOB translates literally "in a besieged city"; another example may be "in the fortified city," and NJB "in a fortified city," referring, perhaps, to Jerusalem. Dahood has "from the fortified city," a reference to the heavenly abode of Yahweh. It is impossible to decide whether the language is meant literally or figuratively.^{3} It seems best to translate either quite literally, "when I was in a besieged city," or else to translate as a simile, "when I was

---

^{3}HOTTP says the expression may be taken literally, "in a besieged (or, fortified) city" or figuratively, of God's grace, "as a fortified city" ("A" decision).

like a besieged city" (FRCL); TEV has understood the Hebrew as a simile but has abandoned altogether the figure of a city under siege.

If the translator wishes to keep something similar to **a besieged city**, it may be necessary to recast this expression as a descriptive phrase and say, for example, "a city that is being attacked by enemies" or "a city that soldiers are attacking to destroy."

In verse 22 Yahweh is addressed in the second person; as often, TEV retains the third person of verse 21.

In verse 22b **I am driven far** translates a Hebrew verb (*garash*) found in two manuscripts (see also Jonah 2.5); the Masoretic text has the verb *garaz*, "be exterminated," while other Hebrew manuscripts have the verb *gazar*, meaning "cut, slaughter." The sense "to be driven out" seems to fit the context better than "be slaughtered." "To be cut off," meaning "to be separated," also fits the context. HOTTP says the Masoretic text means "I found myself left unprovided for." To be **driven far from thy sight** will require some adjustments in translation; for example, "he has sent me away from himself" or "he has made me go far away from him."

31.23-24	RSV		TEV
23	Love the LORD, all you his saints! The LORD preserves the faithful, but abundantly requites him who acts haughtily.	23	Love the LORD, all his faithful people. The LORD protects the faithful, but punishes the proud as they deserve.
24	Be strong, and let your heart take courage, all you who wait for the LORD!	24	Be strong, be courageous, all you that hope in the LORD.

The psalm ends with an exhortation to the people, who are called the Lord's **saints** (see discussion of "the godly" in 4.3) and **the faithful** (see comments at 12.1). **Saints** is often rendered "you who belong to God" or "you who worship God." The command **Love the LORD** in the Bible refers not so much to the emotion as to the willingness and desire to be faithful to him, to obey him, and to do what he commands.

In contrast with the protection he gives to his people, the Lord "pays back liberally to the one who acts proudly." Here the verb "pay back" (RSV **requites**) is used in a bad sense of punishment; in 22.25 it is used in a good sense of "paying" one's promises.

TEV **"as they deserve"** represents the sense of **abundantly**; some idiomatic expressions can be very effective: "pays back in full" (NIV); "repays . . . with interest" (NJB); "pays . . . in full" (NEB); "gives with interest what they deserve" (SPCL).

In some languages it may be possible to command someone to **take courage** but not possible to command anyone to **be strong**. In such cases translators may wish to use a synonym for "be courageous," since strength of courage seems to be implied in this context, or else "Make your courage strong" or "Make the courage of your heart strong."

TEV's **"be courageous"** translates the Hebrew "be courageous in your hearts"; and the verb <u>wait for</u> expresses an attitude of confident expectation (see the synonymous verb in 25.3). The expression <u>wait for the LORD</u> with the sense of hope can often be rendered as "look forward with confidence in the LORD" or "have confidence in God because he is God."

Psalm 32

This psalm is usually classified as a thanksgiving prayer, offered by a man who has had his sins forgiven, as shown by the fact that the Lord had healed him. Illness and trouble were regarded as punishment for sin, requiring confession and forgiveness. Toombs suggests that this psalm was probably composed to be offered in the Temple in connection with the presentation of an offering for sin.

The psalm opens with words of thanks to God for having forgiven sins (verses 1-2), followed by the psalmist's experience in the past, before and after he confessed his sins (verses 3-5). Next the psalmist praises God's protecting care (verses 6-7), relates how God had instructed him to submit to his will (verses 8-9), and concludes with a statement of the spiritual truth he learned in his experience (verse 10) and an exhortation for all to praise the Lord (verse 11).

According to ancient church liturgical usage, this is one of the seven penitential psalms (the others are 6; 38; 51; 102; 130; and 143).

HEADING: "**Confession and Forgiveness**" (TEV); "Repentance and forgiveness"; "Remission of sin"; "Candid admission of sin." The TEV heading must be recast in some languages so that the two nouns are expressed as verb phrases; for example, "The psalmist confesses his sin and asks God to forgive him."

Hebrew Title: **A Psalm of David. A Maskil.**

The Hebrew is literally "By David, *Maskil*." This word, which occurs also in 47.7 and in the Hebrew titles of Psalms 42; 44; 45; 52; 55; 74; 78; 88; 89; 143, is a participle of a verb which means "be wise, prudent"; in 2 Chronicles 30.22 it means to be fit, capable. Some see in the title the indication that the psalm was meant to instruct (Toombs; so verse 8 "I will instruct you"); others see it as indicating the skill with which the psalm was composed (Ewald, Kirkpatrick), while others see it as stressing the element of meditation. NJB translates "Poem"; Mft "Ode."

32.1-2

RSV	TEV
1 Blessed is he whose transgression is forgiven, whose sin is covered.	1 Happy are those whose sins are forgiven, whose wrongs are pardoned.
2 Blessed is the man to whom the LORD imputes no iniquity, and in whose spirit there is no deceit.	2 Happy is the man whom the LORD does not accuse of doing wrong and who is free from all deceit.

For **Blessed is he** see 1.1 and comments. The expression **Blessed is he** refers to the fortunate state of the person whose sins have been forgiven. In some languages the force of the congratulations implied is lost when stated in the third person. Therefore one must sometimes shift to the second person; for example, "How fortunate you are!" or "Congratulations to you!"

In verses 1-2 three synonyms are used for sin: the first one (**transgression**) is generally taken to indicate disobedience, rebellion against the divine will; the second one (**sin**) is misconduct, faulty action; the third one (**iniquity**) is wrong, evil. In verse 2b **deceit** stands for lie, hypocrisy, fraud; and **spirit** represents the inner self, the person's character. In some languages it will not be possible to make the distinction in the nature of sins suggested here. However, in some languages it is possible to qualify evil deeds in order to approximate the suggested differences in meaning. The translator must be careful not to create complex syntactic problems in attempting to make these distinctions.

A poetic device sometimes used in parallelism is matching or contrasting genders. In verse 1, for example, the Hebrew noun translated **transgression** is masculine, and its parallel, **sins**, is feminine. In the following set of parallel lines, **iniquity** is masculine and **deceit** is feminine. One of the functions of this usage of genders in parallelism is to give the impression of completeness or to express harmony. In translation there may be nothing equivalent in the receptor language morphology or in the stylistics of its poetry. However, it is important for the translator to be aware of such Hebrew devices so that equivalent poetic devices may be used when available and appropriate.

In verses 1-2a three verbs are used for forgiveness: (1) "carry away" (the Hebrew for **forgiven**), sin being thought of as a burden; (2) "conceal, hide" (**covered**), sin seen as an imperfection, a defect which must be removed, or else as a stain which must be wiped out; (3) "not to regard as guilty" (**imputes no iniquity**), that is, to consider innocent. Some see in this last one a commercial figure, to cancel a debt (see NEB "the LORD lays no guilt to his account"). In the case of the second verb (verse 1b), the English verbal phrase **is covered** may suggest "covered over," that is, disguised or concealed in such a way that it is not seen. This is not an adequate statement of what forgiveness involves, and a translator must be careful not to give the wrong impression.

Verses 1-2a are quoted in Romans 4.7-8 exactly as they appear in the Septuagint.

32.3   RSV   TEV

When I declared not my sin, my body wasted away through my groaning all day long.	When I did not confess my sins, I was worn out from crying all day long.

The psalmist describes his condition before he had confessed his sins and received forgiveness. He sees his illness and misery as the result of the Lord's punishing him.

The Hebrew of verse 3a is "When I was silent," which is taken by nearly all commentators to mean **"When I did not confess my sins"** (TEV). The psalmist describes his weakened condition as "my bones wasted away" (the same verb is used in 102.26 of clothes that wear out); for the same idea see 31.10. The expression **declared not my sin**, referring to confession of sin, is expressed variously in different languages; for example, "to accuse oneself of sins," "to count up one's sins," "to whiten one's stomach," "to cause one's wrongs to say good-bye," and "to say openly 'I have sinned.' "

The word translated **groaning** is used of a lion "roaring" (see Job 4.10; Isa 5.29); here it may be weeping or else anguished prayer.

32.4   RSV   TEV

> For day and night thy hand was
>   heavy upon me;
> my strength was dried up[o] as by
>   the heat of summer.   *Selah*

> Day and night you punished me,
>   LORD;
> my strength was completely
>   drained,
> as moisture is dried up by the
>   summer heat.

[o] Heb obscure

The psalmist regarded his illness as punishment (line a); literally "your hand was heavy on me," that is, "you beat me severely" (see the same idiom in 38.2b; 39.10).

The second part of the verse is difficult to understand; the Masoretic text is "was changed my moisture by heats of summer." The ancient versions differ from the Masoretic text and from each other. The word translated **strength** (TEV "moisture") occurs only here and in Numbers 11.8, of "bread (or, cake) baked with olive oil." Here it is taken to mean "moisture, sap," in the sense of vitality, strength.

The word translated **heat** occurs only here in the Old Testament. Following one Hebrew manuscript, which has "as the heat" (instead of the Masoretic text "by the heat"), TEV has taken the language to express a simile and filled it out with ". . . as moisture is dried up by the summer heat"; similarly RSV, NEB, NAB, NJV.[1] FRCL has "I was exhausted as a plant by the fierce summer heat"; similarly SPCL. In some languages it is not natural to speak of one's strength drying up. Strength is sometimes said to melt, to wither, or fall down. In languages which employ a different description of failing strength, it will often be necessary to adapt the type of simile used; for example, as in SPCL "as a flower withers from the heat of summer, so I have felt myself fade away."

Some, instead of the Masoretic text "my moisture," make the conjecture "my tongue"; Dahood takes the Masoretic text to be the vocative "O Shaddai," a title for God. These conjectures do not have good support.

---

[1]HOTTP says the Masoretic text means "my strength was dried up in (or, by) the heat of [summer]." One may assume that HOTTP does not mean to say that the psalmist had suffered a sunstroke; but HOTTP does not explicitly state that the statement is to be taken figuratively, not literally.

For _Selah_ see comments on 3.2.

32.5	RSV	TEV

RSV	TEV

I acknowledged my sin to thee,
    and I did not hide my iniquity;
I said, "I will confess my trans-
    gressions to the LORD";
then thou didst forgive the guilt
    of my sin.   _Selah_
	Then I confessed my sins to you;
	    I did not conceal my wrong-
	    doings.
	I decided to confess them to you,
	    and you forgave all my sins.

The turning point in the psalmist's experience was his decision to confess his sins to Yahweh. The vocabulary is much the same as in verses 1-2a. The first two lines of verse 5 say essentially the same thing, first in a positive manner than then negatively.

The psalmist returns to the first verse and picks up three nouns: sin, iniquity, transgressions. However, for the purpose of emphasis these words are placed in a different order from their first occurrence in verse 1. Accordingly the gender matching is different also. In a more formal translation such as RSV, the rearrangement of the same words is more evident than in TEV. The translator should consider the importance of retaining the same terms as used in verse 1 as part of the poet's emphasis through varied repetition. If emphasis is not obtained in this way, it should be done in ways natural to the poetic devices of the receptor language.

In line a the Hebrew verb for **acknowledged** is the causative form of the verb "to know," thus "to make known," that is, to confess, admit, reveal. **I acknowledged my sin** is therefore "**I confessed my sins**" in TEV. In some languages this expression may have to be recast to say, for example, "I told you openly that I had sinned; I did not say that I had not sinned." In some languages an idiomatic example will be more natural; for example, "I carried my evil on my head where you could see it."

In line b the negative counterpart to the verb in line a is **did not hide**; this verb appears only here in the Psalms. These three verbs, **I acknowledged, I did not hide**, and **I will confess**, are an emphatic statement of the supreme importance of confessing one's sins to God. In languages which do not speak of hiding sins, it is sometimes possible to say, for example, "I did not deny that I had sinned" or "I did not say that I had not sinned," or stated in direct discourse, "I did not say, 'I have not sinned.' " In some languages it is not good style to place a negative statement immediately following a positive one with the same meaning, and so the translator will have to modify the form.

In line c the psalmist quotes himself (see RSV). TEV does not preserve this literary form, since it is not natural in English; in many languages, however, it may be quite appropriate and effective. It should be noticed that in line c the third person **the LORD** is used, whereas the second person is used in the other lines. It may be well to keep the second person of address throughout, as TEV has done.

Verse 5 is repetitive for the purpose of emphasizing the psalmist's desire to confess his sin. In some languages this emphasis will be more naturally achieved through other means, for example, the use of adjectival forms. In some languages it will be necessary to supply an address form if RSV is followed. For example, "I said to you, LORD, I will openly tell you the bad things I have done" or "I said, 'LORD, here are the evil deeds I have done, and I told you what they were.' "

If the rather unusual expression **guilt of my sin** is followed by the translator, there are several problems. People in different cultures experience guilt in radically different ways. Grammatically it appears that guilt in **guilt of my sin** is something possessed by sin, whereas semantically it is sin that causes guilt. Guilt is thought of in many cultures as a burden, a mark or stain, a kind of moral indebtedness that must be paid by punishment; guilt includes the damaged relationship between the sinner and God or other people. The psalmist is really saying that the sin which brought about guilt has been forgiven. Therefore the translation can be "you removed my guilt by forgiving my sin," "you forgave me and (thereby) took away my (reason for) guilt," "you forgave me and did not punish me for the wrong I had done," or "you forgave my sin which was a heavy burden" or ". . . which kept me far from you." NEB has "thou didst remit [meaning, pardon] the penalty of my sin" (similarly SPCL).

Proverbs 28.13 offers a good commentary on this verse.

32.6	RSV	TEV
	Therefore let every one who is godly	So all your loyal people should pray to you in times of need;[c]
	offer prayer to thee;	
	at a time of distress,[p] in the rush of great waters,	when a great flood of trouble comes rushing in,
	they shall not reach him.	it will not reach them.

[p] Cn: Heb *at a time of finding only*

[c] *Some ancient translations* need; *Hebrew* finding only.

In verses 6-7 the psalmist instructs his fellow worshipers. For **godly** see comments on 4.3. The expression **who is godly** may require recasting as in the manner of TEV; for example, "those who worship you," "people who follow you," or "people who belong to you."

At a time of distress translates a conjectural Hebrew text; the Masoretic text is "in a time of finding only," which NJV translates "upon discovering [his sin]"; in the margin, "In a time when You may be found," which is how Kirkpatrick, Weiser, TOB and NIV understand it.[2] Some connect the word translated "only" to the following words and translate "surely" (KJV, ASV, *The Holy Sciprtures,* Jewish Publication Society [JPS]). Toombs takes the Masoretic text to mean "at the appropriate times," which is what the Septuagint and Vulgate have; so FRCL. But many prefer to change the Masoretic text "finding only" to "trouble" (Briggs, Oesterley, Anderson; RSV, TEV, NEB, NJB, NAB, SPCL). The TEV rendering **"in times of need"** may have to be recast in some languages to say, for example, "when they

---

[2]HOTTP is less helpful than usual ("C" decision). It states that the Masoretic text may be interpreted in two ways: (1) "at the time he finds [it] (that is, his sin); only . . ."; (2) "for the time [when] he finds the leanness (that is, suffers from famine)"; in this interpretation the Masoretic text punctuation is not maintained.

have difficulties" or "when they are in trouble." It seems best to follow the text translated by the majority.

It should be noted that RSV connects **at a time of distress** with what follows, while TEV's **"in times of need"** is connected with what precedes. The TEV order seems to represent the Masoretic text lines better than does RSV.

The troubles that threaten are likened to **the rush of great waters**, that is, a devastating flood (see also comments on 18.16). RSV translates quite literally, **in the rush of great waters**, but it is quite certain that this is a poetic figure of speech for dangers and troubles. See FRCL "If danger threatens to submerge them . . . ." In some languages it is not natural to speak of **"a flood of troubles"** as in TEV. This expression can sometimes be recast to say "many troubles like the waters of a flood."

32.7	RSV	TEV
	Thou art a hiding place for me, thou preservest me from trouble; thou dost encompass me with deliverance.*q* *Selah*	You are my hiding place; you will save me from trouble. I sing aloud of your salvation, because you protect me.

q Cn: Heb *shouts of deliverance*

In line a **hiding place** means a place where the psalmist can hide from his enemies.

The last line of verse 7 is difficult; the Hebrew is "(with) shouts of deliverance you surround me."[3] TEV has taken the "shouts" to be the psalmist's praise to Yahweh for having protected him (**deliverance**). RSV and NEB omit "shouts" from the text. NJV translates "You surround me with joyous shouts of deliverance," and SPCL "you surround me with shouts of victory," which presumably means that because of the Lord's protection the psalmist's fellow worshipers around him are shouting praises to the Lord; so one may say explicitly "You surround me with the shouts of those who rejoice in my deliverance"—which may be the best way to handle an admittedly obscure text. FRCL has "I will shout with joy for the protection with which you surround me." BJ and NJB translate the Masoretic text quite literally; in a footnote they take "shouts" to be an accidental repetition (dittography) of the preceding three consonants in the Hebrew text. This conjecture may be true but is not a sufficient reason to depart from the Masoretic text.

---

[3] Again, without explaining what the language means, HOTTP says there are two interpretations ("C" decision): (1) "you encompass me with shouts [exhorting me with regard to my] salvation"; (2) "you encompass me with shouts of salvation."

	RSV		TEV
8	I will instruct you and teach you the way you should go; I will counsel you with my eye upon you.	8	The LORD says, "I will teach you the way you should go; I will instruct you and advise you.
9	Be not like a horse or a mule, without understand, which must be curbed with bit and bridle, else it will not keep with you.	9	Don't be stupid like a horse or a mule, which must be controlled with a bit and bridle to make it submit."

TEV, SPCL, GECL, FRCL, and others (Kirkpatrick, Dahood, Anderson) take these two verses to be Yahweh's words to the psalmist; this assumes that the singular "you" in verse 8 is the psalmist being addressed by Yahweh. And in verse 9a, instead of the Masoretic text plural "you," the singular "you" in two Hebrew manuscripts is preferred. Others, however (Briggs, Oesterley, Taylor, Weiser), take the verses to be the psalmist's instructions to his fellow worshipers; in this case the singular "you" in verse 8 is taken to be generic, and the Masoretic text plural "you" in verse 9 is preferred. The statement **my eye upon you** in verse 8 seems to favor Yahweh as the speaker.

Three verbs are used in verse 8: **instruct . . . teach . . . counsel**. In languages which do not have more than one word for teaching, it is sometimes possible to say, for example, "I will show you the way you should go; I will teach you and tell you how to do."

The Hebrew "(with) my eye upon you" carries the idea of concern and care, not of a veiled threat, as the English phrase might be understood. The expression **with my eye upon you** may sometimes be rendered "taking care of you" or "watching out for your safety."

Verse 8 is a case of stair-step parallelism. Each succeeding line adds something to the first. Furthermore, the verse can be analyzed as a tricolon, that is, having three lines: **I will instruct you / and teach you the way you should go / I will counsel you with my eye upon you.**

The last two lines of verse 9 are filled with difficulties, since there is much controversy over the precise form and meaning of the separate words; but the meaning of the whole seems to be that given by RSV and TEV. The last line is translated by Dahood "Then you can approach him"; NEB transposes the words to the end of verse 7 and translates "beyond all reach of harm"; NJV takes the words to be a warning to the hearer: "far be it from you!"; TOB has "and no harm will reach you"; SPCL "or else they will not come to you"; similarly "so that they may not attack you." Any one of these (except, perhaps, NEB) can be defended as a valid translation of the text. The translator faces a great deal of choice in this verse. If TEV and RSV are followed, readers may be surprised to learn that a **horse** or **mule** might be thought of as stupid. On the basis of the Hebrew expression, there is reason to say, for example, "Don't be like a horse or mule; they do not know which way to go without a bit and bridle." In some areas the horse is largely unknown and the mule is totally unfamiliar. In such cases the usual thing is to identify these animals through a borrowed word from a major language, and if necessary, to use a classifier; for example, "an animal called horse." The **bit** is that part of the **bridle** which is inserted in the animal's mouth. Where bit and bridle are unknown, it is best to use a short descriptive phrase (a borrowed word may be too technical). Bridle is sometimes called "animal guiding rope," and a bit is sometimes referred to as "guide thing in the mouth." If more information is required, a note or illustration should be provided.

32.10-11 RSV	TEV
10 Many are the pangs of the wicked; but steadfast love surrounds him who trusts in the LORD. 11 Be glad in the LORD, and rejoice, O righteous, and shout for joy, all you upright in heart!	10 The wicked will have to suffer, but those who trust in the LORD are protected by his constant love. 11 You that are righteous, be glad and rejoice because of what the LORD has done. You that obey him, shout for joy!

The psalm closes with a final lesson (verse 10), followed by an exhortation for all the Lord's faithful people to rejoice (verse 11).

The **many . . . pangs of the wicked** (verse 10a) are the sufferings that come upon those who refuse to obey God. They are contrasted with **the righteous** (verse 11a), **the upright in heart** (verse 11b), who are called upon to **be glad**, **rejoice**, and **shout for joy**.

Steadfast love surrounds must be recast in a number of languages as a clause; for example, "God faithfully loves and protects those who trust him."

The phrase **in the LORD** in verse 11a means "because of what the LORD has done."

The address form **O righteous** may sometimes be rendered "you that are good," or idiomatically, "you that walk straight."

Shout for joy must sometimes be recast to say, for example, "shout and be happy" or "because you are joyful, shout in praise of the LORD."

The phrase **upright in heart** occurs only in Psalms (see 7.10 and comments), and also in 2 Chronicles 29.32.

Psalm 33

In this hymn the psalmist praises Yahweh as Creator of the universe and supreme ruler of humankind. The psalm opens with a call for people to praise Yahweh (verses 1-3) because of who he is (verses 4-5) and what he has done as Creator of the universe (verses 6-9). His complete sovereignty over the destiny of all people is next spoken of (verses 10-15), with particular emphasis on his control over the affairs of nations (verses 16-19). In conclusion the whole congregation expresses its faith in Yahweh (verses 20-21) and prays for his continued blessing (verse 22). Some scholars point out that this psalm contains twenty-two verses, and that number represents the number of letters in the Hebrew alphabet. The psalm is, however, not acrostic (see introduction, "Translating the Psalms.").

HEADING: "**A Song of Praise**" (TEV); "Praise to the Creator and Lord"; "God's word and work." The TEV heading may require some adjustments such as the following: "Sing a song and praise God," "Sing a song to God and say that he is great," or in direct speech, "Sing a song and say 'God, you are wonderful.' "

<u>33.1-3</u>   RSV   TEV

1   Rejoice in the LORD, O you   1   All you that are righteous,
         righteous!   shout for joy for what the LORD
     Praise befits the upright.   has done;
2   Praise the LORD with the lyre,   praise him, all you that obey
         make melody to him with the   him.
         harp of ten strings!   2   Give thanks to the LORD with
3   Sing to him a new song,   harps,
         play skilfully on the strings,   sing to him with stringed in-
         with loud shouts.   struments.
                                          3   Sing a new song to him,
                                                  play the harp with skill, and
                                                  shout for joy!

The people are exhorted to praise the Lord; they are called **the righteous** and **the upright** (see 31.11). As in 31.11, TEV "**for what the LORD has done**" translates **in the LORD** in verse 1a.

In consequence of this it is only right for the people to praise him (verse 1b); in the now quaint language of KJV, "praise is comely for the upright" (see SPCL, "praise is lovely on the lips of good people"). The sense of **befits** can be expressed by "it is right (or, fitting) that those who obey the LORD should praise him."

Instruments were used in public worship, and in verse 2 two stringed instruments are named: the smaller one, the *kinnor*, with two to four strings, and the larger ten-stringed instrument, the *nebel*. Translations vary; **lyre** and **harp** are the two words most often used in English (NEB has "ten-stringed lute" for the second one).

STRINGED INSTRUMENTS

Praise the LORD with the lyre contains two major translation problems. The first is that in many languages the phrase **with the lyre** must be recast as a verb phrase or clause; for example, "praise the LORD by playing music on the lyre" or "make music with the lyre, and praise the LORD." The second problem, which applies also to line 2b, is the term to be used in the translation of the musical instrument. In languages in which there are several stringed instruments, the translator may use one of the smaller ones for the **lyre** (*kinnor*) and a larger one for the second instrument (*nebel*). In languages where there is little or no choice, one must use the known local stringed instrument for the first, and a more generic expression for the second, which may mean simply the plural of the instrument used in line 2a. Where there are no known stringed instruments, it will often be necessary to say, for example, "small instruments with strings" and "large instruments with strings."

A new song (also 40.3; 96.1; 98.1; 144.9; 149.1; see also Rev 5.9) is a new composition celebrating the Lord's never-failing goodness. **Sing a new song** should not be translated as simply "Sing a different song" or "Sing a song again." Where the word **new** carries the meanings of "for the first time" and also "again" and "different," it will often be necessary to say, for example, "Sing a new song which the people have not yet heard."

In verse 3b the Hebrew text says only "play skillfully with a loud noise." The "loud noise" could be of the instrument itself or, more probably, of the accompanying shouts of praise; and the instrument is not named. RSV supplies **on the strings**, and TEV "**the harp**." One can say "Play your instruments skillfully . . . ."

33.4-5	RSV	TEV
4	For the word of the LORD is upright; and all his work is done in faithfulness.	4 The words of the LORD are true, and all his works are dependable.
5	He loves righteousness and justice;	5 The LORD loves what is righteous and just; his constant love fills the earth.

the earth is full of the steadfast
love of the LORD.

Praise is given to Yahweh as the result of his nature and work: his **word . . . is
upright**, that is, Yahweh is always true to his promise and does what he says he will
do; and **all his work is done in faithfulness**, meaning that in all he does he
demonstrates his faithfulness to his people. So SPCL "his works demonstrate his
faithfulness." If TEV is used, in some languages it will be necessary to make explicit
the actor of "depend" in the expression **"his works are dependable"**; for example,
"people can depend on everything he does" or "people can trust all that he does."
Some translations, however, understand the word **faithfulness** to apply to Yahweh's
deeds; NEB "all his work endures," and FRCL "all he does is solid and sure." This is
possible, but the former seems more probable.

The Lord's nature is further revealed (verse 5) by the fact that he **loves
righteousness and justice**, either in the sense that these are the qualities he loves in
people or else the qualities that characterize his own activity. The effect of all this
is that all over the world there is evidence of his concern and care for all people: **the
earth is full of the steadfast love of the LORD**. If the translator follows the suggestion
that God loves righteousness and justice in his people, it will be necessary in some
languages to say, for example, "God loves people who do right and live justly" or
"God loves good and just people." If, on the other hand, these qualities are taken
as applying to God, it is possible to say, for instance, "The LORD loves to do right
and to be just" or, since judgment is such an integral part of God's being, one may
say "the LORD loves to do right and to judge fairly."

In languages where the expression **the earth is full of . . . love** would not be
natural, it is often possible to say, for example, "in all the earth people see the
LORD's faithful love" or "people in all the earth are filled with the LORD's constant
love," or more generally, "everything in the earth receives the LORD's constant love."

33.6   RSV   TEV

By the word of the LORD the   The LORD created the heavens by
heavens were made,   his command,
and all their host by the breath   the sun, moon, and stars by his
of his mouth.   spoken word.

The Lord is the Creator, and he brought the universe into being by his
command (see Gen 1.3,6,9). The universe is spoken of as **the heavens** and **all their
host**, that is, "the sun, moon, and stars" (TEV). In the two parallel lines, **the word
of the LORD** and **the breath of his mouth** mean "his command . . . his spoken word"
(TEV). As commentators point out, **breath** here is not "spirit" or "Spirit," but means
speaking. In some languages instrumental phrases require recasting as time clauses
or as two distinct sentences; for example, "When the LORD commanded, he created
the heavens" or "When the LORD created the heavens, he did this by commanding
it."

33.7   RSV   TEV

He gathered the waters of the sea as in a bottle; he put the deeps in storehouses.	He gathered all the seas into one place; he shut up the ocean depths in storerooms.

In this verse there is a reference to the gathering of the waters of the primeval chaos into a storeroom, reflecting the thought of the time, that above the dome of the sky the upper waters were stored (Gen 1.7) as the source of rain (see Gen 7.11); see also Psalm 148.4b-5.

TEV "**into one place**" translates the Masoretic text "as a heap." NJV translates "He heaps up the ocean waters like a mound." FRCL translates it "behind a dam," and NJB "like a dam." RSV and others use different vowels with the Hebrew consonants to get **as a bottle** (that is, a leather wineskin), which has support from the Septuagint; and see Job 38.37b. NEB translates "in a goatskin."[1] It seems better to follow the Masoretic text.

In line **b** the thought is again expressed, **he put the deeps in storehouses**. (TEV would have done better by saying "reservoirs" instead of "**storerooms**.") All of this demonstrates Yahweh's mighty power; he gathers all the waters of the universe and stores them as easily as a man might store full wineskins in his cellar. SPCL has combined the two parallel lines into one complete statement: "He gathers and stores the waters of the deep ocean." This avoids having to find an equivalent for "heap" and "storehouses."

A special effort will be required to make the concepts in this verse clear in many languages. One may say in line **a** "He dips up the waters of the oceans and pours them into one place" or, following the other interpretation of the Hebrew, "He scoops up the water of the seas and pours them into a container." Line **b** may be translated using a simile based on the verb phrase "putting in storehouses"; for example, "he stores up the waters of the sea like a merchant stores his goods" or "he stores the waters of the sea like a man stores grain in a barn."

33.8-9   RSV   TEV

8	Let all the earth fear the LORD, let all the inhabitants of the world stand in awe of him!	8	Have reverence for the LORD, all the earth! Honor him, all peoples of the world!
9	For he spoke, and it came to be; he commanded, and it stood forth.	9	When he spoke, the world was created; at his command everything appeared.

---

[1]HOTTP follows the Masoretic text, "like a heap" ("B" decision).

All peoples, and not just the Israelites, are called upon to **fear the LORD** (see comments on 5.7; 15.4), to **stand in awe of him**, for his power is unlimited. The two verbs are parallel and practically synonymous, describing that feeling of reverence, awe, respect, and fear, that a devout Israelite felt before Yahweh.

Line b of verse 8 shifts from the general word **earth** in line a to the specific **all the inhabitants of the world**. The sense is that line b heightens the effect of line a and may be translated in English "what is more, let all the people of the world . . . ."

The Hebrew particle which is here translated **For** does not introduce a reason clause. It is rather an extra syllable whose function is to add an extra beat to the line.

When God spoke **it came to be** (TEV **"the world was created"**), literally "it was"; at his command all created things came into being (literally "it stood").

In some languages it will be necessary to avoid the passive construction of the TEV and say "When he spoke, he created the world," "By speaking he created the world," or "He created the world. He did this by speaking."

It seems better in this context to take the verb "to stand" in verse 9b to mean "it was created" (as the Septuagint translates), rather than "it stood firm," as some have it. Briggs: "it sprang into existence and presented itself." FRCL uses a colloquial phrase in verse 9b: "no sooner said than done."

33.10-11   RSV   TEV

10 The LORD brings the counsel of   10 The LORD frustrates the purposes
    the nations to nought;   of the nations;
    he frustrates the plans of the   he keeps them from carrying
    peoples.   out their plans.
11 The counsel of the LORD stands   11 But his plans endure forever;
    for ever,   his purposes last eternally.
    the thoughts of his heart to all
    generations.

The Lord's sovereignty in the affairs of humankind is now stressed. He prevents people from carrying out their **counsel** and their **plans**—it being understood, of course, that these are contrary to his will. The two verbs in verse 10 are synonymous, and the two nouns are also synonymous: "plans, projects, purposes, goals." **Nations** has the specific sense of "pagan nations." **Brings . . . to nought** may sometimes be rendered "causes to fail" or "does not allow to succeed." **The counsel of the nations** may sometimes be rendered "what the nations decide to do" or "the decisions of the tribes." Verse 10a may then be rendered in some languages "The LORD causes the nations to fail in the things they decide to do" or "The LORD does not allow the nations to succeed in their decisions."

But Yahweh's plans are immutable, not subject to change or to interference. In verse 11b the noun in Hebrew for **thoughts** is the same as the noun for **plans** in verse 10b, but "of his heart" is added; so RSV **the thoughts of his heart**. Such a literal translation of the Hebrew is not necessary (see modern dynamic equivalence translations).

In verses 10-11 the second line shows heightening of intensity rather than being statically synonymous. The general expressions in the first lines, **brings to naught** and counsel of the LORD, are intensified in the second lines through **frustrates** and **the thoughts of his heart**. In translation the development in intensity can often be made explicit; for example, "not only that, but also frustrates the plans . . . ." Also in verse 11, "more than that, the thoughts of his heart last forever."

33.12 RSV TEV

> Blessed is the nation whose God is the LORD,
>   the people whom he has chosen as his heritage!

> Happy is the nation whose God is the LORD;
>   happy are the people he has chosen for his own!

From the general truth of God's sovereignty in history, the psalmist passes to the special place occupied by Israel, **the nation whose God is the LORD, the people whom he has chosen as his heritage**. The emphasis is on Yahweh's choice of Israel to be his people; it was not they who elected him to be their God, but he chose them by his own sovereign will. In the last line the word **heritage** stresses this idea; Israel is Yahweh's own particular possession, as no other people are. For a discussion of the word, see 16.6 and 28.9.

Whose God is the LORD requires some recasting in numerous languages; for example, "the God they worship is the LORD," "the God they serve is called the LORD," "who have the LORD as their God" or "who have the LORD as the God whom they worship."

The expression **chosen as his heritage** raises the problem of the metaphor, which, if applied too literally, requires that God die in order that his heirs may receive the inheritance. TEV has solved this problem by avoiding the idea of inheritance. It is possible to retain something of the idea of heir by using such expressions as "the people he has chosen to receive his blessings" or "the people he has chosen to receive the things he has promised to give."

There is no dynamic movement in the parallelism of verse 12. The word pair **nation–people** provides the basis for two statements in parallel and may or may not be joined by a connector such as "and."

33.13-15 RSV TEV

> 13 The LORD looks down from heaven,
>   he sees all the sons of men;
> 14 from where he sits enthroned he looks forth
>   on all the inhabitants of the earth,
> 15 he who fashions the hearts of them all,
>   and observes all their deeds.

> 13 The LORD looks down from heaven
>   and sees all mankind.
> 14 From where he rules, he looks down
>   on all who live on earth.
> 15 He forms all their thoughts
>   and knows everything they do.

As sovereign ruler over history, Yahweh, from where he rules in heaven, sees all the people of the world and knows what they do (for a similar idea see 14.2; see also 11.4). For **the sons of men** see 11.14 and comments.

From where he sits enthroned can often be adapted to local terminology for the position of the ruler; for example, "from his chief's stool," "from the chief's room," and "from the king's court."

Nothing escapes Yahweh's notice; he even **fashions the hearts of them all**. The verb is the one used of a potter fashioning a bowl, and the statement that Yahweh fashions their hearts means that Yahweh not only forms the human body (see the verb in Gen 2.7-8) but also the mind. This does not imply that Yahweh controls a person's thinking, as "**He forms all their thoughts**" (TEV) may appear to say. It simply means that he creates the human mind and therefore knows how it works. The Hebrew word usually translated "all together" (RSV **of them all**) is here somewhat difficult to understand; Briggs and K-B "thoroughly"; NEB "alike"; TOB "the same heart (for them all)"; BJ "only he (forms their hearts)." In some languages it will be necessary to extend the idea of thoughts to include both thinking and willing; for example, "he has given them ability to think and to want," or FRCL, "intelligence and will."

The last line of verse 15, **observes all their deeds**, can be translated "he sees everything they do"; but in parallel with the preceding line, the thought is rather "knows" (TEV), "understands" (NJB), or "discerns" (NJV, NEB).

RSV   TEV

| 16 | A king is not saved by his great army;
a warrior is not delivered by his great strength. | 16 | A king does not win because of his powerful army;
a soldier does not triumph because of his strength. |
| 17 | The war horse is a vain hope for victory,
and by its great might it cannot save. | 17 | War horses are useless for victory;
their great strength cannot save. |

In these verses the psalmist speaks of Yahweh's control over nations at war, affirming that victory in battle is not won because of the size or the strength of armies and the might of war horses; it is God who gives the victory. This is not only a statement of fact; it is a warning to kings and nations (particularly to Israel, Yahweh's people) not to depend on the number and strength of their armies and their war horses, but to depend on God.

In some languages the two lines of verse 16 will have to be recast slightly, otherwise there is likelihood that the reader will understand that the king's powerful army is what causes him to lose, and the warrior's strength likewise causes him to fail. The translation should not mean that they are at the same time the cause of his defeat. Therefore one may sometimes say, for example, "Even if a king has a powerful army, that does not make him win the battle" or "Even if a soldier has great strength, that does not mean he will defeat his enemy."

In verse 17a **a vain hope** translates a word meaning lie, falsehood, delusion (see 7.14); NJV "a horse is a false hope for deliverance." In line b̲ it may be necessary to supply an object for the verb **save**, such as "the rider" (FRCL) or "the soldier," or else make the line parallel with the preceding **victory**: "their great strength cannot win the battle."

33.18-19	RSV	TEV
18	Behold, the eye of the LORD is on those who fear him, on those who hope in his steadfast love,	18 The LORD watches over those who have reverence for him, those who trust in his constant love.
19	that he may deliver their soul from death, and keep them alive in famine.	19 He saves them from death; he keeps them alive in times of famine.

The Lord's providential care extends to those who trust in him (verses 18-19). In verse 18a "his eye is on" expresses care and concern (see 32.8). TEV renders the function of **the eye** with "The LORD watches." **Those who fear him** in line a̲ is parallel with **those who hope in his steadfast love** in line b̲.

In verse 19a the Hebrew "he saves their *nefesh* [see 3.2] from death" means he keeps them from violent or premature death caused by illness, calamity, war, or famine. To translate "he saves their soul from death" in English conveys the wrong idea, suggesting immortality or life eternal. Unlike RSV, modern English translations such as AT, NAB, NEB, NIV, NJB, and NJV do not use the word "soul" in such a context.

33.20-21	RSV	TEV
20	Our soul waits for the LORD; he is our help and shield.	20 We put our hope in the LORD; he is our protector and our help.
21	Yea, our heart is glad in him, because we trust in his holy name.	21 We are glad because of him; we trust in his holy name.

All the worshipers now proclaim their faith in Yahweh. **Our soul** and **our heart** in verses 20a and 21a are parallel, meaning "we"; something like "with all our heart . . . our whole being" may be more effective than the simple personal pronoun. The verb "wait" in verse 20a means to hope, to trust (see similar verbs in 25.3 and 31.24); **shield** in verse 20b is a figure for protection (see 3.3).

Our soul waits for the LORD may sometimes be rendered "We look forward with confidence in what the LORD has promised us." **Help and shield** may be rendered in various ways; for example, "he helps us and protects us like a shield" or "he helps us and protects us as shields protect warriors."

In verse 21a **in him** means "because of him" or "because of what he has done" (see verse 1). This affirmation responds to the exhortation in verse 1a, "Rejoice in the LORD."

His holy name stands for Yahweh himself, who has revealed himself as holy, that is, set apart, which is the one word which best describes his unique character as altogether distinct from human nature. **Trust in his holy name** may sometimes be rendered "we trust in him because he is holy" or "because he is holy, we trust in him."

33.22   RSV   TEV

> Let thy steadfast love, O LORD, be
> > upon us,
> > even as we hope in thee.

> May your constant love be with
> > us, LORD,
> > as we put our hope in you.

The psalm closes with the congregation praying for God's continued love, based on their continued hope in him. Their awareness of God's **steadfast love** for them results from the blessings they receive from him; in a sense, they are praying that God show them his love by helping them, blessing them, causing them to prosper.

The second line may be understood to mean "just as we hope you will do" (see SPCL), or it may indicate the ground or basis for God's activity, that is, that he bless them to the extent that they place their hope in him.

Psalm 34

This psalm, like Psalm 25, is an incomplete acrostic poem, each line beginning with a successive letter of the Hebrew alphabet, from *alef* to *taw* (see the Introduction to Psa 25). The letter *waw* (sixth in the alphabet) is not represented, and the last verse is outside the scheme altogether.

The psalm is a hymn of thanksgiving (see Psa 30; 32) by an individual who has been freed from some unspecified difficulty (verse 4). The requirements of the acrostic scheme caused the author to compose without logical order or progression of thought. The first part (verses 1-3) is a hymn of praise to Yahweh, followed by a tribute to his provident care, of which the psalmist had personal experience (verses 4-10). The main body of the psalm (verses 11-22) is in the form of instruction concerning the right way to live and its rewards, and the punishment awaiting those who disregard God's laws.

HEADING: **"In Praise of God's Goodness"** (TEV); "The goodness of God"; "In praise of God's justice"; "The LORD has freed me from all my fears." The TEV heading will require some adjustments in many languages. Here are two expanded headings based on TEV: "The psalmist worships God and thanks him for being good to him" or "The psalmist speaks well, saying that God is good to his people."

Hebrew Title: **A Psalm of David, when he feigned madness before Abimelech, so that he drove him out, and he went away**.

The title refers to the incident reported in 1 Samuel 21.10–22.1. There is, however, a certain confusion in the statement here, since it was Achish, king of the Philistine city of Gath, who sent David away after he pretended to be crazy. There are several explanations of "Abimelech" here, none of which is convincing. Three men by this name are mentioned in the Old Testament: (1) Abimelech, king of Gerar (Gen 20); (2) Abimelech, son of Gideon (Judges 9); (3) Abimelech as a variant spelling in 1 Chronicles 18.16 of Ahimelech, son of the priest Abiathar (2 Sam 8.17).

34.1-3

	RSV		TEV
1	I will bless the LORD at all times; his praise shall continually be in my mouth.	1	I will always thank the LORD; I will never stop praising him.
2	My soul makes its boast in the LORD; let the afflicted hear and be glad.	2	I will praise him for what he has done; may all who are oppressed listen and be glad!
3	O magnify the LORD with me,	3	Proclaim with me the LORD's greatness; let us praise his name together!

and let us exalt his name together!

The psalm opens with praise. **I will bless the LORD** means "I will praise (or,
thank) the LORD" (see 16.7). If the translator follows the lead of TEV, the words **I
will bless the LORD** will require in many languages some shifting, particularly in
relation to "giving thanks." "Thanks" is often expressed in idiomatic ways; for
example, "My heart is large for the LORD" or "My heart says the LORD is good."
Also in some languages one may speak of kindness and goodness in place of thanks;
for example, "I accept your goodness, LORD," or "I salute your kindness . . . ," or
"I say how good the LORD is."

Line <u>b</u> of verse 1 says the same thing as line <u>a</u>. **His praise** means "praise to
him." Instead of **in my mouth** a more natural English expression is "on my lips"
(NEB, NIV, NJB).

The word translated **LORD** is the key word in this psalm and gives the psalm its
basic cohesion. **LORD** occurs in every verse except verses 5 (where it is replaced by
the pronoun), 12, 13, 14, 20, and 21.

In verse 2a the Hebrew verb *halal* may mean "to boast" (as in 10.3), but more
specifically here it means "to praise," as in 22.22 (so NJB). But SPCL has "I feel proud
of the Lord," and NJB "I glory in the LORD" (see NEB). **My soul** means "I" or, with
more expression, "From my heart, I" (NJB). And **in the LORD** means "because of
what the LORD has done" (see 32.11).

The afflicted in verse 2b are those who have no human help (see comments on
9.12); they are exhorted to **hear**, that is, to listen to what the psalmist is saying (see
FRCL) and to **be glad**, and also to join the psalmist in proclaiming the Lord's
greatness, literally to **magnify** him (verse 3a), which is paralleled in the next line by
exalt his name (see comment on "exalted" in 12.8). **His name** is parallel with **the
LORD** in verse 3a (see comment on "name" in 5.11). Both verbs mean to proclaim
publicly Yahweh's majesty and might, his greatness and glory.

In some languages **the afflicted** are referred to as "those whose heads are held
down" or "people with tied hands." In some languages it is not possible to command
someone to experience an emotional state such as **be glad**. Therefore it is often
necessary to express this type of indirect command as a wish or request; for example,
"I want them to listen and to be glad" or "I ask that the oppressed listen and have
cool hearts." **Magnify the LORD with me** may sometimes be rendered by the same
term used for praise; for example, "say with me that the LORD is great" or "join with
me to speak in honor of the LORD."

34.4-5   RSV   TEV

4   I sought the LORD, and he an-   4   I prayed to the LORD, and he
        swered me,   answered me;
     and delivered me from all my   he freed me from all my fears.
        fears.   5   The oppressed look to him and
5   Look to him, and be radiant;   are glad;
     so your*r* faces shall never be   they will never be disappointed.
        ashamed.

r Gk Syr Jerome: Heb *their*

On the basis of his own experience, the psalmist proceeds to proclaim how Yahweh cares for and protects those who trust in him, call to him for help, honor him.

I sought in verse 4a is used with the meaning to go to (the Lord) in prayer and worship (see comments on "seek" in 9.10). **Answered** means that Yahweh, in response to the psalmist's prayer, did what the psalmist asked him to do.

All my fears in verse 4b are not internal feelings of dread and insecurity, but external terrors which threaten (see "terror" in 31.13). The verb translated **delivered** is the one used in 7.1b. In some languages it is not possible to be "**freed from fears**." However, it is often more natural to say "he freed me from those who caused me to fear."

In verse 5 "**The oppressed**" is supplied by TEV as being implicit in the text. TEV also translates the perfect tense of the verbs in the Masoretic text as present tense: "**look . . . and are glad**" (also NJV, NIV, TOB, BJ, SPCL, Dahood). Some change the vowels in the Hebrew text to make the verbs imperative: RSV, FRCL, NJB, NEB, NAB.

The English expression **Look to** is somewhat idiomatic and must be distinguished from "look at." **Look to** means to place oneself in dependence upon someone, and may be translated in some languages in terms of "trusting." For example, this may be said idiomatically, "They place their hearts on him and are glad" or "Their livers rest with him and they are cool."

The Hebrew "are radiant" (see RSV) expresses gladness, joy; and in verse 5b the verb "be ashamed" (synonymous with the verb used in 6.10) means be disappointed, be disillusioned; see NEB "hang your heads in shame"; NAB "your faces may not blush with shame." The RSV footnote in verse 5b indicates that **your faces** follows the ancient versions; the Masoretic text has "their faces." This departure from the Masoretic text is caused in part by the fact that RSV translates the verbs in line a as imperatives, not indicatives. HOTTP prefers to maintain the Masoretic text ("C" decision).

34.6-7	RSV	TEV
6	This poor man cried, and the LORD heard him, and saved him out of all his troubles.	6 The helpless call to him, and he answers; he saves them from all their troubles.
7	The angel of the LORD encamps around those who fear him, and delivers them.	7 His angel guards those who have reverence for the LORD and rescues them from danger.

Verse 6 is a tricolon, or three-line verse: "The poor man cried / The LORD heard him / and saved him from his troubles." The same thoughts are embodied in a two-line arrangement in verse 17 and have echoes in verses 4 and 19. Such repetition contributes to the unity of the psalm.

RSV **This poor man** in verse 6a takes the phrase to be a reference to the psalmist himself (so NEB, FRCL, SPCL). TEV takes it to be generic, referring to all who are "helpless." The translator will have to decide between **This poor man** referring to people in general or to one specific person, the psalmist. In any event it is important not to translate **poor man** in the sense of a man who owns nothing; rather one must select a term or phrase denoting the unfortunate state of the man.

Saved translates the same verb that in 12.1 RSV translates "Help."

The angel of the LORD is referred to as one who **encamps around those who fear him**. Only here and in 35.5,6 is **the angel of the LORD** referred to in Psalms (see in 91.11 the plural "the angels" of the Lord). It is a concept which finds expression elsewhere, referring to God's heavenly messenger as caring for and protecting his people (see Exo 23.20; Josh 5.13-15 for this same concept; see also Matt 18.10). **The angel of the LORD** is often rendered "heavenly messenger from the LORD."

The verb **encamps** is used in a hostile sense in 27.3; here it means guards, protects, keeps safe. The words **who fear him** can often be rendered "who worship him" or "who honor him." **Delivers** translates the same verb that is used in 6.4.

	34.8-9	RSV	TEV
8	O taste and see that the LORD is good! Happy is the man who takes refuge in him!		8 Find out for yourself how good the LORD is. Happy are those who find safety with him.
9	O fear the LORD, you his saints, for those who fear him have no want!		9 Have reverence for the LORD, all his people; those who obey him have all they need.

The psalmist now exhorts his people to find out by personal trial and experience the goodness of the Lord, literally **taste and see**, which may be translated "Try for yourself and find out" (see FRCL). 1 Peter 2.3 uses the same language, based on the Septuagint translation of this passage. The verb ordinarily translated **see** is derived by Dahood from another root, meaning "drink deeply," but his proposal has not been widely accepted. In many languages it is not possible to use **taste** in any sense other than to savor food or drink. Therefore one must often say, for example, "Look and learn" or "See and find out." In some languages it will be necessary to indicate a relationship of consequence between the second verb and the first; for example, "Look in order to learn" or "Listen so that you can know."

For **takes refuge** see comments on 2.12. In some languages the words **takes refuge in him** must be translated, for example, "who goes to him and he protects them" or "who asks him to defend them."

The people who are faithful to God are called "his holy ones" (RSV **his saints**; see 16.3); usually "the holy ones" in the Old Testament refer to divine beings. They are also called **those who fear him** (verse 9). **Fear the LORD** must often be rendered "Worship the LORD" or "Honor the LORD." Like the psalmist in 23.1, they "have all they need"; **have no want** means "lack nothing" (NEB, NIV, NJV).

34.10　　　　RSV　　　　　　　　　　　　TEV

The young lions suffer want and　　　Even lions go hungry for lack of
　　hunger;　　　　　　　　　　　　　　　food,
but those who seek the LORD　　　　but those who obey the LORD
　　lack no good thing.　　　　　　　　　lack nothing good.

The **lions** in this verse are referred to because they are thought of as the strongest of all animals; but even they **suffer want and hunger**, that is, lack what they need and get hungry; people who **seek the LORD** (see verse 4) **lack no good thing**, that is, they have all their legitimate needs satisfied. The psalmist has in mind not only spiritual needs but bodily needs as well.

TEV "obey" departs rather radically from the notion of "seeking"; something like "those who go to the LORD" would be better (see TEV in 9.10b). NJV here has "those who turn to the LORD."

Following the ancient versions (the Septuagint, Syriac, Vulgate), Dahood, FRCL, and SPCL translate "the rich" instead of **lions**; NEB changes the Hebrew text to get "Unbelievers"; NAB takes "the lions" to be a metaphor for "the great [people]." If the translator follows TEV and RSV **lions**, it will be necessary to substitute another known animal of prey where the lion is unknown. If no local equivalent is available, the translator must then use a foreign word with a classifier such as "powerful animal called lion," or use a generic expression such as "wild animal."

34.11-12　　　　RSV　　　　　　　　　　　　TEV

11　Come, O sons, listen to me,　　　　11　Come, my young friends, and
　　I will teach you the fear of the　　　　　listen to me,
　　LORD.　　　　　　　　　　　　　　　　　and I will teach you to have
12　What man is there who desires　　　　　reverence for the LORD.
　　life,　　　　　　　　　　　　　　12　Would you like to enjoy life?
　　and covets many days, that he　　　　　Do you want long life and hap-
　　may enjoy good?　　　　　　　　　　　piness?

In the second half of the psalm (verses 11-22), the psalmist becomes a teacher, instructing his listeners about the right way to live, that is, the commandments and laws of the Hebrew faith, succinctly expressed as **the fear of the LORD** (see Pro 1.7; 2.5; 9.10; etc.; see also Psa 19.9).

Sons is the traditional term used by a teacher speaking to his students (see Pro 1.8; 2.1; 3.1). Some translations have "children," which, if taken literally, conveys the wrong idea. In some languages unnecessary ambiguities would be created by translating in the manner of TEV or RSV. In order to make clear that those addressed are learners, one must often say, for example, "my students" or "you who learn from me."

The questions in verse 12 are rhetorical and are meant to stimulate the interest of the reader. **Desires** translates the verb that occurs in noun form in 1.2, where it is translated "delight" (RSV) and "finds joy" (TEV). Here NEB has "delights in life." The verb translated **covets** is usually represented by "love"; here it means "desires, wishes, wants." **"Long life and happiness"** (TEV) combines **many days . . . enjoy good** into one phrase; it may be expressed in different ways: "a long and happy life"; see NJV "years of good fortune." Verse 12 may be restated as a negative statement in some languages; for example, "There is no one who does not want to enjoy life . . . ." These two questions may also be translated in some languages as positive statements: "Everyone wants to enjoy life." In languages which require a reply to a rhetorical question, a reply must be given at the end of each question; for example, "Everyone!" Or, if the kinds of questions are used that TEV has, the answer will be "Of course!"

Verses 12-16a are quoted in 1 Peter 3.10-12 essentially as they appear in the Septuagint translation of this passage.

34.13-14 RSV   TEV

13 Keep your tongue from evil, and your lips from speaking deceit.
14 Depart from evil, and do good; seek peace, and pursue it.

13 Then keep from speaking evil and from telling lies.
14 Turn away from evil and do good; strive for peace with all your heart.

The virtues recommended as a prescription for a long and happy life are: avoid malicious talk and lies (verse 13); cease doing evil and do good; and strive for peace (verse 14). In verse 13 **your tongue** and **your lips** are used synonymously and mean "to talk," "to say something." In some languages it may be appropriate and effective to speak of "tongue and lips" (see SPCL). In some languages it will be necessary to give content to **"speaking evil"**; for example, "Do not speak evil words" or "Do not say evil words about other people."

Depart from evil must not be used as if one is departing from a place. In some languages the idea of avoiding evil is "Put your back where people do bad deeds," or stated negatively, "Don't turn your face toward evil." **Do good** must often be completed with some grammatical complement, making explicit what is being done; for example, "Do things that cause good for people" or "Act in the way that is good for people."

The word **peace** here is not merely the cessation of hostility between people; it is the presence of the conditions that make for prosperity, health, happiness, and the common welfare. TEV **"with all your heart"** represents the force of the second verb, "to pursue [peace]"; FRCL has "[Seek peace] diligently." **Seek peace** and **"strive for peace"** must often be restructured so that the actors of peace are made explicit; for example, "work hard so that people will have peace." In some languages having peace is described metaphorically; for example, "work hard so that people's hearts will sit quietly within them" or ". . . so that people's hearts will sit in the shade."

34.15-16 RSV   TEV

15 The eyes of the LORD are toward the righteous,

15 The LORD watches over the righteous

	and his ears toward their cry.		and listens to their cries;
16	The face of the LORD is against evildoers,	16	but he opposes those who do evil, so that when they die, they are soon forgotten.
	to cut off the remembrance of them from the earth.		

The providential care of the Lord for his people is expressed in bodily terms: his **eyes** and his **ears** are **toward** them (verse 15), that is, "**he watches over**" them and "**listens to their cries**" (TEV) for help. In some languages it is possible to keep closer to the Hebrew figurative language than TEV has done; for example, "The LORD puts his eyes on good people" and "he has two ears to hear their cries."

The Lord's hostility toward evildoers is expressed in the same fashion: his **face** is **against** them. The result of God's hostility is that they will die and be forgotten by everyone (see the same ideas in 9.5-6; 109.15b). The expressive verb **cut off** is the one used in 12.3. **The remembrance of them** means the memory that others have of them, the knowledge and awareness that they had ever existed. And **from the earth** means the people of the world will forget them completely.

34.17-18 RSV TEV

17	When the righteous cry for help, the LORD hears,	17	The righteous call to the LORD, and he listens;
	and delivers them out of all their troubles.		he rescues them from all their troubles.
18	The LORD is near to the broken-hearted,	18	The LORD is near to those who are discouraged;
	and saves the crushed in spirit.		he saves those who have lost all hope.

In verse 17 the subject is not explicitly stated in Hebrew (literally, "They cry"), and conceivably it could be the evildoers of verse 16; it seems more reasonable, however, to suppose that **the righteous** are meant (as indeed the ancient versions indicate). RSV and TEV have supplied the subject **the righteous**. An alternate view, however, is that the author is using delayed identification so that the subject is identified after the verb(s) in a later line. Verse 17 is literally "When they cry, Yahweh hears them, and from all their anguish rescues them." Verse 18 "Close is Yahweh to the broken hearted, and those crushed in spirit he saves." In this view the pronouns point ahead to the delayed subject "the broken hearted" and not back to "the righteous." However, the interpretation of RSV and TEV is the one most translations follow.

Delivers is the verb used in verse 7, and **saves** is the one used in verse 6.

The LORD is near in verse 18 is an expressive way of saying that the Lord is attentive and watchful, always ready to help and to save his people. **The brokenhearted** could be repentant and humble people; it seems better, however, to see them as discouraged, just as in line b the **crushed in spirit** are those who have lost all hope. **The crushed in spirit** may sometimes be rendered "those who have nothing good to look forward to," or idiomatically, "those whose stomachs have turned white."

	34.19-20 RSV		TEV
19	Many are the afflictions of the righteous; but the LORD delivers him out of them all.	19	The good man suffers many troubles, but the LORD saves him from them all;
20	He keeps all his bones; not one of them is broken.	20	the LORD preserves him completely; not one of his bones is broken.

In verse 19a **afflictions** means troubles, difficulties, bad things, sufferings, misfortunes. A translation can say "Many bad things happen to good people."

Delivers in verse 19b translates the same verb used in verse 7. The thought is not that Yahweh does not allow bad things to happen to good people, but that he does not let them be defeated or destroyed by them.

In verse 20a **He** refers to Yahweh and **his** to the righteous person. **Keeps** has the meaning "guards."

The expressive language in verse 20 portrays Yahweh's care and concern. Most translations keep the poetic language about **bones**, but there may be some cases in which the figures would be taken literally; in such instances a more general statement can be made, such as "The LORD protects him with great care and does not let him be hurt in the least."

The language of verse 20b is used in John 19.36, but the source of the thought of the quotation is rather Exodus 12.46 and Numbers 9.12, passages which speak of the passover lamb.

34.21 RSV	TEV
Evil shall slay the wicked; and those who hate the righteous will be condemned.	Evil will kill the wicked; those who hate the righteous will be punished.

Evil shall slay the wicked may be a way of saying that the wicked person's own evil plans will eventually destroy him (so SPCL, FRCL, NEB); or else it may be a reference to divine punishment, which is the thought of line **b**: they **will be condemned**, by God, that is. The Hebrew verb translated **condemned** (TEV "punished") occurs very few times and seems to mean "to be held guilty"; the idea may be expressed by "brought to ruin" (NEB), "be ruined" (NJV). NJB translates "will pay the penalty." Because in some languages it is not possible to speak of an abstract quality such as **evil** being the agent of the act of killing, it will be necessary sometimes to translate "The evil person will cause his own death" or, if understood in the sense of God causing his death because of his evil, one may sometimes render it "Because the wicked person is evil, God will destroy him."

RSV	TEV
34.22	

<table>
<tr><td>The L<small>ORD</small> redeems the life of his
servants;
none of those who take refuge
in him will be condemned.</td><td>The L<small>ORD</small> will save his people;
those who go to him for protection will be spared.</td></tr>
</table>

The psalm closes with a final statement of the security of God's people, who are called **his servants**. Only TEV has the future tense of the verb, **"will save"**; all others use the timeless present, which seems better. This can be expressed by "The L<small>ORD</small> always saves . . . ." The verb **redeems** is used also in 25.22; some translate "ransoms," but that term may have some implications not intended by the Hebrew verb. In normal English usage the verb "to ransom" implies a price paid to someone in order to gain the release of a person held captive. This idea should be avoided.

Those who trust in him for protection will not **be condemned**, in contrast with "those who hate the righteous" (verse 21b). For **take refuge in him** see verse 8 and 2.12. And the verb translated **condemned** is used in 5.10, where it has the sense of "bear (their) guilt" (see comments there).

Psalm 35

This psalm is a lament by an individual, like Psalms 17, 22, 28, and 31. The psalmist is persecuted by his enemies, and in his despair he prays to Yahweh for help. There is no clue in the text as to the identity of the writer or the specific circumstances of his desperate situation.

There are three main parts (verses 1-10, 11-18, 19-28), each one of which contains a description of the psalmist's troubles, a denunciation of his enemies, a plea to Yahweh for help, and a promise to praise him.

The first part (verses 1-10) starts with a prayer to Yahweh for vindication (verses 1-6), followed by an accusation against the psalmist's enemies (verse 7) and a renewed plea for vengeance (verse 8), ending with a promise to praise the Lord for his help (verses 9-10).

The second part (verses 11-18) opens with a description of the psalmist's enemies and a declaration of his own innocence (verses 11-16); the psalmist cries for help (verse 17) and promises to praise the Lord (verse 18).

The third part (verses 19-28) contains a description of the psalmist's enemies (verses 19-21), a cry for help (verses 22-27), and a promise to praise the Lord (verse 28).

HEADING: "A Prayer for Help" (TEV); "A plea for vindication"; "Prayer of a virtuous man under oppression"; "A prayer for vengeance." The TEV heading must often be translated by using verb phrases in place of TEV's nominal phrases; for example, "The psalmist prays asking God to help him."

Hebrew Title: **A Psalm of David.**

35.1-3

RSV	TEV
1 Contend, O LORD, with those who contend with me; fight against those who fight against me!	1 Oppose those who oppose me, LORD, and fight those who fight against me!
2 Take hold of shield and buckler, and rise for my help!	2 Take your shield and armor and come to my rescue.
3 Draw the spear and javelin against my pursuers! Say to my soul, "I am your deliverance!"	3 Lift up your spear and war ax against those who pursue me. Promise that you will save me.

328

The psalmist cries out to the Lord to **contend** with his enemies and **fight** against them, using in each instance the same verb to describe the Lord's actions and the actions of his adversaries. The expression **Contend . . . who contend with me** may be difficult to express in some languages. Since the meaning in the context seems to be that of fighting in battle, it is often possible to say "Be an enemy, LORD, against those who are my enemies" or "Fight against those who fight against me." This verb in verse 1a is used also in the sense of "argue with" or "accuse" at a trial, but the figure of physical strife in battle seems more appropriate here.

With **Contend . . . contend** and **fight . . . fight** the psalmist is using a wordplay in the form of repetition in which the identical Hebrew root is repeated in each line. For similar cases see Isaiah 17.12; Jeremiah 3.22. In some languages it will not be possible to maintain the device in the same form as here, since phrases may be required, or because of grammatical considerations. However, the translator should try to use forms that are in some degree repeatable.

In vivid language the psalmist calls on the Lord to arm himself with **shield** (see 3.3), **buckler** (another word for a larger shield, covering the whole body; see 5.12, where the same word is translated "shield"), **spear** (also in 46.9; 57.4), and **javelin**. The last weapon seems to be a double ax used in fighting; the Masoretic text vocalizes the consonants as though the word were an imperative of the verb "close, shut off," that is, destroy;[1] but from Qumran sources it is now established that this is a noun, the name of a weapon. **Shield** often requires some adjustments in translation. If there is no word in the receptor language, it may be desirable, but only rarely, to borrow a foreign term and to add a classifier; for example, "a protection called shield." On the other hand one may find it more convenient to use a descriptive phrase; for example, "body protection board." Often such descriptive phrases can be misleading and therefore must be used with considerable caution. If the translator finds the reader misunderstanding the usage of the expression, an additional note may be given in the glossary. **Buckler** may be distinguished from **shield** as "the big shield." **The spear** is widely known; where it is not, however, one can sometimes use a descriptive phrase such as "sharp stick for throwing."

In verse 2b the command **rise** means that Yahweh is asked to take action (see comments on the same verb in 3.7).

"Promise me" (TEV) in verse 3c translates "say to my *nefesh*" (see 3.2), which in this context means to reassure. So instead of TEV "Promise," something like "Assure me that . . ." may be better. RSV uses direct discourse, quoting the words that the psalmist asks Yahweh to speak; TEV uses indirect discourse, ". . . that you will save me." For the noun **deliverance** see comments on 3.8; here it means to rescue from enemies, not spiritual "salvation." Dahood translates "your victory."

---

[1]HOTTP, however, says the meaning of the Masoretic text imperative "and close" is "and protect"; HOTTP also says that the other interpretation is possible, that is, a "spear."

35.4-6	RSV	TEV

	RSV		TEV
4	Let them be put to shame and dishonor who seek after my life! Let them be turned back and confounded who devise evil against me!	4	May those who try to kill me be defeated and disgraced! May those who plot against me be turned back and confused!
5	Let them be like chaff before the wind, with the angel of the LORD driving them on!	5	May they be like straw blown by the wind as the angel of the LORD pursues them!
6	Let their way be dark and slippery, with the angel of the LORD pursuing them!	6	May their path be dark and slippery while the angel of the LORD strikes them down!

In vivid terms the psalmist prays to Yahweh, asking him to defeat and destroy his enemies, so that they may **be put to shame and dishonor**. For **shame** see comments on "be ashamed" in 6.10; **dishonor** is a synonym, "Let them be . . . humiliated." The expression **put to shame and dishonor** may have to be recast as direct commands; for example, "Defeat and disgrace those who try to kill me," or idiomatically, "Heat their faces with shame and stop those who want to kill me."

He also prays that they may be **turned back and confounded**. **Turned back** uses a military figure, "driven back." For **Let them be turned back** in the sense of repelling an invading force, one may sometimes say "Stop them and send them away" or "Don't let them advance further, but push them back."

Be . . . confounded is the same verb which in 34.5 is translated "be ashamed." **Confounded** can sometimes be rendered idiomatically, "with dizzy heads" or "not remembering who they are." Verse 4 is practically the same as 40.14; 70.2.

The poetic structure of verse 4 is impressive and effective. For readers with a fairly high degree of literary appreciation, the form of RSV may be more appealing; for many readers, however, the gap between **them** and the **who** phrase in each half of the verse may be difficult. For such people the more direct form of TEV may be more appropriate. Or else something like the following:

> LORD, defeat and disgrace
>   those who are trying to kill me!
> Confuse and put to flight
>   all those who make plans to harm me!

For the figure in verse 5a, **like chaff before the wind**, see 1.4 and comments. **Like chaff before the wind** may in some languages require that the verb be explicitly stated; for example, "I ask that they be blown away by the wind as the chaff is blown away."

Angel translates the Hebrew "messenger"; here it is a supernatural being, not a human one (see comments at 34.7).

In verse 6a the adjectives **dark** and **slippery** in Hebrew are two nouns, "darkness" and "slippery places." They portray a difficult and dangerous situation. Dahood takes the nouns as names of Sheol: "Darkness and Destruction"; this, however, is not very likely the primary meaning of the terms. **Let their way be dark and slippery** may have to be recast to say, for example, "May they take a slippery path in the darkness" or "When they go, may the place they walk be slippery and dark."

The verbs used to describe the action of **the angel of the LORD** in verses 5b-6 in the Hebrew text are, respectively, "push, strike down" and "pursue, run after." TEV, following Briggs and others, has transposed the two verbs, since "**pursues**" goes better with "**like straw blown by the wind**" in verse 5, and "**strikes . . . down**" with "**dark and slippery path**" in verse 6.

35.7-8	RSV	TEV
7	For without cause they hid their net for me; without cause they dug a pit*s* for my life.	7 Without any reason they laid a trap for me and dug a deep hole to catch me.
8	Let ruin come upon them unawares! And let the net which they hid ensnare them; let them fall therein to ruin!	8 But destruction will catch them before they know it; they will be caught in their own trap and fall to their destruction!

s The word *pit* is transposed from the preceding line

The Hebrew particle translated **For** in RSV does not necessarily introduce a reason clause, but rather adds an extra beat to the line. TEV has correctly omitted it.

Without cause in lines **a** and **b** means that the psalmist's enemies had no valid reason for trying to harm him; he had done nothing against them.

For the figures **net** and **pit**, see discussion of both 7.15 and 9.15. As the RSV footnote notes, the word **pit** in verse 7b is in line **a** in the Masoretic text, which is literally "they hid a pit for me their net."[2] In verse 7b "for my *nefesh*" (RSV **for my life**) means the same as **for me** in line **a**.

Verse 8 may be understood as a statement (Weiser; TEV, NJB, BJ) or as a wish (RSV, AT, NIV, NEB, NAB, NJV, FRCL, and others). It is probably better to take it as a wish, a prayer. In the expression **Let ruin come**, **ruin** and TEV's "**destruction**" are spoken of as independent agents performing events, something which is unnatural

---

[2]HOTTP claims that the whole verse may be interpreted as "(for in vain they have hidden for me) the pit of their trap (in vain they have dug [it] for my life)." It is hard to figure out what this is supposed to mean, but presumably it intends to say "In vain they have dug a hidden pit in which they want to trap me; in vain they have tried to capture me."

for a large number of languages. In these languages one may sometimes say, for example, "Before they know it they will be destroyed." If it is necessary to use the active voice, the logical agent expressed before and after this verse is the Lord. Therefore one may sometimes say "The LORD will catch them and destroy them." For the preferred form of a prayer or request to God, one may say "Catch them and destroy them . . ." or "Catch them in their own trap." **Unawares** in verse 8a means "by surprise," or else "an unforeseen disaster."

In verse 8b **the net which they hid** is the **net** the psalmist's enemies laid out in a hidden place in order to catch the psalmist.

In verse 8c the Masoretic text is "in ruin they fall in it" ("ruin" being the same word as "ruin" in verse 8a), whereas one expects here "pit" into which they fall, parallel with the **net** in which they are caught in line **b**. Instead of "in ruin" Syriac has "which they dug." NAB, BJ, NJB, follow the Syriac text, while Dahood takes the Masoretic text "in ruin" to mean "the pit" (see Holladay). Others, however, such as RSV, TEV, TOB ("may they fall into this ruin") and others (such as "May they fall into it [the net] and be destroyed"), NIV ("may they fall into the pit, to their ruin"), and NJV ("let them fall into it when disaster [strikes]") stay with the Masoretic text.[3] Either is possible, and the Masoretic text, though a bit strange, can be followed. For the idea expressed in verse 8b-c, see 7.15-16; 9.15 and comments.

35.9-10

RSV	TEV

9   Then my soul shall rejoice in the LORD,
    exulting in his deliverance.
10 All my bones shall say,
    "O LORD, who is like thee,
   thou who deliverest the weak
    from him who is too strong for him,
   the weak and needy from him
    who despoils him?"
	9 Then I will be glad because of the LORD;
	    I will be happy because he saved me.
	10 With all my heart I will say to the LORD,
	    "There is no one like you.
	   You protect the weak from the strong,
	    the poor from the oppressor."

The first part of the psalm concludes with the vow to praise Yahweh for his goodness. In verse 9 the two lines are parallel: **rejoice** and **exulting**; **my soul**, as often, means "I." And **in the LORD** means "because of what the LORD has done." The noun phrase **his deliverance** is best represented as a clause with a verb, "he delivered me." **Rejoice in the LORD** requires some adjustments in translation. In some languages it is possible to say "I will be glad because of what the LORD has done for me" or "because the LORD has protected me."

In verse 10 **All my bones** is a way of saying "my whole being," "my whole self." In English **all my bones** is not a natural expression, but most English translations use

---

[3]HOTTP takes the Masoretic text to mean "in a ruin" and proposes the following: "may he unexpectedly tumble and may his trap which he has hidden catch him; when he tumbles, may he fall down in it" (or "fall down in a ruin").

it. FRCL has "From the depths of my being," and SPCL and TEV have **"with all my heart."**

The rhetorical question in verse 10, **Who is like thee?** is a way of saying **"There is no one like you"** (TEV).

The Hebrew for **the weak** means the poor, the oppressed, the helpless (see comments on the same word, translated "afflicted," in 9.12); **"the strong"** (TEV) translates "the one (who is) too strong for him," leaving implicit their overpowering the poor.

The Hebrew for **deliverest** means to snatch away from the oppressor; TEV **"protect."** In some languages it is necessary to make explicit what it is that the Lord protects; for example, "you protect the weak when the strong abuse them" or "you prevent the strong from harming the weak."

The weak and needy are synonyms here, where **weak** again means "poor"; see 12.5 where they also are used as synonyms, translated "poor" and "needy."

The one **who despoils him** is one who exploits, oppresses, the weak. The Hebrew verb is graphic, "rip off"; in Micah 3.2 there is a vivid description of how violent exploiters "rip off" the skin of their victims. Here it will sometimes be necessary to say, for example, "you prevent powerful people from exploiting poor people" or "you protect the poor when the rich treat them badly."

35.11-12	RSV	TEV

	RSV	TEV
11	Malicious witnesses rise up; they ask me of things that I know not.	11 Evil men testify against me and accuse me of crimes I know nothing about.
12	They requite me evil for good; my soul is forlorn.	12 They pay me back evil for good, and I sink in despair.

The second part of the psalm (verses 11-18) begins with a renewed condemnation of the psalmist's enemies, who are called **Malicious witnesses,** that is, liars who give false testimony against him in court. The Hebrew phrase is "witnesses of violence stand up," which means either "hostile witnesses" or "false witnesses" (TOB, NJB, BJ).

Malicious witnesses may be transformed into a verb phrase as in TEV. If the translator follows TEV, it will be important to give the verb more specific content than "speak" or "tell." The context here is that of the court, and the speaking concerns something of grave importance, and normally something which has been seen by witnesses. However, in the present context these witnesses are telling lies. In some languages "testify" is rendered as "to take words to the people." In this case it will be appropriate to say "take lying words to the people." When following the TEV model, in some languages it will be necessary to say, for example, "they falsely say that I have done evil deeds," or in direct discourse, "they falsely say 'You have done evil deeds.' "

The verb translated **ask** is used here in the context of a trial; these are accusing questions, which imply that the psalmist is guilty of crimes, of which he denies any knowledge (**things that I know not**). So the translation can be **they ask me** or **"accuse me"** (TEV).

In verse 12 their evil character becomes even more evident: **They requite me evil for good**, that is, instead of doing good things for me, in return for the good things I did for them, they do evil things (similarly 38.20). The expression may sometimes be rendered, for example, "I have done good and they do evil to me" or "I have given them good things, but they have given me bad things."

The consequence (verse 12b) is, literally, "bereavement to my *nefesh*." The word "bereavement" is "childless" (RSV **forlorn**); some emend the Hebrew text to get "they seek (for my life)"; so NEB "lying in wait to take my life." TOB translates the Masoretic text "here I am all alone"; another possible version is "they bring desolation upon me"; NJV "[seeking] my bereavement"; NJB "make my life barren." Cohen suggests the phrase is an exclamation, equivalent to "Woe is me!"[4] The meaning represented by RSV and TEV is to be preferred.

35.13-14 RSV	TEV

13   But I, when they were sick—
      I wore sackcloth,
      I afflicted myself with fasting.
      I prayed with my head bowed*f* on
         my bosom,
 14   as though I grieved for my
         friend or my brother;
      I went about as one who laments
         his mother,
      bowed down and in mourning.
	13 But when they were sick, I
	      dressed in mourning;
	      I deprived myself of food;
	      I prayed with my head bowed low,
	 14 as I would pray for a friend or a
	         brother.
	      I went around bent over in
	         mourning,
	      as one who mourns for his
	         mother.

f Or *My prayer turned back*

The psalmist contrasts his own conduct (verses 13-14) with that of his enemies (verses 15-16). Expressing his deep sympathy for their misfortune, he mourned and fasted (verse 13a,b). To wear **sackcloth** and to go without food were ways of expressing grief. The expression **I wore sackcloth** may be expressed without reference to the associated custom of mourning dress; for example, "I showed myself to be in mourning" or, if it can be rendered with more clarity, one may keep the custom and give an explanation of it; for example, "I put on ragged clothes to show I was in mourning" or "I painted my body to show there was a death."

The language in the last part of verse 13 is unclear; the Hebrew text says "and my prayer returned to my bosom." There is much disagreement over the meaning of these words. Some take them to mean unceasing, repeated prayers; others take this as parenthetical, expressing the wish that his prayer for them not be answered (so FRCL); NEB links it with what follows, "When my prayer came back unanswered, I walked with my head bowed . . ." (similarly NIV); NJB has "praying ever anew in my heart"; SPCL "in my inner being I did not stop praying"; NJV "may what I prayed for

---

[4]HOTTP says only that the Masoretic text means "loss of children for my soul" ("A" decision), which is of no great help to translators.

happen to me!"; ZÜR "I prayed with my head bowed." Before such diversity of opinion it is difficult to make a choice; it seems that humility is the emotion indicated, not grief as such.

If the translator follows the suggestion that **head bowed** is here a gesture of humility, then a gesture in the receptor culture which signals humility should be used. In some societies this is placing the hands on the crown of the head, in others crossing the arms over the chest. However, in verse 14 **bowed down** is a gesture of grief at the time of mourning, and an appropriate gesture is called for here also.

Verse 14 continues the idea, showing the psalmist "praying" (TEV) or "grieving" (RSV) for them as he would **for my friend or my brother**, mourning over them as he would for **his mother**.

35.15	RSV	TEV
	But at my stumbling they gathered in glee, they gathered together against me; cripples whom I knew not slandered me without ceasing;	But when I was in trouble, they were all glad and gathered around to make fun of me; strangers beat me and kept striking me.

The conduct of the psalmist's enemies is the opposite of his own; when he was in trouble (literally "stumbled," or "limped" like a wounded animal), "they gathered around (or, against) me"; the verb "gather around" is repeated in the Hebrew text. The picture is that of the psalmist's enemies surrounding him and making fun of him.

Line c is difficult to understand; the Masoretic text has a word occurring only here in the Old Testament and which is taken to mean "beaters, smiters," or else, as RSV has it, a passive form, "smitten, lamed," and so "cripples" (so TOB).[5] Translations differ: NAB has "striking me unawares"; NEB "nameless ruffians jeered at me"; NJB understands the wording of the Hebrew to mean "strangers"; NJV has "wretches"; TOB "my assailants took me by surprise."

It is impossible to say whether the language in line d is a conventional way of talking about slander, criticism, and mockery (so RSV and NIV **slandered me without ceasing**) or refers to physical abuse (TEV). The verb is used elsewhere of "tearing" clothes; so NAB "they tore at me"; NJB "tear me apart incessantly"; and NJV "they tear at me without end." Kirkpatrick, Dahood, and Weiser take it in a figurative sense; SPCL has "they mistreated me without ceasing."

35.16	RSV	TEV
	they impiously mocked more and more,[u]	Like men who would mock a cripple;[f]

---

[5]HOTTP takes the Hebrew to mean "[as] limping men" and suggests this may designate the psalmist's enemies as they mockingly imitated the psalmist in distress.

gnashing at me with their teeth.	they glared at me with hate.

u Cn Compare Gk: Heb *like the pro-fanest of mockers of a cake*   *f* Like . . . cripple; *Hebrew unclear.*

The Hebrew of the first line of this verse is completely unintelligible; literally it seems to say (as the RSV footnote has) "like (or, with) the profanest mockers of (or, for) a cake." There are various explanations of this, most of which seem fanciful rather than possible. NAB has followed the Septuagint: "They made me suffer and jeered at me"; some, with a change in vowels in the first word in the Hebrew text, propose to get "When I faltered, they mocked me unceasingly"; NJB "if I fall they surround me"; NEB has "brutes who would mock even a hunchback." TEV "**Like men who would mock a cripple**" seems to follow HOTTP in part, which says that the Masoretic text says "among the wicked [men], mockers of deformity [that is, of one who is deformed]" ("C" decision).

In line <u>b</u> "they gnash their teeth at me" is an expression of anger and hatred (so also 37.12; 112.10); TEV uses the less specific "**they glared at me with hate**," since the purpose of gnashing of teeth may not be understood by the readers.

<u>35.17-18</u>   RSV   TEV

17	How long, O LORD, wilt thou look on? Rescue me from their ravages, my life from the lions!	17	How much longer, Lord, will you just look on? Rescue me from their attacks; save my life from these lions!
18	Then I will thank thee in the great congregation; in the mighty throng I will praise thee.	18	Then I will thank you in the assembly of your people; I will praise you before them all.

This second part of the psalm closes with a renewed plea to Yahweh to intervene and help the psalmist, and a promise to praise him if he answers his prayer.

The expression **How long, O LORD, wilt thou look on?** will require some shifting in some languages if the meaning of looking without taking an active part in the defense of the psalmist is to be made clear. For example, in some languages it will be necessary to say "How long will you, Lord, just look and not defend me?" or "How long will you do nothing for me but look?" It should be noted that in verse 17a the title "**Lord**" is used, not, as RSV wrongly has it, the name Yahweh.

The meaning of the word translated **ravages** is disputed; NJB "onslaughts"; TEV, NJV "attacks"; NEB "out of their cruel grasp"; Dahood "from their pits"; FRCL, SPCL "from these roaring lions."

In lines <u>b</u> and <u>c</u> of verse 18 (as in 22.20) the Hebrew says "save my *nefesh* . . . my only one," two ways of speaking about his life. Here FRCL expands considerably on "my only one": "Save my life from these roaring lions, my life, which is all that I have."

The figure of <u>lions</u> is often used for enemies (7.2; 10.9; 17.12; 22.13,21). <u>Rescue</u> . . . <u>my life from the lions</u> may have to be shifted to a simile; for example, ". . . from my enemies who attack me like lions."

The psalmist promises to praise Yahweh <u>in the great congregation</u>, that is, in public worship in the Temple (as in 22.22). <u>In the great congregation</u> must sometimes be rendered "where the people meet to praise you." And in line <u>b</u> <u>the mighty throng</u> is another way of speaking of the people gathered in the Temple for worship.

35.19   RSV   TEV

Let not those rejoice over me   Don't let my enemies, those liars,
    who are wrongfully my foes,   gloat over my defeat.
and let not those wink the eye   Don't let those who hate me for
    who hate me without cause.   no reason
                                           smirk with delight over my
                                               sorrow.

Once more the psalmist asks the Lord to rescue him from his enemies. In line a <u>rejoice over me</u> means to be happy because of his, the psalmist's, misfortunes. In line <u>b</u> the Hebrew may mean "(my enemies) those liars" (TEV) or "traitors" (see NEB), or else "those who are wrongfully (my enemies)" (see RSV), as a parallel with the last line, (<u>who hate me</u>) <u>without cause</u> (so NIV). The quotation in John 15.25 comes from this passage or from Psalm 69.5.

The expression <u>wink the eye</u> may mean to gloat gleefully, "**smirk with delight**" (TEV), "leer at me in triumph" (NEB). Or perhaps it is a signal to other enemies of the psalmist, or an evil spell they wish to cast on him. If the translator takes the expression <u>let not those wink the eye</u> to mean "smirk" as in TEV, in some languages this can be rendered "Don't let people smile with satisfaction because I have sorrow" or "Don't let people laugh at me when they see that I am sad."

35.20-21   RSV   TEV

20 For they do not seek peace,   20 They do not speak in a friendly
        but against those who are quiet   way;
        in the land   instead they invent all kinds of
    they conceive words of deceit.   lies about peace-loving people.
21 They open wide their mouths   21 They accuse me, shouting,
        against me;   "We saw what you did!"
    they say "Aha! Aha!
    our eyes have seen it!"

The psalmist's enemies <u>do not speak peace</u>, which means either "do not speak in a friendly way" (TEV; see NEB "No friendly greeting do they give"; FRCL "not a single courteous word") or else "they do not seek peace" (SPCL), that is, do not try to be at peace with others.

Instead, they tell lies against **those who are quiet in the land**. This expression occurs only here in the Old Testament; see NJV "harmless folk"; NEB "peaceable folk"; NJB "the peace-loving people of the land." **Those who are quiet in the land** may in some languages be expressed idiomatically; for example, "people whose hearts sit quietly" or "people who have cool hearts."

In verse 21a "open wide the mouth" may mean shouting (TEV), or else it may portray contempt; Dahood sees it in terms of a ravenous monster, threatening to devour. They falsely accuse the psalmist of a crime: **"We saw what you did!"** (TEV) or, in idiomatic language, "We caught you red-handed!"

This is preceded by a Hebrew expression of mockery, **Aha! Aha!** Many languages have exclamatory expressions used in mockery, particularly among young people; for example, "They mock me and say, 'Bu bu bu bu, we saw what you did!' " The translator must make certain that such expressions are acceptable for public reading.

35.22-23   RSV   TEV

22   Thou hast seen, O LORD; be not   22   But you, O LORD, have seen this.
         silent!   So don't be silent, Lord;
         O Lord, be not far from me!   don't keep yourself far away!
23   Bestir thyself, and awake for my   23   Rouse yourself, O Lord, and de-
         right,   fend me;
         for my cause, my God and my   rise up, my God, and plead my
         Lord!   cause.

Now the psalmist appeals to Yahweh for protection against his enemies. The Lord knows his situation (verse 22a), and so the psalmist asks him to take action (verse 22a,b); see 28.1 for **be not silent**, and 22.1 for **be not far from me**. The initial statement **Thou hast seen** uses the same verb that at the end of verse 21 is used by the psalmist's enemies. Whereas they lie when they say "We saw what you did!" (TEV), the psalmist knows that Yahweh has seen what his enemies are doing. So he asks Yahweh to speak up (**be not silent!**) and denounce his enemies.

In verse 23, with two verbs the psalmist asks Yahweh to **bestir** himself, to **awake** (both verbs also in 44.23); both verbs are used of someone awaking or rousing himself from sleep. **Bestir thyself, and awake** are parallel expressions meaning "Awaken!" This expression has a sense similar to 7.6, "Arise, O Lord . . . awake . . . ." The two verbs in verse 23 give an order for only one action: **awake**. It is not necessary to seek explanation in the Canaanite fertility rites in which the vegetation deity was awakened in the spring. The psalmist is calling on God to act, and he does this through the figure of awakening him from sleep. TEV has translated a parallel line using "**rise up.**" The translator may follow the single figure of awakening as in RSV, which reflects the Hebrew, or the "awake and rise" figures of TEV. If the translator follows TEV, in some languages "rise up" must specify whether from a lying or sitting position.

The two expressions **for my right**, **for my cause** are legal language and mean that Yahweh is to see that justice is done, that right prevail, and that the psalmist's cause be successfully defended in court.

　RSV　　　　　　　　　　　　TEV

24 Vindicate me, O LORD, my God,
according to thy righteousness;
and let them not rejoice over
me!
25 Let them not say to themselves,
"Aha, we have our heart's desire!"
Let them not say, "We have swallowed him up."

24 You are righteous, O LORD, so
declare me innocent;
don't let my enemies gloat over
me.
25 Don't let them say to themselves,
"We are rid of him!
That's just what we wanted!"

Vindicate me in verse 24a is the action that is to follow that of awaking in verse 23, as Yahweh takes the psalmist's side. Here the psalmist asks that Yahweh declare him innocent of all charges. **Vindicate me** in some languages is expressed as "Say that I have done no wrong" or "Tell the people that I am innocent."

According to thy righteousness: "because you are righteous" (see important discussion at 31.1).

For line b see verse 19a.

In verse 25 **we have our heart's desire** means that the enemies would have achieved what they wanted, that is, the psalmist's condemnation, and that is what the psalmist wants Yahweh to prevent. The Hebrew of line b is "Aha, our *nefesh*," the word *nefesh* being used here of desire (see also 3.2). **We have swallowed him up** (see same language used of Yahweh in 21.9) is a picturesque way of saying "We have ruined him completely" (SPCL), "We have gotten rid of him" (see TEV). Many languages, particularly in Africa, use the "swallow" figure for total destruction.

　RSV　　　　　　　　　　　　TEV

Let them be put to shame and
confusion altogether
who rejoice at my calamity!
Let them be clothed with shame
and dishonor
who magnify themselves against
me!

May those who gloat over my
suffering
be completely defeated and
confused;
may those who claim to be better
than I am
be covered with shame and
disgrace.

With a final request concerning his enemies (verse 26) and his friends (verse 27), the psalmist concludes with a promise to praise the Lord for helping him (verse 28).

Parts of the expressions **put to shame and confusion** and **clothed with shame and dishonor** are used in verse 4; they are all used synonymously, indicating total and humiliating defeat.

Calamity translates a Hebrew word that means "evil," "a bad thing," and is applied to any number of undesirable circumstances. Here NJV "misfortune" may be the best word in English.

Clothed with shame as well as the TEV rendering "**covered with shame**" will require some shifting in many languages, particularly in the direction of idiomatic usage; for example, "may their faces burn" or "let them hide their faces."

The enemies **magnify themselves** against the psalmist, that is, they are proud and arrogant, and claim to be better than the psalmist. NEB, NAB "who glory over me"; NJB "who profit at my expense"; another possible version is "act arrogantly toward me." **Who magnify themselves** may be translated in some languages as "people who think they are chiefs and order me about."

35.27-28   RSV   TEV

27 Let those who desire my vindica-   27 May those who want to see me
       tion   acquitted
    shout for joy and be glad,   shout for joy and say again and
    and say evermore,   again,
    "Great is the LORD,   "How great is the LORD!
       who delights in the welfare of   He is pleased with the success
       his servant!"   of his servant!"
28 Then my tongue shall tell of thy   28 Then I will proclaim your righ-
       righteousness   teousness,
    and of thy praise all the day   and I will praise you all day
       long.   long.

Verse 27 describes the reaction of the psalmist's friends, who want to see him declared innocent (**my vindication**—see verse 24).

In verse 27e **welfare** translates the Hebrew *shalom* (see comment on "peace" in 29.11); NJV, NIV, SPCL have "well-being"; NAB "prosperity." **His servant** is the psalmist himself.

Who delights in the welfare of his servant is an expression which poses two major translation problems. The first refers to the translation of the Hebrew word translated **welfare** by RSV and "**success**" by TEV. In many languages this broad concept of well-being and material prosperity can only be summed up in metaphorical terminology; for example, "God delights when people's hearts sit in cool shade" or "God is happy when people's hearts are singing." In the absence of such idiomatic usage, one may in some languages say "God is happy when people are at peace and have all they need."

The second problem in this line is the expression **his servant**, which represents a change to third person reference. In some languages such a switch of pronominal reference will create misunderstandings for the reader. If that is the case, it will be preferable to say, for example, "he is pleased with my success. I am his servant" or "he is pleased with the way I succeed, and I am his servant" or ". . . the way I, his servant, succeed."

In verse 28 the word translated **righteousness** may be taken here in a concrete fashion, such as NJV "beneficent acts," and NJB "saving justice," or else as a moral

340

quality, "goodness" (BJ), "faithfulness" (FRCL). **My tongue shall tell of thy righteousness** may often be translated "I shall tell people how good you are" or "I shall say to the people 'God is good.' "

The expression **My tongue shall tell . . . of thy praise** does not mean that the psalmist will talk about the subject of praising Yahweh, but that he will, in fact, praise Yahweh **all the day long**.

Psalm 36

This psalm does not conform to any one type; it includes a meditation on the nature of evil people (verses 1-4), but without a prayer for their destruction, as is common in laments such as Psalm 35; then there is a hymn in praise of God's goodness (verses 5-9), and the final section is a prayer for God to bless the righteous and punish the wicked (verses 10-12), which is similar to such prayers elsewhere.

HEADING: TEV has two, "**The Wickedness of Man**" for verses 1-4, and "**The Goodness of God**" for verses 5-12; other translations combine both elements in one heading, "Human wickedness and divine providence" (NAB) and "The perversity of sinners and the benevolence of God" (NJB); or else "Man's evil and God's love" (Toombs). TEV's heading may require some adjustments in languages in which "wickedness" must be rendered as a verb phrase; for example, "People do evil deeds" or "The evil things people do."

Hebrew Title: **To the choirmaster. A Psalm of David, the servant of the LORD.**

For **To the choirmaster** see title of Psalm 4. David is called **the servant of the LORD** in 78.70; 89.3; frequently in psalms the authors use this phrase to speak of themselves.

36.1-2

RSV	TEV
1 Transgression speaks to the wicked deep in his heart; there is no fear of God before his eyes.	1 Sin speaks to the wicked man deep in his heart; he rejects God and does not have reverence for him.
2 For he flatters himself in his own eyes that his iniquity cannot be found out and hated.	2 Because he thinks so highly of himself, he thinks that God will not discover his sin and condemn it.

The opening words of the psalm are literally "utterance of sin to the wicked"; with very few exceptions, the noun translated "utterance" is used elsewhere of the voice of God, especially when speaking to the prophets (see 110.1, "Utterance of Yahweh to my lord"). So Dahood translates "Perversity inspires the wicked man"; NJB has "Sin is the Oracle of the Wicked"; another possible version is "Rebellion speaks as an oracle to the wicked man."

At the end of line **b** the Masoretic text has "my heart"; some Hebrew manuscripts and some of the ancient versions have **his heart**, which is followed by most translations.[1] TOB translates the Masoretic text "The impious oracle of the infidel comes to my mind"; NJV "I know what Transgression says to the wicked"; NIV "An oracle is within my heart concerning the sinfulness of the wicked"; FRCL "I keep in mind the maxim that expresses the evildoer's rebellion." It seems best to translate "his heart." In many languages it is unnatural to say that sin can speak, since that is the activity of people. However, it is possible to employ causative constructions which essentially preserve the components of meaning; for example, "Sin causes the wicked to listen deep in his heart," "Sin causes the wicked to listen intently," "Sin makes the wicked person hear the voice of evil in his heart," or "Sin causes people who do evil things to hear bad advice in their hearts." In languages in which sin cannot serve as a subject or as an agent of an event, but only as an event, it may be necessary to say, for example, "When people sin they know what it does to them deep in their heart." It is sometimes possible to employ a simile: "When a person sins, it is like someone speaking to him deep in his heart."

The last part of verse 1 is quoted in Romans 3.18. **There is no fear of God before his eyes** means "in his opinion there is no need to fear God." In this verse the phrase "fear of God" is not the one usually translated "to honor or have reverence for God"; here it means fear, dread, terror. The **wicked** person thinks there is no need to fear God, for God does not punish, God does not act (see related ideas in 10.4; 14.1). The phrase **before his eyes** expresses attitude, opinion; the negative "not to have before one's eyes" means to neglect, disregard, forget, treat as nonsense. So lines c-d can best be translated "in his opinion there is no need to be afraid of God" or "he thinks to himself, 'I don't have to be afraid of God.'"

In verse 2 **he flatters himself in his own eyes** means "he thinks highly of himself." But the subject of the verb could be **transgression** of verse 1, and so the meaning would be (as NJV has it) "its speech is seductive to him"; or else "For rebellion flatters him (and blinds him)." **Flatters himself** may sometimes be rendered "he thinks in his heart what a great chief he is" or "he speaks beautiful words about himself."

The second half of verse 2 is literally "for finding out his sin for hating [it]." It seems best to take God as the implied subject (so Anderson; see TEV), understanding "hate" in the sense of "**condemn**." But there is great variety in the rendering of this line: NEB "and, when he is found out, he does not mend his ways" (following a conjecture, on the grounds that the Masoretic text is unintelligible); TOB takes the sinner himself as the subject in the whole verse, "He sees himself in such a flattering way that he does not discover his own error and hate it"; FRCL: "He has too good an opinion of himself to recognize his own fault and hate it" (so HOTTP).

36.3-4	RSV		TEV
3	The words of his mouth are mischief and deceit; he has ceased to act wisely and	3	His speech is wicked and full of lies; he no longer does what is wise

---

[1]HOTTP, without any comment, recommends "his heart" ("C" decision). It cites factor 12, "Other scribal errors."

	do good.		and good.
4	He plots mischief while on his bed;	4	He makes evil plans as he lies in bed;
	he sets himself in a way that is not good;		nothing he does is good,
	he spurns not evil.		and he never rejects anything evil.

What a wicked person says harms others (**mischief**) and is untrue (**deceit**); see comments on these terms in 5.6b; 10.7. As noted elsewhere, **mischief** in English is not adequate as a description of something that is wrong or harmful to others. **The words of his mouth** may require shifting into an adverbial clause; for example, "When he speaks, his words are evil."

Line <u>b</u> of verse 3 can be translated "he will not consider doing good," as NJV does, or as TEV **"he no longer does what is wise and good"** (so RSV); NEB and NJB "he has turned his back on wisdom"; TOB "he has lost the notion of what is good"; SPCL "he lost his good sense, he quit doing good;" FRCL "Doing good makes no sense to him." It seems best to follow either TEV or FRCL here.

The evil man is further portrayed in verse 4 as one who makes evil plans (**plots mischief**), who "takes his stand on a way that isn't good," that is, whose conduct is always evil (line <u>b</u>), and as one who **spurns not evil** (line <u>c</u>). **He plots mischief** may sometimes be rendered "The things he thinks about doing are evil" or "He thinks of evil things to do." The clause **while on his bed** in line <u>a</u> refers to his time of leisure, or rest. Line <u>b</u> is taken by Dahood to mean "the path of crime," that is, active evil and not just the passive avoidance of good. Both TEV and RSV retain the negative in **he spurns not evil**. In some languages it will be more natural to say, for example, "he always accepts to do evil deeds" or "he always says 'Yes' to evil."

36.5-6   RSV   TEV

5	Thy steadfast love, O LORD, extends to the heavens,	5	LORD, your constant love reaches the heavens;
	thy faithfulness to the clouds.		your faithfulness extends to the skies.
6	Thy righteousness is like the mountains of God,	6	Your righteousness is towering like the mountains;
	thy judgments are like the great deep;		your justice is like the depths of the sea.
	man and beast thou savest, O LORD.		Men and animals are in your care.

In the hymn of praise to God's goodness (verses 5-9), the four basic characteristics of Yahweh as the God of Israel are mentioned explicitly: **steadfast love** (see 5.7 and comments); **faithfulness** (*'emunah*), that is, keeping his promises to his people (see 12.1; 33.4 and comments); **righteousness** (see 5.8 and comments); and **judgments** (see 7.6 and comments). The last one, contrary to the others, appears as a plural in the Masoretic text; Briggs thinks that the original singular form of the text was changed by a copyist to the plural. Since the first three speak of God's attributes and not specifically of his actions, it seems best to follow TEV and NJV here and translate "your justice." All these qualities are manifested in the relation between Yahweh and Israel, as set forth in the covenant that he made with them.

In verse 5a the Hebrew can be translated "in the heavens" (the Septuagint; Briggs); but the parallelism with line b favors the idea of **extends to the heavens** (most translations); Dahood takes it to mean "from heaven." The thought is that his qualities are beyond measuring, without any limits; they cover the whole universe. If the imagery of love having physical extension can be used, it may be possible to say, for example, "you love in such a great way it is like the distance from the earth to the sky." If such a simile cannot be used, it may be necessary to omit the heavens and translate the comparison as "Your constant love is far greater than anything else" or "You always love your people far more than they can imagine."

In verse 6a the Hebrew **the mountains of God** is taken by most to be a Hebrew way of saying "the highest mountains" or something similar (NEB, NAB, NJV, NIV, SPCL); see 68.15a; 80.10; 104.16. The quality evoked here is that of stability and permanence. **Like the great deep** compares God's judgments to the ocean depths, emphasizing the idea of mystery and power. Or else the two lines, verse 6a,b, are an emphatic way of saying that God's righteousness and judgments are all-encompassing, ranging from the highest peaks to the lowest depths of the earth. Poetic imagery is not always subject to logical analysis and definition. Line a may be recast in some languages with less poetic flexibility to say, for instance, "Your way of doing things fairly is as great as a mountain." Line b may be said "you judge everything as fairly as the sea is deep."

It will be noted that the simile is expressed with **like** in both lines of this verse in RSV and TEV. In line b in Hebrew there is ellipsis in the simile, so that **like** in line a is not expressed in line b. In other cases **like** is expressed only in the second line and omitted in the first. Whether or not ellipsis in simile can be retained depends on the poetic usage in the receptor language.

In verse 6c the verb "to save" (see "Help" in 12.1) in this context does not mean to rescue, but means to provide for, care for, supply the needs of. NJB translates "You support," NIV "you preserve," SPCL "You take care of." Yahweh provides for the needs of all living beings, animals and humans alike.

36.7-8	RSV	TEV
7	How precious is thy steadfast love, O God! The children of men take refuge in the shadow of thy wings.	7 How precious, O God, is your constant love! We find[x] protection under the shadow of your wings.
8	They feast on the abundance of thy house, and thou givest them drink from the river of thy delights.	8 We feast on the abundant food you provide; you let us drink from the river of your goodness.

[x] precious, O God, is . . . find; or precious is your constant love! Gods and men find.

The psalmist praises God for his **steadfast love** for his people and for protecting them (**refuge**); for the figure **the shadow of your wings**, see comment at 17.8b. The adjective **precious** in this context means that God's love is worth having, it is valuable; it brings blessings and benefits to people. GECL translates "Your love is incomparable," and SPCL "How marvelous . . . !" In verse 7b the translator may find it necessary to add a simile in order to make the comparison easier for the reader to grasp; for example, "You protect people like a bird protects its young under its wings." For the Hebrew phrase "the sons of men" (RSV **the children of men**), see 11.4 and comments. Instead of "**We**" (TEV), it is better to say "People" or "Everyone."

Instead of **O God! The children of men take refuge** in verse 7a,b, the Hebrew text may be understood to say "gods and men find protection . . ." (so Dahood, NEB). HOTTP regards this as possible, and the form of the Masoretic text seems to make it more probable than the other rendition.

The inexhaustible blessings of God are compared to **abundance of thy house** and **the river of thy delights**. The noun translated **abundance** is "fatness"; it is used to refer to olive oil, food, and rich food. Some take **of thy house** to be the Temple, and that sacrificial feasts are being spoken of (see 23.5,6 and comments); it seems best to understand the expression figuratively.

The river spoken of here is that which flows from the upper waters stored above the heavenly dome (see 33.7 and comments; Job 38.25a), from which come the life-giving rains that cause plants and crops to grow (see 65.9; 104.13). **Delights** translates a noun that is related to the place name Eden. The idea is that which is pleasant and enjoyable. The expression **the river of thy delights** can usually be kept as in RSV and TEV by recasting in the form of a simile; for example, "receive your good things that flow like a river" or "your good things flow like a river, and people drink from it."

36.9   RSV   TEV

> For with thee is the fountain of life;
>   in thy light do we see light.

> You are the source of all life, and because of your light we see the light.

The psalmist speaks of God as **the fountain of life**, that is, "the source of all life"; and **light** is a figure for life (see 18.28; 27.1). The idea in line **b** is that, because God is life and the source of it, human beings are able to have life, a "full and satisfying life" (Anderson). Dahood believes the reference is to eternal life. The expression **with thee is the fountain of life** must be recast in numerous languages. In some it will be necessary to say, for example, "you are the one who creates everything that lives" or "you are the one who gives life to all things." Following the interpretation of light representing life, it is possible to translate line **b** as, for example, "it is your light which illumines our life" (see FRCL). Another suggestion is that followed by SPCL, "in your light we are able to see the light."

36.10-11   RSV   TEV

10   O continue thy steadfast love to   10   Continue to love those who know
        those who know thee,   you
     and thy salvation to the upright   and to do good to those who are
        of heart!   righteous.
11   Let not the foot of arrogance   11   Do not let proud men attack me
        come upon me,   or wicked men make me run
     nor the hand of the wicked   away.
        drive me away.

The psalm closes with a prayer to Yahweh to bless his people (verse 10) and to protect the psalmist from his enemies (verse 11). The final statement (verse 12) expresses the psalmist's conviction that Yahweh will answer his prayer.

In verse 10a **know** means intimate knowledge, a living experience, a close relation, and not mere acquaintance or theoretical knowledge about God (see also comments on 9.10); those who **know** him, that is, **the upright of heart** (see comments at 7.10; 11.2; 32.11), are the people of Israel who obey and serve him. **Thy salvation** in verse 10b is parallel with **steadfast love** of line a; here **salvation** does not mean "rescue" but the blessings and benefits, the "good things" that God gives his people. It is rendered kindness, generosity (Dahood), "beneficence" (NJV), "faithfulness" (FRCL), "justice" (NEB, TOB, SPCL), and "saving justice" (NJB), all of which are better in this context than RSV **salvation**.

In verse 11 **the foot of arrogance** and **the hand of the wicked** are ways of speaking of the psalmist's enemies, who are proud and evil and who oppose and attack him. SPCL uses the language of threshing and winnowing grain, "Don't let the arrogant tread on me, nor the evil winnow me." **Continue** in 10a applies also in 10b, and in some translations will have to be expressed.

In verse 11 the psalmist employs a special Hebrew poetic device. The two lines are parallel with very similar meanings. However, there is a balancing of image and at the same time a balancing of gender. **Foot** and **hand** are both feminine, but **arrogance** is feminine and **wicked** is masculine. Naturally the translator is not expected to imitate such poetic devices unless they are natural in the receptor language. In many languages it will be necessary to depart from the hand and foot figures, as does TEV; however, the translator should not discard figures without first examining alternative figures that keep the poetic tone and which are meaningful in the language.

36.12   RSV   TEV

There the evildoers lie prostrate,   See where evil men have fallen.
   they are thrust down, unable to   There they lie, unable to rise.
   rise.

In this closing verse the psalmist speaks of the future destruction of his enemies as something already accomplished. In a manner of speaking, he points to the fallen enemies and says, "**There they lie**" (see a similar statement in 14.5), defeated and dead, **<u>unable to rise</u>**. Since no definite place has been referred to, however, it is best to avoid saying **<u>There</u>**; something like TEV **"See,"** or "Look at the evil men who have fallen . . . ," is best.

Psalm 37

Like Psalm 34, this psalm is an acrostic poem, the first line of each strophe beginning with a successive letter of the Hebrew alphabet, starting with *alef*, the first letter (verse 1) and ending with *taw*, the last letter (verse 39). Each strophe usually has four lines. The poem consists essentially of twenty-two strophes, each of which is a complete proverb.

The psalm is classified as a wisdom poem, that is, one that teaches truths about God and humankind; the general themes of the providence of God, the punishment of the wicked, and the reward of the righteous are presented in various ways. Given the artificial literary scheme, there is no orderly development of thought in the psalm, and it cannot be outlined. As Weiser says, it is "not so much a psalm as a collection of proverbs."

The only fact about the author is that he is an old man (verse 25); the words do not necessarily mean that he is very old.

HEADING: "**The Destiny of the Wicked and of the Good**" (TEV); "Trust versus envy"; "Trust in the LORD"; "The fate of sinners and the reward of the just." The TEV heading may be adjusted to some languages by translating it as "God rewards good people and punishes evil people."

Hebrew Title: **A Psalm of David.**

37.1-2   RSV   TEV

1   Fret not yourself because of the   1   Don't be worried on account of
         wicked,   the wicked;
     be not envious of wrongdoers!   don't be jealous of those who do
2   For they will soon fade like the   wrong.
         grass,   2   They will soon disappear like
     and wither like the green herb.   grass that dries up;
                                                     they will die like plants that
                                                         wither.

One of the characteristics of this psalm is the occurrence of the same Hebrew consonant repeated in consecutive words or lines. This is a form of alliteration or sound repetition, and no clear patterning is evident. Translators are not expected to imitate alliteration in Hebrew, but the information is called to the translator's attention in case alliteration is used as a poetic device to enhance the sound of poetic lines in the receptor language. Only in verse 20 is the consonant used in alliteration the same as the acrostic consonant. In verse 1 the Hebrew negative *'al* appears as the first word in each line, just as **"Don't"** appears in TEV.

The advice in verse 1 is repeated in verses 7 and 8, dealing with what must have been a real problem at the time. The righteous are not to <u>fret</u> themselves or be <u>envious</u> because of the apparent success of <u>the wicked</u>, or <u>wrongdoers</u>; their success is temporary, and they will soon disappear and die. Each of the two verses consists of two parallel and synonymous lines. The figure of **"grass that dries up"** and of **"plants that wither"** (TEV) under the hot sun is a common one (see 1.3; 90.5-6; 91.5b-6; 103.15). It is a figure of temporary success and prosperity that is quickly ended by harsh conditions. It is not explicitly stated that it is God's punishment that causes the ruin of wicked people, but in the thought of that time, God was ultimately responsible for everything that happened to humankind.

If the translator follows TEV **"jealous"** in verse 1b, it is important not to place in focus the attitude of a lover who resents his rivals, which **"jealous"** in many languages means. **"Jealous"** in this context may be rendered by <u>envious</u> as in RSV, or one may say "don't desire to possess the things that evil people have" or "don't desire to do the things wicked people do."

In verse 2 the psalmist again uses alliteration by using the Hebrew letter *mem* as the initial letter in the words translated "soon" and "wither."

37.3-4	RSV	TEV

3	Trust in the LORD, and do good;
	    so you will dwell in the land,
	    and enjoy security.
		3 Trust in the LORD and do good;
		       live in the land and be safe.

4	Take delight in the LORD,
	    and he will give you the desires
	    of your heart.
		4 Seek your happiness in the LORD,
		       and he will give you your
		       heart's desire.

The best way of avoiding worry and envy is to **trust in the LORD and do good**. Line <u>b</u> of verse 3 is a command in the Masoretic text (so TEV, NEB, SPCL, NJV, BJ), but RSV and others take it as a consequence: "so you will live . . . ." **The land** is Canaan, the Promised Land, where God's people live in safety.

If RSV is followed in verse 3b, it will be necessary in many languages to make the connection between 3a and b clear, as RSV does. Furthermore, it may be necessary further to describe the land in <u>dwell in the land</u> as "the land I have given you."

<u>Enjoy security</u> translates the Hebrew "and pasture on faithfulness"; NJB has "live secure," and FRCL "live in peace"; NAB "enjoy security"; NEB "find safe pasture." The idea of security seems to be required (Briggs); but NJV has "remain loyal," and Kirkpatrick proposes "follow after faithfulness." Dahood seems to follow the Septuagint: "feed on its riches."

The injunction of verse 4 is usually understood as **Take delight in the LORD** (RSV, NIV, NAB, Dahood), that is, seek and find in him the source of happiness and joy, and not in material possessions. But NJV has "Seek the favor of the LORD," and SPCL translates, "Love the Lord with tenderness." **Take delight in the LORD** will require in many languages an explicitly marked relation between <u>delight</u> and <u>LORD</u>.

This may be said, for instance, "Take delight in serving the LORD" or "Take delight in what the LORD has promised you." It is also possible to say, for example, "The LORD gives you joy. Take delight in it."

The desires of your heart: what you want the most.

37.5-6	RSV		TEV
5	Commit your way to the LORD; trust in him, and he will act.	5	Give yourself to the LORD; trust in him, and he will help you;
6	He will bring forth your vindication as the light, and your right as the noonday.	6	he will make your righteousness shine like the noonday sun.

Alliteration in verse 5 is found in the repetition of the Hebrew letter *'ayin*, the first letter of the preposition translated "in" or "on," which occurs twice.

The advice **Commit your way to the LORD** translates the verb "to roll" (see 22.8); it means to turn over to the Lord your whole life—all your desires, problems, anxieties. Let the Lord determine what your life is to be; **trust in him** (see comments on 4.5b and 13.5). **He will act** translates "he will do (it)"—that is, he will take action, he will do whatever is necessary (FRCL), **"he will help you"** (TEV).

Verse 6 states what will happen if the psalmist's advice in verse 5 is followed: "He will cause to appear your *tsedaqah* (line a) . . . and your *mishpat* (line b)." The two nouns seem to refer to the integrity, the upright character of the psalmist (so TEV **"righteousness"**; SPCL "your integrity . . . your justice"; NJB "your uprightness . . . the justice of your cause"). But the nouns may refer to Yahweh's action of successfully defending the cause of the psalmist (so Briggs, Kirkpatrick), **your vindication . . . your right** (RSV), "your vindication . . . the justice of your case" (NJV). Everything considered, it seems that the latter interpretation is to be preferred. God will plainly and publicly demonstrate the justice of the psalmist's cause and prove him to be innocent. So a translation can be "He will clearly prove that you are innocent, he will show that your cause is just."

Verse 6 is chiastic in that **your vindication** comes at the end of line a and **your right** at the beginning of line b. As seen in RSV, there is no verb expressed in line b. However, in translation a verb must sometimes be supplied. Alliteration is present in the Hebrew consonant *kaf*, the prefix meaning "like."

As the light in verse 6a is parallel with **as the noonday** in line b; the two together refer to the sun as it rises in the morning and as it shines with full force at noontime. This is a figure of something that is clear, that is seen by all. If the translator is to keep both characteristics, whether of the psalmist or of the Lord, it is often possible to say "He will make your goodness and your fairness in judging appear as clear as the light of day" or "He will make your goodness appear in the light and your fairness in judging to be seen like the bright sun." It will be noticed that TEV has combined the two parallel lines into one; SPCL has rearranged the material as follows: "He will cause your uprightness and your justice to shine as brightly as the noonday sun"—which may be a model to follow.

RSV   TEV

> Be still before the LORD, and wait
>   patiently for him;
> fret not yourself over him who
>   prospers in his way,
> over the man who carries out
>   evil devices!

> Be patient and wait for the LORD
>   to act;
> don't be worried about those
>   who prosper
> or those who succeed in their
>   evil plans.

This strophe essentially repeats the thought of verse 1; the advice is to wait patiently for Yahweh to act; the success and prosperity of the evil will soon be ended. Yahweh is the one to decide how and when wicked people will be punished, people who now "**prosper**" and "**succeed in their evil plans**" (TEV). **Be still before the LORD** means to be quiet in the Lord's presence and not be constantly and impatiently complaining about the success of the wicked. The command **Be still before the LORD** in the TEV sense of "**Be patient**" is often expressed idiomatically; for example, "Don't cause noise in the heart," "Walk softly," or "Sit coolly."

RSV   TEV

8   Refrain from anger, and forsake   8   Don't give in to worry or anger;
         wrath!   it only leads to trouble.
     Fret not yourself; it tends only   9   Those who trust in the LORD will
         to evil.   possess the land,
9   For the wicked shall be cut off;   but the wicked will be driven
     but those who wait for the   out.
         LORD shall possess the land.

Carrying on the thought of the previous strophes, in this one the psalmist counsels not to nourish **anger** and **wrath** against the evildoers (verse 8a); and again he says **Fret not yourself**, as in verse 1. The last part of verse 8 is difficult; the phrase is literally "to do evil," which is interpreted by most as TEV and RSV have it, "**it only leads to trouble**" (so NJV, NIV, Dahood; SPCL "it makes things worse"); NEB, however, "strive not to outdo in evildoing." In some languages **Refrain from anger, and forsake wrath** are expressed somewhat idiomatically as "Don't let worry and anger hold you."

TEV has represented **anger** and **wrath** by the one word "anger," and uses "worry" to carry the force of **Fret (not) yourself**.

The reason for this advice is given in verse 9: **the wicked shall be cut off**. The verb may mean to be put to death, to be destroyed, or else to be driven out of the land. The thought is that they will suffer the same fate as that of the original inhabitants of Canaan, who were removed from their land either by being killed in battle or else by being put to flight by the invading Israelites.

By contrast, **those who wait for the LORD** (see 25.3 and comment), that is, who trust in him, will **possess the land**, a promise repeated in verses 11, 22, 29, 34 (see also 25.13 and comments). The promise is that they will continue to live safely and in prosperity in Canaan, the Promised Land. Nothing certain can be inferred from this statement as to the time the psalm was written. It seems probable that this was a conventional way of saying that they would continue to be blessed and protected by the Lord in the land of Israel. The expression **possess the land** may be rendered more explicitly as "possess the land the LORD has promised."

37.10-11	RSV	TEV

10 Yet a little while, and the wicked will be no more; though you look well at his place, he will not be there.
11 But the meek shall possess the land, and delight themselves in abundant prosperity.

10 Soon the wicked will disappear; you may look for them, but you won't find them;
11 but the humble will possess the land and enjoy prosperity and peace.

In just a little time **the wicked will be no more**; that is, as a result of God's action, they will disappear completely. **The meek**, however, will receive all that God has promised; they **will possess the land** (as in verse 9).

The meek (NJV "the lowly," NJB "the poor") is one of the many terms used in this psalm to refer to those who trust in Yahweh, obey him, rely completely on him; see "those who wait for the LORD" (verse 9); "the poor and needy" (verse 14); "those who walk uprightly" (verse 14); "the righteous" (verses 16, 17, 21, 25, 29, 30, 33, 39); "the blameless" (verse 18); "those in whose way he delights" (verse 23); "the upright" (verse 37). All these adjectives and phrases refer to the same people, those in Israel who are completely loyal to Yahweh and obey his commands at all times. The term **meek** is expressed in some languages in idiomatic ways; for example, "the one whose heart is low," or "the person who speaks with a soft voice," or "the one who does not have a swollen heart." It is important in translating **humble** not to refer to persons who are classified as having an inferior social status.

Verse 11a, as translated by the Septuagint, appears in Matthew 5.5.

Verse 11b has the additional promise, "They will delight themselves in a great *shalom*" (see comment on "peace" in 29.11), a phrase that succinctly summarizes all the benefits, material and spiritual, enjoyed by those who trust in the Lord. NIV translates "and enjoy great peace." The expression **delight themselves in abundant prosperity** may sometimes be rendered as "will enjoy peace and the good things God gives people."

37.12-13	RSV	TEV

12 The wicked plots against the righteous, and gnashes his teeth at him;
13 but the LORD laughs at the wicked,

12 The wicked man plots against the good man and glares at him with hate.
13 But the Lord laughs at wicked men,

for he sees that his day is com- ing.	because he knows they will soon be destroyed.

In this strophe the psalmist speaks only of the fate of the wicked, whose **plots against the righteous** are useless, because Yahweh **sees that his day is coming**, that is, the day of the final punishment of the wicked will arrive soon. For a discussion of **plots** see 36.4.

For **gnashes his teeth** see comment at 35.16; and for "**the Lord laughs**" (TEV) see 2.4 and comments. It should be noted that here the Hebrew has the title "Lord," not the name Yahweh (as RSV **LORD** wrongly has it).

37.14-15   RSV   TEV

	RSV		TEV
14	The wicked draw the sword and bend their bows, to bring down the poor and needy, to slay those who walk uprightly;	14	The wicked draw their swords and bend their bows to kill the poor and needy, to slaughter those who do what is right;
15	their sword shall enter their own heart, and their bows shall be broken.	15	but they will be killed by their own swords, and their bows will be smashed.

It is impossible to determine whether the language is literal, meaning actual **swords** and **bows**, or figurative, denoting oppression and persecution. It seems better to translate as though actual physical destruction is meant; see 11.2 for similar language. But the wicked will not achieve their aim of destroying **the poor and needy**, **those who walk uprightly** (literally "those whose way is upright"). God will intervene, and the wicked will be killed by their own swords (see the same thought in 7.16), and **their bows shall be broken**.

The expressions **draw the sword and bend their bows** refers to threatening gestures, or else initial movements in preparation for killing. In some languages it will be necessary to say, for example, "Wicked people get their weapons ready to kill" or, if the specific terms are used, "Wicked people prepare their swords and bows to kill."

The expression **the poor and needy** will in many languages be expressed by terms referring to the same persons; for example, "those who have nothing and are in great need."

It will often be clearer to make specific reference to the wicked of verse 14 as the ones who will be killed; for example, "but those wicked people will be killed by their own swords." In languages in which a passive construction cannot be used, and where swords cannot serve as the agent but only the instrument of killing, it will be necessary to make God the agent; for example, "but God will use their own swords to kill the wicked," and in the last line, "he will smash their bows."

	RSV		TEV

37.16-17

16 Better is a little that the righteous has
   than the abundance of many wicked.
17 For the arms of the wicked shall be broken;
   but the LORD upholds the righteous.

16 The little that a good man owns
   is worth more than the wealth of all the wicked,
17 because the LORD will take away the strength of the wicked,
   but protect those who are good.

In this strophe the psalmist expresses a thought found elsewhere in Wisdom literature (see Proverbs 16.8), that **the righteous** person is more fortunate having **a little** than are the **wicked** with all their abundant wealth. True wealth consists in obeying the Lord's commands. To form comparatives in some languages, it is often necessary to repeat phrases; for example, "a good man owns little and the wicked man owns much, but the good man's things are better than the wicked man's things."

The punishment that Yahweh will inflict on the wicked is graphically described: their **arms . . . shall be broken**. Here "arms" is a figure of power (see NIV, FRCL); it is better to say "power" than TEV "**strength**," which is an almost completely physical quality. Dahood takes it to represent "resources." SPCL abandons the figure of breaking arms and translates "will put an end to the wicked." The verb translated **upholds** is the same one used in 3.5 ("sustain").

37.18-19

	RSV		TEV

18 The LORD knows the days of the blameless,
   and their heritage will abide for ever;
19 they are not put to shame in evil times,
   in the days of famine they have abundance.

18 The LORD takes care of those who obey him,
   and the land will be theirs forever.
19 They will not suffer when times are bad;
   they will have enough in time of famine.

In verse 18 the first three words of line a begin with the letter *yod*.

Knows the days of means cares for, is concerned with; FRCL "takes an interest in." For a similar use of the verb "know," see 1.6a. NJV has "The LORD is concerned for the needs of the blameless," and NJB "The lives of the just are in Yahweh's care."

The word for **blameless** is used also in 18.23.

The Hebrew "inheritance" (verse 18b), as in 16.6, refers to the land of Israel; the promise is that it will belong to God's people for all time.

The promise in verse 19 is that in bad times, in times of drought and famine, those who obey the Lord will not be **put to shame**, that is, suffer the humiliation of being in need; instead they will have more than enough.

　　　　RSV　　　　　　　　　　　　　　TEV

But the wicked perish; 　the enemies of the LORD are 　like the glory of the pastures, 　they vanish—like smoke they 　vanish away.	But the wicked will die; 　the enemies of the LORD will 　vanish like wild flowers; 　they will disappear like smoke.

Verse 20 begins with the Hebrew letter *kaf* and proceeds to build up alliteration in lines b and c in the following manner: *Ki . . . kiqar karim kalu beshan kalu* ("But . . . like the beauty of wild flowers they vanish, like smoke they vanish").

In this strophe the lot of **the wicked** is pictured: they will **perish**, that is, they will die prematurely and in disgrace. They will disappear **like the glory of the pastures**, that is, like the beautiful wild flowers, under the burning sun (see verse 2); they will disappear **like smoke** (see 68.2 and 102.3 for the same idea of "smoke" that disappears quickly).

There is no general agreement on the Hebrew phrase translated **the glory of the pastures**. ASV has "the fat of the lambs"; NEB follows a K-B conjecture, "burning ovens"; NJB, NAB are like RSV and TEV; NJV has "like meadow grass consumed in smoke." Anderson proposes "like the best of the he-lambs," meaning that they are alive and well one day, and the next day are slaughtered for sacrifice (they vanish "in smoke"). The similarity to verse 2 makes it probable that "like wild flowers" is the meaning of line b.[1] In some languages it will be necessary to make the agent explicit, where in TEV and RSV **vanish** and "**disappear**" appear to be impersonal. In this case the only one who destroys the wicked is God. Therefore one may have to translate "God will destroy the wicked; he will make his enemies vanish like wild flowers; he will make them disappear like smoke."

　　RSV　　　　　　　　　　　　　　TEV

21　The wicked borrows, and cannot 　　pay back, 　　but the righteous is generous 　　and gives; 22　for those blessed by the LORD 　　shall possess the land, 　　but those cursed by him shall 　　be cut off.	21　The wicked man borrows and 　　never pays back, 　　but the good man is generous 　　with his gifts. 22　Those who are blessed by the 　　LORD will possess the land, 　　but those who are cursed by 　　him will be driven out.

---

[1]HOTTP says two interpretations of the Masoretic text of verse 20 are possible: (1) "and the enemies of the LORD, like the best of lambs (that is, their fat), vanish"; (2) ". . . like the beauty of the pastures (that is, their grass) they vanish, in the smoke they vanish." It should be noticed that the Masoretic text has "in the smoke" (so NEB, FRCL, BJ); many Hebrew manuscripts (and the Septuagint) have "like smoke"— so RSV, TEV, SPCL.

In verse 21 some contend that it is not a matter of the wicked man's being dishonest (so TEV), but of his being unable to repay because of his bad luck (so RSV); it seems preferable to follow the interpretation of TEV (the vast majority of translations).

The thought of verse 22 is similar to that of verse 9. The Hebrew is, literally, "His blessed ones . . . his cursed ones," which most translations understand to mean "those blessed by the LORD . . . those cursed by the LORD." NAB and NJB take the one who blesses to be the good man (of verse 21b): "those he blesses . . . those he curses." It seems better to take the Lord as the one who blesses. The Septuagint translates the two participles not as passives (**are blessed . . . are cursed**) but as actives ("who bless him . . . who curse him").

Those blessed by the LORD may be translated in some languages as "those whom God has favored" or "those who receive good things from God." For **possess the land** see verses 9,11.

Those cursed by him should not be translated as "those whom God has sworn at" but rather "those whom God has put a curse on" or "those whom God has harmed." For **shall be cut off** see verse 9a.

37.23-24   RSV   TEV

23   The steps of a man are from the   23   The LORD guides a man in the
        LORD,   way he should go
     and he establishes him in whose   and protects those who please
        way he delights;   him.
24   though he fall, he shall not be cast   24   If they fall, they will not stay
        headlong,   down,
     for the LORD is the stay of his   because the LORD will help
        hand.   them up.

In this strophe the security of the righteous is emphasized. Verse 23a means that it is the Lord who leads a person in the right way. The psalmist is not saying that, in fact, God guides all people in the way they should go, since it is quite evident that many do not accept God's guidance. To avoid this possible misunderstanding, FRCL translates "When a man's conduct pleases him, the Lord enables him to go through life with confidence," and NIV has "If the LORD delights in a man's way, he makes his steps firm."

He establishes (verse 23b) means that God makes firm, gives security; NEB "holds him firm."

Verse 24 can be translated "If they stumble, they will not fall, for the LORD holds them by the hand" (see NJV).

37.25-26   RSV   TEV

25   I have been young, and now am   25   I am an old man now; I have lived
        old;   a long time,
     yet I have not seen the right-   but I have never seen a good

eous forsaken or his children begging bread. 26 He is ever giving liberally and lending, and his children become a blessing.	man abandoned by the LORD or his children begging for food. 26 At all times he gives freely and lends to others, and his children are a blessing.

The psalmist, an old man, refers to his past experience; he has never <u>seen the righteous forsaken</u> by the Lord <u>or his children begging bread</u>, that is, "**begging for food**." This may be taken as an exaggerated statement, since the psalm speaks often of the troubles that good people encounter; yet the psalmist would say, just as firmly, that the Lord does not forever forsake those who trust in him. See especially Sirach 2.10.

<u>Children</u> translates "seed" (see comments on "descendants" in 18.50).

In verse 26b <u>a blessing</u> may be either a blessing to the man himself or else a help to others. Some take the line to mean "and his children are blessed," that is, they benefit from their father's prosperity; NJB translates "so his descendants reap a blessing" (similarly NIV, FRCL, GECL). It is recommended that the idea that the children will be a blessing to the man himself be expressed in translation. <u>His children become a blessing</u> is difficult to translate in some languages where "blessing" is closely associated with liturgical words. Here one may say, for instance, "his children are the good things God has given him" or "his children are the favor God has done to the good man."

37.27-29   RSV   TEV

27 Depart from evil, and do good; so shall you abide for ever. 28 For the LORD loves justice; he will not forsake his saints. The righteous shall be preserved for ever, but the children of the wicked shall be cut off. 29 The righteous shall possess the land, and dwell upon it for ever.	27 Turn away from evil and do good, and your descendants will always live in the land; 28 for the LORD loves what is right and does not abandon his faithful people. He protects them forever, but the descendants of the wicked will be driven out. 29 The righteous will possess the land and live in it forever.

The command in verse 27a is exactly the same as in 34.14; the promise in line <u>b</u> is literally "and you will dwell forever." The Hebrew verb means to live somewhere, and the sense here is "live in the land," that is, the Promised Land (NIV "you will dwell in the land forever"; also FRCL). TEV has taken <u>for ever</u> to refer to the descendants of those to whom the promise is made. Anderson comments: "the Psalmist is thinking of the descendants of the righteous as being in possession of the ancestral inheritance" (see also Kirkpatrick). It does not seem correct to translate line <u>b</u> "and you will always have somewhere to live" (SPCL, NJB, TOB).

The parallelism on verse 28 is that of a general concept occurring in line a followed in line b by a specific. In this case the second noun **saints** contrasts with **justice** by being both more specific and plural. There is heightening of intensity in line b so that it can be translated in English, for example, as "The LORD loves that which is right, but what is more he will not abandon those who are faithful to him."

In verse 28a **justice** translates *mishpat* (see comments on 7.6); for **saints** see comments on "the godly" in 4.3; **preserved** in 28c means "kept safe, protected"; for verse 28d see verse 9a; and verse 29 repeats the thought of verse 9b.

It should be noted that in verse 28c the Masoretic text is "they are protected forever"; following some manuscripts of the Septuagint, NEB has "The lawless are banished for ever" (similarly BJ, NJB, FRCL, SPCL). This restores to the poem a strophe beginning with the letter *'ayin*, the sixteenth letter, which is otherwise lacking. Though supported by some commentators (see Kirkpatrick, Briggs), this is rejected by HOTTP ("A" decision).

37.30-31	RSV	TEV
	30 The mouth of the righteous man utters wisdom, and his tongue speaks justice. 31 The law of his God is in his heart; his steps do not slip.	30 A good man's words are wise, and he is always fair. 31 He keeps the law of his God in his heart and never departs from it.

Mouth and **tongue**: see similar expressions in 34.13.

In this strophe the speech of **the righteous** is characterized by **wisdom** and **justice**. **Wisdom** here is the kind that is defined in Wisdom literature as being a religious attitude, "the fear of the LORD" (see 34.11 and comments; 111.10). **Utters** translates the same verb which in 1.2 is translated "meditates." If the translator follows TEV, some further adjustments will have to be made in many languages, since words are not always referred to as "wise." Therefore one may have to say "What a good man says is wise," or "A good man speaks wisely," or "The words a good man speaks show that he is wise."

Justice here, as in most passages, is what characterizes Yahweh's laws and commandments; in a very real sense it means "what Yahweh demands." In verse 30b TEV should read "and they are always fair," referring to the "words" of line a, instead of "**and he is always fair.**"

By selective ordering the psalmist has created a special chiastic effect in this verse, based upon the gender pattern:

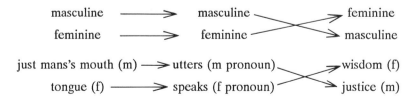

The law of his God (see 1.2) keeps him from sinning, because it is **in his heart**, which means that he is always aware of it and may imply that he has memorized much of it (see 119:11). **The law of his God is in his heart** must be recast in some languages because of the construction **his God**. For example, "He has in his heart the Law from the God he worships" or "He knows in his innermost the words of the Law which the God he obeys gave to him."

His steps do not slip, that is, he stays on the right path and does not stray from it, he does not follow sinful ways. This clause may be rendered nonfiguratively, "and he obeys God's Law," or figuratively, "and his feet walk safely" or "and he is secure where his steps take him."

37.32-33	RSV	TEV

	RSV	TEV
32	The wicked watches the righteous, and seeks to slay him.	A wicked man watches a good man and tries to kill him;
33	The LORD will not abandon him to his power, or let him be condemned when he is brought to trial.	but the LORD will not abandon him to his enemy's power or let him be condemned when he is on trial.

The sense of **watches** in this context is "spies" or even "lies in ambush for" (see K-B); NIV "lie in wait for," and NJB "keeps a close eye on." The Lord protects **the righteous** man and does not **abandon him to his power** (literally "into his hand"), nor does he **let him be condemned when he is brought to trial**, on the supposition, of course, that he is not guilty of any crime.

37.34	RSV	TEV

RSV	TEV
Wait for the LORD, and keep to his way, and he will exalt you to possess the land; you will look on the destruction of the wicked.	Put your hope in the LORD and obey his commands; he will honor you by giving you the land, and you will see the wicked driven out.

For the thought **Wait for the LORD** in line **a**, see 27.14 and comments. The TEV expression **"Put your hope in the LORD"** may often be rendered "Look forward with confidence in the LORD." The injunction **keep to his way** means to obey the Lord's will, his commands and instructions on how a person should live.

The thought of line **b** is the same as verse 9b; here **exalt** means "he will give you the honor (of possessing the Promised Land)."

For the thought of line **c**, see verse 9a and comments; **destruction** translates an infinitive form of the verb "to cut off."

37.35-36	RSV	TEV

35 I have seen a wicked man over-
       bearing,
    and towering like a cedar of
       Lebanon.ᵛ
36 Again Iʷ passed by, and, lo, he
       was no more;
    though I sought him, he could
       not be found.

35 I once knew a wicked man who
       was a tyrant;
    he towered over everyone like a
       cedar of Lebanon;ⁱ
36 but later Iʲ passed by, and he
       wasn't there;
    I looked for him, but couldn't
       find him.

ᵛ Gk: Heb obscure
ʷ Gk Syr Jerome: Heb *he*

ⁱ *One ancient translation* like a cedar of
Lebanon; *Hebrew unclear.*
ʲ *Some ancient translations* I; *Hebrew* he.

This verse is again alliterative in that three of its six Hebrew words begin with
the letter *resh*.

In verse 35a **overbearing** means oppressive, domineering, tyrannical. In some
languages it will be necessary to use a verb phrase for TEV's "**tyrant**." For example,
one may say "a wicked man who terrified people" or "a wicked man who caused
people to tremble."

The Hebrew of verse 35b is obscure. NJV translates "well-rooted like a robust
native tree," saying the translation is problematical; one version may be "flourishing
like a tree luxuriant in its native soil"; NIV "flourishing like a green tree in its native
soil."² Weiser, TEV, RSV, BJ, NJB, and FRCL follow the Septuagint; for comments on
cedar of Lebanon, see 29.5. If the translator follows the suggestion of TEV in regard
to the tree, it may be necessary to say "he was big as the big trees of the mountain
called Lebanon." It is equally possible to use any well-known local tree that is very
large and powerful.

The verb in verse 36a is in the third person singular form, "he passed"; the
verb means "to go, go over, pass, pass by," and it seems more fitting to follow the
ancient versions and read (as do RSV, TEV, NEB, NAB, BJ, NJB, FRCL, GECL) "I passed
by." The Masoretic text, however, is taken by NJV, SPCL, TOB, and Dahood to mean
"he passed away" (that is, he died), which, while admittedly possible, is unusual. See
verse 10 for a similar statement. HOTTP takes the Masoretic text to have an
impersonal sense, "someone passed by."

37.37-38	RSV	TEV

37 Mark the blameless man, and
       behold the upright,
    for there is posterity for the
       man of peace.

37 Notice the good man, observe the
       righteous man;
    a peaceful man has descend-
       ants,

---

²HOTTP says the line can be interpreted as follows: "and rooted/ramifying like a
native [tree] [which] becomes green" ("B" decision).

38 But transgressors shall be alto- gether destroyed; the posterity of the wicked shall be cut off.	38 but sinners are completely de- stroyed, and their descendants are wiped out.

In this strophe the psalmist contrasts the destiny of the good and of the evil. The two verbs **Mark** and **behold** in verse 37a mean "observe carefully, keep a close eye on." Since line 37a consists of two completely parallel statements, in some languages it will be more convenient to reduce them to one; for example, "Notice the good and righteous person." In languages where such a double use of adjectives would make it mean that these are two different persons, one may say, for example, "Notice the person who is both good and righteous."

The Hebrew word translated **posterity** in both verses is "end, result," which some take to mean "their future" (Dahood, NJV, NIV, FRCL, SPCL, NAB); most, however, take it to mean "offspring, descendants."

In verse 37b "a man of *shalom*" indicates not merely one who is easy to get along with, but one whose character is determined by God's greatest gift, *shalom*. The expression **man of peace** may be rendered in idiomatic terms sometimes as "the person whose heart sits coolly" or "a person whose life says 'quiet.' "

Transgressors and **the wicked** will be completely destroyed and leave no descendants. **Transgressors** are those who break God's law. The verb **destroyed** is a strong one, "wiped out, exterminated, obliterated" (used also in 83.10a; 92.7c); and the adverb translated **altogether** may mean "completely, totally" or "all at once" (FRCL), "one and all" (NEB).

37.39-40   RSV   TEV

39 The salvation of the righteous is from the LORD; he is their refuge in the time of trouble. 40 The LORD helps them and delivers them; he delivers them from the wick- ed, and saves them, because they take refuge in him.	39 The LORD saves righteous men and protects them in times of trouble. 40 He helps them and rescues them; he saves them from the wicked, because they go to him for pro- tection.

The final strophe describes in familiar language the security of **the righteous** who **take refuge in** the Lord. In verse 39b **refuge** translates a word meaning "protection, safeguarding."

In verse 40 there is alliteration in the occurrence of *waw yod* "and he," *waw yod* plus *pe, yod* plus *pe*, and *waw yod*.

In verse 40a **helps** translates a verb that is used in 10.14, "helper (of the fatherless)." The verb **delivers** (used twice) is used also in 17.13, and **saves** translates the verb that in 12.1 is translated "Help." For **take refuge** see also 2.12. See comments at these places in the Handbook. In some languages it is necessary to place the reason for the action at the beginning; for example, "They take refuge in the LORD, therefore the LORD helps them . . . ."

Psalm 38

This lament is by an individual suffering from some illness which he regards as punishment inflicted on him by God. So he confesses his sins and asks for God's forgiveness. It is similar to the other psalms which were classified as penitential psalms by the early church (see introduction to Psa 32).

A psalm such as this one with 22 verses is no doubt modelled on an alphabetic acrostic. However, here the psalmist is free from such artificial restrictions.

The psalm opens with a cry for help (verse 1) and then proceeds to an extended description of the psalmist's desperate physical and emotional condition (verses 2-10), which is made worse by the indifference of his friends and the hostility of his enemies (verses 11-12). The psalmist again refers to his pitiful condition (verses 13-14), affirms his faith in the Lord (verses 15-16), asks for forgiveness (verses 17-18), and once more denounces his enemies (verses 19-20). The psalm closes, as it opens, with a cry for help (verses 21-22).

There are no clues as to the author's identity; some take the language here, as elsewhere, to represent the nation's suffering, but it seems more likely that an individual is meant.

HEADING: "**The Prayer of a Suffering Man**"; "The lament and confession of a sick man"; "Under God's wrath"; "Prayer of an afflicted sinner." The TEV heading will require some restructuring in many languages where nouns will have to be shifted to verbs. Examples are "A man who is sick asks God to help him" or "A person who is suffering asks God to forgive the evil he has done."

Hebrew Title: **A Psalm of David, for the memorial offering.**

The Hebrew expression translated **memorial offering** occurs here and in the title of Psalm 70; the word is from the Hebrew root meaning "to remember," and some commentators associate it with "the memorial sacrifice," reminding the Lord of the worshiper (see Taylor). Others take it to mean "for the purpose of making a confession" (see Weiser). It is impossible to state with assurance the exact meaning of the word.

38.1-2	RSV		TEV
1	O LORD, rebuke me not in thy anger, nor chasten me in thy wrath!	1	O LORD, don't punish me in your anger!
2	For thy arrows have sunk into me, and thy hand has come down on me.	2	You have wounded me with your arrows; you have struck me down.

363

The two lines of verse 1 are semantically and syntactically parallel. There is no dynamic movement such as intensification, focusing, dramatization, or specification in line **b**. Clearly the words translated **rebuke** and **chasten** do not have identical meanings, but their differences have not been brought into play. Because of this TEV has shortened and combined the two lines into one. However, since the dominant pattern everywhere in the psalms is for parallel lines, translators should not reduce the two to one unless, of course, parallel lines and poetic form are not being used.

Verse 1 is the same as 6.1, except that in the first line a different word for **anger** is used. Although TEV has combined the two synonymous lines into one, most translations maintain the two lines, using the verb "rebuke, reprimand" in the first line, and "chastise, punish" in the second line. This may be preferable. If the translator follows the model of TEV and reduces the two parallel lines to one line, he may still have to make some adjustments to relate **punish** to **anger**. For example, "Although you are angry LORD, don't punish me." Or it may be possible to imitate TOB: "Lord, punish me without fury; chasten me without anger."

The psalmist considers his illness to be the result of Yahweh's anger; Yahweh has punished him by shooting him with his arrows (literally **thy arrows have sunk into me**). The same figure of "arrows" is used in 7.13; see also Job 6.4. And for the figure **thy hand has come down on me**, the same verb is used, which is rather strange. For the use of "hand" to mean punishment, see 32.4. NJV translates the line "Your blows have fallen upon me." Of the translations consulted TOB is the only one that uses the same verb for both lines: "has descended (or, fallen) . . . have descended." It may be possible in many languages to follow a bit more closely the form of the Hebrew than TEV has done; for example, "Your arrows have gone into me." In line **b** it will often be possible to keep the image of the hand; for example, "your hand has knocked me down."

38.3-4 RSV TEV

	RSV		TEV
3	There is no soundness in my flesh because of thy indignation; there is no health in my bones because of my sin.	3	Because of your anger, I am in great pain; my whole body is diseased because of my sins.
4	For my iniquities have gone over my head; they weigh like a burden too heavy for me.	4	I am drowning in the flood of my sins; they are a burden too heavy to bear.

The psalmist describes his illness as **no soundness in my flesh** and **no health in my bones**. Both **flesh** and **bones** denote the total being, the whole body. It is impossible to say with certainty what his disease was, if, in fact, the language describes an actual disease and is not simply conventional language in a lament of this kind to describe complete physical and emotional distress. Some commentators conjecture a skin disease, such as leprosy. In verse 3b **health** translates *shalom* (see comments on "peace" in 29.11).

The psalmist recognizes his illness as being due to Yahweh's **indignation** and to his own **sin**; there is no contradiction here, since in the thinking of the psalmist

God's anger is caused by the sinning. The translator will notice that TEV has placed the cause, **your anger**, before **great pain** in the first line, and placed the cause, **my sins**, after **diseased** in the second line. The translator should examine which set of relations is most natural in the receptor language, and which provides the reader with the best understanding and poetic effect. The Hebrew order is condition then cause in both lines.

In verse 4 the psalmist likens his sins to a flood which threatens to drown him (literally they **have gone over my head**), and to **a burden too heavy for me**. TEV has taken **my iniquities . . . over my head** to be like a "**flood**." If the translator adopts this possibility, very often some syntactic adjustments will be required; for example, "I am like a man drowning in a flood, my sins are so many" or "My sins are so many they are like a flood and I am drowning." One may prefer to avoid the flood imagery and say, for example, "My sins pile up higher than my head"; see NJB "My sins stand higher than my head." The figure of a **burden**, or a load, is in many languages a natural one to use with sin or guilt, or with unwelcome responsibilities or activities.

38.5-6	RSV		TEV
5	My wounds grow foul and fester because of my foolishness,	5	Because I have been foolish, my sores stink and rot.
6	I am utterly bowed down and prostrate; all the day I go about mourning.	6	I am bent over, I am crushed; I mourn all day long.

The psalmist describes in detail his condition, which is caused by his **foolishness**, which is sin (Taylor: "sin that comes through stupid indifference to discipline"). His **wounds grow foul and fester**, that is, they get worse and they stink. This seems to describe some sort of skin disease; the translation **wounds** (RSV and others) carries the idea, in English, of injuries suffered in a beating, which does not seem to be the case here. Elsewhere the word does mean "blow, stripe" (Gen 4.23; Exo 21.25; Pro 20.30; Isa 1.6, 53.5), and Briggs, noting the similarity of the language here to Isaiah 1.6, says these are "wounds resulting from the divine scourging." Whatever their source, the language clearly seems to be describing the psalmist's physical condition literally; he is not speaking in figurative terms.

The basic element of **foolishness** in the Hebrew Scriptures is a denial of God's rule in human affairs, which leads such a person to folly and sin (see especially 14.1). The term **foolishness** here applies to the moral failing of the writer, and in many languages is rendered idiomatically; for example, "because I have had a bent heart," or "because my heart has lead me on a bad path," or "because I am a failing-heart person."

In vivid language the psalmist, in verse 6, describes his pitiable condition. He has no strength left, all his vitality is gone. He shuffles along **bowed down**, or else lies **prostrate**, so intense is his misery. He is so sad that he cries and weeps all day long.

The translator has two problems with **I am utterly bowed down and prostrate**: first, whether it will be clear to retain the figures; and second, whether it will be necessary in some languages to provide an agent which is the cause of the action. For example, "My pain is so great it has bent me down, down to the dust." If the **bowed**

down figure cannot be used, one may sometimes say "My pain is so great that I cannot stand up."

Here **mourning** is not used in the specific sense of weeping over the death of a friend, but in the general sense of weeping, crying. **I go about mourning** may have to be recast as a simile. For example, "I am like a person in mourning" or "I go about weeping like a person in mourning." In some languages, where there is a single cause followed by two or more consequences, it is often necessary to repeat the cause with each consequence. For example, "Because of my foolishness, my wounds grow foul; because of my foolishness my wounds fester."

38.7-8 RSV   TEV

7   For my loins are filled with   7   I am burning with fever
         burning,   and I am near death.
     and there is no soundness in   8   I am worn out and utterly
         my flesh.   crushed;
8   I am utterly spent and crushed;   my heart is troubled, and I
     I groan because of the tumult of   groan with pain.
         my heart.

In verse 7 **my loins are filled with burning** seems to be a description of fever. **Loins**, which is archaic in English, refers to the region about the hips, and here it is a part of the body used to represent the whole. In languages in which a part of the body is said to be feverish, it is good to translate it in that way; for example, "my neck is hot with fever." In this context, where **loins** is parallel with **flesh**, the whole body is represented by the **loins** ("waist, hips").

Verse 7b is the same as verse 3a. This line goes beyond mere fever to make a more inclusive statement about the whole body, called **flesh**. Instead of TEV "I am near death," it is better to render **no soundness in my flesh** as "I am seriously ill," "I am very sick," or "my health is completely broken," or negatively "I have no health at all," or idiomatically in some languages, "my body is loose" or "my body has drunk tiredness."

In verse 8a the psalmist again describes his condition, using language similar to that used in verse 6a. The verb translated **spent** is used here in the passive voice; elsewhere it is used in the active voice with the sense of becoming numb, insensitive. Some translate here "benumbed" (see NJV, NEB). The verb translated **crushed** is the one that appears in 10.10a. The psalmist uses vivid terms to describe his physical and emotional distress, and a translator should choose equally vivid and extreme terms in the translation of these verses. In languages which must use the active voice, **I am utterly spent and crushed** may be recast to say, for example, "I am so ill I can feel nothing" or "without strength I am broken into pieces."

In verse 8b **the tumult of my heart** is a figure for deep distress rather than a physical symptom of heart trouble. The word translated **tumult** is used of "the roaring of the sea" in Isaiah 5.30. Here it refers to confusion, turmoil; see NJV "the turmoil in my mind." The psalmist's **groan** is the outward expression of his inward feeling. **I groan** translates "I roar" (like a lion) and was used in a similar way in 2.1. This exaggerated expression poetically expresses the degree of anguish experienced by the psalmist. In translation the howl or roar of an animal may be used, if appropriate. **The tumult of my heart** may be expressed sometimes without the figure; for example, "because of the troubles I have" or "because trouble has taken hold of me."

38.9-10   RSV   TEV

9   Lord, all my longing is known to   9   O Lord, you know what I long for;
       thee,   you hear all my groans.
       my sighing is not hidden from   10   My heart is pounding, my
       thee.   strength is gone,
10   My heart throbs, my strength fails   and my eyes have lost their
       me;   brightness.
       and the light of my eyes—it also
       has gone from me.

In verse 9a the usual translation **all my longing** assumes that it refers to the psalmist's wish to be healed; elsewhere RSV has "desire" (see 10.3 and comments); so the word is translated "desires" by SPCL (see FRCL), "entreaties" by NJV; Dahood and TOB have "sighing"; NEB (following G.R. Driver) has "lament." The translator may have to be specific about what the psalmist desires or longs for: "O Lord, you know that I wish to be healed . . . ." In line **b** **my sighing** represents suffering and distress (see the same Hebrew word in 6.6a "moaning"; 31.10b "sighing"; 102.5 "groaning"); so TEV "**groans.**" It does not represent a wish or desire.

The opening words of verse 10 (**My heart throbs**) are taken as a physical symptom by most translations; NJV, however, has "my mind is reeling," which is possible, though not so appropriate here.

Bright eyes (verse 10b) were taken to be a sign of good health (see 13.3 and comments). **The light of my eyes . . . has gone** cannot be rendered literally in many languages without meaning that the person has become blind. Often one must say, for example, "my eyes no longer shine" or "my eyes are no longer clear as they were."

38.11   RSV   TEV

My friends and companions stand   My friends and neighbors will not
    aloof from my plague,   come near me,
and my kinsmen stand afar off.   because of my sores;
                                                          even my family keeps away from
                                                             me.

The psalmist again refers to his disease, using a word which RSV translates **plague** and which in Leviticus 13–14 is used of skin disease ("leprosy") and also of mold and mildew on clothes, materials, houses. So TEV has here "**sores**" (see also SPCL); NAB and NJV, however, translate "affliction"; NEB "sickness." Perhaps some general word like "illness" or "sickness" is the best to use.

His **friends and companions** and his **kinsmen** avoid him (see the similar situation in 31.11). The reason is not only the repulsive nature of his illness (which they probably considered contagious), but also the assumption that a person in such a desperate condition was the object of God's anger and so should be avoided. **Companions** is hardly distinguishable from **friends**; so SPCL joins the two into one phrase, "my best friends"; and FRCL identifies the two, "My friends, my constant companions." The word translated **kinsmen** is literally "those who are near to me" and may mean "neighbors," as some translate it. "**Because of my sores**" in TEV sometimes requires making the reason more explicit; for example, "they will not come near me because they are afraid of my sores" or ". . . because they are afraid of catching my sickness."

One of the tasks of the poet was to use repetition for selected purposes and to avoid it if it did not serve his purposes. Since every word in a language does not have a synonym, it was sometimes necessary for the psalmist to use the same word in parallel lines, but to alter the tense, voice, mood, or conjugation. In this verse the Hebrew verb translated **stand** is such a case. In line <u>a</u> the verb is in the imperfect tense, and in line <u>b</u> it is in the perfect tense. In translation it may be necessary, as in TEV, to use different verbs or verb phrases.

38.12	RSV	TEV
	Those who seek my life lay their snares,	Those who want to kill me lay traps for me,
	those who seek my hurt speak of ruin,	and those who want to hurt me threaten to ruin me;
	and meditate treachery all the day long.	they never stop plotting against me.

The hostility of the psalmist's enemies is described in conventional terms: they **lay their snares** (see similar language in 31.4; 35.7; for **snares** see discussion at 18.5); they **speak of ruin**, that is, discuss how they can ruin him (see similar situation in 35.4), and plot against him (see similar situation in 35.20c). TEV has put into clear, natural English what is expressed in RSV in stilted "biblical" language. NEB takes all three lines of the verse to refer to verbal assaults: "defame me . . . spread cruel gossip . . . mutter slanders."

38.13-14	RSV		TEV
13	But I am like a deaf man, I do not hear,	13	I am like a deaf man and cannot hear,
	like a dumb man who does not open his mouth.		like a dumb man and cannot speak.
14	Yea, I am like a man who does not hear,	14	I am like a man who does not answer,
	and in whose mouth are no rebukes.		because he cannot hear.

The psalmist keeps silent; he pretends not to hear the malicious slander his enemies hurl at him and answers nothing, as though he were **deaf** and **dumb**. TEV, instead of "**I am like . . . and cannot**," should have said "I act like a deaf person, and do not hear, like a dumb person, and do not speak." SPCL has "I act like a deaf man, as though I cannot hear; as though I were dumb, I don't open my mouth." Most languages have special terms for persons who are unable to speak. It is important for users of this volume to remember that **a dumb man** in this context is one who cannot speak.

Verse 14 essentially repeats the thought of verse 13. The phrase **in whose mouth are no rebukes** is not easy to understand; the word translated "rebuke" may mean "argument" or "defense," that is, the psalmist does not attempt to answer the charges brought against him. NAB and NJV have "retort"; NJB "sharp answer"; FRCL "answer"; SPCL, NEB "defense." TEV has reversed the order of the two lines in this verse.

38.15-16	RSV	TEV

15	But for thee, O LORD, do I wait;
	  it is thou, O LORD my God, who
	    wilt answer.
		15 But I trust in you, O LORD;
		  and you, O Lord my God, will
		    answer me.

16	For I pray, "Only let them not
	    rejoice over me,
	  who boast against me when my
	    foot slips!"
		16 Don't let my enemies gloat over
		    my distress;
		  don't let them boast about my
		    downfall.

Now the psalmist affirms his faith in God, confessing his trust in him (literally "I wait for you"; see 31.24 and comments), confident that God will **answer** his prayers. In verse 15b the title "Lord" is used, not the divine name Yahweh. It should be noticed that in Hebrew the verb **answer** has no object (see RSV); so instead of "**answer me**" (TEV) the translation can be "answer my enemies" (see SPCL).

In verse 16 the Hebrew text is "For I say (or, pray), Don't let . . . ." TEV has given the psalmist's request, without using the device of his quoting himself. For the prayer, see similar requests in 13.4; 35.19,25. **Rejoice** and **boast** depict the glee of the psalmist's enemies over his suffering and ruin. **When my foot slips**: a figure for misfortune or ruin (see 13.4, where the same verb is translated "shaken"). **When my foot slips** or TEV "**downfall**" can be rendered in some languages as "when I fail," or "when I stumble and fall," or "when I take a wrong step."

38.17	RSV	TEV

	For I am ready to fall,
	  and my pain is ever with me.
		I am about to fall
		  and am in constant pain.

It is difficult to decide whether **I am ready to fall** refers to the psalmist's physical condition, weakened by his illness ("I am about to die"), or to his situation in face of his enemies (they are about to ruin him). In verse 16b he speaks of his foot slipping, and here he states that at any time he could fall fatally, meaning either total ruin or death (see Anderson). Perhaps something like "I am ready to give up" best expresses the psalmist's feelings. NJV translates "I am on the verge of collapse," and FRCL "I am about to disappear."

My pain is ever with me must often be recast to say, for example, "I suffer all the time," "my pain never leaves me," or sometimes idiomatically, "pain has taken hold of my body and never lets go."

38.18-19   RSV   TEV

18   I confess my iniquity,   18   I confess my sins;
        I am sorry for my sin.   they fill me with anxiety.
19   Those who are my foes without   19   My enemies are healthy and
        cause^x are mighty,   strong;
        and many are those who hate   there are many who hate me for
        me wrongfully.   no reason.

^x Cn: Heb *living*

The psalmist confesses his sins to God (verse 18a), acknowledging that they fill him with anxiety (verse 18b), as TEV translates it (also FRCL, SPCL). RSV translates **I am sorry for my sin** as a close parallel to line a. But the Hebrew verb has the meaning "be anxious about," even "be afraid of" (see Jer 42.16); so NJV here has "I am fearful over my sin"; NIV "I am troubled by my sin"; NEB "I am anxious at the thought of my sin." The expression **"fill me with anxiety"** can sometimes be translated idiomatically; for example, "they hang my heart up" or "they make my heart tremble," or nonfiguratively "they cause me to be afraid."

In verse 19a TEV **"healthy"** translates the Masoretic text "living," which is the sense expressed by TOB "full of life" and NIV "vigorous." NJV and Dahood translate it "mortal."^1 Others conjecture the Hebrew term for "without reason" (as in 35.19), which makes the line a close parallel to the following one (Briggs, Weiser; RSV, NEB, NAB, BJ, NJB). The Masoretic text is somewhat strange. In line b RSV **hate me wrongfully** means "it is wrong for them to hate me"; so TEV **"for no reason."**

38.20   RSV   TEV

Those who render me evil for good   Those who pay back evil for good
    are my adversaries because I   are against me because I try to
    follow after good.   do right.

---

^1HOTTP says only that the Masoretic text means "living" ("A" decision) but does not explain what it means in the context. It cites factor 14, "Conjectural form of the text," which states that the committee does not propose any conjectural emendation (regardless of whether or not the Masoretic text makes sense to the translator).

For the thought of line a, see 35.12a. The verb translated **are my adversaries** in line b is from *satan*, the same root from which the noun "satan" (adversary) is formed. Dahood retains the verb form and translates line b "(they) slander me when I seek their good," a meaning expressed also by NJB and NIV. This is possible and brings the line more into harmony with the preceding one.

38.21-22 RSV TEV

21 Do not forsake me, O LORD!
   O my God, be not far from me!
22 Make haste to help me,
   O Lord, my salvation!

21 Do not abandon me, O LORD;
   do not stay away, my God!
22 Help me now, O Lord my savior!

The psalm concludes with a final plea for the Lord's help. For verse 21a see how the terms are used in 22.1a, and for verse 21b see 22.11a,19a; 35.22b. For verse 22a see 22.19b; and for 22b see comments on "my salvation" in 27.1. The expression **O Lord, my salvation** will sometimes require identifying the Lord in terms of the act of saving; for example, "O Lord, you who have saved me" or "O Lord, you are the one who saves me."

Psalm 39

Like Psalm 38, this psalm is a lament by an individual who in his suffering and sickness is overcome by despair and cries out to Yahweh for justice and mercy. He sees his suffering as punishment for his sins (verses 10-11), and prays the Lord to stop punishing him.

The psalmist begins by recounting how he had resolved to say nothing about his plight, but finally could bear it no longer; so he urgently brings his protest and petition to the Lord (verses 1-6). He prays for mercy, for a stop to his punishment, even though he recognizes it as deserved because of his sins (verses 7-11). With a final plea for mercy, the psalmist concludes his lament (verses 12-13), which is considered by many scholars to be the finest literary expression of its kind in the Psalter.

Psalm 39 as a lament can be compared in a limited way with Psalm 13. (See introduction to Psalm 13.) The present psalm offers the thoughts of the psalmist in a pattern of intensification, but as Alter points out, there is a complex interweaving of the three themes: silence, fleeting existence, and sin-suffering. The first theme is dealt with in verses 1-3, the second in 4-6. Then at the very core of the psalm (verse 7) there is a pivotal point: "My hope is in thee." Verse 8 begins with the third theme, sin-suffering, but verse 9 shifts back to the opening theme of silence. Verse 10 picks up the theme of sin-suffering and maintains it until 11b, when the subject of fleeting existence reappears, "consume like a moth" and "man a mere breath." In 12c the psalmist again echoes the theme of silence when he asks God, "hold not thy peace at my tears," and in 12d,e he evokes once more the matter of his passing existence, and then concludes with a convergence of the two themes of silence and transience when he asks God to "look way from me" and "I . . . be no more."

Theme distribution may be tabulated as follows:

verses 1-3	Silence
verses 4-6	Fleeting existence
verse 7	(Turning point)
verse 8	Sin-suffering
verse 9	Silence
verses 10-11b	Sin suffering
verses 11c-12e	Fleeting existence
verse 13a-b	Silence-Fleeting existence

As the translator will notice, aside from the turning point at the center of the poem, there is little attempt at structural balance. Moreover, the semantic parallelism is characterized by imbalance, a feature that tends to result from the repeated use of three-line parallelism. In contrast with Psalm 13, once the turning point has been reached, there is no steady march toward resolution of the silence, transience, or sin–suffering themes. On the contrary, these themes reappear and disappear, and in the end there is a build-up focusing upon the unbearable lightness of existence, in which the poet asks God to "look away" from him so that he can enjoy his short moment before he becomes a nothing.

HEADING: **"The Confession of a Suffering Man"** (TEV); "The insignificance of man before God"; "The brevity and vanity of life"; "Life is short." The TEV heading can be restructured in some languages to say, for example, "A man who is ill tells God that he has sinned."

Hebrew Title: **To the choirmaster: to Jeduthun. A Psalm of David.**

For **To the choirmaster** see title of Psalm 4. The expression **to Jeduthun** (see also "according to Jeduthun" in the title of Psa 62 and 77) is thought by some to refer to the Jeduthun of 1 Chronicles 16.41, one of David's chief musicians (so Kirkpatrick, who translates, "For the chief musician Jeduthun"); others take the word to mean "confession."

39.1	RSV	TEV

RSV	TEV

I said, "I will guard my ways,
    that I may not sin with my
        tongue;
I will bridle^y my mouth,
    so long as the wicked are in my
        presence."
	I said, "I will be careful about
	        what I do
	    and will not let my tongue make
	        me sin;
	I will not say anything
	    while evil men are near."

^{y} Heb *muzzle*

Although both RSV and TEV have four printed lines, verse 1 is best analyzed as a tricolon, or three-line verse, following the same pattern as verses 2-6. For example, "I said, 'I will guard my ways that I may not sin with my tongue / I will put a muzzle on my mouth / so long as the wicked are in my presence.' " There is characteristic focusing in the second line which carries the meaning of "more than that, I will even put a muzzle over my mouth." The function of the third line is to reveal something about the significance of the first two.

The psalmist had resolved not to say anything, not to complain to God about his suffering (see Job's silence, Job 1.22; 2.10), especially in the presence of **the wicked**, who would use the occasion to pour out their scorn on the suffering man and raise doubts about the goodness of God.

In line a **I will guard my ways** means "I will watch how I behave" (NJB), "I will keep close watch over myself" (NEB), with particular reference to his vow to keep quiet. In some languages it will be clearer for the reader if the quotation is addressed to someone. Here it appears to be to the writer himself. Therefore one may say "I said to myself." Or else one may follow SPCL, "I had promised to be careful about my behavior and not sin with my tongue." The expression **sin with my tongue** will require some adjustment in some languages; for example, "I will not let the words I speak cause me to sin" or "I will not say sinful things."

Line c has a word that appears nowhere else in the Old Testament, "muzzle, bridle," a picturesque description of the psalmist's firm resolve to keep silent. In English it is more natural to speak of a "muzzle" rather than a **bridle** on one's mouth: "I will keep a muzzle on my mouth" (NEB, NJB). Translators who are attempting to keep poetic images will need to find a receptor language equivalent for **I will bridle my mouth**. The context makes it clear that the term refers to keeping silence, not to subjection, as a bridle may imply. In some languages this is expressed "I will keep my hand on my lips" or "I will tie my lips."

39.2-3   RSV   TEV

2   I was dumb and silent,   2   I kept quiet, not saying a word,
         I held my peace to no avail;   not even about anything good!
     my distress grew worse,   But my suffering only grew worse!
3   my heart became hot within me.   3   and I was overcome with anxiety.
     As I mused, the fire burned;   The more I thought, the more
         then I spoke with my tongue: troubled I became;
                                                  I could not keep from asking:

The psalmist kept his promise and said nothing, "**not even about anything good**" (verse 2b, TEV). This translates an obscure Hebrew phrase which appears to say "I was silent from good"; RSV interprets **I held my peace to no avail**.[1] NAB, through a conjecture, gets "I refrained from rash speech"; NJV "I was very still"; and Dahood "I refrained from speaking" (though the meaning is the same, the explanations of the Hebrew text are different). FRCL has "I said nothing at all." NIV and SPCL are like TEV; TOB has "I was silent, even though it did me no good"; Weiser translates "I held my peace, there was no happiness." Everything considered, it seems best for the translator to follow the lead of NJV and FRCL. Line c completes the thought of line b; his situation became worse, not better.

In verse 3a **my heart became hot within me** means he burned with anxiety, with worry, or else with impatience. The expression **my heart became hot within me**, while denoting anxiety in Hebrew, will in many languages suggest anger rather than anxiety, if translated literally.

In verse 3b **the fire burned** carries the idea even farther; the psalmist became even more impatient or worried. NEB takes the line to refer to physical symptoms: "My mind wandered as the fever grew."

No longer able to restrain himself, the psalmist finally spoke up (verse 3c). Weiser, RSV, NIV, and SPCL take the rest of the psalm as what the psalmist says, with

---

[1]HOTTP translates "more [than it was] good," which appears to mean "more than I should have" or "even though it did (me) no good" (as TOB translates).

closing quotation marks at the end of verse 13; NJB places them at the end of verse 6; TEV at the end of verse 4.

39.4	RSV	TEV

"LORD, let me know my end,
  and what is the measure of my
    days;
  let me know how fleeting my life
    is!

"LORD, how long will I live?
  When will I die?
  Tell me how soon my life will
    end."

My end means the end of the psalmist's life; the measure of my days means the length of the psalmist's life. All three lines of the verse are different ways of saying much the same thing (see TEV). GECL translates "Lord show me how brief my life is, and that my end is inevitable; make me aware of how little time is still left." As Anderson points out, the psalmist is really not asking for information as such (after all, the psalmist knows that life is brief); rather he is protesting the unfairness of it all. He is made to suffer, when he should be granted a measure of peace and well-being. In line a it is possible that the psalmist is asking how he will die, what will cause his death; but this does not seem very probable.

If verse 4 is taken in the sense of a protest, translators will in most cases have to make the protest clear. In English this may be done with the use of the auxiliary "should"; for example, "LORD, you should let me know when my life will end" or "LORD, why don't you tell me when I will die?" In some languages the repetition of the same thought in three lines will be stylistically awkward and misleading, and so must be reduced. FRCL uses a legal term in line c meaning a stay of proceedings or even of execution: "May I know the length of my reprieve." SPCL contrasts the third line with the first two by making it an exclamation, "I want to know how short my life will be!"

39.5-6	RSV		TEV

5 Behold, thou hast made my days a
     few handbreadths,
   and my lifetime is as nothing in
     thy sight.
   Surely every man stands as a
     mere breath!   *Selah*
6 Surely man goes about as a
     shadow!
   Surely for nought are they in
     turmoil;
   man heaps up, and knows not
     who will gather!

5 How short you have made my life!
     In your sight my lifetime seems
       nothing.
   Indeed every living man is no
     more than a puff of wind,
6 no more than a shadow.
   All he does is for nothing;
     he gathers wealth, but doesn't
       know who will get it.

In these two verses the psalmist provides, as it were, the answer to his question in verse 4. The language in these verses recalls similar passages in Job and Ecclesiastes (see Job 7.7; 8.9; 10.20; Eccl 2.26; 5.17; 6.12).

Behold is not formally represented by TEV, FRCL, NIV, NJV, SPCL, although the exclamation form in TEV may be considered a functional equivalent. A more natural equivalent in English is "I know . . . ." His life is quite short, literally (some) "handbreadths" (a handbreadth being equivalent to 3 inches, 7.5 centimeters), virtually **nothing** from God's point of view (verse 5b). In languages which will require a verb clause in place of the noun phrase, **my days** in line a of verse 5 may be rendered "What a short time you have given me to live!"

The lifetime of a human being is as frail and transient as **a mere breath**, as insubstantial and unreal as **a shadow** (verses 5c,6a). In verse 5c the verb **stands** is difficult to understand; NJV translates "no man endures any longer than a breath"; NEB "Man, though he stands upright, is but a puff of wind"; NJB "every human being that stands on earth is a mere puff of wind." It seems better to follow TEV or NIV ("Each man's life is but a breath"). Line c may sometimes be rendered "every man's life is like a mere breath."

Selah: see 3.2.

The verb in verse 6a, **goes about**, means activity in general; FRCL translates "his going and coming are no more than a mirage"; NJV "man walks about as a mere shadow." TEV has represented the verb **goes about** in verse 6a by the adjective "**living**" in verse 5c, which carries over to verse 6a. A translation of this line should not make it seem that the psalmist is saying that people look like ghosts when they walk around. In some languages it may be necessary to indicate that, for example, "a man's life disappears like a shadow."

Verse 6b is usually understood to mean "Surely in vain they bustle about"; the plural is used in a generic sense of people's busy lives. NJV has "mere futility is his hustle and bustle," and NIV "He bustles about, but only in vain." But there are problems here, and some (NEB, SPCL, BJ, NJB) conjecture *hamon* "riches" for the Masoretic text *yehemayon* "they bustle."

The sense of verse 6c is that a person will spend all his life and strength in acquiring possessions (**heaps up**), but will die without knowing who will get all he accumulated (**who will gather**). It is all futile, all useless.

Due to the very great differences in the way a dead person's property is disposed of, translators should make clear that **heaps us** refers to becoming the owner of physical property and not to a season's harvest. In some cases it will be necessary to drop the agricultural figures as TEV has done. In order to make clear that **who will gather** takes place after the wealthy man's death, it may be necessary to say, for example, "A person gets wealth while he is alive, but after he dies, he does not know who gets it." Some languages have proverbs which will fit this passage.

39.7-8	RSV	TEV
7	"And now, Lord, for what do I wait? My hope is in thee.	7 What, then, can I hope for, Lord? I put my hope in you. 8 Save me from all my sins,

8	Deliver me from all my transgressions.	and don't let fools make fun of me.
	Make me not the scorn of the fool!	

With verse 7 the three-line structures come to an abrupt halt. The first six verses stepped up progressively the intensification of the psalmist's problems of being silent and living a very short life. Verse 7 shifts the thought and at the same time makes a break with the line pattern. The reason why the build-up of intensification ends as the psalmist takes up the theme of sin-suffering in verse 8 is that he is not depicting the progression of it, but rather is asking to be rescued from it.

Realizing that there is no human endeavor in which he can place his hope (**for what do I wait**, verse 7a; see comments at 25.3; 38.15), the psalmist declares **My hope is in thee**, which can sometimes be rendered "I look to you with confidence."

This affirmation of faith leads him to pray for Yahweh to save him from all his sins, which may be a way of asking God to cure him of his disease, which was caused by his sins, or to free him from the power of sin. Or else, as FRCL translates, the meaning may be "Save me from all who betray me" (so NEB "all who do me wrong"). This healing would then spare the psalmist the mockery of fools (for **fool** see comments on 14.1). **The scorn of the fool** is an expression which can be translated in some languages as "the laughing of persons who have black livers" or "the scorn of gourd-head people."

39.9-10   RSV   TEV

9	I am dumb, I do not open my mouth;	9	I will keep quiet, I will not say a word,
	for it is thou who has done it.		for you are the one who made me suffer like this.
10	Remove thy stroke from me;		
	I am spent by the blows^z of thy hand.	10	Don't punish me any more!
			I am about to die from your blows.

^{z} Heb *hostility*

The psalmist realizes his predicament, since it is his own sin, not God, that is ultimately responsible for his suffering. He must keep quiet and not say a word (verse 9a; see similar expressions in verse 2; 38.13). God punishes a man for his sins, and he is not to question God's justice.

But he can ask God to stop punishing him (verse 10a), literally **Remove thy stroke from me**; the word **stroke** translates the same word which in 38.11 is translated "plague."

In verse 10b the word translated **blows** occurs only here in the Old Testament; it is taken in the general sense of hostility (see RSV footnote), but Anderson suggests that here it probably does mean "blow." See similar ideas in 32.4a; 38.2b.

RSV   TEV

> When thou dost chasten man
>   with rebukes for sin,
> thou dost consume like a moth
>   what is dear to him;
>   surely every man is a mere
>   breath!   *Selah*

> You punish a man's sins by your
>   rebukes,
> and like a moth you destroy
>   what he loves.
> Indeed a man is no more than a
>   puff of wind!

With verse 11 the psalmist joins the themes of sin-suffering and fleeting existence, and in doing so returns to the three-line pattern, which he uses again in verse 12abc before returning in 12de and 13 to the two-line verse.

Lines a and b are circumstantial clauses, as RSV's translation shows. It may be better to translate them as complete statements, as TEV does (also FRCL, SPCL). **When . . . with rebukes for sin** can be rendered in some languages as "You punish a person's sins with your strong words" or "You speak hard words and punish a person for doing wrong things."

The figure in line c, **like a moth**, seems to be applied to God, which is strange (but see Hos 5.12, where it is applied to God). NAB changes the comparison by translating "cobweb": "you dissolve like a cobweb all that is dear to him." But, unusual as it is, "moth" is a valid comparison, since it is a biblical figure for destruction and decay (see Job 13.28; Isa 50.9; Matt 6.19-20). FRCL translates "like a worm in a fruit, you consume what man loves."

What is dear to him probably refers to life, the most precious thing a person owns; NIV, however, has "their wealth," and NJV "what he treasures."

Once more (line d) the psalmist emphasizes how fleeting and frail is human existence (see verse 5c).

Selah: see 3.2.

39.12-13   RSV   TEV

> 12 "Hear my prayer, O LORD,
>   and give ear to my cry;
>   hold not thy peace at my tears!
> For I am thy passing guest,
>   a sojourner, like all my fathers.
> 13 Look away from me, that I may
>   know gladness,
>   before I depart and be no
>   more!"

> 12 Hear my prayer, LORD,
>   and listen to my cry;
>   come to my aid when I weep.
> Like all my ancestors
>   I am only your guest for a little
>   while.
> 13 Leave me alone so that I may
>   have some happiness
>   before I go away and am no
>   more.

The psalm closes with a final plea for the Lord's help (verse 12a-c). Verse 12c means "don't be indifferent to my weeping" (NJV "do not disregard my tears," NJB "do not remain deaf to my weeping") or, as a positive request, "help me when you see me crying." In a striking figure the psalmist speaks of his life on earth as **thy passing guest, a sojourner**, which means that he is a temporary guest in Yahweh's tent. This life, life on earth, was the place where the pious Israelite enjoyed Yahweh's favor, his "hospitality." Like all his ancestors, the psalmist too would soon leave (see 1 Chr 29.15). The expression **thy passing guest** is rendered in some languages as "the stranger who comes and goes quickly."

For the short time he will still be the Lord's guest, the psalmist asks him to spare him further punishment (verse 13). The request **Look away from me** in the sense "**Leave me alone**" (TEV) is strange, since usually a prayer is for the Lord to "look at" a person, to bless and rescue. To bring out the idea here, NEB has "Frown on me no more"; GECL has "turn away your reproachful look from me." In this way the psalmist will **know gladness** before inevitable death comes, **before I depart and be no more**. The pious Israelite believed that in Sheol he would be cut off from any relationship with Yahweh; death was the end of meaningful existence (see 6.5; Job 10.20-22). **That I may know gladness** is expressed in some languages idiomatically; for example, "that my heart may sit quietly" or "that my stomach may feel full." Line b will have to be translated in some languages as simply "before I die."

Psalm 40

This psalm contains a thanksgiving and a lament, and most commentators believe that the two were originally independent compositions which were later joined together. There is a difference of opinion over where the break occurs; some take it to be at the end of verse 11 (Briggs, Taylor, Dentan, Kirkpatrick; see BJ, NJB, NJV, TOB, TEV), others at the end of verse 10 (Anderson, Toombs, Dahood; see RSV, NAB, SPCL). The decision depends in part on whether verse 11 is taken as a statement (thus ending the first part) or as a request (thus beginning the second part).

The first part (verses 1-11, TEV) opens with a statement of the psalmist's experience (verse 1-3), followed by praise to the Lord for his goodness (verses 4-8) and the psalmist's public proclamation of what the Lord has done for him (verses 9-10); it closes with a confession of faith in the Lord (if verse 11 is understood as a statement).

The second part (verses 12-17) opens with a description of the psalmist's condition (verse 12), followed by a cry for help (verses 13-17).

HEADING: TEV has two headings, "**A Song of Praise**" (verse 1) and "**A Prayer for Help**" (verse 12). Other headings are "Gratitude and prayer for help"; "A thanksgiving and a lament"; "It pleases me to do your will, my God." The two headings found in TEV may be restructured in some languages to say "The psalmist sings a song to praise God," and "The psalmist asks God to help him."

Hebrew Title: **To the choirmaster. A Psalm of David.**
For **choirmaster** see title of Psalm 4.

40.1-2   RSV   TEV

1   I waited patiently for the LORD;   1   I waited patiently for the LORD's
        he inclined to me and heard my   help;
        cry.   then he listened to me and
2   He drew me up from the desolate   heard my cry.
        pit,*a*   2   He pulled me out of a dangerous
        out of the miry bog,   pit,
     and set my feet upon a rock,   out of the deadly quicksand.
        making my steps secure.   He set me safely on a rock
                                                          and made me secure.

a Cn: Heb *pit of tumult*

The translator should note in verses 1-3 that parallelism is used to make a series of statements. There is no heightening effect between lines, although there is some semantic sameness between parallel lines; for example, in verse 2 **pit/miry bog**; **feet/steps**; **rock/secure**.

In verse 1 **I waited patiently** translates "Waiting, I waited" (see comments on 25.3a for **I waited**); the Hebrew phrase that follows, "for Yahweh," means "for Yahweh's help." **He inclined** is similar to "he inclined his ear" (see 17.6 and comments) and means "he listened, he paid attention to." SPCL, however, "He bent down to hear my cries"—which the translator may choose to follow.

In figurative language the psalmist describes in verse 2 the danger he was in. It is probable **the desolate pit** and **the miry bog** are metaphors for Sheol, the world of the dead; either because of illness or because of some other dangerous situation, the psalmist was near death, from which Yahweh rescued him, setting his **feet upon a rock** and making his **steps secure**, that is, giving him health and safety. A similar description of deliverance from imminent death is found in 30.3. The word translated **desolate** (TEV "dangerous") is of uncertain meaning; in other contexts the Hebrew word means "tumult, roaring"; for its use here, however, K-B classifies it as a different word, occurring only here in the Old Testament, meaning "desolate, waste," and defines it as a reference to Sheol. Some wish to translate "the noisy pit" believing that this is a reference to "the tumultuous waters in the underworld." Dahood and NAB have "pit of destruction"; NJB "seething chasm"; SPCL "deadly pit." **Desolate pit**, referring to the place of the dead, may be rendered in some languages as "he pulled me up from the pit of death" or "he took me out of the pit where the dead people go." The other expression, **miry bog**, is translated "**deadly quicksand**" by TEV; NJV "slimy clay"; NAB "the mud of the swamp." "**Quicksand**" is not known in some areas; however, a deep bog or place of mud is equally applicable.

The **rock** (verse 2c) is a figure of safety, stability, security, as often in Psalms; **my feet** and **my steps** are parallel. Instead of "**made me secure**" (TEV) the translation can be "and now I walk without fear." One translation preserves the parallelism as follows: "He made me stand on a rock, he made me walk with firm steps."

40.3

RSV	TEV
He put a new song in my mouth, a song of praise to our God. Many will see and fear, and put their trust in the LORD.	He taught me to sing a new song, a song of praise to our God. Many who see this will take warning and will put their trust in the LORD.

As a result of Yahweh's action, the psalmist has **a new song** (see 33.3 and comments), **a song of praise** to sing to God. The expression **our God** is inclusive, that is, it includes the fellow Israelites to whom the psalmist was speaking. **He put a new song in my mouth** means "He gave me a new song to sing." Where intelligible and natural, "He placed a new song on my lips (or, in my mouth)" can be an effective translation of the Hebrew.

A song of praise to our God must be recast in many languages to say, for example, "a song which says our God is great" or, if stated in direct discourse, "a song whose words say 'God, you are great.' "

The result of the psalmist's experience on those who hear about it is that they will **see and fear**. (In Hebrew there is an effective alliteration: *yiru . . . yirau*.) This act of seeing probably is to be understood as a reference to the public recital in the Temple (notice **our God** in verse 3b) of what Yahweh has done for the psalmist. The psalmist's fellow worshipers will be filled with fear, awe, the proper reverence for God that all his people should have (see 34.7,9). FRCL translates **and fear** as a separate line, "they will recognize the authority of the Lord."

40.4   RSV   TEV

Blessed is the man who makes   Happy are those who trust the
    the LORD his trust,   LORD,
who does not turn to the proud,   who do not turn to idols
    to those who go astray after   or join those who worship false
    false gods!   gods.

In lines a-b the verb phrase translated **makes the LORD his trust** is better represented by "trusts the LORD" (see TEV). It is important to use the same word for **trust** here that is used in verse 3.

In lines c and d **the proud** and **false gods** translate the Hebrew "arrogant ones" and "lies"; some commentators (see Anderson) believe that the reference is to pagan gods, as TEV and Dahood translate. Others, however, take it to describe people: NEB "brutal and treacherous men"; NJV "the arrogant . . . followers of falsehood"; AT "idolaters . . . lying apostates"; NJB "rebels and those who have gone astray in falsehood." No certainty is possible; some have suggested placing "arrogant men" in the margin as an alternative for "false gods" in the text. The parallelism seems to favor the TEV rendering. "Idols" are often rendered "things which people worship" or "gods which are not true gods." If the term here is to be understood as "arrogant men," it can sometimes be translated as "men who think they are very important" or, idiomatically, "people who have swollen hearts." In languages which do not use relative clauses, such as those with **who** in RSV and TEV, translators may recast verse 4 to say, for example,

    People trusting in the LORD are happy,
        they do not turn to idols,
        they do not join those who worship false gods.

40.5   RSV   TEV

Thou hast multiplied, O LORD my   You have done many things for
    God,   us, O LORD our God;
    thy wondrous deeds and thy   there is no one like you!
    thoughts toward us;   You have made many wonderful
    none can compare with thee!   plans for us.
Were I to proclaim and tell of   I could never speak of them all—
    them,   their number is so great!

they would be more than can be
numbered.

The structure of the parallelism in verse 5 has two summaries. The first, **none can compare with thee**, refers to God, and the second one, **they would be more than can be numbered**, refers to the great things God has done. In the Hebrew order of the parallelism, line b carries line a forward by expanding it and making it a bit more specific. These lines belong semantically together. However, the summary line c interrupts, since the next line, **proclaim and tell**, refers to the great things. By shifting line c to the position of b, TEV has broken up the first two parallel lines but has related the original line b to the remainder of the verse. Translators may do the same, but they may find that this is not necessary.

The psalmist praises the Lord's goodness, speaking of the **wondrous deeds** on behalf of his people (see comments on 9.1), and his **thoughts toward** them, that is, his purposes and plans for them. RSV **Thou hast multiplied**, besides not being natural English, is not a very good translation of the Hebrew, which is better rendered "Many (or, great) are the wonderful things you have done." TEV has rearranged the material in the first part of the verse for greater ease of understanding (see also FRCL).

RSV **O LORD my God** translates the Masoretic text; TEV follows one Hebrew manuscript (and Syriac) "O LORD our God." Most translations follow the Masoretic text.

The words translated **none can compare with thee** (similarly TEV and others) may mean "they cannot be recounted to you" (see NJV, NIV); the verb translated "compare" means "prepare, set in order." This meaning, while possible, does not seem very probable here.

The Lord's acts of love and kindness are so many that the psalmist would not be able to list them all, if he tried to do so; they are more than can be counted. The passive expression, **they would be more than can be numbered**, may have to be recast to say, for example, "no one could count them," "they would be so numerous no one could say how many they were," or "they would be more than I have numbers for counting." Some languages will prefer to use a direct quotation such as "I will speak of them like this, 'They are too many to count.' "

40.6	RSV	TEV
	Sacrifice and offering thou dost not desire; but thou hast given me an open ear.[b] Burnt offering and sin offering thou hast not required.	You do not want sacrifices and offerings; you do not ask for animals burned whole on the altar or for sacrifices to take away sin. Instead, you have given me ears to hear you,

[b] Heb *ears thou hast dug for me*

The psalmist continues praising the Lord's goodness, and now he speaks of what is the proper response to the Lord's great mercy; it is not sacrifices but obedience.

Four words are used for sacrifices in verse 6: **Sacrifice** (*zevach*) is the regular word for animal sacrifices in general; sometimes it designates a fellowship offering, in which only a part of the animal was burned on the altar; some of it was given to the priest and the rest was eaten by the worshipers. **Offering** (*minchah*) originally was used of both animal and grain offerings, but later was restricted to grain offerings (which is probably what it means here). **Burnt offering** (*'olah*) was the sacrifice of an animal that was completely burned on the altar. **Sin offering** (*chata'ah*) was an offering made in order to have sins forgiven. The list is not complete; there were other sacrifices. The important thing here is that the psalmist, by using these four as representative, is placing sacrifices in their proper perspective (see similar statements in 1 Sam 15.22; Psa 50.8-14; 69.30-31; Amos 5.21-22; Micah 6.6-8); above all, God wants the total and complete obedience of those who worship him, and not just the sacrifices they offer to him.

In some languages it will be difficult to make distinctions between the various kinds of sacrifice, particularly in languages where the term "sacrifice" is translated as "burned gifts offered to God." In such languages one may have to use the term for sacrifice three times, but accompanied by the qualifications provided in lines b and c; for example, "you do not want burned gifts offered to you, and other gifts; you do not ask for animals to be burned in order to take away people's sins."

The psalmist says **thou dost not desire** and **thou hast not required**, but it is probable that these statements are not meant literally; this is rather an emphatic way of saying "Sacrifices are not the *only* thing you want." It is recommended, however, that the translation faithfully represent the meaning of these two absolute statements: God does not want, nor does he require, that his people offer him sacrifices.

As the RSV order of lines shows, line b in Hebrew (literally "you have dug ears for me") has been placed in TEV at the end of the verse, to connect logically with the beginning of verse 7. The meaning is that God gave the psalmist the ability to hear the Lord's command and to obey it (see Isa 50.5). One translation may be "you taught me the meaning of obedience"; NAB "ears open to obedience you gave me." FRCL, however, translates "you have made me understand that very well" (referring to the preceding statement) and NJV is similar; this does not seem very likely.

The Hebrew order of statements as reflected in RSV is negative–positive–negative. TEV shifts this order to become negative–negative–positive. In languages where it is poor style to have the parallelism interrupted by **but thou hast given me an open ear**, it may be clearer in the receptor language to keep them together, as TEV has done.

40.7-8	RSV		TEV
7	Then I said, "Lo, I come; in the roll of the book it is writ- ten of me;	7	and so I answered, "Here I am; your instructions for me are in the book of the Law.*ⁿ*
8	I delight to do thy will, O my God; thy law is within my heart."	8	How I love to do your will, my God!

I keep your teaching in my heart."

[n] your instructions . . . Law; *or* my devotion to you is recorded in your book.

The psalmist's response in verses 7-8 is full of difficulties, and there are various interpretations. Lo, I come in verse 7a indicates readiness to hear and act, better expressed in English by "Here I am."

Verse 7b in Hebrew is "in the roll of the book it is written for (or, about) me." NEB omits this line completely; NJV translates the psalmist's declaration, "See, I will bring a roll recounting what befell me"; SPCL "Here I am, just as the book says about me"; NJB joins the first words of verse 8a to verse 7b, "In the scroll of the book it is written of me, my delight is to do your will"; TOB "Here I come with the roll of a book written for me"; SPCL "Here I am, as it is said of me in the book." All these translations are possible, and complete certainty is impossible. The most difficult decision to make is whether the preposition in Hebrew means "it is written *for* me" (so TEV "your instructions for me") or "it is written *about* me" (so RSV of me and TEV footnote "my devotion to you is recorded in your book").

The roll of the book is taken to refer either to the Torah as a whole (the first five books of the Old Testament) or to the book of Deuteronomy; some take it to refer to the heavenly book, where all human deeds are recorded. FRCL may be recommended: "In the book of the Law I find written what I should do." "The book of the Law" must sometimes be translated "the book which contains the Law," or "the book in which the Law is written," or "the book which teaches the Law."

The psalmist ends his response with a promise to obey the Lord's will completely (verse 8). Thy law is within my heart (verse 9b) means that the psalmist has learned God's Law and cherishes it, that is, he keeps it in mind and obeys it.

Verses 6-8a are quoted in Hebrews 10.5-7 as they appear in the Septuagint, which in verse 7 has "you prepared a body for me" in place of the Masoretic text "you have dug ears for me"; one manuscript of the Septuagint has "ears" instead of "a body." The New Testament quotation joins verse 8a to verse 7b, whereas in the Septuagint, as in the Masoretic text, verse 7b ends with a full stop, and verse 8a is joined to verse 8b. Translators should follow the Hebrew Masoretic text rather than the Septuagint.

40.9-10   RSV   TEV

9 I have told the glad news of deliverance
in the great congregation;
lo, I have not restrained my lips,
as thou knowest, O LORD.
10 I have not hid thy saving help
within my heart,
I have spoken of thy faithfulness and thy salvation

9 In the assembly of all your people, LORD,
I told the good news that you save us.
You know that I will never stop telling it.
10 I have not kept the news of salvation to myself;
I have always spoken of your

I have not concealed thy steadfast
love and thy faithfulness
from the great congregation.

faithfulness and help.
In the assembly of all your people
I have not been silent
about your loyalty and constant
love.

In these two verses the various attributes of Yahweh are praised (see similar lists in 33.4-5; 35.5-6, and the comments there): **deliverance** (*tsedeq*; see comments on "right" in 4.1); **saving help** (*tsedaqah*; see comments on "righteousness" in 5.8); **faithfulness** (*'emunah*; see 36.5); **salvation** (*teshu'ah*; see related noun "deliverance" in 3.8, and the related verb "help" in 12.1); **steadfast love** (*chesed*; see comments on 5.7); and **faithfulness** or "truth" (*'emeth*; see comment on "truth" in 15.2). These are not mutually exclusive qualities; their meanings overlap, and they are all expressive of Yahweh's constant commitment to the covenant he made with his people always to love, bless, and protect them.

The great congregation (verses 9b,10d) is the people of Israel assembled for worship in the Temple (see 22.25; 35.18). **The great congregation** may sometimes be rendered "your people who meet to worship you" or "the great meeting of your people in worship."

In various ways the psalmist declares his firm resolve ever to proclaim Yahweh's saving help. **I have told** (verse 9a); **I have not restrained my lips** (verse 9c); **I have not hid . . . within my heart** (verse 10a), meaning "I have not kept it a secret"; **I have spoken** (verse 10b); **I have not concealed** (verse 10c). Many languages will express verse 10a in a form more closely parallel to the Hebrew than to the TEV; for example, "I have not kept silently in my heart that you save your people." **Thy faithfulness and thy salvation** must often be rendered as verb phrases; for example, "I have always told people how you are faithful to your people and how you help them." In the same way **thy steadfast love and thy faithfulness** must often be recast in some such ways as "how you are always loyal to your people and how you always love them faithfully."

40.11 RSV TEV

Do not thou, O LORD, withhold
thy mercy from me,
let thy steadfast love and thy
faithfulness
ever preserve me!

LORD, I know you will never stop
being merciful to me.
Your love and loyalty will always
keep me safe.

As understood by TEV (see introduction to this psalm), this verse is a statement (Briggs, Oesterley, Kirkpatrick, Dahood; NEB, BJ, NJB, NJV, FRCL, GECL, TOB) and ends the first part of the psalm. Others take it as a request (RSV, NAB, NIV, AT, SPCL). If taken as a request, it should be joined to the next verse.

Do not . . . withhold thy mercy from me must sometimes be rendered idiomatically; for example, "Do not fail to have a white heart for me" or "Do not stop being pained for me."

In many languages it is not possible for qualities like **love** and **faithfulness** (TEV "loyalty") to perform acts. Therefore one must often shift from noun phrases to verb phrases in such cases; for example, "you will always keep me safe because you love me and are loyal to me."

40.12 RSV	TEV
For evils have encompassed me without number; my iniquities have overtaken me, till I cannot see; they are more than the hairs of my head; my heart fails me.	I am surrounded by many troubles— too many to count! My sins have caught up with me, and I can no longer see; they are more than the hairs of my head, and I have lost my courage.

Many consider that the person who brought together the two separate compositions wrote this verse as a joining link between the two. In any case it describes the author's present difficulties, which lead him to ask Yahweh for help (verses 13-17).

The countless **evils** which surround him seem to be the consequences of his sins which, like a flood, **have encompassed** him (see similar idea in 38.4). In some languages it is not natural to say that one is "**surrounded by . . . troubles**" (TEV; RSV **evils have encompassed me**). However, by using a verb phrase it is often possible to say, for example, "Those who cause me trouble are all around me," or it is sometimes possible to maintain the image of being surrounded, through the use of a simile; for example, "I have many troubles, and they have surrounded me like enemies."

The expression **my iniquities have overtaken me** is metaphorical and difficult to reproduce in some languages in that form. The clause seems to have the consequence in the following line of blinding the psalmist so that **I cannot see**. In some languages it is possible to say, for example, "my sins have caught hold of me and I cannot see where I am going" or "my sins have caught up with me and they are so many I cannot see my way." Using the flood image it is sometimes possible to say "my sins are like a flood and have covered me" or "the wrongs that I do are so many they have drowned me like a flood."

Since the statement **I cannot see** is strange in this context, Dahood proposes an emendation by which the text means "I am unable to escape." But the text, as it is, may be taken to refer to the psalmist's constant weeping, which causes his eyesight to fail (see similar expressions in 6.7; 38.10; see also 69.3). FRCL translates "I cannot bear to look at them any longer" (similarly GECL). This makes sense, but it is unlikely that the Hebrew text means this.

With the use of an expressive figure, **more than the hairs of my head**, the psalmist confesses that his sins are many.

My heart fails me means "I have lost my courage (or, hope)."

40.13 RSV TEV

> Be pleased, O LORD, to deliver
> me!
> O LORD, make haste to help
> me!

> Save me, LORD! Help me now!

The psalmist's plea for help (verses 13-17) is almost completely identical with Psalm 70. The translation of the two passages should reflect this identity.

With words that express impatience, the psalmist prays to the Lord to save him from his enemies. **Be pleased** may be represented by a conventional expression such as "Please" (SPCL, FRCL); NEB "Show me favour"; GECL "Be kind." TEV has not represented it formally, since the request itself incorporates the element of an urgent plea.

For the request that the Lord hurry to his aid, see 22.19; 38.22. For **deliver** see 7.1 and comments, and for **help** see 37.40 and comments.

TEV has not shortened the two Hebrew lines when combining them into one, but has translated all the components. It may be best to keep two lines, since **make haste** increases the urgency of the second line.

40.14-15 RSV TEV

> 14 Let them be put to shame and
>   confusion altogether
> who seek to snatch away my
>   life;
> let them be turned back and
>   brought to dishonor
> who desire my hurt!
> 15 Let them be appalled because of
>   their shame
> who say to me, "Aha, Aha!"

> 14 May those who try to kill me
>   be completely defeated and
>   confused.
> May those who are happy because
>   of my troubles
> be turned back and disgraced.
> 15 May those who make fun of me
>   be dismayed by their defeat.

The language of verse 14 is very much like that of 35.4,26 (see also 6.10). "To snatch away my *nefesh*" (see 3.2) means "to kill me."

In verse 14a **put to shame** and in verse 15a **their shame** refer to the shame of defeat (see comments at 6.10).

The requests expressed with **"may"** in TEV and **let** in RSV will have to be shifted in some languages to more explicit requests; for example, "I ask that . . . ."

The passive constructions used in RSV and TEV will in many languages have to be shifted to active constructions; for example, "I ask that you defeat and confuse those who try to kill me." Both TEV and RSV use the expression **be turned back**, which can have several meanings. It is important that the translator not understand this expression in the sense of being refused, but rather with the meaning of being defeated and sent away. In some languages this may be translated as "I ask that they flee," or "I ask that they be chased away" or ". . . that you chase them away."

In some languages **dishonor** is spoken of as "to speak against" or "to take away the praise."

It is impossible to be dogmatic about whether verse 14d means **who desire my hurt** (also NIV, NJV, TOB, SPCL, NEB) or **"who are happy because of my troubles"** (TEV; also NJB, FRCL, GECL). The translator should feel free to choose. Verse 15a **be appalled because of their shame** means "be horrified at their complete defeat." "Dismayed by defeat," as expressed in TEV, will often have to be recast to say "may they be dismayed because God has defeated them."

In verse 15b **who say to me, "Aha, Aha!"** is a vivid description of the psalmist's enemies mocking him (see comments on this expression in 35.21).

The psalmist's prayer for the defeat of his enemies is based on the conviction that, in opposing him, his enemies are showing their hostility toward Yahweh himself.

40.16

RSV	TEV

But may all who seek thee
  rejoice and be glad in thee;
may those who love thy salvation
  say continually, "Great is the
  LORD!"
	May all who come to you
	  be glad and joyful.
	May all who are thankful for your
	  salvation
	  always say, "How great is the
	  LORD!"

The psalmist prays for God's blessings on his faithful people. <u>Seek</u> in line a means to go to the Temple to worship God (see comments on 24.6b). In line <u>b</u> <u>in thee</u> means "because of you," "because of what you have done." This phrase need not be represented formally, since the meaning is inherent in the expression "**come to you**" (see NJB). Parallel lines may be used, as follows: "May all who seek you rejoice; may all who come to you be glad."

<u>Love thy salvation</u> does not mean "love being saved by you"; here it may mean "to wish, desire," or else "who are grateful for" (see TEV). NEB "who long for"; NJV "who are eager for"; SPCL, GECL "desire." FRCL translates "who love you, the Savior." In some languages it will be essential to transform **thy salvation** into a clause; for example, "may all you have saved give you thanks," or "may all the people you have saved show they are thankful," or "may everyone who wants you to save them . . . ."

40.17

RSV	TEV

As for me, I am poor and needy;
  but the Lord takes thought for
  me.
Thou art my help and my deliver-
  er;
  do not tarry, O my God!
	I am weak and poor, O Lord,
	  but you have not forgotten me.
	You are my savior and my God—
	  hurry to my aid!

The psalm closes with a humble prayer. The phrase **poor and needy** translates two synonyms, both of which mean "poor, weak, helpless, oppressed" (see "afflicted" and comments in 9.12; "weak and needy" in 35.10). If the translation uses **poor and needy**, it may sometimes be "I am a have-nothing man," or idiomatically, "I am a man owning only one small pig" or "I am a man living far from the chief's compound."

Takes thought for me (line <u>b</u>) means "is concerned about me," "does not forget me." Some (NEB, SPCL, GECL) translate this as a plea, "Don't forget me, Lord!" Thus it becomes parallel to the plea in line <u>d</u> and may be preferred by translators.

TEV has combined the two synonymous expressions, **my help and my deliverer**, into the one statement, **"You are my savior."** For **help** see comment on the verb "helps" in 37.40, and for **deliverer** see comment on the verb "deliver" in 17.13. Verbal phrases may be preferred: "You are the one who helps me and sets me free" (SPCL).

The last request, **do not tarry**, is a way of asking God to take immediate action on the psalmist's behalf. Most translations follow the Hebrew and use a negative expression, "do not delay"; it may be preferable to use a positive expression, as TEV has done. In most instances it will be helpful to fill out the expression: "do not delay in helping me," "come quickly to help me."

It is better to follow RSV **O my God** as a vocative exclamation instead of TEV **"You are . . . my God."**

Psalm 41

Although some classify this psalm as a thanksgiving (see Toombs; NAB), it seems more appropriate to see it as a lament (see Anderson, Dentan). The psalmist is sick (verse 8) and is insulted by enemies and abandoned by friends, who consider his illness as God's punishment for sin.

The psalm opens with a statement of faith in God (verses 1-3), who protects and blesses those who are concerned for the poor. Then the psalmist describes his situation: ill, abandoned, friendless (verses 4-9); so he prays to the Lord for health, confident that the Lord will answer him because he does what is right (verses 10-12). Verse 13 is not properly a part of this psalm; it forms the conclusion to Book One of the Psalms (Psa 1–41).

HEADING: TEV has "**The Prayer of a Sick Man**"; other headings are "Blessed are the merciful"; "Thanksgiving after sickness"; "Prayer of a sick and lonely man." The TEV heading may sometimes be recast to say "A sick man prays to God for help" or "A sick man asks God for help."

Hebrew Title: **To the choirmaster. A Psalm of David.**
For **choirmaster** see title of Psalm 4.

41.1-2	RSV	TEV
1	Blessed is he who considers the poor!*c* The LORD delivers him in the day of trouble;	1 Happy are those who are concerned for the poor; the LORD will help them when they are in trouble.
2	the LORD protects him and keeps him alive; he is called blessed in the land; thou dost not give him up to the will of his enemies.	2 The LORD will protect them and preserve their lives; he will make them happy in the land; he will not abandon them to the power of their enemies.

c Or *weak*

The psalm opens with an expression of praise for those who are concerned for the poor (or, the helpless; for **Blessed be** see comments on 1.1). This is somewhat strange, since nothing else is said about this in the rest of the psalm. By various means Dahood and Briggs get other meanings from the text; the majority of commentators and translators, however, agree with the meaning expressed by TEV and RSV. Weiser believes that the psalmist is referring to himself, and that the

Hebrew verb **consider** here has the neutral meaning of "pay attention to." The Hebrew word translated **poor** occurs here for the first time in Psalms; it may mean "helpless, weak," being synonymous with the terms used in 40.17. In some languages it is unnatural to express congratulations of happiness when this is addressed in the third person. However, if the translator shifts to the second person in line a, it will be necessary to maintain the second person through the first three verses.

Blessed is he may best be rendered in some languages as "How fortunate is the person" or, in the second person, "How fortunate you are" or "You are truly a happy person if you . . . ."

TEV's **"concerned for"** is rendered sometimes idiomatically as "have a good heart for."

Delivers translates the verb which in 33.17b is translated "save."

In the day of trouble in verse 1b means "in time of trouble," "when he is in trouble (or, difficulty)." The expression **in the day of trouble** is rendered in some languages idiomatically as "when they see trouble" or "when troubles take hold of them."

There is some uncertainty over the exact form and meaning of verse 2b, **he is called blessed in the land**; but in general the thought seems to be that such people will have happiness as they live their lives in the land of Israel (see 37.29 and comments). The Hebrew expression "he will be called" can mean "he will be." But the expression can be taken to mean that such a person will be highly thought of by his fellow citizens. If **land** is not described clearly, it may simply mean in the "country" in contrast to the "city." Accordingly it will sometimes be better to say "land of Israel."

The expression **the will of his enemies** implies what his enemies may do to him, and therefore in some languages it is necessary to say, for example, "he will not abandon them and let their enemies harm them." **Will** translates *nefesh* (see 3.2), which NEB and Weiser translate "greed" (as in the similar passage 27.12). FRCL translates "in the claws of his enemies."

In verse 2c the Masoretic text has the second person of direct address as the psalmist speaks to God (see RSV); TEV has changed it to third person, to be consistent with verse 2a,b and verse 3a (likewise NEB, FRCL, SPCL, GECL). There is no particular merit, as HOTTP proposes, in maintaining the form of the Masoretic text (the same applies to verse 3b). An alternative is to address all the psalm to the Lord in the second person, so as to be consistent with verses 10-12; thus "LORD, you protect him and keep him alive . . . ." However, it may be more important in some languages to address these words to the person who is being congratulated.

41.3   RSV   TEV

> The LORD sustains him on his   The LORD will help them when
>   sickbed;   they are sick
> in his illness thou healest all his   and will restore them to health.
>   infirmities.*d*

d Heb *thou changest all his bed*

In line <u>a</u> the verb translated **sustains** means here "to help," "to strengthen"; NEB "He nurses him"; FRCL "takes care of him."

In line <u>b</u> the Hebrew is "you will change all his bed in his sickness," which means that Yahweh transforms the person's illness into health, he restores him to health; NEB "he turns his bed when he is ill" is hard to understand. One possible version is "when illness befalls him you will make him well." NJV, with a marginal note that the meaning of the Hebrew is uncertain, translates "You will wholly transform his bed of suffering." Instead of using the second person **thou healest** in line <u>b</u>, TEV and others keep the third person used in line <u>a</u>.

41.4-5	RSV	TEV
4	As for me, I said, "O LORD, be gracious to me; heal me, for I have sinned against thee!"	4 I said, "I have sinned against you, LORD; be merciful to me and heal me."
5	My enemies say of me in malice: "When will he die, and his name perish?"	5 My enemies say cruel things about me. They want me to die and be forgotten.

The psalmist describes his condition (verses 4-9), reporting first his confession of sin to the Lord and his prayer for healing (verse 4). For **be gracious to me** see 4.1c and comments. This may be translated "have mercy on me," "take pity on me."

In verse 4b **heal me** translates "heal my *nefesh*" (see 3.2). The psalmist's sickness is the result of his sin, so in confessing his sin he asks for forgiveness and healing. RSV **heal me, for I have sinned** can be misunderstood to mean "God, you must heal me because I have sinned." The **for** is not intended to justify the request but to explain the psalmist's need for healing. A restructuring like the one used by TEV may be helpful.

Sinned against thee must often be recast, since sins are not always spoken of as being **against** God. Accordingly one must sometimes say, for example, "I have sinned and I have offended you, LORD."

The psalmist speaks of his enemies and their cruel taunts. As is common in psalms of lament, the enemies are not specifically identified, and one may only conjecture what was the reason for their hatred of the psalmist. **In malice** means either their attitude ("cruel, hateful") or else refers to what they say: "speak of bad things"; so SPCL "My enemies wish the worst for me."

In verse 5b TEV has put in indirect form what in Hebrew is a direct quotation: **"When will he die, and his name perish?"**

The last part, **his name perish**, may mean simply to die and be forgotten, as TEV has translated (see similar idea in 9.5-6; and see Anderson); or else, which would be worse, it may mean to die childless, leaving no descendants to carry on his name (so NEB "and his line become extinct"; also Dahood). **And his name perish** is difficult to translate in some languages, due to the passive nature of these constructions. One must sometimes say, for example, "they want me to die and people to forget me," or following the other interpretation, "they want me to die without leaving any children."

41.6-7 RSV	TEV
6 And when one comes to see me, he utters empty words, while his heart gathers mischief; when he goes out, he tells it abroad. 7 All who hate me whisper together about me; they imagine the worst for me.	6 Those who come to see me are not sincere; they gather bad news about me and then go out and tell it everywhere. 7 All who hate me whisper to each other about me, they imagine the worst about[P] me.

P imagine the worst about; *or* make evil plans to harm.

Continuing the description of his plight, the psalmist relates how his enemies, hypocrites all, come to see him. But they are really not concerned about him; their pious statements of sympathy and concern are false. All they want to do is find out bad news about him and then leave and spread it everywhere (verse 6).

Empty words seems to mean that their apparent care for the psalmist is false, and what they say does not come from a genuine concern for his welfare. NJB translates "their talk is hollow." **Utter empty words** may sometimes be rendered as "talk without good words" or "talk foolish words." The TEV expression **"not sincere"** can sometimes be translated positively as "double-hearted people" or "people with two tongues."

Line b **his heart gathers** is a bit strange. Some (see Anderson) take "his heart" with the preceding words, "his heart speaks hypocrisy." "Heart" has a variety of meanings; it can denote feeling or thinking, the interior character (as contrasted with the exterior behavior), or even stand for the whole person (as it seems to here). NJV translates line b "his mind stores up evil things," which may be followed; or else SPCL "they keep in mind all the bad things." TEV's **"Gather bad news"** must often be recast, since news in many languages is not something which can be said to be gathered. Accordingly one may often translate "they listen for bad news" or "they learn bad news."

All who hate me is another reference to the psalmist's enemies.

In verse 7b the meaning may be **they imagine the worst for me**, or as the TEV footnote has, "they make evil plans to harm me" (so Weiser, Dahood). The Hebrew verb may mean "imagine" or "plan" (see 35.4d, which is quite similar to this passage). SPCL takes **the worst** to mean that the enemies make the worst of the psalmist's situation, "they think I am suffering because of my guilt." **They imagine the worst for me** may sometimes be recast as "in their hearts they think up the worst things that can happen to me."

41.8 RSV	TEV
They say, "A deadly thing has fastened upon him;	They say, "He is fatally ill; he will never leave his bed

he will not rise again from where he lies."	again."

The first part of this verse in Hebrew is "a wicked thing is poured on him." It is unclear what is the precise force of the words. One suggestion is "An evil power attacks him," and NEB has "An evil spell is cast upon him"; these regard the evil thing either as a demon or as a spell. See also NJV "Something baneful has settled in him." "It is not impossible that the speakers had in mind a curse which, they believe, had been infused into the unfortunate man, operating like a fatal poison" (Anderson; similarly Weiser). Toombs and Taylor also see it as a sorcerer's formula. SPCL has "His illness is caused by the Devil." TEV, NJB, NAB take the phrase "a wicked thing" to mean a disease. **"Fatally ill"** can sometimes be rendered "He is ill and will soon die" or "He is ill and cannot get well again."

Line b means "he will not get well; he is going to die."

41.9 RSV	TEV
Even my bosom friend in whom I trusted, who ate of my bread, has lifted his heel against me.	Even my best friend, the one I trusted most, the one who shared my food, has turned against me.

My bosom friend translates "the man of my peace"; here the word *shalom* (in contrast with 29.11) probably involves the idea of a covenant; see NJV "My ally." Most translations have "My best friend."

Who ate of my bread may be rendered "who used to eat with me" or, as FRCL translates, "with whom I shared my bread." **Bread** stands for food in general.

The expression **lifted his heel against me** may express the idea of violence; most, however, see it in terms of an insult or of betrayal, treachery. NJV has "has been utterly false to me"; SPCL "has betrayed me"; FRCL "turned against me"; also possible is "took advantage of me." **Has lifted his heel against me** with the meaning of "betray" is sometimes expressed idiomatically as "one who eats with you and sells you." In this sense one may translate line b as "he has eaten with me and sold me" or "he has sold me as an enemy."

Part of this verse is used in John 13.18, as a reference to Judas Iscariot.

41.10-12 RSV	TEV
10 But do thou, O LORD, be gracious to me, and raise me up, that I may requite them! 11 By this I know that thou art pleased with me, in that my enemy has not tri-	10 Be merciful to me, LORD, and restore my health, and I will pay my enemies back. 11 They will not triumph over me, and I will know that you are pleased with me. 12 You will help me, because I do what is right;

umphed over me.
12 But thou hast upheld me because
of my integrity,
and set me in thy presence for
ever.

you will keep me in your presence forever.

The psalm closes with a prayer; the psalmist is confident that the Lord will answer him because of his, the psalmist's, righteous character.

For **be gracious** see comments on 4.1; **raise me up** means get me out of my sickbed, that is, restore me to health. The psalmist wants revenge (**requite**; see use of the term in 31.23; 35.12); he is sure that his enemies are the object of Yahweh's anger also.

In some languages **thou art pleased with me** must be recast to say "I have pleased you" or "I have made you glad."

For the psalmist the proof of Yahweh's favor is the defeat of his enemies (verse 11). TEV has reversed the order of the two lines of this verse, as a more natural order in English. **Triumphed** translates a verb that means "to shout in triumph." **My enemy has not triumphed over me** may be recast sometimes as direct speech by saying, for example, "because my enemy has not been able to say 'I have defeated you,' " or indirectly, "because you have not let my enemy say that he won the victory."

In verse 12 **my integrity** describes the psalmist as one who follows the Lord's will in everything (see 7.8c and comments). RSV translates the verbs in verse 12 as perfects, **thou hast upheld me . . . and set me**; SPCL translates them as petitions; FRCL and TEV as future tense; NEB as present tense. **Upheld** translates a verb meaning grab hold of, hold on to, in the sense of helping or rescuing, or else to hold up, to keep from falling (see its use in 16.5b; 63.8b).

The meaning of verse 12b, **in thy presence for ever**, is the same as expressed in 16.11 and 23.6. Anderson comments: "he will be restored to God's favour, and will enjoy his blessings as long as he lives." Some take the word **presence** (literally "face") here to mean the presence of Yahweh in the Temple.

Dahood takes the prayer to mean that the psalmist wants to be taken directly into the presence of Yahweh without dying, as were Enoch and Elijah, and there live forever, but this idea has not been proven. **In thy presence** must sometimes be translated "where you are," or "in the place where you are," or "in the place where people come to worship you."

41.13   RSV

TEV

Blessed be the LORD, the God of
Israel,
from everlasting to everlasting!
Amen and Amen.

Praise the LORD, the God of Israel!
Praise him now and forever!

Amen! Amen!

This verse is not part of the psalm; it marks rather the close of Book One (Psa 1–41). It is a doxology, in which in response to **Blessed be the LORD** (see comments on "bless" in 16.7; 18.46), the congregation answers **Amen and Amen**.

The expression **"Praise the LORD, the God of Israel"** (TEV) can mean in some languages that these are two different gods. Therefore in those cases one may say "the LORD, who is the God of Israel."

Amen and Amen is an expression which has been borrowed by many languages, usually with the meaning "that is the end of the prayer." The word **Amen** means "So be it" or "It shall be so"—a strong affirmation, expressing approval of and agreement with what has been said. If a translation is to be fully meaningful, even such terms as **Amen** should communicate their significance. In some languages it is best to avoid the borrowed form and introduce something equivalent to "This is certainly true" or "Indeed this is true."

Book Two

(Psalms 42–72)

Psalm 42

Psalms 42 and 43 were originally one psalm, composed of three strophes, all of which end with the same refrain (42.5,11; 43.5). It is a lament by a man who in exile longs to be back in Jerusalem and there at the Temple worship God once more. If the geographical data in 42.6 are taken literally, then the psalmist was living in the northern part of the country, near Mount Hermon; some, however, think that the geographical terms are meant figuratively and do not refer to actual places.

In the first strophe (42.1-5) the psalmist pours out his sorrow and his longing for the Temple, which he remembers so fondly (verse 4); the strophe ends with a determination to keep alive his hope in God (verse 5). In the second strophe (42.6-11) he again expresses his deep sorrow and his loneliness, tells of his enemies' cruel taunts, and once more affirms his hope in God in the closing refrain (verse 11). In the third strophe (43.1-5) he asks God to rescue him from his enemies and to take him back to the Temple in Jerusalem; once more he affirms his faith in God.

HEADING: TEV has "**The Prayer of a Man in Exile**" (with the indication that Psalm 43 is a continuation of Psalm 42); other headings are: "Desire for God and his temple"; "Lament of a Levite in exile"; "My hope is in God." The TEV heading can be recast in some languages to say "A man living away from his home prays to return" or "This is the prayer of a man who lives outside of his own country."

A translation should indicate in the heading that the two separate Psalms 42–43 are one composition, either as TEV has done, or else as NEB, NJB, SPCL have, with the one heading, "Psalms 42–43."

Hebrew Title: **To the choirmaster. A Maskil of the Sons of Korah** (TEV "**A poem by the clan of Korah**").

For **choirmaster** see title of Psalm 4; for **Maskil** see title of Psalm 32. **The Sons of Korah** probably indicates that the psalms with this title (42–49, 84, 85, 87, 88) originated in the group of Temple singers known as the Korahites. The word **Sons** here is used in the sense of "descendants" or "members," and a translation that represents this phrase will do better to say either "the clan of Korah" or else "the Korahites" (see NJV). FRCL has "confraternity of Korah."

398

	RSV		TEV
1	As a hart longs for flowing streams, so longs my soul for thee, O God.	1	As a deer longs for a stream of cool water, so I long for you, O God.
2	My soul thirsts for God, for the living God. When shall I come and behold the face of God?	2	I thirst for you, the living God. When can I go and worship in your presence?

It is to be noted that in this Book (Psa 42–72) the personal name of God, "Yahweh," is not often used; instead, the generic term "God" is regularly employed.

As a hart: a simile is sometimes used in Hebrew poetry as a structural feature marking the opening of a stanza; for examples, see Isaiah 54.9; Jeremiah 22.6; 46.7; 25.38; Ezekiel 19.10; Psalm 11.1b.

In English it is preferable to use the more general term **"deer"** (AT, TEV) rather than the masculine **hart** (RSV) or the feminine "hind" (NEB, NAB, NJV). The verb **longs for** in Hebrew is third person feminine, whereas the noun "deer" is masculine; Anderson, however, says that the same word is used of both the male and the female of the species.[1]

The psalmist compares his longing for the Temple, where he can worship God, to the desire a deer has **for flowing streams** (TEV **"a stream of cool water"**).

In verses 1b and 2a **my soul** (*nefesh*) means **"I"** (see discussion at 3.2); a more adequate translation may be "my whole being longs for you."

In some languages it will be necessary to restructure the order of the comparison or simile in this verse; for example, "I long for you, God, as a deer longs for a stream of cool water." In some language areas it will be necessary to substitute an equivalent wild animal for the deer.

My soul thirsts for . . . the living God: verse 2 follows naturally on verse 1, the psalmist using the verb **thirsts** as parallel to and a graphic synonym of **longs** in verse 1. God is called **the living God**, a way of distinguishing the God of Israel from the pagan gods, who were seen as powerless, impotent, dead. In some languages it is not possible to say "I thirst for you." Hence some adjustments will often be required; the most common ways are to use a simile or to use a nonfigurative expression. As a simile one may say, for example, "As a man thirsts for water, I need you." As a nonfigure one may say simply "I long deeply for you" or "I have great need of you."

In verse 2b the psalmist expresses his deep longing for the Temple with the plaintive question "When can I enter and see[2] the face of God?" which means

---

[1] HOTTP says the Hebrew word can be both masculine and feminine. "Here it is certainly feminine and means 'doe' or 'hind.' "

[2] HOTTP points out that the Masoretic text passive form, "be seen (by God)," meaning "to appear before God," represents a scribal correction (*tiqqun soferim*; see footnote 1 at 10.3) of the active form of the verb "see" in the original Hebrew text. Here "there exist ancient text witnesses for the original uncorrected reading," and

"When can I go to the Temple and worship there in God's presence?" To "see the face of God" describes a spiritual experience in which the worshiper realizes he or she is in the immediate presence of the God of Israel (see comment on 11.7). RSV **come** contrasts with TEV "**go**"; it seems preferable to assume that the psalmist is not in the Temple as he composes this poem, and therefore "**go**" is better. It is to be noticed that TEV keeps the second person of direct address to God in verses 1-2. RSV follows the Hebrew text by having the second person in verse 1 and the third person in verse 2.

42.3	RSV	TEV

RSV	TEV
My tears have been my food day and night, while men say to me continually, "Where is your God?"	Day and night I cry, and tears are my only food; all the time my enemies ask me, "Where is your God?"

The psalmist vividly portrays his intense grief with the statement that his tears have been his **food day and night**. In some languages tears cannot be spoken of as food, since they are liquid, or the verb which will be required to express food will have to show that the food in this case is liquid. In some languages one will have to say "my tears are all that I drink," and in others it is possible to say "the only food that I have is my tears."

In verse 3c TEV "**my enemies ask me**" translates "they say," which is the text of a few Hebrew manuscripts; the Masoretic text is "he says," a way of expressing "someone says" or "it is said" (and see also verse 11). NJV and NJB use the passive "I am taunted."

The question "**Where is your God?**" (also verse 10) seems to indicate that the psalmist's enemies are not Jews but Gentiles, who taunt the psalmist for his God's apparent inability to rescue him from his distress. The question means "Why doesn't your God help you?" FRCL has "What is your God doing?"

42.4	RSV	TEV

RSV	TEV
These things I remember, as I pour out my soul: how I went with the throng, and led them in procession to the house of God, with glad shouts and songs of thanksgiving, a multitude keeping festival.	My heart breaks when I remem- ber the past, when I went with the crowds to the house of God and led them as they walked along, a happy crowd, singing and shouting praise to God.

so the committee favors its adoption.

The psalmist's grief is especially sharp as he recalls how in the past he used to go with the crowds to the Temple during the festivals. **"My heart breaks"** translates the Hebrew "I pour out upon me my *nefesh*" (see comments at 3.2); one way of saying it is "I am heartbroken"; NEB has "As I pour out my soul in distress"; the Hebrew can mean "as I give expression to my pent-up feelings" (so Anderson; see SPCL).

I went: in Hebrew this means repeated action: "I used to go."

With the throng translates a word found nowhere else in the Old Testament, and its meaning is uncertain; **and led** also translates a Hebrew form of dubious meaning; the two together are translated by the Septuagint "in the place of the magnificent tabernacle." NEB and Weiser follow a wording found in some Hebrew manuscripts, "in the ranks of the great"; NJB, in part following the Septuagint, "under the roof of the Most High" (that is, the Temple). Most translations which follow the Masoretic text agree with RSV and TEV. Given the difficulty and obscurity of the Masoretic text, the translator may choose to follow the Septuagint, which Toombs translates "how I went into the tent of the Glorious One, in procession to the house of God."[3] It is recommended, however, that the translator imitate the RSV and TEV rendering.

With the throng or **"with the crowds"** must sometimes be rendered "with many people," "with great numbers of people," or idiomatically, "with many other bodies."

Led them in procession: this seems to indicate a group of religious pilgrims making their way to the Temple (**the house of God**) for one of the great annual festivals. **Led them** is sometimes said "I walked before them" or "they followed me as I went ahead." The expression **house of God** in many languages means the Christian church building. Therefore it will often be necessary to qualify the **house of God** so that it will refer to the Temple; for example, "the Jew's big house of God" or "the house of God in Jerusalem."

With glad shouts and songs of thanksgiving represents a combination of two nouns joined by "and," in which the first noun modifies the second—a form of hendiadys. In this case the two nouns can be translated as one event, "a joyful song of thanksgiving." It is often necessary to express the object of shouts and thanksgiving as TEV says, **"to God."**

In the last line, by changing a vowel in the Hebrew word translated **multitude**, it becomes the word for "sound"; so NEB "the clamour of pilgrims." This change, however, is not recommended.

Keeping festival: celebrating a festival, or in a festival procession. **Keeping festival** is a summary way of naming the events of singing and praising in the previous line. The final line of verse 4 may be rendered "many people together remembering the feast" or "crowds of people remembering the day for praising God."

---

[3]HOTTP takes the Masoretic text, as pointed, to mean "in the crowd"; with a change of vowels the Masoretic text means "under the hut," which HOTTP says is more probable and which it identifies with the covered portico mentioned in 2 Kings 16.18. HOTTP also endorses "I led them" as a translation of the second phrase.

42.5 RSV	TEV

| Why are you cast down, O my soul,
and why are you disquieted within me?
Hope in God; for I shall again praise him,
my help [6 and my God.] | Why am I so sad?
Why am I so troubled?
I will put my hope in God,
and once again I will praise him,
my savior and my God. |

RSV represents the form of the Hebrew text, in which the psalmist converses with himself (his *nefesh*). The two questions may be rhetorical, a way in which the psalmist rebukes himself for his sadness and discouragement (**cast down** and **disquieted**). So the translation can be "I shouldn't be so upset, I shouldn't be sad like this." Many languages will find the two questions awkward or unintelligible because they appear to be addressed to no one, and instead of a reply being given, TEV follows them with a statement. Therefore, to avoid possible misunderstanding, it will sometimes be necessary to say, for example, "I ask myself why I am so sad, why I am so troubled?" Or these may be said in direct discourse, "I ask myself 'Why am I so sad?' " or "I ask myself 'Why am I so troubled?' " In some languages it will be possible to say, very similarly to Hebrew, "I ask my heart, 'Why are you so sad?' " In languages where the question forms in this context are not natural, it is possible to recast them as positive statements; for example, "I am so very sad," "I am so very troubled."

The imperative (addressed to his "soul") **Hope in God** is represented by a strong vow in TEV, "**I will put my hope in God.**" FRCL translates "What good does it do for me to be sad, what good does it do for me to complain of my lot? It is better to hope in God . . . ."

The last line in TEV, "**my savior and my God,**" follows the text found in some Hebrew manuscripts (and in the Masoretic text of verse 11 and in 43.5) and is favored by HOTTP ("C" decision). The Masoretic text here is literally "the acts of salvation of his (God's) face, my God," with "my God" at the end of the line but as the beginning of verse 7, not the end of verse 6 (see RSV verse division). The Hebrew plural "acts of salvation" is taken as "salvation, deliverance," and "my face" is preferred to "his face." It also seems better, with TEV, to put the number 6 of the verse at the beginning of the next line.

My help and my God will in some languages be understood as two separate objects of praise. To avoid this possible confusion one may sometimes translate "my God, who is the one who helps me" or "my God, who has saved me."

42.6-7 RSV	TEV

| 6   and my God.

My soul is cast down within me,
therefore I remember thee
from the land of Jordan and of | 6-7   Here in exile my heart is breaking,
and so I turn my thoughts to him.
He has sent waves of sorrow over my soul; |

Hermon,
from Mount Mizar.

7 Deep calls to deep
at the thunder of thy cataracts;
all thy waves and thy billows
have gone over me.

chaos roars at me like a flood,
like waterfalls thundering down
to the Jordan
from Mount Hermon and
Mount Mizar.

As a comparison of RSV with TEV shows, there is considerable difference of opinion about the meaning of verses 6-7. In particular it is difficult to decide about (1) the geographical terms and (2) the meaning of God's **cataracts . . . waves . . . billows**. In verse 6 RSV gives the various clauses and phrases in the same order in which they occur in Hebrew; TEV (see also NEB) has taken **from the land of Jordan and of Hermon, from Mount Mizar** to go with the following **cataracts . . . waves . . . billows**, and not with the preceding **I remember thee** (TEV "I turn my thoughts to you"). TEV has also shifted to the third person, "him" and "he," in place of the second person, **thee** and **thy**. TEV does this in order to maintain the third person reference to God uniformly throughout the psalm.

The land of Jordan could be Canaan as a whole or else the region where the Jordan River rises. Mount Hermon is some 75 kilometers (45 miles) northeast of Lake Galilee, reaching the height of some 2750 meters (8940 feet); the Masoretic text plural "Hermons" is explained as a reference to the whole mountain range, or else to the three main peaks of the Hermon. **Mount Mizar** is unknown; the Hebrew *mits'ar* means "small" (as the Septuagint translates it here); some take it to be a lesser peak near Mount Hermon (GECL translates "the Hermon range with its peaks"); HOTTP recommends **Mizar**; others take it to refer to Mount Zion (see NJB "I think . . . of you, humble mountain.").

One of the difficulties with taking these three geographical terms as defining the psalmist's location arises from the fact that the **deep** (Hebrew *tehom*) is the primeval abyss, the depths of chaos, out of which the earth was formed (Gen 1.2). The statement **Deep calls to deep** is taken to be poetic language; like waterfalls which seem to roar at each other, so the forces of chaos summon other forces to overwhelm the psalmist. That this word **deep** should refer to the torrents of the Jordan River seems unlikely, although some commentators so interpret it. Together with **thy cataracts . . . waves . . . billows** of verse 7, it seems better to take this as figurative language for extreme distress and anxiety. The forces of chaos overwhelm him, and he is near death (see the similar use of these figures in Jonah 2.2). FRCL translates "You make the torrents roar, one flood calls to another, you make them all roll over me, I am completely submerged."

Dahood takes all terms to be mythological allusions to Sheol, the world of the dead. This is quite possible, but the translation should not indicate that this is what the figures mean.

The TEV expression **"sent waves of sorrow over my soul"** may be recast in some languages so that the imagery is preserved in a simile; for example, "he has caused me to feel sorrow like one feels the waves of the sea." In languages where "waves of the sea" are unknown, a different adjustment may be required; for example, it may be necessary to shift to another image: "he has made me feel sorrow like one carried away by a flooding stream."

In many languages it will not be possible to say as in TEV "**chaos roars at me like a flood.**" Such an expression will often require major adjustments; for example, "I hear the roar of confusion; it is like the noise of a flood" or "I hear the noise of confusion which is like the noise of a flood. It is like the rumble of waterfalls falling down from Mount Hermon and Mount Mizar to the Jordan River."

42.8   RSV   TEV

> By day the LORD commands his   May the LORD show his constant
>   steadfast love;   love during the day,
> and at night his song is with   so that I may have a song at
>   me,   night,
> a prayer to the God of my life.   a prayer to the God of my life.

TEV, like NJV and FRCL, takes this verse to be a request; others (RSV, NIV, NJB, NEB, NAB, TOB, SPCL) take it as a statement. Either is possible and the translator should feel free to choose.

In verse 8 what little parallelism exists depends entirely upon the pair **By day** in line <u>a</u> and **at night** in line <u>b</u>. Because of the logical nature of the day–night parallel, the two lines are felt to be balanced. There is a sense of continuity and completion in the use of this pair of words, equivalent to saying "all the time." In translation the poetic order of day and night may have to be reversed in some languages to obtain the equivalent poetic effect. The TEV rendering has moved "**day**" and "**night**" to the end of the lines and thereby shifted the focus to the verbs.

In line <u>a</u> the expression **commands his steadfast love** means "orders his steadfast love to go" (to the psalmist). NAB has "bestows." As a statement this says "by day the Lord shows his constant love for me" (SPCL "By day the Lord sends me his love"); as a request, see TEV. For **steadfast love** see comments on 5.7.

As a consequence of Yahweh's constant love, the psalmist has a song at night, which is in effect a prayer offered to God. **His song is with me** means "I sing a song to him" (see NJV) or "I have a song I (can) sing to him."

The God of my life in line <u>c</u> means "the God who rules my (or, gives me) life." The expression **God of my life** will often require making explicit the relation between God and life; for example, "the God who gives me life" (GECL, FRCL) or "the God who causes me to live."

42.9-10   RSV   TEV

9   I say to God, my rock: 9   To God, my defender, I say,
>   "Why hast thou forgotten me?   "Why have you forgotten me?
>   Why go I mourning   Why must I go on suffering
>   because of the oppression of the   from the cruelty of my ene-
>   enemy?"   mies?"
10 As with a deadly wound in my   10 I am crushed by their insults,
>   body,   as they keep on asking me,
>   my adversaries taunt me,   "Where is your God?"

while they say to me continually,
"Where is your God?"

In verse 9a, for **my rock** see translation and comments at 18.2; 31.2,3.

In perplexity the psalmist wonders why he must go on suffering, and asks God, **Why hast thou forgotten me?** (see similar expressions in 13.1; 22.1). This is a complaint, not a request for information.

For **mourning** in verse 9 see comments at 35.14; 38.6. The psalmist's sorrow is caused by the cruelty of his enemies. **Oppression** is not used very often in the psalms to characterize the psalmists' enemies (43.2; 44.24); the translation can be "persecution."

In verse 10a the Hebrew has "with a crushing of my bones"; the Hebrew verb usually means "to kill," so RSV translates **deadly wound**. Whatever the precise meaning of the words, the general thought is clear enough: the psalmist's enemies, with their jeers and taunts, threaten to make an end of him.[4] FRCL translates "Here I am completely crushed by their insults." In some languages it will be possible to preserve some of the imagery of the Hebrew in line a; for example, "I am pained to the bones" or, as in SPCL, "even my bones ache."

For the end of verse 10 see similar ending of verse 3.

42.11   RSV   TEV

Why are you cast down, O my
   soul,
   and why are you disquieted
   within me?
Hope in God; for I shall again
   praise him,
   my help and my God.

Why am I so sad?
   Why am I so troubled?
I will put my hope in God,
   and once again I will praise
   him,
   my savior and my God.

This verse is exactly like verse 5.

---

[4]HOTTP translates "with death in my bones" and says two interpretations are possible: "it is a deadly wound in my bones" or "because a deadly wound is in my bones."

Psalm 43

See Introduction to Psalm 42.

43.1

RSV	TEV
Vindicate me, O God, and defend my cause against an ungodly people; from deceitful and unjust men deliver me!	O God, declare me innocent, and defend my cause against the ungodly; deliver me from lying and evil men!

The psalmist prays God to deliver him from his enemies. The language used is that of the law court (see the same terms, "vindicate" and "my cause," used in 35.23-24). From the text itself one cannot decide whether the language is to be taken literally or is conventional, that is, a way of asking God to help him against his enemies who torment him with their taunts (42.3,10). The latter seems more probable.

The text does not make clear whether the **ungodly people** are Gentiles or faithless Jews. The phrase is literally "a people not-godly" (see "godly" in 4.3). The Hebrew *goy* (meaning "people") is a collective noun and often means "a nation" (so one possibility is "a disloyal nation"; Dahood "an ungodly nation"; NEB "an impious race"; SPCL "this pagan people"). FRCL, however, has "people who have no pity" (so Briggs "unkind nations"). In the context of the whole psalm (Psa 42⁻43) it seems more likely that pagan Gentiles are meant, who are further characterized as **deceitful and unjust,** that is "treacherous and dishonest" (NJB) or "liars and evildoers" (FRCL). The expression **ungodly people** may often be translated "people who do not worship God." For **deliver** see the same verb in 17.13.

43.2

RSV	TEV
For thou art the God in whom I take refuge; why hast thou cast me off? Why go I mourning because of the oppression of the enemy?	You are my protector; why have you abandoned me? Why must I go on suffering from the cruelty of my enemies?

The psalmist appeals to God as his protector, **in whom I take refuge** (see the same expression in 2.12; 18.2; 31.4), and asks, **why hast thou cast me off?** (see same verb in 44.9,23). To **cast off** means to reject, repel, abandon, discard. Again, this is a complaint, not a request for information.

The psalmist then repeats the question of 42.9.

43.3-4	RSV	TEV

3	Oh send out thy light and thy truth;
	  let them lead me,
	let them bring me to thy holy hill
	  and to thy dwelling!
		3	Send your light and your truth;
			  may they lead me
			  and bring me back to Zion,
			  your sacred hill,*r*
			  and to your Temple, where you live.

4	Then I will go to the altar of God,
	  to God my exceeding joy;
	and I will praise thee with the lyre,
	  O God, my God.
		4	Then I will go to your altar, O God;
			  you are the source of my happiness.
			I will play my harp and sing praise to you,
			  O God, my God.

r SACRED HILL: *See 2.6.*

The psalmist prays that God will send his **light** and **truth** which, like guides, will lead him from exile back to Mt. Zion (**thy holy hill**) and into the Temple (**thy dwelling**), where he will go to the altar and offer a sacrifice of thanksgiving. In many languages it is not possible to speak of sending light and truth. In such cases it will sometimes be necessary to say "show your light to me and speak your truth" or "shine your light for me and speak your true words to me."

Bring me: it would be better if both RSV and TEV had "take me (back)," since the psalmist is not in Israel. TEV has introduced the name "**Zion**" so the reader will know that **thy holy hill** is, in fact, Mt. Zion. **Thy dwelling** is a way of speaking about the Temple. **Thy holy hill** is expressed in some languages as "the hill which is dedicated to you" or "the hill which belongs only to you."

In verse 4 the Masoretic text has **the altar of God** (so RSV); a few Hebrew manuscripts have "**your altar, O God**" (so TEV). It is recommended that translators follow the Masoretic text. The expression **the altar of God** must be rendered in some languages as "the place where people worship God."

In verse 4b **God, my exceeding joy** means "God, who makes me very happy." TEV's "**you are the source of my happiness**" can be rendered in some languages as "you are the one who makes me happy" or idiomatically "you are the one who makes my heart quiet."

For **lyre** see 33.2a. Where the harp is unknown, a local stringed instrument must be substituted, and where no stringed instrument is known, a generic term such as "musical instrument" can be used.

43.3-4

In many languages it is not possible to speak of **my God** as though God were someone's possession. In such cases one may often say, for example, "O God, the God I worship."

43.5   RSV   TEV

Why are you cast down, O my   Why am I so sad?
    soul,   Why am I so troubled?
  and why are you disquieted   I will put my hope in God,
    within me?   and once again I will praise
Hope in God; for I shall again   him,
    praise him,   my savior and my God.
  my help and my God.

See 42.5,11.

Psalm 44

This psalm expresses the people of Israel's distress over a military defeat. The tone is extremely bitter; the psalmist stresses the people's devotion to God and blames him for their defeat. God's action was unjust, and the psalmist cannot understand why God has abandoned his people. Oesterley observes that the irreverent attitude of the psalm toward God (see especially verses 9-12) kept it from being used in the synagogue worship.

The writer (verses 4, 6, 15) either is or speaks in the name of the leader, the king; it is impossible, however, to determine who he was. Nor is there any agreement as to which military defeat would have occasioned this strong protest.

The psalm opens with a description of the great things that God had done for his people in the past (verses 1-3), followed by a song of praise in which the psalmist expresses his confidence in God's power to save (verses 4-8). Then comes the vivid description of the people's present distress (verses 9-16), which the psalmist finds difficult to understand, because they have been loyal to God (verses 17-22). The psalm ends with a fervent cry to God to take action and save his people (verses 23-26).

HEADING: **"A Prayer for Protection."** Other headings are "Wake up, O Lord!"; "National lament"; "Cast off by God?" The TEV heading may require a slight adjustment; for example, "The psalmist asks God to protect him."

Hebrew Title: **To the choirmaster. A Maskil of the Sons of Korah** ("A poem by the clan of Korah").
See title of Psalm 42.

44.1-2	RSV		TEV
1	We have heard with our ears, O God, 　our fathers have told us, what deeds thou didst perform in 　their days, 　in the days of old:	1	With our own ears we have heard 　it, O God— 　our ancestors have told us 　about it, about the great things you did in 　their time, 　in the days of long ago:
2	thou with thy own hand didst 　drive out the nations, 　but them thou didst plant; thou didst afflict the peoples, 　but them thou didst set free;	2	how you yourself drove out the 　heathen 　and established your people in 　their land; how you punished the other na-

409

**tions
and caused your own to prosper.**

The psalm opens with a reminder to God of all the great things that God had done for the people of Israel, particularly how he had driven the heathen nations from the land of Canaan and let Israel occupy it (verses 2-3). The psalmist concentrates on the military victories which God had given his people in the past (**in their days, in the days of old**), because it is a recent disastrous military defeat that causes the psalmist to compose his lament.

Our fathers in verse 1b means "**our ancestors**."

If the translator follows the structure of TEV in verse 1, some recasting may be required, since the referent of "it" in lines a and b occurs in line c. It will be necessary therefore in many languages to place line c first, to be followed by lines a and b; for example, "You did great things for our ancestors when they lived, O God; with our ears we have heard about them, they have told us about them."

With thy own hand means "by means of your own power (or, strength)."

Drive out the nations: this refers to the expulsion of the various Canaanite peoples (**the nations . . . the peoples**) from the land of Canaan as the Israelites, under the leadership of Joshua, invaded the land. The term "**heathen**" or **nations** is rendered in some languages "the people who worship false gods."

In verse 2b the verb **plant** is used figuratively of settling the people of Israel in Canaan (see Exo 15.17; 2 Sam 7.10; Jer 11.17).

The Hebrew term translated **the peoples** and "**the other nations**" is often rendered as "the tribes." The verb translated **afflict** (verse 2c) means literally "to do evil to"—a strong word; and **set free** translates the verb "send out," which is probably the figure of a vigorous tree whose branches grow and spread out, a figure of prosperity (so TEV "**caused . . . to prosper**"). Dahood and NEB take it in the sense of "send out roots," the idea of firmness, stability; NJV takes the verb to refer to the heathen nations, "you drove them out," but the structure of the verse seems to favor taking the Israelites as the object of the verb. TEV's "**caused your own to prosper**" may in some languages be translated "you made your own people have good things" or "you gave good gifts to your own people."

44.3   RSV   TEV

for not by their own sword did
  they win the land,
nor did their own arm give
  them victory;
but thy right hand, and thy arm,
  and the light of thy countenance;
for thou didst delight in them.

Your people did not conquer the
  land with their swords;
they did not win it by their own
  power;
it was by your power and your
  strength,
by the assurance of your presence,
which showed that you loved
  them.

It was God who gave the people of Israel the victory; it was not **their own sword** or **their own arm** that made them victorious; it was God's mighty power and strength (literally **right hand . . . arm**), his favor, his goodness, **the light of thy countenance**; see 4.6). This may be translated "by your constant presence with them" or "because you were always with them."

The expression **not by their own sword** implies that there is some other power that should have the honor for winning battles, even though they did use their swords in warfare to win the land. In some languages where there is no term for sword, one may translate "your people did not win the land with their weapons." Where it is possible to use the term **sword** the expression **by their own sword** requires in some languages that the instrumental use be made explicit; for example, "by fighting with their swords." TEV "**by their own power**" must in some languages be said "because they were strong" or "because they did powerful things."

The expression **the light of thy countenance** and "**your presence**" must sometimes be translated "because they were assured that you were with them."

Thou didst delight in them: "you were pleased with them," "**you loved them**" (so GECL, FRCL, SPCL). Most translations are like RSV, **for**, which gives the reason for the Israelites' victories; FRCL has this line as an additional item, joined to the two preceding lines, "and you loved them."

44.4-5	RSV	TEV

4   Thou art my King and my God,
    who ordainest[e] victories for
    Jacob.
5   Through thee we push down our
    foes;
    through thy name we tread
    down our assailants.

4   You are my king and my God;
    you give[t] victory to your people,
5   and by your power we defeat
    our enemies.

[e] Gk Syr: Heb *Thou art my King, O God; ordain*

[t] *Some ancient translations* and my God; you give; *Hebrew* O God; give.

Speaking for himself (verses 4, 6) and for his people (verses 5, 7-8), the psalmist again affirms his faith that it is God who gives victory to his people.

In verse 4 the Masoretic text is, as the TEV and RSV footnotes show, "You are my king, O God; give victory to Jacob." While this is possible (followed by NJV, TOB, SPCL), the text of the versions (Septuagint, Syriac, Vulgate) seems better in the context and is preferred by TEV, RSV, AT, NIV, FRCL, NEB, BJ, NJB.[1]

In some languages the expression **Thou art my king and my God** must be recast to say, for example, "You are the king I serve and you are the God I worship" or "You are the king who rules over me and the God I worship."

---

[1]HOTTP follows, in part, the ancient versions and recommends "God commanding" (instead of the Masoretic text "God, command"), which it translates as follows: "(it is you, my king, who) are God, deciding."

The Hebrew verb translated **ordainest** means "to command," "to decide to give." The ultimate source of victory is God's decision to make his people win. **Jacob** is a way of speaking of the people of Israel.

Verse 5 has two synonymous parallel lines (see RSV), which TEV has combined and shortened into one. **Through thee** and **through thy name** (see "name" in 5.11) both mean **"by your power,"** by your help. The two verbs **push down** and **tread down** mean to "defeat"; FRCL "we repel . . . we tread upon" (see similar language in 18.38); and **our foes** and **our assailants** are completely synonymous. The verbs evoke a picture of a wild ox goring its opponent (NJV "we gore"; Dahood "we butted"). The expression **through thee we push down our foes** is an event done by the people and through the instrumentality of God. In some languages it is necessary to say, for example, "we defeat our enemies and you enable us to do this" or "because you are powerful we defeat our enemies."

The nature of the parallelism in verse 5 is that of specification in which intensification results. In line <u>a</u> the enemies are "pushed down," but in line <u>b</u> they are dealt with more severely, "trampled down." The two lines may be translated, for example, "You enable us to push our enemies to the ground and even to trample them to death." Translators should consider the dynamic movement between two parallel lines as an essential part of their meaning, and avoid combining and shortening unless there is no alternative.

The translator must decide if the switching between first person singular and first person plural pronouns is an acceptable style in the receptor language. If it is not, and if it will create difficulty in understanding, it will be better to use only the plural pronoun throughout.

44.6-8   RSV   TEV

6   For not in my bow do I trust,
      nor can my sword save me.
	6 I do not trust in my bow
	      or in my sword to save me;

7   But thou hast saved us from our foes,
      and hast put to confusion those who hate us.
	7 but you have saved us from our enemies
	      and defeated those who hate us.

8   In God we have boasted continually,
      and we will give thanks to thy name for ever.   *Selah*
	8 We will always praise you
	      and give thanks to you forever.

In verse 6 the psalmist reaffirms in the first person singular what he had already said in the third person plural in verse 3a,b. The expression **not in my bow do I trust** is an example of a part of a weapon standing for the whole weapon. In some cases it will be necessary to say both "bow and arrows," or if these are unknown, to use the generic "weapon."

In verse 7 **put to confusion** translates the verb meaning "to put to shame" (see 6.10 and comment). It is the shame of defeat that is meant. **Our foes** and **those who hate us** are synonymous.

In verse 8a the verb translated **we have boasted** (see 10.3) can also mean "praise." To boast **in God** means either "to boast of what God has done" or "to be proud of God" (SPCL); or else, "to praise God." Again, in verse 8b, **thy name** stands for "**you.**"

For *Selah* see 3.2.

44.9-10	RSV		TEV
9	Yet thou hast cast us off and abased us, and hast not gone out with our armies.	9	But now you have rejected us and let us be defeated; you no longer march out with our armies.
10	Thou hast made us turn back from the foe; and our enemies have gotten spoil.	10	You made us run from our enemies, and they took for themselves what was ours.

After recalling what God had done for his people in the past, the psalmist now turns to the present. He accuses God of abandoning his people, of deserting them, of letting them be defeated by their enemies. For **cast . . . off** see 43.2. The TEV expression "**you have rejected us**" may sometimes be rendered "you have turned your back on us" or "you have said 'No' to us." **Abased us**: "disgraced us," "put us to shame," "humiliated us" (see comments on "put to . . . shame" in 35.4). The passive construction in TEV "**you . . . let us be defeated**" must be rendered in some languages as an active construction supplying the subject; for example, "you let our enemies defeat us."

In vivid terms he says that God no longer goes out with the Israelite troops to fight the enemy. The Hebrew word for armies recalls the title of God as "Lord of hosts" (see 24.10). The Covenant Box, which accompanied the Israelite army, was the symbol and guarantee of Yahweh's presence with them (see Num 10.35; 1 Sam 4.3). **Armies** is sometimes rendered "soldier companies," or "groups of soldiers," or "companies of fighters."

Because God deserted them, the Israelites fled from their enemies, who captured as **spoil** the belongings and weapons of the Israelites.

44.11-12	RSV		TEV
11	Thou hast made us like sheep for slaughter, and hast scattered us among the nations.	11	You allowed us to be slaughtered like sheep; you scattered us in foreign countries.
12	Thou hast sold thy people for a trifle, demanding no high price for them.	12	You sold your own people for a small price as though they had little value.*u*

^{u} as ... value; *or* and made no profit from the sale.

Verse 11 reports the killing of the Israelites in battle: they were slaughtered **like sheep** and the survivors were taken as prisoners of war to foreign countries. The psalmist continues to insist that God is responsible for these tragic defeats. The TEV expression **"foreign countries"** can sometimes be translated "far away where the other tribes live."

The expression **sold thy people** is a common figure of speech in the Old Testament. If in translation one must indicate to whom the people have been sold, the implication is "sold thy people as slaves to their enemies."

In particularly bitter terms (verse 12) the psalmist says that God has sold his own people **for a trifle**, that is, for an insignificant amount. The second line of verse 12 can be taken to mean "you did not ask a large amount for them" (see RSV) or "you made no profit from the sale" (TEV footnote; see NJB, NEB, NIV, SPCL, FRCL); the latter is probably the best way to translate this line. The verse accuses God of having little, if any, feeling for his people. As Oesterley comments, "Such irreverent sarcasm is without parallel in the psalms."

44.13-14   RSV   TEV

	RSV	TEV
13	Thou hast made us the taunt of our neighbors, the derision and scorn of those about us.	Our neighbors see what you did to us, and they mock us and laugh at us.
14	Thou hast made us a byword among the nations, a laughingstock^f among the peoples.	You have made us a joke among the nations; they shake their heads at us in scorn.

^{f} Heb *a shaking of the head*

The psalmist uses various synonymous terms to describe how neighboring peoples (**our neighbors**) deride and taunt the Israelites for their shameful defeat: **taunt, derision, scorn** (verse 13). In verse 13a the Hebrew is literally "You made us the scorn of our neighbors" (see RSV), which means that the attitude of Israel's pagan neighbors is the result of what God has done to Israel (verses 9-12)—which TEV has represented by "**Our neighbors see what you did to us, and they mock us ....**"

Our neighbors should not be translated in a way as to refer to the people who live next door, nor as mankind in general, but to the people of the other tribes, namely, the Gentiles. Hence one can often say "the other tribes that live around us."

Verse 13 in Hebrew is a case of gender-matched parallelism, in that line a has **taunt** (feminine) and **neighbors** (masculine), while line b has **derision and scorn** (masculine) and "neighborhood" (feminine). Cross gender is used in this manner to make the statement emphatic. Translators should use the poetic devices that are normal for emphasis in the receptor language.

A byword (verse 14a) translates the Hebrew word for "proverb, saying"; in this context it means that Israel is used as a joke, a term of contempt and mockery (see 1 Kgs 9.7; Jer 24.9). **Thou hast made us a byword** can in some languages be translated as "you have made of us two small words" or "you have made us a story to laugh at."

In verse 14b, as the RSV footnote shows, the Israelites have become "a shaking of the head" to their Gentile neighbors. This is a gesture of scorn. All these words are indicative of the attitude of Israel's Gentile neighbors.

44.15-16

RSV	TEV
15 All day long my disgrace is before me,	15 I am always in disgrace; I am covered with shame
and shame has covered my face,	16 from hearing the sneers and insults
16 at the words of the taunters and revilers,	of my enemies and those who hate me.
at the sight of the enemy and the avenger.	

In these verses the psalmist describes his own sense of **disgrace** and **shame** over his people's pitiful condition. **Shame has covered my face** is rendered in some languages, for example, "they have taken away my praise" or "they have caused my face to burn."

In verse 16a "from the voice of" (RSV **at the words of**) refers to the enemies' actual presence; it can be represented by something like "from being confronted by . . . ."

In verse 16b TEV has "**my**" and "**me**" as the object of the enemies' hatred (also NEB, NIV); the Hebrew text has no explicit object, however, and it could well be "our" and "us," that is, the people of Israel, not the psalmist personally.

For **enemy** and **avenger** in verse 16b see 8.2 and comments.

44.17

RSV	TEV
All this has come upon us,	All this has happened to us,
though we have not forgotten thee,	even though we have not forgotten you
or been false to the covenant.	or broken the covenant you made with us.

The psalmist affirms Israel's faithfulness: the people have not **forgotten** God, that is, have not disregarded God's laws, nor have they **been false to the covenant** he had made with them; yet God has severely punished them. As interpreted by RSV, TEV, NAB, and others, the meaning is that God has punished his people even though they had done nothing to merit such treatment. As interpreted by NEB, NJV, Dahood, and others, even though God had punished the people, yet they are not disloyal to him. Either interpretation is allowed by the context and the form of the Hebrew text; the former seems preferable. Anderson says both may be in view.

In some languages it will be preferable to give the ground first and then the result; for example, "We have not forgotten you nor broken the covenant you made with us, yet in spite of all that, this has happened to us."

The term **covenant** is often translated by terms meaning "treaty" or "agreement" (see 25.10). There is little problem in this context because it is clear (in TEV) that the treaty has been God's initiative.

44.18-19　　　RSV　　　　　　　　　　　　　　　TEV

18　Our heart has not turned back,　　18　We have not been disloyal to you;
　　　nor have our steps departed　　　　　we have not disobeyed your
　　　from thy way,　　　　　　　　　　　commands.
19　that thou shouldst have broken us　19　Yet you left us helpless among
　　　in the place of jackals,　　　　　　wild animals;
　　　and covered us with deep　　　　　you abandoned us in deepest
　　　darkness.　　　　　　　　　　　　darkness.

In verse 18 RSV gives the literal form of the Hebrew, **our heart . . . our steps**, which TEV has represented by "**disloyal to you . . . disobeyed your commands.**"

In verse 19 **the place of jackals** and **deep darkness** are figures of desolation and death. **Broken** translates a verb meaning "to crush" (see the passive form in 38.8), and the whole line may be taken to mean "you crushed us and made us a haunt for jackals" (NIV), that is, a wild, uninhabited place. Or else TEV (and FRCL) may be followed.

In the place of the Masoretic text **jackals** (*tannim*), some Hebrew manuscripts have *tannin* "dragon," a reference to the mythological monster of the primeval chaos (see 74.13); so NJV "though You cast us, crushed, to where the sea monster is"; another possible version is "You have crushed us as the Dragon was crushed"; NEB has "sea-serpent"; NAB and SPCL follow the Septuagint "a place of misery."[2] Most translators will find it more intelligible to speak of **jackals** or "**wild animals**" than of dragons. In some languages "river snake" or "sea snake" may be used to translate "dragon," but more often such terms refer to a literal snake. In the Orient the dragon is associated with good fortune. It is sometimes possible to say "a terrible serpent" or "a frightening reptile." Often a note is required if a translation for "dragon" is used. The whole line is a vivid picture of death; the word translated **deep darkness** appears also in 23.4; so NEB here "the darkness of death."

44.20-21　　　RSV　　　　　　　　　　　　　　　TEV

20　If we had forgotten the name of　20　If we had stopped worshiping our
　　　our God,　　　　　　　　　　　　God

---

[2]HOTTP prefers the Masoretic text, "jackals" ("C" decision).

or spread forth our hands to a strange god,	and prayed to a foreign god,
21 would not God discover this? For he knows the secrets of the heart.	21 you would surely have discovered it, because you know our secret thoughts.

Still affirming his people's innocence, the psalmist says that they have not **forgotten the name of our God**, that is, have not stopped worshiping him. For **name** see 5.11. The literal translation of line a will in most languages mean only that the people are not intelligent enough to remember God's name. Therefore the sense of worship should be translated. The expression **our God** must be translated in some languages as "the God whom we worship," since God sometimes cannot be spoken of as being possessed. In this verse it may be appropriate to say, for example, "if we had stopped worshiping you, God."

The gesture of "spreading out the hands" (verse 20b) is that of prayer. In languages where a gesture representing prayer can be expressed, it will be advisable to do so. However, if such gestures, such as "bow the face before," "kneel before" are too limited in their usage, it is better to use the term for prayer. In some languages it is possible to maintain the gesture and to add the word prayer; for example, "we bowed our heads in prayer."

The Israelites had not prayed to false gods (**strange** here means "foreign, of another people"). The expression **a strange god** must often be translated as "gods whom foreign tribes worship."

The rhetorical question (verse 20-21a) is a way of making a strong affirmation: **If we had forgotten . . . would not God discover this?** is a way of saying "If we had quit worshiping God . . . he would certainly have known it." God would have known of his people's idolatry, if they had been guilty of it, because he knows all **the secrets of the heart**. This expression must in some languages be rendered by other idiomatic forms; for example, "white words kept in the stomach" or by nonidiomatic expressions such as in TEV.

44.22 RSV TEV

Nay, for thy sake we are slain all the day long, and accounted as sheep for the slaughter.	But it is on your account that we are being killed all the time, that we are treated like sheep to be slaughtered.

Instead of being unfaithful to God, the people had been faithful, and for this very reason they had been killed, they had been treated as though they were **sheep for the slaughter** (see verse 11a). This made it even harder to understand that God should have punished his people as he did.

For thy sake does not mean here, as the English phrase usually does, that it was "for the benefit" of God that the Israelites had been slaughtered; it was because of their devotion to him (TEV "**on your account**") that they had been defeated and killed. The expression **for thy sake** may be variously translated; for example, "because of you," "because we follow you," or "because we belong to you."

In some languages it will be necessary to shift from the passive to the active in the expression **we are slain**. In this case it will be necessary to introduce a new subject; for example, "our enemies are killing us." The phrase **all the day long** means "all the time," continually. FRCL translates "every day we run the risk of dying."

Since **sheep** figure so dominantly in both the Old and New Testaments, it is assumed that the translator will not need to substitute another animal in the place of sheep. If supplementary information is required for the reader, this may be given in a glossary.

This verse is quoted by Paul in Romans 8.36.

44.23-24   RSV   TEV

	RSV		TEV
23	Rouse thyself! Why sleepest thou, O Lord? Awake! Do not cast us off for ever!	23	Wake up, Lord! Why are you asleep? Rouse yourself! Don't reject us forever!
24	Why dost thou hide thy face? Why dost thou forget our afflic- tion and oppression?	24	Why are you hiding from us? Don't forget our suffering and trouble!

The psalm closes with an urgent cry to God to take action and free his people from their sufferings. Similar protests and requests are to be found in 7.6; 13.1; 27.9; 35.22-23; 59.5; 74.1.

The vivid expressions used—as though God could be sleeping, as though he would hide himself, as though he had forgotten his people in their **affliction and oppression**—should not be weakened in translation. This is a desperate cry born from deepest despair and bewilderment. The rhetorical questions in verses 23a, 24a,b are not requests for information; they are bitter complaints against God's apparent indifference to and neglect of his people as they suffer and die.

For **cast . . . off** see verse 9.

In some languages it will make little sense to speak of God "forgetting our affliction." It is often necessary to speak rather in positive terms; for example, "Help us because we are suffering and our enemies oppress us" or "Listen to us as we suffer and stop our enemies from oppressing us."

44.25-26   RSV   TEV

	RSV		TEV
25	For our soul is bowed down to the dust; our body cleaves to the ground.	25	We fall crushed to the ground; we lie defeated in the dust.
26	Rise up, come to our help! Deliver us for the sake of thy steadfast love!	26	Come to our aid! Because of your constant love save us!

In verse 25 the picture could be that of people bowed down in prayer and supplication (so Taylor, Weiser, Dahood); it seems more likely, however, as TEV has interpreted it, that it is a picture of complete humiliation and defeat.

In both lines **our soul** (*nefesh*, see 3.2) and **our body** are ways of speaking of persons. The picturesque **our body cleaves to the ground** may not be a natural expression in many languages (just as it isn't in English). NEB has "lie prone on the earth", NJD "lie prone on the ground", and Knox has the best rendering of all: "prostrate, we cannot lift ourselves from the ground."

With a final appeal to God's **steadfast love** (see comments on 5.7), the psalmist asks God to take action and save his people. **Deliver** translates the verb which in 25.22 is translated "redeem." See comments there. **For the sake of** in verse 26b means "on account of (your constant love)," that is, "because you love us." The expression **for the sake of thy steadfast love** must often be rendered in translation by a verb phrase; for example, "help us because you have always loved us faithfully."

Psalm 45

This psalm celebrates the wedding of a Hebrew king and a foreign princess. Its author (verse 1) was probably the court poet. It is impossible to identify the king to which the poem is dedicated, or his bride. The mention of "the people of Tyre" in verse 12 is taken by many to indicate that the bride was from that city, and some (see Toombs) identify her as Jezebel, the bride of King Ahab of Israel (see 1 Kgs 16.31).

According to modern categories, this is the most "secular" of all the psalms. Some believe that its inclusion in the final collection is due to the fact that it was later interpreted by Jewish teachers as a messianic psalm (as evidenced by the interpretation of verse 2 in the Targum); according to this view, the king is the Messiah and his bride is Israel.

After the opening dedication (verse 1), the psalm addresses itself to the king (verses 2-9), who is praised in extravagant terms; then the poet addresses the bride (verses 10-15), after which he brings his poem to a conclusion with a final promise to the king (verses 16-17).

This psalm has a minimum of semantic parallelism. Each line is a statement, and apart from verses 12-14 the second line does not emphasize the idea of the first line.

HEADING: Most translations, like TEV, have "**A Royal Wedding Song**"; NAB, however, following later interpretation, has "Nuptial ode for the messianic king." This title will require adaptation in some languages; for example, it may be necessary to say "A song the people sing when a king takes a wife."

Hebrew Title: **To the choirmaster: according to Lilies. A Maskil of the Sons of Korah; a love song** (TEV "**A poem by the clan of Korah; a love song**").

For **choirmaster** see title of Psalm 4; for **A Maskil of the Sons of Korah** see title of Psalm 42. The musical notation **according to Lilies** (which appears also in the titles of Psalms 69 and 80) probably identifies the tune to which the poem was to be sung. The word is taken to be the plural of the Hebrew for "lily," but this is not certain. Some take it to refer to a six-sided musical instrument. **A love song** is not used in any other psalm title.

45.1	RSV	TEV
	My heart overflows with a goodly theme; I address my verses to the king; my tongue is like the pen of a ready scribe.	Beautiful words fill my mind, as I compose this song for the king. Like the pen of a good writer my tongue is ready with a poem.

420

The psalmist begins by stating the nature and purpose of his composition. First (line a) he describes his own feeling as he gets ready to write: his heart is stirred up by the beautiful poem he is about to compose.

Overflows translates a verb that may mean "stir up, excite" ("My heart is stirred by a noble theme").

Goodly theme translates "a good word," variously represented by "a noble theme" (NEB, NIV), "beautiful words" (TEV, SPCL, TOB), or "beautiful speech" (FRCL).

In some languages it is not possible to represent the Hebrew **My heart overflows** nor TEV **"words fill my mind"** without some adaptation. Sometimes it is possible to say idiomatically "My heart is full of good words" or "My heart is speaking good words."

My verses (TEV **"this song"**) translates what is literally "my deeds" in the Masoretic text; with different vowels the Hebrew word can be read as "my deed." Most translate "my poem"; NEB has "the song I have made."

The composition is dedicated to **the king**, and the psalmist compares himself to **the pen of a ready scribe**. The word translated **ready** means quick, skilled, expert (see its use in Ezek 7.6); **scribe** here means "writer."

In some languages it will be necessary to state more explicitly the purpose for the writing of the song; for example, "I write this song the singers will sing to the king." Otherwise the reader may understand that the song is merely for the possession of the king. In some languages it is necessary to place **my tongue** before the thing it is compared with, as in RSV. TEV has reversed the order, which is acceptable in poetic English. The expression **like the pen of a ready scribe** may require some adaptation in translation; for example, "like a person who knows how to write well."

RSV	TEV
You are the fairest of the sons of men; grace is poured upon your lips; therefore God has blessed you for ever.	You are the most handsome of men; you are an eloquent speaker. God has always blessed you.

It was expected that a king be handsome (see the description of Absalom in 2 Sam 14.25), and here the poet describes him in exaggerated terms as **the fairest of the sons of men**, that is, the most handsome man living; for **sons of men** see comment on "children of men" in 11.4. **The fairest of the sons of men** involves a superlative which in some languages is expressed in the following form: "You surpass all men in being fair." **Fairest** or **"most handsome"** must sometimes be rendered as "people like to look at you" or "you are of good appearance."

The Hebrew **grace is poured upon your lips** means, as TEV renders it, that the king is **"an eloquent speaker"** (see NJV "your speech is endowed with grace"; FRCL "you express yourself elegantly"). The meaning can be "grace pours *from* your lips" (so TOB), which would indicate that he is kindly and considerate in talking to people (see SPCL "charm flows from your lips"). It hardly seems likely that the king's lips themselves are being praised, as NEB "your lips are moulded in grace" seems to imply. In some languages "eloquent speaker" is rendered, for example, "you are a man of words" or "you speak the people's words."

RSV **therefore** (also NEB, SPCL) strictly means that God has always blessed the king because of his physical attributes; it seems better to take the Hebrew *'al-ken* as pointing backwards, that is, that the king's beauty and eloquence are evidence of God's favor (Briggs); see NJB and Weiser "for God has blessed you for ever"; FRCL "It is easy to see that God has blessed you forever." The expression **God has blessed you forever** is sometimes rendered "God has always given you good things."

45.3

RSV	TEV
Gird your sword upon your thigh, O mighty one, in your glory and majesty!	Buckle on your sword, mighty king; you are glorious and majestic.

Gird your sword upon your thigh: this means to secure the sword in the sheath, or guard, which hung from a belt around the warrior's waist. In some languages it will be necessary to make one of three possible adaptations in the expression. First, if the sword is unknown, a local instrument for fighting may be substituted. Second, it may be desirable to use a term for sword which needs reinforcement by the use of a classifier, such as "weapon." Third, if neither of the above solutions is satisfactory, one may simply translate sword as "your weapon." If the local weapon is not one that is carried on the hip, further adjustment will be required; for example, "pick up your weapon" or "carry your spear."

The vocative **O mighty one** is applied to the king; it can be translated "mighty warrior" (FRCL), "brave man" (see SPCL), or "warrior king" (NEB).

Line **b** in Hebrew is simply "your glory and majesty"; most connect this with what precedes, **in your glory and majesty**; TEV takes it as an independent statement, **"you are glorious and majestic."** The words can be taken to describe the sword as a symbol of the king's glory and majesty (see SPCL "It is your splendid adornment"; FRCL "a symbol of your splendor and your majesty"). The expression **in your glory and majesty** may sometimes be rendered in reverse order; for example, "you are a great king and do great deeds."

45.4

RSV	TEV
In your majesty ride forth victoriously for the cause of the truth and to defend[g] the right; let your right hand teach you dread deeds!	Ride on in majesty to victory for the defense of truth and justice![w] Your strength will win you great victories!

[g] Cn: Heb *and the meekness of*

[w] *Probable text* and justice; *Hebrew and* meekness of justice.

Some regard the appearance of "and your majesty" in verse 4a (immediately after "and your majesty" at the end of verse 3) as an accidental repetition; and so they connect the last words of verse 3 with the opening words of verse 4, "ride on to victory in majesty and glory." Most stay with the Masoretic text.

The injunction to **ride forth** is not to be understood that the poet wants the king to set out on a military expedition on his wedding day; rather it expresses the poet's wish that the king always be victorious in his campaigns. The king would be riding in a war chariot, or perhaps on a horse.

Victoriously in line a translates a verb form in Hebrew which means "be successful" (imperative); so one may translate "Good fortune be yours" (also Weiser "Good luck!"). But this involves deleting the first word of the verse "and (in) your majesty" as an accidental repetition of the same phrase at the end of verse 3.

In some languages it will be difficult to command the king to **ride forth** without indicating what he is to ride; for example, "ride your horse" or "ride on your wagon of war." The expression **In your majesty ride forth** must in some languages be shifted to an adapted simile; for example, "ride forth like a great chief." **Victoriously** must sometimes be rendered as a verb phrase such as "defeat your enemies."

There is some difficulty in line b, which in Hebrew is "ride on in behalf of truth and meekness (of) justice"; HOTTP prefers this and translates "for loyalty's sake and for mild justice." With a slight change the Hebrew can be made to mean "executing justice on behalf of the humble" (so SPCL); FRCL "in defense of the poor and of justice." Some would translate the Masoretic text "for the cause of faithfulness, meekness, and right" (similarly NIV, NJV). RSV, instead of "and meekness (of) justice," reads "and on account of justice," which is the meaning represented by TEV.

The expression **for the cause of truth** must often be translated as a causal clause; for example, "because you defend truth and justice." TEV's **the defense of truth and justice** must sometimes be rendered "defend the true words you speak and the fairness you judge with" or ". . . and the (right) decisions you make (fairly)."

RSV gives a literal and practically unintelligible translation of the words in line c; it is most unnatural to speak of one's hand teaching one **dread deeds**. **Dread deeds** means "awesome deeds," that is, deeds that strike terror in the hearts of his enemies and evoke awe and respect from his allies. TEV takes the Hebrew as a statement; it can be taken as a wish: see NAB "may your right hand show you wondrous deeds" (similarly NJV). NEB and NJB emend the text to get other meanings. In some languages it will be necessary to shift the noun phrase **your right hand** to a verb phrase which indicates the cause of the action; for example, "because you are strong" or "because you do powerful deeds." Line c may be rendered, for example, "because you are strong you do powerful deeds" or "let your powerful arm show the great acts you do."

45.5 RSV	TEV
Your arrows are sharp in the heart of the king's enemies; the peoples fall under you.	Your arrows are sharp, they pierce the hearts of your enemies; nations fall down at your feet.

This verse is taken as a wish by FRCL and NIV; while possible, it seems better to translate it as a statement, as RSV, TEV, and others do.

In Hebrew the line translated **in the heart of the king's enemies** is the last one of the verse; both RSV and TEV have joined it to the first line, for clarity of meaning. This line refers to the king in the third person, which could be mistakenly understood to be someone other than the king himself, who is addressed in the second person (**Your arrows**); so in this line TEV keeps the second person, "**your enemies.**"

The last line portrays the defeat of the king's enemies.

45.6-7

RSV	TEV

6   Your divine throne*h* endures for ever and ever.
     Your royal scepter is a scepter of equity;
7   you love righteousness and hate wickedness.
     Therefore God, your God, has anointed you
     with the oil of gladness above your fellows;
	6 The kingdom that God has given you*x*
	     will last forever and ever.
	     You rule over your people with justice;
	7 you love what is right and hate what is evil.
	     That is why God, your God, has chosen you
	     and has poured out more happiness on you
	     than on any other king.

h Or *Your throne is a throne of God,* or *Thy throne, O God*

x The kingdom that God has given you; *or* Your kingdom, O God; *or* Your divine kingdom.

The opening words of verse 6 may be understood in a number of ways, depending on how *'elohim* "God" is understood, either as a vocative ("O God") or as a descriptive noun modifying **throne**. The order in Hebrew is "Your throne God forever and ever." It should be noted that **throne** here means "**kingdom**" or "sovereignty"; it is not literally a piece of royal furniture. The possible interpretations are as follows:

(1) Taking *'elohim* as vocative: (a) "Your throne, O God, is . . ." (Briggs; AT, RSV footnote, NIV, TEV footnote, TOB, SPCL); (b) "Your throne, O divine one" (ZÜR), or "Your throne, O divine king" (Weiser); so Taylor, Toombs, and Oesterley, who believe the king is being addressed.

(2) Taking *'elohim* as descriptive: (a) **Your divine throne** (Anderson; RSV, TEV footnote, NJV); (b) or else "Your glorious throne" (taking *'elohim* as superlative); NEB, FRCL "your throne is like God's throne."

(3) Taking *'elohim* as genitive: "Your throne is of God" (Kirkpatrick; BJ, NJB, RSV footnote); GECL "Your throne is God's throne"; TEV "**The kingdom that God has given you**" takes the genitive "of God" as source.

(4) Dahood: "The eternal and everlasting God has enthroned you."[1]

If the vocative "O God" is preferred, it should be noticed that some take it as a title for the king (see NAB footnote), and not as directly referring to God. But some commentators do not believe that the word *'elohim* would be used as a title for the king (so Anderson). Others, however, say that the king could be addressed with this title, since at coronation he became "a son of God" (Toombs; see 2.7-9).

It makes little sense to take *'elohim* as addressed to God; the poem is addressed to the king and his bride, not to God. Between the two alternatives, (1) "God" as a title for the king, and (2) God as the source of the king's power and authority, it seems that the latter is more likely in this context, as shown in TEV. In any case, the translation of this difficult phrase here should not be influenced by the Septuagint translation of verses 6-7, which are quoted in Hebrews 1.8-9. There the words are applied to Christ, and the meaning of the Greek text is quite clear.

TEV's **"The kingdom that God has given you"** will require adaptations in some translations, particularly since kingdom here represents both a place as well as the act of ruling. In some languages it will be possible to say "The country God has given you to be the chief of" or "The country God has given you to rule."

The psalmist continues, praising the king's devotion to **equity** and **righteousness**, on account of which God has made him the happiest of all kings. In verse 6 **scepter** is a figure of the king's power; **a scepter of equity** means that the king is fair and just in ruling his people. In languages where a chief's authority is symbolized in an object associated with him, such as a cane, stool, or scepter, line b can be translated using such symbols of authority; for example, "Your scepter shows that you rule your people fairly."

In verse 7a the abstract qualities **righteousness** and **wickedness** stand for deeds or conduct: "righteous actions . . . evil actions." The expression **you love righteousness and hate wickedness** must be rendered by verb phrases in many languages. It is best in the context to relate these to the acts of the king; for example, "you are a chief who loves to do good things and who hates to see people do bad things."

Has anointed you with the oil of gladness: the king's installation in office included anointing (see 1 Sam 16.13, Samuel anoints David). Here "oil of gladness" means either that this was very happy occasion, or else (as TEV has it) God **"poured out"** happiness on the king, that is, made him very happy. The expression **above your fellows** refers to his fellow kings; less probably, but possibly, it could mean "more than any other man." Or, if "anointed" is taken in a twofold sense, the translation can be "God (has anointed you and) has chosen you (to be king) instead of any other man" (see FRCL). GECL translates the verse, "Therefore God has appointed you as ruler, your God has given you more honor and gladness than to all your people." In many languages it will not be possible to preserve the idea of anointing, as has been done in TEV **"poured out . . . on."** Therefore it may be necessary to say "That is why God has chosen you and placed you higher than any other king."

---

[1]Mft follows a conjectural text, "Your throne shall stand forevermore"; this takes the original Hebrew text to have used a form of the verb "to be" (*yihyeh*), which a later editor mistook for *yhwh* (Yahweh) and which he changed to *'elohim* (God), as it now stands in the Masoretic text.

	RSV		TEV
8	your robes are all fragrant with myrrh and aloes and cassia. From ivory palaces stringed instruments make you glad;	8	The perfume of myrrh and aloes is on your clothes; musicians entertain you in palaces decorated with ivory.
9	daughters of kings are among your ladies of honor; at your right hand stands the queen in gold of Ophir.	9	Among the ladies of your court are daughters of kings, and at the right of your throne stands the queen, wearing ornaments of finest gold.

The poet describes the magnificence of the royal court. The king's robes are **fragrant with myrrh and aloes and cassia**. All three are perfumes derived from vegetable substances (see *Fauna and Flora*, pages 90-91, 104-105, 147-148). TEV has by use of **"perfume of"** indicated the nature of the substances, and names only two of them. The Hebrew text is a bit unusual, and NEB has "powder of aloes" for "aloes and cassia" of most other translations. In languages where there are known substances for making perfume, these may be substituted for **myrrh and aloes and cassia**. Alternatively, the translator must either employ the specific terms with a generic such as "substance," or use some kind of descriptive phrase; for example, "a sweet smelling liquid."

Ivory palaces (see 1 Kgs 22.39) are not palaces completely built of ivory, but palaces decorated with ivory, either in the building itself or in the furniture (see 1 Kgs 10.18; Amos 3.15; 6.4). The expression **ivory palaces** may be rendered in various ways. In some languages one may use a borrowed term for ivory and accompany it with a generic term; for example, "a material called ivory." In other cases where ivory is unfamiliar, it can be compared to other materials such as bone, teeth, and animal horns; for example, "a material that looks like bone." There is little point in using "elephants' teeth" if elephants are unknown.

The **stringed instruments** in verse 8b are not further identified (the word occurs elsewhere only in 150.4); NEB "music of strings." NJV translates "lutes"; NJB "harps." TEV has **"musicians"** instead of musical **instruments**; the translation can be "the music that is played . . . ."

In verse 9 **your ladies of honor** is a rather polite designation of the women of the king's harem. Some of them were royal princesses, **daughters of kings**. The phrase translated **of honor** is taken by some to mean "your prized possessions," "your most valuable belongings." NJV has "Royal princesses are your favorites." In some languages **ladies of honor** may be rendered, for example, "women who have the honor of serving you."

At your right is the place of honor (see 16.11). In some languages the **right hand** is called "the man hand," which is both the position of honor and on the side of power. The word translated **queen** is an unusual one, occurring only here and in Nehemiah 2.6; it can mean "queen mother" (so GECL footnote). Here the queen is the bride herself; the poet is describing the royal court, and not talking about a woman who is already queen, other than the queen-to-be (unless, in fact, the king's mother is being referred to). In some languages no distinction exists between wife, woman, and bride. However, if the queen referred to is to be understood as the bride, it is often possible to qualify by saying "the Queen-woman the king will marry" or "the woman the king will marry."

Gold of Ophir: it is not known exactly where Ophir was; southwest Arabia seems the most likely location. Its gold was the finest (see 1 Kgs 9.28; 10.11; Job 22.24; 28.16), and so TEV has translated the phrase as "**ornaments of finest gold**."

45.10-11	RSV		TEV
10	Hear, O daughter, consider, and incline your ear; forget your people and your father's house;	10	Bride of the king, listen to what I say— forget your people and your relatives.
11	and the king will desire your beauty. Since he is your lord, bow to him;	11	Your beauty will make the king desire you; he is your master, so you must obey him.

The poet now speaks to the bride, addressing her as **daughter**, a term of endearment. He tells her to listen to him carefully (literally "bend the ear"; see 17.6 and discussion). First, he recommends that she no longer be attached to her **people** and to her own relatives (**your father's house**) (verse 10b). This seems to indicate that she is a foreigner; her people would be the people of her own country, and she would have to forsake their customs and religious beliefs. The expression **forget your people** is somewhat metaphorical, since the intention is not one of forgetting, but rather of not obeying. Therefore, in languages where **forget** will only be understood literally, it is better to say "don't be commanded by your people and your relatives" or "no longer follow the advice of your . . . ."

Verse 11a may be read as a clause that is subordinate to the following one: "When the king desires your beauty . . ." (NEB). Such a rendering makes it a specific reference to sexual intercourse (NJV "let the king be aroused by your beauty"). Her new husband is her **lord** and "**master**"; she must obey him (literally "bow down to him"). The expression **he is your lord** may sometimes be rendered "he is the one who rules over you." In some languages one may say "your owner."

45.12-13	RSV		TEV
12	the people*i* of Tyre will sue your favor with gifts, the richest of the people 13 with all kinds of wealth.	12	The people of Tyre will bring you gifts; rich people will try to win your favor.
	The princess is decked in her chamber with gold-woven robes;*j*	13	The princess is in the palace—how beautiful she is! Her gown is made of gold thread.

i Heb *daughter*

j Or *people. All glorious is the princess within, gold embroidery is her clothing*

In verse 12 the Hebrew phrase "the daughter of Tyre" refers to the people of that city (see comments on "the daughter of Zion" in 9.14; "daughter of Babylon" in 137.8). However, by omitting the initial "and" one can take it as a vocative and translate "Tyrian princess" (so TOB, NEB, NJV, SPCL). The explicit reference to Tyre may imply that she was from there. In verse 12b **will sue your favor** translates "will soften (or, flatter) your face," that is, will try to gain her favor.

RSV connects the opening words of verse 13 with the end of verse 12 (also NJV). This is possible but not necessary. The Hebrew phrase that RSV translates **all kinds of wealth** may be taken to describe the bride (so TEV—see next verse). But there are considerable difficulties with the Hebrew text as it now stands, and commentators and translations vary widely.

Verses 13-15 describe the bridal procession into the palace; first **the princess** comes in; TEV **"in the palace"** translates the Hebrew word "within," which RSV **in her chamber** takes to be rather the place where the princess was **decked**. It is better to translate "The princess enters the palace." **"How beautiful she is"** translates a phrase which seems to mean "all glorious" (see RSV footnote); but the noun is taken by RSV to mean "valuable things" (as in Judges 18.21, "goods").[2] NEB, with a change of text, gets "In the palace honour awaits her." The term **princess**, if translated literally as in Hebrew "daughter of the king," will in most cases no longer refer to the bride. Therefore in many languages one must say "the woman the king will marry."

45.14-15	RSV	TEV
14	in many-colored robes she is led to the king, with her virgin companions, her escort,*k* in her train.	14 In her colorful gown she is led to the king, followed by her bridesmaids, and they also are brought to him.
15	With joy and gladness they are led along as they enter the palace of the king.	15 With joy and gladness they come and enter the king's palace.

k Heb *those brought to you*

In verse 14 TEV, RSV, and others take the Hebrew text to mean that only one group of bridesmaids follows her (**her virgin companions, her escort**); but some take these to be two groups, "bridesmaids" and "ladies-in-waiting" (or, less elegantly, her servants). There is no way to be certain; the Hebrew text is none too clear. In some

---

[2]HOTTP understands "all glorious" to mean "the whole glorious (array)" and translates "all glorious, the king's daughter enters."

languages **her virgin companions** may be rendered "the young girls who help her" or "the young women who walk behind her."

TEV **"to him"** translates what is in the Masoretic text "to you" (masculine), that is, the king; two Hebrew manuscripts have "to her" (the princess), which FRCL, RSV, NEB, NJB prefer.[3]

Verse 15 describes how the wedding procession, with great **joy and gladness**, enters the palace for the wedding ceremony.

45.16-17	RSV	TEV

	RSV	TEV
16	Instead of your fathers shall be your sons; you will make them princes in all the earth.	16 You, my king, will have many sons to succeed your ancestors as kings, and you will make them rulers over the whole earth.
17	I will cause your name to be celebrated in all generations; therefore the peoples will praise you for ever and ever.	17 My song will keep your fame alive forever, and everyone will praise you for all time to come.

The poet concludes by addressing the king, promising him that he will have many sons who will, like his ancestors, also be "**kings**" and rule over the whole earth (or, "over all the land of Israel"—see SPCL, NEB). The RSV translation of verse 16a is unintelligible. The Hebrew expression **Instead of your fathers shall be your sons** means that the king's male descendants, his **sons**, will be kings, replacing, as it were, the king's male ancestors (**your fathers**), who also had been kings. **Princes** were a kind of "**rulers**." The title was not limited to sons of a king.

In verse 17 the poet promises that he will keep the king's **name**, that is, his "fame," alive forever (see comments on "name" in 5.12). For all time people will remember the king and praise him. Obviously the poet is referring to this song that he has just composed as the way in which the king's memory will be kept alive forever, not only in Israel but in all the world. In some languages it is not possible to refer to someone's fame as being alive. Therefore one must often say, for example, "I will cause people to remember always what great things you did."

---

[3]HOTTP stays with the Masoretic text, which it translates "for you," referring to the king.

Psalm 46

This psalm is a hymn celebrating the power of God, the mighty defender of his people. The first verse inspired Martin Luther's *Ein' feste Burg ist unser Gott* ("A Mighty Fortress Is Our God"). The psalm is usually classified as a "Hymn of Zion" (together with Psalms 48, 76, and 87).

The psalm is composed of three strophes (verses 1-3, 4-6, 8-10), the last two of which end with a refrain (verses 7,11) which is missing from the first strophe. The first strophe (verses 1-3) proclaims the security of the people of Zion (Jerusalem) even in the greatest of all calamities. Threats from enemy nations will not avail; God is with the city and the enemies will be overcome (verses 4-6). God will finally bring all wars to an end and will command all peoples to honor him as supreme ruler and Lord of the world (verses 8-10).

Psalm 46 is particularly rich in imagery. Furthermore, the distribution of images is structured so that they are all enclosed by "earth": verse 2 "We will not fear though the earth should change," and verse 10 "I am exalted in the earth." The images in verses 1-3 are associated with the physical world: earth, mountains, sea. Those in verses 4-7 form a contrast between the "city of God," blessed by the quiet presence of God symbolized here as "river" and "streams," and the noisy instability of the "nations" and "kingdoms" that rage and totter. The latter is brought to nothing when the "earth" melts at God's "voice." In verses 8-10 the imagery is of war associated with "bows," "spears," and "chariots" (perhaps "shields"), and the universality of it is emphasized by beginning with "earth" in verse 8 and ending with "earth" in verse 10.

The refrain in verses 7 and 11 was probably used for audience participation, but in this psalm the final refrain, "the God of Jacob is our refuge," echoes the opening of the psalm "God is our refuge." Therefore the psalm contains a double envelope structure, one for the imagery outside the refrain and another for the psalm as a whole.

HEADING: "**God Is With Us.**" Other headings are "God is on our side"; "A mighty fortress"; "The mighty God." There is little or no adaptation necessary for this title in most languages.

Hebrew Title: **To the choirmaster. A Psalm of the Sons of Korah. According to Alamoth. A Song** (TEV "A song by the clan of Korah").

For **choirmaster** see title of Psalm 4; for **the Sons of Korah** see title of Psalm 42. **According to Alamoth** is perhaps the name of the tune to which this psalm was sung; the word *'alamoth* means "young women" (so translated by Aquila and Jerome), and Weiser takes it to mean "(the voices of) young women," that is, to be sung in a high pitch. In 1 Chronicles 15.20 the phrase is used of certain harps, "the high-pitched harps." The Septuagint translates "concerning hidden things" (also Vulgate). NJB translates "For oboe."

46.1-3	RSV	TEV

1　God is our refuge and strength,
　　　a very present[1] help in trouble.
2　Therefore we will not fear though
　　　the earth should change,
　　　though the mountains shake in
　　　the heart of the sea;
3　though its waters roar and foam,
　　　though the mountains tremble
　　　with its tumult.　*Selah*

1　God is our shelter and strength,
　　　always ready to help in times of
　　　trouble.
2　So we will not be afraid, even if
　　　the earth is shaken
　　　and mountains fall into the
　　　ocean depths;
3　even if the seas roar and rage,
　　　and the hills are shaken by the
　　　violence.

[1] Or *well proved*

The psalmist's statement of the security of God's people **in trouble** describes such a time in terms of worldwide upheavals and disasters. **God is our refuge**: see the word **refuge** as it is used in 14.6; **God is our . . . strength** means "God keeps us strong," that is, confident, unafraid. The expression **God is our refuge** must often be shifted to a verb phrase; for example, "God is the one who protects us" or "God is the one who shelters us."

In verse 1b **very present** translates a phrase meaning "very accessible"; the verb means "be present, near." The noun **help** is used also in 22.19.

All of the catastrophes listed in verses 2-3 represent the end of the world, with the disappearance of order and the return of the chaos which existed before creation.

In verse 2a RSV translates **the earth should change**; it is better, following Holladay, to see the meaning "shake, quake" for this verb, which in other contexts means "to change, exchange." So most modern translations have "heave, be shaken, reel, quake." NJB translates "be in turmoil"; NJV "reels." The passive constructions used in TEV and implied in RSV will be difficult to use in languages where the passive is nearly nonexistent. In lines 2a and 3b it will be necessary in some languages to say, for example, "even if the earth breaks up" and "the hills move violently."

The second phenomenon, in verse 2b, is that of **mountains** shaking **in the heart of the sea**. This is better represented by "the mountains fall into the depths of the ocean" as the result of a severe earthquake. Or else "the mountains in the depths of the seas totter." These are the mountains reaching down into the underworld, and upon which the earth rests, according to the idea of that time about the structure of the earth.

In verse 3a the psalmist speaks of the seas as they **roar and foam**, and in verse 3b of the hills as they **tremble** from the fury of the waves. RSV **tumult** carries only the notion of noise; the main idea, however, is that of the violence, the fury of the waves as they hurl themselves against the hills. The expression **its waters roar** may in some languages be expressed as a simile; for example, "even if the seas roar like a wild animal and make a great noise."

In verse 3b, instead of **with its tumult** (TEV **"by the violence"**), NEB has "before his majesty"; the Hebrew noun has the meaning of "majesty" in 68.34 (and see also Deut 33.26); most other translations have the same meaning expressed by RSV and TEV.

Translators should be accustomed by now to recognize movement or lack of movement between parallel lines. In verse 2 line a has **the earth**, which is made more specific by **mountains** in line b. In verse 3 line a **waters** picks up from **sea** in 2b, and 3b repeats **mountains** from 2b. The movement through 2ab to 3a is that of a step-up of intensity, both by being more specific in the choice of nouns and by the addition of the verbs. Translators should try to reflect this element of meaning in their translations. In English the step-up can be seen by rendering, for example,

> So we will not be afraid if the earth should shake
>   not even if the mountains should fall into the sea;
>   nor even if the oceans roar and rage
>   and the hills are violently shaken.

For **_Selah_** see 3.2.

46.4-5	RSV	TEV
4	There is a river whose streams make glad the city of God, the holy habitation of the Most High.	4 There is a river that brings joy to the city of God, to the sacred house of the Most High.
5	God is in the midst of her, she shall not be moved; God will help her right early.	5 God is in that city, and it will never be destroyed; at early dawn he will come to its aid.

The figure of **a river** flowing through Jerusalem (**the city of God**) is probably derived from the river in the Garden of Eden (Gen 2.10); there was no river in the city of Jerusalem itself. (For further references to this figure see 65.9; Ezek 47.1-12; Joel 3.18; Zech 14.8.) The flowing waters suggest vitality and life, and they bring joy to the city's inhabitants.

The expression **the city of God** can often be rendered "the city where people worship God." The two parts of 4a can then be combined to say, for example, "There is a river which brings joy to the people in the city where they worship God" or "There is a river that causes the people in God's city to be glad." In some languages it is necessary to make explicit that someone is caused to be joyful; for example, "There is a river which causes the people to be joyful."

In verse 4b **the holy habitation** of God may refer to the Temple or it may be another reference to the city of Jerusalem itself. The Masoretic text has **the holy habitation of the Most High**; the Septuagint represents a slightly different text, which NEB translates "which the Most High has made his dwelling," while NJB translates "it sanctifies the dwelling of the Most High." HOTTP and most translations, like TEV and RSV, follow the Masoretic text.[1]

For **Most High** see comments on 7.17. The expression **the holy habitation of the Most High** can be rendered in some languages as "the house dedicated to God who is above all other gods."

In this context, **not be moved** means "not be defeated," "not be destroyed."

The city's security (verse 5) is assured by the fact that God lives there (a reference to the Temple), and he is ready to defend it every day. The expression **right early** refers to dawn, which is often specified as the time of God's help (see 5.3; 17.15; 30.5; 90.14).

46.6-7	RSV		TEV
6	The nations rage, the kingdoms totter;	6	Nations are terrified, kingdoms are shaken;
	he utters his voice, the earth melts.		God thunders, and the earth dissolves.
7	The LORD of hosts is with us;		
	the God of Jacob is our refuge.[m] Selah	7	The LORD Almighty is with us; the God of Jacob is our refuge.

[m] Or *fortress*

In verse 6a **rage** translates the same Hebrew verb that is translated **roar** in verse 3. The basic idea of the verb is to be in tumult, be noisy; here the emotion is either that of fear or of confusion. TEV **"are terrified"**; NEB "are in tumult"; NIV, NJB "are in uproar." Perhaps something like "The nations roar in fear" or ". . . roar in dismay" is better.

For other references to the thunder of God's voice (verse 6b) see 18.13; 29.3-9 and comments. The result, **the earth melts**, is probably not meant literally, but figuratively of fear and terror on the part of humankind. In some translations it may be useful to follow GECL, which places first "He lets his voice be heard," and then the result of the roar of God's voice, "peoples tremble, kingdoms totter, the whole earth disappears in anguish." The expressions **the nations rage** and **the kingdoms totter** refer to the Gentiles. In languages which require an explicit agent, it is possible to say, for example, "God frightens the countries of the other tribes and shakes their kingdoms." If the translator follows TEV's **"God thunders,"** in many languages it will be necessary to shift to a simile; for example, "God speaks with a noise like thunder makes." If one follows more literally the Hebrew "God gave his voice," it will be possible to translate, for example, "God made his voice heard."

The refrain (verse 7) uses two titles of God: **The LORD of hosts** is a military title, portraying God as the commander of the armies ("Yahweh of armies"). **The God of Jacob** appears often in the psalms; Jacob is either the historical personage, or else a name for the people of Israel (see 20.1).

---

[1]HOTTP translates "the (most) holy of the dwellings of the Most-High."

The expression **LORD of hosts** is sometimes rendered "LORD of the armies." Since the focus is upon the power of the Lord, this title may also be rendered, for example, "the LORD, who is the strongest of all" or "the LORD, who is all powerful" or "the LORD, who has all strength."

As in most first person plural references in the Psalms, it will be necessary to translate **with us** using the inclusive pronominal reference in languages which make a distinction between inclusive and exclusive, in order to include the psalmist and his fellow worshipers who are addressed in this psalm.

The God of Jacob must sometimes be translated as "the God of our ancestor Jacob" or "the God whom our ancestor Jacob worshiped." Otherwise there is the possibility that Jacob will not be sufficiently identified.

For **refuge** see comments on "stronghold" in 9.9.

46.8-9	RSV	TEV
	8 Come, behold the works of the LORD, how he has wrought desolations in the earth. 9 He makes wars cease to the end of the earth; he breaks the bow, and shatters the spear, he burns the chariots with fire!	8 Come and see what the LORD has done. See what amazing things he has done on earth. 9 He stops wars all over the world; he breaks bows, destroys spears, and sets shields on fire.

In the final strophe (verses 8-10) the psalmist portrays the establishment of universal peace, with God bringing wars to an end by destroying all weapons and commanding all nations to submit to him as supreme ruler of the world. The psalmist addresses all peoples everywhere, **Come, behold**, not just his fellow Israelites.

In verse 8a **the works** refers to the actions that follow. In verse 8b **desolations** translates a word meaning an event which evokes terror or wonder from those who see it, an "awesome" or "prodigious" event; so TEV **"amazing things"**; NAB "astounding things"; NJV "astounding deeds"; SPCL "surprising things." This interpretation follows the Septuagint "wonders" and the Vulgate *prodigia*, and is the meaning given by K-B and Holladay. But NEB, NIV, and NJV are like KJV "desolations." It seems best here to follow TEV. The expression translated **"amazing things"** by TEV can be rendered in some languages in idiomatic terms; for example, "eyesore things," "things that stop the heart," and "things that fill up the throat."

In verse 9 the psalmist lists the prodigious things that God has done: he defeats all his enemies and destroys their weapons (bows and arrows, and spears), and thus makes them stop fighting against his people and against one another.

In the expression **He makes wars cease** it is sometimes necessary to render war as "people fighting." Therefore one can sometimes say "He causes people to stop fighting each other."

It is generally agreed by modern commentators and translations (Weiser, Dahood; BJ, NJB, NAB, NEB, FRCL, NIV, GECL) that in verse 9c "shields" (as the Septuagint, Targum, and Vulgate translate) is meant, and not **chariots** (RSV, TOB,

NJV, SPCL); only a slight change of vowels in the Hebrew text is required, and "The War Scroll" of Qumran (6.15) uses the word in the sense of "shields."[2] It is pointed out that the Masoretic text word **chariots** is nowhere used in the Old Testament of war chariots (see FRCL footnote). Ancient shields were made of wood and leather, and frequently rubbed with olive oil; as a result they would burn easily. Where shields are only known to be made of metal, it may be advisable to include a note which will explain how shields can be said to be set on fire.

46.10-11 RSV	TEV
10 "Be still, and know that I am God. I am exalted among the nations, I am exalted in the earth!" 11 The LORD of hosts is with us; the God of Jacob is our refuge*m*　　Selah	10 "Stop fighting," he says, "and know that I am God, supreme among the nations, supreme over the world." 11 The LORD Almighty is with us; the God of Jacob is our refuge.

m Or *fortress*

In verse 10 God himself speaks to the nations (Anderson thinks the words are addressed to the people of Israel): "**Stop fighting**" is what he commands. The traditional **Be still** is widely misunderstood as a command to be reverent (in church) and meditate on God's blessings. The Hebrew verb means to cease, be inactive. SPCL has "Surrender!"; BJ, FRCL "Stop"; NAB, NJV "Desist!"; TOB "Drop your weapons!"; GECL "Make peace."

Know is used in the sense of acknowledge, recognize, admit, confess. **Know that I am God** can sometimes be translated "learn that I am God" or "see that I am God."

I am exalted in verse 10b,c means "I rule" (FRCL), "I am above" (SPCL), "I dominate" (NJV). Some take it as a future: "I will be exalted" (NIV). The expression **I am exalted among the nations** must be shifted to an active construction in many languages; for example, "The nations praise me, the people of the world say that I am great."

The refrain in verse 11 is the same as verse 7.

For *Selah* see 3.2.

---

[2]HOTTP notes that the Hebrew word has two meanings: "chariots of transport" and "round shields." Here the second meaning is the one that fits the context.

Psalm 47

This psalm, like Psalms 93 and 96–99, celebrates the sovereignty of Yahweh over the whole earth. Some commentators, following the lead of Mowinckel, associate these psalms with an annual ritual in which Yahweh was "enthroned" as king of Israel and of the world. But no firm evidence for such an Israelite festival has been brought forward, and many deny that in fact it ever existed, preferring to speak of a celebration of Yahweh's kingship, perhaps at the Festival of Shelters, which took place at the beginning of the Hebrew year (according to earlier usage). Anderson speaks of "an annual renewal of allegiance"; Toombs, while recognizing that there is no direct evidence for the existence of such an enthronement ritual, nevertheless says it provides "a theoretical setting" in which these psalms can be understood. (See the commentaries; for a succinct discussion, see Toombs' "Introduction" in *One-Volume Interpreter's Commentary on the Bible*, page 253.)

Psalm 47 can best be analyzed as consisting of five strophes (also called stanzas). Verses 1-2 make up the first, verses 3-4 the second, verse 5 alone the third, verses 6-7 the fourth, and verses 8-9 the fifth. The arrangement is symmetrical, with four four-line quatrains arranged around a central two-line strophe which is verse 5. The first strophe, verses 1-2, is semantically similar to the fourth, calling upon the people to praise God in shouts and singing. There is a similar correspondence between the second and the final strophes. At the individual verse level, translators should note that verses 2-5 consist of parallel lines in which the following pattern occurs: A-B-C-B'-C', in which C' represents an expansion of C without stepping up intensification.

The psalm opens with an exhortation to all the world to praise Yahweh, king of the universe (verses 1-4); this is followed by a description of Yahweh's taking his place on the throne and ruling over the nations (verses 5-9). This probably was represented symbolically by the entrance of the Covenant Box into the Temple (see 24.7-10).

HEADING: "**The Supreme Ruler.**" Other headings are "Yahweh, king of Israel, Lord of the world"; "God is king of all the earth"; "The LORD the king of all nations." In some languages it will be necessary to make the components of this title more explicit; for example, "God is the supreme ruler," or "God rules above everything," or "God is the greatest chief in the world."

Hebrew Title: **To the choirmaster. A Psalm of the Sons of Korah** (TEV "**A psalm by the clan of Korah**").

See the title of Psalm 42.

RSV   TEV

1   Clap your hands, all peoples!   1   Clap your hands for joy, all peo-
     Shout to God with loud songs of   ples!
     joy!   Praise God with loud songs!
2   For the LORD, the Most High, is   2   The LORD, the Most High, is to be
     terrible,   feared;
     a great king over all the earth.   he is a great king, ruling over
                                                all the world.

The psalm opens with a command to **all peoples** of the world: **Clap your hands**. This indicates some sort of celebration and could well be one similar to the coronation of Josiah as king of Judah (see 2 Kgs 11.12). In some languages it is necessary to relate joy as a sign of **clap your hands**; for example, "All you people clap your hands and show that you are joyful."

The expression **Shout to God with loud songs** (TEV "**Praise God with loud songs**") must in some languages be adjusted so that loud songs are the result of singing; for example, "Praise God by singing loud songs."

TEV has the component "**joy**" in line a, in order to make clear what emotion is expressed by the action of clapping loudly. Some translations, however, will prefer to follow the Hebrew text more closely, and have "**joy**" in line b.

The Most High (see comments on 7.17) "is to be feared." RSV **is terrible** (also SPCL, TOB) does not suit the context, since in modern English the word has a completely negative connotation; NJV, NIV, and NAB "awesome," or else "is to be revered," represent more faithfully the meaning of the Hebrew (NEB "fearful" is ambiguous). Following TEV, "**the LORD . . . is to be feared**," some languages will have difficulty with the passive construction and will therefore have to shift to an active one. In those cases it is often possible to say "show reverence to the LORD, the Most High" or "honor the LORD, who is the Most High."

In line b the adjective **great** means "powerful."

RSV   TEV

3   He subdued peoples under us,   3   He gave us victory over the peo-
     and nations under our feet.   ples;
4   He chose our heritage for us,   he made us rule over the na-
     the pride of Jacob whom he   tions.
          loves.   *Selah*   4   He chose for us the land where we
                                                live,
                                                the proud possession of his
                                                people, whom he loves.

The two lines of verse 3 are syntactically parallel, and in Hebrew there is only one verb for the two lines (see RSV); the **peoples** are the same as the **nations**, both referring to the various gentile peoples who lived in Canaan and who were defeated by the invading Israelites (**us**). However, line b, **under our feet**, is more specific than line a, **under us**. If one follows TEV it is often necessary to say in line a, for example,

437

"He enabled us to defeat our enemies," and in line <u>b</u> "he enabled us to rule over the nations." **Nations** must often be rendered "the other tribes."

In verse 3b <u>**under our feet**</u> is a way of speaking of the defeat of the Canaanites. Yahweh himself is the one who won the victory for his people.

In verse 4a **heritage** refers to the land of Canaan (see discussion at 16.6); the parallel <u>**the pride of Jacob**</u> in line <u>b</u> is also a reference to Canaan, which TEV has represented by "**the proud possession of his people.**" Some (NIV, NJV, SPCL, NEB) take <u>**Jacob**</u> to be the patriarch himself, and so translate "whom he loved." It is better to take <u>**Jacob**</u> to mean the people of Israel (see similar use of the name in 14.7). If one translates literally, it may be important to add a footnote, "that is, the Promised Land."

In some languages it will be necessary to break line <u>b</u> into two sentences. Furthermore, it is not possible in some languages to speak of a possession being qualified as proud, since only people can be proud. Therefore one may translate, for example, "his people are proud to own the land" and "he loves us." In languages which must distinguish between inclusive and exclusive, the inclusive reference will be used for "**us.**"

FRCL translates the verse: "He has chosen our country for us, and we are proud of it, we, the people of Jacob, whom he (God) loves."

For *Selah* see 3.2.

<u>**47.5**</u>   RSV   TEV

> God has gone up with a shout,
>   the LORD with the sound of a
>   trumpet.

> God goes up to his throne.
>   There are shouts of joy and the
>   blast of trumpets,
>   as the LORD goes up.

RAM HORNS

God is portrayed as going "**up to his throne**" (see "his holy throne" in verse 8). As the RSV literal translation shows, the Hebrew text says only "God goes up," with no indication of the place to which he goes; it is most unlikely that "God goes up into heaven" is meant. Perhaps "the Temple" is implied, the place where God was present with his people as king (see 24.3). It seems likely that the words accompanied (or referred to) the taking of the Covenant Box into the Temple (see 24.7-10; 2 Sam 6.15). The Covenant Box was spoken of as the throne of Yahweh, and its entrance into the Temple represented God's taking his seat on the throne. The people in the Temple gave "**shouts of joy**" (RSV <u>a shout</u>), and the Levites blew their trumpets. (The RSV literal rendition wrongly implies, in English, that God shouts and blows a trumpet.) For the blowing of a trumpet at a coronation, see 2 Kings 9.13; 11.14; the trumpet was a ram's horn. If one follows TEV **"goes up to his throne,"** it will be necessary in some languages to specify whether the implied throne is visible or not. Based on the exegesis given here, the throne is present and so is visible. The impersonal expression **"There are shouts of joy"** must often be rendered "The people shout because they are joyful." Likewise "the blast of trumpets" must often be rendered in a more personal manner; for example, "the musicians blow their horns."

47.6-7	RSV		TEV
6	Sing praises to God, sing praises!	6	Sing praise to God;
	Sing praises to our King, sing		sing praise to our king!
	praises!	7	God is king over all the world;
7	For God is the king of all the		praise him with songs!
	earth;		
	sing praises with a psalm![n]		

[n] Heb *Maskil*

In Hebrew verses 6-7 form a chiastic repetition. Verse 6 has **God**, then **King**, while verse 7 has **king**, then **God**. In RSV as well as TEV, the chiasmus disappears. Translators may or may not be able to retain this feature. They should not do so at the expense of naturalness of style.

In these two verses the people are called upon to **Sing praises to God . . . to our King**, and to **sing praises with a psalm**. Hebrew repeats the command **Sing praises** in the two lines of verse 6 (see RSV); TEV has disregarded this repetition, but it may be very effective in some languages. SPCL is good: "Sing, sing hymns to God! Sing, sing hymns to our king!" The expression **Sing praises to God** must often be rendered as "Sing songs and say how great God is."

The expression **God is the king of all the earth** must sometimes be rendered "God is king and rules all the people of the world."

The word translated **psalm** (see RSV footnote) is *maskil*, for which see the title of Psalm 32. NEB translates here "with all your art"; NJB "learn the music"; Dahood "a skillful song"; SPCL "a poem"; NJV "a hymn."

47.8-9	RSV		TEV
8	God reigns over the nations;	8	God sits on his sacred throne;
	God sits on his holy throne.		he rules over the nations.
9	The princes of the peoples gather	9	The rulers of the nations assemble
	as the people of the God of		with the people[a] of the God of
	Abraham.		Abraham.

> For the shields of the earth belong
> to God;
> he is highly exalted!

> More powerful than all armies is
> he;
> he rules supreme.

a *Probable text* with the people; *Hebrew* the people.

In verse 8 TEV has reversed the two lines of the Hebrew verse, for better effect in English.

Seated on **his holy throne**, God **reigns over the nations**. If a specific referent for God's **holy throne** (a phrase found only here in the Old Testament) is to be sought, it probably is the Covenant Box (see discussion at 18.10). In some languages **holy** in the expression **his holy throne** can be translated by the term meaning positive taboo. However, for many languages there is no term that can be used to indicate a holy object which is closely associated with God. Therefore it is often necessary to indicate the holiness of the object through its association with God; for example, "God sits on his own throne" or "God sits on the throne from which he rules."

The princes of the peoples is a way of speaking of the kings, or rulers, of the Gentile nations.

In verse 9 the Masoretic text is "the people of the God of Abraham assemble," which RSV has translated **as the people of the God of Abraham** (similarly TOB, BJ), meaning that the pagan rulers come together as though they were God's people. Though endorsed by HOTTP, this seems rather unlikely; the Septuagint and the Syriac have "with the God of Abraham" (instead of the Masoretic text *'am* "people" they read *'im* "with"). Many commentators believe that the original Hebrew text was *'im 'am* "with the people," and that one of these two words was accidentally omitted by copyists (without the vowel points the text would be simply *'m 'm*). This seems likely and is accepted by TEV, SPCL, FRCL, NAB. NEB emends the text to get "with the families of Abraham's line," that is, "with the Israelites" (see also NJB "rally to the people of the God of Abraham"). The expression **people of the God of Abraham** may in some languages be rendered as "the people of the God whom Abraham worshiped."

Verse 9c in Hebrew is "for to God (belong) the shields of the earth." Many take "shields" as referring to the rulers (NIV, Anderson; NJV "the guardians of the earth"; FRCL "the protectors of the earth"). NEB, instead of the Masoretic text "shields," reads (with no change of consonants) "the mighty ones" (so the Septuagint). TEV has interpreted the Masoretic text to mean that God's power is greater than that of all earthly warriors; this meaning can be expressed by "all earthly power belongs to God" or "all earthly rulers are subject to God."

For **exalted** see the use of the term in 46.10.

Psalm 48

Like Psalm 46, this psalm praises the beauty and strength of Zion, the city of Jerusalem, the place where Yahweh lives as King of the people of Israel. The psalm was probably used during one of the great Hebrew festivals, perhaps the Festival of Shelters.

The nature of the parallelism in Psalm 48 shows considerable variety. Verses 1-3 are statements about Zion in which the elaborations of the names of Zion occur only in the second line of each set. Starting with verse 4 and continuing through verse 11, the parallelism is essentially narrative. However, in verse 6, line b suddenly shifts to focusing by comparing the panic of the invading kings to the "anguish of a woman in travail." In verses 12-13 line b simply adds further to line a, and the final verse again specifies God in line a as "our guide" in line b.

The psalm opens with praise to Yahweh as the God who lives in Jerusalem (verses 1-3); enemy kings with their armies attacked Jerusalem but were defeated (verses 4-7), so God's people are called upon to praise God for his rule (verses 8-11) and to find out for themselves how strong is the city, how mighty is God (verses 12-14).

HEADING: "**Zion, the City of God.**" Other headings may be "The strength of Zion"; "The beauty and security of Jerusalem." In some languages it will be necessary to adjust this title to say, for example, "Zion is the city where people worship God" or "Zion is the name of the city of God."

Hebrew Title: **A Song. A Psalm of the Sons of Korah** (TEV "A psalm by the clan of Korah; a song").

For **the Sons of Korah** see title of Psalm 42.

48.1-3

RSV	TEV

1 Great is the LORD and greatly to be praised
  in the city of our God!
His holy mountain, 2 beautiful in elevation,
  is the joy of all the earth,
Mount Zion, in the far north,
  the city of the great King.
3 Within her citadels God
  has shown himself a sure defense.
	1 The LORD is great and is to be highly praised
	  in the city of our God, on his sacred hill.ᶜ
	2 Zion, the mountain of God, is high and beautiful;
	  the city of the great king brings joy to all the world.
	3 God has shown that there is safety with him
	  inside the fortresses of the city.

^c SACRED HILL: *See 2.6.*

The psalmist begins with an exhortation to praise Yahweh, who lives in Jerusalem. In verses 1-2 he uses four different phrases to speak of Jerusalem: (1) **the city of our God**; (2) **his holy mountain**, a reference to Mount Zion (see 2.6); (3) "the sides of the north" (RSV **in the far north**); and (4) **the city of the great King**. All of these are easily understandable except "the sides of the north" in verse 2. The word translated "north" is *tsafon*, which is the regular Hebrew word for "north." Mount Zion, however, is not in the north of the country but in the south, and most modern commentators believe that the Hebrew word is the name of "Mount Zaphon," in Phoenicia. According to Canaanite mythology their gods lived there, and in this psalm the Hebrew poet has used the Canaanitish phrase to speak of Mount Zion as "the (real) mountain of God." So TEV has "**Zion, the mountain of God.**" Most translations, like RSV, have **in the far north**, usually with a footnote; NJV has "Mount Zion, summit of Zaphon," with a marginal note explaining Zaphon: "A term for the divine abode." FRCL translates "the capital city of the world." NIV has "Like the utmost heights of Zaphon," with a footnote explaining Zaphon as a sacred mountain or the direction north. NEB translates "like the farthest reaches of the north." The translator should feel free to choose whatever rendering best suits the needs of the receptor language.

In many languages it will be necessary in verse 1a to shift to an active voice or to the obligatory; for example, "and people should praise him."

The expression **the city of our God** can be rendered in some languages as "the city where our God is worshiped" or "the city where the people worship God."

For the translation of **holy**, see 2.6.

Two things are said of Mount Zion: (1) it is **beautiful in elevation** (TEV "high and beautiful"), and (2) it **is the joy of all the earth**, that is, it causes people of all the world to be happy, because the blessings of the God who lives there are not reserved for the Israelites alone; they benefit all the peoples of the world. In many languages it is not possible to speak of a city as bringing joy. One must often say "the city of the great king causes the peoples to rejoice" or "the city of the great king causes the people of the world to rejoice."

The city of Jerusalem was protected by **citadels**, that is, "fortified places" or "**fortresses**," and there was safety and security in the city, because God lived there. TEV has reversed the order of the two lines for reasons of style. The expression **within her citadels** may sometimes be translated "inside the place of protection in the city." The expression **has shown himself a sure defense** can sometimes be rendered as "God has shown that where he is there is safety" or "God has shown the people that they are protected when they are with him."

48.4-5   RSV   TEV

4   For lo, the kings assembled,   4   The kings gathered together
        they came on together.   and came to attack Mount Zion.
5   As soon as they saw it, they were   5   But when they saw it, they were
        astounded,   amazed;

they were in panic, they took to flight;	they were afraid and ran away.

These verses tell how Israel's enemies were defeated and fled in terror. It is impossible to know whether a particular military campaign is in the psalmist's mind (such as Sennacherib's unsuccessful attack on Jerusalem in 701 B.C.; so Briggs); in any case, the matter is described as a historical event. Some commentators see this description as part of a ritual recitation whose purpose was to affirm that no enemy, however strong, was ever able to conquer Jerusalem. At the sight of the city's mighty defenses (verse 5, **As soon as they saw it**), they were terrified and fled. Some see here a reference to a frightening manifestation of Yahweh's power, a theophany, which caused the invaders to flee in terror. Such an interpretation can be expressed by "As soon as they saw God manifest (or, show) his power . . . ."

In verse 4b TEV has made explicit that the pagan kings launched an attack on Mount Zion (see GECL "against the city"), and it would be well that translators do something similar. And it may be necessary in some languages to mention explicitly the kings' armies, to avoid giving the impression that the kings alone gathered and marched off to attack Jerusalem.

Verse 4 may need to be adjusted to say, for example, "The kings and their armies gathered together; they came to attack Mount Zion."

The reaction of the enemy forces is graphically described in verse 5. **It** in 5a refers to Mount Zion. It may be clearer to repeat "Mount Zion" in 5a or use another noun substitute such as "that holy place."

48.6-7 RSV	TEV

6   trembling took hold of them there, anguish as of a woman in travail.
7   By the east wind thou didst shatter
       the ships of Tarshish.
	6 There they were seized with fear and anguish,
	       like a woman about to bear a child,
	7 like ships tossing in a furious storm.

The fear of the enemies is compared to that of a woman in labor pains (verse 6). The expression **trembling took hold . . . anguish** (TEV "they were seized by fear and anguish") can be restated "fear and anguish seized them"; more simply, "they became terribly afraid."

Verse 7 is somewhat difficult to understand; the context requires that it be another simile for the **trembling** and **anguish** which overcame Israel's enemies, but the Masoretic text seems to mean what RSV says, "by the east wind you destroyed the ships of Tarshish," which is a statement of fact, not a simile. This is how HOTTP understands the Masoretic text; its translation is "with the east-wind (you break the ships of Tarsis)" (also AT). But instead of the Masoretic text "*by* (the east wind)," some late Hebrew manuscripts have "*like* (the east wind)"; and the Hebrew verb may be pointed to read as a passive, so that the text means "as ships of Tarshish are wrecked by the east wind." This wording of the text better fits the context than to take it as a statement, as RSV does; so the rendering may be "as when an east wind shatters the ships of Tarshish."

The east wind is taken by TEV to be descriptive of a strong wind, not necessarily of a wind from the east (see Anderson). **Tarshish** was probably Tartessus, in Spain, and **ships of Tarshish** may either be ships built in Tarshish or ships sailing to Tarshish; more than likely the phrase here means large, ocean-going ships, with no indication of the place they were sailing to or the place where they had been built (see FRCL, NAB footnote).

Care must be taken to make the comparison intelligible in translation. The "fear and anguish" that Israel's enemies felt was like that of sailors on ships which are being shattered by a furious wind; see FRCL "Trembling seized them there . . . like the east wind when it tosses large ships."

48.8   RSV   TEV

As we have heard, so have we seen   We have heard what God has
   in the city of the LORD of hosts,   done,
in the city of our God,   and now we have seen it
   which God establishes for ever.   in the city of our God, the
                   Selah   LORD Almighty;
                              he will keep the city safe forever.

God's victory over Israel's enemies is celebrated. His presence in Jerusalem guarantees its safety for all time. As RSV shows, no definite object for the verbs **heard** and **seen** is expressed in Hebrew; TEV supplies **"what God has done"** (for his people in the past), which seems clearly implied.

After dividing the first line into two, TEV has combined and shortened the second and third lines into one, **"in the city of our God, the Lord Almighty"**; some translations may prefer to follow more closely the Hebrew form, as RSV has done, **in the city of the LORD of hosts, in the city of our God**. Care should be taken that the reader is not misled to think of two cities.

For **LORD of hosts** see 46.7 and comments there.

The last line, **which God establishes for ever**, means "which God has made secure forever" (NIV) or "whose safety God will guarantee forever."

For *Selah* see 3.2.

48.9   RSV   TEV

We have thought on thy steadfast   Inside your Temple, O God,
   love, O God,   we think of your constant love.
   in the midst of thy temple.

The verb which TEV and RSV translate "to think" or "to reflect," "to meditate" (see NJV, BJ, NJB, NIV, NAB, SPCL; Weiser, Dahood) has the basic meaning of "to be like," and so it can be taken to mean "to compare" or "to make like." Some see here the idea of a representation, a reenactment, in a ritual drama in the Temple, of God's saving acts (and supported by verse 8 "As we have heard, so have we seen"); so NEB "we re-enact the story of thy true love within thy Temple" (also TOB,

FRCL); also possible is "We have commemorated your steadfast love, O God, within your temple." This is attractive and may be the meaning intended (see comments and references in Anderson). A possible model to follow is "In acts of worship and praise in your Temple, O God, we recall the love you have always shown for us."

48.10-11	RSV	TEV
10	As thy name, O God, so thy praise reaches to the ends of the earth. Thy right hand is filled with vic- tory;	10 You are praised by people every- where, and your fame extends over all the earth. You rule with justice;
11	let Mount Zion be glad! Let the daughters of Judah rejoice because of thy judgments!	11 let the people of Zion be glad! You give right judgments; let there be joy in the cities of Judah!

The Hebrew text in the first two lines is "As your name (extends) to the ends of the earth, so does your praise." Here **name** stands for fame, reputation (see 5.11); Yahweh's fame has spread over all the world, evoking praise from all peoples everywhere. **Thy praise** means "praise that people offer you." The expression **thy praise reaches to the ends of the earth** will be difficult to express literally as in RSV or in TEV, since praise is not often said to reach or extend. In many languages it will be necessary to shift to another type of construction; for example, "and people all over the earth praise you because they know that you are great."

In verse 10c the Hebrew *tsedeq* (see comments on "right" in 4.l) is translated **victory** by RSV, JB; "generosity" by Dahood, "salvation" by Weiser, "beneficence" by NJV, all of which are possible. It seems better, however, to join verse 10c to verse 11, as four lines in a chiastic arrangement (a-b-b'-a'): "God's justice . . . Mount Zion is glad; cities of Judah rejoice . . . God's judgments." Thus *tsedeq* in verse 10c is parallel with *mishpat,* **judgments** in verse 11c (see discussion at 7.6); so TEV, BJ, NJB, NAB, NEB.

Right hand in verse 10c is a figure of power, authority; **Mount Zion** in verse 11a stands for the citizens of Jerusalem; and **the daughters of Judah** in verse 11b means the people of the cities of Judah.

The expression **thy judgments** must often be rendered "because you judge people fairly."

48.12-14	RSV	TEV
12	Walk about Zion, go round about her, number her towers,	12 People of God, walk around Zion and count the towers;
13	consider well her ramparts, go through her citadels; that you may tell the next genera-	13 take notice of the walls and examine the fortresses, so that you may tell the next gen- eration:

	tion	14	"This God is our God forever
14	that this is God,		and ever;
	our God for ever and ever.		he will lead us for all time to
	He will be our guide for ever.		come."

It is not certain whether the invitation to the Israelites to walk around Jerusalem and observe its defenses is meant literally or whether it refers to a ritual procession in the Temple in which this action was represented. The **"people of God"** (which TEV has supplied, in order to make explicit to whom the invitation is extended) are called upon to inspect the **towers**, **ramparts**, and **citadels** of Jerusalem—which was very strongly protected and almost impregnable. The expression **towers** can sometimes be rendered as "the highest parts," and **ramparts** as "strong walls." **Citadels** in some languages can be rendered "the strong house that protects people" or "the place people go for protection."

In verse 13b the verb translated **go through** (TEV "examine") occurs only here in the Old Testament, and there is some doubt as to its exact meaning; in the context, however, parallel with the verbs **number** (verse 12b) and **consider well** (verse 13a), something like inspect or consider is meant (so FRCL).

The inspection of Jerusalem's defenses will serve as the basis for passing on to **the next generation** the story about God's faithful care of his people.

Verse 14 in Hebrew is indirect discourse (RSV **that this is**); TEV has used direct discourse, with quotation marks. RSV's literal translation could be understood to mean that the city is God, taking **this** to refer to the description of the city and its defenses. So it is better to follow TEV here.

At the end of verse 14, **for ever** (TEV "for all time to come") translates a Masoretic text phrase of uncertain meaning: *'al-mut*. The consonants can be pointed *'olamot* "forever" (so the Septuagint, NEB) or *'al-mawet*, which may mean "until death" (AT), or "against death," or "beyond death" (Weiser). TOB refuses to translate the phrase, considering the text unintelligible. NJB does not have it in the text; in a footnote it gives "to death," which should go with the following psalm. Some take the Masoretic text as a musical direction (see title of Psa 46), "according to Alamoth," which should go with the next psalm. This was the decision of the majority of HOTTP; the minority took the Hebrew to mean "eternity," which is to be placed at the end of this psalm.

Most translations (see Dahood) understand the Hebrew as RSV and TEV have done, and this seems to be the least unsatisfactory way of handling it.

Psalm 49

Like Psalm 37, this psalm is a wisdom poem, intended to instruct its readers on the futility of wealth as a guarantee of security and true happiness. Death is inevitable; all must die, just like animals. The only sure basis of life is a firm belief in God, who alone can save from death (verse 15).

The progression of thought in the poem is none too orderly; the most that can be done in the way of an outline is briefly to summarize the contents of each strophe. The psalmist calls his readers to pay attention to what he is about to expound (verses 1-4). Riches cannot buy lasting life (verses 5-9); all people alike will finally end in the grave (verses 10-12). The fate of those who trust in riches and of those who trust in God is contrasted (verses 13-15). Once again, wealth cannot stop death (verses 16-20).

The Hebrew text of this psalm is in places impossible to understand, and conjectures must be used in order to make some sense.

HEADING: "**The Foolishness of Trusting in Riches.**" Other headings are "Money isn't everything"; "A riddle of life"; "The delusions of wealth." The TEV title can sometimes be adapted by saying "A person is foolish if he trusts in riches" or "The foolish person is the one who trusts in riches."

Hebrew Title: **To the choirmaster. A Psalm of the Sons of Korah** (TEV "A psalm by the clan of Korah").

For **choirmaster** see title of Psalm 4; for **the Sons of Korah** see title of Psalm 42.

49.1-2　　　　RSV　　　　　　　　　　　　　　　　TEV

1　Hear this, all peoples! 　　Give ear, all inhabitants of the 　　　world, 2　both low and high, 　　rich and poor together!	1　Hear this, everyone! 　　Listen, all people everywhere, 2　great and small alike, 　　rich and poor together.

The poem is addressed to everyone who will listen, **all inhabitants of the world**, since its lesson is universally valid for Israelites and Gentiles alike, whether great or small, rich or poor. The two lines of verse 1 are parallel and synonymous, calling all people of the world to listen to what the psalmist has to say. Line b of verse 1 focuses on **all peoples** of line a by emphasizing it. This results in heightening the effect and may be rendered in English, for example, "Listen to this everyone, let everybody on earth hear it!"

In verse 2a TEV has reversed the two classifications, in accordance with English language usage. The **low** (TEV "**small**") are literally "sons of *'adam* (mankind)"; the **high** (TEV "**great**") are literally "sons of *'ish* (man)" (see the use of "sons of man" in 4.2). SPCL translates "the powerful and the humble"; NJV has "men of all estates." Not all take the two phrases to have distinct meanings; NEB takes them as parallel: "all mankind, every living man."

In some languages it will be necessary to personalize **rich and poor**; for example, "you who are rich and you who are poor." **Together**, verse 2b, in this context is another way of saying **both**, as in line **a**. Both lines include all humankind, all people from one extreme to the other. So a translator may choose to say "all people everywhere," "everyone in the world"; this, however, ceases to be poetry and becomes prose.

49.3-4	RSV	TEV
3	My mouth shall speak wisdom; the meditation of my heart shall be understanding.	3 My thoughts will be clear; I will speak words of wisdom.
4	I will incline my ear to a proverb; I will solve my riddle to the music of the lyre.	4 I will turn my attention to proverbs and explain their meaning as I play the harp.

In verse 3 TEV has reversed the two lines, since words are meant to follow thoughts. The psalmist promises to **speak wisdom**, and his "**thoughts will be clear**" (TEV).

What the psalmist is writing about is not philosophical knowledge but practical, everyday wisdom. To **speak wisdom** must be rendered in some languages as "I will speak words that will make you wise."

Meditation of my heart: the word translated **meditation** occurs only here in the Old Testament; the related verb "to meditate" is used in 1.2 (see comments there).

The word translated **understanding** carries the idea of skill; NJB and FRCL have "good sense"; NJV "my speech is full of insight." Another possible version is "understanding guides my thoughts."

Verse 3 is a clear case of heightening movement from line **a** to line **b**, in which **meditation of my heart** steps up the thought from the physical **mouth** of line **a**. The intensification may be made explicit in English by rendering, for example, "I will not only speak words of wisdom, but what is more, my deepest thoughts will be clearly expressed." Translators may prefer to follow the logical order of thoughts before words, as TEV has done; however, this is not the concern of the psalmist.

In verse 4 **proverb** and **riddle** are parallel. The Hebrew word translated **proverb** is *mashal* (see Howard A. Hatton, *The Bible Translator*, vol. 27, no. 2, April 1976, pages 224-230). **Proverbs** are sometimes called "wise sayings" or "wisdom words of the ancestors." One can also translate verse 4a "I will ponder what I must teach."

The psalmist promises to explain the proverb, calling it **my riddle**. RSV **solve** does not mean that he, the psalmist, is going to discover for himself, for the first time, the meaning of his proverb. Rather, he is going to explain it to his listeners. Anderson suggests "perplexing problem" as the meaning of the latter word here.

Only here in the Old Testament is instruction given to the accompaniment of music, although in places prophetic utterance was so delivered (see 1 Sam 10.5; 2 Kgs 3.15). **To the music of the lyre** may be rendered in some languages "as I play on the stringed instrument called harp" or simply "as I play on the stringed instrument."

<table>
<tr><td>**49.5-6**</td><td>RSV</td><td>TEV</td></tr>
</table>

	RSV		TEV
5	Why should I fear in times of trouble, when the iniquity of my persecutors surrounds me,	5	I am not afraid in times of danger when I am surrounded by enemies,
6	men who trust in their wealth and boast of the abundance of their riches?	6	by evil men who trust in their riches and boast of their great wealth.

The psalmist declares that wealth has no lasting value, and that rich people have no advantage over the poor; so he will not be afraid of his rich enemies. The rhetorical question (see RSV) is a way of affirming the confidence that the psalmist feels.

Times of trouble in 5a is defined in 5b as "**when I am surrounded by enemies** (TEV)." In some languages **times of trouble** must be shifted to a time clause; for example, "when I have troubles," or idiomatically, "when trouble takes hold of my throat."

Iniquity of my persecutors translates a phrase whose meaning can only be guessed at. The literal "iniquity of my heels" (KJV, following the Septuagint and Vulgate) would apply to the psalmist himself and would be most unlikely in this context. Dahood translates "slanderers"; NJV "those who would supplant me"; NIV "wicked deceivers"; NEB "treacherous foes." TEV has "**enemies**" in verse 5b and carries "**evil**" over to verse 6a. The word for "heels" is related to the name "Jacob" (that is, "supplanter"—see Gen 27.36); Cohen explains it here as "wealthy neighbours who deprive him of his rights."

The further description in verse 6 of the psalmist's enemies should offer no difficulty to translators. In some languages **trust** requires a person as object, so it may be necessary to use another verb; for example, "people who love their goods" or "people who like money more than anything." **Boast of . . . riches** is sometimes expressed as "they talk about how much wealth they own" or "they use big words when they talk about their goods."

	RSV		TEV
7	Truly no man can ransom himself,[o] or give to God the price of his life,	7	A person can never redeem himself; he cannot pay God the price for his life,
8	for the ransom of his[p] life is	8	because the payment for a hu-

449

costly,	man life is too great.
and can never suffice,	What he could pay would never be
9 that he should continue to live on	enough
for ever,	9 to keep him from the grave,
and never see the Pit.	to let him live forever.

^o Another reading is *no man can ransom
his brother*
^p Gk: Heb *their*

There are some difficulties in clearly understanding the Hebrew text of verses 7-8. The Masoretic text of verse 7a is "a brother a man cannot redeem" (see RSV footnote); but instead of the Masoretic text "brother" some Hebrew manuscripts have "Surely" (this is the Hebrew wording used by TEV and others). NJV also reads "surely" in the text, with "brother" in the footnote; but it takes "man" as the object of the verb, making "it" (the wealth of verse 6b) the subject. Its translation is "Ah, it cannot redeem a man." In either case the thought is the same: there is not enough money for anyone to buy permanent life insurance; death comes to all, even to the very wealthy. Perhaps FRCL is best, in understanding two different subjects, as follows: "No one has the means to pay God for the life of another person, or to give him the price of his own life."[1] It should be kept in mind that in these three verses what the psalmist is speaking of is earthly life, mortal life, not life after death.

For the verb **ransom** ("**redeem**") see its use in 25.22. The expression **no man can ransom himself** must be said in some languages as "no one can pay for his life" or "no one can pay money in order to live forever."

Verse 8a is literally "the payment for their *nefesh* (see 3.2) is costly." TEV has taken "their" as a general pronoun, that is, anyone's life (so NJV "the price of life is too high"). RSV prefers to follow the Septuagint "his" instead of the Masoretic text "their."

The next line (verse 8b) is in Hebrew "and he (or, it) leaves (or, ceases) forever," which can be taken in at least two ways: (1) as RSV and TEV have done, it refers to the ransom: "**What he could pay would never be enough**" (also Weiser; NEB, BJ, NJB, NAB, NIV, SPCL); or (2) with reference to human life, "and life (or, everyone) will cease forever" (NJV, TOB). The first option seems preferable. FRCL translates "One must give up such an idea once and for all."

In verse 9 the two lines are synonymous (TEV has reversed them); "**the grave**" translates **the Pit**, a name for Sheol (see 16.10); **see the Pit** means to experience death.

---

[1]TOB follows the Masoretic text and translates lines <u>a</u> and <u>b</u> "No one can pay the price for someone else or pay God for his ransom"; a note points out that in the second line "his" may refer to the subject of the verb "pay" or to the "someone else" of the first line. HOTTP follows the Masoretic text in line <u>a</u> ("A" decision) and proposes "Nobody can really ransom a brother."

49.10-11   RSV   TEV

10 Yea, he shall see that even the
      wise die,
    the fool and stupid alike must
      perish
    and leave their wealth to others.
11 Their graves*q* are their homes for
      ever,
    their dwelling places to all gen-
      erations,
    though they named lands their
      own.

10 Anyone can see that even wise
      men die,
    as well as foolish and stupid
      men.
    They all leave their riches to
      their descendants.
11 Their graves*e* are their homes
      forever;
    there they stay for all time,
    though they once had lands of
      their own.

q Gk Syr Compare Tg: Heb *their inward*
(thought)

e Some ancient translations graves; *Hebrew* inner thoughts.

The universality of death is such an obvious fact as to dispense with all comment. But the psalmist's point is that riches are not permanent, and so people should rather put their faith in God. **The wise . . . the fool and the stupid** all must die, and their wealth goes to others (verse 10), while they themselves remain in **their graves** forever (verse 11a,b).

In verse 11a **Their graves** (in Hebrew *qibram*) is the text supported by the ancient Versions; the Masoretic text is *qirbam* "their inner (thoughts)." Practically all modern translations and HOTTP favor the versional text. Line b̲ in Hebrew is exactly parallel to line a̲.

In line c̲ the Hebrew is a bit obscure, but most commentators and translators agree that the meaning is that expressed by RSV and TEV. **Named lands their own** probably refers to obtaining land through a legal transfer of ownership. It is equivalent to saying "though they once held title to their own lands." Translators should use the expression that indicates legal ownership of land; for example, "though they ate in agreement on the land they acquired." NJV sees not the idea of wealth, property, but of importance: "of those once famous on earth." In some languages it may be more effective to imitate FRCL and place as the first line of verse 11, "Even though they had lands of their own, their graves . . . ."

49.12   RSV   TEV

Man cannot abide in his pomp,
  he is like the beasts that perish.

A man's greatness cannot keep
  him from death;
  he will still die like the animals.

Abide is the same word used in 25.13, literally "to spend the night"; a literal translation (such as TOB, "A man, with all his prestige, doesn't last through the night") is liable to be misunderstood. Instead of the Masoretic text "abides," BJ, NJB, and FRCL prefer to follow the Septuagint and Syriac, "understand": "However, in the midst of his wealth, the man does not understand that he is going to his death . . . ."

The word translated **pomp** is literally honor, splendor, and may refer specifically here to wealth (SPCL, NIV, NJB; GECL has "greatness and wealth"). In some languages it will be necessary to shift line <u>a</u> into a reason and result clause; for example, "just because a man is great (or, rich) that will not prevent him from dying."

The idea expressed in line <u>b</u> is the same that is voiced in Ecclesiastes 3.18-21 and should be faithfully and clearly represented in translation.

<u>49.13-14</u> RSV	TEV

13 This is the fate of those who have foolish confidence,
   the end of those*r* who are pleased with their portion.
                                        Selah
	13 See what happens to those who trust in themselves,
	   the fate of those*f* who are satisfied with their wealth—

14 Like sheep they are appointed for Sheol;
   Death shall be their shepherd;
straight to the grave they descend,*s*
   and their form shall waste away;
   Sheol shall be their home.*t*
	14 they are doomed to die like sheep, and Death will be their shepherd.
	   The righteous will triumph over them,
	   as their bodies quickly decay in the world of the dead far from their homes.*g*

r Tg: Heb *after them* *s* Cn: Heb *the upright shall have dominion over them in the morning* *t* Heb uncertain	*f* *One ancient translation* the fate of those; *Hebrew* after them. *g* in . . . homes; *Hebrew unclear.*

The text and meaning of verses 13-14 are hard to determine, and in places the Hebrew text seems so corrupt as to be beyond restoration. Weiser gives no translation to the last half of verse 14, with the comment that "the restoration of the seriously corrupt text is hopeless." There are practically as many proposals for solution as there are commentaries and translations, and it would be futile to multiply examples.

In verse 13a **the fate** is literally "their path," that is, the place to where their path leads them. The expression **This is the fate of those** may sometimes need to be said as "this is what happens to those" or, closer to the Hebrew idiom, "this is the road they go on." **"Who trust in themselves"** (so NJV "self-confident") is taken by some to have the idea of **foolish confidence**.

Verse 13b in Hebrew is "and after them with their mouths they are pleased." This is variously understood. Instead of "and after them" the Targum has "and their end" (parallel with "their path" in line <u>a</u>); TEV, RSV, NJV, FRCL, TOB, and SPCL give this meaning, some without textual note.[2]

---

[2]HOTTP ("A" decision) says there are two interpretations of the Masoretic text: (1) "and the future of those who are pleased with their words"; (2) "and after them,

Who are pleased with their portion translates "with their mouths they are pleased." TEV takes "mouth" in the sense of "mouthful," that is, what is given them, their **portion** (RSV; so Briggs); also possible is "their possessions"; BJ is "happy with their lot" (also NAB). There are other solutions. NJB has "the end of those pleased with their own talk," and NIV "and of their followers, who approve their sayings." FRCL (also TOB, NJV; HOTTP) translates "those who love so much to hear themselves talk."

For **_Selah_** see 3.2.

The first half of verse 14 is fairly straightforward: **Like sheep they are appointed for Sheol**, which TEV translates "**they are doomed to die like sheep.**"

A vivid metaphor follows, **Death shall be their shepherd** (literally, "Death will shepherd them"); see 23.1 for comments on the corresponding noun "shepherd." The expression **Death shall be their shepherd** will be difficult to preserve in this form in many languages where death cannot be spoken of as a shepherd. However, it is often possible to compare death to a shepherd; for example, "they will be led away by death as sheep are led by a shepherd" or "death will take them away as a shepherd leads away the sheep." In languages in which **Death** cannot be personified, it may be necessary to drop both **Death** and **shepherd**. This may require joining line <u>b</u> to line <u>c</u>; for example, "they die and go to the grave" or "they die and are buried."

The next line in verse 14 of the Masoretic text is (or appears to be) "and the righteous will have dominion over them in the morning." TEV (like NJV, NIV, TOB, SPCL) has attempted to stay with the Masoretic text, even though it seems to make no sense, and connects "in the morning" with what follows, not with what precedes (so NJB), taking it in the sense of "**quickly.**" RSV (also FRCL) emends the text (see Anderson), and that yields a satisfactory meaning.[3] Translators may prefer to follow either RSV or TEV.

Their form translates a Hebrew word of uncertain form and meaning; most take the noun to mean **form** (RSV, NIV, FRCL, NJV), which TEV represents by "**bodies**"; BJ "their image"; NJB "all trace of them"; TOB "their features."

TEV "**far from their homes**" translates what in the Masoretic text is (or seems to be) "away from its dwelling" (or "away from its dominion"). NEB has "stripped of their honour"; another suggested translation is "so that they can no longer have any earthly dwelling"; NJV "till its nobility is gone"; TOB "they are far from their palace."[4] NJB (like RSV) connects "Sheol" with these words: "Sheol the home for them!" FRCL translates: "They descend quickly to the grave. Their forms waste away, the world of shadows becomes their home."

---

they are (or, one is) pleased with their words."

[3]HOTTP stays with the Masoretic text ("A" decision), saying that two translations are possible: (1) "and over them the righteous men will reign in the morning"; (2) "and in the morning the righteous will trample them down." HOTTP does not say which one is to be preferred.

[4]HOTTP says the Masoretic text means "far from a lofty abode for them" ("A" decision).

49.15 RSV	TEV

But God will ransom my soul
    from the power of Sheol,
for he will receive me.   *Selah*
	But God will rescue me;
	    he will save me from the power
	    of death.

TEV reverses the two lines of this verse; **"will rescue me"** in line a translates what appears in line b in RSV as **he will receive me**. Verse 15 is an example of untypical parallelism. The usual pattern is for the metaphor to occur in the second line, thus dramatizing the meaning of the first line. Here, however, the figurative language occurs in the first line. TEV has switched lines, and by doing so has recreated the typical order.

The words of this verse are clear: the psalmist knows that he will not share the fate of those who trust in themselves. God will rescue his *nefesh* (see 3.2) from the power (literally "the hand") of Sheol, for he will "take" him from there. The Hebrew verb can mean **receive** (so RSV and others); but in parallel with "rescue, save" of the preceding line (RSV **ransom**, the same verb that is used in verse 7), it seems more likely that here it means "take" (NEB; Dahood and FRCL have "snatch"). **From the power of Sheol** in some languages can be descriptively stated as "from the claws of death." However, in languages where death is not associated with power or with symbols of power such as hands, claws and the like, it will be necessary to simply say "from death."

As to the meaning of the psalmist's assertion, it seems unlikely in this context that it means only that God will save him from untimely death, as in 18.4-6; 30.2-3; were this the meaning, then the ultimate fate of the psalmist (and of those like him) would be no different from that of those who trust in their riches. So it seems that what is meant is that the psalmist expects to be like Enoch and Elijah, who were taken to God without going to Sheol (so Dahood), or else that after he dies (that is, goes to Sheol) God will take him from there into his presence. It seems best to keep as closely as possible to the form of the Hebrew text of this verse, since interpretations of its meaning vary. The translator's task is to represent in the target language, as naturally and clearly as possible, what the Hebrew text says: "Surely God will redeem my *nefesh* from the hand of Sheol, for he will take me" (see NJV).

49.16-17 RSV	TEV

16 Be not afraid when one becomes
    rich,
    when the glory*u* of his house
    increases.
17 For when he dies he will carry
    nothing away;
    his glory*u* will not go down after
    him.
	16 Don't be upset when a man be-
	    comes rich,
	    when his wealth grows even
	    greater;
	17 he cannot take it with him when
	    his dies;
	    his wealth will not go with him
	    to the grave.

u Or *wealth*

In verse 16 the psalmist advises others to be like him (see verses 5-6) and not "**be upset**" because some people prosper. The verb is "to be afraid" (see RSV), which TEV and FRCL take in the sense of being upset, disquieted. NJB and NIV "overawed" is good. But the same Hebrew consonants can be given vowel points to mean "look," possibly yielding "look with envy" (see NEB, Dahood). This makes good sense, and a translator may choose to follow this interpretation.

In verse 16b **the glory of his house** (or, "the honor . . .) may mean "the wealth of his family" (NEB) or "his household goods" (NJV).

The two lines of verse 17 are synonymous: no one takes his riches with him when he "goes down" to Sheol, the world of the dead. RSV has kept the meaning **glory** in the text of verses 16b and 17b, with "wealth" as an alternative translation. It seems best to say "**wealth**" or "riches" in the text (so TEV, NJB; NIV "splendor"; NJV "goods"). In some languages it is not possible to speak of **his glory** going **down** or "**his wealth will not go with him,**" as if wealth had animate characteristics. One may often say "his wealth will not be with him in the grave" or "he will not be able to use his money in the grave."

49.18-19   RSV   TEV

18   Though, while he lives, he counts   18   Even if a man is satisfied with this
          himself happy,   life
      and though a man gets praise   and is praised because he is
          when he does well for him-   successful,
          self,   19   he will join all his ancestors in
19   he will go to the generation of his   death,
          fathers,   where the darkness lasts for-
      who will never more see the   ever.
          light.

Line <u>a</u> of verse 18 is literally "even if he blesses his *nefesh* (that is, congratulates himself—see NJV) while he lives." The psalmist is speaking of the person who in this life has achieved the greatest rewards of all, humanly speaking, that is, inner satisfaction and outer praise. So line <u>b</u> balances line <u>a</u> in portraying this unusually fortunate person, while verse 19 shows the futility of it all.

Line <u>b</u> has some textual problems, especially with the Hebrew personal pronoun suffixes, but it seems that the Masoretic text is a direct statement, as TOB has it, the man speaking to himself: "Everyone praises you because everything goes well with you." Or else (see Anderson) "and though they praise you because you are successful," which is how TEV, NIV, and SPCL have translated it.

In verse 19 the initial verb can be read as third feminine (with *nefesh* as the subject), or second masculine, taking up the "you" of verse 18b, which in Hebrew represents the man saying to himself "You are praised, because everything goes well with you" (FRCL; see NJV). In either case the reference is still to the same person spoken of in verses 16-18, and there is no need to emend the text.

TEV "**all his ancestors**" (RSV **the generation of his fathers**) are in dark Sheol, and that is the eternal destiny of such a person; like them he too will be where they **never more see the light**.

	49.20	RSV	TEV

Man cannot abide in his pomp,
    he is like the beasts that perish.

A man's greatness cannot keep
    him from death;
he will still die like the animals.

The Masoretic text of this verse differs slightly from that of verse 12; instead of **man cannot abide**, reading *yalin* as in verse 12, the Masoretic text here has "man cannot understand" (*yabin*), which HOTTP prefers. So NJV "Man does not understand honor" (which makes little, if any, sense in English), and NJB "In prosperity people lose their good sense," which is a good thought but hardly seems to be what the psalmist was talking about (see TOB, NIV). But some Hebrew manuscripts have *yalin*, and so RSV, TEV, and others translate verse 20 the same as verse 12.

Psalm 50

This psalm proclaims God as the judge of the people of Israel and of all the world. It was used in worship, probably during a festival in which the people renewed their covenant with God. Nothing definite can be said about the time and circumstances of its composition. The psalmist is concerned with the nature of true worship, as opposed to the ritual concept that worship consists of faithfully performing certain prescribed acts. True worship is a matter of a right relationship with God, not ritual practices. Oesterley concludes his discussion on the religious teaching of this psalm with the comment: "For its insistence on the true nature of practical religion, this psalm stands out as second to none."

Through the recurring use of forms alluding to speech, Psalm 50 emphasizes acts of communication. There are some twenty-one occurrences of this in the psalm. Furthermore, the opening of every stanza, except the final one, contains such a reference, always in the second of two parallel lines, and sometimes in both.

The psalm begins with a description of Yahweh's coming to judge Israel (verses 1-6), followed by a lengthy statement about the meaning and purpose of sacrifices (verses 7-15). After this God speaks to the wicked and condemns them for their evil deeds (verses 16-21). In the closing statement (verses 22-23) God repeats his warning to the wicked and his promise to the righteous.

HEADING: "**True Worship**." Other headings are "Worship in spirit and truth"; "God is a just judge"; "Acceptable sacrifice." In some languages it will be necessary to expand the TEV title; for example, "The true way to worship God."

Hebrew Title: **A Psalm of Asaph** (TEV "**A psalm by Asaph**").

This title occurs here and with Psalms 73–83 (in Book Three). Asaph was one of David's chief musicians (1 Chr 6.39; 15.17; 16.5-6; 2 Chr 5.12), the father of four of the leaders of the twenty-four groups of Temple musicians (1 Chr 25.1-2), and the ancestor of a group of Temple musicians (Ezra 2.41).

50.1-2	RSV	TEV

1	The Mighty One, God the LORD,
	   speaks and summons the earth
	from the rising of the sun to its
	   setting.
		1 The Almighty God, the LORD,
		   speaks;
		he calls to the whole earth from
		   east to west.

2	Out of Zion, the perfection of
	   beauty,
	God shines forth.
		2 God shines from Zion,
		   the city perfect in its beauty.

The psalm opens with a solemn declaration about the people of **the earth** being summoned by God, who is spoken of with three names: God (*'el*), God (*'elohim*), and Yahweh. The first two may be taken to mean "the God of gods" (so NJB, TOB), but it is probably better to understand them in the superlative sense, "**The Almighty God.**" RSV translates the first name **The Mighty One**, and joins the second and third names, **God, the LORD. The Mighty One** and "The Almighty God" must in some languages be rendered "the God who is most powerful" or "the powerful God."

Speaks and summons the earth: in some languages it will be necessary to indicate that it is "the people of the whole earth" who are called by God.

The expression **from the rising of the sun to its setting** refers to space, not time, and means "from all the earth," "from everywhere in the world."

The line arrangement in TEV represents the parallelism correctly, since **speaks** in RSV belongs with line **a**. Line **b** of TEV, "**calls to the whole earth,**" makes specific what "**speaks**" refers to in line **a**, and may be rendered, for example, "More than that, he calls to everyone from one end of the world to the other."

God is in his Temple in Jerusalem (**Zion**), whose **beauty** is praised (see 48.2); from there his glory **shines forth** over the world (see 80.1; 94.1; Deut 33.2). **God shines forth** is not an easy form to translate literally, as many languages do not speak of God as shining. However, it is usually possible to make such expressions clear and fairly natural if one uses a comparison; for example, "God shines like a light," or "God shines like the sun," or "God's splendor shines like a light."

50.3-4	RSV		TEV
3	Our God comes, he does not keep silence,	3	Our God is coming, but not in silence;
	before him is a devouring fire,		a raging fire is in front of him,
	round about him a mighty tempest.		a furious storm around him.
4	He calls to the heavens above	4	He calls heaven and earth as witnesses
	and to the earth, that he may judge his people:		to see him judge his people.

Some take verse 3a as a request, a prayer: "May God come . . . !" (NJV, BJ, FRCL, TOB, AT, NAB). It seems better, however, to take it as a statement, describing God's judgment of Israel.

The coming of God (verse 3) is described in terms of **a devouring fire** and **a mighty tempest** (see similar description in Deut 33.1; Psa 18.8-12). If the translator is following TEV, it may be necessary to complete the thoughts of each line more fully; for example, "but he is not coming silently," "a raging fire burns in front of him," and "a furious storm blows around him."

In verse 4 the Hebrew text could conceivably mean that God calls heavens and earth to be judges of his people; but it seems more likely, as the vast majority of commentators and translators believe, that the text means he is calling them "to see him judge his people"; FRCL "to be present at the judgment of his people"; SPCL "to witness the judgment of his people." "**Calls . . . as witnesses**" is a very specialized use of the term "call." In some languages, if the translator follows the lead of TEV, it will be necessary to say, for example, "God tells heaven and earth to witness" or "God makes heaven and earth look on." In many languages it will be difficult to say that heaven and earth are to perform the act of witnessing. Therefore one may need to add a simile; for example, "God calls heaven and earth to watch him, just as a person watches."

50.5-6	RSV	TEV
5	"Gather to me my faithful ones, who made a covenant with me by sacrifice!"	5 He says, "Gather my faithful people to me, those who made a covenant with me by offering a sacrifice."
6	The heavens declare his righteousness, for God himself is judge! *Selah*	6 The heavens proclaim that God is righteous, that he himself is judge.

"He says" (TEV): the Hebrew text does not say to whom God is speaking. But it seems that the imperative **Gather to me** is addressed to the heavens and the earth, as messengers who are to bring God's people to judgment (see Briggs); it is highly unlikely that angels are being addressed. **My faithful ones**: see comments on "godly" in 4.3; here the translation can be "those who are devoted (or, dedicated) to me."

In TEV **Gather** occurs as a command. If the translator follows this wording, it will often be necessary to express the one who is being commanded. Since it is not clear that anyone is being told to do the gathering, it will most often be easier to express line a as a request or command to the people themselves; for example, "God says, 'I want my people to gather to me' " or "God says, 'Let my people come to me.' "

The people are described as those **who made a covenant** with God **by sacrifice**. This could refer to the original ratification of the covenant (Exo 24.5-8) or to a ceremony in which the covenant was renewed, perhaps during the Festival of Shelters. In some languages **covenant** is rendered by such terms as "treaty," "alliance," or "compact" (see 25.10).

The heavens declare: perhaps this means the heavenly beings; more likely, as in verse 4, heaven is here personified. In some languages one cannot say that **the heavens declare** or "proclaim." It is often possible to say, however, "the heavens show that God is righteous."

The initial conjunction in verse 4b may mean "because" or **for** (RSV, NEB, NIV, NJV, NAB) instead of "**that**" (TEV, AT, FRCL, TOB, BJ, SPCL). In some languages it will be necessary to shift from a noun phrase to a verb phrase in the expression **God himself is judge**; for example, "God himself is the one who judges people."

For *Selah* see 3.2.

50.7-8	RSV	TEV
7	"Hear, O my people, and I will speak,	7 "Listen, my people, and I will speak;

O Israel, I will testify against you.	I will testify against you, Israel.
I am God, your God.	I am God, your God.
8 I do not reprove you for your sacrifices; your burnt offerings are continually before me.	8 I do not reprimand you because of your sacrifices and the burnt offerings you always bring me.

God starts the accusation against his people, who are on trial; in solemn terms he reminds them that the one who speaks is none other than **God, your God** (verse 7c). **My people** in line <u>a</u> is the same as **Israel** in line <u>b</u>. In verse 7 line <u>b</u> steps up the intensity by focusing on the kind of speaking God will do, and may be rendered, for example, "I will go so far as to testify against you, Israel" or "I will go even further, Israel; I will testify against you." In some languages the expression **I will testify against you** may be rendered "I will stand and say that you have done wrong."

The expression **I am God, your God** must be adjusted in some languages because one cannot speak of God being possessed. Therefore in those languages it is often possible to say "I am God, the God you worship."

What matters is not the **sacrifices** that they offer to him nor the **burnt offerings** that are continually presented to him (verse 8). The meaning of verse 8 can be better expressed by "When I rebuke you, it is *not* on account of your sacrifices . . . ." God is rebuking his people, not because of what they do (offer sacrifices) but because of what they don't do, namely, offer him their thanksgiving (verse 14). The expression **I do not reprove you for your sacrifices** may be rendered in some languages as "I do not say you do wrong when you burn animals as gifts for me."

50.9   RSV   TEV

I will accept no bull from your house, nor he-goat from your folds.	And yet I do not need bulls from your farms or goats from your flocks;

God explains why animal sacrifices are relatively unimportant to him; he really does not need them, since all animals already belong to him. This idea is radically different from the mythology of the ancient near east, in which the gods go hungry if there are no sacrifices.

Accept: the Hebrew verb ordinarily means to take or to receive (see its use in 49.15b). Here the meaning seems to be something like "need" (TEV, NIV; Weiser), or "ask for" (SPCL; Dahood), or "desire" (Oesterley). But some (FRCL, BJ, TOB) translate "I will not take," like RSV and NJB **I will accept no . . .** ; NJV has "I claim no bull . . . no he-goats"; NEB has "I need [not] take." This makes for a rather strange statement, as though God were abolishing the sacrificial system as such. One must recognize that often in the Scriptures absolute denials or promises are forceful ways of expressing important truths; but such statements are not to be understood in an absolute fashion. The translator, however, must faithfully represent the meaning of the biblical text without trying to tone down or soften what seems to be an exaggeration. So GECL translates, "I do not accept your offering—I do not need the bull from your barn." In some languages it will be clearer to make explicit that the **bulls** and **goats** are not needed as sacrifices; for example, "I do not need sacrificed bulls from your farms or sacrificed goats from your flocks."

<u>**50.10-11**</u>   RSV   TEV

10   For every beast of the forest is   10   all the animals in the forest are
         mine,   mine
      the cattle on a thousand hills.   and the cattle on thousands of
11   I know all the birds of the air,*   hills.
      and all that moves in the field is   11   All the wild birds are mine
         mine.   and all living things in the
                                                                  fields.

ʸ Gk Syr Tg: Heb *mountains*

In these verses God declares that he owns all animals, wild and domestic, and all birds. The Hebrew text of verse 10b is unusual, and the meaning may be "and thousands of cattle in the hills" (see NEB, NJB).

I know in verse 11a is used here in the sense of laying claim to; Anderson explains: "I have both knowledge of and mastery over." GECL translates "All the birds out there belong to me."

TEV "**wild birds**" in verse 11a translates the Masoretic text "birds of the hills" (see RSV footnote; NJV "every bird of the mountains"), which is an unusual phrase; the usual one is "birds of the air," as in the Septuagint, Syriac, and Vulgate. These two verses form a chiasmus in the Hebrew, and the poet undoubtedly used "of the mountains" to correspond to **on a thousand hills** in the previous line.[1] The meaning, however, is the same, namely "**wild birds**."

<u>**50.12-13**</u>   RSV   TEV

12   "If I were hungry, I would not tell   12   "If I were hungry, I would not ask
         you;   you for food,
      for the world and all that is in   for the world and everything in
         it is mine.   it is mine.
13   Do I eat the flesh of bulls,   13   Do I eat the flesh of bulls
      or drink the blood of goats?   or drink the blood of goats?

God does not need sacrifices. It is not a matter of his needs but of his people's needs. If God were to get hungry he wouldn't have to go and ask his people for food, since all the world and everything in it belong to him (see 24.1). So **I would not tell you** in verse 12a does not mean only that he would not inform them of his hunger; rather, God is saying he would not ask them to feed him. FRCL, closer to the Hebrew, translates "If I were hungry, I would not need to tell you about it."

---

[1]HOTTP also prefers the Masoretic text ("C" decision).

In picturesque language God denies the need of sacrifices: he doesn't **eat the flesh of bulls or drink the blood of goats**. This is to be understood against the background of certain primitive beliefs that sacrifices were actually eaten by the gods. The two rhetorical questions in this verse will require replies of "No!" in some languages in which rhetorical questions normally take a reply.

50.14-15

RSV	TEV
14 Offer to God a sacrifice of thanksgiving,*w* and pay your vows to the Most High;	14 Let the giving of thanks be your sacrifice to God,*i* and give the Almighty all that you promised.
15 and call upon me in the day of trouble; I will deliver you, and you shall glorify me."	15 Call to me when trouble comes; I will save you, and you will praise me."

w Or *make thanksgiving your sacrifice to God.*

i Let the giving . . . to God; *or* Offer your thanksgiving sacrifice to God.

The kind of sacrifice that really counts with God is **a sacrifice of thanksgiving** (verse 14a; see also verse 23a). This line is not entirely free of difficulty; as RSV text and TEV footnote show, the meaning can be "offer to God a thanksgiving sacrifice" (also NEB, BJ, NJV, NIV, AT), which was one of the prescribed sacrifices. This actually fits better with the command in verse 14b. But it seems preferable to take it as the TEV and RSV footnotes have it (also TOB, NJB, NAB, SPCL; Dahood, Weiser), with an alternative translation in a footnote. The phrase **a sacrifice of thanksgiving** must in some languages be shifted to a clause; for example, "give God thanks, and this will be your sacrifice" or "your sacrifice should be by saying 'Thank you, God.' "

Both RSV and TEV follow the Hebrew in verse 14 by speaking of God in the third person, changing from the first person in verses 12-13 and 15. This may be difficult to do in some languages, since God is the speaker; so verse 14 can be ". . . be your sacrifice to me, your God, and give me, the Almighty . . . ."

Pay your vows means to keep all the promises you made to offer sacrifices to **the Most High** (see comment on this title in 7.17).

There is no need for elaborate sacrifices; let his people only **call upon** God when trouble comes and he will save them; for **deliver** see the use of the same verb translated "save" in 6.4a. Then they will **"praise"** him for his help (literally "honor"; RSV **glorify**).

50.16

RSV	TEV
But to the wicked God says: "What right have you to recite my statutes,	But God says to the wicked, "Why should you recite my commandments?

<table>
<tr><td>or take my covenant on your
lips?</td><td>Why should you talk about my
covenant?</td></tr>
</table>

God now accuses the wicked (verses 16-21). Some believe that the first line of verse 16 is a gloss, introduced later by a copyist. Such a conjecture makes sense, since the whole purpose of the psalm is to express God's complaint against his people as a whole. But the words stand in our Hebrew text, as well as in the ancient versions, and must be retained in translation.

With two rhetorical questions God begins his accusation of these people. The point is that they were not really interested in obeying his **statutes** (see 18.22b and comments) or in being faithful to his **covenant** (see discussion in 25.10), so they should not be talking about them. Their constant references to them—perhaps involving promises made in public worship to obey them—were hypocritical, as amply demonstrated by their conduct. The expression **recite my statutes** may be rendered in some languages as "you learn and repeat the commands I gave you" or "you say over and over the words of the orders I gave you."

Covenant is here used with the sense of "law or commandments" and is parallel to **statutes** in the previous line. "Why do you talk about my laws?" "Why do you discuss the commands I have given you?"

50.17-18	RSV		TEV

	RSV	TEV
17	For you hate discipline, and you cast my words behind you.	17 You refuse to let me correct you; you reject my commands.
18	If you see a thief, you are a friend of his; and you keep company with adulterers.	18 You become the friend of every thief you see, and you associate with adulterers.

The wicked hate to be disciplined by God and they reject his commandments (literally **words**—see the use of the Hebrew "word" as a commandment in the traditional Ten Commandments, or "Ten Words," Exo 34.28). The first line can be translated "you detest my teaching" (NJB), or "you hate my instruction" (NIV), since the word translated **discipline** can have the broader meaning of "education."

Intensification is used in verse 17 through the use of the figure **cast my words behind you** in line **b**. In some languages an equivalent figure may be used; for example, "you throw away my words" or "you wipe my words away." However, the use of a metaphor in line **b** may not be an intensifying device, and the translator may have to say, for example, "You hate for me to teach you, and more serious than that, you reject what I have ordered you to do."

And instead of condemning such flagrant sinners as thieves and adulterers, these wicked people become their friends and associate with them (verse 18). In verse 18a "**become the friend of**" translates a verb which generally means "be pleased

463

with, be favorable to, approve"; one version may be "you think well of him"; NIV "you join with him"; FRCL "you take his side."[2]

The expression **adulterers** including both sexes is often more difficult than the terms for the female only, which is often expressed by means of idiomatic phrases. In speaking of adulterers one can sometimes say, for example, "men and women who are not faithful to their spouses" or "people who live in other marriages."

50.19-20	RSV	TEV

	RSV		TEV
19	"You give your mouth free rein for evil, and your tongue frames deceit.	19	"You are always ready to speak evil; you never hesitate to tell lies.
20	You sit and speak against your brother; you slander your own mother's son.	20	You are ready to accuse your own brothers and to find fault with them.

God continues his accusation of the wicked: they are guilty of lies, deceit, and slander—all kinds of "sins of the tongue." In verse 19a the text is literally "you send off your mouth with evil," which is strangely like the American slang expression "to shoot off the mouth."

In verse 19b the verb **frames** is "to join to, attach to," which NEB and NIV render "harness to" and NJV "yoke to"—not very successful attempts in English at vividness. NJB is better, "your tongue [is devoted to] inventing lies."

You sit and speak (verse 20a) seems to imply a deliberate, premeditated slander, not just one spoken in the heat of anger. It can mean to **sit** as a judge with others, to hear complaints and accusations that are brought to them for judgment. NJV has "you are busy maligning . . . ," and NEB "You are for ever talking against . . . ."

In verse 20a **brother** could be a fellow Jew; but the parallel in line b makes it probable that the word is meant in the more restricted sense. The two lines, then, may be closely synonymous. But FRCL translates the first line "your neighbor" and the second line "your own brother."

In English **your own mother's son** (also NEB, NJV, NIV, NJB, NAB) in line b is not a natural expression; it would be better to use a personal pronoun. The verbal phrase translated **slander** (TEV **"to find fault"**) uses a noun for "blemish" or "fault" that occurs only here in the Old Testament. NEB translates "stabbing . . . in the back," a vivid, idiomatic phrase in English. Line b steps up the intensity by the use of **slander**, and the two lines may be translated, for example, "You not only say bad things about your own brother, you go so far as to slander him."

---

[2]HOTTP notes that the verb may mean "to run" as well as "to agree with." The rendering "you ran with him" would probably be understood as "you became his partner."

50.21	RSV		TEV

	RSV	TEV
	These things you have done and I have been silent; you thought that I was one like yourself. But now I rebuke you, and lay the charge before you.	˙You have done all this, and I have said nothing, so you thought that I am like you. But now I reprimand you and make the matter plain to you.

The first line of this verse may be translated as a rhetorical question, "When you do such things, shall I keep silent?" (so NEB, TOB, BJ, NJB). The next line is also rendered as a rhetorical question, with good effect: "Do you think that I am really like you?" (NJB, FRCL; also TOB, NAB).

The statement **now I rebuke you** recalls what is said in verse 8. TEV "I . . . make the matter plain to you" translates "I lay it out (in rows, in order) before your eyes." That is, God is plainly stating, as a witness, the charges he brings against them.

50.22-23 RSV TEV

	RSV	TEV
22	"Mark this, then, you who forget God, lest I rend, and there be none to deliver!	22 "Listen to this, you that ignore me, or I will destroy you, and there will be no one to save you.
23	He who brings thanksgiving as his sacrifice honors me; to him who orders his way aright I will show the salvation of God!"	23 Giving thanks is the sacrifice that honors me, and I will surely save all who obey me."

The final two verses bring God's indictment of the wicked to a close, with a warning to them to listen to him or he will destroy them. **Mark this,** "Pay attention to this," "Notice this."

To **forget God** is to disregard him, ignore his commands (see comments on 9.17).

The verb translated **rend** is "to tear to pieces" like a lion; see its use with "lion" in 7.2; 17.12.

For **deliver** (TEV "save") see the use of the same verb in 7.1, and the same verb translated "rescue" in 7.2.

What God wants from his worshipers is a thankful heart (verse 23a; see verse 14a). In many languages it will be necessary to reorder the wording in TEV "**Giving thanks is the sacrifice that honors me.**" This may often be done by saying, for example, "When you give thanks you are giving the sacrifice that honors me" or "By thanking me you give me the sacrifice that honors me."

The phrase **orders his way aright**, while unusual, is readily understood as a metaphor for conduct, behavior; so NJB "the upright," SPCL "who continues (walking) in my way," FRCL "the one who keeps watch over his behavior."

The final **I will show the salvation of God**, it must be remembered, has God as speaker, and he refers to himself in the third person. The noun phrase **the salvation of God** means "God saves people"; and **I will show** means not merely to display or to present, but actually to put into effect. So SPCL "I save," and GECL "and whoever obeys me will experience my help."

Psalm 51

This psalm is a prayer of confession by an individual who has sinned and who comes to God confessing his sin and asking for forgiveness, that is, a restoration of the fellowship with God which has been broken by sin. It is classified as one of the seven penitential psalms (see introduction to Psa 32).

The identity of the psalmist and the reason he composed this prayer are given in the Hebrew title as David's act of adultery with Bathsheba (see below). Most modern commentators do not believe that the title reflects the actual circumstances in which the psalm was written; see commentaries, and see E. R. Dalglish, *Psalm Fifty-One*, page 222. Some, however, strongly defend the traditional view (see Cohen) and, like the others, recognize that the last two verses are a later addition (see Kirkpatrick), since these verses reflect a situation which did not exist in David's lifetime. The Jewish commentator Ibn Ezra, of the twelfth century A.D., suggested that they were added by a Jew who was in exile in Babylonia.

The psalm begins with a prayer for forgiveness (verses 1-2), followed by a confession of sin (verses 3-5). The psalmist prays for a restoration of fellowship with God and a spiritual renewal, ending with a promise to bring sinners back to God (verses 6-13). Then he promises to offer his praise to God and to present the kind of sacrifice that pleases God (verses 14-17). The last two verses are a prayer asking God to restore Jerusalem so that sacrifices may again be offered to him at the Temple (verses 18-19).

HEADING: "**A Prayer for Forgiveness**." Other headings are "O God, have mercy on me"; "Repentance and cleansing"; "A penitent's cry." In some languages it will be desirable and necessary to shift the two nouns in the title to verb phrases; for example, "The psalmist prays asking God to forgive him."

Hebrew Title: <u>**To the choirmaster. A Psalm of David, when Nathan the prophet came to him, after he had gone in to Bathsheba**</u> (TEV "A psalm by David, after the prophet Nathan had spoken to him about his adultery with Bathsheba").

For **choirmaster** see title of Psalm 4. The events referred to are related in 2 Samuel 11.1–12.15. The Hebrew expression "to go in to" means to have sexual intercourse.

51.1-2

RSV	TEV
1 Have mercy on me, O God, according to thy steadfast love; according to thy abundant mercy blot out my transgressions.	1 Be merciful to me, O God, because of your constant love. Because of your great mercy wipe away my sins!

467

| 2 Wash me thoroughly from my iniquity,
and cleanse me from my sin! | 2 Wash away all my evil
and make me clean from my sin! |

The initial verb **Have mercy** (verse 1a) is often used in the Psalms; it means to show favor, to be kindly disposed (see 4.1c, where the same verb is translated "Be gracious"). **Have mercy on me** is sometimes rendered in idiomatic language; for example, "Have a white heart for me" or "Be pained for me."

The two qualities of God on which the psalmist depends for forgiveness are his **steadfast love** (verse 1a; see comments at 5.7) and his **mercy** (verse 1b). The Hebrew word translated **mercy** is plural in form, and when it has this sense it is always plural. In some contexts it means "bowels," and the singular form means "womb." The word carries a sense of intense emotion, of deep-seated feelings, which one has for a person who is especially near and dear.

In the opening prayer for forgiveness, three different words for sin are used: **transgressions** (verse 1b) are primarily acts of disobedience, of rebellion; **iniquity** (verse 2a) is guilt, fault, a deliberate act of misconduct; and **sin** (verse 2b) is the most general word used in the Old Testament; it has basically the idea of going astray, of missing the mark.

The request to forgive is expressed by three verbs: **to blot out** (verse 1b) is to wipe out, like rubbing out an item on a list (see 9.5); **wash** represents sin as a stain that has to be washed out; the verb expresses the way in which clothes were washed by being beaten against rocks to remove the dirt; and **cleanse** means to purify; here sin is thought of as a defilement which renders a person ritually unclean and which must be removed so that he or she can be pronounced clean and rejoin the community.

The figures used of removing sin through wiping and washing may require some adjustments in some languages where these figures are not clear. One may use a simile; for example, "Wipe away my sins like a person wipes up water" and "Wash away my evil like a person washes away dirt."

The two lines of verse 2 form a chiastic structure in Hebrew, with the nouns bracketed by the verbs: wash iniquity: sins cleanse. The parallelism is static, with no heightening effect between the lines. Although the meaning is the same, the word order is different in the two lines, indicating the psalmist's desire to express a totality of action in regard to being relieved of his sins. A chiastic structure in the receptor language may be syntactically impossible or stylistically awkward. The translator should, however, attempt to retain both lines, unless there are very good reasons for reducing them to one.

51.3-4

| RSV | TEV |

| 3 For I know my transgressions,
and my sin is ever before me.
4 Against thee, thee only, have I sinned,
and done that which is evil in thy sight,
so that thou art justified in thy sentence | 3 I recognize my faults;
I am always conscious of my sins.
4 I have sinned against you—only against you—
and done what you consider evil.
So you are right in judging me; |

and blameless in thy judgment.	you are justified in condemning me.

The psalmist confesses his sin to God: **I know my transgressions**; **know** here has the sense of admitting or confessing to oneself; **transgressions** translates the same word used in verse 1b, and **sins** the word used in verse 2b. The expression **is before me** in verse 3b means "I am conscious of," "I am aware of," parallel with **I know** in verse 3a. The psalmist intends to confess all his sins; he will not hide anything. In languages which use a verb phrase for **my sin**, it will often be necessary to say, for example, "I know that I do evil deeds."

He confesses that his sin was against God: **Against thee, thee only** is what he says. Some (see Taylor) point out that it would be difficult for David to have said that, since his sin was against Uriah, Bathsheba's husband, and against Bathsheba as well. But the ardor of the psalmist's confession and his recognition that sin is primarily an offense against God are not the criteria for deciding the historical question of authorship. And it should be noted that David, when confronted with the denunciation of his adultery with Bathsheba and his murder of her husband Uriah, confessed: "I have sinned against the LORD" (2 Sam 12.13). In some languages it is not possible to say that one has **sinned against** someone. To sin against is sometimes rendered "to sin in your eyes;" for example, "I have sinned in your eyes—only in your eyes." It is also possible to say, for example, "I have sinned and offended you."

In thy sentence (verse 4c) translates what is literally "in your speaking," that is, in your pronouncing the sentence of "Guilty!" Some Hebrew manuscripts have "in your words," which Briggs prefers and interprets as a reference to the Ten Commandments. **In thy judgment** in line d is parallel with **in thy sentence** in line c. **Thou art justified** in line c means that God does the right thing; he is not guilty of injustice in condemning the psalmist. The same thought is repeated in line d, **and blameless**, that is, God is not at fault; rather he is innocent of injustice or wrongdoing in his ruling.

Thou art justified in thy sentence may in some languages be rendered "you are right when you say that I am guilty" or, in direct discourse, "you are right when you say to me, 'You are guilty.' " The expression **blameless in thy judgment** can sometimes be translated as "you are fair when you say that I am guilty" or "you judge me fairly when you condemn me."

In Romans 3.4 Paul quotes the second half of verse 4 as translated by the Septuagint, with a meaning quite different from that of the Hebrew text.

51.5 RSV	TEV

Behold, I was brought forth in iniquity, and in sin did my mother conceive me.	I have been evil from the day I was born; from the time I was conceived, I have been sinful.

In vivid language the psalmist confesses that he has been a sinner all his life. The literal language, "In iniquity I was given birth, and in sin my mother conceived me" (see 58.3), is hardly the basis for biological, anthropological, or theological pronouncements about the nature of the human being as sinner. Were the words to be taken literally, they would mean that the psalmist's mother sinned when she became pregnant (which implies either that sexual intercourse as such is sinful or that she was guilty of fornication or adultery), and that at the moment of his birth he was already a sinner. What the psalmist is saying is that he (and so, by implication, everyone) is a sinner; sin is ingrained in human nature and permeates all of human activity. In some languages it may be better to follow the example of TEV or of GECL: "Wrong and guilt have characterized my life ever since my mother gave birth to me."

Verse 5 steps up the intensity in line **b**, in which **mother conceive me** is a specification and dramatization of **brought forth** in line **a**. The two lines may be rendered, for example, "I have been evil from the time of my birth, in fact, ever since I was conceived" or "I have been sinful from my birth, even longer, ever since my mother became pregnant with me."

<u>51.6</u>	RSV	TEV

Behold, thou desirest truth in the
    inward being;
therefore teach me wisdom in
    my secret heart.

Sincerity and truth are what you
    require;
fill my mind with your wisdom.

<u>Behold</u>: see 39.5 and comments.

The opening words of this verse are "Truth (or, faithfulness) you delight in"; these are followed by a phrase whose meaning is unclear. It is usually taken to mean "in the inward parts" (so RSV **inward being**); one possible version is "you desire faithfulness in the heart." NJV translates differently, "Indeed You desire truth about that which is hidden," and TOB has "You love the truth in the darkness," with a footnote: "a word whose meaning and etymology are quite uncertain." TEV has "Sincerity" for the Hebrew phrase; SPCL has "Truly you love a sincere heart," and NJB "You delight in sincerity of heart." If the translator follows TEV in line **a**, "sincerity" is concerned with an absence of hypocrisy or, stated positively, with genuine thoughts and actions. In some languages these qualities are spoken of as being from the heart. **Truth** in the present context refers to the truth of God's wisdom. In some languages it is possible to say, for example, "doing the right thing from the heart and following the true words of God are what God requires."

The second line is likewise difficult; the parallel word is "in a secret place" (or, secretly). Had the psalmist meant "*my* inward parts" and "*my* secret place" as expressions for his mind and heart, one would expect the use of the first person pronominal suffix, but it is missing from both Hebrew terms. So something like NEB may well be the meaning intended for the whole verse: "Yea, though thou hast hidden the truth in darkness, through this mystery thou dost teach me wisdom." For the second line TOB has "in my night you teach me wisdom"; NJV "teach me wisdom about secret things." FRCL translates the whole verse as follows: "But what you like to discover in the human heart is respect for the truth. Make me know wisdom in the depths of my conscience." This is a beautiful statement, but it is not certain that this is what the biblical author meant.

51.7   RSV   TEV

> Purge me with hyssop, and I shall
>   be clean;
> wash me, and I shall be whiter
>   than snow.

> Remove my sin, and I will be
>   clean;
> wash me, and I will be whiter
>   than snow.

The psalmist prays for forgiveness: **Purge me with hyssop**. The verb is the intensive form of the verb "to sin," and means (as Anderson picturesquely puts it) "to de-sin" or "un-sin." Hyssop was a small bush plant used for sprinkling water or blood on things and people in ceremonies of atonement and purification (see *Fauna and Flora*, pages 129-130; Exo 12.22; Lev 14.1-7; Num 19.1-6,16-19). TEV has chosen to abandon the literal language and give the meaning, since it is not ritual purification the psalmist prays for but inner forgiveness. So FRCL "Cause my fault to disappear, and I will be pure."

The verb **wash** is the one used in verse 2a.

In the parallel lines of verse 7, line **b**'s metaphor **whiter than snow** represents going beyond line **a**'s **I shall be clean**. The intensification may be reflected by rendering line **b**, for example, "More than that, wash me and I will be whiter than snow."

The expression **wash me, and I shall be whiter than snow** presents the translator with several problems. In some areas where snow is unknown or where, in spite of the presence of snow, it is not used as a proverbial likeness of something that is very white, it is necessary to avoid the word snow. In some languages it may be satisfactory to use some other article for comparison. However, in this case it is not the suitability of comparison of whiteness so much as it is the meaningful use of the comparison that is important. Consequently the translator must select for his language the solution that is the most natural and meaningful for the readers. One may say, for example, "and I will be white as . . . ," where the dots represent some local object known for its whiteness, or one may say "and I will be very white." It is also appropriate to translate "and I will be very clean," since it is the purification by the removal of sin that is in focus. If it is necessary the translator can also employ a simile to indicate the figurative aspect of the cleanliness.

51.8-9   RSV   TEV

8   Fill[x] me with joy and gladness;
>   let the bones which thou hast
>   broken rejoice.
9   Hide thy face from my sins,
>   and blot out all my iniquities.

[x] Syr: Heb *Make to hear*

8   Let me hear the sounds of joy and
>   gladness;
>   and though you have crushed
>   me and broken me,
>   I will be happy once again.
9   Close your eyes to my sins
>   and wipe out all my evil.

Fill me: RSV and SPCL follow the Syriac; the great majority of translations and HOTTP ("B" decision) follow the Hebrew text, "Make me hear." NJV makes the line more intelligible by translating "Let me hear tidings of joy and gladness," and FRCL

471

does even better: "Tell me that you forgive me, and I will be filled with joy." In some languages it is not possible to speak of joy and gladness having sounds. Therefore if one is following TEV, it may be necessary to say, for example, "Let me feel joy and gladness."

In verse 8b it is difficult to say whether **the bones which thou hast broken** refers to physical illness (see comments on 6.2) or to emotional distress, as TEV has taken it; in either case, God is responsible for the psalmist's condition, and only he can cure it.

Verse 9 is another prayer for forgiveness. First the psalmist asks God to "hide his face" from his sins, and then to **blot out** (as in verse 1b) his **iniquities** (same word as in verse 2a). The first request suggests that the psalmist wants God to quit noticing his sins (see 10.11 and discussion) and not pronounce him guilty of iniquity (see 32.2 and comments).

The expression **Hide thy face from my sins**, if translated literally in some languages, will mean that the psalmist is asking God to be ashamed of his sins. Even the TEV rendering, "**Close your eyes**," will in some languages mean that the psalmist wants to sin and does not want God to notice what he is doing. Therefore, in order to avoid these wrong meanings, it will sometimes be necessary to say "take away my sins" or "forgive the evil things I do."

Verse 9 (also verses 11-12), like verse 2, is chiastic, which is structurally relevant, as this verse falls at the approximate center of the psalm. The psalmist has again employed chiasmus as a poetic device in his petition to God to remove all his sin (see comments on verse 2).

51.10-11	RSV	TEV
10	Create in me a clean heart, O God, and put a new and right^y spirit within me.	10 Create a pure heart in me, O God, and put a new and loyal spirit in me.
11	Cast me not away from thy presence, and take not thy holy Spirit from me.	11 Do not banish me from your presence; do not take your holy spirit away from me.

^{y} Or *steadfast*

The psalmist now pleads for a complete spiritual renewal. He asks for **a clean heart**, by which is probably meant not so much a heart free of impurity as a single-minded, wholehearted devotion to God's will (as in Matt 5.8; see Anderson).

In verse 10b **put a new and right spirit within me** translates "renew a loyal spirit in me." Here "spirit" has to do with attitude, will, desire, and not with "spirit" as opposed to body. The word **right** translates a Hebrew word which means steadfast, firm; so it is a spirit that is constant in its devotion to God. SPCL has "a new and faithful spirit"; another possibility is "a new and constant spirit"; FRCL "renew and strengthen my spirit." In many languages if the local word for spirit is used in line b, the meaning is apt to refer to the spiritual existence in contrast to the physical.

Therefore in those languages it may be advisable to use the word for heart in both a and b; for example, "a heart which is pure and a new heart which is loyal."

The two lines in verse 11 express the same thought. **Cast me not away**: the psalmist prays that God will not abandon him because he has sinned. God's **presence** is the same as his **holy Spirit**, that is, his power, which is called holy because it is God's and accomplishes his will. **From your presence** must sometimes simply be translated "from you."

In many languages the term **holy Spirit** can here be translated as "your spirit." God's breath–spirit is the source of all human life and vitality; in the creation of humankind (Gen 2.7) God breathed life-giving breath into a clay model and it became a living being; in Psalm 104.29-30 it is the breath–spirit of God which gives life to all animals; when he holds it back, they die. So God's breath–spirit is the source of life, not only of physical existence but, in a higher sense, of meaningful life, life in fellowship with and dependent upon God, life that is dedicated to him.

The phrase God's **holy Spirit** does not carry the developed ideas it has in the New Testament and in Christian theology. Only here and in Isaiah 63.10,11 (which see) is the phrase used in the Old Testament. Eaton, who believes the psalm was composed by a king, defines "holy spirit" here as "the power or presence of God at the centre of Israel and working in his chosen ruler" (*Kingship and the Psalms*, page 71).

51.12-13　　　RSV　　　　　　　　　　　　　　　TEV

12　Restore to me the joy of thy salvation,
　　　and uphold me with a willing spirit.

13　Then I will teach transgressors thy ways,
　　　and sinners will return to thee.

12　Give me again the joy that comes from your salvation,
　　　and make me willing to obey you.

13　Then I will teach sinners your commands,
　　　and they will turn back to you.

The psalmist prays for a return of that **joy** which is the result of God's saving action (**thy salvation**). **Of thy salvation** must sometimes be translated "that comes from being saved by you."

He then asks that God provide him with **a willing spirit**, that is, a disposition, a willingness, to obey him. NJV translates "a vigorous spirit." RSV has **uphold**, which is the meaning the Hebrew verb has in 3.5; 37.17,24; also NJV "let a vigorous spirit sustain me," and NJB "sustain in me a generous spirit." If the meaning "uphold" or "sustain" is expressed, then the translator must decide whether the **willing spirit** is the power of God or the psalmist's own inner strength; here, however, it seems better to take the verb in the sense of "to provide" (as in Gen 27.37; see K-B); see NIV "grant me." So Anderson interprets it: "to support him by providing him with a willing spirit." RSV construction makes **a willing spirit** God's attitude, not the psalmist's; it seems that RSV does this unintentionally, unless RSV intends to say "Uphold me *by giving me* a willing spirit." FRCL and SPCL, however, take it to be God's spirit: "sustain me with your generous Spirit" (see TOB footnote).

Verse 13 may be joined to what precedes (as TEV, NJV, AT, NJB, SPCL have done) or to what follows (RSV, NEB, FRCL, NIV, NAB). The former seems preferable.

Some translations (AT, NJV) take verse 13a as a request, "Let me teach"; most take it as a promise, as do TEV and RSV. It should be noted that the vow here is not the usual one, in this kind of psalm, to offer a proper sacrifice, but to **teach transgressors thy ways**. The **transgressors** of verse 13a are the same as the **sinners** of verse 13b; they are not two different groups. **Thy ways** refers to God's require-ments, God's commands for human conduct, especially as they are expressed in the Torah. NEB translates "the ways that lead to thee"; FRCL has "what you expect from them."

To **return** to God implies repentance of sin and a determination to obey God's laws.

51.14-15 RSV TEV

14 Deliver me from bloodguiltiness,[z]
    O God,
    thou God of my salvation,
    and my tongue will sing aloud
    of thy deliverance.

15 O Lord, open thou my lips,
    and my mouth shall show forth
    thy praise.

14 Spare my life, O God, and save
    me,[k]
    and I will gladly proclaim your
    righteousness.

15 Help me to speak, Lord,
    and I will praise you.

[z] Or *death*

[k] Spare my life . . . me; *or* O God my savior, keep me from the crime of mur-der.

It is not certain whether the Hebrew "bloods" (RSV **bloodguiltiness**) in verse 14a refers to the psalmist's own shed blood "death" (see RSV footnote) or to the shedding of the blood of others, "murder." The former is the choice of Kirkpatrick, Anderson; TEV, FRCL, RSV footnote, NEB footnote; the latter the choice of TEV footnote, RSV, NEB, NJV, AT, NAB, SPCL. Some change the Hebrew text slightly (see Oesterley, Taylor) to get "deliver me from silence," either in the sense of the psalmist's being silent, that is, not praising God, or else, the silence of the grave, which seems more likely. (It is assumed that RSV **bloodguiltiness**, NJV, NIV "bloodguilt," NAB "blood guilt," and AT "blood-guiltiness" mean guilt of murder already committed, or murder yet to be committed; the expression is ambiguous.) One possible version is "from deadly sin"; TOB translates literally and in a footnote gives three possible interpretations: (1) exempt me from having to offer sacrifices; (2) don't allow my blood to be shed; (3) purify me from the blood I have shed. Even on the assumption that the psalm was written by David, if "bloods" refers to the murder of Uriah (so some Jewish commentators), the only possible meaning would be that the psalmist is asking forgiveness for the murder; and it seems impossible that the psalmist should ask God to keep him from murdering someone (as Briggs points out, such a meaning is not sustained by usage). On the whole it seems better to understand the words as a request that God spare the psalmist from violent and premature death (see Weiser). So GECL "God, you are my savior! I deserve death, but spare me!"

Thou God of my salvation: "You are the God who saves me" (see 25.5; comments on 24.5).

Deliverance translates *tsedeq* (see comments on "right" in 4.1); NJV "beneficence"; RSV **deliverance** is possible in this context. FRCL has "how you have saved me," NJB "your saving justice." Kirkpatrick defines "righteousness" here as "His faithfulness to His character and covenant . . . exhibited in the pardon of the penitent." The expression "proclaim your righteousness" in some languages must be shifted to a verb phrase; for example, "I will be glad and tell people that you are good."

The psalmist's request in verse 15 is to be understood as a reference to forgiveness; while unforgiven he is unable to praise God, but if God forgives him, then he will be able to praise him. A literal translation of **open thou my lips** could give a totally wrong impression of the psalmist's request, which is a request that God enable him to praise. In 14b **my tongue** is used as a part for the whole person. In 15a,b **lips** and **mouth** again are used as images representing the whole person. The translator should examine carefully the usage of **tongue**, **lips**, and **mouth** to see which organ is most naturally associated with **sing** in 14c and **praise** in verse 15. If none is appropriate the translator may follow TEV, which replaces these images with verbs.

51.16-17 RSV	TEV

16   For thou hast no delight in sacrifice;
      were I to give a burnt offering,
      thou wouldst not be pleased.
	16 You do not want sacrifices,
	      or I would offer them;
	      you are not pleased with burnt offerings.

17   The sacrifice acceptable to God*ᵃ* is
      a broken spirit;
      a broken and contrite heart, O
      God, thou wilt not despise.
	17 My sacrifice is a humble spirit, O
	      God;
	      you will not reject a humble and
	      repentant heart.

ᵃ Or *My sacrifice, O God*

The prayer ends with a recognition of the kind of sacrifice that God approves of; God does not want dead animals burned on the altar or other ritual sacrifices. In a typical way of speaking, the psalmist is not (as it might appear) saying that God wants all sacrifices to cease; he is saying that God prefers the proper attitude which the offering of sacrifices should express and represent (see similar sentiments in 50.8-9). For a discussion of **sacrifice** and **burnt offering**, see 40.6. Here also, the translator should faithfully represent the meaning of the text. TEV has tried to make the meaning clear by placing "**or I would offer them**" at the close of the first line instead of connecting it with the second line, as RSV does (**were I to give . . .**).

In verse 17a the Hebrew text is "The sacrifices of God," which RSV represents by **The sacrifice acceptable to God**; also NJV "True sacrifice to God." NIV "The sacrifices of God (are a broken spirit)" is a most unnatural statement. Dahood takes the word for "God," *'elohim*, here as a superlative, "the finest sacrifices." By a change of the final vowel of the Hebrew word the meaning becomes "My sacrifice, O God" (TEV, FRCL, NEB).[1]

God wants **a broken spirit . . . a broken and contrite heart**, that is, expressions of repentance and humility before the Almighty. In many languages it is not possible to speak of a **spirit** as being "**humble**," much less **broken**. In this context it will frequently be necessary to avoid the word **spirit**, which would mean a kind of inferior, nonphysical being, and say "humble heart." The concept "humble" is sometimes expressed idiomatically as "not making oneself to appear big," or "having a low heart," or "one who speaks softly." In some languages it will be unnatural to follow the Hebrew pattern, which uses a negative to affirm a previous statement. In this way **thou wilt not despise** is more naturally shifted to a positive statement; for example, "O God, you will gladly accept a broken and contrite heart." **A broken and contrite heart** refers to a person who is genuinely sad and repentant for his sin. And so the second half of verse 17 may be rendered, for example, "O God, you will gladly accept a person who is sorry for his sin and has repented."

51.18-19   RSV   TEV

18	Do good to Zion in thy good plea- sure; rebuild the walls of Jerusalem,	18	O God, be kind to Zion and help her; rebuild the walls of Jerusalem.
19	then wilt thou delight in right sacrifices, in burnt offerings and whole burnt offerings; then bulls will be offered on thy altar.	19	Then you will be pleased with proper sacrifices and with our burnt offerings; and bulls will be sacrificed on your altar.

These two verses are generally recognized as being a later addition to the original poem, reflecting a time when Jerusalem and the Temple were in ruins. Some, however, like Briggs, take the verses to be part of the original composition, and thus regard the psalm as having been composed during a time when the city was in ruins and the people in exile.

In verse 18 the psalmist asks God to restore Jerusalem to her former glory; **Zion** and **Jerusalem** both refer to the city. The expression **Zion** meaning **Jerusalem** may often require a classifier such as "city" so that it will not be thought of as distinct from Jerusalem. The **walls** were to surround Jerusalem as fortification against invading armies.

In verse 19 the psalmist tries to counter the antisacrificial tone of verses 16-17 by promising that once again the **right sacrifices**, which are pleasing to God, will be offered on the altar in the Temple in Jerusalem. The word **right** translates *tsedeq*

---

[1]HOTTP stays with the Masoretic text ("A" decision), "God's sacrifices"; in the context "God's sacrifices are a broken spirit" means "the sacrifices God requires (or, desires) are a broken spirit."

(see 4.1); TEV has **"proper"**; FRCL "correct"; NEB "appointed"; and NJV "sacrifices offered in righteousness." For comments on **sacrifices** see 40.6.

Verse 19b in Hebrew is literally "burnt offering and whole (burnt) offering"; some scholars believe this to be an intrusion into the text, and it is omitted by NEB. It is better, however, to follow the Hebrew text.

Verse 19c may be better translated by the use of an active verb, "Then we (or, your people) will sacrifice bulls on your altar." The word translated **bulls** refers to "young bulls," sometimes translated in English as "bullocks" (see also 22.12). Because of the historical situation, translators should retain **bull** in this context. This may mean using a loan word from a major language, or else employing a word meaning cow and qualifying it as "male." If this is not adequate for the context of sacrifice, an illustration may have to be used and either a descriptive term or a loan word used.

Psalm 52

This psalm does not fit easily into any of the various categories in which the psalms are usually classified. It is somewhat like a complaint (lament) by an individual against someone of importance (verse 1) and wealth (verse 7) who has committed some great evil, not specified, and on whom the psalmist calls down God's judgment. The Hebrew title (see below) does not seem to fit precisely with the thrust of the psalm itself and seems clearly to be a later addition. As Anderson points out, Doeg's sin was not that of lying but of being an informer against David and, later, of killing the priests at Nob at the command of Saul.

The psalm opens with a strong condemnation of the psalmist's enemy (verses 1-4), followed by a description of the punishment that God will bring down on him (verses 5-7). The psalmist, confident of his own security, ends with a promise to praise God for his goodness (verses 8-9).

HEADING: **"God's Judgment and Grace."** Other headings are "True and false security"; "The fate of cynics"; "The deceitful tongue." In some languages it will be necessary to substitute verb phrases for the nouns in this title; for example, "God judges people and shows how kind he is."

Hebrew Title: **To the choirmaster. A Maskil of David, when Doeg, the Edomite, came and told Saul, "David has come to the house of Ahimelech"** (TEV "A poem by David, after Doeg the Edomite went to Saul and told him that David had gone to the house of Ahimelech").

For **choirmaster** see title of Psalm 4; for **Maskil** see title of Psalm 32. The account of what Doeg did is found in 1 Samuel 21.7; 22.9-10. He informed King Saul that David had sought help from the priest Ahimelech in the town of Nob (1 Sam 21.1-9); Saul, enraged, ordered his officials to kill Ahimelech and his fellow priests, but none of them dared slay a priest. So Doeg took his sword and killed them all (1 Sam 22.11-19).

52.1-3	RSV		TEV
1	Why do you boast, O mighty man, of mischief done against the godly?*b*	1	Why do you boast, great man, of your evil? God's faithfulness is eternal.
	All the day 2 you are plotting destruction.	2	You make plans to ruin others; your tongue is like a sharp razor.
	Your tongue is like a sharp razor, you worker of treachery.		You are always inventing lies.
3	You love evil more than good,	3	You love evil more than good

478

and lying more than speaking
the truth.   *Selah*

and falsehood more than truth.

b Cn Compare Syr: Heb *the kindness of God*

In some languages **Why do you boast** is expressed in idiomatic language; for example, "Why do you have a swollen heart?" or nonidiomatically, "Why do you make yourself big?"

In his opening words the psalmist calls his enemy **O mighty man**; the Hebrew word *gibbor* is used of a famous soldier, a rich man, a tyrant, or even a gangster. Here there is sharp irony; see TOB *bravache*; NJV "brave fellow." Something like the English slang phrase "You hot shot" may convey the sarcasm of the text. TEV "**great man**" may be understood as a compliment; something like "powerful" or even "notorious" may be better; best of all, however, will be something like "tyrant." And the vocative **O mighty man** may more easily be translated as a descriptive statement, "You are such a tyrant; why do you boast of the evil things you do?"

What follows in the Masoretic text is literally "the constant love of God (is) all day," which TEV has translated "**God's faithfulness is eternal**" (similarly Weiser; TOB, NJV, AT, GECL, SPCL). But this statement seems inappropriate in the context, and other translations are proposed. There are several ways in which the text has been changed: (1) following in part the Syriac, instead of the Masoretic text "constant love of God," read "against the godly," and join the phrase **all the day** with what follows in verse 3 (so Oesterley; RSV, FRCL, NEB; ZÜR also has "against the godly" but keeps "all the day" with this line instead of joining it to the next); (2) following in part the Septuagint, take the Hebrew word *chesed* (see 5.7) in its Aramaic sense of "infamy" and translate "hero of infamy," and join "all the day" with what follows in verse 3 (BJ, NJB, FRCL, NAB); (3) delete "the constant love of God" as a later gloss (Briggs).[1]

The Masoretic text can be translated, but the meaning it provides does not seem as appropriate to the context as that supplied by the proposed changes in the Hebrew text.

The psalmist accuses his enemy of plotting the ruin of other people with his lies (verse 2). In some languages such terms as **destruction** and "ruin" are too highly generic to be used when speaking of action taken against other people. Therefore it is often necessary to say, for example, "you cause people to suffer."

The enemy's tongue is destructive, **like a sharp razor**. In some languages it will be necessary to substitute knife for **sharp razor.**

The vocative phrase **you worker of treachery** can be taken to mean lying (so TEV), slander (FRCL), or else evil deeds (so SPCL "you think only about doing bad things").

In verse 3 the psalmist accuses the tyrant of preferring **evil** over **good**, and **lying** over **truth** (which translates the Hebrew *tsedeq* (see 4.1).

---

[1]HOTTP ("B" decision) follows the Masoretic text and says that two translations are possible: (1) "(why do you boast yourself of your wickedness, O mighty man,) (while) the kindness of God (is over me) all the day?"; (2) "(why do you boast with wickedness, O mighty man,) (saying that) the kindness of God (is over you) all the day?"

52.1-3

For *Selah* see 3.2.

52.4   RSV   TEV

> You love all words that devour,   You love to hurt people with your
>   O deceitful tongue.   words, you liar!

The verb **devour** translates a noun that may mean literally either "(words of) destruction, ruin," or "(words of) confusion," depending on which meaning is assigned to the Hebrew root (see K-B, Holladay); most prefer to take it in the former sense.

It is to be noticed that the meaning of **O deceitful tongue** is expressed in TEV by "you liar"; NEB takes it not as a vocative, as RSV and TEV do, but as another subject of the verb **You love**, that is, "slanderous talk"; also NJV "treacherous speech." If the translator takes **O deceitful tongue** as a vocative, as in RSV and TEV, it may be necessary to translate this synecdoche ("part for the whole" expression) as "you deceitful person" or "you who deceive people."

52.5   RSV   TEV

> But God will break you down for   So God will ruin you forever;
>   ever;   he will take hold of you and
> he will snatch and tear you   snatch you from your home;
>   from your tent;   he will remove you from the
> he will uproot you from the   world of the living.
>   land of the living.   *Selah*

In vivid terms the psalmist predicts the tyrant's ruin: **God will break you down**, that is, God will take away his power and prestige. In some languages **God will break you down** may be expressed figuratively; for example, "God will smash you like a gourd" or "God will crush you like a pot."

God will also **snatch** him (literally "knock down" or "break"—a Hebrew word used only here in the Old Testament), and **tear** him (literally "tear down") from his **tent**. This is a picture of God entering the man's home, knocking him down and dragging him away.

God will **uproot** him from this life; that is, he will remove him from this world and thrust him into Sheol. SPCL has simply "he will end your life." The word translated **land** can mean the land of Israel instead of the world; so FRCL "he will tear you up out of the land where we live." It seems better, however, to understand it in the broader sense of "world." The expression **uproot you from the land of the living** should, if possible, be matched in translation by a poetic or euphemistic manner of indicating death. It is not advisable to say simply that God will cause him to die, unless, of course, there is no alternative in the language.

　　　RSV　　　　　　　　　　　TEV

6	The righteous shall see, and fear, and shall laugh at him, saying,	6	Righteous people will see this and be afraid; then they will laugh at you and say,
7	"See the man who would not make God his refuge, but trusted in the abundance of his riches, and sought refuge in his wealth!"^{c}	7	"Look, here is a man who did not depend on God for safety, but trusted instead in his great wealth and looked for security in being wicked."

^{c} Syr Tg: Heb *his destruction*

The tyrant's destruction will bring fear and joy to God's people (**the righteous**), who will make fun of the man. Here **shall** . . . **fear** has less the idea of being afraid and more that of being "awestruck" (NJB, NEB, NJV), or being "deeply impressed" (see FRCL).

TEV retains the second person of address of verse 5 when it renders "**laugh at you**" instead of switching to third person, as RSV does.

Both RSV and TEV retain the Hebrew expression **laugh at**. The meaning of **laugh at** must be considered in relation to **see, and fear** in the previous line. These persons begin by being "awestruck," which implies tense speechlessness, and then end up laughing. Here **laugh at** does not have the sense of ridicule or making fun of someone, but rather they laugh in amusement at the irony of what happens to a person who does not depend upon God. If **laugh at** means only "to scorn or make fun of," it will be better to use another expression; for example, in some languages it is possible to say "they nod their heads to say yes and say . . . ."

In verse 7 **the man** translates the word *geber*, which means a man in his full strength; the word is akin to *gibbor* of verse 1, and some see here a derisive allusion and translate "the great man," "the brave man" (TOB). The expression **who would not make God his refuge** may in some languages be rendered "who would not let God protect him" or "who would not ask God to defend him."

At the end of verse 7 TEV "**in being wicked**" is a possible translation of the Masoretic text; the Hebrew word elsewhere means "destruction" (see RSV footnote; see verse 2 "to ruin"; also in this sense in 5.9; 38.12; 57.1). In some passages an identical Hebrew word means "desire, lust" (Pro 10.3; 11.6; Micah 7.3), and Anderson takes that to be the meaning here.[2] There is a great variety in the translations: KJV, SPCL "wickedness"; TOB, BJ, NJB "crime"; NAB "harmful plots"; NJV "mischief"; Weiser "and boasted of his malice." Dahood has "his perniciousness." All of these seem probable; less likely is NEB's "wild lies." RSV, FRCL, ZÜR prefer to follow Syriac and Targum "in his wealth" instead of the Masoretic text "in his wickedness."

---

[2]HOTTP says that the word means "the riches acquired to the damage of others," that is, "plunder," and in verse 2 the same word means "destructive plans," "plots."

52.8-9	RSV	TEV
8	But I am like a green olive tree in the house of God. I trust in the steadfast love of God for ever and ever.	But I am like an olive tree growing in the house of God; I trust in his constant love forever and ever.
9	I will thank thee for ever, because thou hast done it. I will proclaim[d] thy name, for it is good, in the presence of the godly.	I will always thank you, God, for what you have done; in the presence of your people I will proclaim that you are good.

[d] Cn: Heb *wait for*

In the final two verses the psalmist contrasts his situation with that of his enemy; the tyrant will be rooted up but the psalmist lives secure, like a healthy **olive tree in the house of God**. (For "olive tree" see *Fauna and Flora*, pages 156-157.) For a similar figure of health and prosperity, see 1.3.

The house of God is usually a way of speaking of the Temple; there is doubt, however, that olive trees actually grew in the Temple area, and some take the phrase here in an extended sense of the land of Israel. Perhaps **in the house of God** should modify **I**, that is, the psalmist himself, and not **olive tree** (see Briggs; so FRCL, which translates "I am in God's house"). In any case it is a figure of prosperity and security (see also 92.13). If the translator takes the meaning of this verse to be the psalmist who is firmly established in the house of God instead of the olive tree, it will be possible to say, for example, "I am secure in the house of God, like an olive tree" or "like a growing olive tree I prosper in the house of God." In many languages the expression **house of God**, if taken to be the Temple in Jerusalem, can be translated "the large worship house in Jerusalem."

Unlike his enemy, who trusts in his wealth (verse 7), the psalmist trusts God's **steadfast love**.

It seems better to translate the last part of verse 9b **"for what you have done"** (also SPCL, FRCL, NIV, NEB, NAB, NJB) than **because thou hast done it**. In the context, **it** can only refer back to the destruction of the psalmist's enemy (verse 5). Or else one may translate "because you have acted" (BJ, TOB, NJV).

The verb translated **proclaim** ordinarily is taken to mean "wait for" (that is, hope; see 25.3 and comments); but the verb with **thy name** as its object appears nowhere else, and it would be rather strange to say "to hope for your name," unless "name" could be taken to mean something like "help, intervention" (see 54.1, where "your name" in line a is parallel with "your might" in line b; and see Briggs). One suggestion has been "I will put my hope in your name" (similarly NJB, NIV). Dahood, in his comments on 19.4, strongly makes the point that the root of the Hebrew verb in the sense of "to collect" has the extended meaning of "to call, proclaim."[3] TEV

---

[3]HOTTP says the verb means "I hope" or "I proclaim," and prefers "I proclaim" as the meaning of the verb here (and in 19.4), not requiring emendation.

and Weiser translate "**proclaim**"; NJV "declare"; NEB "glorify." RSV and NAB resort to an emendation in order to get **proclaim** (see Oesterley).

The final words of the line are "your name because (or, that) (it is) good." "Name" stands for the person (see 5.11). To say "your name is good" in English is meaningless (RSV, NIV, NJV, AT); NJB "your name, so full of goodness," is hardly any better. So it seems best to do as TEV does. The Hebrew conjunction *ki* can mean either **because** or "**that**" (TEV); either meaning makes sense in the context.

For other instances of the promise to praise God in the presence of his people, see 22.22; 26.12; 40.10. The expression **in the presence of the godly** is rendered in some languages as "where your people are" or "where your people gather together."

Psalm 53

This psalm is the same as Psalm 14, with some differences, which are noted and discussed. See the introduction to Psalm 14 and the commentary on it for details of exegesis and translation.

HEADING: the heading should be the same as for Psalm 14.

Hebrew Title: **To the choirmaster: according to Mahalath. A Maskil of David** (TEV "A poem by David").

There is no agreement on the meaning of **Mahalath**, whether as the name of the musical instrument to be used (flute?) or the name of the tune. BJ translates "In sickness." Psalm 88 has this word as part of a longer compound, "Mahalath Leannoth."

53.1

RSV	TEV
The fool says in his heart, "There is no God." They are corrupt, doing abominable iniquity; there is none that does good.	Fools say to themselves, "There is no God." They are all corrupt, and they have done terrible things; there is no one who does what is right.

As RSV shows, instead of "deeds" in Psalm 14, the Hebrew text here has **iniquity** (see comments on the same word translated "wrong" in 7.3).

53.2-3

RSV	TEV
2 God looks down from heaven upon the sons of men to see if there are any that are wise, that seek after God. 3 They have all fallen away; they are all alike depraved; there is none that does good, no, not one.	2 God looks down from heaven at mankind to see if there are any who are wise, any who worship him. 3 But they have all turned away; they are all equally bad. Not one of them does what is right, not a single one.

484

Here **God** is used instead of "Yahweh" ("The LORD") in Psalm 14.

In verse 3 instead of "gone astray" in Psalm 14, here a different verb is used, **fallen away**, with the same meaning of moral and spiritual corruption.

Unaccountably, RSV translates identical Hebrew passages in different ways in these two psalms: verse 2a **sons of men** and "children of men"; verse 2c **that are wise** and "that act wisely"; verse 3b **depraved** and "corrupt."

53.4	RSV	TEV
	Have those who work evil no un- derstanding, who eat up my people as they eat bread, and do not call upon God?	"Don't they know?" God asks. "Are these evildoers ignorant? They live by robbing my people, and they never pray to me."

The only difference between this verse and 14.4 is **God** instead of "the LORD," and "these evildoers" here, whereas Psalm 14 has "*all* these evildoers" (TEV). Again, unaccountably, RSV translates the same Hebrew text in two different ways: in 14.4 "Have they no knowledge, all the evildoers who . . . ?"; here **Have those who work evil no understanding, who . . . ?**

53.5	RSV	TEV
	There they are, in great terror, in terror such as has not been! For God will scatter the bones of the ungodly;*e* they will be put to shame,*f* for God has rejected them.	But then they will become terri- fied, as they have never been before, for God will scatter the bones of the enemies of his people. God has rejected them, and so Israel will totally defeat them.

e Cn Compare Gk Syr: Heb *him who encamps against you*
f Gk: Heb *you will put to shame*

This verse differs considerably from verses 5-6 of Psalm 14. The first word in Hebrew is "There," which seems to indicate location (NJB "There they will . . ."); but in the context it is so vague that RSV has **There they are**, which no longer refers to a specific place. TEV uses the temporal "**then**," connecting it with what follows. The verb itself is translated as present tense by RSV, **are**; it seems better, however, to translate as future tense, as TEV and NJV have done, connecting it with what follows.

The **terror** to which the evildoers will be subjected will be greater than any they have experienced before. Instead of **such as has not been**, one suggested translation has been "they who had not known terror," which is quite possible; SPCL has "Even though there is no reason to tremble" (see also NIV), which is the meaning preferred by HOTTP.[1]

The next line portrays the complete defeat of Israel's enemies: **God will scatter the bones**. The idea is not only that of killing the enemies, but also of leaving their bodies (**bones**) unburied, an added indignity. Some see here a reference to the total destruction of Sennacherib's forces as they were besieging Jerusalem (2 Kgs 19.35).

The Hebrew expression translated "**the enemies of his people**" (TEV) is literally "him who encamps against you (singular)." See RSV footnote. TEV has taken this "you" to be a reference to Israel. By a change of form from the verb *chanah* "encamp" to *chanep*, RSV arrives at **the ungodly** (literally "alienated from God"). It seems best to follow the Masoretic text (in HOTTP this is an "A" decision), perhaps representing the Hebrew more closely than TEV "**the enemies of his people**" has done. See NJV "God has scattered the bones of your besiegers" (see also NJB).

In some languages the expression **God will scatter the bones of the ungodly** may cause problems for the reader who will feel that the transition from bodies to bones is lacking. Therefore it may be necessary to say, for example, "God will kill the enemies of his people and scatter their bones."

In the next line the Hebrew text is "you (singular) will put to shame," without an object; again TEV has taken this as a promise to Israel. RSV has followed the Septuagint **the ungodly . . . will be put to shame**. This **shame** is that of total defeat (see 6.10 and comments).

For the verb **rejected** see 15.4.

53.6   RSV   TEV

> O that deliverance for Israel
>   would come from Zion!
> When God restores the fortunes
>   of his people,
> Jacob will rejoice and Israel be
>   glad.

> How I pray that victory
>   will come to Israel from Zion.
> How happy the people of Israel
>   will be
>   when God makes them prosper-
>   ous again!

The only difference in Hebrew between this verse and 14.7 is the use of **God** here and "the LORD" there.

---

[1]HOTTP proposes "(where) there was (no reason) to fear."

Psalm 54

This psalm is a lament by an individual who feels threatened by enemies and appeals to God for help. The Hebrew title (see below) attributes the psalm to David, written when he was fleeing from King Saul; most commentators, however, hold that there is very little likelihood that the title reflects the actual circumstances of the psalm's composition.

Psalm 54 contains a high percentage of fixed word pairs, which may be an indication that a text originated orally. Word pairs are two words or expressions (or combinations) that became traditionally associated in the minds of composers and listeners, and are known to recur commonly in Old Testament poetry. The idea is that when the composer used one of the pair in line a, the audience normally expected to hear the companion word or phrase in line b. It is suggested that word pairing took place sometimes without regard to context and resulting meaning. Where word pairs occur in parallel lines, there is seldom any dynamic movement at work. Their main function is to maintain static parallelism, increase audience rapport, and provide cohesion between parallel lines.

Using the vocabulary of RSV, the pairings in Psalm 54 may be listed as:

1a:	save me	name
1b:	vindicate	might
2a:	hear	prayer
2b:	give ear	words of my mouth
3a:	insolent men	have risen against
3b:	ruthless men	
4a:	God	helper
4b:	Lord	upholder
5a:	requite with evil	
5b:	put an end	
6a:	sacrifice	
6b:	give thanks	name
7a:	trouble	
7b:	enemies	

The psalmist begins with a cry to God for help (verses 1-2) from his enemies (verse 3). He affirms his faith in God to deliver him (verses 4-5), and promises to offer a sacrifice in gratitude to God for saving him (verses 6-7).

HEADING: "**A Prayer for Protection from Enemies.**" Other headings are "An appeal to the God of justice"; "God is my helper"; "Confident prayer in great peril." In some languages it will be necessary to modify some of the elements of this title; for example, "The psalmist asks God to protect him from his enemies."

Hebrew Title: **To the choirmaster: with stringed instruments. A Maskil of David, when the Ziphites went and told Saul, "David is in hiding among us"** (TEV "A poem by David, after the men from Ziph went to Saul and told him that David was hiding in their territory").

For **choirmaster** and **stringed instruments** see title of Psalm 4; for **Maskil** see title of Psalm 32. The historical reference is to be found in two accounts: 1 Samuel 23.15-24 and 26.1-5. Ziph was a town in the hill country southeast of Hebron, in Judah.

54.1-3	RSV	TEV
1	Save me, O God, by thy name, / and vindicate me by thy might.	1 Save me by your power, O God; / set me free by your might!
2	Hear my prayer, O God; / give ear to the words of my mouth.	2 Hear my prayer, O God; / listen to my words!
3	For insolent men*g* have risen against me, / ruthless men seek my life; / they do not set God before them. *Selah*	3 Proud men are coming to attack me; / cruel men are trying to kill me— / men who do not care about God.

g Another reading is *strangers*

For **Save me** see the same verb translated "Help" in 12.1; the parallel **vindicate me** in the next line translates a verb which means "give a just decision"; most English translations have **vindicate**. The word implies a trial in which the accused person asks the judge to defend him from his accusers; NAB has "defend my cause."

By thy name in verse 1a is parallel to **by thy might** in line **b**; as in 20.1, **name** stands for the personal intervention of God to help. Anderson comments: "The name of God and his might are the manifestation of God in saving the oppressed." The instrumental use of **by thy name** and **by thy might** in some languages requires shifting to a causal clause; for example, "because you are powerful save me" and "because you are mighty set me free." In other languages such instrumental usage can be shifted to a command with a noun phrase; for example, "use your power to save me."

Verse 2 is composed of two parallel and synonymous lines, using language which appears often in the Psalms.

In verse 3a the Masoretic text and the Septuagint have "strangers" (*zarim*), but many Hebrew manuscripts have *zedim* "arrogant men," which fits better with **ruthless men** in line <u>b</u> and is preferred by most translations. Some, including HOTTP,[1] prefer the Masoretic text, taking "strangers" as referring either to fellow Israelites who are rebelling against the God of Israel (see Isa 1.4), or to non-Jews (so NJV, TOB, Weiser, "strangers, foreigners, aliens"). **Insolent men** (TEV "**Proud men**") are sometimes spoken of as "men who say they are great," or idiomatically, "men with swollen hearts."

The Hebrew for **ruthless men** means people who cause terror.

Seek my life means "(they) try to kill me."

In verse 3c **they do not set God before them** means "they ignore God"; so TEV "**who do not care about God**"; NEB "they give no thought to God"; NIV "without regard for God"; FRCL "they take no account of God." NJV's language implies that the psalmist's enemies were Jews: "they are unfaithful to God." Verse 3 is almost exactly the same as 86.14.

For *Selah* see 3.2.

	54.4-5 RSV		TEV

4	Behold, God is my helper;
	     the Lord is the upholder[h] of my
	     life.
		4	But God is my helper.
			     The Lord is my defender.

5	He will requite my enemies with
	     evil;
	 in thy faithfulness put an end to
	     them.
		5	May God use their own evil to
			     punish my enemies.
			 He will destroy them because he
			     is faithful.

[h] Gk Syr Jerome: Heb *of* or *with those who uphold*

Behold: see comments on 39.5.

The psalmist affirms his confidence in God to help and defend him. In verse 4b the Hebrew is "the Lord is with those who sustain my *nefesh*" (see 3.5 for comments on "sustain"), which reads rather strangely. Many take the verbal phrase to be a way of expressing a superlative, "the Lord is my greatest defender"; see NEB "the mainstay of my life"; TOB "my only support"; NJV "my support." Another possible version is "the support of my life." The nominal phrases **my helper** and "**my defender**" in some languages must be switched to verb phrases; for example, "God is the one who helps me" or "God is the one who defends me" or ". . . who defends me from my enemies." The translator can choose to follow TEV "**my defender**" and translate "the Lord defends me" or "the Lord keeps me safe." If the translator

---

[1]HOTTP ("A" decision) points out that in a parallel passage, Psalm 86.14, the Hebrew text has *zedim*, "the insolent people," which is followed by modern translations. And HOTTP remarks: "The difference between the two passages should not be eliminated by assimilating one text to the other."

chooses to represent the meaning "sustain" or "support," one way of saying this is "the Lord keeps me alive" or "the Lord does not allow me to be killed."

In verse 5a the Hebrew text may be understood as a wish (TEV **"May God . . ."**; also NEB, TOB, NIV, Weiser and others) or as a statement, **He will** . . . (RSV, NJV, SPCL). The Hebrew text is, in one form, "He will (or, May he) cause evil to turn on my enemies"—which TEV has taken to mean **"use their own evil to punish my enemies"**; similarly SPCL "He will make the evil of my enemies turn back on them." Another form of the text is "May my enemies' wickedness recoil on them" (similarly NEB).[2] The word translated **enemies** (see 5.8) has the idea of watching, spying; so NJV, NEB "watchful foes"; TOB "those who spy on me."

Verse 5b is translated by TEV as a statement; the other translations consulted all translate it as a direct request, and the translator is advised to do the same. It is to be noticed that this line uses the second person of address, instead of the third person of the previous lines. If the second person is used, the vocative "God" or "Lord" should be used, to make the request quite clear.

54.6-7	RSV	TEV
6	With a freewill offering I will sacrifice to thee; I will give thanks to thy name, O LORD, for it is good.	6 I will gladly offer you a sacrifice, O LORD; I will give you thanks because you are good.
7	For thou hast delivered me from every trouble, and my eye has looked in triumph on my enemies.	7 You have rescued me from all my troubles, and I have seen my enemies defeated.

In verse 6 the Hebrew text may mean **"I will gladly offer"** (TEV; also NJB, TOB, FRCL), or, as RSV has it, **a freewill offering** (also NJV, SPCL), depending on whether the Hebrew word is taken adverbially, to describe the psalmist's attitude, or as an adjective, referring to an offering which is not dictated by law (see Lev 22.18-30; Num 15.1-10).

Verse 6b in Hebrew is "I will give thanks to your name, because it is good" (see the nearly identical expression in 52.9); here, as in 52.9, NEB has "(I will) praise thy name, for that is good," in which "that" refers to the action of praise, not to "name."

For **delivered** in verse 7a see the use of the same verb in 7.1 ("deliver").

Verse 7b is "and my eye has looked on my enemies," which RSV and others fittingly render by **my eye has looked in triumph on my enemies**; so TEV "I have seen my enemies defeated"; also possible is "I have seen the downfall of my enemies."

---

[2]HOTTP ("C" decision) prefers this form of the text.

Psalm 55

This psalm is a lament by an individual who is threatened by enemies and has been betrayed by a friend. The psalmist's emotions run high; he is desperately afraid and cries continuously to God for help. His distress is particularly sharp because of the betrayal by a person who at one time had been his best friend. At times almost incoherent with despair and rage, the psalmist in the most violent terms prays for the immediate death of his enemies.

The irregularities in the progression of thought have led many commentators to conjecture that the work is composite, but there is hardly any agreement on the identification of the two or more separate compositions that might have been brought together in the final form. The Hebrew text is corrupt in many places, and there are many suggestions as to the form and meaning of the original.

The psalm begins with a cry for help (verses 1-2a) and a lengthy description of the psalmist's situation (verses 2b-14): this includes personal threats (verse 3), violence and crime in the city (verses 9b-11), and the treachery of a former friend (verses 12-14). The author prays for his enemies' death (verse 15), and then repeats his cries for help, confident that God will hear him (verses 16-19). Once again he denounces his former friend (verses 20-21), consoles himself with encouraging words (verse 22), and closes the psalm with a final prayer for the death of his enemies (verse 23).

HEADING: **"The Prayer of a Man Betrayed by a Friend."** Other headings are "The prayer of a persecuted man"; "The treacherous friend"; "Oppressed by enemies, betrayed by a friend." The title of this psalm in TEV is more complete than most. However, in some languages further adjustments will be required to make it fully natural; for example, "The psalmist's friend has betrayed him, and so the psalmist asks God for help."

Hebrew Title: **To the choirmaster: with stringed instruments. A Maskil of David** ("A poem by David").

For **choirmaster** and **stringed instruments** see title of Psalm 4; for **Maskil** see title of Psalm 32.

55.1-3	RSV		TEV
1	Give ear to my prayer, O God; and hide not thyself from my supplication!	1	Hear my prayer, O God; don't turn away from my plea!
2	Attend to me, and answer me; I am overcome by my trouble.	2	Listen to me and answer me; I am worn out by my worries.
		3	I am terrified by the threats of my

I am distraught 3 by the noise of
   the enemy,
because of the oppression of the
   wicked.
For they bring[i] trouble upon me,
   and in anger they cherish enmity against me.

   enemies,
crushed by the oppression of
   the wicked.
They bring trouble on me;
   they are angry with me and
   hate me.

[i] Cn Compare Gk: Heb *they cause to totter*

The psalm opens with a cry to God to listen to the psalmist's prayer and answer him (verses 1-2a). For **hide not thyself** in verse 1b, see similar language and comments in 13.1; 27.9a.

Attend to me is a rather old-fashioned form of English; a more normal way of expressing the thought is "**Listen to me**" or "Pay attention to me." When the psalmist asks God to **answer** him, the translator must not think in terms of answering a question. Here the term has the meaning of responding to the psalmist's plea for help. Therefore in translation one must often say, for example, "help me."

Then the psalmist describes his condition: **I am overcome by my trouble** (verse 2b). The Hebrew verb is of uncertain meaning; this form occurs elsewhere only in Genesis 27.40, where it appears to mean "break loose"; see NJV "I am tossed about." The Septuagint has "I am grieved" (also Vulgate); Jerome "I am humiliated." The general idea is clear enough: worry, concern, lack of peace; one possibility is "distraught"; Weiser "restless."

As the RSV verse division shows, the initial verb form of the fifth line of the psalm (RSV **I am distraught**) is in the Masoretic text the end of verse 2, not the beginning of verse 3. For aesthetic reasons TEV has placed the verse number 3 at the beginning of the line.

I am distraught translates a verb which means "be in a stir" (the Septuagint translates "I am troubled"). TEV "**the threats of my enemies**" translates what is literally "the voice of my enemy"; see NJB "outcry" and NJV "clamor," both of which are better than RSV **noise**.

In verse 3b **oppression** translates a word found only here in the Old Testament. TEV in verse 3b supplies the verb "**crushed**" as being more appropriate for **oppression**; the Hebrew text has only one verb for both lines, namely, **am distraught**. The phrase **because of the oppression of the wicked** must be restructured in many languages; for example, "I am crushed by the evil people who oppress me" or "I am defeated because bad people oppress me."

In verse 3c **they bring** translates the causative form of a Hebrew verb which means "to totter, shake" (see "be moved" in 10.6), with the direct object **trouble**. Briggs sees the figure of an enemy force rolling stones down from the heights upon the foe in the valley. There seems to be no need for the kind of a note that RSV has; the other translations do not feel the need of one. NJB translates "they heap up charges against me," and NJV "they bring evil upon me." FRCL may be recommended: "they cause evil to fall upon me."

Cherish enmity translates a verb found only here in the Psalms; it means to nurse a grudge, to cherish hatred (K-B). NEB translates the line "they revile me in their anger" (also NIV). A number of translations see hostile activity expressed by the their anger" (also NIV). A number of translations see hostile activity expressed by the verb; NJV "furiously harass me"; TOB "attack me with fury"; SPCL "attack me furiously."

	RSV		TEV
4	My heart is in anguish within me, the terrors of death have fallen upon me.	4	I am terrified, and the terrors of death crush me.
5	Fear and trembling come upon me, and horror overwhelms me.	5	I am gripped by fear and trembling; I am overcome with horror.

The psalmist describes his distress: he is **in anguish**, crushed by **the terrors of death**; **fear**, **trembling**, and **horror** have overcome him. Verse 4a in Hebrew is "My heart trembles within me"; SPCL has "My heart jumps in my breast."

The translator's main task in these two verses is to find the verbs that go naturally with these intense emotions. TEV in verses 4b-5 uses the active "**crush**" and the passives "**I am gripped . . . I am overcome**." SPCL, in the same lines, has the actives "has fallen on me," "has entered into me," and "I am trembling (with fear)." And FRCL has "they fall on me," "I am seized," and "I am submerged."

Terrors of death are the terrors caused by the danger of death. The nouns **fear and trembling** in many languages must be shifted to verbs; for example, "I am afraid and I tremble." In the same way **horror** may have to be recast as a verb, as in English "I am horrified," or as a figurative expression, "my skin grows cold" or "my heart rattles in me."

	RSV		TEV
6	And I say, "O that I had wings like a dove! I would fly away and be at rest;	6	I wish I had wings like a dove. I would fly away and find rest.
7	yea, I would wander afar, I would lodge in the wilderness, *Selah*	7	I would fly far away and make my home in the desert.
8	I would haste to find me a shelter from the raging wind and tempest."	8	I would hurry and find myself a shelter from the raging wind and the storm.

The psalmist wishes that he could fly far away, **like a dove**, and be out of the reach of his pursuers (verses 6-7). The Hebrew text in verses 6-8 has the psalmist quoting himself (see RSV); TEV here, as elsewhere, has not represented this stylistic device.

In verse 6a some languages may find it better to say "I wish I could fly like a dove." To say "Oh that I had the wings of a dove!" (NJV, NIV, NEB) may sound strange, since a dove's wings could hardly enable a man to fly very far. The is dissatisfied with other wings. If misunderstandings are likely to arise, it may be better to say, for example, "I wish I could fly" or "I wish I could escape."

In verse 7a the verbal phrase means "to be very far away"; see the same verb used in 22.1, "Why art thou so far . . . ?" NEB has "escape far away," others have "flee far away," both of which are better than RSV **wander**, which implies movement without much direction or purpose.

In verse 7b **lodge** translates a verb which means "spend the night" (see its use in 25.13; 30.5).

For *Selah* see 3.2.

Then, changing the figure (verse 8), the psalmist wishes he could find **a shelter** where he would be safe from **the raging wind and the tempest**, a figure for the hatred and fury of his enemies. The word translated **raging** occurs only here in the Old Testament.

55.9-11   RSV   TEV

	RSV		TEV
9	**Destroy their plans,**[j] **O Lord, confuse their tongues;**	9	**Confuse the speech of my enemies, O Lord!**
	for I see violence and strife in the city.		**I see violence and riots in the city,**
10	**Day and night they go around it on its walls;**	10	**surrounding it day and night,**
	and mischief and trouble are within it,		**filling it with crime and trouble.**
11	**ruin is in its midst;**	11	**There is destruction everywhere;**
	oppression and fraud do not depart from its market place.		**the streets are full of oppression and fraud.**

[j] Tg: Heb lacks *their plans*

The first two words in the Masoretic text of verse 9 are "destroy, Adonay," followed by "confuse their tongue." There are several ways in which the text is handled. (1) Some, like NJB, connect the first two words with verse 8 and, by placing different vowels with the same Hebrew consonants, get something like "and from the destructive tempest, Lord"; (2) RSV follows the Targum by adding **their plans** as the object of the verb **destroy** (similarly FRCL); (3) some would take the implied object of the verb "destroy" to be "my enemies" (so SPCL); (4) others, like TEV, take the two verbs as synonymous, with "their tongue" as the object of both (see Anderson).

The first verb in verse 9, "swallow" or **Destroy**, can mean also "**confuse**" (TEV), and the second one means "divide." NJV translates both verbs "confound their speech, confuse it." In English the two verbs are so close in meaning that it may be better to use only one verb, as TEV does. It is recommended that either NJV or TEV be followed. There seems to be a reference to the story about the Tower of Babel, where God scattered the people by "confusing" their speech (Gen 11.7,9). TEV has taken the two verbs to be synonymous; NJV has "confound their speech, confuse it!"; NIV has "Confuse the wicked . . . confound their speech"; Dahood uses other vowels with the consonants of the second verb to get an adjective (instead of the imperative of the verb) and translates "Destroy, O Lord, their forked tongue."[1] If the translator follows TEV, the expression "**Confuse the speech**" may sometimes be rendered "make their tongues thick" or "twist their mouths."

The psalmist describes the conditions that prevail **in the city** (verses 9b-11); this may be Jerusalem, or his home town (unknown), or a generic singular for "cities." The city is full of **violence, strife, mischief, trouble**, and **ruin**. In verse 10a the **violence and strife** of verse 9b are said to be like the guards that patrol the city's walls; instead of protecting, of course, they endanger and harm the city and its inhabitants. If the translator follows TEV "**violence and riots**," these will in some languages require being cast as verb phrases; for example, "I see people committing violent deeds and rioting in the city."

If the translator follows the Hebrew expression **go around it on its walls** in verse 10a, in some languages it will be necessary to say, for example, "go around the top of the wall that surrounds the city." If the knowledge of walled cities is too limited, or if it is impossible to retain the figure, it will be better to follow the model of TEV.

In verse 11a **ruin** (TEV "**destruction**") refers not to the physical destruction or ruin of the city but to violent, lawless people who cause ruin or destruction.

In verse 11b the terms **oppression and fraud** in some languages may be translated as "they take advantage of people through their power and deceive them." **Market place** can be taken to mean the court, the place where trials were held, so that the meaning would be that justice was being corrupted; or else, as TEV has taken it, it is a synonym for "**the streets**" of the city (also SPCL, NIV, TOB), in particular the commercial establishments, where **oppression and fraud** are being practiced by the merchants. NEB has "the public square"; NJV "the square." In some languages it is possible to speak of **the market place** as the "town square" or "the place where the men meet and discuss matters."

	55.12-13 RSV	TEV
12	It is not an enemy who taunts me— then I could bear it; it is not an adversary who deals insolently with me— then I could hide from him.	12 If it were an enemy making fun of me, I could endure it; if it were an opponent boasting over me, I could hide myself from him.
13	But it is you, my equal, my companion, my familiar friend.	13 But it is you, my companion, my colleague and close friend.

The psalmist now speaks of a former friend who had betrayed him (it is

---

[1] HOTTP says the first verb means "cut up, tear up, break, undo," and the second verb means "divide"; the translation proposed is "Undo, O Lord, divide their tongue."

assumed that verses 20-21 refer to the same person). His distress is all the greater because it is not **an enemy** or **an adversary** (literally "one who hates me") who is mocking him.

The two parallel couplets of verse 12 are roughly synonymous; but line d **hide from him** is not the same as **bear it** in line b. Instead of **hide** the translation can be "I would avoid him," "I would be able to stay away from him."

The expression **an enemy who taunts me** in some languages can be translated by terms referring to body gestures; for example, "an enemy who shakes his head at me" or ". . . who points his nose at me." In some languages it is possible to say ". . . who tells funny things about me."

The idea of "**boasting**" (**deals insolently**) is common in all languages and is sometimes said "he makes himself big" or "he looks down on me."

The worst thing about the psalmist's situation is that he is being reviled and mocked by one who used to be an **equal**, a **companion**, a **familiar friend**. NEB translates: "a man of my own sort, my comrade, my own dear friend"; NJV "my equal, my companion, my friend." The three terms **equal, companion,** and **familiar friend** may not be easy to translate in some languages where the people one associates with are almost entirely one's local blood group or persons related by marriage. However, it is sometimes possible to say "you who are like me," "you, the one I go around with," and "you who are like my brother."

55.14	RSV	TEV
	We used to hold sweet converse together; within God's house we walked in fellowship.	We had intimate talks with each other and worshiped together in the Temple.

Now the psalmist speaks of how he and his friend used to go together to the Temple. Line a in Hebrew is "with whom we together enjoyed close fellowship," to be understood either as "have intimate (or, lovely) talks" or "had sweet fellowship" (NJV, NIV), "kept pleasant company" (NEB). The RSV expression **hold sweet converse together** and TEV "**intimate talks**" in some languages can be translated idiomatically; for example, "we put heart stories to each other" or "we laid heart words upon each other."

Line b is "in the house of God we walked in the throng." "Throng" translates the noun *regesh*, which occurs only here; a related noun occurs only in 64.2b ("mobs"); and the verb *ragash* appears only in 2.1 ("plan rebellion"). So it seems that the Hebrew noun means "crowd"; so Dahood "mingle among the throngs" (similarly Oesterley, Weiser; SPCL). Some, however, taking the meaning from the Septuagint "in unity," translate simply "together": so the interpretation of TEV, RSV, BJ, NJB, TOB, NJV. This seems to be the best option.

TEV "**worshiped**" may be a legitimate inference from the context of the passage; it seems better, however, to stay closer to the Hebrew "walked" or "walked about."

55.15   RSV   TEV

> Let death*k* come upon them;
>   let them go down to Sheol alive;
>   let them go away in terror into
>   their graves.*l*

> May my enemies die before their
>   time;
>   may they go down alive into the
>   world of the dead!
> Evil is in their homes and in their
>   hearts.

k Or *desolations*
l Cn: Heb *evils are in their habitation, in
their midst*

The psalmist now prays that sudden death come upon his enemies, like that which came upon Korah and his family, who were swallowed up by the earth and gulped down alive into Sheol (Num 16.31-33).

In line a there are two ways in which the Hebrew text may be divided and understood: "desolations be upon them" (see RSV footnote) or "may death come upon them" (TEV, RSV and most others). The psalmist wants them to die at once, before their appointed time. FRCL says it well: "May death take my enemies by surprise."

For comments on **Sheol** see 6.5. Line b intensifies the request, or malediction, of line a, namely, that his enemies die suddenly and unexpectedly. The form of the request is not logical, inasmuch as Sheol is the world of the dead, and its inhabitants cannot be alive in the normal meaning of the term. But it would be disastrous for a translator to try to make logical prose out of an emotional poetic line, so something straightforward like RSV, TEV, and others is the only way to translate it.

Line c in the Masoretic text is "for evils (are) in their homes, in their insides" (or, "in their midst"); so TEV and the others, including HOTTP ("A" decision). RSV follows a conjecture which is not recommended. NJV has "For where they dwell, there evil is." In some languages it will not be natural to speak of evil as occupying space without some adjustments. For example, one may say "Their homes and their hearts are evil" or "They live in evil homes and think evil thoughts in their hearts (minds, or innermosts)."

55.16-17   RSV   TEV

16 But I call upon God;
      and the LORD will save me.
17 Evening and morning and at noon
      I utter my complaint and moan,
      and he will hear my voice.

16 But I call to the LORD God for
      help,
      and he will save me.
17 Morning, noon, and night
      my complaints and groans go
      up to him,
      and he will hear my voice.

The psalmist takes up his complaint once more and expresses his confidence that God will hear his constant prayer and save him.

In verse 16 **God** in line a is the same as **the LORD** in line b; TEV has chosen to join the two into the one name, "**the LORD God.**" Or else, as FRCL and GECL have it, "I call to God, and he, the Lord, will save me." However it is done, the impression must not be given that **God** and **the LORD** are two different beings.

For **save** in verse 16b, see comments on the same verb translated "Help" in 12.1.

Evening, **morning**, and **noon** were the regular hours of prayer. The order of the words in Hebrew reflects the practice of marking the day's beginning at sundown. TEV has followed the modern way of marking the daily progression of time.

In some languages it will be necessary to shift the nouns in **my complaint** and **moan** to verb phrases; for example, "I complain and I groan"; see NJV "I complain and moan." **My voice** may have to be shifted to "he will hear me" or "he will hear what I say to him."

55.18-19   RSV   TEV

18   He will deliver my soul in safety   18   He will bring me safely back
      from the battle that I wage,   from the battles that I fight
      for many are arrayed against   against so many enemies.
      me.   19   God, who has ruled from eternity,
19   God will give ear, and humble   will hear me and defeat them;
      them,   for they refuse to change,
      he who is enthroned from of   and they do not fear him.
      old;
      because they keep no law,*m*
      and do not fear God.   *Selah*

m Or *do not change*

The meaning of verse 18a in Hebrew is none too clear; it is literally "he will save in peace my *nefesh*." Most commentators and translators give the sense expressed by TEV and RSV.

The expression in line **c** translated **against** seems normally to mean "with," as the Septuagint has it (so NJV "It is as though many are on my side"); but twice in 94.16 the related Hebrew preposition means "against." So the majority take "for there were many (fighting) with me" to mean "fighting against."[2] FRCL has "he (God) comes near me when everybody is against me." In some languages it may be necessary to say, for example, "from fighting people" or "from battling (or, warring)."

Humble in verse 19a translates a verb that can be taken to be the verb "to answer" (so AT). TEV takes **humble** to imply the "**defeat**" of the psalmist's enemies.

The expression **enthroned from of old** or "**from eternity**" in some languages must be rendered "who has always ruled." In some languages eternity is expressed idiomatically in this context as "chair of great age" or "ancient stool."

---

[2]HOTTP ("C" decision) says the Hebrew expression "has a positive meaning of help," and proposes the translation "(has freed . . . my life) of the attack against me, for in great number (they were with me)."

Line c̲ of verse 19 seems in Hebrew to be "there are no changes for them" (or, for him). The noun is defined "substitute, change, relief"; Holladay has "settlement"; K-B "mutual liabilities"; the Septuagint has "retribution." If the Hebrew *lamo* means "to him," the line can mean "for in him (God) there is no variation" (so Dahood; similarly AT); or, as NJV has it, "who will have no successor." But if it means "to them," the line can mean: (1) "they do not change," that is, from their evil ways ("they persist in evil"; similarly TEV, TOD, NJB, NIV, SPCL, NAB), (2) "they have not received retribution" (see Anderson); so, apparently, the Septuagint; (3) FRCL translates "It is impossible to make an alliance with them; they have no respect for God"; (4) Briggs takes it to mean that in the future they will have the same defeats that they have had in the past; (5) Kirkpatrick explains the line to mean that their success is constant, so they don't fear God; (6) others, like NEB, change the text and understand it (in verses 18-19) to refer to various desert tribes. It is difficult to understand how RSV arrived at its rendering of the text. It seems best to take verse 19c as TEV and TOB have.

Selah (see 3.2) in the Hebrew text comes at the end of verse 19b, not at the end of line d̲ (as RSV). It is rather unusual, however, for it to come in the middle of a verse.

55.20-21   RSV   TEV

20 My companion stretched out his   20 My former companion attacked
    hand against his friends,   his friends;
    he violated his covenant.   he broke his promises.
21 His speech was smoother than   21 His words were smoother than
    butter,   cream,
    yet war was in his heart;   but there was hatred in his
    his words were softer than oil,   heart;
    yet they were drawn swords.   his words were as soothing as oil,
                                               but they cut like sharp swords.

In these verses the psalmist refers again to his former friend (see verses 12-14). The Hebrew of verse 20a begins "he stretched out his hand," which most, like RSV and TEV, take to refer to the former friend of verses 12-14; but NEB, NAB, NJB, and SPCL take it to refer to the enemies of verses 18-19. **My companion** may sometimes be rendered "the one I went around with" or "the one who was one heart with me." The expression used should resemble or be the same as the one in verse 13.

He "attacked" (sent out his hand against) **his friends** (literally "those who were at peace with him" or "those who had a covenant with him," that is, his allies).

In this verse **covenant** means the "**promises**" or vows the psalmist and his friend had made to each other, to be friends and to help each other. The verb translated **violated** means basically "to profane"; in this context it means, as TEV, NEB, and NJV translate, "**broke**"; or else "dishonored."

With vivid figures (verse 21) the psalmist accuses his former friend of hypocrisy; his friendly words hide hostility and hatred. **Smoother than butter** as a reference to talking in a hypocritical and deceitful fashion must be translated by an equivalent expression in the receptor language and not simply copied. It may be possible in some languages to say, for example, "his words were heard as smoothly as butter is swallowed" or "he spoke as smoothly as one swallows butter." Likewise **softer than oil** may sometimes be rendered "his words soothed the mind like oil soothes the body." In line **b war** means destructive wishes, or hatred, which he nourished in his heart; so the figure of **drawn swords** follows naturally, meaning destructive curses or wishes. It may be better to use a simile, as TEV does, "**like sharp swords.**"

55.22	RSV	TEV
	Cast your burden[n] on the LORD, and he will sustain you; he will never permit the righteous to be moved.	Leave your troubles with the LORD, and he will defend you; he never lets honest men be defeated.

[n] Or *what he has given you*

There is no clue in this verse as to who is speaking or who is being addressed (**your** and **you** are singular, not plural). Either the psalmist is speaking to himself or to his readers, or a word of assurance is being spoken to the psalmist by a cultic prophet, that is, a prophet serving as a ritual spokesman for God in the Temple; in that case verse 23 would be the psalmist's response.

The word translated **burden** occurs only here in the Old Testament; the word means "burden" in the Talmud, and that is how most modern commentators and translators understand it. The Septuagint and Syriac have "your care"; Jerome "your love"; Targum "your hope"; NEB "your fortunes." There may be an allusion to these words in 1 Peter 5.7. In many languages it is not possible to say **Cast your burden** or "**Leave your troubles.**" In some languages, however, one may translate, for example, "Give the LORD your worries" or "Put on the LORD your troubles." In some languages where it is not possible to speak of transferring such abstract items, one may sometimes say "The LORD will be troubled for you" or "The LORD will have worries in your place."

Sustain in this context means to support, to maintain firm, to provide for one's needs (see its use in 2 Sam 19.32-33).

As frequently in the Psalms, **the righteous** are those who obey God's commandments (so SPCL); FRCL has "a faithful person."

55.23	RSV	TEV
	But thou, O God, wilt cast them down into the lowest pit; men of blood and treachery shall not live out half their days. But I will trust in thee.	But you, O God, will bring those murderers and liars to their graves before half their life is over. As for me, I will trust in you.

The psalmist finishes with a final threat of death against his enemies. God will "push them down into the deepest pit," that is, into Sheol, the world of the dead.

He calls them **men of blood and treachery**, that is, "**murderers and liars.**" The expression **men of blood** or "**murderers**" must sometimes be rendered "men who kill people." Similarly, **men of . . . treachery** may be ". . . who betray people" or ". . . who deceive."

Their final punishment will come "**before half their life is over**" (TEV; see verse 15a-b, where the psalmist prays that his enemies may die suddenly and disastrously, while they are still young and healthy).

The psalm closes with a word of trust in God.

Psalm 56

This psalm is a prayer by an individual who is being persecuted and who turns to God for protection. There is nothing in the text to identify with certainty the author or his circumstances; some commentators take the author to have been the king of Israel (see Dahood, Eaton, Toombs). It is unlikely that the Hebrew title portrays the actual historical setting in which this psalm was composed.

The psalm includes the usual elements of a cry for help to God (verses 1-2), an expression of confidence in God's power to save (verses 3-4), a description of the psalmist's situation (verses 5-6), and a request that God punish his enemies (verse 7). Again the psalmist describes his situation and expresses his trust in God (verses 8-11), and closes the psalm with a vow to offer a sacrifice to God (verses 12-13).

HEADING: "**A Prayer of Trust in God.**" Other headings are "Reliance on God"; "Trust casts out fear"; "The all-sufficient God." This title must in some languages be expressed through the use of verb phrases; for example, "The psalmist prays and places his heart on God."

Hebrew Title: **To the choirmaster: according to The Dove on Far-off Terebinths. A Miktam of David, when the Philistines seized him in Gath** (TEV "A psalm by David, after the Philistines captured him in Gath").

For **choirmaster** see title of Psalm 4; for **Miktam** see title of Psalm 16. The phrase **The Dove on Far-off Terebinths** probably indicates the tune to which the psalm was to be played; there are other suggestions. The terebinth was a tree that in some places was considered an appropriate site for worship to pagan gods; but there is considerable doubt over the form and meaning of the word translated **Terebinths** (see 58.1). HOTTP says that the word refers to the melody, although the meaning is uncertain. Traditionally it has been understood to mean "silence"; and so HOTTP proposes the translation "The dove of silence of the regions far away." NJB translates "Tune: 'The oppression of distant princes.' " Gath was one of the five principal Philistine cities. According to 1 Samuel 21.10-15; 27.1-4, David went there twice in order to escape from Saul.

56.1-2

RSV	TEV

1 Be gracious to me, O God,
    for men trample upon me;
    all day long foemen oppress me;
2 my enemies trample upon me all
        day long,
    for many fight against me
	1 Be merciful to me, O God,
	    because I am under attack;
	    my enemies persecute me all
	        the time.
	2 All day long my opponents attack
	    me.

502

| proudly. | There are so many who fight against me. |

In the psalmist's opening prayer for deliverance, he describes his situation four times (verses 1b,c,2a,b).

For **Be gracious** see the same verb and comments in 4.1c.

In verses 1b and 2a the psalmist twice uses a verb of uncertain meaning: **trample** (RSV), "persecute" (NJV, FRCL, SPCL), "harass" (NEB, TOB), "attack" (TEV, NJB).

Foemen in verse 1c and **fight** (TEV "**who fight**") in verse 2b translate participles of the same verb "to fight."

At the end of verse 2 in Hebrew the word for "a high place" is used, which RSV and SPCL translate **proudly**; NIV "in their pride"; FRCL "(they attack me and) overcome me"; NJB translates "countless are those who attack me from the heights." NEB emends the text to get "Appear on high." Most take it to be a title for God, "O Most High" (Briggs, Dahood, Anderson; TEV, NJV, NAB); TEV translates "**O LORD Almighty**" and places it at the beginning of verse 3.[1] If the translator follows TEV rather than RSV, "**LORD Almighty**" of verse 3 in some languages may be rendered, for example, "Almighty God, you who are powerful" or "Almighty God, you who are great." Note that the name for God, "Yahweh," does not occur here, and so TEV's "**LORD**" should be rendered in some other way, such as "Almighty God."

56.3-4	RSV		TEV
3	When I am afraid, I put my trust in thee.	3	When I am afraid, O LORD Almighty, I put my trust in you.
4	In God, whose word I praise, in God I trust without a fear. What can flesh do to me?	4	I trust in God and am not afraid; I praise him for what he has promised. What can a mere human being do to me?

For a discussion of **I put my trust**, see 4.5.

The psalmist expresses his confidence in God to save him from his enemies. In verse 4a God's **word** means "**what he has promised**" (TEV verse 4b); the psalmist is sure that God will keep his promise to save those who trust in him. If the translator follows TEV "**for what he has promised**," in some languages it will be necessary to make the content of the promise more explicit; for example, "I praise him because he has promised to save me."

In verse 4c **flesh** refers to the human creature in its mortality and weakness, as compared with God. The rhetorical question in verse 4c is the psalmist's way of stating that, with God on his side, he knows that "**a mere human being**" cannot harm him. Most translations in English have "mortal man" or "mortal men." **Flesh** in the

---

[1]HOTTP says there are two ways of interpreting this passage: (1) "for many struggle for me in the heights"—a reference to the angels; (2) "for many struggle against me, O Most High!"

sense of mortal man is sometimes rendered "man who dies." However, a translation which says "What can a man who dies do to me?" may suggest the activities of departed spirits. If so, it will be better to say "What can an ordinary human being do to me?"

56.5-6

	RSV		TEV
5	All day long they seek to injure my cause; all their thoughts are against me for evil.	5	My enemies make trouble for me all day long; they are always thinking up some way to hurt me!
6	They band themselves together, they lurk, they watch my steps. As they have waited for my life,	6	They gather in hiding places and watch everything I do, hoping to kill me.

The psalmist describes how his enemies are trying to bring about his ruin. As RSV shows (verse 5a), the Hebrew text does not explicitly identify the subject of the verbs in verses 5-6; TEV supplies "**My enemies.**" The text is none too clear, and in places is evidently corrupt. Some commentators believe that two separate compositions were brought together, with consequent obscurities.

In verse 5 the first line is literally "All the day they hurt my words" (or, my doings). This can be taken in several ways. RSV, TEV, and NJV take the Hebrew *dabar* to mean here "matter, affair, thing"; RSV **my cause**; NJV "my affairs"; and the verb means "to grieve, to cause hurt." But the verb can be taken to mean "to twist," and *dabar* to mean "word," so it is possible to translate "they twist my words" (Anderson; NIV, FRCL, NJB); SPCL has "they hurt me with words."

The expression **All day long** in some languages will have too limited a meaning, suggesting that the psalmist's enemies trouble him only during the hours of daylight. Therefore in some cases it will be more appropriate to say "My enemies make trouble for me all the time."

Verse 5b is quite straightforward and should offer no translation difficulties; NJV "they plan only evil against me"; NIV "they are always plotting to harm me"; SPCL "all they think about is how to hurt me."

Verse 6 in Hebrew begins with two verbs, usually taken to mean "they gather, they hide"; so TEV "**They gather in hiding places**" and RSV **They band themselves together, they lurk**.

In verse 6b **they watch my steps** can be better rendered "they spy on my movements" (NJB), or "they dog my steps" (NEB), or "they watch my every move" (NJV).

Line c̲ of verse 6, "**hoping to kill me**," is literally "when they wait for my *nefesh*" (see 3.2). TEV and others have joined this line to what precedes; RSV, FRCL, and NEB join it to what follows.

56.7   RSV   TEV

> so recompense^o them for their   Punish^q them, O God, for their
>   crime;   evil;
> in wrath cast down the peoples,   defeat those people in your
>   O God!   anger!

^{o} Cn: Heb *deliver* ^{q} *Probable text* Punish; *Hebrew* Save.

In line a the Hebrew verb *palat* usually means "save, deliver" (see its use in 17.13), a meaning which is inappropriate here, unless the line is taken as a rhetorical question, "Will you save them on account of their evil?" or, as FRCL translates, "After so much injustice will they escape?" This is supported by Weiser and HOTTP.[2] But K-B, from the use of the verb in Job 21.10b (which see), takes the verb to mean here "cast out"—so NJV "Cast them out for their evil" (also NJB "reject"). But many translations prefer to read the verb *palas* (see RSV, TEV, NAB), variously translated "repay," **recompense** (RSV), "keep in view" (NAB), "punish" (TEV).

Cast down translates the causative form of the verb "to go down," so the meaning is "bring them down."

The Hebrew for **peoples** can be understood as foreign nations (Kirkpatrick and others; so RSV, NJB, NIV, NEB, SPCL), or else the psalmist's enemies (so TEV, GECL, TOB, FRCL).

The expression **in wrath cast down the peoples** in some languages will require some adjustment; for example, "show your anger and defeat those people," or idiomatically, "with a hot heart defeat them."

56.8   RSV   TEV

> Thou hast kept count of my toss-   You know how troubled I am;
>   ings;   you have kept a record of my
> put thou my tears in thy bottle!   tears.
> Are they not in thy book?   Aren't they listed in your book?

My tossings translates a Hebrew noun that occurs only here in the Old Testament, and whose form and meaning are quite uncertain: "grief" is one rendering, also "lament" (NEB, Dahood) or "sorrows" (NJB). Anderson takes the word to mean "homelessness," and this is the meaning expressed by NJV "wanderings" (see also TOB, GECL).[3] It indicates some form of distress.

---

[2]HOTTP understands the sentence to be "a bitter ironical question to which the expected answer is of course negative," that is, "For their crime, will there be salvation for them?" If a translator follows HOTTP's interpretation, the translation can be "Surely, O God, you won't reward them for their evil!"

[3]HOTTP also takes the Hebrew to mean "wandering," which "expresses the fugitive's unresting, moving life, its sojourning far away from his home, his family and

If the translator takes line a to refer to distress, in some languages this may be expressed idiomatically; for example, "You know how my heart hangs up" or "You know how my stomach trembles."

The vivid picture "put my tears in your waterskin" (or, wineskin) in line b is a way of telling God (or reminding him, if the verb is understood as indicative, not imperative) to notice how troubled the psalmist is. Dahood takes the word "skin" to mean here a parchment for writing on: "list my tears on your parchment" (see NIV "on your scroll"). This fits well with the next line. TEV has abandoned the figure and translates **"you have kept a record of my tears"** (so SPCL); a similar possibility is "You have taken note of my grief." In some languages, if the expression **put thou my tears in thy bottle** is used, it will be necessary to make explicit the reason for such a request; for example, "put my tears in your bottle so that you can see how much I have cried."

The next line **Are they not in thy book?** is taken by some to have originally been a note in the margin (see NJB, BJ); the copyist wrote, "Shouldn't this [that is, the word for 'your waterskin'] be 'your book'?"—which was introduced into the text by a later copyist (NEB puts this line in a footnote). This is quite possible, but it is best to stay with the traditional interpretation of the Masoretic text.[4]

In some languages line c, if translated as a rhetorical question, will require a reply; for example, "Yes, they are." In many languages it will be necessary to say regarding the tears, lines b and c, "have they not been counted and the number of them written in your book?"

<table>
<tr><td>**56.9-11**</td><td>RSV</td><td>TEV</td></tr>
</table>

	RSV		TEV

9	Then my enemies will be turned back
	  in the day when I call.
	  This I know, that*p* God is for me.
		9	The day I call to you,
			  my enemies will be turned back.
			  I know this: God*r* is on my side—

10	In God, whose word I praise, in the LORD, whose word I praise,	10	the LORD, whose promises I praise.

11	in God I trust without a fear.
	  What can man do to me?
		11	In him I trust, and I will not be afraid.
			  What can a mere human being do to me?

p Or *because*

r I know this: God; *or* Because I know that God.

The author is confident that his enemies will be defeated when he calls to God for help (verse 9). This confidence is based on his assurance that God is on his side (verse 9c). The verb in line a is translated as a passive by RSV and TEV (**will be**

---

his land, as in Ps 11.1."

[4]HOTTP also considers it possible that the line was originally a marginal note, "is it not: 'in your reckoning'?"

turned back); it is better to take it as an active, however, as most translations do: "will turn back." In line <u>c</u>, as elsewhere, the Hebrew conjunction *ki* may be taken as "that" (**This I know, that God** . . .) or as "because" ("I know this because God . . ."); see text and margin of TEV and RSV.

Verse 10 in Hebrew is similar in form and meaning to verse 4a; the statement is repeated, first with **God** and next with **the LORD** (see RSV); TEV has shortened and combined the two lines into one. If the expression **whose word I praise** is repeated twice, it will appear in many languages as needless repetition and so can be reduced to one as in TEV. If the translator follows TEV in translating **word** as "promises," in some languages it will be necessary to say, for example, "I speak well of the things he promises."

Verse 11 is an exact repetition of verse 4b,c, except that in verse 4c "flesh" is used, while here the generic term **man** (*'adam*) is used; the meaning is the same.

<u>56.12-13</u> RSV	TEV
12 My vows to thee I must perform, O God; I will render thank offerings to thee.	12 O God, I will offer you what I have promised; I will give you my offering of thanksgiving,
13 For thou hast delivered my soul from death, yea, my feet from falling, that I may walk before God in the light of life.	13 because you have rescued me from death and kept me from defeat. And so I walk in the presence of God, in the light that shines on the living.

The psalmist closes his psalm with a promise to offer to God the sacrifice he had promised, his thanksgiving offerings (verse 12), in gratitude for having been kept safe. Line <u>a</u> of verse 12 is literally "Upon me, God, (are) your vows"—that is, the psalmist feels the obligation to fulfill the vows he had made to God. See NJV "I must pay my vows to You, O God." In some languages 12a may have to be rendered as "I will give you a sacrifice as payment for what I promised to do." **Render thank offerings** may sometimes be translated "to give sacrifices which show thanks to God."

God had **delivered** him (literally, his *nefesh*—see 3.2) from death (verse 13a); he had kept his **feet from falling**. Some take this second line to be a marginal gloss (like the one in verse 8c; see NEB): "Shouldn't this be 'my feet from falling'?"—which was later made part of the text.[5] Again, it is better to stay with the Hebrew text as generally understood and translated.

As a result of what God has done, the psalmist's life is spent "**in the presence of God**," that is, in the complete assurance of God's power and protection, which is further explained as **the light of life**. This last expression could be understood to

---

[5]HOTTP also admits this possibility; instead of being part of the text, it was a marginal note, "is it not: 'my feet from stumbling'?"

mean "in the life-giving light" or, as TEV has it, **"the light that shines on the living."** Probably the former is preferable. Most translate the phrase quite literally; GECL has "while you also let me see the light." It is possible that the original immediate references of **"the presence of God"** and <u>the light of life</u> were the Temple or the land of Israel as a whole, where God resided and where his light shone on his people.

The expression **that I may walk before God**, if translated literally, may often have the meaning of "walking in front of God." In order to avoid this misunderstanding it will sometimes be necessary to say "I am protected by God" or "I know that God is near me and defends me." Line <u>c</u> can sometimes be rendered, for example, "I am in the light which God causes to shine on the people" or, following the alternative interpretation, "the light which gives life to people."

Psalm 57

This psalm, like Psalm 56, is a cry for help by a man who is threatened by enemies. The Hebrew title gives the circumstances in which the psalm was written; most scholars believe that the statement does not reflect the actual historical setting of the psalm's composition.

The psalm contains the usual elements in this kind of psalm: (1) a cry for help and an expression of trust (verses 1-3); (2) a description of the psalmist's situation (verses 4-6), in which there is a refrain (verse 5) which is repeated later (verse 11); (3) a promise to praise God for his help (verses 7-10); the closing refrain (verse 11).

HEADING: "**A Prayer for Help**." Other headings are "Among ferocious enemies"; "Praise after persecution"; "Faith triumphant." The TEV title in some languages must be adjusted by transforming the nouns into verb phrases; for example, "The psalmist prays to God and asks God to help him."

Hebrew Title: **To the choirmaster: according to Do Not Destroy. A Miktam of David, when he fled from Saul, in the cave** (TEV "A psalm by David, after he fled from Saul in the cave").

For **choirmaster** see title of Psalm 4; for **Miktam** see title of Psalm 16. **Do Not Destroy** is probably the name of the tune to which the psalm was to be sung (it appears also in the titles of Psalms 58, 59, and 75). David's flight from King Saul in the cave is reported in 1 Samuel 24.

57.1-3

RSV	TEV

1 Be merciful to me, O God, be merciful to me,
     for in thee my soul takes refuge;
     in the shadow of thy wings I will take refuge,
     till the storms of destruction pass by.
	1 Be merciful to me, O God, be merciful,
	     because I come to you for safety.
	 In the shadow of your wings I find protection
	     until the raging storms are over.

2 I cry to God Most High,
     to God who fulfils his purpose for me.
	2 I call to God, the Most High,
	     to God, who supplies my every need.

3 He will send from heaven and save me.
     he will put to shame those who trample upon me.   *Selah*
	3 He will answer from heaven and save me;
	     he will defeat my oppressors.

509

> God will send forth his steadfast
> love and his faithfulness!

> God will show me his constant
> love and faithfulness.

This psalm opens with an A-B-A' type structure, that is, the word *'elohim*, God, is preceded and followed by the verb **be merciful**. The purpose of this repetition is to call attention to the psalmist's fears and need of God's protection. Translators should not merely copy this form, but seek to accomplish the psalmist's purpose within the stylistic usage of the receptor language.

For **Be merciful** see comments on 4.1c ("be gracious"); a prayer for God's compassion, God's pity on the psalmist.

The psalmist prays to God for help, because it is God who protects him. The expression **Be merciful to me** in some languages is rendered "be kind to me." It may often be translated by the use of idiomatic phrases such as "have a white heart for me," "let your heart be open for me," or "accept me with your heart."

In thee my soul takes refuge (TEV "**I come to you for safety**") translates "in you my *nefesh* (see 3.2) finds protection" (see comments on "take refuge" in 2.12).

For the figure **the shadow of thy wings**, see 17.8 and comments, and note that **take refuge** is repeated from the previous line. The figurative expression **in the shadow of thy wings** in some languages will require some adaptation. It is sometimes possible to adopt a comparison or simile so that the original form may be preserved; for example, "like a bird I find protection in the shadow of your wings" or "you protect me like a bird protects its young in the shadow of its wings." If the figure of speech must be sacrificed for clarity of meaning, one can say, for example, "close to you I am protected." If **shadow** in some languages carries negative connotations, other possible expressions are "under your wings," "your wings shade me," or "your wings cover me."

The storms of destruction translates the plural of the word "destruction"; for a similar figure for troubles, see 55.8.

For **Most High** in verse 2a, see comments on 7.17. The relative clause **who fulfils his purpose for me** translates a verb which is taken to mean "accomplish"; Dahood and Anderson take it to mean "avenge" here; Briggs, taking his lead from the Septuagint, prefers the sense "deal bountifully with"; so NJB "who has done everything for me"; NJV "who is good to me" (similarly SPCL, TOB). It is difficult to understand precisely what RSV **who fulfils his purpose for me** means (also NIV and NEB); presumably it means that God provides all that is needed for the psalmist to be what God wants him to be.

Some translations, like TOB and NJB, take verse 3 as a request: "May he, from heaven, send me salvation!" RSV **He will send from heaven** is puzzling (also NEB and NIV), since the verb "to send" normally takes a direct object. It is better, like TOB, to join the two verb phrases in the line, "send me salvation."

Put to shame in verse 3b translates a verb which occurs only here in the Old Testament and is taken to mean "confuse" (K-B); so NEB "frustrate." Some, however, prefer the meaning "to reproach, criticize"; so NIV "rebuking," also possible "taunt," and RSV **put to shame**. But the Masoretic text is none too clear, and **my oppressors** can be taken as the subject, not the object, of the verb; so NJV "my persecutor reviles"; Weiser "he who lies in wait for me has slandered (me)." On the whole it seems better to take it as RSV and TEV have.

Who trample (TEV "**Oppressors**") translates a participle of the same verb used in 56.1,2 (TEV "attack"). See comments there.

For *Selah* see 3.2.

The third line of verse 3 is "he will send his *chesed* (see 5.7) and his *'emeth* (see 15.2)," which are like heavenly messengers sent to protect the psalmist (Briggs). The expression **God will send forth his steadfast love and his faithfulness** in some languages can be rendered, for example, "God will always love me, and he will do this with one heart."

<table>
<tr><td>57.4</td><td>RSV</td><td>TEV</td></tr>
</table>

RSV	TEV

I lie in the midst of lions
    that greedily devour*q* the sons
        of men;
their teeth are spears and arrows,
    their tongues sharp swords.
	I am surrounded by enemies,
	    who are like man-eating lions.
	Their teeth are like spears and
	    arrows;
	        their tongues are like sharp
	            swords.

q Cn: Heb *are aflame*

In this verse RSV consistently maintains the metaphor, and some readers, unaware of the figurative nature of the language, may understand the words in a literal fashion.

The verse begins with "My *nefesh*" (see 3.2), which may be emphatic (NJV "As for me . . ."), or else it may go with **in the midst of lions**, while the verb **I lie** goes with "those who devour men." So TOB, which translates, "I am among lions, lying down among creatures . . . ." Most translations are like RSV and TEV. The expression **in the midst of lions** in some languages must be adjusted; for example, where the lion is unknown and there are other large animals that will attack people, such animals may be used in place of lions. If no such animal is known, then the translator may have to say "wild animals."

For other passages in which the psalmist's enemies are compared with **lions** see 7.2; 10.9; 17.12. The Hebrew verb form in line **b** translated "eating" by TEV means "to devour," that is, destructive and greedy eating; it is not necessary, as RSV has done, to supply another Hebrew verb on the supposition that this verb means only "to burn up" (see Anderson). TEV and NJV have "**man-eating lions**." For comments on the phrase **sons of men**, see 11.4.

The psalmist pictures his enemies to be like lions whose **teeth** are **spears and arrows**, whose **tongues** are **sharp swords**—obvious metaphors for ferociousness and destructive fury (see similar language in 52.2; 55.21). **Sharp swords** in some languages where the sword is unknown may be rendered "sharp knives."

<table>
<tr><td>57.5</td><td>RSV</td><td>TEV</td></tr>
</table>

RSV	TEV

Be exalted O God, above the heav-
    ens!
	Show your greatness in the sky, O
	    God,

| Let thy glory be over all the earth! | and your glory over all the earth. |

The symmetry of Psalm 57 is seen in the placement of the refrain at the center and end of the poem. Furthermore, pivot patterns are sometimes used in these places as structural markers. In verse 5 (and verse 11) line **b** lacks the final stress, since the word *'elohim* occurs only at the end of line **a**. A formal translation can be "High above the heavens, God / over all the earth your glory (God)."

The prayer in verse 5 is repeated in verse 11: it is a request that God reveal his "**greatness**" (TEV) and his **glory** (see comments at 3.3) in all the universe. So **above the heavens** in line **a** has its complement **over all the earth** in line **b**; the two together include all of creation. GECL may be followed: "O God, shine upon heaven with your glory, and fill the earth with your might!" In this context the psalmist prays for such a revelation in terms of God's saving him and destroying his enemies. The expression **Be exalted** may be rendered in many languages as in TEV "**Show your greatness**," or shifted to a verb phrase; for example, "Show people how great you are."

57.6   RSV   TEV

| They set a net for my steps; my soul was bowed down. They dug a pit in my way, but they have fallen into it themselves.   *Selah* | My enemies have spread a net to catch me; I am overcome with distress. They dug a pit in my path, but fell into it themselves. |

The psalmist continues by describing how his enemies, like hunters, are trying to capture him with **a net** and **a pit**; but he knows that they will only harm themselves. For similar language see 7.15; 9.15; 31.4; 35.7-8.

TEV "**I am overcome with distress**" in line **b** translates "my *nefesh* is bowed down" (see RSV). NJV, however, on the basis of later Hebrew usage, translates "to ensnare me," while Dahood, from the Akkadian, gets the meaning "a noose for my neck" (also FRCL). NEB has "but I bow my head to escape from it" (that is, "the net" of the preceding line); similarly TOB. It seems best to follow the sense expressed by RSV and say something like TEV: "I have lost all hope" or "I am helpless."

In some languages where the use of nets for catching animals is unknown, the expression **set a net for my steps** can be rendered, for example, "my enemies have set a trap to catch me." In case the idea of catching a person by a trap will be unclear, the translator can add a simile; for example, "my enemies have set a trap to catch me like a hunter sets a trap to catch an animal."

In some languages it may be necessary to make the purpose of the pit explicit; for example, "they dug a pit to make me fall into it."

7	My heart is steadfast, O God, my heart is steadfast! I will sing and make melody!		7	I have complete confidence, O God; I will sing and praise you!
8	Awake, my soul! Awake, O harp and lyre! I will awake the dawn!		8	Wake up, my soul! Wake up, my harp and lyre! I will wake up the sun.

In verses 7-11 (which appear also in 108.1-5) the psalmist promises to praise God for his saving help. **My heart is steadfast** expresses the psalmist's confidence in God; the word means "firm, established." Some (BJ, NJB) have "ready"; most English translations have "steadfast"; NJV "firm." In some languages **My heart is steadfast**, with the meaning of having confidence, is translated idiomatically as "My heart rests on God" or "I have one mind about God."

Make melody can be better translated "I will sing a hymn (or, a psalm)"; the verb is used to refer to vocal music (see comments on "sing praise" in 7.17b).

Then the psalmist summons himself, **my soul** (literally "my glory"—see comment in 7.5; also 16.9; 30.12), and then his musical instruments (see 33.2) to **awake**, that is, to get ready to praise God. Due to the problem of commanding oneself to awaken, it will often be necessary to shift to a parallel expression; for example, "I will awaken myself" or "I will get ready." In some languages it is necessary to complete the expression by making explicit what one is to get ready for; for example, in the present context one may say "I will awaken myself and sing." In languages which can not speak of waking up inanimate objects such as musical instruments, one can sometimes say, for example, "I will awaken and play my harp and lyre." If it is not possible to maintain the poetic imagery of waking inanimate objects, the translator should look for other poetic forms that can be used meaningfully.

The next statement, **I will awake the dawn**, probably means that he will arise before dawn and, so to speak, wake up the sun, instead of letting the sun wake him up (see Anderson). **I will awake the dawn** in some languages can be said, for example, "I will wake up before dawn" or "I will get up before the sun rises."

9	I will give thanks to thee, O Lord, among the peoples; I will sing praises to thee among the nations,		9	I will thank you, O Lord, among the nations. I will praise you among the peoples.
10	For thy steadfast love is great to the heavens, thy faithfulness to the clouds.		10	Your constant love reaches the heavens; your faithfulness touches the skies.
11	Be exalted, O God, above the heavens!		11	Show your greatness in the sky, O God,

> Let thy glory be over all the
> earth!

> and your glory over all the
> earth.

The psalmist's praise to God will be universal: **among the peoples** and **among the nations** (verse 9). Some take the immediate reference here to be fellow Israelites present at a festival in Jerusalem, people who had come from all over the world (see Weiser, Toombs). The expressions **among the peoples** and **among the nations** must in some languages be shifted to clauses; for example, "wherever people live" and "wherever there are nations." In some languages one can say "and all the people will know it" or "and all the nations will hear about it."

Verse 10 is almost identical in form with, and has the same meaning as, 36.5, which see. The expression **steadfast love is great to the heavens** and TEV "**reaches the heavens**" is difficult to translate in some languages. Therefore one can sometimes say "you love so greatly that it is like the distance from earth to sky."

The concluding refrain (verse 11) is a repetition of verse 5. In some languages **over all the earth** can be rendered, for example, "in all the places in the earth," or simply, "everywhere."

Psalm 58

This psalm is a cry to God for help against powerful enemies who are guilty of crimes of violence throughout the country. Unlike other such psalms, there are no personal complaints here; it is on behalf of the whole community that the psalmist writes. By means of fierce denunciations the psalmist calls down divine punishment on his people's enemies; the land is to be rid of these corrupt tyrants.

The psalm begins with a direct accusation of the enemies (verses 1-2), followed by a description of their evil character and conduct (verses 3-5). Then the psalmist, in a series of different figures, prays for God to punish them (verses 6-9). The psalm ends on a note of confidence: the psalmist knows that the righteous will prevail, because God is just (verses 10-11).

HEADING: "**A Prayer for God to Punish the Wicked.**" Other headings are "The judge of earthly judges"; "The wicked and their destruction"; "Against unjust judges." This title is rather full and will require very little adjustment in languages which have a preference for verb phrases rather than nominal ones. In some languages one may say "The psalmist prays that God will punish people who do evil deeds."

Hebrew Title: **To the choirmaster: according to Do Not Destroy. A Miktam of David** ("A psalm by David").

For **choirmaster** see title of Psalm 4; for **Do not Destroy** see title of Psalm 57; for **Miktam** see title of Psalm 16.

58.1-2	RSV	TEV

	RSV	TEV
1	Do you indeed decree what is right, you gods?[s] Do you judge the sons of men uprightly?	1 Do you rulers[u] ever give a just decision? Do you judge all men fairly?
2	Nay, in your hearts you devise wrongs; your hands deal out violence on earth.	2 No! You think only of the evil you can do, and commit crimes of violence in the land.

[s] Or *mighty lords*

[u] rulers; *or* gods.

There is considerable uncertainty over the form and meaning of the Hebrew word translated **you gods**. The Masoretic text has *'elem* (as in the Hebrew title of Psa 56), which cannot be identified with certainty. There are several solutions: (1) Some (following Aquila) change the vowels to *'ilem* "silent, silently" (see BJ, and NJB footnote); so TOB "When you speak, justice is silent." HOTTP prefers the Masoretic text, "silence" ("B" decision) and interprets the text to mean "Do you really speak in order to conceal by silence the righteousness?" (2) Some (following the Septuagint, Syriac, Jerome) change the vowels to *'ulam* "but, instead," a strong adversative (Briggs); this results in something like "Do you, then, indeed decree righteously?" (3) Some read *'elim*, which may be either the plural of *'elah* "terebinth" (a sacred tree; see Hebrew title of Psa 56), or (4) the plural of *'el* "god"; so Weiser, Anderson, Toombs, Oesterley, Taylor; BJ, RSV, AT, TEV footnote; NAB "like gods." NJB has "Divine as you are" in the text but in footnote says the word is here applied to judges and rulers; FRCL has "heavenly powers." (5) Some take *'elim* in the sense of "powerful, mighty men," human, not divine: TEV, NEB, NJV, NIV, GECL, ZÜR, RSV footnote. (6) Dahood takes *'elim* to mean "rams," here understood to refer to "leaders." (7) KJV "congregation" was derived from a twelfth-century A.D. Jewish teacher, Rabbi David Kimchi, who took the word to be from an Aramaic root meaning "to bind." The choice seems to be between (4) and (5); perhaps (5) is better, with (4) as an alternative in a footnote.

The speaker in verses 1-2 is usually taken to be the psalmist; but some take it to be God (see Toombs), addressing the gods in the heavenly council (see 82.1-7).

For comments on **the sons of men**, see 11.4. Instead of being, as they should be, just judges of people, they are guilty of **wrongs** and **violence**; the latter could be taken in a legal sense as injustice, lawlessness, which the rulers (or judges) perpetuate through a corrupt administration of justice. In some languages, particularly in Africa, the TEV expression **"give a just decision"** is said idiomatically as "to cut the words straight." For languages which require a reply to rhetorical questions, TEV provides a model.

If **gods** and not "rulers" is used in verse 1, then at the end of verse 2 it should be "the earth" (see RSV) and not **"the land"** (TEV), that is, the land of Israel. In many languages the expression "in the land" will mean little more than in the ground, or in the country. In these languages it may be necessary to make it clear that the "**land**" refers to the earth generally, or else to the nation Israel.

58.3-5   RSV   TEV

3	The wicked go astray from the womb,	3 Evil men go wrong all their lives; they tell lies from the day they are born.
	they err from their birth, speaking lies.	
4	They have venom like the venom of a serpent,	4 They are full of poison like snakes; they stop up their ears like a deaf cobra,
	like the deaf adder that stops its ear,	
5	so that it does not hear the voice of charmers	5 which does not hear the voice of the snake charmer, or the chant of the clever magician.
	or of the cunning enchanter.	

After addressing the rulers in the second person (verses 1-2), here **the wicked** are spoken of in the third person, which may be understood as a general indictment of all evil people, but more probably is a description of the ones addressed in verses 1-2. Those who take "you gods" as the meaning of the word in verse 1 understand that the wicked people spoken of in the rest of the psalm are the human agents through whom the gods work their evil ways.

In exaggerated language (see similar expressions in 51.5) these people **go astray from the womb**, which translates what is literally "they go astray, the wicked, from the womb they err"; and in line **b** "from the womb they tell lies" (two different Hebrew words for "womb," namely, "belly" and "womb"). TEV has expressed the meaning with one verb in line **a**, "**go wrong**," which is the meaning of the two verbs in the Hebrew text; but most translations, like RSV, take the first verb (**go astray**) with line **a**, the second verb (**err**) with line **b**. Some languages speak of a baby being born from the belly or abdomen, not from the organ known in the language as the "womb."

For the figure of **venom** (that is, "**poison**") as malicious and lying words, see also 140.3.

The figure used in verses 4b-5 of a "**deaf cobra**" (or **adder**) **that stops its ear** is strange. The general sense of the figure is clear enough: these wicked people obstinately refuse to listen to warning or advice. The Hebrew says literally "like the deaf cobra that stops up its ears" (see RSV), which one Jewish commentator ingeniously explained by saying that a snake would lay its head sideways on the ground to stop up one ear and with its tail would cover up the other one! (In fact, snakes do not have the sense of hearing that mammals have.)

It will be noticed that there is quite a variety in translating the name of the animal in verse 4: RSV **serpent . . . adder**; NEB "serpents . . . asp"; NJV "snake . . . viper"; NJB "snake . . . adder"; TEV, NIV "**snakes . . . cobra**." In languages where the cobra or asp are unknown, any other poisonous snake can be substituted. The practice of snake charming, however, will be less recognizable and may require a supplementary note.

In verse 5 **the cunning enchanter** in line **b** is parallel with **the . . . charmers** in line **a**; such people are also spoken of in Ecclesiastes 10.11; Jeremiah 8.17. By means of his music, chants, and body movements, a snake charmer would try to hypnotize a snake so as to make it docile and harmless. In some languages "**snake charmer**" may be rendered, for example, "snake man," "snake show man," or "snake music man." **Enchanter** or "**magician**" should not be identified with one who practices witchcraft. In this context the reference is to casting spells and charming snakes. If a term for one who casts spells is not available, it may be possible to use a phrase; for example, "one who sings his magic" or "one who controls by repeating words."

58.6-7	RSV	TEV
6	O God, break the teeth in their mouths;	6 Break the teeth of these fierce lions, O God.
	tear out the fangs of the young lions, O LORD!	7 May they disappear like water draining away;
7	Let them vanish like water that	may they be crushed like weeds

runs away; like grass let them be trodden down and wither.*t*	on a path.*v* *v Probable text* may . . . path; *Hebrew* *unclear.*

t Cn: Heb uncertain

The psalmist calls down God's vengeance and punishment on the wicked. Verse 6 has two parallel lines, synonymous in meaning, which TEV has shortened and combined into one line (see RSV for the form of the two lines). If a translator prefers to keep the two lines, something like the following can be said: "Break the teeth of these young lions, O God! Pull their teeth out, O LORD!" For **lions** as a figure for the enemies, see 7.2; 10.9; 17.12; 22.13,21; 35.17. (Here, as in 34.10; 35.17, NEB translates "unbelievers.")

Verse 7a is reasonably clear in meaning, and most translations have what RSV and TEV have. But verse 7b is quite different. HOTTP prefers the Masoretic text ("A" decision). Some take the Masoretic text to mean "When he takes aim, let his arrows be as if blunted"; NJV has for the Masoretic text (without any marginal note) "let Him aim His arrows and they be cut down," which makes more sense in the context; NAB translates the Masoretic text, "when they draw the bow, let their arrows be headless shafts" (similarly NIV). As is to be seen, there is much uncertainty, and TEV, like RSV, translates an emended text to get "**may they be crushed like weeds on a path**" (see Anderson). In similar fashion, but with "wither" instead of "**be crushed**," are NEB, NJB, BJ, SPCL.

In verses 7, 8, 9 there is a series of similes, all of which are nearly universally known comparisons: water, weeds, snails, and a newly born child.

58.8-9

	RSV		TEV
8	Let them be like the snail which dissolves into slime, like the untimely birth that never sees the sun.	8	May they be like snails that dis- solve into slime; may they be like a baby born dead that never sees the light.
9	Sooner than your pots can feel the heat of thorns, whether green or ablaze, may he sweep them away!	9	Before they know it, they are cut down like weeds; in his fierce anger God will blow them away while they are still living.*w*

w Verse 9 in Hebrew is unclear.

The two similes in verse 8 are also reasonably clear, but it should be noted: (1) **snail** translates a word found only here in the Old Testament; some take it to mean "beeswax," and others "worm." G. R. Driver takes the word to be synonymous with "abortion" in line **b** (see NEB "like an abortive birth which melts away"); most translate as do TEV and RSV. It seems that it was thought, from the trail of slime left by a snail, that the snail gradually dissolves, and finally there is nothing left but the empty snail shell. (2) The verb translated **dissolves** also occurs only here in the Old Testament, but its meaning is reasonably certain.

The simile in verse 8b is clear enough; see Job 3.16; Ecclesiastes 6.3 for the same figure. **The untimely birth**: a more normal way in English to say this would be either "a stillborn child" or "an aborted fetus."

The difficulty, not to say the impossibility, of translating verse 9 can be demonstrated by the fact that Dahood does not provide a translation of it and confesses: "The Hebrew of this verse is unintelligible to me." He rightly scores RSV for not giving any indication of the impossibility of making sense of the Masoretic text. It would be of little practical use to list the many ways in which the text has been handled. No two translations agree completely, and all (including even NIV) have textual footnotes. Whatever course a translator takes, a note should indicate that the Hebrew makes little sense. Notice how two translations in English have rendered the same Hebrew text: NJV "Before the thorns grow into a bramble, may He whirl them away alive in fury"; NEB "All unawares, may they be rooted up like a thorn-bush, like weeds which a man angrily clears away!"; and one other suggested version, "Before their pots feel the heat of the thorns, whether green or dry, may God sweep them away."[1]

TEV translates an emended text which mostly follows G. R. Driver's reconstruction in "Studies in the Vocabulary of the O.T. V," *Journal of Theological Studies* 34 (1933), page 44; see also Anderson.

58.10-11 RSV	TEV
10 The righteous will rejoice when he sees the vengeance; he will bathe his feet in the blood of the wicked.	10 The righteous will be glad when they see sinners punished; they will wade through the blood of the wicked.
11 Men will say, "Surely there is a reward for the righteous; surely there is a God who judges on earth."	11 People will say, "The righteous are indeed rewarded; there is indeed a God who judges the world."

The psalm closes on a confident note: the psalmist knows that there will be **vengeance**, that is, that God will punish sinners in general, or the people in particular against whom the psalm is addressed.

For the vivid picture in verse 10b, see comments at 68.23; this is an obvious metaphor of the complete destruction of the wicked, by means of which the righteous will be avenged.

God's justice will be seen and proclaimed by everyone (verse 11). The noun translated **reward** is literally "fruit," that is, the outcome of a process. Dahood points

---

[1]HOTTP ("A" decision) says the Masoretic text is difficult and can be interpreted in two ways: (1) "before your kettles were aware of the thorn, the stormwind wipes away, be it green or dry!"; (2) "before your thorns rise to a bush: while it is (still) green, the stormwind wipes it away (as if it were) dried!"

to Proverbs 11.30 for a similar use of the Hebrew noun. The expression **there is a reward for the righteous** in some languages must be shifted to a more active expression indicating explicitly that God is the one who rewards; for example, "God certainly gives a reward to good people."

In the last line **who judges** translates a plural participle, "those who judge," in the Masoretic text. Dahood and TOB say the plural is used here in order to agree with the "plural of majesty" of *'elohim* "God." But there are some who take *'elohim* here to mean "divine beings," in agreement with *'elim* "gods" of verse 1; no translation consulted renders it with the plural "gods who judge on earth." NJV translates "divine justice." One Jewish commentator understood the word to refer to angels. It seems best to say "God."

Psalm 59

This psalm is the prayer of an individual who is in danger of being killed by his enemies. Certain elements in the psalm, especially the references to "the nations" (verses 5,8) and to "my people" (verse 11), lead some commentators to conclude that the psalmist is the king; but nothing definite can be asserted.

Psalm 59 has a poem-length chiastic structure in which the dominant theme of protection from enemies recurs at three structural points: opening, middle, and closure. There are three themes which occur in the following order: 1. plea for protection from enemies; 2. treacherous nature of enemies; 3. plea to God to punish enemies; 2′. treacherous nature of enemies repeated; 3′. plea to God to punish enemies repeated.

Using the vocabulary of RSV the pattern of repetition may be presented as follows:

```
1-2   deliver, protect, deliver, save

      3-4   lie in wait, fierce men band themselves

            5   punish nations, spare none

                  7   snarling with their lips

                        8   hold nations in derision

9   strength, fortress

                              11   make them totter, bring them down

                        12   sin of their mouths, words of their lips

                  13   consume them in wrath

            14   howling like dogs, prowling

16-17   fortress, strength, fortress
```

HEADING: "**A Prayer for Safety**." Other headings are "Against the wicked"; "Against bloodthirsty enemies"; "A Prayer against the nations." In some languages it will be necessary to restructure this title to say, for example, "The psalmist prays and asks God to protect him."

Hebrew Title: **To the choirmaster: according to Do Not Destroy. A Miktam of David, when Saul sent men to watch his house in order to kill him** (TEV "A psalm by David, after Saul sent men to watch his house in order to kill him").

For **choirmaster** see title of Psalm 4; for **Do Not Destroy** see title of Psalm 57; and for **Miktam** see title of Psalm 16. The historical reference is to 1 Samuel 19.11-17; most scholars do not believe that this incident represents the actual circumstances of the composition of this psalm.

59.1-2   RSV   TEV

1   Deliver me from my enemies, O   1   Save me from my enemies, my
       my God,   God;
       protect me from those who rise   protect me from those who
       up against me,   attack me!
2   deliver me from those who work   2   Save me from those evil men;
       evil,   rescue me from those murder-
       and save me from bloodthirsty   ers!
       men.

The opening cry for help (verses 1-2) is made in four lines, all parallel and synonymous. Three verbs are used: **deliver** (verses 1a,2a; see 7.1), **protect** (see 20.1b), and **save** (see 12.1). The **enemies** are described as **those who rise up against me** (verse 1b), **those who work evil** (verse 2a; see 28.3), and **bloodthirsty men** (verse 2b), literally "men of bloods" (see 5.6; 55.23).

Not only is the entire psalm in chiastic arrangement, but verses 1-2, which set forth the major theme, are given emphasis by their particular form. In the Hebrew both verses are built by placing verbs before and after each pair of noun phrases; that is, V1 Np Np V2. Verse 1 uses **deliver** and **protect** respectively before and after **enemies** and **those who rise up against me**. Verse 2 repeats the same structure with **deliver** occurring before **those who work evil** and **save** after **bloodthirsty men**. Translators should not copy these structures but rather determine what devices in their own languages have equivalent stylistic functions. In both verses 1 and 2 there is a step-up of intensity which should be reflected in the translation. TEV has done this to a degree in going from "enemies" in line a to "those who attack me" in line b, and from "evil men" to "those murderers" in line b of verse 2.

59.3-4   RSV   TEV

3   For, lo, they lie in wait for my life;   3   Look! They are waiting to kill me;
       fierce men band themselves   cruel men are gathering against
       against me.   me.
       For no transgression or sin of   It is not because of any sin or
       mine, O LORD,   wrong I have done,
4   for no fault of mine, they run   4   nor because of any fault of
       and make ready.   mine, O LORD,
                                                  that they hurry to their places.

    Rouse thyself, come to my help,
       and see!

The psalmist describes his dangerous situation (verse 3a,b) and then asserts his innocence: nothing he has done justifies his enemies' attempts to kill him. In verse 3a the verb translated **lie in wait** means "to lie in ambush" (see 10.9); and **for my life** means "(in an attempt) to kill me." **Lie in wait for my life** therefore implies hiding and waiting for the psalmist to pass by in order to attack him and kill him. TEV has made the purpose clear with "**to kill me.**" It may be necessary in some languages to say, for example, "they hide and wait for me in order to kill me" or "they are hiding and waiting for me to go by in order to attack me."

Fierce men (TEV "**cruel men**") translates a word meaning "strong (men)," which in this context implies strong enemies intending to do serious harm. **Band themselves against me** must often be recast to make clear the reason; for example, "they gather together to harm me" or "they meet together to attack and injure me."

In verse 3c the two nouns translated **transgression** and **sin** are the two most commonly used for what is generally described as sinful acts against God; and in verse 4a, another word (**fault**) is used (for which see comments on "guilty" in 18.23b and on "iniquity" in 51.2a).

O LORD occurs at the end of verse 3 according to the Masoretic text, but for English style TEV has placed it at the end of the second phrase that claims innocence.

The two verbs translated **they run and make ready** are combined by TEV, "**they hurry to their places,**" that is, to attack. Dahood sees these verbs as denoting military movements, "they charge and take positions," and interprets them as a reference to an attack on the country by foreign enemies; NJB has "they come running to take up position." **They run and make ready** also implies that their purpose is to attack the speaker. Therefore "they run and get ready to attack me."

For comments on the last line of verse 4, see the following verse.

59.5	RSV	TEV
	Thou, LORD God of hosts, art God of Israel.	Rise, LORD God Almighty, and come to my aid;
	Awake to punish all the nations; spare none of those who treacherously plot evil. *Selah*	see for yourself, God of Israel! Wake up and punish the heathen; show no mercy to evil traitors!

TEV has joined the last line of verse 4 (RSV **Rouse thyself, come to my help, and see!**) to verse 5 and rearranged the material for a more natural ordering of the text.

The psalmist says to God **Rouse thyself** (see comments on "awake" in 7.6), **Awake** (see comments on 35.23). Both verbs are used in the same way in 44.23. The psalmist does not thereby imply that God is asleep, but that he is indifferent, he is inactive. **Come to my help** translates "to meet me," but the idea of helping may be implied. And the command **see** is a way of asking God to notice how the enemies are threatening him (or his people). Most translations include the idea of help, as in RSV; but NIV has "look on my plight," and GECL translates the line "Wake up, come, and see for yourself."

In verse 5a, by reminding Yahweh that he is **God of Israel**, the psalmist gives the reason why Yahweh should act and deliver the psalmist from peril. For **LORD**

God of hosts as a title of God, see comments on 46.7. The way in which the psalmist addresses God, LORD God of hosts and God of Israel, favors the idea that the psalmist may be the king, and that it is not just the psalmist who needs help against the attacks of foreign enemies, but the whole nation.

The enemies, **the nations** (TEV "the heathen"), are described as **those who treacherously plot evil** (for comments on the verb "are . . . treacherous," see 25.3b). The translation of **punish all the nations** is in many languages "punish all the other tribes," thus specifying all who are not of Israel. In English **"the heathen"** or "those pagans" better represents the emotional impact of the Hebrew word than **the nations** (see FRCL, SPCL). They are called "treacherous" (**"traitors"**) because they have broken their pact with Israel, or with its king (so Dahood). The translation of "traitors" in some languages is "people who sell their friends" or "people who give friends to their enemies."

For *Selah* see 3.2.

59.6-7	RSV	TEV

	RSV	TEV
6	Each evening they come back, howling like dogs and prowling about the city.	6 They come back in the evening, snarling like dogs as they go about the city.
7	There they are, bellowing with their mouths, and snarling with[u] their lips— for "Who," they think, "will hear us?"	7 Listen to their insults and threats. Their tongues are like swords in their mouths, yet they think that no one hears them.

[u] Cn: Heb *swords in*

The psalmist compares his enemies to a pack of dogs that prowl around the city at dusk. The translation of **they come back** must in many languages have an explicit point of reference; for example, "they come back where they were" or "they return to the place where they had been." **Howling** translates a verb that means simply "be noisy"; NJV "growling"; TEV, NEB, NJB, NIV "**snarling.**"

Prowling: TEV is closer to the Hebrew with "**they go about the city.**" The verb can even be understood as "surround," with the connotation of a siege. However, the translator should be free to use a verb that best fits the context in the receptor language.

The first line of verse 7 is literally "Look, they pour out with their mouths"; the verb "pour out" seems to be used in a figurative sense of unrestrained speech (for example, "they speak without restraint"). TEV has abandoned the figure altogether: "**Listen to their insults and threats.**" Some, however, take the verb to apply to the dogs and translate "they slaver" (see Anderson; SPCL, TOB); this does not seem very probable. In verse 7 the psalmist has abandoned the figure of dogs and is talking about the enemies as such.

Verse 7b is literally "swords (are) in their lips"—an obvious metaphor for cruel and malicious speech; see similar expressions in 52.2; 55.21; 57.4. There is no need to emend the text as RSV has done. For example, it can be rendered "their words are like swords."

The last line in the Hebrew text is "Who will hear?" Most commentators and translations take this to be the thinking of the wicked (see similar statements in 10.11; 64.5); they think that no one, not even God, will know what they are doing. Instead of the rhetorical question, which expects a negative answer (see RSV), TEV has made a statement, which may be clearer to most readers.

<u>59.8-9</u> RSV	TEV

8   **But thou, O LORD, dost laugh at them,**
     thou dost hold all the nations in derision.
9   **O my Strength, I will sing praises to thee;**[v]
     for thou, O God, art my fortress.
	8 **But you laugh at them, LORD;**
	     you mock all the heathen.
	9 **I have confidence in your strength;**
	     you are my refuge, O God.

[v] Syr: Heb *I will watch for thee*

The psalmist is confident that God will defeat his enemies; the two synonymous verbs in verse 8a,b are the same as those used of the Lord in 2.4a,b (see also 37.13). The thought of the wicked, that no one can hear them, provokes God to laughter. Again **the nations** are pagans, heathen, Gentiles.

Verse 9a in the Masoretic text is "His strength, to you I will watch." The initial *'uzo* "his strength" of the Masoretic text is *'uzi* "my strength" (referring to God) in many Hebrew manuscripts and is adopted by practically all commentators and translations, including HOTTP. RSV takes **Strength** as a title for God, **O my Strength** (similarly NIV, NEB).

The Hebrew verb "I will watch (to you)" is somewhat unusual in this construction (see RSV footnote). In other places where this verb is used with an object governed by the preposition *'el*, as here, it means "to watch over, to guard" (see 1 Sam 26.15; 2 Sam 11.16), so that one would expect the meaning here to be "I will watch over the Lord"—which is obviously wrong. Despite the strangeness of the construction, HOTTP, NJV ("wait"), TOB, FRCL, BJ ("look to"), NJB ("keep my eyes fixed"), and TEV ("**I have confidence**") believe the Masoretic text makes sense. So FRCL "I look to you, my protector." RSV (see Briggs, Oesterley, Anderson) has followed the Syriac "I will praise," as in verse 17. SPCL has adopted a suggestion by Dahood; by the use of different vowels for the same consonants, the passive of the verb *shamar* "to keep, guard" is read: "I am guarded." Everything considered, it seems best to follow FRCL in translating this line.

Fortress translates a word that is used also in 9.9, where RSV translates "stronghold" (see comments there).

59.10	RSV	TEV

My God in his steadfast love will
    meet me;
  my God will let me look in tri-
    umph on my enemies.

My God loves me and will come to
    me;
  he will let me see my enemies
    defeated.

My God in his steadfast love is expressed by TEV as "**My God loves me**"; the phrase can be taken to mean "my loving God." NJV has both here and in verse 17 "my faithful God." In some languages it is not possible to speak of "my God," and consequently one must shift to a verb phrase; for example, "the God whom I serve" or "God whom I worship."

Will meet me: that is, he will come and save the psalmist.

The thought of verse 10b is the same as that of 54.7b; literally the Hebrew says "God will cause me to look on my enemies"—an expression of victory in battle. For the word translated **enemies** see comments on 54.5. The expression **look in triumph on my enemies** and the TEV rendering "**let me see my enemies defeated**" in many languages will require shifting so that the two events of allowing to see and defeating are clearly marked as being done by God; for example, "he will defeat my enemies and he will let me watch him" or "he will let me watch him when he defeats my enemies."

59.11	RSV	TEV

Slay them not, lest my people
    forget;
  make them totter by thy power,
    and bring them down,
O Lord, our shield!

Do not kill them, O God, or my
    people may forget.
Scatter them by your strength
    and defeat them,
O Lord, our protector.

The psalmist prays for the punishment of his enemies. The opening petition **Slay them not** reads strangely, and Dahood supposes that, instead of the Masoretic text *'al* "not," the consonants should be given the vowels for *'el* "O God," that is, "O God, slay them" (so NAB). SPCL follows an emended text, "do not have compassion on them" (see Briggs, Weiser). NEB translates the Masoretic text as a rhetorical question, "Wilt thou not kill them . . . ?" But Oesterley and others defend the Masoretic text (so RSV, TEV, FRCL, AT, TOB, NIV, NJV). Taylor explains that they are not to be killed at once but are to be defeated and "left to linger on in weakness" (similarly Kirkpatrick and Anderson). GECL's translation is good, "Do not annihilate them with one blow." But it may be better to emend, as SPCL has done, or else follow the example of NAB.

Slay them not may suggest in some languages that these defeated enemies are to be allowed to linger and die slowly as a form of torture. If that sense is not to be taken, it will often be necessary to make line b a clear alternative to line a by saying, for example, "but rather scatter them . . . ."

Lest my people forget does not say what they are to remember. Perhaps it is the warning as a result of the punishment. In that case one may translate "or my people may forget how you punish your enemies." FRCL says "for fear that my people should forget your victory."

Make them totter in line <u>b</u> translates a verb that means either "to make homeless" (so NJV "make wanderers of them" and NIV "make them wander about") or "to cause to stagger."

By thy power translates a word that could be understood as "your army (of angels)"· so Briggs, Weiser, Kirkpatrick. **By thy power** in some languages must be translated through the use of other kinds of expressions and constructions; for example, "use your power to scatter and destroy them" or "because you are powerful . . . ."

Bring them down translates the causative form of the verb "come down."

For **shield** in line <u>c</u> as a figure for protection, see 3.3. If the translator follows TEV and RSV in this verse, in some languages it will be necessary to mention the thing which is not to be forgotten. In the context it would seem to be God's victory over the psalmist's enemies.

59.12-13	RSV	TEV

12 For the sin of their mouths, the words of their lips,
    let them be trapped in their pride.
    For the cursing and lies which they utter,
13 consume them in wrath,
    consume them till they are no more,
    that men may know that God rules over Jacob
    to the ends of the earth. *Selah*

12 Sin is on their lips; all their words are sinful;
    may they be caught in their pride!
    Because they curse and lie,
13 destroy them in your anger;
    destroy them completely.
    Then everyone will know that God rules in Israel,
    that his rule extends over all the earth.

Line <u>a</u> of verse 12 says the same thing in two ways; SPCL reduces to one statement, "They sin in everything they say." In some languages it is not possible to speak of **the sin of their mouths** nor to say that "sin is on their lips." It is, however, often possible to say, for example, "When they speak they sin," or "All they say is sinful," or "The words they speak show what sinners they are."

In verse 12b the verb **trapped** is the one used of catching animals in a trap (as in 9.15b; 35.8b). The **pride** of the wicked comes from their conviction that God will not act (see comments on "pride" in 10.4; 31.18). It is unnatural in some languages to speak of being **trapped in their pride**. Therefore one must sometimes translate, for example, "may they be caught in their pride, which is like a trap," or "may the trap which is their pride catch them," or "may they be caught in their pride as animals are caught in a trap."

The reason for the psalmist's next request is their **cursing and lies** (verse 12c). In this context **cursing** was not simply the use of profane or obscene language, but the use of certain words which, it was believed, had the power to bring disaster, illness, or death on one's enemies.

For this reason, in verse 13a,b the psalmist asks God to **consume**, that is, to destroy his enemies, to destroy them completely. This hardly accords with verse 11a "Do not kill them," and makes it even more desirable to translate there differently from RSV and TEV.

The psalmist asks for the destruction of his enemies so that everyone will confess that God's rule extends from "**Israel**" (literally **Jacob**; see comments at 46.7) to **the ends of the earth** (see 2.8; 22.27 and comments); so TEV, NJB, NEB, SPCL, TOB. But the text may be taken to mean "that it may be known to the ends of the earth that God does rule in Israel" (NJV, NIV, FRCL). It is preferable to stay with the majority. The expression **to the ends of the earth** in some languages may be translated "God rules the entire earth" or "God rules everyone in the world."

59.14-15	RSV	TEV

	RSV	TEV
14	Each evening they come back, howling like dogs and prowling about the city.	14 My enemies come back in the evening, snarling like dogs as they go about the city,
15	They roam about for food, and growl if they do not get their fill.	15 like dogs roaming about for food and growling if they do not find enough.

Verse 14 is a repetition of verse 6.

It seems better in verse 15 to carry on the figure of dogs and not (as RSV, NJV, NAB; Weiser) speak directly of the psalmist's enemies, as though they were actually scavenging the city for food and would **growl** (RSV), or "howl" (NIV), or "complain," or "whine" (NJV) if they didn't get enough.

Growl translates a verb which means "to murmur"; the form of the verb in the Masoretic text is actually "stand, spend the night" (see the verb in 55.7b), but only a change of vowels is needed to get "murmur." Only TOB, of the translations consulted, tries to stay with the Masoretic text vowels: "they spend the night (complaining)"—and see footnote, which speaks of a "deliberate mistake in the text"![1] It is best to translate **growl**. The alternative translation in the FRCL footnote gives the meaning "they remain the whole night."

59.16-17	RSV	TEV

	RSV	TEV
16	But I will sing of thy might; I will sing aloud of thy steadfast love in the morning.	16 But I will sing about your strength; every morning I will sing aloud

---

[1]HOTTP says the verb has two meanings: "to spend the night" and "to murmur, to growl." The comment is made: "For the interpreters of the Masoretic text tradition, the intended meaning was 'to spend the night,' but the other meaning is well attested also by old witnesses."

For thou hast been to me a fortress
and a refuge in the day of my
distress.
17 O my Strength, I will sing praises
to thee,
for thou, O God, art my fortress,
the God who shows me steadfast love.

of your constant love.
You have been a refuge for me,
a shelter in my time of trouble.
17 I will praise you, my defender,
My refuge is God,
the God who loves me.

The concluding promise to praise God is similar to the closing verses of the first part of the psalm (verses 9-10). The psalmist says he will praise God for his **might** and his **steadfast love**, demonstrated by the fact that God has been his **fortress** (see the word in 9.9) and **refuge**.

In verse 17a **my Strength** is used in the same sense as in verse 9a; verse 17b is the same as verse 9b, and in Hebrew verse 17c is the same as the beginning of verse 10a. In some languages it may be necessary to recast verse 17 to say, for example:

I will sing and say "You are strong,"
that you, O God, are the one who protects me,
that you are the one who loves me faithfully.

Psalm 60

Like Psalms 12, 44, and 58, this psalm speaks for the whole nation of Israel. The people have suffered a military defeat at the hands of their enemy (perhaps Edom; see verse 9) and complain that God has abandoned them. They ask God to change his attitude and once more defeat their enemies.

The psalm opens with a description of the nation's situation (verses 1-4) and a prayer for God's help (verse 5). An answer of assurance comes from God (verses 6-8). Once more the psalmist voices the nation's complaint (verses 9-10) and ends with a prayer for help, confident that God will answer (verses 11-12).

There is no certain indication of the identity of the author or the circumstances of the psalm's composition; most commentators are agreed that the statement in the Hebrew title is not historically accurate.

HEADING: "**A Prayer for Deliverance.**" Other headings are "National prayer after defeat"; "A nation rejected"; "Prayer after defeat in battle." In some languages the TEV title must be recast by replacing nouns with verbs; for example, "The psalmist prays that God will deliver him."

Hebrew Title: <u>**To the choirmaster: according to Shushan Eduth. A Miktam of David; for instruction; when he strove with Aram-naharaim and with Aram-zobah, and when Joab on his return killed twelve thousand of Edom in the Valley of Salt**</u> (TEV "A psalm by David, for teaching, when he fought against the Arameans from Naharaim and from Zobah, and Joab turned back and killed 12,000 Edomites in Salt Valley").

For **choirmaster** see title of Psalm 4; for **Miktam** see title of Psalm 16. The tune, so it seems, was named **Shushan Eduth**. The Hebrew word *shushan* means "lily," or else a six-sided musical instrument (so FRCL; see title of Psa 45). The word *'eduth* means testimony, command (see 19.7b; 25.10; and title of Psa 80). No one knows for certain what the whole phrase means ("The Lily of Testimony"?), and so RSV does not translate but transliterates. NJB has "To the tune 'The decree is a lily.' " Dahood translates "according to 'Lilies.' A solemn commandment." FRCL has "A commemorative poem," and in a footnote gives the alternative: "To be sung to the tune of 'The Lily of Testimony'; a poem."

For instruction indicates the psalm was to be used in teaching, but it is not clear who was to be taught. Cohen suggests army recruits; Kirkpatrick thinks it means that the psalm was to be memorized.

Naharaim, meaning "(two) rivers," was the name of northern Mesopotamia, where the patriarchs had come from (Gen 24.10; Deut 23.4); **Zobah** was a kingdom north of Damascus (see 1 Chr 18.3). David's wars against "**the Arameans**" (Syrians) are related in 2 Samuel 8.3-8; 10.6-18; 1 Chronicles 18.3-11; 19.16-19. **Joab** was the commanding general of David's army; the "**Edomites**" were the descendants of Esau, and their country, **Edom**, was the mountainous region south of Judah. In 2 Samuel 8.13 and 1 Chronicles 18.12, the number of Edomites killed is given as 18,000; in 2 Samuel the slaughter is attributed to David, in 1 Chronicles to Abishai, brother of Joab. **The Valley of Salt** was probably south of the Dead Sea.

60.1-2 RSV	TEV
1 O God, thou hast rejected us, broken our defenses; thou hast been angry; oh, restore us.	1 You have rejected us, God, and defeated us; you have been angry with us— but now turn back to us.[z]
2 Thou hast made the land to quake, thou hast rent it open; repair its breaches, for it totters.	2 You have made the land tremble, and you have cut it open; now heal its wounds, because it is falling apart.

[z] angry with us . . . us; *or* angry with us and turned your back on us.

The psalm begins with a bitter cry of complaint to God for having abandoned his people (see similar language in 44.9-12).

The verb translated **broken our defenses** is taken to mean to break through (enemy lines), to make a breach. So FRCL translates "You have broken through our ranks," and NJV "you have made a breach in us." But many translations, like TEV, use less specific expressions: "broken us," "displaced us."

In verse 1b the verbal form translated **restore us** (TEV "**turn back to us**") may possibly be read as a statement, "you have turned away from us" (so, with variations, Briggs, Dahood, Weiser; AT, NEB, TEV footnote); Anderson is of the opinion that this is not very likely. It is better to translate as a petition.

God's actions are compared to those resulting from an earthquake, in which the land (Israel, that is) trembles and splits open (verse 2a), and God is requested to repair the breaks, for which TEV has "**heal its wounds**." The country "**is falling apart**" (NJV "collapsing"), literally "is shaking, tottering"—see the verb used of mountains in 46.3, where it is translated "tremble." In verse 2b the verb translated "**heal**" (TEV) is not in its normal form, but many take it to be a variant of the verb "to heal." RSV **repair its breaches** keeps the vivid metaphor of an earthquake; so NJB "mend the rifts," and NJV "mend its fissures." The translator must decide whether this will be appropriate and understandable in the receptor language. NEB, however, takes the verb in the sense it normally has of "sink down," and translates "it gives way" (similarly Briggs, Dahood). In many languages it is not possible to speak of healing the wounds of the land. Therefore it may be necessary to say, for example, "make the land strong again," "close the holes in the earth," or "repair the ground that is cut open."

RSV   TEV

> Thou hast made thy people suffer   You have made your people suffer
>   hard things;   greatly;
> thou hast given us wine to   we stagger around as though we
>   drink that made us reel.   were drunk.

The verb translated **Thou hast made . . . suffer** is literally "to see," that is, to experience; but some (NEB, Dahood; see Anderson) take it to be here the equivalent of the verb "to drink," and so understand the line to mean "You have made your people drink (or, drunk with) a bitter drink" (NJB, NEB; Dahood). This is quite attractive, since it supplies a close parallel with the next line, which is **thou hast given us wine to drink that made us reel**.

In some languages the change from **thy people** in line a to **us** in line b may cause considerable misunderstanding and therefore may require that the first person plural be used in both lines; for example, "you have made us who are your people suffer greatly."

The figure of a cup of wine which God forces upon people is a symbol of God's anger (see Isa 51.17,22). A translation of line b should give a closer equivalent of the form of the Hebrew than TEV has done, to show that the wine comes from God; perhaps something like "we stagger around because of the wine you made us drink."

The language of verses 1-3 reflects the belief that Israel's defeat in battle was the result of God's being angry with his people.

RSV   TEV

> 4   Thou hast set up a banner for   4   You have warned those who have
>   those who fear thee,   reverence for you,
>   to rally to it from the bow.*   so that they might escape de-
>   Selah   struction.
> 5   That thy beloved may be delivered,   5   Save us by your might; answer
>   give victory by thy right hand   our prayer,
>   and answer us!   so that the people you love may
>   be rescued.

w Gk Syr Jerome: Heb *truth*

The form and meaning of verse 4 are disputed. The **banner** that God had **set up** could be either a sign for the Israelite forces to rally and fight back at the enemy, or else a sign for them to flee from the enemy (as in Jer 4.6). The verb which RSV translates **rally** occurs only here in this sense; some derive the Masoretic text form from a verb that means "to flee" (see Briggs); others "so that they may flee" (so NEB, NAB).

Instead of the indicative mood, some read the first line of verse 4 as an imperative, a command to God "to raise the banner" (see Dahood; NJV, BJ). In many languages the idea of raising a flag during a battle will be unknown. Therefore the translator normally has three choices: He can keep the flag raising and clarify its meaning with an additional statement; for example, "You have raised a flag to warn those who follow you." Or he can simply state the meaning without reference to a flag, as in TEV. Line 4a may also be rendered, for example, "You have sent a clear signal to those who worship you . . . ." Finally, the translator may use a substitute for flag and translate, for example, "Your drumbeats have warned those who follow you." **Those who fear thee** is expressed in many languages as "those who worship you" or "those who follow you."

The next two words in verse 4b in Hebrew seem to mean "from before the bow." So the translations that understand the preceding verbal form to mean "to flee" translate "to let them escape out of the range of the bow" (NJB); TOB "to flee from the bowman." RSV **to rally to it from the bow** makes no sense in English. But the meaning of the Hebrew word translated **bow** (spelled this way only here in the Hebrew Bible) is also disputed, and some take it to mean "the truth" (see RSV footnote); so NJV translates the verse "Give those who fear You because of Your truth a banner for rallying." SPCL has "Now give a signal to those who honor you so that they may escape from the arrows"; TEV, similarly, "**they might escape destruction.**" TEV would have done better by translating ". . . from defeat."

In face of such variety of interpretations, the translator can only choose one that seems best suited to the context.[1]

For *Selah* see 3.2.

The two lines in verse 5 have been reversed by TEV for a more orderly progression of thought. **Thy beloved** translates "your beloved ones"; this means the people as a whole (FRCL "we, your friends"). **Delivered** in line a translates the verb rendered "save" in 6.4a.

The verb in line b may mean **give victory**; it is the verb which is often translated **save** (see comments on "Help" in 12.1). And **thy right hand** means "your power" (see 18.35; 20.6; 21.8). The final request **answer us** means "answer our prayer." One form of the Masoretic text (*kethiv*) has the plural "us"; the other form (*qere*) has the singular "me," which is preferred by Kirkpatrick and NJV. The expression **answer us** must not be translated normally by the term which is used for answering a question. Many languages make a distinction between answering a question and responding to a request. In some languages it will be necessary to say, for example, "hear us and help us."

In some languages it will be necessary to introduce the first person plural pronoun into line b, if one follows the reordering suggested by TEV; for example, "so that you may rescue us who are your people."

60.6 RSV	TEV
God has spoken in his sanctuary:[x] "With exultation I will divide up Shechem and portion out the Vale of Succoth.	From his sanctuary[a] God has said, "In triumph I will divide Shechem and distribute Sukkoth Valley to my people.

---

[1]HOTTP says the meaning "bow" is to be preferred.

x Or *by his holiness*   *a* From his sanctuary; *or* In his holiness.

Verses 6-8 are God's response to the anguished prayer of his people. God proclaims his victory and his dominion over all countries, especially the ancient enemies of Israel.

The opening words of verse 6 can mean "From (or, In) his sanctuary," that is, the Temple (the "holy place"), or "In (or, By) his holiness." The former seems preferable here. This identifies the oracle that follows as a message of reassurance given the people, perhaps by the priest. But Taylor takes God's message in verses 6-8 to be one which God had given in the past and which is now quoted by the psalmist in order to remind God of how he had failed to keep his promise of victory.

With exultation in line **b** translates the verb "I will exult," which expresses joy over the defeat of the enemy. The expression **With exultation** or "**In triumph**" must sometimes be rendered through a causal clause; for example, "Because I have conquered" or "Because I am powerful."

Shechem was an ancient city some fifty kilometers north of Jerusalem (see Gen 12.6). "**Sukkoth Valley**," on the east side of the Jordan River, was north of the River Jabbok. It is probable that here it is representative of the whole country east of the Jordan, and that Shechem represents the country west of the Jordan. Some see here an allusion to Genesis 33.17-20, which reports Jacob's building a house for himself at Succoth and buying some land in Shechem. In many languages it will be more meaningful to make clear that each of the areas named refers to a geographical region. Otherwise there is the possibility that some readers will understand these names to apply to persons. This is normally done by using a generic classifier; for example, "city of Shechem," "land called Gilead," "land called Manasseh," etc. If further information regarding the location of these places is required, the reader can be referred to a map in the appropriate section of the Bible.

Divide up in line **b** and **portion out** in line **c** are parallel and synonymous, both referring to the division of the land of Canaan among the tribes of Israel. There is no indirect object for either of the two verbs; TEV has interpreted the text as saying that God was assigning these places to his people (so Briggs). It is primarily God's ownership that is asserted, and his right to give these places to the people of Israel.

60.7-8	RSV		TEV
7	Gilead is mine; Manasseh is mine; Ephraim is my helmet; Judah is my scepter.	7	Gilead is mine, and Manasseh too; Ephraim is my helmet and Judah my royal scepter.
8	Moab is my washbasin; upon Edom I cast my shoe; over Philistia I shout in triumph."	8	But I will use Moab as my washbowl, and I will throw my sandals on Edom, as a sign that I own it. Did the Philistines think they would shout in triumph over me?"

Gilead was a country east of the Jordan, in the south, which had been occupied by the tribes of Reuben and Gad. The tribe of **Manasseh** had occupied land in the north (Bashan), also on the east of the Jordan (as well as some land on the west side). So these two represent the area east of the Jordan that was part of Israel. The tribe of **Ephraim** occupied land on the west side of the Jordan, in the north, and quite often **Ephraim** was used to refer to the northern kingdom of Israel. **Judah** was both the southern tribe and the name of the southern kingdom. God says Ephraim is his **helmet**, that is, part of the armor he wears when fighting the enemy; Judah is his **scepter**, that is, the means by which he governs the nations he has conquered. In some languages **helmet** may be rendered by a descriptive phrase; for example, "a protection for my head." **Scepter** is sometimes translated as "chief's stick" or "king's ruling stick." If such descriptive terms or equivalent objects are not found, it may be possible to use a simile; for example, "Ephraim is like my head and Judah is like my authority."

The country of **Moab** was east of the Dead Sea, and it may be that there is an allusion to that fact by God's speaking of Moab as his **washbasin**. The country of **Edom** was south of Judah. The statements in regard to **Ephraim, Judah** and **Moab** are not clear, except to say that God lays claim to them and they serve his purposes.

There is no agreement on what is meant by the Hebrew "on Edom I throw my sandal." (1) Some take it to refer to a custom that is alluded to in Deuteronomy 25.9-10 and Ruth 4.7 of taking off a sandal as a sign of ownership, but there is no firm agreement on this. (2) Dahood takes it to refer to the custom of a victorious king placing his foot on the defeated enemy's neck, as a sign of victory. (3) Others take it that Edom is assigned the menial task of a slave of carrying his master's sandal (see Briggs). Should a translation choose alternative no. 1 (which the majority of commentators and translations favor), there should be a cultural footnote if the figure is kept in the text; it means nothing to the reader to read "I throw my shoe at Edom" (similarly SPCL, RSV, NIV, NEB). Or else the figure and its meaning may be given in the text, as TEV has done. Or the figure may be abandoned altogether and the meaning be expressed by "I am master (or, owner) of the land of Edom."

There is some difficulty with the Masoretic text of verse 8c: "upon (or, over) me Philistia will shout in triumph." The Hebrew text in 108.9 is "I will shout in triumph over Philistia," and this is preferred here by many (note that 108.9 is almost the same as verse 8). Weiser translates the Masoretic text here, "Acclaim me with shouts of joy, Philistia!" which is possible (NJV "Acclaim me, O Philistia!"). TEV translates the Masoretic text as a rhetorical question, expecting a negative answer; NJB translates as irony, "Now try shouting 'Victory' over me, Philistia!" (also BJ). The ancient versions read the text differently; most modern exegetes take the verb to be "to shout in triumph" (see 41.11 and comments). FRCL has "Against Philistia I raise a shout of war," saying that it follows the versions, one Hebrew manuscript, and Psalm 108.9. **Shout in triumph** in some languages must be shifted to a causal clause; for example, "I shout because I have triumphed over the land called Philistia" or "because I have defeated the people of the land called Philistia, I shout."

	RSV		TEV
9	Who will bring me to the fortified city? Who will lead me to Edom?	9	Who, O God, will take me into the fortified city? Who will lead me to Edom?
10	Hast thou not rejected us, O God? Thou dost not go forth, O God, with our armies.	10	Have you really rejected us? Aren't you going to march out with our armies?

The psalm concludes with an assertion of ultimate victory. The speaker (me) is probably the king, as the leader of the army; the fortified city is probably Sela, the strongly defended capital of Edom, the country to the south. The context suggests a military conquest of Edom, but some take the verse to mean a flight to that city, where the king would be safe from his enemies. This does not seem very likely. Fortified city may sometimes be rendered "city which has protection," or "city with strong walls to protect it," or "city which men have built a wall around."

Verse 10 is variously understood; TEV takes it as a double question, by means of which the psalmist expresses his hope that God will change his mind and no longer reject his people (see verse 1) but will once again "march out with our armies" (see 44.9 and comments). But some, like RSV, take the first part as a rhetorical question which affirms God's rejection of his people, and the second part as a statement to the same effect. Others take verse 10 as a continuation of verse 9: "Who else but God, who rejected us, who does not march out with our armies?" (Weiser; BJ, NJB, TOB). NJV takes both parts as statements; Dahood takes the two as questions which indicate a hope that there is a change in God's attitude (so TEV). The choice seems to be between the interpretation expressed by TEV and the one found in NJV. The two are practically the same; it may be that the focus on the question in TEV better suits the context. The verb in the expression go forth . . . with our armies in some languages is insufficient to indicate the purpose of the march. Therefore, sometimes one must translate "Aren't you going to go with our armies to fight our enemies?"

	RSV		TEV
11	O grant us help against the foe, for vain is the help of man!	11	Help us against the enemy; human help is worthless.
12	With God we shall do valiantly; it is he who will tread down our foes.	12	With God on our side we will win; he will defeat our enemies.

The final prayer for God's help recognizes that "human help is worthless" (TEV) and that victory is achieved only with God's help. Vain is the help of man in some languages must be rendered, for example, "the little help people can give is worthless" or, more generally, "all the help that people can give is worthless."

In verse 12a to do valiantly is, in this context, "to gain the victory," "to win the battle," "to triumph."

Tread down in verse 12b is a way of speaking of defeat (as in 44.5b).

536

Psalm 61

In this psalm a man in exile prays for protection from enemies and asks to be allowed to return to Jerusalem, where he will worship God in the Temple. Dahood thinks the psalmist is the king, who speaks of himself in the third person in verses 6-7; others think he is a priest or a Levite who longs to be back at his service in the Temple.

The psalm opens with a cry to God (verses 1-2b), followed by a plea for God to let the psalmist return to the Temple in Jerusalem (verses 2c-5). Then he prays for the king (verses 6-7) and closes the psalm with a promise to offer sacrifices to God in gratitude (verse 8).

HEADING: "**A Prayer for Protection**." Other headings are "God is my refuge"; "A prisoner's lament"; "Prayer of an exile." In some languages the TEV title must be shifted so that the two nouns are represented by verb expressions; for example, "The psalmist asks God to protect him" or, in direct discourse, "The psalmist prays and says 'Protect me, God.' " In some languages one must say "Protect me from my enemies."

Hebrew Title: <u>**To the choirmaster: with stringed instruments. A Psalm of David**</u> (TEV "**By David**").

For **choirmaster** and **stringed instruments** see title of Psalm 4. It should be noted that the Masoretic text here has the singular "stringed instrument," which is unique; many Hebrew manuscripts have the plural "instruments."

61.1-2b	RSV		TEV
1	Hear my cry, O God, listen to my prayer;	1	Hear my cry, O God; listen to my prayer!
2	from the end of the earth I call to thee, when my heart is faint.	2	In despair and far from home I call to you!

The psalm opens with a cry to God for help (verses 1-2b), in which the psalmist pictures himself as being at **the end of the earth** (verse 2a). Most take this to mean, as does TEV, that he is "**far from home**," in exile in some foreign country; Dahood, however, takes it to mean that he is near death, that is, on the brink of Sheol, which the psalmist calls **the earth** (also Taylor and others). It is recommended that the idea of being far away from his own country be represented in translation.

My heart is faint (TEV "**In despair**") indicates lack of courage or of hope; FRCL translates "I can endure no more."

RSV   TEV

2c   Lead thou me   2c   Take me to a safe refuge,
        to the rock that is higher than   3   for you are my protector,
        I;   my strong defense against my
3   for thou art my refuge,   enemies.
        a strong tower against the
        enemy.

In his prayer for protection the psalmist asks God to take him to **the rock that is higher than I**; the Hebrew may mean "a rock too high for me (to climb by myself)"; NJV translates "a rock that is high above me." The figure is a bit strange but its sense seems clear enough: it is a figure of security and safety (see the use of "rock" in 27.5d and discussion). Some translate "Place me safely on a high rock" (SPCL) or "lift me up and set me upon a rock" (NEB, which changes one letter and uses a different word division in the Masoretic text). FRCL and NJB think that it refers to the Temple. TEV **"safe refuge"** in some languages can be rendered "the place where I am safe" or "the place where you protect me."

God is the psalmist's **refuge** (see comments on 14.6 and 46.1), his **strong tower**. A tower was an essential part of a city's defenses (see in 48.12 the towers of Jerusalem), a place which offered protection against the enemy's attack (see the tower at Thebez, in Judges 9.50-57). If **tower** is unknown, a local substitute may be suitable and may be used as a simile; for example, "you are like a strong wall protecting me from my enemies."

RSV   TEV

4   Let me dwell in thy tent for ever!   4   Let me live in your sanctuary all
        Oh to be safe under the shelter   my life;
        of thy wings!   *Selah*   let me find safety under your
5   For thou, O God, hast heard my   wings.
        vows,   5   You have heard my promises, O
        thou hast given me the heritage   God,
        of those who fear thy name.   and you have given me what
                                                     belongs to those who honor
                                                     you.

The psalmist wants to spend the rest of his life in or near the Temple, in Jerusalem; for **dwell in thy tent** see discussion of the identical language in 15.1a, and for **shelter of thy wings** see the similar language in 17.8b; 36.7b. In verse 4a **for ever** means "all my life" (see the similar thought in 23.6). Dahood, however, takes the word to be an adjective which modifies "tent," that is, "your eternal tent." It is best to follow the meaning adopted by RSV and TEV.

For *Selah* see 3.2.

The psalmist justifies his petition by reminding God of the psalmist's vows, which probably are the promises he made to offer sacrifices to God in gratitude for God's answer to his prayers.

It is not clear what **the heritage** in verse 5b means; it is usually taken to be the same as "possession" or "inheritance" (see comments at 16.6), which was originally a way of speaking about the Promised Land, and then was extended to mean all of God's blessings for his people. FRCL translates "their part of the holy land." Here, then, it would mean that God has blessed the psalmist with the blessings that are given to those who obey him. GECL translates "You present rich gifts to all . . . ." It should be noticed that the Masoretic text does not have the personal pronoun **me** (as RSV, TEV, SPCL have); it says simply "You have given the heritage of those who fear your name," which TOB translates "You have given to those who obey your name their heritage." But RSV and TEV can be defended and are probably to be preferred.

Some, however, instead of taking the Hebrew word *yerushah* in its usual sense of "possession," take it to be a variant form of *'areshah* "request, petition" (see 21.2b, the only place where the term clearly occurs) and understand verse 5b to be a request; so NJV "grant the request of those who fear your name." It certainly makes good sense to take verse 5b to mean "You have granted the wish of those who honor you" (NEB), but this involves changing the Hebrew text. NAB, NJB, SPCL, TOB, GECL, and Weiser are like RSV and TEV, and these are preferred.

Those who fear thy name: "those who respect (or, obey) you"; for comments on "name" see 5.11. Line b can sometimes be translated "you have given me the good things you give to those who say you are great" or ". . . to those who worship you."

	RSV	TEV
6	Prolong the life of the king; may his years endure to all generations!	6 Add many years to the king's life; let him live on and on!
7	May he be enthroned for ever before God; bid steadfast love and faithfulness watch over him!	7 May he rule forever in your presence, O God; protect him with your constant love and faithfulness.

The psalmist prays for the king; see the similar prayer in 21.1-7, where one may find most of the petitions made here. The prayer is not just for a long life for the king, but for a long and prosperous reign, and the continuation of his dynasty through descendants who will succeed him on the throne; such is the meaning of **all generations** in verse 6b and **for ever** in verse 7a.

For comments on **before God** (verse 7a) see 56.13. The expression **before God** or "**in your presence**," if translated literally, will often lead to misunderstanding. Therefore it will sometimes be necessary to say, for example, ". . . with God's blessing" or ". . . with God's protection."

Verse 7b in the Masoretic text is literally "appoint constant love and faithfulness to protect him"; some Hebrew manuscripts and ancient versions omit the verb, so that the wording of the text is "May constant love and faithfulness protect" (or, "Constant love and faithfulness will protect"), with very little difference in meaning. For comments see 40.11b,c, and especially 57.3c. **Watch over** translates a verb rendered "guard" in 12.7b.

61.8   RSV   TEV

So will I ever sing praises to thy   So I will always sing praises to
   name,   you,
   as I pay my vows day after day.   as I offer you daily what I have
                                                                                     promised.

The psalm closes with a promise to praise God and offer sacrifices to him. For
<u>thy name</u> in line <u>a</u>, see comments on 5.11.

<u>Pay my vows</u> means the psalmist will keep his promises to offer daily sacrifices
(see verse 5).

Psalm 62

Like Psalms 11, 16, and 23, this psalm is a song of confidence by one who knows from personal experience that only in God, and always in God, are assurance and security to be found. Nothing in the text allows us to determine the psalmist's identity. From verses 3-4 it may be inferred that he was a man of some authority who was being persecuted by enemies; Eaton believes he was the king.

The psalmist begins with a statement of confidence in God (verses 1-2), followed by a denunciation of those who are attacking him (verses 3-4). Once more he affirms his faith in God (verses 5-7) and then counsels his people to trust God, not human power and wealth (verses 8-10). He closes his psalm with a confident statement of trust in God's sovereign power (verses 11-12).

HEADING: "**Confidence in God's Protection.**" Other headings are "What supports trust?"; "Hope in God alone"; "An unshaken faith." In some languages it will be necessary to restructure the TEV title to say, for example, "The psalmist has confidence in God that God will protect him" or, more idiomatically for some languages, "The psalmist places his heart on God and knows God will protect him."

Hebrew Title: **To the choirmaster: according to Jeduthun. A Psalm of David** (TEV "A psalm by David").

For **choirmaster** see title of Psalm 4; for **Jeduthun** see title of Psalm 39.

62.1-2   RSV   TEV

1   For God alone my soul waits in   1   I wait patiently for God to save
        silence;   me;
    from him comes my salvation.   I depend on him alone.
2   He only is my rock and my salva-   2   He alone protects and saves me;
        tion,   he is my defender,
    my fortress; I shall not be   and I shall never be defeated.
        greatly moved.

The psalmist begins with "Surely (or, Only) toward God my soul (in) silence; from him (is) my salvation"—an eloquent statement of trust in the God who alone can save him. The word translated **alone** is used at the beginning of verses 1, 2, 4, 5, 6, and 9, and sets the tone of this confident expression of faith. **Waits**: either for God to speak or to act. If the translator accepts the sense of waiting for God to speak, he may translate 1a as "I wait silently for God to speak" or "I remain quiet waiting for words from God." TEV has taken **in silence** to mean without complaining, that is, "**patiently**"; NJV "quietly"; FRCL "tranquil." Some, however, instead of assuming that

541

a verb like "to wait for" is implied, understand the Hebrew text to mean "Only in God *is* rest (or, peace) for my soul"; so SPCL "Only in God do I find peace," and NJB "In God alone there is rest for my soul" (see FRCL and NIV). Either of the two is possible, and perhaps the latter is to be preferred. The prepositional phrase "in God" indicates that God is the source of peace, and the idea may be expressed by "God alone can give rest (or, peace) to my soul."

Verse 2 begins in the same way: **He only is my rock and my salvation**; for **rock** see 18.2 and comments, and for **salvation** see comments on the related verb translated "Help" in 12.1. For comments on **fortress** see 9.9 ("stronghold"). The translator may be able to preserve the figure of the **rock** by making some adjustments. For instance, it may be possible to say "he protects me like a rock, and he is the one who saves me." If the use of the **rock** as a figure for protection is not meaningful in the language, it may be possible to employ a local equivalent. If that is not possible it is better to shift to a nonfigurative usage such as TEV.

The verb translated **be . . . moved** is found also in 10.6. The word translated **greatly** by RSV is a bit problematic; most (NJV, NAB, NJB, SPCL), like TEV, take it to mean here "not" or **"never"**; so NJV "I shall never be shaken." FRCL has "With him there is no risk of failure." It would seem a bit out of place for the psalmist to state "I shall not be badly shaken," but this could be the meaning intended. Briggs and Weiser omit the word.

62.3-4	RSV		TEV
3	How long will you set upon a man to shatter him, all of you, like a leaning wall, a tottering fence?	3	How much longer will all of you attack a man who is no stronger than a broken-down fence?
4	They only plan to thrust him down from his eminence. They take pleasure in falsehood. They bless with their mouths, but inwardly they curse. *Selah*	4	You only want to bring him down from his place of honor; you take pleasure in lies. You speak words of blessing, but in your heart you curse him.

The psalmist does not identify his enemies who are trying to ruin him. He speaks of himself in the third person as one who occupies a **"place of honor"** (TEV, verse 4a), so he is a man of some importance.

There are two verbs in verse 3a (RSV **set upon . . . shatter**), both of uncertain form and meaning. The first one occurs only here; the second one usually means "to murder," but only Weiser has this meaning ("slay"); also possible, "strike"; NJV "crush"; NEB "battering"; NAB "beat him down." TEV has expressed the meaning of the two verbs by **"attack"**; using the TEV language, the two verbs could be separately expressed by ". . . will all of you attack and do away with a man . . . ?" It should be understood, of course, that the question is rhetorical—it is not a request for information. If a rhetorical question is difficult for most readers, the meaning can be expressed by means of a statement, "All of you must quit attacking a man who is no stronger than a broken-down fence, and trying to do away with him."

The psalmist's enemies are trying to ruin him by bringing him down as though he were **a leaning wall, a tottering fence** (verse 3c). Some (Briggs, Dahood) take these figures to apply to the psalmist's enemies, but most take them to refer to the psalmist himself. TEV has reduced the two synonymous figures to one, "**no stronger than a broken-down fence**." In most language areas both **a leaning wall** and **a tottering fence** are fully understood. The translator must decide if the two expressions really represent mere duplication, or if the reader will think of two distinct types of structures.

The psalmist's enemies are liars and hypocrites (verse 4b-d); see similar language in 12.1; 28.3; 55.21. Here again, **curse** means to use certain words to cause ruin or disaster (see comments at 59.12).

If the use of the third person to refer to the psalmist himself is difficult or strange, it is possible to switch to the first person, as follows (using TEV language): "I am no stronger than a broken-down fence; so how much longer will you attack me? All you want to do is to bring me down from my place of honor . . . ."

It is to be noticed that in verse 4 the psalmist's enemies are spoken of in the third person; for consistency with verse 3, TEV has used the second person.

For *Selah* see 3.2.

62.5-7	RSV	TEV

	RSV		TEV
5	For God alone my soul waits in silence, for my hope is from him.	5	I depend on God alone; I put my hope in him.
6	He only is my rock and my salvation, my fortress; I shall not be shaken.	6	He alone protects and saves me; he is my defender, and I shall never be defeated.
7	On God rests my deliverance and my honor; my mighty rock, my refuge is God.	7	My salvation and honor depend on God; he is my strong protector; he is my shelter.

Again, as in verses 1-2, the psalmist proclaims his confidence. Verse 5 is like verse 1, except that here **hope** is used in line **b** ("salvation" in verse 1b). Verse 6 is like verse 2, except that here the difficult word translated "greatly" is not used.

In verse 7 the psalmist declares that his **deliverance and . . . honor** depend **on God**. For **honor** see comments on "glory" in 3.3; 7.5; here it probably refers to the psalmist's place of "eminence" (verse 4). For **mighty rock** see "rock" in verses 2,6; **refuge** is the same word used in 14.6b (see comments there). The expression **on God rests my deliverance and my honor** must sometimes be shifted to the active voice; for example, "God is the one who saves and honors me" or "God saves me and gives me honor."

Trust in him at all times, O people;
  pour out your heart before him;
  God is a refuge for us.   *Selah*

Trust in God at all times, my
people.
  Tell him all your troubles,
  for he is our refuge.

The psalmist now turns to his people, perhaps his fellow worshipers in the Temple, and urges them to **trust in him at all times**, and to **pour out your heart before him**, that is, to **"tell him all your troubles"**; FRCL "confide in him all that is bothering you." Anderson explains the verb in this way: "give utterance to all your wishes and hopes."

For line c̲ see the same expression in 1.21; 14.6; 18.2.

62.9-10   RSV   TEV

9   Men of low estate are but a
     breath,
       men of high estate are a delu-
       sion;
     in the balances they go up;
       they are together lighter than a
       breath.
10   Put no confidence in extortion,
       set no vain hopes on robbery;
     if riches increase, set not your
       heart on them.

9   Men are all like a puff of breath;
       great and small alike are
       worthless.
     Put them on the scales, and they
       weigh nothing;
       they are lighter than a mere
       breath.
10   Don't put your trust in violence;
       don't hope to gain anything by
       robbery;
     even if your riches increase,
       don't depend on them.

The psalmist shows that it is wrong to rely on human help, because all people, "great and small alike" (TEV), are weak and unreliable. By the use of the figures a̲ breath and a delusion, the psalmist portrays human beings as no more dependable, no more solid and substantial, than a breath. Some take the word delusion in verse 9b as "lie" (as in verse 4), that is, that people are deceptive, they are liars; but as a parallel with breath in line a̲ it seems more appropriate that the word here refers to their lack of value as a dependable object of trust, rather than to their moral character as liars.

"Great and small alike" translates the same two phrases used with the same meaning in 49.2a (see comments there). RSV's of low estate and of high estate shows the meaning but is not a literal translation. In the translation of TEV's "great and small alike" the translator must avoid rendering this expression as big and small in size. In some languages one can say, for example, "people of the front and people of the back," referring to their importance. Other expressions are "people who have much and people who have nothing" or "people with many animals and people with only small animals." SPCL translates "the poor as well as the rich."

In the second half of verse 9 the psalmist uses the expressive figure of a pair of scales; on one plate are placed all people, on the other plate is placed the weight meant to determine how much they weigh. But no matter how small the weight, the plate it is on goes down, while the other plate goes up, which shows that people weigh less than **a breath**. Simply to translate **in the balances they go up** leaves the reader wondering what the psalmist is talking about.

Verse 10, continuing the thought of verse 9, shows the futility of depending on **riches**, on what can be gotten by **extortion** or **robbery**. This verse is the negative equivalent of the positive exhortation in verse 8. The noun translated **extortion**, which means to use threats or force in order to make someone do something (see Lev 6.4), may have the general sense of "**violence**," as TEV, NJV, SPCL, and others translate it. Either meaning makes good sense in the context, and the translator should feel free to choose.

Confidence in extortion and "**trust in violence**" in many languages must be shifted to verb phrases; for example, "don't put your heart on getting things by hurting people."

At the end of verse 10, **set not your heart on them** means not to place your hope, confidence, trust, in wealth.

62.11-12	RSV	TEV
11	Once God has spoken; twice have I heard this: that power belongs to God;	11 More than once I have heard God say that power belongs to him
12	and that to thee, O Lord, belongs steadfast love. For thou dost requite a man according to his work.	12 and that his love is constant. You yourself, O Lord, reward everyone according to his deeds.

This is the first instance in the psalms of number parallelism. As has been pointed out from the beginning of this Handbook, semantic parallelism is not based on the principle of synonymity (words in two lines having the same meanings) but on the idea of dynamic movement from the first to the second line (normally a step up in intensification). Therefore when a number such as **Once** occurs in line a, we should not expect to find the same number repeated like a synonym in line b, but rather an intensifying or step-up, such as **twice**. Thus, when numbers are used in parallel, the second line will always add 1, or be a decimal multiple (1 becomes 10, 2 becomes 20), or a decimal multiple plus the number itself (1 becomes 11). Alter suggests that in this way the "how much more so" operates with numbers the same as with words. In verse 11 the actual application of "how much more so" is to the relation between the pair of parallel statements in 11c and 12a. Therefore in translation the intensification implicit in the number parallelism can be brought out by combining 11a with the first statement and 11b with the second; for example, "God has said that power belongs to him, but he has said even more that steadfast love belongs to him" or "God has made it clear that power belongs to him, and he has made it even clearer that constant love is his."

The psalm closes with a confident statement about God as supreme ruler and just judge of all humankind. The formula **Once God has spoken, twice I have heard this** is what is called a "numerical proverb" (see others in Pro 6.16-19; 30.15-16;

Amos 1.3). The meaning is "often," "repeatedly," "more than once." A literal translation such as RSV, NIV, or NEB ("One thing God has spoken, two things I have heard/learnt") may leave the reader wondering what connection, if any, there is between the two statements. The supreme lesson is that **power** and **steadfast love** (see *chesed* in 5.7) are God's alone. Human beings may have both, but they are always less than and dependent upon God's power and love. In some languages it is not possible to say that **power belongs** to someone. However, one can often say, for example, "God is the only one who is powerful" or "God is the one who can make people strong."

The first line in verse 12 switches from the third person reference to God to the second person of address. TEV keeps the third person and introduces the vocative "**O Lord**" in the next line, addressing God in the second person.

The last two lines in verse 12 may also belong to the things that God has told the psalmist (so NJB, NAB, SPCL), or they may be an independent statement (RSV, TEV). This truth is expressed also in Proverbs 24.12 (and see Rom 2.6). **According to his work** must be expressed in some languages variously; for example, "in the way that people have done," "by seeing the things people have done," or "because you know what people have done."

Psalm 63

This psalm is a prayer of one who is consumed by his longing for a closer relationship with God. He has enemies who threaten him, but his preoccupation with them is slight in comparison with his intense desire for God.

There is no certain clue as to the identity of the psalmist. The reference to the king in verse 11 is taken by some to mean that the psalmist is referring to himself in the third person. This, however, is not accepted by all commentators; it is to be noticed that the psalmist refers to himself in the first person throughout the whole psalm (verses 1-10). Some take verse 11 as a later addition.

The psalm opens with an expression of the psalmist's deep desire to see God's revelation of himself in the Temple (verses 1-5), followed by a statement of trust in God's care (verses 6-8). The psalmist predicts the death of his enemies (verses 9-10) and ends with a prayer for the king (verse 11).

HEADING: "**Longing for God.**" Other headings are "A thirst for God"; "Faith and fellowship"; "God has been my help." If the translator follows the suggestion of the TEV title, it will be necessary in some languages to express the idea of longing idiomatically; for example, "The psalmist's heart desires God" or "The psalmist's insides are open for God."

Hebrew Title: **A Psalm of David, when he was in the Wilderness of Judah** (TEV "A psalm by David, when he was in the desert of Judea").

The historical reference may be to one of several incidents in David's life; some think it refers to the time he was fleeing from his son Absalom (2 Sam 15.23 and following).

63.1

RSV	TEV
O God, thou art my God, I seek thee, 　my soul thirsts for thee; my flesh faints for thee, 　as in a dry and weary land 　where no water is.	O God, you are my God, 　and I long for you. My whole being desires you 　like a dry, worn-out, and water- 　less land, my soul is thirsty for you.

In many languages one cannot say **thou art my God**, as God cannot be possessed like an inanimate object. Hence it is often necessary to say "you are the God I worship" or "you are the God I serve."

In the first line, **I seek thee** is expressed by TEV with "**I long for you.**" The Hebrew verb "to look for" used here is not the usual one which appears in 24.6b or the one in 9.10; 24.6a, but a verb which some take to mean "to look for at dawn"[1] (so NEB "I seek thee early"; the Septuagint has "I rise early for you"). (In the liturgy of the early church, this psalm was read in the morning service.)

The psalmist's desire for God is expressed in terms of thirst (see the same expression in 42.2). It is a longing so intense that he is weak with desire: literally **my flesh faints for thee** (a verb found only here in the Old Testament), which TEV represents by "**my whole being desires you.**" It should be noticed that both **soul** in line b and **flesh** in line c mean the psalmist himself, with no idea of a spiritual or psychological desire as contrasted with one that is only physical or bodily. He compares his thirst and fainting for God to that of **a dry and weary land, where no water is**. It is to be noticed that TEV moves the verb "is thirsty for" to line e, to go with the figure of a dry, arid area. **Weary land** is not a natural English expression; the poet is apparently transferring his own weary feelings figuratively to the land around him. One may speak of "a parched and thirsty land" (NJV) or "a dry and thirsty land" (NEB), to which one may add ". . . where I feel (or, become) so weary."

In some languages it will clearly not be possible to preserve the figures of thirsting and fainting for someone. However, the translator need not discard them without attempting to adjust them through the use of similes and other expressions; for example, "I thirst for you like I thirst for water" or "I desire you like a person thirsts for water." **My flesh faints for thee** in some languages can be said, for example, "so great is my desire for you it is like feeling faint." It is important to phrase the thirsting of the psalmist so that it can be compared to the dry land. For this reason it will sometimes be best to place the line regarding thirst just before or after the comparison of "a dry and waterless land," as TEV has done.

63.2	RSV	TEV
	So I have looked upon thee in the sanctuary, beholding thy power and glory.	Let me see you in the sanctuary; let me see how mighty and glorious you are.

This verse may be understood as a wish (TEV, SPCL; Dahood) or as a reference to a past experience (AT, RSV, NAB, TOB, NJB); NJV takes it as future, "I shall behold you." In the context of the whole psalm, it seems more likely that it expresses a desire for an immediate experience of God's self-revelation. This would be in the form of a vision, in which he saw, or wished to see, some manifestation of God's presence, such as that experienced by Ezekiel (Ezek 1.1,26-28) and Isaiah (Isa 6.1); see also Exo 24.10-11. The translator, however, should represent the text faithfully, using the common words for "see," "look at," "gaze upon," and so forth.

---

[1]TOB translates "Since dawn I long for you" and comments: "The verb translated *long for* is composed of the same consonants as the word for *dawn*. There is a play in the text on this resemblance. The ancient versions have *At dawn* and supply a verb."

The sanctuary ("holy place") is the Temple; Dahood takes it to mean the heavenly sanctuary. In the Temple the psalmist hopes to see a special manifestation of God's **power and glory** (see Isa 6.1-5).

63.3-4	RSV	TEV

3   Because thy steadfast love is better than life, my lips will praise thee.

4   So I will bless thee as long as I live; I will lift up my hands and call on thy name.

3   Your constant love is better than life itself, and so I will praise you.

4   I will give you thanks as long as I live; I will raise my hands to you in prayer.

The psalmist expresses his happiness with God's **steadfast love** and gratefully praises God. **Is better than life** is a way of saying that God's **steadfast love** is the most precious thing there is; without it life is not worth living.

In verse 4a to **bless** used of God means to praise or thank him (see 16.7 and comments), and in verse 4b the Hebrew is "I will lift my hands in your name" (see comments on 28.2), that is, he will pray as he calls on the name of God (see RSV; for "name" see 5.11). People would raise their hands when they prayed, just as today many people will fold their hands. If the translator follows TEV, it may be best to shift to a time clause; for example, "I will lift my hands when I pray" or "when I pray I will lift my hands."

63.5	RSV	TEV

My soul is feasted as with marrow and fat, and my mouth praises thee with joyful lips,

My soul will feast and be satisfied, and I will sing glad songs of praise to you.

The psalmist compares his spiritual experience to a rich feast; **marrow and fat** represent the best food. Actually, animal fat was not eaten but was to be offered to the Lord (Lev 3.16-17; 7.22-25). It seems better to abandon **marrow and fat** and use such expressions as "a rich feast" (NJV), "banquet" (NAB), "a delicious banquet" (SPCL), "the richest of foods" (NIV), "a rich and sumptuous feast" (NEB). Line a can sometimes be rendered "I will be satisfied like one who eats at a feast." In line b **mouth** and **lips** are the usage of a part of the person to represent the person, and may be rendered, for example, "I will praise you joyfully" or "I will say with a joy heart, 'God is great.' "

63.6-8	RSV		TEV
6	when I think of thee upon my bed, and meditate on thee in the watches of the night;	6	As I lie in bed, I remember you; all night long I think of you,
7	for thou hast been my help, and in the shadow of thy wings I sing for joy.	7	because you have always been my help. In the shadow of your wings I sing for joy.
8	My soul clings to thee; thy right hand upholds me.	8	I cling to you, and your hand keeps me safe.

Some (RSV, NJV) connect verse 6 with what precedes; most, like TEV, connect it with what follows. This seems better.

The watches of the night were three periods of four hours each, assigned to watchmen who guarded the city. The psalmist's intense devotion to God is therefore shown by the fact that "**all night long**" (TEV), as he lies in bed, he remembers what God has done for him and thinks about him (**meditate**; same verb as in 1.2).

For comments on **my help** see 33.20; 37.40.

For comments on the phrase **the shadow of thy wings**, see 17.8; 36.7.

In an exquisite statement of dependence and security, the psalmist says to God "**I cling to you**" (literally "my *nefesh* keeps close to you"), and "your right hand holds me fast," a vivid expression of human trust and divine care. **My soul clings to thee** may be rendered, for example, "I hold on to you with all my strength"; negatively this may be said "I will not let go of you." **Thy right hand** as a symbol of God's might may be translated "your mighty hand protects me."

63.9-10	RSV		TEV
9	But those who seek to destroy my life shall go down into the depths of the earth;	9	Those who are trying to kill me will go down into the world of the dead.
10	they shall be given over to the power of the sword, they shall be prey for jackals.	10	They will be killed in battle, and their bodies eaten by wolves.

Verses 9-11 may be understood as a wish, a petition, "May those . . ." (NJV, BJ, TOB, NJB; Dahood), or as a statement of fact (RSV, TEV, NEB, NAB, NIV; Weiser). The initial **But** of RSV, therefore, is useful and should be included in translation, since it contrasts the psalmist's situation (verses 6-8) with that of his enemies (verses 9-10). It seems better to understand verses 9-10 as a wish, a petition. The psalmist prays for the immediate and violent death of his enemies; **the depths of the earth** are Sheol, "**the world of the dead**." **Go down into the depths of the earth** must sometimes be rendered "go to the place where dead people go" or ". . . where the dead are put."

He prays for their death "**in battle**" (literally "given over to the hands of the sword"); and he asks that their bodies, instead of being buried, will be eaten by **jackals,** an especially degrading fate. See similar expressions in Isaiah 18.6; Jeremiah

7.33. The word translated **prey** is "portion, part," here in the sense of food which will be given to the jackals. For **jackals** see *Fauna and Flora*, pages 31-32. In some languages a local animal which scavenges for its food must replace jackal or wolf.

63.11 RSV	TEV
But the king shall rejoice in God; all who swear by him shall glory; for the mouths of liars will be stopped.	Because God gives him victory, the king will rejoice. Those who make promises in God's name will praise him, but the mouths of liars will be shut.

In line a TEV takes **rejoice in God** to mean "rejoice because of what God has done"; in this context it refers to the king's victory over his enemies.

All who swear by him is misleading in English, since "swear" in normal usage means profanity. The meaning is to **"make promises"** or "take an oath" in God's name. FRCL translates "take an oath, calling on God as witness." **By him** can refer either to God (Briggs, Kirkpatrick, Weiser, Dahood; NEB, NJV) or to the king (Anderson, Toombs). Many translations (see NJB, TOB, NAB, AT, RSV, SPCL) leave the phrase ambiguous, which is not to be recommended. One could "swear by the king" (see 1 Sam 17.55; 25.26; 2 Sam 11.11; 15.21), but it seems more likely that here God is meant.

The term **swear** in **all who swear by him** refers to the taking of an oath when making a statement or promise, and is expressed variously in different languages. Such terms are often related to speaking, touching (such as touching an object when taking an oath), and cursing oneself or calling on God or the object touched to curse the speaker if the promise is not kept or the statement is not true. **Swear by him** or "make promises in God's name" must often be recast in translation to say, for example, "everyone who makes a promise and speaks God's name to remove any doubts will praise God" or "all who say 'I will do this,' and confirm it by saying it in God's name, will rejoice."

Shall glory: meaning "will praise God"; or an intransitive verb can be used in translation, "will rejoice, will exult."

TEV makes clear the contrast between those who swear or make promises in God's name in the second line, and the liars in last line. Translators should make the contrast clear.

The mouths of liars will be stopped: this could be a way of speaking about their death (Cohen, Dahood), or else that their lies will be exposed and they will have to keep quiet. It seems more likely that the latter is meant. **Mouths of liars will be stopped** is a passive construction which must be recast in some languages as active. In such cases it is possible to say, for example, "God will close the mouths of liars."

551

Psalm 64

This psalm is a prayer to God for help, by an individual who is threatened by his enemies. Like other psalms of this kind, the psalm begins with a cry for help (verses 1-2), followed by a description of the psalmist's enemies (verses 3-6). Their destruction is predicted (verses 7-8); as a result, all will be afraid, and righteous people will praise God for what he has done (verses 9-10).

Nothing in the text identifies the psalmist or his situation, and the language used is like that of other psalms of lament.

HEADING: "**A Prayer for Protection.**" Other headings are "The punishment for slanderers"; "Divine punishment"; "The destroyer destroyed." The TEV title will often require some adjustment; for example, "The psalmist prays to God and asks that God protect him."

Hebrew Title: **To the choirmaster. A Psalm of David** (TEV "A psalm by David").
For **choirmaster** see title of Psalm 4.

64.1-2

RSV	TEV

1   Hear my voice, O God, in my complaint;
    preserve my life from dread of the enemy,
	1 I am in trouble, God—listen to my prayer!
	    I am afraid of my enemies—save my life!

2   hide me from the secret plots of the wicked,
    from the scheming of evildoers,
	2 Protect me from the plots of the wicked,
	    from mobs of evil men.

The psalmist prays for help because he is "**in trouble**" (TEV). The Hebrew word is used also in 55.2b, where RSV translates "my trouble," while here it translates **my complaint**. The Hebrew word itself is defined as "business, concern," and is variously translated: NJB "as I plead"; NEB "my lament"; SPCL, TOB, and NIV are like RSV (see also FRCL "I complain to you"). And GECL translates "my loud complaint." It may be better to follow the majority and translate something like "Listen to my bitter complaint, O God!"

The phrase **dread of the enemy** means that his enemies make him afraid; the translation can be "terrifying enemies" (see TOB), "the enemy's terror" (NJV), "terrible enemies" (SPCL). Because of the danger they pose, the psalmist asks God to save his life.

In verse 2a the word translated **plots** can also mean a group; that is, it can mean either "counsel" or "council." NJV has "a band"; "that conclave" is also possible; this meaning is more closely parallel to the next line, in which the TEV word "mobs" translates a noun found only here in the Old Testament. In 55.14 a related noun is used, which RSV translates "(we walked) in fellowship." RSV takes the noun in line b as parallel to **secret plots** in line a, and so translates **the scheming of evildoers** (so FRCL, SPCL). NJV translates "a crowd of evildoers," and NJB "the gang." Everything considered, it seems best to follow TEV and NJV here.

64.3-4	RSV		TEV
3	who whet their tongues like swords,	3	They sharpen their tongues like swords
	who aim bitter words like arrows,		and aim cruel words like arrows.
4	shooting from ambush at the blameless,	4	They are quick to spread their shameless lies;
	shooting at him suddenly and without fear.		they destroy good men with cowardly slander.

The psalmist's description of his enemies (verses 3-5) uses the conventional figures of **swords** (see 55.21; 57.4; 59.7), **arrows**, and **ambush** (see 7.15; 9.15; 35.7). The figures are clear enough; what is uncertain is whether they mean accusations, lies, slander, or if they refer to the use of magical formulas and oaths which were thought to have the power to cause disease, disaster, and death.

Some understand **bitter** in verse 3b (TEV **"cruel"**) to mean poison; so Dahood "with poisonous substance (they) tip their arrows." SPCL uses a good simile: "they shoot their poisonous words like arrows." Many languages will be able to maintain the figurative expressions found in verses 3-5, and translators should make an effort to do so, provided ample adjustments are made to make the meaning clear. In some languages it will not be possible to speak of "sharpening the tongue." However, one may sometimes say "they use their tongues like sharpened swords." **Who aim bitter words like arrows** can sometimes be translated "who shoot poison words like a hunter shoots poison arrows."

In verse 4 the enemies are pictured as shooting their arrows from ambush (see the same figure in 11.2), **suddenly and without fear**. TEV has abandoned the metaphor altogether; **"they are quick"** translates **suddenly**, and "shameless" represents the Hebrew "they are not afraid." **"Lies"** and **"slander"** stand for the arrows that are shot. Generally speaking the translator should continue the figurative language, unless the idea of shooting from ambush obscures the developing picture. **Without fear** means that they are not afraid that anyone will see them or accuse them of wrongdoing. Instead of the Masoretic text "they are not afraid," Syriac has "they are not seen," which NEB prefers. The translator should stay with the Masoretic text.

64.5-6	RSV		TEV
5	They hold fast to their evil purpose;	5	They encourage each other in their evil plots;

they talk of laying snares secretly, thinking, "Who can see us?"^{y} 6 Who can search out our crimes?^{z} We have thought out a cunningly conceived plot." For the inward mind and heart of a man are deep!	they talk about where they will place their traps. "No one can see them," they say. 6 They make evil plans and say, "We have planned a perfect crime." The heart and mind of man are a mystery.

^{y} Syr: Heb *them*

^{z} Cn: Heb *they search out crimes*

The first verb in verse 5 can be understood as "they strengthen (for) themselves," which TEV has rendered by "**They encourage each other**," and NJB "They support each other" (see also NIV, FRCL, SPCL). Another possibility is RSV **They hold fast**, or else "they persist."

In verse 5b the Hebrew "they talk about to hide their snares" means that they discuss how to place their traps in such a way that the intended victim does not see them and so will be caught in them.

In verse 5c the question in Hebrew, "Who can see them?" can be understood as an indirect question: "they ask who can see them," that is, who can see the people who are laying the traps, not the traps (so NEB). But the Hebrew interrogative pronoun generally introduces a direct question, and for this reason RSV prefers to emend to **Who can see us?** This is more in line with the usual language in such cases (see 10.11,13; 59.7).^{1} These wicked people think that no one, including God, sees what they are doing.

Verse 6 is particularly difficult as to both the form and the meaning of the Hebrew text. Oesterley does not translate the verse, with the comment that the various drastic emendations proposed "do not inspire confidence." Anderson makes a similar statement: "none of the suggested emendations is really convincing."

(1) The first line in Hebrew seems to mean "they devise evil plans," a translation of the verb meaning "search out, devise" (see its use in 77.7).

(2) The second line in Hebrew seems to mean "we completed a well-planned plot." The verb in the Masoretic text is *tamam*, "be complete, finished"; the noun, which occurs only here in the Old Testament, is related to the verb used in the first line and is taken to mean "plot"; the adjective appears to be a passive of the same verb. But some take the Masoretic text verb to be the equivalent of the third person plural "they completed"; and many Hebrew manuscripts have the similar Hebrew verb *taman*, "to hide" (see 9.15).

(3) The third line in Hebrew is "and the inner part of a man and the heart (are) deep."

Some take the first line as a question and still part of what the wicked say; so RSV, NJB ("who . . . will penetrate our secrets?"). TEV takes it as a statement

---

^{1}HOTTP says the verb *ra'ah* means "to notice, to discover somebody," so that the question means "Who will see them?" It appears, therefore, that "them" refers to the people, not to the traps.

(likewise NEB, NAB, TOB) and takes the verb to mean "devise"; see NIV "they plot" and FRCL "they imagine."

In the second line the verb in the Masoretic text is the first person plural, so TEV translates it as a statement made by the wicked men, **"We have planned a perfect crime"** (so TOB "We have planned well our plot"; see also FRCL, NIV). But many prefer the verb "hide," which is found in many Hebrew manuscripts, and translate "they conceal their cunning plot" (see NAB). NJB takes lines b and c to be the psalmist's reply to the wicked men's question in line a (**Who can search out our crime?**) and translates "He will do that, he who penetrates human nature to its depths, the depths of the heart."

The third line is taken by RSV and TEV to be the psalmist's comment; but TOB takes it to be still a part of what the wicked themselves say ("in man's depths, the heart is impenetrable").

NJV translates the whole verse (reading the verb "to hide" in line b): "Let the wrongdoings they have concealed, each one inside him, his secret thoughts, be wholly exposed" (with a marginal note). NEB has "they hatch their secret plans with skill and cunning, with evil purpose and deep design" (with two textual footnotes). Weiser has "They devise crimes, keep secret their plot; for a man's bosom and heart are deep." SPCL follows NJB, and Dahood's translation is similar to that of NJB.[2]

The translator must make a decision, in the knowledge that any translation is itself conjectural.

	64.7-9 RSV		TEV
7	But God will shoot his arrow at them; they will be wounded suddenly.	7	But God shoots his arrows at them, and suddenly they are wounded.
8	Because of their tongue he will bring them to ruin;[a] all who see them will wag their heads.	8	He will destroy them because of those words;[f] all who see them will shake their heads.
9	Then all men will fear; they will tell what God has wrought, and ponder what he has done.	9	They will all be afraid; they will think about what God has done and tell about his deeds.

---

[2]HOTTP has three separate notes for this verse and concludes: This difficult v. may be understood in two ways: 1. "they plotted crimes: 'we achieved a <cunningly> plotted plot: to man's inward mind <belong> secret plans (lit. a deep heart)!' " The v. contains a quotation of the wicked men's words which are expressed in the manner of a proverb. 2. "they plotted crimes: 'we have achieved a <cunningly> plotted plot: but man's inward mind and his heart <are> deep!' " This second interpretation is less probable, for it does not follow the phrase division of the MT.

a Cn: Heb *They will bring him to ruin, their tongue being against them*

f Probable text He will destroy them because of those words; *Hebrew* They will destroy him, those words are against them.

The psalmist foretells the punishment that God will inflict on the wicked. Weiser believes this section speaks of God's past actions of punishment, but most commentators and translators understand it to refer to God's future action.

God will punish the wicked in the same way they persecute others (verse 4), that is, he **will shoot his arrow at them** (see the same figure in 7.12-13). This may refer to punishment in general or to sickness in particular (as it appears to mean in 38.2).

In verse 7b **suddenly** expresses the idea of surprise on the part of the evildoers, "before they know it . . . ." And **they will be wounded** may be taken to mean "they will be defeated," "they will be shot down" (or, shot dead). See NJV "they shall be struck down."

In verse 8a, as RSV and TEV footnotes indicate, the Masoretic text does not make sense; it seems to say "they make him (or, it) stumble, against (or, upon) them their tongues." HOTTP takes this to mean that they, the wicked, caused their tongue to stumble against themselves, that is, they said things that harmed themselves. TEV and RSV translate the same emended Hebrew text. A rendering that is different: "Their evil speech recoils upon themselves"; NJV translates the Masoretic text, "Their tongue shall be their downfall" (similarly TOB); SPCL "they will fall because of their own words"; NEB (with a correction) is similar, "but their mischievous tongues are their undoing." The translator may prefer to follow HOTTP (see especially NJV), or else follow the RSV and TEV conjecture.

As a result of their punishment everyone else will view them with scorn (verse 8b); they **will wag their heads** (see 22.7), and they **will fear** (verses 8b,9a). Some take the Hebrew verb form translated "they will shake their heads" to be from the verb "to run away" (as in 31.11). In many languages the phrase **wag their heads**, if translated as in TEV "shake their heads," will have an ambiguous meaning, as this gesture can signify many different concepts and attitudes. Therefore it will be necessary to use an appropriate expression to signify "making fun of."

In verse 9a **will fear** could be understood to mean "will be afraid of God"; while possible, the meaning is probably that they will "**be afraid**" of what may happen next, whether it comes from God or from others.

TEV has reversed the two lines in verse 9b,c in order to place "**they will think**" before "**tell**." The verb translated **they will . . . ponder** can be understood to mean "they will understand" (so NJB, SPCL); "they will learn" (so NEB, TOB).

64.10   RSV   TEV

> Let the righteous rejoice in the LORD,
>   and take refuge in him!
> Let all the upright in heart glory!

> All righteous people will rejoice because of what the LORD has done.
> They will find safety in him;
>   all good people will praise him.

The last verse can be taken as a statement of fact (TEV and most others) or as an exhortation (RSV). This verse replaces the standard promise by the psalmist in a psalm like this to thank God (see 59.17) or to offer sacrifices to him (see 61.8).

"**Because of what the LORD has done**" represents <u>**in the LORD**</u>. The verb translated <u>**take refuge**</u> is the same one used in 2.12; and <u>**upright in heart**</u> (as in 11.2) is synonymous with <u>**the righteous**</u> in line <u>a</u>.

Psalm 65

This psalm is a hymn of thanksgiving and praise to God for having blessed his people with abundant harvests. It probably was used at the harvest festival or one of the other regular festivals.

The psalm begins with praise to God as one who answers his people's prayers (verses 1-4), followed by a description of him as savior of his people and creator of the universe (verses 5-8). The last section (verses 9-13) praises God for sending abundant rain and for blessing his people with rich harvests.

HEADING: "**Praise and Thanksgiving**." Other headings are "Creation, providence, and salvation"; "God is worthy of praise"; "A harvest hymn." The TEV title will often require adjustment in translation; for example, "The psalmist praises God and gives him thanks."

Hebrew Title: **To the choirmaster. A Psalm of David. A Song** (TEV "A psalm by David; a song").

For **choirmaster** see title of Psalm 4. The classification **A Song** occurs in the title of some thirty psalms. It seems probable that originally there was a distinction between **Psalm** and **Song**; but the difference, if any, is not known. The noun *mizmor* "psalm" appears some fifty-seven times in the psalm titles and nowhere else in the Old Testament; it is from the verb *zamar* "to praise" (see 7.17b). Some psalms, like this one, are called both a psalm and a song.

65.1-3a RSV		TEV

1	Praise is due to thee,
	    O God, in Zion;
	and to thee shall vows be per-
	    formed,
		1	O God, it is right for us to praise
			    you in Zion
			and keep our promises to you,

2	O thou who hearest prayer! To thee shall all flesh come	2	because you answer prayers. People everywhere will come to you
3	on account of sins.	3	on account of their sins.

The psalm opens with a declaration that it is the duty of God's people to praise him and to keep the promises they made to him. RSV **is due** translates the Hebrew consonants of the Masoretic text with a slight change of vowels (as suggested by the

558

Septuagint, Syriac, and Vulgate); the Masoretic text word means "silence" (so Aquila and Jerome).[1]

Zion, the name of the fortified hill in Jerusalem which David captured from the Jebusites (see discussion at 2.6), was later applied to Mount Moriah, the hill on which the Temple stood, and was extended to mean the city of Jerusalem. In some languages it will be appropriate to use a classifier such as "city" with Zion. In any event, it is advisable to include Zion in the glossary and to indicate that in certain passages it is to be equated with the city of Jerusalem. The vows to God may have been made because of droughts or some other disasters; they are now being fulfilled with the offering of praise and sacrifices.

RSV takes verse 2a as a description of God, **O thou who hearest prayer**; TEV translates it as a statement, connecting it with verse 1 (also NJB, SPCL, FRCL).

In verse 2b **all flesh** is a phrase that usually means "all humankind," "people everywhere," "all the world." But it may be that here it is used somewhat exaggeratedly for all Israelites (so Anderson). "To come (or, go) to God" means to go to the Temple in Jerusalem. **To thee shall all flesh come** will be ambiguous in many languages without stating clearly the purpose in their coming; for example, "all people will come to you to worship you" or ". . . to make sacrifices."

Sins in verse 3a and **transgressions** in verse 3b translate two words that are used also in 51.1-2; see discussion there.

65.3b-4	RSV	TEV
3b	When our transgressions prevail over us,[b] thou dost forgive them.	3b Our faults defeat us,[h] but you forgive them.
4	Blessed is he whom thou dost choose and bring near, to dwell in thy courts! We shall be satisfied with the goodness of thy house, thy holy temple!	4 Happy are those whom you choose, whom you bring to live in your sanctuary. We shall be satisfied with the good things of your house, the blessings of your sacred Temple.

[b] Gk: Heb me

[h] *One ancient translation* us; *Hebrew* me.

For expressions similar to that of verse 3b, see 38.4; 40.12. The meaning is that no one can deal with his or her sins without divine help; only God can deal effectively with them. The expression **When our transgressions prevail over us** may sometimes be rendered "When our sins are too heavy for us to carry" or, expressing sins as a verb phrase, "When we do bad things very much." The Masoretic text in verse 3b has the pronominal suffix "me"; RSV, TEV and others prefer the Septuagint

---

[1]This departure from the Masoretic text is adopted by NJV and TOB and is supported by HOTTP ("B" decision).

and Vulgate "us." TOB, NJV, however, translate the Masoretic text, which HOTTP also prefers.

The Hebrew verb translated **forgive** originally meant either "to cover" or else "to wipe off." In theological usage it means in the Hebrew Scriptures to remove the effects of sin, which are thought of primarily as a blot, or stain, which makes the person spiritually unclean, thus breaking the fellowship which exists between that person and God. The restoration of that broken fellowship can be effected only by God; God alone can remove, remit, cover up, wash away, forgive human sin. **Thou dost forgive them** in RSV and TEV makes the sins the goal of forgiveness. In some languages it is not the sins that are said to be forgiven, but rather the person who does the sin. There are often idiomatic expressions for forgiveness; for example, "heal the neck," "cause one's heart to be soft," "hand back someone's sins to him," and "throw away evil."

Some believe that the text in verse 4 refers to the priests, who actually lived in the Temple area when on duty, but it seems more probable that the worshiping congregation is meant.

In verse 4 the psalmist uses three different expressions to speak of the Temple: **thy courts** (verse 4b), **thy house** (verse 4c), and **thy holy temple** (verse 4d). The expression **to dwell in thy courts** (verse 4b) refers to entering the Temple for the purpose of praise and worship (see 15.1; 24.3).

In verse 4c **the goodness of thy house** means the good things, that is, the blessings, that the people receive in the Temple. This could include sacrificial feasts, of which the people partook, but it seems likely that the spiritual benefits are being spoken of.

In some languages the various terms used referring to the Temple may be rendered, for example, "your holy place," "your house," "your great singing house," or "your big prayer house." In line d TEV has filled out the parallelism with "**the blessings of.**" In some languages it may be helpful to follow this model. If so, it may be necessary to repeat the verb from the previous line. In both lines c and d it will be necessary in many languages to make the relation between "**your house**" and the "**good things**" more explicit than in TEV; for example, "the good things that we receive in your house," and in line c "the blessings you give us in your sacred Temple."

65.5   RSV   TEV

By dread deeds thou dost answer us with deliverance, O God of our salvation, who art the hope of all the ends of the earth, and of the farthest seas;	You answer us by giving us victory, and you do wonderful things to save us. People all over the world and across the distant seas trust in you.

In verses 5-8 the psalmist praises God as the savior of his people and as creator and Lord of the universe. God answers his people's prayers with mighty acts of salvation, which are described in verse 5a as **dread deeds**, and in verse 8a as "signs" which cause fear and terror. They can be called "awesome deeds, mighty acts, wonders, miracles"; TEV has **"wonderful things"** and "great things."

The verb **answer** in verse 5a can be read as indicative (RSV, TEV, FRCL, SPCL) or as imperative (NEB, NJV). The translation of **answer** in such expressions as **By dread deeds thou dost answer us** depends upon the usage in the language. In such an expression the request or prayer to which an answer is expected is implicit. A term which means to reply to a question is not adequate here. A term is needed which means that God responds to the implied petition. In some languages this may be rendered, for example, "You hear us and help us by . . . ." If the translator follows RSV **By dread deeds** or TEV **"wonderful things,"** he may translate, for example, "by doing great things for us."

In verse 5a **deliverance** translates the word *tsedeq* (see comments on "right" in 4.1), as in 40.9; here it is parallel with **salvation** in verse 5b. RSV has kept the parallelism more exact with the nouns **deliverance** and **salvation**. For comments on **God of our salvation**, see 18.46.

The whole inhabited earth is referred to in verse 5c,d by the phrases **all the ends of the earth** and **the farthest seas**; the latter (literally "the sea of those far away") is unusual, and some (Briggs; AT, FRCL, NJB) prefer to read *'iyim* "islands" instead of *yam* "sea." It is better to stay with the Hebrew text, which is the recommendation of HOTTP ("A" decision).

65.6-7	RSV		TEV
6	who by thy strength hast established the mountains, being girded with might;	6	You set the mountains in place by your strength, showing your mighty power.
7	who dost still the roaring of the seas, the roaring of their waves, the tumult of the peoples;	7	You calm the roar of the seas and the noise of the waves; you calm the uproar of the peoples.

God's mighty acts in creation are described in terms of his placing the mountains in place and subduing the raging seas (verses 6-7b). According to the concept of the universe at that time, **the mountains**, which are visible above the surface of the earth, were thought to extend far down into the underworld, serving as the columns on which the surface of the earth rests. The phrase **by thy strength** as the means for putting the mountains in their places must be expressed in some languages as "because you are strong you put the mountains in their places."

God's **might** is spoken of as the belt which he tightens around his waist as he prepares to act (see also 93.1). Verse 6b **being girded with might** may be understood either as "because you clothed yourself with strength" (see FRCL "you are armed with power") or "making a display of your great strength." The former is preferable. **Being girded with might** may be rendered, for example, "because you are very strong."

The seas represent the powers of chaos and disorder that continually threaten the established order of the universe which God brought into being (see 89.9-10; 93.3-4; 104.5-9).

God is also the supreme ruler of all humankind (verse 7c); he calms **the tumult of the peoples**, that is, the angry words and actions of those who rebel against him, just as he calms the rebellious seas. **Tumult** is frequently used to express "rebellion."

65.8	RSV	TEV

RSV	TEV

so that those who dwell at earth's
    farthest bounds
are afraid at thy signs;
thou makest the outgoings of the
    morning and the evening
to shout for joy.
	The whole world stands in awe
	    of the great things that you
	    have done.
	Your deeds bring shouts of joy
	    from one end of the earth to the
	    other.

In this verse the world's inhabitants are described as **those who dwell at earth's farthest bounds**. This phrase is inclusive, not exclusive; that is, it means all people of the world, including those who live in the most distant parts of the earth.

TEV's "**stands in awe**" is often rendered in many languages by idiomatic phrases; for example, "the heart jumps" or "the stomach trembles."

The **signs** are the great deeds, or miracles, that God performed (this is parallel to "dread deeds" in verse 5a).

In line c the psalmist uses the phrase **the outgoings of the morning and the evening** as a way of speaking of the east and the west, the limits of the earth; so TEV "**from one end of the earth to the other.**" NJV has "the lands of sunrise and sunset"; NJB "the gateways of morning and evening"; another possible version is "farthest east and farthest west." The translation of east and west representing the full extent of the earth is expressed variously in different languages, and the form should be the one most natural in the language. In some languages the extremes of distance are expressed in terms of the prevailing winds, in others according to the flow of the river, and in others by the rising and setting of the sun. For instance, in some languages one must speak of "from the mouth of the river to the source of the river," "from the east wind to the west wind," or simply "from upstream to downstream." In some languages this may be rendered, for example, "Because of the great things you do, all the people who live from upstream to downstream shout for joy." It is, of course, people who live in those far-away places who **shout for joy**, not the places themselves.

65.9-10	RSV	TEV

RSV	TEV

9 Thou visitest the earth and water-
     est it,
    thou greatly enrichest it;
  the river of God is full of water;
    thou providest their grain,
    for so thou hast prepared it.
10 Thou waterest its furrows abun-
     dantly,
	9 You show your care for the land
	    by sending rain;
	    you make it rich and fertile.
	  You fill the streams with water;
	    you provide the earth with
	    crops.
	  This is how you do it:
	10 you send abundant rain on the

settling its ridges, softening it with showers, and blessing its growth.	plowed fields and soak them with water; you soften the soil with showers and cause the young plants to grow.

The care and providence of God are shown by his sending the rain to make the earth produce abundant crops. In verse 9a TEV **"You show your care"** translates the Hebrew verb "to visit" (as in 8.4b, where RSV has "care for"; see comments there). To translate literally **Thou visitest** (RSV; also NEB, TOB) gives the wrong idea of God descending from heaven to do the things listed in verses 9-10. It is better, like NJV, to translate "You take care of the earth . . . ." It is possible that in the same line the Hebrew *'erets* means "land" of Israel (AT, NAB) instead of **earth** (RSV and others; TEV **"land"** is probably ambiguous); the majority of translations have "earth."

Some languages do not speak of fertile soil as being "rich," but rather as "dark, deep, good," or "like river-side soil." **Thou greatly enrichest it** may be rendered, for example, "you make the soil good for growing crops" or "you give the soil life and it grows things."

In verse 9c **the river of God** is the heavenly source of the rain which God sends down to earth (see Gen 1.6-7; see similar language in Psa 46.4); NEB translates "the waters of heaven." SPCL understands "of God" here to be a superlative, and translates "roaring streams." TEV has represented the Hebrew by **"You fill the streams with water."** It would be better, however, to stay closer to the Hebrew form, as follows: "Your river, O God, is full of water, to provide the land with crops." The point is that there is a never-failing supply of water for God to send in order to "provide the earth with crops" (or, grain). **Their grain** in line d means "grain for the inhabitants of the earth" (or, of the land). The expression **thou providest their grain** can be rendered in some languages, for example, "you cause the earth to grow crops."

The last line of verse 9 may point backward (so RSV, NJV, NIV) or forward (TEV, NJB, NEB, FRCL). SPCL makes of it a complete sentence, without necessarily pointing backward or forward: "Thus you prepare the field." The context of the translator's own language will determine the best way to render the line.

In verse 10 the effect of the rain on the fields is described. The **furrows** and **ridges** describe a field that has been plowed and sown. In Palestine the rainy season lasted from October to May; the early rains were in the fall, the later rains in the springtime. **Settling its ridges** in line b describes the effects of constant rain, which levels the ridges of the grooves dug in the field by the plow. **Softening it with showers** must sometimes be recast to say, for example, "and sending rain which turns hard clods to soft soil." In the last line, **blessing its growth** means that God blesses the soil by making the plants grow; so a translation can say "you bless the soil by making the plants sprout and grow."

Throughout the whole process it is God who is at work, sending the rain, making the soil rich and fertile, and providing abundant harvests for his people.

	RSV		TEV
11	Thou crownest the year with thy bounty; the tracks of thy chariot drip with fatness.	11	What a rich harvest your goodness provides! Wherever you go there is plenty.
12	The pastures of the wilderness drip, the hills gird themselves with joy,	12	The pastures are filled with flocks; the hillsides are full of joy.
13	the meadows clothe themselves with flocks, the valleys deck themselves with grain, they shout and sing together for joy.	13	The fields are covered with sheep; the valleys are full of wheat. Everything shouts and sings for joy.

The psalmist uses poetic language to picture the large flocks and rich harvests with which God blesses his people. It is recommended that, if possible, a translator read these three verses in a number of different translations in order to get some sense of how these poetic figures hang together. After that a verse-by-verse first draft may be attempted.

In verse 11a **Thou crownest the year with thy bounty** means that God blesses the harvest season with rich crops, as though they were a crown that God places on the land that year (see the verb "to crown" in 8.5b). Here the verb "to crown" is used not in the sense of power and authority, like those of a king, but a wreath, a garland, that indicates victory and celebration. In many languages it will not be possible to speak of **"goodness"** performing an action such as providing rich harvests, as in TEV. However, one may often say "Because you are good you give us rich harvests."

In verse 11b the Hebrew is "your chariot tracks drip with fatness." This pictures God riding around in his chariot, that is, the rain clouds (see 68.4,33), and leaving abundant blessings wherever he goes. But it is not strictly necessary to keep the figure of a chariot. NJV translates "Your paths," and FRCL has "abundance flourishes wherever you have passed." But there are differences of opinion about the word translated "chariot tracks" (used also as "paths" in 17.5; 23.3); Dahood has "pastures," and NEB "palm-trees." SPCL translates "Your clouds." The word **fatness** here indicates abundance of good things.

The same verb, "drip, trickle," is used in verse 12a of **the pastures.** The Hebrew phrase **the pastures of the wilderness** are the open pastures where the flocks graze; for example, "grazing lands." The figure here is that of **"pastures . . . filled with flocks"**; see NJV "The meadows are clothed with flocks." But instead of flocks, perhaps the psalmist is speaking of grass; so SPCL "the pastures of the wilderness are green"; NJB "the pastures of the desert grow moist"; and GECL "The pastures in the wilderness are moist and green." NEB translates in more general terms, ". . . are rich with blessing."

In verses 12b, 13a,b the three verbs "to gird oneself," "to clothe oneself," and "to cover oneself" are used of **the hills,** of **the meadows,** and of **the valleys,** which are covered with **joy**, **flocks**, and **grain**. The poetry is beautiful and highly effective, but a literal translation may communicate very little, if anything, to readers whose way of life is radically different from that of the psalmist and his readers. Verses 12 and 13 are difficult to translate without making several adjustments. The main problem is that in Hebrew a series of inanimate objects are said to be doing things that only humans do. TEV has shifted these to passive constructions and modified the "clothing" verbs. However, in languages which will not take passive constructions here, other changes will be required. One of the most obvious adaptations that can be made would be to switch to active constructions and to supply God as the agent. In addition it will often be necessary to supply some comparisons in order to keep the poetic ideas; for example, "you make the hills like joyful people" or "you cause the hills to look like happy people."

The psalm ends with a portrayal of all of them, the pastures, the hillsides, and the valleys, shouting and singing together for joy in gratitude to God. The referent of **they shout and sing** is inanimate, and in many languages this figurative usage will be misleading. In languages where inanimate subjects cannot perform these events, it will often be necessary to supply a comparison; for example, "everything will be good like people shouting and singing for joy" or "all these things will be like people who shout and sing their thanks to God."

Psalm 66

This psalm is a hymn of thanksgiving by an individual who has been rescued by God (verses 16-19) and is now offering him praise and sacrifice in the Temple. There are several themes which run through the psalm, and this has led some commentators to conclude that it is a composite work.

The psalm opens with a call to all people to praise God (verses 1-4), followed by a recital of his mighty deeds in freeing his people from captivity and preserving them as a nation (verses 5-9). God had put his people to the test but has at last delivered them from troubles (verse 10-12), so the psalmist offers praise and sacrifice to God (verses 13-15). The psalmist calls on his people to join him in worshiping God (verses 16-19), and the psalm closes with one final note of praise (verse 20).

HEADING: "**A Song of Prayer and Thanksgiving.**" Others have "A hymn of gratitude"; "Corporate act of thanksgiving"; "Liturgy of praise and thanksgiving." In many languages it will be necessary to recast the TEV title so as to express the nouns as verb phrases; for example, "The psalmist sings a song to praise God and to give him thanks" or "The psalmist sings and says 'You are great and I thank you.' "

Hebrew Title: **To the choirmaster. A Song. A Psalm** (TEV "A song").
For **choirmaster** see title of Psalm 4; for **Song** see title of Psalm 65.

66.1-2   RSV   TEV

1   Make a joyful noise to God, all the   1   Praise God with shouts of joy, all
          earth;   people!
2   sing the glory of his name;   2   Sing to the glory of his name;
          give to him glorious praise!   offer him glorious praise!

The psalmist calls for **all the earth** (that is, all the people in the world) to praise God, to shout joyfully (**make a joyful noise**), and to **sing** (or, "play music"; see discussion on the verb in 7.17b).

The command **Make a joyful noise to God** is difficult in many languages, as noise is not always thought of as being joyful. However, one can often render the full idea as "praise God by making joyful music," or "make happy music and praise God," or "make joyful music and say 'God, you are great.' "

In verse 2, lines <u>a</u> and <u>b</u> say essentially the same thing in slightly different ways. **Sing the glory of his name** means "sing words that tell how wonderful God is." TEV **"Sing to the glory of his name"** means "sing words that will bring more honor to God." For **name** see comments on 5.11.

The command to **sing the glory of his name** may be rendered in some languages, for example, "sing songs and say that he is glorious," or in direct speech, "sing songs and say 'God, you are glorious,' " or ". . .'God, you are great.' "

Give to him glorious praise means simply to praise him and can often be rendered "Say that God is great" or "Speak well of God."

66.3-4	RSV	TEV
3	Say to God, "How terrible are thy deeds!	3 Say to God, "How wonderful are the things you do!
	So great is thy power that thy enemies cringe before thee.	Your power is so great that your enemies bow down in fear before you.
4	All the earth worships thee; they sing praises to thee, sing praises to thy name."	4 Everyone on earth worships you; they sing praises to you, they sing praises to your name."
	Selah	

In verse 3a **terrible** translates the same word translated "dread" in 65.5 (see comments there); God's mighty deeds provoke fear and awe in those who hear about them (thus "How awesome are your works" is possible). The expression **How terrible are thy deeds**, following the suggestion of TEV **"wonderful,"** can often be translated by idiomatic phrases; for example, "The great things you do cause my insides to tremble" or ". . . make my heart jump."

The verb translated **cringe** in verse 3c is used to describe defeated soldiers unwillingly paying homage to their victorious enemy (see Deut 33.29).

So tremendous and awe-inspiring are God's mighty deeds that the whole world worships him and sings praises to him (verse 4). The last two lines of the verse are almost identical, the only difference being **to thee** in line b and **to thy name** in line c. The two may be combined into one, as SPCL does; if the translator chooses to have two lines, the phrase **to thy name** may be expressed by "in honor of thee."

For *Selah* see 3.2.

66.5-6	RSV	TEV
5	Come and see what God has done: he is terrible in his deeds among men.	5 Come and see what God has done, his wonderful acts among men.
6	He turned the sea into dry land; men passed through the river on foot.	6 He changed the sea into dry land; our ancestors crossed the river on foot.
	There did we rejoice in him,	There we rejoiced because of what he did.

The psalmist, as he offers sacrifice in the Temple, calls on his fellow worshipers to think about God's mighty deeds in saving his people; in a vivid way he calls upon them to **Come and see what God has done** (verse 5a).

For comments on the word translated **terrible**, see verse 3; in English, **terrible** here is a highly inappropriate word. In line <u>b</u> **terrible in his deeds** will in many languages require expressing the adjective phrase as a verb phrase; for example, "he does things that cause people's hearts to tremble." **Men** translates the phrase "sons of man" (see comments on "children of men" in 11.4); a better translation is "people."

The psalmist in verse 6 picks two of the mighty deeds of God: the crossing of the Red Sea (the "Sea of Reeds" in Hebrew; see 106.7), when Yahweh parted the waters for the Israelites to escape from the pursuing Egyptians (Exo 14.21-22), and the crossing of the Jordan River (Josh 3.14-17). It is possible that **the river** in verse 6b is synonymous with **the sea** in verse 6a, so that both lines refer to the earlier event (so Briggs; NEB); but it seems preferable to assume that two separate events are meant. In some languages it is difficult to make a distinction between sea and river. One must often translate, for example, "he turned the big water into dry land" or "he dried up the big water and made it become dry land." The interpretation of line <u>b</u> will affect in some languages the term that is used for "crossing a river," since the term used for making a river crossing on foot may be different from walking across an area of dry land that is referred to as a river.

In the ritual that celebrated these saving events, the psalmist and his contemporaries are joined to their ancestors and can say **There did we rejoice** (verse 6a); the clause **"because of what he did"** (TEV) translates what is literally **in him**.

66.7   RSV   TEV

who rules by his might for ever, whose eyes keep watch on the nations— let not the rebellious exalt themselves. *Selah*	He rules forever by his might and keeps his eyes on the nations. Let no rebels rise against him.

The God who saved his people is described as the one who rules eternally **by his might** and one **whose eyes keep watch on the nations**, that is, who keeps watching the pagan nations so as to notice any hostile actions on their part (see the same verb in 37.32). The verb phrase is not used in the sense of God's guarding or protecting them. So the psalmist warns the nations not to try to rebel against God's rule.

In some languages **by his might** must be translated as a reason clause; for example, "Because he is strong he rules forever." **Nations** refers to the peoples living around Israel and is often rendered as "the other tribes."

The rebellious probably refers to the **nations** in the previous line. In this case it may be possible to translate **the rebellious** as "those who turn against you" or "those who refuse you." The whole line may be translated "Let those who turn against you not think that they are great."

For *Selah* see 3.2.

66.8-9   RSV / TEV

	RSV		TEV

8 Bless our God, O peoples,
let the sound of his praise be
heard,
9 who has kept us among the living,
and has not let our feet slip.

8 Praise our God, all nations;
let your praise be heard.
9 He has kept us alive
and has not allowed us to fall.

The psalmist again calls on the people of other nations to **bless our God**, that is "**Praise our God**" (TEV). The verb **Bless** with God as object means "**Praise**" (see discussion in 16.7). The "our" in **our God** is exclusive, not inclusive; the psalmist is exhorting pagan nations to praise the God of Israel. However, the translator will have to consider how people using the receptor language would speak of "our God" when encouraging those who are not yet worshipers to come and praise him, whether the "our" would be inclusive or exclusive.

In verse 8b **his praise** means "your praise of him." Line b contains two problems for some languages; **let the sound . . . be heard** must often be shifted to another type of expression, and the passive voice must often be changed to the active; for example, "cause people to hear how great you are" or "cause people to hear when they praise God."

God has protected and preserved his people: "he has kept our *nefesh* (see 3.2) among the living," and he **has not let our feet slip** (see 17.5 and comments). Here this may mean protection from disaster or defeat, or, parallel with line a, it may mean protection from death.

Line 9a is positive followed by a negative expression of the same thought in 9b. These lines may sometimes be rendered as two negatives; for example, "He has not let us die, and he has not let us be defeated" or ". . . has not let our enemies defeat us."

66.10-11   RSV / TEV

10 For thou, O God, hast tested us;
thou hast tried us as silver is
tried.
11 Thou didst bring us into the net;
thou didst lay affliction on our
loins;

10 You have put us to the test, God;
as silver is purified by fire,
so you have tested us.
11 You let us fall into a trap
and placed heavy burdens on
our backs.

The psalmist recounts the difficult times the people of Israel have experienced; in all things, whatever happens to Israel is the result of God's will for his people. The psalmist compares those harsh events to the process by which silver is refined, that is, the impurities are removed (see 12.6); the purpose of God in subjecting his people to trials and hardships was to purify them.

As silver is tried will be translated according to the familiarity with this metal and with the refining of metals. Where refining is known but silver is not, another known metal may be substituted. If refining is not known, it is possible to expand the description slightly; for example, "you have put us to the test as a precious metal is melted by fire in order to clean it." Or a supplementary note may be included, such as "Some metals were heated until they melted into a liquid so that the impure parts could be removed."

In verse 11 there is uncertainty concerning the two nouns **net** and **affliction**. The first one means in some instances a hunter's net or trap (Ezek 12.13; 17.20); in other places it means "stronghold, fortress" (see 18.2; 31.2,3). In line with the latter meaning, some take the word here to mean "dungeon, prison" (Weiser; NIV); but most commentators and translators prefer "net."

In verse 11b **affliction** (TEV **"heavy burdens"**) translates a word found only here in the Old Testament; the Septuagint translates "afflictions"; Holladay defines it "misery, hardship"; the Targum translates "chains" (so Oesterley; BJ). NJV has "trammel" (a kind of net); Dahood has "ulcers"; AT "heavy load" (similarly NAB, NJB, TOB, SPCL). Since this **affliction** is something that God laid on the people, the best choice seems to be "heavy loads," an appropriate thing to be placed on a person's back.

Verse 11 should not be understood to mean (as TEV might imply) that God, after catching his people in a trap, laid heavy burdens on their backs. Lines a and b are two different ways of referring to difficulty and suffering.

TEV **"our backs"** translates what is literally **our loins**. The translator should use the expression most suitable to the language and habits of the people.

66.12	RSV	TEV

thou didst let men ride over our heads; we went through fire and through water; yet thou has brought us forth to a spacious place.*c*	You let our enemies trample us; we went through fire and flood, but now you have brought us to a place of safety.*j*

c Cn Compare Gk Syr Jerome Tg: Heb *saturation*

j *Some ancient translations* safety; *Hebrew* overflowing.

The figure in line a seems to be that of enemy horses and chariots running over defeated soldiers (see Isa 51.23). It is a vivid figure of a disastrous military defeat.

Fire and . . . water (that is, **"fire and flood"**) are symbols of hardships and dangers, and are not meant literally. In some languages it will be necessary to make explicit that going **through fire and through water** are comparisons with suffering, and so this can often be translated by the use of a simile; for example, "we suffered like people who suffer from fires and floods" or "we suffered like people who lose their possessions in fires and floods."

But God has always rescued his people (line c). **A spacious place** (TEV **"a place of safety"**) translates the meaning suggested by the Septuagint, Vulgate, Jerome, "relief, respite" (so Weiser; NAB, NEB, BJ, NJB, SPCL, FRCL), which represents a Hebrew word that is used with this meaning in Exo 8.15. The Masoretic text word here means "saturation, overflowing," which Cohen interprets as "abundance" (so NIV); NJV "prosperity," TOB "banquet." Also possible is "plenty."[1]

It seems that the Masoretic text can make sense, and so it is not absolutely necessary to appeal to the ancient Versions. In TEV style the translation can be "but now you have made us prosperous" or "you have given us abundant gifts." Dahood suggests a different meaning: "After you had led us out of abundance," like the "abundance" that the Israelites enjoyed in Egypt (see Num 11.4-6); this, however, does not seem likely.

66.13-15 RSV	TEV
13 I will come into thy house with burnt offerings; I will pay thee my vows,	13 I will bring burnt offerings to your house; I will offer you what I promised.
14 that which my lips uttered and my mouth promised when I was in trouble.	14 I will give you what I said I would when I was in trouble.
15 I will offer to thee burnt offerings of fatlings, with the smoke of the sacrifice of rams; I will make an offering of bulls and goats. *Selah*	15 I will offer sheep to be burned on the altar; I will sacrifice bulls and goats, and the smoke will go up to the sky.

The psalmist now promises to offer his sacrifices to God, in keeping with the promises he had made when he **was in trouble**. The change from the experience and needs of the nation to those of the psalmist himself is abrupt and unexpected, and this leads some to think that this psalm is a composite work. It may be that the psalmist identified the two, so that his troubles and those of the nation were thought of as one.

Thy house (verse 13a) is the Temple in Jerusalem, where the psalmist, in keeping with the promises he had made earlier (**my vows**, verse 13b), offers his sacrifices.

In verse 14 TEV "**I said I would**" reduces to one sentence the double statement in Hebrew, **my lips uttered and my mouth promised**. The chronological sequence of the statements in verse 14 may sometimes require recasting, since the psalmist's troubles came first, followed by the promise he made, and then later his promise to do what he said earlier. In some languages the time sequence following their natural order will make for clearer understanding; for example, "when I was in trouble I made you a promise. Now I will do what I promised."

---

[1]HOTTP prefers the Masoretic text and says it has two well-attested meanings, "abundance" and "rest, free breathing," but makes no recommendation as to which of the two is more suitable in this context. Most translations that follow the Masoretic text prefer the first meaning.

The psalmist offers as **burnt offerings** animals that are identified as **fatlings** (verse 15a). The word can refer to sheep, goats, or bulls which have been especially fattened for sacrifice. Instead of TEV "**sheep**," something like "fat animals" (FRCL) or "fattened animals" (SPCL) would be better. The psalmist also offers **rams** (male sheep) and **bulls and goats**; the word translated **goats** is specifically the male animal.

In verse 15b the Hebrew **with the smoke** is expanded by TEV into "**and the smoke will go up to the sky.**" FRCL is similar: "and their smoke will go up to you."

This is an unusually large number of animals that is being offered; as Anderson suggests, either there is poetic license at work, or else the psalmist was quite a rich person.

66.16-17   RSV   TEV

16   Come and hear, all you who fear God,
     and I will tell what he has done for me.
17   I cried aloud to him,
     and he was extolled with my tongue.

16   Come and listen, all who honor God,
     and I will tell you what he has done for me.
17   I cried to him for help;
     I praised him with songs.

The psalmist now invites all his fellow worshipers (**all you who fear God**) to listen to his recital of what God **has done for me**. **All you who fear God** must sometimes be rendered, for example, "you people who worship God" or "you who revere God."

In verse 17b TEV "**I praised him with songs**" represents the force of the Hebrew "and high praise (was) under my tongue"—which could have been songs (so Briggs) or simply spoken words of praise. Dahood translates "sounds of music were on my tongue." Line b does not seem to fit well with line a, and some have rendered **cried aloud** in line a by "I prayed in a loud voice," with line b giving the content of the prayer. So NJV, "I called aloud to Him, glorification on my tongue"; NEB, somewhat more naturally, has "I lifted up my voice in prayer, his high praise was on my lips." Perhaps SPCL is best: "With my lips and my tongue I called to him and praised him."

66.18-19   RSV   TEV

18   If I had cherished iniquity in my heart,
     the Lord would not have listened.
19   But truly God has listened;
     he has given heed to the voice of my prayer.

18   If I had ignored my sins,
     the Lord would not have listened to me.
19   But God has indeed heard me;
     he has listened to my prayer.

In verse 18 the Hebrew reads "If I had seen iniquity in my heart," by which the psalmist means that if he had been aware of his sin yet done nothing about it; so RSV **If I had cherished iniquity**; TEV **"If I had ignored my sins."** But TOB translates "If I had thought about (doing) evil"; NJV "Had I an evil thought in my mind"; and FRCL "If I had had wicked intentions." This, however, had not happened; the psalmist had confessed his sins or else had not been guilty of any sins; and so his prayer was answered. TEV **"ignored my sins"** is rendered in idiomatic forms in some languages; for example, "If I turned my head from my sins," "If I had shut my eyes on the evil I had done," and "If I had put deaf ears on my sins."

Verse 18b states what would have happened if the psalmist had not been aware of and confessed his sins; God would not have listened to his prayer, that is, God would not have done what he had asked God to do.

Verse 19 shows that the psalmist has repented of his sins and confessed them to God, inasmuch as God has listened to his prayer and answered his pleas. **Voice of my prayer** means "sound of my prayer," but TEV **"my prayer"** is an adequate rendering. Or else, "when I spoke my prayer."

66.20 RSV	TEV

Blessed be God,
    because he has not rejected my
      prayer
    or removed his steadfast love
      from me!
	I praise God,
	    because he did not reject my
	      prayer
	    or keep back his constant love
	      from me.

The psalm ends with praise to God; for comments on **Blessed be God**, see 28.6.

In the last two lines the Hebrew text has only one verb, the causative of "depart, leave," that is, "reject, remove." It is difficult to find one verb that goes naturally with **my prayer** and with **his steadfast love**, and so RSV and TEV use two verbs; see also SPCL "who has not rejected my prayer nor denied me his love," and FRCL "He has not rejected my prayer, he has not deprived me of his goodness."

In some languages **he has not rejected my prayer** can be rendered, for example, "he has not said 'No' to the things I have asked him."

In some languages it is difficult to express removing love or keeping back love. However, one may say, for example, "he has not failed to love me faithfully" or, stated positively, "he has always loved me faithfully."

Psalm 67

This psalm is a thanksgiving hymn to God in praise for a bountiful harvest (see Psa 65). It was probably used in the worship during the Harvest Festival, or some other festival (see Anderson). A decision on the nature of the psalm depends largely on the meaning of the verb in verse 6a (see below).

Psalm 67 is neatly structured into three units or stanzas, each stanza being closed by a recurring refrain. The first stanza (verses 1-2) closes with verse 3, **Let the peoples praise thee . . . .** The second stanza (verse 4) closes with the identical refrain in verse 5. The final stanza (verses 6, 7a) closes with a variation of the refrain in 7b. It is important for translators to recognize the form of a psalm and to reflect its formal features in the printed edition.

HEADING: "**A Song of Thanksgiving.**" Other headings are "A harvest thanksgiving"; "Harvest song"; "Thanksgiving for harvest." The TEV title must often be recast using verb phrases; for example, "The psalmist sings a song and thanks God."

Hebrew Title: **To the choirmaster: with stringed instruments. A Psalm. A Song** (TEV"A psalm; a song").

For **choirmaster** and **stringed instruments** see title of Psalm 4; for **Song** see title of Psalm 65.

67.1-2	RSV	TEV
1	May God be gracious to us and bless us and make his face to shine upon us, *Selah*	1 God, be merciful to us and bless us; look on us with kindness,
2	that thy way may be known upon earth, thy saving power among all nations.	2 so that the whole world may know your will; so that all nations may know your salvation.

The opening prayer seems to reflect the form of the priestly prayer found in Numbers 6.24-26. For comments on the language used in verse 1, see 4.1,6b; 31.16.

TEV has used the direct form of address to God in verse 1 in order to be consistent with its use in verses 2-5; RSV, following the Hebrew text, has the third person in verse 1 and, without a break in the sentence, the second person in verse 2.

The expressions **be gracious** or **"be merciful"** are often expressed idiomatically in many languages; for example, "show us your good heart."

For *Selah* see 3.2.

The request is that all the people in the world (verse 2a **earth**; verse 2b **all nations**) may learn from experience God's will for them (literally, his **way**) and his **saving power**. NJB translates well: "Then the earth will acknowledge your ways and all the nations your power to save." The Hebrew verb "to know" here means not only intellectual knowledge but an experiential knowledge, that is, knowledge that results from experience.

Thy way or TEV's **"your will"** must often be rendered as a verb phrase; for example, "so that all the people will know what you want them to do." **Thy saving power** again must often be translated as a clause; for example, "so that the people of all the nations may be saved by you," or "so that all the nations may be saved" or ". . . know that you have the power to save them."

67.3	RSV	TEV
	Let the peoples praise thee, O God; let all the peoples praise thee!	May the peoples praise you, O God; may all the peoples praise you!

The call for universal praise of God is repeated in a two-line refrain (verses 3,5). The nations are called upon to "be glad and sing for joy" (verse 4) in recognition that God is a just judge and that he guides all nations. He is the ruler of all the world, not only of Israel. The indirect commands expressed in RSV with **let** and in TEV with **"may"** in some languages must be expressed as direct commands or as requests; for example, "Praise God, all you people" or "I ask all you people to praise God."

67.4-5	RSV	TEV
4	Let the nations be glad and sing for joy, for thou dost judge the peoples with equity and guide the nations upon earth. *Selah*	4 May the nations be glad and sing for joy, because you judge the peoples with justice and guide every nation on earth.
5	Let the peoples praise thee, O God; let all the peoples praise thee!	5 May the peoples praise you, O God; may all the peoples praise you!

In some languages it is not possible for impersonal groups such as **nations** to perform acts such as being glad. In some languages, therefore, one must translate "people of all nations, be glad and sing for joy."

For the language of verse 4b, see 45.6b, where the same word translated **equity** is used. And the verb translated **guide** is the same one used in 23.3. **Thou dost judge the peoples with equity** must often be translated idiomatically as "you cut the affairs of people fairly" or "you decide the affairs of men with a straight heart."

Verse 5 repeats the refrain of verse 3.

67.6-7	RSV	TEV

	RSV	TEV
6	The earth has yielded its increase; God, our God, has blessed us.	6	The land has produced its harvest; God, our God, has blessed us.
7	God has blessed us; let all the ends of the earth fear him!	7	God has blessed us; may all people everywhere honor him.

In verse 6a most translations take the perfect tense of the verb (literally "has given") to refer to past action: **"The land has produced"** (TEV; also RSV, FRCL, NEB, TOB, NJB, AT, NAB, GECL, SPCL; Briggs, Weiser). Some, however, contend that this is an example of what is called the precative perfect, that is, the use of the perfect to express a petition, and so should be translated "May the earth yield . . ." (Dahood; NJV, NIV). If so, the psalm is to be thought of as a lament or a petition, not as a prayer of thanksgiving for a good harvest. The clause **The earth has yielded its increase** is difficult in some languages, because the land alone is not said to perform this event. Therefore in some languages one must say, for example, "On the land the harvest has grown."

Line b of verse 6 should be translated like line a, either as a statement or as a petition. **God, our God** must often be translated as "the God whom we worship."

Verse 7 is translated as a prayer by FRCL, TOB, NEB, and SPCL; this makes for a fitting conclusion to the psalm, and translators should feel free to translate the same way.

For comments on the phrase **all the ends of the earth**, meaning "all people everywhere," see 2.8; 22.27; 59.13.

Psalm 68

Both as to text and meaning, this psalm is the most difficult of all psalms to understand and interpret. There is no discernible unity in the composition. Some have suggested that the psalm is no more than a list, a catalogue, of some thirty poems, whose first lines, or strophes, are cited one after the other; or else that separate songs have been brought together for use in worship. The one theme which predominates is that of Yahweh as God of Israel waging war against Israel's enemies and defeating them.

Some procession in the Temple is described in verses 24-27, and the psalm was evidently meant to be used at a celebration by the people in the Temple. Weiser suggests the autumnal Covenant Festival of Yahweh, which he considers to have been the most important of all festivals.

There is no way to show any progression of thought, and no outline is possible. The comments will try to identify separate units for purpose of discussion.

HEADING: "**A National Song of Triumph.**" Other headings are "Israel's triumphant march"; "The might and glory of God"; "God's triumphal procession." The TEV title may sometimes be rendered "A song for the nation that defeats its enemies."

Hebrew Title: **To the choirmaster. A Psalm of David. A Song** (TEV "A psalm by David; a song").

For **choirmaster** see title of Psalm 4; for **Song** see title of Psalm 65.

68.1-3

RSV	TEV
1 Let God arise, let his enemies be scattered; let those who hate him flee before him!	1 God rises up and scatters his enemies. Those who hate him run away in defeat.
2 As smoke is driven away, so drive them away; as wax melts before fire, let the wicked perish before God!	2 As smoke is blown away, so he drives them off; as wax melts in front of the fire, so do the wicked perish in God's presence.
3 But let the righteous be joyful; let them exult before God; let them be jubilant with joy!	3 But the righteous are glad and rejoice in his presence; they are happy and shout for joy.

The verbs in verse 1 may be understood as statements of regularly occurring events, as TEV, NEB, NAB, and TOB translate them (see Weiser, Briggs, Dahood; SPCL has "When God arises . . ."); NJV interprets them as future, "God will arise." RSV, NJB, NIV, and FRCL translate them as petitions. If the understanding is correct that this psalm was used in a service in the Temple celebrating God's victories, then the first interpretation seems more likely. But since this is quite uncertain, perhaps it is better to use the form of petition in verses 1-3.

The words of verse 1 are similar to those in Numbers 10.35, where God is called upon to arise and scatter his enemies. For **arise** see 3.7; 7.6; 9.19; 10.12; 12.5.

God's **enemies** (verse 1a) are called **those who hate him** (verse 1b) and **the wicked** (verse 2c).

In verse 2a God is addressed in the second person; for consistency with verse 1, TEV uses the third person.

Two figures are used in verse 2 to describe how quickly and thoroughly God will win the victory over his enemies: they are like **smoke** that is easily blown away (see 37.20 for the same figure) and like **wax** which the fire quickly melts (see also 22.14 and comments). In languages where the passive voice is uncommon or nonexistent, **smoke is driven away** must often be translated "As wind blows smoke away . . . ."

Perish before God: this describes not only location, that is, that they die in front of God rather than somewhere else; it implies also the effective cause of death, that is, God's presence will slay them.

Because God defeats his enemies, **the righteous** (that is, God's faithful people, the people of Israel) are called upon to rejoice and celebrate **before God**, meaning probably public worship in the Temple. In some languages **before God** or TEV's "in God's presence" may be rendered "where God is."

68.4 RSV	TEV

Sing to God, sing praises to his name;
   lift up a song to him who rides upon the clouds;*d*
his name is the LORD, exult before him!
	Sing to God, sing praises to his name;
	   prepare a way for him who rides on the clouds.*m*
	His name is the LORD—be glad in his presence!

d Or *cast up a highway for him who rides through the deserts*	*m* on the clouds; *or* across the desert.

This verse seems to be the beginning of a hymn celebrating God's power and majesty as "The Rider of the Clouds," with which verses 5-6 do not form a consistent whole. All three verses, however, praise God's power and his care for helpless and oppressed people.

For **name** in line a see 5.11.

The meaning of line b is doubtful. The verb translated "**prepare a way**" by TEV means **lift up** (RSV), and in other contexts it means "build a highway" (see Isa 40.3; 57.14; 62.10). So the Septuagint here has "make a road," and this is the meaning assigned by Oesterley, Dahood, BJ, NJB, RSV footnote. Others, however, take the verb to mean "lift up a song"; so Briggs and Anderson, citing Syriac and Targum (also RSV, NAB, NEB, NJV, NIV, AT, TOB, ZÜR, SPCL). It is up to the translator to decide which meaning to adopt.

Upon the clouds translates a Hebrew word which usually means "in the deserts"—so Oesterley, ZÜR, TOB, NEB, RSV footnote. Some, following the Septuagint, emend the Hebrew text to "on the clouds" (Briggs; NAB). The majority, however, take the Masoretic text word to be a defective spelling for "on the clouds," thus requiring no emendation (so Dahood), and this is the meaning represented by RSV, TEV, BJ, JB, NJV, AT, SPCL. The clouds were thought of as God's chariot (see 18.9-11; Deut 33.26; Isa 19.1).[1]

In line c the name of God is *Yah* (see KJV "JAH"), a shortened form of the usual Yahweh, and one which is found in the exhortation "Hallelujah!" (that is, "Praise Yah!").

68.5-6	RSV		TEV
5	Father of the fatherless and protector of widows is God in his holy habitation.	5	God, who lives in his sacred Temple, cares for orphans and protects widows.
6	God gives the desolate a home to dwell in; he leads out the prisoners to prosperity; but the rebellious dwell in a parched land.	6	He gives the lonely a home to live in and leads prisoners out into happy freedom, but rebels will have to live in a desolate land.

Orphans and widows in the Old Testament are traditionally representative of those who are defenseless, who have no one to take care of them and protect them. For Israelite society, only (adult) males had legal rights, which meant that orphans, widows, and resident aliens had no one in particular to defend their interests. The word protector translates a Hebrew word which means "judge" (see 1 Sam 24.15; see the related verb "to judge" in Psa 7.8). A just and compassionate judge would see to it that a widow's rights were respected by all.

"His sacred Temple" translates his holy habitation, which may be a reference to heaven (so Dahood).

The desolate in verse 6a are other people who, for whatever reason, are also alone; NEB translates "friendless." Instead of a home, perhaps "a family" would be more appropriate (see GECL, NIV).

Prosperity in verse 6b translates a plural word which occurs only here in the Old Testament. NEB has "brings out the prisoner safe and sound"; GECL "in freedom and happiness"; SPCL "he frees the prisoners and makes them prosperous"; and TOB

---

[1]HOTTP gives three possible interpretations of the Masoretic text and recommends the following: "Prepare the highway for him who rides upon the clouds; Lord is his name, and exult before him!"

"he sets free the prisoners by means of a happy deliverance." Dahood and others, on the basis of the Ugaritic, translate "to music" (see NIV); Weiser (footnote) has "accompanied by songs of rejoicing"; Taylor "with jubilations."

A parched land translates another word found only here in the Old Testament; it seems to mean "dry, scorched land." The Septuagint translates "in graves." Dahood takes the word to mean "Wasteland," as one of some thirty biblical names for the world of the dead. **The rebellious** may sometimes be translated in idiomatic terms; for example, "people whose hearts are hard toward God" or "people who say 'No' to God as leader."

68.7-8	RSV	TEV

RSV	TEV
7 O God, when thou didst go forth before thy people, when thou didst march through the wilderness, *Selah*	7 O God, when you led your people, when you marched across the desert,
8 the earth quaked, the heavens poured down rain, at the presence of God; yon Sinai quaked at the presence of God, the God of Israel.	8 the earth shook, and the sky poured down rain, because of the coming of the God of Sinai,*ⁿ* the coming of the God of Israel.

ⁿ GOD OF SINAI: *As the people of Israel went from Egypt to Canaan, God revealed himself to them at Mount Sinai (see Ex 19.16-25).*

In this strophe (verses 7-10) the events of the exodus from Egypt and the trek through the wilderness are recalled as proof of God's care for his people.

The two lines in verse 7 refer to the same event, and the reader should not think that the psalmist is referring to two different matters. So a translation can be "O God, when you led your people on the march through the wilderness . . . ."

For *Selah* see 3.2.

The earth quaked: earthquake and storm are associated with the coming of God to deliver his people (see 18.7-13). In verse 8b God is called **"the God of Sinai."** The Hebrew text is not too clear; it seems to say "God, the one of (or, this) Sinai" (see similar expression in Judges 5.5),[2] and this is the meaning given it by most modern commentators and translators. BJ and NJB omit "the one of Sinai" as a gloss; NEB has "the lord of Sinai." RSV (also SPCL) links the Hebrew phrase "this Sinai" to the verb **quaked** at the beginning of the verse, and repeats the verb (it is not repeated in the Hebrew text), **yon Sinai quaked**. It is best, then, to accept a form of the Hebrew text that appears as follows:

---

[2]HOTTP refers to Judges 5.5 and for both passages suggests "the One of Sinai" as the translation.

8b: before God, the one of Sinai,
8c: before God, the God of Israel.

For translation it is best to follow TEV, or else translate, like NIV, "before God, the One of Sinai"—but this may be awkward and unnatural in some languages, especially in those where the numeral "One" cannot stand alone.

In some languages it may be difficult and unnatural to address God in the second person in verse 7 and then refer to him in the third person in verse 8, so an adjustment may have to be made, such as "because you, the God of Israel came, you came, you who are the God of Sinai." In some languages TEV's **the God of Sinai** may require a more specific relation between Sinai and God. This may often be rendered, for example, "God who appeared at Sinai" or "God who spoke at Sinai." Sinai will be clearer in some languages if used with a classifier; for example, "the mountain called Sinai."

68.9-10	RSV	TEV

	RSV		TEV
9	Rain in abundance, O God, thou didst shed abroad; thou didst restore thy heritage as it languished;	9	You caused abundant rain to fall and restored your worn-out land;
10	thy flock found a dwelling in it; in thy goodness, O God, thou didst provide for the needy.	10	your people made their home there; in your goodness you provided for the poor.

Verses 9-10 can be related to the previous two verses, as RSV, TEV, and others do; they can, however, be separated from them, either as a description of what God customarily does ("You cause abundant rain to fall") or as a petition, "Your generous rain pour down, O God" (Dahood).

Rain in abundance (verse 9a) is the meaning given the Hebrew phrase by most commentators and translators; some, however, take it as a figure of the abundant supplies of manna and quail which God sent down on the Israelites during their years in the wilderness; so BJ, NJB "a shower of blessings."

In verse 9b **thy heritage** means "**your . . . land**" (see 16.6 and comments), a reference to Canaan, the Promised Land.

In verse 10 "**your people**" translates "your living ones," which some ancient versions took to refer to animals. RSV and NAB, **thy flock**, take it as a figure for the people of Israel. Others take it in the sense of "your community" (as "camp" in 2 Sam 21.13); so "thy congregation" (KJV), "your tribe" (NJV), "your family" (BJ, NJB). In any case the reference seems clearly to be to the people of Israel.

In thy goodness must often be recast as a causative clause; for example, "because you are good you provided for the poor."

For **the needy** see comments on "the afflicted" in 9.12.

	RSV		TEV
11	The Lord gives the command; great is the host of those who bore the tidings:	11	The Lord gave the command, and many women carried the news:
12	"The kings of the armies, they flee, they flee!" The women at home divide the spoil,	12	"Kings and their armies are run- ning away!" The women at home divided what was captured:
13	though they stay among the sheepfolds— the wings of a dove covered with silver, its pinions with green gold.	13	figures of doves covered with silver, whose wings glittered with fine gold. (Why did some of you stay among the sheep pens on the day of battle?)

There is no way of finding out what particular event or events verses 11-13 refer to.

In verse 11, at the Lord's **command** (or else, as SPCL has it, "sent a message"), "**many women carried the news**" (see also GECL, SPCL). This translates the Masoretic text, which is a feminine plural participle of the verb "to carry news" (*basar*); see the feminine singular in Isaiah 40.9, applied to Zion. In other places women are cited as those who carried the news of victory or defeat; see Exodus 15.20-21; 1 Samuel 18.6-7.

TEV, RSV, NEB, and SPCL take verse 12a as the message carried by the women; NJV, NIV, and GECL take verses 12-13 to be the message, and NAB and FRCL take verses 12-14 as the message. There is no way of determining which is correct. In some languages it will be necessary to use a term pointing to the next line as containing the content of the news mentioned in line b. Punctuation such as a colon will not suffice in some languages for this purpose.

In verse 12a the Hebrew text is literally **The kings of the armies, they flee, they flee!** But it should be observed that it is not only the kings who flee, but their armies also, as TEV and others make clear.

The women at home translates an obscure phrase which appears to mean "she who remains at home" (see the lexicon of Brown, Driver, and Briggs).

In Hebrew the enigmatic "If you (masculine plural) lie down between the sheep pens" appears as the first line of verse 13. NJV translates "even for those of you who lie among the sheepfolds." Some take the words to have been inserted here from Judges 5.16. It seems to be here a denunciation of those Israelites who did not go to battle but stayed behind in the safety of their homes or their camps. TOB has "Would you remain at ease at the bivouac?"; SPCL "but you stayed back in hiding"; NJB "While you are at ease in the sheepfolds"; and NEB "will you linger among the sheepfolds . . . ?" **Sheepfolds** in some languages may be rendered as "the place where the sheep are kept."

TEV has put this within parentheses, as a prose line, and placed it after the other two lines of verse 13, in order to show its discontinuity from the immediately preceding and following lines. FRCL similarly, translating "Will you remain resting in the camp?"

There are many interpretations of what is meant in verse 13b,c, by **the wings of a dove covered with silver, its pinions with green gold**. The most commonly accepted interpretation is that followed by TEV as a description of the spoil that the women were dividing among themselves. Some take the dove to be a figure for Israel (see 74.19); so NJB "the wings of the Dove are being covered with silver . . . ," with a footnote explaining that the Dove is a symbol for Israel (similarly TOB). In verse 13c **green gold** probably means "yellow gold," that is, "**fine gold**" (so TEV, SPCL). The NJV translation of verses 12-13 (as the message carried by the women) is worth quoting: "The kings and their armies are in headlong flight; housewives are sharing in the spoils; even for those of you who lie among the sheepfolds there are wings of a dove sheathed in silver, its pinions in fine gold."

In some languages it will be necessary to replace the TEV colon at the end of line 12b with a connective showing that the content of the things captured follows in the next line; for example, ". . . divided what was captured and these were figures of doves . . . ."

68.14   RSV   TEV

> When the Almighty scattered kings there,
> snow fell on Zalmon.

> When Almighty God scattered the kings on Mount Zalmon,
> he caused snow to fall there.

The Hebrew title translated **the Almighty** here is *shadday* (also 91.1b), which in Exodus 6.3 is the name by which God made himself known to the patriarchs. The English **Almighty** follows the Septuagint and Vulgate.

The Old Testament makes no mention of a defeat of kings on Mount Zalmon. There was a Mount Zalmon near Shechem (Judges 9.48), a town some 12 kilometers southeast of the city of Samaria, but it does not seem likely that this is the hill referred to here. The name Zalmon means "dark, black." The reference to snow (the Masoretic text "you made it snow") may be understood literally, as RSV, TEV, NAB, TOB, FRCL, and SPCL have done. Others, however, take it to be a figure, perhaps of the bleached bones of the enemy dead scattered on the hillside; NJV "When Shaddai scattered the kings, it seemed like a snowstorm in Zalmon" (similarly NEB, NIV). It may be advisable to follow NJV. In languages where snow is unknown, it is sometimes possible to substitute the morning dew, or hail.

68.15-16   RSV   TEV

15 O mighty mountain, mountain of Bashan;
    O many-peaked mountain, mountain of Bashan!
16 Why look you with envy, O many-peaked mountain,

15 What a mighty mountain is Bashan,
    a mountain of many peaks!
16 Why from your mighty peaks do you look with scorn
    on the mountain[o] on which God

<table>
<tr><td>at the mount which God desired
for his abode,
yea, where the LORD will dwell
for ever?</td><td>chose to live?
The LORD will live there for-
ever!</td></tr>
</table>

^o MOUNTAIN: *See 2.6*

Bashan was a territory on the east side of the Jordan River (see 22.12); other than in this psalm there is no reference to a mountain there or to a conflict between those who claimed that Zion was the holy mountain and those who said that a mountain in Bashan was. Some take this to be a reference to Mount Hermon, which was considered to be the dwelling place of the gods of Canaan. This mountain is here called "mountain of God" (or, the gods), that is, "mountain *'elohim*," which TEV, RSV, SPCL, and Dahood take as a superlative, **mighty mountain**; NIV and NJV have "majestic mountain(s)." But there are translations which have "mountain of God"; some phrase and punctuate verse 15a in a way that implies that the psalmist was stating that Mount Bashan was indeed "a mountain of God" (NJB; NEB "a hill of God"; FRCL "The mountain of Bashan is a sacred mountain").

It seems reasonable to suppose that Mount Bashan is rebuked for its envy of Mount Zion, **"the mountain on which God chose to live"** (TEV), that is, desired or longed for as his dwelling, and where he will live forever. In many languages which have only a term for a hill or slight elevation, there is no term for **"peaks."** However, in such languages one may be able to say "a hill that has many high places." Others say "rugged mountain."

In many languages it will be necessary to make clear that the question is addressed to the mountain of Bashan. Since in many languages it will seem strange to accuse one mountain of being envious of another, it will often be necessary to shift to some kind of simile; for example, "Why do you, Bashan mountain, look with envy at the other mountain where the Lord chose to live, like one person looks at another with envy?" Or we may translate "Why do you people who worship on Bashan Mountain look with envy at those who worship on the mountain where God chose to live?"

68.17-18   RSV   TEV

17 With **mighty chariotry, twice ten thousand,**
    thousands upon thousands,
    the Lord came from Sinai into
    the holy place.^e
18 Thou didst ascend the high
    mount,
    leading captives in thy train,
    and receiving gifts among men,
    even among the rebellious, that
        the LORD God may dwell
        there.

17 With his many thousands of
    mighty chariots
    the Lord comes from Sinai^p
    into the holy place.
18 He goes up to the heights,
    taking many captives with him;
    he receives gifts from rebellious
        men.
    The LORD God will live there.

^p *Probable text* comes from Sinai; *Hebrew* in them, Sinai.

^e Cn: Heb *The Lord among them Sinai in
the holy place*

These two verses speak of Yahweh's victories over his enemies; the thought seems to be that, after defeating the hostile kings and peoples in and around Canaan, Yahweh goes from Sinai to Mount Zion and makes his residence there.

In verse 17a **mighty (chariotry)** translates the superlative force of *'elohim* (as in verse 15); some have "the chariots of God" (NEB, TOB, NIV, NJB, NJV). Following both TEV and RSV the expression **mighty chariotry** must be rendered in some languages as "cars for making war" or "horse wagons for fighting." In many languages an illustration or note will be required in the glossary, as this term occurs several times. The number of the chariots, **twice ten thousand, thousands upon thousands**, is not meant to be exact; it is a way of saying "many thousands" or "the millions" (SPCL). Or else, "too many to count," "more than can be numbered."

Verse 17c in the Masoretic text is unclear: "the Lord (is) in them Sinai in (or, into) the holy place." Anderson quotes with approval Aubrey Johnson's translation of the Masoretic text: "the Lord is amid them, the God of Sinai is in the sanctuary"; but this involves taking the word "Sinai" to mean "the God of Sinai." NJV translates the Masoretic text "the Lord is among them as in Sinai in holiness," and TOB "the Lord is among them; Sinai is in the sanctuary." None of these is very satisfactory, and their explanations seem forced. Most translations (RSV, TEV, NEB, NAB, BJ, NJB, NIV, FRCL) adopt an emended text which is suggested by Deuteronomy 33.2: "The Lord came from Sinai." Instead of **into the holy place**, NEB translates the Hebrew phrase by "in holiness." **The holy place** is the Temple in Jerusalem.

In verse 18 Yahweh is addressed in the second person; TEV has changed to third person, for consistency with verse 17. **The high mount** is probably Mount Zion (see 47.5); some, however, take it to mean heaven. Dahood takes it to mean Mt. Sinai.

Leading captives in thy train is literally "you capture captives." In triumphal procession, like that of a victorious king, Yahweh takes **captives** with him as he goes up Mount Zion; they are his defeated enemies, "**rebellious men**" (TEV) who have to pay tribute (**gifts**) to the victorious God.

The last line of verse 18 is not very clear in Hebrew. Following "even the rebels" come the words "for the dwelling (participle) of Yah Elohim"; but there are other possibilities. SPCL has "and even the rebels surrendered to you, Lord." NEB declares the Hebrew unintelligible and translates the Syriac, "in the presence of the LORD God no rebel could live." BJ has "yes, take rebels to your dwelling, Yahweh!" HOTTP, similarly, "and even the adversaries may dwell with the Lord God." NJV has "even of those who rebel against the Lord God's abiding there." AT, NAB, and Weiser are like RSV and TEV. It is best to follow the example of RSV and TEV.

LORD translates the name *Yah*, as in verse 4c.

In Ephesians 4.8 part of verse 18 is quoted, following the Septuagint, with a change from "you received . . . from" to "he gave . . . to."

RSV   TEV

19   Blessed be the Lord,   19   Praise the Lord,
        who daily bears us up;   who carries our burdens day
        God is our salvation.   *Selah*   after day;
20   Our God is a God of salvation;   he is the God who saves us.
        and to GOD, the Lord, belongs   20   Our God is a God who saves;
        escape from death.   he is the LORD, our Lord,
                                                  who rescues us from death.

The psalmist praises the Lord for his provident care and salvation. For **Blessed be** see 18.46 and comment. **Bears us up** translates the verb "carry a load." And **daily** also can be understood to modify **Blessed be the Lord** (so Anderson; FRCL); but it is best to follow RSV and TEV here.

Salvation in verse 20a translates a word found only here in the Old Testament, literally "saving actions," a word that is related to the verb "to save," which is often used in the psalms (see comments on "Help" in 12.1).

In verse 20b the Hebrew is "Yahweh the Lord" (Dahood "the Lord Yahweh"); he is spoken of as the one to whom belong "the escapes from death," which FRCL translates "he has ways of allowing us to escape from death." TOB has "the gates of death belong to God the Lord." By this is meant that the Lord has the power to save his people from death in battle at the hands of the enemy.

RSV   TEV

21   But God will shatter the heads of   21   God will surely break the heads of
        his enemies,   his enemies,
        the hairy crown of him who   of those who persist in their
        walks in his guilty ways.   sinful ways.
22   The Lord said,   22   The Lord has said, "I will bring
        "I will bring them back from   your enemies back from Ba-
        Bashan,   shan;
        I will bring them back from the   I will bring them back from the
        depths of the sea,   depths of the ocean,
23   that you may bathe*f* your feet in   23   so that you may wade in their
        blood,   blood,
        that the tongues of your dogs   and your dogs may lap up as
        may have their portion from   much as they want."
        the foe."

f Gk Syr Tg: Heb *shatter*

The psalmist proclaims God's power to defeat his enemies and God's promise to his people that they will celebrate his victory over them.

In verse 21a the expression **will shatter the heads of his enemies** may be taken quite literally in the sense of "smashing" or "breaking" their heads, or else as a vivid way of portraying complete victory over the enemies; see in RSV the same verb **shatter** at 62.3; 110.5,6.

In verse 21b **the hairy crown** is parallel to **the heads** in line a. Some take this phrase to refer to the custom of warriors not cutting their hair while engaged in holy wars. NEB has "flowing locks"; NJB "long-haired skull."

In verse 22 the verb **bring back** does not have an object in Hebrew; TEV, RSV, NAB (see Anderson) understand the unexpressed object to be "your enemies"; Toombs and SPCL take "you" (that is, the Israelites) as the object; NJV, BJ, TOB have no object (literally translating the Hebrew); NEB and Weiser emend the text (following the Septuagint) to get "I will return." It seems that "the blood of the enemies" in verse 23 makes it very likely that they, the enemies, are the object in verse 22.

For **Bashan** see verse 15; its significance here, especially with **the depths of the sea** in verse 22b, is difficult to assess. Both lines, b and c, seem to represent, perhaps in general terms, the highest peaks and the lowest depths of the earth to which the enemies had fled in order to escape from God (see the same thought, in similar language, in Amos 9.2-3). Others consider Bashan to be a reference to the mythological Dragon (so NEB), a symbol of the forces of chaos and destruction.

In verse 23a, for TEV **"wade in their blood,"** see the similar image in 58.10. The verb in the Masoretic text is *mahats* "to break" (as in verse 21a), which does not fit the context; Briggs, Oesterley, Weiser, Taylor, RSV, NAB, and others emend, with the Septuagint, Syriac, and Targum, to *rahats* "wade" (as in 58.10). But some (NEB, NJV, TOB, BJ) appeal to an Arabic cognate to get from the Masoretic text the meaning "wade, dabble, churn."

For the picture of dogs lapping up human blood see 1 Kings 21.19; 22.38. RSV translates literally, showing the Hebrew poetic figure of the dogs receiving their share of the victory spoils.

68.24-25 RSV	TEV
24 Thy solemn processions are seen,^{g} O God, the processions of my God, my King, into the sanctuary—	24 O God, your march of triumph is seen by all, the procession of God, my king, into his sanctuary.
25 the singers in front, the minstrels last, between them maidens playing timbrels:	25 The singers are in front, the musicians are behind, in between are the girls beating the tambourines.

^{g} Or *have been seen*

This section (verses 24-27) describes God's **solemn processions** into the Temple, celebrating his victories over Israel's enemies. The order of the procession (verses 25,27) is fairly clearly stated. The entrance of Yahweh into the Temple was probably represented by the priests carrying in the Covenant Box. The plural **processions** may be taken to refer to various processions, or it may be understood as a superlative, "a great procession." **Thy solemn processions** is difficult to express where such formal movements of people are not practiced. However, it is often possible to translate the idea as a time clause; for example, "when you go like a chief" or "when you walk like a soldier." Note that God is referred to as **my King**.

The minstrels (TEV "The musicians") played stringed instruments. In contemporary English **minstrels** (RSV, NAB, NEB) is highly misleading. "**Tambourines**" (RSV **timbrels**) were small one-headed hand drums, sometimes with metallic disks or jingles attached to the sides, which were regularly played by women (see Exo 15.20, of Miriam and her companions).

The Hebrew for **maidens** refers to young girls of marriageable age.

68.26-27	RSV	TEV

| 26 | "Bless God in the great congregation, <br> the LORD, O you who are of Israel's fountain!" | 26 | "Praise God in the meeting of his people;
 praise the LORD, all you descendants of Jacob!" |
| 27 | There is Benjamin, the least of them, in the lead, <br> the princes of Judah in their throng, <br> the princes of Zebulun, the princes of Naphtali. | 27 | First comes Benjamin, the smallest tribe, <br> then the leaders of Judah with their group, <br> followed by the leaders of Zebulun and Naphtali. |

Some device must be used to let the hearer know that verse 26 is the song that is being sung by the people in the procession. A colon or quotation marks, while helpful to the reader, are of no use to the hearer.

The song used in the procession (verse 26) calls on all the people to "**praise God**" (literally, **Bless**—see comments at 16.7) **in the great congregation** (for similar language see 22.25; 35.18; 40.9,10). The Hebrew plural "congregations" is taken as a superlative by RSV, TEV, and others; some, however, take it to refer to different groups: "in choirs" (NAB, NJB), "in assemblies" (NJV).

You who are of Israel's fountain (verse 26b) translates the phrase "from the well, spring, of Israel"; it is a strange expression, but commentators take it to mean "all true Israelites" (so Anderson), with **fountain** referring to the reproductive organs of their common ancestor. In Deuteronomy 33.28 "fountain of Jacob" is parallel to "Israel" (see also Isa 48.1). NJV "you who are from the fountain of Israel" seems to intend to mean "you descendants of Israel." With a slight change in the Hebrew text, the phrase can be read "Fountain of Jacob" as a title of God. NEB considers the Hebrew obscure and emends the text to get "all Israel assembled" (also SPCL). NIV, without any textual footnote, translates "in the assembly of Israel."

The word translated **the least of them** in verse 27a can mean "youngest" (Weiser, BJ, NJB, TOB). **In the lead** translates a verb which may mean "to rule, dominate"; so Jerome, NJV, and Briggs, who sees in it a reference to Saul, Israel's first king. TOB rejects this word as being unintelligible, as well as the word in the next line translated **in their throng**, and places ellipses in the text.

In some languages it will be clearer to say "first come the people of the smallest clan called Benjamin." "Clan," or some other division within the ethnic

588

group, is preferable to "tribe," since the term "tribe" or "race" will imply that the different clans were not related.

In their throng translates another word of uncertain meaning. NJV translates "who command them." One Hebrew manuscript has "in their many-colored garments"; so BJ, NJB, FRCL. It is best to stay with RSV and TEV.

It is not certain why these four tribes are mentioned; **Benjamin** and **Judah** were in the south, and **Zebulun** and **Naphtali** were in the north.

68.28-29   RSV   TEV

28   Summon thy might, O God;   28   Show your power, O God,
        show thy strength, O God, thou   the power you have used on our
        who hast wrought for us.   behalf
29   Because of thy temple at Jerusa-   29   from your Temple in Jerusalem,
        lem   where kings bring gifts to you.
        kings bear gifts to thee.

In this section (verses 28-31) God is called upon to display his power and defeat the enemies of Israel.

In verse 28a the Masoretic text is "Your God has ordered your strength," which is an obscure statement; presumably "your" refers to Israel. TOB ("your God has decided that you will be strong") and NJV ("Your God has ordained strength for you") follow the Masoretic text, which is what HOTTP recommends. But many Hebrew manuscripts have what RSV, TEV, and NAB translate; BJ and NJB emend the text. If the translator follows TEV "**show your power**," it will be necessary in many languages to recast this expression so as to say "show the people that you are powerful" or "show that you are strong."

It seems better to connect the first line of verse 29 to verse 28, as TEV, NJV, BJ, and NJB have done, than to translate **Because of thy temple at Jerusalem**, as RSV has done. Or else, a translator may choose to do what FRCL and SPCL have done and connect verse 29 with verse 30, translating the beginning of verse 29 "From your Temple in Jerusalem . . ." and continuing in the same sentence to verse 30, which begins with the imperative verb "rebuke the beasts . . . ." NEB reverses the two lines of verse 29 and translates "command kings to bring gifts to thee for the honour of thy temple in Jerusalem."

68.30-31   RSV   TEV

30   Rebuke the beasts that dwell   30   Rebuke Egypt, that wild animal in
        among the reeds,   the reeds;
        the herd of bulls with the calves   rebuke the nations, that herd of
        of the peoples.   bulls with their calves,
     Trample*h* under foot those who   until they all bow down and
        lust after tribute;   offer you their silver.
        scatter the peoples who delight   Scatter those people who love to
        in war.*i*   make war!*q*

589

31 Let bronze be brought from Egypt;	31 Ambassadors[r] will come from Egypt;
let Ethiopia hasten to stretch out her hands to God.	the Ethiopians will raise their hands in prayer to God.

[h] Cn: Heb *trampling*
[i] The Hebrew of verse 30 is obscure

[q] *Verse 30 in Hebrew is unclear.*
[r] *Some ancient translations* Ambassadors; *Hebrew unclear.*

Verse 30 is difficult to understand, and the last two lines are incomprehensible in Hebrew; commentators and translators are widely divided in their understanding of the verse.

In line a the Hebrew phrase "the beasts of the reeds" is taken by most commentators to be a reference to the hippopotamus, a symbol of Egypt (see similar language in Ezek 29.3). So NJB "The Beast of the Reeds."

Line b is literally "the groups of bulls with the calves (of) the people," which TEV has taken as a symbol of other nations; some, however, take this to be parallel with line a, as a reference to Egypt. So FRCL, "Hurl your threats at Egypt, that beast of the reeds, that herd of bulls, that lord of peoples . . . ." RSV does not make sense in English. "**Bulls with their calves**" is probably a symbol of more powerful nations ("bulls") accompanied by weaker, dependent nations ("calves"). Dahood takes the last word of the line, "peoples," to go with the following line, thus translating, "who trampled on peoples in his lust for silver," which makes good sense. If the translator follows the lead given by TEV, it will often be necessary to make the comparison more explicit than in TEV; for example, "rebuke Egypt which is like a wild animal . . ." or "rebuke the nations which are like a herd of bulls with their calves."

There are various translations for the third line, as it stands in the Masoretic text; RSV and TEV have two of them. Anderson thinks RSV **tribute** is defensible, representing the Hebrew word "silver." There is much uncertainty over the form and meaning of the first word (RSV footnote "trampling"); Briggs takes it to be a form of the verb "to humble oneself," which TEV has represented by "**until they all bow down**" (similarly Weiser; NJV "till they come cringing with pieces of silver"—and see also NAB, BJ, NJB). SPCL has "who in their lust for silver humiliate the peoples."

By a simple change of vowels in line d, the beginning verb can be read as an imperative: **scatter** (so nearly all translations and commentaries); TOB translates the Masoretic text "he has scattered."[3]

The common noun in the first line of verse 31 appears nowhere else in the Old Testament; it seems to mean bronze objects (so K-B, RSV; Dahood "blue cloth"). It

---

[3]HOTTP says that the meaning of the whole passage, verses 28-30 (verses 29-31 in the Masoretic text) is as follows:

V.29 your God commanded your strength: strengthen, O God, what you have done for us! V.30 in your palace in Jerusalem: to you the kings bring tribute. V.31 rebuke the beast of the reeds, the assembly of the mighty ones with the bulls of the nations (who) bow down with bars of silver (or: [who] trample each other for bars of silver). He has scattered the peoples (which) delight in wars.

seems better to follow the Septuagint, Syriac, and Vulgate, "ambassadors, nobles."[4] If the translator follows TEV, **"ambassadors"** may sometimes be translated "officials sent by the government" or simply "officials."

Ethiopia is the traditional translation of the biblical place name "Cush." But the territory occupied by the modern country of Sudan more nearly corresponds to the territory south of Egypt occupied by "Cush," and so TEV has used "Sudan" to represent the biblical Cush. NEB and TOB translate here "Nubia." It is recommended that the word be translated **Ethiopia**, with a footnote indicating that at that time it was a country on the border of Egypt (see Ezek 29.10).

The verb in verse 31b seems to be the word for "to hurry," and so the phrase seems to mean literally "Cush is to hurry its hands," which HOTTP takes to mean "to bring tribute in haste (to God)" (see the same verb in 1 Sam 17.17, "carry . . . quickly"). But on the basis of Akkadian parallels, the meaning "extend the hands" is possible; this could be **"in prayer,"** as TEV has, or to present gifts (NJV). The context favors the latter.

68.32-33	RSV	TEV
32	Sing to God, O kingdoms of the earth; sing praises to the Lord, *Selah*	32 Sing to God, kingdoms of the world, sing praise to the Lord,
33	to him who rides in the heavens, the ancient heavens; lo, he sends forth his voice, his mighty voice.	33 to him who rides in the sky, the ancient sky. Listen to him shout with a mighty roar.

The final section (verses 32-35) calls on all people everywhere (**kingdoms of the earth**) to praise God. **Kingdoms of the earth** can best be translated in the present context as "the peoples of all the countries of the world." In some languages it is not possible for nations or countries to sing. Therefore it is necessary to say "Sing to God, you people of all nations."

The two verbs in verse 32 are the same as in verse 4a, and verse 33a,b is similar in expression to verse 4b. **The ancient heavens**: created at the beginning of the world (Gen 1.1).

In verse 33, TEV's third line, **"Listen"** translates a word that serves to call attention to what follows; NEB "Hark!" and RSV **lo** are both rather archaic. **His mighty voice** is a way of speaking about thunder (see discussion at 29.3-4), which was thought of as the sound of God's voice.

---

[4]HOTTP says that the meaning of the Hebrew word is no longer clear, and that the two best attested interpretations are "red stuff" and "the great ones."

68.34-35 RSV	TEV
34 Ascribe power to God, whose majesty is over Israel, and his power is in the skies.	34 Proclaim God's power; his majesty is over Israel, his might is in the skies.
35 Terrible is God in his*j* sanctuary, the God of Israel, he gives power and strength to his people.	35 How awesome is God as he comes from his sanctuary— the God of Israel! He gives strength and power to his people.
Blessed be God!	
	Praise God!

j Gk: Heb *from thy*

In verse 34 the people of the world are exhorted to recognize and confess God's power (RSV **Ascribe**; TEV "Proclaim"), whose **majesty** as ruler of the people of Israel has been manifested, and whose **power** is displayed in **the skies** (literally "the clouds," which here is a synonym for "the heavens" in verse 33). In some languages **Ascribe power to God** may be rendered "Say that God is powerful." **Whose majesty is over Israel** must often be recast in translation so that majesty is expressed as a verb phrase; for example, "who rules as king over Israel." **His power is in the skies** may sometimes be rendered in translation as "the skies show his power" or "the skies show how powerful he is."

Terrible (verse 35a) is highly inappropriate; see comments on "dread" in 65.5. The Hebrew text is "God (you are) awesome from your sanctuary," which TEV (with a change to the third person) has translated "**as he comes from his sanctuary**"; RSV **in** is a translation of the Septuagint text (see also NIV). Since the emotion of terror or awesomeness is produced on the people, it is often possible in translation to express this in idiomatic terms such as "how a person's insides tremble . . ." or "how the heart flutters when God comes from . . . ." The Hebrew word is plural, "sanctuaries," which RSV, TEV, and others take to be an intensive plural ("a large/magnificent sanctuary"); NJV and TOB translate it by a plural. Commentators are not agreed whether God's sanctuary here is the Temple in Jerusalem or heaven. **Sanctuary** may be rendered in some languages "God's holy place" or "the place where God lives."

The word **strength** translates a word not found elsewhere in the Old Testament; the related verb "be mighty" is used in 38.19.

For comments on **Blessed be** see 18.46.

Psalm 69

This psalm is a prayer for help to God by an individual who is sick (verse 29), persecuted by enemies (verses 4, 26), and abandoned by family and friends (verse 8). He confesses his sins (verse 5) and asks the Lord to save him and punish his enemies (verses 14-15, 22-29). In return he will praise God and proclaim his greatness (verse 30).

There is no specific information in the psalm that allows us to determine with assurance the time and place of its composition. The psalmist's deep love for the Temple, and his dedication to religious practices, for which he was criticized and ridiculed (verses 9-12), indicate controversy about ritual matters. If verses 35-36 are part of the original composition, it is probable that the psalm was composed during the time when the Israelites were in exile in Babylonia.

The psalm opens with a cry to God for help (verses 1-3), followed by a denunciation of the psalmist's enemies (verse 4), a confession of sin (verse 5), and a prayer for guidance (verses 6-8). The psalmist describes his situation (verses 9-21), alternating between defending himself, asking for help, and picturing his desperate condition. He then prays that God will punish and destroy his enemies (verses 22-28), and again asks God to save him (verse 29). After promising to praise God for his help (verses 30-33), the psalmist closes with a call for all the world to praise God (verse 34), in the confident assurance that God will restore his land and people to peace and prosperity (verses 35-36).

HEADING: "**A Cry for Help.**" Other headings are "A cry of anguish"; "Prayer of the persecuted"; "Piety mocked." The TEV title in some languages will require slight recasting so that verb phrases can be used; for example, "The psalmist cries to God and asks God to help him" or "The psalmist prays and asks God to help him."

Hebrew Title: **To the choirmaster: according to Lilies. A Psalm of David** (TEV "By David").

For **choirmaster** see title of Psalm 4; for **according to Lilies** see title of Psalm 45.

69.1-2

RSV	TEV

1   Save me, O God!
    For the waters have come up to
      my neck.
2   I sink in deep mire,
    where there is no foothold;
	1 Save me, O God!
	    The water is up to my neck;
	2 I am sinking in deep mud,
	    and there is no solid ground;
	    I am out in deep water,

<table>
<tr><td>I have come into deep waters,
and the flood sweeps over me.</td><td>and the waves are about to drown me.</td></tr>
</table>

The psalmist compares his difficult and dangerous situation to that of someone who is about to drown. All the figures used, **waters . . . up to my neck**, **deep mire**, **deep waters**, and **flood**, indicate extreme danger and peril of death; see 18.16; 40.2, for similar descriptions. Either the psalmist is dangerously ill, or his enemies are threatening his life.

The psalmist is using an exaggerated form of imagery here for the purpose of making his plight vivid and picturable. In some languages the imagery used may be so unnatural that it may be necessary to substitute others. To translate the figures of verses 1-2 in nonfigurative language and at the same time keep a semblance of poetic form would be extremely difficult and is not generally recommended.

In verse 1b **neck** translates the word *nefesh*.[1]

In verse 2b the word translated **foothold** (TEV "**solid ground**") occurs nowhere else in the Old Testament. It is related to the verb meaning "to stand" or "to take a stand."

The flood sweeps over me: literally "flowing waters wash over me." The picture may be from either an ocean or a flooded and swiftly-moving river.

The translator may find the logical sequence unclear; for example, in verse 1 the water is said to be up to the psalmist's neck, and it is only later in 2c that the writer is said to be in danger of drowning. This is because verse 1 depicts a general condition, and verse 2, specific aspects of that condition. In order to clarify this picture in some languages, the translator may find it clearer to place lines c and d at the beginning and to follow verse 2 with verse 1; for example, "I am out in deep water, and the waves are about to drown me. I am sinking in deep mud and there is no solid ground; the water is up to my neck; save me, O God!

<u>69.3</u>   RSV   TEV

<table>
<tr><td>I am weary with my crying;
my throat is parched.
My eyes grow dim
with waiting for my God.</td><td>I am worn out from calling for help,
and my throat is aching.
I have strained my eyes,
looking for your help.</td></tr>
</table>

The psalmist has been ceaselessly praying for God to help him, but as yet his prayer has not been answered. For similar language see 6.6-7.

In line b the verb translated **is parched** occurs only here in the Old Testament.

Waiting for my God in line d implies "waiting for my God to save me." For comments on the verb "to wait," see 31.24. It may be better to translate "looking for you, my God, to come and help/save me."

TEV "**for your help**" uses the second person of address, in keeping with the second person of verse 1.

---

[1] See Peacock (1976), page 217.

　　　　　RSV　　　　　　　　　　　　　　　　　　TEV

More in number than the hairs of
  my head
are those who hate me without
  cause;
mighty are those who would destroy me,
those who attack me with lies.
What I did not steal
  must I now restore?

Those who hate me for no reason
  are more numerous than the
  hairs of my head.
My enemies tell lies against me;
  they are strong and want to kill
  me.
They made me give back things I
  did not steal.

The psalmist denounces his enemies, people who hate him **without cause**, that is, people who have no reason to hate him (see 35.19 for a similar statement). They are many, more **than the hairs of my head**, he says (see the same figure used in 40.12).

In line <u>c</u> **mighty** translates a verb that may mean "(they) are many" (see the same verb in 38.19; 40.12). **Destroy** translates a verb which means "put to silence," that is, to put to death; but NEB and Dahood prefer to emend to a form meaning "more than my locks" (parallel to "more than my hairs" in line <u>a</u>); Syriac has "more than my bones." It is best to stay with the interpretation of RSV and TEV.

Those who attack me with lies translates a two-word phrase, "my enemies *sheqer*." Elsewhere this Hebrew word is translated "(who are my enemies) without cause" (see comments on 35.19; 38.19b), and this is probably the meaning here, parallel with line <u>a</u>; so TOB, BJ, NIV, NJV, AT, NAB, SPCL.

The last line in this verse can be understood as a rhetorical question (RSV and others); it implies that the enemies have falsely accused the psalmist of theft and have tried to force him to return what in fact he did not steal. NEB translates "How can I give back what I have not stolen?" Perhaps this was a proverbial statement, used by anyone who had been wrongfully accused of a crime (see a similar situation in 35.11).

What is the first line of the verse in TEV is quoted (from the Septuagint) in John 15.25; see also Psalm 35.19.

　　　　　RSV　　　　　　　　　　　　　　　　　　TEV

O God, thou knowest my folly;
  the wrongs I have done are not
  hidden from thee.

My sins, O God, are not hidden
  from you;
  you know how foolish I have
  been.

The psalmist confesses his **wrongs**, convinced that they are the cause of his misfortune, which is seen as God's just punishment. The **folly** he confesses is his disregard of God's laws (see comments on "foolishness" in 38.5b). TEV has reversed the two lines for greater ease of understanding. **Thou knowest my folly** is sometimes rendered idiomatically as "you know I have had a twisted heart" or "you know that my heart has led me on a bad path."

In some languages it is not possible or at least not natural to say that one's sins **are not hidden from thee**. In such cases it will be necessary to switch to an active expression. However, the sense is that God knows fully the sins of the writer, and therefore one may translate "You know full well all my sins, O God."

69.6   RSV   TEV

> Let not those who hope in thee be
>   put to shame through me,
> O Lord GOD of hosts;
> let not those who seek thee be
>   brought to dishonor through
>   me,
> O God of Israel.

> Don't let me bring shame on those
>   who trust in you,
> Sovereign LORD Almighty!
> Don't let me bring disgrace to
>   those who worship you,
> O God of Israel!

The verse is composed of two parallel and almost synonymous affirmations; **hope in thee** expresses "**trust in you**" (TEV), while **seek thee** means "**worship you**" (TEV); **put to shame** means **brought to dishonor.**

The psalmist prays that God will keep him from bringing **shame** and **dishonor** on his fellow Israelites who are devout like him. What seems to be meant is that if he, the psalmist, is not vindicated, not helped by God, then his fellow Israelites who believe as he does will be disappointed and disillusioned, sharing his shame and disgrace.

Hope in thee translates "wait for you" (see 25.3 and comment); and for **seek thee** see comments on 24.6b. The expression **who hope in thee be put to shame** is often rendered idiomatically; for example, "who place their heart on you should not be caused to have hot faces."

Lord GOD of hosts represents the Hebrew "Lord Yahweh of armies," an unusual combination of divine titles; for comments on "Yahweh of armies," see 46.7. RSV has **Lord GOD** with "GOD" in uppercase letters, to avoid saying "Lord LORD" for "Lord Yahweh." **Lord GOD of hosts** may in some languages be rendered "Lord GOD, you who are the most powerful" or "Lord GOD, you who have the strength of armies."

Dishonor and TEV "**disgrace**" are often rendered idiomatically in some languages; for example, "to speak words against" or "to take away the praise."

69.7-8   RSV   TEV

7   For it is for thy sake that I have
        borne reproach,
    that shame has covered my
        face.
8   I have become a stranger to my
        brethren,
    an alien to my mother's sons.

7   It is for your sake that I have
        been insulted
    and that I am covered with
        shame.
8   I am like a stranger to my
        brothers,
    like a foreigner to my family.

Both verses 7 and 8 show heightening in the second line, in which the poetic movement is from the general to the more particular, and so is more dramatic. In verse 7 line b may be rendered "I am even covered with shame," or in some languages "I even feel the heat on my face."

The psalmist protests that it is because of his devotion to God and the Temple (verse 7, with a more detailed expression of this in verses 9-11) that he is insulted, scorned, mocked, ridiculed. For other comments on the expression **shame has covered my face**, see 44.15. **It is for thy sake** is sometimes rendered, for example, "because of you," "because I worship you," or "in order to please you."

My mother's sons represents a dramatization or intensification of the movement between lines a and b. In line a **brethren** refers to the psalmist's fellow Israelites, while **mother's sons** in line b refers more specifically to his blood brothers and sisters, that is, children of his parents. The two lines are saying, for example, "I have become a stranger to my fellow Israelites; even to my own brothers and sisters I have become a foreigner." In many languages "brothers" will mean brothers and cousins. It may be necessary in line b to say, for example, "the siblings (brothers and sisters) my mother gave birth to."

69.9	RSV	TEV

For zeal for thy house has consumed me, and the insults of those who insult thee have fallen on me.	My devotion to your Temple burns in me like a fire; the insults which are hurled at you fall on me.

In a way which is not clear, it was the psalmist's intense devotion to the Temple in Jerusalem that created trouble for him. Some suggest that he was like the prophets Haggai and Zechariah, whose deep commitment to the rebuilding of the Temple after the Israelites had returned from exile in Babylonia aroused hostility and opposition. The psalmist felt that the Temple was being scorned or misused, and since it was the dwelling of the God of Israel, any insult (from the psalmist's point of view) directed at the Temple was an affront to God; and the psalmist felt as though these affronts had been directed against him personally.

Verse 9a is quoted in John 2.17; verse 9b is also applied to Jesus, in Romans 15.3.

The word translated **zeal** means "ardor, love, passion"; in other contexts it can be used in a bad sense, "jealousy, envy" (as in Pro 6.34; 27.4). The expression **zeal for thy house has consumed me** presents the translator with the problem of expressing adequately the idea of zeal in relation to the Temple, and the consuming effect of such zeal. In some languages the first part may best be translated "my love for your house." In other languages it is possible to say idiomatically, for example, "I am eaten with love for your house" or "like hunger holds a man, I am devoted to your house." Many languages can follow TEV in the second part of this expression, while others will find it more natural to say, for example, "eats up my heart" or "melts my insides."

In many languages it is not possible to speak of insults being hurled or falling. One may sometimes say, for example, "people have insulted you, and their words speak insults to me" or "what people said when they insulted you has now come upon me." **Insult** as a verb may be rendered, for example, "to speak evil words about someone" or "to injure people by speaking bad words about them."

69.10-12 RSV	TEV
10 When I humbled^k my soul with fasting, it became my reproach.	10 I humble myself^t by fasting, and people insult me;
11 When I made sackcloth my clothing, I became a byword to them.	11 I dress myself in clothes of mourning, and they laugh at me.
12 I am the talk of those who sit in the gate, and the drunkards make songs about me.	12 They talk about me in the streets, and drunkards make up songs about me.

^t *Some ancient translations* humble myself; *Hebrew* cry.

^k Gk Syr: Heb *I wept with fasting my soul* or *I made my soul mourn with fasting*

In verse 10a the Masoretic text is "I wept with fasting my *nefesh*" (which is an unusual construction). NJV and SPCL translate "When I wept and fasted"; TOB "I have wept and fasted"; Dahood "I poured out my soul while fasting." But the majority of commentators and translators believe that the text presented by the Septuagint and Syriac "I humble" is preferable;[2] **"myself"** (TEV) represents "my *nefesh*" (see 3.2).

The event of humbling oneself is difficult to express in many languages where it may be confused in the reader's mind with being of low social status. One may say in some languages, for example,"I made myself a person of little importance" or "I placed myself beneath other people." In languages where **fasting** is rendered as "going without food," the meaning should not imply that the reason is scarcity of food. In order to give the concept of fasting its fuller meaning, it will often be necessary to say, for example, "I prayed and refused to eat food" or "I said 'No' to food and worshiped God."

In verse 10b **reproach** (TEV "insult") translates the same word used in verses 7a and 9b.

Sackcloth, a coarse, rough cloth, was worn to indicate the wearer was mourning. Customs associated with mourning vary greatly in different cultures, and in some the clothing or lack of clothing is not relevant. The expression **I made sackcloth my clothing** must in some languages be adapted to reflect other customs; for example, body painting, smearing ashes over the face or chest, and carrying objects such as bags symbolizing a needy widow's mourning. If the translator follows TEV **"clothes of mourning,"** it will often be best to clarify the relation between clothes and mourning; for example, "clothes that show I am mourning for the dead."

---

[2]HOTTP prefers the Masoretic text "I wept."

It is doubtful that the psalmist's fasting (verse 10a) was in repentance for his own sins; it seems better to take it, along with the clothes of mourning he wore (verse 11a), as a sign of his deep distress over certain matters (unknown to us) that were affecting the Temple and its services; or else he was fasting and mourning on behalf of his people, who did not confess the errors of their ways.

In either case, this served only to make him an object of ridicule and mockery; he was insulted (verse 10b) and mocked (verse 11a); literally **I became a byword to them**; for comments on this use of "proverb, saying," see 44.14a.

In verse 12 **the gate** represents the place near the city gates where people met for business and social purposes (see 9.14 and comments), and exchanged information and gossip. The psalmist had become "the talk of the town"; even drunkards composed songs about him. Toombs' comment is worth quoting: "the village wiseacres and tavern haunters made witty songs about him as a pious pretender."

69.13-15	RSV	TEV

	RSV	TEV
13	But as for me, my prayer is to thee, O LORD. At an acceptable time, O God, in the abundance of thy steadfast love answer me. With thy faithful help 14 rescue me from sinking in the mire; let me be delivered from my enemies and from the deep waters.	13 But as for me, I will pray to you, LORD; answer me, God, at a time you choose. Answer me because of your great love, because you keep your promise to save.
15	Let not the flood sweep over me, or the deep swallow me up, or the pit close its mouth over me.	14 Save me from sinking in the mud; keep me safe from my enemies, safe from the deep water. 15 Don't let the flood come over me; don't let me drown in the depths or sink into the grave.

The psalmist renews his prayer to God for help. **At an acceptable time** (verse 13) translates the Hebrew "at a time of goodwill" (see comments on the noun in 19.14). The connection between this phrase and what precedes or what follows is not clear; TEV has supplied the verb **"answer me"** in line b (suggested by its use in the next line), since it feels the word "goodwill" is more appropriately applied to God than to the psalmist (so Briggs, Anderson). NJB connects "at the time of your favour" to the psalmist's declaration "I pray to you"; similarly NJV "at a favorable moment"; TOB has "it is the time (for you) to be favorable."

In verse 13c **steadfast love** translates *chesed* (see 5.7 and comments). **With thy faithful help** does not seem the best translation of the Hebrew "in the faithfulness (*'emeth*; see comment at 15.2) of your salvation." NJB does better by joining the line to what precedes and translating the two lines "O God, in Your abundant faithfulness, answer me with Your sure deliverance."

RSV has joined the last two words of verse 13 ("in the faithfulness of your salvation") to verse 14; this is possible but does not seem to be required by the Masoretic text. The Hebrew "rescue me from the mire" is already quite clear.

From sinking in the mire translates "from the mire and do not let me sink"; the verb "to sink" is used also in verse 2; and for **mire** see the use of the term in 18.42; 40.2; a different Hebrew synonym is used for "mire" in verse 2. It is to be noticed that in verse 14b **my enemies** (literally "those who hate me") does not offer a good parallel to **mire** in verse 14a and **deep waters** in verse 14c. G. R. Driver proposed *mis'on* (another word for "mud") for the Masoretic text *mison'ay* "(from) those who hate me," which is adopted by NEB. Dahood translates "my Enemy" (a reference to death). It seems best to stay with the generally accepted meaning of the text.

The deep waters is the same phrase as in verse 2c.

Verse 15a uses the same language as in verse 2d. **The deep** in verse 15b translates the same word as in verse 2a "deep (mud)"; the verb is literally **swallow**, which is also used in 35.25. **The pit** in verse 15c is the same word used in 55.23. All these figures, as in verses 1-2, represent death, Sheol, destruction, chaos.

In lines <u>b</u> and <u>c</u> the translator must decide to what extent it is possible to retain the figurative language of being swallowed by the **deep,** and having the **pit close its mouth over me.** In some languages it may be possible to maintain the figurative language through the use of an added simile; for example, "don't let the water drown me like a person being swallowed" or "don't let the water drown me like a person swallows food." Line <u>c</u> may be similarly rendered; for example, "don't let the grave eat me like food is eaten in the mouth" or "don't let the grave close over me like a mouth that shuts." In attempting to retain figurative language for poetic effect, the translator must not forget that even poetic language must not be confusing if it is to communicate the author's intent.

69.16-18   RSV   TEV

16 Answer me, O LORD, for thy steadfast love is good; according to thy abundant mercy, turn to me.	16 Answer me, LORD, in the goodness of your constant love; in your great compassion turn to me!
17 Hide not thy face from thy servant; for I am in distress, make haste to answer me.	17 Don't hide yourself from your servant; I am in great trouble—answer me now!
18 Draw near to me, redeem me, set me free because of my enemies!	18 Come to me and save me; rescue me from my enemies.

The psalmist pleads with God, who so far has not answered his prayer (verse 3). He again appeals to God's **steadfast love** (see verse 13 and 5.7) and his **mercy** (see 51.1b). The major problem in the translation of verse 16 is the restructuring of the two nominal clauses of TEV, "in the goodness of your constant love" and "in your great compassion." In some languages both of these may be shifted to causal clauses; for example, "Because you are good and love me faithfully, answer me, LORD; because you have great compassion, turn to me!"

The psalmist begs God not to **hide thy face** (see comments, 13.1), and asks for an immediate answer (**make haste**, verse 17b), that is, immediate help.

His plea is based on the conviction that he, God's **servant**, has been faithful to God and followed his will, and should therefore be given help and protection from his enemies. As Anderson comments, "God's honour would be called in question if his faithful servant were abandoned to the godless."

Draw near to me (verse 18a), he pleads; **redeem me** translates the verb *ga'al* (the noun form, "redeemer," is explained in 19.14), and **set me free** translates the verb rendered "redeem" in 25.22.

In verse 18b **because of my enemies** (also NIV, NJB, FRCL) is a difficult statement; presumably it means "because my enemies are holding me prisoner" or, as NEB, "for I have many enemies." So TOB "I have enemies, set me free." GECL translates "so that my enemies will have to be silent." But it seems better to go with TEV, NJV, SPCL.

69.19-21	RSV		TEV
19	Thou knowest my reproach, and my shame and my dishonor; my foes are all known to thee.	19	You know how I am insulted, how I am disgraced and dishonored; you see all my enemies.
20	Insults have broken my heart, so that I am in despair. I looked for pity, but there was none; and for comforters, but I found none.	20	Insults have broken my heart, and I am in despair. I had hoped for sympathy, but there was none; for comfort, but I found none.
21	They gave me poison for food, and for my thirst they gave me vinegar to drink.	21	When I was hungry, they gave me poison; when I was thirsty, they offered me vinegar.

In strong, bitter language, the psalmist describes his situation, which is well known to God. Words are used that have already appeared in this psalm: **reproach** (verses 7a, 10b); **shame** (verse 7b); **dishonor** (verse 6d); **insults** (verse 9b). But God knows who all his enemies are; he keeps his eye on them (verse 19c; literally "are in front of you").

The figure of a **broken . . . heart** has already been encountered in 51.17b; there it expresses contrition and repentance. Here, however, it means that the psalmist has been deeply offended and hurt by the insults his enemies hurl at him. **Insults have broken my heart** may have to be recast in translation so that two events are depicted. For example, "my enemies insulted me and my head is lowered" or "my enemies have said bad things about me and my heart sits heavy in me."

I am in despair (RSV, TEV, NJV) translates a word found nowhere else in the Old Testament; as used in the Masoretic text, it is of uncertain form and meaning. K-B suggests an adjective, "incurable, desperate." Briggs takes it to be a form of the verb "to be in poor health" (used in 2 Sam 12.15). NJB has a vivid translation, "Insult has broken my heart past cure."

The word translated **pity** describes a shaking of the head from side to side as an expression of condolence, of fellow feeling; no human sympathy, no comfort, for the psalmist! **I looked for pity** in some languages can be rendered idiomatically; for example, "I wanted someone to show me their warm insides." **Comforters** may be rendered as "people who can encourage me" or, idiomatically, "people who can cause my heart to be strong."

It is impossible to decide whether verse 21 is meant literally or figuratively; it probably is the latter, for had the psalmist swallowed **poison**, he would hardly have survived. The word **poison** translates "bitter" (so "gall" in some translations, which is also the Greek word in the Septuagint that is used in Matt 27.34). If the sense of **poison** is not to be taken literally but figuratively, as suggested above, the translator should avoid using a word for **poison** which would mean certain death if eaten. It may be best to translate in such a way as to leave no doubt that the psalmist did not undergo a test by eating poison, as is used in some cultures to establish innocence. For example, "They gave me food that tasted as bad as poison" or "The food they gave me to eat tasted like bitter poison." **Food** occurs only once more, in Lamentations 4.10; it is specifically the meal brought to a mourner by sympathetic friends. **Vinegar** represents a word whose meaning is probably closer to "cheap, sour wine" (as a drink) than to vinegar (as a condiment). But some take it to be vinegar as such, which the psalmist's enemies poured into his drink to make him even thirstier. In languages where **vinegar** is unknown, it is often possible to say "a sour drink."

The language of verse 21, as translated in the Septuagint, is reflected in the accounts of Jesus' crucifixion: see Matthew 27.34,48; Mark 15.36; Luke 23.36; John 19.29.

69.22-23

RSV	TEV
22 Let their own table before them become a snare; let their sacrificial feasts[1] be a trap.	22 May their banquets cause their ruin; may their sacred feasts cause their downfall.
23 Let their eyes be darkened, so that they cannot see; and make their loins tremble continually.	23 Strike them with blindness! Make their backs always weak!

[1] Tg: Heb *for security*

In a series of denunciations the psalmist calls on God to punish his enemies (see a similar series in 58.6-9). There is nothing idle or rhetorical about the language; the psalmist, convinced that his enemies had broken God's law, uses the most extreme language possible in the curses that he hurls at them.

In verse 22a TEV "**banquets**" are the sacrificial feasts at the Temple (verse 22b), where the people were supposedly worshiping Yahweh. The psalmist's wish is that these celebrations be the occasion of their "**ruin**" (**snare**), of their "**downfall**"

(<u>trap</u>, literally "a bird trap"), that is, that God will punish them as they partake of these **sacrificial feasts**. In many languages it will be possible to maintain the figurative language regarding the **snare** and the **trap** through the adaptation of a simile; for example, "when they eat their feasts, may they be caught like birds in a snare; when they eat the meat sacrificed to God, let them be like animals caught in a trap."

In verse 22b **sacrificial feasts** translates the text of the Targum (see RSV); the Masoretic text is "to those who are at peace," that is, their companions; so NJV "their allies"; HOTTP "their guests"; TOB "their friends." NEB reads a slightly different Hebrew text but gets the same meaning; Dahood has "(make) their companions a snare." BJ and NJB translate the Masoretic text by "their abundance." The Septuagint has "for retribution." It is recommended that the translator follow RSV and TEV, or else the translation proposed by HOTTP, "their guests."

In verse 23 the psalmist asks God to punish his enemies with blindness and weakness; in verse 23b the verb is "cause to shake." This may be either a symptom of fear or of a disease. This line is translated in a number of ways: SPCL "may their legs always tremble"; NJV "may their loins collapse continually" is strange, not to say ridiculous. FRCL has "make their backs always bend down," which is better.

As translated by the Septuagint, verses 22-23 are quoted by Paul in Romans 11.9-10; Romans 11.9 is different both from the Masoretic text and from the Septuagint of verse 22; Romans 11.10 is exactly like the Septuagint of verse 23.

69.24-25	RSV	TEV

| 24 | Pour out thy indignation upon them, and let thy burning anger overtake them. | 24 | Pour out your anger on them; let your indignation overtake them. |
| 25 | May their camp be a desolation, let no one dwell in their tents. | 25 | May their camps be left deserted; may no one be left alive in their tents. |

In verse 24a God's **indignation** is parallel with **burning anger** in verse 24b; the word translated **indignation** can be thought of as a curse (so also in 38.3a).

In many languages the expression **Pour out thy indignation** must be recast in terms of punishment; for example, "Punish them in your anger" or "Be angry and punish them." **Let thy burning anger overtake them** can sometimes be rendered "in your hot anger chase them until you catch them."

The language of verse 25, **camp** and **tents**, recalls the time when the Israelites lived in tents, as they journeyed toward the Promised Land; it is probable that here the two words are simply synonyms for "towns" and "homes." The psalmist wants his enemies and their families to be completely exterminated, so that their cities and homes will be left completely empty of inhabitants. In languages which will not express the passive verb constructions in lines <u>a</u> and <u>b</u>, it may be necessary to say "make them abandon their camps; cause everyone in their tents to die."

This verse, changed and adapted to apply to one man (Judas), is quoted in Acts 1.20.

RSV	TEV
For they persecute him whom thou hast smitten, and him *m* whom thou hast wounded, they afflict still more.*n*	They persecute those whom you have punished; they talk about the sufferings of those you have wounded.

m One Ms Tg Compare Syr: Heb *those*
n Gk Syr: Heb *recount the pain of*

In this verse the psalmist interrupts his denunciations in order to provide a justification. The Hebrew text is a bit irregular at the beginning of the verse, but there seems to be no reason to emend. In translation it will be clearer if the translator provides some kind of marker to show that the writer is offering a reason for his attacks on his enemies; for example, one might begin verse 26 with "Do all this because . . . ."

TEV "**those whom you have punished**" takes the Hebrew singular to be generic (so NJV). The singular (so RSV and others) can be taken to refer to the psalmist himself; but in line b̲ the object in the Masoretic text is plural, "**those you have wounded**." One Hebrew manuscript and the Targum have the singular, which RSV prefers, in parallel with line a̲. The psalmist's complaint is that his enemies, not content with the sufferings of those (or, of the one) punished by God, add to those sufferings by their hostile acts.

In verse 26b the Masoretic text is "they recount" (so TEV "**they talk about**"); the Septuagint and Syriac have "they add to," which is preferred by AT, RSV, JB, BJ, NAB; as Anderson points out, this is a closer parallel with line a̲. The Masoretic text, however, does make sense and can be translated.[3]

RSV	TEV
27 Add to them punishment upon punishment; may they have no acquittal from thee.	27 Keep a record of all their sins; don't let them have any part in your salvation.
28 Let them be blotted out of the book of the living; let them not be enrolled among the righteous.	28 May their names be erased from the book of the living; may they not be included in the list of your people.

[3]HOTTP ("C" decision) stays with the Masoretic text "they gossip (about)" and comments: "This expression refers to the discussions about the sins which had caused the suffering of the psalmist, as Job's friends presumed a sin as being the basis for his misfortune."

The first line of verse 27 is literally "Give sin (or, guilt) to their sin (or, guilt)." The noun *'awon* usually means "transgression, guilt" (see comments on "iniquity" in 51.2). It can be used in the sense of "punishment (for guilt)," which is how RSV has interpreted it; similarly NEB "the punishment their sin deserves." Weiser has "Add guilt to their guilt" (also NAB); this is not very satisfactory, unless understood in the sense of convicting them of even worse sins. JB, BJ, NIV, TOB, and Dahood have "Charge them with crime after crime"; this is the sense represented by TEV **"Keep a record of all their sins,"** and FRCL "Make a list of all their faults," taking the verb, literally "to give," in the sense of adding to a list, like a bookkeeper (so Dahood).

In verse 27b "let them not come to your *tsedaqah*" is variously understood (see comments on "righteousness" in 5.8): TEV **"salvation"**; RSV <u>acquittal</u>; SPCL "pardon"; FRCL "approval"; NAB "reward"; NJV "beneficence"; BJ and TOB "justice"; and NJB "saving justice." Any one of these represents some aspect of the word, and every one of them can be defended. "Justice" is the meaning the word has in most contexts, and here it may be preferred, in the sense of "acquittal" or "pardon." The TEV expression **"have any part in your salvation"** is extremely difficult to translate, unless one says simply "do not save them." Other suggestions are "do not pardon them," "do not accept them," or "do not show them justice."

The figure of a heavenly <u>book</u> (or books), in which are listed the names of the righteous, is found in other places in the Bible; it seems obviously derived from the register of citizens in a community, and expresses the idea that God keeps a record of the names of the righteous, of those who are to be given life (or kept alive). See a similar thought in 87.6; and see also Exodus 32.32-33; Daniel 12.1.

<u>The righteous</u> in verse 28b are those who obey God's laws, that is, God's "people" (TEV); see the discussion of the word at 1.5.

69.29 RSV TEV

But I am afflicted and in pain; let thy salvation, O God, set me on high!	But I am in pain and despair; lift me up, O God, and save me!

The psalmist once more reminds God of his desperate situation and prays for help. In Hebrew there is an alliteration in the words translated **I am afflicted**: *wa'ani 'ani*. The passive **afflicted** means to be suffering, to be in pain; see the discussion of the term at 9.12.

The petition **let thy salvation ... set me on high** means "rescue me from danger and put me in a place of safety." Some take line <u>b</u> to be a confident statement (see NJV, FRCL, TOB), "You will lift me up ... ," not a petition. It seems better to understand the line as a prayer, a petition.

69.30-31 RSV TEV

30 I will praise the name of God with a song;	30 I will praise God with a song; I will proclaim his greatness by

I will magnify him with thanks-giving.	giving him thanks.
31 This will please the LORD more than an ox or a bull with horns and hoofs.	31 This will please the LORD more than offering him cattle, more than sacrificing a full-grown bull.

Now the psalmist bursts into praise; evidently he has received some word of assurance that God will answer his prayer (see similar situation in 20.6).

For **the name of God** see comments on 5.11; for **magnify him** see 34.3 and comments.

The Lord is happier with thanksgiving than he is with the offering of animals in sacrifice. TEV makes explicit the implied action of sacrifice by inserting "**offering him**" and "**sacrificing**." TEV "**cattle**" represents the singular **ox** (NEB "bull"), and "**full-grown bull**" stands for the literal **bull with horns and hoofs**. The two singular forms, **an ox** and **a bull**, represent the animals that are offered in sacrifice, and in translation a plural form may be used, if it is more natural. This verse, which minimizes the importance of animal sacrifices (see also 40.6; 50.8-14; 51.16-17), may reveal one of the causes of the hatred directed toward the psalmist. In some languages it may be necessary to show that the cattle in TEV are offered to be sacrificed; for example, ". . . more than offering him cattle to be burned."

69.32-33   RSV   TEV

32 Let the oppressed see it and be glad; you who seek God, let your hearts revive.	32 When the oppressed see this, they will be glad; those who worship God will be encouraged.
33 For the LORD hears the needy, and does not despise his own that are in bonds.	33 The LORD listens to those in need and does not forget his people in prison.

Verse 32 can be taken as a statement (TEV, NJV, FRCL) or as an exhortation (RSV, NEB). Line b has the second person of direct address; TEV uses the third person, parallel with line a. **The oppressed** translates the plural of the same noun rendered "afflicted" in verse 29a (see comments on "afflicted" in 9.12). For **you who seek God** see comments on 9.10b.

To what does **it** in **see it** (TEV "**see this**") in verse 32a refer? It could be the psalmist's act of thanksgiving in the Temple (verse 30; Briggs), or else, as FRCL has it, "The oppressed will see my deliverance," that is, "that God has rescued me." Translators are encouraged to make this meaning explicit.

To "revive the heart" (verse 32b) means to encourage, to give hope. TOB and FRCL translate "A long life to you!" and NJB "let your courage revive."

For translation suggestions on **the needy**, see 9.18.

The verb **despise** means "to ignore, neglect, forget" (see also its use in 22.24; 51.17). **In bonds** in verse 33b indicates they are in prison (same word used in 68.6b). NEB translates "those bound to his service" (similarly Dahood); it seems better, however, to take the word to mean either literal prison or exile, or else to be a figure of the bonds of suffering and oppression.

69.34-36 RSV	TEV
34 Let heaven and earth praise him, the seas and everything that moves therein. 35 For God will save Zion and rebuild the cities of Judah; and his servants shall dwell^o there and possess it; 36 the children of his servants shall inherit it, and those who love his name shall dwell in it.	34 Praise God, O heaven and earth, seas and all creatures in them. 35 He will save Jerusalem and rebuild the towns of Judah. His people will live there and pos- sess the land; 36 the descendants of his servants will inherit it, and those who love him will live there.

^{o} Syr: Heb *and they shall dwell*

The psalm closes with an exhortation for the whole universe to join in praising God. In some languages it will be necessary to say "Everything that is in heaven and earth, praise God," since for those languages heaven and earth cannot themselves perform this event.

In verse 34b **everything that moves** means living creatures; in Hebrew **therein** refers to **the seas**, but by extension it can be made to apply to all three, **heaven**, **earth**, **seas** (so SPCL).

The reason for this universal praise is that God **will save Zion** and **rebuild the cities of Judah** (for comments on **Zion** see 2.6). This clearly points to a time when the country of Israel was under the dominion of foreign forces who had devastated it. The Israelites will return and once more **possess** the land (see 25.13 and comments). In verse 35c RSV adds **his servants** from the Syriac; Hebrew is simply "they will live there," which is clearly a reference to the Israelites, and which TEV translationally represents by "**His people will live there**." This is also the choice of HOTTP ("A" decision).

Children (TEV "**descendants**") translates the Hebrew "seed" (see 18.50). **His servants** in verse 36a are the same as the Hebrew "they" in verse 35c. **The children of his servants** must not be translated in such a way as to mean the small children of his domestic employees, but rather as "the descendants of those who worship him" or "the descendants of those who serve him." The verb **inherit** means to receive, to come into possession of, to be given (by God).

For **who love his name** see "name" in 5.11.

Psalm 70

This psalm is an almost exact replica of 40.13-17. It is a lament by an individual who feels persecuted and oppressed, and who prays to the Lord to help him. See the introduction to Psalm 40 and the comments there; here comments are made only in places where the meaning is significantly different from 40.13-17.

HEADING: "**A Prayer for Help**." Other headings are "A cry of distress"; "Prayer for divine help"; "Come quickly to help me." The TEV title of this psalm, like most of the others, requires recasting the nouns as verb phrases; for example, "The psalmist prays to God and asks God to help him."

Hebrew Title: **To the choirmaster. A Psalm of David, for the memorial offering** (TEV "A psalm by David; a lament").

For **choirmaster** see title of Psalm 4; for **memorial offering** see title of Psalm 38.

<u>70.1-3</u>   RSV   TEV

1   Be pleased, O God, to deliver me!   1   Save me, O God!
        O LORD, make haste to help   LORD, help me now!
        me!   2   May those who try to kill me
2   Let them be put to shame and   be defeated and confused.
        confusion   May those who are happy because
     who seek my life!   of my troubles
     Let them be turned back and   be turned back and disgraced.
        brought to dishonor   3   May those who make fun of me
     who desire my hurt!   be dismayed by their defeat.
3   Let them be appalled because of
        their shame
     who say, "Aha, Aha!"

In verse 1 **God** and <u>LORD</u> are used; in 40.13 "LORD" is used twice. In verse 1a in RSV **Be pleased** is taken from 40.13; the word is not used here. The Hebrew text has simply "O God, to deliver me."

TEV "**who try to kill me**" in verse 2 translates "who seek my *nefesh*," whereas 40.14 has "who seek to snatch away my *nefesh*"; the meaning in both places is the same. And the word translated "completely" in 40.14 is not used here. In languages which do not use passive constructions it will often be necessary to recast line <u>b</u>; for example, "I ask that you defeat and confuse the people who try to kill me."

608

Let them be turned back refers to the defeat of the psalmist's enemies and in some languages may be expressed as "stop them and cause them to run away." **Dishonor** is sometimes translated "to take away their praise" or "to remove their greatness and make them unimportant."

In verse 3b "to me" of 40.15 does not appear, but the meaning is the same. People are making fun of the psalmist. Verse 3 requires considerable restructuring, particularly in languages which do not use the passive voice; for example, one may say "I ask that you defeat people who make fun of me, and cause them to have burning faces."

70.4-5   RSV   TEV

4   May all who seek thee   4   May all who come to you
       rejoice and be glad in thee!   be glad and joyful.
     May those who love thy salvation   May all who are thankful for your
       say evermore, "God is great!"   salvation
5   But I am poor and needy;   always say, "How great is God!"
       hasten to me, O God!
     Thou art my help and my de-   5   I am weak and poor;
       liverer;   come to me quickly, O God.
     O LORD, do not tarry!   You are my savior and my LORD—
                                                         hurry to my aid!

In verse 4 RSV **evermore** translates the same Hebrew word translated **continually** in 40.16; in both places TEV has "**always**." In many languages the request form with **May** must be rendered as an explicit plea; for example, "I ask that . . ." or "I beg that . . . ." In languages where this is not satisfactory, it will sometimes be necessary to use the direct command. In some languages, if one follows TEV "**thankful for your salvation**," it will be necessary to recast this phrase; for example, "May all who thank you that you have saved them . . . ." In languages where there is no term for thanks, it is often possible to say "May all the people who gladly accept your salvation . . . ."

In verse 4c **God** is used, whereas "the LORD" is used in 40.16.

Verse 5 differs a little from 40.17. **Hasten to me, O God** in line b is parallel to line d; and **LORD** is used in line d, whereas in 40.17 it is "my God." In some languages it will be necessary to replace the nominal forms by verb phrases in lines c and d; for example, "You are the one who saves me, and you are the Lord whom I worship; do not delay to come and help me."

Psalm 71

This psalm is a lament by an old man who in spite of adversity, sickness, and persecution remains firm in his faith in God and prays for his help. The language here is much the same as that used in other psalms of this kind, and nothing definite can be stated about the reasons the psalmist was being persecuted.

The psalm opens with a prayer for help in which are statements of trust in God (verses 1-6); next the psalmist denounces his enemies, who say that God has abandoned him (verses 7-11); the psalmist prays for help (verses 12-13) and promises to praise God (verses 14-16). The psalm ends with a reflection on the psalmist's past experience, praise for God's eternal power, and hope for the future (verses 17-24).

HEADING: most translations, like TEV, have "**An Old Man's Prayer**"; other headings are "Humble prayer in time of old age," "Forsake me not, O God." The TEV title will require very little adaptation in translation into many languages; for example, "An old man prays to God" or "An old man worships God."

71.1-3	RSV	TEV

	RSV	TEV
1	In thee O LORD, do I take refuge; let me never be put to shame!	1 LORD, I have come to you for protection; never let me be defeated!
2	In thy righteousness deliver me and rescue me; incline thy ear to me, and save me!	2 Because you are righteous, help me and rescue me. Listen to me and save me!
3	Be thou to me a rock of refuge, a strong fortress,^{p} to save me, for thou art my rock and my fortress.	3 Be my secure shelter and a strong fortress^v to protect me; you are my refuge and defense.

^{p} Gk Compare 31.3: Heb *to come continually thou hast commanded*

^{v} *One ancient translation* a strong fortress; *Hebrew* to go always you commanded.

The psalm opens with a prayer for help; verses 1-3 are practically the same as 31.1-3a. For comments on **In thee . . . do I take refuge**, see 2.12. **I take refuge** can sometimes be rendered in a more active sense as "You protect me."

For a similar translation of **put to shame**, see 6.10. If the passive is to be avoided, it will be necessary to introduce "enemies" as the agent of shame or defeat; for example, "don't allow my enemies to defeat me."

For **righteousness** in 2a, see comments on 5.8.

For **incline thy ear** in verse 2b, see 17.6.

In verse 3a the Masoretic text has "a rock a place"; some Hebrew manuscripts have "a rock of refuge," which most translations follow.[1] For the figures in verse 3, see 18.2; 31.2. In some languages it will be possible to maintain the figure **rock of refuge**, provided some adjustment is made; for example, "be like a rock to protect me" or "protect me as a rock protects a person who hides under it."

In verse 3b the Masoretic text is "to come (or, go) always you have commanded to save me," which is hard to understand. NEB, however, translates the Masoretic text "where I may ever find safety at thy call"; NJV connects "to go always" with the preceding line, as follows: "Be a sheltering rock for me to which I may always repair," followed by the imperative "decree my deliverance." NJB has "you have determined to save me"; TOB and NIV are similar.[2] RSV, TEV, FRCL, and SPCL follow the Septuagint and emend the text to **a strong fortress** (the plural form of the same word in verse 3c; see also 31.2). In some languages it may be possible to say in line b of verse 3 "be like a house with strong walls to protect me" or "protect me as a house with strong walls protects people."

	71.4-5 RSV		TEV
4	Rescue me, O my God, from the hand of the wicked, from the grasp of the unjust and cruel man.	4	My God, rescue me from wicked men, from the power of cruel and evil men.
5	For thou, O Lord, art my hope, my trust, O LORD, from my youth.	5	Sovereign LORD, I put my hope in you; I have trusted in you since I was young.

The psalmist describes his enemies as **wicked**, **unjust**, and **cruel**, all of which are synonymous terms of general meaning, without any specific indication of particular evil traits. In verse 4 **hand** and **grasp** mean "power, control, dominion."

In verse 5 TEV has joined the two divine titles in lines a and b into the one title "Sovereign LORD" (see 69.6 and comments). For **hope** see 62.5, and for **trust** see the translation of the same term as "hope" in 65.5.

Thou, O Lord, art my hope can in some languages be rendered, for example, "You, Lord, are the one I look to with confidence" or ". . . the one I place my heart upon."

---

[1]HOTTP is of the opinion that the Masoretic text should be followed, even though it is not the original text. The ancient versions represent an assimilation to Psalm 31.2c and do not reflect the original text either.

[2]HOTTP also prefers the Masoretic text ("C" decision), which it translates "accessible always, you decided (to save me)."

Verses 5b-6 are very much like 22.9-10. The Hebrew for **from my youth** indicates childhood or adolescence; it can even be applied to a young man old enough to marry. Here it is quite general; NEB and NIV have "boyhood."

71.6　　　　RSV　　　　　　　　　　　　　　　TEV

Upon thee I have leaned from my
　　birth;
　thou art he who took me from
　　my mother's womb.
My praise is continually of thee.

I have relied on you all my life;
　you have protected*ᵂ* me since
　　the day I was born.
I will always praise you.

ᵂ Some ancient translations protected;
Hebrew unclear.

Using language that recalls 22.9-10, the psalmist declares that all his life, from his birth, he has known God's protection and care. Line <u>a</u> in Hebrew is literally "Upon you I have depended from the womb." It is doubtful that the psalmist meant to say that before he was born he already consciously trusted in God, as NJV ("While yet unborn, I depended on You") and SPCL ("while still in my mother's womb I already depended on you") seem to imply. Some languages will prefer an idiomatic rendering such as "Ever since I came out of my mother's womb, I have placed my heart on you."

In line <u>b</u> there is a word in Hebrew whose meaning is not certain; the line is literally "from my mother's womb you *gozi*," which in form is the participle of a verb otherwise unknown. Perhaps it means "cut off," that is, the umbilical cord. TOB has "you took me from my mother's womb" (also NEB footnote). NJV translates "You were my support," and NJB has "you have been my portion." TEV, FRCL, and others follow the Septuagint and Vulgate. Several prefer to emend to *'uzi* "my strength." Briggs prefers to emend to *gohi* ("who took me out"), as in 22.9. RSV and NIV translate as though the Hebrew were identical with 22.9a, which it is not. In light of the difficulty in determining the precise meaning of the Hebrew text, the translator may choose to follow NJV and TEV, "you have taken care of me . . . ," or else render as RSV has done, that God acted as midwife at the psalmist's birth.

71.7-9　　　　RSV　　　　　　　　　　　　　　TEV

7　I have been as a portent to many;
　　　but thou art my strong refuge.
8　My mouth is filled with thy praise,
　　　and with thy glory all the day.
9　Do not cast me off in the time of
　　　old age;
　　forsake me not when my
　　　strength is spent.

7　My life has been an example to
　　　many,
　　because you have been my
　　　strong defender.
8　All day long I praise you
　　　and proclaim your glory.
9　Do not reject me now that I am
　　　old;
　　do not abandon me now that I
　　　am feeble.

It is not easy to understand in what sense the Hebrew word translated **portent** in verse 7a is used here. The same word is generally used of something extraordinary; in Ezekiel 12.6,11; 24.24,27 the word is used of the prophet as a "sign" to Israel. Here it means that the psalmist's experience was either an "**example**" (so NJV, TEV) or "a solemn warning" (NEB), either as a demonstration of God's care (so NJV, TEV in verse 7b) or as the object of God's punishment (so SPCL "a motive of fear"; also BJ, TOB). FRCL expresses this idea with the wording "Many think that you had cursed me." The interpretation depends in part on the meaning attributed to the initial conjunction in line <u>b</u>, which usually means simply "and." RSV, NEB, NAB, NIV, FRCL, BJ, and NJB translate <u>but</u>; TEV "**because**"; NJV "since." If the translator follows the lead of TEV, "**My life has been an example to many**" may in some languages be rendered as "Many people have seen how I lived, and have therefore lived like me" or "Many people have seen how I go, and followed my road."

The two-noun phrase translated **strong refuge** in verse 7b is not found elsewhere in the Old Testament; the two Hebrew nouns "refuge and strength" are used in 46.1.

In verse 8a **My mouth is filled with** means to proclaim, announce, say. The word translated **glory** in verse 8b means "excellence, beauty, adornment," used here in a spiritual sense; the word appears elsewhere in the Psalms at 78.61b; 89.17a; 96.6b. The expression **my mouth is filled . . . thy glory** may be rendered in direct discourse as "I say 'You are wonderful' " or "I say 'You are glorious.' "

The petition **Do not cast me off** in verse 9a is similar to that of 51.11; the verb means "throw off, reject"; and **forsake** in line <u>b</u> is the same verb used in 16.10. Most translations, like TEV, take "**I am old**" and "**I am feeble**" in verse 9 as statements of the psalmist's condition at the time of writing the psalm (see verse 18); some, however, take them to mean that the psalmist is speaking of the time still in the future when he will be an old man. The former seems preferable. **When my strength is spent** is sometimes rendered, for example, "when I am an old man with one hair," "when I am stiff in the body," and "when they lead me by the hand."

<table>
<tr><td>**71.10-11**</td><td>RSV</td><td>TEV</td></tr>
</table>

RSV	TEV

10   For my enemies speak concerning me,
     those who watch for my life consult together,
	10 My enemies want to kill me;
	     they talk and plot against me.

11   and say, "God has forsaken him; pursue and seize him,
     for there is none to deliver him."
	11 They say, "God has abandoned him;
	     let's go after him and catch him;
	     there is no one to rescue him."

My enemies speak concerning me and TEV "**talk . . . against me**" are examples of generic usage which must be made more specific in many languages; for example, "my enemies say threatening words against me" or "my enemies speak evil about me." However, in some languages the use of the more generic level is permissible here, since the specific content of what they speak is stated in verse 11.

In verse 10b **those who watch for my life** means "those who want to kill me"; see the similar "watch my steps" in 56.6.

It is evidently the psalmist's condition, probably sickness, that causes his enemies to conclude that he has been abandoned by God. For **God has forsaken him**, see comments on the verb "forgotten" in 9.10, and on "forsaken" in 22.1. In any case, they feel sure that God will not defend him (for verse 11c see similar expressions using the same Hebrew verb in 7.2; 50.22b), and so they plot his destruction.

In some languages it will be clearer to make the logical relation between lines 11a and 11b more explicit; for example, "Since God has abandoned him, let's go after him" or "God has abandoned him, therefore let's go after him . . . ." It is possible to restructure verse 11 so that the two reason clauses are kept together and the conclusion clause placed after them; for example, "Since God has abandoned him and there is no one to rescue him, let's . . . catch him." It is also possible to reverse the order in languages which would prefer placing the conclusion before the reasons.

71.12-13	RSV	TEV
12	O God, be not far from me; O my God, make haste to help me! 13 May my accusers be put to shame and consumed; with scorn and disgrace may they be covered who seek my hurt.	12 Don't stay so far away, O God; my God, hurry to my aid! 13 May those who attack me be defeated and destroyed. May those who try to hurt me be shamed and disgraced.

The psalmist joins his plea for God's help (verse 12) to a denunciation of his enemies (verse 13), an affirmation of his trust in God (verse 14), and a promise to praise him for his goodness (verses 15-16).

For the language of verse 12a, see 22.1b; 38.21b. Except for the divine name, verse 12b is identical with 40.13b (see also 22.19; 40.17). In some languages it is impossible to say **my God**, since God cannot be possessed like ordinary physical objects. In such cases it is often necessary to shift to a relative clause; for example, "God, whom I worship" or "God, whom I serve."

The language of verse 13 is similar to that of 40.14. **My accusers** translates "the accusers of my *nefesh*" (see 3.2); the verb "accuse" is the same one translated "are my adversaries" in 38.20b. In English "attack" (TEV) may be taken to mean a physical action, so it is better to translate "accuse, slander, denounce."

Put to shame is translated "defeated" in TEV (see comments on 6.10b); and instead of the Masoretic text **consumed**, some translations prefer to follow some Hebrew manuscripts and Syriac, which have "be dishonored" (as in 35.4; 40.14; 70.2; see NEB). In languages which do not use passive constructions, it will be necessary to shift **be put to shame and consumed** to active constructions; for example, "defeat them and destroy them."

With scorn and disgrace may they be covered ("be shamed and disgraced") translates "be covered with reproach and disgrace" (see similar language in 35.26d).

Hurt here is not necessarily physical; something like "harm, damage, ruin," conveys the sense of the word.

71.14-16	RSV	TEV

RSV

14 But I will hope continually,
   and will praise thee yet more
   and more.
15 My mouth will tell of thy righteous acts,
   of thy deeds of salvation all the
   day,
   for their number is past my
   knowledge.
16 With the mighty deeds of the Lord
   GOD I will come,
   I will praise thy righteousness,
   thine alone.

TEV

14 I will always put my hope in you;
   I will praise you more and
   more.
15 I will tell of your goodness;
   all day long I will speak of your
   salvation,
   though it is more than I can
   understand.
16 I will go in the strength of the
   LORD God;
   I will proclaim your goodness,
   yours alone.

The psalmist's **hope** rests on God (verse 14a), for which he will praise him **more and more** (literally "I will add to all your praise"). **I will hope continually** may be rendered "I will always look forward with confidence," or figuratively, "I will always place my heart on you."

Thy righteous acts and **thy deeds of salvation** in verse 15a,b translate the plural of "your righteousness" and "your salvation." This agrees well with the plural "numbers" in line c, but the initial conjunction of that line is used in a concessive sense, "although, even though" (see TEV), and not as RSV has it, **for** (which makes for a contradiction). It seems better, however, to use the plural forms as RSV does, and make the two lines quite synonymous: "your saving actions . . . the things you did to save us."

In some languages **tell of thy righteous acts** requires shifting so that there is a listener; for example, "I will tell the people about the good things you have done." In some languages the noun phrase **deeds of salvation** must be shifted to a clause; for example, "I will tell the people how you have saved us" or "I will tell them how you saved your people." In some languages **all the day**, if translated literally, will mean that the psalmist speaks of God's acts only during daylight hours, whereas the intention is "all the time," and in such languages it will have to be translated by an equivalent expression.

The third line of verse 15 is somewhat strange in Hebrew; the word translated **their number** is understood in different ways. Some take it to be the plural of a word occurring nowhere else in the Old Testament, "numbers"; others take it to be the plural of the word for "list, book." TEV understands the Hebrew to say "for I don't know the number (of them)," in the sense "**it is more than I can understand**" (similarly NAB "though I know not their extent"; also SPCL); see a similar expression in 40.5^3 BJ and NJB take it to be a marginal note by a copyist: "I have not known how to read the letters" (see the Septuagint). NJV has "though I know not how to tell it"; NEB "although I have not the skill of a poet"; and FRCL "even though your good deeds are innumerable." TEV's interpretation seems to be the best one to follow.

In verse 16a **I will come** may imply that the psalmist is talking about going to the Temple to praise God (so FRCL "I will enter your house"; so Anderson). TEV has taken it as an affirmation of the psalmist's determination to praise God (see also SPCL, TOB). It is difficult to make sense of RSV **With the mighty deeds . . . I will come**. TEV **"your power"** translates the singular form "in power" found in many Hebrew manuscripts; RSV follows the Masoretic text plural form **mighty deeds**. Both RSV and TEV take this to refer to God; NJB has "I will come in the power of Yahweh," and FRCL "because of your intervention (on my behalf)." If the translator follows TEV **"praise your power,"** it may be necessary in some languages to shift to a reason-result clause structure; for example, "because you are powerful, Lord, I will praise you," or "I will say you are great, Lord, because you are powerful" or ". . . because you do powerful deeds."

Lord GOD (TEV "Sovereign LORD") translates "Lord Yahweh."

I will praise in verse 16b translates the causative of the Hebrew verb for "to remember"; the causative means "cause to be remembered; to profess, praise." **Righteousness** translates *tsedaqah* (see comments at 5.8); FRCL has "your faithfulness," and NJB "your saving powers." **Praise thy righteousness** must often be shifted into two clauses; for example, "I will say that you are great because you are faithful," or as two coordinate clauses, "you are loyal to your people and I will praise you."

The final words, **thine alone**, express the psalmist's complete dedication to God, which he has expressed so eloquently in verses 14-16. There is no other source, human or divine, from which comes salvation. **Thine alone** may be translated as an exclusive restriction on the psalmist's praise: "I will praise you, and no one else" or "I will praise you only—no one else."

71.17-18   RSV   TEV

17 O God, from my youth thou hast   17 You have taught me ever since I
        taught me,   was young,
    and I still proclaim thy won-   and I still tell of your wonderful
        drous deeds.   acts.
18 So even to old age and gray hairs,   18 Now that I am old and my hair is
        O God, do not forsake me,   gray,
    till I proclaim thy might   do not abandon me, O God!
        to all the generations to come.^{q} Be with me while I proclaim your
    Thy power   power and might
                                                       to all generations to come.

---

^{3}HOTTP calls this a difficult passage and states that the proposed interpretation, "I cannot count them," is the most probable one.

q Gk Compare Syr: Heb *to a generation,*
to all that come

The psalmist declares his dedication to the Law of God with the expressive statement **thou hast taught me**; NJV, however, takes the reference to be to God's goodness (verse 16) and translates "You have let me experience it." But it is better to translate as RSV and TEV have done. For **from my youth** see verse 5, and see 9.1 for the expression **thy wondrous deeds**. The main translation problem in **thou hast taught me** is the absence of an object. In languages which must supply an object, it is most probable that what the psalmist has learned from his youth are the **wondrous deeds** in 17b. These refer to the great acts of God in dealing with Israel. Therefore it may be necessary in some languages to recast verse 17 to say, for example, "O God, ever since I was a child you have taught me your wonderful acts, and I still tell people about them."

The petition in verse 18a,b is similar to that in verse 9. The decision there, whether the psalmist is already old or not yet old, should be reflected here as well. **Gray hairs** in the expression **old age and gray hairs** simply reinforces **old age**. In languages where "gray hair" is not used in this way, it will be necessary to employ a different qualifier or reinforcer; for example, "old age and having only one hair" or "old age and walking with a stick."

In the last half of verse 18, the order of the Hebrew text is "until I proclaim your power (literally 'your arm') to a generation, to all who come your might (literally 'your mighty acts')." **Proclaim thy might** must often be recast; for example, "I will tell everyone that you have done great and wonderful things for your people."

It is not necessary, as RSV has done, to join "your might" (RSV **thy power**) to verse 19 (similarly NAB). But there is quite a variety in the different ways that translations arrange the text of verses 18b-19a. NJV is as follows: "until I proclaim Your strength to the next generation, Your mighty acts, to all who are to come." This is the order favored by HOTTP. SPCL divides and arranges the text as TEV does.

The final **to all the generations to come** is poetic exaggeration; this does not mean, however, that in every case the reader will understand it quite literally. Some translations, however, prefer to be more moderate: FRCL "to young people and to those who will come after them"; GECL "my children and grandchildren."

71.19-21　　　　RSV　　　　　　　　　　　　　　TEV

> Thy power 19 and thy righteous-　19　Your righteousness, God, reaches
> 　　ness, O God,　　　　　　　　　　　　the skies.
> reach the high heavens.　　　　　　　You have done great things;
> 　　　　　　　　　　　　　　　　　　　there is no one like you.
>
> Thou who hast done great things,　20　You have sent troubles and suffer-
> 　O God, who is like thee?　　　　　　ing on me,
> 20　Thou who hast made me see many　　but　you　will　restore　my

617

sore troubles	strength;
wilt revive me again;	you will keep me from the
from the depths of the earth	grave.
thou wilt bring me up again.	21 You will make me greater than
21 Thou wilt increase my honor,	ever;
and comfort me again.	you will comfort me again.

The statement of verse 19a may mean that God's **righteousness**, that is, his saving deeds, includes all creation (see comments at 5.8), or else it means that it is confessed by all creatures. But TOB and FRCL abandon the figure "reaches the skies" and say simply "Your righteousness/faithfulness is so high!" In English, at least, this does not mean much. NEB and TOB make "your righteousness" (together with the preceding "your might" of verse 18) the object of the verb "proclaim" in verse 18; RSV joins **Thy power** of verse 18 to **thy righteousness** of verse 19. It is recommended that the TEV verse division and arrangement of lines be followed.

The expression **righteousness, O God, reaches the high heavens** and TEV's "reaches the skies" must be recast somewhat in many languages, since abstracts such as "righteousness" are not thought of as filling up space. This expression may also mean that God's goodness is beyond understanding (so Anderson). In the light of these various interpretations, the translator will be able to select an expression that is natural and meaningful in the receptor language; for example, "all that you have created tell of your faithfulness," "your faithfulness, God, is so great that it is told all the way to the skies," or "your goodness, God, is beyond (high above) our understanding."

There is none like God (verse 19c); no one can do what God does (see 35.10). The rhetorical question **who is like thee?** is effective if it is not understood as a request for information. If the language requires a reply to the rhetorical question, the reply will be "No one" or "No one at all."

The reflection on God's greatness leads the psalmist to think about his own "great troubles and evils" (verse 20; the Hebrew phrase is alliterative: *tsarot rabot wera'ot*). These **many sore troubles** which God has sent on the psalmist have brought him to death's door, to Sheol, **the depths of the earth** (see 63.9 and comment), but he is sure that God will bring him back, that he will restore him to health and reward him with greater honor, prestige, and eminence than ever before. The literal meaning of the verbs in the Hebrew text in verse 20b,d is "return to life" and "bring back up." It is possible that the psalmist was thinking about resurrection. But verse 21 favors the meaning expressed by TEV (see similar thoughts in 30.3; 40.2).

One form of the Masoretic text in verse 20a,b (*kethiv*) has the plural pronouns "us" instead of **me** in both lines (which Weiser prefers); and in verse 20d some Hebrew manuscripts have the plural pronoun "us." "Return us to life" and "bring us back up" can hardly refer to resurrection; they refer to the restoration of the country's welfare and prosperity. It seems better, however, to translate the text (*qere*) that has the singular "me" and "my" (also the Septuagint and Syriac).

Translators will have to make some adjustments with the expression **the depths of the earth . . . up again**, as does TEV, because this literal expression could easily be misunderstood as referring to being created again out of the earth. TEV's "**keep me from the grave**" will often have to be rendered, for example, "you will not allow me to die."

In verse 21 **my honor** is the psalmist's prestige, greatness, prosperity, power. And **comfort** is the verb that is used in 23.4; see also comments on "comforters" in 69.20. Here something like "make me happy again" may be preferable. GECL and FRCL reverse the two lines, which makes for a more logical statement in these languages.

71.22-24

RSV	TEV
22 I will also praise thee with the harp for thy faithfulness, O my God; I will sing praises to thee with the lyre, O Holy One of Israel. 23 My lips will shout for joy, when I sing praises to thee; my soul also, which thou hast rescued. 24 And my tongue will talk of thy righteous help all the day long, for they have been put to shame and disgraced who sought to do me hurt.	22 I will indeed praise you with the harp; I will praise your faithfulness, my God. On my harp I will play hymns to you, the Holy One of Israel. 23 I will shout for joy as I play for you; with my whole being I will sing because you have saved me. 24 I will speak of your righteousness all day long, because those who tried to harm me have been defeated and disgraced.

The psalmist concludes with a promise always to praise God for his **faithfulness** (verse 22) and to proclaim his **righteous help** (verse 24). For the two instruments named in verse 22 (*nebel* and *kinnor*), see discussion in 33.2. **Praise thee with the harp for thy faithfulness** represents a complex of three events: the psalmist praising God, someone playing the harp, and God being faithful to his people. In translation these three elements may be restructured to say, for instance, "God is faithful to his people, and so I will sing with the harp to praise him."

In verse 22c **sing praises** (TEV "play hymns") translates the same verb used in verse 23b; the verb (*zamar*) is used of singing praises accompanied by instrumental music (see comment at 7.17).

The **Holy One of Israel** is a title for God used frequently in Isaiah, but only twice again in the Book of Psalms (78.41; 89.18). It not only emphasizes the character of God as holy, but also that God brought Israel into an exclusive dedication to himself as his own people; in this sense they are also a "holy" people, who serve and worship Yahweh alone. **Holy One of Israel** must often be recast as "The God who is holy and whom Israel worships."

RSV **my lips** stands for the entire person, not just the mouth; and so TEV "I." **My soul** (TEV "**My whole being**") translates "my *nefesh*" (see 3.2).

In verse 23c "**because**" translates at term that is normally the relative pronoun **which** (so RSV and others); but it is also used as a conjunction, giving the cause of an action, and that is how TEV and TOB interpret it here.

Righteous help in verse 24a translates *tsedaqah* (see 5.8); NJB, as usual, translates "saving justice," and FRCL, as usual, "faithfulness." SPCL has "that you are righteous."

For verse 24c see similar language in 35.26; and for **who sought to do me hurt** in verse 24d see the same clause in verse 13, which is identical in the Hebrew.

Psalm 72

Like Psalm 2, this psalm is a royal psalm, celebrating the coronation of the king of Israel, either at the time of his inauguration as king or at the annual festival in which his coronation was celebrated. There is nothing in the text to indicate the identity of the king; the Hebrew title (see below) attributes the psalm to Solomon, but there is no certainty that this is historically accurate. The language is such as to apply to any of Israel's kings. The psalm was interpreted both by Jewish and Christian teachers as messianic.

The psalm begins with a prayer for the king, that his reign be just and prosperous (verses 1-7), and that his kingdom be universal (verses 8-11). Next the psalmist praises the king's compassion and his readiness to help the oppressed (verses 12-14), and closes the psalm with a prayer for the king's continued success (verses 15-17).

Verses 18-19 are considered a later addition, marking the close of Book Two of the Psalms (Psalms 42–72). Verse 20 is a prose line which may have been added at a different stage of the composition of the whole collection.

HEADING: "**A Prayer for the King.**" Other headings are "A coronation hymn"; "The promised king"; "Long live the king!" The TEV heading may be expressed in some languages as a complete sentence; for example, "The psalmist prays for the king" or "The psalmist asks God to bless the king."

Hebrew Title: **A Psalm of Solomon** (TEV "**By Solomon**").

The form of this title is the same as the titles which say simply "By David" (see Psalms 27, 28). The Septuagint has "for Solomon."

72.1-2

RSV	TEV
1 Give the king thy justice, O God, and thy righteousness to the royal son! 2 May he judge thy people with righteousness, and thy poor with justice!	1 Teach the king to judge with your righteousness, O God; share with him your own justice, 2 so that he will rule over your people with justice and govern the oppressed with righteousness.

The opening prayer for **justice** and **righteousness** for the king uses the two nouns as synonyms. For **justice** (verses 1a, 2b) and the related verb in verse 4a, see 7.6 and comments on "judgment"; for **righteousness** (verses 1b, 2a, 3b) see

621

comments on 4.1 ("right"); 5.8. It should be noted that in verse 1a the Hebrew text has the plural form, which some take to mean "your judgments" (NJV), "your statutes" (Weiser); the Septuagint and Syriac have the singular form, which makes for a better parallel with the singular in line b.

In verse 1 the verb **Give** is used in the sense of "endow" (NEB, NAB, NJV), that is, to confer on the king the qualities mentioned; TEV has used "**Teach . . . to judge**" and "**share**" to express the idea of the Hebrew verb. TEV has thereby restructured **Give the king thy justice**, so that **justice** is the event of judging and **righteousness** is the manner of judging. This model may be followed in many languages. Often **judge** is expressed idiomatically as "cut the words," meaning "to give a decision." In some languages "judge" as a verb combines the notions of "investigation" and "judgment." **Righteousness** is often rendered as "true" or "straightness," or by figurative expressions.

The Hebrew form is "to the king," "to the son of the king," and represents poetic word-pairing in which the noun of line a is paralleled in line b by "son of" plus the word from line a. (For further examples see Amos 1.4; Judges 5.12; 2 Sam 20.2; Num 23.18.) TEV has not attempted to keep the word pair but has replaced "son of the king" in line b with "**him**." Translators should be able to retain the Hebrew order of the lines but should avoid giving the impression that two royal persons are involved. In some languages it will be necessary to say "our king" instead of **the king**; for example, "O God, show our king how you judge matters fairly, and teach our king your goodness."

For the **poor** (verse 2b) see 9.12; the psalmist calls them **thy poor** in parallel with **thy people** in line a. This does not necessarily imply that all the people were poor and oppressed; it recognizes that the oppressed among the people have special need of justice. This psalm stresses what is now called a preferential treatment of the poor. The translator will note that RSV, following the Hebrew, has **thy people** and **thy poor,** whereas TEV has "**your people**" and "**the oppressed**." This may be for stylistic reasons in English; however, in some languages it will be clearer to employ the possessive pronoun, or its equivalent, with both. Otherwise it may appear that "the oppressed" are not God's people. Verses 1 and 2 form a chiastic pattern with the sequence A-B-B'-A': justice, righteousness; righteousness, justice. This is a poetic device used at the opening of the psalm and calls the reader's attention to the major theme running through the psalm. Translators may feel that lines a and b of verse 2 are so similar in content that they should be reduced to one. This is possible. However, if that is done, the translator is obliged to compensate for the loss in emphasis given to the theme, by providing an equivalent device in the receptor language. Since Psalm 72 is a prayer, English "May . . ." is repeated in many stanzas and must be recast in some languages; for example, "I pray that . . ." or "I ask that . . . ."

For the verb **judge** (TEV "**rule**") in verse 2, see 7.8a; it is synonymous with the more frequently used verb in verse 4a (see 7.8b). The traditional translation **judge** may be too limited; the verb applies to all aspects of the king's rule and not just to his function as judge; so TOB, SPCL "govern."

RSV   TEV

| 3 | Let the mountains bear prosperity for the people, and the hills, in righteousness! | 3 | May the land enjoy prosperity; may it experience righteousness. |
| 4 | May he defend the cause of the poor of the people, give deliverance to the needy, and crush the oppressor! | 4 | May the king ·judge the poor fairly; may he help the needy and defeat their oppressors. |

In verse 3 **the mountains** and **the hills** represent the whole country; the verb translated **bear** means "to carry," either in the sense of producing rich harvests or, as messengers, carrying a message of peace (so Briggs). The former seems preferable; the people's well-being and justice will be the harvest that the country will produce as a result of the king's righteous rule.

Prosperity (verse 3a) translates the Hebrew *shalom* (see 29.11 and comment), usually represented by "peace." The parallel **righteousness** in verse 3b shows that the nation's prosperity was not simply a matter of financial well-being but of conformity to the laws of God. The Masoretic text in line a has "peace" as the direct object, but in line b the parallel is "in (or, with) righteousness." TOB translates the whole verse "As a result of justice, may the mountains and hills bear prosperity for the people!" HOTTP says two interpretations of the Masoretic text are possible: (1) "the mountains bring forth peace for the people and the hills (bring it forth) through righteousness"; (2) "the mountains bring forth peace for the people, and the hills (bring with them) righteousness" ("them" refers to the mountains, with which the hills participate in bringing forth righteousness). Some translations (TEV, SPCL, FRCL), following the ancient versions (the Septuagint, Syriac, Vulgate, Jerome), omit the preposition and have "righteousness" as the direct object.

Mountains bear prosperity as well as "enjoy prosperity" and "experience righteousness" are expressions which will often require shifting to a more specific level. Therefore in some languages it will be clearer to say "I pray that the land will give the people good harvests" or ". . . produce good crops." By substituting "**land**" for **mountains** and **hills**, the parallelism is reduced. The problem then is how to express line b **in righteousness**, since the prayer is that the land "**experience righteousness**." In many languages **righteousness** will not be associated with land but rather with the people of the land. If **in righteousness** is understood as instrumentality, then the translator may say, for example, "may the land do this through righteousness," an awkward expression in many languages, since it fails to show who is righteous—the land, the people, or God. Therefore it may be necessary to shift from instrumentality to cause; for example, "may the land . . . because your people are righteous" or ". . . because your people serve you."

In verse 4a **the poor of the people** (see comments on "the afflicted" in 9.12) is parallel with the Hebrew phrase "the sons of the needy" in verse 4b (for which see "needy" and comment in 35.10). In verse 4b **give deliverance** translates the verb "to save" (see "Help" and comments at 12.1).

The needy may sometimes be rendered "people who do not have what they need." **Oppressor** is sometimes rendered "those who hold other people down" or "those who take away other people's rights." In other languages an oppressor is "a person who derides others" or "one who eats on the backs of others," meaning that he exploits them for his own advantage.

72.5

RSV	TEV
May he live*r* while the sun endures, and as long as the moon, throughout all generations!	May your people worship you as long as the sun shines, as long as the moon gives light, for ages to come.

r Gk: Heb *may they fear thee*

In the Hebrew text (followed by Syriac, Targum, Jerome) the psalmist suddenly switches from the king to the people, "may they fear you," which TEV translates **"May your people worship you"** (see also NJV, TOB; SPCL has "may the king fear you"). **"You"** is God, not the king, who is always spoken of in the third person. RSV and most other translations follow the Septuagint, **May he live**, a prayer for the continued reign of the royal dynasty (see 21.4). This makes more sense in the context and may be original.[1]

In translation it is important to avoid a confusion of pronominal reference in this verse, and accordingly one may translate, for example, "I pray that your people, God, may worship you" or "I ask that the people worship God." If translators follow RSV **May he live**, they may refer to Psalm 22.26 for translational suggestions.

While the sun endures translates what is literally "with the sun," and **as long as the moon** translates "in the presence of the moon." For similar language see 89.36-37. The psalmist is not implying by this that some day the sun and the moon will quit shining; he is speaking of a never-ending rule of the royal dynasty, and it may be more effective to state this explicitly, as follows: "May the king and his descendants rule for all time to come, as long as the sun shines, as long as the moon exists." In languages in which **"as long as the sun shines"** would appear to contradict "all time to come," one may say "rule the people forever, until there is no more sun or moon to shine."

72.6-7

RSV	TEV
6 May he be like rain that falls on the mown grass, like showers that water the earth! 7 In his days may righteousness flourish,	6 May the king be like rain on the fields, like showers falling on the land. 7 May righteousness flourish in his lifetime, and may prosperity last as long

---

[1]HOTTP favors the Septuagint ("C" decision), judging that there is an unintentional scribal error in the Masoretic text (factor 12).

and peace abound, till the moon be no more!	as the moon gives light.

The psalmist prays that the king's reign may benefit the people, **like rain that falls on the mown grass, like showers that water the earth**. In verse 6a the Hebrew word translated **mown grass** (NJV "mown field") may refer to a field whose grass has been mown once and needs rain for a second growth (Kirkpatrick; see Amos 7.1); others take it to mean grain that is ready for reaping (Briggs; so NJV "early crops"). This is hardly the sense, since rain on grain that is ready to harvest can cause crop damage. A general term like "planted fields" or "growing crops" will be more effective in translation.

In many languages it will be necessary to make clear in the translation the beneficial purpose of the rain simile; for example, "May the king's rule help the people like rain . . ."; or the purpose may be repeated in both clauses; for example, "May the king's reign provide for the people as the rains provide for the growing crops." In areas where rain does not fall, but where irrigation is based on river water coming from a distant source, the translator may substitute "water" for rain and say, for example, "May he be like the water that nourishes the growing crops, like the river waters that nourish the earth."

In verse 6b the Hebrew term translated **that water** (TEV "**falling on**") occurs only here in the Old Testament and is still somewhat of a puzzle; but the general sense in this context seems clear enough.

In his days (TEV "**in his lifetime**") may also be rendered "as long as he lives."

In verse 7a the Masoretic text is "the righteous person" (*tsadiq*); several Hebrew manuscripts and the Septuagint, Syriac, and Jerome have "righteousness" (*tsedeq*), which better parallels **peace** in line **b** (see verse 3).[2] The expression **may righteousness flourish** may sometimes be rendered as "I pray that straightness (goodness, right living) increase everywhere."

Peace rendered "**prosperity**" in TEV will be translated differently in various languages. Where the focus is upon the happy state of the individuals, many languages express the idea idiomatically; for example, "may people with cool hearts sit well." If the focus is upon material prosperity, many languages may say something like "may the good things the people receive from God increase" or "may God give more and more good things to his people."

Till the moon be no more is a poetic way of saying "for ever."

72.8-9	RSV		TEV
8	May he have dominion from sea to sea, and from the River to the ends of the earth!	8	His kingdom will reach from sea to sea, from the Euphrates to the ends of the earth.
9	May his foes^s bow down before	9	The peoples of the desert will bow

---

[2]Here also HOTTP decides against the Masoretic text, attributing its reading "the righteous person" to assimilation to parallel passages.

<table>
<tr><td>him,
and his enemies lick the dust!</td><td>down before him;
his enemies will throw themselves to the ground.</td></tr>
</table>

him,
and his enemies lick the dust!

down before him;
his enemies will throw themselves to the ground.

^s Cn: Heb *those who dwell in the wilderness*

Verses 8-11 may be understood as a statement (TEV, BJ, NJB, NIV, GECL) or as a petition (RSV, FRCL, NJV, SPCL, Dahood); NEB, NAB, TOB, and Weiser translate verse 8 as a petition and verses 9-11 as statements. The context seems to favor that all four verses be read as petitions.

The psalmist prays that the extent of the kingdom be **from sea to sea**; Exodus 23.31 suggests "from the Gulf of Aqaba to the Mediterranean" (TEV); others think it means "from the Dead Sea to the Mediterranean"; Briggs proposes "from the Mediterranean to the Indian Ocean." Anderson suggests it may mean simply "the whole earth." Many languages will find it awkward to speak of something extending **from sea to sea,** particularly where no seas are known. In such cases the translator must substitute a known extension that represents the greatest distance between two points, or shift to some expression such as "from one end of the land to the other" or "from where the sun rises to where the sun sets."

In verse 8b **the River** is the Euphrates. Translators are advised to follow TEV and other modern versions which specify the **River** as the Euphrates. In most cases it will be necessary to say "from the river called the Euphrates," so that Euphrates is identified as a river, and it should be found on an accompanying map in the Bible.

For **the ends of the earth**, see comments on 2.8; 59.13. **To the ends of the earth** must often be recast in other forms; for example, "to the setting of the sun" or "to the place where the rivers disappear."

Verse 8 is identical with Zechariah 9.10.

"**The peoples of the desert**" (TEV; see RSV footnote) translates a word whose meaning is not clear. The Septuagint translates "the Ethiopians" (so NEB); Dahood and NIV "the desert tribes"; NJV "desert-dwellers"; TOB "nomads." But the word is used also of animals (see 74.14) and of demons (see Isa 13.21; 34.14) that inhabit the desert. So BJ and NJB have "the Beast," which is interpreted as defeated pagan nations. RSV, NAB, and FRCL prefer to emend to **his foes** (so Briggs, Weiser, Anderson), parallel with **his enemies** in the next line; this is possible but not necessary.³

If the translator follows TEV's "**peoples of the desert,**" in some languages it will be difficult to express the idea of "people who live in deserts," since "desert" may have been described in the New Testament as an uninhabited place. Sometimes it is possible to say "people who live out where the wild animals live." This also may be unclear since in many areas such animals live in heavily forested areas. Since the parallel reference is to enemies in 9b, the best solution may be to employ "enemies" in 9a and "they" in 9b.

In verse 9b the expressive **lick the dust** is a figure of defeat and submission. **Lick the dust** should not be used literally, unless it is a genuine idiom for defeat.

---

³HOTTP does not emend but refers to 79.14, where the same word appears, and says that in both passages it may mean "dwellers of the desert" or "navigators."

Some languages distinguish between dust that is on the ground, dust that is in the air, and dust that has settled on objects. In recasting this metaphor to a nonmetaphor, it may be necessary to introduce the agent; for example, "may the king put his enemies low" or "may the king defeat his enemies."

72.10-11   RSV   TEV

10 May the kings of Tarshish and of   10 The kings of Spain and of the
        the isles   islands will offer him gifts;
      render him tribute,   the kings of Sheba and Seba*
    may the kings of Sheba and Seba   will bring him offerings.
      bring gifts!   11 All kings will bow down before
11 May all kings fall down before   him;
        him,   all nations will serve him.
      all nations serve him!

                                            * SHEBA AND SEBA: *Sheba was toward
                                            the south in Arabia and Seba was on the
                                            opposite side of the Red Sea.*

Tarshish is generally taken to mean Spain (see comments on 48.7), the extreme western boundary of the known world at that time. **The isles** are in the Mediterranean; the Hebrew word probably includes also the countries along the seacoasts. **Sheba and Seba** are generally thought to be a kingdom in southern Arabia and a kingdom in north Africa, in the territory now occupied by Ethiopia (see TEV footnote); but this is not certain.

Translators must pay particular attention when transliterating Spain, Tarshish, Sheba, and Seba, to insure that no inappropriate word is created. A transliterated word sometimes sounds very much like another word in the language, and the meaning of the original word attaches to the transliterated word; or, in other cases, a vulgar word may result which makes public reading awkward.

The psalmist sees all foreign nations sending **tribute** and **gifts** to the king of Israel as proof of their submission to him; however, as McCullough points out, nothing is said about their worshiping Yahweh, the God of Israel.

Verse 11 offers no difficulties for the translator; in line **b** **all nations** may be translated "the people of all the countries in the world," or simply "all the tribes."

72.12-14   RSV   TEV

12 For he delivers the needy when he   12 He rescues the poor who call to
        calls,   him,
      the poor and him who has no   and those who are needy and
        helper.   neglected.
13 He has pity on the weak and the   13 He has pity on the weak and poor;
        needy,   he saves the lives of those in
      and saves the lives of the needy.   need.
14 From oppression and violence he   14 He rescues them from oppression
        redeems their life;   and violence;

> and precious is their blood in
> his sight.
>
>   their lives are precious to him.

Verse 12 begins with the conjunction *ki*, which most translate **For** (RSV, NEB, NJV, NIV, NAB, BJ, NJB, SPCL); TOB renders it as an affirmative, "Indeed" (so Anderson); TEV, GECL, and FRCL do not formally represent it. It does not seem likely that the psalmist meant that the king's universal reign (verses 8-11) would be due to the fact that he is kindly and compassionate; it seems rather that the conjunction represents the psalmist's conviction that he is justified in making the prayer for the king (or else, if verses 8-11 are taken as a statement, in predicting his future universal reign), because the king is kindly and compassionate.

In verses 12-13 the psalmist uses a variety of expressions to designate those who are in special need of help: **needy, poor** (the words used in verse 4; the same word **needy** is also used in verse 13a,b). "**Neglected**" in verse 12b translates **him who has no helper**; **the weak** translates a word rendered "the poor" in 41.1, which is another meaning. **When he calls** translates the same verb used in 18.6b; it means to ask for help.

Line **b** of verse 12 in both RSV and TEV is an expansion of the goal, **the needy**, in line **a**. In some languages it will be more natural to keep the compound goal together, that is, "the king rescues the poor and the needy who call on him and who are neglected."

(It should be noted that verse 12a in RSV is ambiguous; generally an expression like **the needy** is collective and refers to many people, not to one person; so this makes it appear that **when he calls** refers to the king instead of the **needy**.)

He has pity in verse 13a is often rendered idiomatically; for example, "the king has a warm stomach . . . ," or "the king has a white liver . . . ," or "the king feels weakness . . . ." In verse 13b **the lives** and in verse 14a **their life** translate "their *nefeshes*" (see 3.2). In verse 13b **saves** translates the verb used in 12.1 ("Help"), and in verse 14a **redeems** translates the verb used in 69.18 (see also "redeemer" in 19.14).

Oppression and violence must often be translated by two clauses, and thus an agent of each verb must be supplied; for example, "he rescues the poor from people who oppress them and who treat them cruelly."

The last line of verse 14, **precious is their blood in his sight**, means that "their lives are precious to him" (see also FRCL, GECL, SPCL), that is, that they have worth, value, in his estimation, which is the opposite of the usual attitude of human rulers toward the poor and the oppressed. Or else, in line with 116.15, it means that the king takes no pleasure in the death of the poor and oppressed; it is a painful experience for him when they die (so NJV "the shedding of their blood weighs heavily upon him").

72.15-16   RSV   TEV

15   Long may he live,   15   Long live the king!
         may gold of Sheba be given to   May he be given gold from She-
         him!   ba;
     May prayer be made for him con-   may prayers be said for him at

	tinually, and blessings invoked for him all the day!		all times; may God's blessings be on him always!
16	May there be abundance of grain in the land; on the tops of the mountains may it wave; may its fruit be like Lebanon; and may men blossom forth from the cities like the grass of the field!	16	May there be plenty of grain in the land; may the hills be covered with crops, as fruitful as those of Lebanon. May the cities be filled with peo- ple, like fields full of grass.

The psalm closes with a final petition for the king's long and prosperous reign (verses 15-17). For a translation of **Long may he live**, see 22.26.

For **Sheba** see verse 10. Both RSV and TEV passive constructions may require shifting to active constructions in translation, in which case the object of **May prayer be made for him** may be stated as "May the people pray for him continually and ask God to bless him always." In languages which do not use a passive, **may gold of Sheba be given** may have to be rendered "may the people of Sheba give him gold."

In verse 15d the Hebrew is "may he be blessed all the day," which may be a prayer for "**God's blessings**" to rest on him (so TEV) or, as RSV has it, the people's **blessings**, that is, their prayers on his behalf, which is parallel with the preceding line (also NJB, NJV, FRCL, NIV). It seems best to follow RSV here.

Verse 16 has some words not occurring elsewhere in the Old Testament, whose meaning is in doubt. In line a the word translated **abundance** is unknown elsewhere; in line b the word translated **wave** means elsewhere "to shake" (usually of earthquakes). In line d the verb translated "be filled" by TEV means "to bloom," used of plants (RSV **blossom forth**). The petition for cities full of people seems a bit odd, and some commentators and translators emend the text to get a reference to crops; so SPCL "may there be ears of grain like grass in the fields" (similarly NEB). But the Masoretic text can be translated; so HOTTP, RSV, TEV; NJV "and let men sprout up in towns like country grass"; NAB "the city dwellers shall flourish like verdure of the fields." (There was no problem of overpopulation at that time.)

If there is no generic term for **grain**, translators may consider using the dominant plant grown in the area. In areas where farming is possible only in the valleys, never on mountain tops, some adjustment may be necessary to express the thought of grain waving **on the tops of the mountains**; either as in TEV or, for example, "may the crops grow everywhere, even on the hill tops." In order to make clear the reference to **fruit be like Lebanon**, it will often be necessary to say "may the grain grow as well as it does on the mountains called Lebanon." (Modern readers may only know Lebanon as the name of a Mediterranean country.)

72.17	RSV	TEV
	May his name endure for ever, his fame continue as long as the sun!	May the king's name never be forgotten; may his fame last as long as the

> May men bless themselves by him,
> all nations call him blessed!

> sun.
> May all nations ask God to bless
> them
> as he has blessed the king.[x]

[x] as he has blessed the king; *or* and may
they wish happiness for the king.

In verse 17a,b the prayer is for the king's perpetual **fame** (in Hebrew the word
"name" is used in both lines); this involves the continuation of the king's royal
dynasty (see discussion of 21.4).

TEV has recast the positive **his name endure for ever** into a double negative,
"**never be forgotten.**" In some languages this expression may be rendered "may
people remember his name forever" or "may people speak well of him forever." In
line **b** the verb translated **continue** occurs nowhere else in the Old Testament; it
seems to mean "sprout forth"; NEB rejects it as unintelligible and translates the
Septuagint "live for ever." HOTTP follows the Masoretic text and translates "may his
name flourish."

Verse 17c in Hebrew is "and they shall bless themselves in him," which may be
interpreted in two ways: (1) "May they ask God to bless them as he has blessed him
(the king)"—so TEV and NEB (which supplies "all people" as the subject, taken from
the Septuagint). As a statement this would be "So shall all peoples pray to be blessed
as he was" (see Kirkpatrick, McCullough). FRCL has "May all people use his name
when they bless one another." (2) "May they be blessed through him," that is, may
the king be the cause or instrument of their blessings (Briggs); so SPCL "May all
nations of the world receive blessings by means of him" (similarly BJ, NJB); NIV "All
nations will be blessed through him." There are good reasons to follow each of the
two interpretations given here; the first one, followed by TEV, NEB, and NJV, seems
preferable, but a translator should feel free to prefer the other interpretation.

Line **d** in Hebrew is "may all nations wish him happiness" (or "call him
happy"); the same form of the verb is translated "called blessed" in 41.2b. NJV has
"let all nations count him happy"; BJ "May all the heathen wish him blessings"; and
NEB "all nations (shall) tell of his happiness."

TEV text has taken the two lines to express one idea, but it is better to translate
as follows: "May all peoples ask God to bless them as he has blessed the king; may
they all pray for his happiness."

72.18-19   RSV   TEV

18   Blessed be the LORD, the God of   18   Praise the LORD, the God of Is-
       Israel,   rael!
     who   alone   does   wondrous   He alone does these wonderful
       things.   things.

19 Blessed be his glorious name for ever; may his glory fill the whole earth! Amen and Amen!	19 Praise his glorious name forever! May his glory fill the whole world. Amen! Amen!

The concluding doxology was added as an appropriate ending for Book Two of the Psalms (Psalms 42–72; see 41.13). For **Blessed be** see comments on 18.46. **Blessed be the LORD** or TEV **"Praise the LORD"** is sometimes rendered "Let all people speak well of the LORD, who is the God of Israel." This may be stated in direct speech as "Let all people say 'The LORD is great' . . . ."

English "alone" in **who alone** and TEV **"He alone"** means "He is the only one who . . . ." For **wondrous things** see comments on the similar expression in 9.1.

To say that God's **name** is **glorious** means that God is great, powerful, and marvelous, who has blessed his people, the people of Israel, in extraordinary ways (verse 18b). For **name** as representing the person, see comments on 5.11.

God's **glory** is his power, majesty, and goodness revealed in what he does, especially in his love and care for his people.

Amen means "So be it" (see 41.13). FRCL translates the whole line "Amen, yes, that it really be thus!"

72.20   RSV   TEV

The prayers of David, the son of Jesse, are ended.	This is the end of the prayers of David son of Jesse.

This prose line, written as the close of an early collection of David's prayers, before the final collection of the Psalms, is not part of this psalm (see Hebrew title of Psa 86). It is omitted by some Hebrew manuscripts and the Syriac. Instead of the Hebrew **prayers** the Septuagint has "songs"; the difference between the two words in Hebrew is of one letter only.

Book Three

(Psalms 73–89)

Psalm 73

Like Psalms 37 and 49, this psalm is a wisdom psalm, designed to instruct the reader about certain basic questions relating to belief in God as a God of justice. The need for this instruction arises from the fact that those who had disobeyed God's laws had not been punished as the psalmist felt they should have been. Toombs describes the psalm as "a journey from the dark night of doubt to the dawn of faith."

There is nothing in the psalm to allow us to identify its author or the circumstances under which it was written. The author was a man who had been faithful to God but had not been rewarded for it (verses 13-14); the prosperity of the wicked (verses 4-8) raised sharp doubts in his mind about the justice of God, and this psalm represents the way in which he tried to settle his doubts. Its inspired insights have been a source of spiritual help and of thanksgiving. Weiser compares it to the book of Job, even though it is not as artistic a composition as Job: "It is the very simplicity with which the psalmist expresses most profound insights which makes his song in this respect unsurpassed in the Old Testament." R. Kittel gave it the title "The Great Nevertheless" (see verse 23).

The psalm begins with a general statement of the psalmist's dilemma (verses 1-3), followed by a description of the good fortune of the wicked (verses 4-12). So the psalmist expresses his doubts (verses 13-16), which are settled when in the Temple he experiences once more the assurance of God's justice: the prosperity of the wicked is temporary (verses 17-20), while the security of the righteous is permanent (verses 21-28).

HEADING: "The Justice of God." "The pilgrimage of a soul"; "The goodness of God"; "The triumph of justice." In many translations the TEV heading must be recast as a full sentence; for example, "God does what is right" or "God decides matters in a just way." (For a similar heading, see Psalm 7.)

Hebrew title: **A Psalm of Asaph** (TEV "**By Asaph**").

There are twelve psalms attributed to **Asaph**; the first one is Psalm 50, which is in Book Two, and the other eleven (Psalms 73–83) are at the beginning of Book Three.

632

RSV   TEV

	RSV		TEV
1	Truly God is good to the upright, to those who are pure in heart.[t]	1	God is indeed good to Israel, to those who have pure hearts.
2	But as for me, my feet had almost stumbled, my steps had well nigh slipped.	2	But I had nearly lost confidence; my faith was almost gone
3	For I was envious of the arrogant, when I saw the prosperity of the wicked.	3	because I was jealous of the proud when I saw that things go well for the wicked.

[t] Or *Truly God is good to Israel, to those who are pure in heart*

The psalm begins with a basic statement of faith, which starts with a strong declaration, **Truly**, "**indeed.**" In the first line of verse 1 RSV, instead of translating the Masoretic text "to Israel," divides the Hebrew text so as to get the phrase **to the upright**, in parallel with the **pure in heart** in the next line (similarly NEB, NAB). This produces a more satisfying parallelism but is not necessary.[1] The translator will note that TEV's "**Israel**" and "**pure hearts**" are not to be taken as parallel and synonymous. The basis for the parallelism is **God is good**, which is elliptical in line b. "Israel" must often be rendered as "the people of Israel."

To be **pure in heart** is not only to be free of hidden sins, but to be faithful in one's devotion to God's Law; it is to be single-minded in one's loyalty to him. **Pure in heart** is sometimes rendered "with a white heart" or "with a full heart." When using such figurative expressions with the sense of "faithful devotion," it may be more accurate to say (as in GECL) "who listen to God with their whole heart" or, as in some languages, "who follow God's way with one heart" or "who walk on God's road with one mouth."

The identity of the speaker in verse 2 may not always be clear to the reader, since the opening statement concerning God's goodness is not attributed to anyone. Therefore in some languages it may be clearer to the reader to open line a of verse 1 by "I say that God is really good to Israel."

In verse 2 the psalmist speaks of his own experience, how his **feet had almost stumbled**, his **steps had well nigh slipped**. This had happened because of his doubts about God's justice and goodness. TEV abandons the metaphors and represents the meaning in terms of losing "**confidence**" and "**faith.**" Most translations retain the metaphors; a translator should be sure that they will not be misunderstood by the readers. SPCL translates "A little more, and I would have fallen; my feet almost slipped."

The psalmist's doubts had been caused by his jealousy of **the arrogant**, as he noticed **the prosperity of the wicked**, literally, "the *shalom* of the wicked" (here, as in 72.3, the word means "success, prosperity"). **The arrogant** are those who believe they have no need to obey God's laws. Both RSV and TEV imply that two different

---

[1]HOTTP sees RSV and NAB as pure conjecture and therefore not to be included in their considerations.

groups are being referred to in verse 30, **"the proud"** and **"the wicked"**; but this is a matter of poetic parallelism, and a better translation would be (following TEV structure) "for I saw that the wicked prosper, and I became jealous of those proud people."

The logical sequence of verses 2 and 3 may cause problems in some languages and thus require shifting, so that the order will then be verse 3 (line b first cause, line a second cause), verse 2 lines a and b result; for example, "When I saw that things go well for the wicked, I was jealous of those proud people; therefore I had nearly lost confidence, and my faith was almost gone."

73.4-5	RSV	TEV
4	For they have no pangs; their bodies are sound and sleek.	4 They do not suffer pain; they are strong and healthy.
5	They are not in trouble as other men are; they are not stricken like other men.	5 They do not suffer as other people do; they do not have the troubles that others have.

The psalmist describes the wicked: they are free from pain, they are strong and healthy, and they are spared the troubles that others have (verses 4-5). In verse 4a the Hebrew word translated **pangs** is the plural of a form meaning "rope, bond" (see Isa 58.6), which is here used figuratively. The whole line a is "For there are no pains (or, ropes) in their death." This is taken to mean that death holds no terror for them (see NJV, SPCL). But the majority of translations prefer to divide the Masoretic text *lemotam* "for their death" into *lamo tam* "to them health," the first word going with line a and the second one with line b (so RSV, TEV, NEB, FRCL, and others).[2]

Verse 4b is literally "their bellies are fat," indicating that the wicked are well-fed and healthy, not that they are necessarily overweight.

In translation it will often be advisable to use the noun phrase "the wicked," since this reinforces the referent for the repeated use of **they** which occurs in verses 4-12. In fact, in many languages it will be necessary to reintroduce the noun referent several times in these verses. In RSV and TEV the two statements of verse 4 are simply in parallel, the first being negative and the second positive. In some languages it will be more natural to place the positive first, and the following negative to be understood as a consequence; for example, "They are sound and healthy and so do not suffer pain" or "Because they are sound and healthy, they do not suffer pain."

In verse 5 the psalmist complains that the wicked escape the troubles and difficulties other people encounter; in line b the verb in Hebrew is "to touch, hit," which means, here, to be struck by blows of misfortune and disaster. The word **trouble** occurs in line a of RSV and line b of TEV. This is because TEV has chosen to

---

[2]HOTTP recognizes that this is a difficult verse and says the Masoretic text may be understood in two ways: (1) "(for there are no bonds) (leading them) to their death"; (2) "(for there are no torments) until their death."

translate the two parallel verbs as **"suffer"** and **"not have troubles,"** whereas RSV translates the second verb by the more literal **are not stricken**. Many languages use terms of perception to express both of these ideas; for example, "to see distress," "to feel trouble," "to taste difficulties," "to smell anxiety."

73.6-7	RSV	TEV
6	Therefore pride is their necklace; violence covers them as a garment.	6 And so they wear pride like a necklace and violence like a robe;
7	Their eyes swell out with fatness, their hearts overflow with follies.	7 their hearts pour out evil,[z] and their minds are busy with wicked schemes.

[z] *Some ancient translations* their hearts pour out evil; *Hebrew unclear.*

Verse 6 is a consequence of verses 4-5 and should be clearly marked as such in translation. RSV **Therefore** may be represented by "That is why" or "That is the reason why . . . ."

In verse 6 the **pride** and the **violence** of wicked people are compared to a **necklace** and a **garment**. The emphasis here is on the fact that these people do not try to hide their pride and their violence; instead they display them openly, unashamedly, as though they were virtues and not defects.

For **necklace** the translator should employ a term that refers to an object worn as a symbol of rank. The Hebrew word suggests a "chain" of gold or jewels worn by high ranking men (see Gen 41.42 for the chain given to Joseph by Pharaoh, or Dan 5.29). The translator must be careful to distinguish between objects worn to symbolize rank, and those worn to symbolize status such as married or single, or associated exclusively with a particular sex. The similes which TEV has used, **"wear pride like a necklace and violence like a robe,"** may have to be recast in some languages to say "their pride can be seen as easily as a necklace, and their violence as easily as the clothes they wear."

The first line of verse 7 in the Masoretic text seems to be "their eye goes out from fatness." A translation such as NJV, "Fat shuts out their eyes," means little, if anything. Some of those who try to translate the Masoretic text take the word **fatness** quite literally; so RSV; NEB "their eyes gleam through folds of fat"; NJB "From their fat oozes out malice"; SPCL "they are so fat that their eyes pop out." Others take the word as a figure of insensitivity, or stubbornness, or unwillingness to submit to God. NIV "From their callous hearts comes iniquity"; and NAB "Out of their crassness comes iniquity." GECL takes "fatness" as a figure of excessive self-indulgence, as follows: "Their luxurious life leads them to sin." Instead of following the Masoretic text "their eye," TEV follows the Septuagint, Syriac, and Vulgate "their iniquity"; and the word for "fatness" is taken in the sense of **"heart"** (see its use in 17.10a). NEB, following G. R. Driver, takes the verb translated **"pour out"** (RSV **swell**) to mean "gleam"; similarly Dahood, who translates "their eyes glisten more than milk." There is hardly any agreement on the form and meaning of the line.

If the translator follows TEV, the metaphor **"hearts pour out evil"** may have to be recast; for example, "their hearts are full of evil thoughts" or "their innermost is full of bad thinking."

The second line is a bit obscure, but the general sense seems clear enough; NEB has "while vain fancies pass through their minds"; NJV "their fancies are extravagant"; FRCL "anyone can clearly see what they are imagining." The word translated "fancies" by NJV (RSV **follies**) is rare and its meaning is uncertain. NIV has "evil conceits," NJB "cunning," and SPCL "evil intentions."

73.8-10   RSV   TEV

8   They scoff and speak with malice;   8   They laugh at other people and
     loftily they threaten oppression.   speak of evil things;
9   They set their mouths against the   they are proud and make plans
     heavens,   to oppress others.
     and their tongue struts through   9   They speak evil of God in heaven
     the earth.   and give arrogant orders to men
                                                on earth,
10   Therefore the people turn and   10   so that even God's people turn to
     praise them;*u*   them
     and find no fault in them.*v*   and eagerly believe whatever
                                                they say.*a*

u Cn: Heb *his people return hither*
v Cn: Heb *abundant waters are drained*   *a* *Verse 10 in Hebrew is unclear.*
by them

The description of the wicked continues. In verse 8a the verb translated <u>scoff</u> occurs nowhere else in the Old Testament. <u>Speak with malice</u> can be understood to mean "plan evil" (NJV); NJB renders the line "Cynically they advocate evil."

Verse 8b is literally "from on high they speak oppression"; the phrase "from on high" denotes pride, arrogance. So RSV and NJB **loftily**, NIV "in their arrogance," and TEV **"they are proud."** These people are proud and they assume that they can, with impunity, carry out their threats to mistreat others.

The language of verse 9 in Hebrew is fairly clear: "they place in heaven their mouth, and their tongue goes about on earth." Most translations, like TEV, RSV, and NEB, take this to mean blasphemy against God (line <u>a</u>) and malicious talk about other people (line <u>b</u>). But some see here mythological allusions in which the wicked are compared to monsters which devour the whole universe, but whose appetite is not satisfied (see Dahood, Anderson). If the translator can maintain the poetic imagery here, he should do so, but not at the expense of falling into a meaningless or misunderstood expression. TEV's **"speak evil of God . . ."** is often rendered "they say evil words about God" or "they say 'God is worthless.'" SPCL has retained the metaphor by saying "they attack the heavens with their lips and go about the earth making idle talk."

Verse 10 in Hebrew is quite unintelligible (see RSV footnote), and most translations resort to emendations. In line <u>a</u> TEV **"God's people"** follows essentially the meaning of the Septuagint, which has "my people." NEB is similar, "And so my people follow their lead" (see also TOB). SPCL has "And so people praise them."

TEV's **"God's people turn to them"** is less specific than RSV's <u>turn and praise them</u>. In most translations it will be best to make the purpose clear; for example, "and so God's people listen to what they say" or ". . . God's people follow their example." Verse 10b in the Masoretic text seems to be "and waters of a full (cup) are drained out to them" (see RSV footnote). TEV has taken the Hebrew as a figure of people "drinking in" whatever the wicked pour out; FRCL "and drink in their words like water." NEB is like AT and RSV: "and find nothing to blame in them."[3]

One translator (Hanson) judged the Hebrew text of this verse so unclear that he did not translate it. However, Bible Society translations are expected to retain it in some form.

73.11-12	RSV	TEV

RSV	TEV
11 And they say, "How can God know? Is there knowledge in the Most High?" 12 Behold, these are the wicked; always at ease, they increase in riches.	11 They say, "God will not know; the Most High will not find out." 12 That is what the wicked are like. They have plenty and are always getting more.

The words in verse 11 are attributed to the wicked; some, however, take the speakers to be the people who are led astray by them in verse 10 (see NJB). The former seems preferable. The idea that **"God will not know"** what they are doing finds expression in such passages as 10.4,11,13. For **the Most High** see 7.17. The purpose of rhetorical questions at this point is to grasp afresh the reader or listener's attention as well as to make an emphatic negative statement. Modification of the rhetorical questions in translation will depend on the function such questions have in the receptor language. They may require an explicit negation to follow, or may be recast as negative statements. In any event, if they are replaced, the attention-getting function should be replaced by an equivalent device in the receptor language. The translation can be "Surely God doesn't know what's happening. The Most High will not discover what we do." It will be necessary in many languages to avoid the ambiguity of reference by making clear the source of this rhetorical question in RSV; for example, "Evil people say . . . ." If the meaning of the two lines is identical in the receptor language, the translator may find it necessary to reduce the two lines to one.

---

[3]HOTTP says that the two different forms of the Masoretic text, the *kethiv* and the *qere*, have two different meanings. The *qere* would be "Therefore his people (that is, God's people) go back to there/to that point (that is, astray from the right road), and water in abundance is (eagerly) absorbed by them (that is, these thoughts of doubt and despair are absorbed by them with eagerness)." The *kethiv* would be "Therefore he brings back his people (that is, God who, for reverence, is not explicitly named, in such a context of rebellion and doubt against his providence) to there/to that point (that is, leading them astray from the right way), and water in abundance is (eagerly) absorbed by them" (with the same explanation as above).

The psalmist's final statement about the wicked (verse 12) sums up his pessimistic conclusion: **always at ease, they increase in riches**. There is nothing that disturbs their ease and well-being, and they keep on getting richer. The Hebrew adjective translated **always at ease** occurs only here in the Psalms; in 30.6 there is a related word, "quietness, ease," which RSV translates "prosperity" and TEV "I felt secure." Here the main idea is that of not having any worries, and so the following may serve as a model for translating this line: "They have no troubles, and keep on getting richer." NJB has "piling up wealth without any worries."

These are the wicked may cause confusion for some readers, since **these** or TEV's **"That is what . . ."** points to the rhetorical questions or negative statements in verse 11. The problem is compounded by the fact that line <u>a</u> points back to verse 11, and line <u>b</u> offers a further amplification on the bad behavior of those people. Therefore translators may find that it is clearer to say, for example, "That is the way evil people talk; and, in addition, they have plenty of wealth and are always getting more."

<u>73.13-14</u> RSV	TEV

13 All in vain have I kept my heart clean
    and washed my hands in innocence.
	13 Is it for nothing, then, that I have kept myself pure
	    and have not committed sin?

14 For all the day long I have been stricken,
    and chastened every morning.
	14 O God, you have made me suffer all day long;
	    every morning you have punished me.

TEV translates verse 13 as a rhetorical question, suggesting the psalmist's anguished perplexity (so NJB, BJ, NAB); most translate as a statement. **All in vain** can be translated "It does me no good (to keep myself pure)." As in 26.6, the figure of **washed my hands in innocence** in verse 13b represents the psalmist's conviction that he is not guilty of any sin which deserves the punishment that he is receiving.

Since verse 13 returns to the first person, and because there is a relation of contrast between 12 and 13, translators should use a natural means in the language to show this; for example, "But on the other hand I have . . ." or "but I have not done like them; I have . . . ." Whether the translator uses a rhetorical question (as in TEV) or a statement (as in RSV), he normally has four choices in handling the metaphor **washed my hands in innocence**: (a) to keep it in its RSV form; (b) to make explicit the meaning of the metaphor; for example, "I have washed my hands to show that I am innocent"; (c) to depart from the metaphor (as in TEV); or (d) to substitute a receptor-language metaphor. In some languages the expression **have I kept my heart clean** is said "I have wiped evil words from my mouth" or "I have kept my heart white."

The expression **all the day long**, if translated literally, will apply in some languages only to one day's time, and therefore should be recast as extended time; for example, "all the time," "every day," or "always."

Verse 14 uses the passive voice of the verb in Hebrew, **I have been stricken** (the same verb is used in verse 5b), and in line <u>b</u> the passive noun phrase "my chastening." Most translations (including FRCL, GECL, SPCL) use the passive voice, leaving it to the reader to decide the source of the psalmist's suffering. TEV understands these passives to refer to God's action and translates with God as the subject of the verbs. But instead of the past tense of TEV, the present tense would be more effective: "O God, you make me suffer all day long; every morning you punish me." The suffering with which the psalmist is being punished could be sickness or some other misfortune. This is the reason for his doubt: the wicked prosper while he, innocent and blameless, suffers. How can a just God allow this to happen?

73.15-17 RSV	TEV
15 If I had said, "I will speak thus," I would have been untrue to the generation of thy children.	15 If I had said such things, I would not be acting as one of your people.
16 But when I thought how to understand this, it seemed to me a wearisome task,	16 I tried to think this problem through, but it was too difficult for me
17 until I went into the sanctuary of God; then I perceived their end.	17 until I went into your Temple. Then I understood what will happen to the wicked.

The psalmist resists the temptation to argue as the wicked do, who say that God has no knowledge of or interest in human affairs (verse 11). Had he so spoken or thought, he would have been guilty of betraying God's people (literally "I would have betrayed the generation of your sons"). The first line of verse 11 can use a direct quote, as TOB does: "If I had said, 'I will reason as they do,' . . ."; and line b can be translated "I would have not been true to your people" or "I would have been unfaithful to your people." This expresses his conviction that, if he had indulged in such a blasphemous statement, he would have been a traitor to his people, which indicates that he would be sinning not only against God but against his people as well. The phrase "your sons" is translated "your disciples" by NJV; FRCL "your sons, my companions." NEB is quite good, "the family of God." It seems better to say "your people" or "the people of God" than to use the word "children" or "sons," which may be misunderstood. Since verse 15 refers to the content of verse 11, readers in some languages may find the referent already too far removed. Something of verse 11 must therefore be reintroduced to build in a bit of redundancy; for example, "If I had said that God can't know things . . . ," or as in direct address, "If I had said, 'God, you have no knowledge of things . . . .' " "The people of God" must often be rendered, not as a possessive, but as a verb phrase; for example, "The people who worship you."

The psalmist remained true to Israel's belief in the rule of God in human affairs and tried to think the matter through, even though it seemed to him to be **a wearisome task** (NJV "a hopeless task"). He went into the Temple (**the sanctuary of God** verse 17a), and there he was given an insight into the fate that awaits the wicked (literally **their end**).

How this insight came to him is not said; the language suggests a special revelation from God, either in a vision or through the inspired word of a priest. Perhaps some ritual was involved.

"**Your Temple**" translates the Hebrew plural "the holy places of God," which HOTTP suggests "may designate the one sanctuary in all its manifold parts." Most take this to refer to the Jerusalem Temple; NJB translates "the sanctuaries of the gods," which in footnote is explained as the ruins of pagan sanctuaries; Dahood and NAB take it to refer to heaven, to which the psalmist was transported in spirit, in a vision or a trance. It seems best to take it to mean the Temple in Jerusalem.

Both RSV and TEV indicate the temporal clause as **until I went into**, which marks the resolution of the psalmist's failure to understand. In some languages it may be necessary to begin a new sentence in 17a and to render this phrase as a means; for example, "Only by going into your Temple did I understand . . ." or "The only way I understood was by going into your Temple."

73.18-19   RSV   TEV

18 Truly thou dost set them in slippery places;
    thou dost make them fall to ruin.
	18 You will put them in slippery places
	    and make them fall to destruction!

19 How they are destroyed in a moment,
    swept away utterly by terrors!
	19 They are instantly destroyed;
	    they go down to a horrible end.

The psalmist describes how God punishes (RSV) or will punish (TEV) the wicked. A translator should feel free to use either the present or the future tense, whichever seems to make better sense. Dahood takes the four nouns in the Hebrew text of verses 18-19 to be titles for Sheol, the world of the dead: "Perdition . . . Desolation . . . Devastation . . . Terrors." For **slippery places** in verse 18a, see similar language in 35.6. **Fall to ruin** and TEV's "**fall to destruction**" must often be recast as simply "to fall" or, in some languages, "to be brought to death." FRCL has "you cause them to fall into a trap."

How they are destroyed in a moment: verse 19 is nearly a repetition of verse 18; the only difference is that the rapidity of the destruction of the wicked is emphasized in verse 19. It is probable that in verse 19b the **terrors** are the terrors of death, that is, "terrible Death" or "Death, the terrible One."

73.20   RSV   TEV

They are[w] like a dream when one awakes,
    on awaking you despise their phantoms.
	They are like a dream that goes away in the morning;
	    when you rouse yourself, O Lord, they disappear.

[w] Cn: Heb *Lord*

This verse is not very clear in Hebrew, but it seems reasonable to understand it to say "(they are) like a dream after one awakes, O Lord; when you rouse, you despise their shadows." The meaning is that the wicked will last no longer than the images in a dream (see similar figures in 39.5-6), that disappear as soon as one wakes up. In line a RSV substitutes the Masoretic text "Lord" by the conjectural text **they are**; this is quite unnecessary.

RSV **phantoms** conveys the notion of something frightening, which is not implied in the Hebrew word. When the Lord rouses himself (see similar expressions in 35.23; 44.23; 59.4-5), he "despises" them; the word here has the idea of "forget intentionally" (see discussion of the same verb in 69.33). TEV **"they disappear"** does not have God as the subject of the action, which is what the Hebrew text does. So something different should be said, perhaps "When you rouse yourself (or, arise), you dismiss them" (or ". . . you forget all about them").

It should be noticed that the first two words of line b in Hebrew can be read "in a city of (their) shadows." Dahood takes "the city of phantoms" (as he translates it) to be another name for Sheol; most take the Masoretic text to be a defective spelling of a form of the verb "to rouse," or else they emend the text slightly to arrive at this meaning (see Anderson). The Septuagint (also Syriac, Vulgate, Jerome) has "in your city."

Perhaps it is best to reverse the two lines, as FRCL and NJV do, and translate "Lord, as soon as you rouse yourself, you forget all about them, just as the images of a dream are forgotten when one wakes up." In translation it may be necessary to reintroduce the subject "evil people." It may, in addition, be necessary to make clearer how it is that the bad dream images depart when the Lord rouses himself. Otherwise the reader may have the impression that the Lord, too, suffers from the dream; for example, "Evil people are like a bad dream that goes away in the morning. The memory of them goes away when you, Lord, come and help me."

73.21-23	RSV	TEV

21	When my soul was embittered,
	     when I was pricked in heart,
		21 When my thoughts were bitter
		         and my feelings were hurt,

22	I was stupid and ignorant,
	     I was like a beast toward thee.
		22 I was as stupid as an animal;
		         I did not understand you.

23	Nevertheless I am continually with
	     thee;
	     thou dost hold my right hand.
		23 Yet I always stay close to you,
		         and you hold me by the hand.

The psalmist reflects on how he had felt at that time in the past, and now regrets his past attitude. At that time, however, he was bitter and hurt (verse 21). The Hebrew text for **soul** is "heart" and for **heart** is "kidneys" (as in 26.2), which represent **"thoughts"** and **"feelings"** (TEV). **Soul . . . embittered** is rendered, as in Hebrew, in many idiomatic ways. In some languages one refers to the "sour throat," in others to a "blackened liver" or a "rotten stomach." **"Were hurt"** (TEV) in line b translates a verb that means "be pierced, run through"; literally, "my kidneys were pierced," which NJV translates "my feelings were numbed," NJB "My heart grew embittered," and NEB "I felt the pangs of envy." FRCL has "I was shocked to the very depths of my being." One may also say "my innermost made me ill" or "I had deep pain in my heart."

In verse 22a the psalmist describes himself as having been **stupid and ignorant**; FRCL has "I was stupid, I understood nothing." The Hebrew word for **stupid** reflects an animal-like stupidity, "brutishness," and this is reflected in **beast** in the next line. In line **b** **a beast** (singular) translates the text of one Hebrew manuscript; the Masoretic text has the plural, "animals, beasts," which NJV translates "I was brutish toward You." It should be noticed that TEV has restructured the two lines, joining **stupid** and **beast** on one line. This verse contains the psalmist's self-understanding, and the translator must decide whether verse 22b describes God's attitude toward him (NEB "I was a mere beast in thy sight, O God") or the psalmist's own behavior toward God, "I behaved like an animal toward you." The latter seems preferable. In some languages the generic "**animal**" may not serve as a comparison for stupidity, since only a specific animal may be so considered. In the absence of such a comparison, it will be better to say "very stupid."

The turning point comes in verse 23, as the psalmist confesses his reliance on God. The thought is similar to that in 63.8. In spite of the psalmist's spiritual stupidity, he was still close to God and was held by him. In the past he was not conscious of this; it is only now that he realizes that he had never been far from God, that God had never let go of him. It is significant that in Hebrew, as well as many other languages, God holds the psalmist's **right hand**. In languages where the right hand is a symbol of honor or strength, it will be best to use the expression as in RSV, unless it will be assumed automatically to be the right hand, even if not specifically stated.

73.24	RSV	TEV

Thou dost guide me with thy counsel, and afterward thou wilt receive me to glory.*ˣ*	You guide me with your instruction and at the end you will receive me with honor.

ˣ Or *honor*

In line **a** the psalmist expresses his confidence in God's guidance; God will always give him the instruction he needs in this life. **With thy counsel** or TEV's "**with your instruction**" states the means by which God leads the psalmist, and may have to be recast in some languages to say, for example, "your teaching shows me the way to go" or "you teach me and I follow your way."

It is disputed whether line **b** refers to eternal life after death as such. It should be noted that the Hebrew word *kabod* "glory" nowhere in the Old Testament has the explicit meaning of "heaven" as the place where God dwells (see comments, 3.3; 7.5). Further, there is no preposition in the Hebrew text that modifies the word "glory"; the Septuagint and other ancient versions have "with glory." The verb **receive** is the one used in 49.15 (see comments there) and is the one which is used of Enoch in Genesis 5.24. The passage here, though not a clear statement of a belief in resurrection or of a bodily assumption into heaven, seems to express a confidence that the psalmist will enjoy unbroken communion with God (Briggs, Dahood, Oesterley, Anderson, Weiser, Toombs, McCullough). Kirkpatrick and Cohen take it to mean vindication in this life. BJ translates "and behind the glory you will take me," taking the word "glory" to mean the brightness hiding God's being, reminiscent of the cloud at the exodus from Egypt. NJV has "You . . . led me toward honor," which is not very clear; FRCL "afterward you will hold me in your glory"; and TOB "you will hold me afterwards, with glory." In some languages **"receive me with honor"** (as in TEV) is to "receive me as a chief," or "welcome me with praise," or "accept me with good words."

TEV's **"and at the end"** suggests a more final state of things than RSV's **and afterward.** In many languages, if the translator follows TEV, it will be necessary to state the end of something. If death is not the primary meaning, this will most often be misleading. Therefore it may be best to say, for example, "and then," leaving open the question of "end of life."

73.25-26	RSV	TEV
25	Whom have I in heaven but thee? And there is nothing upon earth that I desire besides thee.	25 What else do I have in heaven but you? Since I have you, what else could I want on earth?
26	My flesh and my heart may fail, but God is the strength^y of my heart and my portion for ever.	26 My mind and my body may grow weak, but God is my strength; he is all I ever need.

^{y} Heb *rock*

The psalmist is certain that God, in heaven, is for him, that God is with him; in that certainty there is nothing else on earth that he wants. Weiser divides the verse differently from most and translates (following Luther) "As long as I have thee, I wish for nothing else in heaven or on earth"—which is recommended as a good expression of the thought of this verse.

It is only natural that the psalmist would have written "Whom else do I have . . . ?" This, however, does not imply that there might have been other beings in heaven whom he might have; rather, it is a way of saying that having God, in heaven, is all he wants or needs. TEV has tried to express this by saying **"What else . . . what else . . . ?"** It may be better, however, to translate (as SPCL has done) "Whom do I have in heaven? You alone!" Or, as FRCL has done, "Who in heaven will come to my help except you?" Or, as an affirmation, "You are the only one in heaven who is for me" or ". . . who will help me." And line b can be "And since I have you, there is no one else on earth I want."

Whom have I in heaven but thee? must often be recast, since to "have God" would mean possessing God as one possesses an object. The problem is compounded in that the purpose of having God in heaven is not clear. Furthermore, the structure of the question must be shifted in many languages to a statement, "I have no one else in heaven but you" or "You are the only one I have in heaven." More explicit else in heaven but you" or "You are the only one I have in heaven." More explicit is "There is no one in heaven but you, God, who can help me" or "You, God, are the only one in heaven to help me."

In verse 26 the Hebrew for **flesh** and **heart** stand for "**body**" and "**mind**," which TEV has reversed for a more natural order in English. Many languages will be able to retain "body and heart" quite naturally; others may need to shift to other categories that represent the whole human. "**My strength**" translates "the rock of my heart," and "**all I ever need**" represents **my portion for ever** (for comments on **portion** see 16.5). The focus is the contrast between the weakness of the person and the strength of God. **Portion** is correctly taken in the sense of inheritance by SPCL, which says "but God is my eternal inheritance and the one who sustains my heart."

73.27-28	RSV	TEV
27	For lo, those who are far from thee shall perish; thou dost put an end to those who are false to thee.	27 Those who abandon you will certainly perish; you will destroy those who are unfaithful to you.
28	But for me it is good to be near God; I have made the Lord GOD my refuge, that I may tell of all thy works.	28 But as for me, how wonderful to be near God, to find protection with the Sovereign LORD and to proclaim all that he has done!

The psalm ends with a brief statement of the psalmist's faith. Verse 27 begins **For lo**, which indicates the psalmist is about to finish his meditation. Something like "I am certain that" or "I know for sure that" can make this clear. The psalmist knows that the wicked **shall perish** (will be destroyed), the righteous will enjoy God's presence and protection. The fate of the wicked is not simply death; it is destruction (as in 18.40) at the hands of God.

Are far from (TEV "abandon") translates the verb "be far away" (see 22.1 and comments), and **are false** ("unfaithful") is the word used of women guilty of infidelity or of prostitution; so KJV "those that go a whoring from thee" (see similar use of the verb in 106.39b). **Who are false to you** as TEV's "**unfaithful**" may be rendered in some languages "who do not put their heart on you" or "who do not follow your way."

Perish in reference to people is somewhat euphemistic and literary in English and suggests death, but with the focus on the violent or destructive manner of death (see comments on the same Hebrew verb, "destroyed," in 18.40). In some languages it will be necessary to introduce God as the agent of destruction and say, for example, "God will destroy them," or negatively, "God will not allow them to live."

TEV makes all three lines of verse 28 coordinate, "to be near . . . to find . . . to proclaim," whereas RSV and some more recent versions make the second line the means of the final line, "so that I may tell . . . ." **Refuge** is the same word used in 14.6. **Made the Lord GOD my refuge** must often be recast, not as in TEV, where "**protection**" is a noun, but rather, for example, "the Lord GOD has protected me."

Lord GOD translates the combination of the title "lord" and the name "Yahweh" (as in 71.16).

In the last line of verse 28, TEV uses the third person, "**all that he has done,**" for consistency with the first two lines; Hebrew is **all thy works**.

Psalm 74

This psalm expresses the nation's distress and anguish over the invasion of the country by foreign enemies who had destroyed the Temple in Jerusalem (verses 3-7) and other places of worship (verse 8). The people complain that God has abandoned them, and they call on him to change his attitude and save them. There is no confession of sins or request for forgiveness as the basis for the plea to God to act. Instead, God is called upon to fulfill the promise he made to Israel in the covenant (verse 20) and to save his people from their enemies.

The most probable date for the events described in the psalm is 586 B.C., when Jerusalem was captured and the Temple destroyed by the Babylonians. But the statement in verse 9, "there are no prophets left," if taken literally, argues against that date, since there were prophets, such as Ezekiel and Jeremiah, who brought God's message to the people at that time. So some suggest the time of the Maccabees, in the second century B.C. In all, however, the sixth century B.C. date better fits the details of the psalm than any other historical event known to us.

The psalm begins with a cry to God for help (verses 1-3), followed by a description of the destruction wrought by the enemy (verses 4-11). The psalmist interrupts his lament to praise God's power as Creator (verses 12-17), and then resumes his petition for God to act and rescue his people (verses 18-23).

HEADING: "**A Prayer for National Deliverance.**" Other headings are "Lament on the destruction of the Temple"; "Prayer in time of national calamity." TEV's heading must often be recast as a subject and predicate; for example, "The psalmist prays that God will save Israel" or ". . . will rescue the nation from her enemies."

Hebrew title: <u>**A Maskil of Asaph**</u> (TEV "**A poem by Asaph**").
For <u>**Maskil**</u> see title of Psalm 32; for <u>**Asaph**</u> see title of Psalm 50.

<u>74.1-2</u>   RSV   TEV

1 O God, why dost thou cast us off for ever? Why does thy anger smoke against the sheep of thy pasture?	1 Why have you abandoned us like this, O God? Will you be angry with your own people forever?
2 Remember thy congregation, which thou hast gotten of old, which thou hast redeemed to be	2 Remember your people, whom you chose for yourself long ago, whom you brought out of slavery to be your own tribe.

the tribe of thy heritage!   Remember Mount Zion, where
Remember Mount Zion, where   once you lived.
thou hast dwelt.

The psalmist opens with a strong complaint. God has **cast off** his people, he is angry with them, and they do not know why (see similar language in 10.1; 22.1; 44.23-24; 79.5). There is no admission that the people's sins might have been the reason for God's anger.

In verse 1a **cast off** translates a verb meaning "reject" (see its use in 43.2b; 44.23b). **Cast us off** in the sense of discarding something of no value is expressed in some languages as "to throw into the forest" or "to throw into the back place," meaning the place where rubbish is discarded. In the Hebrew text **for ever** comes in line a; TEV places it in line b. A good translation of line a is "O God, why have you rejected us? Will it be for ever?"

In verse 1b the expressive verb "cause to smoke" depicts God's anger as smoke pouring out of his nostrils (see the same image in 18.8). In many languages **anger** is compared to heat or fire in figurative expressions, and in such cases line b may often be rendered "Why has your anger burned . . . ," or "Why are you hot with anger?" or "Why is your heart hot?"

"**Your own people**" represents **the sheep of thy pasture** (see 95.7; 100.3 and comments). **Sheep of thy pasture** refers to the flock which is under God's care. Therefore FRCL says "the flock of which you are the shepherd," and GECL "we are your flock and you are our shepherd." Since the symbolism of sheep and shepherd occurs so frequently throughout the Bible, translators should keep this symbolism if possible. Languages which can maintain **sheep of thy pasture** should do so, provided the expression is fully meaningful to the ordinary readers. If not, it is best to follow TEV's "your own people." It is not recommended that a different animal be used to represent the biblical "sheep."

In verse 2 two expressions are used to speak of Israel as God's people: "your community" (RSV **thy congregation**) and **the tribe of thy heritage**. For comments on **heritage** see 16.6. **The tribe of thy heritage** is a Hebraism that means "the tribe that is your heritage," which does not mean that they are the tribe God inherited from some other god, but that they are the people he chose to be his own. See NJV "your very own tribe that you redeemed." Both expressions stress the exclusive rights that Yahweh has over the people of Israel.

The request **Remember thy congregation** in translation should not imply that God has forgotten. The psalmist calls upon God to "think" about them and their common history. Consequently in languages where "**Remember your people**" will carry the meaning of "Remember who your people are," one may say "Think about your people," or idiomatically, "Put your people into your heart."

The two verbs in verse 2b,c are somewhat parallel: "acquire" and "redeem" (RSV **gotten . . . redeemed**). The first one can be translated "whom you made your own" or "whom you selected to be your own." In the translation of the second one, care should be taken that an equivalent of "redeem" not carry the explicit sense of "to buy" or "to pay for," since that raises questions about whom it was bought from and what was paid for the purchase (see comments at 25.22 and 69.18). A verb such as "save, rescue" is better, since the reference is to Yahweh's delivering his people from bondage in Egypt. Both lines emphasize Yahweh's initiative; it was his choice, his great act of liberation which made Israel his own people. Consequently he is responsible for them, and the people find it impossible to understand why he has now abandoned them. **Of old** (verse 2a) refers back to the time of the exodus from Egypt.

For **Mount Zion** see 2.6.

74.3　　　　　RSV　　　　　　　　　　　　　　TEV

Direct thy steps to the perpetual　　　　Walk over these total ruins;
　　ruins;　　　　　　　　　　　　　　our enemies have destroyed
the enemy has destroyed every-　　　　　everything in the Temple.
　　thing in the sanctuary!

The psalmist invites God to inspect the ruins of the Temple and see for himself what the enemy has done. The ruins are **"total"** (TEV); the Hebrew word "everlasting, perpetual" is not used to indicate that they will never disappear, but to emphasize the fact that the enemy has wrecked and ruined everything. NEB "what was ruined beyond repair"; SPCL, TOB, NJB "endless ruins"; FRCL "ruins already ancient." **Direct thy steps** (TEV **"Walk over"**) translates what is literally "lift up your steps," for which FRCL has "climb up." The meaning may be "rouse yourself to action" (so NJV "Bestir Yourself"). **Direct thy steps** and TEV's **"Walk over these . . ."** imply making a careful inspection of the ruined Temple. Accordingly in some languages it will be necessary to say something more akin to GECL, "Come and see . . . ," or "Climb up and look at . . . ."

Sanctuary: as in 20.2 the Hebrew here is "holy place," which TEV correctly renders "Temple." Elsewhere it is referred to as "house (of Yahweh)" or as "Temple" (as in 5.7), or "meeting place" (as in verse 4a). Translators should determine whether to render all such terms as in the Hebrew and RSV. In any case, the reader must understand clearly that the reference is to the Temple in Jerusalem.

74.4-5　　　　　RSV　　　　　　　　　　　　　　TEV

4　　Thy foes have roared in the midst　　4　　Your enemies have shouted in
　　　　of thy holy place;　　　　　　　　　　triumph in your Temple;
　　they set up their own signs for　　　　　they have placed their flags
　　　　signs.　　　　　　　　　　　　　　there as signs of victory.
5　　At the upper entrance they hacked　　5　　They looked like woodsmen
　　　　the wooden trellis with axes.^z　　　　cutting down trees with their
　　　　　　　　　　　　　　　　　　　　　axes.^c

^z Cn Compare Gk Syr: Heb uncertain

^c *Verse 5 in Hebrew is unclear.*

The psalmist describes how the enemy had completely destroyed the Temple and desecrated it. In verse 4a **roared** refers to the shouts of victory (SPCL has "they sing victory").

TEV's **"shouted in triumph"** may have to be recast in some languages to provide a reason-result clause relationship; for example, "Your enemies shouted in your Temple to show they had triumphed" or, using direct discourse, "Your enemies shouted in your Temple, 'We have conquered you.' "

<u>Thy holy place</u> translates the Hebrew "your meeting place" (so NJV), that is, the place where Yahweh met with his people (see TOB "the very place where you met us"); the same word is used in verse 8b.

Verse 4b in Hebrew is "they placed their signs (for) signs"; although not clear, it seems that this means that the enemy had placed emblems, either religious symbols or military banners, in the Temple. NAB has "tokens of victory"; TEV is like NEB "they planted their standards there as tokens of victory." BJ and NJB follow the ancient versions to get "they fixed their emblems over the entrance," and connect the second "signs" with what follows, "emblems [5] never known before." It is better, however, to follow RSV, NEB, and TEV in their translation of the Masoretic text. In Psalm 20.5 "set up our banners" was translated by TEV as "praising our God," where the meaning is metaphorical. Here, however, the reference is to the objects that were raised in the Temple. In languages where flags or military standards are unfamiliar, it is possible to say, for example, "they have placed their signs of victory here" or "they have put up the signs that show they have defeated us."

Verse 5 is very obscure in the Masoretic text; translators may decide for themselves how to render it, but RSV is not the best model to follow. Weiser does not translate verses 5-6, and those who do translate them differ widely in their rendering of the text. The Masoretic text seems to say "It looked as if (or, It [or, They] became known as) someone raised high in the undergrowth an ax." Or else, as TOB renders line <u>a</u>, "It was known as <u>bringing in on high</u>"; the underlined phrase is translated by RSV (following AT) **At the upper entrance**; no one else does this. The most common emendation is to read "They will be cut off" instead of the Masoretic text "They will be known"; with this emendation, and a change in order of the words, NEB gets "They brought it crashing down, like woodmen plying their axes in the forest." TEV has taken the Masoretic text verb "It is (or, They are) known" in the sense of "It (or, They) looked like"; similarly NAB: "They are like men coming up with axes to a clump of trees" (see Briggs); NJV has "It is like men wielding axes against a gnarled tree."[1] If the translator follows TEV's **"like woodsmen,"** in some languages it will be necessary to say simply "They looked like men in the forest cutting down trees with their axes."

74.6-7	RSV	TEV
6	And then all its carved wood they broke down with hatchets and hammers.	6 They smashed all the wooden panels with their axes and sledge hammers.
7	They set thy sanctuary on fire; to the ground they desecrated the dwelling place of thy name.	7 They wrecked your Temple and set it on fire; they desecrated the place where you are worshiped.

[1]HOTTP ("C" decision) says the text may be interpreted in two ways: (1) "it looked (as if) someone swung the axes high"; (2) "it looked (as if) someone brought axes up."

In verse 6 it is not clear what the Hebrew word translated **carved wood** means; it can mean either carvings on wood or engravings on metal or stone. NJV has "carved work," NEB "carvings," and NAB "paneling." The Septuagint translates "its doors." The two words translated **hatchets** and **hammers** occur only here in the Old Testament, and they are variously translated: NJV "hatchet and pike"; NEB "hatchet and pick"; NJB "axe and pick"; Dahood "hatchets and mattocks." Holladay defines the two as "axes" and "crowbars."[2] The main problem for the translator is to name instruments or weapons that are appropriate for that time. In some languages the means must normally precede the result; for example, "With their axes and hammers they smashed the carved wood."

In verse 7, as RSV shows, **to the ground** is the first word of line b; but it seems better to take it with line a, "They burned your Temple to the ground" or "They razed your Temple and set it on fire." TEV has taken **to the ground** in the sense of "wrecked" (so NEB "tore down"; also TOB) and reversed the order of the two actions as being more natural: "**wrecked . . . and set it on fire.**" 2 Kings 25.9 reports how Nebuzaradan, the commanding general of King Nebuchadnezzar of Babylonia, burned down the Temple and other buildings in Jerusalem in 586 B.C.

It is not stated how the enemy **desecrated** (or "profaned") the Temple, that is, made it unfit for worship. The destruction itself would be an act of desecration, as would be a pagan worship service or the installation of pagan emblems (verse 4). TEV "**the place where you are worshiped**" (verse 7b) translates **the dwelling place of thy name**; NJV has "the dwelling-place of Your presence." This is another way of referring to the Temple, parallel with **thy sanctuary** in line a. **Desecrated the dwelling place of thy name** is sometimes rendered "they dishonored the place where you are worshiped," or "they made filthy the place where you are worshiped," or "they caused the place where you are worshiped to become unclean."

74.8 RSV	TEV

They said to themselves, "We will utterly subdue them"; they burned all the meeting places of God in the land.	They wanted to crush us completely; they burned down every holy place in the land.

This verse in Hebrew has the direct quotation, "They said in their hearts, 'Let us crush them completely!' " In order to avoid confusion of pronouns, TEV has used the indirect form, "**They wanted** (or, decided) **to crush us completely.**"

In line b, instead of the Masoretic text **they burned**, FRCL follows the Septuagint and Syriac "and burn" as a continuation of the direct quotation of line a, so that line b is part of what the enemies said to themselves. TEV has avoided the direct address form in order to preserve the third person plural "**they**" in both lines, thus avoiding possible confusion due to the introduction of **We**.

---

[2]HOTTP says the whole verse should translated "and now—the carvings, at the same time (or, all together), with hatchets and hammers, they smash them."

There is some doubt as to the Hebrew word translated "**crush us**" by TEV (RSV **subdue them**). It may be taken as an irregular form of the verb "to oppress" (AT, RSV, NJV, TEV, NAB); but in the Masoretic text it appears to be "their descendants" (so Dahood, "Let all their progeny be burned"; also Briggs). The translator is advised to follow the lead of RSV, TEV, and others.

TEV "**every holy place**" translates **all the meeting places of God**; the same word is used in verse 4a. SPCL has "all the places where we met to worship you." Some take it here to mean "festivals" (see Briggs). The meaning represented by RSV and TEV is recommended. The "holy places" were shrines (see NJB) or other places where people worshiped God; it is most unlikely that synagogues are meant, in light of the probable time this psalm was composed.

74.9-10	RSV	TEV

| 9 | We do not see our signs; there is no longer any prophet, and there is none among us who knows how long. | 9 | All our sacred symbols are gone; there are no prophets left, and no one knows how long this will last. |
| 10 | How long, O God, is the foe to scoff? Is the enemy to revile thy name for ever? | 10 | How long, O God, will our enemies laugh at you? Will they insult your name forever? |

The psalmist describes the desperate situation of the people of Israel: no **signs**, no **prophet**, no certainty as to **how long** this terrible situation will last. It is not clear what the Hebrew **our signs** in verse 9a refers to: miracles (Dahood); military banners (as the word is used in verse 4; Anderson); the festivals and rituals of the faith (Briggs). There is no way of knowing exactly what the word refers to. HOTTP says it means "our (prophetical) signs"; FRCL has "the signs of your presence," which probably means miracles; see NIV "miraculous signs." Because the interpretation of **our signs** or TEV's "**sacred symbols**" is so uncertain, the translator in smaller languages would be well advised to follow the interpretation given in a major language that people will be reading. (For signs and banners see verse 4.) This is the first mention of **prophet** in the text of the Book of Psalms. (See title of Psalm 51.) In translation it may often be rendered as "one who speaks for God" or "one who speaks God's words to the people." It may be necessary to make clear that it is the situation described in 9a and b that is in doubt. In some languages the expression **who knows how long** may be recast to say, for example, "no one knows when our troubles will end" or "no one knows if this situation will stop or continue."

In verse 10a **scoff** may mean "**laugh at you**" (TEV) or "laugh at us," since there is no direct object in Hebrew; but the parallelism with the next line suggests "you." "Laugh at you" and "insult you" ("revile thy name") are also in verse 18. The two questions in verse 10, while not exactly requests for information, vividly express the people's puzzlement and despair. They can be translated "Surely, O God, you won't let our enemies keep on laughing at you, will you? Surely you won't let them insult your name forever?" **Revile thy name** or TEV "**insult your name**" must be recast in many languages to say "insult you."

74.11 RSV	TEV
Why dost thou hold back thy hand, why dost thou keep thy right hand in*a* thy bosom?	Why have you refused to help us? Why do you keep your hands behind you?*d*
a Cn: Heb *consume thy right hand from*	*d Probable text* Why do you keep your hands behind you; *Hebrew unclear.*

Why dost thou hold back thy hand in line a means "Why do you refuse to help us?" SPCL retains the figure: "Why do you conceal your powerful hand?" FRCL abandons the figure altogether (as does TEV), "Why do you restrain yourself from intervening?" and GECL has "Why do you look on without doing anything?"

Line b is unclear in Hebrew; it seems to be "and your right hand from inside your bosom consume" (see RSV footnote). NJV attempts to translate it "Draw it [your right hand] out of your bosom!" But TEV, RSV, and others prefer to read an emended text; instead of the imperative of the verb "to consume," a form of the verb "to keep" is read, and instead of the preposition "from (your bosom)" the preposition "in" is read. The **bosom** is here the loose fold of the garment into which the wearer could place his hands or some object. TEV has the equivalent cultural gesture of refusing help: "**keep your hands behind you**"; SPCL and FRCL have "with your arms folded." NIV translates "Why do you hold back your hand, your right hand? Take it from the folds of your garment and destroy them!" This is in line with the recommendation of HOTTP.[3] The translator must use expressions in both lines which are entirely natural in the language, and these may have nothing to do with the hands; for example, "Why do you say 'No' when we need help, and shake your head at us?"

74.12 RSV	TEV
Yet God my King is from of old, working salvation in the midst of the earth.	But you have been our king from the beginning, O God; you have saved us many times.

The psalmist praises God as the Creator of the universe, who defeated the forces of chaos and evil. Despite all the defeats of the people at the hands of their enemies, the psalmist knows that God still rules; so he begins with **Yet**, which can be stated more strongly, "But in spite of all this, I know that . . . ." In this verse TEV keeps the second person of address, in line with what comes before and follows after. The psalmist calls God **my King**; in the context it is probable that he is speaking for the nation, and so TEV has "**our king from the beginning**" (see GECL). "The

---

[3]HOTTP says the whole verse (the *qere* form of the Masoretic text) may be interpreted as follows: "Why do you let your hand return, even your right hand? Out of the midst of your bosom put an end (to it)!"

beginning" in this context refers back to the events in Egypt, when Yahweh made the Israelites his own people.

In line **b** the Hebrew is "working deeds of salvation in the middle of the earth (or, land)." The plural of the noun **salvation** may be taken here as "victories" (Briggs, Dahood; TOB); TEV represents the plural by **"you have saved . . . many times,"** and takes the noun "land" to mean the land of Israel, which is represented by "**us**," that is, the people of Israel. NJB takes it to be the world, translating "author of saving acts throughout the earth" (also FRCL). A translation should keep closer to the Hebrew than TEV has, and translate something like "you won many victories (for us) in our land" or "you helped us defeat our enemies here where we live"; see TOB "in the heart (or, center) of our land."

74.13-14 RSV	TEV
13 Thou didst divide the sea by thy might; thou didst break the heads of the dragons on the waters. 14 Thou didst crush the heads of Leviathan, thou didst give him as food _b_ for the creatures of the wilderness. _b_ Heb _food for the people_	13 With your mighty strength you divided the sea and smashed the heads of the sea monsters; 14 you crushed the heads of the monster Leviathan_e_ and fed his body to desert animals._f_ _e_ LEVIATHAN: _A legendary monster which was a symbol of the forces of chaos and evil._ _f_ animals; _or_ people.

Commentators are not agreed whether verses 13-15 refer to creation (Dentan, Fisher, Toombs, Anderson) or to the events of the exodus from Egypt (Briggs). It seems more likely that they refer to creation, using expressions and figures of popular pagan accounts of how the creator God defeated the primeval monsters of the deep. It is significant that seven times in verses 13-17 the psalmist uses the personal pronoun "you" as an emphatic device to assert God's activities; by implication he is denying that some pagan god, Baal or Marduk, had done these things. If the exodus from Egypt is taken as the event being described, then **the dragons** and **Leviathan** are symbols of Egypt.

But on the assumption that creation is being depicted, verse 13a refers to the defeat of the sea, personified as an enemy (see in Gen 1.6-7 the division of the primeval waters into the upper and the lower waters); in some creation accounts the Sea (_Yam_) was a dragon, the opponent of the creator God, who defeated the dragon (see also 89.9-10); so NEB "thou didst cleave the sea-monster in two." In languages where the sea is unknown, it is sometimes possible to speak of a collectivity of waters; for example, "you have divided the places of water in half." Verse 13a may sometimes be rendered as a means-with-result in this way: "by your power you divided the waters in two parts" or "because you are powerful you . . . ."

In verse 13b **the dragons on the waters** may be parallel with **Leviathan** in verse 14a. The Hebrew word is _tanninim_, the plural of _tannin_; in Ugaritic _Tannin_ is another

653

name for **Leviathan**, so here Dahood has "smashed the heads of Tannin." In Job
7.12 "sea" (*yam*) is parallel with "sea monster" (*tannin*).

Verse 14a is parallel with verse 13b; **Leviathan** (also 104.26; Isa 27.1) is the
name of the mythological dragon, which in other places is called by a different name.
Notice that it is thought of as having several **heads**. **Dragons on the waters** may
sometimes be rendered as "great sea snakes" or "big animals that live in the sea."
If such a descriptive expression results in confusion, it is best to provide an
explanatory note.

The creatures of the wilderness (TEV "**desert animals**") translates what is
literally "to the people to the desert dwellers" (see the latter word in 72.9a). The
Septuagint both here and in 72.9a translates "the Ethiopians." The word for
"people" is used in Proverbs 30.25-26 of a group of animals. Here the whole phrase
means either "**desert animals**," as TEV has it (Weiser; SPCL "desert beasts"; BJ and
NJB "wild animals"; NEB and FRCL "sharks"), or "desert people" (see NJV "the
denizens of the desert"; Dahood "desert tribes"). In languages where deserts and
wildernesses are unknown, one may often use a descriptive expression such as
"animals in places where people don't live" or "animals in the lands where no one
grows food."

	74.15-17 RSV	TEV
15	Thou didst cleave open springs and brooks; thou didst dry up ever-flowing streams.	15 You made springs and fountains flow; you dried up large rivers.
16	Thine is the day, thine also the night; thou hast established the luminaries and the sun.	16 You created the day and the night; you set the sun and the moon in their places;
17	Thou hast fixed all the bounds of the earth; thou hast made summer and winter.	17 you set the limits of the earth; you made summer and winter.

Verse 15 seems more naturally to lend itself to the events of the exodus from
Egypt, specifically of the splitting of the rock for water (Exo 17.6; Num 20.7-11); it
is perhaps significant that here the verb "to split" is used. But, in keeping with verses
16-17, this may also refer to the creation of **springs and brooks**. And in verse 15b the
reference can be to the drying up of the Jordan (Josh 3.14-17; 4.23); but in line with
parallels in other creation accounts, this may also refer to acts of creation (see
Anderson). Lines <u>a</u> and <u>b</u> are opposites, and in some languages it is necessary to
mark this kind of shift. For example, "In some places you made springs and streams
flow with water, but in other places you dried up the rivers." **Springs and brooks** may
be rendered "springs and small streams." TEV's "**fountains**" may suggest a jet of
water maintained by a power supply, which is not intended here; "springs and
streams" is better. **Ever-flowing streams** refers to streams or rivers that continually

flow. The focus is not so much on their size (as in TEV) but on their unfailing flow, or as NEB says, "rivers never known to fail."

In verse 16a **the day** and **the night** are said to belong to God. The meaning may be that he rules over them and determines everything that happens in the daytime and at night. Or else it can mean that God created them (as in TEV), and so they belong to him, not to human beings. In line **b** the statement **thou hast established the luminaries and the sun** seems to support the idea that line **a** refers to the creation of **the day** and **the night**, since in the creation story in Genesis the sun and the moon were created to rule over the day and the night (Gen 1.14-18). The word translated **luminaries** may refer to the moon alone, as TEV, NEB, TOB, FRCL, NIV, SPCL, and Dahood translate it. But it may mean "the moon and the stars" (so Weiser, "the stars").

Verse 17a may refer to the boundaries of the land that God gave to his people, or to the division of the surface of the earth among the various nations (see Deut 32.8); but it seems more likely that it refers to the creation of the earth, in line with verse 16, that is, establishing the limits of the dry land as it emerged from the waters (Gen 1.9-10).

Summer and winter in verse 17b stands for the seasons of the year. The verb translated **made** is synonymous with the verb "to create." In many areas **summer and winter** will be rendered "hot season and cold season," "dry season and rainy season," or "light rains and heavy rains."

74.18-19	RSV	TEV

	RSV	TEV
18	Remember this, O LORD, how the enemy scoffs, and an impious people reviles thy name.	But remember, O LORD, that your enemies laugh at you, that they are godless and despise you.
19	Do not deliver the soul of thy dove to the wild beasts; do not forget the life of thy poor for ever.	Don't abandon your helpless people to their cruel enemies; don't forget your persecuted people!

After his eloquent description of God as the Creator, the psalmist returns to his complaint and his pleas.

In translation **remember** is not to be expressed by the verb that implies someone has forgotten a fact. The psalmist is asking God to keep in mind that the enemies scoff. SPCL says "Bear in mind." The verbs in verse 18, **scoffs** and **reviles**, are the same as in verse 10. For translation suggestions on various synonyms of the word translated **scoffs**, see 2.4; 10.5; 22.7. **Impious** translates *nabal* "fool" (see comments on "fool" in 14.1). NJV has "base people"; FRCL "these stupid people"; NIV "foolish people." For the use of **thy name** as a substitute for "you," see 5.11 and 8.1.

In verse 19a TEV "**your helpless people**" translates "the *nefesh* of your dove" (for *nefesh* see 3.2). **Dove** here seems to be a symbol for Israel (see Hos 7.11). SPCL takes it as a metaphor for helplessness and translates with a simile, "We are as weak as doves." FRCL abandons the metaphor: "the life of the people who are so dear to you." Instead of the Masoretic text *toreka* "your dove," the Septuagint and Syriac represent a Hebrew text (also found in one Hebrew manuscript) *todeka* "the one who praises you" (in a collective sense); this is preferred by NEB. Translators should follow the Masoretic text.

TEV **"their cruel enemies"** represents **the wild beasts**. Translators will need to follow the kinds of adjustments made by TEV in order to avoid what may be meaningless renderings based on the delivery of **the soul of thy dove to the wild beasts**.

Do not forget has the meaning of "Do not reject," which is parallel with TEV's **"Don't abandon." "Your persecuted people"** translates **the life of thy poor** (see 9.12). The word translated **life** in verse 19b may here be used in the sense of "community, family" (see comments on this use in 68.10a, "thy people").

The sense of **for ever**, with the negative **do not forget**, is equivalent to "don't keep on forgetting," or "stop forgetting," or "do not neglect."

74.20-21	RSV	TEV
20	Have regard for thy^c covenant; for the dark places of the land are full of the habitations of violence.	20 Remember the covenant you made with us. There is violence in every dark corner of the land.
21	Let not the downtrodden be put to shame; let the poor and needy praise thy name.	21 Don't let the oppressed be put to shame; let those poor and needy people praise you.

^c Gk Syr: Heb *the*

The psalmist prays for God's active intervention in the affairs of the people. In verse 20a the Masoretic text has "the covenant" (see RSV footnote), which translationally TEV renders **"the covenant you made with us"** (for comments on **covenant** see 25.10). The request **Have regard for** means to consider, to pay attention to, to honor.

The Masoretic text of verse 20b is a bit obscure and is variously translated. TEV, RSV, AT, NJV, and SPCL agree substantially on the meaning. **The dark places** may be the hiding places of violent and lawless people, or else the places where the oppressed have tried to hide from their enemies; even there they are persecuted and killed. In any case **the habitations of violence** seems to mean "places where lawless people (criminals) live." In some languages it will be necessary to recast line <u>b</u> to say, for example, "violent people lie in every dark place on earth" or "in all the dark places on earth there are people who do violent deeds."

Three words describe the people of Israel in verse 21: **downtrodden** (see comments on "oppressed" in 9.9; 10.18), **poor** (see comments on "afflicted" in 9.12), and **needy** (see 12.15).

In verse 21a **be put to shame** means to be disgraced, oppressed, persecuted, mistreated (see the verb in 35.4a, RSV 'be put to . . . dishonor," TEV "be . . . disgraced"). The request in the form of a third-person imperative in verse 21b is that the poor and needy be helped and rescued, so that they will once again have reason to praise Yahweh. Instead of **let**, something like "make it possible for . . ." will be better in this context, since **let** here introduces an imperative, not a request for permission.

74.22-23 RSV	TEV
22 Arise, O God, plead thy cause; remember how the impious scoff at thee all the day! 23 Do not forget the clamor of thy foes, the uproar of thy adversaries which goes up continually!	22 Rouse yourself, God, and defend your cause! Remember that godless people laugh at you all day long. 23 Don't forget the angry shouts of your enemies, the continuous noise made by your foes.

The psalmist calls on God to take action against Israel's enemies (verse 22); see similar language in 7.6; 35.23-24; 43.1. The expression **plead thy cause** means for God to put forth the arguments of his case in which he must defend his action or lack of action. **Plead thy cause** is therefore the language of the law court. Israel's cause is God's cause; his interests coincide with those of his people. So when God defends his cause he is defending the cause of his people. In languages where such legal practices are unknown, it may be necessary to say, for example, "defend yourself," "tell your enemies that they are wrong," or "show your people that you are right."

For **impious** see verse 18b; for **scoff at** see verse 18a. For translation suggestions on **all the day**, see 56.5.

The prayer **Do not forget** means "Do not ignore" (NJV, NIV, NEB), that is, pay attention and do something about it. The **clamor** and the **uproar . . . which goes up continually** express the hostility and defiance of God's (and Israel's) enemies.

Psalm 75

In this psalm the people of Israel praise God for his great deeds on their behalf and proclaim him as the supreme judge of all peoples. It is impossible to determine the occasion for the composition of this hymn of worship; perhaps it was after victory in battle.

It opens with praise to God (verse 1), followed by God's affirmation of his power over the physical and moral realms (verses 2-5). There is a warning to all peoples of the punishment that God will send down on the wicked (verses 6-8), and the psalm closes with a word of praise to God, who punishes the wicked and rewards the righteous (verses 9-10).

HEADING: TEV has "**God the Judge.**" Other headings are "Complete and universal judgment"; "God's coming in judgment"; "National thanksgiving for God's mighty acts." The TEV heading must often be recast as a full sentence; for example, "God is the one who judges people," or "God judges people," or "God is the judge."

Hebrew title: **To the choirmaster: according to Do Not Destroy. A Psalm of Asaph. A Song** (TEV "A psalm by Asaph; a song").

For **choirmaster** see title of Psalm 4; for **Do Not Destroy** see title of Psalm 57; for **Asaph** see title of Psalm 50; and for **Psalm** and **Song** see title of Psalm 65.

75.1

RSV

We give thanks to thee, O God; we
   give thanks;
we call on thy name and re-
   count^d thy wondrous deeds.

^{d} Syr Compare Gk: Heb *and near is thy name. They recount*

TEV

We give thanks to you, O God, we
   give thanks to you!
We proclaim how great you are
   and tell of^h the wonderful
   things you have done.

^{h} *Some ancient translations* We proclaim how great you are and tell of; *Hebrew* Your name is near and they tell of.

The psalm opens with praise to God. The verb "praise, give thanks" (see comments at 7.17a) is repeated in line <u>a</u> for emphasis. In languages where the repetition of **we give thanks** will reduce the emphasis, an appropriate emphasizer should be used; for example, "Indeed, we thank you, God."

The second line of this verse in the Masoretic text is "near is your name they tell your wonderful deeds." NJV translates "Your presence is near; men tell of Your wondrous deeds"; similarly TOB, NIV, and NEB. Dahood takes the word "near" to be a title for God, "the Near One." RSV, TEV, BJ, NJB, FRCL, and NAB (also HOTTP) prefer the meaning found in the Septuagint, Syriac and Vulgate.[1] The statement **call on thy name** can mean to ask for God's help; here, however, it seems better to take it as an exclamation of praise, **"We proclaim how great you are"**; FRCL has "we proclaim who you are." For **name** see comments on 5.11. For **thy wondrous deeds** see comments on 9.17.

RSV	TEV
2 At the set time which I appoint I will judge with equity.	2 "I have set a time for judgment," says God, "and I will judge with fairness.
3 When the earth toiters, and all its inhabitants, it is I who keep steady its pillars. *Selah*	3 Though every living creature tremble and the earth itself be shaken, I will keep its foundations firm.

In verses 2-5 God speaks; in the worship service in the Temple these words were probably spoken by a prophet or a priest. This psalm may cause translators problems due to the switching of speakers. Therefore it is important to keep clear the pronominal references when pronouns are used. In order to make clear the change in verse 2 to God as speaker, it will often be necessary to begin by inserting "God says: . . ." or by following TEV.

God announces the coming judgment, which will take place **at the set time**, that is, at the time he chooses. Then he will **judge with equity** (see comments on 9.8; 67.4).

The language suggests a final judgment, when the earth and its inhabitants "dissolve" (RSV **totters**) in fear; the same verb is translated "melts" in 46.6b. TEV uses two synonymous verbs, **"tremble"** for the inhabitants of the world (literally "those dwelling in it," which probably includes all living creatures, and not just human beings), and **"be shaken"** for the earth. Many languages will prefer the active of RSV **the earth totters** rather than the TEV passive.

The last line of verse 3 is literally "I have adjusted its pillars," in the sense of make firm, keep steady. The **pillars** of the earth were thought of as the mountains, which reached down to the underworld, where they were based, and which supported the surface of the earth (see 24.2 and comments). In some languages the clause "though every creature . . ." or "even if every creature . . ." will be placed after the clause "I will keep its foundations."

For *Selah* see 3.2.

---

[1]It should be noticed that Syriac and Vulgate have the plural, "we tell of"; the Septuagint, however, has here the singular, "I will tell of."

4	I say to the boastful, "Do not boast,"	4 I tell the wicked not to be arrogant;
	and to the wicked, "Do not lift up your horn;	5 I tell them to stop their boasting."
5	do not lift up your horn on high, or speak with insolent neck."	

These two verses are parallel and synonymous. Most take the subject of **I say** (verse 4a) to be God; some, however, take it to be the psalmist (see FRCL). RSV represents the form of the Hebrew text. "To lift up the horn" means "to be arrogant," "to show off one's power" (NJB "do not flaunt your strength"). **Horn** was a symbol of strength, power, pride (see 18.2 and comments). In many languages statements made after verbs of communication (**I say to the boastful**) will be more naturally expressed as direct quotations, as in RSV.

The structure of the parallelism in verses 4 and 5 is somewhat different from anything encountered thus far in the psalms. Verse 4 follows the pattern of dramatizing and heightening the impact of line a by the use of a metaphor in line b. However, line 5a then repeats the metaphor and adds **on high**, and then follows with a second figure, **insolent neck.** It may well be that the writer intended the structure to be chiastic ("boast . . . arrogant; arrogant . . . boast"). It is common for such structures to mark off a stanza, as is the case here. The poetic function of the form of these lines is also to give special emphasis to the warnings addressed to the wicked. Translators may contribute to the poetic meaning by employing local metaphors for boasting and arrogance rather than resorting to nonfigures as in TEV.

An **insolent neck** (literally "a stretched-out neck") is another figure for pride, arrogance, stubbornness. For the last line of verse 5 the Septuagint has "do not speak wickedly against God," evidently translating the Hebrew word *tsur* "rock" (instead of the Masoretic text "with the neck"); this is preferred by Briggs, Weiser, and NEB.[2] But there is no need to depart from the Masoretic text.

TEV has shortened and combined the two lines of each verse into one. It may be better in most languages to keep the two lines for each verse, as follows:

> 5 I tell boastful people to stop their boasting,
>   I command those wicked people to stop being proud.
> 6 I say to them, "Do not be proud;
>   quit talking so arrogantly!"

SPCL may also be used as a model:

> 5 To the insolent and wicked I say,
>   "Do not be so arrogant and proud;

---

[2]HOTTP ("C" decision) stays with the Masoretic text, which it translates "do not lift your horns up high (that is, do not regard yourselves as important and full of authority), so as to speak with pride (literally, with neck) arrogantly."

6 do not boast so much of your power,
neither be so insolent as you talk."

75.6-7	RSV	TEV

	RSV		TEV
6	For not from the east or from the west and not from the wilderness comes lifting up;	6	Judgment does not come from the east or from the west, from the north or from the south
7	but it is God who executes judgment, putting down one and lifting up another.	7	it is God who is the judge, condemning some and acquitting others.

i *Probable text* from the north or from the south; *Hebrew* from the wilderness of the mountains.

In these verses the psalmist proclaims God as the only one who judges all humankind. TEV aids the reader in verses 2-5 with quotes and "says God." In many languages it will be necessary to make even more evident that at verse 6 God has ceased speaking and the psalmist now speaks again. In languages which require placing the source of a quotation at the end of the quote, it may be necessary to indicate the switch in speakers with a subtitle before verse 6.

Verse 6 is variously understood: the first line is clearly "not from the sunrise (east) or from the sunset (west)"; the second line seems in the Masoretic text to be "and not from the desert of the mountains" (so the Septuagint, Syriac, and Vulgate). Commentators (Briggs, Weiser, Anderson, Dahood) and translations (TEV, AT, NAB) take this to be a reference to the other two cardinal points: "the desert" represents the south, and "the mountains" (of Lebanon) represent the north. GECL translates this line "neither from the desert nor from the mountains." But the word translated "the mountains" can be read as a form of the verb "to raise"; so Oesterley. RSV has **lifting up** (probably in the sense of "help"; see SPCL); equally NJV "For what lifts a man . . . ," and NEB "raise a man up"; also NIV, TOB.[3] FRCL has "Know that greatness comes neither from the east nor from the west, nor yet from the desert." In Hebrew there may be a play on the words translated **lifting up** in verse 6b and **lifting up** in verse 7b (in Hebrew the two are not identical). This can be carried over into translation, as RSV does; but it should be remembered that the first word may mean "mountains."

Though it is impossible to be dogmatic, TEV is a defensible rendering and can be followed. Otherwise, it is recommended that FRCL be imitated, although the connection between verse 6 and verse 7 is not very clear.

If the translator follows the interpretation of verse 6 as used by TEV, it will not

---

[3]HOTTP says that the Hebrew word may be understood either as "lifting up" or "mountains." In the first case the translation of the line would be "nor from the desert (comes) exaltation"; in the second case it would be "nor from the desert of the mountains."

on the basis of verse 7, by adding "**Judgment.**" TEV's "**Judgment does not come . . .**" must often be recast as "God's judgment . . ." or "the one who judges . . . ." The four directions vary greatly in languages and are often related to local geography; for example, "downstream," "upstream," "toward the mountains," or "toward the sea."

God alone is the judge (verse 7); he condemns (literally "puts down") some and acquits ("raises") others. TEV's "**acquitting**" is sometimes rendered "saying that he is innocent" or "saying that he has done no wrong." Or else the opposites, "honoring . . . humbling," "making important . . . making worthless," may be used.

75.8	RSV	TEV

For in the hand of the LORD there is a cup, with foaming wine, well mixed; and he will pour a draught from it, and all the wicked of the earth shall drain it down to the dregs.	The LORD holds a cup in his hand, filled with the strong wine of his anger. He pours it out, and all the wicked drink it; they drink it down to the last drop.

God's anger is compared to a cup of strong wine, which he makes the wicked drink (see similar language in 60.3b; Isa 51.17; Jer 25.15-16). "**Strong wine**" is literally **foaming wine**, and the word translated **well mixed** occurs nowhere else in the Old Testament; it indicates that spices have been added to the wine to make it even more intoxicating (Briggs).

In line c **he will pour** does not say where God pours it, and it might seem that he is throwing it away. So it may be better to translate "He pours it out for the wicked to drink, and they all drink it." The English word **draught**, in this context, means a quantity that a person drinks.

The Hebrew expression **all the wicked of the earth** should not be taken to contrast with heaven, God's abode. It is simply an emphatic way of saying "all the wicked people in the world."

TEV "**the wicked . . . drink it down to the last drop**" translates what is literally "they drain its dregs, they drink it." The **dregs** (also known as "lees") are the material (sediment) that settles to the bottom of a bottled liquid such as wine. The meaning is that the wicked "drink it to the bottom," that is, they will receive the complete and severe punishment their sins deserve. Translators must judge if the metaphorical use of **a cup** will symbolize anger and judgment naturally. The metaphorical problem is further compounded, since the contents of the cup are poured out "and all the wicked drink it." In some languages it is possible, as in TEV, to define the contents as "**his anger**" and then to continue the unfolding of the metaphor. In some languages it may be necessary to say, for example, "The LORD holds the cup which represents his judgment of the wicked; the cup is filled with strong wine which is his anger. He pours it and all the wicked people drink. They drink it all."

RSV   TEV

	RSV		TEV
9	But I will rejoice*e* for ever, I will sing praises to the God of Jacob.	9	But I will never stop speaking of the God of Jacob or singing praises to him.
10	All the horns of the wicked he*f* will cut off, but the horns of the righteous shall be exalted.	10	He will break the power of the wicked, but the power of the righteous will be increased.

e Gk: Heb *declare*
f Heb *I*

The psalm closes with an affirmation of praise to God, the just judge. Verse 9 returns to the first person, but now it is the psalmist, who continues speaking from verse 6 onward. In some languages it may be necessary to make clear that "I" represents the psalmist; for example, "I who write these words will rejoice . . ." or "the psalmist says, 'I will rejoice . . . .' "

In verse 9a the Masoretic text has "I will tell" (or, proclaim), which TEV has taken to have **the God of Jacob** as object (so NJB, SPCL, NEB); but some take the object to be what precedes (NIV) or what follows, that is, verse 10 (Weiser; TOB, FRCL). The translator is free to follow either.

Instead of the Masoretic text "I will proclaim," RSV follows the Septuagint **I will rejoice** as a closer parallel to **I will sing praises** in the next line. NEB, following a suggestion of G. R. Driver, takes the Masoretic text consonants to represent another verb (not appearing elsewhere in the Old Testament) meaning "magnify, glorify." For **God of Jacob** see comments on 20.1. **The God of Jacob** must often be rendered "the God whom Jacob worshiped." For **sing praises** see 7.17b.

In verse 10 in the Masoretic text, God is the speaker ("I will break" in line a); TEV has translationally used the third person "**He will break**" (likewise SPCL). The translations that have in verse 10 "I will cut off" (NIV, NEB, NJB) take the psalmist to be the speaker (following from verse 9). But the speaker is God. FRCL takes verse 10 to be the song of praise the psalmist sings. Translators should follow TEV and RSV, which have maintained the psalmist's point of view in verse 10. Some modern translations indicate that the Hebrew has "I," but this is probably not necessary.

Horns (as in verses 4-5) means "**power**" and should be so translated; the power of the wicked will be destroyed by God, while that of the righteous "**will be increased.**"

Psalm 76

This psalm is a hymn celebrating God's power and his victory over his enemies. Like Psalms 46 and 48, it praises Jerusalem as the place where God reigns as victorious king. The psalm was probably used in one of the annual festivals, perhaps the Festival of Shelters. There are differences of opinion as to which particular military victory, if any, is the immediate source of this hymn. The opinion that it was the defeat of the Assyrian general Sennacherib in 701 B.C. (2 Kgs 19.35) may receive support from the Septuagint addition to the title, "about the Assyrian."

The psalm begins with the announcement of God's victories (verses 1-3), followed by a hymn of praise to God as victor in battle (verses 4-6) and judge of all humankind (verses 7-9). The psalm ends with an exhortation to offer gifts to God (verses 10-12).

HEADING: "**God the Victor.**" Other headings are "Ode to God the Awe-inspiring"; "The Terrible One"; "Our glorious and terrible God." The TEV heading must often be recast as a full sentence; for example, "God defeats his enemies" or "God is victorious in battle."

Hebrew title: **To the choirmaster: with stringed instruments. A Psalm of Asaph. A Song** (TEV "A psalm by Asaph; a song").

For **stringed instruments** see title of Psalm 4; for the remainder of the title, compare the title of Psalm 75.

76.1-3   RSV   TEV

1 In Judah God is known,   1 God is known in Judah;
      his name is great in Israel.   his name is honored in Israel.
2 His abode has been established in   2 He has his home in Jerusalem;
      Salem,   he lives on Mount Zion.
      his dwelling place in Zion.   3 There he broke the arrows of the
3 There he broke the flashing ar-   enemy,
      rows,   their shields and swords, yes, all
      the shield, the sword, and the   their weapons.
      weapons of war.   *Selah*

The psalmist declares that both in **Judah** and in **Israel** (either the two as separate nations or else the two as encompassing the whole country) **God is known** and **his name is great**. The **name** of God stands here especially for his fame as the triumphant victor over Israel's enemies (see 5.11). So the translation can be "he is famous" or "he is highly respected." Translators may read verse 1 as two lines saying

664

so nearly the same thing that they may wish to reduce the two to one. However, line b raises the impact of line a by being more specific, and this may be reflected in translation by saying, for example, "God is known in Judah, and in Israel his name is really great" or, in languages which must avoid the passive, "In Judah people know God, and in Israel they honor him." Some languages will prefer a direct address form; for example, "The people of Judah know God and the people of Israel even say 'God, you are great.' "

Salem is the older, pre-Israelite, name of Jerusalem (see Gen 14.18), or else is an abbreviation for the full name. The Hebrew reader would see the connection between **Salem** and *shalom* "peace." For comments on **Zion** see 2.6. RSV **has been established** translates the verb "to be"; the line in Hebrew is simply "and in Salem is his tent." In line a the word translated **abode** is "tent, shelter" (as in the Festival of Shelters); and for **dwelling place** see "habitation" in 68.5.

Due to the near identity of both lines in verse 2, it may be best in some languages to reduce these to one line and say, for example, "His house is on Mount Zion in Jerusalem" or "He lives on Mount Zion in Jerusalem." In some languages it will be necessary to qualify Jerusalem as "the city of Jerusalem."

NEB, following Briggs, transposes the first word of verse 3, **There** (*shamah*), to the end of verse 2, and changes the vowels to make *simah* "he placed" and, by taking the two words "tent" and "dwelling place" in a military sense, translates "in Zion his battle quarters are set up" (a rendering which Anderson prefers). This is attractive but not necessary.

The flashing arrows in verse 3a translates "the flames of the bow." This can be a reference to the swiftness of the arrows, or else it describes them as incendiary arrows (see FRCL footnote). So a translation can say "the swift arrows" or "the deadly arrows."

A translation should make clear, as TEV does, that it was the weapons of the enemy that God broke; otherwise it may appear that God was destroying his own weapons.

Besides the two specific weapons, **shield** (see 3.3 and comment) and **sword**, another weapon appears to be indicated by the word which normally means "battle." NJV has "sword of war"; RSV, TEV, and others take it to indicate all other weapons used in war. For a similar statement see 46.9. For translation suggestions regarding bow, arrow, and shield, see 7.10,12,13.

For *Selah* see 3.2.

76.4	RSV	TEV
	Glorious art thou, more majestic than the everlasting moun-tains.*g*	How glorious you are, O God! How majestic, as you return from the mountains where you defeated your foes.

g Gk: Heb *the mountains of prey*

God is praised as the victorious warrior. The word **Glorious** translates what appears to be a form of the verb "to shine"; so NJV "resplendent," NJB "radiant," and NIV "resplendent with light." NEB and others prefer to change the order of the consonants to get the word "terrible" (*nora'* instead of *na'or*; see also 65.5 and comments). <u>Glorious art thou</u> must be rendered in some languages as "How great you are" or "How wonderful you are." If the translator follows RSV and TEV **majestic**, this expression may be rendered in this context as a simile; for example, "Like a great king you return . . . ."

After "**How majestic**" (TEV) the Masoretic text is simply "from the mountains of prey," which TEV has taken to mean "**as you return from the mountains where you defeated your foes**" (the enemy being understood as Yahweh's "prey"). NJV translates this second line "glorious on the mountains of prey"; TOB "because of the mountains of prey." NIV takes "prey" to mean animals to be hunted: "mountains rich with game." RSV translates the Septuagint <u>everlasting</u> instead of the Hebrew "prey" in order to arrive at its text. The Septuagint, however, is not "(more majestic) than the everlasting mountains"; it is "you are marvelously resplendent from the everlasting mountains." FRCL is like RSV.[1] Since the meaning of the original text is so difficult to determine, the translator should feel free to follow either RSV or TEV.

<u>76.5-6</u> RSV	TEV
5 The stouthearted were stripped of their spoil; they sank into sleep; all the men of war were unable to use their hands. 6 At thy rebuke, O God of Jacob, both rider and horse lay stunned.	5 Their brave soldiers have been stripped of all they had and now are sleeping the sleep of death; all their strength and skill was useless. 6 When you threatened them, O God of Jacob, the horses and their riders fell dead.

These two verses are taken by TEV and others to mean that the enemies had been killed (see Briggs, Anderson); some, however, take the verbs to mean that the enemy soldiers were paralyzed with fear, stunned, unconscious, unable to fight (Toombs); see NJV "they were in a stupor." And some take verse 5 to mean death, and verse 6 to mean paralysis (see NJB, Dahood).

In verse 5a **The stouthearted** are the brave enemy soldiers; and **their spoil** are their weapons and armament, which were taken from them. RSV **their spoil** means the weapons and objects these defeated soldiers had plundered from others; but the meaning of the Hebrew is given by TEV, which should be followed. A simpler way to represent the meaning would be "they were despoiled" (so NJV, SPCL). In languages which do not use passive constructions, the active will have to be employed, the agent being the victors in battle; for example, "Those who defeated them have taken from the brave soldiers all they had."

---

[1]Interestingly enough, HOTTP ("C" decision) recommends the RSV conjecture here and says the phrase may be interpreted in two ways: (1) "from the eternal mountains" or (2) "from the mountains of booty."

RSV **they sank into sleep** in verse 5b presumably means death. In languages in which **sleep** is not used as a metaphor for death, it will normally be best to say "they are now dead."

The last line in verse 5 in Hebrew is "they did not find their hands" (see RSV). This is taken by TEV to mean "**all their strength and skill was useless**"; it can mean "they were unable to use their weapons"—either from paralyzing fear (so NJV) or because they were dead (see NIV). NJB has "the warriors' arms have failed them" (also NAB), and NEB "the strongest cannot lift a hand," which provide two different interpretations of the Hebrew word "hands."

For TEV "**threatened**" in verse 6a (RSV **rebuke**) see 18.15 and comments. For **God of Jacob** see comments on 20.1.

The verb in verse 6b is "fall into sleep," which means either "**dead**" (TEV) or **stunned** (NJV, RSV); NEB "fall senseless"; FRCL has "paralyzed." It seems better to follow TEV "**fell dead.**" The nouns in the Masoretic text are "chariot and horse" (so translated by BJ, NJB, TOB, SPCL); but the Hebrew word for "chariot" can, with different vowels, mean **rider** (RSV, TEV, NEB, and most others).

76.7	RSV	TEV

But thou, terrible art thou!
  Who can stand before thee
  when once thy anger is roused?

But you, LORD, are feared by all.
  No one can stand in your presence
  when you are angry.

In verses 7-9 God is praised as judge of all humankind. The word translated "**feared by all**" by TEV means awe-inspiring, fearsome (see comments on "dread deeds" in 65.5); in English the word **terrible** (RSV and others) carries a different connotation and is entirely inappropriate here. No human being can withstand God's anger; all opposition ceases, all resistance disappears. TEV's "**feared by all**" must often be rendered as active, "everyone fears you" or "all people are afraid of you."

The rhetorical question **Who can stand before thee**, if translated literally, may mean only the act of standing, whereas the contextual meaning is that of not being able to endure God's judgment. In some languages this may be expressed "Who can stand up when you judge people?" or "Who can survive when you decide the affairs of people?"

Line c may sometimes be rendered, for example, "when your innermost is hot" or "when your eyes become red."

76.8-9	RSV	TEV

8 From the heavens thou didst utter
     judgment;
     the earth feared and was still,
9 when God arose to establish judg-
     ment
     to save all the oppressed of the

8 You made your judgment known
     from heaven;
     the world was afraid and kept
     silent,
9 when you rose up to pronounce
     judgment,

667

earth.	*Selah*	to save all the oppressed on earth.

Even though God's earthly home is Jerusalem (verse 2), he lives in heaven, and from there he pronounces his sentence as judge of all humankind. **Judgment** is not simply an impartial decision about right and wrong; as verse 9 makes clear, God's judgment is his active intervention on behalf of the poor and the defenseless.

Two different Hebrew words are used in verses 8 and 9 for **judgment**: in verse 8 it is the noun *din* and in verse 9 the verb *shafat*. In 7.8, line a, the verb *din* is translated "judges," and in line b *shafat* is translated "judge me"; similarly, in 9.4a "just cause" translates what is literally "my right (*mishpat*, the noun from *shafat*) and my cause (*din*)" (see comments at both 7.8 and 9.4). In this context RSV and TEV translate both terms identically, and the translator may wish to do so as well.

In languages in which the goal of judgment must be expressed, it is possible in this case to shift the goal from verse 9; for example, "from heaven you decided in favor of the oppressed and saved them all" or, idiomatically, "you cut the words in favor of the poor and saved them all."

In languages in which inanimate objects do not express emotions, it may be necessary to say in verse 8b "the people of the earth." If on the other hand the reference is to all life on the earth, then one may say, for example, "everything on the earth feared God and . . . ." The first interpretation is to be preferred.

Arose in verse 9a takes on added significance if, as maintained by some, at that time the judge would stand "**to pronounce judgment.**" But it is possible that the meaning is not "**pronounce judgment**" but "execute judgment," that is, that God got roused up and went into action to impose justice on the world. For the word translated **the oppressed**, see comments on "the afflicted" in 9.12. **Earth**: here, as elsewhere, the Hebrew word may mean "the land (of Israel)" (so NIV); here, however, it seems best to translate "all the oppressed people in the world" (see the same phrase in 75.8c).

It should be noted that in verse 9 God is referred to in the third person; TEV keeps the second person of address, consistent with the preceding verses.

76.10　　　　RSV　　　　　　　　　　　　　　　TEV

Surely the wrath of men shall praise thee;
the residue of wrath thou wilt gird upon thee.

Men's anger only results in more praise for you;
those who survive the wars will keep your festivals.[k]

[k] *One ancient translation* will keep your festivals; *verse 10 in Hebrew is unclear.*

The psalm closes with an exhortation to offer gifts to God. Verse 10 in Hebrew is quite unclear. The first line is "for (or, surely) human anger praises you"—which TEV takes to mean that, by defeating and overcoming all human opposition to him (**the wrath of men**), God will be praised even more. NIV takes "the anger of man" to mean "your wrath against men"; this is not very likely. TOB has "Even the fury of

668

men contributes to your glory" (so FRCL); SPCL "Man's hatred turns into praise to you." Dahood translates "They (that is, 'the oppressed' of verse 9) will praise you for your rage with other men"; NJV has "The fiercest of men shall acknowledge You"—which is almost identical with AT. If the translator follows either the RSV or the TEV rendering, the problem remains difficult, for it is not at all clear how **the wrath of men** or **"Men's anger"** is made to serve a purpose quite opposite from its usual intention. Furthermore, it is not natural in some languages for an abstract such as anger to **praise**. Therefore it will be necessary in many languages to indicate that it is God who causes it to happen; for example, "God, you cause angry men to praise you even more."

Line b in Hebrew is "the remainder of angers you will put around you" (the same verb is used in 65.12b, "gird themselves"). TEV has taken "the remainder of angers" to mean the enemies **"who survive the wars,"** the wars being the expression of God's anger against them; God's enemies who survive will worship him. **"Keep your festivals"** translates the Septuagint. FRCL is like TEV. TOB translates the Masoretic text: "those who survive this anger (that is, of men, in the previous line), you bind to yourself"; SPCL has "even man's least hatred turns into a crown for you." NJB, somewhat similarly, has "the survivors of your anger will huddle round you."[2] If the translator follows TEV in line b, **"keep your festivals"** may sometimes be rendered "will worship you on your special feast days."

NAB and NEB, using different vowels with the consonants in the Masoretic text, get "wrath of Edom" in line a and "the survivors in Hamath" in line b. Edom was the country south of Israel, and Hamath was a city in Syria, north of Israel.

GECL appears to be following the second interpretation of HOTTP in its translation, "So that the fury of your enemies will cause your fame to increase, and all who have escaped this fury are like a crown with which you adorn yourself." It is recommended that the translator follow either TEV or GECL in translating this very obscure Hebrew verse.

76.11-12	RSV	TEV

11   Make your vows to the LORD your   11   Give the LORD your God what you
         God, and perform them;   promised him;
         let all around him bring gifts   bring gifts to him, all you
         to him who is to be feared,   nearby nations.
12   who cuts off the spirit of princes,   God makes men fear him;
         who is terrible to the kings of   12   he humbles proud princes
         the earth.   and terrifies great kings.

Verse 11a **Make your vows . . . and perform them** is taken to mean "Fulfill now the vows you made when you were in danger" (see the similar command in 50.14b).

---

[2]HOTTP is of the opinion that the verse may be translated as follows: "surely the fiercest men praise you, those who remain angry gird themselves (with sackcloth)." Another interpretation is possible: "surely the fiercest men praise you, you gird (like a diadem) those who have escaped from your wrath."

The psalmist is speaking to the people of Israel, assembled for worship in the Temple.

In verse 11b TEV translates **all around him** as "all you nearby nations," because this seems to be a reference to foreign nations, in contrast with Israel in line a. But it may be that both lines refer to the people of Israel. The TEV interpretation seems to be the better one.

TEV **"God makes men fear him"** in line c translates what is literally "(to) the fear," which is taken to indicate God as the one who causes humankind to fear him; SPCL has "to him who is worthy of fear" (which is like RSV). BJ translates as a title of God, "the Terrible"; Weiser "to the terrible God"; NJV and NJB, more appropriately, "the Awesome One"; HOTTP "the dreadful one." It is recommended that the translator follow either RSV or NJV.

In verse 12 TEV **"he humbles"** translates he **cuts off the spirit** (or, breath). The verb "cut off" is used of gathering grapes at harvest; but K-B conjectures another verb, spelled the same way, meaning "to humble," which appears only here in the Old Testament. The word *ruach* may mean "spirit" in terms of "life," so that the statement may mean "he kills" (so SPCL, BJ, NJB, TOB; presumably this is what RSV means). Or it may mean "spirit" in terms of "pride, courage," so that the meaning is **"he humbles"** (TEV, NIV, NJV, NEB, NAB; Weiser); FRCL has "he deflates the pride of princes." It seems better to take it in the latter sense, since this is more closely parallel to the next line **"and terrifies great kings"** (see similar expressions in 48.4-6). The term **princes** refers to "rulers" and not simply to the sons of kings, and will therefore be translated as "rulers" or "chiefs" in some languages. RSV **terrible** is a translation of *nora'* (see verse 7).

Psalm 77

This psalm is the lament of a faithful Israelite who feels that God has abandoned his people, and in anguish he prays that once again God will lead and help Israel as he did long ago. There are no references in the text to any specific circumstances in which the psalm was composed.

The psalm opens with the psalmist's cry to God for help (verses 1-3) and a statement of his perplexity and despair (verses 4-10). In order to comfort himself, the psalmist recalls God's mighty deeds in the past, in acts of salvation and of creation (verses 11-20).

HEADING: TEV has "**Comfort in Time of Distress**." Other headings are "The mighty God"; "Meditation on Israel's past"; "An appeal to the God who works wonders." The TEV heading may have to be recast in many languages to say, for example, "God comforts people when they suffer" or "God gives a strong heart to those who suffer."

Hebrew title: **To the choirmaster: according to Jeduthun. A Psalm of Asaph** (TEV "A psalm by Asaph").

For **Jeduthun** see title of Psalm 39; for the rest of this title, see Psalm 75.

77.1-3

RSV	TEV

1 I cry aloud to God,
  aloud to God, that he may hear me.
	1 I cry aloud to God;
	  I cry aloud, and he hears me.

2 In the day of my trouble I seek the Lord;
  in the night my hand is stretched out without wearying;
  my soul refuses to be comforted.
	2 In times of trouble I pray to the Lord;
	  all night long I lift my hands in prayer,
	  but I cannot find comfort.

3 I think of God, and I moan;
  I meditate, and my spirit faints. *Selah*
	3 When I think of God, I sigh;
	  when I meditate, I feel discouraged.

The psalmist voices his complaint; in despair he calls to God. In some languages **cry aloud** has the meaning of "shout." In the present context it is often necessary to employ a verb which means to mourn or to lament. In other languages

671

the verb phrase **cry aloud** must be accompanied by a direct object; for example, "I cry aloud my complaint."

TEV **"and he hears me"** at the end of verse 1 is what the form and tense of the Hebrew verb normally mean (see the Septuagint; NEB, NJB, TOB). But the whole strophe (verses 1-3) seems to indicate that God had *not* listened to the psalmist, so AT and RSV **that he may hear me** seems more appropriate (similarly NJV, NIV, FRCL, SPCL). Dahood translates it as an imperative, "give ear at once."

In verse 2, **In the day of my trouble** may also be rendered "When I am in trouble." For **seek**, meaning **"pray to,"** see 9.10 and comments. **My hand is stretched out** (that is, "I lift my hands") is the position for prayer (see comments on 28.2). TEV **"all night long"** (verse 2b) represents the force of **in the night** combined with **without wearying**; see FRCL "without relaxing." In verse 2c **my soul** (see 3.2) is parallel with **my spirit** in verse 3b; both are ways to refer to the psalmist's feelings and emotions. RSV **my soul refuses to be comforted** can be expressed more naturally: "but nothing brings me any comfort." TOB and FRCL translate "I don't let anyone comfort me." Where RSV uses **my soul refuses . . .**, some languages will prefer to represent the whole of the person by means of another part; for example, "my heart, my liver, my throat refuses . . . ." In cases where the part of the body representing the personality does not express volition on its own, it is better to follow TEV. In languages where it is necessary to express the one who fails to provide comfort for the sufferer, it is possible to say, for example, "God does not comfort me."

I moan in verse 3a represents discomfort, despair; SPCL translates "I cry." And in verse 3b **my spirit faints** can be translated "I lose all hope" or "I sink into despair" (FRCL "I lose courage"). In verse 3b **meditate** is parallel with and means the same as **think** in verse 3a, and in many languages they are the same expression. In languages in which **think of God** and **meditate** are expressed in the same way, it may be necessary to say, for example, "When I think of God, I moan and I feel discouraged."

For *Selah* see 3.2.

77.4-6	RSV	TEV

	RSV		TEV
4	Thou dost hold my eyelids from closing; I am so troubled that I cannot speak.	4	He keeps me awake all night; I am so worried that I cannot speak.
5	I consider the days of old, I remember the years long ago.	5	I think of days gone by and remember years of long ago.
6	I commune[h] with my heart in the night; I meditate and search my spirit:[i]	6	I spend the night in deep thought;[m] I meditate, and this is what I ask myself:

[h] Gk Syr: Heb *my music*
[i] Syr Jerome: Heb *my spirit searches*

[m] *Some ancient translations* deep thought; *Hebrew* song.

In verse 4a the psalmist blames God for his sleeplessness; he cannot sleep because he is so upset and discouraged by God's failure to answer his prayers. The Hebrew text has the second person form of address to God (RSV **Thou**); TEV uses the third person for consistency with the preceding verses. But the second person is more direct and vivid and should be retained, if possible. If it is kept, something like "You, LORD . . ." or "You, O God . . ." may be helpful.

I am so troubled is often rendered idiomatically as "I see pain" or "I smell suffering." **I cannot speak**: "I don't know what to say."

Since his present experience provides him with no comfort, the psalmist decides to consider Israel's past history (verse 5).

In verse 5b **remember** translates the verb which in the Masoretic text appears as the first word of verse 6; it seems better to take it with verse 5b, parallel with **consider** in verse 5a (so RSV, TEV, NJB, BJ, NEB, NAB). But some translations take it with verse 6, leaving the one verb **I consider** in verse 5a to govern both lines of verse 5, and translate the word in verse 6a in the Masoretic text by "my song"; so AT "By night I remember my song" (also TOB), and SPCL "I remember when I used to sing at night." NJV translates "my song" as "their jibes at me," which is rather improbable, since no enemies taunting the psalmist are referred to.

It will be noticed that in line <u>a</u> **days** is stepped up in line <u>b</u> to **years**. This follows the same pattern as number parallelism where, for example, "once" in line <u>a</u> will be increased to "twice" in line <u>b</u>. The sense of verse 5 is "I think of days gone by and even remember years of long ago" or "Not only do I remember the days of the past, but I even recall the years long ago." In languages in which one does not remember the years, but rather the events of the years, it may be necessary to say, for example, "I remember the things that happened many years ago."

In verse 6 RSV and TEV follow the Septuagint, Syriac, and Vulgate **I commune (with my heart)**; NEB changes the vowels of the Hebrew word to arrive at the meaning "all night long I was in deep distress."

It is possible that the Masoretic text "I remember my song in the night with my heart" can be translated as AT, TOB, and SPCL do; but the ancient versions, followed by RSV, TEV, and FRCL, make more sense (so Briggs, Oesterley, Weiser, Anderson).[1] Dahood has "through the night I play the lyre, with my heart I commune."

In verse 6b **I meditate** translates the same verb used in verse 3b. TEV "**I ask myself**" translates "my spirit inquires"; there is no need, as RSV **search my spirit** does, to prefer the versions here over the Masoretic text.

<u>77.7-8</u>   RSV   TEV

7   "Will the Lord spurn for ever,   7   "Will the Lord always reject us?
     and never again be favorable?   Will he never again be pleased
8   Has his steadfast love for ever   with us?
     ceased?   8   Has he stopped loving us?
     Are his promises at an end for   Does his promise no longer
     all time?   stand?

---

[1]HOTTP is substantially in favor of RSV.

The psalmist expresses his anguish in six questions which raise doubts about God's love for Israel (verses 7-9). In Hebrew there is no direct object for the verbs, and conceivably the psalmist could be talking about God's attitude in general, or about God's attitude toward him personally; but it is more natural to understand that he is talking about the experience of the whole nation (so NEB, AT, FRCL, SPCL), perhaps a recent military defeat. It may be better to make explicit in all six questions the fact that the object is the people of Israel, as TEV does with the pronoun "**us.**"

It does not seem likely, as Anderson maintains, that these are only rhetorical questions with a negative answer implied, that is, that God really had *not* abandoned his people. The psalmist is puzzled and perplexed, and the questions express his real doubts about God's attitude toward his people. For similar language see 74.1 and the references cited there.

In verse 7a **Lord** translates the title, not the personal name Yahweh. **Spurn** is the same verb translated "cast . . . off" in 43.2b. **Spurn** and TEV's "**reject**" may be rendered in some languages as "say 'No' to his people."

In verse 7b the Hebrew verb translated **be favorable** can indicate God's attitude (see "delight in" in 44.3) or else include the idea of action, "be good to." SPCL has "treat us with kindness."

In verse 8 two synonymous verbs are used for "come to an end, cease, finish." For comments on the noun translated **steadfast love**, see 5.7. In verse 8b **his promises** translates what is literally "word," which may refer to the one "promise" (TEV) expressed in the Covenant, that God would always be with his people, or else be a generic term for all of God's promises. FRCL translates differently: "Has he no longer anything to say to us?" (also TOB), and GECL has "Will his promise in the future no longer be valid?"

In both questions of verse 8, **for ever** and **for all time** emphasize the psalmist's despair. The two questions can be phrased "Will he never love us again? Will he never fulfill his promises to us?" or ". . . keep the promises he made to us?"

77.9-10	RSV		TEV
9	Has God forgotten to be gracious? Has he in anger shut up his compassion?" *Selah*	9	Has God forgotten to be merciful? Has anger taken the place of his compassion?"
10	And I say, "It is my grief that the right hand of the Most High has changed."	10	Then I said, "What hurts me most is this— that God is no longer powerful."[n]

[n] *Verse 10 in Hebrew is unclear.*

In verse 9a **gracious** means "kind, compassionate, merciful." **Gracious** is often rendered idiomatically; for example, "Has God forgotten to have a white stomach for us?"

Verse 9b is literally "Perhaps in anger he has shut out his compassion?" For **compassion** see comments on "mercy" in 51.1. In some languages the noun phrases of both RSV and TEV **in anger** and **his compassion** must be replaced by verb phrases; for example, "Has God become angry with us? Does he no longer feel compassion for us?"

Verse 10 is not very clear in Hebrew. The tense of the initial verb "to say" may be understood as **And I say**; it seems better, however, to take it as a past tense, "And I said." **It is my grief** (TEV **"What hurts me most"**) translates what in the Masoretic text seems to be "my wound" (so RSV, FRCL, BJ, NJB, AT, NAB, SPCL; Weiser); Briggs takes it to be "I begin," that is, "My first word (or, thought)." NJV translates "It is my fault"—which would be an almost unprecedented statement. Dahood derives the form from another Hebrew root and translates "Perhaps his (God's) sickness is this." It is better to follow the majority in their understanding of the Hebrew text.

The second line is taken by most to mean **the right hand of the Most High has changed**, which means, as TEV translates, **"God is no longer powerful"** (similarly NJB) or "God no longer acts the same toward us" (SPCL; see NAB footnote). The word which is translated "has changed" can be understood to mean "has withered" (Dahood); or it can be taken as a noun, "the years" (KJV), but very few follow this interpretation now.[2] NEB emends the text to get "Has his right hand lost its grasp? Does it hang powerless, the arm of the Most High?" The thought appears to be "God no longer helps, protects, saves us as he used to"; so FRCL "The Most High God no longer acts on our behalf," which may be recommended as the best translation of this line.

For translation suggestions for **the Most High**, see 7.17.

77.11-12   RSV   TEV

11   I will call to mind the deeds of the   11   I will remember your great deeds,
         LORD;   LORD;
      yea, I will remember thy won-   I will recall the wonders you did
         ders of old.   in the past.
12   I will meditate on all thy work,   12   I will think about all that you
      and muse on thy mighty deeds.   have done;
                                                           I will meditate on all your
                                                             mighty acts.

In these two verses the psalmist says the same thing in four ways. All the verbs are nearly synonymous: **remember** in verse 11a,b (the same Hebrew verb is used in both lines); **meditate** (see 1.2) in verse 12a; **muse** in verse 12b (the same Hebrew verb as "meditate" in verse 3). Synonymous also in their use here are the expressions **the deeds, thy wonders, all thy work**, and **thy mighty deeds**. There is no intensification in the second line. These are the great victories, miracles, the mighty actions that God performed in order to save his people from Egypt and take them safely to the Promised Land.

Verse 11a in Hebrew refers to God in the third person; TEV uses the second person, for consistency with the next three lines.

LORD here translates *Yah* (see comments at 68.4).

---

[2]HOTTP says the meaning of this verse is "and I said: my wound (literally, my being wounded) is this: the change of the Most High's right hand (that is, of his doings)."

675

In verse 11a TEV, RSV, and others translate one form of the Masoretic text (the *qere*) **I will call to mind** ("**remember**"). Another form of the text (the *kethiv*) is the causative of the same verb, meaning "I will cause to remember," that is, "I will proclaim" (see "praise" and comments at 71.16); this is preferred by Briggs and Weiser. The interpretation of RSV and TEV is recommended.

Because of the closeness of meaning of the four lines and the lack of movement between them, translators may find the lines of verses 11 and 12 overly repetitious; it is possible to reduce them to say, for example, "I will remember the great deeds you did in the past. I will think about all of your mighty acts." SPCL does a good job of reducing the redundancy of the two verses:

> 11 I will recall the wonders
>   that the LORD did in other times;
> 12 I will think of all that he has done.

77.13-15	RSV	TEV

	RSV	TEV
13	Thy way, O God, is holy. What god is great like our God?	13 Everything you do, O God, is holy. No god is as great as you.
14	Thou art the God who workest wonders, who hast manifested thy might among the peoples.	14 You are the God who works miracles; you showed your might among the nations.
15	Thou didst with thy arm redeem thy people, the sons of Jacob and Joseph. *Selah*	15 By your power you saved your people, the descendants of Jacob and of Joseph.

The psalmist praises God for his having saved Israel, his people, from slavery in Egypt. To declare that everything that God does (literally his **way**) **is holy** is to affirm that in all that he does God is true to his nature as a holy God, who is separate from humankind, who maintains the right, who is to be served and worshiped as the only God. He is greater than the gods the other nations claim as their own, the gods other people worship. TEV in verse 13b fails to represent **our God**; the full meaning can be expressed by translating the verse "O God, you are our God, and everything you do is holy; no other god is as great as you are."

The text of verse 13a may mean "your way is in the sanctuary" (KJV; Weiser), which would mean that in the Temple God's will is made known to Israel. This, however, is not very likely. The expression **thy way is holy** is particularly difficult in many languages. In the Bible it is quite common for objects to be called holy, but much less common for an event to be so labeled. Terms commonly used to designate holy, such as "dedicated to God," are obviously unsatisfactory when speaking of the holiness of an event. Also unsatisfactory is "what God does is dedicated to God." It is therefore often necessary to shift to a quality such as "good" or "true." In some languages it will be necessary to make explicit the goal of the action of God; for example, "the way you treat your people" or "everything you do to your people."

The entire expression may sometimes be rendered then as "the way you treat your people is good."

Languages which must express **our God** as including or excluding the persons addressed should use the exclusive pronoun here when addressing God, but inclusive if addressing each other.

English and other languages distinguish between false gods and God by the use of lower case and capital letters. However, in languages where this is not possible, it may be necessary to say, for example, "no false god is great like our God" or, in some languages, "little god some people worship is not great like the God we worship."

Wonders in verse 14a translates the same word used in verse 11b. God's great deeds in saving his people were known by other peoples, the Egyptians, and the various peoples of Canaan. In verse 14b the idea is not only that God caused the miracles to be seen or heard by pagan nations, but that he caused them to know and admit God's power; so NJB "You . . . brought the nations to acknowledge your power." In some languages it will be necessary to make explicit in 14a that God does miracles which people see. In such cases this makes lines a and b very closely parallel, and in some cases it may be best to reduce the parallelism to one line, saying, for example, "You are the God who shows powerful miracles to the other tribes" or ". . . to the peoples who do not worship you."

For the verb **redeem** in verse 15, see "redeemer" in 19.14. TEV "**By your power**" translates **with your arm**, which is a common figure in the psalms. TEV's "**By your power**" expresses the means of God's action. In some languages it will be more natural to shift to a clause and say, for example, "because you are powerful . . . ."

Only here in the Old Testament are the people of Israel called **the sons of Jacob and Joseph**. It is possible that the specific mention of Joseph is intended to emphasize the (northern) kingdom of Israel; the two tribes Manasseh and Ephraim, which were descended from the sons of Joseph, were in the north. In both TEV and RSV **sons of Jacob and Joseph** stand in apposition to **thy people**. However, in many languages it will be necessary to make clear their relationship by saying, for example, "who are the descendants of Jacob and Joseph" or ". . . saved the descendants of Jacob and Joseph, all of whom are your people."

77.16-18   RSV   TEV

	RSV		TEV
16	When the waters saw thee, O God, when the waters saw thee, they were afraid, yea, the deep trembled.	16	When the waters saw you, O God, they were afraid, and the depths of the sea trembled.
17	The clouds poured out water; the skies gave forth thunder; thy arrows flashed on every side.	17	The clouds poured down rain; thunder crashed from the sky, and lightning flashed in all directions.
18	The crash of thy thunder was in the whirlwind;	18	The crash of your thunder rolled out,

thy lightnings lighted up the world; the earth trembled and shook.	and flashes of lightning lit up the world; the earth trembled and shook.

As in the similar passage 74.12-17, it is difficult to decide here whether the psalmist is speaking of creation or of the exodus from Egypt. Certainly in verse 20 the meaning is not in doubt, and some see verses 16-19 as a recital of the events of the exodus. Yet it seems more likely that here, as elsewhere, the biblical writer draws the two themes together: the God who brought the nation Israel into being, defeating Israel's enemies with mighty acts of salvation, is the same God who brought the world into being, defeating the primeval forces of chaos (see Weiser, Anderson, Toombs, McCullough). Some see verses 16-20 as a fragment of an old poem added here either by the psalmist himself or by some later editor (see Dentan, Dahood).

At the coming of God **the waters . . . were afraid, the deep trembled**; these primeval waters (or, the Sea of Reeds, the Red Sea) feared the all-powerful God. **The deep** translates the plural of the word "the deep" used in Genesis 1.2; so TEV "the depths of the sea." As RSV shows, in verse 16 the Hebrew text repeats "when the waters saw you." The poetic expressions **waters saw thee** and **they were afraid** create a translation problem for languages in which the personification of inanimate objects is not natural. In such cases it may be possible to shift to a simile; for example, "like a person sees, when the waters saw you . . . ." In some languages it will be necessary to speak of "all the rivers" or "all the seas." In the same manner it may be necessary in some languages to employ a simile in **the deep trembled** by saying, for example, "the depths of the sea trembled like a frightened person."

God's coming was accompanied by rain, thunder, and lightning (verse 17; see similar accounts in 18.7-15 and 29.3-9 of Yahweh as the God of the storm). In verse 17c God's **arrows** are the **lightnings** of verse 18b (see similar parallel in 18.14a,b). In languages in which arrows are known, it does not automatically follow that the word lends itself for metaphorical use, or that the meaning of "lightning" would be implied. It may be possible to say, for example, "your lightning flashed like flying arrows."

In verse 18a TEV **"rolled out"** translates a word defined as "wheel of a war chariot." TEV takes the line to speak of the thunder as the noise made by the wheels of God's "war chariot" (see 65.11; 68.33). NJV has "Your thunder rumbled like wheels" (same as Weiser); similarly TOB, BJ, FRCL "as it rolled" (also NEB footnote). RSV, NEB, NAB, and SPCL translate **in the whirlwind**; AT "in the cyclone." Dahood takes the word to mean "the dome of heaven," in conjunction with "the world" in line <u>b</u> and "nether world" in line <u>c</u>.

In verse 18c **trembled** translates the same verb as in verse 16c; for **shook** see comments on "quaked" in 68.8.

<u>**77.19-20**</u>   RSV   TEV

19	Thy way was through the sea, thy path through the great waters; yet thy footprints were unseen.	19	You walked through the waves; you crossed the deep sea, but your footprints could not be seen.

| 20 Thou didst lead thy people like a flock
    by the hand of Moses and Aaron. | 20 You led your people like a shepherd,
    with Moses and Aaron in charge. |

These two concluding verses are a poetic description of the crossing of the Sea of Reeds (or the Red Sea; see 106.7). In verse 19a,b, instead of **"the waves"** and **"the deep sea"** of TEV, a better parallelism would be "the sea . . . the deep sea."

The statement **yet thy footprints were unseen** may emphasize the fact that God himself, although present and in action to save his people, was never actually seen; it was faith and trust that made the people know that he was there. Or else, after he used the sea as a path, the deep water hid his footprints from sight (Dahood). In languages which do not use the passive, it will often be necessary to shift to the active; for example, "no one saw your footprints" or "no one could see where you passed by."

In verse 20 the verb "to lead" is the same one used in 23.3. The text says **like a flock**; TEV has **"like a shepherd"** in order to keep the emphasis on God. "You lead your people like a shepherd leads his flock" can be used.

By the hand of means "under the leadership of" or "by means of"—the latter is probably to be preferred. FRCL translates the whole verse "You used Moses and Aaron as shepherds for your people." In languages in which shepherds are unknown, it may be best to avoid the pastoral analogy and say, for example, "you used Moses and Aaron to lead your people." On the other hand, it may be possible to say something like "you caused Moses and Aaron to lead your people as a person leads his animals."

Psalm 78

This psalm is a meditation on Israel's history, from the exodus out of Egypt to the time of King David (see similar Psalms 105, 106, 135, and 136). It is in the style of a wisdom poem (see introduction to Psalm 49) and was probably composed for use in one of the annual festivals celebrated in the Temple in Jerusalem. There is no agreement on the time of its composition; its author may have been from the southern kingdom of Judah (see verses 9, 67-68).

Robert Alter says,

> Perhaps the greatest peculiarity of biblical poetry among the literatures of the ancient Mediterranean world is its seeming avoidance of narrative. The Hebrew writers used verse for celebratory song, dirge, oracle, oratory, prophecy, reflective and didactic argument, liturgy, and often as heightening or summarizing inset in the prose narratives—but only marginally and minimally to tell a tale. (Robert Alter, *The Art of Biblical Poetry,* page 27)

Psalms 78, 105, and 106 are taken as exceptions that confirm the rule.

It is difficult to provide an outline for the psalm. In the opening section (verses 1-4) the author explains the purpose of his composition and the need to instruct succeeding generations about what God has done for his people (verses 5-8). The recital that follows is not developed in chronological order. After having recounted some of the more important events related to the exodus of the Israelites from Egypt and their journey to Canaan (verses 9-39), the psalmist goes back to the events in Egypt (verses 42-51) and the exodus (verses 52-55). Throughout the psalm the main emphasis is on the faithfulness of God and the faithlessness of his people.

McCullough divides the material as follows: (1) Summons to the People to Listen (verses 1-8); (2) Disobedience of the Fathers (verses 9-20); (3) Manna and Quails (verses 21-31); (4) Waywardness of the Nation (verses 32-39); (5) The Exodus in Retrospect (verses 40-55); (6) Israel in Canaan (verses 56-66); (7) God's Continuing Guidance (verses 67-72).

HEADING: TEV has "**God and His People**." Other headings are "The lessons of Israelite history"; "The God behind Israel's history"; "A religious ballad." If the translator follows the TEV heading, it will often be necessary to make explicit the relation between God and the people: "This is how God led his people" or "The history of God's dealing with his people."

Hebrew title: **A Maskil of Asaph** (TEV "A poem by Asaph").
For **Maskil** see title of Psalm 32; for **Asaph** see title of Psalm 50.

	RSV		TEV
1	Give ear, O my people, to my teaching; incline your ears to the words of my mouth!	1	Listen, my people, to my teaching, and pay attention to what I say.
2	I will open my mouth in a parable; I will utter dark sayings from of old,	2	I am going to use wise sayings and explain mysteries from the past,
3	things that we have heard and known, that our fathers have told us.	3	things we have heard and known, things that our fathers told us.

In a manner like the author of Psalm 49 (see 49.1-4), the psalmist begins his work by telling his readers what he is about to do. He instructs them, as a teacher does his pupils. The nominal phrase **my teaching** must be shifted in some languages to a verb phrase; for example, "Listen to the things which I teach you" or "Hear the words that I teach you."

I will open my mouth in verse 2a is a way of calling attention to what follows, and may be translated as TEV has done, or else as NJV has it, "I will expound . . . ."

Parable translates *mashal* "proverb, saying" (see 49.4a and comment), and **dark saying** translates the word "riddle," as in 49.4b; the two words are used synonymously in parallel position. NEB (for *mashal*) has "a story with a meaning"; NJV "I will expound a theme." The meaning is that he will teach by means of proverbs (parables, wise sayings). The meaning of verse 2b is "to expound (or, explain) lessons from the past" (see TOB, FRCL, NJV, NJB). TEV intends to say that the psalmist proposes to explain past mysteries. GECL translates the whole verse as follows: "I will remind you of the past, to point out to you God's guiding instructions."

Verse 2 is quoted in Matthew 13.35. Line a in Matthew 13.35 is exactly the same as the Septuagint translation of this verse; line b translates the Hebrew text differently from the Septuagint.

The term **parable** or TEV's **"wise sayings"** is sometimes rendered as "word examples," "picture words," or "sayings of the old men." RSV's **dark sayings** renders the Hebrew term for riddle, and in the present context refers to secret sayings shared by the people. In the Americas riddles are known and used among nearly all Indian speakers, but in other areas of the world they may be less known or totally absent. In the latter cases it is best to translate as "secret sayings" or "words that hold secrets."

The psalmist is going to deal with the recital of Israel's history as transmitted by succeeding generations (verses 3-4). So he switches from the singular I in verse 2 to the plural we in verses 3-4. As the former generations had done (verse 3), so the psalmist's generation will tell the story of the great deeds of the Lord to the coming generation (verse 4).

RSV   TEV

> We will not hide them from their
> children,
> but tell to the coming genera-
> tion
> the glorious deeds of the LORD,
> and his might,
> and the wonders which he has
> wrought.

> We will not keep them from our
> children;
> we will tell the next generation
> about the LORD's power and his
> great deeds
> and the wonderful things he has
> done.

The Hebrew text in verse 4a is **We will not hide them from their children**, which would, strictly speaking, be the psalmist's own generation (since **them** refers back to "our fathers" of verse 3b). It seems more likely, however, as TEV interprets it, that the meaning is "their descendants," referring to the generation following that of the psalmist. So the translation should be **"our children,"** which is parallel with **the coming generation** in line **b** (see also GECL, FRCL, SPCL). The negative expressions used in RSV and TEV **will not hide them** may have to be recast as positive expressions in some languages; for example, "We will tell them to our children." If this is done, lines **a** and **b** of verse 4 will become fully parallel, and in some languages may have to be reduced to one line, adding an element to emphasize the verb phrase.

The glorious deeds translates "the praises," in the sense of "praiseworthy deeds." So FRCL "the reasons why they should praise the Lord." For **wonders** see comments on "wonderful deeds" in 9.1.

78.5-6   RSV   TEV

> 5 He established a testimony in
>   Jacob,
>   and appointed a law in Israel,
>   which he commanded our fathers
>   to teach to their children;
> 6 that the next generation might
>   know them,
>   the children yet unborn,
>   and arise and tell them to their
>   children,

> 5 He gave laws to the people of
>   Israel
>   and commandments to the de-
>   scendants of Jacob.
>   He instructed our ancestors
>   to teach his laws to their chil-
>   dren,
> 6 so that the next generation might
>   learn them
>   and in turn should tell their
>   children.

The two words **testimony** and **law** are used synonymously here, as they are in 19.7 (see comments there); they both refer to the Torah, God's Law given the people of Israel by Moses. In verse 5 TEV has placed **"the people of Israel"** in line **a** and **"the descendants of Jacob"** in line **b**, for greater ease of understanding. In languages being translated for the first time, it may be necessary to provide a note that identifies the descendants of Jacob with the people of Israel. If this is not done, readers may think that these are two different groups. Alternatively, it is possible to handle this problem in the translation by saying "God gives laws to the people of Israel, who are the descendants of Jacob."

In verses 5c-6 the psalmist again emphasizes the duty of each generation to obey God's command and to transmit to the succeeding generation the story of the great things that God has done for Israel (see Deut 6.7). In verse 6a **the next generation** is further defined as **the children yet unborn**, which TEV does not formally represent, since it is redundant. Should the translator wish to include it, something like the following can serve as a model for verse 6: ". . . so that the next generation, children yet to be born, might learn God's laws and in turn should teach them to their children." In the last line of verse 6 the verb **arise** is used in the sense of beginning an action; it does not mean to stand up.

78.7-8 RSV		TEV
7	so that they should set their hope in God, and not forget the works of God, but keep his commandments;	7 In this way they also will put their trust in God and not forget what he has done, but always obey his commandments.
8	and that they should not be like their fathers, a stubborn and rebellious generation, a generation whose heart was not steadfast, whose spirit was not faithful to God.	8 They will not be like their ancestors, a rebellious and disobedient people, whose trust in God was never firm and who did not remain faithful to him.

RSV has verses 5-8 as one sentence, which is too complex and long for easy reading. It is better to divide the material into several sentences.

The purpose of the instruction in Israel's "history of salvation" is not simply to transmit information; it is to ensure that each generation will **set their hope in God**, **not forget the works of God**, and **keep his commandments**, unlike their ancestors, who proved faithless and fickle. In many languages it will be necessary to shift from the nominal phrases in RSV and TEV to verb phrases in verse 7; for example, "they will hang their hearts on what God has said to them . . . and will obey what he has commanded them to do." In verse 7b **forget** means to ignore, to disregard.

Since verse 8 is a logical conclusion to the preceding verses, it may be clearer in many languages to represent this fact by making that relation explicit; for example, "Because of this . . ." or "Therefore . . . ." In some languages it will be necessary to avoid the apposition of RSV and TEV (**fathers, a stubborn and rebellious generation**) and say, for example, "their ancestors, who were a stubborn . . . ." In verse 8b **rebellious** refers to the tendency of the Israelites to go against God's commands. The expression **heart was not steadfast** is rendered in some languages idiomatically as "they did not rest on God with one heart" or "they did not put their heart in God's hands."

In line c **heart** is parallel with **spirit** in verse 8d; in each case the word denotes qualities of trust and faithfulness.

78.9-11 RSV	TEV
9 The Ephraimites, armed with*ʲ* the bow, turned back on the day of battle.	9 The Ephraimites, armed with bows and arrows, ran away on the day of battle.
10 They did not keep God's covenant, but refused to walk according to his law.	10 They did not keep their covenant with God; they refused to obey his law.
11 They forgot what he had done, and the miracles that he had shown them.	11 They forgot what he had done, the miracles they had seen him perform.

ʲ Heb *armed with shooting*

The reference to the **Ephraimites** is puzzling; there is no record in the Old Testament of their having been cowardly in battle. Many commentators take verse 9 to be a gloss, the origin and purpose of which are variously explained. It could be that Ephraim here stands for the whole northern kingdom of Israel (see Hos 6.4-7). In any case, it introduces an irrelevant bit of information, since the point of the whole passage, both before (verse 8) and after (verses 10-11), is about the generation that was faithless, that did not obey God, and not about a group of cowardly warriors. **The Ephraimites** refers, not to the people generally, but to their soldiers, and may be so represented; for example, "The Ephraimite soldiers."

Armed with the bow translates what is an obscure phrase (see RSV footnote), but on whose meaning there is general agreement. It is better to translate "**bows and arrows**," since obviously the psalmist did not mean the Ephraimites had only bows to fight with.

Turned back or "**ran away**" may require rendering as "ran away from the enemy during the battle."

As the text now stands, verses 10-11 refer to the Ephraimites of verse 9; in fact, the two verses carry on the theme of the "stubborn and rebellious generation" of verse 8. NJV attempts to clarify the matter by starting verse 9 with "Like the Ephraimite bowmen . . . ," but the Hebrew text hardly allows for this. The translation must reflect the meaning of the text as it stands. GECL places verse 10 within parentheses, and in a footnote indicates that this verse anticipates the theme of verses 67 and following.

What was of greater importance about the Ephraimites was their failure to **keep God's covenant** and to obey his laws. For **covenant** see 25.10 and comments. They **forgot** the great deeds God had performed in bringing his people out of slavery in Egypt into the Promised Land. Here it seems that **forgot** implies a deliberate act of not recalling what God had done in the past; it is not a case of a poor memory. Verse 11b does not mean that God **had shown them** certain miracles, and it was these that they **forgot**; rather, it is that they had seen all the miracles he had performed on their behalf, yet still refused to keep their covenant with him, that is, always to obey him. **Miracles** is often rendered as "God's mighty acts" or "the wonderful things God has done."

RSV	TEV

12 In the sight of their fathers he wrought marvels
    in the land of Egypt, in the fields of Zoan.
	12 While their ancestors watched, God performed miracles
	    in the plain of Zoan in the land of Egypt.

13 He divided the sea and let them pass through it,
    and made the waters stand like a heap.
	13 He divided the sea and took them through it;
	    he made the waters stand like walls.

14 In the daytime he led them with a cloud, and all the night with a fiery light.	14 By day he led them with a cloud and all night long with the light of a fire.

The psalmist begins his recital of God's wonderful deeds, the mighty acts and miracles he wrought as he led the Hebrews out of Egypt.

Again in verse 12 **their fathers** seems, because of verse 9, to be the ancestors of the Ephraimites; but it is much more likely that this refers to the ancestors who were a faithless generation (verse 8).

The **marvels in the land of Egypt** (verse 12) are the plagues, described in verses 43-51.

Zoan is identified as the city of Rameses (Exo 1.11), a royal storage city on the eastern side of the Nile Delta; it was also called Tanis (the Septuagint). Zoan is not mentioned in Exodus in connection with the departure from Egypt. In some languages it will often be necessary to identify Egypt as the "country called Egypt."

The account of the parting of the waters for the Israelites to escape safely from the Egyptians is recorded in Exodus 14.21-29. The waters stood "**like walls**" (see Exo 15.8); the Hebrew word for "**walls**" means "barrier, dam," and the same expression is used of the crossing of the Jordan (Josh 3.13,16). RSV **like a heap** is not clear; NJV "stand like a wall" and NIV "stand firm like a wall" can be misunderstood. The picture is that of a path on the sea floor, with the waters of the Sea of Reeds (the Red Sea; see comment at 106.7) standing like walls on either side. The expression **divided the sea** may give a wrong understanding in many languages. Since the sense is that he separated the water in order to make a passage, it will often be better to translate "he made a path through the sea" or "he made a place for them to walk through the sea." The second half of verse 13 may give the reader difficulty, since it is implied that the path through the sea went between the standing walls of water. In order to provide a clearer picture for the reader, it may be necessary to say, for example, "he made the water stand like walls on both sides of the path."

Because of the strangeness of the instrumental use of **a cloud** as an object to lead someone, in some languages it will be clearer to say, for example, "God made a cloud go ahead of them in the daytime to guide them" or "God sent a cloud ahead of them during the day so they would know where to go."

Line b is understood by reading the verb **led** from line a. It will sometimes be necessary to avoid ellipsis and to repeat the verb in the second line, or use a suitable synonym.

What is called in Exodus 13.21-22 "a pillar of fire" is here referred to as **a fiery light**; see NEB "a glowing fire," NJB "the light of a fire."

78.15-16	RSV	TEV

	RSV	TEV
15	He cleft rocks in the wilderness, and gave them drink abundantly as from the deep.	15 He split rocks open in the desert and gave them water from the depths.
16	He made streams come out of the rock, and caused waters to flow down like rivers.	16 He caused a stream to come out of the rock and made water flow like a river.

For these verses see the two incidents narrated in Exodus 17.1-6 and Numbers 20.10-13. **From the deep** in verse 15b translates "as the depths." The same word is used in 77.16 and refers to the underground ocean which supplied the water of rivers and seas (see related ideas in 33.7); TOB "as from the source of the large Abyss," NJV "as if from the great deep." **From the deep** may sometimes be rendered "from deep in the earth."

In verse 15b, to make the text clear, instead of **gave them** it is better to say "gave the people" or "gave his people."

Verse 16 refers to the same incidents as in verse 15 (see also verse 20a,b). The two parallel lines describe the same event; **waters** in line b is parallel to **streams** in line a.

78.17-18	RSV	TEV

	RSV	TEV
17	Yet they sinned still more against him, rebelling against the Most High in the desert.	17 But they continued to sin against God, and in the desert they rebelled against the Most High.
18	They tested God in their heart by demanding the food they craved.	18 They deliberately put God to the test by demanding the food they wanted.

In spite of God's care and providence, the people still rebelled against him. Here the two basic themes are repeated: Israel has always been faithless, though God is always faithful. For the repeated accusation of rebellion, see verses 8, 40, 56.

Exodus 16.1-3 and Numbers 11.4-6 tell how the Hebrews rebelled in the desert against God and demanded food. In verse 17a it is better, with TEV, NEB, SPCL, NIV,

NJV, and TOB, to translate "**continued to sin**" or "sinned again," rather than **sinned still more**, which has the idea of a greater number of sins than before. For comments on **the Most High**, see 7.17. As in other cases of parallelism, it should be clear to the reader that **him** in verse 17a and **the Most High** in verse 17b are the same one.

They tested God: they demanded that he prove that he cared for them and was able and willing to provide for their needs. TEV "**deliberately**" (also NJB) translates **in their heart**. It is not that their sin was inward, hidden; rather, it was a conscious, deliberate act. See NIV and NEB "wilfully"; TOB "consciously."

The food they craved (verse 18b) translates "food for their *nefesh*"; here *nefesh* (see 3.2) has the meaning of craving, desire, appetite. NJV, however, has "food for themselves." Some languages have special terms for food cravings, depending on the desire for sweet, sour, salty, and other tastes. Here the most generic of these may be used.

	78.19-20 RSV	TEV
19	They spoke against God, saying, "Can God spread a table in the wilderness?	They spoke against God and said, "Can God supply food in the desert?
20	He smote the rock so that water gushed out and streams overflowed. Can he also give bread, or provide meat for his people?"	It is true that he struck the rock, and water flowed out in a torrent; but can he also provide us with bread and give his people meat?"

In verse 19a **spoke against God and said** is better translated "insulted God by saying" (NJB).

In verse 19b TEV "**supply food**" is literally **spread a table**, as in 23.5; it would be better to say "supply food for us" or ". . . food for us to eat." FRCL has "serve us a meal." In some languages the use of the rhetorical question will require a negative reply. If the rhetorical question here is not natural, the translator may shift to a negative statement; for example, "Certainly God cannot set a table in the desert" or "Certainly God cannot provide food in the desert."

Verse 20a,b repeats, with a different phraseology, what is described in verses 15-16. Here it is better to treat it as concessive, as TEV, NJV, and SPCL do; something like "Even though he . . . torrent, can he now also . . . ?" In verse 20c,d **bread** and **meat** are the two staple foods; the same two words are used in Exodus 16.12. The answer to their demand came in the form of manna and quails. It should be clear in translation that "**us**" in verse 20c is the same as "**his people**" in verse 20d. In language areas where **bread** is largely unknown or used only for special ceremonial purposes, it will be better to substitute the staple food of the local diet.

RSV   TEV

21	Therefore, when the LORD heard, he was full of wrath; a fire was kindled against Jacob, his anger mounted against Israel;	21	And so the LORD was angry when he heard them; he attacked his people with fire, and his anger against them grew,
22	because they had no faith in God, and did not trust his saving power.	22	because they had no faith in him and did not believe that he would save them.

The Lord's reaction to his people's lack of faith is described. It is not certain whether verse 21b **a fire was kindled** is to be taken literally of a consuming fire or is a figure for God's fierce anger. Numbers 22.20 has "the anger of the Lord blazed hotly," and it may well be that in verse 21b **fire** is synonymous with **anger** in verse 21c (so SPCL). But Numbers 11.1-3 speaks of the fire of the Lord destroying parts of the camp. The psalmist may have intended the meaning to be ambiguous, so that both **anger** and real **fire** are referred to by the combined figures. If the receptor language cannot duplicate this effect, it is better to select either one meaning or the other for clarity.

Jacob in verse 21b and **Israel** in verse 21c are two ways of speaking of the Hebrews. TEV replaces both proper nouns with "**his people**" and "**them**" in order to avoid the repetition.

It was their lack of confidence, of trust, that roused God's anger (verse 22); they had to have proof that he would keep his promise. In verse 22b **his saving power** translates the noun "deliverance, salvation" (see comments on 3.8).

78.23-25   RSV   TEV

23	Yet he commanded the skies above, and opened the doors of heaven;	23	But he spoke to the sky above and commanded its doors to open;
24	and he rained down upon them manna to eat, and gave them the grain of heaven.	24	he gave them grain from heaven, by sending down manna for them to eat.
25	Man ate of the bread of the angels; he sent them food in abundance.	25	So they ate the food of angels, and God gave them all they wanted.

Exodus 16.13b-15 and Numbers 11.7-9 describe the sending of **manna** to the people in the wilderness.

In verse 23a instead of **the skies above** the meaning may be "the clouds above" (TOB; FRCL, GECL, and SPCL have "the clouds"). The word **above** can be misunderstood to mean "above God," so it may be well not to represent it formally in translation. **The skies above** refers to the sky above the people, not above God.

Only here (verse 23b) is there a reference to **the doors of heaven**; elsewhere "gate" or "windows" are spoken of. The passage says literally **he . . . opened the doors of heaven**; this is probably to be taken with line a to mean that God ordered the doors to be opened. Most translations, however, have two different actions in verse 23, an oral command in line a and the action of opening the doors in line b. The translator will have to determine to what extent it is possible to apply the figurative language **opened the doors of heaven**. Where such a metaphor creates misunderstanding, nonmetaphorical language will have to be used; for example, "he ordered the sky to open," or with a simile, "he commanded the sky to open like a door."

Part of verse 23, as translated by the Septuagint, is quoted in John 6.31.

In verse 24 TEV has reversed the order of the two lines for greater ease of understanding. "Sending down" in verse 24b is literally **he rained down** (as in verse 27a). The Hebrew word for **manna** is *man*; in Exodus 16.15 the people ask: "What is it?" (*man-hu*)—and it appears that this is the origin of the name. Again the two lines of verse 24 should not appear to refer to two different things. Most translations transliterate the term **manna**, or adapt it in some other way, if the resultant transliteration may be confused with a word in the receptor language. It may be useful to provide an explanatory footnote for **manna**.

In verse 25a the Hebrew is **Man ate**, which may mean "they ate" (TEV), or "each one ate" (TOB), that is, everyone there ate. Or else it may emphasize that mere human beings ate **the bread of the angels**; so NJB "mere mortals."

The word translated **angels** is literally "strong ones"; most take the word to refer to heavenly beings (so the Septuagint translates "bread of angels"; and see in 103.20b where this same word is parallel with "angels" in verse 20a). TOB has "the Strong Ones," with a footnote explaining that this means the powers who unite to form the heavenly court; NJB and NAB translate "the Mighty," explaining in a footnote that they are angels. NJV has "Each man ate a hero's meal," which is quite unlikely. If the translator follows TEV or RSV **bread of the angels**, in many languages where bread is not used, the common local food should be substituted, or a generic term for food. Whether the translator translates **angels** or follows one of the other suggestions, the main concern will be to avoid giving the reader the impression that the people were given the food that the angels were intending to eat. This may be done by saying, for example, "they ate the same kind of food that the angels eat," or if the translator follows the interpretation which contrasts mortals with angels, it may be possible to say, for example, "ordinary people ate the same kind of food that angels eat."

78.26-28	RSV	TEV
26	He caused the east wind to blow in the heavens, and by his power he led out the south wind;	26 He also caused the east wind to blow, and by his power he stirred up the south wind;
27	he rained flesh upon them like	27 and to his people he sent down

dust,	birds,
winged birds like the sand of the seas;	as many as the grains of sand on the shore;
28 he let them fall in the midst of their camp,	28 they fell in the middle of the camp all around the tents.
all around their habitations.	

It is possible that **the east wind** in verse 26a and **the south wind** in 26b are a poetic way of speaking of the southeast wind (Briggs, Anderson). Numbers 11.31 speaks of "wind from the LORD" which blew in "quails from the sea" (RSV), by which is meant the Gulf of Aqaba, which was to the south and east of the camp of the Hebrews. In some languages **east wind** must be designated by a local directional term; for example, "He caused the wind to blow from the mountainside," ". . . from the waterside," or ". . . from the side of the rising sun." Similar terminology also applies to **south** and other directions. In some languages the direction from which the wind blows is related to the seasons of the year.

In verse 26a RSV **in the heavens** probably should be "from heaven" (NEB, NIV; see Dahood, Anderson). SPCL combines the two lines, as follows: "The east wind and the south wind blew in the sky; God brought them with his power!" TEV considers **in the heavens** to be redundant information and so does not represent it formally. But a translation can do so, either by following NEB, or else by translating "He caused the east wind to blow high above the camp; by his power he stirred up the wind from the south."

"**Sent down**" in verse 27a translates the same verb used in verse 24a "rained down"; RSV uses the same verb **rained**. The use of **flesh** here is most inappropriate; "meat" (NJB, NJV, NEB, etc.) is the right word in English. TEV "**birds**" combines "meat" in line <u>a</u> and **winged birds** in line <u>b</u>.

In verse 27 **like dust . . . like the sand of the seas** refers to the huge quantity of quails that fell on the Israelite camp.

In verse 28 a translation should not give the impression that the birds fell in two distinct locations, **the camp** and **their habitations**; the two refer to the tents of the Hebrews in the camp. "They fell in the camp where the people had their tents" or "they fell around the people's tents where they were camped." (It should be noted that in verse 28 RSV **their . . . their** could mistakenly be taken to refer to **winged birds** of verse 27b.)

78.29-31   RSV   TEV

29 And they ate and were well filled, for he gave them what they craved.	29 So the people ate and were satisfied; God gave them what they wanted.
30 But before they had sated their craving, while the food was still in their mouths,	30 But they had not yet satisfied their craving and were still eating,
31 the anger of God rose against them and he slew the strongest of	31 when God became angry with them and killed their strongest men,

them, and laid low the picked men of Israel.	the best young men of Israel.

In verses 29b,30a **what they craved** and **their craving** translate the same noun, "desire, craving." The Hebrew word *ta'awah* is represented in Numbers 11.34 as part of the name given the place, "Kibroth-hattaavah" (RSV), "graves of craving." The verb phrase **they ate** here refers to the Hebrews eating the birds, whereas in verse 25 it refers to their eating the bread or grain. In some languages the verb will differ in these two verses. Verses 29 and 30 in both RSV and TEV make it appear that the people were satisfied, but that their craving was not satisfied. If this is followed, in many languages the reader will be confused. It may be preferable therefore to say in verse 29 "And so the people ate the meat and filled their stomachs. God had given them what they wanted. (verse 30) But they still had their desire for meat and were still eating it when . . . ."

No specific reason is given why God suddenly got angry with them and killed **the strongest of them**. Numbers 11.31 reports that it was with "a very great plague" (RSV) that the Lord killed them. But the lesson the psalmist is seeking to teach is that it was lack of trust, it was rebellion and disobedience, that caused God's anger. In verse 31c **the picked men of Israel** is parallel to **the strongest of them** in verse 31b and means "the best young men," young men in the prime of life.

78.32-33   RSV   TEV

32	In spite of all this they still sinned; despite his wonders they did not believe.	32	In spite of all this the people kept sinning; in spite of his miracles they did not trust him.
33	So he made their days vanish like a breath, and their years in terror.	33	So he ended their days like a breath and their lives with sudden disaster.

Neither God's anger nor his goodness could guarantee the people's faithful obedience. They **still sinned** and did not believe in him, even after the miracles he had performed. Verse 32b could mean, as NJV, TOB, FRCL, SPCL translate, "they did not believe his miracles." If this is the meaning adopted by the translator, the sense would be "they did not believe that these were miracles performed by God."

Again God's anger at them flared up, and he killed them (verse 33). **Like a breath** translates a word (*hebel*) that means primarily a breath, a puff of wind (see 39.5c,11c; 62.9a,d); it also means in vain, for nothing (see 39.6b)—a key word in Ecclesiastes. Here it may mean, as RSV and TEV have it (also Weiser, Dahood, SPCL), that God destroyed them as though they were no more substantial or lasting than a breath, a puff of wind (NAB "quickly"; so Briggs). But this does not offer as close a parallel with the next line as "*with* a breath" (see FRCL), that is, "he snuffed out their lives" (NEB). NJV has "He made their days end in futility."

The poetic euphemism for killing, **made their days vanish**, is a case of substituting **their days** for "the days of their lives." In some languages it will be necessary to avoid the euphemism and repeat "God killed them" from verse 31. There is a poetic progression from **their days** to **their years**.

In verse 33b TEV "**sudden disaster**" translates a word rarely used in the Old Testament; RSV has **in terror**, and NJV has "sudden death"; FRCL "he put an end to their life with a sudden disaster."

78.34-35 RSV	TEV
34 When he slew them, they sought for him; they repented and sought God earnestly.	34 Whenever he killed some of them, the rest would turn to him; they would repent and pray earnestly to him.
35 They remembered that God was their rock, the Most High God their redeemer.	35 They remembered that God was their protector, that the Almighty came to their aid.

In verse 34 it is obvious that the psalmist is not saying that dead people sought God, as the RSV literal translation of the Hebrew says (similarly BJ, NJB, NIV, TOB, NAB, SPCL, Dahood). NEB and NJV translate "When he struck them," but the verb is the same one used in verse 31b. The meaning is quite clearly that, when God killed some of them, then the others would "search for him" (see Anderson).

The action of the survivors is described by three verbs: "search . . . turn . . . look for" (RSV **they sought** . . . **they repented and sought**). For "search" see "seek" and comments at 9.10, and for "look for" see comments on "seek" at 63.1. "Turn" (or, return) is the word generally used for repentance in the Old Testament. TEV has expressed the meaning of the verbs by "**turn to him . . . repent . . . pray earnestly to him.**" FRCL "they turned to God, they returned to him and sought his help."

Their repentance lasted only as long as there was danger of punishment. They would remember that God was **their rock** (see 18.2 and comments), **their redeemer** (see the comment on *go'el* in 19.14). Here **remembered** means they thought about the fact that God was, indeed, their protector and savior. But this conscious awareness did not for long sustain them, and they went back to their sinful ways. Instead of the Masoretic text "their rock," NEB changes the vowels that go with the Hebrew consonants to get "their Creator." NJB, SPCL, TOB, and NEB join verse 35 to verse 34 as one sentence; this makes good sense, and translators may find it useful to follow their example.

For comments on **Most High** see 7.17; here the full title *'el 'elyon*, "God the Mighty One" is used.

78.36-37 RSV	TEV
36 But they flattered him with their mouths;	36 But their words were all lies; nothing they said was sincere.

they lied to him with their tongues.	**37** They were not loyal to him; they were not faithful to their covenant with him.
37 Their heart was not steadfast toward him; they were not true to his covenant.	

The psalmist says that their change of heart was not genuine (verse 36); all their professions of repentance were lies, intended to deceive God. RSV **flattered him** follows KJV and ASV; the Hebrew verb, however, means to lie to, to deceive, to act the hypocrite. FRCL translates the verse "But they were not sincere, what they said was not true."

Their heart was not steadfast toward him: they were disloyal to God and disregarded the obligations they should have kept under the terms of the covenant (see verses 8c and 10). In verse 37b **his covenant** means either "the covenant he made with them" or "the covenant they made with him"—the former is to be preferred. For comments on **covenant** see 25.10.

78.38-39   RSV   TEV

38 Yet he, being compassionate, forgave their iniquity, and did not destroy them; he restrained his anger often, and did not stir up all his wrath.	**38** But God was merciful to his people. He forgave their sin and did not destroy them. Many times he held back his anger and restrained his fury.
39 He remembered that they were but flesh, a wind that passes and comes not again.	**39** He remembered that they were only mortal beings, like a wind that blows by and is gone.

The psalmist emphasizes God's "compassion" for his people (see comments on "abundant mercy" in 51.1). Although their sins deserved it, he did not **destroy them** totally; instead he **forgave** them (see 65.3b for comments on "forgive"; and for **iniquity** see comments on 51.2). Often "**he held back his anger**" (TEV) and did not arouse all his fury. The psalmist uses vivid human language to describe God's emotions, and a translation should use the same kind of language.

The connection between the last part of verse 38 and verse 39 can be made clearer by ending verse 38 with a comma, and starting verse 39 "because he remembered . . ." (see FRCL, NJV).

TEV "**only mortal beings**" in verse 39a translates the Hebrew word **flesh**, a word which is used to characterize human beings as weak, frail, mortal. The expression "**mortal beings**" of TEV is sometimes rendered "people who die" or "people and nothing more." **Wind** in verse 39b translates *ruach,* which may mean also "breath" or "spirit." Here it is a figure for how easily and quickly a person disappears, ceases to be, dies (see related thoughts, 103.14-16); NJV has "a passing breath that does not return."

In line b it may be necessary in translation to repeat the subject pronoun, "they are like a wind . . . ." If the figure of the wind is unclear, it is possible to say, for example, "they live a short while and then die" or "their lives do not last very long."

78.40-41   RSV   TEV

40   How often they rebelled against   40   How often they rebelled against
        him in the wilderness   him in the desert;
     and grieved him in the desert!   how many times they made him
41   They tested him again and again,   sad!
     and provoked the Holy One of   41   Again and again they put God to
        Israel.   the test
                                              and brought pain to the Holy
                                                 God of Israel.

Once more the psalmist stresses the fickleness, the faithlessness, of the Hebrews. They **rebelled against him** (see verse 17b) and **tested him** (see verse 18a); they **grieved him** and **provoked** him. The latter verb occurs only here in the Old Testament; RSV, NJB, and NEB have **provoked** (which connotes anger, not grief); NJV "vexed"; SPCL, NIV, and TOB "grieved"; FRCL "offended." It seems that the idea of sadness is the one intended. **They rebelled against him** is sometimes rendered idiomatically as "they made their hearts hard against God" or "they said 'No' to God."

In verse 40 TEV has used the one word "**desert**" for the two synonymous words in lines a and b, **wilderness** and **desert**.

For comments on **the Holy One of Israel**, see 71.22.

78.42-43   RSV   TEV

42   They did not keep in mind his   42   They forgot his great power
        power,   and the day when he saved
     or the day when he redeemed   them from their enemies
        them from the foe;   43   and performed his mighty acts
43   when he wrought his signs in   and miracles
        Egypt,   in the plain of Zoan in the land
     and his miracles in the fields of   of Egypt.
        Zoan.

The psalmist returns to the initial act of salvation in Egypt (see verses 11-12). Here again "**forgot**" (TEV) is a deliberate act of disregarding (see verse 11). In verse 42a **his power** translates "his hand." The translation of the nominal phrase **his power** in **they did not keep in mind his power** must often be translated by a verb phrase; for example, "they forgot how powerful he was." **Signs** in verse 43a means "mighty acts," and **miracles** translates a word rarely used (see 71.7, where RSV translates it "a portent"). **Redeemed** in verse 42b is the verb used in 25.22. The reference here is to the plagues (verses 44-51).

For **fields of Zoan** see verse 12b. A translation should avoid suggesting, as does the RSV literal translation, that **Egypt** and **the fields of Zoan** are two different places where God performed his miracles.

78.44-51 RSV	TEV
44 He turned their rivers to blood, so that they could not drink of their streams.	44 He turned the rivers into blood, and the Egyptians had no water to drink.
45 He sent among them swarms of flies, which devoured them, and frogs, which destroyed them.	45 He sent flies among them, that tormented them, and frogs that ruined their land.
46 He gave their crops to the caterpillar, and the fruit of their labor to the locust.	46 He sent locusts to eat their crops and to destroy their fields.
47 He destroyed their vines with hail, and their sycamores with frost.	47 He killed their grapevines with hail and their fig trees with frost.
48 He gave over their cattle to the hail, and their flocks to thunderbolts.	48 He killed their cattle with hail and their flocks with lightning.ᵖ
49 He let loose on them his fierce anger, wrath, indignation, and distress, a company of destroying angels.	49 He caused them great distress by pouring out his anger and fierce rage, which came as messengers of death.
50 He made a path for his anger; he did not spare them from death, but gave their lives over to the plague.	50 He did not restrain his anger or spare their lives, but killed them with a plague.
51 He smote all the first-born in Egypt, the first issue of their strength in the tents of Ham.	51 He killed the first-born sons of all the families of Egypt.
	ᵖ hail . . . lightning; *or* terrible disease . . . deadly plague.

In these verses the psalmist recalls the plagues in Egypt (Exo 7–12).

Verse 44, the first plague: water into blood (Exo 7.17-21; see Psa 105.29). **Their rivers** are the rivers of the Egyptians; and **their rivers** in line a and **their streams** in line b refer to the same bodies of water. Both TEV and RSV make line b a consequence of line a. However, the use of "**and**" in TEV is also coordinate and therefore more ambiguous. Most languages will require making line b explicitly a consequence of line a; for example, "and because of this the Egyptians could not drink the water."

Verse 45a, the fourth plague: flies (Exo 8.20-24; see Psa 105.31a). The Hebrew text is "they ate them up" (RSV **devoured**), which is not to be taken literally. FRCL has "sucked their blood." TEV **"tormented them"** may be a bit weak; perhaps "caused them great suffering" or something similar would be better. Again it is to be noticed that **them** refers to the Egyptians.

Verse 45b, the second plague: frogs (Exo 8.1-7; see Psa 105.30). The use of the verb **destroy** does not mean that the frogs killed the Egyptians but that they "ruined the land" (the same Hebrew verb is used in Exo 8.24, "the land was ruined" by the flies); FRCL has "laid waste to everything." SPCL handles this verse well: "He sent among them flies and frogs, which ate and destroyed everything." In languages in which frogs, locusts, grapevines, and fig trees are unknown, local objects may have to be used or illustrations provided, particularly if the book of Exodus has not yet been translated.

Verse 46, the eighth plague: locusts (Exo 10.1-20; see Psa 105.34-35). The Hebrew text has two different words, which RSV translates **caterpillar** and **locust**, but it is probable that the two are synonymous, both referring to locusts (TEV, SPCL; see *Fauna and Flora,* pages 53-54). **Their crops** in line <u>a</u> is parallel with **the fruit of their labor** in line <u>b</u>, both referring to their cultivated fields, with all the plants and fruit trees they (the Egyptians) grew.

Verse 47, the seventh plague: hail and thunderstorms (Exo 9.18-26; see Psa 105.32-33). **Frost** in line <u>b</u> translates a word found only here in the Old Testament; the ancient versions so understood it, but the account in Exodus does not mention frost. The psalmist no doubt selected it as a suitable term to be in parallel position with **hail**. Some take the word to mean "deluge" (K-B, Holladay "devastating flood"; NEB "torrent of rains"; NIV "sleet"; FRCL "torrential rains"; Oesterley "hailstones"). **"Fig trees"** (also SPCL) represents the Hebrew word usually rendered **sycamores** (RSV), which also produce figs, but here it probably refers to fig trees (see 105.33; *Fauna and Flora,* pages 179-181).

Verse 48: it is difficult to determine whether this verse continues from verse 47 as a reference to the seventh plague, or is a description of the fifth plague, pestilence (Exo 9.1-7). **He gave over to** is a way of saying that God caused the hail to fall on the cattle (see similar language in verses 46a and 50c). The Masoretic text in line <u>a</u> has **hail**, the same word used in verse 47a; and in line <u>b</u> the word is *reshep,* which means "flames" (as in 76.3a), and so TEV **"lightning"** (RSV **thunderbolts**). The account in Exodus 9.22,25 specifies that the hail destroyed not only the vegetation but also the animals, and so verse 48 may be the same plague as verse 47 (so TEV, RSV, NJB, TOB, NJV, NAB, Dahood, Weiser).

But two Hebrew manuscripts, instead of "hail" in verse 48a, have *deber* "pestilence" (the same word in verse 50c); and in line <u>b</u> of the Masoretic text the word *reshep* may mean "plague" (see Hab 3.5 where *reshep* in line <u>b</u> is parallel to *deber* "pestilence" in line <u>a</u>). So verse 48 may refer to the fifth plague (Exo 9.1-7; in Exo 9.3 the word is *deber*); so Briggs, TEV footnote, NEB.

Their flocks in both RSV and TEV refer to sheep. SPCL provides a good translation model here: "Their cows and their sheep died under the hail and the lightning." Many languages will require an active voice, "He killed the cows and sheep with hail and lightning."

Verses 49-51 describe the last plague, the worst one of all: the death of all the first-born sons of the Egyptians (Exo 11.1–12.30; see Psa 105.36). The Hebrew text is very full: "the heat of his anger, rage, and indignation, and distress"; TEV has taken "**distress**" to be that of the people, as the result of God's fury. But it is better to take the word as applying to God, and translate "trouble" (NJV) or "anguish" (SPCL). The psalmist calls these passions God's **company of destroying angels**; see NJB "a detachment of destroying angels"; NJV "a band of deadly messengers." If the translator follows the restructuring of TEV, it is possible that some translation problems will remain. The figure of "**pouring out his anger and fierce rage**" must often be recast to say, for example, "he struck them in his anger" or "because he was angry at them, he struck them. His anger was like a messenger bringing news of death" or ". . . like messengers who have come to kill people."

In verse 50a the Hebrew text is "he prepared a way for his anger," which NJB translates "he gave free course to his anger." God let loose his anger to go where it would. Line b is "he did not hold back the death of their *nefesh*" (see 3.2). And in line c **but gave their lives over to the plague**. For the verb see also verses 48 and 62. The word **plague** in **gave their lives over to the plague** is sometimes rendered "a terrible disease that kills people." Line c of verse 50 may then be rendered "but killed them by giving them a terrible disease."

In verse 51 the two phrases **all the first-born** and **the first issue of their strength** (see also 105.36) refer to the oldest son of every Egyptian family. (Exo 12.29 adds also "the first-born of the cattle.") It is better to shorten and combine the two, as TEV, SPCL, and GECL have done, than to have both phrases, as RSV does.

Many languages designate the first-born child, whether son or daughter, by special terms.

In verse 51b **the tents of Ham** is a way of speaking about Egypt (see 105.23,27; 106.22, where Egypt is called "the land of Ham"). Ham, one of the sons of Noah, was regarded as the ancestor of the Egyptians (see Gen 10.6).

78.52-53	RSV	TEV
52	Then he led forth his people like sheep, and guided them in the wilderness like a flock.	52 Then he led his people out like a shepherd and guided them through the desert.
53	He led them in safety, so that they were not afraid; but the sea overwhelmed their enemies.	53 He led them safely, and they were not afraid; but the sea came rolling over their enemies.

In verses 52-55 the psalmist gives a succinct account of the exodus from Egypt, the journey through the wilderness, the entry into Canaan, and the settlement of the tribes in the conquered land.

In verse 52 **like sheep** and **like a flock** are rendered by TEV by the single "like a shepherd," applying the figure to God. Three different verbs are used in verses 52a,b, 53a for "guide, lead, drive (like a flock)." Verse 53b refers to the crossing of the sea and the drowning of the Egyptians (see verse 13). In languages in which the herding of sheep is familiar, the figurative language in this verse will normally be clear. However, in many languages some recasting will be necessary. If possible the figure of sheep should be maintained. Where pastoral care of sheep is unknown, it may be better to shift to a different simile; for example, "he led his people out of Egypt like a chief and guided them through the desert." It is also possible to drop the shepherd image and say, for example, "he led his people out of Egypt and guided them through the desert."

The expression **the sea overwhelmed** or TEV's **"came rolling over"** may not suggest in some languages that the enemies were actually drowned by the sea. Therefore it may be necessary to say, for example, "but the sea drowned their enemies" or "but their enemies were drowned in the sea."

78.54-55	RSV	TEV

	RSV	TEV
54	And he brought them to his holy land, to the mountain which his right hand had won.	54 He brought them to his holy land, to the mountains which he himself conquered.
55	He drove out nations before them; he apportioned them for a possession and settled the tribes of Israel in their tents.	55 He drove out the inhabitants as his people advanced; he divided their land among the tribes of Israel and gave their homes to his people.

Verse 54 speaks of the land of Canaan as God's **holy land** and **the mountain which his right hand had won**. **Land** translates a word meaning "border, frontier"; by extension it means the territory enclosed within the borders. **Holy** in **his holy land** extends the use of "holy" to still another aspect of things which are in relation to God. (For a more detailed discussion of the concept of "holy," see 28.2.) **Holy land** may sometimes be rendered "land that belongs to God," "God's own land," or "land that God has set apart."

The mountain (singular in Hebrew) can be a reference to Mount Zion (so FRCL) or else is a term for the whole land. NJV, NEB, and Dahood take the word "border" in line a as a synonym of "mountain" in line b. Oesterley thinks the verse speaks of Mount Sinai, but this does not seem very likely; most commentators take the singular **the mountain** to mean Mount Zion.

His right hand means "his power"; so TEV "**he himself conquered**."

Nations in verse 55a are the pagan nations defeated by the Hebrews; Deuteronomy 7.1 names seven of them.

Since there are two plurals in verse 55, one referring to the Hebrews and the other to the Canaanites, care must be taken that the two are clearly distinguished. **Them** in line a refers to the Hebrews; in line b it refers to the Canaanites.

TEV "**divided their land**" in verse 55b translates "apportioned by lot," a reference to the division of the land of Canaan among the tribes of Israel (see Josh 23.4). **Apportioned them** is misleading, since in the context **them** can refer only to the people (the Canaanites); the meaning is (in RSV terms) "he apportioned their lands." For **possession** see 16.6; here it means "for the Hebrews to possess."

In line c **their tents** is too literal a translation of the Hebrew; "**homes**" or "houses" would be better (the Canaanites were not nomads).

This verse presents a problem for some languages in respect to the sequence of events. If the translator follows TEV, the structure is that of simultaneous action in line a, "as the people advanced God drove out the inhabitants." Lines b and c are subsequent actions of God, and in many languages it will be necessary to make this clear by saying, for example, "and then . . . ," or "and after that . . . ," or "after driving out the inhabitants . . . ."

78.56-58 RSV   TEV

56 Yet they tested and rebelled against the Most High God, and did not observe his testimonies,
57 but turned away and acted treacherously like their fathers; they twisted like a deceitful bow.
58 For they provoked him to anger with their high places; they moved him to jealousy with their graven images.

56 But they rebelled against Almighty God and put him to the test. They did not obey his commandments,
57 but were rebellious and disloyal like their fathers, unreliable as a crooked arrow.
58 They angered him with their heathen places of worship, and with their idols they made him furious.

The psalmist now speaks of the Hebrews settling in Canaan and gives a summary of the history of the people's repeated infidelities against their God.

He repeats the language already used: they **rebelled** (verses 17,40a), "**put him to the test**" (verses 18a,41a). For **Most High God** see verse 35; for **testimonies** see verse 5a. If the translator has followed TEV and ended verse 55 with two pronominal references, it will often be clearer to begin verse 56 by avoiding the pronoun and saying "But the people of Israel rebelled."

In verse 57a TEV "**were rebellious**" translates the verb "turn away" (see the passive use, "turned back," in 35.4); and **they acted treacherously** means they "**were . . . disloyal**" (NIV, NJV, TEV; NJB "treacherous," NIV "faithless"; see comments on "untrue" in 73.15b).

Verse 57b is not easy to understand; the Hebrew seems to say "they changed like a loose bow" (see the same language in Hos 7.16). The Hebrew adjective may mean "deceitful" (see "deceit" and comments in 32.2b) or "slack, loose." The idea seems to be of a defective, unreliable bow, either because the bowstring isn't tight or for some other reason; and so it could not shoot an arrow accurately. TEV has changed the figure to "**a crooked arrow**" as being more easily understood by most of its readers; other translations may find **bow** more natural. NJB has "like a faulty bow"; Dahood and NAB have "they recoiled like a treacherous bow" (see also NJV "a treacherous bow"). Anderson suggests "they were perverse like a slack bow," and FRCL translates "like a bow with a slack cord." If **bow** is to be kept, something like "unreliable" or "defective" is more natural. NIV does it well: "as unreliable as a faulty bow." In languages where the bow is not known, another weapon may be substituted. If that solution is unsatisfactory, it will be best to drop the simile and say, for example, "they were unreliable" or "God could not depend upon them."

In verse 58 **high places** refers to pagan shrines, which were usually located on elevated places such as mounds or hills. These were the places of worship of the native Canaanites and which the Hebrews adopted, along with their idols, which were **graven** (or carved) **images** of the fertility god Baal and the goddess Astarte. In verse 58 the verb **provoked . . . to anger** ("**angered**," TEV) translates "to vex, irritate" (see 106.29) and **moved him to jealousy** ("**made him furious**") is the causative of the verb "be jealous" (see comments on "envious" in 37.1; 73.3). This attribute of God is used quite often and quite naturally in the Old Testament of Yahweh's reaction to his people's idolatry. See Exodus 20.5, TEV "I tolerate no rivals." It is an expression of God's exclusive rights to his people's devotion and loyalty. The current idea of jealousy is a bit narrow, and its application to God may carry some wrong connotations. If the translator follows the TEV handling of the two Hebrew terms rendered "angered him" and "made him furious," the parallelism of the two halves becomes very closely equivalent and in that case may have to be reduced to one; for example, "they made God terribly angry with their heathen places of worship and their idols" or "the false gods they worshiped and their worship places caused God to be very angry."

78.59-61	RSV	TEV

	RSV	TEV
59	When God heard, he was full of wrath, and he utterly rejected Israel.	God was angry when he saw it, so he rejected his people completely.
60	He forsook his dwelling at Shiloh, the tent where he dwelt among men,	He abandoned his tent in Shiloh,*q* the home where he had lived among us.
61	and delivered his power to captivity, his glory to the hand of the foe.	He allowed our enemies to capture the Covenant Box, the symbol of his power and glory.

q SHILOH: *The central place of worship for the people of Israel before the time of King David.*

More of Israel's calamities are cited as examples of God's anger with his people. Verse 59 begins **When God heard**; TEV substitutes "saw" as being less difficult for the reader (also SPCL). The main idea, in any case, is God's awareness of what the Israelites were doing. NJB has "God listened and . . . ," and FRCL "When he became aware of this . . . ."

The Hebrew **full of wrath** in verse 59a is the verb used in verses 21a, 62b. For comments on **rejected** see 15.4 ("despised") and 53.5.

Shiloh was a city in the territory of the tribe of Ephraim, some 32 kilometers north of Jerusalem, where the Covenant Box was kept in the early days of Israel's history (see Josh 18.1; 1 Sam 1.3). Verse 60b TEV has "**where he had lived among us**": the Hebrew word translated "**us**" is generic, *'adam,* "humankind, humanity," but the reference is specifically to Israel, not to the human race as a whole (so GECL).

However, a translator may prefer to retain the idea of humankind and translate "the place where he had lived among human beings" or "the place where he had lived on earth." NJB avoids the problem by translating "the tent where he used to dwell on the earth."

In verse 61 it is agreed that **his power** and **his glory** which God allowed to be taken captive refer to the Covenant Box, which the Philistines captured in battle (1 Sam 4.1-22). TEV, OECL, and FRCL name the Covenant Box; SPCL says only "the symbol of his glory and power." TOB and NJV have footnotes to indicate that the language refers to the Covenant Box. **Glory** here translates a word meaning "beauty, ornament" (see also comments at 71.8b). If the translator follows TEV's "**Covenant Box**," this expression may be rendered "the box that held God's agreement with his people" or "the box containing the writing of the agreement between God and his people."

<table>
<tr><td>**78.62-64**</td><td>RSV</td><td>TEV</td></tr>
</table>

62 He gave his people over to the sword, and vented his wrath on his heritage.	62 He was angry with his own people and let them be killed by their enemies.
63 Fire devoured their young men, and their maidens had no marriage song.	63 Young men were killed in war, and young women had no one to marry.
64 Their priests fell by the sword, and their widows made no lamentation.	64 Priests died by violence, and their widows were not allowed to mourn.

TEV has restructured the two lines in verse 62: "**his own people**" translates both **his people** and **his heritage** (see comments at 16.6). **Vented his wrath** ("He was angry") translates the same verb used in verse 59a.

The sword (verse 62a) represents death in battle. The reference is probably to the same battle with the Philistines (1 Sam 4.10-11; see the commentaries). **Gave . . . over to the sword** means "let them be killed."

In verse 63 **Fire** means war, battle, in parallel with **sword**. Care should be taken lest the modern notion of "firearms" be inadvertently expressed. It is doubtful that the text means the young men were burned to death (so NJB, NIV, SPCL, and others).

TEV "**young women had no one to marry**" translates **their maidens had no marriage song**, which is a reference to the songs at the wedding which praised the bride's beauty and charms. NJV translates "their maidens remained unwed." SPCL "there were no wedding songs for the brides" could be misleading. **Maidens had no marriage song** is, of course, a consequence of their future husbands being killed in battle. In many languages it will be necessary to make explicit the logical relationship between line a and line b; for example, "because the young men were killed in war, the young women had no one to marry."

In verse 64 the statement about **priests** being killed may refer to Hophni and Phinehas, the two sons of Eli (1 Sam 4.11). **Their widows made no lamentation** in line b means either that so many priests were killed that there was no time for proper burial rites for each dead priest, or else that the widows were not permitted to have public mourning for their dead husbands (as TEV expresses it; also Weiser, NEB, NJV), or that the conditions of war made normal mourning impossible. It does not mean that the widows were unmoved by the death of their husbands.

78.65-66   RSV   TEV

65   Then the Lord awoke as from sleep,
     like a strong man shouting because of wine.
66   And he put his adversaries to rout;
     he put them to everlasting shame.

65   At last the Lord woke up as though from sleep;
     he was like a strong man excited by wine.
66   He drove his enemies back in lasting and shameful defeat.

In these two verses the psalmist seems to be describing military victories over the Philistines during the time of Saul and David. The psalmist uses the figure of a warrior waking up from sleep and going into battle. For similar language about God waking up, see 35.23; 44.23. It is not clear what line b of verse 65 means, because the verb is of uncertain form and meaning. Some take it to be a figure of a man who is stimulated by wine and roars into action (RSV **shouting**; TEV **"excited"**; NEB "heated"; NJB "fighting-mad with wine"; so Anderson and Kirkpatrick). Others take the verb to represent a man sobering up after having drunk too much (AT "overcome with wine"; NJV "like a warrior shaking off wine"; SPCL "like a warrior who sobers up"; NIV "as a man wakes from the stupor of wine"; so Briggs and McCullough). Dahood has "like a warrior resting after wine." There is hardly any way of deciding which interpretation is correct; possibly the first one better fits the context. In many languages it will be necessary to say, for example, "excited from the wine he has drunk" or "the wine he has drunk has made him excited."

He put his adversaries to rout (verse 66a): some take the word translated **to rout** (TEV "back") to be "the back" of the enemies, an allusion to the tumors (or hemorrhoids) inflicted on the Philistines (1 Sam 5.6-12); so KJV, NJB, NEB, and Dahood. The **everlasting shame** God brought upon them was "**lasting and shameful defeat.**"

78.67-69   RSV   TEV

67   He rejected the tent of Joseph, he did not choose the tribe of Ephraim;
68   but he chose the tribe of Judah, Mount Zion, which he loves.
69   He built his sanctuary like the high heavens,
     like the earth, which he has

67   But he rejected the descendants of Joseph;
     he did not select the tribe of Ephraim.
68   Instead he chose the tribe of Judah
     and Mount Zion, which he dearly loves.

<table>
<tr><td>founded for ever.</td><td>69</td><td>There he built his Temple
like his home in heaven;
he made it firm like the earth
itself,
secure for all time.</td></tr>
</table>

These verses describe how the central place of worship was moved from Shiloh (see verse 60), which was in the territory of the tribe of Ephraim. Ephraim was one of the sons of Joseph, and the tribe was made up of his descendants; so in verse 67 **tent of Joseph** and **tribe of Ephraim** are parallel and used synonymously. After having been captured in battle by the Philistines, the Covenant Box, once it had been returned to Israel, was not taken back to Shiloh. It would be impossible to make clear the significance of the relation of Joseph and Ephraim and the historical implication of the removal of the Covenant Box without building a commentary into the translation. However, any translation of this passage should contain adequate cross references to assist the reader, and perhaps a supplementary note. In regard to the translation of this verse, it may be possible to keep only "**descendants of Joseph**" or "**tribe of Ephraim**." Since verse 68 continues with reference to the "tribe of Judah," it may be better to keep "**tribe of Ephraim**" only, in verse 67.

Mount Zion (see information at 2.6) was in Jerusalem, in the territory of **the tribe of Judah**. David placed the Covenant Box there, after the original inhabitants, the Jebusites, were driven out.

The Temple (**his sanctuary**, verse 69) was built by Solomon on nearby Mount Moriah; the name **Mount Zion** was applied to that hill and also to the whole city of Jerusalem.

In verse 69 it is not clear what the simile **like the high heavens** means; either "high as the heavens" (NEB) or "like the high hills" (NJB). Most translations follow the RSV interpretation. Perhaps the idea of permanence, which is explicitly expressed in line b, is meant also in line a (Anderson); so FRCL "There he built his temple, solid like heaven, and like the earth, which he set in place forever." For translation suggestions on **sanctuary** see 20.2; 28.2. At the end of verse 69, **which he has founded for ever** refers to **the earth**; consequently TEV should be ". . . the earth, which he made to last forever" or ". . . the earth, which he set in place forever."

78.70-72	RSV	TEV

	RSV		TEV
70	He chose David his servant, and took him from the sheep- folds;	70	He chose his servant David; he took him from the pastures,
71	from tending the ewes that had young he brought him to be the shepherd of Jacob his people, of Israel his inheritance.	71	where he looked after his flocks, and he made him king of Israel, the shepherd of the people of God.
72	With upright heart he tended them,	72	David took care of them with unselfish devotion and led them with skill.

> and guided them with skilful
> hand.

The psalm closes with the choice of David as king of Israel. Verses 70-71 in RSV give the form of the Hebrew text, whose meaning TEV has tried to express in less literal fashion: **"pastures"** for the sheepfolds and **"flocks"** for the ewes that had young; **"king of Israel"** and **"the shepherd of the people of God"** for shepherd of Jacob his people, of Israel his inheritance.

In the translation of verses 70-71, translators will have to decide first if the pastoral analogies can be meaningfully kept. If not, they may be substituted. However, in most cases it will be possible to maintain the reference to David as one who cared for his animals. The second decision will be regarding the purpose for which God chose David. In many languages it will be clearer to say "God chose David who was his servant to be king of Israel." The second statement, which contains the circumstances under which David was chosen, can more naturally be followed by the shepherd analogy; for example, "God took David from the pastures, where he looked after his flocks, and made him the shepherd of the people of God." SPCL translates the two verses as follows:

> 70 He chose his servant David,
>   who was a shepherd of sheep;
> 71 he stopped him from walking behind the flocks
>   that he might take care of his people,
>   that he might be the shepherd of Israel.

In verse 72a TEV **"unselfish devotion"** translates what is literally "perfection of heart." RSV and others take it to refer to David's upright character. The idea of sincerity or devotion is expressed by TEV and others; NAB and SPCL have "sincere heart"; NIV "integrity of heart"; NEB "singleness of heart." See 1 Kings 9.4.

In verse 72b skilful hand (TEV "skill") portrays David as a wise and competent king, who provided his people the leadership they needed. In some languages to guide with skilful hand may be translated "he led them well because he knew how," "he showed them what to do and they did it well," or idiomatically, "he went ahead of them and showed them how to follow him."

Psalm 79

This psalm, like Psalm 74, is a prayer by the people of Israel and is made because of a military defeat, the destruction of Jerusalem, and the desecration of the Temple. It is probable that this psalm, like Psalm 74, has for its background the Babylonian invasion in 587 B.C.

The psalm opens with a description of the devastation wrought by the enemy (verses 1-4); this is followed by a prayer to God for forgiveness and help (verses 5-12); and the psalm closes with a promise to praise God forever for his goodness (verse 13).

HEADING: TEV "**A Prayer for the Nation's Deliverance**." Other headings are "Grief over the destruction of Jerusalem"; "National lament"; "Prayer in national disaster." The TEV heading may have to be recast in some languages to change the two noun phrases into verb phrases; for example, "The psalmist prays that God will deliver the nation" or "The psalmist prays asking God to save Israel."

Hebrew title: **A Psalm of Asaph** (TEV "A psalm by Asaph").
For **Asaph** see title of Psalm 50.

79.1-2	RSV	TEV
1	O God, the heathen have come into thy inheritance; they have defiled thy holy temple; they have laid Jerusalem in ruins.	1 O God, the heathen have invaded your land. They have desecrated your holy Temple and left Jerusalem in ruins.
2	They have given the bodies of thy servants to the birds of the air for food, the flesh of thy saints to the beasts of the earth.	2 They left the bodies of your people for the vultures, the bodies of your servants for wild animals to eat.

The psalmist describes the destruction wrought by the invading enemy. For <u>the heathen</u> see comments on 2.1, where the same Hebrew word is rendered "the nations." In this verse <u>heathen</u> refers to foreigners, invaders, and in some languages a term such as "foreign enemies," "other tribes," or "strangers" may be used. "**Invaded your land**" may sometimes have to be recast to say "have attacked us to take away your land" or "have come to take away the land you gave us." For

inheritance see 16.6; however, here it is the property of God, not of the people, and so TEV has "**your land.**"

Line <u>b</u> of verse 1 has the same meaning as 74.7b; **defiled** translates a different verb, but the meaning is the same. We can only speculate about the specific things the enemy did to make the Temple unfit for worship to Yahweh. But if the whole city was in ruins, the Temple could hardly have escaped destruction. **Defiled** in the sense of making taboo or unfit for worship may be rendered "they have made your holy Temple unclean so that people cannot worship you." If the sense of such a translation refers to physical uncleanliness, then it is better to say "they have destroyed your holy Temple." For translation suggestions on "holy" related to the Temple, see comments on "holy sanctuary" in 28.2.

The corpses of the dead Israelites had been left unburied, which was a final indignity and disgrace (see Eccl 6.3; Jer 14.16; Tobit 1.17-18). In verse 2 **thy servants** and **thy saints** are synonymous; they refer to the people of Israel in general, not to any specific group. For **thy saints** see comments on the same term translated "the godly" in 4.3. TEV has "**your people**" first, in order to help the reader understand that "**your servants**" in the next line means the same thing. If the translator finds it difficult to avoid **servants** and **saints** being understood as two different groups, it may be necessary to reduce them to one and say, for example, "They left the bodies of your people for the vultures and the wild animals to eat" (see SPCL).

The birds of the air in verse 2a are birds of carrion, such as "**vultures.**" **Of the air** and **of the earth** are set expressions used many times in the Old Testament. These qualifiers do not specify the kinds of birds or animals, but the context makes clear that they refer to "**vultures**" and "**wild animals.**"

79.3-4	RSV		TEV
3	They have poured out their blood like water	3	They shed your people's blood like water;
	round about Jerusalem,		blood flowed like water all through Jerusalem,
	and there was none to bury them.		and no one was left to bury the dead.
4	We have become a taunt to our neighbors,	4	The surrounding nations insult us;
	mocked and derided by those round about us.		they laugh at us and mock us.

The slaughter was so terrible that "**blood flowed like water**" in Jerusalem. TEV and RSV begin verse 3 with **They**, which may be slightly ambiguous due to the references in verse 2 to the vultures and wild animals. The referents in verse 3 should be clear: **They have** refers to the enemies; **their blood** refers to the Israelites, and **them** are the dead Israelites. In languages where the degree of ambiguity would be increased, it will be better to begin verse 3 with the noun subject.

Round about Jerusalem does not mean outside the city but all through the city. SPCL translates "through all Jerusalem." TEV has repeated the simile "**like water**" in connection with the killing of the people and its location in Jerusalem. This is not necessary. If the expression **poured out . . . blood** or "**shed . . . blood**" has the wrong meaning, it will be better to say "they have killed the people all around Jerusalem." If the simile is to be kept, one may say, for example, "the blood of the dead has flowed like water in Jerusalem."

Verse 3c emphasizes again the fact that so many Israelites were slaughtered that there were hardly any survivors to bury the dead.

Verse 4 is practically identical with 44.13, except that here God is not specifically the one who caused the mocking. **Our neighbors** are the surrounding heathen nations, often translated as "the other tribes" or "the tribes around us who do not worship God."

79.5-7	RSV	TEV
5	How long, O LORD? Wilt thou be angry for ever? Will thy jealous wrath burn like fire?	5 LORD, will you be angry with us forever? Will your anger continue to burn like fire?
6	Pour out thy anger on the nations that do not know thee, and on the kingdoms that do not call on thy name!	6 Turn your anger on the nations that do not worship you, on the people who do not pray to you.
7	For they have devoured Jacob, and laid waste his habitation.	7 For they have killed your people; they have ruined your country.

In conventional language the people ask God how long this situation will continue (see similar passages in 13.1; 74.1,10). Their defeat by the enemy is seen as a result of God's anger with them, and they plead with God to turn his anger from them and vent it on their enemies. The two questions in verse 5 vividly express the people's dismay and perplexity.

In verse 5b **jealous wrath** translates a noun that is related to the verb "to be jealous" (see discussion at 78.58b). Yahweh's jealousy was usually aroused when his people worshiped the gods of other nations. The expression **wrath burn like fire** must often be recast in idiomatic speech in some languages; for example, "Will you continue to have a hot heart against us?" or "Will you continue to look at us with red eyes?"

In verse 6 the enemy is described as **the nations that do not know thee** and **the kingdoms that do not call upon thy name**: these are pagan nations, and the two nouns **nations** and **kingdoms** are synonymous. SPCL combines the two as follows: "Discharge your fury on pagan kingdoms who do not know you or pray to you." The negative **not know** can be translated "disregard, ignore, not pay attention"; and **not call upon** means not to pray to, or not to worship (for discussion of **name** see 5.11).

In verse 7a **Jacob** designates the people of Israel, and **his habitation** in verse 7b means the country. Instead of TEV "**your country**" in verse 7b, "our country" matches the Hebrew more closely. A literal rendering of verse 7 (RSV, NJB, NJV) may lead the reader to think of **Jacob** as a person and **his habitation** as his home. **Devoured** your people is a common Hebrew expression for "killing" or "destroying" and is used in many languages with the same basic meaning of "to eat," particularly in certain African languages. Verse 7 may be rendered, for example, "They have killed the descendants of Jacob and have destroyed their country" or "Those tribes have killed your people and destroyed your nation."

Verses 6-7 are practically the same as Jeremiah 10.25.

79.8-9	RSV		TEV
8	Do not remember against us the iniquities of our forefathers; let thy compassion come speedily to meet us, for we are brought very low.	8	Do not punish us for the sins of our ancestors. Have mercy on us now; we have lost all hope.
9	Help us, O God of our salvation, for the glory of thy name; deliver us, and forgive our sins, for thy name's sake!	9	Help us, O God, and save us; rescue us and forgive our sins for the sake of your own honor.

The people pray that God not punish them for the sins of their ancestors. The Hebrew **Do not remember against us** can be translated somewhat idiomatically, "Don't hold the sins of our ancestors against us" or, as SPCL translates, "Do not make us pay for the sins of our ancestors." The word TEV translates "**ancestors**" (so most commentators and translators) is taken by some to mean "earlier, former" (see McCullough). So NJV "Do not hold our former iniquities against us." This makes sense, but the other makes just as much sense: one generation does not want to pay for the sins of former generations.

For **compassion** see comments on "abundant mercy" in 51.1. TEV "**we have lost all hope**" translates "We are very low"; Dahood translates "We are down and out." In some languages it may be necessary to place the reason for the psalmist's plea before the plea; for example, "we are brought very low; therefore let your compassion come . . . ." **Brought very low** is sometimes rendered "we are weakened," "our hearts are low," "trouble fills our hearts," or "trembling takes hold of us." **Let thy compassion come speedily to meet us** translates the Hebrew closely in form but will need to be recast in many languages, similarly to TEV, or, for example, "quickly show us your good face," "make us see now your warm heart," or "have a warm heart now for us."

God of our salvation in verse 9a means "the God who saves us" (see translations and comments at 18.46; 24.5; 25.5; 27.9; 65.5).

The people plead to be saved **for the glory of thy name** . . . **for thy name's sake**. The two expressions here are synonymous, which TEV has represented by one line, "**for the sake of your own honor**," and SPCL by "for the glory of your name." Yahweh's fame and reputation were affected by his people's situation: when they were humiliated, so was he; when they were praised, so was he. So it is not only for their own sake but also for God's sake that the people pray for the defeat of their enemies, the enemies of God. The expression "**for the sake of your own honor**" must often be recast to say, for example, "so that the other tribes will honor you" or "so that other people will respect you."

79.10   RSV   TEV

> Why should the nations say,   Why should the nations ask us,
>   "Where is their God?"   "Where is your God?"
> Let the avenging of the outpoured   Let us see you punish the nations
>   blood of thy servants   for shedding the blood of your
>   be known among the nations   servants.
>   before our eyes!

The opening sentence is a question that includes a question, both of which are rhetorical. It may be better to use a negative statement for the larger question, as follows: "The people of other nations should not say . . ." or "God, don't let the people of other nations ask us . . . ." The enemies of the Israelites should not be able to put them to shame by asking **"Where is their God?"** (see 42.3,10; 115.2). TEV has the question addressed to the Israelites. FRCL translates "What is their God doing?" Such a question was humiliating in the extreme, because there was no answer they could give; God had remained silent, impassive, inactive, while his people suffered.

So they pray for vengeance (verse 10c,d). The language of these two lines can be hard to understand if a literal translation is attempted (see RSV). For comments on "vengeance" in the sense of "punish," see 18.47. **The outpoured blood of thy servants** means "the killing of your servants (or, your people)." **Let the avenging . . . be known among the nations** means "let the nations experience (or, feel)." Most translations take "know" to mean "learn, realize"—so FRCL, TOB; SPCL translates "Allow us to see the death of your servants avenged! And may the pagans also know it!" But it seems better to see here the meaning "to experience," that is, that they, the pagans, suffer God's punishment; so NEB "Let thy vengeance . . . fall on those nations," and NJB "Let us see the nations suffer vengeance for shedding your servants' blood." **Before our eyes** means "while we look on." In some languages it may be necessary to render the second half of verse 10 as "Let us watch you as you kill the other tribes for having killed your people," or "We pray that we may be able to see . . . ," or "We ask you to allow us to see . . . ."

79.11-13   RSV   TEV

11 Let the groans of the prisoners   11 Listen to the groans of the prison-
       come before thee;   ers,
    according to thy great power   and by your great power free
    preserve those doomed to die!   those who are condemned to
12 Return sevenfold into the bosom   die.
       of our neighbors   12 Lord, pay the other nations back
    the taunts with which they have   seven times
       taunted thee, O Lord!   for all the insults they have
13 Then we thy people, the flock of   hurled at you.
       thy pasture,   13 Then we, your people, the sheep of
    will give thanks to thee for ever;   your flock,
    from generation to generation   will thank you forever

| we will recount thy praise. | and praise you for all time to come. |

In verse 11 (whose vocabulary is similar to that of 102.20) the people pray for **prisoners** and for **those doomed to die**. This probably refers quite explicitly to prisoners of war; it could, in more general terms, refer to Israelites in exile, doomed to die in a foreign country. In many languages it will be necessary to shift from the passive **"condemned to die"** and say, for example, "those of our people whom the enemy has decided to kill."

Into the bosom in verse 12a means directly, individually, personally. Folds in the garment made it possible to carry precious things as well as money in the **bosom**. The idea of repayment is also present; so TEV **"pay . . . back."** NEB has "on their own heads." NIV "into the laps of our neighbors" is not a natural idiom in English. **Our neighbors** are the surrounding nations. The people pray for complete and full punishment of the enemy: may they suffer seven times as much as they have made the Israelites suffer. **"Pay . . . back seven times"** need not be rendered literally as in RSV and TEV. The expression **"seven times"** suggests "again and again" or "many times." For parallel usages see Job 5.19; Proverbs 24.16; 26.25.

The psalm closes (verse 13) with a promise of eternal praise and thanksgiving to God for answering his people's prayer. For **the flock of thy pasture**, see comments on the similar phrase in 74.1. In some languages it will be necessary to introduce a simile; for example, ". . . your people, who are like the sheep of your pasture." In the last line, **from generation to generation** is simply a Hebrew way of saying "for all time" (NJV), "throughout all centuries" (SPCL), "from age to age" (NJB). **Recount thy praise** is an elaborate way of saying "repeatedly praise you," "keep on praising you." NJV makes the two lines closely parallel: "shall glorify you forever, for all time we shall tell your praises."

Psalm 80

In this psalm the people of Israel complain to God about their situation: their country has been devastated by enemies and Israel is in bondage. The people pray to God that he change his attitude from anger to concern and save them.

The refrain that appears three times (verses 3, 7, 19) marks the end of three strophes. In the first strophe (verses 1-2) the psalmist cries to God to save the nation; in the second one (verses 4-6) he describes the desperate situation of the Israelites; this same description continues by means of an allegory which recounts the nation's history (verses 8-13). In the final strophe (verses 14-18) once more the psalmist appeals to God for help.

HEADING: "**A Prayer for the Nation's Restoration**." Other headings are "A prayer for restoration"; "Look at us with favor!"; "A prayer in behalf of the nation." If the translator follows the TEV heading, the noun phrases may have to be recast as verb phrases; for example, "The psalmist prays that God will save Israel."

Hebrew title: **To the choirmaster: according to Lilies. A Testimony of Asaph. A Psalm** (TEV "A psalm by Asaph; a testimony").

For **choirmaster** see title of Psalm 4; for **according to Lilies** see title of Psalm 45; for **Asaph** see title of Psalm 50. And for **Testimony** see title of Psalm 60, where "Shushan Eduth" (RSV) is taken to be the name of the tune. Here NJB joins the two words *Shoshanim 'eduth* as the title: "Tune: 'The Decrees are lilies.' " (RSV has **. . . Lilies. A Testimony . . .**). The Septuagint adds here, as it does at Psalm 76, "concerning the Assyrian." The translator should feel free to follow either RSV or TEV.

80.1-2   RSV   TEV

1   Give ear, O Shepherd of Israel,   1   Listen to us, O Shepherd of Is-
          thou who leadest Joseph like a   rael;
          flock!   hear us, leader of your flock.
      Thou who art enthroned upon the   Seated on your throne above the
          cherubim, shine forth   winged creatures,
2   before Ephraim and Benjamin   2   reveal yourself to the tribes of
          and Manasseh!   Ephraim, Benjamin, and
      Stir up thy might,   Manasseh.
          and come to save us!   Show us your strength;
                                                     come and save us!

711

The psalmist appeals to God, the **Shepherd of Israel**, to listen to his people. In verse 1b **Joseph** is synonymous with **Israel** in verse 1a as a designation of the people of Israel. But since two of the northern tribes are named in verse 2, perhaps **Joseph** here stands specifically for the northern tribes (Joseph was the father of Ephraim and Manasseh; see discussion at 78.71). TEV does not formally represent **Joseph** in verse 1b, since it means simply "people of Israel," and few readers will know that; if the text says only **Joseph**, they will probably think of the person, not the tribe.

In languages in which the figure of the shepherd is understandable, it will often be necessary to recast the opening of verse 1 to say, for example, "Shepherd of the people of Israel, listen to us." If the shepherd image is not fully meaningful, the translator may say, for example, "you who take care of the people of Israel . . . ." Line **b**, if it is to be kept as a parallel line, may require using a different verb, particularly if the object of the verb is the same as in line **a**. In some cases the two lines may best be reduced to one; for example, "Listen to us, you who lead the people of Israel" or "You who lead the people of Israel like a flock, listen to us." It is possible to retain the name **Joseph** as follows: "Listen to us, O Shepherd of Israel, you who lead the descendants of Joseph like a flock."

For **the cherubim** see the description in 18.10. Here they denote the Covenant Box, which was regarded as the earthly throne of God. If the word **cherubim** is transliterated, it will be essential to provide the reader with a note or a reference to the earlier verse where the note may be found. Most attempts at rendering this word by means of a descriptive phrase result in confusing the reader, due to the very large number of winged creatures he already knows.

The psalmist asks God to **shine forth**, that is, to **"reveal"** his power and might by coming to save his people.

Ephraim and **Manasseh** were the two most important northern tribes; **Benjamin**, a southern tribe, was often associated with them. It is to be remembered that Joseph (the father of Ephraim and Manasseh) and Benjamin were the two sons of Rachel. In translation it is advisable to provide the reader with a note explaining these three tribes, particularly if **Joseph** is kept in verse 1. Without a note it may not be clear in what way the prayer is directed toward the saving of the three tribes and at the same time **save us**. This problem may also be handled within the text by saying, for example, "reveal yourself to our people of the tribes of . . . ."

Stir up thy might (TEV **"Show us your strength"**) translates "Rouse your power" (see Dahood), which is practically equivalent to the plea in 44.23 for the Lord to wake up, to rouse himself. It seems to the people of Israel that Yahweh has been inactive, and so they ask him to take action on their behalf. The final **save us** means to free the people from their enemies (as in verses 3, 7, 19).

80.3   RSV   TEV

Restore us, O God;   Bring us back, O God!
let thy face shine, that we may   Show us your mercy, and we
be saved!   will be saved!

The prayer in the refrain (verses 3,7,19) is that God restore his people to their former condition as a strong and prosperous nation. SPCL translates "Make us become what we used to be." The Hebrew verb is the causative form of "turn, return," the verb regularly used of repentance, and some take it here to mean "cause us to repent." This is possible but not very probable. The expression **Restore us** or TEV "**Bring us back**" implies returning to a previous condition and must in some languages be rendered as a clause; for example, "make us great like we used to be" or "return our good fortune to us."

For comments on **let thy face shine**, see 31.16; see also 67.1. In many languages the passive structures of TEV and RSV must sometimes be recast as imperatives; for example, "be merciful to us and save us."

80.4-6	RSV	TEV

	RSV	TEV
4	O LORD God of hosts, how long wilt thou be angry with thy people's prayers?	4 How much longer, LORD God Almighty, will you be angry with your people's prayers?
5	Thou hast fed them with the bread of tears, and given them tears to drink in full measure.	5 You have given us sorrow to eat, a large cup of tears to drink.
6	Thou dost make us the scorn[k] of our neighbors; and our enemies laugh among themselves.	6 You let the surrounding nations fight over our land; our enemies insult us.

[k] Syr: Heb *strife*

For translation suggestions on **LORD God of hosts**, see 46.7. Note also that this is the final, fully expanded name for God as it appears in verse 19.

The psalmist cries to Yahweh in protest against what he has done to his people (for similar language see 74.10-11; 79.5). He cannot understand why God has punished Israel so harshly. Even the people's prayers of confession and repentance are rejected by God (verse 4a). **Be angry** translates the verb "to smoke" (see comments, 74.1); FRCL translates "how long will you smoke (or, fume) in anger?" and NJB "how long will you flare up?" Instead of **with thy people's prayers**, some interpret the Hebrew phrase as a temporal clause, "while your people pray" (Briggs, Dahood). The sense of this passage is that God is angry and will not answer the prayers of the people; it may be rendered "how much longer will you be angry with us and refuse to answer our prayers?"

In verse 5a TEV "**sorrow to eat**" translates **the bread** (or, food) **of tears**; see a similar expression in 42.3. In verse 5b TEV "**a large cup**" translates "one-third of a measure," which is otherwise unspecified; it indicates a large amount (RSV **in full measure**). TOB translates "a triple measure of tears"; NEB "tears of threefold grief." It is sometimes necessary to recast verse 5 to say, for example, "You have given us sorrow for bread to eat and tears to drink" or "You have given us sorrow to eat just as we eat bread, and tears to drink just as we drink water." In languages in which bread is not known, it is possible to say ". . . given us sorrow for the food we eat."

In verse 6a the Hebrew text is "You made us a contention to our neighbors," which means that Israel is an object of contention among the surrounding nations, who compete with each other for the possession of the land. Some prefer the conjecture **scorn** (*manod*, "shaking" of the head, as in 44.14) in place of the Hebrew "strife" (*madon*); this offers a better parallel with the next line (so RSV, SPCL) but does not seem necessary. If the translator follows TEV, **"nations fight over our land"** may be rendered in some languages as "the other tribes fight each other to take away our land."

In verse 6b the Masoretic text has **laugh among themselves** or, as HOTTP interprets it, "laugh for themselves," that is, for their own amusement. Two Hebrew manuscripts (and the Septuagint and Syriac) have "laugh at us," which is preferred by TEV (**"insult us"**); NJB, NJV, NIV, and NEB have "mock us," and SPCL "laugh at us." It seems best to follow the majority in their rendering of the text.

80.7   RSV   TEV

Restore us, O God of hosts;   Bring us back, Almighty God!
  let thy face shine, that we may   Show us your mercy, and we
  be saved!   will be saved!

This verse is like verse 3, except that it has the title **God of hosts** (see verse 4) instead of **God**. This enlarging of the title represents the first intensification added to verse 4. Verse 19 will add further intensification.

80.8-9   RSV   TEV

8 Thou didst bring a vine out of   8 You brought a grapevine out of
     Egypt;   Egypt;
   thou didst drive out the nations   you drove out other nations and
     and plant it.   planted it in their land.
9 Thou didst clear the ground for it; 9 You cleared a place for it to grow;
   it took deep root and filled the   its roots went deep, and it
     land.   spread out over the whole
                                               land.

In his attempt to get God to change his attitude and save his people, the psalmist recalls Israel's history, how God had cared for them, led them into the Promised Land, and made them prosper. The psalmist uses the allegory of a grapevine as a figure for Israel; this figurative language often appears in the Bible (see especially Isa 5.1-7). In graphic language he describes how God brought the Israelites out of Egypt into Canaan (verse 8); in verse 8b he departs from his allegory and uses literal language in the first half of the line (see the same expression in 78.55). **The nations** are the original inhabitants of the land of Canaan. In verse 9a, in the metaphor of a farmer clearing a field, the psalmist uses figurative language to repeat what was said literally in verse 8b; and in verse 9b the strength and expansion of Israel in Palestine are described.

Because the events in line <u>b</u> follow those in line <u>a</u>, it may be necessary to make this clear by saying, for example, "You brought a grapevine out of Egypt, and when you had driven out the other nations you planted it."

In some languages it will be necessary to substitute another fruitbearing vine for the grapevine of TEV. In some cases, even where the vine image is retained, it will be necessary to make the allusion clear by shifting to a simile; for example, "You brought your people like a grapevine out of Egypt."

The translator will have to determine whether these agricultural figures of clearing the land, planting the shoot of a grapevine, and the sprouting and growth of the vine will make sense to readers. If not, something like the following may serve as a model:

> 8 You brought your people out of Egypt;
>   you expelled the peoples who lived in Canaan
>   and let your people take possession of the land.
> 9 After you drove out those other nations,
>   your people settled in Canaan
>   and spread out over the whole land.

<u>80.10-11</u> RSV	TEV
10 The mountains were covered with its shade, the mighty cedars with its branches; 11 it sent out its branches to the sea, and its shoots to the River.	10 It covered the hills with its shade; its branches overshadowed the giant cedars. 11 It extended its branches to the Mediterranean Sea and as far as the Euphrates River.

These verses describe the extension of Israel's dominion over all the country as far west as the Mediterranean Sea and as far east as the Euphrates River. It is probable that in verse 10a **the mountains** refer to the southern part of the country, and **the mighty cedars** in verse 10b refer to the northern part, that is, Lebanon (see 29.5; 37.35 and comments).

In verse 10b the Hebrew is "and its branches the cedars of God," which is taken by most to follow the structure of verse 10a, meaning, "its branches overshadowed the mighty cedars." RSV does not repeat the verb in this line; the sense is "the mighty cedars *were covered* with its branches." Some, however, have "its branches were like giant cedars" (also NEB), indicating the size of the vine. The Hebrew for **mighty cedars** is an example of the use of *'el* "God" as a superlative; see 36.6 for further discussion.

For **the sea** (the Mediterranean) and **the River** (the Euphrates), see discussion at 72.8.

Should the figurative language in verses 10-11 also be difficult, the following may be attempted:

10 They took possession of the whole country, .
    from the south all the way north to the Lebanon Mountains.
11 They extended the country's borders
    from the Mediterranean Sea
    all the way to the Euphrates River.

80.12-13

RSV	TEV

12   **Why then hast thou broken down its walls,**
    so that all who pass along the way pluck its fruit?
	12 **Why did you break down the fences around it?**
	    Now anyone passing by can steal its grapes;

13   **The boar from the forest ravages it,**
    and all that move in the field feed on it.
	13 **wild hogs trample it down,**
	    and wild animals feed on it.

After expending so much care and attention on his grapevine, why did God abandon it and let it be destroyed? He broke down **"the fences"** (made of stone, not wood or wire) that protected it, and now any passerby can **pluck its fruit**, that is, "steal its grapes," and the wild animals are busy destroying it—a figure of the enemies of Israel invading the land and looting and destroying.

In verse 13a **boar** (TEV "hogs") translates the word for swine, pig (see *Fauna and Flora,* pages 80-81); only here are **"wild hogs"** (**boar from the forest**) referred to in the Old Testament. The Hebrew singular for **boar** represents pigs in general. The verb translated **ravages** occurs only here in the Old Testament; it means "cut in pieces," either by eating (so most translations) or by trampling on the vine (Briggs; TEV; see SPCL). If the parallelism with the next line is purely synonymous, the meaning "consume, eat up" seems more likely; NJV and NEB have "gnaws"; another possible version is "tears at." Something like **ravages** (RSV, TOB, FRCL, NIV) expresses well the idea of the destruction caused by a wild animal. But it is more likely that the two verbs describe the devastation caused by wild hogs, or boars, as they trample down and devour the vegetation.

TEV **"wild animals"** in verse 13b translates "what moves in the field" (see RSV), a word that occurs only here and in 50.11b; NEB translates here "swarming insects from the fields," which seems unlikely.

Due to the poetic extension of the vine, it is likely that many readers will have lost or forgotten the original reference to the vine in verse 8, and particularly to the symbolism of the vine as representing Israel. Therefore it may be necessary to repeat the referent; for example, "Why did you break down the fences around your vine which is the people of Israel?" or simply "Why did you break down the fences around your vine?" If the analogy with the vine has to be sacrificed in translation for the clarity of meaning, the translator may say something like:

12 Why did you let Israel's enemies invade her land?
    Now foreigners go through the land
    looting and destroying it.

13 Like wild pigs they trample it,
   and like wild animals they destroy it.

80.14-15 RSV	TEV

14 Turn again, O God of hosts!
   Look down from heaven, and
   see;
   have regard for this vine,
15 the stock which thy right hand
   planted.[1]
	14 Turn to us, Almighty God!
	   Look down from heaven at us;
	   come and save your people!
	15 Come and save this grapevine that
	   you planted,
	   this young vine you made grow
	   so strong!

[1] Heb *planted and upon the son whom thou hast reared for thyself*

The psalmist, still using the language of the allegory of the grapevine, prays for God to save his people. In verse 14a the Hebrew is simply "turn" (without an object); this may mean "relent." Verse 14c in Hebrew is "and visit this grapevine"; for "visit" see comments on "care for" in 8.4b. TEV does not use the figure **this vine** in verse 14c, but "**your people.**"

In verse 15a TEV repeats "**Come and save**" for emphasis and clarity. "**This grapevine**" (RSV **the stock**) translates a word found only here in the Old Testament; it is variously translated "sapling" (Weiser), "stock" (NJV, NEB), or else as a verbal phrase, "what (your right hand) has planted"; so NAB, NJB, FRCL, Dahood. In any case, it refers to the grapevine. If the translator has had to avoid the analogy of the grapevine from verse 8, it will be necessary to continue in that manner through 16a. TEV provides the substitute "**your people**" in this verse and returns to the grapevine in verse 15a. If the vine is to be avoided, verse 15 (including RSV footnote) may be rendered:

Come and save your people whom you have placed here
   and made into a strong nation.

Verse 15b in the Masoretic text is similar to verse 17b; it reads "upon the son you made strong" (see RSV footnote; verse 17b is "upon the son of man you made strong"). RSV, NEB, BJ, and NJB omit it as an accidental repetition of verse 17b (so Oesterley, Anderson). Dahood takes "son" here to be the king (see TOB footnote); Weiser takes it to represent the people. But the word "son" is also used in connection with a plant (see Gen 49.22), and TEV "**this young vine**" takes it to be still another reference to the grapevine (see SPCL, GECL "sprout"; NJV "the stem"; Kirkpatrick, Cohen; KJV).[1] It is recommended that translators follow TEV here.

---

[1]HOTTP recognizes that "this expression is secondary in its present position," but there is no textual basis for omitting it. It interprets "the son" to mean "the sprout."

	RSV		TEV
16	They have burned it with fire, they have cut it down; may they perish at the rebuke of thy countenance!	16	Our enemies have set it on fire and cut it down; look at them in anger and destroy them!
17	But let thy hand be upon the man of thy right hand, the son of man whom thou hast made strong for thyself!	17	Preserve and protect the people you have chosen, the nation you made so strong.
18	Then we will never turn back from thee; give us life, and we will call on thy name!	18	We will never turn away from you again; keep us alive, and we will praise you.

The psalmist closes with a final plea to God. The enemies have ruined the nation, and the psalmist asks God to destroy them.

Cut it down in verse 16a is taken by most to be from a verb meaning "to cut down," but BJ and NJB take the form to be "like dung": "They have thrown it on the fire like dung." It is better to translate **cut it down**. SPCL reverses the two verbs as being a more natural order of events: "they (who) cut it and burn it."

Most translations take verse 16b to refer to the enemies; some, however, instead of **may they perish**, translate "they perish," that is, the Israelites themselves (Weiser; TOB, NJV, NIV); this, however, seems unlikely. **Rebuke of thy countenance** or TEV's **"look at them in anger"** must be recast in some languages where the sense of judgment is not conveyed by "angry looks." In such cases 16b may be rendered, for example, "look at them and judge them" or "judge them and destroy them."

RSV gives the form of the Hebrew text in verse 17; **the man** in line a̲ is parallel with **the son of man** in line b̲. **The son of man** here has the meaning "the human being." TEV interprets **the man** and **the son of man** as references to the nation of Israel (so Kirkpatrick, Cohen, McCullough, Weiser, Dentan). But some (Dahood, Toombs, Anderson, Briggs) take them to refer to the king (see GECL, SPCL, FRCL; NJB footnote); see 110.1, where the king is spoken of as at the right side of God. It is impossible to be dogmatic, and a personal reference may be intended. But the lack of mention of the king in the rest of the psalm may argue against this interpretation.

Let thy hand be upon means **"Preserve and protect,"** and **of thy right hand** means "the one you have chosen." In the way in which TEV has structured verse 17, line b̲ does not repeat the verbs from line a̲. If the translator follows TEV, it will be necessary in some languages to repeat the verbs from line a̲. It is also possible to say, for example, "Protect the people you have chosen, preserve the nation you made so strong."

At the end of verse 17, **for thyself** may be the meaning intended by the Hebrew; NJV, somewhat differently, translates the line "the one You have taken as Your own." And NEB has "the man whom thou hast made strong for thy service." But the Hebrew may be simply emphatic; in TEV language it would be "the nation you yourself made so strong."

Dahood takes verse 18a not as a promise but as a statement: "We have never turned away from you" (similarly AT, NEB). It is better to take it as a statement.

Give us life is a plea for the restoration of the nation, that it may continue to exist. **We will call on thy name** is a promise to praise and worship God.

80.19 RSV	TEV
Restore us, O LORD God of hosts! let thy face shine, that we may be saved!	Bring us back, LORD God Almighty. Show us your mercy, and we will be saved.

The concluding refrain is like verses 3 and 7, except for the title, **LORD God of hosts** here; "God" is used in verse 3 and "God of hosts" in verse 7, and this verse has the final expansion of the title.

Psalm 81

This psalm has two main parts: the first one (verses 1-5b) is closely related to a festival in Jerusalem, while the second part (verses 5c-16) is a message from God for his people, recalling his constant goodness (verses 6-10) and their frequent disobedience (verses 11-16). There is no natural connection between the two parts, and some think that they are parts of what were originally two separate compositions.

The festival referred to (verse 3a) seems to be the Festival of Shelters (traditionally known as Feast of Tabernacles); see Deuteronomy 16.13-15. It was one of the three main festivals in Israel and was the most joyful of them all.

Nothing definite can be said about the time and place of the composition of this psalm.

HEADING: "**A Song for a Festival**." Other headings are "A call to obedience"; "For the Feast of Tabernacles"; "An appeal to experience"; "God's goodness and Israel's wickedness." If the translator follows the TEV heading, it may be necessary in some languages to recast this heading as an imperative; for example, "Sing songs to celebrate the feast" or "Sing songs and praise God." Some translations represent the two themes in one title. Some translators may prefer to place the second heading before verse 5c.

Hebrew title: **To the choirmaster: according to The Gittith. A Psalm of Asaph** (TEV "By Asaph").

For **choirmaster** see title of Psalm 4; for **Gittith** see title of Psalm 8; for **Asaph** see title of Psalm 50. A few Hebrew manuscripts add the word **Psalm**; it is not in the Masoretic text.

81.1-3

RSV	TEV
1 Sing aloud to God our strength; shout for joy to the God of Jacob!	1 Shout for joy to God our defender; sing praise to the God of Jacob!
2 Raise a song, sound the timbrel, the sweet lyre with the harp.	2 Start the music and beat the tambourines; play pleasant music on the harps and lyres.
3 Blow the trumpet at the new moon, at the full moon, on our feast day.	3 Blow the trumpet for the festival, when the moon is new and when the moon is full.

The psalm opens with a command to the people to **sing aloud** and **shout for joy** to God; the two verbs are used synonymously (see 20.5 and comments on "shout"). **Our strength** means **"our defender"** or "our protector"; for **God of Jacob** see 20.1 and comments. The two noun phrases, **God our strength** and **God of Jacob** may have to be recast in some languages as verb phrases; for example, "to God who defends us from our enemies" and "to God whom the descendants of Jacob worship" or "to God whom the people of Israel worship."

The music (verse 2) is both vocal and instrumental. **Raise a song** may be vocal music (see SPCL "Sing to the sound of the tambourine"), but the Hebrew verb may mean to start the instrumental music that accompanied the singing. NIV has "Begin the music." According to some, **"tambourines"** (TEV; RSV **timbrel**; see 68.25 and comment) were not allowed to be played inside the Temple; if this is so, the music was played as the people approached the Temple. For **lyre** and **harp** see comments on 33.2. RSV **the sweet lyre** is an odd phrase in English; it is the music that has the sweet quality. Something like "melodious" or "tuneful" would be better, or else TEV's restructuring is useful.

For **trumpet** see 47.5 and comments. It should be noted that here the trumpet is not being used to play a tune, but to give the signal for the festival to begin. **Blow the trumpet . . . on our feast day** (TEV **"blow the trumpet for the festival"**) means to blow the trumpet to begin the festival, and in many languages the expression will have to be rendered in some such manner.

The new moon and **the full moon** probably indicate the first and the fifteenth days of the lunar month. The Festival of Shelters (also known as Sukkoth) began on the 15th of Tishri, the seventh month of the Jewish calendar; in later times there was a blowing of trumpets on the first day of this month (see Num 29.1). Most commentators believe that the Festival of Shelters (**our feast day**) is the one referred to here; some believe it was Passover. Many Hebrew manuscripts (also Syriac and Targum) have the plural "our festivals."

Many commentators take verse 1 to be directed to the people, verse 2 to the Levites, and verse 3 to the priests (see a similar scheme in 150.3-5).

81.4-5b	RSV	TEV
4	For it is a statute for Israel, an ordinance of the God of Jacob.	4 This is the law in Israel, an order from the God of Jacob.
5	He made it a decree in Joseph, when he went out over*ᵐ* the land of Egypt.	5 He gave it to the people of Israel when he attacked the land of Egypt.

ᵐ Or *against*

These two verses give the reason for the festival: it was commanded by God. In verses 4a,b, 5a three synonymous terms are used for this command: **statute** (see "decree" and comments at 2.7), **ordinance** (see "judgment" and comments at 7.6), and **decree** (see "testimony" and comments at 19.7). TEV's **"This"** points back to the content of the first three verses. In some languages it will be necessary to make explicit the relation of verse 4 to verses 1-3; for example, "Do all this because it is the law of Israel" or "The law of Israel requires that you do this."

In verse 5a TEV "**the people of Israel**" stands for **Joseph**; this may be used in the more restricted sense of the northern kingdom, but more likely it is a synonym for **Israel** in verse 4a (see discussion at 80.1).

In verse 5b TEV "**when he attacked**" translates the Hebrew "in his going out upon (or, over)." Thus understood, the subject is God and the phrase alludes to his punishing Egypt with the plagues. But the preposition translated "over" (or, "against"; see RSV footnote) may also mean "from" (see Anderson, Dahood); in this case the subject is "**the people of Israel**" (that is, **Joseph**) in verse 5a and refers to the exodus (so the Septuagint, Jerome; Dahood, NEB, NJV; Briggs, Oesterley and NAB follow the Septuagint). Either of the two is possible; the more usual meaning of the Masoretic text would be "over" in the sense of "against" (so RSV, TEV, AT, NJB, SPCL, NIV; Kirkpatrick, Weiser, McCullough, HOTTP).

	81.5c-7 RSV		TEV
5c	I hear a voice I had not known:	5c	I hear an unknown voice saying,
6	"I relieved your[n] shoulder of the burden;	6	"I took the burdens off your backs;
	your[n] hands were freed from the basket.		I let you put down your loads of bricks.
7	In distress you called, and I delivered you;	7	When you were in trouble, you called to me, and I saved you.
	I answered you in the secret place of thunder;		From my hiding place in the storm, I answered you.
	I tested you at the waters of Meribah. *Selah*		I put you to the test at the springs of Meribah.

[n] Heb *his*

Most modern commentators and translators take verse 5c as the introduction of God's message that follows in verses 6-16. But the meaning in the context is not very clear, and some take it as a marginal note in which the copyist indicated that he did not understand the meaning of the text. Most take it to be the words of the psalmist himself, or else of a priest or a prophet who is delivering God's message. Dahood, however, takes it to be God speaking: "I heard the speech of one unknown to me"—a reference to the people of Israel in Egypt, who were "unknown" to God before he chose them. NEB omits the line as a later gloss. The Septuagint translates "he [Joseph, that is, the people of Israel] heard a language he did not understand"; this is the sense given by NIV, but without a textual footnote. It is best to take it as referring to the psalmist himself. In many languages it is unnatural to "hear a voice." One must in such cases say, for example, "I hear someone I do not know saying."

The burden and **the basket** (verse 6) are metaphors for the tasks of the people of Israel in Egypt, where they were forced to work as slaves; TEV takes **the basket** to refer to "**loads of bricks**" (see Exo 1.11-14; 5.6-9). The Hebrew text has "his back" and "his hands" (see RSV footnote), which TEV has represented by "**your backs**" and "your loads of bricks," in order to make clear that the reference is to the people of Israel, not to the psalmist (as RSV might be taken to mean). It is not necessary to specify the content of the baskets as TEV has done. SPCL recasts this as "hard labor." This verse may also be rendered "I have taken the loads off your backs and freed you from hard labor."

God's act of salvation (verse 7a) was to take his people out of Egypt. He is the God whose shelter is a storm (verse 7b; see 18.11-14; 77.17-18, Exo 20.18-20), FRCL translates "from the heart of the storm," NIV "out of a thundercloud." RSV **in the secret place of thunder** should not be taken to mean that the Israelites were also there. God put his people to the test at **Meribah**, where there was no water for them to drink (see Exo 17.1-7; Num 20.2-13; Psa 95.8-9).

In some languages it will not be clear to say **I answered you** when no question had been asked. **I answered you** is synonymous with **I delivered you** in the previous line and may therefore be translated "I helped you" or "I rescued you."

For *Selah* see 3.2.

81.8-10 RSV	TEV
8 Hear, O my people, while I admonish you! O Israel, if you would but listen to me! 9 There shall be no strange god among you; you shall not bow down to a foreign god. 10 I am the LORD your God, who brought you up out of the land of Egypt. Open your mouth wide, and I will fill it.	8 Listen, my people, to my warning; Israel, how I wish you would listen to me! 9 You must never worship another god. 10 I am the LORD your God, who brought you out of Egypt. Open your mouth, and I will feed you.

God admonishes his people; he tells them to be faithful to him and he will provide for their needs.

In verse 8 **Israel** in line b is parallel with **my people** in line a. The two can be joined as follows: "My people Israel, listen to my warning! How I wish you would listen to me!" However, it may be best to keep both forms in order to retain the complete parallel.

The nature of the parallelism in verse 9 is the heightening of effect between **there shall be no strange god** in line a and **you shall not bow down to . . .** in line b. Line b steps up the intensity from the mere presence of foreign gods to the worship of them. For this reason the intensification should be reflected in the translation; for example, "not only must you not have strange gods among you, but you must never bow down and worship them" or "you must not have strange gods among you; even more, you must never bow down to them."

Verse 10a can be rendered "I, the LORD (or, Yahweh), am your God" or "I am the LORD, the God you worship." He is contrasting himself here with the gods of other nations in verse 9.

Some believe that line c of verse 10 belongs at the end of verse 7 (see NEB). This line states that God longs to fulfill the physical and spiritual needs of the people (see verse 16). If the metaphor of a mother bird feeding her young is inappropriate in the receptor language, the translator will normally have to use a nonfigure which may have to favor either physical or spiritual filling. It is probably best to keep the content as general as possible and say, for example, "If you are faithful, I will bless you" or ". . . give you good gifts."

81.11-12   RSV   TEV

RSV	TEV
11 "But my people did not listen to my voice; Israel would have none of me.	11 "But my people would not listen to me; Israel would not obey me.
12 So I gave them over to their stubborn hearts, to follow their own counsels.	12 So I let them go their stubborn ways and do whatever they wanted.

Yahweh regrets his people's disobedience, but he allows them to reap the fruit of their own stubbornness (verses 11-12). Here God does not directly address the people, as he does in verses 6-10; he seems to be speaking to himself. It would be very odd if the psalmist thought of God speaking to someone else, someone not identified. If this constitutes a problem for the readers, the best thing to do is to change to the second person of direct address; for example, "So you, God, let them go their stubborn ways . . . ," or omit "you" and say, for example, "So God let them go their stubborn ways . . . ."

In verse 11b the Hebrew is "Israel did not want me," that is, would have nothing to do with me, which TEV represents by "**would not obey me**," parallel with "**would not listen to me**" in line a.

Stubborn hearts in this context is rendered idiomatically in many languages as "I let them follow their blindness," ". . . their hard hearts," or ". . . their closed ears."

Follow their own counsels: instead of coming to the Lord for advice and guidance, they guide themselves and ignore God.

81.13-14   RSV   TEV

RSV	TEV
13 O that my people would listen to me, that Israel would walk in my ways!	13 How I wish my people would listen to me; how I wish they would obey me!
14 I would soon subdue their enemies,	14 I would quickly defeat their enemies and conquer all their foes.

> **and turn my hand against their**
> **foes.**

In verse 13 there is again the parallelism **my people** and **Israel**, here in reverse order from the order in verse 11. FRCL combines the two as follows: "Ah, if my people, if Israel would listen to me, if they had followed the way I drew for them . . . ." In line b **walk in my ways** means to live as God wants his people to live (see 119.3; 128.1).

It would be well to make clear the connection between verse 13 and verse 14 by beginning verse 14 with "If they did, I would . . . ."

In verse 14b **turn my hand against** means "fight," "strike" (NJV), "punish" (SPCL), "**conquer**" (TEV).

81.15-16	RSV	TEV

	RSV	TEV
15	Those who hate the LORD would cringe toward him, and their fate would last for ever.	15 those who hate me would bow in fear before me; their punishment would last forever.
16	I would feed you*o* with the finest of the wheat, and with honey from the rock I would satisfy you."	16 But I would feed you with the finest wheat and satisfy you with wild honey."

o Cn Compare verse 16b: Heb *he would feed him*

Most commentators and translators take verses 15-16 also to be the Lord's words (despite the various changes in pronouns); SPCL and FRCL, however, take the words to be the psalmist's own comment.

In verse 15a the Hebrew is "Those who hate Yahweh would cower before him," which TEV has represented with the first person pronoun "me . . . me," since it takes Yahweh to be the speaker. Many emend the text from "those who hate Yahweh" to "those who hate him" (that is, Israel), but this does not seem necessary. For **cringe toward him** see comments on 18.44.

In verse 15b the Hebrew is "their time would last forever," which is taken to mean **their fate** (RSV), their doom, "**their punishment**." Some take "their time" to be a reference to Israel's good times, which would last forever (so FRCL; see also Briggs, Kirkpatrick, McCullough); this is possible but does not seem probable. If the translator follows TEV's "**their punishment would last forever,**" it will be necessary in some languages to shift to a verb phrase, which will mean introducing God as the agent; for example, "I will punish them forever."

Verse 16a in Hebrew is "he would feed him," which TEV and others take to refer to God feeding Israel, parallel with **I would satisfy you** in verse 16b.[1] In languages in which **wheat** is unknown, a local grain of importance to the diet may be substituted, or in the absence of that, it is possible to use a generic term for grain.

Honey from the rock is taken by most to mean wild honey (see Deut 32.13); Dahood, however, translates "essence of honey." NEB transfers verse 16 to follow immediately after verse 7; this is not recommended.

---

[1]HOTTP considers two textual questions in verse 16 ("I/he would make him eat" and "I/he would satisfy you") and sets forth its interpretation of verses 14-16. The meaning given for verses 14-15 (Hebrew verses 15-16) is quite clear, but that of verse 16 (Hebrew verse 17) is most unclear: "while he had fed them with a flour of wheat, and I would fill you with honey of the rocks." In the context "he" seems to be (the people of) Israel; "them" is the enemies of Israel; "I" is God; and "you" is the people of Israel.

Psalm 82

This psalm, which proclaims God as supreme, has been interpreted in different ways, depending on how the word *'elohim* in verse 1a is understood (see exegesis below). The interpretation most favored by modern commentators and translators is that they are the gods of the various nations, who are here portrayed as subordinate to the God of Israel and responsible to him for the way in which they have failed to carry out his purposes. In the heavenly council God calls them to account and rebukes them (verses 1-4); after accusing them of injustice, he pronounces their doom (verses 5-7). The psalm closes with a prayer asking God to manifest his power and rule the world (verse 8).

HEADING: TEV has "**God the Supreme Ruler.**" Other headings are "Against pagan princes"; "Against corrupt judges"; "A scene in heaven"; "The judgment of the gods." (It is to be noticed that these headings reflect different opinions on the meaning of the psalm.) If the translator follows the TEV heading, it may be necessary in some languages to say "God is the greatest ruler" or "God rules over all others."

Hebrew title: **A Psalm of Asaph** (TEV "A psalm by Asaph").
For **Asaph** see title of Psalm 50.

82.1-2

	RSV		TEV
1	God has taken his place in the divine council; in the midst of the gods he holds judgment:	1	God presides in the heavenly council; in the assembly of the gods he gives his decision:
2	"How long will you judge unjustly and show partiality to the wicked? *Selah*	2	"You must stop judging unjustly; you must no longer be partial to the wicked!

The psalm opens with the scene in heaven where God takes his place in the heavenly council, that is, his place as chief; before him are assembled all the *'elohim* to hear his decision. It seems fairly evident that the *'elohim* in line b are the gods of the other nations (see discussion of "sons of gods" in 29.1). Some take them to be Israel's judges (so the Targum; see Kirkpatrick), while others think they are Israel's foreign oppressors (see Briggs). But the language of verses 6-7 makes it quite clear that these are divine beings. (For a similar depiction of the heavenly council, see Job 1-2; and see references in commentaries.) NJV has "divine beings," and SPCL "heavenly judges" (in verse 6 it has "gods"); it is better to translate "gods" both in verse 1 and in verse 6. The focus in this verse is upon God, who speaks to the assembled gods, and the picture may be represented in some languages as "God sits on his stool (royal throne) before the gods." Translators may have difficulty indicating the nature of the gods in this psalm. They are not looked upon by the writer as simply "false gods," but rather divine creatures that have responsibilities but have failed in their duties under God.[1] In some languages there is no term to represent a "god," whether in the singular or plural. It is, however, sometimes possible to make a contrast between the "great chief spirit," which is "God," and the "small spirit," which is "god." In the present context it may be possible to speak of "heavenly beings" or "angels." Since the reference is to the **gods** in the **divine council**, some translators find it more convenient to speak of "God's servants," "God's messengers," or "the ones who serve God in heaven."

He holds judgment translates the verb *shafat* (see 7.8); it may mean here "judges" (NAB), "pronounces judgment" (NJV), "hands down sentence" (SPCL), or "administers justice." **Holds judgment** is sometimes rendered idiomatically as "he cuts the affairs" or "he cuts the words."

Verse 2 in Hebrew is in the form of a question; it is not, however, a request for information, but a rebuke for the failure of the gods to judge justly, which TEV has represented by a command for them to stop acting as they have. Most translations keep the rhetorical question. **Show partiality to the wicked** must often be recast in translation, and sometimes expressed as a negative; for example, "not take the side of the wicked" or "not give your hand to the wicked." This may also be rendered as "how long will you treat the wicked as though they were not wicked?"

For *Selah* see 3.2.

82.3-4	RSV		TEV
3	Give justice to the weak and the fatherless; maintain the right of the afflicted and the destitute.	3	Defend the rights of the poor and the orphans; be fair to the needy and the helpless.
4	Rescue the weak and the needy; deliver them from the hand of the wicked."	4	Rescue them from the power of evil men.

Instead of favoring the wicked, the gods in their position as judges are to provide help for those most in need of it: **the weak**, **the fatherless**, **the afflicted**, **the destitute** (verse 3), and **the weak and the needy** (verse 4a). All these terms apply to the poor and powerless people in that society at that time.

---

[1]NIV in verses 1 and 6 translates "gods" with quotation marks around the word (verse 1: he gives judgment among the "gods"; verse 6 "I said, 'You are 'gods' "). The function of these quotation marks is to indicate that the word is being used in a sense different from its normal one. What this device means here is that the psalmist (in verse 1) and God (verse 6) address these beings as "gods" when they really are not gods (see the explanatory footnote in the NIV Study Edition). Such a device in translation should not be imitated (NIV uses it also elsewhere).

The two verbs in verse 3, **Give justice** and **maintain the right**, are not used here in the sense of a rigorous and impartial application of the law, but of active help for those who are being oppressed and mistreated by wicked people. **Give justice** may be rendered, for example, "Do what is right," "Be fair to," "Act in a right way toward." **Maintain the right** is closely synonymous to the first expression. Other suggestions are "defend," "help," "protect."

TEV has combined and shortened the two lines in verse 4. "**Rescue**" represents the two synonymous verbs in lines <u>a</u> and <u>b</u>: for **Rescue** see "deliver" and comments on 17.13, and for **deliver** see comments on 7.1. TEV "**them**" refers to the helpless and oppressed people cited in verse 3. But a translation may wish to maintain two synonymous lines, and so the following may serve as a model:

> Rescue those poor people,
>> free them from the power of evil men.

82.5	RSV	TEV

They have neither knowledge nor understanding, they walk about in darkness; all the foundations of the earth are shaken.	"How ignorant you are! How stupid! You are completely corrupt, and justice has disappeared from the world.

RSV and some other translations take verse 5 to be the words of the psalmist; most take them still to be the words of God, even though there is a change (which is not uncommon) from the second person of direct address to the third person. TEV, for consistency, has kept the second person (also NEB, FRCL, GECL, SPCL). It is possible, however, that the third person in verse 5 refers to "the evil men" of verse 4; but most take verse 5 to refer to the gods themselves. (Some, like Oesterley, believe verse 5 to be a later comment.)

The gods are accused of being ignorant and stupid, that is, they persistently ignore God's laws, his will for humankind. In verse 5b **they walk about in darkness** does not mean the darkness of ignorance, but of unrighteousness, corruption, evil, as a result of which **all the foundations of the earth are shaken**. See a similar figure in 11.3. It is the moral universe which is in focus here, not the physical universe; FRCL "the world is threatened with ruin." Weiser's comment on verse 5 is worth quoting: "No wonder that the foundations of the moral order on earth are shaken when those who had been appointed to act as the heavenly guardians of God's order of the universe themselves do not even know and obey that order!" If the translator follows TEV's "**justice has disappeared . . . ,**" it will often be necessary to change this expression from a noun to a verb phrase; for example, "you do nothing justly anywhere in the world," or "nothing that you do brings justice to the world," or "you do nothing to help people everywhere live right."

6	I say, "You are gods, sons of the Most High, all of you;	6 'You are gods,' I said; 'all of you are sons of the Most High.'
7	nevertheless, you shall die like men, and fall like any prince."*P*	7 But you will die like men; your life will end like that of any prince."

P Or *fall as one man, O princes*

Dahood and RSV take verses 6-7 to be the psalmist's words, not God's. It seems better to take them as God's words.

Verse 6a is quoted in John 10.34.

In these two verses God, in a slightly ironic fashion, admits to having once acknowledged their divine status: **gods . . . sons of the Most High**. It is not necessary to think that the language of verse 6b means that God acknowledges the gods as his own "sons"; here, as often, **sons of** denotes membership in a class. But GECL translates quite straightforwardly, "You are gods, you are my sons, sons of the Most High!" They are divine beings, they are gods, as is God himself (see Job 1.6). For **the Most High** see comments on 7.17.

Verse 7 would make no sense if the *'elohim* who are being addressed are human beings, since death is the inescapable lot of all human beings. The gods are reduced to mortal beings. In verse 7a **like men** could be "like Adam" (NEB footnote); the Hebrew *'adam* can be generic "humankind" or specifically "Adam." In verse 7b **fall** is parallel with **die** in verse 7a. The word **prince** in RSV and TEV does not necessarily mean the son of a king, but rather a "ruler," and probably focusing upon the ordinariness of the ruler. GECL has "incapable official," and FRCL has "an ordinary minister of government."

Arise, O God, judge the earth; for to thee belong all the nations!	Come, O God, and rule the world; all the nations are yours.

The psalmist prays for God to manifest his power (**Arise**) and "rule the world," since **all the nations** belong to him. As often, the Hebrew verb for **Arise** does not mean specifically to stand up from a sitting or reclining position, but to take action (see 3.7). The verb "rule" (TEV) translates the Hebrew *shafat,* which may be rendered **judge**. The verb translated **belong** is related to the noun "inheritance, heritage" (see discussion at 16.6). For a discussion of God's "inheritance," see comments on 28.9. G. R. Driver, however, relates the verb here to an Assyrian verb "to sift"; so NEB "thou dost pass all nations through thy sieve"—a figure of judgment. This does not seem likely.

Psalm 83

In this psalm the people of Israel pray that God save them from their enemies, of whom ten are listed by name. They threaten to invade the land and destroy the people. No such specific coalition against Israel can be cited from the known history of that time. The reference to Assyria, in verse 8, would place the composition of the psalm sometime between the ninth and the seventh centuries B.C.; but some hold that the reference is more symbolic than actual. All the other peoples listed were from neighboring nations.

The psalm begins with a plea for help (verse 1), followed by a description of the danger that confronted Israel (verses 2-8). The psalm ends with a prayer asking God to defeat the nations and demonstrate his sovereign power (verses 9-18).

HEADING: "**A Prayer for the Defeat of Israel's Enemies.**" Other headings are "Prayer against a hostile alliance"; "Enemies on all sides"; "National prayer for divine aid." The TEV heading must often be recast to replace the noun phrases by verb phrases; for example, "The psalmist prays that God will defeat Israel's enemies."

Hebrew title: **A Song. A Psalm of Asaph** (TEV "A psalm by Asaph; a song").
For **Asaph** see title of Psalm 50; for **Song** and **Psalm** see title of Psalm 65.

83.1   RSV   TEV

> O God, do not keep silence;   O God, do not keep silent;
>   do not hold thy peace or be still,   do not be still, do not be quiet!
>   O God!

The psalm opens with a plea to God to change from his apparent indifference and inactivity, and to intervene on Israel's behalf. The verse is chiastic in structure. For similar language addressed to God, see 28.1; 35.22; 39.12; 44.23-24.

83.2-4   RSV   TEV

2 For lo, thy enemies are in tumult;   2 Look! Your enemies are in revolt,
     those who hate thee have raised   and those who hate you are
     their heads.   rebelling.
3 They lay crafty plans against thy   3 They are making secret plans
     people;   against your people;
   they consult together against   they are plotting against those

thy protected ones.	you protect.
4 They say, "Come, let us wipe them out as a nation; let the name of Israel be remembered no more!"	4 "Come," they say, "let us destroy their nation, so that Israel will be forgotten forever."

The people remind God that those nations conspiring against Israel are for that very reason his enemies and hate him (verse 2; see the similar expression in 68.1). The initial **For lo** is a way of calling God's attention to what the psalmist is about to say. In verse 2b **raised their heads** is a figure of defiant behavior, parallel with **in tumult** (in line <u>a</u>), which means "stir themselves up" (FRCL), that is, are in a state of hostility and hatred. NJV "assert themselves" seems a bit too mild. Both lines of this verse have much the same meaning. However, line <u>b</u> shifts from the common term **enemies** to the more specific **those who hate you**, and **tumult** in line <u>a</u> is raised in intensity by means of the poetic figure **raised their heads**. Therefore it is not advisable to reduce the two lines to one, but rather to translate the element of intensification in the movement from line <u>a</u> to line <u>b</u>; for example, "Your enemies are becoming hostile; but even more, the people who hate you are defying you."

Israel's enemies have joined forces and are plotting the destruction of Israel (verses 3-4). The purpose is not to kill all Israelites but to conquer the country and reduce it to a vassal state, no longer a free and independent nation. The destruction they plan will be so complete that even the existence of Israel as a country "**will be forgotten forever**" (see similar language in 9.6).

In verse 3b **thy protected ones** is parallel with **thy people** in verse 3a; Dahood, however, takes it as a singular (so Jerome, Symmachus), perhaps a reference to the Temple. This does not seem very likely. The Hebrew verb translated "**protect**" means "to hide," and the meaning may be "your treasured ones" (NJV), "your treasure" (TOB, NEB), "those you cherish" (NJB, NIV).

In many languages the source of the quote in verse 4 (**They say**) cannot be inserted into the quote, as in TEV. It may be necessary in some cases to avoid the use of the second pronoun and say, for example, "Come, let us destroy Israel." Line <u>b</u> must often be recast with an active verb; for example, "so that no one will ever remember Israel."

<u>83.5-8</u> RSV	TEV
5 Yea, they conspire with one accord; against thee they make a covenant—	5 They agree on their plan and form an alliance against you:
6 the tents of Edom and the Ishmaelites, Moab and the Hagrites,	6 the people of Edom and the Ishmaelites; the people of Moab and the Hagrites;
7 Gebal and Ammon and Amalek, Philistia with the inhabitants of Tyre;	7 the people of Gebal, Ammon, and Amalek, and of Philistia and Tyre.
8 Assyria also has joined them;	8 Assyria has also joined them

they are the strong arm of the children of Lot. *Selah*	as a strong ally of the Ammonites and Moabites, the descendants of Lot.

The enemies are named. They are "of one heart" (RSV **with one accord**) in their plan (verse 5a), that is, **they agree on their plan** to conquer the land of Israel; NJV "unanimous in their counsel"; NEB "With one mind." **They make a covenant**, that is, they make a treaty among themselves to act together against Israel, and so their covenant is an alliance against God himself. Many languages use the same idiom as Hebrew in this context, "one heart." Other languages use such expressions as "one word," "one mouth," or "one stomach." The expression **they make a covenant** in some languages must include the purpose. In the present context it is to make war against Israel, and therefore against God. Here it is possible to say "with one mouth they agree to attack you." If "you" would appear to be unclear, then one can say ". . . attack you, God." The literal Hebrew expression is "cut a covenant" and is expressed in some languages in the same manner.

Edom was the territory to the south of Israel, occupied by the descendants of Esau (for **the tents of Edom** see comments on the similar expression "the tents of Ham" in 78.51). Although in Hebrew the expression **the tents of . . .** represents the people living in each of the named areas, in translation it will most often be best to speak of "the people of . . . ." **The Ishmaelites**, who lived on the east side of the Jordan, were descendants of Ishmael, son of Abraham by Hagar (see Gen 25.12-18). **Moab** was the territory on the east side of the lower Jordan. **The Hagrites** were a nomadic tribe living east of Gilead, on the east side of the Jordan (see 1 Chr 5.10).

Gebal is taken by most commentators to be a region south of the Dead Sea; some think it is the Phoenician city Byblos (see Dahood), but this is disputed. **Ammon** was on the east side of the Jordan, north of the territory of Moab. **Amalek** was a nomadic tribe living south of Judah. **Philistia** was the territory along the Mediterranean coast, west of the territory occupied by the Israelites. And **Tyre** was a Phoenician city on the Mediterranean, some fifty-five kilometers north of Mount Carmel.

Assyria was the mighty empire in Mesopotamia, in the north; its capital was Nineveh. Some take the Hebrew name here to refer to the Ashurites, a tribe living east of the Jordan (see 2 Sam 2.9); Briggs emends to "Samaria," but this is not necessary. **The children of Lot** are the descendants of Moab and Benammi, the sons of Lot (see Gen 19.36-38), that is, "the Ammonites and Moabites" (already referred to in verses 6,7). TEV has inserted their names to make this information explicit. The Hebrew **strong arm** means "strong ally," "strong supporter."

Translators who are transliterating any of these names for the first time must be careful to insure that no undesired meaning is created, for example, due to identity or similarity to a word in the receptor language. Translators should make certain that adequate maps are printed to enable the reader to know the location of these places.

For *Selah* see 3.2.

RSV   TEV

9   Do to them as thou didst to   9   Do to them what you did to the
       Midian,   Midianites,

	as to Sisera and Jabin at the river Kishon,			and to Sisera and Jabin at the Kishon River.
10	who were destroyed at En-dor, who became dung for the ground.		10	You defeated them at Endor, and their bodies rotted on the ground.
11	Make their nobles like Oreb and Zeeb, all their princes like Zebah and Zalmunna,		11	Do to their leaders what you did to Oreb and Zeeb; defeat all their rulers as you did Zebah and Zalmunna,
12	who said, "Let us take possession for ourselves of the pastures of God."		12	who said, "We will take for our own the land that belongs to God."

In verses 9-18 the psalmist calls down on Israel's present enemies the same defeats suffered by their enemies in the past. "The Midianites" (verse 9) were defeated by Gideon (Judges 6-8); **Oreb and Zeeb** were two Midianite princes killed by the Ephraimites (Judges 7.24-25); **Zebah and Zalmunna** were two Midianite kings whom Gideon killed personally (Judges 8.21).

Sisera was the commander of the army of **Jabin**, king of Hazor; Jabin's army was defeated by Barak and Deborah at **the river Kishon**, while Sisera was killed by Jael, as he hid in Jael's tent (Judges 4.1-24). **Endor** is not mentioned in the account of the defeat of the Midianites in the book of Judges; it was a town near Mount Tabor, where the Israelites gathered before the battle against Sisera (Judges 4.12), and this may be the reason why it is mentioned here. Some emend the text to "En-Harod," the place where Gideon camped with his army (Briggs; NEB; see Judges 7.1). It is better to stay with the Hebrew text as it is.

In verse 10b **who became dung for the ground** is a vivid way of expressing the fact that the corpses were not buried but left to rot where they fell (see similar expressions at 79.2-3).

If the one sentence of verses 11-12 is too long for a given language, a full stop can be placed at the end of verse 11, and verse 12 can begin "They said . . . ." Verse 13 can then begin "Therefore" or "And so."

The phrase **pastures of God** in verse 12b for the land of Israel recalls the idea of Israel as the flock of God, grazing in his pastures. AT and Dahood take *'elohim* here as a superlative: "the very finest meadows."

83.13-15   RSV   TEV

13	O my God, make them like whirling dust,[q] like chaff before the wind.		13	Scatter them like dust, O God, like straw blown away by the wind.
14	As fire consumes the forest, as the flame sets the mountains ablaze,		14	As fire burns the forest, as flames set the hills on fire,
15	so do thou pursue them with thy tempest and terrify them with thy hurricane!		15	chase them away with your storm and terrify them with your fierce winds.

q Or a *tumbleweed*

There is some uncertainty over the precise meaning of the word translated **whirling dust**, which occurs only here and in Isaiah 17.13; NIV and RSV footnote have "tumbleweed"; NJV, NJB, NEB, "thistledown"; NAB "leaves." KJV "wheel" is wrong. For the translator the important thing is a natural figure employing some object readily blown away by the wind. See similar language in 1.4; 35.5.

And for the language of verses 14-15 see 21.9; 58.6-9. The two nouns in verse 15, **tempest** and **hurricane**, are synonymous; NJB "tempest" and "whirlwind"; NJV, NIV "tempest" and "storm." The verbs used in verse 14, **consumes** and **sets . . . ablaze**, mean to destroy completely. In verse 15 the psalmist goes on to ask God to get rid of his people's enemies as fire and flames get rid of vegetation: **pursue them** and **terrify them**. Here **pursue** means more precisely "drive away" (NJB; TEV "chase . . . away"). **Terrify** comes almost as an anticlimax, but that is what the psalmist wrote. Verses 14 and 15 may have to be restructured in some languages in order to maintain the connection between the two parts of the simile. For example, in some languages it may be necessary to join 14a with 15a and 14b with 15b: "Chase them away with your storm, like fire burning the forest. Terrify them with your fierce winds, like flames setting the hills on fire."

83.16-18	RSV	TEV

	RSV	TEV
16	Fill their faces with shame, that they may seek thy name, O LORD.	16 Cover their faces with shame, O LORD, and make them acknowledge your power.
17	Let them be put to shame and dismayed for ever; let them perish in disgrace.	17 May they be defeated and terrified forever; may they die in complete disgrace.
18	Let them know that thou alone, whose name is the LORD, art the Most High over all the earth.	18 May they know that you alone are the LORD, supreme ruler over all the earth.

The psalm concludes with the final prayer for the complete destruction and everlasting shame of the enemies of Israel (see similar language in 35.26; 40.14-15; 70.2-3). In verse 16a the psalmist asks Yahweh to disgrace them; better than RSV or TEV, the NEB phrase here is more natural in English, "Heap shame upon their heads"; SPCL "Put them to shame." For some idioms on **shame** see 6.10.

In language that is not very logical, the people pray for the destruction of their enemies (verse 17b) so that they, the enemies, will **seek thy name** (verse 16b). This could mean "turn to you," that is, either for help (SPCL) or to obey and worship (FRCL); or else, as NEB has it, "confess the greatness of thy name," or TEV **"acknowledge your power."** If the translator follows TEV, this phrase will have to be recast in some languages to say, for example, "make them acknowledge that you are powerful" or, as direct address, "make them say, 'God, you are powerful.' "

Verse 17 intensifies the request for the complete and disgraceful extermination of Israel's enemies, so that in verse 18 they may realize that God alone is the Lord, the supreme ruler of all the earth (see 59.13).

Let . . . put to shame in the Hebrew is not a passive but an active form, "be ashamed." The thought is parallel and synonymous with verse 16a, although a different term for **shame** is used there. Languages such as English use the passive, but in languages in which the passive cannot be used here, it will be necessary to shift to the active and introduce God as the agent of the action; for example, "Make them ashamed for ever, and terrify them."

The Hebrew verbs in verse 17b have been reversed because of English style, in both RSV and TEV. **In disgrace** translates a verb, a third term for deep shame. The prayer is that the enemies may suffer such shame that they will **perish**. This is the final and deepest stage of their disgrace.

Verse 18 returns to the thought of verse 16b, but in greater detail. In Hebrew it can be understood in slightly different ways. For an Israelite to write "you alone are named Yahweh" seems trite, superficial, since there was no other god who claimed the name Yahweh. So it may be better, with RSV and NIV, to say "you alone, whose name is Yahweh, are the supreme ruler of all the earth"; or else, as FRCL has it, "So that they may know who you are, Yahweh, the only God Most-High over all the earth."

Only here in the Psalms does KJV translate the divine name by "JEHOVAH"; elsewhere it is always "the LORD." Only three times elsewhere in the Old Testament does KJV use "JEHOVAH" by itself, and three other times in combination with other names.

Here again, **the Most High** translates *'elyon*, one of the names for God in the Hebrew Bible (see 7.17 and comments).

Psalm 84

This song of praise for the Temple is sung by pilgrims as they come to Jerusalem for one of the great festivals of faith, perhaps the Festival of Shelters (also known as Sukkoth); see reference to "the early rain" in verse 6, which may indicate the season of the year when this was used. The Temple is praised as the dwelling place of God, as the most desirable place in all the world. Some, noting a resemblance between this psalm and Psalm 42–43, suggest that the same person wrote both. However that may be, the sentiments are the same.

The psalm opens with praise for the Temple and for those who live there (verses 1-4); praise is also expressed for the pilgrims as they come to the Temple (verses 5-7). A prayer for the king follows (verses 8-9), after which God is praised as the source of all happiness and security (verses 10-12).

HEADING: "**Longing for God's House.**" Other headings are "A saint's delight in the sanctuary"; "Pilgrimage song"; "Happy are those who live in God's house." The TEV heading may have to be expanded in translation to say, for example, "The psalmist desires to live in the temple" or "The psalmist wishes he could be in God's worship house."

Hebrew title: <u>**To the choirmaster: according to The Gittith. A Psalm of the Sons of Korah**</u> (TEV "A psalm by the clan of Korah").

For **choirmaster** see title of Psalm 4; for **<u>Gittith</u>** see title of Psalm 8; for <u>**the Sons of Korah**</u> see title of Psalm 42.

84.1-2	RSV		TEV
1	How lovely is thy dwelling place, O LORD of hosts!	1	How I love your Temple, LORD Almighty!
2	My soul longs, yea, faints for the courts of the LORD; my heart and flesh sing for joy to the living God.	2	How I want to be there! I long to be in the LORD's Temple. With my whole being I sing for joy to the living God.

The psalmist begins by expressing his fervent desire to be in the Temple. The Hebrew adjective in verse 1 may mean <u>lovely</u> (RSV and others), an expression of the beauty of the Temple, or else "beloved," which expresses the psalmist's feelings for the Temple (see Briggs). So TEV has "**I love**" (also FRCL, GECL); or else, in a general way, "How people love . . ." (TOB, BJ). (KJV "amiable," in the sense of "lovable," is now archaic.) "**Temple**" translates the plural "dwelling places," which is probably used for emphasis. For translation suggestions on **"Temple"** see 2.6; 5.7; 20.2. LORD **of hosts** translates "Yahweh of armies" (see 46.7 and comments).

In verse 2 the Temple is again spoken of, this time as **the courts of the LORD** (see 65.4 and comments). **My soul** in verse 2a (see *nefesh* in 3.2) and **my heart and flesh** in verse 2c are ways of speaking of the individual, as expressions of deep feelings and emotions (see comments on "heart" and "body" in 16.9). **Faints** in verse 2a is a way of reinforcing the emotion expressed by **longs**. In English **my soul . . . faints** is not a natural expression; a translation should not make it appear that the psalmist had a fainting spell. So NJV "I long, I yearn," and NJB "My whole being yearns and pines."

In the expression **sing for joy to the living God, for joy** is the manner of singing, and in some languages this structure must be shifted to a causal clause; for example, "with my whole heart I will sing to God who lives, because I am glad." **The living God** means not only that God lives but that he is source and sustainer of all life. The expression **the living God** must often be recast as "the God who gives life" or "the God who causes everything to live."

For similar expression of deep longing for the Temple, see 42.1-2.

84.3-4   RSV   TEV

3	Even the sparrow finds a home, and the swallow a nest for herself, where she may lay her young, at thy altars, O LORD of hosts, my King and my God.	3 Even the sparrows have built a nest, and the swallows have their own home; they keep their young near your altars, LORD Almighty, my king and my God.
4	Blessed are those who dwell in thy house, ever singing thy praise! *Selah*	4 How happy are those who live in your Temple, always singing praise to you.

The psalmist proclaims the happiness of those who live in God's Temple. Even the sparrow and the swallow (see *Fauna and Flora*, pages 77, 80) are to be envied; they live in the Temple, with their nests near the **altars**. The text of verse 3 is not altogether clear; Briggs and Dahood rearrange the text in two different ways. But the Masoretic text as it is may be taken to mean what RSV, TEV, and others have. Kirkpatrick refers to the fact that in ancient times birds which had their nests in temples were considered sacred.

There were two altars in the Temple built by Solomon: the altar for burnt offerings, at the entrance to the Temple, and the gold altar for burning incense, in front of the Most Holy Place. Here the plural **altars** may simply be emphatic; some, like NJV, translate "Your altar."

In languages where the **sparrow** and **swallow** are not known, other local birds may be substituted, provided they are birds which are known for building their nests inside buildings. It is also possible to employ a generic term for birds, even as the

Hebrew term translated **sparrow** may be generic. In areas where birds are not known to build nests in buildings, an explanatory note may be required.

Lay her young at thy altars refers to the laying of the eggs in the nest near the altar and not the placing of the young near the altar for sacrifice, as TEV makes clear.

The double form of address, **my King and my God**, should not be taken by the reader as two persons. It may be necessary therefore to say, for example, "my king who is my God," or in some languages "the king who rules over me and who is the God I worship."

For translation suggestions on **Blessed are** in verse 4, see 1.1. The words **those who dwell in thy house** may be meant literally, referring to the permanent staff of priests and Levites; or else, in a more general sense, it means all people who regularly worshiped in the Temple (see Anderson; see the language in 15.1; 24.3). **Thy praise** means "praise (offered) **to you.**"

For **Selah** see 3.2.

84.5-7	RSV	TEV
5	Blessed are the men whose strength is in thee, in whose heart are the highways to Zion.*r*	5 How happy are those whose strength comes from you, who are eager to make the pilgrimage to Mount Zion.
6	As they go through the valley of Baca they make it a place of springs; the early rain also covers it with pools.	6 As they pass through the dry valley of Baca, it becomes a place of springs; the early rain fills it with pools.
7	They go from strength to strength; the God of gods will be seen in Zion.	7 They grow stronger as they go; they will see the God of gods on Zion.

r Heb lacks *to Zion*

Now the psalmist sings the happiness of the pilgrims, as they make their way through dry, desolate regions to Mount Zion, where they will see God in the Temple. They start on their way strengthened by God himself; by his strength they begin the pilgrimage (verse 5a) and **"they grow stronger as they go"** (verse 7a). But the word translated **strength** in verse 5a may mean "refuge" (NEB, FRCL, NJV). It is better to translate **strength**, as RSV and TEV have done. The expression **whose strength is in thee**, or TEV's **". . . comes from you,"** must sometimes be shifted to say, for example, "who receive their strength from you" or "who are strong because you give them their strength."

Verse 5b in Hebrew is "the highways (are) in their hearts," which TEV has taken to mean that they have a deep desire to travel the roads that lead to Mount Zion; NJV "whose mind is on the [pilgrim] highways." NEB "whose hearts are set on the pilgrim ways!" may be ambiguous. SPCL has "those who want to make the pilgrimage to your mountain," and NAB "their hearts are set on the pilgrimage" (similarly NJB, NIV).

Instead of the Hebrew **highways** the Septuagint has "ascents," which BJ prefers, explaining the word as a reference to the "Psalms of Ascent" (Psalms 120–134), which the pilgrims sang as they made their way up to Mount Zion. TEV supplies translationally "**(make the pilgrimage) to Mount Zion**"; SPCL "to your mountain"; and GECL "to your sanctuary." It is recommended that the translator imitate TEV. In verse 5b, if the translator is to retain the sense of making a pilgrimage, this may be rendered sometimes as "people who wish to walk up the paths to worship you in Mount Zion."

In verse 6a the Hebrew for **the valley of Baca** is hard to understand. The Masoretic text is *baka'*, "balsam tree," a tree that grows in dry places; seven Hebrew manuscripts have *bekeh*, which is taken to mean "weeping" (so the Septuagint, Syriac, Targum, and Vulgate). AT, RSV, TEV, NIV, and NJV translate as a proper name, a name that appears nowhere else in the Old Testament; Weiser and SPCL have "Valley of Tears"; NEB "the thirsty valley"; NJB "Valley of the Balsam"; BJ, FRCL, and TOB "valley of balsam trees." It seems preferable either to translate the Masoretic text by "valley of balsam trees," or else to translate the variant reading in the Hebrew manuscripts and the ancient versions, "Valley of Tears." Nothing much is gained by transliterating the Hebrew word as a place name, **Baca**. In any case, as the context shows, it was an arid place.

Verse 6b in Hebrew is "they make it (a place of) springs," which is what most translations say. TEV has taken the plural active form as an impersonal plural, "**it becomes**"; FRCL translates "God transforms it into an oasis." If an active plural form is used in translation, **they make**, it should not appear to the reader that by means of hard work and irrigation the pilgrims transformed the place from a desert into a well-watered valley. So something like TEV or FRCL may be preferable. As the next line shows, it is **the early rain** (that is, the rains in autumn) that **covers it with pools**. The word translated **pools** involves a change of vowels in the Hebrew text; the Masoretic text has the vowels that make the word "blessings" (Briggs, Oesterley, Kirkpatrick; NJV, SPCL, TOB, BJ, NJB).[1]

NJV, with a footnote, "Meaning of Heb. uncertain," translates the verse as follows: "They pass through the Valley of Baca, regarding it as a place of springs, as if the early rains had covered it with blessing." This is as good a model as any for the translator to follow.

In verse 7a TEV "**They grow stronger**" translates **they go from strength to strength**. But the noun may be taken to mean "a strong place," that is, a fortified wall, a rampart (so NJV "from rampart to rampart"), or "high place, height" (so BJ, NJB); NEB translates "They pass from outer wall to inner wall" (that is, of Jerusalem).

The verb (he) **will be seen** in verse 7b may be translated to mean "they (that is, the pilgrims) will appear (or, present themselves)"; so Weiser, TOB, and NJV. TEV and SPCL transform the passive "he will be seen" into the active "they will see." The phrase **God of gods** is a superlative, that is, "the supreme God" (SPCL). But the vowels in the Masoretic text make the first word mean "before (God)"; so NJV "appearing before God in Zion" (similarly TOB, FRCL, NIV); the Septuagint, however,

---

[1]HOTTP translates the whole verse as follows: "When they wander through the Baka Valley, they change it into a spring, and moreover the early rain envelopes it with blessings."

translates as though it were "God (of gods)"—so RSV, TEV, NEB, and others.[2] If the translator follows RSV and TEV **God of gods**, it will be necessary in some languages to recast this expression to say, for example, "God who is above all other gods" or "God who rules over all other gods."

84.8-9	RSV		TEV
8	O LORD God of hosts, hear my prayer; give ear, O God of Jacob! *Selah*	8	Hear my prayer, LORD God Almighty. Listen, O God of Jacob!
9	Behold our shield, O God; look upon the face of thine anointed!	9	Bless our king, O God, the king you have chosen.

This prayer for the king changes the subject abruptly from the pilgrimage to Mount Zion, and some consider these two verses to be a later addition to the text.

LORD God of hosts translates "Yahweh God of armies" (see comments on "LORD of hosts" in 46.7). This is the same expression as in verses 1 and 3, but with **God** inserted. For **God of Jacob** see also 46.7.

In verse 9a the Hebrew is "Look at our shield." Many take **shield** here as a reference to God himself (as often in the Psalms; see 3.3); so SPCL "O God, our protector, look . . ." (similarly BJ, NJB). But TEV, TOB, NEB, NAB, and others take **shield** to refer to the king as the protector of the people (parallel with **thine anointed** in line b), as in 89.18. So FRCL "O God, look at the king, our shield."

The two verbs **Behold** and **look upon** mean to regard with kindness, favor, goodwill; so SPCL, using one verb, translates "Look with favorable eyes at the one you have chosen as king," and TEV has "**Bless**." For translation suggestions on "**Bless**" see 3.8; 16.7; and 21.3.

In verse 9b **thine anointed** is taken by most to be the king; BJ and NJB (footnotes) take it to refer to the High Priest. For comments on **anointed** see 2.2.

84.10	RSV	TEV
	For a day in thy courts is better than a thousand elsewhere. I would rather be a doorkeeper in the house of my God	One day spent in your Temple is better than a thousand anywhere else; I would rather stand at the gate of

---

[2]Here HOTTP prefers the versional reading "God" and not the Masoretic text's "toward." It justifies its decision by saying that there was an interpretive modification by ancient editors or scribes (Factor 7).

than dwell in the tents of wick- edness.	the house of my God than live in the homes of the wicked.

In the final section (verses 10-12) the psalmist praises the Temple and the God who dwells there, as the source of happiness and security. To live in the Temple was the greatest blessing a pious Israelite could imagine.

In verse 10a,b there is some obscurity, inasmuch as the Hebrew text is simply "For better is a day in your courts than a thousand"—without indicating where those thousand days would be spent. Most translations, like TEV and RSV, just assume a normal ellipsis, with **"anywhere else"** or <u>elsewhere</u> implied. Simply to translate "a day in your courts is better than a thousand" (KJV, TOB) is quite inadequate; taken literally, it seems to say that the fewer days spent in the Temple, the better.

The word that follows in the Masoretic text is read as the form of the verb "to prefer" (<u>**I would rather**</u>) and goes with the following words. But some emend the word represented in RSV and TEV by **I would rather** so as to get "on my own" (BJ), "at home" (NEB), and put it on the previous line, after **than a thousand**. Dahood proposes "How much better is one day in your court than a thousand in the Cemetery" (that is, Sheol)—which, to say the least, is not very complimentary of the Temple.

In the second half of verse 10, the same idea is expressed in terms of standing at the Temple gate. Anderson considers RSV <u>**doorkeeper**</u> to be misleading, since that was the title of a high official among the priests or Levites (see 2 Kgs 12.9; 23.4). It seems to imply a Levite guard stationed at the Temple; the figure would then be that of service in the Temple. But it seems better to take the expression in a more general way, parallel with line a; that is, the psalmist is speaking of standing at the entrance to the Temple, ready to go in and worship God. What is here portrayed is a pilgrim asking permission to enter the Temple and worship there. TEV's **"gate of the house . . . ,"** if translated literally, may be misleading. In some language areas, gates are primarily for keeping animals out. A better translation may be "entrance" or "door."

The comparison **"than live in the homes of the wicked"** (literally <u>**than dwell in the tents of wickedness**</u>) does not seem very fitting, and so some propose to emend to "homes of the wealthy." Again Dahood's translation is somewhat of an insult to the Temple: "To stand on the threshold of your house, my God, than to abide in the Tent of the Wicked One" (another name for the world of the dead). TEV's **"stand at the gate"** does not carry a very clear contrast with **"live in the homes of the wicked."** In some languages a contrast is made by saying, for example, "I would rather stand outside the Temple than sit in the homes of wicked people," where "sit" carries the meaning of live or dwell.

84.11-12   RSV   TEV

11 For the LORD God is a sun and
     shield;
     he bestows favor and honor.
     No good thing does the LORD
	11 The LORD is our protector and
	     glorious king,
	     blessing us with kindness and
	     honor.

<table>
<tr><td>

     withhold
  from those who walk uprightly.

12 O Lord of hosts,
    blessed is the man who trusts
    in thee!

</td><td>

He does not refuse any good thing
  to those who do what is right.

12 Lord Almighty, how happy are
    those who trust in you!

</td></tr>
</table>

In verse 11 the figures **sun and shield** may stand for guidance and protection; see SPCL "God . . . shines on us and protects us." See similar language, "my light and my salvation," in 27.1. TEV **"glorious king"** is meant to represent the might and splendor of the sun. But **sun** is nowhere else in the Old Testament used as a figure for God, and some have proposed that the word here, *shemesh,* means "bulwark, battlement" (NEB, BJ, NJB; Weiser; NJV footnote). In Isaiah 54.12 the word *shemesh* does mean "bulwark," and that may well be the most probable meaning here. K-B and Holladay define it here as "sun-shaped shield." The idea of **"protector"** is to be preferred. Verse 11a may be translated, for example, "The LORD is the one who protects us and rules over us" or "The LORD defends us from our enemies."

God blesses his people with **favor and honor**, that is, he shows his love for them and brings honor, or glory, to them by causing them to prosper and succeed. God gives good things **"to those who do what is right"** (literally, "who walk blamelessly"; see 15.2 and comments). RSV **who walk uprightly** may be ambiguous.

Although GECL retains the idea of **sun** and **shield**, it provides a good example of a dynamic equivalence translation:

> Yes, God, the Lord, is the sun,
> > who gives us light and life.
> He is the shield,
> > who protects us.
> He gives us his love,
> > and receives us with honor.
> To all who live blameless lives
> > he gives the greatest good fortune.

The final praise (verse 12) is reserved for those who trust in God. **LORD of hosts** translates "Yahweh of armies" (as in verses 1, 3, 8).

Psalm 85

This psalm is a group prayer: the people pray to God, who in the past had been gracious to them and blessed them, but who is now angry with them. We do not know what event in Israel's life would provide the reason for such a prayer, and no firm statement can be made about the time and occasion of the psalm's composition. Some, like Weiser, think it reflects a situation shortly after the people returned from the exile in Babylonia.

The psalm begins with a reminder to God of how he had saved Israel in the past (verses 1-3), followed by a plea that in the present he once more show his love for his people and save them (verses 4-7). The rest of the psalm (verses 8-13) is a response made to the people, either by a prophet or a priest, or perhaps by the psalmist himself: God in the future will relent, and once more his people will experience blessings and prosperity.

HEADING: "**A Prayer for the Nation's Welfare.**" Other headings are "Prayer for peace"; "Save us once more!"; "Comfort and hope." The TEV heading may be adjusted for some languages to say, for example, "The people pray that God will save Israel" or "The people pray that God will give good things to Israel."

Hebrew title: **To the choirmaster. A Psalm of the Sons of Korah** (TEV "A psalm by the clan of Korah").

For **choirmaster** see title of Psalm 4; for **the Sons of Korah** see title of Psalm 42.

85.1-3   RSV   TEV

1   LORD, thou wast favorable to thy   1   LORD, you have been merciful to
        land;   your land;
    thou didst restore the fortunes   you have made Israel prosper-
        of Jacob.   ous again.
2   Thou didst forgive the iniquity of   2   You have forgiven your people's
        thy people;   sins
    thou didst pardon all their sin.   and pardoned all their wrongs.
                                Selah   3   You stopped being angry with
3   Thou didst withdraw all thy wrath;   them
    thou didst turn from thy hot   and held back your furious
        anger.   rage.

The psalm begins with the people reminding Yahweh of how in the past he had once changed from his anger toward them, had forgiven their sins, and had made

744

them prosperous again. The most common interpretation is that this refers to the return of the Israelites from the Babylonian captivity; God's anger toward them had ceased and he had saved them. Some think the reference is to the exodus from Egypt, but this seems unlikely. It is impossible to determine for sure what the present distress is; Dahood thinks the whole setting of the psalm is a devastating drought from which the people are suffering and on account of which they pray for rain. In Hebrew there is a play on the sound of the words **favorable** and **land** in line a, and **restore** and **fortunes** in line b.

The verbs in these verses are understood by most commentators as equivalent to past-time actions (either perfects or simple pasts); NJV translates as futures; BJ and NJB translate by the present tense; Dahood takes them as imperatives. According to the interpretation favored here, the simple past tense (RSV, NIV) is the most suitable one; the perfect tense (NEB, FRCL, TOB, NAB, SPCL) makes the shift to the imperative verb in verse 4 difficult, for the perfect tense implies that the effects of the past actions still continue in the present. Why, then, the plea for the Lord to change? TEV attempts to meet this problem by using the perfect in verses 1-2 and the past in verse 3, but it may be better to use the simple past tense in all three verses, or else the past perfect (pluperfect), as follows: "LORD, you had been merciful . . . you had made . . . You had forgiven . . . You had stopped . . . and had held back . . . ." Then the change in verse 4 is natural and understandable.

The verb translated **wast favorable** is used in 44.3, "didst delight"; see comments. **Thy land** in verse 1a is parallel with **Jacob** in verse 1b; together they refer to the land and the people of Israel. In some languages it is not natural to speak of being merciful to an inanimate object such as land, and in such cases it may be necessary to say "you have been merciful to the people of your land," or idiomatically, "you have had a warm heart for the people who live in your land." The phrase **restore the fortunes** is the same as the one in 14.7; 53.6. But one form of the Hebrew text (the *qere*) yields the meaning "you brought back the Israelite captives"; so BJ, NJB, TOB. **Restore the fortunes** may sometimes be rendered "you have given Israel back its wealth" or "you have made Israel rich (or, prosperous) again."

In verse 2a **forgive** translates the verb "lift away, remove," and in verse 2b **pardon** translates the verb "cover" (see 32.1b and comments). The two nouns **iniquity** and **sin** are the same two used in 51.2.

For *Selah* see 3.2.

The two lines of verse 3 are parallel and synonymous; at one time God had "stopped being angry" (TEV) with his people, that is, he had quit punishing them for their sins, and so they had had a change in their condition.

85.4-5	RSV	TEV
4	Restore us again, O God of our salvation, and put away thy indignation toward us!	4 Bring us back, O God our savior, and stop being displeased with us!
5	Wilt thou be angry with us for ever?	5 Will you be angry with us forever? Will your anger never cease?

> Wilt thou prolong thy anger to
> all generations?

There are various ways of understanding the exact force and meaning of the initial plea in verse 4: TEV **"Bring us back"** (so BJ, NJB, TOB); <u>Restore us again</u> (AT, RSV, FRCL, NIV, NAB; Weiser); "Save us now also" (SPCL); "Turn back to us" (NEB). The usual interpretation, represented by the majority, is that the people are asking God once again to intervene and save them (here the same verb is used as in verse 1a). For **God of our salvation** see comments at 18.46; 79.9. RSV <u>Restore us again</u> and TEV **"Bring us back"** do not indicate the nature of this process, which in many languages will have to be more explicit than either of these versions. If this restoration is to Israel's preexilic condition, the translator may say, for instance, "make us strong (or, prosperous) the way we once were."

For the sentiment expressed in verses 4b, 5, see similar language in 74.1; 79.5. The verb in verse 4b is somewhat unusual; the Masoretic text is a form of the verb "to break, invalidate," thus "break your anger." It appears that RSV has followed the Septuagint (so Anderson) and translates a causative verb which means "get rid of, remove" (see "depart," 6.8). NEB has "cancel," TOB "renounce," and NJV "revoke" for the Masoretic text. The Masoretic text does make sense and should be followed.

The rhetorical questions in verse 5 are a familiar way of protesting God's seemingly perpetual anger with his people and asking him to relent. The two questions are parallel and synonymous. <u>**To all generations**</u> in line <u>b</u> means the same as <u>**for ever**</u> in line <u>a</u>. SPCL has reduced the two rhetorical questions to one: "Can it be that you will prolong forever your anger against us?" In some languages it may be more natural to express the two rhetorical questions as negative commands in which the two lines may, if necessary, be reduced to one; for example, "Don't be angry with us for ever."

     RSV   TEV

	RSV		TEV
6	Wilt thou not revive us again, that thy people may rejoice in thee?	6	Make us strong again, and we, your people, will praise you.
7	Show us thy steadfast love, O LORD, and grant us thy salvation.	7	Show us your constant love, O LORD, and give us your saving help.

Verse 6 in Hebrew is a negative question, which expects an affirmative answer: "Will you not revive us?" demands the answer "Yes, I will revive you." TEV has represented the meaning by a direct request; NJV by a strong affirmative, "Surely You will revive us again." The plea is "Give us life once again," that is, make us prosperous, strong, happy once more (see the same verb in 80.18, "give us life"). In verse 6b <u>rejoice in thee</u> (see RSV, NIV, NEB, NJV) may mean "be happy because of what you have done" or **"praise you"**; TOB "and you will be the joy of your people"; FRCL "that we may again find joy in you."

The people ask the Lord to reveal to them his <u>**steadfast love**</u> (see 5.7 and comments), that is, by giving them his <u>**salvation**</u>. The two may be combined as SPCL has done: "Show us your love and save us!" The verb **show** in this context means to manifest, to reveal, by acting, by doing something; it is by saving his people that Yahweh will show to them, prove to them, that he loves them.

85.8-9	RSV	TEV
8	Let me hear what God the LORD will speak, for he will speak peace to his people, to his saints, to those who turn to him in their hearts.^{s}	8 I am listening to what the LORD God is saying; he promises peace to us, his own people, if we do not go back to our foolish ways.
9	Surely his salvation is at hand for those who fear him, that glory may dwell in our land.	9 Surely he is ready to save those who honor him, and his saving presence will remain in our land.

^{s} Gk: Heb *but let them not turn back to folly*

Verses 8-13 are God's answer to his people's prayer. It is delivered through a prophet or a priest in the Temple, or else by the psalmist himself. The Lord's promise is **peace** (for *shalom* see also comments on 29.11), which includes both spiritual and material well-being, health, soundness; Weiser translates here "salvation"; also possible is "well-being."

Verse 8 begins with the psalmist's determination to hear God's message. A better translation than RSV or TEV may be "I will now listen . . . ." The present tense **"is saying . . . promises"** (TEV; see TOB, FRCL, GECL) seems preferable to the future **will speak . . . will speak** (RSV, NEB, SPCL, NIV), since it provides at once the message which comes from God in response to the people's prayer. The sudden injection of the first person into the psalm will create some misunderstanding for the reader, unless an explanation is provided. This may be done in one of three ways: a) by introducing the speaker into the text; for example, "the psalmist says to the people . . . ;" b) by means of a subtitle placed at the beginning of verse 8; for example, "The psalmist speaks to the people for God"; and c) by means of a note. The translator should evaluate for his language which of the foregoing will be most appropriate for the reader.

The people of Israel are spoken of as **his people** and his **saints** (for **saints** see comments on "godly" in 4.3); TEV has shortened and combined the two into **"us, his own people."**

The line that follows is not easy to understand; the Hebrew text seems to mean "and they do not turn to folly" (see also RSV footnote). TEV (also BJ, NJB, NJV, TOB, SPCL; Weiser) represents the Masoretic text (with a change in person from the third plural to the first plural) by **"if we do not go back to our foolish ways"**; RSV, NEB, and NAB follow the Septuagint, emending the text to get **who turn to him in their hearts**. This makes sense; but, as McCullough states, it is not exact to say that the

747

Masoretic text does not make sense. It is not necessary for the translator to depart from the Masoretic text.[1]

In verse 9 the people are assured that God will save them; TEV "**those who honor him**" (or, who obey him) represents the meaning of **those who fear him** (see 15.4 and comments).

In verse 9b **glory** represents the revealed presence of God with his people; so TEV "**his saving presence**" (see Toombs "his authoritative presence"). The presence of God was manifested by a shining light that filled the Tent of the Lord's Presence, where God met with his people (Exo 40.34-35), and later the Temple (see 2 Chr 7.1-3); here the promise is made that this same visible presence of God will remain in Israel. In many languages it is unnatural to speak of an abstract such as **glory** "living in the land." At the same time TEV's "**saving presence**" presents an equally difficult expression. However, it is often possible to reformulate the TEV expression as two clauses; for example, "he will show himself to us and save us in Israel."

85.10-11   RSV   TEV

	RSV		TEV
10	Steadfast love and faithfulness will meet; righteousness and peace will kiss each other.	10	Love and faithfulness will meet; righteousness and peace will embrace.
11	Faithfulness will spring up from the ground, and righteousness will look down from the sky.	11	Man's loyalty will reach up from the earth, and God's righteousness will look down from heaven.

Translations vary in their understanding of the verbs in verses 10-13; some have the future tense (RSV, NAB, TEV, SPCL; Weiser, Dahood); NEB has the perfect tense in verse 10, the present tense in verse 11, and the future tense in verses 12-13; NJB, FRCL, NJV have the present tense for all four verses; TOB has the perfect tense in verse 10 and the present tense in verses 11-13. There is no way of proving which is right, but in the context it seems more reasonable to suppose that the psalmist (or whoever is the speaker in verses 8-13) is announcing what will happen in the future, as God answers his people's prayers (so McCullough and others).

In poetic language the psalmist speaks of **steadfast love** and **faithfulness** (see the same pairing in 25.10; 40.10,11; 57.3; 61.7); he then speaks of God's **righteousness** and **peace**. These may be taken to be attributes of God, not of human beings, which are spoken of as God's representatives, or messengers. They **meet** and greet each other with a **kiss** as they prepare to go and bless God's people. In languages in which abstract qualities can be quite readily personified, it is fairly simple to represent the Hebrew text as NJB has done: "Faithful Love and Loyalty join together, Saving Justice and Peace embrace." A footnote explains: "Personified attributes of

---

[1]Here HOTTP ("C" decision) splits; of the committee members, the majority prefers the Masoretic text, translating "provided they do not go back to folly!"; the minority votes for the Septuagint, "and to (those who) turn to him with their heart."

748

God; these will inaugurate the kingdom of God on earth and in human hearts." For the average English-speaking reader this is a satisfactory translation.

Others, however, see in verse 10 the divine initiative and the human response (as in verse 11); God's **steadfast love** is met by his people's **faithfulness**, and human **righteousness** is rewarded by God's **peace** (a chiastic arrangement). This seems to be the best way to read the verse. God's **steadfast love** is the way in which God maintains the promise he made when he established his covenant with the people of Israel, the promise always to be their God and to bless them, if they faithfully obeyed his laws. Line a, then, speaks of God and the people of Israel keeping their terms of the covenant. And in line b, God's **righteousness** represents God's way of making right and justice prevail among his people; when this happens, the people know **peace**, that is, the full blessings of a community in which God's will prevails. These abstract qualities, both human and divine, refer to God's deeds in blessing his people and making right prevail, and the people's response in keeping God's laws and so enjoying **peace** (see 29.11).

The translation problem in verses 10-11 concerns the personification of abstracts where such qualities as **love and faithfulness** perform human events. In languages in which abstracts are not allowed this kind of poetic privilege, it is often possible, even if a bit awkward, to shift to a simile; for example, "like two people meet each other, God's love and faithfulness will meet each other" or "God sends his messengers of love and faithfulness to meet each other." Verse 10b may be expressed in a parallel manner. In those languages in which these abstracts are not spoken of as nouns but rather as events, the restructuring must be more radical. Some interpreters see "faithfulness" as Israel's relation to God, and "righteousness" as Israel's keeping of the law, and "peace" as God's reward to Israel. This view lends itself more easily to translation where noun phrases are not possible. For example, in such languages it may be possible to say "God who loves Israel and Israel who is faithful to God will meet. Israel who is loyal to God will have the peace which God gives like a kiss."

In verse 10b the verb may be understood as "**embrace**" (TEV, JB, BJ, TOB) or **kiss** (RSV, GECL, NJV, NIV, SPCL); NEB has "join hands."

In verse 11, by use of **from the ground** and **from the sky**, it is quite clear that it is the people's **faithfulness** (or, "loyalty") which responds to God's **righteousness**. Verse 11 must be restructured in some languages somewhat in the manner of verse 10. Here, however, it is possible to shift the focus to "man" and "God" as in TEV, with a further adjustment in which the subject switches to "man" and "God," who are characterized as "loyal" and "faithful"; for example, "Israel, who is loyal to God, will reach up from the earth and God, who is faithful to Israel, will look down from heaven."

85.12-13	RSV	TEV

	RSV	TEV
12	Yea, the LORD will give what is good, and our land will yield its increase.	12 The LORD will make us prosperous, and our land will produce rich harvests.
13	Righteousness will go before him,	13 Righteousness will go before the

and make his footsteps a way.	**Lord** **and prepare the path for him.**

In verse 12 TEV "**The Lord will make us prosperous**" translates <u>the Lord will</u> <u>give what is good</u>; this can be understood as "give blessings." NJB has "give prosperity"; GECL "success." Dahood takes "the good" here to mean rain (also SPCL), as a result of which the land will "**produce rich harvests.**" <u>Yea</u> at the beginning of the verse represents an emphatic "Certainly," "Surely," of the Hebrew text.

In verse 13a <u>righteousness</u> is seen as a herald going ahead of Yahweh, preparing the way for him. This is the third occurrence of the term (after verses 10 and 11), marking this verse as the conclusion of a minor unit in the psalm.

Verse 13b is somewhat unclear; it seems to mean "**and prepare the path for him,**" giving the purpose of the verb in line <u>a</u>. RSV makes no sense in English; NIV "and prepare the way for his steps" is, presumably, what RSV intends to say (so NJB "treading out a path"). Briggs and others emend to "and peace walks (in) his footsteps," that is, either preceding him (so NEB) or following him (so NAB; Weiser). This makes better sense than the Masoretic text, even though the Masoretic text can be understood as TEV and SPCL have translated. NJV has "as He sets out on His way." In languages in which <u>righteousness</u> as a noun can be used, it is possible to adjust line <u>a</u> to a simile to say, for example, "righteousness goes like a guide ahead of the Lord to prepare his path" or ". . . to prepare the path for him to come on."

Psalm 86

This psalm is an individual's prayer for help against enemies who threaten to destroy him. He knows that he is a devoted and faithful servant of God, and thus he confidently expects God to answer him and defeat his enemies. There is nothing in the psalm to enable us to ascertain the time and circumstances of its composition. The language is conventional, that is, it is the kind of language commonly used in psalms like this; most of the text, as the commentators point out, is paralleled in other psalms and other Old Testament writings. Cohen assumes the psalm was not written out of the psalmist's own experience, but as a prayer to be used by those who faced difficulties and dangers.

The order of the psalm as we now have it is not very logical, and some would place verses 8-13 after verses 14-17.

The psalm begins with a cry to Yahweh for help (verses 1-7), in which the psalmist bases his request on his own good character (verse 2) and on the Lord's goodness (verse 5). Next the psalmist proclaims Yahweh's greatness (verses 8-10), and then, mixing praise with petition, he promises to serve God and follow his ways (verses 11-17). Only in verses 14 and 17 does the psalmist refer to his enemies and their desire to kill him.

HEADING: "**A Prayer for Help.**" Other headings are "The prayer of a needy man"; "From self to God"; "Prayer in time of distress." The TEV heading may be modified for some languages to say "The psalmist prays to God for help" or "The psalmist prays that God will help him."

Hebrew title: **A Prayer of David** (TEV "**A prayer by David**").
For **Prayer** see title of Psalm 17.

86.1-2	RSV		TEV

	RSV		TEV

1	Incline thy ear, O LORD, and answer me,
	    for I am poor and needy.
		1	Listen to me, LORD, and answer me,
			    for I am helpless and weak.

2	Preserve my life, for I am godly;
	    save thy servant who trusts in thee.
	Thou art my God; 3 . . .
		2	Save me from death, because I am loyal to you;
			    save me, for I am your servant and I trust in you.

The structure of the first four verses is that of requests supported by reasons. In all there are six requests and five reasons, unless **poor and needy** in verse 1 can be taken as two. In this kind of structure it is possible, but not always necessary or

751

desirable, to list the request as a series and then to follow with the reasons. The only utterance which is neither request nor reason is **thou art my God**, which occurs more or less at the mid point. Such restructuring will not disturb the parallelism, since no semantic parallelism is involved.

The psalmist cries for help (verse 1); for **Incline thy ear** see 17.6 and comments. **Poor and needy** translates two words often used in this kind of prayer (see "afflicted" in 9.12; "weak and needy" in 35.10). The expression **answer me** does not mean that the psalmist seeks a reply to a question, but rather is a plea that God respond to his prayer. In many languages this may be expressed as "help me" or "save me."

In verse 2 "Preserve my *nefesh*" (see 3.2) means "don't let me die." For **godly**, that is, pious, devoted, faithful, see 4.3 and comments. NEB has "constant and true"; FRCL "one of your faithful ones"; SPCL "I am faithful to you."

The second half of verse 2 in Hebrew is "save your servant, you are my God, who is loyal to you." In some languages it will be necessary to relate **thy servant** in verses 2 and 4 to the psalmist; otherwise it is possible to understand that the psalmist is making the pleas for himself and someone else. TEV does this in verse 2 and, having established the identity of the writer and "your servant," does not need to do it again in verse 4. It may be necessary in some languages to say again in verse 4 "make me, your servant, glad" or "make me, who serves you, glad."

Both RSV and TEV transpose "you are my God" to the end of the verse, joining it to what follows. For aesthetic reasons TEV has kept verse number 3 at the beginning of the line; RSV places it in the middle, at the exact beginning of the verse.

86.3-5	RSV		TEV
	. . . 3 **be gracious to me, O Lord,**	3	**You are my God, so be merciful to**
	for to thee do I cry all the day.		**me;**
4	**Gladden the soul of thy servant,**		**I pray to you all day long.**
	for to thee, O Lord, do I lift up	4	**Make your servant glad, O Lord,**
	my soul.		**because my prayers go up to**
5	**For thou, O Lord, art good and**		**you.**
	forgiving,	5	**You are good to us and forgiving,**
	abounding in steadfast love to		**full of constant love for all who**
	all who call on thee.		**pray to you.**

As RSV shows, in verses 3, 4, and 5 the vocative **O Lord** (the title, not the name Yahweh) occurs once in each verse; for stylistic reasons TEV has it only once. For **be gracious** see 4.1 and comments. In verse 3b **all the day** is not meant literally; "constant," or "insistent," or "continual" prayer is meant.

In verse 4a (as in verse 2b) the psalmist refers to himself as **thy servant**. "The *nefesh* of thy servant" is the psalmist's way of referring to his innermost self. In verse 4b the Hebrew is "I lift my *nefesh* to you," which TEV takes to mean prayer (see 25.1 and comments). It is not necessary to have the prayers **"go up to you"** as in TEV, and in many languages this figure **lift up my soul** may be rendered "I pray to you" or "I worship you."

In verse 5 the adjective **forgiving** in Hebrew occurs only here in the Old Testament; the related verb is frequently used, always with God as subject (see comment on "pardon" in 25.11).

It should be noted that TEV "**good to us and forgiving**" is used to avoid the phrase **good and forgiving** (RSV, NJV, AT), which could be wrongly understood, since "good and . . ." is often used as an intensifier, as in "he is good and mad." TEV has supplied "**us**" as the object of God's goodness and forgiveness. However, there is nowhere in this psalm a mention of "us," and translators may find that "me" is more in keeping with the rest of the individual and personal style of the prayer.

For **steadfast love** see 5.7.

86.6-7	RSV		TEV
6	Give ear, O LORD, to my prayer; hearken to my cry of supplication.	6	Listen, LORD, to my prayer; hear my cries for help.
7	In the day of my trouble I call on thee, for thou dost answer me.	7	I call to you in times of trouble, because you answer my prayers.

For verse 6 see similar language in 28.2; 55.1.
For verse 7a see 50.15a; 77.2a.

86.8-10	RSV		TEV
8	There is none like thee among the gods, O Lord, nor are there any works like thine.	8	There is no god like you, O Lord, not one has done what you have done.
9	All the nations thou hast made shall come and bow down before thee, O Lord, and shall glorify thy name.	9	All the nations that you have created will come and bow down to you; they will praise your greatness.
10	For thou art great and doest wondrous things, thou alone art God.	10	You are mighty and do wonderful things; you alone are God.

The psalmist breaks into praise to God, proclaiming him as supreme and unique, doing what no other god can do. In verse 8 **the gods** are the gods of the other nations. Those nations were created by the God of Israel, not by their own gods, so they will worship him and praise his greatness (**glorify thy name**), that is, they will praise him because he is great. None of the gods is able to do what the Lord of Israel has done (verse 8b). This line may be translated, as RSV does, as an absolute statement of the great deeds of the Lord or, as TEV has it, as a continuation of the thought of line a, that none of the gods has done what the Lord has done. In either case, **works** here refers to God's deeds on behalf of Israel, not to the works of creation (also **wondrous things** in verse 10a). Translators should refer to the translation comment on **gods** in 82.1. There the gods were related to God. In 86.8 **the gods** are related to the pagan nations. Therefore it may be necessary to make clear that these are gods worshiped by the other nations; for example, "The gods others worship are not like you, O Lord," "You, O Lord, are greater than the gods other nations pray to," or "Others pray to spirits, but none of these is great as you are, Great Spirit."

It should be noted that in verse 9a both RSV and TEV say that only those nations that God has created will come, implying that there are nations that God did not create. So it is better, with SPCL, GECL, and FRCL, to translate "You have created all the nations, so they will come to you . . . ."

For verse 8b and verse 10a compare similar language in 72.18; 77.14. In verse 10b the psalmist declares **thou alone art God**, that is, he has the rank and nature that none of the other gods has. The words may be translated "you alone, O God, do wonderful things," proclaiming what he alone does, not that only he is God; so BJ, NJB, Dahood. But the translation preferred by the majority is recommended.

86.11-13 RSV	TEV
11 Teach me thy way, O LORD, that I may walk in thy truth; unite my heart to fear thy name. 12 I give thanks to thee, O Lord my God, with my whole heart, and I will glorify thy name for ever. 13 For great is thy steadfast love toward me; thou hast delivered my soul from the depths of Sheol.	11 Teach me, LORD, what you want me to do, and I will obey you faithfully; teach me to serve you with complete devotion. 12 I will praise you with all my heart, O Lord my God; I will proclaim your greatness forever. 13 How great is your constant love for me! You have saved me from the grave itself.

In verse 11 the psalmist prays for God's guidance; line <u>a</u> is exactly like 27.11a; line <u>b</u> is almost exactly like 26.3b: "and I will walk in your *'emet*" (see 15.2 and comments). Some, as in 26.3, take the word here to mean "your truth" (RSV, BJ, TOB, NAB, NIV, NJV). Others, like TEV, take it to mean "loyalty, faithfulness," and take the phrase "your faithfulness" to mean "faithfulness to you"; so NJB, FRCL, NEB, SPCL, Dahood. In this context TEV may have the better interpretation.

The last line of verse 11 in Hebrew is **unite my heart to fear thy name**. TEV and others take the verb **unite** here to signify single-hearted, complete devotion; NIV "an undivided heart," NEB "let me be one in heart." Some, following the Septuagint and Syriac, use different vowels for the Hebrew consonants, so that instead of "unite (my heart)" the text reads "(my heart) will rejoice" (Briggs, Oesterley; AT). But the Masoretic text does make sense. And **to fear thy name** may mean either "to serve you" or "to worship you" (so NJV); many have "to revere your name," which means "to honor you" (see 85.9). FRCL translates "Place in me this one preoccupation: to remain submissive to your authority"; and GECL, "Let my only concern be to honor you and to obey you." In line c̲ TEV has repeated "**teach me**" for clarity and emphasis.

Verse 12a is almost exactly the same as 9.1a; and verse 12b makes use of words found in verse 9c. **My whole heart** in line a̲ repeats the idea of "an undivided heart" in verse 11c. The expression **glorify thy name** may be rendered in some languages as "I will always tell everyone that you are great," or in direct address, "I will always tell the people 'You, God, are great.' "

For **steadfast love** in verse 13a, see 5.7 and comments.

The language of verse 13b ("you rescued my *nefesh* from the depths of Sheol"), if taken literally, means that God saved the psalmist from what seemed to be certain death, either from a near-fatal illness or else at the hands of his enemies (see next verse). It is possible that the language is figurative and that the psalmist is praising God for having saved him from a very difficult situation that did not necessarily threaten his life. In some languages "**saved me from the grave itself**" would be taken to mean that the psalmist was somehow resurrected from death. Since this can hardly be the meaning, it is better in many languages to avoid a figurative expression and to say, for example, "you kept me from dying" or "you rescued me when I was about to be killed." For **delivered** see the same verb in 7.1.

86.14-15 RSV	TEV

14 O God, insolent men have risen up against me;
    a band of ruthless men seek my life,
    and they do not set thee before them.
	14 Proud men are coming against me, O God;
	    a gang of cruel men is trying to kill me—
	    people who pay no attention to you.

15 But thou, O Lord, art a God merciful and gracious,
    slow to anger and abounding in steadfast love and faithfulness.
	15 But you, O Lord, are a merciful and loving God,
	    always patient, always kind and faithful.

Verse 14, the only place in which the psalmist refers to his enemies' actions, is practically identical with 54.3. Line c **they do not set thee before them** means "they have no regard for you"; NEB "give no thought to thee," NJV "they are not mindful of You."

In the midst of his difficulties the psalmist knows that God is with him (verse 15); he is **merciful and gracious** (the latter word is related to the verb "to be kind"— see 4.1). God is **slow to anger** (TEV "**always patient**," NEB "forbearing"), that is, not quickly aroused to punish sinners. The expression **slow to anger** is sometimes rendered "you, God, do not get a hot heart quickly." He is full of **steadfast love and faithfulness** (see comments on 5.7 and on "truth" in 15.2).

	RSV		TEV
16	Turn to me and take pity on me; give thy strength to thy servant and save the son of thy hand-maid.	16	Turn to me and have mercy on me; strengthen me and save me, because I serve you just as my mother did.
17	Show me a sign of thy favor, that those who hate me may see and be put to shame because thou, LORD, hast helped me and comforted me.	17	Show me proof of your goodness, LORD; those who hate me will be ashamed when they see that you have given me comfort and help.

Verse 16a is similar to 25.16a. In this verse the psalmist refers to himself as **thy servant** (as in verses 2,4) and **the son of thy handmaid** (as in 116.16). RSV **handmaid** is an archaic term for "maidservant" or "servant girl." The second phrase may be nothing more than the equivalent of the first; so SPCL shortens and combines the two into one, "this servant of yours" (see Anderson, McCullough). Others take the expression to mean that, just as the child of a slave was a slave for life (see Exo 21.4), so the psalmist considered himself to be a permanent slave of God. So FRCL "I am your servant . . . I belong to you." TEV has taken the expression to be a reference to the devoutness of the psalmist's mother as an additional reason for God to save him; no other translation consulted, however, gives this meaning.

The psalmist asks for a clear indication, a proof, of God's goodness, of God's approval (**a sign of thy favor**), either some favorable sign or else the deliverance itself from his difficulties. Such a demonstration of the Lord's goodness would **put to shame** the psalmist's enemies, for they would see that by his intervention God had proven the psalmist's claims to be true. And the psalmist himself would have received God's comfort and help. In some languages the expression **show me a sign** or "proof" must be rendered as "do something so that I will know . . . ," or specifically, "help me so that . . ." or "save me so that . . . ." For **comforted** see comments on 23.4; 71.21.

Psalm 87

This psalm, like Psalms 46, 48, and 76, celebrates the greatness of Jerusalem as the place where God dwells and as the capital for the future kingdom which God will establish. Anderson entitles the psalm, "Zion as the Spiritual Centre of the World."

The present order of the lines of the Hebrew text seems illogical, and there are several proposals for changes; but there is no widespread agreement on what might have been the original order of the composition. Dentan's brief comment is apt: "The text of this psalm is damaged and disarranged." NEB has this footnote: "The text of this psalm is disordered, and several verses have been rearranged." NJV has a footnote: "The meaning of many passages in this psalm is uncertain."

Anderson thinks it wiser to keep the line order of the Masoretic text, which is supported by the ancient versions. The notes and comments will follow the order of the Masoretic text, and no proposals will be made for rearranging the lines. NEB restructures as follows: 2, 1, 5c, 4a,b, 5a,b, 6, 7, 3; Weiser has the following order: l, 5c, 2, 3, 6, 4, 5a,b, 7.

The structure of the psalm, as it stands in the Masoretic text, seems quite obvious: 1) verses 1-3: God's choice of Zion; 2) verses 4-6: Zion, mother of all; 3) verse 7: closing expression of praise. The Masoretic text itself supports this division of the psalm by placing *Selah* at the end of verses 3 and 6. Most commentators and translations follow this division of the psalm. TOB, however, has: 1-3, 4-5, 6-7. It does this by omitting the *Selah* (Pause) at the end of verse 6 and running verses 6-7 together as one sentence. This seems quite arbitrary.

The main problem is to decide who is the speaker in verses 4 and 5. TEV takes verse 4 as the Lord's words, and verse 5 as the psalmist's (so Kirkpatrick, McCullough, Dahood; BJ, NJB, SPCL); Briggs and FRCL have God as speaker in verses 4-5; NEB has the psalmist as speaker in both verses. In verse 4 God is clearly the speaker: **those who know me** in line a is decisive. In verses 5 and 6, however, God is referred to in the third-person forms: **the Most High** in verse 5c and **The LORD** in verse 6a. Of course God can speak of himself in the third person, but it seems reasonable to assume that the speaker here is either the psalmist himself or a priest or a prophet in the Temple liturgy.

It is recommended that the translators make quite clear that God is the speaker in verse 4, and that the psalmist is the speaker in verses 5 and 6.

There is nothing in the text that allows us to determine the time and circumstances of the composition of this psalm. It may have been sung by pilgrims as they went to Jerusalem for a festival.

HEADING: "**In Praise of Jerusalem.**" Other headings are: "Zion, mother of nations"; "Zion the home of all nations"; "Praise to the city of God." In some languages the TEV heading may be recast as "The psalmist says that Jerusalem is the great city" or "The psalmist says that God loves the city of Jerusalem."

<u>Hebrew title</u>: **A Psalm of the Sons of Korah. A Song** (TEV "A psalm by the clan of Korah; a song").

For **the Sons of Korah** see title of Psalm 42; for **Psalm** and **Song** see title of Psalm 65.

87.1-3	RSV		TEV
1	On the holy mount stands the city he founded;	1	The LORD built his city on the sacred hill;[a]
2	the LORD loves the gates of Zion more than all the dwelling places of Jacob.	2	more than any other place in Israel he loves the city of Jerusalem.
3	Glorious things are spoken of you, O city of God. *Selah*	3	Listen, city of God, to the wonderful things he says about you:

[a] SACRED HILL: *See 2.6.*

The first line in Hebrew is simply "His foundation on the hills of holiness." The meaning expressed by RSV and TEV is found also in SPCL, FRCL, TOB, Dahood. It is possible to take "his foundation" as a reference to the Temple as Yahweh's dwelling place; but the psalm is in praise of the city of Jerusalem, not of the Temple as such. **The holy mount** is Mount Zion (see 2.6). It may be preferable to translate the Hebrew plural "sacred hills" (literally, "hills of holiness") as a reference to the various hills on which Jerusalem was built (so TOB, FRCL). GECL's rendering of this verse is recommended as a good model: "The Lord has built his city, its foundation is his holy mountain." In many languages it will be more understandable to render **holy mount** as "God's Mount Zion" or "the mountain called Zion which belongs to God."

In verse 2 TEV **"the city of Jerusalem"** translates **the gates of Zion**, and **"any other place in Israel"** translates **all the dwelling places of Jacob**. Here **dwelling places** may mean towns and cities, in a general sense (so TEV, FRCL), or it may have the more restricted sense of sanctuaries, temples, as "dwelling places of God" (so Anderson). Of course the two are not mutually exclusive, but again the emphasis seems to be on Jerusalem, the city, and not on the Temple in particular. In some languages the comparative degree must be structured to say, for example, "God loves all the places in Israel, he loves most the city of Jerusalem."

In verse 3 Jerusalem is called **city of God**, which may be taken to mean the city that belongs to God or the city in which God lives; in this case both are true (see 46.4; 48.1,8). The Hebrew passive **are spoken of you** in line <u>a</u> may be an impersonal passive: "people say," "everyone says" (SPCL); but in light of what follows in verse 4, where God is the speaker, it seems preferable to understand that God is here the speaker (so TEV, BJ, NJB, GECL, FRCL). Most translations have the plural active form ("people say") or the passive ("are said"). For languages in which it is awkward to say **"Listen, city of God,"** it is often possible to recast this as a simile and say "Listen, people of God's city," or more in the RSV style, "God says good things about you, Jerusalem," or ". . . people of Jerusalem."

For *Selah* see 3.2.

87.4   RSV   TEV

Among those who know me I men-   "I will include Egypt and Babylo-
   tion Rahab and Babylon;   nia
behold, Philistia and Tyre, with   when I list the nations that
   Ethiopia—   obey me;
"This one was born there," they   the people of Philistia, Tyre, and
   say.   Ethiopia
                                            I will number among the inhab-
                                                itants of Jerusalem."

The Hebrew text says quite simply that the various nations mentioned
acknowledge, or will acknowledge, Yahweh, and they are counted as belonging to the
people of God. This may have been the intention of the author (see 86.9); or else
the text means that Yahweh includes all Jews who live in those countries, the Jews
of the Diaspora (Dispersion); or else it means that the people in those countries who
have converted to Judaism (proselytes) are included among God's people. Whatever
interpretation, the translator should give either the names of the countries, or else
their inhabitants, with no further restrictive description.

Translations vary on the time references of the verbs in verse 4: TEV, NJB, NIV,
and Dahood have the future; RSV, BJ, TOB, FRCL, NJV, and SPCL have the present.
Translators should follow the best tense or mode that fits the local language.

RSV shows the form of the Hebrew text. The meaning of the first two lines is
fairly clear; **those who know me** designates people who worship, obey, serve Yahweh
(NEB "my friends"; NJB, NJV "those who acknowledge me").

"Egypt" translates **Rahab**, a poetic name for the country (see Isa 30.7). The use
of this name recalls Egypt as the monster that devoured Israel (see 89.10). For
Ethiopia see comments at 68.31.

The third line of the verse is obscure; the Hebrew text says simply **This one was
born there**, without any indication of who **this one** is or where **there** is; nor does the
Hebrew have **they say** of RSV. TEV takes the text to mean that the people born in
those countries are listed as having been born in Jerusalem, so that they are full-
fledged citizens, belonging to the people of God. One possible version is "will be
reckoned as citizens of Zion"; SPCL "all of them were born in you" (that is,
Jerusalem).

It is possible, as some do, to take this verse to mean that the people of those
countries were all born in those countries (so FRCL); but of all it will be said "They
were born in Zion" (verse 5). In either case the meaning is the same. The Septuagint
has in verse 5 "Everyone will say, 'Zion is our mother.' " It is possible that Paul had
this passage in mind when writing Galatians 4.26.

87.5-6   RSV   TEV

5   And of Zion it shall be said,   5   Of Zion it will be said
        "This one and that one were   that all nations belong there
           born in her";   and that the Almighty will make
     for the Most High himself will   her strong.
        establish her.   6   The LORD will write a list of the
6   The LORD records as he registers   peoples

| the peoples,
"This one was born there."
<center>*Selah*</center> | and include them all as citizens
of Jerusalem. |

These verses repeat the thought of verse 4. In verse 5 **This one and that one** is an idiomatic phrase meaning "everyone"; TEV **"all nations"**; NEB "men of every race"; TOB, NJV "Every man." But the reference may be restricted to those people listed in verse 4 (so FRCL). It seems better to take the text to mean that all peoples will be among God's people. They are all "reckoned as citizens of Zion"; the thought, on the surface at least, is that all peoples (or, all those people) will be counted as belonging to God's people. Both TEV and RSV express the first line as a future passive, which in many languages must be recast as a future active. Since it is God who makes these statements, the translator may say, for example, "God will say about Zion . . . ."

The third line of verse 5 bears no logical relationship to the first line; it is more appropriate with verse 1 (so Weiser, NEB). Some treat it as a relative clause, "the city which the Most High himself has established"; TOB "and it is the Most High who strengthens her." Dahood is like TEV: "and the Most High will make her secure." In English "her" is used to refer to cities and localities as if they were female.

For comments on **the Most High**, see 7.17.

The Lord is pictured in verse 6 as making a register of all the citizens of Jerusalem, in which he includes all peoples. See 69.28 for a similar figure of a list of citizens. RSV **The LORD records as he registers the peoples**, followed by a direct quotation, is an unclear use of the verb "to record." NJV "The LORD will inscribe in the register of peoples that each was born there" is clear (see also NEB, NJB, NIV).

87.7   RSV   TEV

| Singers and dancers alike say,
"All my springs are in you." | They dance and sing,
"In Zion is the source of all our
blessings." |

In this verse the Hebrew is simply "And singers like dancers all my springs in you." It is assumed that the words "all my springs (are) in you" represent what "singers and dancers" say. But some Hebrew manuscripts have "princes" instead of "singers"; so BJ and NJB. And the Hebrew word translated "(like) dancers" is taken by BJ and NJB to be from another root, "to beget"; so NJB translates, "princes no less than native-born."

Springs is used figuratively as a source; so TEV **"the source of all our blessings"**; or else "Zion is the source of all our blessedness." Toombs refers to 46.4, which speaks of the river "that brings joy to the city of God" (see also 36.8,9).[1]

Instead of **my springs** the Septuagint and Vulgate have "dwelling place," which SPCL and NAB adopt: "My home is in you" (so Briggs). Actually the Septuagint is

---

[1]HOTTP gives the following translation of this verse: "and singing as well as dancing (they say) 'all my springs (are) in you.' " In this context, HOTTP says, "springs" refers to origin.

"and they all rejoice (whose) dwelling (is) in you." NEB emends the Hebrew "all my springs" to "they all chant"; Dahood emends to "all who have suffered."

The least that can be said is that verse 7 in the Masoretic text is difficult and obscure, and that it takes a bit of good will to make sense of it without any changes in the Hebrew text. If the translator follows the lead of TEV, **"source of all our blessings"** will have to be recast in some languages to say, for example, "Zion is the place from which we receive all good things" or "We get all the good things from Zion." Probably the best model to follow is GECL: "All dance for joy and sing, 'Zion, in you we are at home!' "

Psalm 88

Of all the psalms of lament this one is the most despairing. There is not one word of joy, or hope, or confidence; unrelieved gloom is not pierced by a single ray of light. The last word of the psalm is "darkness."

But the first words are "Yahweh God, my Savior"; even where there is no hope, the psalmist cries to Yahweh, whom he calls "my Savior." The prayer is not an exercise in futility; the psalmist must pray, even though, humanly speaking, there is no reason to pray. This psalm has traditionally been used by Christians for reading on Good Friday.

The language indicates that the psalmist suffered from an incurable disease that had afflicted him all his life (verse 15), perhaps leprosy. It caused him to be shunned by all (verses 8, 18). The psalmist considered his hopeless situation to be God's punishment (verses 7, 14, 16-17), and so in his despair he cries to God to relent and save him; his death, which seemed imminent, would take him to Sheol, the place where he would be cut off completely from any fellowship with Yahweh (verses 5, 10-12).

The psalm opens with a cry to God for help (verses 1-2), followed by a description of the psalmist's hopeless condition (verses 3-9). Again he cries to God for mercy, mixing petition with a description of his pitiful condition (verses 10-18).

HEADING: **"A Cry for Help."** Other headings are: "Unrelieved sorrow"; "Lament and prayer in affliction"; "A cry from the depths"; "A stubborn faith." The TEV heading may be filled out, for the requirements of some languages, to say "The psalmist cries out to God for help" or "The psalmist prays that God will help him."

Hebrew title: **A Song. A Psalm of the Sons of Korah. To the choirmaster: according to Mahalath Leannoth. A Maskil of Heman the Ezrahite** (TEV "A psalm by the clan of Korah; a song. A poem by Heman the Ezrahite").

For **Song** and **Psalm** see title of Psalm 65; for **the Sons of Korah** see title of Psalm 42; for **choirmaster** see title of Psalm 4; for **Maskil** see title of Psalm 32. There is no agreement on the meaning of **Mahalath Leannoth** (see "Mahalath" in title of Psa 53). The Hebrew *leannoth* may mean "for affliction" or "for singing." NJB translates here "In sickness In suffering"; Kirkpatrick suggests it may mean "for singing antiphonally."

It is not certain who **Heman the Ezrahite** was. 1 Chronicles 6.33 names Heman son of Joel as one of the music leaders in the Temple. The designation "the Ezrahite" is also given to Ethan in the title of Psalm 89; probably he is the one referred to in 1 Kings 4.31 (nowhere else other than in these three passages does "the Ezrahite" occur); he is there associated with Ethan and two other men. There is no certain way of identifying the Heman in this title or the Ethan in the title of Psalm 89 with any of the other men who have these names in Kings and Chronicles.

It is supposed that "Ezrahite" means "son of Zerah" (see in 1 Chr 2.6 Ethan and Heman, two of the five sons of Zerah). Dahood, BJ, and NJB translate the title "Ezrahite" by "the native-born," by which is meant someone whose ancestors had been native Canaanites (that is, aborigines), not Israelites.

How the same composition is called **A Psalm of the Sons of Korah** and **A Maskil of Heman the Ezrahite** cannot be explained.

	88.1-2 RSV		TEV
1	O LORD, my God, I call for help[t] by day; I cry out in the night before thee.	1	LORD God, my savior, I cry out all day, and at night I come before you.
2	Let my prayer come before thee, incline thy ear to my cry!	2	Hear my prayer; listen to my cry for help!

[t] Cn: Heb *O LORD, God of my salvation.*

In the opening cry for help the psalmist addresses God as "Yahweh, God of my salvation." After this the Masoretic text has "by day I cry (and) at night before you," which Dahood translates "day and night I cry to you" (so SPCL, NIV, TOB); NJV translates as a temporal clause, "when I cry out in the night before You . . . ." Many emend the text as RSV has done, **I call for help by day; I cry out in the night before thee** (also AT, NEB, NAB, NJB). Weiser and FRCL are like TEV. Although not free of difficulty, the Masoretic text can be translated; see Anderson, Dahood.[1] **"My savior"** must be expressed as a verb phrase in some languages; for example, "God who saves me" or "God the one who rescues me." For the verb "to save" see comments on "Help" in 12.1. **Cry out** should not be translated by a term for "shout" but rather by one which carries the element of sadness and distress. In some languages the equivalent is to mourn. If the verb to mourn is only used in connection with a death, then it is sometimes possible to say, for example, "I cry out in my sadness," or as a simile, "I cry like one who is mourning for the dead."

In verse 2 TEV **"Hear"** stands for "May (my prayer) come before you" (see RSV), and **"listen"** translates "bend your ear" (see 17.6). **Let my prayer come before thee** may sometimes be rendered as "Hear the words that I pray to you."

	88.3-5 RSV		TEV
3	For my soul is full of troubles, and my life draws near to Sheol.	3	So many troubles have fallen on me that I am close to death.
4	I am reckoned among those who		

---

[1]HOTTP says there are two possible interpretations of the Masoretic text: (1) "God of my salvation during the day I cried and in the night before you"; (2) "God of my salvation when (literally, the day when) I cried in the night before you."

	go down to the Pit; I am a man who has no strength,	4	I am like all others who are about to die; all my strength is gone.[c]
5	like one forsaken among the dead, like the slain that lie in the grave, like those whom thou dost remem- ber no more, for they are cut off from thy hand.	5	I am abandoned among the dead; I am like the slain lying in their graves, those you have forgotten com- pletely, who are beyond your help.

[c] all my strength is gone; *or* there is no help for me.

The psalmist graphically describes himself as practically a dead man, one whose life has been crushed out by the Lord's punishment. In verses 3-4 he uses a variety of words and phrases to describe his condition: his *nefesh* (see 3.2) is **full of troubles**, and his life **draws near to Sheol** (see description of **Sheol** in 6.5). In some languages **troubles** are grammatically considered to be active agents which perform events; for example, "troubles have taken hold of me" or "troubles hang about my head." TEV's "**close to death**" is often expressed as "**I am about to die**," as in TEV verse 4a.

The psalmist is regarded as being **among those who go down to the Pit** (see comments on 28.1; 30.3). The verb translated **reckoned** means "to count, to number"; that is, others include him among people who are about to die. So FRCL "Everybody considers me as a man who has reached the end (of his life)." **The Pit** (verses 4a, 6a) is a synonym for Sheol, the world of the dead. In the first line of verse 4, RSV employs the passive voice **I am reckoned**, which must be expressed in the active voice in many languages, as FRCL has done; for example, "people look upon me like a corpse" or "people think of me as a dead man."

In verse 4b the Hebrew word translated **strength** occurs only here in the Old Testament; it may mean "help" (so McCullough; TEV footnote; NJV "helpless"; FRCL "one for whom nothing more can be done"). It is recommended that the word be translated **strength**.

The psalmist compares himself to a lifeless corpse left unburied (verse 5a); he is like a dead man already buried (verse 5b). In line a the word translated **forsaken** (a noun in Hebrew) means in other contexts "free, released" (so KJV here "free among the dead"). Anderson suggests "unclean among the dead"; Oesterley thinks that the similarity of this word to the word for a leper's house in 2 Kings 15.5 (which RSV translates "a separate house") implies that the psalmist was a leper. It may be that the psalmist meant that the dead are "freed" from God, no longer obliged to serve and worship him. The meaning "abandoned," that is, like a corpse that is not buried, seems to fit the context better.[2]

In verse 5b the word **grave** in Hebrew is singular, and some think the picture is that of a number of dead bodies on the battlefield being buried in one grave. If the

---

[2] HOTTP says the word means "freed, exempted," and seems to refer to the total "freedom" that death brings "from the bonds and obligations of life, society, bondage, and labor."

translator follows the suggestion of **like the slain** referring to the bodies of slain soldiers, one may say, for example, "I am like one of the dead warriors in a common grave."

In verse 5c,d the psalmist strikes the first note of the mournful theme that he has been rejected by God: the dead are "**forgotten completely**" (TEV) by God (see in verse 12b where Sheol is called "the land of oblivion," that is, the land whose inhabitants are forgotten by God); here "**forgotten**" means ignored, disregarded, overlooked. FRCL translates "you no longer have any regard for them." The dead are beyond his help (literally **cut off from thy hand**); SPCL "they have lost your protection"; NJV "cut off from Your care." **Cut off from thy hand** may be rendered, for example, "you do nothing more for them" or "you help them no more."

88.6-7   RSV   TEV

6   Thou hast put me in the depths of   6   You have thrown me into the
         the Pit,   depths of the tomb,
     in the regions dark and deep.   into the darkest and deepest pit.
7   Thy wrath lies heavy upon me,   7   Your anger lies heavy on me,
     and thou dost overwhelm me   and I am crushed beneath its
         with all thy waves.   *Selah*   waves.

These two verses are even more explicit: it is God who has placed the psalmist **in the depths of the Pit**, that is, Sheol, a dark and deep abyss (see similar language in 69.2,15). FRCL translates verse 6b "in the deep darkness of death." In many languages RSV **Pit** will not signify death or near death. TEV's "**tomb**" suggests in English a structure for burial of the dead, either in the ground or particularly above the ground. In languages in which burial is not in the ground, some adaptation is required; for example, "You have thrown me into the place of dead bodies, into the darkest and deepest hole."

The psalmist feels on himself the full weight of God's **wrath**, which crushes him as though it were giant **waves** (see 42.7; Jonah 2.2-3 for similar language). TEV has related "**waves**" to "**Your anger**" and made the two halves of verse 7 parallel. FRCL, in a similar way, says "your anger has crushed me in waves that overwhelm me." In some languages the idea of verse 7 may be expressed as a simile; for example, "Your anger has been like sea waves crushing me" or "You have been angry at me like sea waves knocking me down." In languages in which "waves" are meaningless, the translator may be able to accomplish the same poetic effect with wind or some other natural force.

For *Selah* see 3.2.

88.8-9   RSV   TEV

8   Thou hast caused my companions   8   You have caused my friends to
         to shun me;   abandon me;
     thou hast made me a thing of   you have made me repulsive to
         horror to them.   them.

765

I am shut in so that I cannot escape;	I am closed in and cannot escape;
9 my eye grows dim through sorrow.	9 my eyes are weak from suffering.
Every day I call upon thee, O LORD;	LORD, every day I call to you
I spread out my hands to thee.	and lift my hands to you in prayer.

The psalmist seems to refer to his physical condition, which causes his friends to shun him (verse 8a,b); this may have been leprosy or some other loathsome disease (see Job 19.13-19; Psa 31.11). In verse 8b **a thing of horror** is variously translated: "loathsome" (NEB); "abhorrent" (NJV); "unbearable" (SPCL); "a disgusting thing" (FRCL); **"repulsive"** (TEV, NJB, NIV). The statement in verse 8c **I am shut in** may be literal, perhaps meaning prison (NEB, NAB, NJB) or quarantine (NIV "confined"; RSV, AT, NJV **shut in**); or it may be figurative, that is, he is hemmed in by his troubles and cannot escape (so FRCL). Briggs and Dahood believe the psalmist is speaking of himself as a prisoner in Sheol. Toombs interprets the words as a figure of deprivation, restriction, the contrary to that of salvation, which is characterized by openness, space (see 18.19).

For verse 9a see similar language in 31.9b; 38.10b. It is more natural in English to refer to one's **"eyes"** (TEV) when both are meant, than to one's **eye** (RSV).

Despite the Lord's fury and anger, the psalmist persists in praying to him for help (verse 9b,c); **Every day** (or "all day long," that is, insistently, continually) he cries out to the Lord. For **spread out my hands** see comments on "lift up my hands" in 28.2.

<u>**88.10-12**</u>   RSV   TEV

10 Dost thou work wonders for the dead?	10 Do you perform miracles for the dead?
Do the shades rise up to praise thee? *Selah*	Do they rise up and praise you?
11 Is thy steadfast love declared in the grave,	11 Is your constant love spoken of in the grave
or thy faithfulness in Abaddon?	or your faithfulness in the place of destruction?
12 Are thy wonders known in the darkness,	12 Are your miracles seen in that place of darkness
or thy saving help in the land of forgetfulness?	or your goodness in the land of the forgotten?

In these three verses, by means of rhetorical questions the psalmist gives expression to the belief that the dead in Sheol are completely cut off from Yahweh's care and concern. Yahweh performs no **wonders** there (verses 10a,12a), as he had when he freed his people from Egypt. His **steadfast love** (*chesed*; see comments, 5.7), his **faithfulness** (*'emunah*; see 36.5), his **saving help** (*tsedaqah*; see 5.8) are all absent from Sheol, which is called **the grave** (see verse 5b), **Abaddon**, which means "destruction" (the Hebrew name comes from the verb "to perish"—see comments on "broken" in 31.12), **the darkness** (see verse 6), **the land of forgetfulness** (verse 12b), that is, the land where the inhabitants are forgotten by God (see verse 5c). It is less likely, as SPCL has it, that **the land of forgetfulness** means "the land where everything is forgotten." All these names and phrases accurately portray the concept of Sheol, the world of the dead, which was prevalent at that time. TEV has imitated the Hebrew in using rhetorical questions in verses 10-12 as an effective way of expressing the despairing, hopeless attitude of the psalmist. In some cases strong negative statements may be more effective; for example:

> You make no miracles for the dead,
>   and they do not rise up and praise you.
> Your constant love is never mentioned in the grave,
>   and no one speaks of your faithfulness in the place of destruction.
> No one sees your miracles in that place of darkness,
>   nor your goodness in the land of the forgotten.

Abaddon or TEV's **"place of destruction"** is synonymous with **the grave,** and the translator should avoid giving the impression that they refer to different places. **Wonders known** must often be recast as active; for example, "Do the dead in the grave see the great works that you do?" **Land of forgetfulness** may sometimes be rendered as "that place of the dead where God is no longer concerned with dead people" or "in the grave where God pays no attention to the dead."

In line 10a the psalmist speaks of **the dead**, but in line **b** he uses the more dramatic **shades**. In 11a the ordinary term **grave** is paralleled in 11b by the more literary level **Abaddon**, and in 12a the common **darkness** is matched by the more imaginative **land of forgetfulness**. In this series of parallel lines the writer is moving the idea of death forward toward the point of total extinction. Translators should pay particular attention to see that the terms they use and the poetic devices they employ reflect this movement.

In verse 10b the dead are called **the shades**. The Hebrews did not speak of the "souls" or "spirits" of the dead surviving in Sheol, as did the Greeks; the "shades" or "shadows" were pale, lifeless, ineffectual, shadowy images or replicas of the former living, active, robust self. Care should be taken not to picture them as ghosts, however, since this introduces elements not present in the Hebrew concept.

In the translation of the rhetorical questions in verses 10-12, the translator must first decide if such a sequence of questions is natural in the receptor language. If the questions are natural, do they require responses, since they assume a negative reply? Are there implicit elements that need to be made explicit in the receptor language? If the keeping of the question form will result in an unnatural style, the translator may have to recast these questions as statements. Examples are given here of two ways to handle the questions of verse 10 and three ways to treat them in verse 11. The same applies equally well to verse 12 or to any other rhetorical question. Verse 10: "Do you make miracles for the dead? No! Do the dead praise you? Never!" or, as negative statements, "You do not perform miracles for the dead, and they do not get up and praise you." In verse 11: "Is your constant love spoken of in the grave? No! Is your faithfulness spoken of in the place of the dead? Never!" As negative statements: "Your constant love is not spoken of in the grave, nor is your faithfulness spoken of in the place of the dead." With further adjustments for implicit information: "Do the dead in their graves speak about how you always love them, or do they talk about how faithful you are to them in the world of the dead?" Each question in the last rendering may in turn be followed by a negative reply or may be transformed into a negative statement, each case depending on the requirements of the receptor language.

88.13-14   RSV   TEV

	RSV	TEV
13	But I, O LORD, cry to thee; in the morning my prayer comes before thee.	13 LORD, I call to you for help; every morning I pray to you.
14	O LORD, why dost thou cast me off? Why dost thou hide thy face from me?	14 Why do you reject me, LORD? Why do you turn away from me?

Once again the psalmist cries to the Lord for help. **In the morning** (that is, "**every morning**") he prays to him—but in vain! See similar statements about morning prayer in 5.13; 55.17; 82.2.

For verse 14 see similar language in 10.1; 13.1; 22.1; 27.9; 44.23; 74.1. For **cast me off** see 43.2 and comment; and for **hide thy face** see 13.1 and comments. The psalmist feels completely rejected and abandoned by God; and the absence of any confession of sin in this psalm makes even more poignant the psalmist's desperate situation. The questions in verse 14 are real; the psalmist would like to know why Yahweh is treating him like this.

88.15-18   RSV   TEV

	RSV	TEV
15	Afflicted and close to death from my youth up, I suffer thy terrors; I am help- less.[u]	15 Ever since I was young, I have suffered and been near death; I am worn out[d] from the bur- den of your punishments.
16	Thy wrath has swept over me; thy dread assaults destroy me.	16 Your furious anger crushes me; your terrible attacks destroy me.
17	They surround me like a flood all day long; they close in upon me together.	17 All day long they surround me like a flood; they close in on me from every side.
18	Thou hast caused lover and friend to shun me; my companions are in darkness.	18 You have made even my closest friends abandon me, and darkness is my only com- panion.

[u] The meaning of the Hebrew word is uncertain

^d *Probable text* I am worn out; *Hebrew unclear.*

In verse 15a the psalmist alludes to his life-long illness, which we cannot identify with certainty; he sees it as coming from God (verse 15b). **Thy terrors** means the terrifying things Yahweh has done; FRCL "the terror that you impose on me"; SPCL "I have endured terrible things you have done to me." TEV **"your punishments"** may imply that these things happen as a result of sin, but that idea does not occur in the Hebrew of this psalm. SPCL "terrible things" is better. **I am helpless** translates a word found only here in the Old Testament and whose meaning is uncertain; SPCL "I can't take it any more!"; NJB "I am finished"; NIV "and am in despair." NJV, following the Jewish commentator Saadia, translates "wherever I turn."

The psalmist feels crushed and destroyed (literally "silenced"; so Weiser) by the blows which God, in his anger, rains down on him (verse 16). In line a **swept over** translates a verb meaning to assail or overwhelm, like a strong wind that blows everything down (see its use in 103.16a). There is no escaping from God's attacks (verse 17; see similar language in verse 7). They are like enemies all around him who are moving in to kill him.

Verse 18a repeats the thought of verse 8a; although RSV (also NEB) **lover** is a possible translation of the Hebrew word, it is not suitable in the context. It may be that the psalmist was referring to his wife; it is certain he would not have meant "lover" in the common meaning of the word today. NIV has "my companions and loved ones"; FRCL "all my friends"; GECL and NJV "friend and neighbor"; and SPCL "friends and companions."

The last line in Hebrew is "my acquaintances darkness," which TEV and others understand to mean **"and darkness is my only companion"** (Dahood, Weiser, Cohen; HOTTP; BJ, NJB, FRCL, GECL, NIV, TOB, NAB, SPCL; Dahood takes "Darkness" as a name for Sheol). It does not seem probable that the Hebrew means, as AT and RSV have, **my companions are in darkness**. For languages in which an abstract such as **darkness** could not naturally be said to be a companion, it is possible to recast this figurative expression to say something like "every place I go there is only darkness" or "wherever I am it is always dark."

NEB places different vowels on the Hebrew consonants to get the meaning "and deprived me of my companions"; this is exactly parallel with line a and may be the meaning intended; but the Masoretic text does make sense, and it is to be preferred.

769

Psalm 89

This psalm has three clearly marked sections: (1) Verses 1-18 are a hymn in praise of Yahweh as supreme Lord and Creator of the universe. (2) Verses 19-37 are an oracle in which God restates the eternal covenant he made with David, that there would always be a descendant of David's as king of Israel; even if David's descendants proved unfaithful, God would not break his promise and he would ensure the perpetuity of the Davidic dynasty. (3) Verses 38-51 are a lament over the defeat of the king and a prayer for his deliverance. The lament (verses 38-45) seems to be a community lament; the prayer for deliverance (verses 46-51) is by an individual, who in verse 50 is identified as the king himself. Verse 52 is not part of the psalm; it is a concluding doxology for Book Three (Psalms 73–89).

Most scholars believe the psalm is a composite work, bringing together three or more separate compositions. The final part (verses 38-51) clearly reflects a recent defeat of the king of Israel. There is no complete agreement on which national defeat is meant; most believe that it is either the defeat of Jehoiachin in 597 B.C. or the defeat of Zedekiah and the fall of Jerusalem in 587 B.C. It would have been such an event as this which would have provided the occasion for the psalm's composition.

Psalm 89 is particularly instructive from the point of view of its parallelism and recurring themes of steadfast love, faithfulness, and covenant. A large majority of the verses are characterized by two (and sometimes three) lines in which the second line completes the first by carrying it to a more dramatic, specific, or concrete level. In this way line b tends to go beyond line a, raising the idea in line a to a more intense poetic level, and thereby expressing the thought "A is so, and what is more, B is so." A typical representative of this kind of parallelism in Psalm 89 is verse 25: line a **I will set his hand on the sea**; line b **his right hand on the rivers**. (See also verse 9, where **sea** in line a is matched in line b by **waves**.) In verse 12 **north and south** are matched by the names of places, **Tabor and Hermon**. Although this is the predominant pattern in Psalm 89, there are always exceptions which confirm the rule; in verse 21 **hand:arm**; verse 40 **walls:strongholds**. Since the themes are built into the parallel lines, it is not possible to modify one without affecting the other. For example, reducing parallel lines to a single line may mean that a key word at the theme level is deemphasized or removed completely. How the translator will render parallel lines in which the second line intensifies the whole parallel unit depends upon the poetic resources of the receptor language. At the same time the translator has the task of giving the themes the prominence the psalmist has given them.

HEADING: TEV has four headings, marking the various sections of the psalm. The first one is "**A Hymn in Time of National Trouble.**" Headings in other translations are: "The covenant of God with David"; "A crisis of the old covenant"; "The sorrow of Judah." If the translator follows the TEV headings, the first may be recast in some languages to say, for example, "This is a hymn to be sung when Israel is in trouble." The other TEV headings will be discussed at their place in the text.

<u>Hebrew title</u>: **A Maskil of Ethan the Ezrahite** (TEV "A poem by Ethan the Ezrahite").

For comments see title of Psalm 88.

89.1-2	RSV	TEV

	RSV	TEV
1	I will sing of thy steadfast love, O LORD,^v for ever; with my mouth I will proclaim thy faithfulness to all generations.	1 O LORD, I will always sing of your constant love; I will proclaim your faithfulness forever.
2	For thy steadfast love was established for ever, thy faithfulness is firm as the heavens.	2 I know that your love will last for all time, that your faithfulness is as permanent as the sky.

^v Gk: Heb *the steadfast love of the LORD*

The psalm begins with praise to Yahweh. In Hebrew verse 1a is "I will sing of Yahweh's constant love forever," with Yahweh referred to in the third person, whereas in line <u>b</u> the second person of direct address is used. For consistency RSV and TEV use the second person in both lines; it is not necessary (like RSV footnote) to treat this as a textual matter. In Hebrew the word for **steadfast love** is plural (see 5.7 and comments), which may mean "acts of constant love" (FRCL "your acts of kindness"); but here (as in the Hebrew of 17.7; 25.6) the plural is probably used for emphasis. For **faithfulness** see 36.5 and comments; **to all generations** translates "to generation and generation" (TEV "**for ever**"), which is a phrase meaning "for all time" (parallel with **for ever** in line <u>a</u>), which is a more suitable translation in English than **to all generations**.

With my mouth I will proclaim in line 1b is parallel with **I will sing** in line <u>a</u>. This is typical heightening of poetic effect through the use of a more concrete or picturable level of vocabulary in <u>b</u>. Since this dynamic kind of parallelism must be taken as a unit, translators should not normally reduce such lines to one. Not only is the poetic heightening lost, but the key words (in this case, **steadfast love** and **faithfulness**) are not brought to the foreground. However, if the parallel line structure does not serve the poetic function intended, then the translator should find an alternative solution for the receptor language.

In some languages **steadfast love** and **faithfulness** must be recast as verb phrases. Such recasting often requires the introduction of a goal such as "a song" and "the people" (here meaning Israel); for example, "I will sing a song telling how you always love your people; even more, I will proclaim to the people that you are always faithful to your people."

Verse 2 begins in Hebrew with "For I said" (or, say), which TEV represents by "**I know that**"; also possible is "I acknowledge that"; NIV has "I will declare." RSV and others follow the Septuagint, Syriac, and Vulgate in reading "you said," and transfer the phrase to the beginning of verse 3 (strangely enough, RSV has no textual footnote). The verb translated **was established** means "to build"; here it is better to say, like NEB, "is firm" (see NIV); SPCL has "is eternal."

In line **b** the Masoretic text is "you establish in the heavens your faithfulness"; two Hebrew manuscripts, instead of "in the heavens," have "as the heavens," which TEV and others follow. The verb in the Masoretic text has vowels for the second singular active "you establish"; but other vowels may be used to make the verb a third person singular passive, "is established." NJV translates the Masoretic text "there in the heavens You establish Your faithfulness." Parallel with line **a**, however, it seems better to translate like RSV, **is firm as the heavens**; so Weiser, TEV, NEB, SPCL. But most translations have "in the heavens." If this is preferred, a translation can say "heaven is (the place) where your constant faithfulness is to be found." In languages in which verb phrases will be required, as in verse 1, one may say, for example, "I know that you will love your people forever." The second line will require further adjustment in some languages where the verb phrase will be accompanied by the simile **as the heavens**. For example, "I know that you will be as faithful to your people as the sky, which they can always see."

89.3-4   RSV   TEV

	RSV		TEV
3	Thou hast said, "I have made a covenant with my chosen one, I have sworn to David my servant:	3	You said, "I have made a covenant with the man I chose; I have promised my servant David,
4	'I will establish your descendants for ever, and build your throne for all generations.' " *Selah*	4	'A descendant of yours will always be king; I will preserve your dynasty forever.' "

In verse 3 God is the speaker, which RSV indicates by **Thou hast said** (also TEV **"You said"**); it should be noted that the Hebrew text does not have these words here (see comments on verse 2, above). The psalmist recalls God's promise to King David that the throne of Israel would always be occupied by a descendant of David's (see 2 Sam 7.16, God's message to David by the prophet Nathan). **My chosen one** in line **a** is a reference to **David my servant** in line **b** (see also verses 19-20). The translator cannot assume in every case that **my chosen one** and **David my servant** will be understood to be the same person. In order to avoid the reader's thinking of these as two different persons, it may be necessary to say, for example, "I have made a covenant with David whom I chose, and what is more, I have sworn to be faithful to him." For comments on **covenant** see 25.10.

In verse 4a the Hebrew "I will forever establish your seed" (see "descendants" and comments in 18.50) is to be understood in light of **and build your throne for all generations** in line **b**. It is not simply a promise that David will always have descendants, but that the Davidic dynasty will never end; descendants of David will always be the kings of Israel. SPCL translates the verse "I will ensure that your descendants will always succeed you as king." It is to be noticed that in verse 2 the Hebrew verbs are "build . . . be firm," and in verse 4 "be firm . . . build."

TEV's **"preserve your dynasty"** simply repeats line a in reference to the throne. Although the two lines appear to say much the same thing, the poetic movement is from **establish your descendants**, a somewhat abstract idea, to the more concrete image **build your throne**. Translations such as SPCL and TEV translate the message of the verse, but sacrifice the poetic "going beyond" which is an integral part of the parallelism. The two lines as a unit may be rendered, for example, "Not only will I always make a descendant of yours to be king, I will also keep your dynasty forever" or ". . . I will make them rule after you forever."

For **Selah** see 3.2.

89.5-7	RSV	TEV

	RSV	TEV
5	Let the heavens praise thy wonders, O LORD, thy faithfulness in the assembly of the holy ones!	The heavens sing of the wonderful things you do; the holy ones sing of your faithfulness, LORD.
6	For who in the skies can be compared to the LORD? Who among the heavenly beings[w] is like the LORD,	No one in heaven is like you, LORD; none of the heavenly beings is your equal.
7	a God feared in the council of the holy ones, great and terrible[x] above all that are round about him?	You are feared in the council of the holy ones; they all stand in awe of you.

[w] Or *sons of gods*
[x] Gk Syr: Heb *greatly terrible*

Verses 5-18 are a hymn praising Yahweh's greatness as supreme over all creation. The psalmist calls upon the beings in heaven to proclaim God's greatness. They are called **the holy ones** (verses 5b,7a) and "sons of gods" (verse 6b). They form an **assembly** (verse 5b), a **council** (verse 7a) around God (verse 7b); they are subordinate to him (verse 6) and fear him (verse 7b).

In verse 5a **the heavens** means "all heavenly beings," "all creatures (or, living beings) in heaven," in parallel with **the holy ones** in line b.

The holy ones in verses 5b,7a are thought of either as the gods of other nations, as in 82.1 (so Oesterley and others), or as the angels (Briggs, FRCL, and others); McCullough calls them angels and demigods. Dahood defines them as "the divine beings who comprise the court of Yahweh." The "sons of gods" in verse 6b are to be identified as gods (see also 29.1); Anderson defines them as "those belonging to the class of gods." Translations vary: "the sons of gods" (Weiser, BJ), "sons of God" (NAB), "the gods" (Dahood, SPCL, TOB), "divine beings" (NJV). If the translator does not use "angels," some expression for "divine beings" may be used. In many languages a term for such beings will be associated with the idea of "idols." However, these are not idols, and the translator should not identify them as being part of the unseen world of evil. In some languages a generic term for God may be used, while in others a term for spirit, or "heavenly spirit" can be used, provided, of course, that this word does not refer to evil spirits. Therefore one can say, for example, "the spirits in heaven sing of the wonderful things which you do." The second line of verse 5 may be rendered "the spirits sing and tell in their heavenly meeting how faithful you are."

RSV shows that the Hebrew of verses 6-7 is in the form of a rhetorical question which refers to God in the third person; TEV uses declarative statements, addressed to God in the second person, in keeping with the second person in verse 5. If the translator uses the rhetorical question, the answer "no one" may have to be provided in some languages. SPCL does a good job of shortening and combining the two lines of verse 6: "No god, no one in heaven, can be compared to you, Lord!" FRCL has "Lord, you have no peer, up there; in the world of the gods, none is equal to you."

Yahweh is greater than any of the gods, and they all respect and fear him (verses 6-7). The two passive adjectives used to characterize God in verse 7 are "dreadful" and "fearful"—that is, God inspires dread and fear in those around him. TEV **"feared"** and **"stand in awe"** is rather weak; see NJV "greatly dreaded . . . awesome." Verse 7a may require recasting as an active verb; for example, "the spirits in the heavenly council fear you, God."

As the footnote in RSV verse 7b indicates, the Hebrew word "greatly" is not the normal form used in a context like this, and some translators feel the need to emend, following the Septuagint; so RSV, NEB, BJ, NJB, NAB. Others, like Dahood, SPCL, and TEV, believe that the Masoretic text, though unusual, does make sense.[1]

89.8-10 RSV   TEV

8   O LORD God of hosts,
     who is mighty as thou art, O
     LORD,
     with thy faithfulness round
     about thee?
9   Thou dost rule the raging of the
     sea;
     when its waves rise, thou stillest
     them.
10   Thou didst crush Rahab like a
     carcass,
     thou didst scatter thy enemies
     with thy mighty arm.
	8 LORD God Almighty, none is as
	     mighty as you;
	     in all things you are faithful, O
	     LORD.
	9 You rule over the powerful sea;
	     you calm its angry waves.
	10 You crushed the monster Rahab^f
	     and killed it;
	     with your mighty strength you
	     defeated your enemies.
	
	f RAHAB: *A legendary sea monster which*
	represented the forces of chaos and evil.

TEV restructures the three lines of RSV verse 8 as two lines. The psalmist (or the congregation) praises God's power as Creator (verses 8-14). For translation

---

[1] HOTTP criticizes both RSV and NEB translations of the Masoretic text and says the translation should be "(very fearful), in the council of saints, greatly, and terrible."

suggestions on the title "Yahweh God of armies" in verse 8a (LORD God of hosts), see 46.7. LORD in verse 8b translates *Yah* (see 68.4 and comments).

The word translated **mighty** occurs only here in the Old Testament. Some (Briggs, Weiser), instead of the Masoretic text **mighty**, read "your constant love," which offers a more satisfactory text but is not necessarily the true text.

TEV "**in all things you are faithful**" translates "your faithfulness (is) around you." It is difficult to understand the precise notion of **faithfulness** here (in verse 2 it is joined to "steadfast love," both of which are the main characteristics of God's attitude toward his people). Here Yahweh's role as Creator is in focus, and it is hard to understand why the psalmist singled out this particular characteristic. Cohen explains: "loyalty to his promises enwraps him like a garment." The word is probably to be understood as speaking of Yahweh's constancy, his consistency; all he does is in keeping with his character as sovereign Lord of the universe and of his people.

Verses 9-10 describe the creation in language similar to 74.13-14 (see comments there). **The raging of the sea** represents the primeval force of chaos, the watery abyss, which God subdued at creation. The expression **rule the raging of the sea** should not be translated by a term that refers to ruling as an administrator, but rather to controlling or subduing. In language areas in which the sea is unknown, a large body of water will have to be substituted, such as "the water of the lake" or "the water of the biggest river."

The mythological sea monster **Rahab** is referred to also in Job 9.13; 26.12; Isaiah 51.9. Unlike its use in 87.4, **Rahab** here refers to the mythological sea serpent. **Rahab** will require a footnote as in TEV, and cross references.

In 10b **scatter thy enemies** is the literal translation. TEV renders the practical effect: "defeated your enemies." TEV "**your mighty strength**" translates **thy mighty arm**.

89.11-12   RSV   TEV

11 The heavens are thine, the earth   11 Heaven is yours, the earth also;
    also is thine;   you made the world and every-
    the world and all that is in it,   thing in it.
    thou hast founded them.   12 You created the north and the
12 The north and the south, thou   south;
    hast created them;   Mount Tabor and Mount Her-
    Tabor and Hermon joyously   mon sing to you for joy.
    praise thy name.

God's role as Creator receives more praise. To him belong **the heavens** and **the earth**, because he created them; he created **the world and all that is in it**. The verb translated **founded** in verse 11b is used in similar contexts in 24.2a; 78.69b; 102.25a ("lay the foundation"). The sense is to build firmly, securely, parallel with the verb **created** in verse 12a.

It is not certain how **the north and the south** in verse 12 are to be understood; perhaps the phrase indicates the whole world, from one end to the other (so Anderson). Others (Dahood) see **north** (*tsafon*) as a reference to Mount Zaphon (see comments on 48.2), the sacred mountain of Baal, and the word translated **south** as the name of Mount Amanus (in southern Turkey); so NEB "Thou didst create Zaphon and Amanus." But this explanation has found little acceptance; HOTTP says it is possible. In some languages it is unnatural to speak of creating **the north and the south**. One must recast this expression to say sometimes "You created all that is in the north and all that is in the south" or "You created the land to the north and the land to the south."

Tabor was a mountain west of the south end of Lake Galilee, rising to a height of some 555 meters; for **Hermon** see 42.6 and comments. Both of them were considered sacred by the Canaanites. In verse 12b **"sing to you for joy"** may be taken to mean "praise you" (Hebrew "your name"; see RSV). In some languages it will be necessary to add a simile in order to translate verse 12b; for example, "like people singing, Mount Tabor and Mount Hermon sing joyfully to you."

89.13-14   RSV   TEV

13   Thou hast a mighty arm;   13   How powerful you are!
        strong is thy hand, high thy   How great is your strength!
        right hand.   14   Your kingdom is founded on
14   Righteousness and justice are the   righteousness and justice;
        foundation of thy throne;   love and faithfulness are shown
        steadfast love and faithfulness   in all you do.
        go before thee.

God's power and strength are spoken of in verse 13 as his **mighty arm**, **strong . . . hand**, and **high . . . right hand**, that is, the right hand lifted up as a gesture of power. The poetic movement is from **mighty arm** to **hand**, and finally **right hand**. However, in most languages these metaphors will be translated as nonmetaphors.

God's "kingdom" (RSV **throne**) is his rule over the whole universe; the four divine qualities, **righteousness** (see 5.8), **justice** (see 7.6), **steadfast love** and **faithfulness** (see verse 2), characterize his rule. The verb in verse 14b can be understood to mean either "go in front of, precede" (so NAB, RSV, NEB, GECL, FRCL, NJB, NIV, TOB, BJ) or "attend, wait on" (NJV "stand before you"); SPCL translates "come out to meet you." TEV **"are shown in all you do"** may be defended as an attempt to provide a meaningful statement; it may have been better, however, to say "your love and faithfulness go ahead of you as your messengers" (see similar language in 85.13). The passive construction of TEV will often have to be recast as active; for example, "You have built your kingdom on righteousness and justice" or, in some languages, "You have built your kingdom by being good and treating people justly."

89.15-16   RSV   TEV

15   Blessed are the people who know   15   How happy are the people who
        the festal shout,   worship you with songs,
        who walk, O LORD, in the light   who live in the light of your
        of thy countenance,   kindness!

16 who exult in thy name all the day, and extol*y* thy righteousness.	16 Because of you they rejoice all day long, and they praise you for your goodness.
y Cn: Heb *are exalted in.*	

In verses 15-18 the psalmist celebrates Yahweh's relationship to his people Israel. In verse 15a we are not sure exactly how **the festal shout** was expressed in Temple worship, but it certainly involved praise. The same term is used for the shout of the Israelites when the walls of Jericho fell, so it may have implied victory (Josh 6.20). It seems best to express the function of the words **know the festal shout** as "know how to sing praises to you," "know how to praise you with songs." NJB has "the nation that learns to acclaim you." And in verse 15b **who walk . . . in the light of thy countenance** means "who live in the light of your presence" (see NJV, NJB, NIV, NEB); see comments on 4.6; 44.3. Here **countenance** (that is, "face") is a way of indicating God's favor; God looks kindly, lovingly, approvingly on his people. So instead of TEV "**your kindness,**" something like "approval" or "favor" would be better.

In verse 16a TEV "**Because of you**" translates **in thy name**. In verse 16b RSV indicates there is a problem in the Hebrew text; but this may be more apparent than real. Anderson and others say that the Masoretic text may mean (parallel with line a) "they rejoice in your righteousness," that is, "they rejoice because you are righteous." The noun is *tsedaqah*, which TEV here translates "**goodness**"; Dahood has "generosity." But the line can be understood to mean "they are exalted through Your righteousness" (NJV; see also NEB, NAB), a thought similar to that of verse 17b. One cannot be dogmatic, but it would appear that this line is parallel with line a, as TEV and RSV translate it.[2] **Extol thy righteousness** or TEV "**. . . for your goodness**" must be recast in some languages to say "because you are good to them."

89.17-18	RSV	TEV

17 For thou art the glory of their strength; by thy favor our horn is exalted.	17 You give us great victories; in your love you make us triumphant.
18 For our shield belongs to the LORD, our king to the Holy One of Israel.	18 You, O LORD, chose our protector; you, the Holy God of Israel, gave us our king.

Verse 17a **thou art the glory of their strength** seems to mean "You give them your wonderful strength" (GECL); **glory** translates the same word used in 71.8; 78.61 (see comments there). NJV (similarly NEB) translates "You are their strength in which they glory"; another possible version is "Their splendor and their strength come from you" (similarly SPCL, NIV); FRCL "You are their sovereign strength." Dahood "you are our glorious triumph" is like TEV. It may be that the line means

---

[2]HOTTP translates "and in your righteousness they stand."

that Israel's power and her fame come from Yahweh, parallel with line **b** "**in your love you make us triumphant**" (literally <u>**our horn is exalted**</u>—see 75.4).

TEV uses the first person plural "**us**" in verse 17a in place of the third person (RSV **their**), to make the line consistent with line **b**, which uses the first person, <u>**our**</u>. TEV's "**You give us great victories**" must be recast in some languages to say, for example, "You powerfully enable us to defeat our enemies."

In verse 18a the two lines are synonymous: "For to Yahweh (is) our shield, to the Holy One of Israel (is) our king." As **shield** the king is the protector of Israel (see discussion under 47.9; 84.9). TEV understands the Hebrew "is to" or **belongs to** (RSV) to mean that it was Yahweh who chose and gave the people of Israel their king; it is in this sense that the king "belongs to" Yahweh. SPCL, however, takes the verse to mean "Our protector is the Lord! Our king is the Holy One of Israel" (so NEB, NJV). It seems better to follow TEV here. TEV has recast the verb structures into active verbs, thus providing a good model for many translations.

For a discussion of **the Holy One of Israel**, see 71.22.

<u>89.19-21</u> RSV	TEV
	God's Promise to David
19 Of old thou didst speak in a vision to thy faithful one, and say: "I have set the crown^z upon one who is mighty, I have exalted one chosen from the people.	19 In a vision long ago you said to your faithful servants, "I have given help to a famous soldier; I have given the throne to one I chose from the people.
20 I have found David, my servant; with my holy oil I have anointed him;	20 I have made my servant David king by anointing him with holy oil.
21 so that my hand shall ever abide with him, my arm also shall strengthen him.	21 My strength will always be with him, my power will make him strong.

^z Cn: Heb *help*

HEADING: the second TEV heading may be adapted for some languages as "God promises to keep his covenant with David" or "God will keep the promises he made to David."

The second section of the psalm (verses 19-37) has to do with God's promise to make David and his descendants kings of Israel. The psalmist recalls what God had said long ago (**Of old**) in **a vision** to his "**faithful servants**," the prophets. Most take this to refer to what is related in 2 Samuel 7.14-17, God's message to David through the prophet Nathan. The Masoretic text is plural "your faithful ones" (see comments on "the godly" in 4.3); this could mean "your faithful people" (NIV), but this is not very likely. Many Hebrew manuscripts have the singular "your faithful one" (see RSV), presumably a reference to Nathan. It is better to translate the Masoretic text.

In a vision suggests a supernatural intervention in which the recipient sees and hears a message. A dream may serve the same purpose, and in many languages "vision" is translated "dream." It is also possible to avoid the word "dream" and to say "you showed yourself and spoke to your faithful servants long ago."

In verse 19c the Hebrew text is "I have placed help upon," which TEV and others translate "**I have given help to.**" The Hebrew is somewhat unusual, and instead of *'ezer* "help," some emend to *nezer* **crown** (RSV, BJ, NAB, AT). NJV translates the Masoretic text "I have conferred power on" (see NJB "I have given strength to"). TEV "**a famous soldier**" translates a word meaning "hero, warrior" (RSV **one who is mighty**; see translation of "warrior" in 33.16b).

In verse 19d **I have exalted** may mean, as TEV translates, "**I have given the throne.**" The translation can be "I have made (him) king." It is also possible to take verse 19d to mean "I have exalted a youth above the people" (similarly NEB; somewhat differently, Dahood). NAB has "Over the people I have set a youth" (also FRCL, NIV, TOB). In this instance the Hebrew word is taken to mean "young person" and not "chosen one." TEV is like NJV. TEV's "**I have given the throne**" is idiomatic in English and, if followed by the translator, may require recasting as "I have made the one I chose from the people to be king," which is nearly parallel with the wording of verse 20a in TEV.

In verse 20a the Hebrew is **I have found David my servant; with my holy oil I have anointed him**. This seems to refer to what the prophet Samuel did, as related in 1 Samuel 16.1-13. For "anoint" see comments at 2.2; **holy oil** was olive oil especially used for the ritual of anointing. For translation suggestions on **holy** see 28.2. Instead of TEV "**I have made my servant David king,**" it may be better to say "I have found my servant David and made him king"; and in verse 20b the translation should read **my holy oil**.

In verse 21 **my hand** and **my arm** mean "**my strength**" and "**my power.**" The order **hand** in line a and **arm** in line b is the reversal of the usual direction of poetic movement.

89.22-23   RSV   TEV

22   The enemy shall not outwit him,   22   His enemies will never succeed
        the wicked shall not humble   against him;
        him.   the wicked will not defeat him.
23   I will crush his foes before him   23   I will crush his foes
        and strike down those who hate   and kill everyone who hates
        him.   him.

In verse 22 **outwit** translates a word whose form and meaning are disputed. The Brown-Driver-Briggs lexicon (BDB) derives it from the verb *nasha'* [I], "to be a creditor"; McCullough and others relate it to *nasha'* [II], "to deceive" (so RSV, NJB, GECL **outwit**; NAB "deceive"; TOB and FRCL "take by surprise"). K-B derives it from a verb meaning "treat badly, oppress" (NJV, NIV); NEB "strike at" (similarly SPCL). The best thing to do is use a word that gives the general idea of "oppress" or "conquer." TEV's **"succeed against him"** is somewhat elliptical and difficult to translate, as it does not make clear what they will not succeed in doing against him. If the translator follows TEV, it may be necessary to say, for example, "his enemies will not succeed in their battles against him."

In verse 22b **the wicked** translates a Hebrew idiom, "son of wickedness." The verb **(not) humble** means (not) to inflict a shameful defeat on him. Here there is no particular poetic movement between lines a and b. Both say very much the same thing. It is in such cases as this that translators may want to reduce the two lines to one by saying, for example, "His enemies who are wicked people will not be able to defeat him."

God promises to defeat David's enemies and destroy them completely (verse 23). The word translated **crush** is a process in which pressure is brought to bear on two sides of an object. However, in this context the sense of this action is in its results. The thing is crushed, destroyed, collapsed, broken to pieces. When the object is animate, crushing refers to disabling or to destruction. The sense here is to destroy, do away with. In some languages line 23a may be rendered "While he is watching I will wipe out his enemies" or ". . . do away with his enemies." In some languages this expression may best be handled as a simile, "I will crush his enemies as a person smashes an egg." In verse 23 **before him** has not been included by TEV; something like the following can be done: "In his presence (or, As he looks on) I will destroy his foes." In line b **strike down** translates a verb that is used only here in the Psalms in this sense; see its use in 91.12b "strike (your foot)."

89.24-25	RSV		TEV
24	My faithfulness and my steadfast love shall be with him, and in my name shall his horn be exalted.	24	I will love him and be loyal to him; I will make him always victorious.
25	I will set his hand on the sea and his right hand on the rivers.	25	I will extend his kingdom from the Mediterranean to the Euphrates River.

In verses 24-29 God promises to be with David always, to uphold him, bless him, and make him king over a mighty empire. The direct quotation of what God said to David is a long one (verses 19-37), and in some translations it may be helpful to make a break and reintroduce God as speaker; verse 24 can begin: "God also said, 'I will love David . . . .' "

In verse 24, as in verses 2, 14b, God's **faithfulness and steadfast love** are spoken of; here he pledges them to David for all time. In verse 24b the Hebrew is **and in my name shall his horn be exalted** (see verse 17b). **In my name** means "by means of my power (or, presence) with him." **His horn** is a figure for power, strength (see also comments on 18.2; 75.4,5). GECL translates "Because I will be with him, his power will grow," and SPCL has "and by means of me his power will grow"; FRCL translates "I am the one who will make his power grow." TEV has shifted from the noun phrases in RSV to verb phrases, just as many translators will be required to do. "**I will make him always victorious**" must in many languages be recast to say, for example, "I will always enable him to defeat his enemies."

One of the typical devices for heightening poetic effect in parallel lines is the use of a metaphor in the second line, here **horn be exalted**. This effect may be translated by saying, for example, "Not only will I love him and be loyal to him, I will always help him defeat his enemies."

David's kingdom will reach from **the sea** to **the rivers**. TEV and others take this to mean "**from the Mediterranean to the Euphrates River**" (see discussion of similar expressions in 72.8; 80.11). Some take the language to mean that David's reign will be universal, **the sea** and **the rivers** standing for the limits of the whole world (see 24.2 and comments). It is probable, as Dahood maintains, that here, as in verse 13b, **hand** and **right hand** mean "left hand" and "right hand." It is also possible that the psalmist is dealing more with poetic word pairs than with geographical space.

89.26-27	RSV	TEV
26	He shall cry to me, 'Thou art my Father, my God, and the Rock of my salvation.'	26 He will say to me, 'You are my father and my God; you are my protector and savior.'
27	And I will make him the first-born, the highest of the kings of the earth.	27 I will make him my first-born son, the greatest of all kings.

Since David has not been mentioned since verse 20, it may be necessary to reintroduce him by name. David will acknowledge Yahweh as his **Father** and his **God** (see 2 Sam 7.14). The word **Father** here indicates a special relationship with God which the king enjoys by virtue of the fact that he has been anointed; God "adopts" him as his son (for a similar statement see 2.7 and comments). **My God** will sometimes have to be rendered as "the God whom I worship." TEV "**my protector and savior**" translates **the Rock of my salvation** (see 62.2 for comments on a similar expression); TOB translates "the rock that saves me," and FRCL "the rock where I find salvation." If the translator follows TEV, "**my protector and my savior**" may have to be shifted to say "the one who protects and saves me."

In verse 27a **the first-born** is a title that distinguishes the one so named as having rank and privileges above all others. The oldest son received a greater share of his father's property than any of the other sons and became the head of the family upon the father's death. SPCL translates "I will give him the rights of the oldest son." The promise here is that David will be a king greater than all other kings. The major problem for the translator in connection with this verse is the ambiguity in **make him the first-born**. Since the meaning focuses upon the rights of this particular son, it will in most cases be best to follow the model of SPCL or to say, for example, "I will give him all the things the oldest son should receive."

In line **b highest** means "greatest, most powerful, most famous." As God is the Most High (see 7.17), so David is also the "most high" king (the same Hebrew word *'elyon*).

28 My steadfast love I will keep for him for ever, and my covenant will stand firm for him.	28 I will always keep my promise to him, and my covenant with him will last forever.
29 I will establish his line for ever and his throne as the days of the heavens.	29 His dynasty will be as permanent as the sky; a descendant of his will always be king.

In verse 28a the word *chesed* is used, which TEV usually translates "constant love" (so RSV here has **steadfast love**); but in parallel with **covenant** in line <u>b</u>, the word here is probably to be understood as loyalty (so Anderson, commenting on the word in verse 24: "loyalty to the Covenant promises"). So one possibility is "my faithfulness" (also TOB). But the usual meaning "love" may be the one intended here and is what most translations have (see the similar verse 33a). NJB has "I shall maintain my faithful love for him always."

In languages in which **covenant** is represented by a verb phrase ("the promise I have made" or "what I have promised to do"), the translation of this verse will produce two lines with almost identical meanings, and in some cases it may be preferred to reduce them to one line.

Verse 29 **I will establish his line for ever, and his throne as the days of the heavens** is a promise that the Davidic dynasty will always endure, that Israel will always have as king a descendant of David's. The same thought is expressed in verses 4, 36-37. SPCL has here "His descendants will reign in his place forever, as long as the sky lasts."

The days of the heavens is a phrase found nowhere else in the Old Testament; Anderson takes it to mean "time that is practically endless." A literal translation, such as RSV, is practically meaningless; NIV has "as long as the heavens endure"; NJV "as long as the heavens last."

30 If his children forsake my law and do not walk according to my ordinances,	30 "But if his descendants disobey my law and do not live according to my commands,
31 if they violate my statutes and do not keep my commandments,	31 if they disregard my instructions and do not keep my commandments,
32 then I will punish their transgressions with the rod and their iniquity with scourges;	32 then I will punish them for their sins; I will make them suffer for their wrongs.

Yahweh warns that he will punish any disobedience on the part of David's descendants (**his children**, verse 30), but their sins will not cancel the promise he made to David, that his dynasty would always continue to reign over Israel.

RSV and TEV render verses 30-32 as one sentence, which in some languages may be too long. In that case each verse can be rendered as a separate sentence; for example, "30 It may be that his descendants will . . . commands. 31 Or it may be that they will . . . commandments. 32 If that happens, I will . . . ."

In verses 30-31 four synonymous terms are used: **law**, **ordinances**, **statutes**, **commandments** (see similar list in 19.7-9). All of these are the laws that are part of the covenant between God and his people. In verse 30b the verb **walk** means, as it often does, to conduct oneself, to live. Verses 30-31 are two conditions followed in verses 32-37 by continued promises. With verse 30 the psalmist shifts to a chiastic arrangement, which here serves the function of grasping the reader's attention. The translator should not simply employ a Hebrew chiasmus, but whatever device in the receptor language which serves an equivalent function. By contrast with verse 30, in verse 31 both lines follow the same word order. The first line of verses 30 and 31 is positive, while the second line in each verse is negative. The second line does not go beyond the first line in terms of heightening the poetic effect. It merely restates it in a negative way. How the translator handles these two verses will depend largely on the effect of combining positive and negative conditions. It is possible that the two lines will have to be reduced to one.

In verse 31 **violate** translates a verb that usually means "to profane, to desecrate"; see in 55.20b its use with a covenant as the object, and 74.7b with the Temple as the object ("desecrated"); and see verse 34 below.

In verse 32, for the word translated **transgression** see 19.13; and for **iniquity** see 51.2. **The rod** and **scourges** are figures for harsh punishment (see 2 Sam 7.14); SPCL shortens and combines the two lines into one: "I will punish their rebellion and wrongdoing with lashes of a cane." **The rod** was probably a straight, pliable stick, chosen and prepared to serve as a cane for whipping people; **scourges** are to be thought of as flexible whips made of vines or ropes. If the figurative language is to be kept, as well as the two lines, the following may be said:

> I will beat them on account of their sins,
> I will whip them because of their wrongdoing.

89.33-34	RSV		TEV
33	but I will not remove from him my steadfast love, or be false to my faithfulness.	33	But I will not stop loving David or fail to keep my promise to him.
34	I will not violate my covenant, or alter the word that went forth from my lips.	34	I will not break my covenant with him or take back even one promise I made him.

God will punish those who do not keep the covenant, but he will not break the covenant: he will remain faithful to his promises. In verse 33 **him** refers to David, which TEV makes explicit (see 2 Sam 7.15). In verse 33a the Masoretic text is "I will not break off"; many Hebrew manuscripts have the verb "take away," as in 2 Samuel 7.15. In this verse again **steadfast love** and **faithfulness** are paired as the two outstanding characteristics of Yahweh in dealing with his people.

The translator should coordinate the rendering of **violate my covenant** with the expressions used and discussed at verse 31.

In verse 34b the Hebrew word translated **the word that went forth** is, like the English word "utterance," derived from a verb meaning "to go out, emit." Here, in parallel with **my covenant** in line a, it means "the promise I made (to him)."

89.35-37 RSV	TEV
35 Once for all I have sworn by my holiness; I will not lie to David.	35 "Once and for all I have promised by my holy name: I will never lie to David.
36 His line shall endure for ever, his throne as long as the sun before me.	36 He will always have descendants, and I will watch over his kingdom as long as the sun shines.
37 Like the moon it shall be established for ever; it shall stand firm while the skies endure."*ᵃ* *Selah*	37 It will be as permanent as the moon, that faithful witness in the sky."

ᵃ Cn: Heb *the witness in the skies is sure*

God repeats his promise, taking a vow **by my holiness**, that is, by his holy name, that he **will not lie to David**. **By my holiness** means that God guarantees that what he says is true and trustworthy. This may be translated, for example, "I have sworn by my own name" or "I have promised and will do what I say because I am God." The promise **"by my holy name"** may be translated as FRCL has done, "as sure as I am God." Here **not lie** may be translated as "not be unfaithful (or, disloyal)," as some do; or else, "not deceive" or "not break my promise."

The promise in verse 36a repeats the promise made in verse 29a; it may be well to use the same noun here as in verse 29, as SPCL does.

In verse 36b the Hebrew is "and his throne (will last) like the sun before me." TEV joins **before me** to the verb (which carries over from the first line), and understands **before me** to mean God's care and protection. Most translations have simply **before me**, joining it either to **his throne** or to **the sun**. It may well be that **before me** adds little to the thought, and that the line means only "and his kingdom will last as long as the sun" (see verse 4b). SPCL translates the verse "His descendants will reign in his place always, as long as the sun exists."

It may be necessary in translation to reintroduce the subject "David's kingdom" at the beginning of verse 37. Verse 37a repeats the thought of permanence, the same idea expressed in different words in verse 29b. Verse 37b in Hebrew is "and a witness in the sky (is) sure." TEV **"that faithful witness in the sky"** is like BJ, NAB, JB, NJB, NIV, TOB, Weiser; NJV has "an enduring witness in the sky." FRCL has "a faithful witness behind the clouds." RSV emends the Hebrew text (so Briggs; AT, NEB, SPCL) to get **it shall stand firm while the skies endure**.[3]

Some take "the witness" to be God himself; others take it to be the rainbow, but this seems rather unlikely. If the translator follows TEV and others, taking the moon to be the "**faithful witness in the sky**," it may be necessary to recast this expression to say, for example, "the moon in the sky that is always watching" or "the moon in the sky that sees everything."

89.38-39 RSV	TEV
	Lament over the Defeat of the King
38 **But now thou hast cast off and rejected, thou art full of wrath against thy anointed.**	38 **But you are angry with your chosen king; you have deserted and rejected him.**
39 **Thou hast renounced the covenant with thy servant; thou hast defiled his crown in the dust.**	39 **You have broken your covenant with your servant and thrown his crown in the dirt.**

HEADING: the third TEV heading may be recast in some languages to say, for example, "The psalmist mourns because the king has been defeated" or "The psalmist laments because the king's enemies have defeated him."

In verses 38-45 the psalmist accuses God of having broken his covenant with the king and having caused his defeat and humiliation. In order to make it clear that the psalmist is addressing God, it may be well to say "But you, LORD, are angry . . . ." Kirkpatrick notes that the harshness of the language of these verses scandalized many ancient Jewish commentators; one of them, Aben-Ezra of Toledo, Spain (twelfth century A.D.), reported that there was "a certain wise and pious man in Spain who would never read nor listen to this Psalm."

TEV has reversed the two lines of verse 38 for a more natural development of thought. For a similar expression of God's anger, see 78.59,62. "**Your chosen king**" translates **thy anointed** (see 2.2). There is no certain way of identifying the king. He has suffered military defeat, and Jerusalem has fallen to enemy forces and been

---

[3]HOTTP says the whole verse can be interpreted: (1) "as the moon, (which) is established for ever and (which) is faithful (as) witness in the clouds"; or (2) "as the moon (which) is established for ever, and the witness (which) is faithful in the clouds."

ransacked (verses 40-41). The king has been deposed and stripped of his royal symbols (verses 39b,44).[4]

The boldness of verse 39 is extraordinary: God is accused of having gone back on the promise he made to the king: "**You have broken your covenant with your servant.**" The verb translated **renounced** occurs only here and in Lamentations 2.7b ("disowned"). In verse 39b TEV "**thrown**" translates a verb which means "to pollute, defile, desecrate" (see its use in 74.7b, "desecrated"). The crown was the symbol not only of the king's power but also of the holiness of his office, as the anointed of God. The Hebrew word here translated **crown** is not the usual one; *nezer* is related to the verb "to dedicate, consecrate," and the Septuagint translates the word here "his holiness"; NJV has "his dignity." It may be well to follow the example of TOB, "You have thrown his diadem to the ground and profaned it," or FRCL "you have dirtied his crown by throwing it on the ground." In languages in which **defiled his crown in the dust** carries little or no meaning, it will be necessary to shift to another symbol and say, for example, "you have taken away his chief's stool," or to a nonmetaphorical rendering, "you have taken away his authority as chief" or ". . . removed the symbol of his authority." In languages in which the leader's symbols of authority are in objects very different from crowns, these symbols should be employed.

89.40-41   RSV   TEV

40 Thou hast breached all his walls; thou hast laid his strongholds in ruins.	40 You have torn down the walls of his city and left his forts in ruins.
41 All that pass by despoil him; he has become the scorn of his neighbors.	41 All who pass by steal his belongings; all his neighbors laugh at him.

Jerusalem has been captured by the enemy and its defenses destroyed (verse 40). The land is open to neighboring peoples, who plunder it and mock the king and his people (verse 41). All of these misfortunes are God's doing; and in the whole bitter narrative, not once is there any admission of sin which might account for God's anger.

In verse 40a the word translated **breached** means to break through the walls, normally by destroying a section so as to gain entrance into the city through the break in the wall. Here, however, **all his walls** shows that the walls have been broken down completely; thus TEV "**You have torn down the walls of his city.**" The same Hebrew word occurs in 80.12a, "broken down." **His walls** (TEV "**walls of his city**") may have to be recast to say, for example, "the walls that protect his city."

For translation notes on **strongholds** (TEV "**forts**") see 18.45, "fastnesses."

---

[4]It should be noted that some believe that these verses do not express a concrete historical situation but are part of a cultic act in which the king underwent a ritual degradation; see A. R. Johnson, *Sacral Kingship in Ancient Israel,* pages 103-104.

All that pass by, verse 41, is the same expression as in 80.12b. **Despoil** means to take away everything that belongs to someone else, to plunder.

He has become the scorn of his neighbors resembles the scene pictured in 44.14; 79.4; 80.6. It would be better to translate **neighbors** as "all the neighboring peoples" or "the people of all the nearby nations . . . ."

89.42-43	RSV	TEV

	RSV	TEV
42	Thou hast exalted the right hand of his foes; thou hast made all his enemies rejoice.	42 You have given the victory to his enemies; you have made them all happy.
43	Yea, thou hast turned back the edge of his sword, and thou hast not made him stand in battle.	43 You have made his weapons useless and let him be defeated in battle.

Instead of fighting on behalf of his servant, the king of Israel, Yahweh took the side of his enemies; he made them victorious (literally "lifted high the right hand") and made them all **rejoice**.

In verse 43a the Hebrew text is "you turned back the rock of his sword." Most commentators associate "rock" here with flint (stone) knives (see Exo 4.25; Josh 5.2,3) and translate the phrase "the blade of his sword" (so NJV) or **the edge of his sword** (so AT, RSV); NEB, NAB have "his sharp sword." BJ and NJB emend the text to get "you have snapped off his sword on a rock"; this emendation, however, is not necessary. The figure is that of God himself foiling the king's attack and allowing the enemy to defeat him. TEV has shifted to the generic "**weapons**." In those languages which have no generic term such as weapons, it will be necessary to shift to a descriptive clause and say, for example, "You have taken away from him the things he uses in fighting" or "You have ruined for him the things he uses in fighting."

Line **b** means "you have not given him victory in battle" or "you have not supported him in battle" (FRCL, NIV).

89.44-45	RSV	TEV

	RSV	TEV
44	Thou hast removed the scepter from his hand,*ᵇ* and cast his throne to the ground.	44 You have taken away his royal scepter and knocked his throne to the ground.
45	Thou hast cut short the days of his youth; thou hast covered him with shame. *Selah*	45 You have made him old before his time and covered him with disgrace.

ᵇ Cn: Heb *removed his cleanness*

ᵍ Probable text royal scepter; *Hebrew* purity.

Verse 44a in Hebrew is unclear. The text seems to mean "You removed his splendor" (or, purity); so AT, NAB, SPCL. There is much uncertainty over the form and meaning of the noun, which appears nowhere else in the Old Testament. NJV translates "his splendor" with a note, "Meaning of Heb uncertain." TOB, GECL, and NIV have "You have put an end to his splendor." Many commentators and translators emend the text to get "**his royal scepter**" (TEV; also BJ, NJB, NEB); RSV has **the scepter from his hand** (see Oesterley). Although an impressive number of translations find that the Masoretic text makes sense, it must be admitted that the Hebrew word as it appears in the Masoretic text has not yet been satisfactorily explained.[5] If the translator preserves the use of symbols of authority, these should be used as are known in the local language. Otherwise the translation can say "royal power," "his power as king," in line a.

Verse 44b should not be understood literally; so a translation can be "you removed him from his position as king" or "you brought his kingdom to an end." Or else a translation that uses one of the symbols of kingship may be a good parallel to line a. The language vividly expresses the way in which God has shamed and humiliated the king.

As a result of all this, the king has aged prematurely (verse 45a), his health and vigor are gone, and he is **covered . . . with shame**. SPCL has "you have taken years away from his life"; FRCL "you have shortened his youth." In some languages "**You have made him old**" would be the equivalent of having made him wise. For this reason it may in such cases be better to follow the model of such versions as SPCL and FRCL.

89.46-48   RSV   TEV

A Prayer for Deliverance

46 How long, O LORD? Wilt thou hide thyself for ever?
    How long will thy wrath burn like fire?

47 Remember, O Lord,[c] what the measure of life is,
    for what vanity thou hast created all the sons of men!

48 What man can live and never see death?
    Who can deliver his soul from the power of Sheol?   *Selah*

46 LORD, will you hide yourself forever?
    How long will your anger burn like fire?

47 Remember how short my life is; remember that you created all of us mortal!

48 Who can live and never die?
    How can man keep himself from the grave?

[c] Cn: Heb *I*

---

[5]HOTTP ("A" decision) says the word may mean "splendour" or "purity"; the former is more probable.

HEADING: since this portion of the psalm appears to have two speakers, it may be necessary to include both in the heading and say, for example, "The psalmist and the king pray that God will save them." Verses 46-51 are a prayer for deliverance; verses 50-51 appear to identify the speaker as the king himself.

The opening cry (verse 46) is phrased in familiar language; see 79.5 and references.

The psalmist appeals to the Lord to take into account his frailty and mortality; should Yahweh continue to punish him, he will surely die.

Verse 47a in Hebrew is obscure; the Masoretic text seems to say "**Remember how short my life is**" (TEV; similarly NJV, NIV, NAB, SPCL); Weiser and RSV emend; NEB also emends, but differently. HOTTP translates "remember me: of what duration (am I)?" This meaning is well represented by FRCL: "Remember me; life is so short!"

And the meaning of verse 47b is also debated. Some punctuate it as a question: NEB "hast thou created man in vain?"; similarly NJV. BJ has "For what vain purpose have you created man?" (similarly NJB, Dahood). Others translate it as an affirmation, "(remember) for what nothingness you created humankind." The noun "vanity, fraud, deception" (see "lies" and comments at 12.2) here indicates human frailty, weakness, and particularly mortality (so TEV, SPCL). In the context the idea of mortality seems to be the most probable one. The Hebrew phrase **the sons of men** means humankind, the human race (see 11.4). If the translator follows TEV's "**mortal**," in some languages this may be rendered as "remember that you created people that live and then die."

In verse 48 **see death** means "**die**"; **deliver his soul** translates "save his *nefesh*" (see 3.2); and "**the grave**" translates what is literally "the hand of Sheol" (see comments at 6.5); FRCL has "the claws of death"; NJV "the clutches of death." Line b steps up the negative **never see death** through the use of the positive expression "deliver his soul from the hand of Sheol." If the poetic heightening is to be reflected in the translation, it may be necessary to change from questions to emphatic statements; for example, "No one can live and never die, nor can anyone ever escape from the power of the grave."

	RSV		TEV
89.49-51			
49	Lord, where is thy steadfast love of old, which by thy faithfulness thou didst swear to David?	49	Lord, where are the former proofs of your love? Where are the promises you made to David?
50	Remember, O Lord, how thy servant is scorned; how I bear in my bosom the insults of the peoples,	50	Don't forget how I, your servant, am insulted, how I endure all the curses[h] of the heathen.
51	with which thy enemies taunt, O LORD, with which they mock the footsteps of thy anointed.	51	Your enemies insult your chosen king, O LORD! They insult him wherever he goes.

^d Cn: Heb *all of many*   ^h *Probable text* curses; *Hebrew* crowds.

The psalmist's prayer concludes with one final plea for Yahweh's love and mercy. And the psalmist reproaches Yahweh for having gone back on his promises to King David.

It should be noted that **Lord** in verses 49 and 50 translates the Hebrew title *adonai*; in verses 46, 51, and 52 "LORD" translates the Hebrew *Yahweh*.

Verse 49 is a long, rather complex rhetorical question, and it is advisable to divide it into two separate questions, as in TEV. Or else "Where are your former acts of steadfast love . . . your faithful promises which you made to David?" (similarly FRCL, NEB, NJV). SPCL and NIV are like RSV, with the one subject (**thy steadfast love**) for the two lines. In verse 49a the plural of *chesed* (see 5.7) is translated by TEV "**proofs of (your) love**," and in verse 49b *'emunah* (see 36.5) is represented by "**the promises**," as in verse 33b. In some languages it is not possible to ask where abstracts such as love and promises are. If the translator follows the lead of TEV, it may be necessary to render this as, for example, "What can you do to show us that you love us as you used to do, and that you have kept the promises you made to David?"

In verse 50 the first person singular is the subject of the verb in line b; TEV, for clarity, has also included it in line a, "**I, your servant**." The Masoretic text is plural "your servants" (so NJV, TOB, NAB, SPCL), which probably means the people of Israel; many Hebrew manuscripts have the singular "**your servant**" (TEV, RSV, AT, GECL, FRCL, NEB, BJ, NJB). Dahood understands the plural as "plural of majesty," a reference to the king. It seems better to follow the Hebrew manuscripts that have the singular.

In verse 50b the Masoretic text seems deficient; literally it is "I bear in my bosom all the many peoples." TOB understands the Masoretic text to mean "all these people of whom I am in charge." Most translations emend the text to get "all the curses" or "all the insults" (AT, RSV, TEV, NEB, NJB, NIV, NAB; Weiser). NJV translates line b as a relative clause, "that I have borne in my bosom [from] many people."[6] It seems best to go with the majority here. If "**the heathen**" are taken as the ones who insult and curse the king, then in many languages which do not use the passive, verse 50a may be rendered "Do not forget how the tribes who do not worship you insult and curse me, your servant." In this way the two lines may have to be reduced to one.

In verse 51a **thy enemies** refers to **the peoples** (that is, the pagan Gentiles) of verse 50b. In verse 51a there is no object for the verb **mock**; TEV takes it to be **thy anointed** of line b, and so transfers it to line a, "**your chosen king**" (see verse 38a) and uses "him" in line b. The same Hebrew verb is used in both lines; RSV varies with **taunt** and **mock**.

---

[6]HOTTP gives two possible interpretations of this verse, without indicating which one is preferable: (1) "remember, O Lord, the shame of your servants, what I bear in my bosom, (from) all the numerous peoples"; (2) "remember, O Lord, the shame of your servants, all the numerous peoples (which) I bear (with love) in my bosom."

TEV takes **the footsteps** to mean "**wherever he goes**" (see Anderson); so SPCL "at every step." TOB understands the verbal clause in line <u>b</u> to mean "by spitting on the footsteps of your anointed one." It is not clear how this meaning was arrived at.

89.52	RSV	TEV

Blessed be the LORD for ever! Amen and Amen.	Praise the LORD forever! Amen! Amen!

This verse is not part of the psalm; it is the concluding doxology of Book Three (Psalms 73–89); see similar concluding doxologies in 41.13; 72.18-19.

Book Four

(Psalms 90–106)

Psalm 90

This psalm, as it now stands, is a prayer by the community, Israel, a prayer that reflects suffering and distress. There has been some unspecified disaster (verses 13,15), and the people pray to God to have pity on them and bless them.

Many scholars believe that this psalm is made up of two separate compositions: verses 1-12, a meditation on human mortality in the light of God's eternity; and verses 13-17, a community lament occasioned by some tragedy which was interpreted as God's punishment of the people. Yet it can be shown from the recurrent images and the poetic structure that the psalm is an integral unit. The psalm is viewed by Alter as consisting of four segments: (1) verses 1-2, introduction addressing God and stressing his eternal nature; (2) verses 3-6, characterization of mankind's limited existence; (3) verses 7-11, the community's confession of their sinfulness in their temporal existence; (4) verses 12-17, prayer of short-lived creatures for wisdom and God's grace. Aspects of the poetic structure will be dealt with in the text.

HEADING: "**Of God and Man.**" Other headings are "The eternal God and mortal man"; "The human condition"; "God's eternity and man's frailty." The TEV heading in the form of two noun phrases will have to be recast if used in translation in some languages; for example, "Men are weak but God is strong" or "The psalmist prays that God will have mercy on people because they are weak."

Hebrew title: **A Prayer of Moses, the man of God** ("A prayer by Moses, the man of God").

For **Prayer** see title of Psalm 17; for Moses as **the man of God**, see Deuteronomy 33.1; Joshua 14.6. This title probably has the sense of "prophet" (see Elijah, 1 Kgs 17.18; Elisha, 2 Kgs 4.7).

90.1-2 RSV	TEV

1 Lord, thou hast been our dwelling place*e*
   in all generations.
2 Before the mountains were brought forth,
   or ever thou hadst formed the
	1 O Lord, you have always been our home.
	2 Before you created the hills
	   or brought the world into being,
	   you were eternally God,
	   and will be God forever.

> earth and the world,
> from everlasting to everlasting
> thou art God.

e Another reading is *refuge*

The opening statement reflects confidence which is based on the knowledge of God's eternal nature. Always he has been the **dwelling place** of his people. Instead of the Masoretic text **dwelling place**, some Hebrew manuscripts and the Septuagint have "refuge" (so NEB, BJ, NJB, TOB, SPCL). It may well be that the word in the Masoretic text has here the meaning "place of safety"; FRCL has "our place of security."[1] **Lord** translates the title, not the personal name Yahweh. The Hebrew "for generation and generation" in verse 1b means "for all time, forever." In some languages it will not be natural to speak of the Lord being a place, and the noun phrase must therefore be recast as a clause and in some cases as a simile; for example, "Lord, you have always protected us" or "Lord, you have always been like a home to us."

In verse 2 the Hebrew text is literally "before the hills were born, before you gave birth to the earth and the world." The language is poetic, portraying God as giving birth. The second verb means "to have labor pains" (see also comments on "whirl" in 29.9). The birth imagery functions poetically here to hint at the birth of humankind, which suggests the limitations of time that are imposed on humans in contrast with God, who is eternal. NIV approximates the female imagery: "were born . . . you brought forth"; TOB "were born . . . you gave birth to"; and NJB "were born . . . came to birth." TOB provides a good model to follow.

It is not certain what difference, if any, is intended between the two words **earth** and **world**; it seems that the two are quite synonymous here (see 19.4; 24.1; 33.8; 77.18b,c, where they are parallel). Perhaps something like "the earth and (the rest of) the universe" can be said. In English **the earth and the world** is repetitious and redundant, as will be the case in most languages. FRCL has only "the world," and GECL "the earth."

The Hebrew phrase translated **from everlasting to everlasting** in verse 2c expresses all time, past and future (see the same idea in 102.27). The emphasis in the Hebrew "you (are) God" is better brought out by "you are the one who is God" (see FRCL). If the translator follows the restructuring of TEV in this verse, it may be necessary to place "you were eternally God" at the opening and "will be God forever" at the conclusion. For example, "You always were God" or "You always were the God we worship, even before you created the hills and the world, and you will always be the God we worship."

90.3-4	RSV	TEV
3	Thou turnest man back to the dust,	3 You tell man to return to what he was;

---

[1] HOTTP gives both alternatives, without expressing a preference.

and sayest, "Turn back, O children of men!"	you change him back to dust.
4 For a thousand years in thy sight are but as yesterday when it is past, or as a watch in the night.	4 A thousand years to you are like one day; they are like yesterday, already gone, like a short hour in the night.

Verse 3 opens the second segment of the poem, which calls attention to mankind's mortality, and this theme will be sustained to the end.

Verse 3 in Hebrew is "you turn man to dust, and you say, 'Return, humankind.'" By most commentators and translators the two lines are taken as synonymous, indicating God's activity in deciding a person's time to die, by which that person returns to the **dust** from which God made the human race (Gen 3.19). The time of a person's death is God's decision. Some have understood the word translated **dust** to mean "destruction" (KJV, RV) or else "contrition" (see JPS; NJV footnote); the majority, however, take it to mean the soil, the earth. Some take "return" in verse 3b to mean "repent"; this is possible but does not seem likely. Most understand the two lines to be parallel. TEV reverses the two lines for greater ease of understanding.

Briggs and Dahood change the vowel mark for the last word of verse 2 in the Hebrew text from 'el "God" to 'al "not," and connect it with what follows: "Do not turn man back to dust." This is possible, but it is not widely accepted.

For comments on **children of men** in verse 3b, see 11.4.

The whole verse may be translated as follows:

> You order human beings to return to the soil,
> you change them back to the soil they came from.

Verse 4 extends the meditation on mankind's limited existence by looking at time as it were from God's point of view. The poetic process is that of narrowing time from **a thousand years** to a day (**yesterday**) to a single **watch in the night**. The end point of this shortening of time is **night**, which prepares the reader for the next line, which is about sleep. In this way cohesion between the two verses is established.

TEV has added, for clarity, "one day" in verse 4a, but this may not be necessary. The following may be said: "For a thousand years to you are as brief as yesterday, which is already gone . . . ." A confusion which may arise in some languages in this verse is related to **in thy sight** or TEV's **"to you."** In some cases it will be clearer to say, for example, "A thousand years of ours is like one day of yours" or "The way people count time, a thousand years is the same as one day in the way you count time." The Hebrew for "**a short hour in the night**" (TEV) is "a night-watch," which was a period of four hours (see also comments on 63.6); for a person asleep, this is a short time.

There may be an allusion to this verse in 2 Peter 3.8.

90.5-6 RSV   TEV

5 Thou dost sweep men away; they   5 You carry us away like a flood;
     are like a dream,   we last no longer than a dream.
   like grass which is renewed in   We are like weeds that sprout in
     the morning: the morning,
6 in the morning it flourishes and is   6 that grow and burst into bloom,
     renewed;   then dry up and die in the eve-
   in the evening it fades and with-   ning.
     ers.

These two verses are not clear in Hebrew, and there are different explanations of the text. The verb in verse 5a appears in this form nowhere else in the Old Testament; K-B says only "unexplained"; Holladay defines it "stop, put an end to life." RSV has **sweep**; SPCL "you drag men away violently"; NJV "you engulf men in sleep"; and NJB "you flood them with sleep." The expression **sweep men away** must not be rendered so that the reader pictures God busy with a broom. In the same way TEV's **"carry . . . away"** may produce a picture of God carrying people away in his arms. Other expressions may be used; for example, "You bring people's lives to a sudden end" or "You cast people aside as if they were nothing." See FRCL "You put an end to human life."

The word translated **dream** is literally "sleep" (see 76.5 and comments), and some translate the Hebrew "You make an end to them in their sleep" (NAB; similarly Dahood). Most, however, interpret as do RSV and TEV, comparing a human being's frail and transitory existence to a dream that is quickly gone. TEV uses the exclusive plural **"us"** and **"we"** in verses 5-6 for greater ease of understanding, and also to be consistent with the first plural in verses 7-12.

The author reaches for another image of brief human life, which he finds in a fragile grass that withers between morning and evening. **Grass**, that is, weeds, last only one day, sprouting **in the morning** and dying **in the evening**. See similar language in 37.2; see also 103.15-16; Job 14.1-2.

90.7-8 RSV   TEV

7 For we are consumed by thy an-   7 We are destroyed by your anger;
     ger;   we are terrified by your fury.
   by thy wrath we are over-   8 You place our sins before you,
     whelmed.   our secret sins where you can
8 Thou hast set our iniquities before   see them.
     thee,
   our secret sins in the light of
     thy countenance.

With verse 7 begins the confession of the community, and again there is cohesion, as the image of the withering grass in verse 6 is carried forward by the terms **anger** and **wrath**, which in Hebrew suggest heat and "hot breath of the nostrils." The translator should note how the confession in verses 7-11 is enclosed in an envelope; that is, 7 opens with "anger/wrath," and 11 closes with "anger/wrath." The imagery of verses 7-11 continues the central theme of mankind's fragile and brief span of life.

In a melancholy mood the psalmist sees life as trouble and sorrow, spent under the attacks of God's anger and fury. Human life is not only short, it is also a wearisome burden. The relation between verses 7 and 8 seems to be that it is human sin which provokes God's destructive **anger**, his terrifying **wrath**. People cannot hide their sins from God, and so they suffer God's punishment. For the verb **consumed** in verse 7a, see 18.37b and comments; and the verb in verse 7b is "terrified, terror-struck" (see its use in 2.5b). Through its parallelism verse 7 emphasizes God's anger at the people's sin, and the translator should use the device which will communicate the equivalent function. This need not necessarily be by keeping the two synonymous lines. In some languages it may be necessary to reduce verse 7 to a single line by saying, for example, "we are destroyed and terrified by your anger." SPCL translates "Truly your anger consumes us, it leaves us confused." The more logical order is "terrified and destroyed." In languages which do not use the passive, the rendering may be "your anger terrifies and destroys us."

In verse 8b **in the light of thy countenance** ("your face") is synonymous with **before thee** in verse 8a; it is quite appropriate for **our secret sins**, that is, those that are kept hidden from others. Intensification in parallel lines is not common in Psalm 90. However, in 8b **secret sins** steps up what is **iniquities** in line a and can be rendered, for example, "You place our sins before you, even our secret sins you put where you can see them." In many languages it will not be possible to **set** . . . **iniquities** as if they were physical objects. Therefore it will sometimes be necessary to say, for example, "You not only see us when we sin, you even see us when we commit secret sins" or ". . . when we try to hide our sins from you."

90.9-10   RSV   TEV

9   For all our days pass away under   9   Our life is cut short by your an-
       thy wrath,   ger;
     our years come to an end^f like a   it fades away like a whisper.
       sigh.   10   Seventy years is all we have—
10   The years of our life are three-   eighty years, if we are strong;
       score and ten,   yet all they bring us is trouble and
     or even by reason of strength   sorrow;
       fourscore;   life is soon over, and we are
     yet their span^g is but toil and   gone.
       trouble;
     they are soon gone, and we fly
       away.

^{f} Syr: Heb *we bring our years to an end*
^{g} Cn Compare Gk Syr Jerome Tg: Heb *pride*

The psalmist now produces a contrast in time. In verse 4 he looked at time from God's view, which moved from years to yesterday to a watch in the night. Now looking at mankind's time the movement is in the opposite direction: **our days . . . our years.**

In verse 9 **all our days** and **our years** are parallel expressions, meaning "our lifetime, our life." In verse 9a RSV **our days pass away under thy wrath** misses the point that God's wrath is the cause of our days ending. Furthermore, the verb is used with a poetic connotation that calls to mind the ending of a day. TEV **"cut short"** misses that connotation. FRCL translates "Under the effect of your anger our life wanes," and SPCL has "In truth, our whole life ends because of your anger." In verse 9b **comes to an end** is parallel with **pass away** in verse 9a; the form of the verb in Hebrew is "we end (our years)" (see RSV footnote). It is not necessary to depart from the Masoretic text and follow the Syriac, as RSV does, in order to make sense of the passage. NJV translates the Masoretic text "we spend our years like a sigh." The emphasis appears to be on the brevity of human life, so a better translation can be "our life goes by as quickly as a sigh."

Even when a person lives out the full life span of seventy years—and, in exceptional cases, eighty years—all that person experiences is **toil and trouble**; life is over quickly **and we fly away**. Again, this is poetic language, and nothing is to be inferred from this passage as to what happens at death. FRCL has "we fly toward death."

TEV's **". . . years is all we have"** is idiomatic in English and will have to be recast in many languages to say something like "A person only lives seventy years, or if he is strong, he may live eighty years."

TEV **"all they bring"** in verse 10c translates what seems to be "and their pride." The noun is variously defined by the lexicons: BDB has "pride"; K-B "eagerness, insistence"; Holladay "crowding, hurry." One possible translation is "but at best they bring only"; SPCL "yet pride in living so long (only brings illnesses and toil)"; NJV "but the best of them" (with a note: "meaning of Heb uncertain").

RSV, NAB, AT, and NJB follow the Septuagint and other ancient versions in reading "their extent." Anderson says the RSV emendation is not needed; the meaning of the Masoretic text is "even the best years of our life . . . are characterized by toil and trouble."[2]

90.11-12	RSV	TEV
11	Who considers the power of thy anger, and thy wrath according to the fear of thee?	11 Who has felt the full power of your anger? Who knows what fear your fury can bring?
12	So teach us to number our days that we may get a heart of wisdom.	12 Teach us how short our life is, so that we may become wise.

---

[2]HOTTP suggests "and their turmoil (or, hurry)" ("B" decision).

As suggested in the introduction above and in the comment on verse 7, verse 11 is the end of the confessional unit, and translators may wish to make the division into units in that way rather than as found here.

The meaning of the two rhetorical questions in verse 11 is not at once apparent. The first one seems to mean that no one has ever really experienced the full effect of God's anger against human sin; consequently a person should always be conscious of the punishment that awaits sin. **Considers** is "knows" in Hebrew—a verb for deep, intimate knowledge. Thus the request in verse 12 comes as a consequence of acknowledging the need for such knowledge. But verse 11b, if parallel with verse 11a, is quite obscure in Hebrew: "as your fear (so is) your rage." RSV is unintelligible. TEV takes "your fear" to be an objective genitive phrase, that is, fear of God, produced by his fury. NJV has "Your wrath matches the fear of You" (similarly NIV). TOB is "The more we fear you, the more we know your fury," which it explains in a footnote: "your fury is up to the measure of the fear you inspire." NJB has "who fears you, your wrath?" Another possible rendering is to carry over the verb "who understands" from line a and translate line b "and (who understands) your fury, so that he shows you due reverence?" NAB is different: "or (who knows) your indignation toward those who fear you?" And Dahood translates "or (who can understand) that those who fear you can be the object of your fury?" In face of such diversity, the most a translator can do is choose the rendering that seems to fit the context best. If the translator follows TEV and RSV **power of thy anger**, in many languages this noun phrase will have to be recast as a clause, "Who has felt the powerful effect when God is angry?" In languages in which an object must be associated with God's anger, it is possible to say ". . . when God is angry at the bad things which people do?"

Verse 12 begins the series of petitions found in each succeeding verse. The verse is a plea; the psalmist asks God to make him realize how short life is, so as to **get a heart of wisdom** (see Deut 32.29). The literal translation **to number our days** in line a would mean "to keep an account of the days (already lived)," so as to be aware of how many are still left. FRCL translates, "Make us understand that our days are numbered."

Wisdom, as elsewhere in Psalms and Proverbs, here includes heavy emphasis on reverence for God. In languages in which "**become wise**" merely means to be bright and intelligent, it will be better to make the content of such wisdom associated with God; for example, "so that we may have God's wisdom in our hearts."

90.13-14   RSV   TEV

13   Return, O LORD! How long?   13   How much longer will your anger
     Have pity on thy servants!   last?
14   Satisfy us in the morning with thy   Have pity, O LORD, on your
     steadfast love,   servants!
     that we may rejoice and be glad   14   Fill us each morning with your
     all our days.   constant love,
                                               so that we may sing and be glad
                                               all our life.

As indicated in the introduction, the fourth segment of the psalm is an integral part of the whole in the following way: In verse 13 the psalmist prays for God to **return** to man. This responds in the hopeful prayer to verse 4, where mankind was made to "turn back" to the dust. Where mankind was like grass that withered from morning to evening in verse 5b and 6, the prayer in 13 is **Satisfy us in the morning**. In 9a the people's "days pass away under thy wrath," but now in prayerful hope they ask that they **may rejoice . . . all our days**. In fact, the only temporal terms that are not repeated in the final prayer are the evening and night associated with sleep and death; however, **the morning** is set in contrast with them.

In this part of the psalm the people, in conventional language, ask God to change from anger to kindness, to stop punishing his people, and to give them as much happiness as the sadness he had brought them in the past.

The petition **Return** means "change your attitude, relent," in anticipation of line b (see comments on "Turn" in 6.4). And for ideas on translating **How long?** see 79.5; 89.46. **Thy servants** are, as nearly always, the people of Israel. TEV fails to represent formally **Return** in line a; the translation could be

> How much longer, LORD, will your anger last?
> Relent, and have pity on us, your servants!

For **steadfast love** in verse 14a, see 5.7 and comments. The verb **satisfy** ("fill up"; see 17.14 and comments) may not be appropriate in some languages with the object **love**; so some other verb, such as manifest, show, reveal, make known, may be better.

The verb for **rejoice** includes singing—a loud cry of joy.

90.15-17 RSV	TEV
15 Make us glad as many days as thou hast afflicted us, and as many years as we have seen evil.	15 Give us now as much happiness as the sadness you gave us during all our years of misery.
16 Let thy work be manifest to thy servants, and thy glorious power to their children.	16 Let us, your servants, see your mighty deeds; let our descendants see your glorious might.
17 Let the favor of the Lord our God be upon us, and establish thou the work of our hands upon us, yea, the work of our hands establish thou it.	17 LORD our God, may your blessings be with us. Give us success in all we do!

In verse 15 the people ask God to be fair and give them as much time of happiness as the time of troubles he had brought on them. The language suggests that the time of troubles was quite long (**as many days . . . as many years**), which seems best understood as a reference to foreign oppression. As usual, such suffering is God's doing: **thou hast afflicted us**.

In verse 15b RSV **we have seen evil** is quite literal; the meaning is "we have experienced troubles," "we have suffered."

Days and **years** are parallel and express poetically how the **evil** has lasted from **days** on into **years**; SPCL shortens and combines the terms as follows: "Give us as many years of happiness as the years of suffering that we have had." FRCL has a more logical order: "For a long time you have humbled us. Give us now as many years of joy as those we have had of trouble."

In verse 16 Yahweh's **work** and his **glorious power** are probably to be understood as acts of salvation; the people ask the Lord once more to save them and give them and their descendants freedom and prosperity. In line a the Masoretic text is singular, "your deed" (so RSV **thy work**); some Hebrew manuscripts, the Septuagint, and the Syriac have the plural (TEV "**mighty deeds**"). **Thy servants** and **their children** are not parallel in the sense of being the same people. Here the community that had no future because of the limitations imposed upon its existence, takes on new hope in prayer and goes ahead confidently into the future. If it is necessary to reduce the two lines to one, the two may be rendered, for example, "Let us who are your servants and our children also see the great things which you do."

In verse 17a **favor** translates the word which in 27.4 RSV translates "beauty." The word means pleasure, good will; SPCL "kindness" is good. **Lord** is the title, not the name Yahweh (TEV is wrong here). In some languages verse 17a may be rendered "may the goodness of the Lord, who is the God we worship, be with us," or in languages in which an abstract such as "goodness" cannot be said to be with someone, "Lord, you who are the God we worship, be kind to us."

The last line of the psalm is repeated in the Masoretic text (so RSV and others); some Hebrew manuscripts and the Septuagint omit the repetition (so TEV and NEB; see NAB). Most translations follow the Masoretic text. The request is "make all our endeavors last for us"; RSV **upon us** is hardly appropriate. It is a prayer for continued success and prosperity in the national life.

Psalm 91

This psalm is a meditation, in a serene and confident mood, on the security of the person who trusts in God. There is nothing in the text that provides a clue as to the time and circumstances of its composition. Dahood and others take it to be a royal psalm, understanding the participle in verse 1a to mean "he who sits enthroned," that is, the king.

Verses 1-13 are an extended commentary on how God protects those who trust him; here the psalmist speaks of God's angels as guaranteeing their safety, a concept rarely found in the psalms. In verses 14-16 God speaks, confirming the words of the psalmist and promising safety and long life to those who trust him and obey him.

It is possible to place in the left-hand margin the speakers, as follows: verse 1, a priest; verse 2, the worshiper; verses 3-8, priest; verse 9a, worshiper; verse 9b, priest; and verses 14-16, God.

HEADING: "**God Our Protector.**" Other headings are: "Under the divine wings"; "Security in God"; "My refuge and my fortress." The TEV heading may be recast for adaptation to other languages in such forms as the following: "God is the one who defends us," "God, you are the one who takes care of us," or "God is our defender."

The Hebrew text has no title for this psalm.

91.1-2	RSV	TEV

1 He who dwells in the shelter of the Most High,
   who abides in the shadow of the Almighty,
2 will say to the LORD, "My refuge and my fortress;
   my God, in whom I trust."

1 Whoever goes to the LORD for safety,
   whoever remains under the protection of the Almighty,
2 can say to him,
   "You are my defender and protector.
   You are my God; in you I trust."

The psalm opens with a statement of assurance of God's protection, which he provides for all who avail themselves of it. The two lines of verse 1 are synonymous: **dwells** and **abides**; **shelter** and **shadow**; **the Most High** (see 7.17) and **the Almighty** (see 68.14). The verb in verse 1b translated **abides** means "spend the night" (see 55.7b). In verse 1b **shadow** is probably an allusion to "the wings" of Yahweh (see comments on 17.8b, and on verse 4, below). **Shelter** and **shadow** may be references

801

to the Temple (Toombs). Translators in some languages may find it best to reduce both lines of this verse to one, as does SPCL, which says "He who lives under the protecting shadow of the Most High and Almighty." In some languages "to be in the shadow" is more related to being hidden than protected. In such cases it will be better to follow the lead of TEV. However, in some languages a more active construction will be required; for example, "Whoever the Almighty protects" or "Anyone whom God takes care of." TEV **"goes to the LORD"** is not good, and something like the following can be said:

> Whoever lives under the protection of the Most High,
> whoever is kept safe by the Almighty . . .

In verse 2 TEV uses the second person of direct address, **"You are."** For **refuge** and **fortress** see comments on similar language in 14.6; 18.2. In verse 2 the Masoretic text has "I say"; RSV, TEV, and others (following the Septuagint) mark the verb with other vowels to get the third person singular, "he will say." It is possible to retain the first person, identifying the speaker as a worshiper. TOB, NIV, and NJV take the psalmist to be the speaker and translate "I (will) say of the Lord . . . ." In many languages **my refuge and my fortress**, as well as TEV's **"my defender and protector,"** will have to be recast as verb phrases; for example, "you are the one who defends me and protects me." **My God** must often be rendered "you are the God I worship." **I trust** is often rendered idiomatically; for example, "I hang my heart upon you" or "I place you in my liver."

91.3-4   RSV   TEV

3	For he will deliver you from the snare of the fowler and from the deadly pestilence;	3
4	he will cover you with his pinions, and under his wings you will find refuge; his faithfulness is a shield and buckler.	4

3 He will keep you safe from all hidden dangers and from all deadly diseases.
4 He will cover you with his wings; you will be safe in his care; his faithfulness will protect and defend you.

The dangers listed in verses 3-5, 6 seem to include both human and nonhuman forces. The latter appear to include demons, but there is no agreement on their identification. In its footnote to verses 5-6, TOB points out that the ancient Greek, Aramaic, and Syriac versions used "demon(s)" or (evil) "spirit" in verse 5b.

In verse 3 TEV **"all hidden dangers"** in line a translates "the bird-catcher's trap" (RSV **the snare of the fowler**). Many languages will prefer to retain the image of "hidden traps" rather than TEV's more generic "**hidden dangers.**"

"**All deadly diseases**" in line b translates "the pestilence of destruction" (RSV **deadly pestilence**). The word for "destruction" is used in 5.9b. (KJV "noisome pestilence" means "a stinking plague.") The reference is probably to epidemics. Some, however, following the Septuagint and other ancient versions, use other vowel marks with the Hebrew consonants of the word **pestilence** to get the word "word," and understand the phrase to mean a plot, or a false accusation, or a witch's spell.[1] Dahood uses still other vowels to get the meaning "venomous substance"; NEB translates the text "raging tempest." It seems best, however, to follow the example of RSV (and TEV) here.

The first two lines of verse 4 are synonymous: **his pinions** and **his wings** are figures of God's protection. In many languages it will be necessary to recast the imagery in the form of a simile, for example, "he will cover you like a bird covers its young under its wings."

In verse 4c God's **faithfulness** in keeping his promises is the source of security; **shield** (see 5.12 and comments) and **buckler** provide protection. The Hebrew word translated **buckler** occurs only here in the Old Testament; it is variously defined as "tower, bulwark, wall." Briggs and NJV explain the term as the participle of the verb "to surround," and NJV translates "an encircling shield." It is recommended that translators follow RSV **buckler**, which was a small shield carried in the hand or worn on the arm, for protecting the body. **His faithfulness is a shield** must sometimes be recast as two clauses; for example, "God is faithful and will protect you like a shield" or "God keeps his promises and will protect and defend you."

91.5-6	RSV		TEV
5	You will not fear the terror of the night, nor the arrow that flies by day,	5	You need not fear any dangers at night or sudden attacks during the day
6	nor the pestilence that stalks in darkness, nor the destruction that wastes at noonday.	6	or the plagues that strike in the dark or the evils that kill in daylight.

In verse 5a **the terror of the night** may be a reference to night demons, such as Lilith, the name of a female demon in ancient Semitic legends. NEB understands it to mean "hunters' trap"; Dahood takes it to mean a pack of wild dogs; it is also possible to simply translate "an attack." TEV's **"dangers at night"** may suggest in some languages only physical dangers. Since the meaning appears to be the unseen evil associated with darkness, it may be better to render this more specifically as such; for example, "you need not fear evil spirits that go about at night." **The arrow** in verse 5b may be human or demonic dangers; Anderson suggests a sunstroke may be meant.

In verse 6 **the pestilence** and **the destruction** are identified by many as demonic forces (see Oesterley). In verse 6b the Septuagint translates "from the calamity and the demon of midday." The Hebrew noun for **destruction** is explained in later Rabbinical commentaries as a demon, "covered with scales and hair, and which sees out of only one eye," that stalked abroad between 10:00 A.M. and 3:00 P.M. (cited in Oesterley). FRCL translates "sunstroke." But it is possible that the words in verses

---

[1]HOTTP agrees with the change: "from the word (of calamity)." In support of its decision it cites factor 12, "scribal errors."

5-6 are used in a general sense of natural dangers and epidemics, with no thought of demons as their cause. If **pestilence** and **destruction** are taken to be evil spirits, then verses 5 and 6 are nearly synonymous and may be combined into one; for example, "the evil spirits that attack people and kill them in the dark or in the light" or "the evil spirits that go about during the night and the day to attack people and destroy them."

91.7-8   RSV   TEV

7   A thousand may fall at your side,   7   A thousand may fall dead beside
        ten thousand at your right   you,
        hand;   ten thousand all around you,
     but it will not come near you.   but you will not be harmed.
8   You will only look with your eyes   8   You will look and see
        and see the recompense of the   how the wicked are punished.
        wicked.

In exaggerated fashion the psalmist promises absolute safety to those who trust in Yahweh. The figures **thousand** and **ten thousand**, which represent step-up parallelism, if taken literally, suggest either warfare or an epidemic; but it is probable that no specific danger is intended. Dahood, NJV, and SPCL translate, in verse 7a,b, "at your left" and "at your right." **"You will not be harmed"** translates it will not come near you, in which it refers to whatever may have caused the deaths of the others.

In verse 8a **only** may be translated "Just open your eyes and you will see . . ." or "All you have to do is look, and you will see . . . ."

In verse 8b **recompense** translates a word found nowhere else in the Old Testament; it is here used in a bad sense of punishment, destruction; see a similar statement in 54.7b. In languages in which the passive is not used, God will have to be introduced as the subject of the action; for example, "see how God punishes wicked people."

91.9-10   RSV   TEV

9   Because you have made the LORD   9   You have made the LORD your[x]
        your refuge,[h]   defender,
     the Most High your habitation,   the Most High your protector,
10   no evil shall befall you,   10   and so no disaster will strike you,
     no scourge come near your tent.   no violence will come near your
                                                    home.

[h] Cn: Heb *Because thou, LORD, art my fuge; you have made*

[x] *Probable text* your; *Hebrew* my.

Verse 9 in Hebrew begins with *ki* **Because**; this may relate the verse either to what precedes (so BJ, NJB, NAB) or to what follows (RSV, TEV, TOB, FRCL, SPCL, and others).

Verse 9 in Hebrew is addressed to Yahweh in line <u>a</u> and to an Israelite in line <u>b</u>, with no marking to make the change explicit: "For you, Yahweh, (are) my refuge, the Most High you made your habitation." NJV's handling of the Masoretic text is not convincing: "Because you took the LORD—my refuge, the Most High—as your haven." TOB is better: "Yes, Lord, you are my refuge! You have made the Most High your habitation." (It is understood, of course, that "you" in the second line is addressed to someone other than "you" in the first line.) RSV emends the text to make line <u>a</u> parallel with line <u>b</u>. It seems better to follow RSV in line <u>a</u> and read **your refuge**, as do TEV, SPCL, FRCL, and take "Yahweh" as accusative, the object of the verb, and not vocative (that is, not "You, O LORD").[2] The expression **you have made the LORD** ... may be misinterpreted by some translators for whom English is a second language. The meaning is "you have accepted the LORD as the one who defends you" or "you have allowed the LORD to be your defender."

For **the Most High** see verse 1; TEV **"protector"** translates the word which in 90.1 appears as "home." Here the parallel with **refuge** (as in verse 2) makes it likely that the meaning is "safeguard, protection," and not "dwelling place" or **habitation**. This verse is a reference to the words in verse 2.

In verse 10b **scourge** translates a word meaning "stroke, blow, plague"; in 38.11 the word is used with the specific meaning of "disease, plague," but here, in parallel with **evil** in line <u>a</u>, it probably has the general meaning of "calamity" (NEB), "evil" (TOB); NJV, however, has "disease"; SPCL "illness"; and NJB "plague." **Tent** in verse 10b means "dwelling place, home."

91.11-12   RSV   TEV

11 For he will give his angels charge   11 God will put his angels in charge
    of you   of you
    to guard you in all your ways.   to protect you wherever you go.
12 On their hands they will bear you   12 They will hold you up with their
    up,   hands
    lest you dash your foot against   to keep you from hurting your
    a stone.   feet on the stones.

Verses 11-12 are quoted in Matthew 4.6 and Luke 4.10-11 as they appear in the Septuagint; the quote in Matthew omits verse 11b, and in Luke the words "in all your ways" in verse 11b are omitted.

Verse 11 in the Masoretic text is "For he will order his angels concerning you, to protect you in all your ways." The meaning is quite clear: "God will give his angels orders to protect you wherever you go." Dahood takes **in all your ways** to mean "in all your marches," in a military sense of the king in his campaigns; and in verse 10b he takes "the tent" to be the king's military headquarters. This is not very convincing.

It is not easy to decide the exact sense of verse 12a; the text may mean that the angels carry the person in their arms (TOB, NJB, NIV) or else help support him as he

---

[2]HOTTP proposes either (1) "for you, O LORD, (are) my refuge . . ." or (2) "for you, (with your) 'LORD my refuge' you have made the Most High your shelter."

walks (so TEV and most others). Some commentators refer to the language in Exodus 19.4, where God reminds the people of Israel, "I bore you on eagles' wings." Weiser comments that the language expresses "the almost motherly solicitude of God." The angels "will carry him like a child, carefully and protectively." For comments on **angels** see 34.7; 35.5,6.

The language of verse 12b reflects the harsh and sometimes dangerous condition of the roads in Palestine; the figure is probably used in a general way of not coming to any harm. See the language of slipping and stumbling in 35.15; 37.31; 38.16.

A literal translation of **your foot** may give the reader the impression that the angels are providing protection for only one part of the body, something like a restricted insurance policy. It may be clearer to say "to keep you from hurting yourself on the stones" or "to keep the stones from hurting you."

91.13   RSV   TEV

> You will tread on the lion and the   You will trample down lions and
>   adder,   snakes,
>   the young lion and the serpent   fierce lions and poisonous
>   you will trample under foot.   snakes.

The language in this verse is symbolic, the various animals representing enemies and other dangers. The two lines are synonymous; for **lion . . . young lion** see *Fauna and Flora*, pages 50-51; for **adder . . . serpent** see *Fauna and Flora*, pages 72-73. It should be noted that the word in verse 13b for **serpent** is *tannin* (see its use and meaning in 74.13b). In verse 13b the psalmist has chosen not to parallel line a syntactically. Because there are only two lines in most parallel verses, the result of not paralleling line a produces a form of chiasmus. Therefore, while the meaning of the two lines is nearly the same, the word order makes them different. In some languages the chiastic form will not be possible, and thus the parallel meaning plus the parallel word order may strike the reader as unnecessarily repetitive, and the translator may prefer in such a case to reduce the two lines to one. SPCL has "You will be able to walk among lions, among wild animals and snakes."

NEB translates all the animals in verse 13 as snakes: "asp . . . cobra . . . snake . . . serpent." This is possible, and a translator may choose to do the same, if there are four different words for "snakes" in the receptor language.

In Luke 10.19 there seems to be an allusion to the language of this verse.

91.14-16   RSV   TEV

14   Because he cleaves to me in love,   14   God says, "I will save those who
>   I will deliver him;   love me
>   I will protect him, because he   and will protect those who ac-
>   knows my name.   knowledge me as LORD.
15   When he calls to me, I will answer   15   When they call to me, I will an-
>   him;   swer them;

806

I will be with him in trouble, I will rescue him and honor him. 16 With long life I will satisfy him, and show him my salvation.	when they are in trouble, I will be with them. I will rescue them and honor them. 16 I will reward them with long life; I will save them."

In these verses God is the speaker, which TEV has made explicit (see also NIV, GECL, FRCL). The Hebrew text throughout has the personal object, **me**, in the singular (see RSV), which TEV has taken as generic and so translated by plural forms, "those who"; Dahood interprets the Hebrew singular as reference to the king.

In verse 14a **cleaves to me in love** is parallel with **knows my name** in verse 14b; here the verb "know" is used in the sense of "confess, accept." The two verbs **deliver** (see 17.13) and **protect** (see 20.1b) are parallel.

It is possible to reduce verse 14 to say, for example, "I will save and protect those who love me and know me."

For **rescue** in verse 15c see "save" and comments in 6.4. **Honor** means that God will provide blessings, such as victory or success, that will bring honor and fame to the person.

A long life (verse 16a) is an indication of God's pleasure (see 21.4); Dahood takes it here to refer to immortality, which is possible. The verb **satisfy** is the one used in 90.14a.

Show . . . my salvation in verse 16b may mean, as TEV has it, "I will save." FRCL translates "I will make him see that I am his savior." However, the verb form translated **show** is understood by many to mean "drink deeply" in a figurative sense of "enjoy to the fullest" (NEB, SPCL, Dahood); this provides a better parallel for the verb in line a.

Psalm 92

This psalm is a hymn of praise by an individual who knows from personal experience that the Lord is righteous, punishing the wicked and rewarding the good (see verses 4 and 10). In joy and gratitude the psalmist sings to the Lord.

There is nothing in the text that indicates the time of the composition or the identity of the author.

The introduction states the psalmist's reason for praising God (verses 1-4); this is followed by a statement of God's power and justice, particularly as revealed in the punishment and destruction of the wicked (verses 5-9). The psalmist thanks God for giving him victory over his enemies (verses 10-11), and the psalm ends with a description of the prosperity and long life of the righteous (verses 12-15).

HEADING: "**A Song of Praise.**" Other headings are: "The virtuous man rejoices"; "Righteousness rewarded"; "The sabbath hymn." The TEV heading must be adapted for some languages to say, for example, "The psalmist sings and says that God is great" or "The psalmist praises God."

Hebrew title: **A Psalm. A Song for the Sabbath** (TEV "A psalm; a song for the Sabbath").

For **Song** see title of Psalm 65. **For the Sabbath** indicates the psalm was used in public worship. Jewish tradition held that this psalm was composed by Adam on the first Sabbath of creation (Cohen). According to the Mishnah, this psalm was sung on the Sabbath by the Levites in the Temple.

92.1-3

RSV	TEV

1 It is good to give thanks to the LORD,
    to sing praises to thy name, O Most High;
2 to declare thy steadfast love in the morning,
    and thy faithfulness by night,
3 to the music of the lute and the harp,
    to the melody of the lyre.
	1 How good it is to give thanks to you, O LORD,
	    to sing in your honor, O Most High God,
	2 to proclaim your constant love every morning
	    and your faithfulness every night,
	3 with the music of stringed instruments
	    and with melody on the harp.

In verse 1 Yahweh is spoken of in the third person in line a and addressed in the second person in line b; for consistency TEV uses the second person in both lines.

The psalmist begins on a note of joy; it is **good** (that is, either enjoyable or right) to praise Yahweh. Instead of the impersonal form of the declaration (**It is good to give thanks**), a personal form may be better: "It is good (or, right) for people (or, me) to give thanks . . . ." In languages which require an explicit object for giving thanks, it may be possible to say ". . . I give you thanks for the good things you have done."

In verse 1b **to thy name** means "in honor of you" (see 5.11); for **Most High** see 7.17. The two verbs **give thanks** and **sing** are the same ones used in 7.17a,b. The occasion for such joyful praise was probably the daily services or the annual festivals in the Temple. The expression **sing praises to thy name** may also be rendered "sing praise to you" or "sing and say that you are great."

For **steadfast love** in verse 2a, see 5.7, and for **faithfulness** in verse 2b, see 36.5. In some languages **steadfast love** and **faithfulness** require an object such as "declare every morning that you always love us, and every night that you are faithful to us."

It is not entirely clear in verse 3 whether two or three instruments are named; in verse 3a the Hebrew is "upon a ten (-stringed instrument) and upon a harp," which RSV translates as **the lute and the harp**. It is probable, however, that the meaning is "a ten-stringed harp" (NJV; see NAB, NEB, NJB, NIV); see the terms in 33.2. In verse 3b **melody** translates the word that is used in the sense of "meditation" in 19.14 and appears as a musical term in 9.16. NJV translates it here as vocal music, "with voice and lyre together"; most take it to refer to the instrument's sound. Verse 3 shows the manner in which verse 2 is to be performed, and in some languages it will be necessary to switch the position of the two verses, placing verse 3 before verse 2.

92.4	RSV	TEV

For thou, O LORD, hast made me glad by thy work; at the works of thy hands I sing for joy.	Your mighty deeds, O LORD, make me glad; because of what you have done, I sing for joy.

In line **a** for **thy work** the Masoretic text has the singular "your mighty deed"; many Hebrew manuscripts have the plural, which TEV prefers, "**Your mighty deeds**" (parallel with the plural **works** in line **b**). There is no way of knowing for sure the exact nature of the Lord's "**mighty deeds**" which the psalmist praises, whether they are those that he himself experienced (see verses 10-11), or whether they are Yahweh's acts of salvation in Israel's history. Line **b** steps up line **a** by making **work** become **work of thy hands** and **glad** become **sing for joy**. Therefore, to reflect this intensifying movement in line **b**, the two lines may be translated, for example, "O LORD I am glad because of your mighty deeds; I even sing for joy because of the wonderful things you have done" or ". . . even more than that, I sing for joy . . . ."

92.5-6	RSV		TEV

5 How great are thy works, O
  LORD!
  Thy thoughts are very deep!
6 The dull man cannot know,
  the stupid cannot understand
  this:

5 How great are your actions,
  LORD!
  How deep are your thoughts!
6 This is something a fool cannot
  know;
  a stupid man cannot understand:

The psalmist praises God for his power and for his wisdom. Yahweh's **works** are **great**, that is, they are mighty, wonderful; and his **thoughts are very deep**, that is, profound, mysterious, hard to understand. NJV translates "subtle." And instead of **thoughts**, "plans, designs" may be more appropriate (see the word in 33.10b); God's plans are beyond human understanding. The expression **thy thoughts are very deep** may be rendered in some languages "the things you think, LORD, are difficult for us to understand."

The psalmist speaks particularly of the inevitable punishment of the wicked; they may prosper for a while, but they cannot escape their eventual destruction.

In verse 6 **dull man** and **stupid** are the words used in 49.10b; it is not lack of intelligence the psalmist is talking about, but lack of discernment about God's power and justice (compare 10.4). TEV's "**This**" points to verse 7. However, it is only the colon after "**understand**" in the second line that signals the beginning of what "**This**" refers to. RSV has the advantage of keeping **this:** at the end of verse 6. SPCL reduces the two lines to one and says "Only fools cannot understand it," referring back to verse 5. But RSV and TEV make verse 6 point forward to verse 7, which seems better.

92.7-8	RSV		TEV

7 that, though the wicked sprout
  like grass
  and all evildoers flourish,
  they are doomed to destruction for
  ever,
8 but thou, O LORD, art on high
  for ever.

7 the wicked may grow like weeds,
  those who do wrong may prosper;
  yet they will be totally destroyed,
8 because you, LORD, are supreme forever.

These verses state what the fool cannot understand, that is, how God's power and justice operate: though **the wicked** and **evildoers** may prosper and succeed, their final fate is **destruction** and death (see similar expressions in 37.35-36; 73.18-20). Yahweh is supreme ruler of the universe, and sinners are punished and destroyed.

"Totally" in verse 7c translates a Hebrew phrase which means "eternal, forever," parallel with **for ever** in verse 8 (which translates a different Hebrew expression). NJB translates "eternally destroyed."

Verse 7 consists of a concessive clause followed by a result, "although the wicked flourish, they will be destroyed." In some languages it is necessary to restructure this type of sentence in two contrasting statements; for example, "the wicked grow like weeds and prosper, but in spite of that they will be forever destroyed." In some languages it will be necessary to avoid the passive and say "but God will destroy them forever."

In Hebrew verse 8 begins with the connective "and," which most translate as **but**, in contrast with the fate of the fools in verse 7c. **On high** represents complete authority and power. TEV's **"supreme"** avoids a term referring to space, **on high**. In some languages this may be rendered "because you are the one who rules over all others forever."

92.9   RSV   TEV

For lo, thy enemies, O LORD,   We know that your enemies will
  for lo, thy enemies shall perish;   die,
  all evildoers shall be scattered.   and all the wicked will be de-
                                                 feated.

Some translations join verse 9 to verse 8 as the last part of the strophe that includes verses 5-9 (see introduction); but TEV, NJV, NAB, NJB, BJ join the verse to what follows: the defeat of Yahweh's enemies (verse 9) is balanced by the success of the psalmist (verses 10-11). Either division is possible.

RSV reproduces the form of the Masoretic text in verse 9, with its buildup to the climax **shall perish** in line b; TEV has followed the Hebrew manuscripts that omit the first line. TEV **"We know that"** translates the Hebrew "look, see" (RSV **lo**); NEB has "surely," which may weaken, not strengthen, the statement that follows. SPCL has "One thing is certain . . . ."

The Lord's **enemies** in verse 9 are also the psalmist's "enemies" in verse 11. **Scattered** means to be driven away in defeat.

92.10-11   RSV   TEV

10   But thou hast exalted my horn   10   You have made me as strong as a
       like that of the wild ox;   wild ox;
     thou hast poured over me[i]   you have blessed me with happi-
       fresh oil.   ness.
11   My eyes have seen the downfall of 11   I have seen the defeat of my ene-
       my enemies,   mies
     my ears have heard the doom of   and heard the cries of the
       my evil assailants.   wicked.

[i] Syr: Heb uncertain

For the figure in verse 10 **exalted my horn**, see 75.4,5. As the context shows, here **exalted my horn** means "made me powerful." For **wild ox** see *Fauna and Flora*, page 63; as a figure of brute strength, "wild bull" may be more appropriate. In many languages the comparison with the **wild ox** will have to be shifted to some other strong animal. Translators must make certain that unintended comparisons, such as sexual virility, are not introduced. In languages where there is not a suitable animal denoting strength, the simile may be dropped and the idea may be rendered "You have made me very strong."

The verb in verse 10b in Hebrew seems to mean "I am anointed"; RSV appeals to the Syriac for "you have anointed me," but most translations follow the Masoretic text. TEV has made explicit the actor implicit in the passive "I am anointed," that is, "You anointed me." The figure of "anoint with fresh olive oil" is taken by TEV to mean causing happiness, rejoicing (see 23.5; 45.7); Anderson and others think it indicates strengthening, empowering; Briggs believes it has to do with a celebration of victory. The literal rendering "you poured fresh oil over me" (RSV; similarly NJV, NEB, NIV, NJB, NAB) conveys no sensible meaning to readers today.

Verse 11 in Hebrew is somewhat wordy and confused: "my eye saw my enemies, my ear heard (of) the wicked who rise up against me." The word translated **enemies** occurs only here in the Old Testament; it is taken to be an alternate form of the word which means "enemy, foe" (see 5.8). The meaning of the verse seems clear enough, and most translations render the text as do RSV and TEV. For language similar to that in line a, see 54.7b. In languages in which a noun phrase such as **downfall of my enemies** will have to be shifted to a verb phrase, it may be necessary to introduce God as the agent of the actions; for example, "I have seen God defeat my enemies." In line b the psalmist speaks of having heard the cries of defeat sounded by his evil attackers. TEV fails to represent the first personal pronoun; "*my* wicked foes" would be better. Or else something like SPCL will serve: "I shall see how my enemies fall; I shall hear the complaints of those evil men!"

92.12-14

	RSV		TEV
12	The righteous flourish like the palm tree, and grow like a cedar in Lebanon.	12	The righteous will flourish like palm trees; they will grow like the cedars of Lebanon.
13	They are planted in the house of the LORD, they flourish in the courts of our God.	13	They are like trees planted in the house of the LORD, that flourish in the Temple of our God,
14	They still bring forth fruit in old age, they are ever full of sap and green,	14	that still bear fruit in old age and are always green and strong.

The psalm closes with a confident statement about the prosperity and success of **the righteous**. They are compared to a **palm tree** (see *Fauna and Flora,* pages 160-162), which is productive for many years (see similar figure in 1.3); they are also compared to **a cedar in Lebanon** (see 29.5; 37.35; see *Fauna and Flora,* page 108). In languages in which the palm tree and the cedar of Lebanon are unknown, trees with similar characteristics will have to be substituted. If such substitutes are not available, then the comparisons may shift to other plants that are known for these qualities, and, lacking that, the comparisons will have to be dropped.

For language similar to verse 13, see 52.8. Since it is uncertain whether trees actually grew in the Temple precincts, some understand **the house of the LORD** here to mean the land of Israel, not the Temple (see Kirkpatrick); but the parallel with **the courts of our God** in line **b** makes this unlikely. Dahood thinks the language refers to the heavenly habitation of God. It is best to keep verse 13 as a simile, "like trees that are planted," instead of the metaphor, **They are planted . . . they flourish** (and on through verse 14). By using complete statements, **They are planted** and **They still bring forth**, the subject is **the righteous** of verse 12; so it is better to imitate TEV, which uses a simile.

The comparison continues in verse 14; righteous people are like trees that **bring forth fruit**, and so forth. In verse 14b **full of sap and green** (TEV "green and strong") can be rendered "fresh and green" (Dahood, NJB, NIV), "vigorous and sturdy" (NAB), "strong and flourishing" (BJ).

92.15	RSV	TEV
	to show that the LORD is upright; he is my rock, and there is no unrighteousness in him.	This shows that the LORD is just, that there is no wrong in my protector.

The prosperity of the righteous demonstrates the Lord's character as being "**just**" and free of "**wrong**" (or **unrighteousness**); for similar language see Deuteronomy 32.4. RSV connects verse 15 to verse 14 by **to show**, which indicates purpose; it seems better to understand verse 15 as result: "**This shows**"; FRCL has "living proof that . . ."; NJV "attesting that." Some, because of the first person singular **my** in verse 15b, take verse 15 to be a quotation of the affirmation of the righteous; so NIV "proclaiming, 'The Lord is upright; he is my Rock, and there is no wickedness in him' " (see also NEB, TOB). TEV's "**the LORD is just**" must be rendered in some languages as a verb phrase; for example, "the LORD does things in a fair way" or "the LORD's way of doing things is good." **My rock** (TEV "**my protector**") must sometimes be rendered as "the one who takes care of me." See comments on "rock" in 18.2.

Psalm 93

This psalm, like Psalm 47, celebrates the majesty of Yahweh as king of the universe. For this type of psalm see introduction to Psalm 47.

There is no certain indication as to when the psalm was used; most commentators think the Festival of Shelters (Sukkoth) was the most likely occasion. The Septuagint has the title "For the day before the Sabbath, when the land was resettled; a hymn of praise by David." The Talmud states that this psalm was sung every Friday by the Levites in the Temple.

Verses 1-2 praise Yahweh's kingship over the world, and verses 3-4 proclaim his permanent victory over the forces of chaos and destruction. The psalm closes (verse 5) with praise for Yahweh's laws and his Temple.

HEADING: "**God the King**." Other headings are: "The majesty of God"; "The Ruler of the universe"; "The majestic King." The TEV heading for this psalm may require recasting in the form "God is our king," or in some languages, "God is the one who rules us."

<u>93.1-2</u>   RSV   TEV

1   The LORD reigns; he is robed in   1   The LORD is king.
        majesty;   He is clothed with majesty and
     the Lord is robed, he is girded   strength.
        with strength.   The earth is set firmly in place
     Yea, the world is established; it   and cannot be moved.
        shall never be moved;   2   Your throne, O LORD, has been
2   thy throne is established from   firm from the beginning,
        of old;   and you existed before time
     thou art from everlasting.   began.

The psalm begins with an acclamation of Yahweh as king. The first line of verse 1 in TEV will be rendered in some languages in the form suggested for the heading. Only in verse 1 is God spoken of in the third person. TEV retains the third person here. However, in many languages, for consistency it will be better to switch to second person. The verb is in the perfect tense, which some believe means here "has become king," with reference to an enthronement ritual in which Yahweh was depicted as taking his place on his throne (see Taylor; Weiser has "is become King"). But translations uniformly have "**is king**" or **reigns**.

His royal robes are described as **majesty** and **strength**. Two verbs are used in Hebrew: "clothe oneself" and "gird oneself"; for the latter verb see 65.6; see also 18.32,39. In most translations the metaphors **is robed in majesty . . . is girded with**

strength will have to be changed into similes: "his divine majesty and strength are to him like the splendid robes worn by a king," or "he is dressed like a king and is powerful," or "he is strong and wears the robe of a chief."

The statement about **the world** is a consequence of Yahweh's power as king; at the time of creation he set it firmly in place, and so it **shall never be moved** (see 96.10a,b). There is no power, human or otherwise, which can threaten the Lord's sovereignty over the world (see also 104.5-9). The passive construction of RSV and TEV will have to be recast in many languages so that God is the agent; for example, "you have set the earth firmly in place and nothing can move it."

In verse 2 **throne** is a figure for Yahweh's kingly power; he has been king **from of old**, from a very long time ago, that is, from the time he created the world.

God's eternal existence is stated in verse 2b. The Hebrew is simply "you (are) from all time (past)" (see 90.2); this can be stated "You have always existed."[1] SPCL, instead of repeating **established from of old**, says "ever since then . . . ." One may also translate "and since then you have been king." The expression "**existed before time began**" may be rendered in some languages as "you were there before people began counting years."

<table>
<tr><td>93.3</td><td align="center">RSV</td><td align="center">TEV</td></tr>
<tr>
<td></td>
<td>

The floods have lifted up, O LORD,
    the floods have lifted up their
      voice,
    the floods lift up their roaring.

</td>
<td>

The ocean depths raise their voice,
    O LORD;
    they raise their voice and roar.

</td>
</tr>
</table>

Yahweh's power over the unruly powers of chaos and destruction is celebrated; **the floods** (verse 3), the "many waters" (verse 4a), and "the sea" (verse 4b) all refer to the primeval chaos which Yahweh conquered at creation (see comments on 74.13-14; 89.9-10). Some commentators take these to be symbolic references to the nations which were Israel's enemies, such as Egypt and Assyria (see Kirkpatrick); but it is more likely that the reference is to the powers defeated at creation.

In verse 3c **roaring** translates a word found nowhere else in the Old Testament; NEB and Dahood have "pounding waves." It should be noted that the verb **lift up** in line c is in the imperfect tense, whereas in lines a and b it is in the perfect tense. Some take this change of tense to mean that **the floods** continue to rage and roar (for example, "the floods keep raging"; also RSV **lift up**; TOB). But most take the change to be simply stylistic.

The three lines in verse 3 may be represented as following:

The ocean depths, O LORD,
    the ocean depths roar;
    they let out a mighty roar.

---

[1] Instead of the Masoretic text "you (are)," the Targum has "you (are) God"; so NEB, FRCL. But it is not necessary to abandon the Masoretic text (so HOTTP).

In languages in which oceans are unknown, other bodies of water such as rivers will have to be used. One difficulty is that deep rivers tend to flow quietly. Consequently it may be necessary to say, for example, "the rushing rivers roar."

93.4   RSV   TEV

Mightier than the thunders of many waters,	**The LORD rules supreme in heaven,**
mightier than the waves[j] of the sea,	**greater than the roar of the ocean,**
the LORD on high is mighty!	**more powerful than the waves of the sea.**

[j] Cn: Heb *mighty the waves*

This verse in Hebrew is somewhat unusual, but most translations handle it without emending the text (see RSV footnote).[2] TEV has altered the order of the lines, placing line c of the Hebrew text first for greater ease of understanding. TEV **"The LORD rules supreme in heaven"** translates "majestic on high is Yahweh" (see the similar terms in 92.8). He is **mightier** than the forces of chaos and destruction, whether thought of as mythological beings or as human kingdoms. TEV line b **"greater than the roar of the ocean"** is better translated "mightier (or, more powerful) than the raging ocean." In languages which cannot use **waves of the sea** as a metaphor for power, very often the swirling of rapids on rivers is a close substitute.

93.5   RSV   TEV

Thy decrees are very sure;	**Your laws are eternal, LORD,**
holiness befits thy house,	**and your Temple is holy indeed,**
O LORD, for evermore.	**forever and ever.**

The psalm closes with praise for Yahweh's laws and Temple. For **decrees** see 19.7c, where RSV has "testimony" in the same expression; **are very sure** means that Yahweh's laws are unchangeable, they apply for all time.

The statement about the **holiness** of the Lord's **house** is made by use of a verb which means "to be seemly, proper, fit" (see "befits" also in 33.1); **holiness** is the outstanding characteristic of the Temple. FRCL translates "your temple should be a holy house." It is holy because the Lord, who dwells there, is holy.

But instead of reading the Hebrew word for **befits** as a verb, some translations (NEB, TOB, NJB, SPCL) read it as a noun, "holiness is the beauty of your house." NIV translates "holiness adorns your house." Dahood translates the line differently: "in

---

[2]HOTTP says the verse has two comparisons; the sense of the HOTTP rendering is "mightier than the noise of many waters, the waves of the sea are mighty; even more mighty is the LORD on high."

your temple the holy ones will laud you" (see his comments; see also Anderson). He takes "your temple" to be heaven, and "the holy ones" to be the gods. It is better not to follow Dahood here. (For a translation discussion of "holy" in relation to the Temple, see 28.2.)

The last line in Hebrew can be taken to mean "Yahweh (is) forever and ever," similar to verse 2b, with **LORD** understood as nominative. Most, however, understand **LORD** as vocative, as RSV and TEV do. **For evermore** is literally "for length of days," meaning that the statement will always be true.

Psalm 94

This psalm is the prayer of an individual who calls to the Lord for help against his enemies. They are not foreign oppressors but are leaders in Israel (see verses 4-7, 20-21).

The change in subject clearly evident between verse 15 and verse 16 has led many to consider that two separate compositions have been joined together (verses 1-15 and verses 16-23). Certainly verses 1-15 are a complete poem, and from verse 16 on, the subject becomes intensely personal, as the psalmist contemplates his own troubles and the eventual punishment of his enemies. In any case, as it now stands the psalm speaks for the entire community.

The psalm opens with an appeal to God to act (verses 1-4), followed by a description of the wicked leaders of the people (verses 5-7). Next the psalmist denounces these people, rebuking them for not recognizing that God is wise and just (verses 6-11); this is followed by praise for those who obey the Lord and trust in him (verses 12-15). The psalmist then describes his own troubles (verses 16-19) and closes the psalm with a declaration of his faith in God's justice (verses 20-23).

The Septuagint has as title "A psalm of David, for the fourth day of the week." The Mishnah states that the psalm was sung in the Temple on Wednesdays (the fourth day of the week) by the Levites.

HEADING: "**God the Judge of All.**" Other headings are: "The justice of God"; "The LORD is the judge of the world"; "God the avenger of injustice." The TEV heading must be recast for some languages; for example, "God judges all people," or "God is our judge," or "God judges us."

<u>94.1-2</u>	RSV	TEV
1	O LORD, thou God of vengeance, thou God of vengeance, shine forth!	1 LORD, you are a God who punishes; reveal your anger!
2	Rise up, O judge of the earth; render to the proud their deserts!	2 You are the judge of all men; rise and give the proud what they deserve!

Verses 1 and 3 contain stairstep parallelism; that is, the <u>a</u> line is repeated and then completed in <u>b</u>. The function of such parallelism is to catch the listener or reader's attention with an incomplete statement, which is then completed in the second line. The purpose is to move the listener or reader to want to see the undeveloped thought brought to completion.

818

The psalm begins with an urgent plea to God to act: he is called **God of vengeance**, that is, a God who takes vengeance on his enemies, the enemies of Israel, by punishing them (see "vengeance" in 18.47). In many languages the expression **God of vengeance** will carry the meaning of "vengeful vindictiveness." For this reason it will often be better to follow the example of TEV's **"God who punishes."** However, in some languages it will be necessary to make explicit the ones who receive this punishment. In the present context it refers to those in power who oppress others.

TEV **"reveal your anger"** translates the causative form of the verb "to shine": "cause to shine forth" (see 50.2; 80.1). In the context this "shining forth" is the manifestation of God's anger, or at least his justice, his determination to avenge. NJV translates "appear," which is better, in English at least, than "show yourself" (NAB; also NEB); FRCL has "manifest yourself." The verb in Hebrew is in the perfect tense, not the imperative;[1] NEB is the only translation to change the Hebrew text to justify using the imperative (see L. H. Brockington, *The Hebrew Text of the Old Testament*, page 146). Because both lines of verse 1 are closely synonymous, some translations such as SPCL reduce them to a single line, "Show yourself, Lord, God of vengeances." (The Spanish keeps the plural form, as in Hebrew.)

In verse 2 God as **judge of the earth** is asked to stand up and pass sentence on **the proud** and punish them as they deserve (see similar expression in 28.4d). **The proud** are people who disregard God (see verse 7). **Rise up** means "Take action" (see 3.7; 9.19). In languages in which **rise up** from a lying and sitting position are different, the expression as used here probably means that the psalmist is asking God to stand up (from his throne) and pronounce his verdict. **The proud** is often rendered by means of idiomatic expressions; for example, "give to people with swollen hearts the things they should get." **Their deserts** means **"what they deserve"** (TEV, NJB, NIV); NEB has "punish the proud as they deserve."

94.3-4	RSV	TEV
3	O LORD, how long shall the wicked, how long shall the wicked exult?	3 How much longer will the wicked be glad? How much longer, LORD?
4	They pour out their arrogant words, they boast, all the evildoers.	4 How much longer will criminals be proud and boast about their crimes?

In verse 3 the same construction is used as in verse 1: the first line is incomplete, lacking a verb; the second line repeats the first line and completes the thought with a verb: "How long (will) the wicked, Yahweh, how long will the wicked be glad?" The question is not a request for information; it is a way of reminding Yahweh that it is time he stop the boasting of **the wicked**. Instead of TEV "be glad,"

---

[1]The Greek translations of Aquila, Symmachus, and Theodotion, and Jerome and the Syriac, have the imperative; some believe the Masoretic form is simply a scribal error and that the imperative form is intended; see 80.1.

the verb "to gloat" better suits the context. In languages in which the question **How long shall** . . . will be interpreted as a request for information, it will be necessary to recast this to say, for example, "the wicked should stop being glad for the evil they do." or "evil people should stop boasting about the wicked things they do."

RSV takes verse 4 as declarative, placing it at the beginning of the next strophe (so NEB, NIV, SPCL); but TEV, AT, NAB, NJB, NJV, and Dahood take it as parallel with verse 3 (see Briggs, Kirkpatrick). In verse 4 TEV has used the word **"criminals"** to describe those people (RSV **evildoers**). The verse in Hebrew is "They pour out, they speak insolence, they boast, all the doers of evil." TEV **"be proud and boast"** translates the three verbal phrases; the verb **pour out** is used here figuratively, as in 19.2; 79.6. Weiser translates "they foam with rage," which is possible but does not seem likely. The verb **they boast** in Hebrew does not have a complement; TEV has supplied **"about their crimes"**; however, a translation can be "they are boastful" or "they brag about themselves."

94.5-7	RSV	TEV
5	They crush thy people, O LORD, and afflict thy heritage.	5	They crush your people, LORD; they oppress those who belong to you.
6	They slay the widow and the so- journer, and murder the fatherless;	6	They kill widows and orphans, and murder the strangers who live in our land.
7	and they say, "The LORD does not see; the God of Jacob does not perceive."	7	They say, "The LORD does not see us; the God of Israel does not notice."

The psalmist exposes the evil actions of the Israelite leaders: they are heartless, cruel, and unjust.

Verse 5 is an example of the way in which the poet sometimes places the metaphor (**crush**) in the first line and the general term (**afflict**) in the second. This, however, applies only to the event words. The objects of these events follow the more common positioning, with the general term **people** in the first line and the more specific **heritage** in the second line. This combination tends to remove the intensification, but not so much as to encourage the translator to reduce them to a single line, unless, of course, there is no alternative.

In verse 5a **crush** is used in the sense of "persecute," "destroy," "oppress," as in 10.10; 72.4. In verse 5b **thy heritage** is parallel with **thy people** in verse 5a.

Some consider the denunciations in verse 6 to be poetic exaggeration (see Oesterley), but it would not be proper to tone down the harsh language in translation. For **"widows and orphans"** see 68.5; see also 82.3-4 for comments on a similar passage that sheds light on this one. TEV **"the strangers who live in our land"** (RSV **the sojourner**) translates the Hebrew term for resident aliens, whose rights were protected by Israelite law. TEV has kept **"widows and orphans"** together as a common class of those who are often oppressed. Many translators will also prefer to do so, although in the Hebrew text "widows and foreigners" are together.

For statements similar to the thought expressed in verse 7, see 10.4,11. Such people act as if God does not exist, as though he has no interest in what is going on (see also 14.1; 53.1). In verse 7a **the LORD** translates *Yah* (as in 68.4); and for comments on **the God of Jacob**, see 46.7. Verse 7 closes the stanza and contains a degree of intensification in the second line which may be rendered, for example, "They say, 'The LORD does not see what we do; the God of Israel does not even pay any attention to us.'" **God of Israel** may have to be recast as "The God whom the people of Israel worship."

94.8-9	RSV	TEV
8	Understand, O dullest of the people! Fools, when will you be wise?	8 My people, how can you be such stupid fools? When will you ever learn?
9	He who planted the ear, does he not hear? He who formed the eye, does he not see?	9 God made our ears—can't he hear? He made our eyes—can't he see?

The psalmist rebukes the evil Israelite leaders for their stupidity. As often, this is lack of spiritual perception, not a lack of intelligence. The Hebrew for verse 8a is a command, as in RSV, while verse 8b is a rhetorical question. TEV has made both lines rhetorical questions. TEV's **"My people"** is too mild an expression to fit the context of rebuke being uttered by the psalmist. "You evil people" would be a more appropriate address form. TEV **"stupid fools"** translates the Hebrew for **dullest** and **fools**, two words used also in 92.6.

How can these people think that God will not see them or take notice of what they do (verse 7), when he is himself the Creator, who **planted** the ears and **formed** the eyes? (See comments on 33.15, "fashions the hearts.") Indeed God hears and sees. Where rhetorical questions may be misunderstood as requests for information, it may be better to use strong assertions: "Of course God hears! . . . Of course God sees!" Such assertions will also avoid the danger posed by the TEV rhetorical questions in verses 9 and 10, which may be understood as statements of despair or frustration.

94.10-11	RSV	TEV
10	He who chastens the nations, does he not chastise? He who teaches men knowledge,	10 He scolds the nations—won't he punish them?[x] He is the teacher of all men—
11	the LORD, knows the thoughts of man, that they are but a breath.	hasn't he any knowledge? 11 The LORD knows what they think; he knows how senseless their reasoning is.

[x] them?: *or* our wicked leaders?

In verse 10a the two verbs are practically synonymous; both mean "to discipline, admonish, rebuke, reprove" and occur in parallel lines in 6.1a,b; 38.1a,b (see also 39.11). The argument is as follows: the people whom the psalmist is accusing admit that Yahweh rebukes the pagan **nations** (the Hebrew term used in 2.1); will he not surely punish others as well, including the Israelite leaders themselves? So TEV **"punish them"** (also AT, NEB) is inadequate, since **"them"** here may be taken to refer to **"the nations"** in the same line, when it should refer to the wicked Israelite leaders (see TEV footnote). In the context it may be better to translate "He rebukes the nations—won't he punish our wicked leaders?" GECL has "He who disciplines all people, should he not also surely be able to punish you?"

The next line (verse 10b) is in Hebrew simply "he who teaches people knowledge." AT, NJV, and NAB connect it with the preceding line as a further description of God ("He who instructs man in knowledge"); RSV, BJ, NJB, GECL and TOB connect it with the following line. But others, like TEV, assume that there is an ellipsis of **"hasn't he any knowledge?"** (parallel with verses 9a,b, 10a) and so translate the line as a complete rhetorical question (so TOB, NEB, FRCL, SPCL, and Dahood). Translators may wish to do the same.

The thought of verse 11 finds a parallel in 39.5c; here the psalmist is talking about human thoughts, human reasoning. Most translations take **they are but a breath** (*hebel*; see 78.33) to refer to **thoughts**, despite the fact that in Hebrew "thoughts" is feminine and the pronoun "they" is masculine. But the context seems to require that it is human reasoning which God considers to be "vapid" (Dahood), "futile" (NJV, NIV); it is not likely that here the focus is on human mortality. If the translator interprets line <u>b</u> to refer to human thoughts, in some languages a simile can be used to denote their insubstantial existence; for example, "he knows their thoughts are like smoke that vanishes" or ". . . like clouds that pass by."

Verse 11 is quoted in 1 Corinthians 3.20 as it appears in the Septuagint, except that instead of "people" in the psalm, the word "the wise (people)" is used by Paul.

94.12-13 RSV	TEV
12 Blessed is the man whom thou dost chasten, O LORD, and whom thou dost teach out of thy law	12 LORD, how happy is the person you instruct, the one to whom you teach your law!
13 to give him respite from days of trouble, until a pit is dug for the wicked.	13 You give him rest from days of trouble until a pit is dug to trap the wicked.

After having condemned the wicked leaders in Israel (verses 4-11), the psalmist now turns to the righteous. In verse 12a the verb is the same as the first verb of verse 10a (RSV **chasten**). Here the parallel with the verb **teach** in line <u>b</u> makes it probable that the meaning is **"instruct"** (TEV, NEB, NAB, NJB), or else "discipline" (NJV, TOB) or "correct" (SPCL, TOB). <u>Law</u> translates *torah,* the special characteristic of Israel's religion, that is, Yahweh's instructions or commandments. Many times the specific reference is to the Pentateuch (see comments at 1.2), the written record of

Yahweh's *torah*; here the wider meaning of "instruction" or "commandments" is intended. LORD translates *Yah* (see verse 7a). In languages in which there are no synonyms for **teach**, and in which **teach** requires an object, it may be necessary to reduce verse 12 to a single line and to say, for example, "LORD, how happy is the person to whom you teach your law."

Respite from days of trouble is what the Lord gives to those who obey his law; they will be protected from their enemies, who will be caught like animals (see 57.6 and the references there). The nominal expression **days of trouble** will have to be recast in some languages as a verb phrase or clause; for example, ". . . rest from the times in which the wicked trouble you." **Days of trouble**, if translated literally, in some languages will imply that the person is free from such troubles at night.

It is clearly divine retribution at work in verse 13b, but a translation should not keep the figure of digging a pit if God is named as the subject of the active verb; it would be better to abandon the figure and say something like "until you are ready to punish the wicked." It is possible that here **pit** means the grave, so that it is the death of the wicked that is in view.

94.14-15   RSV   TEV

RSV	TEV
14 For the LORD will not forsake his people; he will not abandon his heritage;	14 The LORD will not abandon his people; he will not desert those who belong to him.
15 for justice will return to the righteous, and all the upright in heart will follow it.	15 Justice will again be found in the courts, and all righteous people will support it.

In verse 14 **his people** and **his heritage** mean the same as in verse 5; and the two verbs are also synonymous. They can be translated by the present tense (so TOB, FRCL).

Verse 15 is difficult to understand. Dahood comments that it is "the thorniest line in the entire psalm, grammatically and lexically." Line a seems to say "for judgment (*mishpat*; see 7.6) will turn back to righteousness (*tsedeq*; see 4.1)." RSV emends *tsedeq* to *tsadiq*, **the righteous**, which parallels **the upright in heart** in line b. Perhaps the most natural way to understand the line is as SPCL has done: "Justice will once again be just"; see NJV "Judgment shall again accord with justice" (so also TOB). TEV has expressed this meaning in a concrete form, "**Justice will again be found in the courts**" (see NAB footnote explanation: "The decisions of the judges will again be just").[2] In languages in which it is not possible to speak of **justice** as an abstract noun but rather as an event, it may be possible to say, for example, "judges will decide matters in a fair manner" or "rulers will judge the people fairly." GECL

---

[2]HOTTP says "judgment" here means "the practice or the exercise of justice," and "righteousness" means "the rule or norm of justice." It recommends: "for to righteousness the judgment comes back," which makes very little sense in English.

translates "Soon the judges themselves will judge again according to what is right [or, just], and all honest people will be pleased."

In verse 15b TEV **"will support it"** translates the Hebrew "after it," which seems to have the idea of acceptance, conformity, or approval (RSV **will follow it**; see NJV "shall rally to it").

<table>
<tr><td>94.16-17</td><td>RSV</td><td>TEV</td></tr>
</table>

16	Who rises up for me against the wicked? Who stands up for me against evildoers?	16 Who stood up for me against the wicked? Who took my side against the evildoers?
17	If the LORD had not been my help, my soul would soon have dwelt in the land of silence.	17 If the LORD had not helped me, I would have gone quickly to the land of silence.[k]

[k] LAND OF SILENCE: *The world of the dead (see 6.5).*

The psalmist refers to his own troubles, during which he had no human help or support; it was the Lord, and the Lord alone, who gave him comfort and aid.

The language in verse 16 suggests a trial (so TOB "plead my cause"), at which no one came to the psalmist's help. But the language may be general, not specific, and may indicate simply the lack of human help when the psalmist was being attacked by his enemies.

TEV translates the verbs in verse 16 in the past tense, as most fitting in the context (similarly Dahood); many translators, however, use the future tense (NJV, SPCL, NIV, NAB, TOB); a few, like RSV and NEB, use the present tense. But verses 17-18 definitely refer to past experience, so that the past tense seems best in verse 16.

Instead of the general **the wicked** . . . **evildoers**, it may be better to be specific, "these wicked people . . . these evildoers" (see TOB, FRCL). In languages in which legal proceedings cannot be reflected in the language (for lack of a legal tradition), it will be better to make the statements general. The question form implies that "No one" is the answer, and so in some languages these two questions may be recast as statements, that no one intervened. Since the two lines are fully synonymous and without intensification, they may require in some languages being reduced to a single line; for example, "Only the LORD helped me against those evil people" or "No one but the LORD helped me against those bad people."

The psalmist was in mortal danger; only the Lord's timely help kept him from dying (verse 17). "I" (**my soul**) translates the Hebrew "my *nefesh*" (see 3.2). In verse 17b **the land of silence** is the world of the dead, Sheol (see 6.5). The expression **land of silence**, if translated literally in some languages, may refer to local inhospitable and uninhabited areas. "World of the dead" in many languages means the local cemetery. It will be best in some cases to say simply "I would have died."

RSV   TEV

18 When I thought, "My foot slips,"   18 I said, "I am falling";
    thy steadfast love, O Lᴏʀᴅ, held   but your constant love, O Lᴏʀᴅ,
    me up.   held me up.
19 When the cares of my heart are   19 Whenever I am anxious and wor-
    many,   ried,
    thy consolations cheer my soul.   you comfort me and make me
                                               glad.

In parallel with verse 17, it seems that **"My foot slips"** in verse 18a means imminent death and not simply danger (see 18.36b; 38.16b-17a). Verse 18 begins literally "When I said." In the context it seems that "shouted" or "called out" would be more appropriate, but most translations keep it as in TEV. RSV has chosen **I thought** (NJV "I think"), which is suitable. NEB is good, "When I felt that my foot was slipping."

In verse 19 TEV **"I am anxious and worried"** translates "the many thoughts in my heart." The Hebrew word for "thoughts" is found only here and in 139.23; here the thoughts are clearly disquieting and worrisome. In verse 19b **thy consolations** is best represented by a verb phrase, "you console (or comfort, or reassure)"; and "my *nefesh*" (**my soul**) is again a way of saying "**me.**"

94.20-21   RSV   TEV

20 Can wicked rulers be allied with   20 You have nothing to do with cor-
    thee,   rupt judges,
    who frame mischief by statute?   who make injustice legal,
21 They band together against the   21 who plot against good men
    life of the righteous,   and sentence the innocent to
    and condemn the innocent to   death.
    death.

In the final verses the psalmist sums up his faith in the Lord's justice: Yahweh is with the righteous and against the wicked. In verse 20, by means of a rhetorical question, the psalmist declares that Yahweh is in no way on the side of "**corrupt judges**" (TEV), which translates "throne of destruction." RSV takes this to mean **wicked rulers**, but as Anderson points out, it is more likely that in this context judges are meant (see SPCL, FRCL). For a translation discussion of "**corrupt**," see 14.1. The Hebrew phrase translated by TEV as "**You have nothing to do with . . .**" is rendered by SPCL as "you cannot be the friend of . . . ," which may serve as a better model for many languages. RSV **mischief** (also NEB, NJV) does not seem adequate for the Hebrew word, which indicates rather "wrong, disorder, wickedness"; so TEV "injustice." The Hebrew phrase translated **by statute** can be taken to mean "against the law," as SPCL translates it. TOB and FRCL translate "who create misery by flouting the law." TEV's "**who make injustice legal**" will often have to be shifted to two clauses; for example, "who do things which the law is against" or "who do wrong acts which the law says people should not do."

In verse 21a **band together** translates a verb form found only here in the Old Testament, which is defined as "gather together (against)." **Against the life** implies that they plan to kill him. **Condemn the innocent to death** translates "condemn innocent blood" (see similar language in 106.38).

94.22-23   RSV   TEV

22   But the LORD has become my   22   But the LORD defends me;
         stronghold,   my God protects me.
     and my God the rock of my   23   He will punish them for their
         refuge.   wickedness
23   He will bring back on them their   and destroy them for their sins;
         iniquity   the LORD our God will destroy
     and wipe them out for their   them.
         wickedness;
     the LORD our God will wipe
         them out.

In this closing statement the psalmist reaffirms his faith in Yahweh's justice.

For **stronghold** and **the rock of my refuge** in verse 22, see 9.9; 14.6; 18.2. Only here does the particular combination **the rock of my refuge** occur.

The thought of verse 23a is similar to that found in 54.5 (see also 5.10); **wipe ... out** in line <u>b</u> translates a verb meaning "to put to silence," that is, to kill (see 18.40b). NJV translates "annihilate."

The TEV expressions **"for their wickedness"** and **"for their sins"** are synonymous and must be recast in many languages to say, for example, "because they have done evil acts" or "because they have been bad people."

The Masoretic text repeats the verbal phrase in lines <u>b</u> and <u>c</u>, "he will destroy them" (so RSV, TEV, and others); some Hebrew manuscripts and the Septuagint omit the first one, so that the text reads "and Yahweh our God will destroy them for their sins" (so NEB).

Psalm 95

This psalm praises Yahweh as King of the earth. It was sung in worship, probably in one of the great festivals of faith, perhaps the Festival of Shelters, at which occasion, according to many scholars, there was a ritual in which Yahweh was represented as seated on his throne as king. Consequently this psalm, like the following Psalms 96–99 (and Psalms 47, 93), is called an "enthronement psalm." See introduction to Psalm 47.

The psalm clearly divides into two parts: the first (verses 1-7c) is a call to worship, sung either by pilgrims coming to the Temple or else by the whole congregation; and the second (verses 7d-11) is a message from the Lord, delivered either by a priest or a prophet, warning against rebellion and disobedience.

HEADING: "No worship without obedience"; "A call to praise and obedience"; "Worship of the creator–king." The TEV heading "**A Song of Praise**" may be adapted for translation into many languages by recasting it as a full sentence; for example, "The psalmist calls the people to sing and praise the LORD" or "The psalmist invites the people to worship God."

95.1-2   RSV   TEV

1	O come, let us sing to the LORD; let us make a joyful noise to the rock of our salvation!	1	Come, let us praise the LORD! Let us sing for joy to God, who protects us!
2	Let us come into his presence with thanksgiving; let us make a joyful noise to him with songs of praise!	2	Let us come before him with thanksgiving and sing joyful songs of praise.

In the opening strophe (verses 1-5) the people are called upon to worship Yahweh (verses 2-3), because he is the ruler of the world (verses 3-5).

The two verbs **sing** and **make a joyful noise** are used synonymously; they translate the Hebrew "shout for joy" (see 20.5a) and "shout" (see 66.1). For **the rock of our salvation** in verse 1b, see 62.6; 89.26b. SPCL translates "our protector and savior"; FRCL "our keeper, our Savior"; GECL "our strong helper."

Come into his presence in verse 2 means to enter the Temple, where Yahweh is worshiped. Again two terms are used synonymously, **thanksgiving** and **songs of praise**; the latter term is used in 81.2 of instrumental music, but here, in parallel with the preceding line, it indicates vocal music. In many languages the word **come** in **come into his presence** is used differently, depending upon the position of the speaker. In the context of this verse the psalmist calls for the people to enter the place from which he calls them. This probably means from inside the Temple. If it is from outside the Temple, then "go" or "enter" would be appropriate in English. SPCL has "let us enter his presence with gratitude." TEV's **"come before him"** implies for the purpose of worship, which will have to be made explicit in many languages. Accordingly it will often be necessary to say, for example, "Let us go in where he is and worship him" or "Let us go into the Temple and worship him."

95.3-5	RSV		TEV
3	For the LORD is a great God, and a great King above all gods.	3	For the LORD is a mighty God, a mighty king over all the gods.
4	In his hand are the depths of the earth; the heights of the mountains are his also.	4	He rules over the whole earth, from the deepest caves to the highest hills.
5	The sea is his, for he made it; for his hands formed the dry land.	5	He rules over the sea, which he made; the land also, which he himself formed.

Yahweh's greatness is acclaimed in verse 3; he is <u>**a great God**</u>, superior to <u>all gods</u>, whether real or imaginary (see 96.4-5). He is the Creator God who rules over all that he has made. The expression <u>**King above all gods**</u> or TEV's "over all the gods," if translated literally, in many languages will refer to space only. Therefore it will often be necessary to recast this expression to say, for example, "He is a great king who rules over all other gods," or in some languages to make a comparison; for example, "He is a powerful king, but all other gods are weak."

In verse 4a <u>**In his hand**</u> indicates not only possession but sovereignty. <u>**The depths of the earth**</u> and <u>**the heights of the mountains**</u> are picturesque phrases used to indicate the whole earth.

Instead of the Masoretic text "depths" in verse 4a (a word which occurs nowhere else in the Old Testament), one Hebrew manuscript and the Septuagint have "the far places," which NEB prefers; but <u>**depths**</u> better parallels <u>**heights**</u> in the next line. Dahood takes <u>**the depths of the earth**</u> to mean Sheol. The "mountain heights" were thought of by many as the places where the gods dwelt (see 68.15-16), and the idea may be in the background of the language here.

In verse 5 Yahweh's power over both <u>**the sea**</u> and <u>**the dry land**</u> (TOB "the continents") is asserted, for he created both (see 24.1-2). The verb in verse 5b, <u>**formed**</u>, represents God as fashioning, molding, the dry land with his own hands (see the verb also in 94.9b).

95.6-7c	RSV		TEV
6	O come, let us worship and bow down, let us kneel before the LORD, our Maker!	6	Come, let us bow down and worship him; let us kneel before the LORD, our Maker!

7	For he is our God, and we are the people of his pasture, and the sheep of his hand.	7	He is our God; we are the people he cares for, the flock for which he provides.

In these verses Yahweh is praised as Creator and Lord of his people. Once again the people are exhorted to worship him. The first verb in verse 6, **Come**, is not the same as the first one in verse 1; it means "enter," and some see here not just a synonym but a progression. Here the worshipers are called upon to enter the Temple; TOB and FRCL have "Enter in"; Dahood "Come in" (see Taylor). The other two verbs in verse 6a are used synonymously, **worship** and **bow down**, and they are followed by the verb **kneel** in verse 6b. The noun phrase **our Maker** must often be recast as a verb phrase; for example, "he is the one who created us" or ". . . the one who has given us life."

In verse 7 TEV **"the people he cares for"** translates the phrase **the people of his pasture**, which is paralleled in the next line by **the sheep of his hand**. Israel is the flock, Yahweh is their shepherd. One Hebrew manuscript and the Syriac have a slightly different text: "We are his people and the flock of his pasture" (as in 100.3c), which NEB prefers. In line **b** **the people of his pasture** (see comments at 74.1b; 79.13a) at once identifies God as the shepherd and the people as his flock. The meaning may be expressed by "we are the flock of which you are the shepherd." In the next line **sheep** makes specific the idea of a flock, which has been already suggested by **pasture** of the previous line. **His hand** is a figure for protection and provision; the shepherd protects his sheep and provides for their needs. HOTTP prefers the idea of guidance: "the flock which he leads." The expression **he is our God** must often be shifted to a verb phrase in some languages in which God cannot be "possessed"; for example, "he is the God we worship." **Of his pasture** and **his hand** may be kept as synonyms as in TEV or reduced to one. In some languages it may be best to shift to a simile; for example, "we are his people whom he cares for as a shepherd cares for his sheep" or "we are his people and he cares for us as he cares for sheep."

95.7d-9	RSV		TEV

7d	O that today you would hearken to his voice!	7d	Listen today to what he says:
8	Harden not your hearts, as at Meribah, as on the day at Massah in the wilderness,	8	"Don't be stubborn, as your an- cestors were at Meribah, as they were that day in the desert at Massah.
9	when your fathers tested me, and put me to the proof, though they had seen my work.	9	There they put me to the test and tried me, although they had seen what I did for them.

In the second part of the psalm, a message from Yahweh is delivered to the people, probably by a prophet or a priest, warning them not to be disobedient, as their ancestors had been. TEV has placed the content of verses 8-11 in quotes. In some languages it will be necessary to make even clearer that God is now the speaker, and to indicate this by placing a subheading before 7d; for example, "God speaks to the people."

The message begins, "If today you would listen to his voice!"—a wish, which TEV expresses by a command (also GECL, SPCL).[1]

The warning comes in verses 8-10, reminding the people of the incidents in **Meribah** and **Massah** (see Exo 17.1-7; Num 20.1-13; Deut 6.16; 33.8). According to Exodus 17.7 the two names were given to the one place where the people put God to the test by asking for water; but it is possible that two separate incidents have been combined into the one account; or else there were variant traditions of the same event. **Meribah** means "quarrel" and **Massah** means "testing" (see the verb in verse 9a). See also 106.32-33; and see 81.7, where it is said that God put the people to the test at Meribah.

It should be noticed that the Hebrew text in verse 8a is "Don't be stubborn as you were at Meribah," and only in verse 9a are the ancestors referred to. TEV has accordingly made "**your ancestors**" the subject in verse 8a, since that is what is meant. The Hebrew phrase "harden the heart" means "be stubborn."

For the language of verse 9 see 78.18,41,56. The two verbs **tested** and **put to the proof** are synonymous. Even though the Israelites had seen what God had done for them, they wanted further proof of his love for them; in this way they put him to the test. Translators should provide cross references to verses 8-9 and a brief explanatory note.

95.10-11	RSV	TEV

10	For forty years I loathed that generation and said, "They are a people who err in heart, and they do not regard my ways."	10	For forty years I was disgusted with those people. I said, 'How disloyal they are! They refuse to obey my commands.'
11	Therefore I swore in my anger that they should not enter my rest.	11	I was angry and made a solemn promise: 'You will never enter the land where I would have given you rest.' "

In verse 10a **loathed** translates a verb expressing deep dislike, revulsion, disgust. The sentiment is not as much of anger or indignation (NIV, NEB) as it is of disgust; see this verb in 119.158a; 139.21b. For **forty years** see Numbers 14.33-34.

---

[1] It should be noticed that NEB, following its textual decision in the first part of verse 7, begins the passage in Hebrew with "his hand," which it translates "his power," supplying "You shall know" with which to begin the sentence: "You shall know his power today if you will listen to his voice."

In verse 10b **err in heart** means to be "**disloyal**" (TEV), perverse, fickle (NJB), parallel with line c **they do not regard my ways**, that is, "**They refuse to obey my commands.**"

God was angry with them and swore that **that generation**, that is, all the adults who had left Egypt, would never enter the Promised Land, Canaan, which is here called **my rest**, that is, "my resting-place." This is the place where God "rests" (see also 132.8,14), and where the people would also enjoy rest after their years of wandering in the wilderness (see Deut 12.9). In some languages it will be best to avoid TEV's "**those people**," verse 10a, and to speak of "your ancestors" as in verse 8. Modern translations are divided in the expression of **my rest**. Many express it as "God's rest," while others, like TEV, FRCL, and GECL, render it as giving rest to the people.

Verses 8-11 are quoted in Hebrews 3.7-11, substantially as they appear in the Septuagint; references are made to the same passage in the rest of the chapter and in the following chapter in Hebrews.

Psalm 96

This psalm, like Psalm 95, praises Yahweh as king and judge of the universe. Its theme is the same as that of Psalms 97–99, and some believe that they were all composed by the same person.

The text of this psalm is found, with some variations, in 1 Chronicles 16.23-33; it is the opinion of most commentators that the author of Chronicles used and adapted this psalm, not vice versa. The translation of the two passages should reflect their similarities and their differences.

Like other psalms of this kind, Psalm 96 was composed to be sung at one of the festivals where Yahweh was acclaimed as king, probably the Festival of Shelters (see introduction to Psalm 47).

The psalm is an invitation for all the peoples of the world to praise Yahweh as king. It begins with a call for universal praise (verses 1-3), followed by the reason for this: Yahweh is the Creator God (verses 4-6). Again all the nations are called upon to praise Yahweh (verses 7-9), and the psalm closes with the call to the whole universe, including inanimate creation, to praise Yahweh, who is also the judge of all humankind (verses 10-13).

HEADING: "**God the Supreme King**." Other headings are: "Yahweh is king and judge"; "The universal king"; "God comes to judge." The headings of Psalms 96–99 in TEV are essentially the same and may be adapted to many languages by saying, for example, "God is the greatest king," or "There is no chief like God," or "God rules the people of the world."

96.1-3   RSV   TEV

RSV	TEV

1   O sing to the LORD a new song;
      sing to the LORD, all the earth!
	1 Sing a new song to the LORD!
	      Sing to the LORD, all the world!

2   Sing to the LORD, bless his name;
      tell of his salvation from day to
      day.
	2 Sing to the LORD, and praise him!
	      Proclaim every day the good
	      news that he has saved us.

3   Declare his glory among the na-
      tions,
      his marvelous works among all
      the peoples!
	3 Proclaim his glory to the nations,
	      his mighty deeds to all peoples.

BJ and NJB bring out the strophic arrangement of verses 1-3 by printing them as two strophes of three lines each.

All humankind is exhorted to praise the Lord. The **new song** (see 33.3; 40.3) is probably this psalm itself, which is offered as one more hymn in praise of Yahweh. **All the earth** must in many languages be expressed by "all the people in the world."

Bless his name in verse 2a means "**praise him**"; for **bless** see 16.7, and for **name** see 5.11. FRCL translates "thank him for being your God." In verse 2b TEV interprets **his salvation** as a reference to Israel's own experience, "**he has saved us**"; but the text may mean either Yahweh's power to save, his nature as savior, or else his future victory over all the enemies of Israel. NEB has "triumph," and NJV "victory"; FRCL "that he is the Savior." In any case **his salvation** in verse 2b is parallel with **his glory** in verse 3a and **his marvelous works** in verse 3b. In this context **his glory** can be translated "his fame" or "his greatness." All three describe Yahweh as a God who manifests himself (**glory**) by means of his mighty deeds on behalf of his people (**his salvation**). For **marvelous works** see "wonderful deeds" in 9.1. It should be noted that the verb translated **Declare** in verse 3a is a synonym of the verb **tell of** in verse 2b; the verb in verse 2b means "tell good news," so TEV translates "**Proclaim . . . the good news.**"

The announcement of Yahweh's great deeds is to be made **to the nations**, **among all the peoples** (verse 3). The expression **his glory among the nations** and **his marvelous works** may be handled as synonymous and may be rendered, for example, "tell all the tribes how great he is."

96.4-5 RSV	TEV
4 For great is the LORD, and greatly to be praised; he is to be feared above all gods.	4 The LORD is great and is to be highly praised; he is to be honored more than all the gods.
5 For all the gods of the peoples are idols; but the LORD made the heavens.	5 The gods of all other nations are only idols, but the LORD created the heavens.

Verse 4a is identical with 48.1a, and here it gives the reason why Yahweh should be praised by all peoples. The statement "**is to be highly praised**" may be expressed by "should be . . . ," or "is worthy of being . . . ," or "deserves to be . . . ." "**Honored**" translates the verb "to fear" (RSV; see 15.4); here, in the contrast between Yahweh and all the gods, the meaning is better expressed by "awe" or "reverence," or even "fear"; see NEB "he is more to be feared than all gods" (also Dahood). The impersonal construction of both TEV and RSV **he is to be feared** will have to be recast in many languages to say, for example, "people should worship the LORD" or "people should have reverence for the LORD."

The word **gods** (Hebrew *'elohim*) refers to supernatural powers that are recognized as existing, but inferior to Yahweh. Therefore translators should not translate **gods** by a term meaning "evil spirits" or "demons." In some languages **gods** may be called "strong spirits." The **gods** should not be translated by the term used for "angels" or "God's messengers." In some languages **gods** may be rendered by a phrase meaning "the little gods" or "the spirits that are not the great spirit."

Implicitly the psalmist acknowledges the reality of **the gods** of other nations (verse 4a), but at once he declares that they **are idols**, in no way to be ranked with Yahweh, who **made the heavens**. The Septuagint translates the Hebrew word by "demons," but the word means essentially "nothing, nobody," a term of contempt which is better represented by **idols**. In speaking of Yahweh as Creator, the psalmist seems to single out **the heavens**, perhaps because it was believed that the act of creating them was the greatest of all (see 8.3). In some languages **idols** are referred to as "things which people worship" or, depending on the local practice, "wooden things people pray to" or "things people make and pray to." Accordingly verse 5 may sometimes be rendered "the gods which some tribes worship are nothing more than things made by people for worship, but the LORD made the heavens." If the contrast must be made more explicit, the translator may say ". . . but the LORD is so great he made the heavens."

96.6 RSV	TEV
Honor and majesty are before him; strength and beauty are in his sanctuary.	Glory and majesty surround him; power and beauty fill his Temple.

Yahweh as king possesses **honor and majesty**, the two greatest attributes of a king (see the same nouns translated "splendor and majesty" in 21.5b, and "glory and majesty" in 45.3b). **Strength** and **beauty** are the two terms used to describe the Covenant Box in 78.61 (where RSV translates "power" and "glory"), and they are two other characteristics of Yahweh as king. In other words, the psalmist is saying that, because of the presence of the Covenant Box in the Temple, God's **strength** and **beauty** are there; he is not saying that the Temple itself is strong and beautiful. **Before him** in line a (TEV "surround him") may be represented by "He radiates greatness and majesty" (FRCL); NEB's use of the verb "attend" represents the two characteristics as royal servants that wait upon Yahweh. In line b **his sanctuary** may be Yahweh's heavenly dwelling; given the probable reference to the Covenant Box, however, it more likely refers to the earthly Temple, where he dwelt with the people of Israel.

The major translation problem in this verse is the handling of abstract nouns as though they were objects. SPCL says "there is great splendor in his presence." In languages which permit a passive, it is possible to say "Glory and majesty can be seen around him." Where the passive is not possible, this may be rendered, for example, "People in his presence can see how great and like a king he is." Line b can sometimes be rendered "People can see in his Temple that he is strong and beautiful" or "the things in his Temple remind people that he is strong and beautiful."

RSV   TEV

7 Ascribe to the LORD, O families of the peoples, ascribe to the LORD glory and strength!	7 Praise the LORD, all people on earth; praise his glory and might.
8 Ascribe to the LORD the glory due his name; bring an offering, and come into his courts!	8 Praise the LORD's glorious name; bring an offering and come into his Temple.
9 Worship the LORD in holy array; tremble before him, all the earth!	9 Bow down before the Holy One when he appears;¹ tremble before him, all the earth!

l when he appears; *or* in garments of worship.

Again all the nations are called upon to praise Yahweh. The verb used in verses 7a,b,8a and translated **Ascribe** is the imperative form of "to give." It is as though the worshipers are to bring into the Temple with them Yahweh's **glory and strength**, **the glory due his name**. Most English translations use the verb **Ascribe**, since obviously "bring" is not appropriate in the context. "Give" (NJB, SPCL, TOB, Dahood) or "offer" seems better. Since these "offerings" are worship and praise, TEV uses the verb "**Praise**"; "proclaim" or "announce" would also serve. FRCL has "come to honor . . . come to proclaim."

In verse 7 the same stylistic device (called a staircase arrangement) is used that was noted in 94.1,3. In verse 7a **families of the peoples** is a way of speaking of humankind in terms of national or racial groups. Except for this phrase, verses 7a,b, 8a are exactly like 29.1,2a (which see); the translation should reflect this identity.

FRCL offers a good dynamic equivalence translation of verse 8:

Come and proclaim his glory,
enter the courts of his temple
as you carry your gifts.

In verse 8b the word for **offering** is general (see 20.3) and is applicable to any offering, of animals or cereals. **His courts** refers to the open areas within the Temple grounds.

Verse 9a is identical with 29.2b, which see. In verse 9b the verb translated **tremble** is taken by some to mean "dance" (see Briggs; NEB). For translation suggestions on **tremble before him**, see 2.11.

96.10   RSV   TEV

Say among the nations, "The LORD reigns! Yea, the world is established, it shall never be moved;	Say to all the nations, "The LORD is king! The earth is set firmly in place and cannot be moved;

| he will judge the peoples with equity." | he will judge the peoples with justice." |

In verses 10-13 the psalm closes with an exhortation for all creation, human and nonhuman, animate and inanimate, to worship and praise the universal Lord.

The command **Say** is apparently addressed to the worshipers. In the context of communicating a message to someone, "Tell" in English would be more appropriate. The message **The LORD reigns** is to be proclaimed to **the nations**. The contents of the message in verse 10a,b are phrased in language used in 93.1a,c (which see). And in verse 10c **judge . . . with equity** uses the same terms as in 9.8b.

96.11-13   RSV   TEV

11   Let the heavens be glad, and let   11   Be glad, earth and sky!
         the earth rejoice;   Roar, sea, and every creature in
      let the sea roar, and all that   you;
         fills it;   12   be glad, fields, and everything in
12   let the field exult, and every-   you!
         thing in it!   The trees in the woods will shout
      Then shall all the trees of the   for joy
         wood sing for joy   13   when the LORD comes to rule
13   before the LORD, for he comes,   the earth.
      for he comes to judge the earth.   He will rule the peoples of the
      He will judge the world with   world
         righteousness,   with justice and fairness.
      and the peoples with his truth.

In verses 11a,b, 12a the whole universe is called upon to praise Yahweh: **heavens, earth, sea, field,** together with all the living beings that inhabit the seas and the fields. Four verbs are used synonymously: **be glad** (see 9.2), **rejoice** (see 9.14), **roar** (see 46.3), and **exult** (see 28.7). For **sing for joy** in verse 12b, see "shout for joy" in 20.5. In languages in which inanimate objects do not express human emotions, it may be necessary to add a simile; for example, "earth and sky be glad as people are glad." The same is true for sea, fields, and trees.

In verse 12b the form of the Hebrew is not an exhortation, as in verses 11a,b, 12a, but a declaration; so TEV, RSV, NJV, NEB, NAB, NIV, Dahood; but BJ, NJB, TOB, FRCL, and SPCL disregard the difference and translate the line as though it were like the preceding three.

The Hebrew in the first part of verse 13 is repetitious: "before Yahweh, for he comes, for he comes to rule the earth." TEV has expressed it more succinctly, "**when the LORD comes to rule the earth.**"

The verb translated "**rule**" by TEV in verse 13a,b is *shafat* (not the same verb used in verse 10a), which in many contexts has the precise meaning of **to judge** and is so translated here by RSV and others. But here more is implied than the exercise of judgment: Yahweh as king (verse 10) is coming to rule, to govern, the world (so TEV, SPCL, TOB, NJV, NAB, Dahood); see the verb in 72.2. TEV "**justice**" translates *tsedeq* (see 4.1), and "**fairness**" translates *'emunah* (see 36.5). RSV and others translate the latter word by **truth** or "faithfulness." Anderson defines the phrase here: "with self-consistency and without arbitrariness."

Psalm 97

This psalm, like Psalm 96, celebrates Yahweh as supreme ruler of the universe. The language is similar to that used in other psalms which praise Yahweh's sovereignty.

The psalm opens with a description of the power and majesty of Yahweh (verses 1-6); idolaters are condemned, while the faithful worshipers of Yahweh rejoice (verses 7-9). The psalm closes with praise for Yahweh's righteousness and his love for his people (verses 10-12).

Several commentators see this psalm as eschatological, that is, a description of the Lord's final victory, not an account of his present activity (so Dahood, Fisher, McCullough; NJB).

HEADING: **"God the Supreme Ruler."** Other headings are: "King above the gods"; "The triumph of Yahweh"; "The universal king." The TEV heading must often be recast as a full sentence; for example, "God is the greatest ruler" or, in some languages, as a negative comparison, "There is no ruler like God."

97.1   RSV   TEV

The LORD reigns; let the earth rejoice; let the many coastlands be glad!	The LORD is king! Earth, be glad! Rejoice, you islands of the seas!

The opening words **The Lord reigns** are the same as those of 93.1 (which see). In verse 1b **the many coastlands** translates the phrase "many islands"; as in 72.10, the word translated "islands" may include coastal settlements as well (TEV "islands of the seas," SPCL "the many islands," and NEB "coasts and islands"). Anderson takes the phrase here to mean "the remotest parts of the earth"; another option is to say in a footnote "the coastal settlements in distant parts of the Mediterranean." FRCL has "all distant peoples," and NIV "the distant shores."

In verse 1 the common term **earth** in line a is paralleled in line b by the more specific **coastlands**, which represents a heightening of poetic effect. In many languages **the earth rejoice** will have to be recast as "the people of the earth rejoice." Accordingly the intensification may be represented by saying, for example, "The LORD rules everywhere; so let the people of the earth rejoice; let even the people in the distant islands be glad!"

RSV	TEV
2 Clouds and thick darkness are round about him; righteousness and justice are the foundation of his throne.	2 Clouds and darkness surround him; he rules with righteousness and justice.
3 Fire goes before him, and burns up his adversaries round about.	3 Fire goes in front of him and burns up his enemies around him.
4 His lightnings lighten the world; the earth sees and trembles.	4 His lightning lights up the world; the earth sees it and trembles.
5 The mountains melt like wax before the LORD, before the Lord of all the earth.	5 The hills melt like wax before the LORD, before the Lord of all the earth.

For a similar description of the Lord's presence as described in these verses, see 18.7-15; 50.3. In verse 2 the psalmist uses physical phenomena (**clouds and thick darkness**) and moral attributes (**righteousness and justice**) to describe Yahweh's reign. **Clouds and thick darkness** may be represented by "dark clouds"; see SPCL "thick clouds," and GECL "thick dark clouds." **Clouds and thick darkness** may carry meanings in the translator's language which are not associated with the hiddenness and mystery of God's rule. In such cases it may be necessary to make this clear in the text in order to prevent the reader from misinterpreting the expression. It will also be advisable to provide the reader with cross references such as Deuteronomy 4.11; 5.22.

The Hebrew phrase **the foundation of his throne** in verse 2b refers to the basis on which Yahweh's rule is exercised; so TEV "**he rules with righteousness and justice**"; or else, "righteousness and justice are the basis of his rule" (see FRCL). The same language occurs in 89.14a. **Righteousness and justice** describe how God rules, in much the same way that **clouds and thick darkness** describe the location of his rule. In some languages it will be more understandable to reverse the biblical order and say, for example, "He rules people in a way that is right and just, and he rules them from behind clouds and darkness."

Fire and **lightnings** (verses 3,4) are manifestations of God's power and anger; the language used of **the earth** in verse 4b is identical with that used of the sea, the "deep," in 77.16; and see also 77.18b,c. The expression **Fire goes before him** will require recasting in languages in which an agent who is causing the fire to move must be expressed; for example, "God sends his fire ahead of him."

Verses 3-5 describe the effects of the Lord's presence upon **his adversaries**, **the earth**, and **the mountains**. Yahweh's power is overwhelming, and nothing or no one can resist him (see similar language in 68.2). In verse 4 **the world** and **the earth** are exact synonyms; most translations feel comfortable with using both words. The metaphor **the earth sees and trembles** may have to be recast as a simile; for example, "just as a person sees, the earth sees the lightning and trembles." In languages where a simile would not serve to make the metaphor clear, it may be necessary to use a nonmetaphor; for example, "the lightning flashes on the earth, and the earth shakes."

In verse 5 for **melt like wax**, see 46.6b, "the earth melts." The translator should make certain what the basis for the comparison is in his language in the simile **melt**

like wax; for example, some languages use "sugar" as the basis for the comparison. In verse 5a the name Yahweh is used; in verse 5b the title "lord" is used. **Before the LORD** means "in the presence of the LORD" or "when the LORD is near." **Lord of all the earth** must often be rendered, for example, "the Lord who rules all the people of the earth."

97.6   RSV   TEV

> The heavens proclaim his right-
>   eousness;
> and all the peoples behold his
>   glory.

> The heavens proclaim his right-
>   eousness,
> and all the nations see his
>   glory.

Some (see RSV) place verse 6 at the beginning of the next strophe; it seems better, however, to include it as the last verse of the first strophe (Dentan, Anderson; NAB, NIV, NJB).

The heavens, like messengers, **proclaim** Yahweh's **righteousness** (see identical language in 50.6), while on earth **all the peoples** (or "all the nations") see **his glory**. The two attributes, **righteousness** and **glory**, here in parallel lines, may refer specifically to Yahweh's saving activity, whereby he manifests himself as a God who protects and rescues his people. The expression **The heavens proclaim** may have to be shifted in some languages to say, for example, "The heavens show that God is good." **Behold his glory** may sometimes be rendered "the people see that God is great."

97.7   RSV   TEV

> All worshipers of images are put
>   to shame,
> who make their boast in worth-
>   less idols;
> all gods bow down before him.

> Everyone who worships idols is
>   put to shame;
> all the gods bow down[m] before
>   the LORD.

> [m] all the gods bow down; *or* bow down,
> all gods.

The psalmist now describes the effect of Yahweh's sovereignty on Gentiles and Israelites alike. The former are **put to shame**, that is, "dismayed" (NJV), "humiliated" (Dahood). For **put to shame** see comments on "ashamed" in 6.10. The Hebrew text of verse 7a,b is composed of two synonymous lines (see RSV) which TEV has shortened and combined into one line. But it may be better to have three lines in translation, as follows:

> All who worship false gods,
>   who are proud of those worthless idols,
>   are put to shame.

In line a the word **images** (found only here in the Psalms) is the artifact itself, either of metal or of wood, while in line b the word translated **idols** is the same one used in 96.5. For translation notes on **idols**, see 96.5. RSV, TEV, and others translate the two verbs **put to shame** and **bow down** as statements of fact; some, however, translate the first one as indicative and the second one as imperative (Dahood, TOB, NEB; see TEV footnote).

The Septuagint translates the Hebrew *'elohim* in line c by "his angels"; but it seems preferable to take it here in the same sense it has in verse 9b, the **gods** of the other nations (see 96.4-5).

In languages where **bow down before** does not have the meaning of "worship," it will be necessary to make the component of worship explicit; for example, "bow down in order to worship" or "worship by bowing down."

97.8-9	RSV	TEV
8	Zion hears and is glad, and the daughters of Judah rejoice, because of thy judgments, O God.	8 The people of Zion are glad, and the cities of Judah rejoice because of your judgments, O LORD.
9	For thou, O LORD, art most high over all the earth; thou art exalted far above all gods.	9 LORD Almighty, you are ruler of all the earth; you are much greater than all the gods.

In verse 8a the Hebrew text is **Zion hears and is glad**; it is not clear what the verb **hears** refers to; it is either the preceding statement concerning the idolaters and the gods, or else Yahweh's **judgments** in verse 8c. Toombs takes it to be the proclamation in the Temple of Yahweh's supreme power (as described in verse 7). So TOB places verse 7 within quotation marks. McCullough speculates that "some recent demonstration of the Lord's power" is meant. It seems best to refer the word forward to **thy judgments**. **Zion** stands for the inhabitants of the city of Jerusalem; and **the daughters of Judah** in verse 8b are the other cities (see GECL, SPCL, FRCL; NIV "the villages of Judah"); NJV has in the margin the alternative rendering "women (of Judah)," which does not seem likely here. The **judgments** of Yahweh are probably his condemnation and punishment of the enemies of Israel. It will be noted that TEV and SPCL have not translated **Zion hears**. NEB implies that the hearing and rejoicing refer to the "judgments" of God. GECL makes it refer to the preceding statement in verse 7. In many languages it will be necessary to make clear what is heard by the people of Zion; for example, "The people of Zion hear that the gods bow down" or "The people of Zion learn that God judges their enemies." In some languages TEV's **"cities of Judah rejoice"** will have to be kept parallel with **"the people of Zion,"** and in this case it can often be translated, for example, "the people of Zion and those of Judah."

For TEV **"LORD Almighty"** see 7.17; RSV takes *'elyon* here not as a title ("the Most High") but as a superlative adjective, **most high** (so SPCL, NEB; also NJV "supreme"). In Hebrew there is a play on the words *'elyon* in verse 9a and a form of the verb *'alah* "to be exalted" in verse 9b. Yahweh is the supreme ruler of the world, far greater in power than the pagan gods. In languages in which the earth may not be said to be ruled, this statement can be recast as "you are the one who rules all the people of the earth." For translation suggestions on **gods**, see 40.4 and 96.5.

97.10 RSV TEV

> The LORD loves those who hate evil;[k]
>   he preserves the lives of his
>   saints;
>   he delivers them from the hand
>   of the wicked.

> The LORD loves those who hate evil;
>   he protects the lives of his peo-
>   ple;
>   he rescues them from the power
>   of the wicked.

[k] Cn: Heb *You who love the LORD hate evil*

[n] *Probable text* The LORD loves those who hate evil; *Hebrew* Hate evil, you who love the LORD.

The first line of this verse in Hebrew is "Hate evil, (you) lovers of Yahweh." This is strange, because it switches abruptly from Yahweh to the people. The change which is made in the text by RSV, TEV, NEB, NAB, BJ, NJB, and SPCL involves two slight alterations, one of which, from the imperative plural "(you) hate" to the plural participle "(you) haters," is supported by several Hebrew manuscripts and the Syriac. NJV, GECL, NIV, and TOB, however, follow the Masoretic text.[1] Translators should feel free to follow the emended text. **The lives** in line **b** translates the plural of *nefesh* (see 3.2), and for **his saints** see comments on "the godly" in 4.3. In line **c** **the hand** means the power (of the wicked). In some languages **who hate evil** must be recast to say, for example, "who hate the things evil people do." Likewise, in the last line **hand of the wicked** must be recast to say "from the power of wicked people."

97.11-12 RSV TEV

> 11 Light dawns[l] for the righteous,
>   and joy for the upright in heart.
> 12 Rejoice in the LORD, O you right-
>   eous,
>   and give thanks to his holy
>   name!

> 11 Light shines on the righteous,
>   and gladness on the good.
> 12 All you that are righteous be glad
>   because of what the LORD has
>   done!
>   Remember what the holy God has
>   done,
>   and give thanks to him.

[l] Gk Syr Jerome: Heb *is sown*

In verse 11a the Masoretic text has "Light is sown," a statement found nowhere else in the Old Testament; TEV follows one Hebrew manuscript (and the Septuagint, the Syriac, Targum, and Vulgate) "shines" (so BJ, NJB, SPCL, FRCL, RSV, and others);

---

[1]HOTTP prefers the Masoretic text.

NEB has "A harvest of light is sown for the righteous"; NJV has "Light is sown for the righteous."[2] NIV translates "Light is shed upon the righteous," without indicating any textual problem. **Light** here is, as elsewhere, a figure for God's salvation, his goodness, his blessing on his people (see 27.1). In verse 11b **the upright in heart** (see 7.10) is parallel with **the righteous** in verse 11a.

In languages in which **light dawns for the righteous** will simply mean that "the sun comes up where there are righteous people," the clause must be recast as in TEV. However, in some languages the metaphor of light shining on someone without naming the source of the light will likely be misunderstood. Therefore it may be necessary to shift to a simile and say, for example, "God's goodness shines like a light on his righteous people." Line b may be taken as a consequence of line a; for example, "and this brings joy to those who are good."

In verse 12 TEV, as elsewhere, represents **in the LORD** by "**because of what the LORD has done.**" And the Hebrew of the last part of verse 12 is "and give thanks to his holy memorial," which TEV translates "**Remember what the holy God has done, and give thanks to him**" (see similar language in 30.4b). But many take the Hebrew "memorial" here to be the equivalent of "name" (as in Exo 3.15; so Anderson); so RSV, NEB, NJV, NIV, NAB, SPCL, Dahood. This may be preferable. NJB has "his unforgettable holiness" (similarly, KJV "give thanks at the remembrance of his holiness"). In some languages it will be necessary to go further than TEV by saying "because of what the LORD has done for you." Lines 12a and b as restructured in TEV are a command followed by a reason. In some languages this order will be more natural when reversed.

---

[2]Again HOTTP ("C" decision) opts for the Masoretic text, justifying its decision by referring to Factors 12 ("Other scribal errors") and 4 ("Simplification of the text").

Psalm 98

This psalm, which is much like Psalm 96, praises Yahweh's power as ruler of the world. The events described in verses 1-3 are spoken of as past, but some commentators understand the language to be prophetic in style, in which future events are portrayed as having already taken place. It seems better to assume, however, that the references are to events in Israel's history.

On the basis of Yahweh's great deeds in the past (verses 1-3), the whole world is exhorted to praise him as king (verses 4-6), and all inanimate creation is called upon to join in the chorus of praise to Yahweh, who is coming to rule the world (verses 7-9).

HEADING: "**God the Ruler of the World.**" Other headings are: "God comes to rule"; "God has won the victory"; "The warrior king." The TEV heading, if followed, may be recast to say, for example, "God rules the world" or "God rules all the people of the world."

Hebrew title: **A Psalm** (TEV "A psalm").

Because the title in Hebrew is only **A Psalm**, this psalm has sometimes been called an orphan psalm. The Septuagint has "A psalm by David."

98.1-2   RSV   TEV

1   O sing to the LORD a new song,
        for he has done marvelous
        things!
    His right hand and his holy arm
        have gotten him victory.
2   The LORD has made known his
        victory,
    he has revealed his vindication
        in the sight of the nations.

1   Sing a new song to the LORD;
        he has done wonderful things!
    By his own power and holy
        strength
        he has won the victory.
2   The LORD announced his victory;
        he made his saving power
        known to the nations.

The psalm begins as does Psalm 96, **Sing to the Lord a new song**. The **marvelous things** (see 9.1b) done by Yahweh are not here explicitly described (for an example, see 78.12-16). Some think **the victory** spoken of in verse 1 is a reference to creation, when Yahweh defeated the powers of chaos and destruction (see Fisher); or else the word may be generic, referring to all the victories won by Yahweh over Israel's enemies (so most commentators). GECL makes explicit that it was for the Israelites that Yahweh did those things: "He has accomplished wonders for us." Dentan takes the text to mean future victories.

844

The translator will note that RSV makes the relation of line 1b to 1a an explicit reason: **for he has done marvelous things!** TEV leaves the relation between those two lines implicit and therefore somewhat ambiguous.

TEV **"his own power and holy strength"** translates the Hebrew **His right hand and his holy arm** (see 44.3c). Here **holy** serves to emphasize the fact that God singlehandedly won the victory, without help from any other source; FRCL translates "divine power," and GECL "by means of his powerful, godly might." **Holy arm** is rendered **"holy strength"** by TEV. Both expressions are difficult to translate in many languages where the idea of holy is related to that of taboo. This association can often be avoided here by associating the object or, in this case, the abstract of strength, with God himself; for example, "by means of God's own power and his strength." In many languages these will be expressed as one rather than as a doublet. **Have gotten him victory** refers to the defeat of his enemies and in many languages will be expressed as "God has defeated his enemies."

In verse 2a **victory** is parallel with **vindication** (*tsedeq*), which NEB translates "righteousness"; NAB "justice"; NJB "saving justice"; FRCL "faithfulness"; NJV "triumph." RSV **vindication** emphasizes the element of retribution and can be represented by "the punishment he inflicted (on his enemies)." The last phrase, **in the sight of the nations**, means that all the world saw that Yahweh had defeated his enemies. FRCL translates the last line "To the ends of the earth everyone has been able to see that God has saved us." Line a must often be recast in more specific terms; for example, "God has made his people know that he defeats his enemies."

98.3 RSV	TEV
He has remembered his steadfast love and faithfulness to the house of Israel. All the ends of the earth have seen the victory of our God.	He kept his promise to the people of Israel with loyalty and constant love for them. All people everywhere have seen the victory of our God.

In this verse the psalmist tells how Yahweh "remembered his *chesed* (see 5.7) and his *'emunah* (see 36.5) for the house of Israel" (see RSV). TEV takes this to mean that the Lord **"kept his promise"** to his people, the promise contained in the covenant always to show them "constant love" and "loyalty." For the pairing of these two characteristics, see also 89.2,14b,24,33; 92.2. FRCL translates "he has not forgotten to be good and faithful (to the people of Israel)." Dahood assigns other vowels to the verb to make it imperative and translates "Remember his love and his fidelity, O house of Israel!" For **all the ends of the earth**, see 2.8.

He has remembered his steadfast love and faithfulness becomes more specific in TEV's rendering. The problem for many languages is contained in **"with loyalty and constant love for them."** In some languages this expression of manner must be shifted to clauses; for example, "God has always loved them and has been faithful to them." The expression **have seen the victory** may be understood in some languages to be limited to the physical act of seeing. Since the intention is that of experiencing God's delivery, it may be necessary in some cases to say "God has made it clear to all peoples that he saves his people" or "God has shown everyone how he saves his people."

RSV	TEV
4 Make a joyful noise to the LORD, all the earth; break forth into joyous song and sing praises!	4 Sing for joy to the LORD, all the earth; praise him with songs and shouts of joy!
5 Sing praises to the LORD with the lyre, with the lyre and the sound of melody!	5 Sing praises to the LORD! Play music on the harps!
6 With trumpets and the sound of the horn make a joyful noise before the King, the LORD!	6 Blow trumpets and horns, and shout for joy to the LORD, our king.

All the people on earth are called upon to praise Yahweh (verse 4). The expression **all the earth** must often be rendered as "all people everywhere" or "all people living on the earth." Verse 4b in Hebrew is a succession of three verbs: "break forth (in song) and shout for joy and sing praise," which NJV renders "break into joyous songs of praise!" In verse 5 the Hebrew is "Sing praises to the LORD with the harp, with the harp and the sound of a song," a command to use both vocal and instrumental music in praise of Yahweh. Some Hebrew manuscripts omit the second "with the harp," which TEV and others follow; SPCL translates "Sing hymns to the Lord to the sound of the harp, to the sound of string instruments." For **lyre** see 33.2a.

Line 4b and 5a echo line 4a and in some languages may need to be reduced to avoid the repetition. **Sing praises** may have to be translated in some languages as "Sing songs and praise God" or "Sing songs and say that God is great."

Trumpets in verse 6 are metal instruments (see "silver trumpets" in Num 10.2), mentioned only here in the Psalms. For **horn** (*shofar*) see 47.5. In some languages it will not be possible to make a distinction between the two Hebrew terms translated **trumpets** and **horn**. In such cases the local term for a horn will be used. The Greek Old Testament used only one term. In verse 6b the phrase translated **before the King** (or "in the presence of") is translated by NEB "ac-

TRUMPETS AND RAM HORNS

claim the presence of the Lord our king" (similarly NJB). This is a command to praise Yahweh in the Temple, where he is present with the people. For similar exhortations see 47.6; 81.2-3. In languages which must distinguish between inclusive and exclusive first person plural, TEV's **"our king"** should be rendered to include the writer and his readers.

RSV		TEV
7 Let the sea roar, and all that fills it; the world and those who dwell in it!	7	Roar, sea, and every creature in you; sing, earth, and all who live on you!
8 Let the floods clap their hands; let the hills sing for joy together	8	Clap your hands, you rivers; you hills, sing together with joy before the LORD,
9 before the LORD, for he comes to judge the earth. He will judge the world with righteousness, and the peoples with equity.	9	because he comes to rule the earth. He will rule the peoples of the world with justice and fairness.

The psalm closes with an invitation for all creation to join in praising Yahweh: <u>sea</u>, <u>world</u>, <u>floods</u> and <u>hills</u> (see similar passage in 96.11-13). Verse 7a is exactly like 96.11b. In Hebrew there is no verb in verse 7b; TEV has supplied "sing" as a synonym of "roar" in line <u>a</u>. RSV uses the third person imperative <u>Let</u> in verses 7-8; TEV uses the second person imperative, directly addressing the various parts of the world.

<u>Clap their hands</u> in verse 8a translates a Hebrew verb used only here and in Isaiah 55.12 and Ezekiel 25.6 (in 47.1 a different verb is used). Verses 7-8 are filled with personifications which are problematic in many languages, particularly when an inanimate object is commanded to perform human actions. These may sometimes be shifted to similes, as suggested in 96.11.

The phrase <u>before the LORD</u> in the Hebrew text is at the beginning of verse 9; TEV has placed it at the end of verse 8, since it goes with the verb <u>sing</u>. For a discussion of the verb translated <u>judge</u> ("rule") see 96.13. Line 9a (as arranged in TEV) provides the reason for the preceding imperatives. In some languages it will be clearer to state the reason before the commands of verses 7-8. <u>Judge the earth</u> in some languages will have to be shifted to "the people of the earth," in spite of the personifications in verses 7-8.

Although verse 9c,d resembles 96.13c,d closely, <u>equity</u> translates a different word from the one used in 96.13d; it is used in 96.10c and is a close synonym of *tsedeq*, <u>righteousness</u>.

Psalm 99

This psalm is the last one of the psalms whose main theme is the proclamation of Yahweh as king (see introduction to Psalm 47). Its distinctive note is the emphasis on Yahweh's holiness (verses 3,5,9); the Lord is different and separate from humankind, and his worshipers are to acknowledge that quality which sets him apart. But at the same time he is a God who is interested in what is right, is concerned with justice and fairness; he is a God who forgives his people and gives them guidance.

The psalm opens with a description of Yahweh's greatness (verses 1-3), followed by a statement of his concern for justice and righteousness (verses 4-5). The last part of the psalm (verses 6-9) concentrates on the love and care he has shown for his people.

HEADING: "**God the Supreme King**." Other headings are: "The holy king"; "The LORD, the holy king"; "The God of holiness." For adaptation of the TEV heading, see the heading of Psalm 97.

<u>**99.1-3**</u>   RSV   TEV

1	The LORD reigns; let the peoples tremble! He sits enthroned upon the cherubim; let the earth quake!	1	The LORD is king, and the people tremble. He sits on his throne above the winged creatures, and the earth shakes.
2	The LORD is great in Zion; he is exalted over all the peoples.	2	The LORD is mighty in Zion; he is supreme over all the nations.
3	Let them praise thy great and terrible name! Holy is he!	3	Everyone will praise his great and majestic name. Holy is he!

For **The LORD reigns** see 93.1. The verbs at the ends of the two lines of verse 1 are translated by TEV (and NEB, NAB, NJV, BJ, NJB, FRCL, SPCL) as statements, "**the people tremble**," "**the earth shakes**." RSV, NIV, AT, and Dahood translate as exhortations, <u>let . . . tremble</u>, <u>let . . . shake</u>. For TEV "**his throne above the winged creatures**," see 80.1; 18.10. In verse 1b <u>quake</u> translates a verb found nowhere else in the Old Testament. Whether the translator follows TEV or RSV, the implied logical relation between each set of lines is that of statement followed by consequence. In some languages it will be clearer to make this relationship explicit. Therefore one may say, for example, "the LORD is king, therefore the people tremble; he sits on . . . , therefore the earth shakes." The translator must be careful not to give the

848

impression that it is the weight of the Lord on his throne that causes the earth to shake.

Zion in verse 2 stands for Jerusalem and its inhabitants; Yahweh is supreme not only over Israel but also over **all the peoples**. **Exalted over all the peoples** and TEV's "supreme over all" may be rendered sometimes "he is the most powerful" or "he rules all the other people."

As a result all peoples **"will praise his great and majestic name"** (verse 3a). Hebrew has "your name"; for consistency TEV has used the third person, **"his . . . name."** TEV **"majestic"** translates the passive verbal adjective "fearful." The best English equivalent is "awesome" (so NJV, NIV, NAB, NJB); **terrible** (AT, RSV, NEB) is highly unsatisfactory in current English. Some languages use figures of speech to refer to "awe-inspiring" reactions, for example, "heart stopping" or "inside melting."

The word **holy** (verse 3b) is used to describe the divine nature, the essential attribute that makes God what he is, the conviction that there is an "otherness" to God, a mode of being which is different from that of all living creatures and which makes him unique. In various places in the Bible, several consequences are drawn from this central fact, the main one being that of reverence, awe, fear, that a person feels when confronted by the holy God; the feeling of unworthiness, of inferiority, before the awesome mystery of the God of Israel. For translation suggestions regarding **holy**, see 22.3; 28.2.

99.4-5	RSV	TEV

	RSV	TEV
4	Mighty King,*ᵐ* lover of justice, thou hast established equity; thou hast executed justice and righteousness in Jacob.	4 Mighty king,*ᵒ* you love what is right; you have established justice in Israel; you have brought righteousness and fairness.
5	Extol the LORD our God; worship at his footstool! Holy is he!	5 Praise the LORD our God; worship before his throne! Holy is he!

ᵐ Cn: Heb *and the king's strength*

ᵒ Probable text Mighty king; *Hebrew* The might of the king.

Verse 4 in Hebrew begins "and the might of the king." Some, by a change of vowels, get the adjective "mighty" and connect it with the last part of verse 3, "he is holy and mighty" (Briggs; NJB, NEB). Others, with the same change of vowels but maintaining the Masoretic text division of verses, translate "and a mighty one is king" (Weiser). Another way to render the Masoretic text may be "Strong as he is, the king . . . ." TEV and RSV change the Hebrew text to get **Mighty King**; NJV translates in the same way, with a footnote, "Meaning of Heb uncertain."[1]

---

[1]TOB, without indicating any textual problem, translates "The strength of a king is to love justice." This is a beautiful statement but does not seem to be the meaning

Three synonymous words are used in verse 4: *mishpat* **justice** (see 7.6) is used twice; *tsedaqah* **righteousness** (see 5.8), and *mesharim*, which RSV consistently translates **equity** (TEV "**fairness**"; see 96.10c; 98.9c). All of these refer to the qualities which should govern the life of the community of Israel (literally **Jacob**), in people's relations one with another. Yahweh is a God concerned with social justice and morality. FRCL translates "You have prescribed the rules that govern our lives, you have established law and order in Israel."

In some languages it will not be possible to say **lover of justice** or "you love what is right." Instead one must sometimes translate "you love those who do things that are right." **Established equity** and TEV's "**established justice**" intend to say that God is the giver of justice, and may be rendered "you have given the rules that show people how to do the right things."

In verse 5b **footstool** could refer to Jerusalem or to the Temple; it probably refers to the Covenant Box, in the Most Holy Place in the Temple, which was considered God's "**throne**" (see verse 1). In many languages it will be necessary to express God as the object of the act of worship; for example, "worship God before his throne" or "worship God at the place from which he rules the people."

99.6-7 RSV	TEV

6   Moses and Aaron were among his priests,
      Samuel also was among those who called on his name.
      They cried to the LORD, and he answered them.
 7   He spoke to them in the pillar of cloud;
      they kept his testimonies, and the statutes that he gave them.
	6 Moses and Aaron were his priests, and Samuel was one who prayed to him;
	      they called to the LORD, and he answered them.
	 7 He spoke to them from the pillar of cloud;
	      they obeyed the laws and commands that he gave them.

Moses is not elsewhere called a priest, but the plain meaning of the Hebrew text here is "Moses and Aaron (were) among his priests." Some commentators explain that when Moses interceded on behalf of the people, he was acting as priest. The three great figures in Israel's history, **Moses**, **Aaron**, and **Samuel**, are listed to recall the times of crisis, when God answered their cries for help. In verse 6b **called on his name** means that they prayed, and here it refers specifically to intercessory prayer on behalf of the people (see 1 Sam 7.8-9; 12.18).

---

of the Masoretic text. FRCL assumes an ellipsis of the verb "Praise" of verse 3 and translates "Let all praise your might, you a king who loves justice." HOTTP says there are two possible interpretations of this passage: (1) "and the might of the king who loves justice, you did (or: do) establish it with equity"; (2) "and the might is for the king who loves justice. You have established equity firmly, and . . . ."

In verse 7 **He spoke to them** has as its natural antecedent the three men in verse 6; but since there is no record of God's speaking to Samuel from **the pillar of cloud**, some would take **them** to mean the people as a whole. This is possible but not very probable. For Moses and the pillar of cloud, see Exodus 33.9; for Aaron see Numbers 12.5. RSV's **in the pillar of cloud**, if translated literally, in some languages will mean that the people were inside the pillar, too. TEV's **"from the pillar"** must sometimes be rendered "from the pillar of cloud where God was." For **testimonies** see 19.7, and for **statutes** see 18.22. In some languages it will not be possible to give both **testimonies** and **statutes**; these may have to be reduced to one.

99.8-9	RSV	TEV
8	O LORD our God, thou didst answer them; thou wast a forgiving God to them, but an avenger of their wrongdoings.	8 O LORD, our God, you answered your people; you showed them that you are a God who forgives, even though you punished them for their sins.
9	Extol the LORD our God, and worship at his holy mountain; for the LORD our God is holy!	9 Praise the LORD our God, and worship at his sacred hill!ᵖ The LORD our God is holy.

ᵖ SACRED HILL: *See 2.6.*

In verse 8a the object in Hebrew of the verb **"you answered"** is **them**, which could still refer to Moses, Aaron, and Samuel. But it is clear that **them** and **their** in lines b and c are the people as a whole and not the three men, and so it seems preferable to take **them** in line a as **"your people"** (so Anderson and others). Most translations, however, have simply "them." **Forgiving** translates the verb *nasah*, which in most contexts has the sense of "to carry, bear"; and **avenger** translates the verb *naqam*, which has the sense of "take vengeance" (see 94.1). Here it refers to God punishing the people for **their wrongdoings**. For translation suggestions on **forgiving** see 25.18. Line 8c is a concession clause in TEV, and if it is used as a model, in some languages it may have to be moved ahead of 8b.

The psalm closes with a final exhortation for the people to praise Yahweh as the holy God of Israel. **Extol** means to acclaim or announce the greatness of Yahweh: "Proclaim that the LORD our God is mighty."[2] For Yahweh's **holy mountain** see 2.6. Here, as throughout Psalm 99, the psalmist refers to the God of Israel, and in languages which must make a distinction between inclusive and exclusive first person plural pronouns, **our God** will require an appropriate form for including the hearers as fellow Israelites.

[2]The 1976 British edition of TEV switches in verse 8 to "my God"; this was corrected to "our God" in later editions.

Psalm 100

This is a hymn of praise to Yahweh, used in worship in the Temple. The Hebrew title stresses this fact (see below). Some believe that this psalm serves, so to speak, as the doxology of the preceding psalms (93; 95–99), which praise Yahweh as king.

There is no obvious division into strophes. It is suggested by some that verses 1-3 were sung by the pilgrims as they approached the Temple, while verses 4-5 were sung by the choir inside the Temple.

HEADING: "**A Hymn of Praise.**" Other headings are: "Processional hymn"; "Invitation to praise God"; "The LORD has made us, and we are his." The TEV heading may be adjusted for some languages by saying, for example, "This is a song to praise the LORD" or "The psalmist sings this song to praise God."

Hebrew Title: **A Psalm for the thank offering** (TEV "A psalm of thanksgiving").

The word *todah* may mean **thank offering**, as RSV translates it; in verse 4 it means "thanksgiving" (parallel with "praise" in line b), and so "thanksgiving" is taken by TEV and NJB to be the meaning in the title. NJV translates "A psalm for praise."

100.1-2	RSV		TEV
1	Make a joyful noise to the LORD, all the lands!^{n}	1	Sing to the LORD, all the world!
2	Serve the LORD with gladness! Come into his presence with singing!	2	Worship the LORD with joy; come before him with happy songs!

^{n} Heb *land* or *earth*

All people of the world are called upon to worship and praise Yahweh with songs. In verse 1a **Make a joyful noise** translates a verb which means "to shout" (see its use in 47.1b; 98.4a), and so it may be preferable to translate "Sing loudly." NJV translates "Raise a shout." **All the lands**, or TEV's "**all the world**," must often be rendered by "everyone" or "all the people of the world." In this psalm only one subject actor, **all the lands**, is expressed, but it is implied with each of the commands found in verses 2a, 2b, 3a, 4a, 4c. In some languages it will be necessary to repeat the ones to whom the commands are addressed.

In verse 2a TEV "**Worship**" translates a verb which in most contexts means "to serve" (RSV); here, however, in connection with the Temple worship (parallel with

852

come into his presence in line b), it is clear that the "service" is that of worship (so NEB, NJV, FRCL, NIV, SPCL). The phrase his presence refers specifically to the Temple, where Yahweh was present with his people. It will be noted that TEV has "come before him" in 2b and "go into" in 4b. In many languages it will be necessary to maintain a consistent speaker point of view.

100.3	RSV	TEV

RSV	TEV
Know that the LORD is God! It is he that made us, and we are his;⁰ we are his people, and the sheep of his pasture.	Acknowledge that the LORD is God. He made us, and we belong to him; we are his people, we are his flock.

⁰ Another reading is *and not we ourselves*

"Acknowledge" (TEV) translates the imperative of the verb "to know" (RSV); the verb here means to "recognize" (SPCL, TOB) or "confess" (see 91.14 "knows my name"). The term "recognize" is translated through figurative expressions in some languages; for example, "Say 'Yes' in your heart" or "Put this word in your mouth." "Yahweh is God" is the fundamental creed of the Hebrew faith, confessed by his people, who proclaim It is he that made us. This does not mean creation, in terms of God creating humankind; it means that Yahweh had created a nation out of the slaves in Egypt, choosing them as his own people, a people who belonged to him alone. We are his translates one form of the Masoretic text (which is represented in the Targum and the Vulgate, and is followed by nearly all translations, and by HOTTP as well); another form has "and not ourselves" (represented in the Septuagint and the Syriac, and followed by KJV). Dahood, as often, goes his own way; he prefers the reading "not" and translates "He himself made us when we . . . were nothing."

The phrase the LORD is God makes little sense in many languages without making explicit the specific-to-generic relation of the two terms; Yahweh is the specific and God the generic. Accordingly it is possible to say, for example, "the God we worship is called Yahweh" or "Israel's God (that is, Yahweh) is the one true God."

For "his flock" (literally the sheep of his pasture) see 74.1; 95.7. In some languages it may be necessary to recast and the sheep of his pasture to say, for example, "and the people whom he cares for."

100.4-5	RSV	TEV

RSV	TEV
4 Enter his gates with thanksgiving, and his courts with praise! Give thanks to him, bless his name!	4 Enter the temple gates with thanksgiving; go into its courts with praise. Give thanks to him and praise him.

5	For the LORD is good;	5	The LORD is good;
	his steadfast love endures for ever,		his love is eternal
	and his faithfulness to all generations.		and his faithfulness lasts forever.

The pilgrims are exhorted to go through "**the Temple gates**" into the Temple **courts** with songs of **thanksgiving** and **praise**. In languages where the expressions **gates** and **courts** are difficult to represent, it will be possible to say, for example, "Enter his temple . . ." and "enter the inside." It may be necessary in some languages to adjust **with thanksgiving** and **with praise** by saying, "be thankful" and "praise God." In verse 4c TEV "**praise him**" translates **bless his name** (for **bless** see 16.7, and for **name** see 5.11).

The reason for praising Yahweh is given in the concluding verse. Again the two words are used which most aptly describe Yahweh's relation with his people: his **steadfast love** and his **faithfulness** (for *chesed* see 5.7; for *'emunah* see 36.5). In some languages it will be necessary to recast **his steadfast love** and **his faithfulness** as clauses; for example, "he loves his people for ever and is faithful to them for ever."

Psalm 101

Like Psalms 2, 18, 20, 45, and 71, this is a royal psalm; perhaps it represents the promises made by the king at his coronation. There is no way of telling by whom it was composed or when it was first used. It is possible that the psalm was used during an annual celebration of the king's enthronement, which some scholars believe took place each year at the beginning of the Festival of Shelters.

The king's concerns are social and moral; he himself sets the standards that his people should follow, and these standards are defined by conformity to the Law of God.

The Hebrew text is composed of 14 lines, each line divided into two half-lines. RSV and NJB print the psalm in seven strophes, each strophe consisting of two principal lines and two secondary lines. This may be as good a way as any to print the text, except that this division does not correspond to the verse division in verses 2 and 3. Translators will notice in this psalm that RSV and TEV do not always handle parallelism in the same way. RSV consistently prints the Hebrew half lines as line a over indented line b. TEV does the same, provided the second line is in some way parallel in meaning to the first, or when the second line is nearly as long as the first. In the remainder of cases TEV makes a single line (see verses 2, 3a, 7a, 7b). These are not lines that have been shortened and combined, but simply a clause that has been placed on a single line. In verse 5a and 5b, TEV has for syntactic reasons reversed the order of the lines.

HEADING: "**A King's Promise.**" Other headings are: "The ideal prince"; "The ideal ruler"; "The king's promise to God"; "The moral code of a king." The TEV heading may be adapted in some translations by saying, for example, "What the king said when he made promises to God" or "This is what the king promised to do."

Hebrew Title: **A Psalm of David** (TEV "A psalm by David").

101.1-2b   RSV   TEV

1   I will sing of loyalty and of justice;   1   My song is about loyalty and jus-
        to thee, O LORD, I will sing.   tice,
2   I will give heed to the way that is   and I sing it to you, O LORD.
        blameless.   2   My conduct will be faultless.
    Oh when wilt thou come to me?   When will you come to me?

It is uncertain whether **loyalty** and **justice** are meant to be God's attributes or human qualities; in this context the latter seems preferable, and the king is talking about his own **loyalty** to Yahweh's will for him, and the **justice** that he, the king, will

855

practice. As a human quality, *chesed* (see 5.7) is better represented by **loyalty** (RSV, TEV, NEB), or "faithful love" (NJB), or "faithfulness" (NJV, TOB), rather than "goodness" (FRCL, GECL), "kindness" (NAB), or "love" (SPCL, BJ). Dahood takes the words to refer to God: "Your love and justice will I sing." If the translator takes **loyalty** and **justice** to refer to the king's actions, it will be necessary in some languages to switch to clauses and say, for example, "I will sing about how I will be loyal to God and how I will treat people fairly."

Two synonymous verbs for **sing** are used in verse 1; NJV and Dahood translate "sing" and "chant."

The king's first promise is in verse 2a: the Hebrew verb has a variety of meanings; the idea of "to understand, consider, ponder" seems basic. RSV **I will give heed to**; NJV "I will study the way of"; FRCL "I will apply myself to understand." Briggs prefers "I will behave myself wisely" (so KJV), which McCullough rejects. TEV has taken the verb to express a promise concerning the king's own conduct; see SPCL "I want to live," NEB "I will follow (a wise and blameless course)," NAB "I will persevere." The complement of the verb is "in a perfect way" (NAB "the way of integrity"). The king promises to be **blameless** in his behavior.

Line 2a in both RSV and TEV is generic but may require more specific content in some languages, if it is to have any meaning. One may say, for example, "No one will be able to criticize the way I live" or "The way I live will not cause people to find fault with me."

The question in verse 2 seems out of place, and some emend the Hebrew to get "Truth will abide with me" (so Weiser); NEB emends to get "whatever may befall me." NJV translates the Masoretic text "when shall I attain it?"; it does this by taking the verb as third feminine singular, referring to "way," which is feminine, instead of second masculine singular "you" (the two forms in Hebrew are identical). But it is strange to speak of a way "coming" to someone. It seems better, with the vast majority of translations, to render "When will you come to me?"—an expression of the king's desire to have an immediate and personal revelation of God's power and guidance.

101.2c-3   RSV   TEV

	I will walk with integrity of heart within my house;	I will live a pure life in my house and will never tolerate evil.
3	I will not set before my eyes anything that is base.	I hate the actions of those who turn away from God; I will have nothing to do with them.
	I hate the work of those who fall away; it shall not cleave to me.	

The king promises to "**live a pure life**" (so TEV; literally "walk with a perfect heart") in his **house**, which is, of course, the royal palace. His private conduct will be moral and pure. **Integrity of heart** is often translated by figures of speech; for example, "with one heart" or "with a straight liver." **Within my house** focuses upon the king's activity. The same expression in some languages may be too limiting and will have to be recast to say, for example, "where I rule the people" or "from the place where I govern the people."

In verse 3a **I will not set before my eyes** means "I will not allow to appear in my presence." FRCL has "I refuse to become involved in (anything dishonest)." **Base** translates the phrase "a thing of Belial," something worthless, or else something bad; the same phrase occurs in 41.8 (where RSV translates "A deadly thing"). TEV's "tolerate" is rather general in sense, and RSV's **set before my eyes** suggests entirely a visual avoidance of evil. This may be recast in some languages to say, for example, "Where I am I will allow no evil." In some languages it may not be possible to treat "evil" as a thing occupying space. One must switch, therefore, to "evil things" or, more commonly, to "evil people."

In verse 3c **those who fall away** translates a word found only here in the Old Testament; the Septuagint translates "transgressions"; K-B labels the word "unknown," but Holladay defines it as "deviation, transgression." Dahood takes it to mean "(the making of) images"; NEB "disloyalty"; Briggs, TOB, and FRCL take it to mean apostasy; NJV "crooked dealing," and NJB "act crookedly." Toombs explains it as a violation of the covenant. TEV takes it to mean apostasy, "**turn away from God**"; equally SPCL "those who are not loyal to God."

In verse 3d the verb **(not) cleave** (see 22.15b) here means to avoid altogether, to get rid of. FRCL has "I will have nothing in common with that," and NEB "I will have none of it." The reference may be to the people, "**them**" (TEV, NAB, SPCL), or to the evil itself, **it** (RSV, NJV, NEB, TOB, FRCL, NJB). A translator may feel free to choose.

101.4-5   RSV   TEV

	RSV		TEV
4	Perverseness of heart shall be far from me; I will know nothing of evil.	4	I will not be dishonest[s] and will have no dealings with evil.[t]
5	Him who slanders his neighbor secretly I will destroy. The man of haughty looks and arrogant heart I will not endure.	5	I will get rid of anyone who whispers evil things about someone else; I will not tolerate a man who is proud and arrogant.

[s] not be dishonest; *or* stay away from dishonest people.
[t] evil; *or* evil men.

In verse 4a it is not certain whether the psalmist is talking about himself or of others in the statement "A crooked heart will depart from me"; the former is favored by the majority of commentators and translators. And in verse 4b the Hebrew for **evil** may be evil people or evil as such. The Hebrew verb "to know" in this line has the meaning of "to have experience of, to participate in"; so NEB and TEV "**have no dealings with**."

In verse 5 the king promises to **destroy** slanderers in his court (literally "to silence"—see "wipe them out" in 94.23). The meaning of "to silence" in other contexts makes it likely that here the meaning is also "to destroy, to kill," which seems harsh (see "destroyed" in 18.40; "put an end to" in 54.5 and 73.27; "wipe them out" in 94.23; and "destroy" in verse 8, below). Some (NEB, FRCL, NIV, SPCL, TOB) have simply "I will silence."

In the second part of verse 5 the king promises to banish from his court anyone who is **"proud and arrogant"** (literally "haughty eyes and a proud heart"). **Endure** translates the Masoretic text verb *yakal* "to be able, to endure"; by using other vowels with the same Hebrew consonants, NEB (following the Septuagint) gets a form of the verb *'akal* "to eat": "I will not sit at table with proud and pompous men." Most translations have "endure, tolerate." The proud person in verse 5 is described twice with expressions having the same meaning, and in some languages it may be necessary to have only one term or figure of speech.

<table>
<tr><td>__101.6__</td><td>RSV</td><td>TEV</td></tr>
</table>

RSV	TEV

I will look with favor on the faith-
    ful in the land,
  that they may dwell with me;
he who walks in the way that is
    blameless
  shall minister to me.
	I will approve of those who are
	    faithful to God
	  and will let them live in my
	    palace.
	Those who are completely honest
	  will be allowed to serve me.

This verse is the complement of verse 5; the king will **"approve of"** (literally "my eyes are on") **the faithful in the land**, that is, the faithful Israelites; and they will be his associates and advisors. In languages where **dwell with me** or "live in my palace" will be taken only in a literal sense, it will be better to say, for example, "will work for me in my palace." The second half of verse 6 repeats the promise in a different way: **"completely honest"** people (or "of blameless conduct"; literally, "walk in a perfect way"—see verse 2a) will minister to the king as officials in the government.

<table>
<tr><td>__101.7-8__</td><td>RSV</td><td>TEV</td></tr>
</table>

RSV	TEV

7 No man who practices deceit
    shall dwell in my house;
  no man who utters lies
    shall continue in my presence.
 	
8 Morning by morning I will destroy
    all the wicked in the land,
  cutting off all the evildoers
  from the city of the LORD.
	7 No liar will live in my palace;
	  no hypocrite will remain in my
	    presence.
	8 Day after day I will destroy
	    the wicked in our land;
	  I will expel all evil men
	  from the city of the LORD.

The psalm closes with the king's promise to expel from his service every liar and hypocrite. TEV seems to make a sharper distinction between the two than the Hebrew allows: "one who does deceit" in line a and "speaker of falsehoods" in line c may be strictly synonymous. (See in 52.2,3 "lies" and "falsehood" in TEV; in that passage RSV has "worker of treachery" and "lying.") But it may be that the first one involves deceitful actions, the second one falsehoods (so RSV, NIV; also NJV "deals deceitfully" and "speaks untruth"). For translation suggestions on "**hypocrite**" see 26.4.

Finally the king promises to put to death (literally "to silence" as in verse 5a) **all the wicked** in Israel and to "cut off" from Jerusalem ("the city of Yahweh") **all the evildoers**. He will do this "in the mornings," that is, every morning, the usual time of day when cases were tried and judgment administered. The king himself would normally judge cases of greater importance. The promise seems exaggerated; as Anderson remarks, "The destruction of *all* the wicked in the land is an ideal rather than a fact." And Weiser says "he expresses the lofty ideal principles whereby the conduct of a ruler shall be guided." The expression **Morning by morning** or TEV's "**Day after day**" may suggest that the same people are daily destroyed. If this is a serious problem, it may be necessary to say something like "Each day I will destroy those who do evil things," it being assumed that evil never ceases to flourish.

Psalm 102

This psalm is a lament by an individual, a young man (verse 23) who is ill, lonely, and threatened by enemies (verses 3-11). He prays for help for himself (verses 1-2) and for Jerusalem (verses 13-17). The psalm mixes personal matters with concern for Jerusalem, and also includes a hymn of praise to God (verses 12-22). Some commentators, noting the different subject matters, believe that verses 12-22 are from a different author and have been included in the original psalm (verses 1-11, 23-28). Others defend the unity of the composition (Dahood, Anderson, Cohen). It is a matter of conjecture who the author was (Dahood believes it was the king) and when the psalm was written (Cohen and Kirkpatrick take it to be during the Exile; Briggs dates it in the Maccabean times).

The psalm clearly divides along the lines mentioned above. It begins with a cry to the Lord for help (verses 1-2), followed by a description of the psalmist's pitiable condition (verses 3-11). Next, in a hymn of praise to God, a prayer is made on behalf of Jerusalem (verses 12-17), which concludes with a confident assertion that God will intervene and save his people (verses 18-22). Once more the psalm deals with the psalmist's own sufferings, contrasting the brevity of human life with the eternity of God (verses 23-27). The psalm closes on a confident note of the future prosperity and security of God's people (verse 28).

This psalm is one of the seven classified in church liturgy as penitential psalms (see introduction to Psalm 32); but it is noted that nowhere does the psalmist explicitly confess any sins. In Jewish liturgy the psalm was used on days of fasting.

HEADING: "**The Prayer of a Troubled Young Man.**" Other headings are: "The prayer of a suffering man"; "Prayer in time of distress"; "An exile's plaint." The TEV heading may be adapted for some languages by saying, for instance, "A young man who is suffering prays to God" or "A young man in trouble asks God for help."

Hebrew title: **A prayer of one afflicted, when he is faint and pours out his complaint before the LORD** (TEV "**A prayer by a weary sufferer who pours out his complaints to the LORD**").

The title is unique in that it describes the condition of the author without attempting to identify him. He is "**a weary sufferer**" (literally "oppressed, when he grew faint"), and so he prays to Yahweh for help.

102.1-2	RSV		TEV

1   Hear my prayer, O LORD;
    let my cry come to thee!

1   Listen to my prayer, O LORD,
    and hear my cry for help!

2	Do not hide thy face from me in the day of my distress! Incline thy ear to me; answer me speedily in the day when I call!	2 When I am in trouble, don't turn away from me! Listen to me, and answer me quickly when I call!

The opening cry to the Lord for help is couched in the familiar language of laments. See similar and sometimes identical language: for verse 1, see 39.12; 18.6; for verse 2a,b see 13.1; 27.9a; 69.17a; for verse 2b, see 13.1b; 27.9a; 69.17a; for verse 2c (in TEV), see 17.6b; 31.2; 71.2b; and for verse 2d, see 69.17b. In some languages **my prayer** and **my cry** may have to be recast as verbs; for example, "Listen to me when I pray and when I cry for help."

102.3-4   RSV   TEV

3	For my days pass away like smoke, and my bones burn like a furnace.	3 My life is disappearing like smoke; my body is burning like fire.
4	My heart is smitten like grass, and withered; I forget to eat my bread.	4 I am beaten down like dry grass; I have lost my desire for food.

The psalmist describes his pitiable condition: he is ill and lonely, and is being attacked by enemies. His **"life"** (literally **days**) is vanishing **like smoke** (see 37.20; 68.2). The Masoretic text is "in smoke," but many Hebrew manuscripts, the Septuagint, and Jerome have "like smoke."[1] In some languages it is not possible to speak of one's life disappearing. Instead it is often necessary to say, for example, "I am dying, just like rising smoke disappears." His whole body (literally **bones**) "is **burning like fire**," which sounds like a high fever (if meant as a physical symptom). The word translated **"fire"** is an unusual one; it usually means "burning coals" (so Dahood "brazier"), or "hearth" (NJV), or "oven" (NEB: "burn up as in an oven"; NJB "burning like an oven"; RSV **furnace**).

In verse 4a the psalmist compares himself to **grass** (or weeds) that has dried up and is beaten down; Hebrew has **My heart** (so RSV), which is taken by most to represent the whole person (see NEB, NJV). It is hard to understand how the psalmist could have spoken of the bodily organ, his heart, as being like dried grass (see NAB). In a psychological sense the figure could be descriptive of his feeling of despair and loneliness. In languages which cannot employ the passive, it may be necessary to recast the verb phrase "beaten down" and say, for example, "I feel like I have become like dry grass" or "I am like dry grass that someone has beaten down."

In verse 4b **I forget to eat my bread** means that his sickness has caused him to lose his appetite. Most translations are quite literal; TEV and SPCL indicate loss of appetite as the reason the psalmist does not eat. The verbal form translated **I forget**

---

[1]HOTTP ("C" decision) stays with the Masoretic text.

is taken by some, on the basis of a Ugaritic parallel, to mean "be wasted, emaciated, weak"; so NJV "too wasted to eat my food"; NEB "I cannot find the strength to eat." The interpretation of TEV seems preferable. Although the Hebrew term used is the regular word for **bread**, it is also used generically for "**food.**" In the present context, if the translator uses the term for the most commonly eaten food (equivalent to **bread**), the translation will have more emotive impact on the intended readers.

102.5	RSV	TEV

RSV	TEV

Because of my loud groaning
  my bones cleave to my flesh.
	I groan aloud;
	  I am nothing but skin and bones.

In this verse the relation between the psalmist's groaning in line a and his emaciated condition in line b is taken by RSV and others to be that of cause and effect, which seems strange. (But see Delitzsch: "Continuous straining of the voice . . . does really make the body waste away.") Briggs takes line a to explain the reason for forgetting to eat food (in verse 4b). But it seems better (with NEB) to take the literal "From the voice of my groaning" in a general sense, to indicate the suffering, the illness, which makes him groan and which is the reason for his emaciated condition.

TEV "**nothing but skin and bones**" translates "my bones stick to my flesh"; most take this to mean complete emaciation. The English expression "skin and bones" is a doublet indicating an emaciated physical condition. In some languages such a condition is spoken of as "having a stick body," "having sunken eyes," or "body of ribs."

102.6-8	RSV	TEV

RSV	TEV

6 I am like a vulture[p] of the wilderness,
    like an owl of the waste places;
7 I lie awake,
    I am like a lonely bird on the housetop.
8 All the day my enemies taunt me,
    those who deride me use my name for a curse.
	6 I am like a wild bird in the desert,
	    like an owl in abandoned ruins.
	7 I lie awake;
	    I am like a lonely bird on a housetop.
	8 All day long my enemies insult me;
	    those who mock me use my name in cursing.

[p] The meaning of the Hebrew word is uncertain

The psalmist compares himself to **a vulture** (verse 6a), **an owl** (verse 6b), **a lonely bird** (verse 7b). As the RSV footnote indicates, there is uncertainty over the identification of the bird in verse 6a (see *Fauna and Flora*, "Pelican," page 65); the Septuagint has "pelican"; NEB, NJB, and NAB "desert owl"; NJV "great-owl." The bird in verse 6b is **an owl** (*Fauna and Flora,* page 61); in verse 7b **bird** translates the word which in 84.3a is translated "sparrow." For translation suggestions for **wilderness** (TEV "**desert**") see comments on 29.8. The Hebrew for **waste places** (TEV "**abandoned ruins**") most likely refers to abandoned cities or buildings that have been destroyed, where an **owl** may live, but there are no people. **Waste places** and "**desert**" must sometimes be rendered "places where people do not live."

In verse 7b the Masoretic text is "and I am"; some emend this to "I wail" (NEB), or "I moan" (NAB), or "I groan" (BJ, NJB), joining it to the preceding **I lie awake**. This does make for a better balanced line, but the Masoretic text as it is can be translated. **A lonely bird on the housetop** may be understood by readers in some cultures to refer to witchcraft. Where this idea is common, it may be necessary to add a note to explain that the psalmist is speaking of his lonely condition, in which he has no one to comfort him.

In verse 8 the psalmist complains of his enemies, who scoff at him (see similar language in 89.51). In some languages **All the day** or "**All day long**" may be taken as excluding the night-time. In such cases it may be better to say "All the time" or "Day and night." In line **b**, instead of the Masoretic text **those who deride me**, the Septuagint, Syriac, and Vulgate have "those who (used to) praise me," which is followed by BJ, NJB; but the Masoretic text better parallels the preceding line.[2]

Use my name for a curse means that the psalmist's enemies call down upon others the same misfortunes and disasters that have befallen him; for an example of this see Jeremiah 29.22. Some, however, take it to mean that they curse the psalmist himself. **For a curse** and "**in cursing**" are both ambiguous. Therefore it will be necessary in some languages to adjust this statement by saying, for example, "curse others by using my name" or "when they curse other people, they do it by pronouncing my name."

102.9-11	RSV		TEV
9	For I eat ashes like bread, and mingle tears with my drink,	9-10	Because of your anger and fury, ashes are my food, and my tears are mixed with my drink.
10	because of thy indignation and anger; for thou hast taken me up and thrown me away.		You picked me up and threw me away.
11	My days are like an evening shadow; I wither away like grass.	11	My life is like the evening shadows; I am like dry grass.

TEV has joined verses 9-10, placing first what is verse 10a in Hebrew; see RSV, which follows the order of the Hebrew text. Translators will be well advised to follow the reordering of verses 9-10 as in TEV, providing the cause at the beginning, unless, of course, this order is not natural in the language.

---

[2]HOTTP prefers the Masoretic text, which it translates "those who become mad against me."

The psalmist attributes his misfortune to Yahweh's **indignation and anger**, which (though not here explicitly stated) are regarded as God's way of punishing him for his sins. The word translated **indignation** has sometimes the meaning of "curse" (see comment on "indignation" in 69.24a). The psalmist's only food is **ashes**, and his **tears** pour down and mingle with his **drink** (see similar language in 42.3; 80.5). During times of fasting and mourning, it was the custom either to place ashes on the head (see 2 Sam 13.19) or to sit on ashes (see Job 2.8; Jonah 3.6). Some, like Oesterley, see **ashes** and **tears** as a sign of the psalmist's repentance. In some languages it may be clearer to say, as in SPCL, "in place of bread, I eat ashes."

In the most abject language possible, the psalmist states that God has picked him up and thrown him away like a worthless object (verse 10b). The expression **taken me up and thrown me away**, if translated literally, may in some languages miss the point of being rejected and without help or healing. Accordingly it may be necessary in some languages to employ a simile in translation; for example, "you have picked me up and thrown me away as a person throws away refuse" or ". . . as people get rid of dirt."

The psalmist compares himself to **an evening shadow** of a day that is coming to its end; he is growing weaker, like **grass** that dries up. In languages in which **an evening shadow** may not carry the meaning of approaching the end, it will be necessary to use a different figure or to say, for example, "my life will soon finish like the evening shadow disappears with the coming of dark." RSV **wither away like grass** is a better model than TEV, which contains no verb and leaves the reader to wonder what the nature of the comparison with dry grass may be.

102.12-14	RSV	TEV
12	But thou, O LORD, art enthroned for ever; thy name endures to all generations.	12 But you, O LORD, are king forever; all generations will remember you.
13	Thou wilt arise and have pity on Zion; it is the time to favor her; the appointed time has come.	13 You will rise and take pity on Zion; the time has come to have mercy on her; this is the right time.
14	For thy servants hold her stones dear, and have pity on her dust.	14 Your servants love her, even though she is destroyed; they have pity on her, even though she is in ruins.

In the hymn of praise (verses 12-22) the psalmist proclaims Yahweh's power as king, a fact never to be forgotten. In verse 12a TEV **"are king"** translates the verb "to sit"; as in 9.7 (which see), the idea may be "to remain, abide," and that is how NAB translates it here. But it is better to understand it to mean "sit (on your throne as king)," that is, to be **enthroned** (RSV).

In verse 12b **name** translates the Hebrew "memorial, remembrance," as in 97.12 (see also 30.4); NEB and NJV have here "fame." Instead of the Masoretic text "your memorial," some Hebrew manuscripts have "your throne" (as in Lam 5.19). The statement "your memorial (or, fame) (is) to generation and generation" means "your fame will last forever." GECL translates "all generations will speak of you" (similarly TOB). SPCL is like TEV: "your name will always be remembered." **All generations**, as used in the TEV sense, may be rendered "all people not yet born" or "everyone still to be born."

The psalmist's thoughts now turn to Jerusalem (**Zion**); she is destroyed (verse 14a) and in ruins (verse 14b), but the Israelites (**thy servants**) love her and have pity on her. In verse 13b,c **time** and **appointed time** are synonymous; the situation seems to be the Babylonian exile, and the expectation is that God will take the exiles back home. The words **her stones** and **her dust** indicate that Jerusalem has been destroyed, and so the psalmist affirms that now is the right time for Yahweh to act, for him to restore Jerusalem (see verse 16a). For **arise**, used of God, see 3.7; 7.6. For idiomatic translation suggestions concerning **have pity**, see 72.13.

Favor her in the expression **it is the time to favor her** means "to comfort, be kind, be merciful, to treat tenderly," and in some languages it may be expressed, for example, "to cause her to be happy," "to make her feel good," or idiomatically sometimes, "to give her a cool heart."

The translator will note how TEV has restructured verse 14 by comparing it with RSV. **Stones** and **dust** have been made into two concessive clauses related to "servants love" and "they have pity." Some such restructuring as this is necessary if the reader is not to think of literal **stones** and **dust**.

102.15-17 RSV	TEV
15 The nations will fear the name of the LORD, and all the kings of the earth thy glory.	15 The nations will fear the LORD; all the kings of the earth will fear his power.
16 For the LORD will build up Zion, he will appear in his glory;	16 When the LORD rebuilds Zion, he will reveal his greatness.
17 he will regard the prayer of the destitute, and will not despise their supplication.	17 He will hear his forsaken people and listen to their prayer.

The psalmist speaks of the effects of Yahweh's intervention, when he will restore the power and prosperity of the people of Israel. There will be universal fear: all peoples **will fear the name of the LORD** and "all the kings of the earth will fear his power." Here "**his power**" translates the Hebrew **thy glory**, that is, the revelation of himself as a God who acts to save his people and defeat their enemies. "Majesty" or "might" may serve here as a translation of the word **glory**. TEV maintains the third person reference in verse 15b; the Hebrew text has the second person, "your glory." In some languages it will be clearer to say "all the kings of the earth will fear the powerful things that God does."

In verse 16b the psalmist speaks again of Yahweh's **glory** (TEV "**greatness**"), which will be evident when he rebuilds Jerusalem, that is, brings the people out of exile back to the city. **Will appear in his glory** may also be readjusted to say, for example, "he will show the people how great he is" or "he will appear in his brightness."

In verse 17a **the destitute** are Israelites in exile. **Destitute** may sometimes be rendered as "people who have nothing," "homeless people," or "people who live like animals." In verse 17b, for **he will not despise** see 69.33, which is quite similar to this verse. **Supplication** means prayer, request, petition.

There are different ways in which verses 15-17 can be joined together. TOB and SPCL make of the three verses one sentence: "15 All the nations will fear . . . 16 when the Lord rebuilds . . . 17 when the Lord answers the prayers . . . ." NEB joins verses 15-16 in one sentence: "15 Then shall the nations revere . . . 16 when the Lord builds up . . . ." Perhaps the best way to handle the text (using TEV vocabulary) is as follows: "15 All the nations will fear . . . (16) when the LORD rebuilds Zion and reveals his greatness. 17 For he will hear . . . prayer."

18 Let this be recorded for a genera-
      tion to come,
      so that a people yet unborn may
      praise the LORD:
19 that he looked down from his holy
      height,
      from heaven the LORD looked at
      the earth,
20 to hear the groans of the prison-
      ers,
      to set free those who were
      doomed to die;
	18 Write down for the coming gener-
	      ation what the LORD has
	      done,
	      so that people not yet born will
	      praise him.
	19 The LORD looked down from his
	      holy place on high,
	      he looked down from heaven to
	      earth.
	20 He heard the groans of prisoners
	      and set free those who were
	      condemned to die.

The psalmist consciously regards his work as a written record of Yahweh's soon-to-come intervention. There is uncertainty over what **this** in **Let this be recorded** in verse 18a refers to. Some take it to mean the author's own words in verses 13-17 (so SPCL, which places verse 18 as the last verse of the preceding strophe). TOB and NIV take it to refer to verses 19-20; RSV, BJ, NJB and Dahood take it to be verses 19-22; TEV takes it to refer to the coming intervention of Yahweh on behalf of his people—"**what the LORD has done.**" The author is writing of the future event as though it had already taken place, and this is the meaning the translator should try to convey. In verse 18b **people yet unborn** (literally "a created people") is parallel with **a generation to come** in line a; some take it to mean "a recreated people" (see FRCL), that is, the Israelites freed from exile and once again a nation (see Cohen). In verse 18b the name *Yah* is used (see 68.4). The sudden insertion of a command in verse 18a will cause problems of understanding in many languages, as it is necessary to make clear who is making the command as well as who is addressed. Therefore it may be necessary to say "I the psalmist say 'Write down . . .' " or " 'Let someone write down,' I, the psalmist, say this." **A people yet unborn** may be misunderstood by readers as "before birth people will praise the LORD." To avoid this problem it may be necessary to say, for example, "people who will be born later" or "people who will come after us."

What the Lord will do is to be written down as though it were in the past, because it will have happened when future people read it; it is described in verses 19-20. He will look down from his dwelling place in heaven (**from his holy height, from heaven**) to earth, to the place where his people are (see similar language in 14.2; 33.13-14); he will take notice of the suffering of his people and set them free. The translator should make certain that the reader understands that the two halves of verse 19 are parallel and do not refer to two different kinds of height.

In verse 20 **the prisoners** and **those who were doomed to die** (literally "the sons of death," as in 79.11) are the Israelites in exile. **Who were doomed to die** will have to be recast in languages which do not use a passive; for example, "those of our tribe whom the enemy has decided to kill."

102.21-22   RSV   TEV

21 that men may declare in Zion the   21 And so his name will be pro-
        name of the LORD,   claimed in Zion,
    and in Jerusalem his praise,   and he will be praised in Jeru-
22 when peoples gather together,   salem
    and kingdoms, to worship the   22 when nations and kingdoms come
        LORD.   together
                                             and worship the LORD.

RSV keeps verses 21-22 in the one long sentence that begins in verse 18. It is better to break up the material into several sentences.

As a result of the Lord's activity, there will be rejoicing in Jerusalem, where **peoples** and **kingdoms** will gather to **worship** (literally "serve") Yahweh. In verse 21a to **declare . . . the name of the LORD** means to acclaim him, to proclaim the great things he has done; and in verse 21b **(declare) . . . his praise** may be simply "praise him," or else "declare why he must be praised." It should be clear in verse 22 that this universal gathering of **peoples** and **kingdoms** will take place in Jerusalem. In many languages it will be preferable for the translator to avoid the exclusivist language of **men may declare** and say "people will . . . ." In verse 22 it will often be necessary to express the subject as "people from many nations and kingdoms."

102.23-24b   RSV   TEV

23 He has broken my strength in   23 The LORD has made me weak
        mid-course;   while I am still young;
    he has shortened my days.   he has shortened my life.
24 "O my God," I say, "take me not   24 O God, do not take me away now
        hence   before I grow old.
    in the midst of my days,

Once more the psalmist describes his own situation (see verses 3-11); the natural implication of verse 23 is that he is still young but does not expect to live to a ripe old age. Line a is literally "He has brought down my strength in the way"; "way" here is taken to mean "**while I am still young**" (RSV **in mid-course**). One form of the Hebrew text has "his strength" (so the Septuagint); TEV, RSV, and the majority of modern texts read the form of the text which has "my strength." In languages where **broken my strength** or **"made me weak"** will refer only to sexual vitality, it may be necessary to say, for example, "has brought me close to death." In some languages such a notion may be expressed better in figurative language.

In verse 24 the psalmist quotes himself, his prayer that God not let him die but allow him to live a normal life span. TEV, as usual, does not represent this form but has the prayer, with the second person address to God. "**Before I grow old**" translates **in the midst of my days**.

Most translations limit the prayer to verse 24; some take it to the end of the psalm (see NIV, NJV).

The last line in verse 24 (see RSV) is taken by TEV to go with what follows, not with what precedes. It seems difficult to take it to mean, as RSV and others render it, that the psalmist is saying, in effect, that it is unfair for God, whose existence has no end, to cut him off in mid-life. So TEV, SPCL, GECL, and TOB connect it with what follows. Briggs takes the whole strophe (verses 24c-27) to be a fragment of a lost psalm, incorporated into this psalm.

<u>102.24c-27</u>   RSV   TEV

thou whose years endure
  throughout all generations!"
	O LORD, you live forever;
	25 long ago you created the earth,
	    and with your own hands you
	      made the heavens.

25 Of old thou didst lay the founda-
      tion of the earth,
    and the heavens are the work of
      thy hands.
	26 They will disappear, but you will
	    remain;
	    they will all wear out like
	      clothes.

26 They will perish, but thou dost
      endure;
    they will all wear out like a
      garment.
    Thou changest them like raiment,
      and they pass away;
	You will discard them like clothes,
	    and they will vanish.
	27 But you are always the same,
	    and your life never ends.

27 but thou art the same, and thy years have no end.	

In the last part of the psalm (as understood by TEV), the psalmist, in a hymn to Yahweh, praises his eternal being, which is without beginning or end; this is the basis for the security of those who trust in him (verse 28). In contrast with mortal humankind and transient creation, Yahweh endures forever (see 90.2 for the same affirmation).

The psalmist begins (verse 24c) "for all generations (are) your years," meaning "your years have no end" (SPCL) or **"you live forever"** (TEV). This is balanced in the last line of the strophe (verse 27b) by "your years do not end."

The Lord created the universe (**the earth . . . the heavens**); for **lay the foundation of the earth** in verse 25a, see 89.11; and for verse 25b see 8.3. Unlike Yahweh, **the earth and the heavens** are temporary and will vanish (verse 26). The psalmist compares them to clothes which get worn out and so are discarded (see Isa 51.6). In verse 26c **Thou changest them** (NJV "You change them") may appear to mean that Yahweh would replace the old ones with new ones (so Briggs). But it seems better to understand the text as TEV and NEB have done. The analogy of the earth and the heavens wearing out like clothes may not be clear. Therefore it may be necessary to recast this expression to say, for example, "they will become old and useless like old clothes" or "they will wear out and be discarded like old clothes."

Verse 27a in Hebrew is simply "you are he," a way of speaking of Yahweh's uniqueness as one who does not change or grow old; verse 27b matches verse 24c.

Verses 25-27 are quoted in Hebrews 1.10-12 substantially as they appear in the Septuagint; in verse 26a the Septuagint has "you will change them," while Hebrews 1.12 has "you will fold them" (or "roll them up").

102.28 RSV	TEV
The children of thy servants shall dwell secure; their posterity shall be established before thee.	Our children will live in safety, and under your protection their descendants will be secure.

The psalm closes with the confident assurance that future generations of Israelites will dwell securely in rebuilt and restored Jerusalem. RSV **shall be established** in line **b** is meant to be parallel with **shall dwell secure** in line **a**. A better way to say this may be "endure" (NJV), or "continue," or "survive." TEV **"under your protection"** translates **before thee**; as Anderson says, "in Yahweh's land and in his care" (see FRCL "under your care"). The expression **children of thy servants** refers to the descendants of Israel, and to avoid possible misunderstanding may have to be recast to say, for example, "We are your servants, and our children will live in safety," or "The children of those who worship you will . . . ," or more directly as in TEV, **"Our children . . . ."**

Psalm 103

This psalm is a hymn of thanksgiving to God for his love and care; it calls on the whole universe to join the psalmist in praising the all-merciful Lord. McCullough aptly describes it as "one of the noblest hymns in the Old Testament."

The psalm opens with the psalmist's exhortation to himself to praise Yahweh (verses 1-2) because of Yahweh's goodness to him (verses 3-5). The Lord's love and compassion for his people are praised (verses 6-14), and the finite life of human beings is contrasted with the Lord's eternal love (verses 15-18). Using the same words as in the opening, the psalm closes with an eloquent call for all creation to join in praise of the all-powerful King (verses 19-22).

There is no way of determining who wrote the psalm or the precise date of its composition.

HEADING: "**The Love of God.**" Other headings are: "A father's compassion"; "God is love"; "Praise of divine goodness." The TEV heading may be adapted to some languages by saying, for example, "God loves his people" or "This song shows how much God loves his people."

<u>Hebrew Title</u>: **A Psalm of David** (TEV "By David").

It should be noted that the Hebrew says only "by David"; the word "psalm" is not used.

103.1-2   RSV   TEV

	RSV		TEV
1	Bless the LORD, O my soul; and all that is within me, bless his holy name!	1	Praise the LORD, my soul! All my being, praise his holy name!
2	Bless the LORD, O my soul, and forget not all his benefits,	2	Praise the LORD, my soul, and do not forget how kind he is.

The psalmist exhorts himself, **O my soul** (see 42.5,11; 43.5), to praise Yahweh, literally **Bless** (see 16.7). This dialogue of the psalmist with his inner self may be impossible or unnatural to represent in other languages; SPCL, FRCL, and GECL translate "I will praise the Lord . . . ." This may be a good model to follow; or else, "I promise that I will praise the LORD . . . ." The expression **all that is within me** is sometimes rendered "all my innermost," "all my heart," or other body parts that represent the whole person.

In verse 1b, for **his holy name** FRCL has "the holy God." For translation suggestions on **his holy name** see 33.21.

Bless the LORD in verse 2 is the third occurrence of this expression in the first three lines of this psalm. The repetition is for emphasis, but in some languages that stylistic device will take a different form than mere repetition. The translator must use the structure that most naturally gives emphasis.

In verse 2b TEV **"how kind he is"** translates a word which means "(good) deed." In the Masoretic text the word is in the plural (so most English translations, **his benefits**; NJB has "his acts of kindness"); one Hebrew manuscript has the singular. It may be better to be specific, "and do not forget all the good things he has done." The negative "do not forget" can be expressed by the positive "always remember."

103.3-5	RSV	TEV

3	who forgives all your iniquity, who heals all your diseases,	3 He forgives all my sins and heals all my diseases.
4	who redeems your life from the Pit, who crowns you with steadfast love and mercy,	4 He keeps me from the grave and blesses me with love and mercy.
5	who satisfies you with good as long as you live*q* so that your youth is renewed like the eagle's.	5 He fills my life*w* with good things, so that I stay young and strong like an eagle.

w Probable text my life; *Hebrew unclear.*

q Heb uncertain

The psalmist gives a list of Yahweh's acts of kindness toward him: forgiveness, healing, protection from death, and spiritual and material blessings. In Hebrew these verses follow without a break from verses 1-2 (see RSV) as a lengthy description of the kind of God Yahweh is, in terms of what he does for the psalmist. TEV has started a new sentence with verse 3 and changed the personal references to "me," "my," and "I," in place of the second person form of address, "you" (that is, referring to "my soul" in verses 1-2). NEB does the same.

Forgives translates a verb found in the Psalms only here and in 25.11; the related adjective "forgiving" is used in 86.5. For translation suggestions on **forgives all your iniquity**, see 25.18.

In verse 4a the verb *ga'al* "redeems" is used in the sense of rescue (see comments on the noun, 19.14, and the verb, 25.22; 69.18). Together with **the Pit**, a synonym for Sheol (see 6.5; 16.10), these terms are taken by most as a deliverance from death. Dahood understands the words to mean resurrection. In verse 4b TEV **"blesses"** translates the verb **crowns** (see comments at 8.5), an expression which describes an unusual honor and favor. The two outstanding blessings are Yahweh's **steadfast love** (see 5.7) and his **mercy** (see 40.11) for the psalmist. The TEV expression **"keeps me from the grave,"** which makes clear the meaning of **redeems from . . . the pit**, must often be recast as "who does not let me die." The expression **"blesses me with love and mercy"** must often be recast as phrases showing manner; for example, "he gives me good things by loving me and being kind to me."

871

In verse 5a, for TEV **"my life,"** the Masoretic text has a word that seems to mean "your ornaments" (see 2 Sam 1.24), which makes no sense here (KJV "your mouth" is wrong). Most emend to a word meaning "your lifetime" (see Briggs, Anderson; see 104.33; 146.2) or else translate the Masoretic text as "the prime of life" (NEB, NJV). The Septuagint has "your desire" (so Weiser, "your longing"); NAB translates the Masoretic text "your lifetime"; Dahood translates it "your eternity," as a reference to the blessed afterlife in heaven; TOB has "your strength."[1] If the translator follows the TEV model, the expression **"fills my life with . . ."** may have to be recast to say "he gives me good things as long as I live."

The **eagle** was famous for its strength (see Isa 40.31) and long life (see *Fauna and Flora,* pages 82-85). If the eagle is unknown, a local bird of prey which is known to live to old age should be used.

<table>
<tr><td colspan="2">103.6-7</td><td>RSV</td><td>TEV</td></tr>
</table>

	RSV		TEV
6	The LORD works vindication and justice for all who are oppressed.	6	The LORD judges in favor of the oppressed and gives them their rights.
7	He made known his ways to Moses, his acts to the people of Israel.	7	He revealed his plans to Moses and let the people of Israel see his mighty deeds.

Turning from Yahweh's goodness to him personally, the psalmist now describes the qualities of Yahweh as revealed in his relation to the people of Israel. First there is the manifestation of his righteousness and justice toward the oppressed. In verse 6 the psalmist uses the plural of *tsedeq* and *mishpat* (see 4.1; 7.6), perhaps to stress the various deeds of the Lord in favor of his people. NJV translates "executes righteous acts and judgments," and TOB translates the verse "The Lord accomplishes deeds of justice, he does what is right to all who are exploited." But it is not necessary to use a plural in translation; see RSV and Dahood, **vindication and justice**. **All who are oppressed** is sometimes rendered as "those who have no rights, "people who have no power," or "those who have no one to defend them."

The righteousness of Yahweh is manifest also in his relation to the people of Israel (verse 7), who saw **"his mighty deeds,"** primarily the great **acts** of salvation (verse 7b). The **ways** which he revealed to Moses (verse 7a) were his will, his purpose, his plans, for the people of Israel. **Made known his ways to Moses** may be recast to say, for example, "he showed Moses what he planned to do."

103.8-10	RSV		TEV
8	The LORD is merciful and gracious,	8	The LORD is merciful and loving, slow to become angry and full

---

[1]HOTTP says the meaning of the Hebrew expression is no longer known with certainty; the most probable interpretation is "your vitality."

slow to anger and abounding in steadfast love.
9 He will not always chide,
   nor will he keep his anger for ever.
10 He does not deal with us according to our sins,
   nor requite us according to our iniquities.
	of constant love.
	9 He does not keep on rebuking;
	   he is not angry forever.
	10 He does not punish us as we deserve
	   or repay us according to our sins and wrongs.

Verses 8-12 reflect the thinking and vocabulary of Exodus 34.6-7 (which see). Verse 8 is similar in thought to 86.15 and uses the same vocabulary. **Merciful and gracious** translates a phrase with a play on word sounds in Hebrew, *rachum* and *chanun*. Yahweh is not quick to punish but is patient and always acts with love toward his people (verse 8b).

Nor does he persist in rebuking the sinner (verse 9a); the verb reflects court procedure (see its use in 35.1a, "contend"). Neither does he stay angry forever; the verb, used only here in Psalms, means to hold a grudge against someone. In many languages it will be necessary to express the object of God's actions of rebuking and being angry; for example, "God will not keep on rebuking his people; he will not stay angry at them for ever."

The psalmist goes a step farther; from Yahweh's feelings he goes on to Yahweh's deeds and asserts that he never punishes his people as severely as their sins deserve (verse 10). Here the psalmist starts using the first person plural, referring to himself and his fellow Israelites. The verb translated **deal** means literally "do." That is, he does not take action toward us **according to our sins** (TEV "He does not punish us as we deserve"). The verb translated **requite** means to reward when used in a good sense (see 18.20a); when used in a bad sense, as here, it means to punish (so Dahood). **Sins** and **iniquities** translate the two most common words in the Old Testament for sin (see 51.1-2). Another way in which verse 10 may be translated is:

> He punishes us for our sins and wrongdoings,
> but never as much as we really deserve.

103.11-14   RSV   TEV

11 For as the heavens are high above the earth,
   so great is his steadfast love toward those who fear him;
12 as far as the east is from the west,
   so far does he remove our transgressions from us.
13 As a father pities his children,
   so the LORD pities those who fear him.
	11 As high as the sky is above the earth,
	   so great is his love for those who honor him.
	12 As far as the east is from the west,
	   so far does he remove our sins from us.
	13 As a father is kind to his children,
	   so the LORD is kind to those

14 For he knows our frame;
     he remembers that we are dust.
	who honor him
	14 He knows what we are made of;
	     he remembers that we are dust.

The psalmist uses two figures (verses 11-12), the distance that separates **the heavens** from **the earth** and the distance from **the east** to **the west**, in order to illustrate Yahweh's great love for his people and his readiness to forgive them. For **steadfast love** see 5.7, and for **those who fear him** see 15.4.

In verse 11 the greatness of the distance of the sky from the earth is used as the basis for comparing the greatness of God's love. In this case distance is compared with intensity. In some languages it will not be clear how two such different things can be said to be alike; in such languages it may be necessary to say something like "God loves those who honor him; he loves them so greatly, it is like the greatness with which the sky covers the earth."

Verse 12 speaks of forgiveness in terms of Yahweh's taking the people's sins and placing them as far away as possible. The Hebrew uses the word "distance" as a noun and as a verb, as follows: "As is the distance from the east to the west, so he distances our sins from us" (see similar language in Micah 7.19). The meaning is that Yahweh frees his people from the power and consequences of their sins by granting them full pardon. **As far as the east is from the west** will have little or no meaning in some languages. It will be necessary in some cases to say, for example, "God removes our sins from us as far as the place where the sun rises is from the place where the sun sets."

Yahweh's mercy is compared to that of a kind father, who **pities his children**. The Hebrew verb means "show love, tenderness, kindness" (see 102.14b; 116.5b, "merciful"). The verb "to pity" has too great an element of sorrow in it and is not the best English equivalent of the Hebrew verb. NJB is good: "As tenderly as a father treats his children, so Yahweh treats those who fear him" (see SPCL).

Yahweh's attitude of love and kindness (verse 13) is based on his intimate knowledge of people (verse 14); he knows that they are weak and prone to failure, creatures made of **dust** (see the creation story, Gen 2.7; see also Psa 90.3). TEV **"what we are made of"** translates the noun for **our frame**, which is related to the verb "to form" used in Genesis 2.7; so NJV "He knows how we are formed"; NEB, NAB "he knows how we are made." The expression **that we are dust** will often have to be recast to say, for example, "that we have been created from dust," and a cross reference to Genesis 2.7 provided. The expression **he remembers that** should not be translated by a term which implies that he forgot and then recalled, but by a term that indicates knowing. SPCL says "he well knows that . . . ."

103.15-16   RSV   TEV

15 As for man, his days are like
     grass;
     he flourishes like a flower of the
     field;
16 for the wind passes over it, and it
	15 As for us, our life is like grass.
	     We grow and flourish like a wild
	     flower;
	16 then the wind blows on it, and
	     it is gone—

is gone,   no one sees it again.
and its place knows it no more.

Having said in verse 14 what human beings are made of (dust), the psalmist now expands on this theme, contrasting human frailty and mortality (verses 15-16) with the Lord's eternal love and goodness (verses 17-18). The word for **man** in verse 15a is the same as in 8.4a: a mortal, weak creature, whose life span is compared to that of **grass**, of **a flower of the field**, which is dried up by the hot desert wind and is seen no more. See the same figure in 90.5-6; Isaiah 40.6-8. As in TEV 90.5, here "weeds" would be more appropriate in English than **grass**. TEV has avoided the possibility of **man** being interpreted in exclusivist terms, by using "us." In translation, if "**us**" is used, it will be necessary to make it inclusive, since the psalm is addressed to people, not to God. In languages where the comparison may not be recognized, it may be necessary to say, for example, "a person's life is short, it passes quickly away like grass."

Since it is the drying or withering effect of the wind that causes the flower to disappear, it may be necessary in translating verse 16a to say, for example, "then the wind blows and dries it up, and the flower disappears" or "the drying wind blows on the flower and soon it is gone."

In verse 16b the Hebrew is **and its place knows it no more**, a way of saying that it is completely gone, never to return; see FRCL "it disappears without leaving a trace." Some translations (BJ, NJB, NAB, Dahood) take the pronouns in verse 16 to refer to **man**; it seems better to take them to refer to "the wild flower" (RSV, TEV, NJV, TOB, NIV, SPCL).

103.17-18   RSV   TEV

17   But the steadfast love of the LORD   17   But for those who honor the
     is from everlasting to ever-   LORD, his love lasts forever,
     lasting   and his goodness endures for all
     upon those who fear him,   generations
     and his righteousness to chil-   18   of those who are true to his cove-
     dren's children,   nant
18   to those who keep his covenant   and who faithfully obey his
     and remember to do his com-   commands.
     mandments.

Yahweh's "**love**" (*chesed*) and his "**goodness**" (*tsedaqah*) last forever for those who **fear him**, those who **keep his covenant** and **remember to do his commandments**. In some languages the expression "**his love lasts forever**" will have to be recast to say "he will love them for ever." The word translated **righteousness** by RSV may be taken to mean "beneficence"(NJV), "loyalty" (FRCL), "saving justice"(NJB), "goodness" (TEV). The Hebrew expression "to the sons of sons," which is represented by RSV's **to children's children** and TEV's "**for all generations**," is parallel with "**forever**" in 17a and may be translated in the same way. Alternatively, the translator may prefer to combine the second part of the parallelism with the first part and say, for example, "he will love them and be good to them for ever."

The **covenant** (verse 18a) is the one Yahweh made with his people in Sinai, in which he promised to be their God, to protect and to prosper them, if they obeyed him and kept his commandments (see 25.10). The Hebrew **remember to do** is a way of saying "are careful to obey." And the word translated **commandments** is the one used in 19.8a, "precepts." Verse 18 expands the recipients of God's love in verse 17. In some languages it will be clearer to keep these persons together by combining them with verse 17; for example, "those who honor the LORD, are true to his covenant, and obey him . . . ."

<u>103.19-22</u>   RSV   TEV

19   The LORD has established his   19   The LORD placed his throne in
       throne in the heavens,   heaven;
     and his kingdom rules over all.   he is king over all.
20   Bless the LORD, O you his angels,   20   Praise the LORD, you strong and
       you mighty ones who do his   mighty angels,
       word,   who obey his commands,
     hearkening to the voice of his   who listen to what he says.
       word!   21   Praise the LORD, all you heavenly
21   Bless the LORD, all his hosts,   powers,
       his ministers that do his will!   you servants of his, who do his
22   Bless the LORD, all his works,   will!
       in all places of his dominion.   22   Praise the LORD, all his creatures
     Bless the LORD, O my soul!   in all the places he rules.
                                                  Praise the LORD, my soul!

The psalm closes with an exhortation for all to join in the chorus of praise to Yahweh. The psalmist first asserts God's universal power (verse 19; see similar statements in 47.8; 93.2; 102.12); Yahweh, the King of Israel, is king of all creation. NJV joins verse 19 to the preceding strophe, but it seems better to make it the first verse of the final strophe. For translation suggestions on **throne** see 2.4.

TEV **"Praise"** in verses 20-22 translates the verb **Bless** (see verse 1). The heavenly powers, God's heavenly court, are addressed as **angels** (verse 20a), who are described as **you mighty ones**, a term for heroes in an army, "mighty warriors" (TEV "strong and mighty"; Dahood, NJB "mighty warriors"; TOB "elite troops"). The angels are also called **hosts** (verse 21a), a translation of the noun "armies" found in the title "Yahweh of armies" (see 46.7). **Ministers** in verse 21b translates the same word used as a verb in 101.6 of the king's officials, who "shall minister," and here the celestial beings are likened to officials in the royal court who carry out the king's wishes. In some languages it will be necessary to place the persons addressed before the command; for example, "You strong and mighty angels . . . , praise the LORD." Where this order is more natural, it will also be followed in verses 21-22.

In verse 22 all creation throughout Yahweh's dominion is called upon to praise him. In line **a his works** are everything that Yahweh has created; this may include inanimate things as well as all living creatures; so SPCL "the entire creation." And the psalm closes as it begins, with the psalmist exhorting himself to "**praise the LORD.**" See verse 2 for **Bless the LORD, O my soul!**

Psalm 104

This hymn of praise to God as creator and sustainer of the universe is similar in style to Psalm 103, and many think the two psalms were composed by the same person. This psalm was also used in the Temple worship during one of the great festivals, perhaps the New Year Festival in the fall of the year (see Anderson).

Similarities are noted between this psalm and other creation accounts, both biblical (in Genesis 1) and nonbiblical, particularly the Egyptian hymn to the sun, attributed to King Akhenaton of the 14th century B.C. (see McCullough).

There are differences of opinion about the strophic arrangement. RSV and TEV are quite close. McCullough proposes the following division: verses 1-4, 5-9, 10-13, 14-18, 19-23, 24-26, 27-30, 31-35. Toombs sees a seven-fold description of creation, as follows: (1) the heavens (verses 1-4); (2) the earth (verses 5-9); (3) water (verses 10-13); (4) food (verses 14-18); (5) organization of time (verses 19-23); (6) the sea (verses 24-26); (7) control of life (verses 27-30). Verses 31-35 form the conclusion.

HEADING: "**In Praise of the Creator**." Other headings are: "The wonder of creation"; "God's creation"; "The glories of creation." The TEV heading may be adjusted for use in some languages by saying, for example, "I will praise the Creator" or "Sing a song to praise the Creator."

104.1-4 RSV   TEV

RSV	TEV
1 Bless the LORD, O my soul!	1 Praise the LORD, my soul!
O LORD my God, thou art very great!	O LORD, my God, how great you are!
Thou art clothed with honor and majesty,	You are clothed with majesty and glory;
2 who coverest thyself with light as with a garment,	2 you cover yourself with light.
who hast stretched out the heavens like a tent,	You spread out the heavens like a tent
3 who hast laid the beams of thy chambers on the waters,	3 and built your home on the waters above.[x]
who makest the clouds thy chariot,	You use the clouds as your chariot and ride on the wings of the wind.
who ridest on the wings of the wind,	4 You use the winds as your messengers
4 who makest the winds thy messengers,	and flashes of lightning as your servants.
fire and flame thy ministers.	

> ^x THE WATERS ABOVE: *A reference to the waters above the celestial dome (Genesis 1.6-7).*

The psalmist begins with an exhortation to himself to **Bless the LORD** (see 103.1). In languages in which God cannot be possessed, it is often possible to translate **my God** as "the God whom I worship." This is followed by a description of Yahweh's greatness: **honor and majesty** (see 96.6; 93.1) are his clothing (verse 1c), the **light** is his mantle (verse 2a; see 71.13 for the verb "to cover"). **Garment** (verse 2a) is not meant to be a different piece of clothing from what is implied by the verb **clothed** in verse 1c; but a word like "robe" or "mantle" would be quite appropriate (NJV and NEB "wrapped in a robe of light"). In some languages it will be possible to translate lines 1c and 2a by means of a simile; for example, "As a person wears clothing, you wear honor and majesty and light." It may also be possible to translate this difficult figure by saying, for example, "You are surrounded by honor and majesty and wear light as a person wears clothing." In languages in which **honor** and **majesty** cannot be expressed as nouns, it may be necessary to replace the figure by a nonfigure and say, for example, "people honor you and treat you like a chief, you are covered with light" or ". . . light shines on you."

The psalmist then compares the creation of the heavens (verse 2b) to a man putting up his tent, literally the curtains or flaps of a tent (a Hebrew word used only here in Psalms). In languages where the tent is not known, it may be possible to use some other local structure, employ a generic term, or use such a term as "roof."

In verse 3a TEV "**home**" translates a plural word which means either the upper stories or the rooms on top of the house (see 1 Kgs 17.19; 2 Kgs 1.2; 4.10); "**built**" translates a verb that means "to build with beams." Some take the plural to refer to the successive layers of heaven, either three or seven. In any case, they are Yahweh's heavenly habitation. RSV **laid the beams of thy chambers** is unnecessarily cumbersome and difficult; similarly NJV "He sets the rafters of His lofts in the waters." The implication that Yahweh put the **beams** or the "rafters" in place, and nothing else, is rather ridiculous. The psalmist is saying that Yahweh built his dwelling place like the living quarters on top of a house. NJB translates "your palace." "**The waters above**" (TEV) are the waters above the heavenly firmament, separated at creation from those below (see Gen 1.6-7); simply to translate **waters**, as RSV and NJV do, is not enough; NIV "their waters" is even less adequate. FRCL abandons the concept altogether: "You have placed your dwelling place even higher than the sky."

Translators in Middle Eastern languages will be familiar with rooms built on the flat roofs, and terms for these are available; however, since the reference is to God's abode, it will be better to follow TEV "**home**," or say "palace," or "the place where you live."

The natural phenomena, **the clouds** and **the wind**, serve as Yahweh's **chariot** as he comes to visit the earth (see 18.10; 68.4,33; Isa 19.1). For translation suggestions on **chariot** see 20.7. In languages in which the figure of speech **wings of the wind** does not make sense, it may be necessary to drop the figure and say, for example, "you ride on the wind" or "the wind carries you."

Yahweh uses **the winds** and the "**lightning**" to carry his messages and otherwise perform duties of servants as he rules the world. The Hebrew phrase translated "**flashes of lightning**" is literally "a flaming fire" (RSV **fire and flame**); this is taken to mean lightning (see NAB footnote; Briggs, Cohen). Most translations, however, by saying only "fiery flames" (NJV), "flames of fire" (NIV, NEB), or "fire" (FRCL), lead the reader to think of fire, not of lightning. For comments on **ministers** see 103.21.

Verse 4 is quoted in Hebrew 1.7 as it appears in the Septuagint, which takes "angels" and "servants" as the direct objects of the verbs, and "winds" and "flames of fire" as the complements. Some, like Kirkpatrick and Briggs, believe that this is the proper meaning of the Hebrew text itself: "You make your angels winds, and your servants flashes of lightning" (see KJV). But no modern translation consulted follows this interpretation of the verse. In some languages it will be clearer to avoid the nominal forms in the figures of the wind and lightning, as suggested above, and say, for example, "You use the wind to carry your messages, and the lightning to serve you."

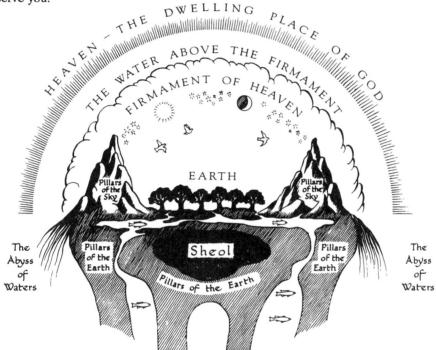

ANCIENT HEBREW CONCEPT OF THE UNIVERSE

104.5-6	RSV		TEV

RSV	TEV

5   Thou didst set the earth on its foundations,
     so that it should never be shaken.
 6   Thou didst cover it with the deep as with a garment;
     the waters stood above the mountains.
	5 You have set the earth firmly on its foundations,
	     and it will never be moved.
	 6 You placed the ocean over it like a robe,
	     and the water covered the mountains.

In this strophe (verses 5-9) the psalmist describes the creation of the earth in terms of the defeat and control of the watery chaos (see Gen 1.2) which prevailed before creation (see 74.13-15; 89.9-10).

Yahweh placed **the earth** solidly **on its foundations** (see 24.2; 102.25a); this reflects the idea that the earth was a flat disk that rested on pillars under the ground, which reached down into the underworld. (Note the illustration on page 878.) In some languages it will be necessary to shift from the noun **foundations** to a clause; for example, "You have firmly built the earth" or "You . . . founded the earth."

TEV, RSV, and others (NJV, BJ, NJB, TOB, NAB, Dahood) take the Hebrew text of verse 6 to mean that Yahweh spread the ocean (the primeval **deep**) over the earth as part of the creative process. But this seems strange, since it implies that the surface of the earth lay submerged under the primeval waters, which would have to refer back to the condition of the earth before creation; or else it would have to refer to the Flood, which seems most unlikely (see Kirkpatrick). It seems preferable, with Weiser, NEB, FRCL, GECL, and SPCL, to make a slight change in the Masoretic text (from *kisito* "you covered it" to *kisatah* "it covered"), and to understand the text to refer to the condition of the earth before creation, and then to connect verse 6 with verse 7, which tells what happened when the Lord's creative word was uttered.[1] This interpretation would lead TEV to be:

> 6 The ocean was lying over the earth like a robe,
>   and the water covered the mountains;
> 7 but when you rebuked the waters, they fled . . .

If the translator follows RSV or TEV, it may be necessary to say, for example, "You put the ocean over the earth as a person puts on clothing" or "You laid the ocean over the earth, covering it as with a cloth." The second line is understood as consequence, "and water covered the mountains," or "so that the water covered the mountain," or "and the mountains were beneath the water." If the second interpretation is followed, it may be necessary to make the time reference explicit; for example, "When you began to create, the ocean was lying over the earth . . ." or "Before you created the world, the ocean covered . . . ."

104.7-9

RSV	TEV
7 At thy rebuke they fled; at the sound of thy thunder they took to flight.	7 When you rebuked the waters, they fled; they rushed away when they heard your shout of command.
8 The mountains rose, the valleys sank down to the place which thou didst appoint for them.	8 They flowed over the mountains and into the valleys, to the place you had made for them.
9 Thou didst set a bound which they should not pass,	

---

[1]HOTTP does not consider this possibility.

| so that they might not again cover the earth. | 9 | You set a boundary they can never pass, to keep them from covering the earth again. |

In verse 7 the primeval waters flee and rush away at Yahweh's command; the two lines of the verse are synonymous. See in 76.6 another instance of Yahweh's **rebuke**. In line **b** TEV **"your shout of command"** translates a phrase that elsewhere means **sound of thy thunder** (see "thunder" in 77.18; 81.7).

Verse 8 is understood in different ways by RSV and TEV. TEV, along with BJ, NJB, NJV, FRCL, NIV, NEB, TOB, SPCL (Briggs, Oesterley, McCullough, Anderson, Dahood), takes **"the waters"** of verse 7 as the subject of the verbs in verse 8. NJV does this by setting off verse 8a between dashes ("—mountains rising, valleys sinking—") and connecting verse 8b directly to verse 7, with "the waters" of verse 6b as the subject of verse 8b, "(They rushed away) . . . to the place you established for them." RSV, however, follows AT (see Kirkpatrick, Weiser). TEV's interpretation is preferred, since this continues the description of water from verse 7 through verse 9.

In verse 9 Yahweh is pictured as confining the primeval waters to a closed space, so that never again would they **cover the earth**, as they did before creation (see Gen 1.6-9). Beginning with line 7b, TEV uses **"they"** and **"them"** six times to refer to **"the waters."** In many languages it will be necessary to reintroduce the subject **"waters."**

104.10-12   RSV   TEV

10	Thou makest springs gush forth in the valleys; they flow between the hills,	10	You make springs flow in the valleys, and rivers run between the hills.
11	they give drink to every beast of the field; the wild asses quench their thirst.	11	They provide water for the wild animals; there the wild donkeys quench their thirst.
12	By them the birds of the air have their habitation; they sing among the branches.	12	In the trees near by, the birds make their nests and sing.

TEV (also SPCL, TOB, FRCL, NEB, NJB, BJ) ends this strophe with verse 12; RSV, McCullough, and Toombs end it with verse 13.

Yahweh provides water for the animals. In verse 10a the word translated **the valleys** is understood by NJV to mean "in torrents" (Weiser "in streams"). NEB has "gullies" and NJB "ravines." It may mean either the course taken by the water as it rushes down, or else the water itself (Dahood has "springs and torrents"). TEV in verse 10 supplies **"rivers"** as the subject, for a more natural sequence; this may not be necessary in some languages. Or else, "their water" (referring back to "springs" of the preceding verse) may be more satisfactory.

In verse 11a **every beast of the field** means all the wild animals; and in line b, for **wild asses** see *Fauna and Flora,* pages 5-7. In languages in which the donkey is not known, the translator has the following choices: (a) borrow the term from a major language; (b) use a generic term with some kind of qualifier; (c) substitute a local animal. If the animal is unfamiliar, it is usually recommended that an illustration be provided somewhere in the publication, particularly near the first occurrence of the word. The importance of providing such an illustration is due to the repeated references to this animal.

The pastoral picture of peace and plenty includes the birds (literally "the birds of the heavens") building their nests and singing in the nearby trees. Notice that RSV **By them** in verse 12a could be taken to mean "By the wild asses"; it should be clear to the reader that it means "By the streams." It is important in the process of editing a translation to read the text aloud. Readers sometimes fail to observe punctuation, and they run lines together, so that TEV's ". . . **donkeys quench their thirst**" may be read together with the following line, "**In the trees near by.**" If this is a common problem, this kind of misreading can be avoided in the present case by switching lines 12a and 12b.

104.13-15 RSV	TEV
13 From thy lofty abode thou waterest the mountains; the earth is satisfied with the fruit of thy work.	13 From the sky you send rain on the hills, and the earth is filled with your blessings.
14 Thou dost cause the grass to grow for the cattle, and plants for man to cultivate,ʳ that he may bring forth food from the earth,	14 You make grass grow for the cattle and plants for man to use, so that he can grow his crops
15 and wine to gladden the heart of man, oil to make his face shine, and bread to strengthen man's heart.	15 and produce wine to make him happy, olive oil to make him cheerful, and bread to give him strength.

ʳ Or *fodder for the animals that serve man*

RSV joins verse 13 to the preceding strophe, as seen in the paragraphing; most translations, like TEV, join it to what follows.

Yahweh provides food for animals and human beings by sending rain from the sky (literally "his upper chambers," as in verse 3), which waters the ground so that the soil brings forth abundant crops. Verse 13b is not very clear; the Hebrew seems to say "the earth is satisfied (or, filled) from the fruit (or, result) of your deeds." This seems to mean that, as a result of what Yahweh does, the earth is completely filled with good things, or else the earth is completely satisfied. There are various conjectures; many believe the phrase **the fruit of thy work** refers specifically to the rain itself (Briggs, Oesterley; SPCL); Kirkpatrick has "fruit produced by God's manifold operations" (also Cohen); NEB has "the earth is enriched by thy provisions"; SPCL has "with the streams of heaven you satisfy the earth."

Verses 14-15 list the crops of the fields and how they benefit humankind. Verse 14b in Hebrew seems to be "and plants (or, vegetation) for the service of man," which RSV takes to mean **and plants for man to cultivate.** TEV has **"plants for man to use,"** that is, with reference to the items listed in verse 15, the basic foods needed to sustain him (so Anderson, "plants for the sustenance of man"). NAB has "and vegetation for men's use." NEB has "for those who toil for man" (a reference to work animals), which involves assigning other vowels to the Hebrew consonants (see also RSV footnote). Perhaps the best way to translate is to imitate TOB, FRCL, SPCL: "You make the grass grow for the cattle, and the plants that people cultivate." So line c can follow: "In this way they can get their food from the earth."

Both RSV and TEV employ ellipsis in 14b. In some languages it will be necessary to say in 14b, for example, "you cause plants to grow for people . . . ."

Verse 15 lists the basic crops which are cultivated; they include grapevines (**wine**), olive trees (**oil**), and wheat or barley (**bread**). The wine makes a person happy, and the olive oil makes a person's face shine (verse 15a,b). The latter may be meant quite literally (so Cohen, Briggs, Toombs), since olive oil was applied to the face and the head to cleanse the skin and restore the scalp. TEV takes it in a figurative sense, **"to make him cheerful"** (see comments at 92.10). Dahood takes it to mean "glowing health." Perhaps it is best to take it literally; so FRCL "a good appearance," and NJB "to make their faces glow" (see also NIV). The last item is **bread** (or better, perhaps, "food"—so Dahood), which sustains a person's strength (see the same verb in 41.3a; 94.18b; so NEB, FRCL, SPCL). NJV has "that sustains man's life."

104.16-18	RSV		TEV
16	The trees of the LORD are watered abundantly, the cedars of Lebanon which he planted.	16	The cedars of Lebanon get plenty of rain— the LORD's own trees, which he planted.
17	In them the birds build their nests; the stork has her home in the fir trees.	17	There the birds build their nests; the storks nest in the fir trees.
18	The high mountains are for the wild goats; the rocks are a refuge for the badgers.	18	The wild goats live in the high mountains, and the rock badgers hide in the cliffs.

The psalmist now describes Yahweh's provision for the needs of plants and animals. In verse 16 TEV has reversed the lines in order to make easier the identification of "the LORD's own trees" as **the cedars of Lebanon** (for which see 29.5). Some take the Hebrew "the trees of Yahweh" to mean "gigantic trees" (as "mountains of God" in 36.6 is interpreted). The verb in verse 16a is simply "are satisfied" (as in verse 13b), which is taken by most to refer to plentiful rain; but NEB has "are green and leafy." NJV and NJB translate "drink their fill."

Line 16b picks up the subject from line 16a and identifies it further. In many languages this technique requires a different kind of structure from that found in English. It is often possible to say, for example, "The cedars of Lebanon are the LORD's own trees, which he planted; these trees get plenty of rain."

See *Fauna and Flora* for the identification of the following: **birds**, page 77 ("sparrow"); **stork**, pages 78-79; **fir trees**, pages 162-163. There are differences of opinion about the trees in verse 17b; some think they are junipers (NJV, Dahood), others, cypresses (FRCL, TOB) or pines (NIV). Some (Weiser; NEB, BJ, NJB, SPCL) emend the Hebrew text to get "on top of them" (that is, on top of the cedars of Lebanon of verse 16).[2]

Further information on the animals includes the following: Hebrew *tsippor* may mean "sparrow"; however, there are numerous varieties of this small bird, which belongs to the weaverbird family. The translator may use the term for the common house or English sparrow. Although this bird is found across the world, it is largely restricted to the temperate zones. Where the sparrow is not known, a commonly known local bird which nests where people live may be used. It is always possible to use the generic term for birds (see RSV and TEV). In areas where some variety of the **stork** is not found, the translator may use another long-legged, long-necked bird, preferably one that nests in twig platforms built at the tops of trees, on rock ledges, or on roof tops. In many language areas the **wild goat** will not be familiar, and a substitute animal may not be available. In such cases it may be necessary to borrow the term from another language and to provide an illustration. It should be noted that **badgers**, or even "**rock badgers**" (NJV, TEV, NEB), is not quite accurate, since the badger is a carnivorous, burrowing animal; the more accurate name in English is "hyrax," a herbivorous animal, that does not burrow; it lives in colonies in rocky regions (see Pro 30.26). The translation adaptation made for wild goat also applies to badgers.

For further information on **wild goats**, see *Fauna and Flora,* pages 46-47.

104.19-21	RSV	TEV
19	Thou hast made the moon to mark the seasons; the sun knows its time for setting.	You created the moon to mark the months; the sun knows the time to set.
20	Thou makest darkness, and it is night, when all the beasts of the forest creep forth.	You made the night, and in the darkness all the wild animals come out.
21		The young lions roar while they hunt,

---

[2]HOTTP ("C" decision) favors the emendation "on their top," in justification of which it refers to Factors 8 ("Misunderstanding of linguistic data") and 9 ("Misunderstanding of historical data").

| 21 | The young lions roar for their prey,
seeking their food from God. | looking for the food that God provides. |

Time is also part of Yahweh's creation and is a provision for the needs of all living beings. The moon marked the time of the festivals (see Gen 1.14); the Hebrew word for **seasons** in verse 19a does not mean precisely what we call the four seasons of the year. The Hebrews followed a lunar calendar, the beginning of each month being determined by the new moon; so TEV translates "**months**"; TOB has "the festivals"; FRCL "the dates"; NEB "to measure the year"; and SPCL "to measure time."[3] Verse 19b refers to the day, which began at sunset. If the translator follows TEV, it may be necessary in some languages to say, for example, "You created the moon to show when each month begins." In some languages the personification of the sun in **the sun knows** . . . may have to be recast to say, for example, "the sun sets when it should" or "the sun sets at the right time."

Darkness and **night** (verse 20) were thought of as having real existence, and not simply as the absence of light. They also are part of God's beneficent creation, a time when the wild animals leave their dens and roam about. Verse 21 speaks specifically of the young lions as they hunt, **seeking their food from God**, that is, "**the food that God provides**" for them. All of the natural order depends on God's sustenance, care, and provision.

104.22-23   RSV   TEV

| 22 | When the sun rises, they get them away
and lie down in their dens. | 22 | When the sun rises, they go back and lie down in their dens. |
| 23 | Man goes forth to his work
and to his labor until the evening. | 23 | Then people go out to do their work
and keep working until evening. |

At sunrise the young lions go back to **their dens**, where they stay the whole day (verse 22). Sunrise, also, is the time for people to start working, and they stay at it until sunset (verse 23). Verse 23 must not be related to verse 22 in such a way as to imply that people don't leave their homes for work until the lions have gone back to their dens (because they are afraid the lions will attack them). This is hardly a problem in urban industrial societies, but it can be a real problem in some parts of the world.

[3]The Hebrew of verse 19a is "He made" (see TOB, NJV, BJ); many translations (see RSV, TEV, FRCL, GECL, SPCL) have "You made," without a textual note. NAB, however, reads the participle "making" (only a change of vowels in the Hebrew text) and provides a note. NIV, quite alone, has "the moon" as the subject: "The moon marks off the seasons."

	RSV		TEV

24   O LORD, how manifold are thy
works!
In wisdom hast thou made them
all;
the earth is full of thy creatures.

25   Yonder is the sea, great and wide,
which teems with things innumerable,
living things both small and
great.

26   There go the ships,
and Leviathan which thou didst
form to sport in it.

24   LORD, you have made so many
things!
How wisely you made them all!
The earth is filled with your
creatures.

25   There is the ocean, large and
wide,
where countless creatures live,
large and small alike.

26   The ships sail on it, and in it plays
Leviathan,
that sea monster which you
made.*y*

y in it plays . . . made; *or* Leviathan is
there, that sea monster you made to
amuse you.

Now the psalmist (verse 24) breaks into praise of Yahweh's wisdom in creating
so many different things. The expression **In wisdom** and TEV's **"How wisely"** will have
to be recast in some languages to say, for example, "You were very wise when you
made . . ." or "Because you are very wise, you made . . . ." In line c the word
creatures translates a Hebrew word which occurs in Psalms only here and in 105.21;
it seems to mean possessions, property. Most translations have **creatures** or
"creations." The verb related to **creatures** can mean either "acquire" or "create"
(see 139.13a); and in Genesis 14.22 the verb is used to speak of God as the Creator.
In some languages **creatures** will have to be rendered as "the animals which you
created" or "the things you gave life to."

In verse 25 **the sea, great and wide**, is singled out, emphasizing the fact that,
like the moon and the sun in verse 19, it too is a part of God's creation and is
entirely subordinate to him. Likewise all living beings in the seas are God's creation.

The mention of **ships** in verse 26a is rather strange, since they can hardly be
counted as Yahweh's creation; some (see Weiser) have proposed to change to a word
meaning "monsters," but this has not been widely accepted. Briggs attributes the line
to a later unimaginative editor. These are, of course, sailing ships.

For **Leviathan** see 74.14; this huge sea monster is also God's creation. The
Hebrew text may mean either (1) "Leviathan, that one you made to play in it [that
is, in the ocean]" (RSV, TEV, NIV, NEB footnote); or (2) "Leviathan, that one you
made to play with" (Weiser; NEB, BJ, NJB, FRCL, GECL, NAB, NJV, TOB, SPCL, TEV
footnote, Dahood; see Job 41.5). The majority favor (2), and the translator may
prefer it.

104.27-28   RSV   TEV

	RSV		TEV

27	These all look to thee,
	    to give them their food in due
	    season.
		27	All of them depend on you
			    to give them food when they
			    need it.

28	When thou givest to them, they
	    gather it up;
	    when thou openest thy hand,
	    they are filled with good
	    things.
		28	You give it to them, and they eat
			    it;
			    you provide food, and they are
			    satisfied.

All living creatures depend on Yahweh for their food (verses 27-28) and their continued existence (verses 29-30). For passages similar to verses 27-28, see 145.15-16; 147.9. **In due season** in verse 27b means "at the right time," "at the proper time" (NEB, NIV), "**when they need it**" (TEV, NJB). In verse 28a TEV "**eat**" translates the verb which means to "**gather**," pick up; and in verse 28b "**you provide food**" translates "you open your hand" (see RSV). In simple and graphic language the psalmist portrays all living creatures looking to God for their food and God giving it to them. The translation should do its best to represent faithfully this poetic language.

104.29-30   RSV   TEV

	RSV		TEV

29	When thou hidest thy face, they
	    are dismayed;
	    when thou takest away their
	    breath, they die
	    and return to their dust.
		29	When you turn away, they are
			    afraid;
			    when you take away your
			    breath, they die
			    and go back to the dust from
			    which they came.

30	When thou sendest forth thy
	    Spirit,[s] they are created;
	    and thou renewest the face of
	    the ground.
		30	But when you give them breath,[z]
			    they are created;
			    you give new life to the earth.

[s] Or *breath*

[z] give them breath; *or* send out your spirit.

In verse 29a **When thou hidest thy face** means to withdraw, to leave, to turn away from. FRCL translates "But if you refuse (to give them their food), they are terrified." God's presence is essential to the animals' continued existence. When the animals sense that Yahweh is abandoning them, they become terrified.

In verse 29b the Masoretic text has **their breath** (or "their spirit," or "their life"); it is God who gives *ruach* (breath, spirit) to all living beings, and should God withhold it, they die, and their *ruach* returns to God (Gen 2.7; Eccl 12.7).[4] SPCL,

---

[4]See R. G. Bratcher, "Breath, life, spirit," and D. C. Arichea, "Translating breath and spirit," in *The Bible Translator* 34, no. 2 (April 1983), pages 201-213.

FRCL, and GECL translate "When you withhold from them the life-giving breath, they die." Dahood argues that the Masoretic text is identical in meaning with the parallel **thy face** in verse 29a, though here the word has the pronoun suffix for **their** instead of **thy**. But it should be noted that the Qumran manuscript of the Psalms has "your breath." So the meaning may be "when you hold back your life-giving breath, they die" (see TEV). This seems preferable and better parallels the thought of verse 30a.

For verse 29c see the parallel in 90.3. NEB and others consider this line to be a later gloss. The Hebrew **their dust** means "the dust they were made of."

In verse 30a the translation of "your *ruach*" should use the same word as in verse 29b, "your life-giving breath." TEV here should be "your breath." RSV and NIV have **thy Spirit**, which introduces a nuance that is lacking in the Hebrew; see NJV "send back Your breath, they are created." **They are created** means that the successive generations of animals are all acts of divine creation; God is the one who brings them into being and thus continually renews life on earth (literally "you renew the face of the earth"). FRCL has "everything on the surface of the earth becomes new." GECL has "you give the earth a new appearance" (similarly SPCL). Care must be taken in translation not to lead the reader to think that verses 29b and 30a speak of the death and resurrection of the same animals; it is rather the successive generations of living beings, each new generation replacing the old one that has died. The expression **thou renewest the face of the ground** or TEV's **"you give new life to the earth"** must often be recast to say, for example, "you cause new life to be born on the earth," or "you make new creatures to be born . . . ," or "you make everything on the earth new."

104.31-32　　　RSV　　　　　　　　　　　　　　　　　　TEV

RSV	TEV
31 May the glory of the LORD endure for ever,	31 May the glory of the LORD last forever!
may the LORD rejoice in his works,	May the LORD be happy with what he has made!
32 who looks on the earth and it trembles,	32 He looks at the earth, and it trembles;
who touches the mountains and they smoke!	he touches the mountains, and they pour out smoke.

The psalmist prays that Yahweh's **glory** will last forever. Here **glory** is his power and majesty as revealed in his creation of and dominion over all living creatures (see in 19.1 where God's glory is parallel with his works). Verse 31b recalls the repeated assertion in Genesis 1 that God was pleased with all that he had created. The wish expressed in the English expression **May the glory of the LORD endure** must often be recast in other languages, sometimes as a direct imperative, or by such expressions as "I pray that . . ." or "I wish that . . . ."

Verse 32 emphasizes Yahweh's complete power and dominion; he has only to look at the earth, **and it trembles**, only to touch the mountains, **and they smoke** (that is, they pour out smoke, or burst into flames). The two seem to refer, respectively, to earthquakes and the eruptions of volcanoes.

104.33-35   RSV   TEV

33 I will sing to the LORD as long as   33 I will sing to the LORD all my life;
    I live;   as long as I live I will sing
    I will sing praise to my God   praises to my God.
    while I have being.   34 May he be pleased with my song,
34 May my meditation be pleasing to   for my gladness comes from
    him,   him.
    for I rejoice in the LORD.   35 May sinners be destroyed from
35 Let sinners be consumed from the   the earth;
    earth,   may the wicked be no more.
    and let the wicked be no more!
    Bless the LORD, O my soul!   Praise the LORD, my soul!
    Praise the LORD!   Praise the LORD!

The psalm closes with the psalmist's promise to **sing to the LORD** all his life, to praise him as long as he lives (verse 33). The two lines of verse 33 are parallel and synonymous. Concerning the translation of **my God**, see verse 1.

Then in verse 34 the psalmist prays that Yahweh be pleased with his composition. The word translated "song" by TEV means "that which concerns one, which occupies one's time," and it takes its precise meaning from the context. Here it may be understood as prayer (NJV), **meditation** (RSV, NEB, NIV), poem (TOB, FRCL), "song" (TEV, GECL), thoughts (SPCL), musings (NJB), language (BJ), theme (NAB). Perhaps **meditation** (RSV) or "thoughts" best fits the context here. In verse 34b **I rejoice in the LORD** can be translated "I find my happiness in the LORD" (SPCL) or "Yahweh gives me joy" (NJB).

The last petition (verse 35) is for the complete destruction of **sinners**, which introduces a somber note in a psalm otherwise filled with joyous themes. In some languages which do not use the passive, the expression **Let sinners be consumed** must be recast to say, for example, "I ask that you destroy sinners . . ." or "I pray that you get rid of sinners . . . ."

Bless the LORD, O my soul! The psalm closes (verse 35a) as it began (verse 1a).

In the Septuagint **Praise the LORD** is placed at the beginning of the following psalm (so Dahood, BJ, NJB). This Hebrew phrase has, in transliteration, entered the English language as "Hallelujah" (see NJV) or "Alleluia" (see NJB, NAB); the Hebrew *hal^e lu-yah* is the second person plural of the imperative of the verb *halal* "to praise," plus *Yah* "the LORD" (see 68.4).

Psalm 105

This psalm is a hymn of praise to Yahweh as the savior and protector of his people. Like Psalm 78 it describes the major events in Israel's history (except the events at Mount Sinai) from Abraham to the entry of the people into Canaan. It was probably composed to be used at a festival celebrating the Covenant. The first fifteen verses appear in 1 Chronicles 16.8-22 almost exactly in the same form as here.

The psalm begins with a call to the people to praise God for all he has done (verses 1-6), and recalls his initial covenant with Abraham, Isaac, and Jacob (verses 7-11). Then follows a brief reference to the time of the patriarchs (verses 12-15), after which comes the story of Joseph, son of Jacob, in Egypt (verses 16-22). The history continues: the Israelites in Egypt (verses 23-25); Moses and Aaron, and the plagues in Egypt (verses 26-36); the Israelites' departure from Egypt and their being led through the wilderness (verses 37-42) until they enter the Promised Land (verses 43-45).

HEADING: "**God and His People**." Other headings are: "The wonderful history of Israel"; "The divine covenant." The TEV heading can be adapted into other languages by saying "God saves his people" or "God protects his people."

105.1-4	RSV		TEV
1	O give thanks to the LORD, call on his name, make known his deeds among the peoples!	1	Give thanks to the LORD, proclaim his greatness; tell the nations what he has done.
2	Sing to him, sing praises to him, tell of all his wonderful works!	2	Sing praise to the LORD; tell the wonderful things he has done.
3	Glory in his holy name; let the hearts of those who seek the LORD rejoice!	3	Be glad that we belong to him; let all who worship him rejoice.
4	Seek the LORD and his strength, seek his presence continually!	4	Go to the LORD for help; and worship him continually.

The psalmist begins by calling on the people to praise Yahweh and to proclaim to everyone all that he has done (verses 1-2); see similar statement in 75.1. **Call on his name** is an exhortation to worship and praise Yahweh (for **name** see 5.11). The translation can be "worship him" or "praise him." FRCL has "Say in a loud voice that he is God." In verse 1c **the peoples** are the Gentile nations, and it may be better to translate "the other nations" or "all other peoples."

890

In verse 2a the Hebrew has two synonymous verbs for "sing" (see Dahood "sing . . . chant"); Briggs says the two refer to vocal and instrumental music. TEV has expressed the command with one verb phrase, "**Sing praise.**" Verse 2b repeats, in essence, what is said in verse 1c; the people are exhorted to proclaim the great deeds of God in the history of Israel.

Verse 3a is literally **Glory in his holy name** (similarly NAB, NJB, NIV, Dahood), which SPCL renders "Be proud of his holy name" (also TOB). TEV has taken the verb *halal* "to glory" (reflexive form) to indicate not just pride but happiness as well (see NEB, NJV "Exult";) see the same form in 63.11b and 106.5c, parallel with "rejoice" in 63.11a and 106.5b. **His holy name** is Yahweh's character revealed to his people in choosing them and making them his own. Briggs explains differently: "make boast of the majestic sacredness of the renown won by Yahweh." Perhaps "Be proud of what the holy God has done!" best expresses the meaning of the Hebrew; GECL and FRCL have "Be proud of him, the holy God."

In verse 3b **Seek the LORD** translates the verb occurring also in 24.6b, and **seek his presence** (literally "his face") in verse 4b uses the same verb; in verse 4a the verb is the same as in 9.10. In all instances the meaning is to go to the Temple and worship Yahweh. In verse 4a the Hebrew is "Seek Yahweh and his strength," which TEV takes to mean his help. NJV takes **his strength** to be a reference to the Covenant Box (as in 78.60-61; see 132.8). FRCL has "Turn to the almighty Lord," and NEB "Turn to the LORD, your strength." The expression **Seek the LORD** should not be rendered in such a way that the reader may get the impression that the Lord has become lost. TEV's **"Go to the LORD"** is particularly appropriate, containing as it does both the idea of going to the place where God was to be found, and worshiping him.

105.5-6	RSV	TEV
5	Remember the wonderful works that he has done, his miracles, and the judgments he uttered,	5-6 You descendants of Abraham, his servant; you descendants of Jacob, the man he chose:
6	O offspring of Abraham his servant, sons of Jacob, his chosen ones!	remember the miracles that God performed and the judgments that he gave.

TEV has reversed verses 5 and 6 for greater ease of understanding, and these comments will follow the order of TEV.

In verse 6 the Israelites are called **offspring** (literally "seed") **of Abraham** and **sons of Jacob**. For "seed" see 18.50. Following **Jacob**, the Masoretic text has **his chosen ones** (so RSV); it seems better, however, to prefer two Hebrew manuscripts and the Qumran manuscript, which have the singular "his chosen one" (that is, Jacob), which better parallels **his servant** in the preceding line (so TEV, BJ, NJB). Most translations, however, follow the Masoretic text.[1] The address form **O offspring** and **sons of Jacob** may have to be recast in some languages to say, for

---

[1]HOTTP prefers the Masoretic text.

example, "Listen, you descendants of Abraham, who was God's servant" and "Listen, you descendants of Jacob, the man God chose." Another restructuring is possible: "Abraham was God's servant, so listen, you who are his descendants" and "Jacob is the man God chose, so listen, you who are his descendants." If necessary it may be possible to combine the two vocative expressions; for example, "Abraham was God's servant, and Jacob was the one God chose. So listen, you who are their descendants."

In verse 5a **Remember** may be better translated "Commemorate" or "Celebrate" (see Briggs).

In speaking of what Yahweh has done, the Hebrew uses two synonymous terms: **wonderful works** (as in verse 2) and **miracles** (see verse 27b and 78.43b). TEV has combined the two into one, "**the miracles**"; perhaps "the great miracles" is better; SPCL has "his great and marvelous deeds." **Judgments** probably refers to God's condemnation of Israel's oppressors, not to the laws and commandments given at Sinai (see Anderson). The expression **the judgments he uttered** may have to be recast in some languages as a clause, in which case it may be necessary to make explicit the goal of the judgment; for example, "remember . . . how he judged our enemies."

105.7-8   RSV   TEV

7 He is the LORD our God;   7 The LORD is our God;
   his judgments are in all the   his commands are for all the
   earth.   world.
8 He is mindful of his covenant for 8 He will keep his covenant forever,
   ever,   his promises for a thousand
   of the word that he commanded,   generations.
   for a thousand generations,

This strophe (verses 7-11) relates how Yahweh made a covenant, successively, with the patriarchs Abraham, Isaac, and Jacob. In verse 7a the translation can be "Yahweh is our God" (TEV) or, better, GECL "He, Yahweh, is our God," or "He is Yahweh, our God" (most translations). GECL's rendering seems preferable (see Briggs). In verse 7b **judgments** (TEV "commands") translates the same Hebrew word used in verse 5. The meaning may be the same; here the emphasis is on their universal application, **in all the earth** (see SPCL "he rules over all the earth"; similarly Dahood, TOB). The psalmist is speaking of himself and his intended audience, those who shared the experiences alluded to. Therefore in languages in which exclusion or inclusion is obligatory, the translator must use the inclusive form for **our God**.

In verse 8 **covenant** in line **a** is parallel with "**his promises**" (literally **the word that he commanded**) in line **b** (NEB, NJB, and NJV have "the promise"). **For ever** and **for a thousand generations** are also used synonymously (see Deut 7.9). For translation suggestions regarding **covenant** see 25.10. **He is mindful of** means that he always keeps the terms of the covenant he made with his people. **For ever** and **for a thousand generations** are parallel expressions, the latter intensifying the poetic effect by being more specific. The meaning, however, is for an unlimited time, endlessly, and it is semantically equivalent to **for ever**. The two lines should be translated as a single unit; for example, "He will keep his covenant for ever, and will never, never forget the promises he has made to you." Duplication is used here as an example of heightening the intensity in line b.

105.9-11	RSV		TEV
9	the covenant which he made with Abraham, his sworn promise to Isaac,	9	He will keep the agreement he made with Abraham and his promise to Isaac.
10	which he confirmed to Jacob as a statute, to Israel as an everlasting covenant,	10	The LORD made a covenant with Jacob, one that will last forever.
11	saying, "To you I will give the land of Canaan as your portion for an inheritance."	11	"I will give you the land of Canaan," he said. "It will be your own possession.'

In the Hebrew text verses 9-11 follow verse 8, "He is mindful of . . . ," without a break (see RSV); the subject discussed throughout is the agreement made with Abraham and confirmed in turn with Isaac and Jacob (see similar language in 89.3 of the covenant with David). TEV has started a new sentence in verse 9, supplying "He will keep."

In verse 10 the lines are synonymous, **Jacob** in line a and **Israel** in line b, both referring to the patriarch (see also verse 23). For Yahweh's promise to **Abraham** see Genesis 12.7; 17.8; to **Isaac**, Genesis 26.3-4; to **Jacob**, Genesis 28.13-14). The verb **confirmed** translates "made stand"; NJB has "he established." Most translations in English use the verb "to confirm."

In verse 10 TEV has "**covenant**" in line a to represent **statute** and **covenant** in lines a and b of the Hebrew text, since they both refer to the same agreement Yahweh made with Jacob. But if a more formal translation is preferred, the following can be said (following TEV style):

> With a law Yahweh confirmed to Jacob
> the promise of a covenant that will last forever.

In verse 11 the pronoun **you** in line a is singular in the Masoretic text; in line b **your** is plural. The Qumran manuscript has the plural form in both lines. In any case the promise was made to Jacob and to his descendants (see Gen 28.13; 35.12). But it could be that the Masoretic text singular "you" (in line a) and plural "your" (in line b) indicates that in verse 10 **Jacob** is the patriarch, and **Israel** is the people of Israel. If this interpretation is adopted, the translation can be as follows:

> With a law the LORD confirmed his promise to Jacob,
> and made an eternal covenant with the people of Israel.

In verse 11b "**your own possession**" translates "your share of the inheritance" (see 16.6 for the two Hebrew words, translated there as "lines" and "heritage"). In languages which distinguish formally between "you" singular and "you" plural, some confusion for the reader may be introduced by making the second "you" plural. If the translator wishes to indicate the plural in the second line, it may be better to say, for example, "it will be a possession for your (singular) descendants."

105.12-15 RSV   TEV

	RSV		TEV
12	When they were few in number, of little account, and sojourners in it,	12	God's people were few in number, strangers in the land of Canaan.
13	wandering from nation to nation, from one kingdom to another people,	13	They wandered from country to country, from one kingdom to another.
14	he allowed no one to oppress them; he rebuked kings on their account,	14	But God let no one oppress them; to protect them, he warned the kings:
15	saying, "Touch not my anointed ones, do my prophets no harm!"	15	"Don't harm my chosen servants; do not touch my prophets."

These verses describe the condition of the Hebrews during the patriarchal age, **when they were few in number** and had no settled residence in Canaan (verse 12), but wandered from place to place (see Gen 12–35). RSV **of little account** (verse 12b) seems not quite accurate for the Hebrew, which means "only a few" (in number); NAB, NJB, and NJV have "a handful"; NIV "few indeed"; Dahood, "a mere handful"; see also NEB and FRCL, and see the same Hebrew phrase in Genesis 34.30. In verse 12b **sojourners** is better represented by "temporary residents" or "resident aliens" than by TEV "**strangers**"; see TOB "a handful of immigrants." In some language areas there are known groups of nomadic wanderers who may come and go according to the seasons, and terms for such groups may be applicable to these **sojourners**.

Verse 13 describes the situation of the Hebrews nomads, **wandering** from place to place. Verses 14-15 seem to refer to the incidents with the king of Egypt (Gen 12.17) and with Abimelech, king of Gerar (Gen 20.1-8), both involving Sarah, Abraham's wife; but here these incidents are made more general. As may be seen from the reading of the two passages, the meaning of **he rebuked kings on their account** in verse 14b is that God warned foreign kings not to harm his servants. **On their account** can be represented by "on their behalf" or "in order to defend them." The TEV phrase in verse 15a "**my chosen servants**" is literally **my anointed ones**—see discussion at 2.2. Only here and in the parallel 1 Chronicles 16.22 is the plural of this word used in the Old Testament. Here it refers to the patriarchs, as does **my prophets**. **My prophets** is used in the general sense of people who speak for God, and not in the specific sense of the great figures in Israel's history usually called the prophets. Abraham is called a prophet in Genesis 20.7.

Translators in languages deeply influenced by Islam will recognize that many of their readers will know that Abraham, Isaac, and Jacob are referred to as *ambiya'* "prophets" in the Koran. The task of the translator is to determine the popular meaning of the Arabic words *rasuul* and *nabi*, if these are used. In some cases it is best to avoid terms of Koranic origin and to employ descriptive phrases.

105.16-19	RSV	TEV

	RSV	TEV
16	When he summoned a famine on the land, and broke every staff of bread,	16 The LORD sent famine to their country and took away all their food.
17	he had sent a man ahead of them, Joseph, who was sold as a slave.	17 But he sent a man ahead of them, Joseph, who had been sold as a slave.
18	His feet were hurt with fetters, his neck was put in a collar of iron;	18 His feet were kept in chains, and an iron collar was around his neck,
19	until what he had said came to pass the word of the LORD tested him.	19 until what he had predicted came true. The word of the LORD proved him right.

In this strophe (verses 16-22) the psalmist tells the story of Joseph (see Gen 37 and 39–50). In verse 16 TEV **"their country"** (RSV the land) is Canaan, where the Hebrews (Jacob and his descendants) were living. It is better to be specific: "The LORD sent a famine on the land of Canaan" or ". . . caused a famine in the land of Canaan" (see Gen 41.53-57). The expression **summoned a famine** or TEV's "sent famine" must often be recast in other languages to say, for example, "God caused the people to be hungry."

In verse 16b the Hebrew is literally **he . . . broke every staff of bread**; some take **staff** here to refer to the small wooden stake on which loaves were carried (Oesterley, Toombs; see FRCL footnote, and K-B *mateh* 2), but it seems more probable that the word is used figuratively (McCullough, Cohen, Anderson). So NEB "cut short their daily bread," NJB "took away their supply of food," and TOB "he cut short all their food." Some take **staff** in the sense of a stalk (of wheat); NAB has "ruined the crop that sustained them"; Dahood has "broke every stalk of grain."

Joseph, sold by his brothers into slavery, was taken to Egypt and there was made a prisoner when his master's wife falsely accused him of trying to rape her (Gen 39.7-20). Verse 17 is none too explicit, and only a reader who knows the Genesis story will understand what **he had sent a man ahead of them** means; so it may be necessary to be explicit:

But in order to save his people
   he had sent a man ahead of them to Egypt;
that man was Joseph,
   who had been sold as a slave.

The account in Genesis does not mention **fetters** or **a collar of iron**. In translating verse 18a it must not be implied that Joseph was placed in chains in order to **hurt** his feet, as RSV seems to imply; the text means "His feet were bound (or, tied up) in chains." NJV has "his feet were subjected to fetters." In verse 18b **neck** translates *nefesh* (see 3.2), which in places means neck or throat (see 69.1). Since readers may not find the information in verse 18 familiar, it may be helpful to make explicit in the text that this refers to his being put in prison; for example, "When he was put in prison . . . ."

Verse 19a in Hebrew is "until his word came," which could refer to Yahweh's promise (Briggs, Kirkpatrick, Oesterley). Most, however, take it to refer to Joseph's prediction of the famine in his interpretation of the king's dream (Gen 41.1-36). NJV translates "Until his prediction came true."

In verse 19b **the word of the LORD** is taken to refer to Yahweh's message to Joseph in the dreams he had had while still at home (Gen 37.5-10). And the verb in Hebrew for **tested** is "refine" (see 12.6), which is here taken to mean "**proved him right**" (also NAB, NIV, BJ, NJB); others (TOB, NEB, SPCL) take it as RSV has done, **tested him** or "purged him" (NJV); see Anderson. Kirkpatrick comments: "purified and refined his character." A translator should feel free to choose either possibility.

The relation between verse 19a and verse 18b and possibly verse 19b is variously understood. In what follows it should be remembered that the verb in verse 19b is translated in several different ways, and the verb tense in verse 19a is also variously understood. (1) Verse 19 is a complete sentence: RSV, NJB, NJV, SPCL, TOB; NEB reverses the two lines, achieving thereby a clear, coherent statement. (2) Verse 19a goes with verse 18, and verse 19b is a separate statement: TEV. (3) The two lines of verse 19 are parallel and depend on verse 18: "till . . . till" (NIV). Everything considered, it seems best to follow NJB or NEB:

> In due time his prophecy was fulfilled,
>   the word of Yahweh proved him true. [NJB]

> He was tested by the LORD's command
>   until what he foretold came true. [NEB]

If the translator follows TEV's "**The word of the LORD proved him right**," this expression may have to be recast to say, for example, "What the LORD had told Joseph . . . ."

<table>
<tr><td colspan="2">105.20-22   RSV</td><td>TEV</td></tr>
<tr><td>20</td><td>The king sent and released him,
    the ruler of the peoples set him
    free;</td><td>20 Then the king of Egypt had him
      released;
      the ruler of nations set him
      free.</td></tr>
<tr><td>21</td><td>he made him lord of his house,
    and ruler of all his possessions,</td><td>21 He put him in charge of his gov-
      ernment</td></tr>
<tr><td>22</td><td>to instruct^f his princes at his plea-
    sure,
    and to teach his elders wisdom.</td><td>   and made him ruler over all the
      land,</td></tr>
</table>

t Gk Syr Jerome: Heb *to bind*	22	with power over the king's officials and authority to instruct his advisers.

The "**king of Egypt**" released Joseph from prison and put him in charge of Egypt (verses 20-22; see Gen 41 37-45); in verse 20b the Egyptian king is called **the ruler of the peoples**. This may be taken as an honorific title, not in the technical sense that he was an emperor ruling over many nations. **Ruler of peoples** in line b is not a literary expression raising the poetic effect of line b. Neither does the expression make more specific or dramatic the title **king** in line a. Accordingly the two lines are semantically equivalent, and therefore in some languages it may be desirable to adjust the two titles by placing one in apposition to the other, as SPCL has done: "The king, who ruled many people, commanded that Joseph should be set free."

In verse 21a **his house** means the palace, that is, the government, and in verse 21b **all his possessions** means the land of Egypt (see Gen 41.39-41).

In verse 22a the Masoretic text has the verb "to bind," which TEV translates "**with power over**"; but many prefer to follow the ancient versions, which have "to instruct," which is a better parallel to the next line (see RSV **to instruct**; also AT, NJB, ZÜR, NEB, BJ, NIV).[2] NJV takes the Masoretic text to mean "to discipline." RSV **at his pleasure** translates the Hebrew "in his *nefesh*," a figure of complete authority. **Princes** and **elders** are the king's high officials and the royal counselors. The literal language, as reflected in RSV **to instruct** and **to teach . . . wisdom**, makes it appear that Joseph's role was that of a teacher or instructor (see SPCL, FRCL); but in line with the events as reported in Genesis, it seems better to understand the language to mean that Joseph was given the authority to command the Egyptian officials and tell them what was the wisest course to follow in order to keep the country from being ruined by the seven years' famine.

105.23-25	RSV	TEV

	RSV	TEV
23	Then Israel came to Egypt; Jacob sojourned in the land of Ham.	23 Then Jacob went to Egypt and settled in that country.
24	And the LORD made his people very fruitful, and made them stronger than their foes.	24 The LORD gave many children to his people and made them stronger than their enemies.
25	He turned their hearts to hate his people, to deal craftily with his servants.	25 He made the Egyptians hate his people and treat his servants with deceit.

[2]HOTTP ("B" decision) prefers the Masoretic text "to bind" and explains it: "The expression 'to bind' means here the exercise of authority and power . . . ."

For the events referred to in verse 23, see Genesis 46.1-27; the story of the lengthy stay of the Israelites in Egypt (verses 24-25) is found in Exodus 1.7–2.25 (see in Exo 12.40 "430 years"). Since the writer is retelling a series of episodes from Old Testament history, it will often be important for the translator to pay special attention to the marking of transitions, which in many languages requires repeating part of the previous episode; for example, "After Joseph instructed the king's advisers, Joseph's father, whose name was Jacob, went . . . ."

In verse 23 TEV has combined the two synonymous lines (see RSV) into one; "Jacob" represents both **Israel** and **Jacob**, and **"that country"** translates **the land of Ham** (see 78.51b). In line **b** the verb **sojourned** comes from the same root as the noun used in verse 12b ("sojourners"). Here the idea does not seem to be that of a temporary residence; TOB has "emigrated," NEB "came to live," NJB "settled."

The birth rate of the Israelites was greater than that of the Egyptians (see Exo 1.7), and eventually they became more powerful than the Egyptians (verse 24).

The Egyptians' hatred of the Israelites was God's doing (verse 25a; literally **He turned their hearts to hate his people**). But the Hebrew text can be translated "Their hearts turned" (so the Targum; and see NJV footnote), which Briggs prefers; but all translations consulted have Yahweh as subject. The Israelites are Yahweh's **servants** (verse 25b), and the Egyptians treated them deceitfully (see Exo 1.10-14), which included not only making slaves of them but also scheming to have Israelite male babies put to death at birth (Exo 1.15-16; see also Acts 7.19). It is important in verse 25 that the reader understand that **his people** and **his servants** refer to the Israelites; for example, "he made the Egyptians hate his people, who served him, so that they treated the Israelites with deceit" or ". . . deceived the Israelites."

105.26-27	RSV	TEV
26	He sent Moses his servant, and Aaron whom he had chosen.	26 Then he sent his servant Moses, and Aaron, whom he had chosen.
27	They wrought his signs among them, and miracles in the land of Ham.	27 They did God's mighty acts and performed miracles in Egypt.

In verses 26-36 the psalmist recounts the plagues that Moses and Aaron inflicted on the Egyptians (Exo 7–12); see the similar account in Psalm 78.44-51.

In verse 26 it may be well to introduce "Egypt" as the place to which Yahweh sent Moses and Aaron, as follows:

Then the Lord sent to Egypt his servant Moses,
together with Aaron, whom he had chosen.

The meaning of verse 27a is disputed. AT, NJV, NAB, NIV, Weiser are like RSV and TEV. The Hebrew phrase translated **"God's mighty acts"** (TEV) and **his signs** (RSV) is literally "words (or, matters) of his signs," which is taken by some to be the predictions of Moses and Aaron concerning the plagues (NEB "They were his mouthpiece to announce his signs"); by others it is taken to refer to God's commands to Moses and Aaron for them to inflict the plagues (BJ "they performed among them the plagues he had spoken of"; FRCL "Among the Egyptians the two performed the prodigies that God had commanded them to do"; see NJB). TOB translates "Their command brought down signs on Egypt." The Hebrew phrase is unusual, but see the similar phrase in 143.5b, literally "the words of your wonderful deeds." It appears that the rendering of RSV and TEV is defensible.

The verb in verse 27a in Hebrew is plural "**They did**"; the Septuagint and Syriac have the singular "He did," a reference to God (so Briggs, Weiser); most follow the Masoretic text. For <u>land of Ham</u> in verse 27b see verse 23.

105.28-36   RSV   TEV

28   He sent darkness, and made the   28   God sent darkness on the country,
     land dark;   but the Egyptians did not obey[a]
     they rebelled[u] against his   his command.
     words.   29   He turned their rivers into blood
29   He turned their waters into blood,   and killed all their fish.
     and caused their fish to die.   30   Their country was overrun with
30   Their land swarmed with frogs,   frogs;
     even in the chambers of their   even the palace was filled with
     kings.   them.
31   He spoke, and there came swarms   31   God commanded, and flies and
     of flies,   gnats
     and gnats throughout their   swarmed throughout the whole
     country.   country.
32   He gave them hail for rain,   32   He sent hail and lightning on
     and lightning that flashed   their land
     through their land.   instead of rain;
33   He smote their vines and fig trees,   33   he destroyed their grapevines and
     and shattered the trees of their   fig trees
     country.   and broke down all the trees.
34   He spoke, and the locusts came,   34   He commanded, and the locusts
     and young locusts without num-   came,
     ber;   countless millions of them;
35   which devoured all the vegetation   35   they ate all the plants in the land;
     in their land,   they ate all the crops.
     and ate up the fruit of their   36   He killed the first-born sons
     ground.   of all the families of Egypt.
36   He smote all the first-born in
     their land,   [a] *Some ancient translations* did not obey;
     the first issue of all their   *Hebrew* obeyed.
     strength.

[u] Cn Compare Gk Syr: Heb *they did not
rebel*

These verses report eight of the plagues, as follows:

Verse 28: the ninth plague, **darkness** (Exo 10.21-23). In verse 28b the Hebrew text is "and they did not rebel against his word." Briggs says this refers to the Israelites, and HOTTP says it refers to Moses and Aaron. Weiser, ZÜR, and others change the Hebrew *lo' maru* "they did not rebel" to *lo' shamru* "they did not obey." The ancient versions omit the negative adverb, and this text (**they rebelled**) is preferred by AT, RSV, TEV, NAB, BJ, NJB, SPCL. NJV translates the Masoretic text by "did they not defy His word?" with a marginal note "Meaning of Hebrew uncertain." This rendering (similarly NIV) is none too convincing. FRCL takes the third person plural "they did not oppose" in an impersonal sense, "and no one was opposed to his command."

Verse 29: the first plague, **waters into blood** (Exo 7.17-21; Psa 78.44).

Verse 30: the second plague, **frogs** (Exo 8.1-7; Psa 78.45b). In verse 30b the Hebrew is "in the rooms of their kings" (see RSV, AT, TOB, NAB), which NEB renders "even their princes' inner chambers," and NIV "the bedrooms of their rulers." NJB and FRCL have "royal apartments"; TEV **"the palace"**; NJV "the rooms of their king." It seems best to follow TEV here.

Verse 31: line <u>a</u> the fourth plague, **flies** (Exo 8.20-24; Psa 78.45a) and line <u>b</u> the third plague, **gnats** (Exo 8.16-19). There is a difference of opinion over the exact identification of the latter; NJV has "lice," NEB "maggots," and NJB "mosquitoes." See *Fauna and Flora,* pages 35-36. It is recommended that **gnats** be chosen.

Verses 32-33: the seventh plague, **hail** and **lightning** (Exo 9.18-26; Psa 78.47). **Lightning** translates what is literally "fire of flames" (see similar phrase in 104.4b), which Weiser and NJV translate "flaming fire" (as though it were a firestorm); FRCL has "and lightning, that spread fire throughout the land." The narrative in Exodus 9.23-24 includes thunder and lightning with the hail. Verse 33 describes the ruinous effects of the hail and lightning as Yahweh's act: **he smote . . . and shattered**.

Verses 34-35: the eighth plague, **locusts** (Exo 10.1-20; Psa 78.46). It is most unlikely that the two different words used in verse 34 refer to two different insects; this is poetic parallelism. See similar usage in 78.46; see *Fauna and Flora,* pages 53-54. NJV, NAB, NIV, and Dahood have "locusts" and "grasshoppers." In verse 35b **the fruit of their ground** means their **"crops"**; NJB translates "all the produce of the soil."

Verse 36: the tenth plague, the death of the first-born sons of all the Egyptian families (Exo 11.1–12.30; Psa 78.49-51). This verse employs much of the language used in 78.51 (which see). In verse 36a the Masoretic text has **in their land** (see RSV); many Hebrew manuscripts have "in Egypt" (which TEV prefers).[3]

105.37-38	RSV	TEV

RSV	TEV
37 Then he led forth Israel with silver and gold, and there was none among his tribes who stumbled.	37 Then he led the Israelites out; they carried silver and gold, and all of them were healthy and strong.

---

[3]HOTTP ("C" decision) prefers the Masoretic text.

| 38 | Egypt was glad when they departed,
for dread of them had fallen upon it. | 38 | The Egyptians were afraid of them and were glad when they left. |

In this strophe (verses 37-42) the psalmist recounts the departure of the Israelites from Egypt and some of the events during the forty years' wandering in the wilderness. As they left they carried with them **silver and gold** jewelry and ornaments gotten from the Egyptians (see Exo 3.21-22; 11.2; 12.35-36). Their physical well-being is described: "no one among his tribes stumbled" (see RSV). In translating **silver and gold** it should be clear to the reader that the text is talking about jewelry and ornaments, not bars of silver and of gold. And should the word **tribes** as a subdivision of the whole group be difficult to represent, a translation may imitate TEV. In order to keep the possessive **his (tribes)**, the translation can be "Then the LORD led his people out . . . ."

In verse 38 TEV has reversed the order of the lines to put first the cause (fear; see Exo 1.12) and second the effect (gladness). But the order of the Hebrew may be maintained:

> The Egyptians were glad when they left,
> because they were afraid of the Israelites.

105.39-42 RSV TEV

39	He spread a cloud for a covering, and fire to give light by night.	39	God put a cloud over his people and a fire at night to give them light.
40	They asked, and he brought quails, and gave them bread from heaven in abundance.	40	They[b] asked, and he sent quails; he gave them food from heaven to satisfy them.
41	He opened the rock, and water gushed forth; it flowed through the desert like a river.	41	He opened a rock, and water gushed out, flowing through the desert like a river.
42	For he remembered his holy promise, and Abraham his servant.	42	He remembered his sacred promise to Abraham his servant.

[b] *Some ancient translations* They; *Hebrew* He.

For the pillars (or, columns) of **cloud** and of **fire** to guide the Israelites (verse 39), see Exodus 13.21-22. Here the cloud is spoken of as a protective cover for them.

In verse 40a the Hebrew is "He asked," which could refer to Moses. RSV, NJV, NEB, GECL, NIV, SPCL (all without textual note), and TEV, NAB, FRCL, NJB, TOB, Weiser (all with textual note) follow the ancient versions, which have the plural, **They asked**. HOTTP says that "He asked" means the Israelites; but it should be noticed that nowhere in this strophe are they referred to by a singular pronoun or verb.[4] It may be necessary to make 40a clear by saying, for example, "Moses asked God for meat . . . ." or, if the plural is used, "the people asked Moses for meat . . . ."

For the **quails** see 78.26-28; and for **bread from heaven**, that is, the manna, see 78.23-25.

The incident in verse 41 is probably what happened at Rephidim (Exo 17.1-6); see 78.15-16. The reader who is not acquainted with the historical account in Exodus may not know what **opened a rock** means, so it may be well to say "He caused a rock to split open . . . ." In any case, a cross reference to Exodus 17.1-6 should be provided.

In verse 42 the psalmist recalls Yahweh's **holy promise** to Abraham (see verse 9) as the reason for his continued help and sustenance to the people of Israel. RSV **he remembered his holy promise, and Abraham** (following KJV) is a possible translation of the Hebrew, but it seems more natural to read the text "his holy promise to Abraham," as most translations do (see McCullough). The expression **his holy promise** must be recast in many languages, as it is difficult to speak of "holy" in relation to an utterance. However, here the meaning is God's promise in the form of the covenant, and can be translated, for example, "he remembered his covenant with his servant Abraham" or "he did not forget what he had promised Abraham who served him."

105.43-45   RSV   TEV

43 So he led forth his people with   43 So he led his chosen people out,
        joy,   and they sang and shouted for
      his chosen ones with singing.   joy.
44 And he gave them the lands of the   44 He gave them the lands of other
        nations;   peoples
      and they took possession of the   and let them take over their
        fruit of the peoples' toil,   fields,
45 to the end that they should keep   45 so that his people would obey his
        his statutes,   laws
      and observe his laws.   and keep all his commands.
    Praise the LORD!

                                             Praise the LORD!

The whole exodus event is summarized in these last verses. In verse 43 it should be clear that **with joy** and **with singing** refer to the Israelites, not to Yahweh. In verses 43 and 44 the two lines of each verse are synonymous; TEV has not formally represented the poetic parallelism **his people** and **his chosen ones** in verse 43.

In verse 44a **the lands of the nations** are the lands occupied by the various people in Canaan and on the east side of the Jordan, which the invading Hebrews conquered. In verse 44b **the peoples' toil** refers to the cultivated fields of the

---

[4]HOTTP ("C" decision) adds that the singular form could have God as subject, "God called," or could be impersonal, "one asked/they asked."

Canaanites, on which they had toiled. A translation can be "and they took over what other people had worked for." NJV, however, has simply "the wealth of the peoples." For the historical account of the conquest under Joshua, see Joshua 11.16-23.

Yahweh's purpose in giving Canaan to the Israelites was that they should be his people, obeying **his statutes and** . . . **his laws**. In languages in which there are no synonyms to represent **statutes** and **laws**, it will often be necessary to say, for example, "obey God's laws and do all the things he had ordered them to do."

For the closing words, **Praise the LORD!** see 104.35.

Psalm 106

This psalm, like Psalm 105, is also a recital of Israel's history, but the dominant theme here is Israel's consistent unfaithfulness, the people's persistent rebellion against God. But God's love and mercy did not change; he was faithful to his covenant, and time and again he saved his people from their enemies.

Israel's sin has continued down to the time of the psalmist (verse 6), and this national confession of sins leads to the impassioned prayer that God bring his people out of exile back to their land, so that once more they may worship him in Jerusalem.

Following the opening call to praise Yahweh (verses 1-3), the psalmist offers a personal prayer (verses 4-5). The long confession of Israel's sins (verses 6-46) includes many specific instances of disobedience and rebellion as well as general statements. The psalm closes with a prayer that God free his people from captivity and lead them back to the land of Israel (verse 47). The final verse (verse 48) is not part of the psalm but the conclusion of Book Four (Psalms 90–106).

HEADING: "**The LORD's Goodness to His People.**" Other headings are: "Israel's confession of sin"; "National confession"; "A record of rebellion." Translators wishing to adapt the TEV heading may often be required to recast it as a full sentence; for example, "The LORD is good to his people" or "This psalm tells how good the LORD is to his people."

106.1-3	RSV	TEV

106.1-3   RSV

1   Praise the LORD!
O give thanks to the LORD, for he
   is good;
   for his steadfast love endures
    for ever!

2   Who can utter the mighty doings
    of the LORD,
   or show forth all his praise?

3   Blessed are they who observe
    justice,
   who do righteousness at all
    times!

TEV

1   Praise the LORD!

   Give thanks to the LORD, because
    he is good;
   his love is eternal.

2   Who can tell all the great things
    he has done?
   Who can praise him enough?

3   Happy are those who obey his
    commands,
   who always do what is right.

For the opening words **Praise the LORD!** see 104.35; several Hebrew manuscripts and the Syriac omit them. **Steadfast love** translates *chesed* (see 5.7). **His steadfast love endures** must often be recast to say "he loves people forever."

By means of the form of a question (verse 2), the psalmist declares that human words cannot describe **"the great things"** that Yahweh has done for his people, and no one can offer him all the praise he deserves. As is often the case, the question is rhetorical; it does not ask for information but is a way of making an emphatic statement. Rhetorical questions, their structure and use, vary considerably from language to language. The purpose of these questions in this verse is to make a negative emphatic statement. Accordingly, if the question form is retained, in some languages it is necessary to give a negative reply such as "No one!" In languages where this kind of rhetorical question is not used, it will be better to recast these as negative statements; for example, "No one can tell all the great things God has done; no one can praise him enough!"

In verse 3 the psalmist praises those who always obey Yahweh's law; in line a the word is *mishpat* (see 7.6), literally "guard justice," and in line b it is *tsedaqah* (see 4.1), literally **do righteousness**. The two are parallel and used synonymously. Instead of TEV **"his commands"** in line a, a translation may prefer to say "Happy are those who act justly" (NEB, NJV).

	RSV		TEV
106.4-5			

<table>
<tr><td>4</td><td>Remember me, O LORD, when thou showest favor to thy people;
help me when thou deliverest them;</td><td>4

5</td><td>Remember me, LORD, when you help your people;
include me when you save them.
Let me see the prosperity of your people</td></tr>
<tr><td>5</td><td>that I may see the prosperity of thy chosen ones,
that I may rejoice in the gladness of thy nation,
that I may glory with thy heritage.</td><td></td><td>and share in the happiness of your nation,
in the glad pride of those who belong to you.</td></tr>
</table>

The psalmist prays to live to see and share in the deliverance of his people, when Yahweh will take them out of exile to their own land (see verse 47). Instead of the Masoretic text **me** twice in verse 4, two Hebrew manuscripts and the Septuagint have the plural "us" (which FRCL prefers). The Masoretic text should be followed here. In verse 4a the verb "show favor" is defined as "deliver" in line b; and in line b the verb translated by RSV **help** has the sense of "look in on" (see comments on "care for" in 8.4). The sense of line b is that the psalmist wants to be among the people when Yahweh saves them.

In verse 5a TEV **"your people"** translates **thy chosen ones**, and "those who belong to you" in line c translates "your inheritance" (see 28.9). **That I may glory** translates the same form of the verb *halal* used in 105.3a. But it is desirable to translate line c in a clearer and more understandable manner than TEV has done—at least to make clear that the verb **"share"** is implicit before **"in the glad pride."** Or, joining verses 4 and 5, it may be better to translate as follows:

4 Remember me, LORD, when you help your people;
  when you save them, also save me,
5 so that I may see your people prosper again,
  and I may be happy together with them,
  and share the pride of those who belong to you.

In some languages **Remember me** will carry the force of "recall who I am," which presupposes that the person to be remembered has become forgotten. In such cases it may be better to say "Do not forget me . . . ."

<u>106.6-7</u>   RSV   TEV

| 6 | Both we and our fathers have sinned; we have committed iniquity, we have done wickedly. | 6 | We have sinned as our ancestors did; we have been wicked and evil. |
| 7 | Our fathers, when they were in Egypt, did not consider thy wonderful works; they did not remember the abundance of thy steadfast love, but rebelled against the Most High at the Red Sea. | 7 | Our ancestors in Egypt did not understand God's wonderful acts; they forgot the many times he showed them his love, and they rebelled against the Afmighty at the Red Sea. |

^{c} *probable text* the Almighty; *Hebrew* the sea.

^{v} Cn Compare 78.17, 56: Heb *at the sea*

The psalmist begins the recital of Israel's constant acts of rebellion with a confession of national sin; his own generation also is guilty of sin and disobedience, as were their ancestors. The psalmist uses three verbs in verse 6 to describe the depth and extent of the sins of his contemporaries and their ancestors. In such a context the verbs are practically synonymous, serving to reinforce one another and emphasizing how terribly sinful the Israelites had been and were. The first verb is the most common one for "to sin." The other two appear with this meaning in the Psalms only in this verse. The second verb means, quite generally, "to do wrong," and the third one, more specifically, "to be (or, become) guilty." A translator will choose whatever terms are available in the target language that will express wilful and serious acts of sin.

The long record of Israel's rebellion begins at the exodus from Egypt; while still in Egypt the Israelites failed to understand God's wonderful acts (see 9.1b), which here refer to the plagues Yahweh inflicted on the Egyptians through Moses and Aaron. The verb translated **consider** means to pay attention, to reflect upon, to understand.

In verse 7a,b the Hebrew text uses the second-person singular pronoun "your wonderful acts . . . your love" (see RSV); for consistency TEV uses the third person.

Thy wonderful works or "**God's wonderful acts**" must be recast in many languages to say "the wonderful things God did for us."

Beginning at verse 7d the psalmist recalls the departure of the Israelites from Egypt (see Exo 14). In verse 7c the Hebrew text is unusual: "they rebelled against the sea at the Sea of Reeds"; instead of the Masoretic text *'al-yam* "against the sea," some change the Hebrew text to *'elyon* "the Almighty" (see 7.17); so Briggs, Oesterley, McCullough, Anderson; AT, RSV, TEV, NAB, NIB, NEB changes to *'aleyhem* "in spite of all." NJV translates the Masoretic text "at the sea, at the Sea of Reeds"; TOB "near the sea, the sea of Reeds" (similarly NIV), which is what HOTTP favors. It may be best to stay with the Masoretic text. For this act of rebellion see Exodus 14.12. For translation suggestions on "the Almighty," see 7.17.

In naming the body of water the Israelites crossed, translators must decide whether to use the Hebrew name, *yam suf* "Sea of Reeds" or "Reed Sea," or the name used in the Greek Septuagint and the New Testament, *eruthra thalassa* **Red Sea**. Many scholars are sure that two bodies of water are involved. The modern "Red Sea" itself is divided into two branches by the Sinai Peninsula, and these are the Gulf of Aqaba and the Gulf of Suez. The Gulf of Suez is the western branch and is referred to as "Sea of Reeds" in the Hebrew of Exodus 10.19; Numbers 33.10-11; similarly the Gulf of Aqaba is the eastern branch of the Red Sea and is likewise called "Sea of Reeds" in Exodus 23.31; Numbers 14.25; 21.4; Deuteronomy 1.40; 2.1; 1 Kings 9.26; Jeremiah 49.21. It may be appropriate to translate using "Red Sea" at these places, but it is better to use the known name for each respective gulf, whether the Gulf of Aqaba or the Gulf of Suez, for that will identify the body of water for today's reader (note the respective passages in TEV). However, since there are no reeds growing on the shores of the Red Sea, and because of the geography and the routes to be taken into the wilderness, it seems evident that the name was derived from one of the smaller bodies of water north of the Red Sea. That body has not yet been identified, but some of the lakes there are large enough to have been an obstacle and a danger to the escaping Israelites, and their size would not diminish or belittle the significance of a miracle. To say the crossing took place at the body of water that is today known as the Red Sea is to go against the weight of good biblical scholarship. (See TEV footnote, Exo 13.18.)

There are three alternatives that translators may take in naming the body of water the Israelites crossed: (1) They may follow the example of Martin Luther, who in his German translation called it *Schilfmeer*, "Reed Sea," in all Old Testament occurrences, but *das rothe Meer*, "the Red Sea," in the two New Testament occurrences (so FRCL, TOB, ZÜR; also NJV in its translation of the Hebrew Bible; Dahood uses "Sea of Reeds" regularly in the Psalms). This has the advantage of representing the exact differences between the Hebrew and the Greek terms. However, it runs counter to the principle of using the same proper noun in translation for identical people and places that occur in both Testaments, and it does not distinguish between the real bodies of water. (2) They may use "the Red Sea" throughout the Bible (so RSV, NEB, NAB, SPCL). While this uses one proper noun for both Testaments, it too does not distinguish between the actual bodies of water. (3) They may use "Sea of Reeds" for the body of water the Israelites crossed, but "Red Sea" for all other occurrences where it is certain the larger body of water is meant (so, in varying ways, NJB, BJ, GECL, although all use "Red Sea" in the New Testament for the waters Israel crossed). This third alternative is recommended, for to translate mechanically either "Red Sea" or "Sea of Reeds" in all passages fails to represent the meaning of the text. All occurrences of the term in the Book of Psalms are references to the Sea of Reeds.

106.8-12 RSV		TEV
8	Yet he saved them for his name's sake, that he might make known his mighty power.	8 But he saved them, as he had promised, in order to show his great power.
9	He rebuked the Red Sea, and it became dry; and he led them through the deep as through a desert.	9 He gave a command to the Red Sea, and it dried up; he led his people across on dry land.
10	So he saved them from the hand of the foe, and delivered them from the power of the enemy.	10 He saved them from those who hated them; he rescued them from their enemies.
11	And the waters covered their adversaries; not one of them was left.	11 But the water drowned their enemies; not one of them was left.
12	Then they believed his words; they sang his praise.	12 Then his people believed his promises and sang praises to him.

In verse 8a TEV **"as he had promised"** translates "on account of his name" (see 23.3). Or else the translation can be "to maintain his fame (or, honor)"—see FRCL "in concern for his honor"; SPCL "bringing honor to his name." **Make known his mighty power** may be recast in some languages to say, for example, "so that the people could see how powerful he was."

In verse 9a the verb **rebuked** portrays God as angrily commanding the Sea of Reeds to part in order to let the people walk through; see a similar use of the related noun in 104.7. The sea is treated like a disobedient servant (Briggs). TOB has "he threatened," and NJV "He sent His blast against the Sea of Reeds." In line b **the deep** (Hebrew "the deeps") is the same as the Sea of Reeds in line a; and **desert** here stands for "dry land" (see Exo 14.22). **He rebuked the Red Sea** and TEV's **"gave a command to . . ."** must sometimes be modified to include the content of the rebuke or order; for example, "he ordered the Red Sea to dry up, and it dried up."

In verses 10-11 the Egyptians are identified as **the foe . . . the enemy . . . their adversaries**. In both lines of verse 10 Hebrew has **from the hand of**, that is, from the power of. Two different verbs are used: the common verb *yasha'* for **saved** (see "Help" in 12.1) and *ga'al* for **delivered** (TEV "rescued"; see "redeemer" in 19.14 and "redeemed" in 74.2). Both lines in verse 10 are the same in meaning and may need to be reduced to one line in some languages.

In some languages it will not be natural to say in verse 11 that "**the water drowned their enemies,**" but rather "their enemies drowned in the water" or "their enemies drowned."

Momentarily the people believed Yahweh (Exo 14.31) and sang praises to him (verse 12). Soon, however, they forgot what he had done. It should be clear that the subject of verse 12 is the Israelites, not the Egyptians.

106.13-15 RSV	TEV
13 But they soon forgot his works; they did not wait for his counsel.	13 But they quickly forgot what he had done and acted without waiting for his advice.
14 But they had a wanton craving in the wilderness, and put God to the test in the desert;	14 They were filled with craving in the desert and put God to the test;
15 he gave them what they asked, but sent a wasting disease among them.	15 so he gave them what they asked for, but also sent a terrible disease among them.

In these verses the psalmist recalls the time when the people **put God to the test** (see 78.18,41,56; 95.9) by asking for food, which he gave in the form of manna and quails (Num 11.4-6,31-35; Psa 78.17-31). In verse 13b **counsel** or "plan" (NJV) reflects the people's unwillingness to follow God's will. Here GECL, TOB, and FRCL translate "they did not wait for God to act," which fits very well with what follows. **Wait for his counsel** must often be recast as a verb phrase; for example, "They did not wait to see what God wanted them to do."

In verse 14a the **wanton craving** in the Hebrew is the intense craving they felt for the good, fresh food they used to eat in Egypt (see Num 11.4-6, and see comments on Psa 78.29-31). The Hebrew has two completely synonymous words in verse 14, which RSV translates **wilderness** and **desert** (see NJV "wilderness" and "wasteland"); there is no difference in meaning between the two words. **Wanton craving** and TEV's "**filled with craving**" do not indicate the nature of the desire. In languages in which the object of such a desire must be expressed, it will be necessary to say, for example, "they craved food" or "they had a great desire for food." Many languages have specific words for various kinds of hunger: for meat, salty food, sweet, or sour foods. Here the most generic should be used. For **put God to the test**, see comments on this statement in 78.41.

God answers their request (verse 15a) but also does something else. In verse 15b **among them** translates "in their *nefeshes*" (see 3.2); some take it here to mean "their throats" (NEB footnote). TOB translates the line "but he sent far too little for their appetite" (that is, too little to satisfy their hunger), but this interpretation is not recommended. FRCL prefers the Septuagint and Syriac: "he satisfied them until they were nauseated" (see Num 11.19-20).

106.16-18 RSV	TEV
16 When men in the camp were jealous of Moses and Aaron, the holy one of the LORD,	16 There in the desert they were jealous of Moses and of Aaron, the LORD's holy servant.
17 the earth opened and swallowed up Dathan, and covered the company of Abiram.	17 Then the earth opened up and swallowed Dathan and buried Abiram and his family;
18 Fire also broke out in their company; the flame burned up the wicked.	18 fire came down on their followers and burned up those wicked people.

These verses allude to a revolt that broke out in the wilderness, narrated in Numbers 16.1-35. It appears that the narrative there combines two separate incidents: the revolt led by Dathan and Abiram (and On), of the tribe of Reuben, and the revolt led by Korah, a Levite. The first group was swallowed up by the earth (Num 16.25-34), while the 250 followers of Korah were burned to death by fire from heaven (Num 16.35).

The Hebrew **in the camp** in verse 16a can be translated "when they were camped in the desert" or "in their camp in the wilderness." Either one of these is better than TEV **"in the desert."**

Moses' brother Aaron is called **the holy one of the LORD** because he was a priest; see NEB "who was consecrated to the Lord." **Holy one of the LORD** or TEV's **"holy servant"** must often be adjusted in translation, due to the use of "holy" in relation to a person. Accordingly it is sometimes possible to say, for example, "Aaron who belonged to God and served him" or ". . . was dedicated to serving God."

In verses 17b and 18a TEV **"family"** and **"followers"** translate the same Hebrew word, **company** (RSV), or else "party" (NJV), or "adherents, followers." The fire that **broke out** (verse 18a) came down from heaven (Num 16.35), that is, it was sent by God. In many languages it is necessary to specify who caused the fire to break out. In this case one may say "God sent fire down on . . . ."

106.19-20 RSV	TEV
19 They made a calf in Horeb and worshiped a molten image.	19 They made a gold bull-calf at Sinai and worshiped that idol;
20 They exchanged the glory of God for the image of an ox that eats grass.	20 they exchanged the glory of God for the image of an animal that eats grass.

For the events referred to in verses 19-23, see Exodus 32.1-14. *Horeb* in Hebrew is another name for Mount Sinai, where the people asked Aaron to make

<u>a molten image</u> in the form of a <u>calf</u> (or TEV "**bull-calf**," or NIV "bull")[1] from the gold jewelry they took to him; then they worshiped that idol. See Exodus 32.4 for the way in which the people's gold jewelry was melted and used to make the gold idol.

It remains to be noticed that nearly all translations consulted translate verse 19a quite literally, **They made a calf**; and in line b, RSV, at least, can be read as referring to something quite separate from line a. Of the translations consulted only GECL (besides TEV) avoids the ridiculous implication that the Israelites made a live animal.

In verse 20 **the glory of God** translates the Hebrew text "his glory"; the Hebrew copyists made a deliberate change in the text, changing "his glory" to "their glory" (that is, of the Israelites), which is what the Masoretic text has. The change was made presumably on the ground that the original text was offensive to God (see Cohen, McCullough). BJ, NJB, and NJV translate the Masoretic text; FRCL translates the Masoretic text "They replaced God, who was their glory, for the statue of a bull"; NIV and TOB have "their Glory," a reference to God. The recommendation here is that a translation follow RSV and TEV. **Exchanged the glory of God for** is a difficult expression which must be recast in many languages to say "they stopped worshiping God, who is great, and began to worship . . . ."

RSV **calf** in verse 19 and **ox** in verse 20 translate two different Hebrew words; but in the nature of the case, it was one and the same animal, and in English at least, a calf and an ox are two different animals altogether. TEV has avoided saying "a bull that eats grass" in verse 20b, since the phrase implies that this is one particular species of bulls, different from others that do not eat grass.[2] NJV is like RSV: ". . . for the image of a bull that feeds on grass."

106.21-23	RSV	TEV

	RSV	TEV
21	They forgot God, their Savior, who had done great things in Egypt,	21 They forgot the God who had saved them by his mighty acts in Egypt.
22	wondrous works in the land of Ham, and terrible things by the Red Sea.	22 What wonderful things he did there! What amazing things at the Red Sea!
23	Therefore he said he would destroy them— had not Moses, his chosen one, stood in the breach before him,	23 When God said that he would destroy his people, his chosen servant, Moses, stood up against God

---

[1]The usual translation of 'egel is "calf," but since "calf" can be either a male or a female, it does not serve here, since it must be clear that the animal was a male; nor is "bull" quite right, since it is a fully-grown animal. For this reason TEV has "**bull-calf**," although no standard dictionary recognizes the existence of this word.

[2]The Hebrew word here is *shor*, which Holladay defines as "a fully-grown male bovine, whether castrated or not: *bull, ox, steer* . . . ."

to turn away his wrath from destroying them.	and kept his anger from destroying them.

Verses 21-22 flow together (see RSV), and a translation may seek to preserve this form, if it is not too difficult for the readers.

In verse 21a **forgot** repeats the accusation made in verse 7. In verse 22a **the land of Ham** is the same as **Egypt** in verse 21b (see 78.51). And **great things** . . . **wondrous works** . . . **terrible things** (verses 21b, 22a,b) all mean the same thing, the miracles, the marvelous things that God did. **Terrible things** (verses 22b) is most inappropriate in English; it is better to say "surprising" (SPCL) or "awesome" (NJV, NJB, NIV); see 99.3. For **Red Sea** see verse 7.

Verse 23 relates how Moses persuaded God to change his mind and not destroy the people of Israel for their idolatry (see Exo 32.9-14). There is an ellipsis in RSV (also NIV and others) which may be misleading. The thought is that God actually did threaten to **destroy them**, and **would** have done so **had not Moses** . . . . The figure used, **stood in the breach**, is that of warfare, where a soldier might stand in a break made in the wall by enemy soldiers, so as to keep them from entering the city. The figure **stood in the breach** and TEV's "**stood up against**" are picturable images of Moses' action; however, the action consisted mainly in speaking to God on behalf of the people. Accordingly, in many languages it will be clearer to say something like "Moses stood up and argued with God" or "Moses spoke with God and persuaded him." The expression **turn away his wrath from destroying them** may have to be recast to say, for example, "to keep God, who was angry with them, from killing them" or "to convince God in his anger that he should not kill them."

106.24-27   RSV   TEV

24 Then they despised the pleasant land,
   having no faith in his promise.
25 They murmured in their tents,
   and did not obey the voice of the LORD.
26 Therefore he raised his hand and swore to them
   that he would make them fall in the wilderness,
27 and would disperse _w_ their descendants among the nations,
   scattering them over the lands.

24 Then they rejected the pleasant land,
   because they did not believe God's promise.
25 They stayed in their tents and grumbled
   and would not listen to the LORD.
26 So he gave them a solemn warning
   that he would make them die in the desert
27 and scatter their descendants among the heathen,
   letting them die in foreign countries.

_w_ Syr Compare Ezek 20.23: Heb _cause to fall_

These verses relate the Israelites' refusal to try to enter Canaan, after the spies returned from exploring the land, and a majority of them advised the people not to attempt to enter the land because of the size and strength of the inhabitants (Num

13.1–14.10). Since this happened years after the events related in the preceding verses, it is better to begin verse 24a with "Later" (SPCL) instead of RSV and TEV **Then**. And the verb **"rejected"** or **despised** may not be natural in the context, so perhaps something like "they refused to enter" or "they were afraid to enter" may be better.

Verse 25 portrays the people in their tents, in the wilderness, refusing to advance into the land of Canaan.

Angry with their lack of faith in him, God **"gave them a solemn warning"** (literally "lifted his hand to them," the gesture which accompanied an oath) **"that he would make them die in the desert"** (verse 26; literally, **make them fall**).

Verse 27 in Hebrew begins "and to make fall," the same verb as in the preceding line. The verse is otherwise the same as Ezekiel 20.23, which has the verb "and to disperse," which is followed here by RSV (similarly NIV, NEB, NJV). TEV (also TOB, FRCL) has followed the Masoretic text but reverses the two lines, since it is rather ludicrous to speak of God killing their descendants and then scattering them in foreign countries (see SPCL). It may well be that there is a scribal error in the Masoretic text, and that the verb in verse 27a should be, as in Ezekiel 20.23, "to disperse" (parallel with "to scatter" in the following line).[3] For translation suggestions concerning **the nations** (TEV **"the heathen"**), see 9.5.

106.28-31	RSV		TEV
28	Then they attached themselves to the Baal of Peor, and ate sacrifices offered to the dead;	28	Then at Peor, God's people joined in the worship of Baal and ate sacrifices offered to dead gods.
29	they provoked the LORD to anger with their doings, and a plague broke out among them.	29	They stirred up the LORD's anger by their actions, and a terrible disease broke out among them.
30	Then Phinehas stood up and interposed, and the plague was stayed.	30	But Phinehas stood up and punished the guilty, and the plague was stopped.
31	And that has been reckoned to him as righteousness from generation to generation for ever.	31	This has been remembered in his favor ever since and will be for all time to come.

---

[3]HOTTP ("B" decision) prefers the Masoretic text and explains, somewhat redundantly, that "to make fall down" means "to cast down." But in this passage "to make fall down" means "to kill" and not "throw down," which is what "cast down" means in English. Here HOTTP cites TOB as following the Masoretic text (which is correct), but gives *disperser* as the TOB translation of the verb of the Masoretic text, not realizing that TOB, like TEV, has reversed the two lines and translates the verb of the Masoretic text by *abattre*.

These verses report the events narrated in Numbers 25.1-13. **Peor** was a mountain in Moab, on the east side of the Jordan. The name **Baal** means "lord, master," and is the name often given in the Old Testament to the gods of other nations. The Hebrew verb translated **attached themselves to** (TEV "**joined in the worship of**") is the one used in Numbers 25.3. Something like "committed themselves to" or "pledged their allegiance (or, loyalty) to" may be better. In verse 28b **the dead** are the idols, the pagan gods themselves, which the psalmist considers to have no real existence (see the description in 115.4-8). NJB and NIV translate "lifeless gods." Dahood, however, takes the meaning here to be funeral sacrifices, offerings for the dead (so Oesterley, Weiser). A translator may choose to follow this interpretation. **Baal** may require some identification; for example, "the god called Baal" or "the god the other nations worshiped, called Baal."

In verse 29b the **plague** (same word used in Num 25.8-9) is unspecified; it is a disease or epidemic of some sort. It should be clear that this happened as a result of Yahweh's anger.

In verse 30a TEV **"punished the guilty"** translates a verb which means "sit in judgment" or "arbitrate, intervene." So RSV **interposed**; NJV, NJB, and NIV have "intervened." Phinehas killed an Israelite man and the Midianite woman he had taken into his tent; this "intervention" caused God to stop the plague (which had killed 24,000 people). Instead of "intervened" the Septuagint has here "made atonement," the same word used in Numbers 25.13. The use of the passive in **the plague was stayed** will have to become active in many languages, in which case the subject supplied will be God; that is, "God stopped the plague" or "God stopped the sickness that was killing them."

In verse 31 the Hebrew is "this is accounted to him as righteousness" (*tsedaqah*); TOB translates "This was reckoned as a righteous deed." The text can be understood to refer to divine approval (so FRCL); the same phrase is used of Abraham in Genesis 15.6. Or it can mean the high regard in which Phinehas was held by the people of Israel ever since the original event, and which will continue for all time to come. In translation this may be stated "people have always remembered this good act and will go on remembering it always."

106.32-33   RSV   TEV

| 32 | They angered him at the waters of Meribah, and it went ill with Moses on their account; | 32 | At the springs of Meribah the people made the LORD angry, and Moses was in trouble on their account. |
| 33 | for they made his spirit bitter, and he spoke words that were rash. | 33 | They made him so bitter that he spoke without stopping to think. |

For the incident reported in these verses, see Numbers 20.1-13; see further references in Psalms 81.7; 95.8. At the beginning of verse 32 it is important to specify that it was the Lord whom the people made angry; otherwise, as RSV shows, **him** could be taken to refer back to Phinehas.

The historical narrative in Numbers is not too clear as to the precise nature of Moses' sin; here the text says it was his rash words which brought him trouble, that is, God kept him from entering Canaan. **On their account** may be stated more clearly "because of what they did."

Verse 33a has been taken in different ways. The Masoretic text is "they rebelled against his spirit," the verb *marah* here being the same as the one in verse 7; **his spirit** is probably Yahweh's (so NJV, NIV, TOD; Dahood, Kirkpatrick, Briggs), although it could be Moses' (who is the subject of the following line).

But the Masoretic text consonants can be assigned other vowels to become a causative form of the verb *marar* "be bitter" (so two Hebrew manuscripts, and the Septuagint, Syriac, and Jerome); in this case **they made his spirit bitter** refers to Moses (RSV, TEV, NEB, NAB, BJ, NJB, GECL, FRCL, SPCL). Either interpretation is possible; the majority prefer the second one. In either case the subject of verse 33b is Moses, not God. In many languages **made his spirit bitter** or TEV's **"made him so bitter"** must be recast to say "they made him so angry . . . ."

106.34-36 RSV	TEV
34 They did not destroy the peoples, as the LORD commanded them,	34 They did not kill the heathen, as the LORD had commanded them to do,
35 but they mingled with the nations and learned to do as they did.	35 but they intermarried with them and adopted their pagan ways.
36 They served their idols, which became a snare to them.	36 God's people worshiped idols, and this caused their destruction.

Verses 34-39 summarize a long history of Israel's repeated periods of idolatry, as related in the book of Judges. Yahweh ordered his people to get rid of the Canaanites and not intermarry with them, for that would cause the Israelites to adopt their pagan ways (Exo 34.11-16; Deut 7.1-6; 20.16-18). Instead of obeying Yahweh's order, however, they did intermarry with the Canaanites and began to practice their pagan rites (verses 34-35). The Hebrew verb translated by TEV as **"intermarried"** means to mix, mingle; it can mean here "lived (peaceably) with them" or "had dealings with them" (so TOB); NJB and Dahood also have "intermarried." In verse 35b **learned to do as they did** refers specifically to their pagan religion. **Mingled with the nations** or TEV's **"intermarried with them"** will have to be recast in some languages to say, for example, "the men got their wives from them" or "men took wives from the pagan tribes."

Idolatry brought about the downfall of the Israelites (verse 36b); literally, it "was a snare to them" (see 69.22). SPCL has "this caused their ruin." In verse 36a TEV **"idols"** is not enough; it should be explicit that these are the idols of the Canaanites. For translation suggestions on **idols** see 31.6; 96.5. In languages in which the terms for snares and traps are used metaphorically, the translator will give his translation more emotive value by using such expressions.

106.37-39 RSV	TEV
37 They sacrificed their sons and their daughters to the demons;	37 They offered their own sons and daughters as sacrifices to the idols of Canaan.
38 they poured out innocent blood, the blood of their sons and daughters, whom they sacrificed to the idols of Canaan; and the land was polluted with blood.	38 They killed those innocent children, and the land was defiled by those murders.
39 Thus they became unclean by their acts, and played the harlot in their doings.	39 They made themselves impure by their actions and were unfaithful to God.

In verse 37b the word translated "**idols**" by TEV is found only here and in Deuteronomy 32.17; it is taken by most to mean **demons** (so the Septuagint). The reference is still to the pagan deities, whom the psalmist calls demons (as in Deut 32.17). FRCL "false gods" is better than "**idols**"; NEB "foreign demons" is not very satisfactory. Briggs defines the word as meaning the ancient gods of the Canaanites.

Verse 38 is long and wordy in Hebrew (see RSV); TEV has expressed the meaning more concisely. Because the Israelites had offered their innocent children as sacrifices, both the land (verse 38b) and they themselves (verse 39a) were made **polluted** and **unclean**, that is, unfit to worship Yahweh, to have fellowship with him.

If a translator wishes to reproduce the rather repetitious character of the Hebrew text in verses 37-38, the following may serve as a model:

37 They offered their own sons and daughters
as sacrifices to those false gods.
38 They killed those innocent children—
their own sons and daughters—
and offered them as sacrifices
to the idols of the Canaanites;
these killings made the land impure.

Idolatry is compared here, as often elsewhere in the Old Testament, to marital infidelity; Israel was Yahweh's "wife," and when she worshiped foreign gods she was being unfaithful to him. RSV's quaint **played the harlot** is from KJV; see NJB's more vigorous "their behavior was that of a harlot."

106.40-43 RSV	TEV
40 Then the anger of the LORD was kindled against his people, and he abhorred his heritage;	40 So the LORD was angry with his people; he was disgusted with them.

41	he gave them into the hand of the nations, so that those who hated them ruled over them.	41	He abandoned them to the power of the heathen, and their enemies ruled over them.
42	Their enemies oppressed them, and they were brought into subjection under their power.	42	They were oppressed by their enemies and were in complete subjection to them.
43	Many times he delivered them, but they were rebellious in their purposes, and were brought low through their iniquity.	43	Many times the LORD rescued his people, but they chose to rebel against him and sank deeper into sin.

In verses 40-46 the psalmist summarizes a long history of Israel's constant sins, their punishment, their repentance and cries for help, and the Lord's recurring mercy—a theme which runs through the historical books of the Old Testament, especially Judges.

Verse 40 describes Yahweh's reaction: he became angry with his people, and he **abhorred** them. For the verb "despise, detest, loathe," see 5.6b. In verse 40b, for Israel as Yahweh's **heritage** see verse 5.

It was because of God's anger that the Israelites were time and again defeated by their enemies and ruled by them (verses 41-42). TEV's **"abandoned them to the power of the heathen"** must be recast in many languages to say, for example, "He allowed the other nations to conquer them." It should be clear that **the nations** in line a and **those who hated them** in line b both refer to the same people, the Gentile powers that time and again oppressed the people of Israel.

RSV in verse 42b is unnecessarily wordy; see NJV "and they were subject to their power," NIV "and subjected them to their power," and NJB "crushing them under their rule."

In verse 43a **delivered** translates the verb used in 7.1. In verse 43b TEV **"they chose to rebel"** translates "they rebelled in their plans" (see RSV); it indicates a deliberate, wilful act (NJV "they were deliberately rebellious"; NJB "they still defied him deliberately"). In verse 43c the Hebrew verb is rather unusual, occurring in this form only here in the Old Testament. Verse 43c is literally "and were brought low in their sin," forming a parallel with line b. "In their sin" can be understood as TEV has, **"sank deeper into sin"** (also BJ, NJB, SPCL, TOB, FRCL), or else as RSV and others, "because of their sin." The latter may be preferable. In this case the translation can be "and were ruined (or, brought to ruin) because of their sins" "or . . . because they had sinned."

106.44-46	RSV		TEV

44	Nevertheless he regarded their distress, when he heard their cry.	44	Yet the LORD heard them when they cried out, and he took notice of their distress.
45	He remembered for their sake his		

	covenant,	45	For their sake he remembered his
	and relented according to the abundance of his steadfast love.		covenant, and because of his great love he relented.
46	He caused them to be pitied by all those who held them captive.	46	He made all their oppressors feel sorry for them.

In verse 44 TEV has reversed the order of the lines for greater ease of understanding. Yahweh heard the people's prayers for help and took pity on them. **He regarded their distress**; "he took notice of their suffering."

For verse 45a see Leviticus 26.40-42. **For their sake** means "because of them," that is, because they were his people; it can be translated "in order to help them." For the thought expressed in verse 45b, see Jonah 3.9-10. The verb translated **relented** may mean "have pity" (see 90.13b) or "regret, repent" (see its use in Gen 6.6, "was sorry"; see also "change his mind" in Psa 110.4). Here "changed his mind" may be the better translation.

In verse 46a **"their oppressors"** translates **those who held them captive** (see the verb *shabah* also in 68.18b); foreign domination is likened to captivity. Yahweh made the foreign masters take pity on the Israelites (see 1 Kgs 8.50).

106.47   RSV   TEV

Save us, O LORD our God,
    and gather us from among the
        nations,
that we may give thanks to thy
    holy name
and glory in thy praise.

Save us, O LORD our God,
    and bring us back from among
        the nations,
so that we may be thankful
    and praise your holy name.

The psalm ends with a prayer for Yahweh to deliver his people from exile and take them back to their land, where once again, in the Temple, they will praise his **holy name**. If the translator follows TEV's **"bring us back,"** the verb used will in many languages represent a speaker point of view, and in languages which require stating the place, it will be necessary to say, for example, "return us to our land" or "take us back to our country."

Lines c and d are "to give thanks to your holy name, and to take pride in praising you." The verb "take pride" (or, boast) in line d further defines the gratitude expressed in line c; see similar language in 105.3.

Verses 47-48 appear also in 1 Chronicles 16.35-36.

106.48   RSV   TEV

Blessed be the LORD, the God of
    Israel,
    from everlasting to everlasting!

Praise the LORD, the God of Is-
    rael;
    praise him now and forever!

And let all the people say, "Amen!" Praise the LORD!	Let everyone say, "Amen!" Praise the LORD!

This verse is the conclusion of Book Four (Psa 90–106); see the conclusion of Books One (41.13), Two (72.18-19), and Three (89.52).

For **Blessed be** in line a, see 18.46.

For **Amen** in line c see 41.13; 72.19.

For the final **Praise the Lord!** see 104.35.

Book Five

(Psalms 107–150)

Psalm 107

This psalm is composed of two main parts: a hymn of thanksgiving (verses 1-32) and a song of praise (verses 33-43). Many believe that the two parts were originally independent compositions which were later brought together; others think the psalm was an original composition as it now stands. There is no denying that verses 33-43 are different in style from verses 1-32, and it seems more likely that they were originally part of another poem.

The psalm seems to be intended for use by pilgrims who have come to Jerusalem for one of the great festivals. It opens with a general call to praise Yahweh (verses 1-3), followed by four strophes in which Yahweh is thanked by different groups for what he has done for them: people who have traveled across deserts (verses 4-9); people who have been prisoners (verses 10-16); people who have been sick (verses 17-22); and people who have traveled across the sea (verses 23-32). In each strophe there is a double refrain: the people's cry for help (verses 6, 13, 19, 28) and the exhortation to praise Yahweh (verses 8, 15, 21-22, 31-32). Some commentators take the four strophes to indicate the four directions from which people came (see verse 3), but this seems rather far-fetched. The psalm closes with praise to Yahweh for what he has done for his people (verses 33-43).

HEADING: "**In Praise of God's Goodness.**" Other headings are: "God, a refuge in all dangers"; "The LORD's constant love"; "Divine providence." The TEV heading may be adapted for use in some languages by recasting it to say, for example, "Let us thank God because he is good" or "God is good; so let us thank him."

<u>107.1-3</u>   RSV   TEV

1   O give thanks to the LORD, for he   1   "Give thanks to the LORD, be-
        is good;   cause he is good;
     for his steadfast love endures   his love is eternal!"
        for ever!   2   Repeat these words in praise to
2   Let the redeemed of the LORD say   the LORD,
        so,   all you whom he has saved.
     whom he has redeemed from   He has rescued you from your
        trouble   enemies
3   and gathered in from the lands,   3   and has brought you back from

920

from the east and from the west,	**foreign countries,**
from the north and from the south.	**from east and west, from north and south.**[d]

[d] *Probable text* south; *Hebrew* the Mediterranean Sea *(meaning "west")*.

The psalm opens with a call to thank Yahweh (verse 1), which is exactly like the opening call in 106.1. "**His love is eternal**" must often be recast to say "he loves people for ever." For comments on **love** see 5.7.

All **the redeemed** are to repeat these words of thanksgiving (verse 2). The Hebrew verb for "to save" is used twice in this verse (see 69.18; 19.14). TEV has translated "the redeemed of Yahweh" by "**all you whom he has saved**," and "say" by "**Repeat these words**." If the translator follows TEV "**Repeat these words . . . ,**" it will be necessary in some languages to make certain that the pointing device that is used points back to the words in verse 1. English "**these**" may refer forward as well as backward. In many languages it will be more natural to place "**all you whom he has saved**" before the command.

The people whom Yahweh has saved are to thank him because he rescued them from their enemies—literally, "the hand of the enemy" (verse 2b). The Hebrew word can be taken to mean **trouble**, as RSV has done (see NJV "adversity"); most take it in a personal sense as "**enemies**" (TOB, FRCL, NIV, NEB, NAB, NJB, BJ, SPCL).

Yahweh has brought his people **from the lands** (that is, from exile in "**foreign countries**"; see the prayer in 106.47) to Jerusalem, where they are gathered to worship him in the Temple.

In Hebrew the last word in verse 3 is "and from the sea"; such directional use of the word means "the west," the sea being the Mediterranean. Since **the west** has already been mentioned in the verse, the Masoretic text *miyyam* "from the sea" is changed to *miyamin* "**from the south**" (TEV, NAB, BJ, NJB, FRCL, NIV, NEB, all with textual footnotes; RSV and SPCL do not have footnotes). NJV translates the Masoretic text "from the sea," and Dahood translates it "from the southern sea," taking it to refer to the Gulf of Aqaba.[1] It seems better to emend the text (see Anderson, Kirkpatrick). For translation suggestions regarding geographic directions, see 75.6; 89.12; 103.12. It may be more suitable in some languages to say, for example, "from every direction" or "from every place in the world."

107.4-6   RSV   TEV

4 Some wandered in desert wastes, finding no way to a city to dwell in;	4 Some wandered in the trackless desert and could not find their way to a city to live in.
5 hungry and thirsty, their soul fainted within them.	5 They were hungry and thirsty and had given up all hope.
6 Then they cried to the LORD in	

[1]HOTTP sees no reason to depart from the Masoretic text.

their trouble,		6 Then in their trouble they called
and he delivered them from		to the LORD,
their distress;		and he saved them from their
		distress.

In this first strophe (verses 4-9) people who have **wandered in desert wastes** are singled out as the object of Yahweh's care. It is not certain whether this actually refers to lost travelers in general, or is intended to refer to the exodus from Egypt or to the return of the Israelites from exile. **A city to dwell in** is the way most translations render the Hebrew phrase "a city of dwelling" in verse 4b; but it may mean "an inhabited city" (NAB; similarly TOB, FRCL, BJ, NJB; NJV "settled place"). This may better fit the context, the meaning being that the lost travelers found no city where they could get help (so Anderson).

In verse 5 TEV **"had given up all hope"** (see also GECL) translates "their *nefesh* fainted in them" (see the verb "to faint" in 77.3b); the words can mean "they were about to die" (see SPCL, Dahood, TOB, NIV, NAB). FRCL has "they were about to lose courage"; perhaps the best translation is "they became discouraged" or "they were plunged into despair."

The language of verse 6 is repeated in verses 13, 19, and 28; in verses 13 and 19 the verb translated "called" is different but has the same meaning; and the verb "to save" in verses 13 and 19 is a different verb from the one used in verse 6, and in verse 28 still another verb is used; all three are closely synonymous. Each of these four verses serves as a transition from the first part of the stanza (which describes the plight of the people) and the second part (which tells how Yahweh saved them). The verb **cried** (for help) in line a appears also in 34.17; 77.1; and **delivered** is used in 7.1.

107.7-9	RSV	TEV
7	he led them by a straight way, till they reached a city to dwell in.	7 He led them by a straight road to a city where they could live.
8	Let them thank the LORD for his steadfast love, for his wonderful works to the sons of men!	8 They must thank the LORD for his constant love, for the wonderful things he did for them.
9	For he satisfies him who is thirsty, and the hungry he fills with good things.	9 He satisfies those who are thirsty and fills the hungry with good things.

In verse 7b the same phrase "a city of dwelling" is used, as in verse 4b. Those who translate it here, as there, "an inhabited city," see this primarily as a reference to Canaan, with its towns and cities, after the years of wandering in the wilderness (see NJB). In verse 7a the meaning can be expressed by "He led them directly" or "He led them on a road that went straight to . . . ."

Verse 8 is repeated in exactly the same words in verses 15, 21, and 31. It is a command expressed in the third person form. The **wonderful works** of Yahweh are the mighty deeds, the miracles through which Yahweh saved them (see 9.1 for comments on the root verb). The Hebrew phrase **the sons of men** usually means all of humankind (see 11.4), so here the meaning may be quite general, "what Yahweh does for people"; or it may refer specifically to the people who are the subject of this strophe (so Kirkpatrick; see Anderson). GECL translates "Now you must thank the Lord for his benefits, praise him for your wonderful deliverance."

In verse 9 **him who is thirsty** translates "the longing *nefesh*," which NJB takes to mean "hungry"; most take it to mean thirsty. **The hungry** in verse 9b translates "the hungry *nefesh*." Instead of the singular "the one who is thirsty and the one who is hungry," TEV has used the plural forms, **"those who are thirsty . . . the hungry,"** to avoid the possibility of misunderstanding the text to refer to one person. **Good things** here means food. In some languages it will be necessary to be more specific in both lines 9a and 9b; for example, "he gives water to those who are thirsty and food to the hungry."

107.10-13 RSV		TEV	
10	Some sat in darkness and in gloom, prisoners in affliction and in irons,	10	Some were living in gloom and darkness, prisoners suffering in chains,
11	for they had rebelled against the words of God, and spurned the counsel of the Most High.	11	because they had rebelled against the commands of Almighty God and had rejected his instructions.
12	Their hearts were bowed down with hard labor; they fell down, with none to help.	12	They were worn out from hard work; they would fall down, and no one would help.
13	Then they cried to the LORD in their trouble, and he delivered them from their distress;	13	Then in their trouble they called to the LORD, and he saved them from their distress.

In this strophe (verses 10-16) the psalmist describes how God set prisoners free; they also are called upon to thank him for having saved them. The **prisoners** may be thought of in literal terms as people in prison; it is probable, however, that the general thought is that of Israelites in exile, perhaps in Babylonia. In verse 10a **gloom** translates the word used in 23.4. The two-word phrase in Hebrew for **in darkness and in gloom** means "deepest darkness" or "a very dark place." The verb **sat** is here used in the sense of "to live," as is often its meaning. In line **b** instead of TEV "suffering" it is better to translate "bound in" or "tied up with"; see NJV "bound in cruel irons." Verse 10 can then be rendered "Some people were living in a very dark place; they were prisoners bound with chains."

923

The reason for their condition is given in verse 11; this makes it even more probable that the exile in Babylonia is meant. Their disobedience to God was the cause of their being taken away as captives by their enemies. **Words** can also mean "commandments," as in Exodus 34.28. **Spurned** translates a verb meaning "to despise, to treat with contempt" (see "revile" in 74.10b,18b). For **the Most High** in verse 11b, see 7.17. In some languages it will be more natural to place the cause (verse 11) before verse 10.

Verse 12 in the Masoretic text begins "he crushed" (so NJV, NAB, Dahood "he humbled"; similarly AT, BJ, NJB, GECL, NIV, TOB, SPCL). The same Hebrew consonants are assigned other vowels to give the meaning "they were crushed" (so the Septuagint; RSV, TEV, NEB; Weiser). Either interpretation is possible and equally fitting in the context. Following the latter interpretation, **Their hearts** is taken as a way of speaking of the people themselves, "**They were worn out,**" or else, as NEB has it, "Their spirit was subdued." But it seems better to translate "Their spirit was crushed." In some cases, however, it may be better to translate as an active verb, with God as subject, "He crushed their spirit with hard labor" or "hard labor crushed their spirits." This is probably not to be understood literally of physical weakness, but of moral and spiritual despair.

Verse 13 is like verse 6; the two Hebrew verbs translated **they cried** and **he delivered** are not the same but are close synonyms of the verbs in verse 6, with no difference in meaning. Like verse 6, this verse marks the change from a description of the people's suffering to a statement of how Yahweh rescued them.

RSV	TEV
14 he brought them out of darkness and gloom, and broke their bonds asunder.	14 He brought them out of their gloom and darkness and broke their chains in pieces.
15 Let them thank the LORD for his steadfast love, for his wonderful works to the sons of men!	15 They must thank the LORD for his constant love, for the wonderful things he did for them.
16 For he shatters the doors of bronze, and cuts in two the bars of iron.	16 He breaks down doors of bronze and smashes iron bars.

In verse 14 God responds. In verse 14a the phrase **darkness and gloom** translates the same two words used in verse 10a; for the expression in verse 14b, see 2.3. **Broke their bonds** or "their chains" must often be recast in other languages to say, for example, "the chains that bound these people."

Verse 15 is the same as verse 8.

Yahweh's action in setting prisoners free is described in vivid language in verse 16; the verb "**smashes**" in line b may be understood as **cuts (in two),** as RSV translates it; see its use in 75.10a. Instead of **doors of bronze** it may be better to translate "gates of bronze"; the iron bars in the next line are those that reinforce either the prison gates or the gates of the cities where the Israelites were exiled.

The verse uses the language found in the promise in Isaiah 45.2. RSV and TEV use the timeless present tense; also NJV, NJB, FRCL, NEB, SPCL, TOB. Verse 16 returns abruptly to extend the description of Yahweh's acts of salvation in verse 14. In some languages readers will fail to understand this amplification without some clue being added; for example, it is possible to say "he breaks down the enemies' doors made of bronze and smashes their iron bars, to set his people free."

107.17-19   RSV

17   Some were sick*x* through their
      sinful ways,
      and because of their iniquities
      suffered affliction;
18   they loathed any kind of food,
      and they drew near to the gates
      of death.
19   Then they cried to the LORD in
      their trouble,
      and he delivered them from
      their distress;

x Cn: Heb *fools*

TEV

17   Some were fools, suffering because
      of their sins
      and because of their evil;
18   they couldn't stand the sight of
      food
      and were close to death.
19   Then in their trouble they called
      to the LORD,
      and he saved them from their
      distress.

This strophe (verses 17-22) takes up the plight of those who had been sick and near death; these people also are exhorted to thank Yahweh for having saved them. Verse 17 begins in Hebrew with the word "fools": "fools because of their evil ways and because of their iniquities they suffered." This construction is rather strange, and so there are many who replace the Masoretic text "fools" with the word "sick, feeble": Briggs; RSV, NAB, SPCL. The majority follow the Masoretic text; Dahood takes the Masoretic text to mean "enfeebled." HOTTP prefers the Masoretic text, and FRCL translates the Masoretic text as follows: "Others showed they had gone out of their minds, for they behaved so badly. On account of their wrong they were crushed with suffering." NEB translates "Some were fools, they took to rebellious ways, and for their transgressions they suffered punishment." This, however, in line a disregards the preposition "from (their sinful way)," which ties the phrase to the preceding "fools." NJV is best: "There were fools who suffered for their sinful way, and for their iniquities." "Fools" here are people who are spiritually and morally foolish, that is, who disregard God's laws; and so these people suffered because of their sins and their evil.

In their wretched condition they (literally, "their *nefesh*") "hated" **any kind of food**, and they **drew near to the gates of death** (see similar idea in 9.13). The figure pictures the world of the dead, Sheol, as a city with gates, waiting to receive those who die. For the verb "hated" (**loathed**) in the sense of "abhorred," see 106.40b.

Verse 19 is exactly like verse 13.

RSV   TEV

	RSV		TEV
20	he sent forth his word, and healed them, and delivered them from destruction.	20	He healed them with his command and saved them from the grave.
21	Let them thank the LORD for his steadfast love, for his wonderful works to the sons of men!	21	They must thank the LORD for his constant love, for the wonderful things he did for them.
22	And let them offer sacrifices of thanksgiving, and tell of his deeds in songs of joy!	22	They must thank him with sacrifices, and with songs of joy must tell all that he has done.

The use of the verb **healed** in verse 20 shows that the people in this strophe are sick as a result of their sins. Yahweh's spoken command is literally **he sent forth his word**. That word **healed them** and **delivered them**. **He sent forth his word** indicates an action, whereas TEV **"with his command"** serves as an instrumental phrase. In many languages it will be better to recast the speaking and the healing and say, for example, "he spoke and they were healed" or "the word which he spoke healed them." The verb **delivered** (TEV **"saved"**) here is the same as the one used in 41.1b and is different from the ones used in verses 6 and 9. **Destruction** in line b translates a word whose form and meaning are in doubt; but most commentators take it to mean "their pits," a synonym for Sheol. Most translations have either "the grave" or "death." NEB, BJ, and NJB follow an emended text which means "(he saved) their lives from the abyss." The expression **delivered them from destruction** ("saved them from the grave") will have to be adjusted in some languages to say "he did not let them die" or "he kept them alive."

Verse 21 is exactly like verse 15.

Sacrifices of thanksgiving refers to offerings which expressed the gratitude of the people. Verse 22 specifies that such sacrifices should be offered (see "Sacrifice" in 40.6), as the healed worshipers joyfully proclaim in the Temple what Yahweh has done for them.[2]

RSV   TEV

	RSV		TEV
23	Some went down to the sea in ships, doing business on the great waters;	23	Some sailed over the ocean in ships, earning their living on the seas.
		24	They saw what the LORD can do,

---

[2]In the Masoretic text, in the margin of verses 21-26 and of verse 40, there is an inverted letter *nun*. There is no certain knowledge of the meaning of this. Some take it as an indication that the verses are out of place (see Kautzsch-Cowley *Gesenius' Hebrew Grammar,* page 31).

24   they saw the deeds of the LORD,
    his wondrous works in the deep.
25   For he commanded, and raised the
    stormy wind,
    which lifted up the waves of the
    sea.
	his wonderful acts on the seas.
	25 He commanded, and a mighty
	    wind began to blow
	    and stirred up the waves.

In this strophe (verses 23-32) the psalmist calls upon those who sailed over stormy seas, and says they should thank Yahweh for keeping them safe. These were not just occasional travelers but people who were "**earning their living on the seas**" (verse 23b, TEV). It is to be noticed that the Hebrews as a whole were not a seafaring people; most of the Mediterranean seacoast was controlled by the Phoenicians or others. In some languages it will be necessary to make clear that the reason for sailing on the seas was to earn their living; for example, "In order to earn their living, some people sailed in ships on the ocean" or "Some people worked on ships sailing on the sea to make their living."

Yahweh's **wondrous works in the deep** (verse 24b) are his power to bring on furious storms (verse 25) and then to calm them down (verse 29). For **wondrous works** see the similar "wonderful works" in verse 8a. The Hebrew term for **the deep** here emphasizes the depth of the ocean, but it is not the same as the primeval "deep" of 104.6 **The stormy wind** in verse 25a translates a two-word phrase, "a wind of a tempest," "a tempestuous wind"; NJV translates "a storm wind." For people unfamiliar with the sea, the expression **his wondrous works in the deep** may require adjusting to something like "the great storms he caused on the big waters." In the same manner, **lifted up the waves of the sea** may have to be recast to say, for example, "which made the waters move" or "which caused the big waters to flow."

107.26-28   RSV   TEV

26   They mounted up to heaven, they
    went down to the depths;
    their courage melted away in
    their evil plight;
27   they reeled and staggered like
    drunken men,
    and were at their wits' end.
28   Then they cried to the LORD in
    their trouble,
    and he delivered them from
    their distress;
	26 The ships were lifted high in the
	    air
	    and plunged down into the
	    depths.
	  In such danger the men lost their
	    courage;
	27 they stumbled and staggered
	    like drunks—
	    all their skill was useless.
	28 Then in their trouble they called
	    to the LORD,
	    and he saved them from their
	    distress.

Verse 26 describes the effects of the furious storm, as the ships wildly tossed and pitched. The subject is not formally expressed in Hebrew, but it is understood to be the sailors, not the waves; but since the sailors are in ships, it is better to make "**The ships**" the subject (so TEV, FRCL, GECL).

In verse 26a TEV **"high in the air"** translates what is literally to heaven. If the translator follows the pattern of TEV, and the passive cannot be used, the waves can serve as the agent of the action; for example, "the waves lifted the ship into the air and . . . ." Here the term for the primeval **depths** is used, probably for poetic effect and variety. The language used does not mean the ships were sunk, but that they plunged down into the trough between the mountainous waves.

In verse 26b TEV **"lost their courage"** translates "their *nefesh* melted," which most take to mean a loss of courage (RSV, TEV; see NAB, BJ, NIV, SPCL); NJV, however, understands the Hebrew to mean seasickness, "disgorging in their misery" (also FRCL). NJB has "Their stomachs were turned to water." The situation was so dangerous that the sailors lost all hope.

In verse 27b the Hebrew is "and all their wisdom was swallowed up"; the word "wisdom" here means their skill as sailors. See NJV "all their skill to no avail"; NEB "their seamanship was all in vain" (see FRCL, SPCL). TEV **"all their skill was useless"** may have to be recast to say, for example, "although they were good sailors, they didn't know what to do next."

Verse 28 is like verse 6, except that the Hebrew verb "to save" is different (and different also from the verb used in verses 13 and 19).

RSV	TEV
29 he made the storm be still, and the waves of the sea were hushed.	29 He calmed the raging storm, and the waves became quiet.
30 Then they were glad because they had quiet, and he brought them to their desired haven.	30 They were glad because of the calm, and he brought them safe to the port they wanted.
31 Let them thank the LORD for his steadfast love, for his wonderful works to the sons of men!	31 They must thank the LORD for his constant love, for the wonderful things he did for them.
32 Let them extol him in the congregation of the people, and praise him in the assembly of the elders.	32 They must proclaim his greatness in the assembly of the people and praise him before the council of the leaders.

In these verses the psalmist describes how Yahweh saved the seafarers. In verse 29 the text does not say how the Lord made the storm be still; presumably it was with a command, as in verse 25 (and also verse 20). In line **b** the appropriate verb would be "and the waves *subsided*"; more popularly, "the waves calmed down."

In verse 30a the subject is still the same, that is, the men on the ships (see verse 26a in TEV); it may be better to reintroduce the subject, since "the waves" of verse 29b is the nearest plural antecedent. In line **b** **haven** translates a word found only here in the Old Testament; it is an Akkadian loanword meaning "city." The verb phrase **he brought them** must not be translated in such a way as to picture Yahweh

928

carrying the ship into port. The picture is that God guided and led them to a safe harbor; "caused them to reach their destination-port."

Verse 31 is like verse 8.

For **extol him** in verse 32a, see "exalt" in 34.3 and 12.8, and for **the congregation of the people**, see 22.22,25. The psalmist calls upon the people who have been rescued by the Lord to praise him in public worship in the Temple. The **elders** are the leaders of the people, or perhaps more specifically the male heads of families.

107.33-35 RSV   TEV

33 He turns rivers into a desert,	33 The LORD made rivers dry up
springs of water into thirsty	completely
ground,	and stopped springs from
34 a fruitful land into a salty waste,	flowing.
because of the wickedness of its	34 He made rich soil become a salty
inhabitants.	wasteland
35 He turns a desert into pools of	because of the wickedness of
water,	those who lived there.
a parched land into springs of	35 He changed deserts into pools of
water.	water
	and dry land into flowing
	springs.

In the last part of the psalm (verses 33-42), Yahweh is praised for all he does for his people. RSV and others (NJV, NEB, FRCL, GECL, SPCL) use the present tense of the verbs throughout the section, which serves to portray God in terms of his continual deeds of goodness; TEV and others (AT, BJ, NJB, NIV, NAB, Dahood) use the past tense, which serves to speak of Yahweh's actions in the past on behalf of his people. Considering the nature of this song of praise (see introduction to this psalm), it seems that the present tense is more appropriate. Dahood, however, argues for the unity of the psalm, holding that the psalmist is here referring to happenings in the past. This same viewpoint is expressed in the footnote to verse 36 in NAB: "the psalmist probably has in mind the settlement and development of the Promised Land (36ff), the hard times caused by the Assyrian and Babylonian invasions (39), the humiliation and exile of the last kings of Judah (40), and the restoration of Zion after the exile (41)."

Verses 33-34 speak of how Yahweh punishes wicked people: he ruins their fertile soil by drying up their rivers and springs; verse 35 shows the opposite action. Perhaps, as Dahood contends, the language is figurative, describing how Yahweh punished the original inhabitants of Canaan and blessed his people Israel. However that may be, the translation should be quite faithful in representing the language of the text.

At the same time care should be taken to describe in a natural manner what is actually reported. In verse 33 it is not natural to say that **rivers** become **a desert**; in straightforward terms, the rivers stop flowing and so the land they run through becomes a desert. In the same way **springs of water** do not become **thirsty ground;**

929

the springs dry up and the land becomes "thirsty." Something like the following can be said:

> The Lord makes rivers dry up
>   and makes springs stop flowing,
>   so the land becomes a barren desert.

In verse 34a the language of the text is quite natural and should offer no difficulty. For the language **salty waste** see Deuteronomy 29.23; Job 39.6; **a salty waste** is a place where no trees or plants will grow because of the saltiness of the soil. Land that has become a **salty waste** is not known in some areas. It will be necessary in some languages to say, for example, "land that has become useless" or "land that will produce no crops."

Since verse 34b supplies the reason for Yahweh's actions in verses 33a,b and 34a, it may be well to combine the two verses and give first the reason for Yahweh's actions.

Verse 35 describes the opposite of verse 33; here the translation can be:

> He makes pools of water appear in deserts,
>   and makes springs flow in dry places.

	RSV	TEV
36	And there he lets the hungry dwell, and they establish a city to live in;	He let hungry people settle there, and they built a city to live in.
37	they sow fields, and plant vineyards, and get a fruitful yield.	They sowed the fields and planted grapevines and reaped an abundant harvest.
38	By his blessing they multiply greatly; and he does not let their cattle decrease.	He blessed his people, and they had many children; he kept their herds of cattle from decreasing.

A city (verse 36b) may be generic for "cities" (SPCL, FRCL); the Septuagint has the plural "cities." The word recalls verses 4 and 7. The verb **establish** means to found, to build.

Because of the Lord's blessings, their **fields** and **vineyards** produce abundant harvests (verse 37). In areas where the grapevine and grapes are unknown, it may be necessary to say, for example, "planted crops that produce fruit called 'grapes.' " In this case the term for grapes may have to be a loan word.

Verse 38 describes the increase in the number of people (line a) and of cattle (line b). Both are due to Yahweh's **blessing** (see Deut 7.12-13). The verb **multiply** in line a means, as often, an increase in population due to a high birth rate. In line b **cattle** includes cows and bulls, goats and sheep. TEV's "**he blessed his people**" is difficult to define with any precision. The essential meaning is that God causes good things to happen to the ones he blesses, often through a spoken formula. In the present context it is possible to say, for example, "God made his people to be fortunate" or "God gave his people good things and they . . . ."

107.39-42   RSV   TEV

39   When they are diminished and   39   When God's people were defeated
        brought low   and humiliated
     through oppression, trouble,   by cruel oppression and suffer-
        and sorrow,   ing,
40   he pours contempt upon princes   40   he showed contempt for their
     and makes them wander in   oppressors
        trackless wastes;   and made them wander in
41   but he raises up the needy out of   trackless deserts.
        affliction,   41   But he rescued the needy from
     and makes their families like   their misery
        flocks.   and made their families in-
42   The upright see it and are glad;   crease like flocks.
     and all wickedness stops its   42   The righteous see this and are
        mouth.   glad,
                                                but all the wicked are put to
                                                silence.

It is not certain how verses 39-40 relate to what precedes or to what follows. TEV, AT, RSV, NIV, and SPCL join the two verses and connect them with what follows. NJV, TOB, and Dahood connect verse 39 with verse 38, and verse 40 with verse 41; NJV makes the action of verse 40 come before that of verse 39. NAB and FRCL make a full stop at the end of verse 39, and connect verse 40 with verse 41. BJ and NJB take verses 39-40 as a quatrain, describing how Yahweh dealt with his people. Some commentators believe that the two verses 39-40 should be reversed, and verse 39 joined to verse 41. Verse 40 is an exact replica of Job 12.21a,24b, and ZÜR here puts the verse in quotation marks and refers in a footnote to the Job passage (see Kirkpatrick).

Everything considered, it seems best to follow the example of RSV and TEV in the division of the strophes, using the present tense of the verbs, as RSV does.

TEV begins verse 39 by making the subject explicit, **"God's people."** FRCL has "But others . . . ." SPCL has the subject of verse 38 as the subject of verse 39. NEB, by conjecture, supplies the noun "Tyrants" as the subject (parallel to "princes" in verse 40a). It is recommended that the subject be made explicit, as TEV has done.

In verse 39a **diminished** translates the verb used in verse 38b; FRCL takes it to mean the same: "But others see their number decrease." But in connection with **brought low**, this describes the shameful condition of the Israelites when they are under foreign oppression. In many languages it will not be possible for "**cruel oppression and suffering**" to serve as the agents which bring about defeat. Accordingly verse 39 may have to be recast to say, for example, "When the enemies of God's people defeated them, the people were humiliated; they were oppressed and made to suffer."

In verse 40a TEV **"their oppressors"** translates the word **princes**. It is uncertain whether this refers to the leaders of the Israelites (so Anderson, who thinks the psalmist is alluding to the fate of Judah's last two kings, Jehoiachin and Zedekiah) or to foreign leaders who oppressed Israel (so Kirkpatrick, Cohen; Dahood, SPCL). It is possible that no particular historical events are alluded to, but that in general terms the psalmist is speaking of how the Lord reverses human conditions, bringing down the mighty and exalting the lowly (a common theme in Wisdom literature). This being so, the present tense of the verbs is much more appropriate. Verse 40b is similar in thought to verse 4a.

In verse 41a the verb **raises up** means to restore to well-being and prosperity; God comes to their aid and delivers them from their miserable situation (see 113.7-9). **The needy** are the Israelites who are poor and in want.

In verse 41b **makes their families like flocks** is a figure of a high birth rate and a rapid increase in numbers. Although TEV has made it clear that the analogy **makes their families like flocks** refers to population increase, this will not help where people do not raise flocks of animals. In such cases it will be better to say "he made their families have many children" or "he made their families become very numerous."

In verse 42a the verb **see** does not imply that **the upright** are actual spectators of all the events described; it is rather that they know what Yahweh has done, they perceive the meaning of the events reported. In some languages it will be necessary to say, for example, "good people understand these things and are glad." It is important in line **b** to avoid the abstract **all wickedness**, and say "all wicked people," "all wrongdoers." In TEV the last verb phrase **"are put to silence"** implies an external agent that silences the people; something like NJV "have nothing to say" or "the wicked can say nothing against it."

TEV, AT, RSV, NIV, and SPCL join the two verses of verse 39, NIV, TOB, and Dahood connect verse 39 with verse 38, and verse 40 with verse 41. NIV makes the action of verse 40 come before that of verse 39, NAB and FRCL make a full stop at the end of verse 39, and connect verse 40 with verse 41. B1 and NEB treat verses 39-40 as a quatrain, describing how Yahweh dealt with his people. Some

107.43   RSV   TEV

> **Whoever is wise, let him give heed**   verse 39   **May those who are wise think**
> **to these things;**   is an exact replica of Job 12.2.   **about these things;**
> **let men consider the steadfast**   refers back and relates to the passage (see   **may they consider the LORD's**
>   love of the LORD.   Kirkpatrick).   **constant love.**

Everything considered, it seems best to follow the example of RSV and TEV in

The psalm closes with an appeal (RSV, NIV, TEV, NEB) for the listener (or reader) to pay attention to what the psalmist has written, and to reflect on Yahweh's **steadfast love** for his people. The verb in line **b** means "consider, ponder, think about"; see its use in 28.5a, "regard." In Hebrew **steadfast love** is the plural of *chesed* (see 5.7); NAB has "the favors," Dahood "the mercies," Weiser "gracious deeds" (see comments on 89.1).

NJV joins verse 42 to verse 43 as the closing strophe and translates as statements, not as wishes: "The upright see it . . . . The wise man will take note . . . . he will consider." The meaning may also be "Whoever wishes to be wise should think about these things." It seems better to follow the example of RSV and TEV.

Psalm 108

This psalm is composed of material found also in two other psalms: verses 1-5 are identical with 57.7-11, and verses 6-13 are the same as 60.5-12. As it stands here the psalm is a prayer to God for Israel's victory over foreign enemies. In verses 1-4 the psalmist expresses his purpose to praise God for his goodness, and then prays for victory in verses 5-6. God's answer is given in verses 7-9, after which the psalmist once more prays for God's help (verses 10-12), closing the psalm with a confident statement that God will answer his prayer (verse 13).

HEADING: **"A Prayer for Help against Enemies."** Other headings are: "Morning hymn and national prayer"; "Prayer for victory"; "A prayer for God's help." The TEV heading can be adapted to other languages by saying, for example, "The psalmist asks God to defeat Israel's enemies."

Hebrew Title: **A Song. A Psalm of David** (TEV "A psalm by David; a song").

For **Song** see title of Psalm 65.

For comments on this psalm see the text and commentary of 57.7-11 and 60.5-12. Here, only the passages in this psalm that are different from those in the other two psalms will be commented on.

108.1-4 RSV TEV

1	My heart is steadfast, O God, my heart is steadfast! I will sing and make melody! Awake, my soul!	1	I have complete confidence, O God! I will sing and praise you! Wake up, my soul!
2	Awake, O harp and lyre! I will awake the dawn!	2	Wake up, my harp and lyre! I will wake up the sun.
3	I will give thanks to thee, O LORD, among the peoples, I will sing praises to thee among the nations.	3	I will thank you, O LORD, among the nations. I will praise you among the peoples.
4	For thy steadfast love is great above the heavens, thy faithfulness reaches to the clouds.	4	Your constant love reaches above the heavens; your faithfulness touches the skies.

At the end of verse 1a, RSV **my heart is steadfast** is not in the Masoretic text but is found in five Hebrew manuscripts, the Septuagint, and the Syriac (in these it appears as it is in the Masoretic text of 57.5b). TEV here follows the Masoretic text

933

(which is what HOTTP recommends). The expression "**I have complete confidence**" in many languages is expressed by means of figurative language; for example, "My heart lies down on," "My innermost rests on," or "My liver sits on."

In verse 1c **Awake** translates the verb that is in 57.8; the Hebrew text here says simply "now."[1]

Verses 2 and 3 are the same as 57.8b-9, except that LORD in verse 3a translates the divine name, while in 57.9 the title is used.

In verse 4a the Hebrew is "reaches above the heavens"; in 57.10 it is "reaches the heavens." The difference should be reflected in translation. Here the text means that Yahweh's love is so vast that the earth cannot contain it; he extends not only to heaven but goes beyond it.

108.5-6   RSV   TEV

5   Be exalted, O God, above the   5   Show your greatness in the sky, O
       heavens!   God,
       Let thy glory be over all the   and your glory over all the
       earth!   earth.
6   That thy beloved may be delivered,   6   Save us by your might; answer my
       give help by thy right hand, and   prayer,
       answer me!   so that the people you love may
                                                   be rescued.

Verse 5 is exactly like 57.11.

For verse 6 see 60.5. In 6b RSV **give help** translates the same Hebrew verb translated "give victory" in 60.5. The Masoretic text at the end of verse 6b is **answer me**; in 60.5 it is "answer us." It should be noticed that one form of the Hebrew text here has the reading "answer us."

108.7-9   RSV   TEV

7   God   has   promised   in   his   7   From his sanctuary[g] God has
       sanctuary:[y]   said,
       "With exultation I will divide up   "In   triumph   I   will   divide
       Shechem,   Shechem

---

[1]HOTTP translates the phrase "also my glory" and says its function is to make explicit the subject of the two preceding verbs, "I will sing, I will make melody." The phrase is probably a gloss, and translators who use notes may wish to indicate this in a note. In terms of TEV language, the HOTTP suggestion seems to be:

    I have complete confidence, O God!
    And so I myself[*] will sing and praise you.

[*]This phrase, "And so I myself," was probably added to the text to make it more emphatic; the original was "I will sing and praise you."

and portion out the Vale of Succoth.

8 Gilead is mine; Manasseh is mine; Ephraim is my helmet; Judah my scepter.

9 Moab is my washbasin; upon Edom I cast my shoe; over Philistia I shout in triumph."

y Or *by his holiness*

and distribute Sukkoth Valley to my people.

8 Gilead is mine, and Manasseh too; Ephraim is my helmet and Judah my royal scepter.

9 But I will use Moab as my washbowl, and I will throw my sandals on Edom, as a sign that I own it. I will shout in triumph over the Philistines."

g From his sanctuary; *or* In his holiness.

Except for verse 9c, verses 7-9 are exactly the same as 60.6-8.

In verse 7a RSV has **has promised**, whereas it translates the same Hebrew text in 60.6a as "has spoken." The translation should be the same in both passages.

In verse 9c the Hebrew has "I will shout over Philistia"; in 60.8 the Hebrew text is "Philistia will shout over me." (HOTTP does not consider this difference between the two passages.) TEV reflects the difference between the two passages, while RSV has the same translation for the two.

108.10-13   RSV   TEV

10 Who will bring me to the fortified city?
Who will lead me to Edom?

11 Hast thou not rejected us, O God?
Thou dost not go forth, O God, with our armies.

12 O grant us help against the foe, for vain is the help of man!

13 With God we shall do valiantly; it is he who will tread down our foes.

10 Who, O God, will take me into the fortified city?
Who will lead me to Edom?

11 Have you really rejected us? Aren't you going to march out with our armies?

12 Help us against the enemy; human help is worthless.

13 With God on our side we will win; he will defeat our enemies.

Verses 10-13 are the same as 60.9-12, except that in verse 10a **fortified** translates a different word from the one used in 60.9; there is, however, no difference of meaning between the two.

Psalm 109

This psalm is a lament by an individual who is being hounded by his enemies and who cries to the Lord for help. In unusually strong and vivid language he prays that the Lord destroy them—not only them but their whole families as well. The whole list of the evils (verses 6-19) that he prays may fall on his enemies is so awful, in fact, that some commentators and translations take the position that in these verses the psalmist is quoting his enemies' words against himself (Cohen, Weiser, Fisher, Murphy, Toombs). So TOB, BJ, NJB have verses 6-15 as what others are saying against the psalmist; FRCL and GECL have verses 6-19; NIV, in a footnote, proposes this as an alternative.

While this interpretation cannot be ruled out, the following considerations make it quite improbable: (1) there is no indication in the Hebrew text itself that the author's own words stop at verse 5, that he begins to quote his enemies' words at verse 6 and continues through verse 19 (or 15), to resume his own words at verse 20 (or 16). In support of his position, Cohen says that something like "saying" must be understood before verse 6 (see NEB, which limits the "quotation" to verse 6). (2) Much is made of the fact that in verses 1-5 and 20-29 the psalmist speaks of his enemies (plural), while verses 6-19 are directed against one person (who would be the psalmist himself). But it is almost past belief that in verses 16-19 the psalmist would, without a word of protest, quote his enemies' words as though they were a true statement of what he had done (which is probably why some limit the "quotation" to verses 6-15). It seems better to take the singular in verses 6-19 as generic, or else as directed against the leader of the psalmist's enemies. (3) Even if it be granted that verses 6-19 are spoken by the psalmist's enemies, in verse 20 the psalmist prays that the same curses fall on them that they have called down on him—which puts him on an equal footing with them. (4) Although these curses are especially strong, they do not differ in kind from language already encountered elsewhere in Psalms (see, for example, 35.4-6; 58.6-9; 69.22-28). Such language reflects the basic attitude that the psalmist's enemies are, by definition, Yahweh's enemies, and so the psalmist has not only the right but the duty to pray for their defeat and death (see Briggs, Kirkpatrick, Oesterley, McCullough, Anderson, Dahood).

The psalm begins with a cry to God for help (verses 1-5), followed by a long list of punishments the psalmist prays that God inflict on his enemies (verses 6-20). The psalmist renews his cry to God (verses 21-29), and ends the psalm with a promise to praise God for having answered his prayer (verses 30-31).

There is nothing in the text to identify the author or the time when the psalm was composed.

HEADING: **"The Complaint of a Man in Trouble."** Other headings are: "Cursed but confident"; "Imprecatory psalm"; "Prayer against a slanderous enemy."

The TEV heading can be adapted to other languages often by recasting it to say "A man complains to God because he is in trouble."

Hebrew Title: **To the choirmaster. A Psalm of David** (TEV "A psalm by David").

For **To the choirmaster** see title of Psalm 4.

109.1-3 RSV		TEV
1	Be not silent, O God of my praise!	1	I praise you, God; don't remain silent!
2	For wicked and deceitful mouths are opened against me, speaking against me with lying tongues.	2	Wicked men and liars have attacked me. They tell lies about me,
3	They beset me with words of hate, and attack me without cause.	3	and they say evil things about me, attacking me for no reason.

The psalmist begins with a prayer that God not keep quiet or remain inactive in response to his pleas, but that he take action against his enemies (see 28.1; 83.1). **O God of my praise** means "O God, whom I praise." **Be not silent** may have to be recast positively in some languages to say, for example, "God, please do something" or "Answer my plea, God."

The psalmist's enemies are **wicked**; with no reason for doing so, they lie and say evil things about the psalmist (verses 2-3); see similar language in 69.4. In verse 2 the Hebrew has **mouths** as the subject; it is better to speak of people who accuse and revile the psalmist; and in line **b** the expression **lying tongues** can be represented by "liars" or "they tell lies," instead of TEV "have attacked me," which may be taken to mean physical assault. A better translation, for example, may be ". . . say bad things about me" or ". . . slander me."

In verse 3 **words of hate** can be translated "hateful words"; TEV "evil things" is not adequate, since the same Hebrew word "hatred" is used also in verse 5b, and the verb **beset** means surround, encircle.

109.4-5 RSV		TEV
4	In return for my love they accuse me, even as I make prayer for them.[z]	4	They oppose me, even though I love them and have prayed for them.[i]
5	So they reward me evil for good, and hatred for my love.	5	They pay me back evil for good and hatred for love.

[i] *Probable text* have prayed for them; *Hebrew unclear.*

[z] Syr: Heb *I prayer*

Although his enemies attack him for no reason at all, the psalmist loves them and prays for them (verse 4). In verse 4a **accuse** translates the verb *satan* (the synonymous verb translated "contend" in 35.1 may also mean to accuse in a trial). Ordinarily, in English the verb "accuse" is transitive, that is, the one accused must be mentioned, and something like "they accuse me of doing evil things" (or the like) must be said. SPCL has "they attack me," which is better than TEV **"They oppose me."**

Verse 4b in Hebrew is strange; it seems to say simply "and I a prayer." NEB emends the text to get "though I have done nothing unseemly"; NJV translates the Masoretic text "and I must stand judgment" (with the footnote "Or 'but I am all prayer.' ") The majority render the text as RSV and TEV do; HOTTP says the Masoretic text means "while I did but pray." NIV "but I am a man of prayer" does not fit in the context.

The psalmist protests that he is completely innocent and has given his enemies no reason for their hatred (verse 5); for similar language see 35.12; 38.20. Instead of abstract nouns, verbal phrases may be better in translating this verse:

> I do good things for them,
>> but they pay me back with bad things;
> I love them, but they hate me.

109.6-7

	RSV		TEV
6	Appoint a wicked man against him; let an accuser bring him to trial.[a]	6	Choose some corrupt judge to try my enemy, and let one of his own enemies accuse him.
7	When he is tried, let him come forth guilty; let his prayer be counted as sin!	7	May he be tried and found guilty; may even his prayer be considered a crime!

[a] Heb *stand at his right hand*

The psalmist begins the long list of misfortunes he calls down upon his enemy by praying that the man will be brought to trial before a corrupt judge. It is to be noticed that the singular "enemy" is used throughout (see introduction to this psalm); Dahood believes that the setting of the psalm is a court where the psalmist is standing trial, and that his prayer is directed against the judge and the false witnesses, who are bent on his destruction.

In verse 6a TEV **"corrupt judge"** translates "an evil man" (NIV); the rest of the line in Hebrew may be translated either "over him" (NJV), which indicates a judge (so Kirkpatrick, Briggs; TEV, GECL, SPCL), or **against him** (RSV), which indicates an accuser, parallel with line b (so RSV, BJ, NJB, NEB, TOB). If the translator follows TEV **"corrupt judge,"** it will be necessary in some languages to say, for example, "a judge whose eyes are closed with money."

Verse 6b is literally "and make an accuser stand at his right," the Hebrew word for "accuser" being *satan,* which KJV translates "Satan." Dahood does the same, taking "the Evil One" in line a to be parallel to "Satan" in line b; Dahood believes that the trial takes place after death. Most commentators believe that the Hebrew noun *satan* in the Old Testament refers to a nonhuman being only in 1 Chronicles

21.1; Job 1.6-12; 2.1-7; Zechariah 3.1,2. It appears that the accuser stood at the right of the person on trial (see Zech 3.1; but see verse 31, below). SPCL translates "May his own lawyer condemn him" (similarly GECL).

Verse 7b is difficult to understand; the Masoretic text appears to mean "and let his prayer be for sin." Some take the word translated "prayer" to mean the plea to the judge (see NAB "may his plea be in vain"; SPCL "may his defense result in his condemnation"); but nowhere else in the Old Testament does the Hebrew word for **prayer** mean anything other than prayer addressed to God. The general sense can be that the man's protestations of innocence, in which he would invoke the name of God, would only add to his guilt, since they would obviously be false. In some languages the two requests in English beginning in TEV with **"May he . . . may even his . . ."** must be shifted to imperatives, in which case God will have to be introduced as the primary or secondary agent who will perform the requested action. For example, "God, try him and declare him guilty, consider even his prayer a crime!" or "I ask God to try him and find him guilty, to consider even his prayer a crime."

<u>109.8-10</u>   RSV   TEV

8   May his days be few;   8   May his life soon be ended;
       may another seize his goods!   may another man take his job!
9   May his children be fatherless,   9   May his children become orphans,
       and his wife a widow!   and his wife a widow!
10   May his children wander about   10   May his children be homeless
       and beg;   beggars;
       may they be driven out of^b the   may they be driven from^j the
       ruins they inhabit!   ruins they live in!

^{b} Gk: Heb *and seek* ^{j} *One ancient translation* be driven from;
                                              Hebrew seek.

In verses 8-9 the psalmist prays for his enemy's premature death, with its devastating consequences on his family. In verse 8b **"his job"** (or NJV, BJ, TOB "his position," or NJB, NAB, Dahood "his office") is one possible meaning of the Hebrew word; it can be taken to mean **goods** (RSV, SPCL) or "hoarded wealth" (NEB). In any case, the petition has in view the man's death. This line is quoted in Acts 1.20b as it appears in the Septuagint (except for a difference in the mood of the verb **"take"**); the Greek word *episkopē* means "place of oversight," "office." (Because of the application of this line to Judas Iscariot in Acts 1.20, this psalm has been called *Psalmus Ischarioticus*.)

Verse 9 repeats the request for the man's premature death, so that his children will become orphans and his wife a widow.

Verse 10 concentrates on the situation of the man's children after his death. Line <u>b</u> in Hebrew is difficult to understand; it seems to mean "may they seek from their ruins"; NJV takes it to mean "from their hovels . . . in search of [bread]." TOB has "may they beg outside of their ruins." But the majority, instead of the Masoretic text "may they search," prefer to follow the Septuagint **"may they be driven from"** (so RSV, TEV, NAB, NIV, TOB, BJ, NJB); NEB manages to represent the Masoretic text by translating the verb "may they seek" by the noun "beggars," and taking "from their ruins" to mean "driven from their ruins."[1]

It is uncertain what is the exact force of **the ruins** in this context; either it is their ruined homes, or else other ruins in which they are forced to live. The following verse makes the second choice the more likely one.

109.11-13 RSV   TEV

11 May the creditor seize all that he	**11 May his creditors take away all**
has;	**his property,**
may strangers plunder the	**and may strangers get every-**
fruits of his toil!	**thing he worked for.**
12 Let there be none to extend kind-	**12 May no one ever be kind to him**
ness to him,	**or care for the orphans he**
nor any to pity his fatherless	**leaves behind.**
children!	**13 May all his descendants die,**
13 May his posterity be cut off;	**and may his name be forgotten**
may his name be blotted out in	**in the next generation.**
the second generation!	

The prayer continues in the same mood; the psalmist hopes that after his enemy's death "his creditors" (or **the creditor**), that is, the people or the person he owed money to, will come and take possession of all his belongings. And in the next line (verse 11b) even **strangers** are to get "everything he worked for" (Hebrew **the fruits of his toil**). For an example of the power of creditors, see 2 Kings 4.1.

In verse 12a **kindness** translates *chesed* (see 5.7), which usually is an attribute of God, "constant love." In verse 12b the verb "to have pity" may have the active sense of "be kind to," "be concerned about."

Not only does the psalmist pray for his enemy's death, but also for the death of his descendants, so that the family line will disappear (verse 13). For similar language see 9.5. In verse 13b the Masoretic text has "their name," that is, the name of his descendants (verse 13a); many Hebrew manuscripts and the Septuagint have **his name**, which is preferred by RSV, TEV, and SPCL. NJV, NIV, TOB, and NEB follow the Masoretic text—either reading makes good sense. **The second generation** means the one following the generation of the man himself; so TEV "the next generation." In languages which do not use the passive, it will be necessary to adjust the expression "may his name be forgotten . . ." to say, for example, "may the people in the next generation forget about him," or negatively, ". . . not remember who he was."

---

[1] HOTTP ("C" decision) stays with the Masoretic text. The whole line is then to be translated "and may they beg far from their ruins."

109.14-15 RSV   TEV

14 May the iniquity of his fathers be remembered before the LORD, and let not the sin of his mother be blotted out!	14 May the LORD remember the evil of his ancestors and never forgive his mother's sins.
15 Let them be before the LORD continually; and may his^c memory be cut off from the earth!	15 May the LORD always remember their sins, but may they themselves be completely forgotten!

^c Gk: Heb *their*

Even his enemy's ancestors are included (verse 14). In the two lines of verse 14, **be remembered** and **not . . . be blotted out** are both ways of asking God not to forgive those people. For a similar use of the verb "blot out" in this sense, see 51.1d. Because of the mention of **his mother** in line **b**, some either change the Masoretic text **his fathers** in line **a** to "his father" (Oesterley), or else, like Dahood (also SPCL), take the Masoretic text **his fathers** to be a plural of excellence, meaning "his father." It is recommended that the Masoretic text be followed, taking it in the sense of "his ancestors"; "his father" requires a textual footnote. NJV, strangely enough, has the singular "his father's iniquity" without textual footnote (similarly SPCL); FRCL translates **his fathers** by "his father and his grandfather."

In verse 15a **them** means **the iniquity** and **the sin** of verse 14a,b; to **be before the LORD** here means that the Lord is not to forget or forgive.

In verse 15b TEV **"they themselves"** translates the Masoretic text and ancient versions "their memory"; here "memory" (as in 9.6) means what people remember about the **fathers** and the **mother**. RSV prefers to follow one manuscript of the Septuagint that has the singular **his memory**, referring to the memory of the psalmist's enemy (so Briggs, Oesterley). **Be cut off** translates the passive form of the verb "cut off," which appears in two Hebrew manuscripts, the Septuagint, and Jerome; the Masoretic text has the active form "may he cut off," that is, may Yahweh do it (the only difference between the two forms of the verb is in the vowels used). NJV, NEB, NAB, NJB, BJ, FRCL, GECL, NIV, TOB, SPCL all follow the Masoretic text, which is probably to be preferred.

109.16-17 RSV   TEV

16 For he did not remember to show kindness, but pursued the poor and needy and the brokenhearted to their death.	16 That man never thought of being kind; he persecuted and killed the poor, the needy, and the helpless.
17 He loved to curse; let curses come on him! He did not like blessing; may it be far from him!	17 He loved to curse—may he be cursed! He hated to give blessings—may no one bless him!

941

Verse 16 in Hebrew begins with "Because" (or "On account of"), stating the reason why the psalmist is calling down God's punishment on his enemy. **To show kindness** translates the phrase "to do *chesed*" (see verse 12a); NEB has "never set himself to be loyal to his friend." **Pursued . . . to their death** is well rendered by TEV, **"persecuted and killed."** In line c TEV **"the helpless"** translates **brokenhearted**, which indicates either intense suffering, or else discouraged, disheartened, dispirited, which seems more likely here (NJV "one crushed in spirit," FRCL "a deeply depressed man").

Some take verses 17-18 to be purely descriptive, with no wishes expressed by the psalmist; so Briggs, Kirkpatrick; AT, TOB, Dahood. Actually the vowels provided in the Masoretic text do make them descriptive; but it only requires a change of vowels to make them wishes (following the Septuagint, Jerome) (so RSV, TEV, NEB, NAB, BJ, NJB, FRCL, SPCL).[2]

In verse 17 **to curse** and **curses** do not mean the use of vulgar or obscene language, but a plea to God to send misfortunes on another person. SPCL is able to do it well: "Since he preferred to pronounce malediction, may others do the same to him!" (*la maldicion . . . maldigan*). **"To give blessings"** may sometimes be rendered "to ask God to do good to other people" or "to ask God to give good things to others."

	RSV		TEV
18	He clothed himself with cursing as his coat, may it soak into his body like water, like oil into his bones!	18	He cursed as naturally as he dressed himself; may his own curses soak into his body like water and into his bones like oil!
19	May it be like a garment which he wraps round him, like a belt with which he daily girds himself!	19	May they cover him like clothes and always be around him like a belt!

In verse 18a the psalmist compares his enemy's cursing to wearing clothes; TEV takes this to mean **"He cursed as naturally as he dressed himself"**; but the language may be a figure for the constancy, not the ease, with which he uttered curses on others. So a translation can be "He cursed others all the time" or "He never stopped cursing others." NJB translates "Cursing has been the uniform he wore." But NJV and SPCL translate this as a plea: "May he be clothed in a curse like a garment," which means that the curses against him are to cling to him like the clothes he wears (as

---

[2]HOTTP proposes the following as the translation of verses 16-19:

16 because he did not remember . . . , (because) he persecuted the poor man . . . , 17 (because) he loved cursing (so much so) that it went far from him, 18 (because) he clothed himself with the cursing . . . (so much so) that it came like . . . , 19 (for all that,) may that become for him a garment . . . .

in verse 19, but this interpretation is not preferred). In verse 18b,c, by the use of a rather unusual figure, the psalmist hopes that those curses the enemy pronounced on others might **soak into his body like water** and **like oil**. Of course water can enter the body (literally "the inside"; see "within me" in 103.1) when someone drinks it, but olive oil is spread over the body and was thought to seep into the bones. So GECL has ". . . like water that one drinks, like oil which one rubs on oneself." SPCL translates "may it [the malediction] enter his stomach and his bones as though it were water and olive oil." Some see in this figure a reference to the ritual described in Numbers 5.11-31, in which a married woman suspected of adultery had to drink a liquid which contained a curse (see especially verses 23 and 27). There is perhaps a degree of intensification involved in the movement through the lines in this verse. This is contained mainly in the process of moving from the outside of the body (the garment) to the inside of the body, and finally into the bones. A suggested rendering can be:

> He cursed as regularly as he put on his clothes.
> May his curses even enter his body like the water he drinks,
> And may they go on to reach like oil down to his bones.

The same wish is expressed in another fashion in verse 19, that these curses always cover the enemy **like a garment** and **like a belt**, that is, that they hang on to him and never let go of him.

109.20-22 RSV	TEV
20 May this be the reward of my accusers from the LORD, of those who speak evil against my life!	20 LORD, punish my enemies in that way— those who say such evil things against me!
21 But thou, O GOD my Lord, deal on my behalf for thy name's sake; because thy steadfast love is good, deliver me!	21 But my Sovereign LORD, help me as you have promised, and rescue me because of the goodness of your love.
22 For I am poor and needy, and my heart is stricken within me.	22 I am poor and needy; I am hurt to the depths of my heart.

In verse 20 the psalmist, in summary, asks the Lord to punish his enemies with all the misfortunes listed in verses 6-19. Some translations attach this verse to the end of the preceding strophe (RSV, NJV, SPCL); TEV, NIV, BJ, NJB, FRCL, NAB connect it to what follows; TOB separates it from both. Perhaps it is better to join it to verse 19 as the summary of the preceding verses.

TEV uses the second person of address to God, consistently with the second person in the next verse. **Accusers** in line a translates the same word used in verse 6b. It should be noted that RSV's placing of **from the Lord** may make it appear that it goes with **accusers**; of course it goes with **the reward**.

In verse 20b TEV **"against me"** translates "against my *nefesh*"; RSV <u>against my life</u> is an unnatural, literal rendition of the Hebrew.

In verse 21 <u>GOD my Lord</u> translates the unusual "Yahweh, my lord"—the divine name and the title; for **thy name's sake** (TEV **"as you have promised"**) see 23.3 and comments. In the last line of verse 21, <u>thy steadfast love is good</u> is a rather unusual statement; something like "because of your love and your goodness" or "because you are good and you love me" may be a good translation; see NJV "Good and faithful as you are." **Deliver** translates the verb used in 7.1.

In verse 22b TEV **"I am hurt"** translates the verb "to be pierced" (see NJV, NJB, NAB, Dahood); this means distress, anguish, emotional turmoil and pain. The ancient versions presuppose another Hebrew verb, "to writhe (in pain)," which Briggs prefers.

<u>**109.23-25**</u>　　　　RSV　　　　　　　　　　　　　　　　　TEV

23　I am gone, like a shadow at eve-　23　Like an evening shadow I am
　　　　ning;　　　　　　　　　　　　　　　　about to vanish;
　　I am shaken off like a locust.　　　　I am blown away like an insect.
24　My knees are weak through fast-　24　My knees are weak from lack of
　　　　ing;　　　　　　　　　　　　　　　　food;
　　my body has become gaunt.　　　　　I am nothing but skin and
25　I am an object of scorn to my　　　　bones.
　　　　accusers;　　　　　　　　　25　When people see me, they laugh at
　　when they see me, they wag　　　　　me;
　　　　their heads.　　　　　　　　　　they shake their heads in scorn.

The psalmist is near death; he compares himself to <u>a shadow at evening</u> (see 102.11 and comments); the Hebrew is "like a lengthening shadow," a way of referring to the end of the day, when the shadows grow longer. In verse 23b the psalmist compares himself to <u>a locust</u> (see 78.46) that is **"blown away"** by the wind. But the verb translated **"blown away"** (TEV, SPCL) may be taken to mean <u>shaken off</u> (RSV), in which case the figure is that of locusts being shaken off the plants (see NAB footnote) or off a garment (Cohen, McCullough; FRCL footnote). The Hebrew verb in other places means "shake" (Neh 5.13; Job 38.13; Isa 33.9; Psa 136.15 "over-threw"), and that is probably the meaning intended here (RSV; also NEB, FRCL, NJB, NJV, NIV). **"I am blown away like an insect"** may have to be shifted to an active construction; for example, "I am like a locust which the wind blows away," or if the locust is unknown and the verb is interpreted as <u>shaken off</u>, the translator may prefer to say "I am like an insect that a farmer shakes off a plant."

The psalmist speaks of his feeble condition (verse 24). The **"lack of food"** here may be a reference to the loss of appetite (see 107.18); some think this is voluntary fasting, which the psalmist underwent as he awaited his trial (see Dahood, Anderson). Most translations, like RSV, have <u>fasting</u>. In verse 24b the text can be understood in two different ways, depending on whether the final Hebrew phrase *mishshamen* means "from fatness" or "from olive oil." In the former case the line means "my body is lean from lack of fat" (that is, either the body fat as such or nourishing food); in the latter case, "my body is lean from lack of olive oil." A mourner refrained from rubbing olive oil on the body (see 2 Sam 14.2). The former is favored by RSV, TEV, NEB, NAB, NJV, SPCL, NIV, NJB, FRCL; the latter by Briggs, Kirkpatrick; AT, BJ, TOB. TEV has chosen to express the meaning quite idiomatically (as in 102.5b).

For expressions similar to that in verse 25a, see 22.6; 31.11; 89.41. At the end of the line the Hebrew text has "to them," which RSV takes to mean **to my accusers**; TEV takes it to mean people in general. For language similar to verse 25b, see 22.7.

109.26-27 RSV TEV

26 Help me, O LORD my God!   26   Help me, O LORD my God;
    Save me according to thy   because of your constant love,
    steadfast love!   save me!
27 Let them know that this is thy   27   Make my enemies know
    hand;   that you are the one who saves
    thou, O LORD, hast done it!   me.

For the plea in verse 26, see similar requests in 6.4; 31.16b. Line <u>b</u> can be translated "Your love is constant (or, never stops); therefore, help me!"

In verse 27a the Hebrew is "and may they know that this is your hand," followed by "(that) you, Yahweh, did it." Perhaps the psalmist is referring to his distress (so Anderson), but it seems more likely he is absolutely certain that Yahweh will answer his plea and save him, and so he prays that his enemies will see and recognize that Yahweh has saved him. The expression **this is thy hand** may be represented more explicitly than TEV has done, as follows: "May my enemies know that you have acted, that you are the one who saved me." It seems best to say, at the end, "who saved me," rather than "who did it." TEV omits as unnecessary the vocative **O LORD** in verse 27b; translators are advised to include it.

109.28-29 RSV TEV

28 Let them curse, but do thou bless!   28   They may curse me, but you will
    Let my assailants be put to   bless me.
    shame;^{d} may thy servant be   May my persecutors be
    glad!   defeated,^{k}
29 May my accusers be clothed with   and may I, your servant, be
    dishonor;   glad!
    may they be wrapped in their   29   May my enemies be covered with
    own shame as in a mantle!   disgrace;
                                may they wear their shame like
^{d} Gk: Heb *they have arisen and have*   a robe.
been put to shame

                            ^{k} *One ancient translation* May my perse-
                            cutors be defeated; *Hebrew* They perse-
                            cuted me and were defeated.

Verse 28a in Hebrew has no direct object for the verbs **curse** and **bless**; TEV, SPCL, and GECL provide the direct object "**me**."

Verse 28b in Hebrew is "they arose and were put to shame"; TEV, RSV, NEB, and NAB follow the Septuagint. Other translations in various ways represent the Masoretic text: FRCL "If they attack me, they will be made to look ridiculous"; TOB "They raised themselves up, (and) this proved to be their shame"; NIV translates "when they attack they will be put to shame." HOTTP ("C" decision) says the Masoretic text means "they may stand up, but they will be put to shame." The Masoretic text can make good sense in the context, if the verb "they arose" can be understood as a precative perfect (Dahood), that is, as expressing not a statement of fact but a desire: "let them arise." This is how it is translated by NJV, "let them rise up, but come to grief," and by Dahood, "Let them rise up, only to be humiliated." This seems to be the best way to translate this line. In languages which do not use the passive, the plea "**May my persecutors be defeated**" will have to be recast to say something like "God, defeat the people who persecute me." At the end of the verse, TEV "**I, your servant**" makes the identification explicit, that the psalmist is talking about himself.

The prayer in verse 29 is similar to those in 35.26c,d; 71.13. The figure of clothing is like that in verses 18a,19a. For **accusers** in line a see verses 4 and 20.

RSV	TEV
30 With my mouth I will give great thanks to the LORD; I will praise him in the midst of the throng.	30 I will give loud thanks to the LORD; I will praise him in the assembly of the people,
31 For he stands at the right hand of the needy, to save him from those who condemn him to death.	31 because he defends the poor man and saves him from those who condemn him to death.

The psalm closes with a promise to praise the Lord publicly, in the Temple, because he answered the psalmist's prayer (see similar language in 22.22; 107.32).

In verse 30a **give great thanks** means to be lavish and persistent in praising Yahweh; "I will praise him greatly." This does not necessarily involve "**loud thanks**," as TEV says. **The throng** in verse 30b is the people assembled in the Temple for worship.

In verse 31a TEV "**he defends**" translates "he stands at the right of" (see 16.8b; 110.5a). Here it appears that the person's defender stood at that person's right (see verse 6, above). Or the meaning may be "he stands ready to help the needy." **The needy** (see 12.5) translates the singular form in Hebrew; here a plural form, "the needy" (NJV, NJB), is better than TEV's generic singular "**the poor man**."

In verse 31b the Hebrew is "to save him from those who judge his *nefesh*," which is taken by most as RSV and TEV have done. NEB emends the text to get "from his accusers," but this seems hardly necessary.

Psalm 110

This royal psalm, like Psalm 2, was composed to celebrate the enthronement of a king, who is chosen by Yahweh and is promised victory over his enemies.

There is much disagreement concerning the time of its composition, with opinions ranging from the tenth century B.C. to the Maccabean age, in the second century B.C. By and large modern scholarship tends to regard it as an ancient composition; Anderson says that it "may well be one of the oldest poems in the Psalter" (see also Dahood, McCullough, Weiser).

By the time of Jesus it was interpreted as referring to the Messiah; it is clear from the passages in the Gospels (Matt 22.41-46; Mark 12.35-37; Luke 20.41-44) that Jesus' hearers agreed with him that the psalm spoke of the Messiah. In the New Testament this psalm (verses 1,4) is applied to Christ and is quoted more often than any other Old Testament passage.

The text, as Dentan says, is unusually corrupt, and there is little if any general agreement on its meaning in several places, especially verses 2-4.

HEADING: "**The LORD and His Chosen King**." Other headings are: "The priest-king"; "The LORD gives power to the king"; "The Messiah: king and priest." The TEV heading may be adjusted to use in other languages by saying, for example, "The LORD makes promises to the king he has chosen" or "The LORD promises his king the victory."

Hebrew Title: **A Psalm of David** (TEV "A psalm by David").

110.1 RSV	TEV
The LORD says to my lord: "Sit at my right hand, till I make your enemies your footstool."	The LORD said to my lord, the king, "Sit here at my right side until I put your enemies under your feet."

The psalm begins with Yahweh's command to the psalmist's **lord**. The Hebrew word translated **says** is a noun which is often used of God's message, "utterance, saying"; the Hebrew phrase "utterance of Yahweh" occurs only here in Psalms. Some translations therefore avoid using a verb: AT "An oracle of the Lord"; Dahood "Yahweh's utterance"; FRCL "Statement of the Lord God." Most translations that have a verb, use the past tense "**said**," as TEV has done; RSV and NIV have **says**. The past tense is preferable. GECL translates "God, the Lord, has sent word to you, to you, my lord and king . . . ."

Yahweh speaks to **my lord**, who is the king (see commentaries, and footnotes to TOB, RSV Oxford Edition, NEB Oxford Edition). TEV, FRCL, and GECL make this explicit.[1] In many languages the term often used for God (Lord) cannot be used to refer to the king; for this reason the confusion that appears in English and other languages may not be present. However, if the same term is used, it is best, as in TEV, to add "the king." Yahweh invites him to sit at the place of honor, "my right side" (see 45.9 and comments). In languages in which the right side does not carry the meaning of "place of honor," it is sometimes advisable to say, for example, "on my right side, which is the place of honor" or "to my right, where I give you honor."

The preposition translated **till** (verse 1c) may be rendered "while" (NJV); NEB has "when," with two alternatives, "until" or "while." BJ translates "since I have made." **Till** or "**until**" implies that the command to the king to sit at Yahweh's right is good only until the complete victory over his enemies; in order to avoid this implication, TOB has "for I am about to make," FRCL "I am going to compel," and GECL "I will submit your enemies to you." The Hebrew **footstool** is used here as a symbol of the complete victory of the king over his enemies; see the passage where the victorious captains place their feet on the necks of their defeated foes (Josh 10.24). In some languages the figurative language may not be appropriate, so something like "I will place your enemies under your power" or "I will make you defeat your enemies" may be better.

In the New Testament this passage is applied to the risen Christ, who reigns in power at God's right side in heaven (Acts 2.32-36; Eph 1.20-21; Col 3.1; Heb 1.13; 8.1; 10.12-13).

110.2

RSV	TEV
The LORD sends forth from Zion your mighty scepter. Rule in the midst of your foes!	From Zion the LORD will extend your royal power. "Rule over your enemies," he says.

Line **a** is a promise that the king's rule will extend from Jerusalem (**Zion**), where he reigns. **Your mighty scepter** is a figure of domination, of the king's power; but it is not clear how the Hebrew "from Zion" is to be understood. TEV takes it to mean that the king's dominion will reach out from Jerusalem, the capital city, to other lands; see NJB "from Zion you will rule your foes all around you." It may mean, as NEB and SPCL have it, that Yahweh, who is in Zion, gives to the king the symbol of his power, the royal scepter. Some translate the words as a wish, not a

---

[1]It should be noted that FRCL has *à mon Seigneur, le roi*; it is not certain what the capital letter *S* indicates—presumably a royal title, without any intimations of divinity; but TOB has only *à mon seigneur*. GECL is *meinem Herrn und König*; but since nouns in German are capitalized, this presumably means "my lord and king." Both the Brazilian and the Portuguese Common Language translations have "my lord, the king." NIV has "The LORD says to my Lord." The Living Bible makes the psalmist write like a Christian: "Jehovah said to my Lord the Messiah."

statement (Crim; TOB, FRCL): "May the LORD extend your power . . . ." "**From Zion . . . will extend**" may also be rendered "The LORD will make you powerful beyond the city of Zion."

TEV has taken the command "**Rule over your enemies**" to be spoken by Yahweh; most translations take it to be addressed to the king by the psalmist. Some translate this line as a statement (see NJB, NIV); but it is better to keep it as a command (if by Yahweh) or a fervent wish (if by the psalmist). In the coronation ritual it would have been spoken by a priest (see Anderson). The Hebrew "in the middle of your enemies" may be translated "(rule) over the enemies who surround you" (FRCL).

110.3	RSV	TEV

RSV	TEV
Your people will offer themselves freely	On the day you fight your ene-mies,
on the day you lead your host upon the holy mountains.^{e}	your people will volunteer.
From the womb of the morning like dew your youth^f will come to you.	Like the dew of early morning your young men will come to you on the sacred hills.^{m}

^{m} *Verse 3 in Hebrew is unclear.*

^{e} Another reading is *in holy array*
^{f} Cn: Heb *the dew of your youth*

There is no way adequately to summarize the many reasons for the varied interpretations of this verse. HOTTP has six separate notes on this one verse, and the majority of the Committee recommends the following translation: "With you the princely dignity on the day <when> you <display> your power, on the holy mountains; from the womb of the dawn go forth as dew (or: <I said> of you: as dew), I have begotten you." The comment follows: "This is the most probable interpretation according to the criteria of textual analysis." A minority of the Committee recommends: "Your people follows willingly on the day <when> your power <is displayed> in holy splendor. From the womb of the dawn, to you <belongs> the dew of your youth!" And the minority states: "This is the form of the Masoretic text." Neither interpretation is presented in clear language.

Let us examine the Hebrew text and the various proposals offered.

The first half-line is "your people (are) voluntary offerings." The noun means "free will" (see "freewill offering" in 54.6); here RSV translates **will offer themselves freely**; TEV "**will volunteer**"; NJV "come forward willingly." **Your people** translates *'amka*; but the Septuagint and Vulgate "with you" translate *'imka*, which involves only the change of a vowel. And the next word, "voluntary offerings," is changed by some to a form meaning "the princes," with the resultant meaning "with you are the princes" or "with you is princely power" (so, approximately, the Septuagint and Vulgate). NEB translates this half-line "you were endowed with princely gifts."

The next half-line is "on the day of your power." The last noun in the Hebrew can mean "power, strength, wealth, army, nobility." Here it is taken to mean battle, both by RSV **on the day you lead your host** and by TEV "**On the day you fight your** enemies"; SPCL has "On the day of your victory," NJV "on your day of battle," and FRCL "on the day you mobilize your army." Anderson thinks that "the day of your power" refers to "the day of the enthronement of the King." But the word translated "your power" may be given different vowels to mean "your birth"; so NEB "at birth." (If the text is understood to mean "your birth," it could refer to the day of the enthronement; see similar language in 2.7.) BJ, NJB, and NAB follow this interpretation: "Royal dignity has been yours from the day of your birth" (NJB).

Dentan says that the meaning of the second half of the verse "can no longer be recovered with certainty."

The next line in the Masoretic text begins "in holy ornaments" (or, in holy array); BJ "the holy honors"; NJV "In majestic holiness"; TOB "with holy splendor." But instead of *behadrey* "ornaments" of the Masoretic text, many Hebrew manuscripts have *beharrey* "mountains"—which RSV, TEV, FRCL, and others prefer. TEV, FRCL, and SPCL connect it with what follows, while RSV connects it with what precedes.

The next phrase in the Masoretic text means "from the womb from the dawn"; it is possible to take it to mean, as most do, **from the womb of the morning**. There is much disagreement over the meaning of the phrase in this context; there are probably mythological allusions whose exact significance now escapes us. See Weiser, who speaks of "the magnificent word-pictures, borrowed from myth, of the dew that abundantly flows from the womb of the dawn and refreshes Nature in the early morning."

The rest of the line is "to you the dew of your young men." It is probable that "dew" is a figure of freshness and vigor. (1) Some, like RSV, TEV, and Weiser, prefer to change to "**Like the dew**." (2) The Masoretic text *leka* "to you" can have its vowels changed to *lak* "go" (so HOTTP). (3) Instead of the Masoretic text "your young men," some Hebrew manuscripts and early versions have "I have begotten you." (It is to be noted that RSV **your youth** means "your young people," not "your young age"; the word **youth** here is ambiguous.)

Probably the best way to show how this second part of the verse may be understood is to cite some of the translations. NEB has "At your birth you were endowed with princely gifts and resplendent in holiness. You have shone with the dew of youth since your mother bore you." NJV has "In majestic holiness, from the womb, from the dawn, yours was the dew of youth." NJB has "Royal dignity has been yours from the day of your birth, sacred honor from the womb, from the dawn of your youth." SPCL "on the sacred hills, and like the dew that appears at dawn, your youth renews itself from day to day." FRCL "On the sacred mountains your young men come to you, like the dew born from the dawn." And GECL has "Festively adorned, as fresh as the day at dawn, your young recruits gather themselves to you." If nothing else, TEV makes sense; but it cannot be proven that it correctly translates the text.

It should be added that Dahood's translation of this verse bears little resemblance to those cited.

110.4   RSV   TEV

The LORD has sworn   The LORD made a solemn promise
  and will not change his mind,   and will not take it back:
"You are a priest for ever   "You will be a priest forever
  after the order of Melchizedek."   in the priestly order of Melchi-
                               zedek."[n]

> [n] in the priestly order of Melchizedek;
> *or* like Melchizedek; *or* in the line of
> succession to Melchizedek.

It is commonly assumed that these words are also addressed to the king; some, however, believe that this is a promise which the king, who speaks in Yahweh's name, makes to the priest.

In line a the verb **sworn** means "took a solemn vow" or "**made a solemn promise**" (TEV), and not "cursed."

Most translations are like RSV and TEV in the interpretation of the promise; this interpretation goes back to the Septuagint, which is also quoted in the New Testament (Heb 5.6; 7.17,21). The word translated by TEV "**in the priestly order**" means "manner" (so TOB "in the manner of") and is generally translated **order** (following the lead of the Septuagint); SPCL has "of the same category as Melchizedek." NEB has "in the succession of Melchizedek," and FRCL "in the tradition of Melchizedek." But the form of the Hebrew word is such that some understand it to mean "because of me" (so AT "You shall be a priest for life, a Melchizedek, because of me"; also NJV). **After the order of . . .** or TEV's footnote "**in the line of succession to . . .**" may also be rendered in some languages "like those who followed behind Melchizedek" or "like others who came after . . . ."

Melchizedek was the Canaanite king and priest of Jerusalem, when it was still a Jebusite city (Gen 14.18-20). The name is a compound: the first element, *malki*, means "my king"; the second element, *tsedeq*, means "righteousness" (see the point made in Heb 7.2). Some doubt that the Hebrew word is a proper name; Dahood translates "his legitimate king," and NJV "a rightful king (by My decree)." It seems better to understand it as a proper name.

110.5-6   RSV   TEV

5 The Lord is at your right hand;   5 The Lord is at your right side;
    he will shatter kings on the day   when he becomes angry, he will
      of his wrath.   defeat kings.
6 He will execute judgment among   6 He will pass judgment on the
      the nations,   nations
    filling them with corpses;   and fill the battlefield with
  he will shatter chiefs[g]   corpses;
    over the wide earth.   he will defeat kings all over the
                              earth.

[g] Or *the head*

The king is promised God's protection: the Lord will win victory for him over his enemies. The Lord stands by him, at his right side, to protect him. The **day of his wrath** in verse 5b further defines **He will execute judgment** in verse 6a; these refer to the day of the Lord, when he will judge all peoples on earth. The verb translated "defeat" in verse 5b (literally "break in pieces") is in the perfect tense (see TOB, NEB "has broken"); some translate it as a timeless present (NJV, BJ, NJB, TOB, FRCL); it seems better to take it to speak of future action, as the tense is sometimes used (RSV, TEV, SPCL, NIV).

This psalm is particularly difficult to hear read and to read in most translations. For example, in TEV verse 1 God tells the king to sit at God's right hand. In verse 4 it is God (The LORD) who makes a solemn promise (to the king), but in verse 5 it is the Lord (king) who is at "**your** (God's) **right side**." In 5b it is the king who will defeat his enemies, but in verse 1 it is God who will put the king's enemies under the king's feet. There are two principal sources which create the confusions which arise in reading this psalm: the use of "Lord" referring to God and to the king, and the change in speakers. In languages in which a single term such as "Lord" is used for both God and the king, it is possible to identify the Lord as being God, and not depend entirely on the use of capitals, as TEV and RSV do; for example, "God, who is the Lord, said to my lord the king." In line 2a the translator may again say "God, the Lord . . . ." The same may be repeated in lines 4a and 5a. *The Living Bible* has "Jehovah said to my Lord the Messiah." This is a case of reading Matthew back into the Psalm and then translating it from Matthew's perspective. The task of the translator is to translate the text of the Old Testament, not to revise it in the light of the New Testament.

Most traditional and modern versions provide quotes to indicate that God is the speaker of "Sit at my right hand" (verse 1) and "You are a priest for ever . . ." (verse 4). However, TEV alone makes God the speaker of "Rule over your enemies" (verse 2). GECL continues the quote from verse 1b to the end of verse 3. This does not seem to be satisfactory, for the subject in verse 2 is clearly Yahweh, and by including verse 2a in the quote, Yahweh is made to speak of himself in the third person. It is, however, possible to consider verse 3 as a continuation of the quote in verse 2b. In any event the translator should make an effort to make clear the words spoken by God and to identify them as such.

Again it can be helpful for the reader if the translator considers adjusting line 5a to say, for example, "God, who is the Lord, is at your right side, King," or in some languages, "God the Lord is close to you, King, to help you."

Verse 6b translates the Hebrew "he will fill with corpses"; TEV supplies "**the battlefield**," while RSV has **them**, referring back to **the nations** of the preceding line. Instead of the Masoretic text **corpses**, some ancient versions have "valleys." NEB emends to "majesty."

In verse 6c **he will shatter chiefs** translates "he will shatter the head" (see RSV footnote), which some take literally (NAB, SPCL, TOB, NJV, NJB, BJ; see 68.21); others, like RSV, TEV, NIV, GECL, and FRCL, take the word as a figure for rulers.

RSV   TEV

He will drink from the brook by the way; therefore he will lift up his head.	The king will drink from the stream by the road, and strengthened, he will stand victorious.

The meaning of this verse is not clear in the context of the psalm. The subject of the action is not made explicit in the Hebrew, but it is most certainly the king, not Yahweh, as RSV has it. TEV, FRCL, GECL, and TOB footnote make this explicit: "**The king will drink.**" Some conjecture the verse to be a fragment of another composition. It may refer to a part of the ritual of enthronement (see Toombs, Anderson).

To **lift up his head** (line **b**) is probably a sign of victory (see 3.3; 27.6). Most, like RSV, translate quite literally; SPCL has "and the water will renew his strength." **He will lift up his head**, which TEV renders "**strengthened, he will stand victorious,**" can be expressed in some languages as "he will be great because he has defeated his enemies." It is possible that in the last line **therefore** refers not just to the preceding line but to the whole psalm. Following this interpretation the last line may stand as a complete sentence (with a full stop at the end of the first line): "For all these reasons the king will be victorious."

Psalm 111

This psalm, a hymn of praise, is an acrostic poem; every one of the twenty-two lines begins with a successive letter of the Hebrew alphabet, from *alef* in the first line to *taw* in the last. This artificial device is somewhat restrictive and does not allow the composer much freedom or originality.

The division into strophes is quite arbitrary: RSV, NAB, NJV, and NEB provide no breaks; SPCL divides into verses 1b-4a, 4b-9, 10.

There is no way of determining the time of the psalm's composition; as for its purpose, it was perhaps intended to be used at one of the annual festivals. Because of its similarity with Psalm 112, some think that both of them were composed by the same person.

HEADING: "**In Praise of the LORD.**" Other headings are: "The wonderful works of God"; "God's saving acts"; "The beginning of wisdom." The TEV heading may be adapted for use in other languages by saying, for example, "I will thank God," "Let people praise God," or "I will say that God is great."

111.1-3	RSV	TEV

1	Praise the LORD!
	I will give thanks to the LORD
	  with my whole heart,
	  in the company of the upright,
	  in the congregation.
		1 Praise the LORD!
		
		With all my heart I will thank the
		  LORD
		  in the assembly of his people.

2	Great are the works of the LORD,
	  studied by all who have pleasure
	  in them.
		2 How wonderful are the things the
		  LORD does!
		All who are delighted with them
		  want to understand them.

3	Full of honor and majesty is his
	  work,
	and his righteousness endures
	  for ever.
		3 All he does is full of honor and
		  majesty;
		his righteousness is eternal.

For **Praise the LORD!** see comments at the end of 104.35. This stands as a title in Hebrew; it is not part of the acrostic structure.

In verse 1c **in the company of the upright, in the congregation** is better rendered by TEV as "the assembly of his people"; this translates "the council of the righteous and the congregation"—by which one group is meant, not two different groups, as NIV has it ("in the council of the upright and in the assembly"; see also TOB); see similar language in 22.22. NJV has "in the assembled congregation of the upright," and FRCL "among the assembled faithful." SPCL keeps the redundancy, "in the meeting of the honorable men, in the whole community."

The **great . . . works** that Yahweh does (verse 2) are here his deeds on behalf of his people, and not creation. In verse 2b **studied** translates a form of the Hebrew verb meaning "to seek"; BJ translates "worthy of study." The verb form translated **who have pleasure in them** is translated by BJ, TOB, and SPCL "who love them": "all who love them study them." But it may be difficult to use the verb "to study" with the object "the wonderful works of Yahweh"; what is meant is "to study the record (or, history) of his wonderful works"; or else, meditate upon, think about (NIV "they are pondered"). NJV "within reach of all who desire them" is not too good; NJB is better: "to be pondered by all who delight in them."

In verse 3a the psalmist attributes the abstract qualities of **honor and majesty** to Yahweh's deeds. This may be difficult to express in some languages, and a more natural statement may be "Yahweh's works reveal (or, demonstrate) his honor and majesty." In some languages it will be necessary to shift from the noun forms **honor and majesty** to verbs; for example, "All he does shows how people respect him and that he is powerful like a king."

In verse 3b **his righteousness** is parallel with **his work** in line a; NJV has "beneficence," Dahood "generosity," and FRCL "he is always true to himself." **His righteousness endures** must sometimes be recast to say, for example, "his goodness lasts for ever" or "he is good to people always."

111.4-6	RSV	TEV

4	He has caused his wonderful works to be remembered; the LORD is gracious and merciful.	4	The LORD does not let us forget his wonderful actions; he is kind and merciful.
5	He provides food for those who fear him; he is ever mindful of his covenant.	5	He provides food for those who honor him; he never forgets his covenant.
6	He has shown his people the power of his works, in giving them the heritage of the nations.	6	He has shown his power to his people by giving them the lands of foreigners.

The statement in verse 4a probably refers to the festivals, during which there was a recital of Yahweh's miracles and actions on behalf of his people; this was the way in which he constantly reminded his people of what he had done for them. But the Hebrew "He made a memorial for his wonderful deeds" can be understood to mean "He wants his wonderful deeds to be commemorated" (FRCL) or "He has won renown for His wonders" (NJV; similarly, NEB). GECL has "he has himself provided that his wonders should not be forgotten."

Verse 4b uses the same two words that are used in 103.8a, but in reverse order.

The statement in verse 5a probably has as its background the quails and the manna that Yahweh gave to his people during the years of wandering in the wilderness. And in verse 5b the force of the statement is that Yahweh never fails to keep the promises he made in his covenant with Israel at Mount Sinai (see 25.10).

In verse 6 the psalmist singles out the conquest of Canaan as the supreme example of Yahweh's **power**. The Hebrew phrase **the power of his works** may be taken to mean "his greatest power, his mighty power," or (NJV) "His powerful works"; NEB has "what his strength could do." **Shown his people the power of his works** must often be recast to say, for example, "He has shown his people how powerful he is." If the translator is following TEV, care must be taken that "**his people**" in verse 6a not conflict with "**us**" in verse 4a; if "**us**" is used in verse 4a, perhaps verse 6a should read ". . . to us, his people."

The word **heritage** in line **b** refers to the territory occupied by the peoples of Canaan; **the nations** are the Canaanite people. In some languages "lands of foreigners" must be adjusted to say "lands that had belonged to foreigners" or "land that belonged to people of other nations."

<table>
<tr><td>**111.7-8**</td><td>RSV</td><td>TEV</td></tr>
</table>

	RSV		TEV
7	The works of his hands are faithful and just; all his precepts are trustworthy,	7	In all he does he is faithful and just; all his commands are dependable.
8	they are established for ever and ever, to be performed with faithfulness and uprightness.	8	They last for all time; they were given in truth and righteousness.

In verses 7-9 the psalmist remembers the giving of the Law at Sinai (**his precepts**, verse 7b) and the covenant Yahweh made with his people there.

In verse 7a TEV "**all he does**" translates the Masoretic text **The works of his hands** (some Hebrew manuscripts and early versions have "the work . . ."). **Faithful and just** translates *'emet* (see comments on 15.2) and *mishpat* (see 7.6); **trustworthy** (verse 7b) translates a form of the verb *'aman* "be sure, firm, dependable" (see 36.5). The word for **precepts** is used also in 19.8a; 103.18b ("commandments"). For translation suggestions regarding "faithful" see discussion on "loyal" in 18.25. **His precepts are trustworthy** must be recast in some languages to say, for example, "when he orders people to do something, they can trust what he says."

In verse 8a **established** translates the passive participle of the verb "to support"; here it means "firm, immovable, unshakable." If the translator has used a clause in verse 7 to express "his commands," it may be necessary to switch to "words" in verse 8; for example, "his words last forever."

In verse 8b the Hebrew verb is the passive participle of the verb "to do." RSV takes the people as the implied agent of the passive **to be performed**; TEV has Yahweh as the agent of the action "**they were given**" (also NEB, NIV, NAB, BJ, NJB, FRCL, NJV, TOB, SPCL, Dahood; see NAB "wrought in truth and equity"). **Faithfulness** (TEV "**truth**") here translates *'emet* (as in verse 7a), and **uprightness** (TEV "**righteousness**") translates a term for "straight, upright" (see "upright in heart" in 7.10; 11.2). The statement "**they were given in truth and righteousness**" can be stated "Yahweh acted in a true and righteous manner when he gave his commands," or in some languages, "God did what was true and right when he told his people what to do."

9   He sent redemption to his people;   9   He set his people free
     he has commanded his covenant   and made an eternal covenant
     for ever.   with them.
     Holy and terrible is his name!   Holy and mighty is he!
10   The fear of the LORD is the begin-   10   The way to become wise is to
     ning of wisdom;   honor the LORD;[o]
     a good understanding have all   he gives sound judgment to all
     those who practice it.   who obey his commands.
     His praise endures for ever!   He is to be praised forever.

[o] The way . . . the LORD; *or* The most important part of wisdom is honoring the LORD.

In verse 9a the Hebrew noun translated **redemption** is used only here, in 130.7, and in Exodus 8.23 (8.19 in the Hebrew) and Isaiah 50.2. The reference is probably to the deliverance from Egypt. Although the noun can mean "payment," it stands here for deliverance as such, without suggesting that Yahweh paid someone to set the people free.

In verse 9b the verb **commanded** with the object **his covenant** does not sound very natural; the line can be translated "he commanded that his covenant should last forever" (see NEB) or "he established his covenant forever" (see SPCL).

For **name** in verse 9c see 5.11 and comments. TEV "**mighty**" translates a verbal participle rendered "feared by all" by TEV in 76.7; as observed elsewhere, **terrible** is not a good translation of this word. "Awesome" or even "fearful" (that is, that causes fear) is better.

In verse 10 the Hebrew noun translated **the beginning** is "head"; so it may mean here the start of wisdom or the most important part of wisdom (see NJV footnote, TEV footnote); NJB has "The root of wisdom is fear of Yahweh," and SPCL has "the greatest wisdom consists in honoring the LORD." For comments on **fear of the Lord**, see 19.9; and for the whole maxim see Proverbs 1.7; 9.10; Job 28.28. **The fear of the LORD is the beginning of wisdom** must be recast in many languages so that someone is doing the "fear of the LORD." For example, "When a person honors the LORD, that person is starting to be wise" or "The person who respects the LORD is beginning to be a wise person." (Or see TEV Pro 1.7.)

In verse 10b **all those who practice it** translates the Masoretic text "all who do them" (plural, referring back to Yahweh's "precepts" in verses 7-8); some ancient versions have "all who do it" (singular, referring to **wisdom** in the preceding line), and this is preferred by TOB, NEB, NAB (with textual footnotes), and by RSV and SPCL (without footnotes). HOTTP, however, says the plural form (which it prefers) does not refer back to the commands in verses 7-8, but "in a general way, the fear of the Lord with all its multiple aspects and commandments." If the translator follows TEV, it will be necessary in some languages to recast verse 10b to say, for example, "God enables people who obey his words to decide matters well."

In verse 10c **His praise** means "The praise to be given Yahweh" (Yahweh is the receiver, not the doer, of the praise). SPCL has "God will be praised always!" TEV's "**He is to be praised**" must be recast in languages which do not use the passive; for example, "People should always praise God" or "People should always say that God is great."

Psalm 112

This psalm, like the preceding one, is an acrostic poem consisting of 22 lines, each of which begins with a successive letter of the Hebrew alphabet. It is to be classified as a wisdom psalm (see Psa 1, 27, 49, 73), providing instruction on the rewards of obeying the laws of God. It is to be noticed that these rewards all belong to this life. Those who fail to obey God's laws are the wicked (verse 10), and they are doomed to disappear.

As in the case of Psalm 111, the division into strophes is quite arbitrary. RSV, NEB, NAB, NJV, SPCL provide no breaks; TOB divides into verse 1, verses 2-4, 5-8, 9-10.

HEADING: "**The Happiness of a Good Person**." Other headings are: "In praise of the virtuous"; "The blessings of the just man"; "The good fortune of an honorable man." The TEV heading may be adjusted for use as a heading in some languages by saying, for example, "These are the things a good person does" or "A good person does these things and is happy."

112.1-3   RSV   TEV

1   Praise the LORD!   1   Praise the LORD!
    Blessed is the man who fears the
        LORD,   Happy is the person who honors
        who greatly delights in his com-   the LORD,
        mandments!   who takes pleasure in obeying
2   His descendants will be mighty in   his commands.
        the land;   2   The good man's children will be
        the generation of the upright   powerful in the land;
        will be blessed.   his descendants will be blessed.
3   Wealth and riches are in his   3   His family will be wealthy and
        house;   rich,
        and his righteousness endures   and he will be prosperous for-
        for ever.   ever.

For **Praise the LORD!** see 104.35.

Verse 1 sets the tone for the whole psalm. To "fear Yahweh" is to honor and respect him, to obey him. For **Blessed** see 1.1, where TEV also translates as "Happy." In verse 1b the meaning of **delights in his commandments** is "is happy to obey his commandments," "takes pleasure in doing what Yahweh commands."

The rewards for obeying Yahweh's commands are prosperity and wealth, not only for the man himself but also for his family and descendants (verses 2-3). In verse

959

2a the Hebrew word translated **mighty** is generally used of military might, but here it may mean prosperity, wealth. In the same line **in the land** is the land of Israel; the Hebrew does not mean "on earth" (as TOB, SPCL have it).

It seems probable that in verse 2b **the generation of the upright** means the descendants of the good man referred to in the preceding line (see NEB, JB, NJV); SPCL combines the two lines as follows: "The descendants of the honorable man will be blessed and will be powerful on earth." The verb translated **blessed** is not the same as the word so translated in verse 1b by RSV; here it means "will be blessed by God" (see comments on the verb in 16.7).

Three Hebrew words are used in verses 2a-3 to speak of the family and descendants of the righteous man: "seed . . . generation . . . house." **Generation . . . will be blessed** must often be recast to say "God will give good things to his descendants." **Wealth and riches** are synonymous and in many languages will be translated by a single term.

It is not easy to determine the precise meaning in verse 3b of *tsedaqah* (usually translated **righteousness**). The exact same statement is made of Yahweh's *tsedaqah* in 111.3b; in both instances the line starts with the letter *waw*, the sixth letter of the Hebrew alphabet. It is better to take it here to refer to the reward for being righteous (see Anderson, Briggs, Kirkpatrick), that is, prosperity (as in Pro 8.18). NAB, NJV, SPCL, and Dahood take the meaning to be "generosity, beneficence," but it seems rather strange to switch so suddenly from the good man's rewards (verses 2-3a) to one of his virtues. So FRCL translates here "God's approval is his forever." GECL, however, has "his faithfulness to the Lord lasts forever."

112.4	RSV	TEV

Light rises in the darkness for the upright; the LORD[h] is gracious, merciful, and righteous.	Light shines in the darkness for good men, for those who are merciful, kind, and just.

[h] Gk: Heb lacks *the LORD*

The translation of this verse is doubtful, because it is not certain what the subject of the verb **rises** (TEV "shines") is, nor who is referred to in the Hebrew of line **b**. RSV, TEV, NJV, FRCL, GECL take the subject of line **a** to be **Light**; but others take it to be the righteous man, who is the subject of the preceding and the following verses (see Kirkpatrick, Weiser; AT, NEB, NAB, BJ, NJB, SPCL). So SPCL translates "He is like a light in the darkness, that shines for the honorable men." This is a possible rendition of the Hebrew and is probably to be preferred; Anderson, however, favors the other interpretation, as do Toombs and McCullough. See similar language in 97.11. **Light**, in this context, would be a symbol of prosperity (Oesterley). The verb in line **a** is "shines, breaks forth, dawns." In languages in which it is not possible to say "Light shines in the darkness" without specifying who caused the light to shine, it will be necessary to recast verse 4a as a simile in the direction of SPCL and to say something like "The good man is like a light that shines in the darkness for the benefit of honorable people," or as two coordinate clauses, "A good person is like a light that shines in the darkness, and so good people are helped by it."

In line b the adjectives are all singular, whereas in line a the plural **the upright** (TEV "**good men**") is used. Following the interpretation that makes the righteous man the subject in line a, these three adjectives, as they are in the Masoretic text, are further descriptions of him. RSV supplies **the LORD** as the subject. NEB translates the verse "He is gracious, compassionate, good, a beacon in darkness for honest men." Everything considered, it seems preferable to translate the whole verse as a description of the person who obeys God's laws, as NEB, SPCL, FRCL, and others do. The following may serve as a model: "He is (like) a light shining in the darkness on good people; he is always merciful, kind, and just."

Dahood takes **darkness** to be a name for the world of the dead, and interprets the verse to mean that after death the righteous "will enjoy happiness with Yahweh in the life to come." He translates the verse "In the Darkness will dawn the Sun for the upright, The Merciful and Compassionate and Just One!" However, this interpretation is not normally followed by translators.

112.5-6

RSV	TEV
5 It is well with the man who deals generously and lends, who conducts his affairs with justice. 6 For the righteous will never be moved; he will be remembered for ever.	5 Happy is the person who is generous with his loans, who runs his business honestly. 6 A good person will never fail; he will always be remembered.

Prosperity is further promised for the person who lends generously and is honest in his business affairs (verse 5). Verse 5 begins with "Good (or, Well) man," which may be taken to mean "The good man" (SPCL, Dahood) or **It is well with the man who** (RSV; similarly NJV; TEV "**Happy is the person**"; ZÜR "Fortunate the man"), or "it is right for a man" (NEB, TOB). TEV's "**who is generous with his loans**" must be readjusted in some languages to say, for example, "who is generous and lends his money to other people." The word "**honestly**" in TEV translates "with *mishpat*" (RSV **with justice**; see 7.6).

For verse 6a see similar language in 15.5c, in a similar context. **The righteous**, as elsewhere, means primarily one who faithfully obeys God's commands as found in the Law of Moses. So something like "A person who obeys God's laws" will be better than TEV's "**a good person**." **Never be moved** in this context means never fail in his personal and business dealings. The expression **he will be remembered for ever** means that the family and friends of the good man will remember him, and in languages which do not use the passive, it may be said "people will always remember him" or "people will never forget him."

	RSV		TEV

7	He is not afraid of evil tidings; his heart is firm, trusting in the LORD.	7	He is not afraid of receiving bad news; his faith is strong, and he trusts in the LORD.
8	His heart is steady, he will not be afraid, until he sees his desire on his adversaries.	8	He is not worried or afraid; he is certain to see his enemies defeated.
9	He has distributed freely, he has given to the poor; his righteousness endures for ever; his horn is exalted in honor.	9	He gives generously to the needy, and his kindness never fails; he will be powerful and re- spected.

Verses 7-8 speak of the security of the person who trusts in Yahweh. He knows that Yahweh will take care of him, and so he is not worried or afraid, and even **evil tidings** strike no terror in his heart. His confidence and assurance are described in two ways: **his heart is firm** (verse 7b) and **his heart is steady** (verse 8a). In verse 8a the same verb is used that appears in 111.8a ("are established").

Verse 8b **until he sees his desire on his adversaries** is literally "until he looks upon his enemies" and is much like 54.7b; the meaning is "until he sees their defeat." NJV translates "in the end he will see the fall of his foes," NIV "in the end he will look in triumph on his foes," and NEB "in the end he will gloat over his enemies" (similarly NJB). **Sees his desire on his adversaries** is not clear; the meaning is expressed better by TEV's **"see his enemies defeated."** This passive form may have to be transformed in some languages into the active, in which God will have to be introduced as the subject; for example, "he will see God defeat his enemies."

The Hebrew text in verse 9a is "he scatters, he gives to the poor"; and in verse 9b the Hebrew is the same as in verse 3b (except for the initial "and" in verse 3b): "his *tsedaqah* endures forever." In the context here the Hebrew word probably means **"kindness"** (TEV), or "generosity" (NAB, SPCL, Dahood), or "beneficence" (NJV). FRCL translates the same as in verse 3b: "God's approval is his forever." Verse 9a,b is quoted in 2 Corinthians 9.9.

For **horn** in verse 9c, a symbol of power, see 18.2; 75.4-5,10. "To exalt the horn" is to make someone powerful, proud, victorious. NEB has "in honor he carries his head high," and FRCL "His strength increases with his glory." TOB translates "his forehead is held high in pride," and GECL "Therefore power and honor will be bestowed on him."

	RSV		TEV

112.10

The wicked man sees it and is angry; he gnashes his teeth and melts away;	The wicked see this and are angry; they glare in hate and disap- pear; their hopes are gone forever.

    the desire of the wicked man
      comes to nought.

This verse describes how the wicked react to the success and prosperity of the righteous: they are **angry**; **"they glare in hate"** (literally "they grind their teeth"; see 35.16; 37.12); and then they disappear. **The wicked man sees it . . .** and TEV's ". . . sees this"** will have to be recast in some languages to say "Wicked people see how the good person prospers, and they become angry." The second verb in line b translates the Hebrew verb "to melt," which is variously understood: "illness" (Anderson), "pines away" (NAB, Dahood), "despair" (NEB), loss of courage (NJV), dismay (Weiser), or "loss of power," "loss of reputation." It is quite likely, however, that it means death (Toombs).

In verse 10c TEV and NEB take the Hebrew **desire** to mean **"hopes"**; SPCL has "ambition." Anderson comments: "the plans and the things coveted by the wicked come to nothing." **The desire of the wicked man comes to nought** and TEV's "their hopes are gone . . ."** may sometimes be rendered as "what wicked people plan to do does not succeed" or "the hopes of wicked people are bound to fail."

Psalm 113

This hymn of praise is the first of the "Egyptian Hallel" ("Praise") psalms (Psa 113–118), so called because of the mention of Egypt in 114.1. These psalms were used at the great annual festivals; Psalms 113–114 were sung before the meal, during the family celebration of Passover, and Psalms 115–118 were sung after the meal (see Mark 14.26).

The psalm opens with a call to the people to praise Yahweh (verse 1) and repeats the call in various ways (verses 2-4). This is followed by a description of Yahweh's incomparable greatness and his mercy toward the needy and deprived (verses 5-9). The psalm closes with the same word of praise with which it opens.

It will be noticed that RSV and TEV disagree slightly on the division of the psalm into strophes: RSV separates verse 1 from verses 2-4, while TEV does not. Others divide the psalm into verses 1-3, 4-6, 7-9, while still others have verses 1-3, 4-9.

HEADING: "**In Praise of the LORD's Goodness.**" Other headings are: "To God the glorious, the merciful"; "God's sovereignty and compassion"; "The generous deeds of God." The TEV heading may be recast in some languages to say "I will praise the LORD because he is good."

113.1-4   RSV   TEV

1   Praise the LORD!   1   Praise the LORD!
     Praise, O servants of the LORD,
        praise the name of the LORD!   You servants of the LORD,
                                                   praise his name!

2   Blessed be the name of the LORD   2   May his name be praised,
        from this time forth and for   now and forever.
        evermore!   3   From the east to the west
3   From the rising of the sun to its   praise the name of the LORD!
        setting   4   The LORD rules over all nations;
     the name of the LORD is to be   his glory is above the heavens.
        praised!
4   The LORD is high above all na-
        tions,
     and his glory above the heav-
        ens!

For the initial **Praise the LORD!** see comments on 104.35.

In verse 1b the **servants of the LORD** are the people of Israel, gathered for worship. The verb *halal* "to praise" is used twice in verse 1; in verse 2 the passive form of the synonymous verb *barak* "to bless" is used (see comments on 18.46). The translator has the option in verse 2a of using the passive form, as RSV and TEV have done; if it is preferred, however, the active form may be used, "Praise the name of the LORD," which repeats exactly the language of verse 1c.

In verse 3a **from the rising of the sun to its setting** is probably to be taken in a spatial sense, "**From the east to the west**," that is, all over the world (see 50.1); some, however, take it in a temporal sense, "from morning until night." If the translators interpret **from the rising of the sun . . .** to be spatial, they will have to employ the local designations used for the extremes of east and west. If it is taken as referring to time, in most languages the Hebrew form as found in RSV will most often serve. In verse 3b the verb *halal* is used again, this time in the passive voice: "praised be the name of Yahweh." "**Praise the name of the LORD**" (TEV) is the same as "Praise the LORD."

In verse 4a "Yahweh is high above all the nations" means that he rules (from heaven) over the nations (see the similar expression in 99.2b). For Yahweh's **glory** in verse 4b, that is, his majestic presence, see 26.8b and comments; and for the expression **above the heavens**, see text and comments at 8.1; 57.5,11; 108.5.

113.5-6   RSV   TEV

5   Who is like the LORD our God,   5   There is no one like the LORD our
        who is seated on high,   God.
6   who looks far down   He lives in the heights above,
        upon the heavens and the   6   but he bends down
        earth?   to see the heavens and the
                                                       earth.

Verses 5-6 are a rhetorical question, **Who is like . . . ?** (see RSV), which TEV represents in the form of a statement, "**There is no one like . . . .**" If the translator chooses to use rhetorical questions (as RSV does), it should be kept in mind that **who . . . who** in 5b, 6a are relative pronouns and are not the same as the interrogative pronoun in 5a. The expression **the LORD our God** must often be recast to say "the LORD, who is the God we worship." In verse 5b "**lives**" translates the verb "to sit" (see RSV); here perhaps the better translation is "he is enthroned" or "he reigns" (see NAB, NJB, NJV, NIV, Dahood).

In an unusual figure the psalmist declares in verse 6 that Yahweh is so high above all creation that he must bend down in order to see **the heavens and the earth**. This not only locates his dwelling as being in the heights above, but emphasizes his care for the universe (verses 7-9 give specific examples of his mercy and help); see also 138.6 for similar language. The verb in line a is better translated "**bends down**" or "stoops down" (see NJB, SPCL, TEV, NIV) than RSV **looks far down**. Dahood, however, translates in verse 6 "stoops to look from heaven to earth," that is, locating Yahweh in heaven, not above the heavens. It seems better to follow TEV.

RSV   TEV

7	He raises the poor from the dust, and lifts the needy from the ash heap,		7	He raises the poor from the dust; he lifts the needy from their misery
8	to make them sit with princes, with the princes of his people.		8	and makes them companions of princes, the princes of his people.
9	He gives the barren woman a home, making her the joyous mother of children. Praise the LORD!		9	He honors the childless wife in her home; he makes her happy by giving her children.

Praise the LORD!

In verse 7 the two lines are synonymous; **the dust** in line a represents either poverty (as in line b) or defeat. **The ash heap** in line b translates the Hebrew "garbage dump." At that time poor people would live near the town's garbage dump, searching through the refuse for items of food and shelter (see Job 2.8). The synonymous verbs **raises** and **lifts** are used figuratively here, and the translator should look for an equivalent figure in the receptor language. If there is no meaningful figure to use, it may be necessary to shift to nonfigurative terms to avoid being taken in a purely literal sense; for example, the translator may have to say "He improves the lives of poor people." This one line will stand for the original two lines, if the repetition must be avoided.

Verses 7-8a are the same as 1 Samuel 2.8a-c. In verse 8a **to make them sit** means that Yahweh gives these people the same honor and dignity that **princes** enjoy. Just as in verse 7, the translator will have to decide if the metaphor **sit with princes** or to be "**companions of princes**" carries the meaning of being honored and given dignity. In many languages "to be a companion of a prince" would be translated as "to be a friend of a chief's son," which may not be associated with honor and dignity. Accordingly the translator may have to use a nonfigure and say sometimes "he makes them to be honored by the people," or "he causes the people to respect them," or "he gives them the kind of honor people give their leaders." SPCL avoids the use of "princes" and says "important people"; similarly FRCL "to place him in the highest rank, with the nobles of his people." In verse 8b **his people** means Yahweh's people.

Verse 9 describes Yahweh's care for **the barren woman**, who in Hebrew society at that time was regarded as a failure and as one whom God was punishing; by giving children to her the Lord brought her happiness and honor in her family. RSV's translation of line a can be misunderstood; **He gives the barren woman a home** implies that such a woman has no home to live in. But the point is that Yahweh gives her happiness in her home. NEB is a good translation: "who makes the woman in a childless home a happy mother of children." In many languages a clear understanding of verse 9 depends on the way in which the relation between lines is stated. SPCL does this by placing the giving of a home at the end, that is, "to the woman who has not had children he gives the joy of being a mother and of having her own home."

The psalm closes with the same call to praise, **Praise the LORD!** with which it begins. Since this phrase usually occurs at the beginning and not the end of a psalm, some, following the Septuagint, place it at the beginning of the following psalm (NEB, NAB, BJ, NJB).

Psalm 114

This psalm praises God for having set his people free from slavery in Egypt, and calls upon all the people on earth to await, with fear and trembling, the coming of Yahweh. The psalm is the second of the so-called "Egyptian Hallel" psalms (see introduction to Psa 113).

It seems to divide naturally into four strophes of two verses each (so RSV, TEV, SPCL, TOB); some translations, however, provide no breaks (NJV, NEB, NAB). Particularly obvious in the structure of this psalm, made up of quatrain (four-line) strophes, is the way in which every line of verses 3 and 4 is echoed in verses 5 and 6. The other characteristic feature of this psalm is the repeated use of ellipsis. Every second line in each verse is the elliptical line, depending on the first line to complete its meaning. This is the only psalm in which ellipsis is so consistently employed.

HEADING: "**A Passover Song**." Other headings are: "Hymn for the Passover"; "The LORD's wonders at the exodus"; "Memories of the exodus from Egypt." The TEV heading may be adjusted for some languages by saying "The psalmist sings to remember when the people left Egypt" or "This is a song about leaving Egypt."

114.1-2   RSV   TEV

1	When Israel went forth from Egypt, the house of Jacob from a people of strange language,	1	When the people of Israel left Egypt, when Jacob's descendants left that foreign land,
2	Judah became his sanctuary, Israel his dominion.	2	Judah became the Lord's holy people, Israel became his own possession.

It was at the exodus from Egypt that the Israelites became Yahweh's people. The two lines of each of the two verses are parallel and synonymous; in verse 1 **Israel** in line a is the same as **the house of Jacob** in line b, and **Egypt** in line a is **a people of strange language** in line b. Some translators may prefer to combine elements of line b with line a; for cxample, "When the Israelites, who were Jacob's descendants and who were living in Egypt, left that foreign country." On the other hand, the basic pattern of each verse in this psalm is two parallel lines or versets, the second lacking the verb that is expressed in the first line. The psalmist does not attempt to heighten the poetic intensity, but prefers to vary the key terms in each set of parallel lines. If ellipsis is not a commonly used feature in the receptor language,

968

the translator may have to supply the verb in the second line, either by repeating it from the first, or by using a synonym.

In verse 2 **Judah** and **Israel** are also synonymous. They may refer to the land itself that the Israelites occupied, or to the people; it seems more probable that they refer to the people. In this case the Hebrew "his holy thing" (or "his holy one") in line a means, as TEV (also NJV) has it, "**the Lord's holy people**." But if **Judah** and **Israel** are taken to designate the land (so Briggs, Dahood and others), then RSV's **sanctuary** (also NEB, TOB, FRCL) is preferable. The word characterizes the land as the place where Yahweh lived and was worshiped. In line b **dominion** means either the people or the land that Yahweh rules. If the translator follows TEV's expression "Lord's holy people," in some languages that phrase will have to be recast to say, for example, "the people who belong to the Lord" or "the Lord's own people." If RSV is followed, **sanctuary** may be translated as "place where the people worship God."

114.3-4	RSV	TEV

	RSV	TEV
3	The sea looked and fled, Jordan turned back.	3 The Red Sea looked and ran away; the Jordan River stopped flowing.
4	The mountains skipped like rams, the hills like lambs.	4 The mountains skipped like goats; the hills jumped round like lambs.

At the mere presence of Yahweh **the sea** (see 106.7) **fled**, a poetic description of the parting of the waters of the Sea of Reeds, or Red Sea (Exo 14.10-22). For the crossing of the Jordan River, see Joshua 3.7-17; the water "**stopped flowing**" and the people crossed on dry land. The psalmist speaks poetically of the Jordan flowing upstream (**turned back**).

In verse 3a the verb "to see" has no direct object in Hebrew; NJV supplies "them," that is, the Israelites (also SPCL "Israel"). In 77.16 the direct object is God, and this can be the implied object here. **The sea looked**, while possible in many languages, may provoke laughter when read. Where the personification of inanimate objects is not natural in the language, it is better to shift to another kind of expression. For example, it is often possible to say "God appeared before the sea" or "God came to where the sea was." In the same way in some languages **the sea . . . fled** must be shifted to say "and disappeared" or "and the sea dried up."

Verse 4 refers perhaps to Mount Sinai (see Exo 19.18; Judges 5.5; Psa 68.8); the emotion described is that of fear, not of joy (see 29.6, where the same figure is used).

For English readers the verb **skip**, used in both RSV and TEV in verses 4 and 6, indicates movements of the legs and feet used in dancing and play, and suggests anything but fear. Translators may have to make the element of fright explicit.

RSV   TEV

5	What ails you, O sea, that you flee?	5 What happened, Sea, to make you run away?
	O Jordan, that you turn back?	And you, O Jordan, why did you
6	O mountains, that you skip like rams?	stop flowing?
	O hills, like lambs?	6 You mountains, why did you skip like goats?
		You hills, why did you jump around like lambs?

In Hebrew these two verses form one sentence, with the initial "**What happened . . . ?**" carrying over into the next three lines. The Hebrew is simply "What to you?" SPCL translates it as "What happened to you?" NJV "What alarmed you?" NEB "What was it?" TOB "Why . . . ?" The psalmist mocks them for their fear of Yahweh. RSV and some others use the present tense (NAB, BJ, NJB, TOB), as though the psalmist were present and seeing the events; this is a superb poetic device, but in translation it may convey the idea that the events are still taking place. So it is better to use the past tense, as TEV and others do. In languages in which the asking of questions to inanimate objects is not a familiar poetic device, it may be necessary to say "Why did the sea dry up, and why did the River Jordan stop flowing?"

RSV   TEV

7	Tremble, O earth, at the presence of the LORD,	7 Tremble, earth, at the Lord's coming,
	at the presence of the God of Jacob,	at the presence of the God of Jacob,
8	who turns the rock into a pool of water,	8 who changes rocks into pools of water
	the flint into a spring of water.	and solid cliffs into flowing springs.

The verb translated **Tremble** may mean "dance" (as in 87.7; NEB, TOB); most, however, take it to represent fright, not joy. In both lines of verse 7 the Hebrew says **the presence of**, which TEV has represented in two different ways. It should be noticed that in line a the Hebrew has the title "Lord," not the divine name (RSV **LORD**). **Of Jacob** may stand for the patriarch himself, or else for the people of Israel as a whole (see 20.1; 46.7,11; 75.9; 76.6; and others). In this context the former is preferable. In languages in which the earth cannot be told to tremble, it may be possible to switch to a statement, that is, "when the God whom Jacob worshiped is near, the earth trembles."

In verse 8b TEV "**solid cliffs**" translates the Hebrew word for **flint** (which occurs only in four other places in the Old Testament); as a parallel for "rocks" in line a, however, **the flint** (RSV) is not appropriate in the context. In this verse the psalmist is alluding to the events at Kadesh (Exo 17.1-7; Num 20.1-13; see also Psa 78.13-16,20). RSV, TEV, TOB, FRCL, BJ, NJB use the present tense for the verb in verse

8, as a description of Yahweh's power; NIV, NJV, SPCL use the past tense as a statement of what Yahweh had actually done, and this may be more appropriate. Verse 8 should be accompanied by a cross reference to assist the reader in understanding the allusion.

Psalm 115

In this hymn of praise (see introduction to Psa 114) the psalmist contrasts the power of Yahweh, the God of Israel, with the weakness of idols, the gods of other nations. Yahweh's power is manifested especially in his care for his people, and for this reason they are called upon to praise him.

Dentan suggests the following liturgical setting of the psalm: in verses 1-2 the choir praises God; then in verses 3-8 a soloist proclaims God's power, to which the choir responds (verses 9-11) by exhorting all the worshipers to trust in the Lord. In verses 12-13 the worshipers respond, and then a priest pronounces a blessing on the people (verses 14-15); the psalm closes with a hymn of praise (verses 16-18).

HEADING: "**The One True God.**" Other headings are: "A liturgy of praise"; "God and the idols"; "National trust in God." The TEV heading of this psalm may be adapted for other languages by saying, for example, "There is only one God who speaks words that are true."

---

115. 1-2　　　　RSV　　　　　　　　　　　　　　　　　　TEV

1　Not to us, O LORD, not to us,
　　but to thy name give glory,
　　for the sake of thy steadfast
　　love and thy faithfulness!
2　Why should the nations say,
　　"Where is their God?"

1　To you alone, O LORD, to you
　　alone,
　　and not to us, must glory be
　　given
　　because of your constant love
　　and faithfulness.

2　Why should the nations ask us,
　　"Where is your God?"

The psalm opens with the declaration that to Yahweh alone, and not to the people of Israel, must **glory**, that is, praise and honor, be given. This is an exhortation for the people assembled for worship in the Temple to praise Yahweh (see NIV). They are to do so because of his **steadfast love** and **faithfulness**, the two words that most accurately describe Yahweh's attitude toward his people. The Hebrew says "you (Yahweh) to your name give glory," which does not mean that Yahweh is to boast about himself or to glorify himself (so SPCL), but that he is to act in such a way that his people will glorify him; so NJV "bring glory." Here, as elsewhere, **thy name** means Yahweh himself (see comments on 5.11). In verse 1c **for the sake of** may be taken to mean "in order to promote (or, advance)"; it seems better to translate "**because**," giving the reason why Yahweh should receive glory. Both TEV and RSV are difficult models in this verse. This is due to the contrastive expressions "**you alone . . . not to us**," the use of the passive without a subject, and the reason held for the conclusion. For some languages an easier model to follow may be "Because you are loyal and always love us, we must honor you and you only, LORD; we must not honor ourselves." Or else, "You are loyal and always love us; therefore . . . ."

The question in verse 2 introduces the long response in verses 3-8, and for this reason TEV (also TOB, NEB) joins it to the second strophe and not to the first, as RSV does. The Hebrew text has **their God**, but the question, of course, is addressed to Israel, so TEV has "**ask us, 'Where is your God?'** " This is a question not about the whereabouts of the God of Israel but about his activity. A colloquial way of phrasing the question is "What's happened to their God?" The taunting question implies that something has happened to raise doubts about the concern and power of God (see the same question in 42.3; 79.10), but this psalm has nothing that indicates a recent calamity or defeat. Perhaps the word translated **the nations** would be better translated "the heathen" (see 2.1 and comments); Weiser has "the Gentiles." In this psalm, where the people are addressing Yahweh, not each other, it will be necessary to use appropriate forms of the exclusive first-person plural pronouns.

115. 3-7   RSV   TEV

	RSV		TEV
3	Our God is in the heavens; he does whatever he pleases.	3	Our God is in heaven; he does whatever he wishes.
4	Their idols are silver and gold, the work of men's hands.	4	Their gods are made of silver and gold, formed by human hands.
5	They have mouths, but do not speak; eyes, but do not see.	5	They have mouths, but cannot speak, and eyes, but cannot see.
6	They have ears, but do not hear; noses, but do not smell.	6	They have ears, but cannot hear, and noses, but cannot smell.
7	They have hands, but do not feel; feet, but do not walk; and they do not make a sound in their throat.	7	They have hands, but cannot feel, and feet, but cannot walk; they cannot make a sound.

The power of the invisible God of Israel is contrasted with the weakness of the gods of the Gentile nations, who are lifeless, powerless, ineffective.

In verse 3 the psalmist proclaims Yahweh as the all-powerful God **in the heavens**, who **does whatever he pleases**; his will is supreme, his power is limitless.

The "gods" of the heathen are only **idols** that people manufacture; they are objects made of **silver and gold** (verse 4). **Their idols** stands in sharp contrast to **Our God** in the previous verse, and in some languages it may be necessary to mark the contrast. They have no life in them, no power to act, no feeling (verses 5-7); see a similar passage in 135.15-17. Since verse 5a describes the idols' inability to **speak**, it may be that in verse 7c **they do not make a sound in their throat** means that there is no breath going in and out of their windpipe; they do not breathe, they are dead (as the different language in 135.17b means). But no translation consulted gives this meaning. (As commentaries point out, this extra line in verse 7 departs from the pattern used and repeats, so it seems, the thought of verse 5a. It looks like a later addition to the text.)

115.8	RSV	TEV

RSV	TEV
Those who make them are like them; so are all who trust in them.	May all who made them and who trust in them become*p* like the idols they have made. *p* May all . . . become; *or* All who made them and who trust in them will become.

This verse may be taken as a wish, that is, a curse, as TEV, TOB, and FRCL have it, or else as a statement (RSV and others). As a statement the verse means that the heathen who make and trust in idols are like them, without any value or power; they can accomplish nothing. "Those who trust in idols, which are nothing, are bound to become as nothing themselves" (Anderson). Or else, "Those who trust in idols, which have no power, will themselves become powerless." The verse speaks of two different groups: (1) those who make the idols, and (2) those who trust in them. This is clear in RSV but not in TEV. The two are not distinct, however, as though the idols' makers (line <u>a</u>) did not trust in them (line <u>b</u>). So a translation should read "May all who made them become powerless like them, as well as all others who also trust in them."

115.9-11	RSV	TEV

RSV	TEV

9   O Israel, trust in the LORD!
    He is their help and their shield.
10   O house of Aaron, put your trust in the LORD!
    He is their help and their shield.
11   You who fear the LORD, trust in the LORD!
    He is their help and their shield.
	9 Trust in the LORD, you people of Israel.
	    He helps you and protects you.
	10 Trust in the LORD, you priests of God.
	    He helps you and protects you.
	11 Trust in the LORD, all you that worship him.
	    He helps you and protects you.

The threefold call to **trust in the LORD** is addressed to **Israel**, to the **house of Aaron**, and to **You who fear the LORD**. The second group, **house of Aaron**, clearly means priests, and some conjecture that **Israel** stands for the lay Israelites assembled in worship, while **You who fear the LORD** indicates the whole group, including the proselytes who may be present. Some think that **You who fear the LORD** means only Gentile proselytes (so FRCL "recent converts"); for **fear** see comments on 15.4. For

<u>trust</u> see 13.5 and comments. **House of Aaron**, which TEV translates "**priests of God**," may have to be shifted in some languages, since "**priests of God**" may imply a retinue of priests that are with God. It may be possible to say, for example, "priests who serve God in the Temple."

Line <u>b</u> of all three verses is **He is their help and shield**; this sounds like a response sung by another group. The third person **their** can be misunderstood to refer to some other group, so TEV uses the second person plural; SPCL uses the first person plural. For comments on **shield** see 3.3; the two words **shield** and **help** are used together, as here, in 33.20. TEV has translated **shield** in verses 9-11 as "**protects**." Translators may prefer to do the same, or to keep the term **shield** (provided, of course, that it is a commonly known object) and to supply the function, which is to protect or defend.

The verb **trust** appears in the Masoretic text as an imperative; the Septuagint, Syriac, and Jerome, however, have the indicative (so NAB, NEB), which agrees better with the third person suffix *their* **help and shield**. TEV follows the Masoretic text imperative, and in line <u>b</u> of every stanza it uses the second person "**you**" to agree with the second person of the verb in line <u>a</u>.

115.12-13 RSV	TEV

12   The LORD has been mindful of us;
     he will bless us;
     he will bless the house of Israel;
     he will bless the house of
     Aaron;
13   he will bless those who fear the
     LORD,
     both small and great.
	12 The LORD remembers us and will
	     bless us;
	     he will bless the people of Israel
	     and all the priests of God.
	13 He will bless everyone who honors
	     him,
	     the great and the small alike.

These two verses are the response to the previous three verses: Yahweh is mindful of his people and will answer their prayers. When used of God the verb "remember" means more than merely an act of recalling something that happened in the past; it is not just a fleeting recollection but a positive activity. It is to become aware of, to adopt an attitude that will lead God to take action on behalf of his people. So the translation can be "The LORD will not forget our needs."

All three groups of verses 9-11 are included: **the house of Israel**, **the house of Aaron**, and **those who fear the LORD**. For verse 13a TEV has the verb "honors," whereas in verse 11a the same Hebrew verb is translated "worship." Either "worship" or "reverence" should be used in both places. To the last group is added the all-inclusive **both small and great**, that is, everyone, regardless of status or social position. **Both small and great** in modern English appears to embrace people who are small in stature and those who are great in renown. In many languages this may be translated, for example, "important and unimportant people" or "high people and low people."

14	May the LORD give you increase, you and your children!	14	May the LORD give you children—you and your descendants!
15	May you be blessed by the LORD, who made heaven and earth!	15	May you be blessed by the LORD, who made heaven and earth!

In verse 14a the verb "to increase" or "to add" is taken by most to mean "**give you children**," which was regarded as one of the greatest of all blessings (see 127.3-5); GECL translates "May the Lord give you large families." NAB, however, has "bless you more and more," and TOB translates "make you prosper."

Yahweh is addressed as the one **who made heaven and earth**, that is, the Creator of the universe (see 121.2; 124.8; 134.3).

115.16-18   RSV   TEV

16	The heavens are the LORD's heavens, but the earth he has given to the sons of men.	16	Heaven belongs to the LORD alone, but he gave the earth to man.
17	The dead do not praise the LORD, nor do any that go down into silence.	17	The LORD is not praised by the dead, by any who go down to the land of silence.^{q}
18	But we will bless the LORD from this time forth and for evermore. Praise the LORD!	18	But we, the living, will give thanks to him now and forever. Praise the LORD!

^{q} LAND OF SILENCE: *The world of the dead (see 6.5).*

In this closing hymn of praise, Yahweh is praised as the one to whom the heavens belong; he alone is supreme in his realm, but he has entrusted the earth to humankind. In the Masoretic text verse 16a reads "the heavens (are) heavens of Yahweh"; the ancient versions translated "the heaven of the heavens," that is, "the highest heavens," which is probably what the Hebrew phrase means. Most translations have either "the heavens" or "heaven." For comments on the Hebrew phrase **the sons of men**, meaning humankind, see 11.4, "children of men."

For the idea in verse 17 that the dead do not or cannot praise Yahweh, see 6.5; 30.9; 88.10. Line **b** is strictly synonymous with line **a** and does not speak of a separate group, as RSV and NJV imply. Here Sheol, the world of the dead, is called ("the land of") silence (see 94.17 and comments). Verses 16-17 reflect the concept of the whole universe as consisting of heaven, the earth, and the underworld. In verse 17 **the LORD** translates the name *Yah* (see comments on 68.4).

In verse 18 TEV, in order to make clear the contrast with **the dead** of verse 17, translates the pronoun <u>we</u> by "**we, the living**" (as is done in the Septuagint and Vulgate; so BJ, NJB); for <u>**bless**</u> meaning "**to give thanks,**" see comments on 16.7.

For the concluding **Praise the LORD!** see 104.35.

Psalm 116

In this psalm a man who has been saved from death goes to the Temple in Jerusalem and fulfills the promises he had made to the Lord when he was sick. This expression of thanksgiving begins with a description of the psalmist's brush with death (verses 1-4), followed by a statement of Yahweh's goodness and compassion (verses 5-7), shown by the way in which he had kept the psalmist from dying (verses 8-11). The psalmist offers the sacrifices he had promised (verses 12-14) and expresses his dedication to the Lord (verses 15-19b). The psalm closes with a call for the people to praise Yahweh (verse 19c).

The Septuagint, followed by the Vulgate, divides the psalm into two psalms: verses 1-9 and verses 10-19. Most commentators believe the psalm is a unity.

HEADING: "**A Man Saved from Death Praises God.**" Other headings are: "A psalm of thanksgiving"; "Gratitude for deliverance"; "A prayer of gratitude." The TEV heading of this psalm is one that can be used in most languages with little or no transformation. However, in languages which do not use the passive, it may be necessary to say "A man whom God saved from death . . . ."

116.1-2　　　　RSV　　　　　　　　　　　　　　　TEV

1　　I love the LORD, because he has
　　　　heard
　　　　my voice and my supplications.
2　　Because he inclined his ear to me,
　　　　therefore I will call on him as
　　　　long as I live.

1　　I love the LORD, because he hears
　　　　me;
　　　　he listens to my prayers.
2　　He listens to me
　　　　every time I call to him.

The psalm begins with an expression of gratitude to the Lord because he listens to and answers the psalmist's prayers. The first line of verse 1 in Hebrew is somewhat unusual in that the verb **I love** is followed by "because (or, that) he hears me," after which comes the name Yahweh: "I love because (or, that) hears me Yahweh"; but commentators and translations generally agree that the meaning is that given by RSV and TEV; BJ, however, translates "I love, for Yahweh listens . . . ." RSV, NIV, and SPCL use the past tense of the verb; TEV, TOB, FRCL, BJ, NJB use the present tense, which seems more fitting. The noun **supplications** in verse 1b can be translated "my pleas" (NJV), "my cries for help." GECL has "when I cry to him for help."

In verse 2b TEV **"every time"** translates "in my days"; so NEB and NJV have "whenever," and JB, FRCL "when," NJB "as." TOB, NIV, GECL, FRCL, SPCL, and RSV have **as long as I live**, which the translator is encouraged to follow.[1]

RSV and others translate the verb in verse 2b as future, **I will call**; but it can be translated as a timeless present, indicating repeated or habitual action, as TEV has done.

116.3-4	RSV	TEV
3	The snares of death encompassed me; the pangs of Sheol laid hold on me; I suffered distress and anguish.	3 The danger of death was all around me; the horrors of the grave closed in on me; I was filled with fear and anxiety.
4	Then I called on the name of the LORD: "O LORD, I beseech thee, save my life!"	4 Then I called to the LORD, "I beg you, LORD, save me!"

For verse 3a,b see similar language in 18.4-5. The two lines are parallel: **the snares of death** in line <u>a</u> is synonymous with **the pangs of** (that is, caused by) **Sheol** in line <u>b</u>. Death is pictured as a hunter with nets and traps trying to catch its victim. In line <u>b</u> the word translated **the pangs** occurs elsewhere in the Old Testament only in 118.5 and Lamentations 1.3 (RSV "distress"), and seems to have the general meaning of "distress, anguish" (the Septuagint translates "dangers"); so TEV **"horrors."** It does not seem precisely parallel to **snares**, but the Hebrew for **pangs** resembles **laid hold on me**, so a play on words may be involved. Some propose the conjecture "hunting-net" (so BJ; NJB translates the two figures "bonds of death" and "snares of Sheol"). Dahood translates "emissaries of Sheol." In some languages where snares and traps are common, it may be possible to keep the figurative language, provided, of course, that it is natural to speak of **snares of death**. In some languages it will be necessary to shift to a simile; for example, "death surrounds me like a snare." In languages in which a simile will not serve, it may be possible to say "death is trying to destroy me." In languages in which death cannot be an active agent, it may be necessary to say "I was always in danger of dying." Line 3b may sometimes be rendered "I was filled with the fear of dying" or "I was afraid that I would die."

Both lines portray the psalmist as almost dead; it seemed that death had caught him and would not let him go. This vivid language emphasizes how desperate the psalmist was; he felt that he would soon die. But in verse 4 the psalmist **"called to the LORD"** (literally "the name of Yahweh"; for "name" see 5.11) and begged him to save him (Hebrew "save my *nefesh*"—see 3.2).

---

[1] HOTTP says "and in my days" means "during my life."

RSV   TEV

5   Gracious is the LORD, and righ-
       teous;
      our God is merciful.
6   The LORD preserves the simple;
      when I was brought low, he
      saved me.
7   Return, O my soul, to your rest;
      for the LORD has dealt bounti-
      fully with you.

5   The LORD is merciful and good;
      our God is compassionate.
6   The LORD protects the helpless;
      when I was in danger, he saved
      me.
7   Be confident, my heart,
      because the LORD has been
      good to me.

The psalmist praises Yahweh for his mercy, goodness, and compassion. The word translated **gracious** is used in 103.8, and the word translated **merciful** appears in 102.13 ("have pity") and 103.13 ("pities"). The word that TEV translates "**good**" is *tsadiq*, which most translations render "just" or **righteous**; here, however, the meaning seems to be more in the nature of kindness or goodness; so NJV "beneficent"; TOB "does mercy"; SPCL "compassionate"; FRCL "faithful." As Toombs says, this is "justice which saves the oppressed."

In verse 6a **the simple** are people who are inexperienced, untried (so SPCL), who are not yet able to take care of themselves. NEB and NIV translate "the simplehearted," Dahood "the innocent." NAB (like the Septuagint) has "the little ones"; it does not seem, however, that children as such are meant. Translators should take special care when translating **the simple** so that the word or phrase used does not denote a person who is mentally impaired or stupid. If the translator follows TEV, it may be more natural to say "The LORD protects those who cannot help themselves" (so GECL). It seems that the psalmist includes himself among **the simple**, since in the next line he refers to his own experience.

I was brought low in verse 6b is a way of speaking of "**danger**" (TEV) or weakness (TOB, GECL, SPCL), perhaps weakness caused by illness (see the same verb in 79.8). For **saved** see "Help" and comments in 12.1.

In verse 7a the text is "Return to your resting place, my *nefesh*," the psalmist's way of exhorting himself to "**be confident**," to rest assured, to be serene (NJB "be at peace once again"). The noun "resting place" is the one used in 23.2, "still waters," or "waters of rest." For the difficulty of a dialogue with one's own "soul" or "heart," see comments on 103.1-2. Here FRCL has "Therefore I must be calm again, for the Lord has been good to me." Another model which translators may want to consider is SPCL, which has "Now I can indeed again feel at ease because the Lord has been good to me."

In verse 7b the verb translated **has dealt bountifully** (TEV "**has been good**") appears with the same meaning in 13.6.

RSV   TEV

8   For thou hast delivered my soul
      from death,
    my eyes from tears,

8   The LORD saved me from death;
      he stopped my tears
      and kept me from defeat.

	my feet from stumbling;	9	And so I walk in the presence of
9	I walk before the LORD		the LORD
	in the land of the living.		in the world of the living.

In these verses the psalmist relates how Yahweh saved him; they are similar to 56.13. TEV uses the third person of address in verse 8 in order to keep it consistent with verse 9. No particular significance in terms of intensity or logic seems intended in the sequence **death . . . tears . . . stumbling**. In Hebrew the one verb "save, deliver" (see 6.4a) in line <u>a</u> governs the three objects in lines a,b,c, **soul . . . eyes . . . feet**. The noun translated **stumbling** in line <u>c</u> occurs elsewhere in the Old Testament only in 56.13. Here, as there, it may mean death (so FRCL "the fatal slip"). BJ and NJB consider "my *nefesh* from death" in line <u>a</u> to be a later addition; NEB, on the basis of the Syriac, omits "my eyes from tears," but there is no good reason to depart from the Masoretic text (so HOTTP). SPCL expresses lines <u>a</u> through <u>c</u> as two additional reasons to line 7b for the statement in 7a; that is, "because he has freed me from death, because he has freed me from crying and falling," a structure which other translators may wish to consider.

In verse 9 to **walk before the LORD** means to live one's life conscious of his will, "to live obediently before Yahweh" (Anderson). So SPCL "I will be obedient to the Lord." FRCL has "I will walk under the Lord's surveillance." RSV, TEV, TOB, and ZÜR translate the verb as a present tense, **I walk**; many, however, take the verse to be a promise and translate the verb as future (NJV, Dahood, AT, NAB, NEB, FRCL, BJ, NJB, SPCL). In many languages a literal rendering of **walk before the LORD** will mean nothing more than to pass on foot in front of the Lord. Accordingly this expression must be avoided in favor of one explicitly referring to "living" or "existing." GECL has "I want to remain in the land of the living and to go on living close to you." **Land of the living** is in contrast to Sheol, the land of the dead, and can be expressed in some languages as "in this world where people live."

116.10-11   RSV   TEV

10	I kept my faith, even when I said,	10	I kept on believing, even when I said,
	"I am greatly afflicted";		"I am completely crushed,"
11	I said in my consternation,	11	even when I was afraid and said,
	"Men are all a vain hope."		"No one can be trusted."

In the Septuagint and Vulgate verse 10 marks the beginning of another psalm.

In verses 10-11 the psalmist tells how through all his trials and miseries he had not lost his faith. There is considerable difference of opinion over the form and meaning of verse 10 in the Masoretic text. NAB, BJ, NJB, TOB, FRCL, SPCL, and Weiser agree with RSV and TEV. But NEB has "I was sure I should be swept away, and my distress was bitter"; NJV is "I trust [in the Lord]; out of great suffering I spoke." The Septuagint translates verse 10a "I believed, and so I spoke," which is how the passage is quoted in 2 Corinthians 4.13.[2] In both verses **I said** may be translated "I thought to myself." The psalmist was not necessarily talking to someone.

The object of the psalmist's faith, of course, was the Lord; and some translations will need to make this explicit (as GECL does, "I have trusted the Lord"). **I am greatly afflicted** is rendered by TEV's idiom "I am . . . crushed." In many languages it will be necessary to say "I suffer pains," but in some languages "pain" serves as an agent in such expressions as "pain took hold of me" or "pain would not give me rest."

Verse 11 reveals how disillusioned the psalmist became with all human help: "Everyone is false!" he declared—by which he meant **"No one can be trusted"** (TEV, FRCL). NJV has "All men are false," and Weiser "All men are liars." In line a RSV **in my consternation** translates a verbal form which means "be in a hurry"; NEB translates "panic," and NJV "rashly." SPCL "I was desperate," FRCL "I was so upset," TOB "Forsaken." Either "too quickly" or "in a panic" is a better translation than RSV, or than TEV **"I was afraid."**

116.12-14	RSV	TEV
12	What shall I render to the LORD for all his bounty to me?	12 What can I offer the LORD for all his goodness to me?
13	I will lift up the cup of salvation and call on the name of the LORD,	13 I will bring a wine offering to the LORD, to thank him for saving me.
14	I will pay my vows to the LORD in the presence of all his people.	14 In the assembly of all his people I will give him what I have promised.

The psalmist now offers to Yahweh the sacrifices he had promised when he was in need of Yahweh's help. The question form of verse 12 is not a request for information; either it is a rhetorical device, designed to dramatize the psalmist's concern, or else an interior dialogue, as the psalmist considers how best to express his thanks to the LORD. In verses 13-14 he answers his own question. The word translated **render** in line a is the verb normally meaning "to turn, return"; so AT, NEB, NIV, NJV "How can I repay . . . ?" The word translated **bounty** occurs only here in the Old Testament.

In verse 13a **the cup of salvation** refers to the wine offering, which was part of the ritual of thanksgiving; as Briggs says, "it expresses thanksgiving for the blessings of salvation received and enjoyed." TOB translates "the cup of victory." In verse 13b **call on the name of the LORD** means, in this context, a prayer of praise and thanksgiving, not a petition for help. GECL has "I will confess it before the assembly, and raise the goblet in order to thank him." The expression **"will bring a wine**

---

[2]Here, as elsewhere, NIV disregards the context of the Hebrew passage in order to make it conform verbally with the way in which the Septuagint version of the passage is quoted in the New Testament. Such a practice is dictated by a particular doctrinal view of Scripture, not by sound scholarly principles.

offering . . ." must be recast in many languages to say, for example, "I will offer the LORD a gift of wine to thank him . . . ."

It is in public worship in the Temple (verse 14) that the psalmist offers his sacrifice to Yahweh (see comments on 22.25; 66.13). Verse 14 is repeated as verse 18; many manuscripts of the Septuagint omit verse 14.

116.15-16   RSV   TEV

15   Precious in the sight of the LORD   15   How painful it is to the LORD
        is the death of his saints.   when one of his people dies!
16   O LORD, I am thy servant;   16   I am your servant, LORD;
        I am thy servant, the son of thy   I serve you just as my mother
        handmaid.   did.
        Thou hast loosed my bonds.   You have saved me from death.

Verse 15 seems to have little relation to the context; it is best understood as a statement arising from the psalmist's narrow escape from death (verses 2-3, 8-9). The meaning of the Hebrew word for **Precious** in this context is a matter of dispute; it is used in other places of precious stones, and in 36.7a it appears in an easily understood context, "How precious, O God, is your constant love!" (and see similar meaning for the related Hebrew verb in 72.14b). But here it seems odd to assume that the psalmist is saying that the death of Yahweh's people is a precious thing, a desirable thing, in his sight, unless one follows Dahood, who says "This statement that Yahweh puts great value on the death of his faithful assumes that he will take them to himself when they die." This is possible, but it seems more in keeping with the context of the psalm and of other passages in the Old Testament to take the word **Precious** here to mean "costly." So Toombs: "the Lord is not indifferent to whether or not his faithful servants are killed." Cohen says "God does not regard their death lightly and therefore hastens to protect them." Fisher has the note "their death is precious, i.e., costly to him." So TEV **"How painful it is to the LORD"**; TOB "It costs the Lord to see his faithful ones die"; SPCL "It costs the Lord a lot to see those who love him die"; NJV has "is grievous in the LORD's sight"; and FRCL "The Lord sees with sorrow the death of his faithful ones."

Here **saints**, as elsewhere, are "God's own people" (see comments on "godly" in 4.3).

In verse 16 the psalmist appeals to his life-long devotion to Yahweh, a devotion he inherited from his mother (see similar language in 86.16). The expression **I am thy servant** should not be translated so as to imply that the psalmist is a domestic employee of the LORD. If this is a likely understanding, it will be better to use a verb form; for example, "O LORD, I am the one who serves you" or ". . . I am the one who worships you." It seems that the double expression **servant, the son of thy handmaid** implies an inherited slave status metaphor, and in that case a stronger term than **servant** is required; for example, "I am your slave, just as my mother was." If this is too strong, TEV will serve as a good model. In verse 16c **Thou hast loosed my bonds** most likely refers to the psalmist's deliverance from death (verses 2-3, 8-9); some, however, take it literally to mean to be set free from prison. Dahood takes the verb here to be an imperative, "Loose my fetters!"

983

	RSV		TEV
17	I will offer to thee the sacrifice of thanksgiving and call on the name of the LORD.	17	I will give you a sacrifice of thanksgiving and offer my prayer to you.
18	I will pay my vows to the LORD in the presence of all his people,	18-19	In the assembly of all your people, in the sanctuary of your Temple in Jerusalem,
19	in the courts of the house of the LORD, in your midst, O Jerusalem. Praise the LORD!		I will give you what I have promised.

Praise the LORD!

Verse 17 is similar to verse 13 and refers to the same thanksgiving sacrifice the psalmist is offering in the Temple to the Lord. **Sacrifice of thanksgiving** is a complex expression made up of two events connected by **of**. In many languages this expression will have to be expressed as two clauses; for example, "I will offer you a sacrifice to show you my thanks" or "I will offer you a sacrifice to thank you."

Verse 18 is identical with verse 14. TEV has combined verses 18-19 in order to place the promise "I will give you" last, which makes the two verses easier to read; but translators may prefer to keep the form of the Hebrew. **The house of the LORD** is the Temple, and the outside court (see RSV **the courts**) was the place where the altar stood. So TEV **"sanctuary"** is misleading. Verses 18-19 become difficult because three locations, although related, are named where the psalmist will pay his vows. In languages which find it confusing to have a series of locations related to one event, it is possible to restructure these verses by repeating the main event; for example, "I will pay my vows to you, LORD, in Jerusalem. I will do this in the Temple courts, where all your people assemble for worship."

For the concluding **Praise the LORD!** see 104.35.

Psalm 117

This hymn of praise is the shortest of all the psalms. It is a call for all people everywhere to praise Yahweh because of his love for and faithfulness to his people. It was probably used for the beginning of a service in the Temple. Some commentators think that originally it was the opening of a larger unit, but that it became detached from the rest of that psalm. This is unlikely, however, since the psalm embodies perfectly the structure of a hymn of praise: the call to praise (verse 1), the reason for the praise (verse 2a,b), and the concluding praise (verse 2c).

HEADING: "**In Praise of the LORD.**" Other headings are: "Doxology of all the nations"; "Summons to praise"; "Praise to the LORD." Translators who wish to use the TEV heading may often adapt it to their language by filling it out to say, for example, "All people should praise the LORD" or "Let everyone praise the LORD."

117.1-2   RSV   TEV

1 Praise the LORD, all nations!
   Extol him, all peoples!
2 For great is his steadfast love
   toward us;
   and the faithfulness of the
   LORD endures for ever.
   Praise the LORD!

1 Praise the LORD, all nations!
   Praise him, all peoples!
2 His love for us is strong,
   and his faithfulness is eternal.

   Praise the LORD!

All people everywhere are called upon to **praise the LORD** (verse 1). Two different Hebrew verbs are used, both of which are translated "**Praise**" by TEV; the first one is *halal* (as in the final **Praise the LORD!**); the second one, *shabach*, is used very few times and is here rendered **Extol** by RSV. In 147.12 the same two verbs are used, but in reverse order. The second line can be translated "Praise his greatness." This verse is quoted in Romans 15.11.

The reason given for the call to praise Yahweh (verse 2) is **his steadfast love** and his **faithfulness** toward his people. It seems to imply that the other peoples of the world are or will be in some way associated with the people of Israel in acknowledging Yahweh as the supreme God of all. For *chesed* "constant love" see 5.7 and comments; and for *'emeth* "faithfulness" see 15.2 and comments. TEV "**is strong**" (also BJ, NJB, NEB) translates a verb meaning "to be over, be superior." FRCL has "strongest," and NJV "great." As is often the case in many languages, TEV's "**his faithfulness is eternal**" must be recast to say, for example, "he is loyal to his people forever."

For the concluding **Praise the LORD!** see 104.35.

Psalm 118

This is the last psalm in the group known as the Hallel Psalms (see introduction to Psa 113). It is a hymn of thanksgiving to God for having given his people victory in battle against their enemies. Most commentators agree with the ancient Jewish tradition that the psalm was used in the annual Festival of Shelters (see Lev 23.33-36, 39-43). Verses 19-20 show that at least part of the psalm was sung in front of the Temple gates, as the people entered to worship.

It is difficult to decide on the division of the psalm into strophes. In verses 1-4 all the people are called upon to give thanks to Yahweh; in verses 5-21 an individual is the speaker; he seems to be the king, thanking God for giving him victory in battle (verses 5-16) and for sparing his life (verses 17-18). In verse 19 the speaker requests permission to enter the Temple, and in verse 20 the answer comes from inside the Temple as to who may enter; the speaker responds (verse 21) by proclaiming Yahweh's greatness. Verses 22-25 seem to be from the people, or the choir, as they give thanks to Yahweh; in verses 26-27 the blessing is probably spoken by the priest, and in verse 28 the speaker begins his act of thanksgiving. The psalm ends with a call for all to give thanks to Yahweh (verse 29).

Fisher constructs the following scenario:

> . . . a procession forms outside the Temple and is invited to praise the Lord (verses 1-4); the king or another individual in the name of the group describes dramatically how God came to the rescue when the nation confidently implored his help (verses 5-18); a dialogue between the leader of the procession outside the Temple gates and the priests within (verses 19-25); the blessing given by the priest to the procession gathered around the altar (verses 26-27); resumption of the invitation (verse 1) to praise the Lord (verses 28-29).

HEADING: "**A Prayer of Thanks for Victory**." Other headings are: "Processional hymn for the Feast of Tabernacles"; "Hymn of thanksgiving to the savior of Israel"; "A liturgy of thanksgiving." The TEV heading may require some adaptation if used in some languages; for example, "The psalmist thanks God for defeating Israel's enemies."

118.1-4   RSV   TEV

1   O give thanks to the LORD, for he   1   Give thanks to the LORD, because
        is good;   he is good,
     his steadfast love endures for   and his love is eternal.
        ever!   2   Let the people of Israel say,
                                                    "His love is eternal."
2   Let Israel say,   3   Let the priests of God say,

986

> "His steadfast love endures for
>   ever."
> 3 Let the house of Aaron say,
>   "His steadfast love endures for
>   ever."
> 4 Let those who fear the LORD say,
>   "His steadfast love endures for
>   ever."

> "His love is eternal."
> 4 Let all who worship him say,
>   "His love is eternal."

The people of Israel, assembled in the Temple for worship, are called upon to thank Yahweh for his goodness and his **steadfast love** (for comments on **steadfast love** see 5.7, and for the whole statement see 107.1). The same three groups that appear in 115.9-11—**Israel . . . the house of Aaron . . . those who fear the Lord**—are called upon in verses 2-4 to proclaim **"His steadfast love endures for ever."** The expression **His steadfast love endures for ever** will often have to be recast to say, for example, "He loves eternally," "The LORD loves his people forever," or "His love for his own people never ceases." In verse 4a TEV **"all who worship him"** can be "all who honor (or, reverence) him."

118.5-6   RSV   TEV

> 5 Out of my distress I called on the
>   LORD;
>   the LORD answered me and set
>   me free.
> 6 With the LORD on my side I do
>   not fear.
>   What can man do to me?

> 5 In my distress I called to the
>   LORD;
>   he answered me and set me
>   free.
> 6 The LORD is with me, I will not be
>   afraid;
>   what can anyone do to me?

The psalmist recounts how Yahweh has protected him. In verse 5a **distress** translates the same word translated "pangs" in 116.3b; and **LORD** translates *Yah* (see comments on 68.4). **Set me free** translates "in a roomy (or, large) place" (see 18.19; 31.8), thus contrasting with the word for **distress**, which means a narrow, confined place. From such a restrictive place of imprisonment the psalmist was given freedom to roam about (see comments on 4.1). The language is figurative; the psalmist is not talking of having been released from prison.

The psalmist knows that Yahweh is with him, and so he is not afraid of anyone or anything (verse 6a). The rhetorical question **What can man do to me?** in verse 6b is a way of stating that he is certain no one can harm him (see 56.4,11). Verse 6 is quoted in Hebrews 13.6. **With the LORD on my side I do not fear** is a statement consisting of a reason followed by a conclusion. In some languages this relationship will need to be more clearly marked than in RSV and TEV; for example, "Because the LORD is with me, I will not be afraid" or "The LORD is with me; therefore I will fear nothing." In many languages a literal translation of **What can man do to me?** will be misunderstood. It will very often be necessary, accordingly, to make explicit that the generic **do to me** means "do evil" or "do harm"; for example, as a statement, "No one can do me any harm" or "No one can harm me"; as a rhetorical question, "Who can do any evil to me?"

	RSV		TEV
7	The LORD is on my side to help me; I shall look in triumph on those who hate me.	7	It is the LORD who helps me, and I will see my enemies defeated.
8	It is better to take refuge in the LORD than to put confidence in man.	8	It is better to trust in the LORD than to depend on man.
9	It is better to take refuge in the LORD than to put confidence in princes.	9	It is better to trust in the LORD than to depend on human leaders.

In verse 7a the psalmist repeats what he said in verse 6a about Yahweh being his helper. Certain of this, the psalmist is able to say **I shall look in triumph on those who hate me**. This means not only that the psalmist's enemies will be defeated by Yahweh, but that he, the psalmist, will see this happen (see the similar language in 54.7b; 112.8b). If the speaker is the king—which is probable—then his enemies are foreign armies that threaten the nation (verse 10), and not personal enemies as such. "**See my enemies defeated**" will often have to be recast in other languages to say "I will see God defeat my enemies."

Verses 8-9 both state the same truth: Yahweh offers greater security and protection than any human being. The verbal phrase **to take refuge** means to seek protection, safety, security (see 2.12 and comments); and **put confidence in** translates the verb meaning "rely on, depend on, trust in" (see comments on "trusted" in 13.5).

In verse 9b the Hebrew word translated **princes** (see 113.8) does not necessarily imply royalty, but means people who are powerful and influential; so NJV "the great"; FRCL "influential people"; SPCL "great men."

	RSV		TEV
10	All nations surrounded me; In the name of the LORD I cut them off!	10	Many enemies were around me; but I destroyed them by the power of the LORD!
11	They surrounded me, surrounded me on every side; in the name of the LORD I cut them off!	11	They were around me on every side; but I destroyed them by the power of the LORD!
12	They surrounded me like bees, they blazed[i] like a fire of thorns; in the name of the LORD I cut	12	They swarmed around me like bees, but they burned out as quickly as a brush fire;

them off!

by the power of the LORD I
destroyed them.

i Gk: Heb *were extinguished*

In these verses the representative of the people (probably the king) relates how Yahweh saved him in battle and gave him the victory. In verse 10a he says that he was surrounded by **all nations** (or, "all the heathen"; see FRCL "the pagans") This is not to be taken literally but is an exaggerated way of describing the danger he was in. In verses 10-12 he tells how they had surrounded him completely and were about to defeat him; but **in the name of the LORD** he **cut them off**. The phrase "in (or, by) the name of Yahweh" does not mean here that he acted as Yahweh's representative; it means that because of the power that Yahweh gave him he defeated the enemy. FRCL has "thanks to the Lord . . . ." **In the name of the LORD I . . .** must be recast in many languages. The TEV expression **"by the power of the LORD"** equally requires some adjustment in translation; for example, "I destroyed them; I did this because the LORD enabled me to do it" or, more simply, "the LORD helped me destroy my enemies."

The Hebrew verb translated **cut . . . off** everywhere else in the Old Testament means "to circumcise." Some take that to be the meaning here (Briggs, Dahood; see NJB footnote). Dahood refers to 1 Samuel 18.25-27 and believes that the psalmist was referring to the Philistines, who did not practice the rite of circumcision. Although possible, it does not seem probable that the meaning of the Hebrew verb is "circumcise." Most translators follow the suggestion in K-B and Holladay that the verb used here, though the same in form, differs in meaning. So NJB, NJV "cut down"; NEB "drive away"; GECL "drive back"; SPCL "defeat." In English "to cut off" in this kind of context is none too appropriate, for in terms of a military engagement it means to separate and isolate troops from the rest of the attacking force and thus be able to defeat them; thus "to cut off" in modern English does not mean to defeat, as intended by the Hebrew.

A few Hebrew manuscripts have a form of another verb that is similar to the verb in the Masoretic text, and which Oesterley translates "tread down," and NAB "crush."

The psalmist compares the enemies to a swarm of bees (verse 12a). In line <u>b</u> the Hebrew has the passive "they were extinguished" (see RSV footnote). This seems to indicate, by the figure used (Hebrew "like a thorn bush on fire"), the quickness with which their furious attack was stopped. So SPCL "but their fury burned out like a thornbush on fire." RSV and others follow the Septuagint **they blazed**, which describes the fury of their attack. Although this seems to make better sense in the context, the Hebrew text can be translated and should be followed (so HOTTP). **Fire of thorns** refers to the use of the dry, combustible thorn bushes in the Middle East, which ignite quickly and burn out quickly. In many language areas the thorn is equivalent to "dry grass," used very often to start a fire. GECL translates "straw fire."

RSV and TEV agree on translating the verbs in verses 10-12 by the past tense: **surrounded . . . cut them off**; some, however, represent the attack of the enemies as a present fact and their defeat as a future event. So NEB "surround . . . I will drive them away" (see also NJV). The former seems preferable, since the psalm as a whole appears to celebrate a victory already won.

989

	RSV		TEV
13	I was pushed hard,*ʲ* so that I was falling, but the LORD helped me.	13	I was fiercely attacked and was being defeated, but the LORD helped me.
14	The LORD is my strength and my song; he has become my salvation.	14	The LORD makes me powerful and strong; he has saved me.

ʲ Gk Syr Jerome: Heb *thou didst push me hard*

In verse 13 the Hebrew text begins "You pushed me hard" (see RSV footnote). This can scarcely be addressed to Yahweh, so most take it to be addressed to the enemy. Dahood, who agrees with this view, takes the enemy to be death. NJV translates "You pressed," with a note identifying the pronoun as the enemy; TOB has a note which says that "You" refers either to God or to the enemy. TEV assumes the enemy is meant, and represents the meaning by an impersonal passive; others use the impersonal third person plural (see GECL, SPCL); RSV and other translations follow the Septuagint, Jerome, and Syriac, which have the passive, **I was pushed hard**. The psalmist refers to his near defeat, with the statement **I was falling**. This can be translated "I was about to be defeated."

In verse 14a the Hebrew seems to mean **The LORD is my strength and my song**. Some suggest, however, that the noun translated **song** means "strength" here and in the similar passages Exodus 15.2; Isaiah 12.2 (see K-B, Holladay). So FRCL "The Lord is my mighty strength." If the meaning is taken to be **song**, the sense is that the Lord is the subject of the psalmist's song of praise (see Anderson). TOB takes **song** to mean a war cry: "He is my strength and my war cry!" **The LORD** in this verse translates *Yah*, as in verse 5.

In verse 14b **he has become my salvation** is parallel with **the LORD helped me** in verse 13b.

	RSV		TEV
15	Hark, glad songs of victory in the tents of the righteous: "The right hand of the LORD does valiantly,	15	Listen to the glad shouts of victory in the tents of God's people: "The LORD's mighty power has done it!
16	the right hand of the LORD is exalted, the right hand of the LORD does valiantly!"	16	His power has brought us victory— his mighty power in battle!"

In these verses Yahweh is praised for having won the victory for his people. In verse 15a **the righteous** are the Israelites as such, not just those who were particularly law-abiding. These are the Israelites as contrasted with their enemies, the pagans. But the Hebrew word often has the sense of "victory," and NJV translates "the victorious," NEB "the victors," and Dahood "the triumphant." It seems better to follow either FRCL "the faithful," or else TEV, GECL "**God's people.**"

The tents may refer in a general sense to houses or homes (so SPCL), but it is more likely that these are military tents, in which the men lived while on military campaigns (so NEB "the camp"); or else they are the temporary shelters which the people built and in which they lived during the week-long Festival of Shelters. **Songs of victory** or TEV's "**shouts of victory**" along with line <u>b</u> must be shifted in many languages to say "Listen to God's people shouting in their tents because they have defeated their enemies."

The right hand represents Yahweh's strength, his power, used to defeat the enemy (see Exo 15.6). **Does valiantly** in verses 15c, 16b means "won the victory" (SPCL) or "is triumphant" (NJV, NJB, FRCL). TEV "**it**" at the end of verse 15 anticipates "**has brought us victory**" in verse 16a. In some languages "**the LORD's mighty power**" cannot be the agent of the action; therefore one must often say, for example, "Our victory came from the LORD's powerful help" or "We won because the LORD is powerful and helped us." In verse 16a **the right hand of the LORD is exalted** may refer to a gesture that the winner would make as a sign of victory, or else it portrays Yahweh's mighty hand lifted up in a threatening gesture against the enemy.

118.17-18　　RSV　　　　　　　　　　　　　　TEV

17　I shall not die, but I shall live, 　17　I will not die; instead I will live
　　and recount the deeds of the 　　　and proclaim what the LORD
　　LORD. 　　　　　　　　　　　　has done.
18　The LORD has chastened me 　18　He has punished me severely,
　　sorely, 　　　　　　　　　　　but he has not let me die.
　　but he has not given me over to
　　death.

Here the psalmist states how Yahweh saved him from death, probably death in battle. So he is able now, and will be able in the future, to proclaim what Yahweh has done for him, **recount the deeds of the LORD**. This he will do in public worship in the Temple.

In the context of this psalm, the statement in verse 18, **The LORD has chastened me sorely**, seems to refer to the battle against the enemies; this is seen as Yahweh's punishment of the speaker (so TEV, NJV "**punished me severely**"). Ordinarily this kind of expression refers to some other disaster that was nearly fatal, such as a grave illness or an attack by personal enemies. In any case the psalmist's life has been spared; Yahweh has not let him die (verse 18b).

118.19-21　　RSV　　　　　　　　　　　　　　TEV

19　Open to me the gates of right- 　19　Open to me the gates of the
　　eousness, 　　　　　　　　　　　Temple;

that I may enter through them and give thanks to the LORD.	I will go in and give thanks to the LORD!
20 This is the gate of the LORD; the righteous shall enter through it.	20 This is the gate of the LORD; only the righteous can come in.
21 I thank thee that thou hast answered me and hast become my salvation.	21 I praise you, LORD, because you heard me, because you have given me victory.

As noted in the introduction, in these verses the speaker (presumably the king) stands in front of the Temple and requests admission (verse 19); a voice from inside (perhaps Levites, who were the gatekeepers) states the condition for entering the Temple (verse 20); the king is admitted and praises Yahweh for having given him victory (verse 21).

It is better to keep each of the three verses in a separate paragraph, as TEV does. In RSV verse 21 is joined to verses 22-25, but it should be noted that in verse 21 the speaker is one person (**I**), while in verses 22-25 several persons are speaking ("our . . . us . . . we").

TEV has taken **the gates of righteousness** in verse 19a to mean "**the gates of the Temple**" (also SPCL). FRCL translates "the gates reserved for the faithful" and in a footnote identifies them as the Temple gates. See GECL "Open to me the gate of the Temple, through which the faithful are allowed to enter." As in the case of verse 15b, NJV translates "the gates of victory" here and "the victorious" in verse 20b; NEB has "the gates of victory" and "the victors"; Dahood has "the gates of victory" and "the triumphant." This may be the meaning of the phrase, but it seems better to follow either TEV "**the righteous**" in verse 15b, or FRCL and SPCL "the faithful"; or, best of all, translate here as TEV has done in verse 15a, "God's people."

The expression **the gate of the LORD** in verse 20a may be understood as synonymous with **the gates** in verse 19a, emphasizing here that the gates lead to the sanctuary of Yahweh, according to Anderson. In some languages **gate of the LORD** suggests a gate that has the purpose of keeping the Lord out. Therefore it may be necessary to say "This is the door you enter to go to the LORD."

The same verb "to thank" is used in verses 19b and 21a. **Answered me** in verse 21a means, as very frequently in the Psalms, "you responded to my request," "you did what I asked you to do."

Verse 21b is like verse 14b; in both places the psalmist is talking about the victory that God has given him in his battle against his enemies.

118.22-23 RSV TEV

22 The stone which the builders rejected has become the head of the corner.	22 The stone which the builders rejected as worthless turned out to be the most important of all.

23 This is the LORD's doing;	23 This was done by the LORD;
it is marvelous in our eyes.	what a wonderful sight it is!

Verses 22-25 were probably spoken or sung by the choir or the congregation as the procession filed into the Temple.

It is difficult to understand the meaning of verse 22 in this context; some suggest it was a proverbial saying which is here applied to the king. He had been near defeat and death, but now Yahweh has granted him victory and success. If a translator accepts this interpretation, then the saying may be enclosed within quotation marks, to show it is a proverbial saying. Others take the stone to represent Israel, rejected as unimportant by the great empires (see Dahood). In later times Judaism applied this verse not only to the king but also to the expected Messiah, an interpretation adopted by the Christian church. Verse 22 is applied to Jesus in Luke 20.17; Acts 4.11; 1 Peter 2.7; and it is perhaps alluded to in Ephesians 2.20; and verses 22-23 are quoted in Matthew 21.42 and Mark 12.10-11. There is no sure way of identifying **the builders**, and the proverbial nature of the saying must be preserved in translation. **The stone which the builders rejected** clearly refers to a stone used in construction of buildings, but in languages where the use of stones for construction purposes is unknown, it may be necessary to say "The stone used in building a house, and which the builders refused to use . . ." or ". . . considered to be worthless."

Has become (or TEV "**turned out to be**") indicates the change in the opinion of the builders. The stone itself did not change, but the builders' evaluation of it did. Originally they thought it was worthless, but when the building was being finished, they discovered it was the cornerstone (or capstone).

The Hebrew phrase **the head of the corner** probably refers to the large stone placed at the corner of the foundation, where two rows came together (see Isa 28.16); some think it would be the keystone (or, capstone) which completed the arch of the structure. NJV and NEB have "chief cornerstone," and NIV "capstone." TEV is not specific: "**the most important of all**" (similarly SPCL); FRCL has "the most important one, the cornerstone." GECL translates "The stone which the builders had thrown away now crowns the whole building."

Verse 23a means that it was Yahweh who had brought about this unexpected change of events. The original readers (or hearers) of the psalm would know what **This** refers to; it is no longer the figurative stone and building, but the event which the figure represented. And verse 23b **it is marvelous in our eyes** can be represented simply by "how wonderful (or, marvelous) it is"; see SPCL "we are amazed." GECL translates "The Lord has accomplished this wonderful thing and we have seen it."

118.24-25 RSV	TEV
24 This is the day which the LORD has made; let us rejoice and be glad in it.	24 This is the day of the LORD's victory; let us be happy, let us celebrate!
25 Save us, we beseech thee, O LORD! O LORD we beseech thee, give us success!	25 Save us, LORD, save us! Give us success, O LORD!

This is the day which the LORD has made is the literal form of the Hebrew; the meaning is well represented by NEB, "This is the day on which the LORD has acted" (also SPCL). TEV has **"the day of the LORD's victory,"** since the whole psalm celebrates Yahweh's victory over the enemies of Israel. FRCL translates "This feast day is the Lord's doing" (similarly GECL). In the celebration in the Temple **the day** once more becomes real and actual as the worshipers praise Yahweh for his victory. If the translator follows TEV, it may be necessary to recast this expression and to say "This is the day we remember when the LORD defeated our enemies."

In the prayer in verse 25 the congregation or the choir asks God to continue giving the people victory over the enemy (**Save us**) and to bless the people with **success** and prosperity (see NJV, NEB) in all they do. **Success** is rendered in some languages as "help us accomplish what we hoped to do."

It should be noticed that part of verse 25a and verse 26 seem to be alluded to in Matthew 21.9; Mark 11.9-10; Luke 19.38; John 12.13, on the occasion when Jesus entered Jerusalem; allusion to verse 26 alone is found in Matthew 23.39; Luke 13.35. The Hebrew phrase in verse 25a, "Save, we pray," is transliterated in the Greek text of the New Testament by *osanna*, which appears in many translations as "Hosanna" (RSV and others), an expression of acclamation and praise.

<u>**118.26-27**</u>   RSV   TEV

26   Blessed be he who enters in the   26   May God bless the one who comes
          name of the LORD!   in the name of the LORD!
     We bless you from the house of   From the Temple of the LORD
          the LORD.   we bless you.
27   The LORD is God,   27   The LORD is God; he has been
          and he has given us light.   good to us.
     Bind the festal procession with   With branches in your hands,
          branches,   start the festival
     up to the horns of the altar!   and march around the altar.

From inside the Temple the priests pronounce a blessing on the king, **who enters in the name of the LORD**. Here **in the name of the LORD** may mean "as the LORD's representative," but it probably means, as in verses 10-12, "by the power of the LORD." In verse 26b **you** is plural, not singular, and indicates that the blessing is for the whole group that is entering the Temple. Some take "in the name of Yahweh" to go with **Blessed be he**, and not with the verb **enters**; so NEB "Blessed in the name of the LORD are all who come." But the RSV and TEV understanding of the phrase seems preferable. In order to distinguish between the blessing offered to **he who enters** in line **a** and **you** in line **b**, it may be clearer to say "May God bless the king who comes . . ." and "We bless you people" or "We bless you (plural)."

In verse 27a **he has given us light** refers to the blessings of prosperity and success which God has bestowed on his people; it may explicitly refer to victory (so Anderson).

Verse 27b,c contains directions about the festival procession in the Temple, but there is some uncertainty as to the exact meaning of the Hebrew, which seems to say "Bind up the festival with branches to (or, as far as) the horns of the altar." NJV translates "bind the festal offering to the horns of the altar with cords." But this seems rather doubtful (see Anderson), and the TEV translation may be recommended as a reasonable representation of the meaning of the text. SPCL has "Begin the festival, and take boughs up to the horns of the altar"; AT "Arrange the festal dance with branches, up to the horns of the altar"; NJB "Link your procession, branches in hand, up to the horns of the altar," and explains in a footnote: "Ritual of the *lulab,* branch of myrtle or palm, waved as the procession circled the altar." The **horns** were small projections at the four corners of the altar (see Exo 27.2), which were regarded as particularly holy (see 1 Kgs 1.50). HOTTP says the Hebrew text can be taken in two different ways: "bind up the feast victim(s) with ropes as far as the horns of the altar"; or, "line up the feast <pilgrims> with ropes at the horns of the altar," meaning that the worshipers were enclosed within ropes to set them off as a holy people (see Weiser). HOTTP follows NJV in translating "ropes" instead of "branches" (or, boughs).

118.28-29   RSV   TEV

28   Thou art my God, and I will give   28   You are my God, and I give you
        thanks to thee;   thanks;
     thou art my God, I will extol   I will proclaim your greatness.
        thee.
                                           29   Give thanks to the LORD, because
29   O give thanks to the LORD, for he   he is good,
        is good;   and his love is eternal.
     for his steadfast love endures
        for ever!

In verse 28 the king once more gives thanks to God. **Thou art my God** must often be rendered in translation as "You are the God whom I worship." "**Proclaim your greatness**" in TEV must often be recast to say, for example, "I will tell everyone how great you are."

The psalm closes with a final call to thanksgiving, sung by the choir or the congregation, which is exactly like the opening call in verse 1.

BJ and NJB follow the Septuagint and at the end of verse 28 repeat verse 21.

Psalm 119

This psalm, in praise of the Law, is an acrostic poem (see Psa 9–10, 25, 34, 37, 111, 112). It consists of twenty-two strophes of eight lines each. Each strophe has the same Hebrew letter at the beginning of every one of its eight lines, going in succession, by strophes, from *alef*, the first letter of the Hebrew alphabet, as the first letter of each line in the first strophe, to *taw*, the last letter of the Hebrew alphabet, as the first letter of each line in the last strophe.

Corresponding to the eight lines of each strophe is the fact that eight different Hebrew words are used to speak of the Law (see 19.7-9 for a similar device, where six different words are used). Originally, perhaps, it was intended to have these eight words in each and every strophe, with one of the eight used in each verse. In the Hebrew text that we have, however, this is not the case. Only three strophes (verses 33-40; 57-64; 73-80) have all eight words, one for each verse.[1] All of these eight words are synonyms; they all refer to God's Law as contained in the Mosaic legislation recorded in the first five books of the Scriptures. The Law is not seen as having a human origin, but always a divine origin; Yahweh is the author of the Torah. It should be noticed that in every one of the 176 verses in this psalm, God is either addressed or referred to.

RSV is quite consistent in its translation of these eight words, as follows: law; testimony; ordinance (or, judgment); commandment; statutes; precepts; word; word (or, promise). NJV is thoroughly consistent, as follows: teaching; decree; rule (or, rulings); commandment; laws; precepts; word; promise. TEV is less consistent: for *torah* it always has "law," and for *mitswah* (the next most commonly used word) TEV has "commandment." The other Hebrew terms are rendered "judgment, instruction, teaching, promise, commands, rules." A translator should not feel bound to try to maintain complete consistency; the context in which a given Hebrew word appears should determine which particular word will be used. But where consistency can be maintained without violating normal language usage, the translator will do well to use the same word for a given Hebrew word. This assumes, of course, that there are

---

[1]The following Hebrew words are used: (1) *torah* (see "law" and comments, 1.2); (2) *'eduth* (see "testimony" and comments, 19.7c); (3) *mishpat* (see "judgment," 7.6); (4) *mitswah*, always in the plural, except in verses 96, 98 (see "commandment," 19.8c); (5) *choq*, always in the plural (see "decree" and comments, 2.7; "statutes," 18.22); (6) *piqudim*, a plural form (see "precepts," 19.8a); (7) *dabar*; (8) *'imrah* (see "promises," 12.6; 18.30). *Torah* is always singular and means the whole law of God, the Mosaic Law; *dabar* and *'imrah* mean "word, saying," and sometimes have the specific meaning of "promise." The other words refer to rules or commands or instructions.

996

eight different and synonymous words or phrases within the reach of the average reader of the translation. The translator who wishes to maintain verbal consistency can follow RSV.

The artificial device followed by the psalmist in composing this psalm naturally restricts him as to content and expression. Perhaps better than any other strophe, the fourth one (verses 25-32) illustrates the difficulty of trying to start each verse with the same letter—in this case the letter *daleth*. Verses 26, 27, 29, 30, and 32 all begin with the word *derek*, "way," and verses 25 and 31 begin with the verb *dabaq*, "to join." It is not possible for the psalmist to develop a consistent line of thought; and many of the verses have little if any connection with the preceding or the following verses.

The psalm is to be classified as a wisdom psalm, that is, one that teaches ethical and moral conduct in keeping with the Law of God, the Torah. There are traces in it of lament; the psalmist sometimes complains about his enemies and prays that God will rescue him (see verses 21-23, 42, 51, 61). The psalmist's enemies are never clearly identified (but see verses 23, 161); probably they were not Gentiles but fellow Israelites who were not as dedicated as he was to the Law (see verse 53).

The dominant theme running through this long psalm is that of joy. Despite his enemies and his own shortcomings, nowhere does the psalmist complain about having to obey God's Law. He never finds the Law restrictive or galling or negative; it is always a source of life, wisdom, comfort, and hope. No wonder again and again he exclaims "In your Torah I find joy!" (see verses 14, 16, 24, 35, 47, 70, 77, 92, 111, 143, 162, 174). Oesterley states the matter well:

> It is perfectly true that the main purpose of the psalmist is the glorification of the Law, and the setting forth of the joy that he, as a truly godly man, experiences in observing its precepts; but, as he constantly emphasizes, the Law is the expression of the divine will; it is not the Law, *per se*, that he loves . . . ; he loves the Law because it tells of God's will; and he loves it because he loves God first. Unless this fact is recognized all through, we shall neither do justice to the writer, nor apprehend the deeply religious character of the whole psalm.

No exact time can be determined for the composition of this psalm; most commentators place it quite late.

HEADING: "**The Law of the LORD.**" TEV has supplied a heading for each of the twenty-two strophes. Other translations have one heading: "Praises to the Law of God"; "In praise of the Divine Law"; "Meditation on the Law of the LORD." Translators wishing to provide a heading for each set of eight verses may consider those found in TEV. These will often require some adaptation for use in many languages. The first heading is general and may be recast to say, for example, "This song is about the Law of the LORD" or "The psalmist tells about God's Law."

119.1-3	RSV		TEV
1	Blessed are those whose way is blameless, who walk in the law of the	1	Happy are those whose lives are faultless, who live according to the law of

	LORD!		the LORD.
2	Blessed are those who keep his testimonies, who seek him with their whole heart,	2	Happy are those who follow his commands, who obey him with all their heart.
3	who also do no wrong, but walk in his ways!	3	They never do wrong; they walk in the LORD's ways.

In the opening strophe (letter *alef*, verses 1-8) the psalmist praises the law of Yahweh as the sure way to happiness, and pledges himself to obey it faithfully.

The psalm opens, as does Psalm 1, praising **those whose way is blameless**. For **Blessed** see 1.1. **Way** in line a is used synonymously with **walk in** in line b (see "walk" in 78.10); both mean conduct, behavior, manner of life. The word **blameless** (or "faultless") indicates total conformity with the requirements of the Torah, which is the complete and perfect expression of the will of God. The Hebrew word for **law**, *torah*, is derived from the verb "to teach," so Torah is to be thought of in terms of "teaching" or "instruction" (see 78.1, where the same word is translated "teaching"); NJV "the teaching of the Lord." Yahweh's "teaching," of course, has the full force of command. **Whose way is blameless** or TEV's **"whose lives are faultless"** must often be recast in other languages to make explicit either the words of blame or the people who express the blame; for example, "Happy are the people against whom no bad words are spoken," or sometimes idiomatically, "How fortunate are people when no one puts their tongues against them." **Law of the LORD** must often be expressed as a clause; for example, "who live the way the LORD has commanded them."

In verse 2a **keep** means to protect, to guard (see 12.7b); but "to keep God's law" means to obey it, follow it, practice it (see 78.7).

To **seek** Yahweh means to ask for his guidance, his instructions, and so to obey him (see comments on 9.10; 14.2). It may be necessary in some languages to reduce verse 2 to one line by saying "Happy are the people who obey with all their heart what God commands them to do."

In verse 3b the Lord's **ways** signifies Yahweh's will for his people; those who **walk** in them are living as Yahweh wants them to live (see 81.13). **Who also do no wrong** must often be translated in other languages as "who do nothing evil" or "who do not do bad things."

119.4-6   RSV   TEV

4	Thou hast commanded thy precepts to be kept diligently.	4	LORD, you have given us your laws and told us to obey them faithfully.
5	O that my ways may be steadfast in keeping thy statutes!	5	How I hope that I shall be faithful in keeping your instructions!
6	Then I shall not be put to shame, having my eyes fixed on all thy commandments.	6	If I pay attention to all your commands, then I will not be put to shame.

It is to be noticed that in verse 4 the Hebrew word translated **precepts** appears only in the Psalms. The Hebrew verb "to keep" is used in verses 4b and 5b (see its use in verse 2a); again, it means to follow, to "**obey.**"

In verse 5 the wish represented by **O that . . .** may be expressed by "I hope that" or "I wish that." NJB has "May my ways be steady in doing your will."

In verse 6 **be put to shame** is the public shame to which a pious Israelite would be subjected who did not fully obey the law of Yahweh; failure to obey the Law would be obvious from the disgrace or the suffering which would overtake such a person. TEV in verse 6 has inverted the order of the Hebrew text, putting first line **b**, "**If I pay attention to all your commands,**" so as to make the psalmist's statement easier to understand. RSV **having my eyes fixed on** means "because I have my eyes fixed on." The Hebrew phrase "fix one's eyes on" means to "**pay attention to,**" to observe, to obey. In some languages the expression **be put to shame** will have to be expressed in the active. Furthermore, in some languages an idiomatic phrase will be more natural; for example, "people will not cause my face to burn" or "people will not heat my blood."

119.7-8   RSV   TEV

7   I will praise thee with an upright   7   As I learn your righteous judg-
       heart,   ments,
    when I learn thy righteous ordi-   I will praise you with a pure
       nances.   heart.
8   I will observe thy statutes;   8   I will obey your laws;
    O forsake me not utterly!   never abandon me!

In these two verses the psalmist makes two promises. The first one is **I will praise thee with an upright heart**; the phrase **an upright heart** means "a pure heart" (TEV), "a sincere heart" (NJV, SPCL; see NEB). FRCL uses an expressive idiom, "without second thoughts," that is, totally, completely, without hesitation or reservations.

When I learn in verse 7b is better translated "**As I learn**" (TEV, NIV, NEB, NJV). Yahweh's **righteous ordinances** are his "just rules" (NJV), "just decrees" (NEB), or "fair decisions." In many languages **learn** often suggests a process of rote memorization, a product of formal schooling. In order to avoid this kind of misunderstanding, it may be better to say something like "as you teach me your righteous judgments." **Righteous ordinances** may have to be shifted to a verb form; for example, "the way in which you judge matters fairly." The two lines may then be translated "As you teach me the way in which you judge matters fairly, I will praise you . . . ."

Verse 8a contains the psalmist's second promise: **I will observe thy statutes**, that is, "**I will obey your laws**" (for **observe** see 78.56).

The first strophe ends with a fervent prayer: **O forsake me not utterly!** In English it is more natural to say "do not abandon me wholly" (NJB); better still, "**never abandon me!**" (TEV).

Obedience to the Law of the LORD

9   How can a young man keep his
        way pure?
    By guarding it according to thy
        word.
10 With my whole heart I seek thee;
        let me not wander from thy
        commandments!
11 I have laid up thy word in my
        heart,
    that I might not sin against
        thee.

9   How can a young man keep his
        life pure?
    By obeying your commands.
10 With all my heart I try to serve
        you;
    keep me from disobeying your
        commandments.
11 I keep your law in my heart,
    so that I will not sin against
        you.

Perhaps the dominant note in this strophe (letter *beth*, verses 9-16) is that of joy, happiness (verses 14, 16), and eagerness to obey completely the law of Yahweh (verses 10, 11, 15). It can be inferred from verse 9a that the psalmist himself was <u>a young man</u> (and see verse 100), but this is not necessarily so. The TEV heading may have to be adapted for use in other languages by saying something like "The person who obeys the LORD's Law will be happy," or "I will obey the LORD's Law," or "I will do what the LORD teaches."

In verse 9a <u>way</u> means conduct, behavior, way of living (see verse 1a); <u>pure</u> here means free from sin, free from fault. In verse 9b the form of the Hebrew text seems to be "to keep according to your word"; so RSV <u>By guarding it according to thy word</u>, supplying <u>it</u> (that is, his <u>way</u> of the preceding line) as the object of the verb. But the Hebrew preposition that RSV translates <u>according to</u> may be regarded as an emphatic particle (see Anderson), in which case "your word" is taken as the direct object; so TEV **"By obeying your commands"** (see NEB, NAB, BJ, NJB, NIV, SPCL, FRCL). The Masoretic text has the singular "your word"; many Hebrew manuscripts have the plural, which TEV prefers, **"your commands."** It is important that the translator use the format in the receptor language which will make clear that the psalmist is first asking a question, then answering his own question. In some languages this requires putting the question and reply in a different form from the English; for example, "I ask myself . . ." and "I say in reply . . . ."

For verse 10a see verse 2b. Translators should note that RSV **keep** in verse 2b has a different meaning from TEV verse 10b. In the former it means to obey. In the latter **"keep me from"** means "do not let me" or "prevent me from"; therefore "do not let me disobey your commands." The negative request <u>let me not wander</u>, that is, depart from, abandon, disregard, can be expressed in a positive way, "keep me true (or, faithful) to your commandments."

In verse 11 the psalmist proclaims his determination not to sin against Yahweh, that is, not to disobey any of his commands; so he treasures Yahweh's <u>word</u> in his heart. The verb RSV translates **I have laid up** means "store up, treasure, hide away"; here it may mean to memorize the Law. This meaning seems to be supported by verse 13, which speaks of the recitation of all the laws that Yahweh has given his people (see also verse 15a). The singular <u>thy word</u> in verse 11a may mean "your promise" (so NEB; NJV "In my heart I treasure Your promise"). In languages in which it will not be natural to "store things in the heart," it may be necessary to say, for example, "I have memorized your words" or "I have learned your words and put them in my heart."

	RSV		TEV
12	Blessed be thou, O LORD;	12	I praise you, O LORD;
	teach me thy statutes!		teach me your ways.
13	With my lips I declare	13	I will repeat aloud
	all the ordinances of thy mouth.		all the laws you have given.

For **Blessed be** in verse 12a, see comments on 18.46; 16.7. FRCL translates "Thank you, Lord," and NIV "Praise be to you." And for **statutes** in verse 12b, see the same word in verses 5b, 8a.

Verse 13 is a declaration, not a promise. The psalmist states that he likes to recite Yahweh's laws, **With my lips I declare**. The Hebrew verb may mean to tell or to number (see its use in 9.1b, "I will tell"). See the instruction in Deuteronomy 6.7, "you . . . shall talk of them," that is, of Yahweh's commandments. In order to make clear that this is not a silent procedure, TEV has "**I will repeat aloud . . . .**" NEB is good: "I say them over, one by one"—which includes the idea of numeration (see BJ, "I will enumerate them all").

The literal translation of verse 13b in RSV is not normal English idiom. NJV is "all the rules You proclaimed"; NJB "all the judgments you have given"; NEB "the decrees that thou hast proclaimed." If the translator follows TEV's "**all the laws you have given**," in some languages it will be necessary to specify the receivers and say "given to your people."

	RSV		TEV
14	In the way of thy testimonies I delight	14	I delight in following your commands
	as much as in all riches.		more than in having great wealth.
15	I will meditate on thy precepts,		
	and fix my eyes on thy ways.	15	I study your instructions;
16	I will delight in thy statutes;		I examine your teachings.
	I will not forget thy word.	16	I take pleasure in your laws;
			your commands I will not forget.

In verses 14 and 16 the psalmist describes his great pleasure in doing Yahweh's will; and in verse 15 he promises to study God's laws. The literal form of the Hebrew in verse 14b seems to mean **as much as in all riches** (so HOTTP; NIV "as one rejoices in great riches"). But this may be a way of saying "**more than . . . ,**" as TEV, SPCL, BJ, and NJB translate (see verses 72, 127); NEB follows the Syriac, which has "more than." The Hebrew phrase **all riches** is a way of saying "many riches, great wealth."

Both RSV and TEV contain ellipses, which in many other languages must be filled out, repeating the verb element in both lines; for example, "more than I delight in having great riches."

In verse 15 the two lines are parallel and synonymous, which is unusual in this psalm; **thy precepts** in line <u>a</u> is a synonym of **thy ways** in line <u>b</u>. Yahweh's **ways** are his commands, his rules, for his people to follow. The two verbs are also parallel and synonymous: **meditate** (literally "be concerned with, be occupied with"—see its use in 77.3b, 12a) and **fix my eyes on**, that is "pay attention to" (as in verse 6b; see SPCL). Accordingly, in some languages it may be preferable to reduce the two lines to one.

Again, exceptionally, verse 16 has two synonymous words, **statutes** and **word**. The Masoretic text in line <u>b</u> has the singular **thy word**, but many Hebrew manuscripts and ancient versions have the plural, which TEV prefers (as in verse 9b). For verse 16a see the similar statement in 1.2a. In line <u>b</u> the verb **forget** is better translated "neglect, disregard" (see NJV, NIV).

119.17-18	RSV	TEV

Happiness in the Law of the LORD

17	Deal bountifully with thy servant, that I may live and observe thy word.		17	Be good to me, your servant, so that I may live and obey your teachings.
18	Open my eyes, that I may behold wondrous things out of thy law.		18	Open my eyes, so that I may see the wonderful truths in your law.

In this strophe (letter *gimel*, verses 17-24) the psalmist reaffirms his pleasure in obeying God's laws, even though he is persecuted and reviled by his enemies. The TEV heading may require some modification for translation; for example, "The Law of the LORD makes a person happy."

The psalmist's very life depends on God's continued blessing, and he promises that he will live in obedience to God's law (verse 17). In line <u>a</u> he asks Yahweh to be good to him (NJV "Deal kindly"; FRCL "Be good to me"). The request can be translated "Do me this favor" (so NEB; see SPCL), with the following "let me live" as the favor requested. But the way RSV and TEV translate the verse seems to be better. The psalmist calls himself Yahweh's **servant**, a common way for a pious Israelite to refer to himself. RSV **with thy servant** is recast by TEV **"me, your servant"** to avoid the use of third person reference to the speaker. A similar adjustment will have to be made in many languages. To **live** here is to continue living, to have a good life. For **observe** see verse 8a.

Insight into the meaning of God's law depends not only on prolonged study and meditation; it depends also on God's guidance. So the psalmist prays **Open my eyes**; only in this way can he discover the wonderful truths, or teachings, in the Law. It is God who will enable him to appreciate and understand the Law. It is better to use an expression like "wonderful teachings" than to have **wondrous things** or "wonderful things" (NIV), which may not be clearly understood by the reader. In some languages one does not "see the truth" but rather "understands" it or "hears" it. Therefore the expression **Open my eyes** will not serve in 18a. Sometimes one must translate "Open my ears," or "Help my mind," or "Make my mind strong," followed by "so that I may understand the wonderful true words of your teaching."

119.19-20

RSV	TEV
19 I am a sojourner on earth; hide not thy commandments from me! 20 My soul is consumed with longing for thy ordinances at all times.	19 I am here on earth for just a little while; do not hide your commands from me. 20 My heart aches with longing; I want to know your judgments at all times.

In these verses the psalmist recognizes that his life will last for only a little time (see similar language in 39.12). Instead of **I am a sojourner** in verse 19a, the translation can be "I am here on earth for a short time." Many translations have "I am a stranger" (see NIV), but this can be misunderstood by the readers. **On earth** can be taken to mean "in the land (of Israel)," but **earth**, meaning the world, seems better.

The request to Yahweh that he not **hide** his commandments from the psalmist seems strange. It is a negative way of asking Yahweh to reveal, or explain, his commands, and balances the positive request "Open my eyes" in verse 18a. In some languages it will be more natural to use a positive request such as "show me your teachings" or "make me understand your teachings."

Verse 20 expresses the psalmist's great love for the Torah. He says that his *nefesh* (see 3.2) is "crushed with desire." The verb translated **consumed** occurs only here and in Lamentations 3.16 ("made my teeth *grind*"); and the noun translated **longing** appears only here in the Old Testament. NJV and NIV are exactly like RSV. TOB translates "I love passionately." "Aches" in TEV is a natural English idiom to express a deep, abiding passion or sentiment. **At all times** is represented by NEB "day and night."

119.21-23

RSV	TEV
21 Thou dost rebuke the insolent, accursed ones, who wander from thy command- ments; 22 take away from me their scorn and contempt, for I have kept thy testimonies. 23 Even though princes sit plotting against me,	21 You reprimand the proud; cursed are those who disobey your commands. 22 Free me from their insults and scorn, because I have kept your laws. 23 The rulers meet and plot against me, but I will study your teachings.

**thy servant will meditate on thy
statutes.**

In these verses the psalmist complains of his enemies, who insult and scorn him, and who plot against him. Nothing definite is said why they do this, but the context seems to imply that it was because he was so devoted to God's law, while they disregarded it altogether. The psalmist calls his enemies **the insolent, accursed ones**. He thus portrays them as proud and arrogant. Their pride is the kind which rejects God's claim to govern and control human conduct; it is a denial of God's sovereignty over humankind, and as such deserves God's condemnation. They are **accursed**, which is to say, they deserve God's curse, God's punishment. They **wander from thy commandments** (see verse 10b). In some languages it will be necessary to express **accursed ones** as those who receive God's punishment for disobedience; for example, "You punish those who disobey your commands" or "You condemn those who do not obey your commands."

The request in verse 22a is based on the psalmist's claim (in verse 22b) that he has obeyed God's laws: **I have kept thy testimonies** (see verse 2a). "**Free me from their insults . . .**" must sometimes be recast to say, for example, "Do not let them insult me and make fun of me."

The enemies are **princes**, men of power and influence (see 118.9b and comment). But the psalmist knows that God will protect him and that he will be able to continue studying and obeying God's laws. For **meditate** see verse 15a.

119.24   RSV   TEV

Thy testimonies are my delight,   Your instructions give me plea-
    they are my counselors.   sure;
                                                   they are my advisers.

The strophe closes with another expression of pleasure in being able to know God's laws. Line a is similar to verse 14a; and **my counselors** in line b translates the Hebrew phrase "my men of advice." The meaning is "my teachers, my instructors," but in some languages it may be necessary to say "I am instructed (or, made wise) by studying them." NJV translates the phrase "my intimate companions."

119.25-27   RSV   TEV

*Determination to Obey the Law
of the LORD*

25 My soul cleaves to the dust;   25 I lie defeated in the dust;
        revive me according to thy   revive me, as you have prom-
        word!   ised.
26 When I told of my ways, thou   26 I confessed all I have done, and
        didst answer me;   you answered me;
        teach me thy statutes!   teach me your ways.

| 27 | Make me understand the way of thy precepts, and I will meditate on thy wondrous works. | 27 | Help me to understand your laws, and I will meditate on your wonderful teachings.^{r} |

^{r} teachings; *or* deeds.

This strophe (letter *daleth*, verses 25-32) includes lament and petition. The TEV heading may need to be adjusted for translation; for example, "The psalmist decides to obey the LORD's Law."

In verses 25 and 28 the psalmist refers again to his situation (see verses 21-23), which he describes poetically, **My soul cleaves to the dust** (verse 25a, RSV). This is a way of saying that he is close to death (NAB "I lie prostrate in the dust"); see similar language in 44.25. So he prays **revive me**, that is, restore me to health and prosperity. **According to thy word** probably means, as TEV has it, "as you have promised" (also NJB, GECL, SPCL, FRCL); it is doubtful that **word** here refers specifically to a commandment in the Law. **My soul cleaves to the dust** has been restructured by TEV as "**I lie defeated . . . .**" The problem with the TEV model is the use of the passive, and it is difficult to know who defeated him—a question which is not at all implied in the Hebrew. In many languages "lying in the dust" will be unclear. Therefore it will usually be better to say something similar to SPCL, "I am about to die."

In verse 26a **told of my ways** has "you" as the implied indirect object, that is, Yahweh. The Hebrew word for **ways** means way of life, conduct, behavior (see verses 1a, 5a). Here, then, the psalmist says he told God everything he had done (see NEB); SPCL "I have revealed to you my conduct," FRCL "I have recounted my life to you." This does not seem to be only a confession of sins, as TEV "**I confessed all I have done**" could be understood. It seems better to use a more neutral verb, "I told, narrated, related, recited." Yahweh's answer, then, may be encouragement, or reprimand, or instruction.

The request in verse 26b is the same as in verse 12b.

The request for understanding in verse 27a is like the ones in verses 12b, 18a. It is somewhat unusual for the phrase **the way of thy precepts** to be the object of **Make me understand**, but here this phrase seems to mean "the meaning (or, purpose) of your laws" or possibly "the way of life your precepts demand"; SPCL has simply "your laws"; FRCL has "the meaning of your requirements"; NIV "the teaching of your precepts."

For **meditate** in verse 27b see verse 15b. RSV **wondrous works** (also NAB) may be what the psalmist means: "the wonderful things you have done" (see NJV). In the context of the psalm, however, TEV "**your wonderful teachings**" seems preferable. No other translation consulted, however, expresses this meaning.

| **119.28-29** | RSV | | TEV |

| 28 | My soul melts away for sorrow; strengthen me according to thy word! | 28 | I am overcome by sorrow; strengthen me, as you have promised. |
| 29 | Put false ways far from me; | 29 | Keep me from going the wrong |

and graciously teach me thy law!	**way, and in your goodness teach me your law.**

In verse 28a the psalmist again refers to his situation: **My soul melts away for sorrow**. The Hebrew verb may mean "to weep, fill with tears" (see FRCL), or else "be sleepless" (see NEB "I cannot rest"; NIV "weary"). Delitzsch explains: "melting away in the trickling down of tears." The meaning can be expressed, somewhat idiomatically, "My sadness is about to kill me"; SPCL has a vivid expression: "I have drowned in tears of pain." In some languages there are idiomatic expressions for 28a; for example, "My heart melts like sugar because I am sorrowful." In some languages strong emotions act as agents of events; for example, "Sorrow takes hold of me" or "Sorrow strangles me."

Verse 28b is similar to verse 25b; here the verb **strengthen** suggests the psalmist's condition is not as serious as portrayed in verse 25a.

Once more (verse 29) the psalmist pleads with Yahweh to keep him faithful to his law. Line a is somewhat like verse 10b; the psalmist asks Yahweh to keep him from wrong conduct, deceitful practices. Line b, which is like verses 12b, 26b, may be rendered as NJV has it, "Favor me with your teaching" (also SPCL); NJB "grant me the grace of your Law," and NEB "grant me the grace of living by your law." **Graciously teach me thy law** may have to be recast as another kind of command, saying, for example, "be good to me and teach me your law."

119.30-32	RSV	TEV

	RSV		TEV
30	I have chosen the way of faithfulness, I set thy ordinances before me.	30	I have chosen to be obedient; I have paid attention to your judgments.
31	I cleave to thy testimonies, O LORD; let me not be put to shame!	31	I have followed your instructions, LORD; don't let me be put to shame.
32	I will run in the way of thy commandments when thou enlargest my understanding!	32	I will eagerly obey your commands, because you will give me more understanding.

In verse 30a the psalmist affirms he has **chosen the way of faithfulness** (as opposed to the "false ways" of verse 29a). This is translated by Dahood, SPCL, NEB, NAB, and BJ "the way of truth." NJB, NJV, FRCL, RSV, and TOB, however, take it to mean **faithfulness** (to Yahweh), which TEV renders "**to be obedient.**" This seems preferable; TEV would be better if it were "to be obedient to you." In line b the Hebrew is simply "I have placed your judgments," which most take to mean, as NJV has it, "I set Your rules before me" (see RSV). The meaning is that he pays attention to, is always conscious of, God's laws.

The verb **cleave** in verse 31a is the same as the one in verse 25a; to "cling" to God's laws means to value them, to try to remember and obey them.

In verse 31b **let me not be put to shame** refers to the shame suffered by those who are abandoned by Yahweh and so suffer public disgrace or defeat (see verse 6a; 25.2).

In verse 32a **I will run in the way of thy commandments** means that the psalmist is eager to direct his life in accordance with God's laws; so SPCL "I hurry to obey your commands." FRCL "I run on the way that you order me to" (also GECL). The verb in verse 32b is "to make large," and the direct object is "heart." RSV, NJV, TEV, and Oesterley take the phrase to mean ability to understand: **"you will give me more understanding."** GECL has "because you help me to understand it (that is, the way) correctly." Others, however, interpret differently: freedom (NJB, NIV); gladness (NEB, SPCL); docility (NAB); encouragement (Briggs). It seems better to interpret the Hebrew as RSV, TEV, and NJV have done.

119.33-34	RSV	TEV

A Prayer for Understanding

RSV	TEV
33 Teach me, O LORD, the way of thy statutes; and I will keep it to the end. 34 Give me understanding, that I may keep thy law and observe it with my whole heart.	33 Teach me, LORD, the meaning of your laws, and I will obey them at all times. 34 Explain your law to me, and I will obey it; I will keep it with all my heart.

The main theme of this strophe (letter *he*, verses 33-40) seems to be a desire to understand God's laws; to the prayer for understanding is joined the promise to keep God's law at all times. A suggested adaptation of the TEV heading may be "The psalmist prays that God will help him to understand God's Law" or "The psalmist asks God to teach him what God's Law means."

In verse 33a **the way of thy statutes** is like the phrase in verse 32a. TEV translates **"the meaning of your laws."** In line b the Hebrew word translated **to the end** (it appears also in verse 112) may mean "reward" (as in 19.11); so TOB "my reward will be in keeping them" (also NEB). It is better to follow RSV and TEV here.

Verse 34 practically repeats verse 33; the two verbs **keep** and **observe** are also used (in reverse order) in 105.45. It is probably better to follow RSV in line a and translate **Give me understanding**, instead of TEV "Explain your law to me." So the translation can be "Make me able to understand your law, so that I will be able to obey it . . . ." See GECL "Enable me to understand clearly your rules (laws)." **Observe it with my whole heart** may have to be recast, using a different body part to represent the whole person.

119.35-37	RSV	TEV

RSV	TEV
35 Lead me in the path of thy commandments,	35 Keep me obedient to your commandments,

for I delight in it.	because in them I find happiness.
36 Incline my heart to thy testimonies, and not to gain!	36 Give me the desire to obey your laws rather than to get rich.
37 Turn my eyes from looking at vanities; and give me life in thy ways.	37 Keep me from paying attention to what is worthless; be good to me, as you have promised.

These verses are petitions to God to guide and direct the psalmist; he prays for guidance (verse 35), for a right attitude (verse 36), and to be kept from giving his attention to what is of no value (verse 37).

The request in verse 35a, **Lead me in the path of thy commandments**, is well expressed in FRCL, "Make me follow the way that you order me to." Perhaps it will be better to say "Lead me in the way indicated (or, prescribed) by your commandments," "Help me follow the path that your laws say I should take." As always, **path** is conduct, behavior, manner of life. TEV's **"keep me obedient"** may have to be shifted to a negative command; for example, "do not let me be disobedient."

For verse 35b see the similar statement in verse 14a.

In verse 36a **Incline my heart** means "Make me willing to," "**Give me the desire to.**" **Gain** in verse 36b means "profit" (used also in 30.9a); the idea of its being illegal or shameful is not necessarily implied (as NEB "ill-gotten gains"; also SPCL). NJV and NJB have "selfish gain," which may be better. But others have simply "profit" or "riches" (BJ, TOB, TEV); GECL "great wealth."

Vanities in verse 37a means "worthless things" (NIV), or else "falsehood" (NJV; TOB "illusion"). But the word may refer to idols (see TEV in 24.4; see also 31.6a, where the word functions as an adjective, modifying "idols"). So SPCL has here "Don't let me put my faith in false gods," and NJB "Avert my eye from pointless images."

In verse 37b the Masoretic text is **give me life in thy ways**; TEV has followed the text of the Qumran manuscript for the verbal phrase **"be good to me."** TEV has followed the same manuscript, plus two other Hebrew manuscripts, for the reading "by your word" (NEB "by thy word"; TEV **"as you have promised"**; see also BJ, NJB).[2] As in verse 35, it may be necessary in some languages to say, for example, "Do not let me pay attention to . . . ."

119.38-40   RSV

TEV

38 Confirm to thy servant thy promise, which is for those who fear thee.	38 Keep your promise to me, your servant— the promise you make to those who obey you.

---

[2]HOTTP prefers the Masoretic text "on your ways"; but it should be noticed that this is a "C" decision.

dread; for thy ordinances are good. 40 Behold, I long for thy precepts; in thy righteousness give me life!	39 Save me from the insults I fear; how wonderful are your judg- ments! 40 I want to obey your commands; give me new life, for you are righteous.

In verses 38-39 the psalmist again appeals to God to keep his promise and save him from his enemies (see verses 21-22). The plea in verse 38a **Confirm . . . thy promise** means "Keep your promise," "Do what you promised to do"; NJV and NIV "Fulfil your promise." For **thy servant** see verse 17a. "Keep your promise . . ." must often be recast to say, for example, "Do what you told me you would do." In line b, where "**promise**" is repeated in TEV, it may be necessary to say "as you do it to everyone who obeys you."

In verse 38b **those who fear thee** can be translated "who worship you" (NJV), "honor" (SPCL), "obey" (TEV). FRCL offers a good model for the whole verse: "Do for me, your servant, what you have promised to your faithful ones."

The request in verse 39a concerning **the reproach which I dread** has in mind the taunts and insults the psalmist's enemies were pouring out on him (see in verse 22 "their scorn," which translates the same Hebrew noun used here). This is not God's censure but the enemies' scorn that is directed at him because he, the psalmist, is so devoted to the Torah.

In verse 39b the Hebrew word translated **ordinances** may refer here specifically to God's judgments on the psalmist's enemies, and not to God's laws in general. But if the meaning is taken to be God's laws, the connection of this line with the one preceding it is not altogether clear. "Because your laws are good" does not seem a natural justification for the request in line a. TEV shows no formal relationship between the two lines; neither do TOB or GECL.

In verse 40a the Hebrew verb translated **long for** occurs only here and in verse 174 (see the related noun in verse 20). The qualifying phrase **in thy righteousness** may mean "because you are righteous" (FRCL, SPCL, TEV) or "by means of your righteousness" (TOB, NJV; see NJB). **Give me life** translates the same verb phrase found in verse 37b. This expression should probably not be translated here by "do not let me die," since the primary meaning is "**give me new life**" or "restore me to new life."

119.41-42   RSV   TEV

Trusting the Law of the LORD

41 Let thy steadfast love come to me, O LORD, thy salvation according to thy promise;	41 Show me how much you love me, LORD, and save me according to your promise.
42 then shall I have an answer for those who taunt me, for I trust in thy word.	42 Then I can answer those who insult me because I trust in your word.

In this strophe (letter *waw*, verses 41-48), each line in Hebrew begins with the letter *waw*, which often functions as the conjunction "and." The TEV heading will require adjustment for translation into some languages; for example, "The psalmist trusts the Law of the LORD," or sometimes "The psalmist rests his heart on the words the LORD teaches him."

In verse 41 the psalmist prays for Yahweh's **steadfast love** (see 5.7) and his **salvation**; the two words are used here as synonyms (see 40.10 and comments). The specific meaning here is probably deliverance or rescue from the psalmist's enemies. **Let . . . come to me** is a way of asking Yahweh, who loves the psalmist, to act on his behalf. TEV **"Show me . . ."** is a way of asking for God's action, that is, to prove through his saving action that he loves the psalmist. In verse 41b the Hebrew "word" means **promise**. In some languages it will be necessary to translate 41a as "Show me your love," and line **b** as "and show me your salvation as you said you would." These lines may also be rendered as in SPCL, which says "Lord, show me your love and salvation just as you have promised." Where verb phrases must be used in place of nouns, it is possible to say, for example, "Love me and save me . . . ."

In verse 42 the psalmist states the result of Yahweh's activity: he, the psalmist, will be able to refute his enemies (see verses 21-22), who say that Yahweh has abandoned him. **Word** in line **b** means Yahweh's promise to save; it is not a reference to the Torah as such, although the Torah is the written record of Yahweh's promises to the people of Israel.

119.43-45

	RSV		TEV
43	And take not the word of truth utterly out of my mouth, for my hope is in thy ordinances.	43	Enable me to speak the truth at all times, because my hope is in your judgments.
44	I will keep thy law continually, for ever and ever;	44	I will always obey your law, forever and ever.
45	and I shall walk at liberty, for I have sought thy precepts.	45	I will live in perfect freedom, because I try to obey your teachings.

In verse 43a the phrase **the word of truth**, which the psalmist begs Yahweh not to remove from his mouth, probably means the truth about Yahweh's faithfulness in keeping his promise to save those who trust in him. Should Yahweh not save him, the psalmist's message about Yahweh's love would not be true. **Word of truth** or TEV's **"the truth"** must often be rendered as "the true words" or "words that speak straight." The adverb **utterly** seems a bit awkward; it means "completely, entirely," and as represented in RSV it seems to give the wrong impression that a partial "removal" of **the word of truth** from the psalmist's **mouth** would be all right. So NEB and SPCL omit the word, and BJ, NJB, following the Septuagint and Syriac, transfer the word to verse 47. It is better to represent the word by a negative expression such as "Never keep me from being able to speak the truth (about you)" or, as TEV does it in a positive expression, **"at all times."** Verse 43b repeats the statement of verse 42b; both "trust" and **hope** represent a confidence, an assurance, that Yahweh's laws are true. **My hope is in thy ordinances** must sometimes be rendered as "I have confidence in the way you judge matters."

As a result of his promise always to obey Yahweh's **law** (verse 44), the psalmist knows that he will be at **liberty** (literally "a broad place"; see comments, 18.19; 118.5), free from his enemies' attacks and other difficulties (verse 45a). **Walk at liberty**, or TEV's "**in perfect freedom**," must sometimes be expressed negatively and idiomatically; for example, "I will not be tied up by my enemies." In verse 45b the psalmist's statement that he has **sought** God's **precepts** means that he has tried to keep them, to obey them (see similar language in verses 15-16).

119.46-48   RSV   TEV

46   I will also speak of thy testimonies   46   I will announce your commands to
        before kings,   kings
     and shall not be put to shame;   and I will not be ashamed.
47   for I find my delight in thy com-   47   I find pleasure in obeying your
        mandments,   commands,
     which I love.   because I love them.
48   I revere thy commandments,   48   I respect and love your command-
        which I love,   ments;
     and I will meditate on thy stat-   I will meditate on your instruc-
        utes.   tions.

It is not clear who are the **kings** (verse 46a) to whom the psalmist will proclaim Yahweh's laws; in any case, he will not be refuted and so will **not be put to shame** (see verses 6a, 31b).

The sentiment expressed in verse 47a is like what is said in verses 14a, 16a, 24a; in verse 47b the psalmist's declaration of his **love** for Yahweh's laws appears for the first time in this psalm (see especially verse 97a).

In verse 48 **I revere** translates the Hebrew phrase "I raise my hands," a gesture of prayer, indicating reverence and devotion (see 28.2 and comments; FRCL "While praying to you, with hands raised"). NJV, however, translates "I reach out for Your commandments," which is none too clear. NIV, TOB, NJB, and BJ translate rather literally. For verse 48b see verse 15a.

119.49-50   RSV   TEV

                                               Confidence in the Law of the LORD

49   Remember thy word to thy ser-   49   Remember your promise to me,
        vant,   your servant;
     in which thou hast made me   it has given me hope.
        hope.   50   Even in my suffering I was com-
50   This is my comfort in my affliction   forted
     that thy promise gives me life.   because your promise gave me
                                                       life.

The main theme that runs through this strophe (letter *zayin*, verses 49-56) is the psalmist's persecution from his enemies, people who do not obey Yahweh's laws, and the psalmist's confidence that his faithfulness to the Law will save him from them. A suggested adaptation of the TEV heading here is "The psalmist has confidence in the Law of the LORD," or idiomatically, "The psalmist rests his heart on the LORD's Law."

The strophe opens with the prayer that God will **remember** his **word** (that is, his "promise") to the psalmist; it was through that promise that God had given him **hope**. The statement in verse 49b, **in which thou hast made me hope**, should not be taken to mean that Yahweh had forced the psalmist to hope in Yahweh's promise; it is a way of saying that Yahweh's promise to the psalmist had given him hope (see NIV "for you have given me hope"; NJV "through which You have given me hope"; NJB "on which I have built my hope"). **Remember thy word** may be rendered sometimes negatively: "Do not forget what you said you would do."

The same thought is expressed differently in verse 50. The psalmist's **affliction** was caused by his enemies; but he did not despair, because God's **promise** was a source of life to him (see similar language in verse 37b). NJV has "that Your promise has preserved me." In languages which will not use the passive here, it may be necessary to say, for example, "When I was suffering, you comforted me." The relation between lines a and b is stated differently by RSV **that** (which gives the content of the psalmist's **comfort**) and TEV "**because**" (which gives the reason for the psalmist's comfort). Should the translator wish to follow RSV here, something like the following can be said: "When I am in trouble, I take comfort from the fact (or, knowledge) that your promise gives me life (or, keeps me alive)." Line b may sometimes be rendered "because what you told me you would do enabled me to live."

	119.51-53 RSV		TEV
51	Godless men utterly deride me, but I do not turn away from thy law.	51	The proud are always scornful of me, but I have not departed from your law.
52	When I think of thy ordinances from of old, I take comfort, O LORD.	52	I remember your judgments of long ago, and they bring me comfort, O LORD.
53	Hot indignation seizes me because of the wicked, who forsake thy law.	53	When I see the wicked breaking your law, I am filled with anger.

The same **godless** (that is, arrogant, proud) people referred to in verse 21 scorn the psalmist and mock him, but he continues to obey God's **law**, the Torah (verse 51). It is not apparent why RSV has **Godless men** as a translation of the word which in verse 21 is translated "insolent"; it is better to translate here "insolent" (SPCL), "arrogant" (NJV, NJB, NIV), or "**proud**" (TEV, NEB). To **not turn away** from God's **law** means to continue to obey it, faithfully doing what the Law commands.

1012

The Torah reminds the psalmist of God's **ordinances**, which are **from of old,** that is, they were given a long time ago (verse 52). RSV **When I think of** (also FRCL) translates the verb usually translated "**remember**" (TEV, NJV, NIV, TOB, BJ, NJB, SPCL), the verb which is the first word in verses 49, 52, 55. The word **comfort** here means reassurance, a sense of safety and well-being.

The psalmist again expresses his anger at those who break God's law (verse 53; see verses 21-22, 51). TEV **"When I see"** can be replaced by "When I hear of" or "When I think of." **Forsake thy law** and TEV's "**breaking your law**" must often be rendered as "disobeying, refusing, saying 'No' to your law."

119.54-56	RSV	TEV

54 Thy statutes have been my songs
    in the house of my pilgrimage.
55 I remember thy name in the night,
    O LORD,
    and keep thy law.
56 This blessing has fallen to me,
    that I have kept thy precepts.

54 During my brief earthly life
    I compose songs about your
    commands.
55 In the night I remember you,
    LORD,
    and I think about your law.
56 I find my happiness
    in obeying your commands.

The psalmist's anger toward his enemies (verse 53) is contrasted with the **songs** he composes about Yahweh's **statutes** (verse 54). The Hebrew word for "song" here is taken by some in the same sense it has in 118.14a (which see); the meaning then would be "your commands give me strength" (so NJV; Dahood "my defenses"). The meaning of the line is well expressed by FRCL: "your decrees are the theme of my songs." The Hebrew phrase **the house of my pilgrimage** may be taken to indicate that the psalmist was living in exile (so NJB, NAB; see SPCL "in this land where I am a foreigner"); or the meaning may be the same as in verse 19, that is, the expression is a way of speaking of life here on earth as a temporary abode. The latter seems more probable; see GECL "So long as I am a guest on this earth." TEV has reversed the order of the two lines in this verse for greater ease of understanding.

In verse 55 the psalmist speaks of **the night**, the time when he would feel fears and anxieties; he comforts himself by remembering Yahweh (literally "your name, Yahweh"). In line <u>b</u> the verb "to keep" means to obey (see verses 4b, 5b). NEB, however, has "and dwell upon thy law," and TEV "**and I think about your law.**"

Verse 56 in Hebrew begins with "This has happened to me"; what "This" refers to is left undefined. It may point forward to line <u>b</u>, "that I keep your commands," or else it may refer generally to the psalmist's confidence, or to the **blessing** (RSV) or "**happiness**" (TEV) that is his in obeying Yahweh's commands. NJV uses a neutral term, "This has been my lot"; NIV has "this has been my practice." SPCL, TOB, BJ, and FRCL give the general sense of "this is what is expected of me" or "this has been my privilege" (so Kirkpatrick). GECL is more explicit: "Always to live according to your laws is my charge and my greatest good fortune." Dahood understands it to mean "this indignity" (that is, the scorn of the psalmist's enemies).

119.57-59 RSV	TEV
	Devotion to the Law of the LORD

57 The LORD is my portion;
    I promise to keep thy words.
58 I entreat thy favor with all my
    heart;
    be gracious to me according to
    thy promise.
59 When I think of thy ways,
    I turn my feet to thy testimo-
    nies;
	57 You are all I want, O LORD;
	    I promise to obey your laws.
	58 I ask you with all my heart
	    to have mercy on me, as you
	    have promised!
	59 I have considered my conduct,
	    and I promise to follow your
	    instructions.

In this strophe (letter *cheth*, verses 57-64) the psalmist declares his deep and constant devotion to the Law. The TEV heading can be rephrased as "The psalmist promises to obey God's Law."

Yahweh represents all that the psalmist wants (verse 57a), literally "My portion is Yahweh"; for comments on **portion** see 16.5; 73.26. The division of lines in the Hebrew text makes **to keep thy words** the object of the verb "I say" (RSV and TEV **I promise** in line b). FRCL, however, divides differently and translates "I repeat: the portion that falls to me, Lord, is to put into practice what you have said." Similarly NJB, "My task, I have said, Yahweh, is to keep your word." The translator may choose to follow this interpretation.

TEV has Yahweh as second person (direct address) in both lines, to keep line a consistent with all the other lines of this strophe. In languages in which "to love" and "to want" are the same, it may be best, if following TEV, to translate "You are all I need." SPCL has "you are all I have."

In verse 58a **I entreat thy favor** translates a verb meaning "to put (someone) in a good mood, to conciliate" (see its use in 45.12, "will sue your favor"). **Be gracious to me** means "be kind to me, bless me." For **according to thy promise** see verse 41b and comments.

In verse 59a the Hebrew text has "my ways" (TEV "my conduct"); RSV **thy ways** translates the Septuagint. **I turn my feet** in line b may mean repentance, since the Hebrew verb "to turn" is often used for repentance; so NJV has "I . . . have turned back to Your decrees," and SPCL "I returned to obeying your laws" may be understood to imply repentance. TEV takes the Hebrew verb here to mean a decision, a resolution, to follow God's laws. Perhaps the better interpretation is one that implies repentance and a resolve once again to obey God's laws. It is to be noticed that, since RSV follows the Septuagint in line a, the statement in line b cannot be understood as implying repentance but expresses the psalmist's decision to obey God's laws at all times. If the translator follows "**my conduct**" as in TEV, it may be necessary to say in line a, for example, "I began to think about the way I was living."

119.60-61 **119.60-61** RSV TEV

60 I hasten and do not delay 60 **Without delay I hurry**
   to keep thy commandments.   **to obey your commands.**
61 Though the cords of the wicked 61 **The wicked have laid a trap for**
   ensnare me,   **me,**
   I do not forget thy law.   **but I do not forget your law.**

In verse 60 the psalmist promises that he will immediately put God's laws into practice. In line a two verbal phrases say exactly the same thing: **I hasten . . . (I) do not delay**. Saying something positively and then the same thing negatively is in Hebrew a stylistic means for adding emphasis. The translator should find an equivalent style structure to do the same, and if there is none, it may be wise to avoid the repetition.

In verse 61 the psalmist again refers to his enemies, who have tried to catch him with their **cords** (literally "they surround me with cords"). The figure is that of hunters who are trying to trap animals with their nets (see 18.5). It is not clear whether the Hebrew means that his enemies have caught him (as RSV, NIV, and others interpret) or that they are trying to catch him and he avoids their trap (as TEV and SPCL interpret). Either is possible, and one cannot be dogmatic about the matter.

In verse 61b **forget** means to disregard, neglect, pay no attention to (see verse 16b).

119.62-64 RSV TEV

62 At midnight I rise to praise thee, 62 **In the middle of the night I wake**
   because of thy righteous ordi-   **up**
   nances.   **to praise you for your righteous**
63 I am a companion of all who fear   **judgments.**
   thee, 63 **I am a friend of all who serve you,**
   of those who keep thy precepts.   **of all who obey your laws.**
64 The earth, O LORD, is full of thy 64 **LORD, the earth is full of your**
   steadfast love;   **constant love;**
   teach me thy statutes!   **teach me your commandments.**

The psalmist is so grateful to Yahweh for his **righteous ordinances** that even at nighttime he wakes up and praises Yahweh (verse 62; see verses 55, 147-8). In languages in which **righteous ordinances** will have to be translated by a verb phrase, it may be necessary to say "I praise you because you judge matters fairly."

The psalmist's friends, like himself, are devoted to Yahweh's commandments (verse 63). For comments on **fear** see 2.11; 15.4; for **keep thy precepts** see comments on verse 4b.

The strophe closes (verse 64) with praise to Yahweh, whose **steadfast love** fills **the earth**, that is, includes all people everywhere (see 33.5b). TEV's "the earth is full of your constant love" must be recast in many languages to say "you faithfully love all the people of the world." Again the psalmist asks Yahweh to **teach** him his **statutes** (see verse 12b).

RSV   TEV

The Value of the Law of the LORD

65 Thou hast dealt well with thy   65 You have kept your promise,
        servant,   LORD,
    O LORD, according to thy word.   and you are good to me, your
66 Teach me good judgment and   servant.
        knowledge,   66 Give me wisdom and knowledge,
    for I believe in thy command-   because I trust in your com-
        ments.   mands.

A new note is struck in this strophe (letter *teth*, verses 65-72), with the recognition that the psalmist's sufferings are of value to him because they turn him even more strongly to obeying God's laws (verses 67, 71). He sees his sufferings as divine punishment, and so he does not complain.

Each verse in this strophe begins with the letter *teth*; verses 65, 66, 68, 71, and 72 start with the word *tob*, "good." The TEV heading in more complete form can be "The Law of the LORD is the most valuable thing" or "The psalmist says the Law of the LORD is worth more than wealth."

The psalmist confesses that Yahweh has been good to him, has blessed him: **Thou hast dealt well with thy servant**. The verbal phrase in Hebrew is "You have done good"; a more natural English idiom is "You have treated (your servant) well." NJB has "You have been generous." For **thy servant** see verse 17a; and **according to thy word** in line **b** means "as you have promised." NIV takes line **a** as a request: "Do good to your servant"; this does not seem likely. TEV and FRCL reverse the two lines of verse 65, for a more natural statement.

The request in verse 66a is for **good judgment and knowledge**; in the context this is a request for greater knowledge of God's Law and for good sense in applying it in daily life. FRCL translates "Teach me to value and to know your command-ments." **Teach me good judgment** must be adjusted in some languages to say, for example, "Teach me how to decide matters well" or "Show me how to make good decisions."

In verse 66b the Hebrew verb "to be firm" may be translated as **"trust"** (TEV, NJV, NEB, SPCL), "have confidence" (FRCL), or **believe** (RSV, NIV); NJB has "rely."

RSV   TEV

67 Before I was afflicted I went   67 Before you punished me, I used to
        astray;   go wrong,
    but now I keep thy word.   but now I obey your word.
68 Thou art good and doest good;   68 How good you are—how kind!
    teach me thy statutes.   Teach me your commands.

In verse 67 the Hebrew verb RSV translates **I was afflicted** is translated "you punished me" by TEV (see NEB, NJB "I was punished"), since the psalmist regards his distress not as the result of human circumstances alone but of divine judgment (also verse 71). **I went astray** means "I disobeyed your commands," "I stopped following the way you want me to go." For **I keep thy word** see similar expressions in verses 4b, 5b. SPCL and FRCL all understand the affliction in verse 67 to be the act of God upon the psalmist, and accordingly translate **afflicted** as "humbled." If translators follow those versions, in some languages idiomatic expressions must be used; for example, "Before you brought my heart low, I disobeyed your teachings" or "I used to disobey your words, then you lowered my head."

Line a of verse 68 is a statement about Yahweh's nature (**Thou art good**) and his activity (**and doest good**). This can be represented as a cause and effect: "Because you are good, everything you do is good." GECL translates "Always you are good and you do me such great good!" For **teach me thy statutes** see verse 12b.

119.69-70	RSV		TEV
69	The godless besmear me with lies, but with my whole heart I keep thy precepts;	69	Proud men have told lies about me, but with all my heart I obey your instructions.
70	their heart is gross like fat, but I delight in thy law.	70	These men have no understanding, but I find pleasure in your law.

Once again in verse 69 the psalmist refers to his enemies. For RSV **The godless** see verse 51; it is better to translate "proud, insolent, arrogant." They spread malicious **lies** about the psalmist, but he is confident of his complete devotion to God. To **besmear** is to damage the reputation of, give a bad name to, insult. In some languages it is possible to remain closer to the Hebrew "smear" or "plaster" than does TEV; for example, "Proud people cover me with lies" or "Proud people lay their lies on my head." For verse 69b **I keep thy precepts**, see verse 56b; for **with my whole heart** see verses 2b, 10a.

In verse 70 the psalmist says of his enemies: "their hearts are thick like fat" (RSV **gross like fat**). This probably refers to their lack of understanding, of insight into the meaning of God's law (see similar language in Isa 6.10). See FRCL "they are stupid." Some take it to mean lack of sympathy or kindness; they are unfeeling and cruel (NIV "callous and unfeeling"). In some languages it will be necessary to qualify **"These men have no understanding"** as "They do not understand your law" or "They do not understand what you have taught the people." For **I delight in thy law**, see verses 24a, 35b.

119.71-72	RSV		TEV
71	It is good for me that I was afflicted, that I might learn thy statutes.	71	My punishment was good for me, because it made me learn your commands.
72	The law of thy mouth is better to me	72	The law that you gave means more to me

than thousands of gold and silver pieces.	than all the money in the world.

In verse 71 the psalmist repeats the thought already expressed in verse 67: the punishment he received from Yahweh was for his own good. It gave him even greater understanding of Yahweh's **statutes**, in the sense that by means of this experience he learned that God's laws are good. For **learn** GECL has "reflect on"; TOB "to study."

In verse 72 the psalmist expresses his high regard for the Torah: it is worth more to him than **thousands of gold and silver pieces**. He compares the law of the Lord to riches. Comparisons are structured differently in various languages. In some languages it will be necessary to translate, for example, "The law you gave me is worth much. All the money in the world is worth little" or "The law you gave me is very good; all the wealth in the world is good a little bit."

The phrase **The law of thy mouth** in line a emphasizes the fact that the Torah is the personal expression of Yahweh's will for his people. NJV translates "the teaching you proclaimed."

119.73-74   RSV   TEV

The Justice of the Law of the LORD

	RSV		TEV
73	Thy hands have made and fash-ioned me; give me understanding that I may learn thy command-ments.	73	You created me, and you keep me safe; give me understanding, so that I may learn your laws.
74	Those who fear thee shall see me and rejoice, because I have hoped in thy word.	74	Those who honor you will be glad when they see me, because I trust in your promise.

In this strophe (letter *yod*, verses 73-80) the psalmist prays for Yahweh's love and mercy and confesses that Yahweh is just and right in all he does. He also prays that he may perfectly obey God's laws and that his enemies may be defeated. The TEV heading may have to be recast slightly for translation in some languages; for example, "The Law of the LORD is fair" or "What the LORD teaches is just."

In verse 73 the psalmist confesses his absolute dependence on Yahweh, who created him: **Thy hands have made and fashioned me**. The second verb, "to make firm, establish," may be understood to mean **fashioned** (RSV, NJV, NAB; NEB "Thy hands molded me and made me what I am"). But it may be understood to mean "to keep safe, preserve"; so TEV "**you keep me safe**"; FRCL "keep me standing up"; NJB "held me firm." Probably the first meaning better fits the context here (see similar language in Job 10.8). For verse 73b see similar thought in verse 34a. Where RSV and TEV have **understanding**, SPCL has "intelligence," and FRCL "discernment." In some languages **give me understanding** is rendered "put thinking into my heart" or "open up my innermost."

Those who, like the psalmist, obey Yahweh's commands will share the psalmist's joy when they see how Yahweh has blessed him (verse 74a). For **who fear thee** see verse 63a. In verse 74b **thy word** may mean the Law as such, or else in a more restricted sense it may refer to Yahweh's promise (see the same language in verse 43b).

119.75-77 RSV		TEV
75	I know, O LORD, that thy judgments are right, and that in faithfulness thou hast afflicted me.	75	I know that your judgments are righteous, LORD, and that you punished me because you are faithful.
76	Let thy steadfast love be ready to comfort me according to thy promise to thy servant.	76	Let your constant love comfort me, as you have promised me, your servant.
77	Let thy mercy come to me, that I may live; for thy law is my delight.	77	Have mercy on me, and I will live because I take pleasure in your law.

God's punishment is motivated by his **faithfulness**, that is, he keeps his promise, as expressed in his covenant with his people, to reward the righteous and punish the wicked. So the psalmist does not complain: **I know . . . that thy judgments are right**. TEV's **"your judgments are righteous"** will have to be shifted in some languages to say, for example, "I know that you judge things in the right way."

In verses 76-77 the psalmist appeals to Yahweh to show him **steadfast love** and **mercy**, because of Yahweh's **promise** and the psalmist's devotion to Yahweh's **law**. For **to comfort me** in verse 76a, see verse 52b; and for verse 76b see similar language in verses 41b, 58b.

For verse 77a see similar request in verse 41a; for **that I may live** see verse 17b; and for verse 77b see verse 70b.

119.78-80 RSV		TEV
78	Let the godless be put to shame, because they have subverted me with guile; as for me, I will meditate on thy precepts.	78	May the proud be ashamed for falsely accusing me; as for me, I will meditate on your instructions.
79	Let those who fear thee turn to me, that they may know thy testimonies.	79	May those who honor you come to me— all those who know your commands.
80	May my heart be blameless in thy statutes, that I may not be put to shame!	80	May I perfectly obey your commandments and be spared the shame of defeat.

Verse 78 is another plea that Yahweh will punish the psalmist's enemies, **the godless** (that is, "the arrogant"; see verse 51); for **be put to shame** see verse 31b. In languages which will not use the passive in **godless be put to shame**, it will be necessary to say something like "God, put the proud to shame," or idiomatically sometimes, "God, make the proud have burning faces." They accuse the psalmist falsely. RSV **they have subverted me with guile** is not easy to understand. A clearer and more natural translation is provided by NEB, "with their lies they wrong me" (also NAB "for oppressing me unjustly"; NIV "for wronging me without cause"; NJV "they have wronged me without cause"). For verse 78c see verse 15a.

In verse 79 the psalmist prays that faithful fellow Israelites come to him to be instructed about God's laws. RSV, TOB, FRCL, and Dahood in verse 79b follow one form of the Masoretic text, **that they may know**; TEV, NEB, NIV, NJV, SPCL, NJB, and BJ follow another form of the text, "even those who know."[3] **Turn to me** and TEV's **"come to me"** may have to be recast to avoid ambiguity. In some languages one may say, for example, "bring to me those who honor you" or "let those . . . unite with me."

The strophe closes (verse 80) with a fervent resolution to obey Yahweh's commandments. RSV's language in line a is unnecessarily unintelligent and unnatural; the meaning is clearly expressed in normal English by NJV, "May I wholeheartedly follow Your laws." **Be put to shame** echoes the same verb in 78a.

119.81-83   RSV   TEV

A Prayer for Deliverance

81	My soul languishes for thy salvation; I hope in thy word.	81	I am worn out, LORD, waiting for you to save me; I place my trust in your word.
82	My eyes fail with watching for thy promise; I ask, "When wilt thou comfort me?"	82	My eyes are tired from watching for what you promised, while I ask, "When will you help me?"
83	For I have become like a wineskin in the smoke, yet I have not forgotten thy statutes.	83	I am as useless as a discarded wineskin; yet I have not forgotten your commands.

In this strophe (letter *kaf*, verses 81-88) the psalmist complains that Yahweh has abandoned him, and so he prays insistently that he will come to his help and save him from his enemies. The TEV heading may have to be modified if used; for example, "The psalmist asks God to deliver him from his enemies."

Verse 81 begins "My *nefesh* is worn out for your salvation" (see RSV); SPCL has "I anxiously await for you to save me." See similar language in verse 20a, "My soul

---

[3]"That they may know" is *kethiv* (also Targum); the appositional "and those who know" is *qere* (also the Septuagint, Syriac, Jerome).

is consumed with longing," and in verse 28a "My soul melts away." The psalmist is in despair, but still he trusts Yahweh to save him; for verse 81b see verse 74b. The relation of **my soul languishes** to **for thy salvation** is that of result to reason. In some languages this relationship will require shifting the clauses to say "I have waited for you to save me, and now I am worn out" or "I have waited so long for . . . that now I am worn out."

Verse 82 repeats the same complaint (see similar language in 69.3); **My eyes fail** is an expressive way of saying that he has kept on waiting, in vain, for God's help (see the same expression in verse 123). **Thy promise** as the object of the verb "to watch" means "what you have promised," that is, deliverance from enemies or illness. In verse 82b the verb "to comfort" implicitly includes the idea that Yahweh will deliver the psalmist from his enemies; for other passages where the verb is used, see 23.4; 71.21; 119.76.

In verse 83 **a wineskin in the smoke** refers to a wineskin (usually made of goatskin) that has been hanging up near the ceiling and which the smoke has blackened and shriveled to such an extent that it is no longer useful and should be thrown away. SPCL discards the figure altogether and translates "I am an old man, useless and forgotten." The only trouble with this is that the figure does not necessarily mean that the psalmist was an old man; and the claim in verse 100 has no validity to it if the psalmist himself was an old man (and see verse 9). In many languages TEV's **"useless as a discarded wineskin"** will have little or no meaning. Accordingly the translator has two choices: either to say something like "I am of no account," or to use a local object such as a woven bag that hangs in a smokey kitchen hut. For **forgotten** see verses 16b, 61b.

119.84-85	RSV	TEV

	RSV	TEV
84	How long must thy servant endure? When wilt thou judge those who persecute me?	84 How much longer must I wait? When will you punish those who persecute me?
85	Godless men have dug pitfalls for me, men who do not conform to thy law.	85 Proud men, who do not obey your law, have dug pits to trap me.

Verse 84a in Hebrew is "How many are the days of your servant?" (RSV **How long must thy servant endure?**). This can mean "How much longer will I live?" (so NJB, NJV, FRCL, Dahood); in the context, however, it seems better to understand it to mean **"How much longer must I wait?"** (that is, for Yahweh to save him, as in verses 81, 82). So TEV, NEB, NIV, GECL, SPCL, TOB. For **thy servant** see verse 17a. The psalmist is impatient for God to **judge** his persecutors (verse 84b); in the context the verb **judge** implies punishment. NJV and NJB translate well: "When will You bring my persecutors to judgment?"

The psalmist's enemies are again called **Godless men**, or better, **"Proud men"** (verse 85a; see verse 51). They **have dug pitfalls**, which is another figure taken from hunting, in which a pit is dug into which the animal will fall (see similar figure in verse 61a). They are trying to trap the psalmist, either to take him prisoner or else to lead him to wrong conduct (see similar language in 35.7 and 57.6). SPCL translates "grave" (and not "**pits**"), which does not seem likely.

In verse 85b **who do not conform to thy law** translates the Hebrew "which (or, who) not according to your law." This can mean that what they do is contrary to Yahweh's law (NIV, NJV); but it seems better, with the majority, to take this as a description of the enemies: they disregard God's law.

119.86-88 RSV	TEV
86 All thy commandments are sure; they persecute me with false-hood; help me!	86 Your commandments are all trustworthy; men persecute me with lies— help me!
87 They have almost made an end of me on earth; but I have not forsaken thy precepts.	87 They have almost succeeded in killing me, but I have not neglected your commands.
88 In thy steadfast love spare my life, that I may keep the testimonies of thy mouth.	88 Because of your constant love be good to me, so that I may obey your laws.

The adjective **sure** in verse 86a means "**trustworthy**," dependable; some translations express the idea of truth (see SPCL); NEB has "stand for ever."

In verse 86b the psalmist again accuses his enemies of telling lies about him (see verse 69a). It is to be noticed that RSV, by following the order of the Hebrew, makes **they** in line **b** refer back to **thy commandments** in line **a**. It is better to reverse the lines (SPCL, NEB), or else to make explicit the subject of line **b**. The psalmist's cry to God, **help me!** is a plea for God to keep him safe from his enemies.

In verse 87 the psalmist speaks of actual physical danger he runs; his enemies have almost killed him, either through sudden violence or else (which is more likely) through constant harassment and threats. He, however, has been faithful in obeying Yahweh's laws: **I have not forsaken thy precepts.** For similar language see verse 53b; verse 51b "turn away from"; verses 16b, 61b "forget."

In verse 88a the Masoretic text has the verb "to live" (RSV **spare my life**); the Qumran manuscript has the verb "be kind to," which TEV prefers (as in verse 37b). RSV **spare my life** may sound as though God were threatening to kill him; it seems better to translate "preserve my life" (see NJV, NIV) or "save me from death." The psalmist is confident that Yahweh's **steadfast love** will lead him to answer the psalmist's prayer.

In verse 88b the Hebrew says "the testimony of your mouth"; see the similar expression in verse 72a. Both RSV (**testimonies**) and TEV ("**laws**") use the plural form; but it is preferable to use a singular noun. For the verb **keep** see verses 55b, 67b.

Faith in the Law of the LORD

	RSV		TEV
89	For ever, O LORD, thy word is firmly fixed in the heavens.	89	Your word, O LORD, will last for- ever; it is eternal in heaven.
90	Thy faithfulness endures to all generations; thou hast established the earth, and it stands fast.	90	Your faithfulness endures through all the ages; you have set the earth in place, and it remains.
91	By thy appointment they stand this day; for all things are thy servants.	91	All things remain to this day be- cause of your command, because they are all your ser- vants.

In this strophe (letter *lamed*, verses 89-96) the psalmist praises Yahweh's law as perfect and eternal, and again asks him to save him from his enemies. The TEV heading may need to be restated for translation; for example, "The psalmist has faith in the Law of the LORD" or "The psalmist believes in the LORD's teachings."

In verse 89a **thy word** is synonymous with Torah, the complete expression of Yahweh's will. In Hebrew there is only the one verb "is firm" in line b; TEV uses two synonymous verbs for a better balance of the lines. NJV, however, translates line a "The LORD exists forever," taking the word "LORD" as nominative, not vocative. None of the other translations consulted does this. The Hebrew text in line b is **in the heavens**; NAB adopts a conjecture, "(it is as firm) as the heavens"; Dahood translates the Hebrew text "more stable than the heavens." In many languages it is not possible to speak of a word lasting for a long time, since a word is not thought of as having that kind of duration. Accordingly line a must often be shifted to something like "your word will always be true" or "what you have said will always be true; it will be true for ever in heaven."

In verses 90b-91 the author speaks of the created universe, which is fixed and permanent. First (verse 90a) he refers to Yahweh's **faithfulness** (see 36.5 and comments), which will last forever (**to all generations**); this line balances verse 89, which speaks of the eternity of Yahweh's law. In verse 90b the verbal phrase **thou hast established the earth** means "you have set the earth firmly in its place." It is to be noticed that the text in verse 90 does not mention the Law, and some, instead of the Hebrew "your faithfulness," conjecture "your word" (Briggs; see NEB "Thy promise"). In place of **Thy faithfulness endures**, it will often be necessary in translation to say, for example, "You will be faithful for ever," or in some languages, "You will always be faithful to people."

In verse 91a RSV does not make clear who **they** (the subject of **stand**) refers to; in line b the reader may be able to infer that **all things** is the subject of **stand** in line a. It is better to make the subject explicit in line a and then use the pronoun in line b. **By thy appointment** means "Because of your command," "In obedience to your command." The noun in Hebrew is plural, so TOB has "according to your decisions."[4]

The subject of the verb in verse 91b in Hebrew is simply "all (things)," which most translations take to mean "all created things" (see TOB "the universe"). But NEB has for line a "This day, as ever, thy decrees stand fast," which is possible; it seems more likely, however, that the reference is to "all created things." **All things are thy servants** and TEV's **"they are all your servants"** must often be shifted to a verb phrase by saying, as does NEB, "for all things serve you" or "everything obeys your commands."

119.92-94

RSV	TEV
92 If thy law had not been my delight, I should have perished in my affliction.	92 If your law had not been the source of my joy, I would have died from my sufferings.
93 I will never forget thy precepts; for by them thou hast given me life.	93 I will never neglect your instructions, because by them you have kept me alive.
94 I am thine, save me; for I have sought thy precepts.	94 I am yours—save me! I have tried to obey your commands.

In verses 92-93 the psalmist describes how his faithfulness to the Torah has kept him alive. For the expression of Yahweh's **law** as the psalmist's **delight**, see verses 47a, 70b, 77b. The psalmist's **affliction** (verse 92b) is his persecution by his enemies. The negative form of the assertion may be recast in a positive way: "Because your law was my delight, I did not die from my sufferings" (or ". . . I remained alive despite all my sufferings").

For verse 93a see verses 61b, 83b; and for verse 93b (**thou hast given me life**) see the plea in verses 37b, 40b.

The psalmist asks Yahweh to **save** him from his enemies, basing his request on the assurance that he belongs to Yahweh (**I am thine**). In languages in which **I am thine** is not possible, it may be necessary to shift to "I belong to you" or "You are the one who owns me." For verse 94b see verse 45b.

119.95-96

RSV	TEV
95 The wicked lie in wait to destroy me;	95 Wicked men are waiting to kill me, but I will meditate on your laws.

---

[4]NJV, however, takes the Hebrew preposition to mean "to" (and not "by" or "according to") and translates the line "They stand this day to [carry out] your rulings." This does not seem very probable.

	but I consider thy testimonies.	96	I have learned that everything has limits;
96	I have seen a limit to all perfection,		but your commandment is perfect.
	but thy commandment is exceedingly broad.		

Again the psalmist refers to his enemies (verse 95); for **wicked** see verse 53a. The verb translated **lie in wait** may mean simply "wait for," but followed in this context by an expression of purpose; see NJV "The wicked hope to destroy me." In line **b** the phrase **consider thy testimonies** means to think about them, meditate upon them, reflect on what they mean.

The Hebrew of verse 96 is somewhat difficult to understand: in line **a** there are two words which seem to be complete synonyms: "I have seen that there is a limit to everything, an end"; RSV **a limit to all perfection** (also TOB, GECL, BJ, NJB) is possible (see HOTTP).[5] But it seems better to translate as NJV does, "I have seen that all things have their limit" (see FRCL, GECL "I have seen that all things have an end"). The TEV expression "**everything has limits**" must be recast in some languages to say, for example, "everything comes to an end," "everything finishes" or, idiomatically in some languages, "all things sit down and die." In contrast with the imperfection of everything else is the perfection of Yahweh's **commandment**. The phrase **is exceedingly broad** (NJV "is broad beyond measure") is probably best represented by FRCL "is without limits," that is, is not limited either by time or by any flaw. Briggs comments: "All things else, however complete, have their limit; they come to an eventual end; but in antithesis the Law is **broad**, limitless in breadth, without end in time, past, present, or future."

119.97-100	RSV		TEV

Love for the Law of the LORD

	RSV		TEV
97	Oh, how I love thy law! It is my meditation all the day.	97	How I love your law! I think about it all day long.
98	Thy commandment makes me wiser than my enemies, for it is ever with me.	98	Your commandment is with me all the time and makes me wiser than my enemies.
99	I have more understanding than all my teachers, for thy testimonies are my meditation.	99	I understand more than all my teachers, because I meditate on your instructions.
100	I understand more than the aged, for I keep thy precepts.	100	I have greater wisdom than old men, because I obey your commands.

---

[5]The word translated **perfection** occurs only here in the Old Testament; the related word "completeness" is used in 139.22 ("*perfect* hatred").

In this strophe (letter *mem*, verses 97-104) the psalmist expresses his deep love for the Law and how it has blessed him. The heading of this strophe may be lightly recast for translation in some languages to say "The psalmist loves the Law of the LORD."

For verse 97a see similar statements in verses 47b, 48a, 113b, 163b. The psalmist is always studying the Torah (verse 97b); for **meditation** see verses 15a, 27b. **All the day** is not to be understood literally to mean 24 hours a day. His continued study of the Torah has made him **wiser** than his **enemies** (verse 98a), his **teachers** (verse 99a), and **the aged** (verse 100a). For translation notes on comparatives see verse 72. When translating **the aged** or TEV's **"old men,"** some languages distinguish between old people who are senile and elders who are mentally alert; the first group would be inappropriate in this context.

In verse 98a the Hebrew text has the plural "your commandments"; by a change of vowels, however, the singular **"Your commandment"** is read, which many prefer.

In verse 98b **it is ever with me** expresses the same thought as **It is my meditation all the day** in verse 97b; and verse 99b **thy testimonies are my meditation** is another way of saying the same thing. FRCL translates verse 98b "because I reflect a long time on your commands."

The psalmist's **teachers** (verse 99a) were those who had taught him the Torah; and in Israelite society older people were regarded as especially wise, so that the psalmist's claim to **understand more** than them (verse 100a) is quite surprising. The implication here is that he is not an old man.

119.101-102   RSV   TEV

101 I hold back my feet from every evil   101 I have avoided all evil conduct,
          way,   because I want to obey your
     in order to keep thy word.   word.
102 I do not turn aside from thy ordi-   102 I have not neglected your instruc-
          nances,   tions,
     for thou hast taught me.   because you yourself are my
                                                                  teacher.

In these two verses the psalmist once more states that he has avoided **every evil way** and that he does **not turn aside** from Yahweh's laws. **I hold back my feet from** in verse 101a means "I do not walk in," "I do not follow." For **way** see verses 1a, 3b; for **keep thy word** see verse 67b.

To **turn aside from** Yahweh's commands (verse 102a) means to disregard them, to quit obeying them (see "forsaken" in verse 87b). **I do not turn aside from thy ordinances** or TEV's **"I have not neglected . . ."** may be better expressed positively in some languages; for example, "I have obeyed your teachings" or "I have kept your laws." For **thou hast taught me** see the plea "Teach me" in verses 33a, 64b. The statement that Yahweh has taught him means that in his study of the Torah he has learned Yahweh's will.

119.103-104   RSV   TEV

103 How sweet are thy words to my taste, sweeter than honey to my mouth! 104 Through thy precepts I get understanding; therefore I hate every false way.	103 How sweet is the taste of your instructions— sweeter even than honey! 104 I gain wisdom from your laws, and so I hate all bad conduct.

For the thought of verse 103, see similar language in 19.10b. In this verse the word translated **sweet** occurs only here in the Old Testament. In verse 103a the Masoretic text has the singular "your word"; a few Hebrew manuscripts and the ancient versions have the plural "your words," which RSV, TEV, and others prefer. The concept of "sweetness" as applied to Yahweh's laws means that they are pleasant to learn, to memorize, to practice. In some languages it is natural to speak of some events as being sweet to experience. It is less common for words to be spoken of as sweet; however the expression is sometimes used with the meaning of deception. In languages where this metaphor will have no meaning or will suggest a wrong meaning, it will be best to use a nonmetaphor; for example, "How happy it makes me to learn your law." Alternatively, the translator may consider adapting the metaphor to the most delicious local food (not all peoples value sweetness as the best taste).

Again in verse 104 the psalmist uses the concept of **way** to speak of conduct (as in verse 101). Through his study of the Torah he has gained wisdom, and so he hates all bad conduct, that is, all behavior that does not conform to God's laws. **Every false way** and TEV's "**all bad conduct**" may appear abstract to the translator in those languages where this expression must be rendered, for example, as "I hate the crooked path that some people go on" or "I hate the evil way some people live."

119.105-106   RSV   TEV

Light from the law of the LORD

105 Thy word is a lamp to my feet and a light to my path. 106 I have sworn an oath and confirmed it, to observe thy righteous ordinances.	105 Your word is a lamp to guide me and a light for my path. 106 I will keep my solemn promise to obey your just instructions.

This strophe (letter *nun*, verses 105-112) contains the usual elements of praise, complaint, petition, and expression of devotion to God's law. The TEV heading may require adjusting for translation to something like "The LORD's Law is like a light" or "The Law of the LORD shines like a light."

Verse 105 is perhaps the best known verse of the whole psalm. The figures of **lamp** and **light** express the blessings of Yahweh, the guidance that he provides by means of his **word**, that is, the Law; **my feet** and **my path** are synonyms, meaning the psalmist's behavior, his conduct, his life as a pious Israelite. **A lamp to my feet** means "a light that lights up the path I walk on." In some languages it will be necessary to make explicit the function of the light, that is, to shine; for example, "a light to shine on my path" or "a light to shine in the place where I walk."

In verse 106 the psalmist promises to obey Yahweh's **righteous ordinances**. For comments on **righteous ordinances** see verse 7; for **observe** see verse 8a. In line a, instead of RSV **I have sworn an oath and confirmed it**, it is better to say "I have made a solemn promise and I will keep it" or, as FRCL has it, "I will keep the promise I have made"; NJV has "I have firmly sworn to . . . ."

119.107-109   RSV   TEV

107 I am sorely afflicted;   107 My sufferings, LORD, are terrible
    give me life, O LORD, according   indeed;
      to thy word!   keep me alive, as you have
108 Accept my offerings of praise, O   promised.
    LORD,   108 Accept my prayer of thanks, O
    and teach me thy ordinances.   LORD,
109 I hold my life in my hand continu-   and teach me your commands.
    ally,   109 I am always ready to risk my life;
    but I do not forget thy law.   I^s have not forgotten your law.

                                          ^{s} I am always ready to risk my life; I; *or*
                                       My life is in constant danger, but I.

In verse 107 the psalmist once more complains of his troubles: **I am sorely afflicted**; see "affliction" in verse 92b. His prayer for help, **give me life according to thy word**, is like the one in verse 25b; see also similar pleas in verses 28b, 37b, 40b).

In verse 108 **my offerings of praise** translates "the voluntary offerings of my mouth"; the psalmist's prayer is likened to a sacrifice which he offers to God. NIV translates "the willing praise of my mouth," and NEB "the willing tribute of my lips." For verse 108b see verses 12b, 26b, 64b.

Line a in verse 109 in Hebrew is "My *nefesh* is in my hand always," a way of saying "I risk my life" (see Judges 12.3; 1 Sam 28.21); see NAB "constantly I take my life in my hands." NJV has "my life is always in danger," and SPCL "I am always in danger of death." The psalmist's life is in danger because of his devotion to the law of God (see verses 23, 161). RSV's literal translation **I hold my life in my hand continually** carries little meaning. TEV has an alternative rendering in the footnote, which may be preferable to the rendering in the text (see NJV, GECL, FRCL, SPCL). For verse 109b see verse 61b.

119.110-112   RSV   TEV

110 The wicked have laid a snare for   110 Wicked men lay a trap for me,
    me,   but I have not disobeyed your

but I do not stray from thy
precepts.
111 Thy testimonies are my heritage
for ever;
yea, they are the joy of my
heart.
112 I incline my heart to perform thy
statutes
for ever, to the end.

commands.
111 Your commandments are my eternal possession;
they are the joy of my heart.
112 I have decided to obey your laws
until the day I die.

In verse 110 the psalmist uses the familiar figure of a **snare** (which is used to catch a bird) to describe his enemies' attempts to destroy him (see similar language in verses 61, 85). He repeats that he has not disobeyed Yahweh's commands (verse 110b); see similar expressions in verses 87b, 102a.

In the last two verses of this strophe the psalmist promises to obey God's laws all his life. For **heritage** in verse 111a, see 28.9. **Heritage** as used in this verse normally refers to the land in terms of the covenant. Here, however, the psalmist speaks of God's **testimonies** being his **heritage for ever**. The problem for the translator is to make clear how **testimonies** can be said to be inherited. In many languages this requires shifting away from the idea of inheritance to a valuable possession; for example, "Your laws are a valuable gift to me for all times," or "Your laws teach me things I will value for ever," or "I will keep for ever the things you teach me in your laws." For **the joy of my heart** in verse 111b, see similar expressions of "delight" in verses 47a, 70b, 77b. **They are the joy of my heart** must often be recast to say "they cause my heart to be glad" or "they make me very happy."

I incline my heart in verse 112a means "**I have decided**," "I have made up my mind." NJV has "I am resolved." In verse 112b the Hebrew reads "forever to the end" (see a similar expression in verse 44). The Hebrew word translated **to the end** (so AT, RSV, NIV, TEV, SPCL) may mean "reward," as in verse 33 (so NEB "they are a reward that never fails"; similarly Weiser, BJ, NJB, GECL, TOB, FRCL); NJV translates "to the utmost," and NAB "to the letter." It may be best to translate "reward."

119.113-115   RSV   TEV

Safety in the Law of the LORD

113 I hate double-minded men,
but I love thy law.
114 Thou art my hiding place and my
shield;
I hope in thy word.
115 Depart from me, you evildoers,
that I may keep the commandments of my God.

113 I hate those who are not completely loyal to you,
but I love your law.
114 You are my defender and protector;
I put my hope in your promise.
115 Go away from me, you sinful
people.
I will obey the commands of my
God.

In this strophe (letter *samek*, verses 113-120) the psalmist denounces his enemies, prays to Yahweh for help, and expresses his love for God's law. The TEV heading may have to be recast for translation. One possibility is "The psalmist is safe because he obeys the Law of the LORD."

In verse 113a the psalmist uses a word not found elsewhere in the Old Testament to describe those he hates; the Septuagint translates "transgressors (of the Law)"; Vulgate has "wicked." Most translations are like RSV **double-minded men** or "double heart"; SPCL has "hypocritical people," and FRCL "duplicity." Kirkpatrick defines them as "unstable waverers, half Israelites, half heathen." The word seems to describe those whose religious commitment is not total; they do not have "pure hearts," that is, single-minded devotion to Yahweh. For **I love thy law** in verse 113b, see verse 97a. Verse 113 is structured in Hebrew as a contrast: this I hate, but that I love. It can also be translated as two coordinate statements: "I love people who are fully loyal to you, and I love your law." However, it will be best to maintain the stylistic device of the psalmist, unless, of course, such contrast carries an unwanted meaning.

In verse 114a, for **hiding place** see 32.7, and for **shield** see 3.3; 28.7; both indicate protection and safety. Verse 114b is identical with verse 81b.

For verse 115a see 6.8; here **you evildoers** are the psalmist's enemies, of whom he repeatedly complains in this psalm. They try to keep him from obeying the commands of the Torah. For verse 115b see similar statements in verses 55b, 67b. **My God** can be translated "the God I serve (or, worship)."

<hr/>

119.116-117   RSV   TEV

116 Uphold me according to thy   116 Give me strength, as you prom-
     promise, that I may live,   ised, and I shall live;
     and let me not be put to shame   don't let me be disappointed in
     in my hope!   my hope!
117 Hold me up, that I may be safe   117 Hold me, and I will be safe,
     and have regard for thy statutes   and I will always pay attention
     continually!   to your commands.

In these two verses the psalmist appeals to Yahweh for help; the two verbs in verses 116a and 117a are synonymous, "sustain, uphold, support" (see RSV **Uphold** and **Hold . . . up**). For **according to thy promise** in verse 116a, see verse 58b; and in verse 116b **be put to shame** means "be disillusioned, be disappointed." NJV has "do not thwart my expectation." In this line **hope** translates a noun found only here and in 146.5b in the Old Testament; the related verb is found in verse 166. **In my hope** in both RSV and TEV does not make clear the object of the hope, which many languages will require. Accordingly one may need to say ". . . in my hope that you will save me."

In verse 117b the verb **have regard for** translates the Hebrew "regard, look at"; some prefer to emend the text to read the verb "be pleased with, take delight in" (as in verses 16a, 47a), but this does not seem warranted.

RSV   TEV

| 118 | Thou dost spurn all who go astray from thy statutes; yea, their cunning is in vain. | 118 | You reject everyone who disobeys your laws; their deceitful schemes are useless. |

118 Thou dost spurn all who go astray
      from thy statutes;
      yea, their cunning is in vain.
119 All the wicked of the earth thou
      dost count as dross;
      therefore I love thy testimonies.
120 My flesh trembles for fear of thee,
      and I am afraid of thy judg-
      ments.

118 You reject everyone who disobeys
      your laws;
      their deceitful schemes are
      useless.
119 You treat all the wicked like rub-
      bish,
      and so I love your instructions.
120 Because of you I am afraid;
      I am filled with fear because of
      your judgments.

In verses 118-119 the psalmist describes Yahweh's attitude toward those who do not keep the Law. **Spurn** means to reject, to disapprove of, not accept. For **go astray from** see the similar expressions, "stray from" in verse 110b and "forsake" in verses 53b, 87b.

In verse 118b **their cunning is in vain** means that their deceitful plans will fail. SPCL translates "their thoughts are senseless." But the Hebrew word translated **in vain** can be taken to mean "false, a lie"; so NJV translates "they are false and deceitful." FRCL translates "their plots cover up falsehood."

In verse 119a the psalmist says Yahweh looks upon **the wicked** as garbage; **dross** is the worthless material which is thrown away in the process of smelting ore or metal (see the word further in Pro 25.4; Isa 1.22,25). In languages where metal smelting is well known, the translator must make certain that the term for **dross** is not a technical term known only to a handful of specialists. If it is, there are two choices: he may employ a more generic term such as TEV's "**rubbish**," or use a descriptive phrase such as "worthless things that are thrown out." The verb in this line of the Masoretic text is "to stop, put away" (see its use in 8.2; 46.9a); a few Hebrew manuscripts and some ancient versions have the verb "consider, **treat**," which RSV, TEV, and SPCL follow, and which is also the preference of the majority of the HOTTP committee.[6]

In verse 120 the verb translated **trembles** is found only here and in Job 4.15 ("hair . . . stood up"); the related word "bristly" is found in Jeremiah 51.27. This verse is unusual in that the psalmist expresses fear and apprehension, instead of pleasure and delight as he usually does. The psalmist's strong expressions should not be softened in translation. FRCL renders **trembles** as "respect which you inspire," which is something of an attempt to give a positive basis for the psalmist's fear. However, this may not be the reason for his fear. TEV has translated **my flesh** as "I." Many translators will want to follow TEV here. However, if it is natural to express

---

[6]The HOTTP committee not only divided on whether to follow the Masoretic text or some Hebrew manuscripts and ancient versions, but of those who were in favor of the verb "consider," a majority were for the second person singular "you consider"; the minority were for the first person singular "I consider" (as in the Qumran manuscript and the Septuagint).

fear as "my body . . . ," "my skin (or some other body part) trembles," this should, of course, be done.

Obedience to the Law of the LORD

121 I have done what is just and right; do not leave me to my oppressors.	121 I have done what is right and good; don't abandon me to my enemies!
122 Be surety for thy servant for good; let not the godless oppress me.	122 Promise that you will help your servant; don't let arrogant men oppress me!

In this strophe (letter '*ayin*, verses 121-128) the psalmist affirms his innocence and asks Yahweh to rescue him from his enemies. The words suggest that he is on trial, a setting often found in psalms of lament. The TEV heading may be revised to say "The psalmist obeys the Law of the LORD" or "The psalmist obeys what the LORD teaches him."

In these two verses the psalmist pleads with Yahweh to rescue him from his **oppressors**, for he has always **done what is just and right** (verse 121). He calls his enemies **my oppressors** because they persecute and mistreat him; the same verb **oppress** is used in verse 122b. In verse 122a the Hebrew verb form translated **Be surety** by RSV is a legal term describing the action of someone who makes himself responsible for another's debts; here the term has the general sense of helping. The meaning of the line is well expressed by NJV, "Guarantee your servant's well-being" (also NJB); FRCL has "Guarantee me that everything will end well." **Be surety for thy servant** may also be rendered, for example, "Be my protector and helper" or simply "Protect me and help me." For **thy servant** see verse 17a; for **the godless** see verse 51a. (It is to be noticed that in verses 121-122 there is no reference to God's law.)

123 My eyes fail with watching for thy salvation, and for the fulfilment of thy righteous promise.	123 My eyes are tired from watching for your saving help, for the deliverance you promised.
124 Deal with thy servant according to thy steadfast love, and teach me thy statutes.	124 Treat me according to your constant love, and teach me your commands.
125 I am thy servant; give me understanding, that I may know thy testimonies!	125 I am your servant; give me understanding, so that I may know your teachings.

For verse 123a see similar language in verse 82a; for **thy salvation** see verse 81a. In verse 123b the Hebrew is simply "for the word (or, promise) of your righteousness." Here "righteousness" is parallel to **salvation** in line a and means "deliverance, rescue" (NJV "victory"); and "word" here could be "message," but more likely, as often, it means "promise." RSV, however, translates the phrase **for the fulfilment of thy righteous promise** (similarly NEB). SPCL is "waiting for you to free me, according to your promise"; FRCL "and the salvation that you have promised." Thus understood and interpreted, there is no reference in this verse to the Law. **Watching for thy salvation** may have to be recast to say "watching for you to come and save me." TEV's **"for the deliverance you promised"** may have to be recast as "and to save me as you said you would do."

In verse 124 the psalmist appeals to Yahweh's **steadfast love**. In line a TEV has not represented the often-used phrase "your servant." It is better to say "Treat me, your servant . . . ." Verse 124b is the same as verses 12b, 26b, 64b, 68b.

Verse 125 is similar in thought to verse 34; only with the Lord's help and guidance can the psalmist **know** Yahweh's teachings, that is, understand them and put them into practice.

119.126-128   RSV   TEV

126 It is time for the LORD to act,   126 LORD, it is time for you to act,
        for thy law has been broken.   because people are disobeying
127 Therefore I love thy command-   your law.
        ments   127 I love your commands more than
        above gold, above fine gold.   gold,
128 Therefore I direct my steps by all   more than the finest gold.
        thy precepts;^{k} 128 And so I follow all your instruc-
     I hate every false way.   tions;^{t}
                                                I hate all wrong ways.

^{k} Gk Jerome: Heb uncertain

                                           ^{t} *Some ancient translations* all your in-
                                           structions; *Hebrew unclear.*

In verse 126 the psalmist calls upon Yahweh **to act**, that is, to punish those who are not obeying the Law. TEV has line a in the second person, for consistency with line b; an incautious reader of RSV might think that in line b someone other than **the LORD** of line a is being addressed.

The Hebrew text begins verse 127 with a phrase ordinarily translated **Therefore** (RSV), which makes for a strange connection with verse 126, since it implies that because the Law is being broken the psalmist loves it. (This Hebrew phrase begins with the letter *'ayin,* just like the other lines in this strophe; matching lines may have been more important to the psalmist than making the discourse flow smoothly.) So some take the Hebrew as an affirmation: "Rightly" (NJV), "Truly" (NEB). For the thought of this verse, see verses 14, 72.

The Hebrew text of verse 128a is hard to understand; it seems to mean "Therefore all precepts (of) all I follow." The Hebrew "all precepts (of) all" seems to be an error for **"all your instructions"** (see Anderson, Briggs). The Septuagint and

BJ, NJB, SPCL. But HOTTP prefers the Hebrew text, saying it means "all the precepts in their totality or in every domain whatsoever, without exception." This is how TOB translates: "Thus I find all the precepts just in all points."

There is also considerable difference of opinion over the meaning of the Hebrew verb "be straight" in this context. RSV has **I direct my steps**, and TEV "**follow**." Holladay defines it here "keep precisely"; NAB has "go forward," and NEB "find the right way." NJV translates "Truly by all [Your] precepts I walk straight," and NJB "I rule my life by all your precepts." For verse 128b see 104b.

<table>
<tr><td>**119.129-131**</td><td>RSV</td><td>TEV</td></tr>
</table>

119.129-131	RSV	TEV

Desire to Obey the Law of the LORD

	RSV		TEV
129	Thy testimonies are wonderful; therefore my soul keeps them.	129	Your teachings are wonderful; I obey them with all my heart.
130	The unfolding of thy words gives light; it imparts understanding to the simple.	130	The explanation of your teachings gives light and brings wisdom to the ignorant.
131	With open mouth I pant, because I long for thy commandments.	131	In my desire for your commands I pant with open mouth.

In this strophe (letter *pe*, verses 129-136) the psalmist praises the Law, prays for Yahweh's mercy, and asks to be saved from his enemies. Here the heading may be adjusted to say "The psalmist wants to obey the Law of the LORD."

The psalmist praises Yahweh's laws as **wonderful** ("marvelous, excellent"), and so he obeys them; for **keeps them** see verse 67b. The phrase "my *nefesh*" in verse 129b is a way of saying "I."

In verse 130a the first word in the Hebrew text occurs nowhere else in the Old Testament and is generally taken to mean "disclosure, communication"; so RSV **unfolding**, TEV "**explanation**" (also SPCL, GECL); NAB has "revelation," and NJB translates "As your word unfolds it gives light." But some take the word to be derived from a verb meaning "engrave"; so NJV has "The words You inscribed give light," which is probably a way of referring to the Ten Commandments, which in Hebrew are "The Ten Words." It seems better to follow the interpretation of the majority. TEV's "**explanation of your teachings gives light**" is a difficult model to follow in translation, because it does not say who explains nor to whom the light is given. In languages in which it will be necessary to make the agent of the first verb explicit, it will often be clearer to say, for example, "You reveal your words and they give light," "You show your teaching to people and they receive light," or, without God as the agent of the action, "People discover your teaching and this gives them light."

In verse 130b **the simple** are unlearned, uninformed people who do not know the Torah; see similar idea in 19.7; 116.6. **It imparts understanding to the simple** may be recast sometimes to say, for example, "and makes ignorant people wise" or "enables people who know nothing to be wise people."

"enables people who know nothing to be wise people."

TEV has reversed the two lines in verse 131 for greater ease of understanding. The expressive figure used by the psalmist indicates his eagerness to know and obey Yahweh's commands. **With open mouth I pant** (see Job 29.23b) suggests to the modern reader the picture of an animal panting in eagerness to be fed; it is a figure of a very strong desire. FRCL takes it as a figure of drinking, "I avidly drink in your words." The verb translated **I long for** is found only here in the Old Testament. In languages in which the panting image obscures the meaning of great desire, it will be best to say something like "I have a very great desire for your commands" or "I wait with great desire for you to command me." The translator may find another metaphor more suitable to express this desire. SPCL adapts the panting figure by saying "I open my mouth with great desire because I desire your commandments."

<u>119.132-133</u>   RSV   TEV

132 Turn to me and be gracious to me,   132 Turn to me and have mercy on me
        as is thy wont toward those who   as you do on all those who love
        love thy name.   you.
133 Keep steady my steps according to   133 As you have promised, keep me
        thy promise,   from falling;
        and let no iniquity get dominion   don't let me be overcome by
        over me.   evil.

In these two verses the psalmist asks God to be kind to him and keep him from sinning. In verse 132a **Turn to me** means "Look at me, pay attention to me, listen to me"; for **be gracious** see verse 58b. In verse 132b **as is thy wont** translates the Hebrew "according to your *mishpat*." This Hebrew word normally means "justice" or "righteousness," but here it is used in the sense of "manner, custom" (see NJV "as is your rule"; NIV "as you always do"); see this use of the word, translated "custom," in 1 Kings 18.28; 2 Kings 11.14. **Those who love thy name** is a way of saying "those who love you" or "those who love to obey you."

In verse 133a **Keep steady my steps** (or, feet) may be understood as TEV has it, "**keep me from falling**"; but it may be taken to mean "guide me" (see Anderson); so SPCL "Make me walk." NEB has "make my steps firm" (similarly NJB). The phrase **according to thy promise** translates the text in many Hebrew manuscripts and the Septuagint, "according to your word"; the Masoretic text has "by your word," which NJV translates "through your promise," and TOB "by your commands."

In verse 133b the psalmist prays to be kept from the power of evil, or sin, or wrongdoing. In many languages it is difficult to speak of evil or the power of evil as the agent of an action. In this verse there is support for assuming the power of evil is that of the psalmist's enemies mentioned in 134a. Accordingly we may suggest, for example, "Do not let evil men dominate me," "Do not let those who are wicked have power over me."

RSV	TEV

134 Redeem me from man's oppression,
    that I may keep thy precepts.
135 Make thy face shine upon thy servant,
    and teach me thy statutes.
136 My eyes shed streams of tears,
    because men do not keep thy law.
	134 Save me from those who oppress me,
	    so that I may obey your commands.
	135 Bless me with your presence
	    and teach me your laws.
	136 My tears pour down like a river,
	    because people do not obey your law.

Once more the psalmist asks God to rescue him from his enemies (verse 134). For the noun **oppression** see the verb "oppress" in verses 121-122; and for **keep thy precepts** see verses 55b, 67b.

Then he prays for the blessing of Yahweh's presence (verse 135), **Make thy face shine upon thy servant** (see the same request in 31.16a). This is a figure of Yahweh present to bless and to guide. For verse 135b see verse 124b.

The strophe closes with an expression of the psalmist's deep grief over the fact that **men do not keep thy law**. He is thinking about his fellow Israelites who are not as faithful as he is in obeying all the commands of the Law. If the metaphor **My eyes shed streams of tears** will suggest a wrong meaning in the receptor language, then a suitable figure should be found, or the translator may have to say "I cry very much because . . . ."

The Justice of the Law of the LORD

RSV	TEV

137 Righteous art thou, O LORD,
    and right are thy judgments.
138 Thou hast appointed thy testimonies in righteousness
    and in all faithfulness.
	137 You are righteous, LORD,
	    and your laws are just.
	138 The rules that you have given
	    are completely fair and right.

The main theme of this strophe (letter *tsade*, verses 137-144) is the justice of God's laws, which the psalmist loves and wants to obey. The TEV heading may have to be adapted for translation by saying "The Law of the LORD is fair."

In verses 137-138 the psalmist praises Yahweh's laws as just, fair, and right, which reflects the fact that Yahweh himself is **righteous** (see 116.5). Verse 137b speaks of Yahweh's laws as **right**, that is, just and fair. RSV's use of **righteous** in line **a** and **right** in line **b** seems to imply that in Hebrew the two Hebrew words are related, which they are not. NEB seems better: "How just thou art, O Lord! How straight and true are thy decrees!"

In verse 138a **Thou hast appointed thy testimonies** is better translated "You have given your instructions" or "You have given your laws." RSV **in righteousness and in all faithfulness** makes the two words "righteous" and "faithful" attributes of

Yahweh (also FRCL). This is possible, but it seems better to take them as attributes of Yahweh's laws, as TEV, NEB, NIV, NJV, and SPCL do. TEV has **"fair and right"**; see NIV "fully trustworthy," and NJV "firmly enduring."

119.139-141   RSV   TEV

139 My zeal consumes me,   139 My anger burns in me like a fire,
       because my foes forget thy   because my enemies disregard
       words.   your commands.
140 Thy promise is well tried,   140 How certain your promise is!
       and thy servant loves it.   How I love it!
141 I am small and despised,   141 I am unimportant and despised,
       yet I do not forget thy precepts.   but I do not neglect your teach-
                                                                     ings.

In verse 139 the psalmist expresses his anger at those who disregard Yahweh's commands (see the same thought in verse 53, and see similar language in 69.9). The word translated **zeal** by RSV has in places the idea of jealousy or fury (see 78.58b, where it is parallel to "anger" in line a). The psalmist says that his anger **consumes** him; it is like a fire that is so intense that it is about to destroy him. For **forget thy words** see verses 83b, 109b.

In verse 140 the phrase **well tried** translates the verb "refine"; see a similar use of the word in 12.6; 18.30 ("proves true"). The idea here seems to be that of dependability, trustworthiness; see NJB "Your promise is well tested"; NEB "tested through and through." But NJV has "is exceedingly pure." TEV **"How certain"** expresses the idea that God always keeps his promise. For **thy servant loves it** see similar expression in verse 97a. In some languages the nominal expression **Thy promise** may have to be rendered as a verb phrase, "What you have promised," and thus saying, for example, "What you have promised me is very certain" or "The words you have told me are very true."

In verse 141 the psalmist refers to himself as **small and despised** (see 68.27 ["the least"] and 22.6). **Small** here means **"unimportant"**; NJV has "belittled"; NEB "of little account." For 141b see verses 61b, 83b, 109b.

119.142-144   RSV   TEV

142 Thy righteousness is righteous for   142 Your righteousness will last for-
       ever,   ever,
       and thy law is true.   and your law is always true.
143 Trouble and anguish have come   143 I am filled with trouble and anxi-
       upon me,   ety,
       but thy commandments are my   but your commandments bring
       delight.   me joy.
144 Thy testimonies are righteous for   144 Your instructions are always just;
       ever;

give me understanding that I may live.	give me understanding, and I shall live.

In verse 142a the psalmist speaks of Yahweh's outstanding characteristic— **righteousness**—as eternal. It is better simply to say "Your righteousness is eternal" (NJV; similarly NIV) than to represent the Hebrew literally, as RSV does. In languages in which **Thy righteousness** must be rendered as a verb phrase, one will often have to say, for example, "You are righteous and you will be righteous for ever" or "You are good and you will be good for ever." In verse 142b **is true** may be too narrowly understood as meaning there are no errors or mistakes in the Torah. FRCL has "is immutable" (that is, it is always in force); GECL uses two adjectives "true and trustworthy."

In verse 143 the psalmist again complains of his troubles (line a); but Yahweh's laws bring him happiness (line b; see verses 24a, 47a, 77b).

In verse 144a the psalmist praises Yahweh's commandments as **righteous for ever**. The meaning can be, as NJV translates, "Your righteous decrees are eternal," but the former seems preferable. A translation can be "Your commandments (or, laws) are always right (or, just)." GECL has another interpretation: "through your command justice stands forever."

The strophe closes with a prayer for **understanding**, so that the psalmist will **live** (see similar requests in verses 17, 77, 116). For **give me understanding** see verse 125a.

119.145-147   RSV

TEV

A Prayer for Deliverance

145 With my whole heart I cry; answer me, O LORD! I will keep thy statutes.	145 With all my heart I call to you; answer me, LORD, and I will obey your commands!
146 I cry to thee; save me, that I may observe thy testimonies.	146 I call to you; save me, and I will keep your laws.
147 I rise before dawn and cry for help; I hope in thy words.	147 Before sunrise I call to you for help; I place my hope in your promise.

In this strophe (letter *qof*, verses 145-152) the psalmist pleads with Yahweh to save him from his enemies, and once more he affirms his devotion to the Law. The TEV heading may require some adjustment for translation. It may be possible to say, for example, "The psalmist prays that God will save him."

In verses 145-147 the psalmist calls to Yahweh for help. Again we must suppose that his enemies are fellow Israelites who do not obey the Law (verse 150). In contrast with the psalmist's enemies, who are far from the Law, Yahweh is **near** the psalmist (verse 151a), to protect and help.

In verse 145a **cry** does not mean "weep"; it means to call out to Yahweh, an urgent plea for him to save the psalmist. And **answer me** is a request that Yahweh do what the psalmist is asking him to do. For **I will keep thy statutes** in verse 145b, see similar statements in verses 55b, 67b, 134b.

Verse 146 is practically the same as verse 145; for **observe** see verse 8a. In both verses 145 and 146, **I cry** translates the same verb "to call," which is the first word in the line (it begins with the letter *qof*).

In verse 147a **cry for help** translates a different Hebrew verb; the meaning, however, is the same as **cry** in verses 145, 146. For verse 147b see the same language in verses 81b, 114b. One form of the Hebrew text has the plural "your words" (RSV, TOB, NAB); another form of the text has the singular "your word," which the majority of translations prefer.[7]

119.148-149   RSV   TEV

148 My eyes are awake before the   148   All night long I lie awake,
       watches of the night,   to meditate on your instruc-
    that I may meditate upon thy   tions.
       promise.   149   Because your love is constant,
149 Hear my voice in thy steadfast   hear me, O LORD;
       love;   show your mercy, and preserve
    O LORD, in thy justice preserve   my life!
       my life.

In verse 148a **My eyes are awake before the watches of the night** means that the psalmist lies awake the whole night; at the start of each of the periods into which the night was divided (usually reckoned as three), the psalmist still had his eyes open. Even during the night, when most people sleep, the psalmist lay awake to think about Yahweh's laws (see similar statement in verse 55; for the verb **meditate** see verses 15a,27b). GECL translates line a "even at nighttime I still lie awake."

In verse 148b the Masoretic text has the singular "your word," which RSV (**thy promise**) and others prefer; TEV, TOB, NIV, FRCL follow some Hebrew manuscripts, the Septuagint, and Jerome, which have the plural "your words."

In verse 149 the two lines are parallel: "according to your steadfast love" in line a is parallel with "according to your justice" in line b. It is not easy to decide what the Hebrew word translated "justice" (*mishpat*) means here; most translate as does RSV. NJV translates "as is Your rule," taking the word to mean what it does in verse 132b. FRCL has "your decisions"; GECL "through your righteous decision"; NEB "by thy decree." TEV has taken the word here to mean what often the synonymous *tsedeq* means in similar contexts, "kindness, mercy, help." It seems better to follow the other translations, especially GECL. If the translator follows the model of GECL, it may be necessary to recast this expression to say, for example, "keep me safe by deciding things fairly" or "preserve my life by making just decisions." Instead of the

---

[7]The plural "your words" is *qere* (also many Hebrew manuscripts, Syriac, Targum); the singular "your word" is *kethiv* (the Septuagint).

singular form (as the Hebrew text can be read), some Hebrew manuscripts have the plural for "justice," which Briggs, TOB, BJ, NJB, FRCL, and NIV prefer; here the singular seems preferable (RSV, NJV, NEB, NAB, TEV, SPCL).

119.150-152 RSV   TEV

RSV	TEV
150 They draw near who persecute me with evil purpose; they are far from thy law.	150 My cruel persecutors are coming closer, people who never keep your law.
151 But thou art near, O LORD, and all thy commandments are true.	151 But you are near to me, LORD, and all your commands are permanent.
152 Long have I known from thy testimonies that thou hast founded them for ever.	152 Long ago I learned about your instructions; you made them to last forever.

Once more the psalmist complains about his enemies (verse 150) but relies upon the Lord's presence to save him. In the Hebrew text they are described as "those who pursue wicked plans"; see NJV "those who pursue intrigue" (also HOTTP). But with the change of one vowel (as in a few Hebrew manuscripts), the text means "those who wickedly persecute me," which most translations prefer. RSV **persecute me with evil purpose**; NAB "malicious persecutors"; TEV and SPCL "cruel persecutors." In line **b** the statement **they are far from thy law** means they have no use for the Law; they disregard it altogether.

In contrast with the psalmist's enemies, who are far from the Law, Yahweh is **near** the psalmist, to protect and help him (verse 151a).

In verse 151b the adjective translated **true** can be understood to mean "firm, steadfast" (TEV, NAB); or else the translation can be "reliable, trustworthy." The translation here should be the same as in verse 142b.

The strophe closes with the confession that the Law (**thy testimonies**) is eternal. The verb in verse 152b means "to establish, found, appoint," as though the Law were part of God's universe, which he created to last forever. In line **a** the preposition "from (your testimonies)" seems to indicate that it was in the Torah itself that the psalmist had learned that Yahweh's laws are meant to last forever; but the sense may be, as FRCL has it, "For a long time I have known about your orders, that you issued them to last forever" (see TOB). SPCL has "Since a long time ago I have known your rules, established by you eternally."

119.153-154 RSV   TEV

A Plea for Help

RSV	TEV
153 Look on my affliction and deliver me, for I do not forget thy law.	153 Look at my suffering, and save me, because I have not neglected

| 154 | Plead my cause and redeem me;
give me life according to thy
promise! | | your law. |
| | | 154 | Defend my cause, and set me free;
save me, as you have promised. |

The main theme of this strophe (letter *resh*, verses 153-160) is again the psalmist's cry to God to save him from his enemies. The TEV heading may have to be restated for translation in some languages as, for example, "The psalmist asks God to help him."

The plea in verse 153 is like the one in verse 107. The request **Look on my affliction** means "Pay attention to my sufferings (or, troubles)." For **affliction** see verse 107a. The expression **Look on my affliction** or TEV's "**Look at my suffering**" may have to be recast in other languages in some such manner as "Look and see how much I am suffering" or "Look at me and you will see how much I suffer." For verse 153b see verses 83b, 109b, 141b.

In verse 154 the Hebrew expression translated **Plead my cause** is the language of a law court, where the psalmist sees himself on trial (see 35.23-24; 43.1); he is asking God to defend him against his accusers. **Redeem me** (see comment, 19.14; 69.18) is parallel to **give me life** in line **b** (used also in verses 156b, 159b). In the context of this strophe, in which the setting of a trial is the background of the language, the meaning "save me from being condemned" or "preserve my life" seems preferable (see NJV "preserve me"; Dahood "preserve my life"). For **according to thy promise** see verses 58b, 116a. In languages where no set legal expressions are available, the translator will often have to say, for example, "Defend me" or "Protect me."

155	Salvation is far from the wicked, for they do not seek thy stat- utes.	155	The wicked will not be saved, for they do not obey your laws.
156	Great is thy mercy, O LORD; give me life according to thy justice.	156	But your compassion, LORD, is great; show your mercy and save me!
157	Many are my persecutors and my adversaries, but I do not swerve from thy testimonies.	157	I have many enemies and oppres- sors, but I do not fail to obey your laws.

In verse 155 the psalmist refers to his enemies as **the wicked** (see verses 53a, 95a); the statement that **salvation is far from** them means that they have little if any chance at all of being rescued from their troubles by Yahweh. For **seek thy statutes** in verse 155b, see verses 45b, 94b. **Salvation is far from the wicked** has been restructured by TEV as a sentence with a passive verb, "**will not be saved.**" If the translator follows this model, it may be necessary to use an active verb and say, for example, "God, you will not save wicked people."

In the first part of verse 156, the psalmist praises Yahweh's **mercy** (kindness, compassion; FRCL "You have a heart full of love").

The second part of verse 156 is similar to verses 40b, 107b, which see. Here the Masoretic text has the plural of *mishpat* (so TOB, BJ, NJB, FRCL, NIV), but a few Hebrew manuscripts and the Septuagint have the singular (which is followed by RSV, TEV, SPCL, GECL). For **according to thy justice** see verse 149b for the same phrase.

In verse 157 the psalmist complains once more about his many enemies; despite all of them, he does not **swerve from** Yahweh's **testimonies**. For similar language see "turn aside from" in verse 102a; "forsaken," verse 87b; "stray from," verse 110b.

119.158-160   RSV   TEV

158 I look at the faithless with disgust,   158 When I look at those traitors, I
     because they do not keep thy   am filled with disgust,
     commands.   because they do not keep your
159 Consider how I love thy precepts!   commands.
     Preserve my life according to   159 See how I love your instructions,
     thy steadfast love.   LORD.
160 The sum of thy word is truth;   Your love never changes, so
     and every one of thy righteous   save me!
     ordinances endures for ever.   160 The heart of your law is truth,
                                                   and all your righteous judg-
                                                   ments are eternal.

It is generally agreed that **the faithless** in verse 158a are fellow Israelites who do not keep Yahweh's laws. The verb translated **I look . . . with disgust** appears also in 95.10 ("I loathed"). For verse 158b see similar but positive language in verses 67b, 134b, 145b.

For the sentiment in verse 159a, see verses 97a, 113b. With the verb **Consider** the psalmist calls Yahweh's attention to his love for the Law. TEV inserts the vocative "LORD" here, to make clear whom "**Your**" in line <u>b</u> refers to. For verse 159b see verses 40b, 107b, 156b; for **according to thy steadfast love** see verse 124a.

In verse 160 the Hebrew reads "The head of your word is *'emet*," the word "head" here having the meaning of "sum, totality, substance, essence." NJV has ". . . the essence of Your word" (also NJB). And the Hebrew word *'emet* is taken here by most commentators and translators to mean **truth**. NAB, however, has "permanence," and Briggs and NJB "faithfulness." This may be preferable, since biblical writers rarely if ever speak of **truth** as an abstract concept (see Anderson). GECL translates "Your word, Lord, is true and trustworthy" (as in verse 142b). In many languages it is nearly impossible to find an expression for such abstract notions as "essence" or "totality." Accordingly one must sometimes say, for example, "What you say, LORD, is true," "Your words, LORD, are true," or idiomatically sometimes, "LORD, your words are straight."

Dedication to the Law of the LORD

161 Princes persecute me without cause, but my heart stands In awe of thy words. 162 I rejoice at thy word like one who finds great spoil. 163 I hate and abhor falsehood, but I love thy law.	161 Powerful men attack me unjustly, but I respect your law. 162 IIow happy I am because of your promises— as happy as someone who finds rich treasure. 163 I hate and detest all lies, but I love your law.

In this strophe (letter *sin/shin*, verses 161-168) the psalmist expresses his deep devotion to the law of God. The TEV heading may be adjusted for translation by saying, for example, "The psalmist loves and obeys the Law of the LORD."

Once again he refers to his enemies as **Princes** (verse 161; see verse 23) who **persecute** him **without cause** (see similar statements about his enemies in verses 69a, 86b, 95a, 110a, 150a). But he feels safe because of his **awe** for Yahweh's law. The verb translated **stands in awe** has elsewhere the meaning of "be afraid, terrified" (see 14.5), and the meaning here may be "but I am afraid only of your law" (so TOB, Anderson). The idea of fear and trembling is inherent in the word (see similar language in verse 120); so NIV "but my heart trembles at your word." NJV and NEB, however, have "my heart thrills at your word," which strikes a note of joyous anticipation; but nowhere else in the Old Testament does the verb or the related noun have any idea other than fear. So TEV **"respect"** may not be strong enough; perhaps "deep reverence for" is better.

One form of the Masoretic text of verse 161b has the singular "your word" (so TEV and others), while another form has the plural "your words" (so RSV and others). The same variation occurs in verse 162a.

The psalmist (verse 162) likens his happiness to that of a man who discovers a great treasure, literally "a large amount of booty" (RSV **great spoil**), which means wealth captured from a defeated enemy after a battle. But **"treasure"** well expresses the essential meaning of the word (TEV, FRCL, SPCL, NJB).

In verse 163 the psalmist repeats his feeling of hatred of **falsehood** and his love for the Torah. **Hate and abhor** may have to be reduced to a single verb in some languages.

164 Seven times a day I praise thee for thy righteous ordinances. 165 Great peace have those who love thy law; nothing can make them stumble.	164 Seven times each day I thank you for your righteous judgments. 165 Those who love your law have perfect security, and there is nothing that can make them fall.

In verse 164 the psalmist expresses his gratitude to Yahweh for his **righteous ordinances** (see similar phrase in verse 62b). **Seven times a day** may be meant literally, or else it may mean "many times."

In verse 165 **peace** translates the word *shalom* (see 29.11), which is how most translate it. NJV, however, has "well-being" (see FRCL *bonheur*), and Dahood "prosperity." The basic idea of wholeness, or completeness, means not only absence of conflict but the positive qualities of security and prosperity. So GECL has "prosperity and peace." In verse 165b **stumble** (or "**fall**") refers to error or to misfortune in general. NJV has "they encounter no adversity."

119.166-168   RSV   TEV

166 I hope for thy salvation, O LORD,   166 I wait for you to save me, LORD,
       and I do thy commandments.   and I do what you command.
167 My soul keeps thy testimonies;   167 I obey your teachings;
       I love them exceedingly.   I love them with all my heart.
168 I keep thy precepts and testimo-   168 I obey your commands and your
       nies,   instructions;
       for all my ways are before thee.   you see everything I do.

In verse 166a **I hope for thy salvation** means "I am trusting in you to save me" (see similar statement in Gen 49.18); as elsewhere in this psalm (verses 41b, 123a) **salvation** is deliverance from enemies or from troubles in general. In line **b** he affirms once again that he obeys Yahweh's **commandments**.

For verse 167a see similar expression in verse 129b; and for verse 167b see verse 159a.

It is to be noticed that in verse 168a the psalmist uses two synonyms in the same line, **thy precepts and testimonies**, which happens nowhere else in this psalm. In verse 168b **my ways** means behavior, conduct; SPCL "you know all my conduct!"; and **before thee** is a way of saying that everything he does is seen by Yahweh.

119.169-170   RSV   TEV

                                                      A Prayer for Help

169 Let my cry come before thee, O   169 Let my cry for help reach you,
       LORD;   LORD!
       give me understanding accord-   Give me understanding, as you
       ing to thy word!   have promised.
170 Let my supplication come before   170 Listen to my prayer,
       thee;   and save me according to your
       deliver me according to thy   promise!
       word.

In this final strophe (letter *taw*, verses 169-176) the psalmist mixes petition for God's help with praise for the Law. The heading of this strophe is essentially the same as the heading of verses 153-160.

The first two verses are parallel; the first line of both is a prayer for help, and in the second line are additional requests, based on Yahweh's promise to save. The verb in verse 169a "to bring near" is used also of sacrifices, and the psalmist may have thought of his prayer as a sacrifice offered to God (see verse 108). NEB takes **cry** in verse 169a to be "cry of joy." The Hebrew verb in verse 170a is not the same as in verse 169a; the two, however, are synonymous. And in both lines **before thee** translates "before your face," that is, "into your presence." This is a way of asking Yahweh to hear and respond to the psalmist's plea. **Let my cry come before thee** will often have to be recast in translation to say, for example, "Hear my cry," or "**Listen to my prayer**" as in TEV verse 170. For **give me understanding** in verse 169b, see verses 125a, 144b.

For **deliver me** in verse 170b, see synonymous verbs in verses 153a and 146a. TEV's "**according to your promise**" must often be recast to say "because you have promised me."

119.171-173 RSV	TEV
171 My lips will pour forth praise that thou dost teach me thy statutes.	171 I will always praise you, because you teach me your laws.
172 My tongue will sing of thy word, for all thy commandments are right.	172 I will sing about your law, because your commands are just.
173 Let thy hand be ready to help me, for I have chosen thy precepts.	173 Always be ready to help me, because I follow your commands.

Verses 171-172 both express the psalmist's promise to **praise** Yahweh because of his **statutes** and because his **commandments are right**. **My lips** in verse 171 and **My tongue** in verse 172 are figures of speech for the psalmist himself. For **teach me thy statutes** in verse 171b, see verses 64b, 68b, 124b. For **all thy commandments are right** in verse 172b, see similar expressions in verses 137b, 144a, and especially in verse 151b.

In verse 173 the psalmist again appeals to Yahweh for **help**; in this verse **thy hand** is also a figure of speech, denoting Yahweh himself. In verse 173b **I have chosen** describes a deliberate decision by the psalmist to obey Yahweh's laws.

119.174-176 RSV	TEV
174 I long for thy salvation, O LORD, and thy law is my delight.	174 How I long for your saving help, O LORD! I find happiness in your law.
175 Let me live, that I may praise thee, and let thy ordinances help me.	175 Give me life, so that I may praise

176 I have gone astray like a lost
    sheep; seek thy servant,
    for I do not forget thy com-
    mandments.

    you;
    may your instructions help me.
176 I wander about like a lost sheep;
    so come and look for me, your
    servant,
    because I have not neglected
    your laws.

For verse 174a see the similar thought in verse 81a; and for verse 174b see verse 77b.

In verse 175 **Let me live** translates "Give life to my *nefesh*" (see 3.2). And the request in verse 175b may be translated "may your laws support me" (see NIV "sustain"), that is, in the sense that they will provide him with wisdom and strength to live in accordance with Yahweh's will.

In verse 176 the psalmist compares himself to **a lost sheep** that has strayed away from the flock and the shepherd. He sees his sins not as a deliberate act of disobedience but as the result of ignorance and carelessness; and so he prays, not for forgiveness, but that Yahweh will look for him. Surely Yahweh will answer his prayer, because he has not disregarded his laws (for **forget thy commandments** see similar language in verses 61b, 83b, 109b, 141b).

Psalm 120

Psalms 120–134 all have a title in the Hebrew text which is translated by RSV as **A Song of Ascents** (TEV does not include this title). The collection is also called "The Book of Pilgrim Songs." The Hebrew word translated **Ascents** comes from the verb "to go up," but other than this there is no agreement as to what the phrase means. Some take it to indicate the return of the Hebrew exiles from Babylonia; others take it to refer to a stylistic feature found in some of the psalms, in which the order of the statement progresses in a step-like fashion from one verse to the other; others take it to refer to the steps in the Temple precincts which led from one court to the other; the majority take it to refer to the ascent up the mountain on which the Temple was built (Mount Moriah, known as Mount Zion). Thus understood, these psalms are songs which the pilgrims sang as they came to Jerusalem for one of the three major annual festivals (see GECL).

Psalm 120 is a lament, a complaint by an individual who is persecuted by enemies. But verse 1 may be understood to mean that his prayer has already been answered, which would mean that the psalm is a thanksgiving for answered prayer (so Fisher). If so, however, it is strange that the psalmist does not actually thank God for answering his complaint.

HEADING: "**A Prayer for Help.**" Other headings are: "The enemies of peace"; "A warning to liars"; "Prayer in face of danger." The TEV heading may be recast for translation into some languages as "The psalmist asks God to help him" or "The psalmist asks for God's help."

Hebrew Title: **A Song of Ascents.**
See the first paragraph of comments on this psalm.

120.1-2

	RSV		TEV
1	In my distress I cry to the LORD, that he may answer me:	1	When I was in trouble, I called to the LORD, and he answered me.
2	"Deliver me, O LORD, from lying lips, from a deceitful tongue."	2	Save me, LORD, from liars and deceivers.

As shown by the difference between RSV and TEV, there is no agreement whether the verbs in verse 1 are to be understood as present, **I cry . . . he may answer**, or as past "I called . . . he answered." Like TEV are Dahood, NJV, TOB, NEB, NAB; like RSV are AT, BJ, NJB, NIV, SPCL; but these, unlike RSV **that he may answer**, have "and he answers." There is no way of being dogmatic, but it seems that the verbs should be taken as past tense (see Weiser, Anderson, Taylor, Kirkpatrick). **Cry** means to call for help, and **answer** implies that Yahweh will help. In some languages it will be necessary to make clear the purpose of calling to the Lord; for example, "I called to the LORD for help" or "I asked the LORD to help me." "He answered me" may be taken to mean that he replied to my question. If this is the case, it is better to say "and he helped me" or "and he answered me by helping me."

RSV places verse 2 in quotation marks, thus making it the prayer that the psalmist refers to in verse 1; NEB does the same, and this is probably correct. The words of the psalmist's prayer are inserted in an unusual way. In languages in which verse 2 may not fit well, it may be necessary to make clear that these are the words which the psalmist uses to ask God for help in verse 1. Accordingly it may be necessary to say, for example, "I prayed saying this . . ." or "I said to the LORD." In some languages quotation marks will be sufficient. **Deliver me** represents the Hebrew "save my *nefesh*" (see 3.2). For the verb see 7.1. The psalmist's prayer is that Yahweh save him **from lying lips, from a deceiving tongue** (see similar language in 52.3-4), by which the psalmist means his enemies, who tell lies about him. See FRCL "people who lie and take false oaths." It is uncertain who these enemies are, but probably they are fellow Israelites, not Gentiles. **Lying lips and deceitful tongue** represent the entire person or persons, which TEV correctly renders as "liars" and "deceivers."

<u>120.3-4</u>   RSV   TEV

3   **What shall be given to you?**   3   **You liars, what will God do to**
     And what more shall be done to   **you?**
        you,   **How will he punish you?**
     you deceitful tongue?   4   **With a soldier's sharp arrows,**
4   **A warrior's sharp arrows,**   **with red-hot coals!**
     with glowing coals of the broom
        tree!

By means of the rhetorical device of a question and an answer, the psalmist describes how God will punish his enemies. Verse 3 in Hebrew is literally "What will he give to you and what will he add to you?" This question reflects the language used in a curse: "May God do so to you, and add to you" (see Ruth 1.17; 1 Sam 3.17; 14.44; 25.22). Here the question means "How will he punish you?"[1] See FRCL "What punishment will God inflict on you . . . ?" and GECL "How will God punish you . . . ?"

As RSV shows, only in line <u>c</u> of verse 3 are the psalmist's enemies named, **you deceitful tongue**. In most cases it will be better to place this first, as TEV does: "**You liars . . .**" And RSV, by using the passive voice of the verb, translates in an impersonal sense, **What shall be given . . . what more shall be done . . . ?** (see also TOB). It is preferable to take it in a personal sense, as TEV, FRCL, GECL, and others

---

[1]NJV, however, translates "What can you profit, what can you gain?" This is possible but not very probable.

do. As in the case of all rhetorical devices, the translator must ask what the function of the question is in this verse, and supply a structure which will serve the same purpose in the receptor language. The question form in verse 3 represents an emphatic statement whose content comes in verse 4. Accordingly in many languages a question in verse 3 will be wrongly understood. In such cases it may be better to say, for example, "You liars, God will do something awful to you; he will certainly punish you."

The answer (verse 4) may be taken literally, but more probably **sharp arrows** and **glowing coals** are figures for harsh punishment, extreme suffering. Weiser comments: "The two metaphors . . . are as much as to say 'murder and fire,' that is, death and destruction." The Hebrew text in verse 4a identifies the coals as being of **the broom tree**; see *Fauna and Flora,* page 100, for the identification of this bush, which is mentioned in 1 Kings 19.4-5; Job 30.4. It is not necessary to identify the tree, unless the broom tree is well known to the readers. So TEV **"red-hot coals,"** and NJB and NEB "red-hot charcoal." In many languages the punishment of **sharp arrows** and **glowing coals** will not be clear. Therefore it may be necessary to make explicit who is to be punished, either in generic or in specific terms; for example, "by shooting you with sharp arrows and burning you with hot coals."

120.5   RSV   TEV

Woe is me, that I sojourn in Meshech, that I dwell among the tents of Kedar!	Living among you is as bad as living in Meshech or among the people of Kedar.*u*

u MESHECH . . . KEDAR: *Two distant regions whose people were regarded as savages.*

The language of the Hebrew text of verse 5 is difficult to understand; its literal translation makes it appear that the psalmist at the time he wrote the psalm was living in **Meshech** and in **Kedar** (see RSV; also AT, NEB, NAB, NJV, NJB, NIV, SPCL). This was obviously impossible, since Meshech, a region between the Black Sea and the Caspian Sea, was a long distance from Kedar, the region of a desert tribe living south of Damascus, in Syria. So most commentators take the names, not as actual places where he was then living (or had lived), but as figures for "barbarians" or "savages." So FRCL, "How terrible for me to have to live among barbarians, and to dwell in the midst of savages!" This seems to be the best way to represent these name places. Taylor suggests that the names are mysterious references to some well-known Jewish center of population in some foreign country. TEV has followed the interpretation favored by most commentators, but retains the names of the two places. Similar is "My plight is like exile in Meshech, like living among the tents of Kedar." In verse 5 the translator must decide whether to use a note, as in TEV, or to give the meaning suggested by the TEV note and by FRCL in the text. This decision will depend in part upon how familiar readers are with notes and how effectively they are used. Since the meaning of "barbarian" and "savage" are essentially the same, it is not necessary to use both. "Savages" may sometimes be rendered "cruel people" or "people who practice cruel customs."

120.6-7   RSV   TEV

6   Too long have I had my dwelling   6   I have lived too long
        among those who hate peace.   with people who hate peace!
7   I am for peace;   7   When I speak of peace,
        but when I speak,   they are for war.
        they are for war!

The people the psalmist denounces are hostile and quarrelsome: they **hate peace** and **they are for war**, and the psalmist laments that he has to live among them. For a discussion of **peace** see 29.11. **Those who hate peace** is difficult to express in many languages, because **peace** is sometimes not found as a noun. Accordingly verse 6b must sometimes be rendered "with people who love to fight each other" or "with people who hate to live with others peacefully," or idiomatically, "with people who are opposed to having cool hearts with others." In verse 7b **when I speak** probably has "**of peace**" as the implied subject of his conversation (so FRCL, SPCL, GECL, TEV). TEV has shortened and combined **I am for peace; but when I speak** into one line, "**When I speak of peace.**" If the translator follows TEV in this, it may be necessary to recast the expression to say, for example, "When I tell people they should live together peacefully," or idiomatically sometimes, "When I speak of people living together with cool hearts."

Psalm 121

This second psalm in the collection of "Pilgrim Psalms" (see introduction to Psa 120) has for its setting a journey, and in general it is thought that it is a journey to Jerusalem, to one of the annual festivals in the Temple (see Anderson; Taylor takes **the hills** in verse 1 to be the hills along the pilgrim's route to Jerusalem). But there is nothing specific in the psalm itself to indicate that Jerusalem is the goal of the journey, and some believe that the journey is away from Jerusalem (Toombs, Anderson).

There is an obvious dialogue pattern, but there is no certainty as to who are the participants in the dialogue, whether it is an inner dialogue conducted by the psalmist, or a dialogue between a parent and a child or a priest and a pilgrim. Most believe it to be between a priest and a pilgrim. In the Hebrew text the psalmist himself speaks in verses 1-2, while the words of reassurance, from someone else, come in verses 3-8.

HEADING: **"The Lord Our Protector."** Other headings are: "The guardian of Israel"; "The guardian God"; "God the helper." The TEV heading may be recast for translation in some languages by saying "The Lord is our protector" or "The Lord is the one who protects us."

Hebrew Title: **A Song of Ascents** (TEV **"By David"**).
    For the title **A Song of Ascents**, see introduction to Psalm 120.

121.1-2	RSV		TEV
1	I lift up my eyes to the hills. From whence does my help come?	1	I look to the mountains; where will my help come from?
2	My help comes from the Lord, who made heaven and earth.	2	My help will come from the Lord, who made heaven and earth.

The psalmist begins by saying **I lift up my eyes to the hills**, and then asks where his help will come from. There is no certainty about the location of these hills; Anderson thinks they are the mountains on the route from Jerusalem to the psalmist's home, and Taylor takes the journey to be the reverse of this. Some believe that these are the hills of or near Jerusalem, while others see an allusion to the "high places" where the pagan gods were believed to live. Dahood takes it to be heaven itself, where Yahweh lives. The only way to translate the Hebrew is to say "the mountains" (or, the hills), without any specific identification. The Hebrew phrase "to lift up one's eyes" means, in English, "to look up at." The question in verse 1b is a way of introducing the information that comes in the answer, in verse 2. It should be translated as a question whose answer is supplied by the psalmist himself. FRCL translates it "Is there anyone who will be able to help me?" (It should be noticed that RSV **from whence** is redundant; **whence** already means "from where.") The relation of the answer in verse 2 to the question in verse 1b will be determined by what one understands **the hills** in verse 1a to represent. If they represent heaven, as Dahood believes (and see 123.1), or the mountains near Jerusalem, then the question implies that the psalmist's help will come from those hills, for that is where Yahweh lives. But if **the hills** are understood as the dwelling place of pagan gods, the question implies that the psalmist's help will not come from those hills but will come from Yahweh, who created **heaven and earth.**

GECL and POCL (Portuguese Common Language Version) translate verse 1 as a statement: "I look to the hills, where my help comes from." This is possible and in some languages may be the best way to translate the verse. Line a of verse 1 appears in many translations as a statement unrelated to the rest of the psalm. If the translator follows such versions as TEV, it may be necessary to make the connection between the two lines of verse 1 clearer; for example, "When I look to the mountains, I ask myself where my help will come from," or as direct address, "**Where will my help come from?**" (see SPCL). In some languages it will be necessary to ask the question as "Who will help me"?

The answer to the question comes in verse 2, with the psalmist himself as the speaker. It would be more natural if the answer were given by someone else; so some commentators (Taylor, Dentan), instead of the Hebrew **my help**, change the text to "your help." NEB tries to achieve the same result by translating "Help," without any possessive adjective. But the Hebrew text should be translated as it is. Yahweh is the psalmist's helper; he is the Creator of heaven and earth (see the same phrase in 115.15) and so has all the power needed to protect the psalmist. If the question in verse 1 is made in personal terms, "Who will help me?" the answer in verse 2 should also be personal: "The LORD will help me" or "The LORD is the one who will help me."

121.3-4 RSV TEV

	RSV		TEV
3	He will not let your foot be moved, he who keeps you will not slumber.	3	He will not let you fall; your protector is always awake.
4	Behold, he who keeps Israel will neither slumber nor sleep.	4	The protector of Israel never dozes or sleeps.

The statement in verses 3-8 seems to be made by a different speaker from the one in verses 1-2. If these verses are thought of as a blessing, the speaker is probably a priest. Some would like to read in verse 3 the first person pronoun instead of the second person of the Hebrew text (see Taylor), so that it also would be, as in verse 1, the psalmist's words: "May he not let me fall, may my protector stay awake!" This is very attractive but has no support in the text. The switch in pronouns may cause some problem in understanding. If the understanding of the psalm is seriously affected, the translator may introduce a subtitle before verse 3; for example, "This is how the LORD protects you" or, since this part of the psalm is a benediction, "God's protection is a blessing."

He will not let your foot be moved means "He will not let you stumble (or, fall)," a figure for "falling" into misfortune or trouble (see 66.9). The TEV expression **"not let you fall"** may be rendered idiomatically in some languages; for example, "He will not let you see misfortune" or "He will not let trouble grab hold of you."

Some take the negative **not** in the Hebrew of verse 3 to be an interrogative particle (see Briggs, Oesterley, Weiser, Taylor, Kirkpatrick); so NEB "How could he . . . ?" (so the Septuagint); TOB and FRCL have "May he not let . . . ." Most translate as RSV and TEV do. In verse 3b **he who keeps you** means "your guardian," "**your protector**"; and **slumber** means "sleep, fall asleep."

The reassurance in verse 4 picks up the language of verse 3 and makes it even more emphatic, **neither slumber nor sleep**. This can be expressed in a positive way, "is always awake and alert." And here Yahweh is called **he who keeps Israel** (like **he who keeps you** in verse 3). **Israel** is the people of Israel, not the country as such.

121.5-6	RSV	TEV
5	The LORD is your keeper; the LORD is your shade on your right hand.	5 The LORD will guard you; he is by your side to protect you.
6	The sun shall not smite you by day, nor the moon by night.	6 The sun will not hurt you during the day, nor the moon during the night.

In verse 5 **your keeper** uses the same word "to keep" used in verses 3b, 4a; and **your shade** means "your protection," a meaningful figure of speech in a land where the shade of a tree would protect the traveler from the harmful effects of the hot sun (see "shadow" in 91.1b). **On your right hand** means "close to you, near you, at your side."

In verse 6 Yahweh is said to afford protection from **the sun** and **the moon**. The sun's intense heat can be harmful, and it was believed that the rays of the full moon were dangerous, causing epilepsy and other diseases. (A reflection of this belief is seen in the word "lunacy," which comes from the Latin word for "moon.") The verb **smite** can be translated in a more general way, "hurt, harm, injure." It may be necessary to be specific in regard to the harm of the sun and say, for example, "The sun will not burn you in the daytime." Both TEV and RSV use ellipsis in **nor the moon by night**. Obviously, if the translator has used "burn" in connection with the sun, it cannot be used with the moon. This is the advantage of using a generic verb with the sun. In languages where ellipsis cannot be used, the translator must consider carefully the use of a specific verb in relation to the moon. Since a great variety of beliefs and customs are associated with the moon and its phases, it may be necessary to provide a note to say that verse 6 means that God protects people both day and night.

	RSV		TEV
7	The LORD will keep you from all evil; he will keep your life.	7	The LORD will protect you from all danger; he will keep you safe.
8	The LORD will keep your going out and your coming in from this time forth and for evermore.	8	He will protect you as you come and go now and forever.

The final two verses repeat in more emphatic and general terms the promise that Yahweh **will keep you**. It is to be noticed that the verb "to keep" is used in verses 3, 4, 6, 7, 8. **All evil** in verse 7a includes all kinds of danger and harm; this is not a reference to moral evil or sin. In verse 7b **he will keep your life** means "he will keep you safe (from harm)."

In verse 8 the Hebrew phrase **your going out and your coming in** is taken by TEV and others in the sense of journeys or of activity in general, that is, from the time the man left the house in the morning until he returned in the evening (see the use of the phrase in this sense in Deut 28.6). It may also be translated "wherever you go" or "wherever you may be." Some take the phrase to be quite specific: "when you leave here and when you arrive at your destination," that is, for the whole journey. The general sense seems to be preferable.

Line c is an emphatic assertion of the fact that Yahweh's protection lasts forever.

Psalm 122

In this psalm a pilgrim arriving in Jerusalem for one of the major annual festivals in the Temple (see introduction to Psa 120) breaks into a song of thanksgiving and praise. The psalm opens with the arrival at the Temple (verses 1-2), which is followed by a song of praise to Jerusalem (verses 3-5). The psalm closes with a prayer for the peace and prosperity of the city (verses 6-9).

HEADING: "**In Praise of Jerusalem.**" Other headings are: "The pilgrim's joy"; "A prayer for Jerusalem"; "Hail, Jerusalem!" The TEV heading may have to be adjusted for translation into some languages as "The psalmist speaks well of Jerusalem" or "The psalmist says that Jerusalem is great."

Hebrew Title: **A Song of Ascents. Of David** (TEV "By David").
For **A Song of Ascents** see introduction to Psalm 120.

122.1-2	RSV		TEV
1	I was glad when they said to me, "Let us go to the house of the LORD!"	1	I was glad when they said to me, "Let us go to the LORD's house."
2	Our feet have been standing within your gates, O Jerusalem!	2	And now we are here, standing inside the gates of Jerusalem!

The psalm opens with a statement of the joy the psalmist felt when he was asked to join his friends on the pilgrimage to the Temple in Jerusalem (verse 1); the occasion would have been one of the three major annual festivals. If the indefinite **they said** needs to be modified, something like "I was glad when my friends (or, companions) said to me . . . ." FRCL uses the indefinite "someone said to me"; or the passive voice can be used, ". . . when I was invited to go to the house of the LORD." Some, however, translate line **b** not as an invitation but as a statement, "We are going to the house of the LORD" (FRCL, NJV); in this case "We" includes the psalmist as the person spoken to. It seems better to translate as an invitation, as do the majority. **The house of the LORD** is the Temple in Jerusalem, and this may need to be made explicit.

In verse 2 the psalmist addresses Jerusalem directly (see RSV); he has now arrived in the city. TEV has represented the meaning by use of a declarative statement; but if direct address to the city is meaningful, then it may be used in translation. The verb can be understood as referring to past time, "(Our feet) stood" (or, were standing); so Dahood, NJV. It seems preferable to take it as TEV, NEB, NIV, NAB, and others have done, "We are standing." RSV **have been standing** implies they have been there quite some time. FRCL has "At last our feet stand in your house, Jerusalem," and NJB has "At last our feet are standing at your gates, Jerusalem!" In some languages it is necessary to mark clearly the transition from the invitation in verse 1 to the arrival at the Temple in verse 2; for example, "Let us go to the LORD's house. We went there, and now we are standing inside . . . ."

	122.3-4 RSV		TEV

3	Jerusalem, built as a city
	  which is bound firmly together,
		3	Jerusalem is a city restored
			  in beautiful order and harmony.

4	to which the tribes go up,
	  the tribes of the LORD,
	as was decreed for Israel,
	  to give thanks to the name of
	  the LORD.
		4	This is where the tribes come,
			  the tribes of Israel,
			to give thanks to the LORD
			  according to his command.

In these verses the psalmist praises Jerusalem. It is to be noticed that in verses 3-5 Jerusalem is referred to in the third person; in verses 7-9 it is addressed in the second person. If the change from third to second person is likely to cause confusion, it may be best to use the second person throughout (see GECL).

The Hebrew verb in verse 3a can mean "to build" or "to rebuild"; most translations take it to mean "built" or "built up," without any reference to its restoration (see Anderson, Taylor). TEV and BJ have the idea of "rebuilt" (see Briggs, Kirkpatrick). In verse 3b **which is bound firmly together** translates what seems to say "which is joined to itself together." The idea is that of the city built (or, rebuilt) firmly and compactly (see NAB "with compact unity"; NJB "one united whole"; NJV "knit together"). But some, following in part the meaning found in some of the versions, take the words to refer to the people; so NEB "where people come together in unity" (also SPCL, Taylor). TOB translates "a city with only one defender" (Yahweh, that is). FRCL has "securely surrounded by its walls." Translators may find TEV's rendering a difficult model due to the abstractness of "**beautiful order and harmony.**" If it refers to the people, SPCL offers this: "Jerusalem, the city built so that the community can gather together in it."

In verse 4a,b the subject is repeated, **the tribes . . . the tribes of the LORD**; if the repetition is not effective, this can be reduced to one subject, "the tribes of the LORD." Here **LORD** translates *Yah* (see 68.4 and comments). TEV "**tribes of Israel**" should not be imitated; something like "the tribes that belong to (or, worship) the LORD" would be better. If the word for **tribes** is used in verse 4, it will be taken in many languages to mean that Israel is made up of different ethnic groups speaking different languages. Since the reference is to the people of Israel, it may be best to use a term denoting clans or some other subdivision within a tribe, such as "families." Or else one may say "all the people who belong to (or, worship) the LORD." If **tribes of the LORD** is used, it may be necessary to recast this as "the clans that belong to the LORD." In verse 4c **as was decreed for Israel** translates "a law for Israel." The Qumran manuscript has "the community of Israel," which in the context seems to make more sense; but the translations follow the Masoretic text. TEV's **"according to his command"** may have to be recast to say "in the way he has told the people to do." See Deuteronomy 16.16-17 for the law requiring people to go to the Temple. **To give thanks to the name of the LORD** means to praise the LORD.

122.5	RSV	TEV
	There thrones for judgment were set, the thrones of the house of David.	Here the kings of Israel sat to judge their people.

Thrones for judgment were set means that Jerusalem was the place where the kings of Israel sat on their thrones to judge the people. It seems better to speak of the kings sitting on their thrones (to judge) instead of speaking of **thrones for judgment** as such. "To judge" means "to rule with justice" or "to render justice." See FRCL "It is also in you where the throne of the descendant of David is located, where he sits to render justice." In verse 5b **the house of David** means the Davidic dynasty, that is, the descendants of King David who succeeded him as king of Israel. TEV's **"Here,"** of course, refers to Jerusalem, and in many languages it will be clearer to mention Jerusalem. In languages in which sitting on a throne is meaningless, it will be best to omit it and say "In Jerusalem the Kings of Israel judged the people."

122.6-7	RSV	TEV
6	Pray for the peace of Jerusalem! "May they prosper who love you!	6 Pray for the peace of Jerusalem: "May those who love you prosper.
7	Peace be within your walls, and security within your towers!"	7 May there be peace inside your walls and safety in your palaces."

In these two verses a prayer is offered for Jerusalem. The psalmist asks his readers to wish Jerusalem peace. The verb translated **Pray for** may be rendered "Ask for" (FRCL, BJ), "Wish" (GECL), "Say from your heart" (SPCL). In verse 6a **peace** translates the word *shalom* (see 29.11 and comments); NJV translates "well-being"; GECL "prosperity and peace." The prayer itself is verses 6b, 7. Line **b** in verse 6 provides the content of the prayer mentioned in line **a.** In some languages it will be necessary to make clear that this is the relation between the two lines by saying, for example, "Pray for the peace of Jerusalem by saying" or "Pray for the peace . . . and say . . . ." **Peace of Jerusalem** may have to be recast as "Pray that God will give Jerusalem peace," ". . . that the people of Jerusalem will live in peace," or idiomatically sometimes, ". . . that the people of Jerusalem will sit down with cool hearts."

In verse 6b **prosper** translates a verb which may be taken to mean "live in peace" (so NJV, SPCL, TOB); NIV "be secure." **They . . . who love you** translates the

Masoretic text; one Hebrew manuscript has "your tents" for this phrase, which is followed by BJ and NJB; it seems better to stay with the Masoretic text (so HOTTP).

In verse 7 **peace** in line <u>a</u> is paralleled by **security** in line <u>b</u>, which translates a noun that is related to the verb used in verse 6b; so NJV has "well-being . . . peace." In verse 7b the word RSV translates **towers** (that is, fortresses; NIV "citadels") may be translated **"palaces"** (TEV, NJV, TOB, NEB, BJ, NJB). See 48.13, where the two nouns arc used together (RSV **ramparts . . . citadels**). In many languages it is difficult to give a command to an abstract noun such as **peace**. Accordingly it is often necessary to say, for example, "May everyone in Jerusalem live peacefully." TEV's **"safety in your palaces"** may have to be shifted somewhat to say, for example, "and may those in the chief's houses live in safety."

122.8-9   RSV   TEV

8   For my brethren and companions'   8   For the sake of my relatives and
        sake   friends
     I will say, "Peace be within   I say to Jerusalem, "Peace be
        you!"   with you!"
9   For the sake of the house of the   9   For the sake of the house of the
        LORD our God,   LORD our God
     I will seek your good.   I pray for your prosperity.

In verse 8 **brethren and companions** are the psalmist's fellow Israelites who live in Jerusalem; and it is for their sake and for the sake of the Temple (verse 9a) that the psalmist wishes peace for the city and prays for her prosperity (**your good**). **For the sake of** may be rendered here "Because I love . . ." or "Because I am concerned for . . . ." As in verse 7, the command **Peace be within you** will have to be shifted in some languages to say, for example, "People of Jerusalem, live in peace" or ". . . live peaceably together."

In verse 9b **I will seek** may be taken to indicate activity; it seems more likely, however, that here, as elsewhere, the word is a synonym for prayer (so Cohen, Anderson); see BJ "I pray," FRCL "I ask for." **Your prosperity** refers to the city of Jerusalem. As Toombs says, "He values the city, not because it is the nation's capital, but because it is the place where God's temple, his earthly home, is established." **For the sake of the house of the LORD our God** may be recast in some languages to say "Because I love the Temple of the LORD, who is the God we worship" or "I love the LORD our God's Temple; therefore I pray that God will make Jerusalem prosper."

Psalm 123

This pilgrim psalm (see introduction to Psa 120) is a lament by a group who complain to God about their enemies and pray for his mercy. The language of verses 3-4 implies that the enemies are foreigners, not fellow Israelites. This suggests that these pilgrims are people returning home from exile in a foreign country (Fisher). After expressing their humble submission to Yahweh (verses 1-2), the group prays for his mercy (verses 3-4).

HEADING: **"A Prayer for Mercy."** Other headings are: "Israel's prayer in persecution"; "A song of sighs"; "Hymn of faith." The TEV heading may have to be adjusted for translation into other languages by saying, for example, "The psalmist asks God to be merciful to his people" or "The psalmist prays 'Be merciful to us, God.' "

Hebrew Title: **A Song of Ascents**.
For **A Song of Ascents** in the title, see introduction to Psalm 120.

123. 1-2	RSV	TEV

1	To thee I lift up my eyes,
	  O thou who art enthroned in the heavens!
		1 LORD, I look up to you,
		    up to heaven, where you rule.

2	Behold, as the eyes of servants
	  look to the hand of their master,
	as the eyes of a maid
	  to the hand of her mistress,
	so our eyes look to the LORD our God,
	  till he have mercy upon us.
		2 As a servant depends on his master,
		    as a maid depends on her mistress,
		  so we will keep looking to you, O LORD our God,
		    until you have mercy on us.

The psalm begins with an individual speaking (verse 1), but in the rest of the psalm (verses 2-4), the group speaks. The language **To thee I lift up my eyes** (that is, "I look up to you") represents the posture of prayer. For the figure of Yahweh's throne in heaven, see 2.4; 11.4. Instead of TEV **"heaven, where you rule,"** it is possible to say "heaven, where you sit on your throne." But if the verb "rule" or "govern" is used, a direct object may be needed, in which case it will be "over the earth" or "over all the world."

In English **"I look up to you"** has a double meaning; the unintended meaning is "I admire you." The intended meaning is "I pray to you," and in many languages it will be best to translate it that way. In languages in which "**I look up**" will not signify prayer, it may be best to reverse the two lines and say, for example, "You are in heaven, where you rule, and I pray to you."

It is not easy to understand precisely what is meant in verse 2 by "as servants look at their master's hand, as a maid servant looks at her mistress' hand" (RSV **as the eyes of servants look to the hand of their master, as the eyes of a maid to the hand of her mistress**). It can be an attitude of waiting for a command, or waiting for reward or for punishment; it seems better, however, to take the language as a figure of trust and dependence (Kirkpatrick, Taylor, Anderson). With such an attitude the people look to Yahweh their God for his **mercy** (NJV "favor"; NEB "kindness"). TEV keeps the second person of address in verse 2, to keep it consistent with verse 1. TEV has dropped the image of the eyes that are looking and switched to "**depends**" in lines <u>a</u> and <u>b</u>, and returns to the image in line <u>c</u>. Translators may find the poetic effect is enhanced by keeping the imagery intact. However, this should not be done if it distorts the meaning. In Hebrew the double simile followed by the conclusion (*ke . . . ke . . . ken*) has more alliteration than in English (**As . . . as . . . so**). In many languages the opposition of **servants–master** and **maid–mistress** is unknown. In such cases it may be possible to say, for example, "as a worker depends on the one who pays him." It may be convenient in some languages to reduce the male–female lines to one by saying "as a man or woman worker depends . . . ." Some translators may find the structure of verse 2 is too cumbersome, in which two comparisons are followed by a conclusion containing a time element. This may be overcome by reducing the two comparisons to a single line, as indicated above, or it may be necessary to place the comparison at the end; for example, "We will keep looking to you, LORD, our God, until you have mercy on us. We will do this as a servant or a maid looks to the one in charge of them."

<u>123.3-4</u>　　　　　RSV　　　　　　　　　　　　　　　　　TEV

| 3 | Have mercy upon us, O LORD, have mercy upon us, for we have had more than enough of contempt. | 3 | Be merciful to us, LORD, be merciful; we have been treated with so much contempt. |
| 4 | Too long our soul has been sated with the scorn of those who are at ease, the contempt of the proud. | 4 | We have been mocked too long by the rich and scorned by proud oppressors. |

In the prayer for mercy (verses 3-4) the people complain of the **contempt** and **scorn** to which they have been subjected. Verse 3b in Hebrew is "we have been completely filled with contempt," not their contempt for others but the contempt with which others treat them. For translation suggestions on **have mercy upon us**, see "Be gracious" in 4.1; 9.13; 27.7; "Be merciful" in 57.1. It may be necessary to avoid the passive in "**we have been treated with so much contempt**" and say "people have treated us with so much contempt." "Treated with contempt" may be rendered sometimes as "treated us as if we were nothing" or "treated us as if we were not people."

The same idea is expressed in verse 4a, where "our *nefesh*" stands for "**We**" (see 3.2). In this same verse **those who are at ease** are the rich people, self-satisfied people who have all they want and are happy with things as they are (see Amos 6.1); NJV and NJB translate "the complacent."

In verse 4c one form of the Hebrew text has **the proud** (so RSV and the majority of translations); the Hebrew word occurs nowhere else in the Old Testament. Another form of the Hebrew text has the phrase "**proud oppressors**" (so TEV); both are equally fitting in the context. For translation suggestions concerning "**oppressors**" see "him who despoils" in 35.10.

Psalm 124

This psalm is a hymn of thanksgiving in which the community, the people of Israel, thank God for rescuing them from their enemies. The psalm opens with someone (probably a priest) asking the people what would have happened if Yahweh had not defended Israel (verse 1). The answer comes in verses 2-5, after which the people express their thanks to Yahweh for his help (verses 6-8).

There is no way of determining what is the specific danger referred to in the psalm.

HEADING: "**God the Protector of His People**." Other headings are: "A victory song"; "God, the savior of Israel"; "A song of gratitude." The TEV heading may be slightly adjusted for translation by saying "God protects his people."

Hebrew Title: **A Song of Ascents. Of David** (TEV **"By David"**).
For **A Song of Ascents** see introduction to Psalm 120.

124.1-5

	RSV		TEV
1	If it had not been the LORD who was on our side, let Israel now say—	1	What if the LORD had not been on our side? Answer, O Israel!
2	if it had not been the LORD who was on our side, when men rose up against us,	2	"If the LORD had not been on our side when our enemies attacked us,
3	then they would have swallowed us up alive, when their anger was kindled against us;	3	then they would have swallowed us alive in their furious anger against us;
4	then the flood would have swept us away, the torrent would have gone over us;	4	then the flood would have carried us away, the water would have covered us,
5	then over us would have gone the raging waters.	5	the raging torrent would have drowned us."

TEV sets forth the dialogue pattern of these verses by separating verse 1 from verses 2-5, and by placing verses 2-5 within quotation marks as the people's answer to the priest's question. RSV preserves the form of the Hebrew, where verse 2a repeats exactly verse 1a; between the two comes verse 1b with the direction <u>let Israel now say</u>. Of the translations consulted, only TEV uses the question and answer form;

all the others follow the Hebrew form. Verses 1 and 2 are an example of staircase parallelism in which the second line (2a) repeats line 1a and then adds something further, **when men rose up against us**. The Hebrew form is used here as an opener with the purpose of catching the reader's attention. A translator must decide whether the form of the Hebrew will be easily understood by the readers. As the form stands (see RSV), some adjustment may be required to make the meaning of the opening lines clear. See suggestions below.

RSV **If it had not been the LORD** . . . (in verses 1a, 2a) is fairly high-level language; a simpler form is "If the LORD had not been on our side" (NEB, NIV) or "Unless the LORD had not been on our side . . . ." The opening question (as found in TEV) implies a background which is supplied in 2b. In some languages the question will remain obscure without the background. It is possible to supply that information in the opening question; for example, "When our enemies attacked us, what if the LORD had not been on our side?" **Who was on our side** translates what is literally in Hebrew "who was for us" and may have to be recast as "who helped us" or "who fought for us." In verse 1b **Israel** may be represented by "the people of Israel." It should be noted that **now** in RSV is not meant to represent "at the present time"; it translates a Hebrew particle which is used for emphasis, indicating a note of urgency, "Say it, Israel!"

In verse 2b **men** translates the Hebrew *'adam*, "people" (see NJB); NEB has simply "they."

The destructive force of the enemy is depicted in terms of a ferocious monster (verse 3) and a devastating flood (verses 4-5). All three verses begin with a Hebrew word translated **then**, which is found only here in the Old Testament; this word sets off each verse as a description of what would have happened had it not been for Yahweh's help. In the event that **swallowed . . . alive** does not carry the meaning of destroying, it will be necessary to use a different metaphor or to use a nonmetaphor; for example, "they would have killed us."

For other passages where the language of verse 3a is used, see 35.25; Proverbs 1.12; Jeremiah 51.34.

The language of verses 4-5 recalls passages elsewhere in which the waters, the sea, the floods, are representative of the chaos and destruction which Yahweh defeated at creation (see 74.12-14; 89.9-10; 93.3-4). In verse 4a **the flood** is the same as **the torrent** in verse 4b and **the raging waters** in verse 5b. These vivid figures emphasize the hostility and the power of Israel's enemies. In verses 4b, 5a **over us** translates the Hebrew "over our *nefesh*" (see 3.2); verse 5a picks up the words of verse 4b and repeats them for dramatic effect. In verse 5 **raging** translates a word found nowhere else in the Old Testament. Verses 4 and 5 make up a three-line parallelism. There is a degree of heightening suggested in the Hebrew terms for the flood, which are "waters," "stream," "raging waters." However, the accompanying verbs do not support the movement. Lines 4a and 4b have essentially the same word order, while verse 5 reverses the order, creating thereby a chiasmus with the first two lines. The function of this poetic reversal is to bring the strophe to a sharp halt. Translators should consider what poetic device in the receptor language serves best in this context as a climax to the parallelism, and at the same time marks the end point of a strophe or stanza. In cases where the imagery of flood, water, and raging torrent do not adequately represent the enemies who destroy Israel, it may be necessary to employ a series of similes; for example, "Our enemies would have carried us away like a flood; they would have flowed over us like water, and they would have drowned us like a rapid river."

RSV   TEV

	RSV			TEV

6	Blessed be the LORD,
	   who has not given us
	   as prey to their teeth!
			6	Let us thank the LORD,
				   who has not let our enemies
				   destroy us.

7	We have escaped as a bird
	   from the snare of the fowlers;
	the snare is broken,
	   and we have escaped!
			7	We have escaped like a bird from
				   a hunter's trap;
				the trap is broken, and we are
				   free!

In these verses the people give thanks to Yahweh for having saved them from their enemies.

For **Blessed be** in verse 6a, see 18.46. The enemy is compared to a wild animal whose teeth quickly kill its victim (see similar language in 7.2).

In verse 7 the enemy is compared to a hunter who sets out his trap to catch birds (see 91.3; 119.110). RSV **fowlers** is the name given those who trap birds (see comments at 91.3). The Hebrew is plural, **fowlers**; but it is more natural to translate by a singular, "fowler" (so most English Versions). Yahweh has set his people free from their enemies: **the snare is broken, and we have escaped!** The language as such does not directly say that Yahweh broke the trap (**the snare is broken**), but that is probably implied (Briggs). It may be necessary to recast **"from a hunter's trap"** to say "caught in a hunter's trap." Many languages have specific terms which apply to bird snares, according to their construction and according to the types of birds they are used for. A snare appropriate for small birds will be adequate. If the active is used with the LORD as the agent, it will probably be well to use it in both parts; for example, "The LORD has broken the snare and has freed us."

RSV   TEV

RSV	TEV

Our help is in the name of the
   LORD,
who made heaven and earth.
	Our help comes from the LORD,
	   who made heaven and earth.

The psalm closes with an affirmation of faith in Yahweh (literally "the name of Yahweh"—see 5.11), creator of **heaven and earth** (see 121.2). **Our help is in the name of the LORD** means "Our help comes from the LORD himself" (FRCL). The phrase **is in the name of** (RSV, NEB, NIV) is not natural English idiom; it is translationese. NJV has "Our help is the name of the LORD." In languages in which a verb must be used for help, it may be necessary to say, for example, "The LORD is the one who helps us. He is the one who made the heavens and the earth."

1064

Psalm 125

In this psalm the people express their confidence in God's power. Even though their enemies may win or have won (depending on the meaning of verse 3), the people know that the enemies will be defeated, because Yahweh protects his people. Together with the statement of confidence (verses 1-3) is a prayer that God bless the righteous (verse 4) and punish the wicked (verse 5a,b). The psalm closes with a prayer for the welfare of Israel (verse 5c).

HEADING: "**The Security of God's People**." Other headings are: "The LORD the protector of Israel"; "God protects his own"; "Unshakable faith." The theme of this psalm is essentially the same as 124, and the TEV heading differs from 124 by viewing God's protection from the people's point of view. Here we may suggest for translation purposes "God makes his people secure" or "God's people know they are safe."

Hebrew Title: **A Song of Ascents.**
For **A song of Ascents** in the Hebrew title, see introduction to Psalm 120.

125.1-2   RSV   TEV

1   Those who trust in the LORD are   1   Those who trust in the LORD are
        like Mount Zion,   like Mount Zion,
    which cannot be moved, but   which can never be shaken,
        abides for ever.   never be moved.
2   As the mountains are round about   2   As the mountains surround Jeru-
        Jerusalem,   salem,
    so the LORD is round about his   so the LORD surrounds his
        people,   people
    from this time forth and for   now and forever.
        evermore.

The psalmist in verse 1 compares the security of **those who trust in the LORD** to the strength and stability of **Mount Zion** (see 2.6). It is unshakable (**cannot be moved**) and will never disappear (**abides for ever**). TEV's passives "**never be shaken, never be moved**" must sometimes be recast as "no one can shake it or move it."

In verse 2 the psalmist compares the protection provided by Yahweh to **the mountains** around **Jerusalem**. In the same way Yahweh surrounds his people, that is, protects them from danger. For verse 2c see 121.8c. In some languages it will not be possible to say "**the LORD surrounds his people**." It may be necessary, therefore, to make a comparison in the following way: "As the mountains are around

Jerusalem, so the LORD puts his arms around his people" or "The LORD protects his people like the mountains protect Jerusalem."

125.3	RSV	TEV

<table>
<tr><td>

For the scepter of wickedness
shall not rest
upon the land allotted to the
righteous,
lest the righteous put forth
their hands to do wrong.

</td><td>

The wicked will not always rule
over the land of the right-
eous;
if they did, the righteous them-
selves might do evil.

</td></tr>
</table>

In line a it is not certain whether the Hebrew verb here means "to come down on" or "to rest upon"—that is, whether it means (in this context) "rule" or "continue to rule." TEV takes it in the latter sense (also Anderson, Briggs, Toombs; NAB, SPCL, NIV, FRCL, Weiser); the former is the choice of NJV, BJ, NJB, TOB, Dahood. RSV seems to mean the latter, but **rest** can be taken to mean "remain." It is not possible to be dogmatic, but probably **"will not always rule"** is the meaning to be preferred. **The scepter of wickedness** means "a wicked ruler" or "wicked rulers." A scepter was a symbol of power, and it is used as a figure for the person who wields power.

In this same line **the land allotted** translates the Hebrew word for "lot," that is, the means by which ownership of a parcel of land was decided ("casting the lots"; see the same Hebrew word in 16.5; 22.18); SPCL translates "the land that God has given to his people."

In the last part of the verse, **lest the righteous put forth their hands to do wrong** implies that, should wicked rulers, that is, heathen kings, rule the land of Israel, the Israelites themselves might adopt the pagan ways of their conquerors, especially their religion. **The righteous** refers to the faithful in Israel and may be translated as "people who are loyal to God" or "people who trust in God."

125.4-5	RSV	TEV

<table>
<tr><td>

4   Do good, O LORD, to those who
      are good,
    and to those who are upright in
      their hearts!
5   But those who turn aside upon
      their crooked ways
    the LORD will lead away with
      evildoers!
    Peace be in Israel!

</td><td>

4   LORD, do good to those who are
      good,
    to those who obey your com-
      mands.
5   But when you punish the wicked,
    punish also those who abandon
      your ways.

    Peace be with Israel!

</td></tr>
</table>

In verse 4 **those who are good** in line a is parallel with **those who are upright in their hearts** in line b. Both are ways of describing people who obey the Torah, the law of God. NJB and SPCL translate line b "to the sincere at heart." The prayer **Do good** translates "Give good things," which may be represented by "Bless."

1066

TEV (also SPCL) has represented the language of verse 5 by a direct petition addressed to Yahweh, and not by a wish, in which he is spoken of in the third person, which is how the Hebrew text has it. **Those who turn aside upon their crooked ways** are those who abandon the good way that Yahweh sets out for them, and follow their own evil ways; these are Israelites who have turned away from Yahweh. The prayer is that Yahweh punish them at the same time that he punishes the **evildoers**, that is, Gentiles, the heathen. Here the punishment (**lead away**) is either exile (NIV "banish") or death (NEB "destroys"). SPCL is good: "make them suffer the fate of evildoers." TEV's **"those who abandon your ways"** may sometimes be rendered, for example, "people who do not trust you," or idiomatically, "people who do not walk on your road."

The concluding words are a prayer for the *shalom* of Israel (see 29.11), which NJV translates "May it be well with Israel!" and GECL "May prosperity and peace come upon Israel!"

Psalm 126

The understanding of the whole purpose of this psalm depends in large measure on the precise meaning of the opening words of verses 1 and 4 (see below). The majority of commentators take it that the people refer to a time in the past when Yahweh had rescued them (verses 1-3), and they now pray that he will do the same once more (verses 4-6). But some take verses 1-3 as an expression, not of a fact in the past, but of a present hope, "When the LORD restores . . ." (Briggs, Oesterley, Weiser).

It is impossible to specify what particular event is referred to or the situation in which the people find themselves now. Some commentators take it to mean that the people remember the joy that was theirs when they returned to the land of Israel from exile; but now there are difficulties of various sorts, troubles and enemies, and the people pray that Yahweh will once again save them from their distressing situation.

HEADING: "**A Prayer for Deliverance.**" Other headings are: "The people's prayer for full restoration"; "Song of the returning exiles"; "A disappointed hope." The TEV heading must be adjusted for translation in some languages by saying, for example, "The psalmist asks God to rescue Israel."

Hebrew Title: **A Song of Ascents.**
For **A Song of Ascents** see introduction to Psalm 120.

126.1-3

RSV	TEV
1 When the LORD restored the fortunes of Zion,^{l} we were like those who dream.	1 When the LORD brought us back to Jerusalem,^{x} it was like a dream!
2 Then our mouth was filled with laughter, and our tongue with shouts of joy; then they said among the nations, "The LORD has done great things for them."	2 How we laughed, how we sang for joy! Then the other nations said about us, "The LORD did great things for them."
3 The LORD has done great things for us; we are glad.	3 Indeed he did great things for us; how happy we were!

^{x} brought us back to Jerusalem; or made Jerusalem prosperous again.

1068

¹ Or brought back those who returned to Zion

In verse 1 the Hebrew phrase translated **restored the fortunes of Zion** uses the same language that appears in 14.7; 53.6; 85.1 (and which RSV translates also "restores [or, restore] the fortunes of . . ."). TEV has here "**brought us back to Jerusalem**," but in the other passages it has "makes (or, have made) . . . prosperous again" (as in the footnote here). It is generally agreed that the Hebrew phrase as such means to reverse an unhappy situation to a prosperous situation formerly enjoyed (so NEB "turned the tide of Zion's fortune"). But its precise meaning in a given passage must be determined by the context. Here there is not enough evidence one way or the other to determine whether it means the return of the Jews from exile, as TEV, NAB, NIV, BJ, NJB, GECL, and Mft have it, or, in a general sense, the restoration of Israel's former prosperity (so NJV, SPCL, FRCL, ZÜR, NEB, Dahood). No final decision is possible, and commentators are as much divided on the matter as are translators. Some believe that the words express a hope, not a fact, and so translate "When the LORD restores . . ." (AT, NJV, Weiser); but it seems preferable to take it as a statement of past fact. If the translator follows TEV and other translations which understand verse 1 to refer to the return from exile, it may be necessary in some languages to make explicit the place from which they were brought back; for example, "When the LORD brought us back from captivity to Jerusalem" or "When the LORD returned us to Jerusalem from the place we were in exile."

Zion here stands for the city of Jerusalem (see 2.6).

Line b of verse 1 can be translated "we thought we were dreaming."

In verses 2-3 the psalmist describes the happiness of the people whom the Lord had rescued. Lines a and b of verse 2 are synonymous, both indicating great joy. The two lines of verse 2 are semantically but not syntactically parallel. Line b also depends on the verb from line a to complete its sense. The two lines form a poetic unit and should normally be retained in translation, unless, of course, it suits the style of the receptor language to dissolve them into one, as in TEV. In the next line **they said among the nations** means "people of other nations said to one another." The phrase **the nations** can be translated "the foreign nations" or "the heathen" (see 2.1). The Gentiles recognized what Yahweh had done for the Israelites; it may be necessary to make this quite clear and translate "The LORD has done great things for his people." In verse 3a the psalmist takes up their statement and repeats it, adding **we are glad** or, as NJB has it, "we were overjoyed."

126.4-5	RSV		TEV
4	Restore our fortunes, O LORD, like the watercourses in the Negeb!	4	LORD, make us prosperous again,ʸ just as the rain brings water back to dry riverbeds.
5	May those who sow in tears reap with shouts of joy!	5	Let those who wept as they planted their crops, gather the harvest with joy!

> ^y make us prosperous again; *or* take us
> back to our land.

The psalmist begins the prayer in these verses with the same language used in verse 1. It is possible that the words in verse 4a mean the same as in verse 1a, that is, "take us back to our land" (TEV footnote); but it seems preferable to do as NJB and Mft have done, either "Bring back our people from captivity" (NJB) or "bring back now the rest of our exiles" (Mft). RSV, NAB, and NIV have the general sense, **Restore our fortunes**. Whatever the circumstances, the people are in need once more of Yahweh's saving help. The translator must be careful in translating verse 4 not to give the impression that the psalmist is asking God to take the people back again into captivity, particularly if he follows TEV. Readers may be confused, since in verse 1 the Lord has already brought the people back to Zion. The recommendation of following Mft or particularly NJB will avoid the likely confusion. As an alternative translators may say, for example, "Restore us to our former glory" or "make us great as we were in former times."

In verse 4b **like the watercourses in the Negeb** refers to the arid desert country south of Judah, where the dry riverbeds would be suddenly turned into rushing streams by a heavy rainfall. The language may have been proverbial, indicating a sudden change of fortune from bad to good. TEV has used analogous expressions of bringing people back to the land, and bringing water back to dry river beds. If the translator has followed the model of NJB in 4a, it may be possible in line 4b to say "just as you bring water to the dry river beds" or "like you bring water to fill the dry river beds."

It is not easy to understand in verses 5a,6a why the people wept as they planted their crops (**those who sow in tears**). Commentators suggest that this weeping reflects an ancient pagan belief that the sowing of the seed had to be marked by weeping for the death of the nature god of fertility, who was thought to die when the dry season arrived and come back to life when the rains returned (see Taylor, Weiser, Anderson; see Ezek 8.14). As Taylor says, "Such a custom could linger on in Israel long after its primitive origin had been forgotten." Or the saying may depict a time of famine, when the seed that could be used to feed a hungry family had to be planted in the earth. In any case, the figure of sorrow, or hard work, at seedtime and joy at harvest dramatically describes a change of fortune, which the people fervently hope will happen to them. None of the translations consulted gives a footnote to explain this saying. Translators may consider doing so, if the saying is obscure. They may be able to adapt this saying to the receptor language. The saying consists of verb-noun : noun-verb: *hazor'im bedim'ah : berinah yiqtsoru*, in which the two noun phrases "in tears" and "with shouts" sound similar.

126.6   RSV   TEV

He that goes forth weeping,   Those who wept as they went out
  bearing the seed for sowing,   carrying the seed
shall come home with shouts of   will come back singing for joy,
  joy,   as they bring in the harvest.
bringing his sheaves with him.

In verse 6, **bearing the seed for sowing**, it is uncertain what the Hebrew word translated **the seed** means; most take it to mean a leather bag in which the seed was carried (so NJV "carrying the seed-bag"; Dahood "seed pouch"; similarly SPCL). Others, like RSV, have **the seed for sowing**, but this seems less likely (see Anderson). Given the uncertainty of meaning of the specific term, TEV has expressed the essential meaning of the Hebrew by having "**carrying the seed**," which means, of course, in order to plant the seed. Care should be taken in this verse not to lead the reader to think that the going out to sow and the returning home with the harvest happened on the same day. The time of sowing was in late winter, and harvest began in mid-April. In languages in which there is no generic term for **seed**, it will be necessary to specify the kind of seed, such as corn. TEV has avoided the picture of sheaves of grain by substituting "**bring in the harvest**," which many other languages can do. If this is not possible, the translator will have to specify the nature of the harvest according to the seed.

Psalm 127

This psalm is classified as a wisdom psalm, its purpose being to teach people rather than to praise God or ask for his help. In the first part (verses 1-2) the psalmist stresses the fact that all human labor is useless unless Yahweh is involved; and in the second part (verses 3-5) he speaks of the blessing of having many children. Some commentators believe that the two parts were originally independent compositions; this is reasonable but cannot be proved. The particular purpose for which the psalm was composed and the time of its composition are impossible to determine. Dahood takes "house" in verse 1 to mean "palace" and understands that the psalm was composed for a king; in his view, the many children spoken of in the second part are the king's children.

HEADING: **"In Praise of God's Goodness."** Other headings are: "Trust in providence"; "Unless the LORD is there"; "Everything comes from the LORD." In some languages the TEV heading may be adjusted for translation by saying, for example, "The psalmist praises God who is good" or "The psalmist says God is great because he does good things."

Hebrew title: **A Song of Ascents. Of Solomon** (TEV **"By Solomon"**).

Some believe that **Solomon** is named as author because this is a wisdom psalm, or else because it was thought that **the house** in verse 1 was the Temple that Solomon built. The Hebrew preposition attached to **Solomon** can be taken to mean this psalm is written in honor of Solomon or is dedicated to Solomon. Some also have thought that **his beloved** in verse 2 is a reference to Solomon's name "Jedidiah," which means "beloved of Yah" (see 2 Sam 12.25), and that **sleep** in verse 2 refers to the incident narrated in 1 Kings 3.5. For **A Song of Ascents** see introduction to Psalm 120.

127.1   RSV   TEV

> Unless the LORD builds the house,
>   those who build it labor in vain.
> Unless the LORD watches over the
>   city,
>   the watchman stays awake in
>   vain.

> If the LORD does not build the
>   house,
>   the work of the builders is use-
>   less;
> if the LORD does not protect the
>   city,
>   it does no good for the sentries
>   to stand guard.

It is not certain whether **the house** in line a refers literally to a home or some other building, or figuratively to a family; some take it to mean the Temple (SPCL), others the palace (Dahood). Possibly the double sense of family and home is intended; but it seems best to translate quite generally "house" or "building." In languages where there is no general word for building, **house** will normally be used. In some languages there are many specific terms for "house" according to structure, use, and occupancy. In such languages the translator should use a word for house which is occupied by a family or extended family group. **It is in vain** or TEV's ". . . is useless" may be rendered in some languages, for example, as "It is of little value," "It does not help," or "It is worth nothing." Human labor is **in vain** unless it is in keeping with the Lord's sovereign purpose and will.

In the same way the vigilance of **the watchman** is useless if Yahweh himself does not watch **over the city**. The form followed by RSV **Unless . . .** or TEV "**If . . .**" is rather difficult; perhaps it is better to imitate GECL and translate "The LORD himself must build the house; if he doesn't . . . The LORD himself must watch over the city; if he doesn't . . . ." **The watchman** or TEV's "sentries" will have to be rendered in some languages as "people who guard the village." Instead of the literal **stays awake** in line d, it is better to say "**stand guard**" (TEV, NIV), "keep watch" (NJB, NEB), or something similar.

127.2   RSV   TEV

> It is in vain that you rise up early
>   and go late to rest,
> eating the bread of anxious toil;
>   for *ᵐ* he gives to his beloved
>   sleep.
>
> *ᵐ* Another reading is *so*

> It is useless to work so hard for a
>   living,
>   getting up early and going to
>   bed late.
> For the LORD provides for those
>   he loves,
>   while they are asleep.

The same theme is expressed in an even more general way in this verse: all human toil **is in vain** unless Yahweh is involved, that is, unless his will and purpose are being followed. There is no point in getting up early to work and working until late at night. The Hebrew phrase **the bread of anxious toil** means the food which one has had to work hard to earn; one possible version is "toiling to earn your food"; NEB "toiling for the bread you eat"; see NJB "sweating to make a living."

The last part of the verse is not easy to understand. The initial word in the Hebrew text is *ken*, "thus, so," but two Hebrew manuscripts (see also the Septuagint) have *ki*, "for," which RSV, TEV, and others follow. HOTTP prefers the Masoretic text, translating it "thus" or "as much" (so NJV, FRCL). The second difficulty is found in the word translated **sleep**, which occurs nowhere else in the Old Testament. The NEB footnote says the word is unintelligible, and omits it in translation. In the Hebrew text the word seems to function as the direct object of the verb "to give," and so RSV translates **he gives . . . sleep** (also AT). But most take the word in an adverbial sense; TEV "**while they are asleep**" (also NAB, BJ, NJB, NJV, SPCL; so HOTTP "in <his> sleep"). NJV translates "He provides as much for His loved ones while they sleep," and FRCL "The Lord gives as much to those he loves while they are asleep." What this expressive language means is that all anxious toil is of little value, since it is ultimately the Lord who makes provision for people's needs. What is needed is not anxious care but faith and trust. The Hebrew text has the singular "the one he loves," but this is probably meant generically, not specifically; two Hebrew manuscripts (and the Septuagint, Syriac) have the plural, "those he loves." TEV has "provides for," which is general and fits with "work for a living." If, however, the translator says in line a something like "It is useless to work so hard to get food to eat," in line c he can then say "The LORD will give it (food) to those he loves."

127.3-4	RSV		TEV
3	Lo, sons are a heritage from the LORD, the fruit of the womb a reward.	3	Children are a gift from the LORD; they are a real blessing.
4	Like arrows in the hand of a warrior are the sons of one's youth.	4	The sons a man has when he is young are like arrows in a soldier's hand.

In this strophe (verses 3-5) the psalmist speaks of the happiness of having many children. The two lines of verse 3 are parallel and synonymous. **Sons** parallels **the fruit of the womb**, and **heritage** parallels **reward**. For **heritage** see 16.6. The parallel **reward** translates a word that means "wages"; there may be the connotation of being a payment for good deeds, but in parallel with **heritage** the word stresses the idea of an unearned gift. TEV's **"a real blessing"** tries to bring out the idea of the LORD's generosity in giving children. It is better to translate **"children"** in verse 3a instead of **sons**, since the parallel **fruit of the womb** includes both male and female offspring. In some languages it may be necessary to recast TEV's **"gift from the LORD"** and say, for example, "The LORD blesses people with children" or "The LORD gives people children, and these are a blessing."

In verse 4 a man's **sons** are compared to the soldier's **arrows**; they are a guarantee of security. Naturally they are of greater benefit if they are born when the father is young (**the sons of one's youth**), because they will be old enough to provide him real security when he is old. In languages in which **arrows** are unknown, the simile may not be useful. The translator may search for an equivalent comparison or avoid the comparison and say, for example, "(they) can defend him from his enemies."

127.5	RSV	TEV
	Happy is the man who has his quiver full of them! He shall not be put to shame when he speaks with his enemies in the gate.	Happy is the man who has many such arrows. He will never be defeated when he meets his enemies in the place of judgment.

In this verse the psalmist continues with the figure of arrows, speaking of a **quiver full of them**. TEV does not refer to a quiver, since the word would be difficult for many readers (similarly SPCL); but TEV has retained the figure, "**who has many such arrows.**" In those languages in which **quiver** cannot be used and no adequate substitute is available, the translator may say, for example, "Happy is the man who has many sons."

The last part of verse 5 in Hebrew has the verbs in the plural, "They will not be ashamed when they speak," and some take the subject to be **the sons** of verse 4 (NJV, NIV, BJ, NAB); but most translations take the plural as a general way of speaking (so NEB "such men"), referring to the fathers of many sons (see Cohen; so RSV, TEV, SPCL, TOB, NJB), not to the sons themselves. This seems preferable, since it maintains the same subject in verses 4-5. To **be put to shame** is to experience the shame of defeat. TEV's "**never be defeated**" will in some languages require recasting; for example, "His enemies will never defeat him."

The **enemies in the gate** are a man's adversaries in a legal dispute; the open space near the inner gate of the city was the place where legal disputes were settled (see Ruth 4.1-2; Job 29.7-17). If he had a number of grown sons with him, a man would be more likely to win in a legal dispute with his adversaries. In some languages there is a term for a designated place in the village where village elders meet for hearings. In cases where there is no such customary place, **in the gate** is sometimes rendered, for example, "the place where men meet to decide matters," or idiomatically, "the place where people meet to cut words."

Psalm 128

This psalm praises the blessings that come to those who obey Yahweh: they will be prosperous and will have large and healthy families (verses 1-4). The blessing in verses 5-6 was probably spoken by a priest, and it seems that it was given as the pilgrim started back home from the Temple in Jerusalem, where he had gone for one of the annual festivals (see Anderson); Toombs believes it was spoken at the arrival of the pilgrim at the Temple.

HEADING: "**The Reward of Obedience to the LORD.**" Other headings are: "The happy home of the just man"; "The truly happy man"; "A priestly blessing." The TEV heading may be restructured for translation into some languages as "People who obey the LORD will be happy" or "People who obey the LORD will receive good gifts."

Hebrew Title: **A Song of Ascents.**
For **A Song of Ascents** see introduction to Psalm 120.

128.1   RSV   TEV

| Blessed is every one who fears the LORD, | Happy are those who obey the LORD, |
| who walks in his ways! | who live by his commands. |

For the language of line a see 1.1 and 15.4; and for line b see 119.3b. It should be noticed that in this verse RSV **Blessed** translates the same word that in 127.5 it translates "Happy," which is a better translation of the Hebrew word. For the verb "to fear (the LORD)," see comments at 5.7. Here TEV "**obey**" seems to miss the intended meaning, and something like "have reverence for" may be better. **Who walks in his ways** may be rendered also as "a person who does what he wants him to do." This line is well translated by NEB, "who live according to his will."

128.2-4   RSV   TEV

2	You shall eat the fruit of the labor of your hands;	2	Your work will provide for your needs;
	you shall be happy, and it shall be well with you.		you will be happy and prosperous.
		3	Your wife will be like a fruitful vine in your home,
3	Your wife will be like a fruitful		

vine
within your house;
your children will be like olive
  shoots
around your table.

4   Lo, thus shall the man be blessed
who fears the LORD.

and your sons will be like young
  olive trees around your table.

4   A man who obeys the LORD
will surely be blessed like this.

It should be noticed that the rest of the psalm (verses 2-3, 5-6) is in the form of direct address to some person; the personal pronoun **you** is singular. The psalmist could have someone specifically in mind; it is more likely that this is a way of addressing the reader. Where this literary device is fairly common, the translator should use it. Otherwise it is possible to go to the third person; in this case verse 2 would begin (in the language of TEV): "That man's work will provide for his needs . . . ."

In verse 2 the Hebrew **the fruit of the labor of your hands** means the result of your work, whether thought of in terms of wages, crops, or food. The thought of the whole line is that the man who obeys Yahweh's laws will earn enough from his work to provide for his needs at all times. In some languages 2a may need to be recast to say, for example, "the work you do will give you what you need to live" or "you will enjoy the results of your work." Such a man will **be happy** and all will **be well** with him, that is, he will be prosperous. In some languages to "prosper" is rendered idiomatically; for example, "you will sit well" or "you will see goodness."

In verse 3 the psalmist compares such a man's **wife** to **a fruitful vine**, that is, a grapevine that bears many grapes, and his **children** to young olive trees. It is possible that the psalmist had in mind "sons" (TEV, NEB, NJV) and not **children** in general. His wife will bear him many children and they will all be strong and vigorous (see 52.8). The figure of **olive shoots** is that of the shoots that grow up around a cultivated olive tree. Understanding the comparisons in verse 3 depends on familiarity with the grape vine and the olive tree. In languages in which these are unknown, it may be necessary to substitute other vines and trees which are locally cultivated. In the absence of such, it may be necessary to avoid the comparison. In the latter case one may translate, for example, "At home your wife will give you many children; and the children around your table will be many." **Around your table** may be a meaningless picture in languages in which children do not sit at a table to eat. Accordingly one may translate "and there will be many children around the fire."

Verse 4 closes this part of the psalm by repeating the thought of verse 1. It should be noticed that **shall . . . be blessed** translates a different Hebrew term from the one used in verse 1. In some languages it will be necessary to shift from the passive to the active and say, for example, "In this way the LORD will surely bless the person who obeys him."

128.5-6   RSV   TEV

5   The LORD bless you from Zion!
May you see the prosperity of
  Jerusalem

5   May the LORD bless you from
  Zion!
May you see Jerusalem prosper

	all the days of your life!		all the days of your life!
6	May you see your children's children!	6	May you live to see your grandchildren!
	Peace be upon Israel!		
			Peace be with Israel!

The blessing pronounced in these verses seems to be given in **Jerusalem** itself (for **Zion** as a name for the Temple or for the city, see 2.6). In some languages **from Zion** may require additional information to prevent misunderstanding; for example, "May the LORD who lives in his Temple bless you" or "May the LORD bless you from his Temple in Zion." In verse 5b, instead of **see the prosperity of Jerusalem**, NJV and NEB translate "share the prosperity of Jerusalem" (see Briggs). **All the days of your life** comes at the end of verse 5; NIV places it after the prayer in line a; this is possible and may be followed.

The final wish (verse 6) is that the man live long enough to see his grandchildren. Long life and descendants are considered a blessing from God, as is true in many cultures today.

For the final **Peace be upon Israel!** see 125.5.

Psalm 129

In this psalm the people pray to God to punish their enemies. The language of verses 2b, 4 seems to imply that the people were not at that time under foreign domination, but the danger always existed that their enemies would prevail, and so they pray to Yahweh for help, confident that he will answer them.

The first part of the psalm is a song remembering the past (verses 1-4), and the second part is a prayer for God to destroy the enemy (verses 5-8).

HEADING: "**A Prayer against Israel's Enemies**." Other headings are: "The fleeting fortune of the wicked"; "So far and no farther"; "The LORD gives freedom." The TEV heading may have to be recast for translation; for example, in some languages it may be necessary to provide one heading for verses 1-4 and a second one for verses 5-8. In languages in which it will appear strange for Israel to speak in the first person, it may be necessary to use such a heading as "The people of Israel tell how they have suffered." The second heading may be "The psalmist asks God to defeat Israel's enemies."

Hebrew Title: **A Song of Ascents**.
For **A Song of Ascents** see introduction to Psalm 120.

129.1-2   RSV   TEV

1   "Sorely have they afflicted me   1   Israel, tell us how your enemies
         from my youth,"   have persecuted you
     let Israel now say—   ever since you were young.
2   "Sorely have they afflicted me
         from my youth,   2   "Ever since I was young,
     yet they have not prevailed   my enemies have persecuted me
     against me.   cruelly,
                                              but they have not overcome me.

The same rhetorical device is used in the beginning of this psalm as in Psalm 124; someone, probably a priest leading the liturgy, calls out the first line and commands the people to repeat it (verse 1), which they do (verse 2a) and then continue in the description of past sufferings. **Israel** is addressed as a person and is asked to recite the story of how he has been cruelly persecuted **from my youth**, that is, from the very beginning of Israel's history as a nation, when the people came out of Egypt (see Hos 11.1). In languages in which it will not be possible to ask "Israel" as a nation to speak, it will often be necessary to say "You people of Israel" or "You who belong to the nation of Israel." The expression **from my youth** should not refer to the lives only of the people responding, but to the entire history of the nation. Accordingly one may have to say "ever since Israel began as a nation" or "since the very beginning of Israel." **Sorely have they afflicted me** means "My enemies made me suffer cruelly." The chant and response structure of verses 1a and 2a is helped by such headings as in FRCL "The Chant of Pilgrims." TEV has made this type of structure clear through "**Israel, tell us,**" and by putting the response in quotes. If translators can follow this model, some problems will be avoided. TEV's "**tell us**" requires the use of the exclusive form in languages which must make a choice. This is because the liturgical leader does not include the group of pilgrims in the pronoun "us."

In verse 2b they state that, even though the enemies were powerful, they were not able to destroy Israel; it still survived as a nation. **Have not prevailed** or TEV's "**have not overcome me**" may be rendered "they have not destroyed me."

129.3	RSV	TEV

RSV	TEV
The plowers plowed upon my back; they made long their furrows."	They cut deep wounds in my back and made it like a plowed field.

The language in this verse is the figure of a farmer plowing his field: the sharp end of the plow cuts deep furrows in the earth and leaves ridges behind. In the same way (by a change of metaphor) the cruel oppressors of the Israelites had been like slave overseers whose whips would leave deep welts on the slaves' backs. The figure is not one easily portrayed in translation, and it may be necessary to abandon it altogether. SPCL translates "They have wounded my shoulders with whips, opening large welts in them"; FRCL has "They have left deep furrows in my back, like a man plowing a field." The most cruel and painful kind of suffering is indicated. In translation it may be necessary to make clear that the image refers to suffering; for example, "They made me suffer, like a farmer plowing a field they made deep wounds in my back." In some languages it will be necessary to adapt the plowing metaphor to say in line 3b, for example, "and made my back like a hoed field" or "tore open my back like a farmer works a field."

129.4	RSV	TEV

RSV	TEV
The LORD is righteous; he has cut the cords of the wicked.	But the LORD, the righteous one, has freed me from slavery."

This verse is placed outside the quotation marks of verses 1-3 by RSV; TEV includes it as part of what the congregation recited in verses 2-4.

In line <u>a</u> the Hebrew text may be read **The LORD is righteous** (RSV, NIV) or "**the LORD, the righteous one**" (TEV, NJV, NJB). **The LORD is righteous** or TEV's rendering may be translated as "The LORD, who is faithful" or "The LORD, who is loyal to his people."

The language of line b is not quite clear; TEV takes **the cords of the wicked** as a figure of slavery (see the use of "cords" in 2.3). Cohen suggests that the figure is that of an ox, tied by cords to a plow (see Job 39.10). SPCL translates "has freed me from the domination of the wicked." In languages in which the figure of being freed from slavery is not clear, it will be better to follow such a model as SPCL or say, for example, "he has freed me from wicked people." Or else GECL can be followed: "He has cut the cords of my enemies, with which they force me to work as a slave."

129.5   RSV   TEV

> **May all who hate Zion**   **May everyone who hates Zion**
>   **be put to shame and turned**   **be defeated and driven back.**
>   **backward!**

The people pray for the destruction of their enemies (probably foreigners), those who hate **Zion**, here either Jerusalem or the whole land of Israel (see 2.6 and comments). Here it is probable that the city of Jerusalem is meant, or more specifically, the Temple. Again, as often, the verb translated **be put to shame** (line b) is used in the sense of "be defeated" (see 6.10).

The literal rendition of RSV is unnatural: **be put to shame and turned backward**; see NEB "be thrown back in shame"; NJV "fall back in disgrace"; and NJB "be thrown back in confusion."

129.6-7   RSV   TEV

> 6 **Let them be like the grass on the**   6 **May they all be like grass growing**
>   **housetops,**   **on the housetops,**
>   **which withers before it grows**   **which dries up before it can**
>   **up,**   **grow;**
> 7 **with which the reaper does not fill**   7 **no one gathers it up**
>   **his hand**   **or carries it away in bundles.**
>   **or the binder of sheaves his**
>   **bosom,**

In these verses the psalmist pictures the destruction of the enemies in terms of the grass and weeds which grew wild on the flat roofs of the houses, roofs made of branches or reeds with mud spread over them. The hot sun and scorching wind would kill the growth before it reached maturity (see similar language in 37.2; 103.15-16). The verb translated **grows up** can be taken to mean "pull up"; so "which withers before it is pulled up" (SPCL, NJV, FRCL). Given the uncertainty of the meaning of the Hebrew text, Oesterley and Weiser change it to read "grass . . . which the east wind withers" (see NJB footnote), but this does not seem necessary. The picture of grass sprouting on a house top will make little sense in some areas. SPCL says "weeds that grow on the roof tiles." It may be more satisfactory to say "like grass that grows where there is not enough soil for its roots." It may be necessary in some cases to supply an illustration or a note.

Reaping is described in verse 7: the reaper held the stalks of grain in one hand and cut them with the scythe which he held in the other hand; then he would hold the stalks against his chest while tying them up in a sheaf. The psalmist is saying in verse 7 that **the grass** that grows on housetops is not cut and tied up, because it is of no value. This is the fate he wishes on the enemies of Israel. In many languages it will be necessary to make the connections between verse 7 and verse 6 clearer by saying, for example, "reapers who gather up stalks of grain and tie them in bundles do not gather up the worthless weeds that grow on the roof of a house."

129.8	RSV	TEV
	while those who pass by do not say, "The blessing of the LORD be upon you! We bless you in the name of the LORD!"	No one who passes by will say, "May the LORD bless you! We bless you in the name of the LORD."

This verse portrays the normal situation at harvest time, which the psalmist prays will **not** happen. The passersby would greet the reapers with the words **The blessing of the LORD be upon you! We bless you in the name of the LORD!** This was the regular harvest blessing (see Ruth 2.4).

The psalmist has extended the figure almost beyond normal application to the situation. Verses 5-8 are the prayer against the enemies of Israel; the psalmist wishes that the enemies, instead of being like a normal growth and harvesting of grain (verses 7-8), may be like short-lived grass and weeds on the roofs of the houses (verses 6-7). In order to keep the picture clear for the readers, considerable restructuring in translation may be necessary. Because the custom of greeting the reapers may not seem to relate to the imaginary reapers in verse 7, it may be necessary to say, for example, "When people go past and see reapers at work, they say 'May the LORD bless you.' " If verse 8c is to be taken as the response of the reapers to the passers-by, it may be necessary to insert this here; for example, "and the reapers reply 'We bless you in the name of the LORD.' " Since this imaginary salutation between reapers and passers-by is an event which will not take place, it will be necessary to make this clear at the end by saying, for example, "and none of this will happen" or "no neighbor will greet you as you harvest, nor will you greet them, wishing them the LORD's blessing."

Some (BJ, FRCL, SPCL, TOB) take the last line to be the psalmist's own words, not a part of the blessing of the passers-by; this, however, does not seem very likely. NJV and Weiser place this last line in separate quotation marks, as the answer of the reapers to the passers-by's greetings; this may quite likely be correct. **We bless you in the name of the LORD** means "Acting as Yahweh's representatives we wish his blessings on you."

Psalm 130

This psalm, which is included among the seven Penitential Psalms (see introduction to Psa 32), is a cry of despair by an individual. It is to be inferred from the language of verses 3-4 that the cause of his despair was sin—his own and that of his people. After expressing his despair (verses 1-4), the psalmist gives voice to his impatience as he waits for Yahweh's help (verses 5-6). The psalm closes with an exhortation for Israel to place its complete trust in Yahweh, who will save his people (verses 7-8).

Nothing explicit can be determined as to the psalmist's circumstances or the time of the writing of this psalm.

HEADING: "**A Prayer for Help**." Other headings are: "A sinner's cry"; "Out of the depths"; "Prayer for pardon and mercy." The TEV heading may be recast for translation in some languages by saying, for example, "The psalmist asks God to help him."

Hebrew Title: **A Song of Ascents.**
For **A Song of Ascents** see introduction to Psalm 120.

130.1-2	RSV		TEV
1	Out of the depths I cry to thee, O LORD!	1	From the depths of my despair I call to you, LORD.
2	Lord, hear my voice! Let thy ears be attentive to the voice of my supplications!	2	Hear my cry, O Lord; listen to my call for help!

In the opening verse **the depths** translates the Hebrew "the deep" (see its use in the phrase "deep waters" in 69.2,14). The language resembles passages where the writer sees himself near death, almost drowning in the deep waters of the underworld (see 124.4-5; Jonah 2.2-3). **Out of the depths** should not be translated so as to give the impression that the psalmist cries to the Lord from a deep hole. In many languages it is not possible to speak metaphorically of the "depths" of trouble or despair. Accordingly it is often necessary to say "because I have many troubles . . . ."

The psalmist fervently pleads with Yahweh to answer his desperate cry for help (verse 2). In verse 2a **Lord** translates the title "Adonai," not the name "Yahweh." The two lines are synonymous: **hear** and **let thy ears be attentive**; and **my voice** and **the voice of my supplications**. The latter phrase is better translated "my plea for mercy" (NJV, NEB) or "my cry for mercy" (NIV). In some languages it will be necessary to recast TEV's **"I call"** and **"my cry"** in more specific terms; for example, in verse 1, "I beg you, LORD," and in 2a, "Listen to what I say."

130.3-4

RSV	TEV
3 If thou, O LORD, shouldst mark iniquities, Lord, who could stand?	3 If you kept a record of our sins, who could escape being condemned?
4 But there is forgiveness with thee, that thou mayest be feared.	4 But you forgive us, so that we should reverently obey you.

In verse 3 the psalmist acknowledges his sin, and the sins of all. Were the Lord strict in his judgment, no one would escape punishment. In line <u>a</u> of this verse <u>O LORD</u> translates the name *Yah* (see 68.4); <u>Lord</u> in line <u>b</u> translates "Adonai." **"Kept a record"** (RSV **mark**) translates the verb "to keep"; it could mean "keep in mind, remember" (see its use in Gen 37.11), but here it probably means keep an account, a list (see Mft "keep a strict tally"). The verb **stand** at the end of the verse can mean "stay alive" (Anderson; see TOB, FRCL, NJV, BJ, Dahood "survive") or "remain in the Lord's presence" (GECL), or "escape being condemned" (by the judge in court; Toombs, Taylor). TEV has taken it in this last sense. If the translator follows TEV's **"kept a record,"** this will be rendered in some languages as "wrote a list." If the translator follows TEV's **"escape being condemned,"** this expression may have to be recast as a question; for example, "is there anyone you would not condemn?" As a statement it can be "there is no one you would not condemn," or better, "you would have to condemn everyone."

But Yahweh is not a strict, merciless judge; he is always ready to forgive (verse 4; see 103.3). He does this so that his people should "fear" him (see 15.4). For translation suggestions on **be feared**, see 65.8.

130.5-6

RSV	TEV
5 I wait for the LORD, my soul waits, and in his word I hope;	5 I wait eagerly for the LORD's help, and in his word I trust.
6 my soul waits for the LORD more than watchmen for the morning, more than watchmen for the morning.	6 I wait for the Lord more eagerly than watchmen wait for the dawn— than watchmen wait for the dawn.

In these verses the psalmist expresses his deep longing for Yahweh to rescue him from his distress. The Hebrew in verse 5a is emphatic, "I wait for Yahweh, my *nefesh* waits"—with his whole being he waits. See NEB "I wait for the LORD with all my soul"; also possible is "I wait for the Lord; I wait eagerly." Or the translation can be "I wait longingly" or ". . . with deep longing." But his waiting is not hopeless, for he trusts **in his word**, that is, in Yahweh's promise to save those who turn to him. Both in verses 5 and 7 TEV **"trust"** translates the verb which may be rendered **hope** (RSV and others) or "wait" (NJV and others). There is no sure way of deciding which word in English better represents the original; but it may be said in general that in English, at least, the distance between the attitude of "hope" (for which there is no objective support in the facts) and of "trust" (which generally implies an assumption that the facts warrant it) is greater than in the biblical concept, where "hope" is in many places practically a synonym for "faith, assurance." So it seems better to translate "trust" here. Certainly the sentries guarding the walls of a city (verse 6) know that day will eventually come, even though the sun may seem to be taking a long time finally to appear on the horizon. For **in his word I hope** see 119.74b, 81b, 114b. **In his word I hope** must sometimes be recast to say, for example, "I trust in what he has said."

In the Hebrew text verse 6 begins "my *nefesh* for the Lord," without a verb; the verb is implied from the previous verse. (Here the Masoretic text has the title "Adonai," not the proper name "Yahweh"; many Hebrew manuscripts, including the Cairo Geniza manuscript, have the proper name.) Some (SPCL, NAB, NEB, BJ, NJB) join the last line of verse 6 to the first line of verse 7, as follows: "As sentries wait for the morning, wait, O Israel, for the Lord" (SPCL). This is possible, but it seems better to take verse 6c with verse 6b, as a poetic device for emphasis, a stylistic "step-like" feature (see introduction to Psa 120 on the meaning of **A Song of Ascents**).

130.7-8	RSV		TEV
7	O Israel, hope in the LORD! For with the LORD there is steadfast love, and with him is plenteous re-demption.	7	Israel, trust in the LORD, because his love is constant and he is always willing to save.
8	And he will redeem Israel from all his iniquities.	8	He will save his people Israel from all their sins.

In the last two verses the psalmist exhorts the people of Israel to **hope in the LORD** because of his **steadfast love** (see 5.7) and his **plenteous redemption**, that is, his willingness to save. This phrase can be taken to mean "complete freedom" (SPCL) or "great power to redeem" (NJV; similarly NEB); FRCL has "he has a thousand ways to set you free." TEV takes it to refer to his attitude, his constant willingness to save his people. In some languages it may be necessary to switch to a verb phrase and say in line b "because he always loves you," and in line c it may be necessary to make explicit the goal of saving; for example, "and always wants to save you."

In verse 8 the Hebrew is emphatic: "He (and none other) will save" (see NEB), or "It is he who will save" (see NJV, TOB, BJ). This emphasis is worth representing in translation. Salvation **from all his iniquities** seems to include both forgiveness of sins and deliverance from their consequences (so Cohen, Anderson).

Psalm 131

In this short psalm the writer expresses in eloquent terms his complete trust in the Lord and his willing submission to God's will. He exhorts his fellow Israelites to imitate him and trust completely and always in Yahweh.

HEADING: **"A Prayer of Humble Trust."** Other headings are: "The secret of inward peace"; "Humility"; "A prayer of confidence." The TEV heading may be recast for translation into some languages as "The psalmist trusts God as would a child."

Hebrew title: **A Song of Ascents. Of David** (TEV **"By David"**).
For **A Song of Ascents** see introduction to Psalm 120.

131.1   RSV   TEV

O LORD, my heart is not lifted up,   LORD, I have given up my pride
　my eyes are not raised too high;   　and turned away from my arro-
I do not occupy myself with things   　gance.
　too great and too marvelous for   I am not concerned with great
　me.   　matters
                                            　or with subjects too difficult for
                                            　me.

In the first part of this verse the psalmist confesses himself to be free of all "pride" (**my heart is not lifted up**) and "arrogance" (**my eyes are not raised too high**); see similar language in 18.27; 101.5. Expressions of pride are rendered by many idiomatic terms; for example, the translator may render line **a** "I am not a person with a swollen heart" or "I do not have big thoughts about myself."

It is not easy to determine precisely what the psalmist means in the last part of this verse. He writes: "I do not walk in things too great or wonderful for me." TEV **"great matters"** and **"subjects too difficult"** is a possible interpretation; NJV has "I do not aspire to great things or to what is beyond me"; SPCL "I do not attempt great and extraordinary accomplishments which are beyond my reach"; another possible version is "affairs which are too great or too difficult for me." It is possible to infer from this that the psalmist was a man of some importance and power; Dahood believes he was the king. **I do not occupy myself** or TEV's **"I am not concerned with great matters"** may sometimes be rendered "I do not try to do things that are too difficult for me." TEV's **"subjects too difficult"** may sometimes be rendered "I do not think about things that are for wise old men" or, stated positively, "I think only about things that are simple." It is possible that the Hebrew term translated **(things)** . . .

1086

<u>too marvelous</u> refers to God's great deeds, so that the psalmist is saying he does not attempt to deal with God's wonderful deeds, which are beyond his comprehension. This interpretation is not defended by many.

131.2　　　RSV　　　　　　　　　　　　　　TEV

> But I have calmed and quieted my
>   soul,
> like a child quieted at its moth-
>   er's breast;
> like a child that is quieted is my
>   soul.

> Instead, I am content and at
>   peace.
> As a child lies quietly in its moth-
>   er's arms,
> so my heart is quiet within me.

The psalmist says he has **calmed and quieted** his *nefesh*, that is, himself, his inner being. Briggs comments: "the soul . . . was by deliberate action reduced to a calm, gentle, submissive, patient, and contented state." TEV **"content and at peace"** seems to represent the meaning. In some languages it is possible to use a direct address form and say, for example, "I said to my heart, 'Sit down and be cool.' "

Child translates a Hebrew word that means "a weaned child" (so NJV, NEB, NIV, NAB, JB; Dahood translates "infant"). The Hebrew says "like a weaned child with its mother." But RSV (**like a child quieted at its mother's breast**) and SPCL take the meaning to be a younger child, before weaning, who has just finished nursing at its mother's breast. This seems to make more sense and is supported by Briggs and Taylor; but others (Anderson, Weiser, Kirkpatrick, Cohen, Delitzsch) quite strongly reject this view and take the picture to be that of a child who has already been completely weaned and is content to be with its mother, without desiring any longer to be suckled. NIV is "like a weaned child with its mother," and FRCL "like a child with its mother." Translators in many languages will have to choose a form of **child** which indicates sex as well as age.

The next line in Hebrew is somewhat difficult to understand: "like a child upon me (is) my *nefesh*." This is generally taken to mean, as TEV has it, a comparison with the former line: his inner being, his spirit, is as content as a child with its mother is content. NJV translates "like a weaned child am I in my mind." NEB omits this line, which it translates in a footnote, "as a weaned child clinging to me." NAB translates "so is my soul within me," but places the line within brackets.

131.3　　　RSV　　　　　　　　　　　　　　TEV

> O Israel, hope in the LORD
>   from this time forth and for
>   evermore.

> Israel, trust in the LORD
>   now and forever!

For line <u>a</u> see the same exhortation in 130.7; for line <u>b</u> see 121.8c; 125.2c.

Psalm 132

This psalm is a hymn of praise in which several themes appear: the Temple, the Covenant Box, the city of Jerusalem, and King David and his royal descendants. The majority of commentators believe the psalm was used during the Festival of Shelters, in the fall, when Yahweh's sovereignty as king of his people was celebrated. In some ways it resembles the royal psalms (see Psa 2, 28, 20, 21) and the psalms in praise of Jerusalem (see Psa 46, 48, 76, 87).

In verses 1-5 Yahweh is reminded of David's determination to build the Temple, and verses 6-10 relate how the Covenant Box was taken into the sanctuary. Verses 11-12 speak of God's promise to King David that his descendants would succeed him as kings of Israel, and verses 13-18 praise the Temple (or the city of Jerusalem) as the place where Yahweh dwells with his people. Verse 10 is a transition between the first and the second strophes; TEV joins it to the following verses, while RSV joins it to the preceding ones.

Most commentators date the psalm in the time when one of David's descendants ruled as king in Jerusalem; some place it in the time of King Solomon, and Dahood thinks it belongs to the time of King David.

HEADING: "**In Praise of the Temple.**" Other headings are: "The pact between David and the LORD"; "The ancient promise"; "Dedication of the Temple." The TEV heading may have to be recast for translation into some languages as "The psalmist praises the Temple" or "The psalmist says good words about the Temple."

Hebrew Title: **A Song of Ascents**.
For **A Song of Ascents** see the introduction to Psalm 120.

132.1-2

RSV	TEV
1 Remember, O LORD, in David's favor, all the hardships he endured;	1 LORD, do not forget David and all the hardships he endured.
2 how he swore to the LORD and vowed to the Mighty One of Jacob,	2 Remember, LORD, what he promised, the vow he made to you, the Mighty God of Jacob:

The psalm begins with a plea to Yahweh to **Remember . . . all the hardships he [David] endured** (verse 1), and also the promise that David had made (verse 2). The verb **Remember** is a way not simply of asking Yahweh to keep something in mind, but for him to take the necessary action in light of what he is to remember.

RSV (**Remember** . . .) **in David's favor** is a possible translation of the Hebrew (so AT "for David's sake"; NJV "count in David's favor"). Most translate as does TEV (see TOB, FRCL, NIV, NEB, BJ, NJB, SPCL). The word translated **hardships** can be taken in the sense of "difficulties, troubles"; they are those David **endured** in his attempt to return the Covenant Box to Jerusalem and to build a temple for Yahweh where the Box would be kept. TEV has restructured verses 1 and 2 by beginning verse 1 with **"do not forget,"** and verse 2 with **"Remember."** In Hebrew, as in RSV, verse 2 does not repeat the command to remember but leaves it implied from verse 1. Translators in many languages will make the relation between verses 1 and 2 clearer by following the model of TEV. In languages in which a command to remember something or to not forget something would imply that God is something less than intelligent, it may be necessary to say, for example, "LORD, do not set aside (from your mind)," "Do not ignore," or idiomatically sometimes, "Do not take out of your heart" or "Do not turn your back on."

Verse 2 is composed of two lines which are synonymous and parallel. TEV in verse 2 uses the second person of address to God to prepare for the direct quotation in verse 3. The translator should note that verses 2, 4, and 5 consist of two lines each, the second line being semantically parallel to the first line. However, there is little if any intensification in the second line. Such poetic lines are sometimes referred to as static parallelism, and if the apparent repetition is not stylistically acceptable in the receptor language, it may be necessary to reduce the two lines to one, as TEV has done in verses 3 and 4.

The title **the Mighty One of Jacob** is an ancient one (see its use in Gen 49.24); **Jacob** here may be the patriarch himself or the people of Israel (see 46.7 and comments). The word translated **Mighty** is used of angels in the Hebrew of 78.25. In this context **swore** and **vowed** are used as exact synonyms: "promised . . . pledged." If it should be necessary to reduce the two lines to one, the translator may say, for example, "LORD, remember what David promised to you, who are the Mighty God of Jacob" or ". . . the Mighty God whom Jacob worshiped."

132.3-5	RSV		TEV
3	"I will not enter my house or get into my bed;	3 4	"I will not go home or go to bed; I will not rest or sleep,
4	I will not give sleep to my eyes or slumber to my eyelids,	5	until I provide a place for the LORD,
5	until I find a place for the LORD, a dwelling place for the Mighty One of Jacob."		a home for the Mighty God of Jacob."

David's vow (verses 3-5) is not recorded elsewhere in the Old Testament. Each one of the three verses is composed of two parallel and synonymous lines; TEV has reduced verses 3-4 to one line each, without omitting any of the semantic content of the text.

In verse 3 **my house** translates the Hebrew "the tent of my house" (see NAB "the house I live in"), and **my bed** translates the Hebrew "the bed of my couch" (see 6.6). In English the word "couch" today is not used as a precise synonym for "bed."

For nearly the same expression as that in verse 4, see Proverbs 6.4; Anderson suggests the language may have been proverbial. For translators who wish to keep the poetic parallelism by having two synonymous and parallel lines, NJB offers a good model: "will not allow myself to sleep, not even to close my eyes."

Verse 5 is also composed of two parallel and synonymous lines; **find** in verse 5a does not mean to try to locate a place, as though it were unknown or had been lost, which "find" in English suggests. Briggs, however, takes it in this sense, believing it means the attempt to find the place where the Covenant Box was before David took it to Jerusalem. It seems best to take it in the sense of preparing a tent where the Covenant Box was to be placed (see 1 Chr 15.1–16.1). The translator should stay with the language of the text and represent David as trying to build or provide a place for Yahweh to live in; it would not be advisable to expand the text and say "until I prepare a place for *the Covenant Box of* the LORD, the Mighty God of Jacob." In verse 5b **a dwelling place** is synonymous with **a place** in verse 5a. Some modern versions keep both "a place" and "a home," as in TEV. Others such as SPCL have only "a home," and GECL has "a place where the Lord . . . can live." The manner in which this is handled depends largely on whether or not the translator keeps the parallelism.

The language of verse 5 is used in Acts 7.46, but there are textual problems in the New Testament passage.

	RSV		TEV
6	Lo, we heard of it in Ephrathah, we found it in the fields of Jaar.	6	In Bethlehem we heard about the Covenant Box, and we found it in the fields of Jearim.
7	"Let us go to his dwelling place; let us worship at his footstool!"	7	We said, "Let us go to the LORD's house; let us worship before his throne."

These verses speak of the transfer of the Covenant Box from Kiriath Jearim to Jerusalem (see 1 Sam 7.1-2; 2 Sam 6.2-15; 1 Chr 13.5-8). **Ephrathah** seems to have been the older name of Bethlehem (see Ruth 1.1-2; Micah 5.2); Kiriath Jearim (here called **the fields of Jaar**) was a town some fourteen kilometers northwest of Jerusalem, where the Covenant Box stayed for some twenty years, after having been returned by the Philistines, who had captured it in battle (1 Sam 4.1–6.16). KJV "fields of the wood" is a possible translation of the Hebrew phrase; most modern scholars are convinced that the Hebrew phrase is a variant for Kiriath Jearim (which means "the city of woods").

For the sake of intelligibility TEV has introduced "**Covenant Box**" in verse 6a from its first mention in verse 8b; the Hebrew text in verse 6a is simply "we heard about it." This is not to be understood to mean that it was only on that specific occasion when David and his men were in Bethlehem that they heard about the Covenant Box for the first time; it means that when they decided to return the Box to Jerusalem, they got the news about where the Box was while they were in

Bethlehem (David's birthplace). AT, TOB, NJV, and FRCL translate "We heard that it was in Ephrathah," but this makes for difficulties, since Ephrathah (on the supposition that it is Bethlehem) was not near Kiriath Jearim. Delitzsch takes Ephrathah to be the name of the district to which Kiriath Jearim belonged. FRCL says that Ephrathah here does not mean Bethlehem, but is another Ephrathah, which was a short distance from Bethel. Others say that Ephrathah here means Ephraim, and take the meaning of verse 6a to be "We heard that it was in Shiloh." It seems best to translate as TEV has done; GECL has "In Ephrathah we received the news about the Covenant Box of the Lord, and we found it in the vicinity of Jaar." TEV's "**Covenant Box**" may sometimes be rendered "the box that held God's agreement with the people" or "the box that held the written pact between God and the people." If transliteration of these place names must be avoided, for example, to avoid confusion with other words in the receptor language, the translator may follow the KJV translation, or NJB "Forest-Fields."

In verse 7 the scene shifts to Jerusalem: the Covenant Box has been installed in the tent that David prepared for it (2 Chr 1.4); some, however, take **his dwelling place** in verse 7a (the same Hebrew word used in verse 5b) to be the place in Kiriath Jearim where the Covenant Box was (see Toombs). Others take it to be the Temple in Jerusalem (Taylor, Weiser, Anderson), so that the words are spoken by the worshipers as they sing the psalm in the festival. This is probably correct. In verse 7b **his footstool** is a reference to the Covenant Box (see 99.5). The Hebrew verb translated **worship** can mean "to bow down in subservience before someone," and hence GECL's rendering "we throw ourselves at his feet." In languages where this picture has the appropriate meaning, it should be used. If not, it is best to follow RSV and TEV. **Footstool** may have to be replaced by another image, unless it very clearly is associated with the throne or place where the ruler sits.

132.8-9	RSV	TEV
	8 Arise, O LORD, and go to thy resting place, thou and the ark of thy might. 9 Let thy priests be clothed with righteousness, and let thy saints shout for joy.	8 Come to the Temple, LORD, with the Covenant Box, the symbol of your power, and stay here forever. 9 May your priests do always what is right; may your people shout for joy!

In these verses the scene is the Temple (see parallel in 2 Chr 6.41), and Yahweh is invited to enter, both he and the Covenant Box, which is here described as **the ark of thy might**. In 78.61 the ark is referred to as "his power" and "his glory"; here, as there, TEV has expressed the meaning of the Hebrew by "**the symbol of your power**"; FRCL has "the place where your power resides." TEV "**and stay here forever**" (that is, in the Temple) translates the meaning of the Hebrew **your resting place**; see the same word in verse 14. In some languages "stay" or "remain here" will be sufficient. The idea of "resting" is not that of complete cessation of work, as though Yahweh would do nothing else; it is rather the idea of having a permanent place in which to live (see 95.11 and comments). If the translator follows TEV's "the symbol of your power," it may be necessary to recast this expression as "that shows how powerful you are." Since the psalmist speaks from the Temple, the invitation is expressed in TEV as "Come"; RSV has **go**. However, since the permanent resting place was the innermost room, the Holy of Holies, where only the high priest entered, most priests and Israelites would have to say "go."

It is not easy to determine precisely what is meant in verse 9a **be clothed with righteousness** (for **righteousness** see comments at 4.1). TEV has taken it to mean "do ... what is right" (see Cohen, Anderson). SPCL translates "be clothed in kindness," NJV "are clothed in triumph." Thus translated, "righteousness" or "kindness" is seen as a moral quality that is compared to a robe, a "habit" that is worn. FRCL translates "May your priests carry salvation with them in the same way they carry their robes . . . ." The language may be taken to mean the "righteousness" (and, in verse 16, the "salvation") of Yahweh which the priests mediate to the people (Briggs, Toombs); see GECL "Give your priests the authority to secure your help for us." Weiser takes the word here to mean "salvation," as in verse 16, and that it refers to the blessing which the priests pronounced on the people. Crim understands the phrase to mean "sacred garments that express God's righteous dealings with his people." The expression **clothed with righteousness** will have to be recast in many languages. If it is desirable to retain the poetic image of clothing, it may be possible to say, for example, "May your priests cover themselves with goodness the way they wear their garments" or ". . . wear kindness as a person wears a garment."

In verse 9b **saints** are the people of Yahweh (see comments on "the godly" in 4.3). **Shout for joy** must often be translated, for example, "shout because they are happy" or "because they are joyful let them shout."

132.10	RSV	TEV
	For thy servant David's sake do not turn away the face of thy anointed one.	You made a promise to your servant David; do not reject your chosen king, LORD.

In verses 10-12 the psalmist speaks of Yahweh's promise to David that his descendants would rule as kings over Israel. TEV connects verse 10 with what follows. The verse begins, "For the sake of your servant David," which TEV takes as a reference to the promise given in verse 11; in verse 10b **thy anointed one** (see 2.2) is probably not David himself (as Dahood interprets it) but the reigning king at the time the psalm was used (Anderson and others). The language **do not turn away the face of** means "do not reject" (TEV, NIV, NJV, NEB), but instead accept, that is, bless and help. TEV's "**do not reject your chosen king, LORD**" may be recast in some languages as "LORD, do not say 'No' to the man you have chosen to be king" or ". . . the king you have chosen."

RSV   TEV

11   The LORD swore to David a sure   11   You made a solemn promise to
        oath   David—
     from which he will not turn   a promise you will not take
        back: back:
     "One of the sons of your body   "I will make one of your sons
     I will set on your throne.   king,
12   If your sons keep my covenant   and he will rule after you.
        and my testimonies which I   12   If your sons are true to my cove-
        shall teach them,   nant
     their sons also for ever   and to the commands I give
        shall sit upon your throne."   them,
                                              their sons, also, will succeed
                                                 you for all time as kings."

In these verses the psalmist refers to Yahweh's promise to David (see 2 Sam 7.12-16). TEV, connecting verse 10 to verses 11-12, has kept in verse 11 the direct form of address, "**You**," that is used in verse 10; in Hebrew Yahweh is spoken of in the third person. The sense of verse 11a,b is that Yahweh made a firm promise to David which he will not break.

The language in verse 11c,d is literally "from the fruit of your body I will place on your throne," which means that one of David's sons, or a succession of David's direct male descendants (**your sons** in verse 12a), will succeed David as king of Israel. The translation should not appear to mean that David would be replaced in his own lifetime by one of his sons; this is why TEV has "**he will rule after you.**"

The promise is extended to later descendants of David (verse 12); the Davidic dynasty will continue forever to rule the people of Israel. In verse 12 the plural **your sons** (RSV and TEV) may be difficult, for in the nature of the case only one son at a time was to succeed David as king. If necessary, the verse can read "If your son who succeeds you as king is true to my covenant and to the commands I give him, then the succeeding male descendants will succeed you as king for all time." But it may not be worth the trouble to make it that clear and explicit.

The divine promise will be kept on condition that David's descendants always keep Yahweh's covenant with them and obey his commands. Yahweh himself will **teach** them his **testimonies**, that is, the rules and laws the people of Israel must follow. For the sake of clarity it may be necessary in some languages to modify the order in verses 11-12 so that "**a promise you will not take back**" is placed at the end of verse 12. In this way the quoted promise follows directly; that is, "You swore to David when you said 'I will make one of your sons king . . . for all times as kings'; this is an oath that you will not break."

132.13-14   RSV   TEV

13   For the LORD has chosen Zion;   13   The LORD has chosen Zion;
        he has desired it for his habita-   he wants to make it his home:
        tion: 14   "This is where I will live forever;

1093

14   "This is my resting place for ever;   this is where I want to rule.
        here I will dwell, for I have
        desired it.

In the final strophe (verses 13-18) the psalmist praises Jerusalem as the place in which Yahweh chose to live; Yahweh will bless and protect the city and its people, and will guarantee the success of David and his male descendants as kings of the people of Israel.

In verse 13 **Zion** is the city of Jerusalem (see 2.6); SPCL takes it to be the mountain on which the Temple was built. Yahweh chose it because he wanted it to be **his habitation** (verse 13b); in verse 14a **resting place** is the same word used in verse 8a. In verse 14b **I will dwell** translates the verb "to sit, to dwell" which may mean "sit on the throne," that is, "to rule" (see Briggs, Anderson; see the verb in 29.10; 33.14a; 55.19b; 102.12). Most, like RSV, translate "I will live there."

132.15-16   RSV   TEV

15   I will abundantly bless her provi-   15   I will richly provide Zion with all
        sions;   she needs;
        I will satisfy her poor with   I will satisfy her poor with food.
        bread.   16   I will bless her priests in all they
16   Her priests I will clothe with sal-   do,
        vation,   and her people will sing and
        and her saints will shout for   shout for joy.
        joy.

In verse 15 Yahweh promises to supply the needs of the people of Jerusalem, including the **poor**. In verse 15a, instead of the Hebrew text **her provisions**, NEB prefers to change the text to read "her needy"; K-B changes the text to "her virtuous"; neither is necessary (so HOTTP). In verse 15b **bread** stands for "**food**" in general.

Verse 16 is similar to verse 9 except that here the priests have **salvation** for their garment, which means either that they mediate God's salvation to the people (see Toombs), or else that they enjoy his salvation, that is, his blessings. It is not easy to translate in such a way as to convey some meaningful concept. The usual translation "I will clothe her priests with salvation" (RSV, NEB, NAB, BJ, NJB, TOB, FRCL, SPCL) doesn't mean much except that the priests will be saved (see Taylor). NJV and Mft translate "triumph," which in the context doesn't make much more sense. GECL translates here as it does verse 9, "I give her priests authority to secure my help for her."

For verse 16b see verse 9b.

132.17-18   RSV   TEV

17   There I will make a horn to   17   Here I will make one of David's
        sprout for David;   descendants a great king;

I have prepared a lamp for my anointed.	here I will preserve the rule of my chosen king.
18 His enemies I will clothe with shame, but upon himself his crown will shed its luster."	18 I will cover his enemies with shame, but his kingdom will prosper and flourish."

In verse 17 the figure **I will make a horn to sprout** means to give power to, or else, to cause a son to be born who will be powerful; and **I have prepared a lamp** means to give life, continuity, success (Dahood: "a natural metaphor for the preservation of the dynasty"); see 1 Kings 11.36. For **horn** see 18.2 (and see Ezek 29.21). The parallels **David** and **my anointed** stand for the Davidic dynasty, that is, David's direct royal descendants: Yahweh guarantees that they will continue to be kings of the people of Israel. FRCL translates "I will cause to be born in Zion a powerful king of the descendance of David. Like a lit lamp I will maintain there the king I have consecrated." And SPCL translates "There I will bring about the rebirth of David's power. I have prepared a lamp for the king I have chosen." **There** and TEV's "**Here**," repeated in the next line, refer to Zion, the place where God rules. It may be clearer to say "In Zion . . . ." TEV's "**preserve the rule . . .**" may sometimes be rendered "I will make his rule to go on and on." If the translator wishes to combine the metaphor with its meaning, one may say, for example, "like a lamp that will burn forever," as GECL does.

The psalm closes with Yahweh's promise to defeat (**clothe with shame**) the enemies of the king and to make his kingdom prosper and flourish. The word translated **crown** here is the same one used in 89.39 (which see). If the figure of a **crown** is maintained in translation, a natural way of translating will be "but the crown he wears will shine (or, sparkle) brightly." Translators should attempt to maintain the parallelism of **clothe with shame** and to wear a crown. In many languages this will not be possible, particularly in languages where the crown will have to be substituted by some other symbol of authority which is not "worn" on the body.

Psalm 133

This wisdom psalm praises fellowship and harmony, but we cannot be certain what specific kind of harmony is meant. Some take it to be literally that of brothers living together on their ancestral land (see Toombs, Taylor, Weiser); others take it to be of the nation as a whole (Fisher); while others take it to mean the Jewish pilgrims staying in Jerusalem during one of the annual festivals (Briggs, Anderson). Kirkpatrick and Cohen take the situation to be that of Nehemiah in his attempt to build up the restored community in Jerusalem.

HEADING: **"In Praise of Brotherly Love."** Other headings are: "Blessing of unification"; "The unity of the family"; "Brothers together." If the translator wishes to follow the TEV heading, it may be necessary to recast it to say something like "The psalmist says it is good for God's people to live in peace" or ". . . to live together peacefully."

Hebrew title: **A Song of Ascents** (TEV **"By David"**).

For **A Song of Ascents** see introduction to Psalm 120. RSV, on the basis of two Hebrew manuscripts and some ancient versions, omits "By David." It should be noted that this phrase is found in the Qumran manuscript.

133.1　　　　RSV　　　　　　　　　　　　　　TEV

> Behold, how good and pleasant it
> is
> when brothers dwell in unity!

> How wonderful it is, how pleasant,
> for God's people to live together
> in harmony!

The adjective **pleasant** (see note at 16.6) means that what is so characterized brings joy, causes pleasure, and is by its very nature good.

In this verse all translations consulted have the sense of **when brothers dwell in unity** or "when people live together as brothers" (see NJB). Only TEV translates the Hebrew **brothers** by **"God's people."** Instead of "to live" as the translation of the form of the Hebrew verb meaning "to sit" or "to live," NJV and BJ have "sit together," which implies a communal meal as part of the festival; and NEB footnote has "to worship together." FRCL has simply "to be together." Any of these is a defensible translation of the Hebrew text. In some languages the expression "sit together" is idiomatic, meaning to live harmoniously. In other languages an expression such as "tie themselves to one thing" or "tie their hearts together" carries the same meaning.

133.2   RSV   TEV

It is like the precious oil upon the   It is like the precious anointing oil
   head,   running down from Aaron's
   running down upon the beard,   head and beard,
   upon the beard of Aaron,   down to the collar of his robes.
   running down on the collar of
   his robes!

The comparison in verse 2 to **the precious oil** that ran down from "**Aaron's head**" to his **beard** and on down to **the collar of his robes** is a strange one for today's readers (it sounds rather messy); but it was meaningful to the original readers. The anointing of the High Priest with the special olive oil was an occasion of great solemnity and joy. Perhaps, as one commentator proposes, it suggests "the pervasive influence of good will." Fisher thinks that the anointing of the High Priest brought him into "a brotherly relationship of Temple ministers." Kirkpatrick sees the High Priest as the chief religious representative of Israel and so the symbol of national unity. There is no way to determine the specific application of the figure. The last line of verse 2 is taken by TEV and most other translations as a reference to the olive oil, and since this is the focus of the simile, it is the interpretation to be preferred. NJV, TOB, and Weiser, however, following the accent in the Masoretic text, refer it to Aaron's beard, running down to the collar of his robes.[1] SPCL takes **Aaron** to mean the priests; FRCL translates it "the High Priest." In some languages it may be necessary to repeat the subject "harmony" as the thing that is to be compared; "Such harmony is like . . . ." For a comparison to be understood, there must be a recognized point of similarity. This is hardly the case in verse 2 and may require a footnote to provide the basis for the comparison. "**Anointing oil**" may have to be recast while still retaining the poetic imagery; for example, "It is like the precious oil poured on Aaron's head at his consecration; the oil ran down his beard, down to the collar of his robe."

133.3   RSV   TEV

It is like the dew of Hermon,   It is like the dew on Mount
   which falls on the mountains of   Hermon,
   Zion!   falling on the hills of Zion.
For there the LORD has com-   That is where the LORD has
   manded the blessing,   promised his blessing—
   life for evermore.   life that never ends.

---

[1]FRCL takes the first two lines as a reference to the olive oil provided a guest in the home (see Psa 23.5): "It is like the precious olive oil that is poured on the head of a guest and that goes down to his beard." The second part, then, is about the beard of the High Priest: "It is like the beard of the High Priest, that goes down to the collar of his robes."

The figure of **the dew of Hermon which falls on the mountains of Zion** can hardly be taken literally, given the great distance between Mount Hermon, in Syria, and Mount Zion (some 200 kilometers). Some take **the dew of Hermon** to mean "very heavy dew" (see Briggs), which seems reasonable (see NAB "It is a dew like that of Hermon, which comes down upon the mountains of Zion"). It was believed that dew, like rain, fell from the clouds (Pro 3.20) or from the sky (Zech 8.12). Since the comparison in verse 3 is still with living harmoniously, it may be necessary to repeat "living together in unity" at the beginning of verse 3. **Hermon** or TEV's "**Mount Hermon**" may have to be recast to say "the mountain called Hermon." It is possible to translate verse 3a as a parallelism; for example, "It is like the dew on the mountains called Hermon, heavy as the thick dew on Mount Zion."

In the last part of this verse **there** refers to Jerusalem, where Yahweh dwells, and where he bestows **(has commanded)** the **blessing** of **life for evermore**. Few believe, as does Dahood, that this refers to individual immortality; most take it as meaning "a very long life" (see SPCL), or else the perpetuity of the nation, a promise that Israel will never cease to exist. With less probability Cohen takes "forever" to modify the verb "commanded," not the noun "life." If there is any doubt as to the referent of **there**, the translator should use "in Zion" or "in Jerusalem;" FRCL says "for it is there, in Zion . . . ."

Psalm 134

This short hymn was probably used for the evening service in the Temple (Toombs) or else for the final evening service at the Festival of Shelters (Taylor, Anderson). It is the last of the fifteen psalms which are called "A Song of Ascents" (see introduction to Psa 120).

Verses 1-2 are a call for all present to praise Yahweh, spoken either by the worshipers to the priests or else by the priests to all those present; verse 3 is a priestly blessing upon the people.

HEADING: "**A Call to Praise God**." Other headings are: "Evening worship"; "For the evening festival"; "A night hymn for the Temple." The TEV heading may require slight modification for translation; for example, "The psalmist calls the people to come and praise God" or ". . . to say that God is great."

Hebrew Title: **A Song of Ascents.**

For **A Song of Ascents** see introduction to Psalm 120.

134.1	RSV	TEV

	Come, bless the LORD,
	  all you servants of the LORD,
	  who stand by night in the house
	    of the LORD!
		Come, praise the LORD, all his
		  servants,
		all who serve in his Temple at
		  night.

For **bless the LORD** see 16.7; the meaning is "**praise the LORD**."

It is not certain whether **all you servants of the LORD** means all the worshipers, as in 113.1, or the priests, spoken of in the next line as **who stand by night in the house of the LORD**. It seems preferable to take the two lines to refer to the priests and Levites; but some (see Toombs) take it to refer to the worshipers, the verb **stand** meaning not Temple service, as TEV, NIV, and FRCL have it, but prayer. Translators may find that it is more natural to use the address form **all you servants of the LORD** than "**all his servants,**" as in TEV. This expression may also be recast as "all you who serve the LORD." If the second person plural form is used in line b, it will be well to continue it in line c, "all you who serve in his Temple . . . ."

In this verse BJ and NJB follow the Septuagint (which is like 135.2), which after "who stand in the house of the LORD" adds "in the courts of the house of our God." HOTTP and the other translations prefer the Hebrew text.

134.2-3 RSV	TEV
2 Lift up your hands to the holy place, and bless the LORD!	2 Raise your hands in prayer in the Temple, and praise the LORD!
3 May the LORD bless you from Zion, he who made heaven and earth!	3 May the LORD, who made heaven and earth, bless you from Zion!

In verse 2 **to the holy place** may mean, as TEV, NIV, and NEB have it, "**in the Temple**" (NEB "sanctuary"); most translate as does RSV, **to** (or, toward) **the holy place**, which indicates the Most Holy Place in the Temple, where the Covenant Box was kept. In some languages **Lift up your hands to the holy place** will have to be rendered "Stretch out your arms towards the most holy place" or "Turn your face toward . . . and raise your hands in prayer." TEV has added "**in prayer**" to make clear the purpose of raising the hands, which many translators will also have to do.

The blessing in verse 3 is pronounced on the worshipers; for line a see 128.5a; for line b see 121.2b. It should be noted that **you** in Hebrew is singular; it is used generically and includes all the worshipers, not just one in particular. **Bless you from Zion** may have to be recast in some languages to say "May the LORD, who lives in Zion, bless you."

Psalm 135

This hymn of praise to Yahweh proclaims him as the greatest of all gods, Lord of the universe and savior of his people. The psalm was probably used during one of the festivals in the Temple, perhaps Passover (Anderson), or New Year, or Shelters (Taylor).

The psalm opens with a call to the worshipers in the Temple to praise Yahweh (verses 1-4), followed by praise of his power as lord of nature and savior of his people (verses 5-12). After a short general statement of Yahweh's greatness (verses 13-14), the gods of the heathen are portrayed as weak and ineffective (verses 15-18). The final strophe is another call to praise (verses 19-21). The psalm ends as it begins, with **Praise the LORD!**

Much of the language in this psalm is paralleled in various psalms and other passages in the Old Testament.

HEADING: "**A Hymn of Praise.**" Other headings are: "The great acts of God"; "Lord of nature and history"; "Creation and election." Translators wishing to follow the TEV heading may refer to similar titles found in such psalms as 33, 40, 92, 95, 100, 111, 117.

135.1-2

	RSV		TEV

1	Praise the LORD.
	Praise the name of the LORD,
	    give praise, O servants of the
	      LORD,
		1	Praise the LORD!
			
			Praise his name, you servants of
			    the LORD,

2	you that stand in the house of the
	      LORD,
	    in the courts of the house of
	      our God!
		2	who stand in the LORD's house,
			    in the Temple of our God.

For the opening **Praise the LORD!** see 104.35. Verses 1b-2 are similar to 134.1; here is added a parallel line for the Temple as **the courts of the house of our God** (verse 2b). As in 134.1 it is impossible to say whether **the servants of the LORD, you that stand in the house of the LORD** (verses 1b-2a) are the officiating priests and Levites or the worshipers as such. TEV here has taken it in the more general sense (so Anderson). TEV, which did not use "you servants" in 134.1, uses that form here, thus providing a better model for many translations. **Our God** refers to the God of the priests and the Temple worshipers, and will have to be rendered in an inclusive form in languages which must make that kind of distinction, for it includes the worshipers being addressed. One may have to avoid the possessive pronoun and say instead "the God we (inclusive) worship."

It is much more common for the vocative (the persons addressed) to be placed immediately before or after the command, or in the following line. Here it is placed in the third line and expanded in both lines of verse 2. In languages which must place the vocative first, some adjustments will be required. For example, "You servants of the LORD, praise the LORD . . . ." In the same way it may be necessary to repeat the command to praise the LORD in verse 2; for example, "You who serve (or, worship) in the LORD's Temple, praise the LORD."

135.3-4	RSV		TEV

3 Praise the LORD, for the LORD is good;
   sing to his name, for he is gracious!
4 For the LORD has chosen Jacob for himself,
   Israel as his own possession.

3 Praise the LORD, because he is good;
   sing praises to his name, because he is kind.[b]
4 He chose Jacob for himself,
   the people of Israel for his own.

[b] he is kind; *or* it is pleasant to do so.

In verse 3b **gracious** translates an adjective which in 133.1 is translated "pleasant"; so here (see TEV footnote) the Hebrew may mean "it is pleasant to do so" (see NIV), or "it brings joy" (NJB). Or else, as NJV has it, "for it (that is, Yahweh's name) is pleasant."[1] **Sing to his name** may need to be rendered "sing to Yahweh," in which **his name** stands for Yahweh.

In verse 4 **the LORD** translates *Yah* (see 68.4). The two lines are synonymous; **Jacob** and **Israel** are the people of Israel. **As his own possession** in line b translates a noun meaning "private property" (see its use in Exo 19.5; Mal 3.17). NEB has "his special treasure" (see SPCL). If the translator must reduce verse 4 to one line, it may be rendered "He chose the people of Israel to be his own property."

135.5-7	RSV		TEV

5 For I know that the LORD is great,
   and that our Lord is above all gods.
6 Whatever the LORD pleases he does,

5 I know that our LORD is great, greater than all the gods.
6 He does whatever he wishes in heaven and on earth,
   in the seas and in the depths below.

---

[1] In verse 3a, on the basis of the Syriac and one Old Latin manuscript, NEB omits the second **the LORD** and translates "Praise the LORD, for that is good" (as an exact parallel, line b is translated "honour his name with psalms, for that is pleasant"). HOTTP stays with the Hebrew text ("C" decision).

		7	He brings storm clouds from the ends of the earth;
	in heaven and on earth, in the seas and all deeps.		he makes lightning for the storms,
7	He it is who makes the clouds rise at the end of the earth, who makes lightnings for the rain and brings forth the wind from his storehouses.		and he brings out the wind from his storeroom.

Yahweh's power as lord of the universe is praised in these verses. **I know**: the speaker here is probably a priest. Yahweh is greater than all the heathen **gods** (verse 5; see comments on 96.5; 97.9b). The psalmist takes it for granted that these gods do exist, but Yahweh is more powerful than all of them.

Yahweh's power is unlimited (verse 6; see 115.3b). He does what he wishes, that is, he carries out his purposes, he accomplishes what he plans to do, **in heaven and on earth**. If a distinction is to be made between **the seas** and **all deeps**, the latter (the plural of *tehom*; see comments on 104.6) represents the primeval waters which Yahweh conquered at creation (so commentaries). Most translations make the two parallel. By using the four spacial terms **heaven**, **earth**, **seas**, and **deeps**, the psalmist is expressing poetically the limitless extent of God's dominion. The images move from the highest point to the lowest point, passing through the intermediate points of earth and seas. **All deeps** may be rendered "to the bottom of the seas" or "to the deepest parts of the seas." In languages unfamiliar with seas, adjustments to lakes or rivers will have to be made, if the images are to be kept.

Yahweh is also lord of the storms: the storm **clouds**, the **lightnings**, and **the wind** are all under his control (verse 7). **The end of the earth** and TEV "the ends . . ." is somewhat idiomatic, meaning from the most distant parts, and must often be translated in that way. Instead of the Masoretic text **lightnings**, NEB reads another word, "rifts" ("he opens rifts for the rain"), but without any justification (so HOTTP). For the idea of Yahweh's **storehouses** where he keeps the wind, see similar language in 33.7. See also Jeremiah 10.13; 51.16, for almost identical language.

135.8-9   RSV   TEV

8	He it was who smote the first-born of Egypt, both of man and of beast;	8	In Egypt he killed all the first-born of men and animals alike.
9	who in thy midst, O Egypt, sent signs and wonders against Pharaoh and all his servants;	9	There he performed miracles and wonders to punish the king and all his officials.

In verses 8-12 the psalmist chooses three events from Israel's history to illustrate the unlimited power of Yahweh: the plagues which were sent on Egypt (verse 8-9), the defeat of kings (verses 10-11), and the conquest of the land of Canaan (verse 12).

For the death of **the first-born of Egypt**, human and animal, see 78.51; 105.36; and for the other **signs and wonders**, that is, the plagues, see 78.42-49; 105.27-35. It may be helpful in some translations to specify that only the Egyptians suffered the loss of their first-born sons (and of their domestic animals).

It is to be noticed that in verse 9 the Hebrew text has "in your midst, Egypt," changing from the third person in verse 8 to the second person of direct address, which seems to emphasize the importance of Egypt. The majority of translations preserve this form, but there is no need to do so (see NJV text "against Egypt"; see GECL, SPCL, NJB, NEB). **Pharaoh** is not a proper name but a title, like "Czar" or "Augustus." Pharaoh's **servants** are the court officials (see NJB, SPCL); NEB, however, has "his subjects."

135.10-12 RSV TEV

10 who smote many nations
    and slew mighty kings,
	10 He destroyed many nations
	    and killed powerful kings:

11 Sihon, king of the Amorites,
    and Og, king of Bashan,
    and all the kingdoms of Ca-
    naan,
	11 Sihon, king of the Amorites,
	    Og, king of Bashan,
	    and all the kings in Canaan.

12 and gave their land as a heritage,
    a heritage to his people Israel.
	12 He gave their lands to his people;
	    he gave them to Israel.

These verses are paralleled in 136.17-20. For the defeat of **Sihon** see Numbers 21.21-24; Deuteronomy 2.30-33; and for the defeat of **Og** see Numbers 21.33-35; Deuteronomy 3.1-6. **Amorites** is a general term for the original inhabitants of the land of Canaan; Sihon's kingdom was north of Moab, on the east side of the Dead Sea; **Bashan** was a territory further north, east of Lake Galilee. These two kings, on the east side of the Jordan River, were the first two rulers defeated by the Israelites in their conquest of Canaan. The psalmist adds (verse 11c) **and all the kingdoms of Canaan**, thinking probably of those whose lands were on the west side of the Jordan River. In some languages it may be necessary to begin verse 11 by saying "those kings' names were: . . . ."

For **heritage** in verse 12 see 16.6. The Hebrew text repeats **heritage** in both lines, which TEV maintains as "he gave." It is not always necessary to preserve the parallelism, and in such cases one may translate "He gave their lands to his people" or ". . . to his people called Israel."

135.13-14 RSV TEV

13 Thy name, O LORD, endures for
    ever,
    thy renown, O LORD, through-
    out all ages.
	13 LORD, you will always be
	    proclaimed as God;
	    all generations will remember
	    you.

14 For the LORD will vindicate his
    people,
	14 The LORD will defend his people;
	    he will take pity on his servants.

and have compassion on his servants.

These two verses, which praise Yahweh for his power and his compassion, serve as an interlude, a transition to the next section. In both verses the two lines are parallel and synonymous. In verse 13a the Hebrew is simply "Yahweh, your name (is) eternal," which TEV has represented by "LORD, **you will always be proclaimed as God**"; for **name** see 5.11. Most translations use the two abstract nouns, **name . . . renown** (or, fame). Verse 13b is the same in Hebrew as 102.12b, which see; see also Exodus 3.15. Translators may wish to reduce the two lines of verse 13 to one, in which case they may say, for example, "Your fame will last forever," "People will always know you," or "No one will ever forget you." Or, like GECL, a translation may express the meaning in two different linguistic forms, "Lord, your fame will never end; all generations will speak about you!"

Verse 14 is the same as Deuteronomy 32.36a,b. The Hebrew verb in line a means "to judge" (see 72.2); here it has the specific meaning of acquitting, declaring innocent (see its use in 54.1b). The translation can be "will render justice to his people" (FRCL, SPCL); NJV has "will champion His people"; and TEV "**will defend**" (similarly NAB, Dahood). In verse 14b **his servants** are the people of Israel, parallel with **his people** in line a.

135.15-17

RSV	TEV
15 The idols of the nations are silver and gold, the work of men's hands.	15 The gods of the nations are made of silver and gold; they are formed by human hands.
16 They have mouths, but they speak not, they have eyes, but they see not,	16 They have mouths, but cannot speak, and eyes, but cannot see.
17 they have ears, but they hear not, nor is there any breath in their mouths.	17 They have ears, but cannot hear; they are not even able to breathe.

In these verses the psalmist describes the pagan **idols** as completely powerless and ineffective, in contrast with the all-powerful Yahweh, the God of Israel. For translation suggestions regarding **idols** see 31.6; 96.5; 106.38; 115.4. **The nations** refers, of course, to foreign nations, and must sometimes be rendered "the nations that do not worship you." **The work of men's hands** is sometimes translated as "they are things that people make." Verses 15-17a repeat the thought and the language of 115.4-6a. Verse 17b has no parallel in 115.4-8; the meaning of **nor is there any breath in their mouths** is that the gods of the other nations are lifeless, inert, dead (see SPCL "They even have no life!"). The Hebrew has "mouth"; there is no need to change the text, as NEB does, to "nostril" (see HOTTP).

135.18   RSV   TEV

> Like them be those who make   May all who made them and who
>   them!—   trust in them
> yea, everyone who trusts in   become[c] like the idols they have
>   them!   made!

> [c] May all . . . become; *or* All who made
> them and who trust in them will be-
> come.

Verse 18 is like 115.8, which see. RSV, TEV, FRCL, GECL, and TOB translate it here as a wish; but it can be a statement (TEV footnote; NJB, BJ, NEB, NIV, SPCL, NJV).

135.19-21   RSV   TEV

19   O house of Israel, bless the LORD!   19   Praise the LORD, people of Israel;
     O house of Aaron, bless the   praise him, you priests of God!
     LORD!   20   Praise the LORD, you Levites;
20   O house of Levi, bless the LORD!   praise him, all you that worship
     You that fear the LORD, bless   him!
     the LORD!   21   Praise the LORD in Zion,
21   Blessed be the LORD from Zion,   in Jerusalem, his home.
     he who dwells in Jerusalem!
     Praise the LORD!   Praise the LORD!

All the people are called upon to <u>bless the LORD</u>, that is, to praise him (see 16.7). There are four groups mentioned: first, the <u>house of Israel</u>, that is, all the "people of Israel"; then the "priests" (<u>house of Aaron</u>); then the "Levites" (<u>house of Levi</u>); and finally all the worshipers (<u>You that fear the LORD</u>); see 115.9-11; 118.2-4, where the Levites are not mentioned by name. The Levites assisted the priests in the Temple services; among other duties they served as musicians and guards.

The Hebrew text in verse 21a has "Blessed be Yahweh from Zion," which, as Kirkpatrick points out, corresponds to 134.3, "May Yahweh bless you from Zion." The thought here is that from Zion (Jerusalem, or the Temple), where the worshipers have come together, praise must be offered to Yahweh. Since both the worshipers and Yahweh are in Zion, the easiest way to represent the meaning of the text is to say simply "in Zion."

For the concluding **Praise the LORD!** see 104.35.

Psalm 136

This psalm is a hymn of praise to Yahweh for his power as Creator of the universe and savior and protector of his people. The psalm was used in the celebration of one of the major annual festivals in the Temple; most commentators associate it with Passover. It is traditionally known as "The Great Hallel" (see introduction to Psa 113) and was sung after "The Egyptian Hallel" at the Passover meal. The second half of each verse, **his steadfast love endures for ever** (TEV **"his love is eternal"**) was sung either by the congregation or the choir, in response to the first half, which was probably sung by a priest, a Levite, or a choir.

The psalm opens with a call for all people to give thanks to Yahweh (verses 1-3); he is praised for having created the universe (verses 4-9), for having rescued his people from Egypt (verses 10-15), and for leading them safely into the Promised Land (verses 16-22). The last strophe recalls Yahweh's continuing care (verses 23-25), and the psalm closes with a final call to praise him (verse 16).

HEADING: **"A Hymn of Thanksgiving."** Other headings are: "God's saving love"; "Litany of thanksgiving"; "God's eternal love for Israel." Translators wishing to use the TEV heading may refer to the suggestions on the same heading found in Psalms 65, 66, and 67.

136.1-3	RSV		TEV
1	O give thanks to the LORD, for he is good, for his steadfast love endures for ever.	1	Give thanks to the LORD, because he is good; his love is eternal.
2	O give thanks to the God of gods, for his steadfast love endures for ever.	2	Give thanks to the greatest of all gods; his love is eternal.
3	O give thanks to the Lord of lords, for his steadfast love endures for ever;	3	Give thanks to the mightiest of all lords; his love is eternal.

The first strophe (verses 1-3) calls upon all people to **give thanks to the LORD, for he is good** (see 106.1); he is **the God of gods** (verse 2) and **the Lord of lords** (verse 3), a Semitic way of saying "the greatest of all gods" and "the mightiest of all lords" (see similar language in Deut 10.17). **Lords** is to be taken as a synonym of **gods**, referring to supernatural beings (see 135.5). **God of gods** and **Lord of lords** has been handled in TEV by use of the superlatives "greatest" and "mightiest." In languages which form the superlative in very indirect ways, one may have to say this by way of contrast; for example, "God is very great; the gods are not great. Give thanks to God" or "the gods are great a little bit; God is very great. Give thanks to the great God."

The repeated refrain "his *chesed* is everlasting" uses the one word which more than any other expresses Yahweh's attitude toward his people (see 5.7). The word is variously translated: **steadfast love** (RSV, NJV), "**love**" or "constant love" (TEV, NEB, NIV, BJ, FRCL, GECL, SPCL), "mercy" (NAB), "kindness" (Dahood), "faithfulness" (TOB), "faithful love" (NJB). The two primary components are Yahweh's love and his faithfulness in keeping his covenant with the people of Israel. TEV's "**his love is eternal**" may have to be recast in some languages to say, for example, "he loves his people for ever" or "God will love his people forever."

In printed editions of this psalm, it will be helpful for public reading to print the refrain (line **b**) in each verse differently from the way in which line **a** is printed. Several editions of the Hebrew Bible print each verse on a single line, but the repeated refrains are printed at the ends of the lines against the margin, so that they form a column. There are many other possible formats.

136.4-9

RSV	TEV
4 to him who alone does great wonders, for his steadfast love endures for ever; 5 to him who by understanding made the heavens, for his steadfast love endures for ever; 6 to him who spread out the earth upon the waters, for his steadfast love endures for ever; 7 to him who made the great lights, for his steadfast love endures for ever; 8 the sun to rule over the day, for his steadfast love endures for ever; 9 the moon and stars to rule over the night, for his steadfast love endures for ever;	4 He alone performs great miracles; his love is eternal. 5 By his wisdom he made the heavens; his love is eternal; 6 he built the earth on the deep waters; his love is eternal. 7 He made the sun and the moon; his love is eternal; 8 the sun to rule over the day; his love is eternal; 9 the moon and the stars to rule over the night; his love is eternal.

RSV, following the Hebrew, begins each verse from verse 4 to verse 17 with **to him**, with the implied **O give thanks** carrying over from verse 3. This may be effective in other languages, but in some it may be difficult for the reader. Others have "who" (see NJV), without a break in the sentence. NIV displays the antiphonal character of the psalm by printing "His love endures forever" in italics.

In this strophe Yahweh's power as Creator of the universe is praised: **great wonders** (verse 4) summarizes all his wonderful works (see comments on "wonderful deeds" in 9.1). Most translate either "great marvels" or "great wonders"; usually the word refers to Yahweh's marvelous deeds in rescuing his people from Egypt and leading them to Canaan. Here it refers to creation: **the heavens** (verse 5), **the earth** (verse 6), **the great lights, the sun, the moon and stars** (verses 7-9). The psalm follows the order and language of Genesis 1.1-19.

It should be noted than in verse 4 BJ and NJB, on the authority of the Qumran manuscript (and the Septuagint), omit "great," which omission Anderson endorses (see also Dahood). The HOTTP committee was divided on this: half approved the omission, regarding the Masoretic text as an expansion (which ruins the meter); the other half of the committee preferred the Masoretic text. It is possible that in many languages the translation will be the same in either case.

Who alone in verse 4 is to be taken in the sense "only he, and no one else," not in the sense "by himself."

The idea of Yahweh's **understanding** (or "wisdom") in creation (verse 5) is expressed also in 104.24; see also Proverbs 8.27-30. **By understanding** and TEV's "**by his wisdom**" may be considered the instrumental or expressive function of God's wisdom. In some languages this may have to be shifted to a causal relation; for example, "Because God is wise he could make the heavens," or "God is wise, therefore he made the heavens," or "God showed his wisdom when he made the heavens."

In verse 6 the creation of the earth is described by the use of the verb "to spread out"; the picture is that of the earth as a solid layer that was spread out **on the waters**, that is, on the watery abyss which Yahweh conquered at creation (see 24.2); the same verb is used in Isaiah 42.5; 44.24.

In verse 7 **the great lights** (see Gen 1.16) are **the sun**, which here is portrayed as ruler of **the day** (verse 8), and **the moon**, ruler of **the night** (verse 9). The psalmist also includes the **stars**, although in the Genesis account they are not spoken of as rulers over the night (see Gen 1.16). Nearly all the translations consulted use the verb "to rule" or "to govern"; SPCL and POCL, however, use the verb "to illuminate, light up." Because of the interruption of sequence caused by the refrain, it may be necessary in such verses as 8 and 9 to repeat the verb "made" from verse 7. In languages in which it may not be possible to speak of the sun "ruling," the translator may have to say, for example, "he made the sun to be the great one during the day." And in verse 9 "He made the moon and the stars to be the great ones at night." Alternatively, the translator may have to say "God made the sun to shine during the day," and in verse 9, ". . . the moon and stars to shine in the night."

136.10-15   RSV   TEV

10   to him who smote the first-born of   10   He killed the first-born sons of the
        Egypt,   Egyptians;
     for his steadfast love endures   his love is eternal.
        for ever;   11   He led the people of Israel out of

11 and brought Israel out from among them, for his steadfast love endures for ever;	Egypt; his love is eternal;
12 with a strong hand and an out-stretched arm, for his steadfast love endures for ever;	12 with his strong hand, his powerful arm; his love is eternal.
13 to him who divided the Red Sea in sunder, for his steadfast love endures for ever;	13 He divided the Red Sea; his love is eternal;
14 and made Israel pass through the midst of it, for his steadfast love endures for ever;	14 he led his people through it; his love is eternal;
15 but overthrew Pharaoh and his host in the Red Sea, for his steadfast love endures for ever;	15 but he drowned the king of Egypt and his army; his love is eternal.

In these verses the psalmist praises Yahweh for having safely brought the Hebrews from slavery in Egypt. He begins with the killing of **the first-born of Egypt** (verse 10), the last of the plagues (see 78.51; 135.8). It is possible that here **the first-born** includes both human beings and animals, as in Exodus 12.29; Psalm 135.8.

In verse 11 RSV's literal translation **from among them** (also NIV) can only refer back to **the first-born of Egypt**; it means, of course, "from among the Egyptians." Translators in some languages may experience difficulty in showing the relationship between verses 10-12. This is because the two episodes in verses 10 and 11 are separated by the refrain, and verse 12 particularly, because it provides the manner in which the two episodes are carried out. Therefore, in order to give coherence to these three verses, it may be necessary to omit the refrain after verses 10 and 11; for example, "He killed the first-born sons of the Egyptians; he led the people of Israel out of Egypt. He did this with his strong hand, his powerful arm. His love is eternal." In some languages it may be necessary to recast **strong hand** and **outstretched arm** as instrumental, "with great power" or "showing his great power."

In verse 13 the Hebrew verb means "to cut in two" or "to cut in pieces." NJV has "split apart," and NJB "split . . . in two." It is possible to translate "He made a path through the Red Sea." For **the Red Sea** (that is, the Sea of Reeds) see 106.7.

Yahweh led his people safely through the sea (verse 14), but he drowned the Egyptian king and his army, who were pursuing the Hebrews (verse 15). The verb translated **overthrew** (NJV "hurled") is literally "shake off" (see its use in 109.23b); the same verb is used in Exodus 14.27 (where TEV has "threw them into the sea"). For **Pharaoh** see comment at 135.9. In languages in which the sequence of related events must remain without the interruption of the refrain, verses 13-15 can, if necessary, be handled the same as suggested for verses 10-12.

RSV   TEV

16	to him who led his people through the wilderness, for his steadfast love endures for ever;	16	He led his people through the desert; his love is eternal.
17	to him who smote great kings, for his steadfast love endures for ever;	17	He killed powerful kings; his love is eternal;
18	and slew famous kings, for his steadfast love endures for ever;	18	he killed famous kings; his love is eternal;
19	Sihon, king of the Amorites, for his steadfast love endures for ever;	19	Sihon, king of the Amorites; his love is eternal;
20	and Og, king of Bashan, for his steadfast love endures for ever;	20	and Og, king of Bashan; his love is eternal.
21	and gave their land as a heritage, for his steadfast love endures for ever;	21	He gave their lands to his people; his love is eternal;
22	a heritage to Israel his servant, for his steadfast love endures for ever.	22	he gave them to Israel, his servant; his love is eternal.

In this strophe the psalmist relates the journey **through the wilderness**, on the way from Egypt to Canaan (verse 16), the defeat of enemy kings (verses 17-20), and the conquest of Canaan (verses 21-22).

Verses 17-18 are parallel and synonymous; for **Sihon** and **Og** (verses 19-20) see 135.11.

For verses 21-22 see 135.12. **Israel his servant** (verse 22) is not a common phrase in the Psalms but occurs often in Isaiah (see 44.1,2). Here **Israel** means the Israelites. It is to be noticed that in verse 21 it is not said to whom Yahweh gave the lands of the defeated kings; this information is given only in verse 22 (see RSV). TEV introduces in verse 21 "**his people**" as a parallel to "**Israel, his servant**" in verse 22. In verse 22 the expression **Israel his servant** may have to be recast to say, for example, "the people of Israel, who serve him."

The sequence of events in verses 16-22 may again require omission of the refrain until the end of verse 22. However, here the sequence is not as fixed as in the previous verses.

RSV   TEV

| 23 | It is he who remembered us in our low estate, for his steadfast love endures for ever; | 23 | He did not forget us when we were defeated; his love is eternal; |
| | | 24 | he freed us from our enemies; |

24 and rescued us from our foes,
     for his steadfast love endures
     for ever;
25 he who gives food to all flesh,
     for his steadfast love endures
     for ever.
 	
26 O give thanks to the God of
     heaven,
     for his steadfast love endures
     for ever.
	his love is eternal.
	25 He gives food to every living crea-
	     ture;
	    his love is eternal.
	
	26 Give thanks to the God of heaven;
	    his love is eternal.

Verses 23-25 refer to Yahweh's constant care for his people. It is not certain if **in our low estate** (FRCL "in our misfortune," NEB "when we were cast down," NJB "when we were humbled") refers to a particular event; if so, it is probably the exile in Babylonia (see Taylor, Anderson). The Hebrew word means "low place, humiliation"; it occurs elsewhere only in Ecclesiastes 10.6. If the translator follows the TEV model, it may be necessary to avoid the passive and say, for example, ". . . when our enemies defeated us."

In verse 24 the verb translated **rescued** occurs elsewhere in Psalms only in 7.2b.

In verse 25 **all flesh** is taken by TEV to mean "**every living creature**," humans and animals alike (see 104.27-28); it can be taken to mean "all human beings." **All flesh** or TEV's "**every living creature**" may have to be recast in some languages as "people and animals," "everything that eats," or "all living creatures."

The psalm concludes, as it begins, with a call to **give thanks** to Yahweh. Only here in Psalms is he called **the God of heaven**, by which is meant "the God who lives in heaven" or "the God who rules from heaven"; see its use in Ezra 1.2; Nehemiah 1.4; and Jonah 1.9.

Psalm 137

In this psalm an Israelite, possibly in exile in Babylonia, laments the sad fate of his people, far from their homes and the Temple. It is not certain whether the writer was still in exile when he composed the psalm, or whether he had recently returned to Jerusalem (after the edict of Emperor Cyrus of Persia in 538 B.C.); commentators are divided, but a decision on the matter will determine the translation of verse 4 (see below). The language of verses 5-6 seems to indicate that the psalmist was still away from Jerusalem.

The psalm begins with a lament over the sad situation of the exiles (verses 1-3). In the next strophe (verses 4-6) the psalmist calls down upon himself a curse, should his love for Jerusalem ever lessen; this is followed by a curse on the Edomites (verse 7) and one on the Babylonians (verses 8-9).

HEADING: "**A Lament of Israelites in Exile**." Other headings are: "The song of an exile"; "Revenge upon Israel's foes"; "No song of Zion." The TEV heading may be adapted for translation by saying, for example, "People of Israel show their sorrow in Babylon" or "This song tells of the sadness of the Israelites in a foreign land."

137.1-2   RSV   TEV

1   **By the waters⁰ of Babylon,**   1   **By the rivers of Babylon we sat**
      there we sat down and wept,   **down;**
      when we remembered Zion.   **there we wept when we remem-**
2   **On the willows ᵖ there**   **bered Zion.**
      we hung up our lyres.   2   **On the willows near by**
                                                          we hung up our harps.

⁰ Heb *streams*
ᵖ Or *poplars*

In verse 1 **the waters of Babylon** include not only the Tigris and the Euphrates and their tributaries, but also the extensive irrigation canals in the country. The picture is that of a group of people seated on the ground and mourning. **Zion** here is probably the Temple or the city of Jerusalem, not the land of Israel as such (see also comments at 2.6). The use of the plural "**By the rivers**" will mean in many languages that the event took place many times beside many rivers, and require that the verb "**sat down**" reflect this. Babylon may have to be adjusted as "the country called Babylon," or in languages with a name for the country, "Babylonia," that is different from the name of the city, "Babylon." In languages in which first person plural shows exclusion or inclusion, here **we sat down** will be exclusive if the psalm was composed after the exile, for the exiles are then speaking to people who were

1113

not with them in Babylon. However, if the psalm was composed in Babylon, the exiles are speaking to each other, and the pronoun is inclusive. In cases where it is not sufficiently clear that the weeping was caused by the sad memory, it may be necessary to say, for example, "when we thought about the destruction of Zion, we cried." It is important that the verb "remember" not suggest that the people had forgotten, but then suddenly recalled it.

There is a difference of opinion whether the trees named in verse 2 are willows (RSV, TEV, NEB) or poplars (NJV, NJB, Dahood); see *Fauna and Flora,* pages 169-170. NAB says the tree (whose Latin name is *populus euphratica*) is the Mediterranean aspen. For **harps** see "lyre" and comments, 33.2. The figure of hanging the harps on the trees is metaphorical; it meant, of course, that their owners were setting them aside and did not plan to play them again. If the translator finds that hanging an instrument on a tree does not express the idea of ceasing to play, it will be better to say, for example, "We never played our harps (or musical instruments) again," or "We never made any more music with our instruments," or "We put away . . . ."

137.3   RSV   TEV

> For there our captors
>   required of us songs,
> and our tormentors, mirth, saying,
>   "Sing us one of the songs of
>   Zion!"

> Those who captured us told us to
>   sing;
> they told us to entertain them:
>   "Sing us a song about Zion."

This verse describes how their Babylonian masters tried to make the Israelite captives sing the sacred songs used in worship in the Temple. There is considerable uncertainty over the meaning of the Hebrew word that RSV and NJV translate **tormentors**; the word occurs only here in the Old Testament. Holladay and HOTTP propose "oppressors"; SPCL "our despoilers"; FRCL "our persecutors." The Septuagint translates "those who led us away" (parallel with "those who made us prisoners"). In any case the word is synonymous with the previous **our captors**. TEV has shortened and combined the two, since it is not necessary to supply an exact synonym.

The Hebrew "they demanded of us . . . happiness" can be understood either "they demanded that we be happy" (see NEB) or ". . . sing happy songs" (FRCL, SPCL); or else, "they demanded that we make them happy," that is, **"entertain them"** (by singing); so TEV, NJV, and BJ. In some languages it may be necessary to recast **"those who captured us"** as "the Babylonians who captured us." This helps avoid giving the impression that the captors and the Babylonians are two separate groups. TEV's **"they told us to entertain them"** may sometimes be recast as "sing for them and make them happy."

In the last line **one of the songs of Zion** can be, as TEV has it, **"about Zion"**; or else, "one of the songs you used to sing in Jerusalem (or, in the Temple)." The latter is more likely.

137.4   RSV   TEV

> How shall we sing the LORD's   How can we sing a song to the
>   song   LORD
> in a foreign land?   in a foreign land?

The separation of verses 4-6 from the preceding strophe helps identify a structural change. Here the psalmist seems to be addressing his question to Zion, rather than as a reply to the Babylonian captors. This becomes clear in verse 5 with "If I forget you, Jerusalem." This transition may need to be made more explicit in some languages. One way is to introduce a second heading before verse 4.

In verse 4a "a song of Yahweh" refers to the same song as **one of the songs of Zion** in verse 3, that is, one of the Temple songs. The phrase **a foreign land** here has the added implication of "a pagan land"; away from their sacred city (made sacred by the Temple, Yahweh's earthly dwelling) the Israelites could not sing one of their sacred songs. If, as some believe, the psalmist was already back in Israel when he wrote the psalm (see Cohen, Dahood), verse 4 would be translated "How could we sing . . . ?" Most believe the psalmist was still in exile in Babylonia, but this view overlooks the significance of the change in verb forms. The question in verse 4 is rhetorical and can be translated as a negative statement; for example, "We cannot sing a song to the LORD in a foreign land."

137.5-6   RSV   TEV

5   If I forget you, O Jerusalem,   5   May I never be able to play the
        let my right hand wither!   harp again
6   Let my tongue cleave to the roof   if I forget you, Jerusalem!
        of my mouth,   6   May I never be able to sing again
    if I do not remember you,   if I do not remember you,
    if I do not set Jerusalem   if I do not think of you as my
        above my highest joy!   greatest joy!

There is a play on words in the Hebrew text of verse 5; the same verb is used in both lines. In line a RSV has **If I forget**, and **wither** in line b; it is contended by many that the verb has both meanings (see Anderson, Dahood; so RSV, NJV). It seems no longer necessary, as NJB does, to change the Hebrew in line b to another verb. KJV "forget her cunning" in line b is from the Great Bible of 1540. NIV follows KJV's lead by translating "If I forget . . . may my right hand forget [its skill]." The Septuagint has the verb in the passive, "let my right hand be forgotten," which requires only a change of vowels in the Hebrew text (so NAB). TEV takes the language to mean **"May I never be able to play the harp again."**

In verse 6 TEV **"May I never be able to sing again"** (literally "May my tongue stick to the roof of my mouth") parallels verse 5b. Both verses 5 and 6 represent a curse the psalmist calls upon himself, a punishment he prays be sent upon him by God: total or partial paralysis, in which he would lose control of his hands and tongue.

The last clause in verse 6 is literally "if I do not place Jerusalem above the top of my joy" (RSV **if I do not set Jerusalem above my highest joy**). The meaning is either to place Jerusalem's happiness, prosperity, joy, above that of the psalmist, or else to consider Jerusalem the source of the psalmist's greatest happiness. The latter seems more probable.

The structure of this kind of curse upon oneself must often be recast. This may require adjusting verses 5 and 6 so that the conditions for the curse are stated first, and introducing God as the operator of the curse; for example, "If I forget you, Jerusalem, if I do not think of you as my greatest joy, may God prevent me from playing the harp or singing again." This kind of polite language will be stylistically inappropriate for a curse formula in many languages where one must follow the Hebrew formulation as seen in RSV.

137.7

RSV	TEV
Remember, O LORD, against the Edomites the day of Jerusalem, how they said, "Raze it, raze it! Down to its foundations!"	Remember, LORD, what the Edomites did the day Jerusalem was captured. Remember how they kept saying, "Tear it down to the ground!"

In this verse the psalmist prays that Yahweh punish (**Remember . . . against**) **the Edomites** for the help they gave to the Babylonians in the capture and destruction of Jerusalem in 587 B.C. (see Obadiah 10-14; Ezek 25.12-14; 35.5-9). The Edomites, who lived to the south of Judah (in Edom), were descendants of Esau and thus were related to the Israelites. **Day of Jerusalem** has been rendered clearly by TEV's **"the day Jerusalem was captured."** In languages which will not use the passive here, it may be necessary to say "Remember what the people of Edom did the day the Babylonians captured Jerusalem." The Hebrew word translated <u>raze</u> means "to lay bare, uncover." It is quite possible that there is a play on words here and, as Dahood suggests, Jerusalem is compared to a woman; the command reads "strip her to her buttocks" (see NJV "Strip her, strip her, to her very foundations!"). In any case, the capture and destruction of Jerusalem by the Babylonians in 587 B.C. is meant.

137.8-9

	RSV		TEV
	RSV		TEV
8	O daughter of Babylon, you devastator!^q Happy shall he be who requites you with what you have done to us!	8	Babylon, you will be destroyed. Happy is the man who pays you back for what you have done to us—
9	Happy shall he be who takes your little ones	9	who takes your babies and smashes them against a rock.

> **and dashes them against the
> rock!**

q Or *you who are devastated*

In these verses the psalmist wishes a curse on Babylon, called here either
"Daughter Babylon" (Dahood) or **Daughter of Babylon** (RSV); NJV has "Fair
Babylon" (see the same idiom discussed in 9.14; 45.12). **Daughter of Babylon** can
refer to the people of Babylon, and in many languages it will have to be translated
in that manner. On the basis of a possible allusion of **the rock** to Petra, the capital
of Edom, some take **daughter of Babylon** to refer to Edom (see footnote "g" to
verse 9 in TOB). This does not seem very likely.

After **Babylon** the Hebrew has the passive form of the verb "to destroy"; so
TEV **"you will be destroyed"** (also SPCL, FRCL, BJ; similarly TOB "destined to
destruction"; and NJB "doomed to destruction"). Some of the ancient versions read
the active form "destroyer" (so RSV, NJV, NEB, NAB, Dahood, Weiser). Either sense
is appropriate; as Anderson says, however, the active form seems more appropriate.
HOTTP prefers the passive form of the Hebrew text: "you who are to be devastated."

Line b is an example of the law that required that the punishment fit the crime,
the *lex talionis*, a "tit for tat" (see Lev 24.19-20). TEV would have done better by
translating "Happy is the one who does to you what you did to us." For **Happy** see
the comments on "Blessed" in 1.1. A possible translation here is "He will do well
who . . . ."

The gruesome "blessing" (curse) pronounced in verse 9 is to be understood in
its context; it was not uncommon for victorious armies to kill the children—especially
the male children—of their conquered enemies (see 2 Kgs 8.12; Isa 13.16; Hos 13.16;
Nah 3.10). TEV has connected verse 9 with verse 8, to form one sentence; it is better
to make verse 9 a complete and separate sentence, another "blessing." Verse 9
contains two wishes for vengeance. These are the same as curses, but their result is
intended to bring happiness to the avenger. In some languages it will be necessary
to appeal to God as the one who will provide the reward of happiness; for example,
"Let God make the person happy who does to you the bad things you did to us. Let
God make the person happy who takes your babies and smashes them against a
rock."

Psalm 138

In this hymn of thanksgiving an individual praises Yahweh's power and love, and thanks him for his protection and care. Nothing can be inferred as to the particular circumstances in which the psalm was composed; it appears that, because he had been delivered from some difficulty, the psalmist went to the Temple in Jerusalem and offered his thanks to Yahweh.

The psalm begins with a statement of praise and thanksgiving (verses 1-3), after which the psalmist declares that all the rulers on earth will also praise Yahweh for his greatness and kindness (verses 4-6). The psalm closes with a statement of trust in Yahweh's protective care (verses 7-8).

HEADING: "**A Prayer of Thanksgiving.**" Other headings are: "Hymn of a grateful heart"; "The help of God"; "The divine presence." For headings similar to Psalm 138, see 65, 66, 67, 118, 136.

Hebrew title: **A Psalm of David** (TEV "By David").

It is to be noticed that Psalms 138–145 are ascribed to King David.

138.1	RSV	TEV

I give thee thanks, O LORD, with my whole heart;	I thank you, LORD, with all my heart;
before the gods I sing thy praise;	I sing praise to you before the gods.

The psalm begins with the psalmist's prayer of thanksgiving; he stands in front of the Temple in Jerusalem, bows down, and praises Yahweh **before the gods**. It is not clear what this means; the most probable explanation is that the language reflects the concept of Yahweh's sitting on his throne in heaven as the supreme God, surrounded by the other gods, who are part of his court (see 29.1; 58.1; 82.1; 97.7). The ancient versions had various translations: the Septuagint and Vulgate had "angels"; Syriac "kings"; the Targum "judges." NJV translates "the divine beings"; BJ and NJB "angels"; FRCL "the powers in heaven."[1] Translators in many languages

---

[1]GECL translates "with my song I will praise you, you—and not the other gods!" NEB has "boldly, O God, will I sing . . . ." NIV reads "before the 'gods' I will sing your praise." The quotation marks around "gods" indicates the word is used with a meaning other than its normal one. One wonders what the NIV translators meant to say.

will have little choice but to say **"before the gods"** or "before the false gods," which may seem contradictory in the context. Some languages say idiomatically "where the gods sit."

It should be noted that in verse 1 the Masoretic text does not have the vocative LORD; but many Hebrew manuscripts (including the Qumran manuscript) have it, as well as the versions; translational needs may require it, whether or not it has a textual basis.[2]

138.2 RSV TEV

I bow down toward thy holy temple and give thanks to thy name for thy steadfast love and thy faithfulness; for thou hast exalted above everything thy name and thy word.[r]	I face your holy Temple, bow down, and praise your name because of your constant love and faithfulness, because you have shown that your name and your commands are supreme.[e]
[r] Cn: Heb *thou hast exalted thy word above all thy name*	[e] *Probable text* your name and your commands are supreme; *Hebrew* your command is greater than all your name.

In verse 2a **toward thy holy Temple** may indicate, as Dahood thinks, that the psalmist is not in Jerusalem but in some foreign country, and is bowing in the direction of Jerusalem. But verse 1a seems to indicate that he is in Jerusalem (see also comments on 5.7).

In verse 2b **thy name** is synonymous with **thee** in verse 1a. TEV's **"praise your name"** may also be rendered "praise you."

In verse 2c the two key words **steadfast love** and **faithfulness** are again used (see comments on "steadfast love" in 5.7 and 136.2, and on "truth" in 15.2; for the two terms used together, see also 57.3; 61.7).

The rest of verse 2 in the Hebrew text is "for you have exalted your word above all your name" (see RSV footnote). This, as Anderson says, sounds odd. Commentators try to make sense out of this. Cohen explains: "God's name, His revealed nature . . . gave us confidence that He would honor his plighted word to us; but what he has actually done for us exceeds what we anticipated." So NJB "your promises surpass even your fame." FRCL also follows this line of reasoning in its translation: ". . . for you have done more than to keep your promise, more than we expected from you." HOTTP has two possible renderings of the Hebrew text, of which the clearer is "you

---

[2]HOTTP prefers the Masoretic text ("C" decision), citing Factor 4: "simplification of the text (easier reading)." This is a rule that says that a difficult reading is more likely to be original than an easy reading, since a copyist would more likely try to make a difficult text easy than make an easy text difficult.

have exalted your word more than your former reputation."[3] NJV translates "You have exalted Your name, Your word above all," in which "Your word" is in apposition to "Your name," which is also odd. Dahood also makes "your promise" to be in apposition to "your name." TOB translates "you have made promises that are greater than even your name." NAB adds the conjunction "and" before "your word"; so TEV **"you have shown that your name and your commands are supreme."** It is possible to take "your word" to mean "your promise," as it often does. If translators follow TEV's rendering of the final line in verse 2, it may be necessary to recast this to say ". . . that you and what you have commanded people to do are above all other things" or ". . . and what you have said you would do are . . . ."

138.3 RSV	TEV
On the day I called, thou didst answer me, my strength of soul thou didst increase.[s]	You answered me when I called to you; with your strength you strengthened me.

[s] Syr Compare Gk Tg: Heb *thou didst make me arrogant in my soul* with strength

There is difficulty in understanding the Hebrew text of verse 3b: the verb is defined by lexicons as meaning "to make proud" (see RSV footnote). RSV, SPCL, BJ, and NJB follow Syriac "you have increased my strength" (which may be the best course to follow). TEV takes the meaning to be **"with your strength you strengthened me,"** while NJV and TOB understand the Hebrew to mean "you inspired me with courage" or "you have stimulated my strength." HOTTP prefers the Hebrew text, which it translates "you made me bold by giving me strength in my soul." FRCL has "you have filled me with courage and strength." For translation suggestions related to **"answered me"** and **"called you,"** see 120.1.

138.4-5 RSV	TEV
4 All the kings of the earth shall praise thee, O LORD, for they have heard the words of thy mouth;	4 All the kings in the world will praise you, LORD, because they have heard your promises.

---

[3]HOTTP says: "This part of the V. may be understood in two ways: either 'you have exalted, more than all your name, your word / promise' (i.e. you have exalted your word more than your former reputation), or: '(more than your steadfast love, and more than your truth,) indeed, you have exalted—more than all your name!—your word / promise', understanding thereby the former part (quoted in brackets) with the latter part as *one* phrase."

| 5 | and they shall sing of the ways of the LORD, for great is the glory of the LORD. | 5 | They will sing about what you have done and about your great glory. |

This strophe (verses 4-6) begins with the statement that Yahweh will be praised by **all the kings of the earth** because **they have heard the words of thy mouth**. This seems to mean that those kings actually heard Yahweh give his laws and promises; it seems best to assume that the meaning is "they have heard about your laws." GECL and SPCL translate "when they hear . . . ," but the Hebrew *ki* normally means "for, because, that." NIV, NEB, and FRCL translate the verse as a plea, "May all the kings of the earth praise you, O LORD, when they hear the words of your mouth." It seems best to follow RSV and TEV, but say "heard about (or, of)."

In verses 5-6 the Hebrew speaks of Yahweh in the third person; TEV, in order to keep the verses consistent with verse 4, uses the second person of direct address.

In verse 5a **the ways of the LORD** are his actions, his deeds: "**what you have done.**" In verse 5b the initial *ki* is taken by RSV, SPCL, and NEB to mean "for"; BJ, NJB, NJV, NAB, FRCL, and Dahood take it to introduce direct discourse, and so end line a with a colon and place line b within quotation marks, as the content of the song of the kings. TEV has done this but uses indirect discourse, "**and about your great glory.**" For **glory** see 3.3. TEV's "**about your great glory**" may have to be recast in some languages as "and sing about how great you are."

	RSV		TEV
	For though the LORD is high, he regards the lowly; but the haughty he knows from afar.		Even though you are so high above, you care for the lowly, and the proud cannot hide from you.

This verse is taken by BJ, GECL, TOB, and FRCL to be part also of the song of the kings; it seems better, however, to take it to be the psalmist's own words, in which he proclaims that though Yahweh is in heaven, far above everything and everyone (see 113.4-8), still **he regards the lowly**, that is, he is aware of their needs and provides for them (see 106.44).

The last part of the verse is variously interpreted; most take **the haughty** to be in contrast with **the lowly** of the preceding line. NJV and Dahood, however, take it to be parallel with **high**, which modifies Yahweh in the preceding line; so NJV "lofty, He perceives from afar"; Dahood translates the word as a title of Yahweh, "the Lofty." The second difference is to be found in the translation of the verb, which is normally rendered **he knows** or something similar (RSV, NAB, NJV, TOB, SPCL, FRCL, Dahood). Some take the verb here as the form of a homonym of the Hebrew "to know" that means "to humble, bring down" (see references in Anderson); so "he humbles the proud." This makes excellent sense but has not been widely adopted by translators; most take the verb to mean "know," parallel with "see" in the preceding line. The sense would be "but from afar Yahweh knows what the proud are doing"—so TEV "**and the proud cannot hide from you.**" Many languages, unlike Hebrew and

English, will not contrast that which is high with that which is low, meaning humble. Accordingly one must sometimes say, for instance, "even though you are above everything, you care for people who are not proud," or idiomatically in some languages, "people who do not have swollen hearts."

138.7-8	RSV	TEV

	RSV	TEV
7	Though I walk in the midst of trouble,	7 When I am surrounded by troubles,
	thou dost preserve my life;	you keep me safe.
	thou dost stretch out thy hand against the wrath of my enemies,	You oppose my angry enemies and save me by your power.
	and thy right hand delivers me.	8 You will do everything you have promised;
8	The LORD will fulfil his purpose for me;	LORD, your love is eternal.
	thy steadfast love, O LORD, endures for ever.	Complete the work that you have begun.
	Do not forsake the work of thy hands.	

The psalm closes with a confident affirmation of Yahweh's power and care. He will not abandon the psalmist in his **trouble** but will save him from his angry enemies (verse 7c). In verse 7c,d the psalmist uses the figure of Yahweh's **hand . . . right hand** as symbols of his care and power. There is no way of knowing what specific **trouble** the psalmist had, other than **the wrath** of his **enemies**. NEB, NJV, and Dahood take the Hebrew word in verse 7a which TEV translates "**troubles**" to mean "adversaries, foes," parallel with **enemies** in verse 7c. TEV has adjusted the Hebrew image of **walk in the midst of trouble** as "surrounded by troubles," both being metaphors. In some languages one must say "when trouble grabs me" or "when trouble strangles me." In languages in which "raise the hand" carries the meaning of stopping someone (in verse 7c), the figure should be used. If not, it is best to follow TEV. "**Save me by your power**" must sometimes be rendered "you save me because you are powerful" or "you are powerful and so you save me."

It is to be noted that in verse 8 TEV has kept the second person of direct address, in harmony with verse 7; the Hebrew has the third person in verse 8.

In verse 8 the verb translated **fulfil** is used only in the Book of Psalms (7.9 "let . . . come to me"; 12.1 "there is no longer"; 57.2 "fulfils"; 77.8 "at an end"). The context here is similar to that in 57.2. TEV has omitted the personal **for me**; it should read "You will do *for me* everything you have promised." Verse 8b uses the statement found in the repeated refrain in Psalm 136.

It is not clear what is specifically meant by **the work of thy hands**; probably it refers to the people of Israel. FRCL has "Do not abandon now those you have made with your own hands." Dahood takes it to be the king, the author (as he supposes) of the psalm. NJB seems to restrict the sense to created things: "do not abandon what you have made." It may refer in a more general way to everything that Yahweh has planned: so TEV, NEB, SPCL, and GECL. GECL has "Finish what you have begun!" It seems best to take it as a reference to the people of Israel.

Psalm 139

This prayer of confidence and trust comes from a man who has been wrongly accused by his enemies of some sort of wrongdoing. So the psalm includes a prayer that his enemies be destroyed, and the claim that the psalmist himself is innocent of any sin against Yahweh. He is certain that he will be acquitted, because Yahweh knows him completely.

The psalm begins with a description of Yahweh's complete knowledge of the psalmist (verses 1-6), followed by an eloquent statement of Yahweh's presence in the whole universe (verses 7-12). In the next strophe (verses 13-18) the psalmist meditates on the wonders of his own creation by God. In verses 19-22 the psalmist prays that Yahweh will kill his enemies, and the psalm closes with the confident assurance that Yahweh's judgment of him will show him to be innocent (verses 23-24).

HEADING: "**God's Complete Knowledge and Care.**" Other headings are: "The ever-present God"; "God omniscient and omnipresent"; "The all-knowing and ever-present God." The TEV heading may be adjusted for translation into some languages by saying, for example, "God knows everyone and cares for them."

Hebrew Title: <u>**To the choirmaster. A Psalm of David**</u> (TEV "A psalm by David").
For <u>**To the choirmaster**</u> see title of Psalm 4.

139.1-2	RSV		TEV
1	O LORD, thou hast searched me and known me!	1	LORD, you have examined me and you know me.
2	Thou knowest when I sit down and when I rise up; thou discernest my thoughts from afar.	2	You know everything I do; from far away you understand all my thoughts.

The first strophe (verses 1-6) describes Yahweh's altogether incomprehensible knowledge of the psalmist; nothing he does or says or thinks escapes Yahweh's notice. In verse 1 he succinctly states the case: Yahweh has **searched** him and so he knows him (see similar language in 17.2-3; 26.2; and also verse 23, below). "To search" means "to investigate, examine." **Searched me** or TEV's "**examined me**" may be rendered in some languages as "you have looked into my innermost" or "you have seen inside my heart." **And known me** will sometimes be rendered "you know everything about me" or "there is nothing about me you don't know."

In verse 2a **when I sit down and when I rise up** is a way of describing the whole of the psalmist's activity, everything he does. Not only his activities but all his **thoughts** are known by God, even though God is far away, either in his Temple or in the heavens (verse 2b). The Hebrew word translated **thoughts** occurs only here and in verse 17. In some languages TEV's **"from far away"** may have to be recast as a concessive clause; for example, "even though you are far away, you know everything I think about."

139.3-5	RSV	TEV

<table>
<tr><td>3</td><td>Thou searchest out my path and my lying down,
and art acquainted with all my ways.</td><td>3</td><td>You see me, whether I am working or resting;
you know all my actions.</td></tr>
<tr><td>4</td><td>Even before a word is on my tongue,
lo, O LORD, thou knowest it altogether.</td><td>4</td><td>Even before I speak,
you already know what I will say.</td></tr>
<tr><td>5</td><td>Thou dost beset me behind and before,
and layest thy hand upon me.</td><td>5</td><td>You are all around me on every side;
you protect me with your power.</td></tr>
</table>

Verse 3 repeats essentially the thought of verse 2. The verb translated **searchest out** comes from a root, found only here in the Old Testament, meaning "to measure off, determine" (see K-B, Holladay). In verse 3a **my path and my lying down** is parallel with **all my ways** in verse 3b and means all activities, one's "entire life" (Anderson). NJB translates "when I walk or lie down," and Dahood translates "my departure and my arrival" and "all my travels." Briggs explains the verse as follows: "the path he followed when he rose in the morning and the resting place to which he returned for the night," while **"all my ways"** indicates everything that happened between morning and night.

Yahweh's knowledge extends also to the psalmist's unspoken words (verse 4); Yahweh knows what the psalmist will say even before he says it.

In verse 5a the Hebrew verb (RSV **beset**) usually means "besiege" in a hostile sense; here it obviously means "surround," but in a protective, benevolent sense. In some languages TEV's **"You are all around me"** will be expressed as a simile; for example, "You are like a fence (hedge) that protects me." In verse 5b "you lay your hand on me" is also used in a good sense of protection and care.

139.6	RSV	TEV

<table>
<tr><td>Such knowledge is too wonderful for me;
it is high, I cannot attain it.</td><td>Your knowledge of me is too deep;
it is beyond my understanding.</td></tr>
</table>

Such knowledge is Yahweh's complete knowledge of the psalmist, and it is well to make this explicit. So FRCL "That you know me to this degree is too wonderful for me." The phrase **too wonderful for me** requires a complement, specifically ". . . for me to understand." So TEV **"is too deep"**; NJB is better, "is beyond me," and NEB even better, "is beyond my understanding."

This meaning of line a is made clear in line b, where the dimension **high** is applied to God's knowledge of the psalmist. This may have to be modified in those languages where **high** does not fit with **knowledge**. For example, some other kind of dimension may supply the normal adjective, such as "deep," "wide," or "large."

139.7-8	RSV	TEV
7	Whither shall I go from thy Spirit? Or whither shall I flee from thy presence?	7 Where could I go to escape from you? Where could I get away from your presence?
8	If I ascend to heaven, thou art there! If I make my bed in Sheol, thou art there!	8 If I went up to heaven, you would be there; if I lay down in the world of the dead, you would be there.

In verses 7-12 the psalmist praises Yahweh's power to be present everywhere; this thought is not only a comfort but a warning as well, since it reminds him that nowhere can he escape Yahweh's notice. In verse 7 the two lines are parallel and synonymous: **go from** and **flee from**, and **thy Spirit . . . thy presence**. The question in Hebrew is a way of saying that it is impossible to get away from Yahweh's presence; it does not imply, however, that the psalmist wants to get away from him.

Yahweh's "spirit" is his presence and power. TEV has not used the word "spirit" here, since the Hebrew *ruach* in this context, parallel with "face" in the next line, means Yahweh himself, not the use of his power to give life and strength (see its use in 51.11; 104.29-30). See also FRCL "you . . . your presence"; GECL "you . . . you"; TOB "your breath . . . your face." It should be noticed that in English there is a considerable difference of meaning between "spirit," with a lower-case initial letter, and "Spirit," spelled with a capital initial letter. Especially in the context of the Bible, "the Spirit of God" will be understood by the Christian reader to mean "the Holy Spirit," in terms of Christian theology. So RSV and NIV **Spirit** should not be imitated; NEB and NJV "spirit" is better. But best of all is to say "you" or "your presence." The two questions in verse 7 may require a reply, namely "Nowhere." In some languages it will be more natural to recast these questions (or this single question if reducing the two to one) as negative statements; for example, "There is nowhere I could go where you will not also be" or "No matter where I go you will always be there."

The psalmist speaks of the most distant places in the universe, in all of which Yahweh is present; neither in **heaven** above nor in **Sheol** below (see 6.5 and comments) would he, the psalmist, be beyond Yahweh's knowledge and care.

	139.9-10 RSV		TEV
9	If I take the wings of the morning and dwell in the uttermost parts of the sea,	9	If I flew away beyond the east or lived in the farthest place in the west,
10	even there thy hand shall lead me, and thy right hand shall hold me.	10	you would be there to lead me, you would be there to help me.

In verse 9 the psalmist refers to the extreme east and the extreme west. RSV gives the wrong impression that the actions of the two lines are part of one event, **take the wings . . . and dwell**. The Hebrew lines show two distinct events, "If I take . . . , if I dwell . . . ." The exact meaning of the language in verse 9a, **If I take the wings of the morning**, is in dispute; in parallel with verse 9b (which clearly refers to the farthest west) it seems probable that the language is a figurative way of speaking of going to the east, where the sun comes up (so SPCL "if I were to fly away to the east"; GECL has "Were I to fly to where the sun rises"; and FRCL is similar). In verse 9b **the uttermost parts of the sea** means as far as one could go to the west; the **sea** is the Mediterranean, which is west of Palestine. In many languages the directions in verse 9 can best be expressed as "where the sun rises" and "where the sun sets." However, if the translator wishes to keep the geography of Palestine in view, he may translate "west" as does SPCL, "the borders of the western sea." GECL has "to the end of the seas, where the sun sinks."

Wherever he may go, the psalmist knows that Yahweh is there **to lead** him and **to hold** him (verse 10); the second verb in Hebrew is "to hold, grasp," in the positive sense of helping or sustaining, not in the negative sense of seizing or arresting.

	139.11-12 RSV		TEV
11	If I say, "Let only darkness cover me, and the light about me be night,"	11	I could ask the darkness to hide me or the light around me to turn into night,
12	even the darkness is not dark to thee, the night is bright as the day; for darkness is as light with thee.	12	but even darkness is not dark for you, and the night is as bright as the day. Darkness and light are the same to you.

In these verses the psalmist uses the figures of **darkness** and **light** to show how impossible it is to hide from Yahweh. In verse 11a the Hebrew verb translated **cover** is found elsewhere in the sense of crush, bruise (Gen 3.15; Job 9.17); here this is taken to mean, in a general sense, to overwhelm or to hide. NJV has "conceal," and NEB "steal over me." Some, however, propose to change the Hebrew to a form of the verb which means "to cover" (so NAB). Most translations find that the Hebrew text as it is yields a satisfactory sense. In verse 11b instead of the Masoretic text "and the light around me (become) darkness," the Qumran manuscript has "the night (become) a belt around me," which BJ, NJB, and NEB follow.[1] The TEV form "ask the darkness to hide me" presents difficulties in translation, in that an inanimate object is being asked to perform an action. SPCL provides a model that may be more easily followed: "If I thought of hiding in the darkness, or that the light that surrounds me be turned into darkness . . . ."

Not even the possibility of changing light into darkness would be of any help to the psalmist, were he to attempt to flee from Yahweh, for with Yahweh there is no difference between **darkness** and **light** (verse 12). SPCL goes on to say in verse 12a "the darkness would not hide me from you," which can also be rendered "but I could not hide from you in the darkness."

139.13 RSV	TEV
For thou didst form my inward parts, thou didst knit me together in my mother's womb.	You created every part of me; you put me together in my mother's womb.

In this strophe the psalmist meditates on the mystery of his creation by God (verses 13-16); in verses 17-18 he exclaims in wonder and awe at his inability to understand God's ways.

In verse 13 the psalmist says Yahweh created him in his mother's womb; **my inward parts** in line a translates what is literally "my kidneys" (see comments on the figurative use of the word translated "heart" in 7.9; 16.7; 26.2); most translate **my inward parts** or "my inmost self" (AT "my vitals" is now quite old-fashioned). Only BJ and TOB translate "my kidneys." SPCL has "my whole body." NJV has "my conscience," and FRCL "my personality," both of which may introduce rather modern concepts into this ancient Hebrew document.

The Hebrew verb in line b is defined by BDB and Holladay as "weave, shape" (K-B says "block"). Most English translations, like RSV, have **knit me together**; see similar language in Job 10.11. The sense of "protect" is preferred by Briggs (protecting the psalmist in his mother's womb) and by Dahood (protecting the psalmist since birth). It is better to stay with the sense of "fashion" or "make." In languages in which some inner part of the body is not in this context equated with the whole body, it will be better to say, for example, "you created me" or "you made my body." "Womb" is translated in some languages by the more generic "abdomen" or "belly," "womb" being used as a technical term.

---

[1]HOTTP says: "There are two possible ways of interpreting this part of the V., either: '(. . . even darkness covers me,) and the light is night around me', or: '(. . . even in darkness he [i.e. God] watches me,) and during the night he is light about me . . .'"

I praise thee, for thou art fearful
    and wonderful.[t]
Wonderful are thy works!
Thou knowest me right well;

I praise you because you are to be
    feared;
all you do is strange and won-
    derful.
I know it with all my heart.

[t] Cn Compare Gk Syr Jerome: Heb
fearful things I am wonderful

This verse in Hebrew is hard to understand; after considering three different textual problems in this verse, HOTTP proposes the following translation: "I praise you that I am so dread-fully distinguished, marvelous are your works, and I know that with all my being/I (lit. my soul) know it perfectly well."

The first line (following the RSV division of the verse) seems to mean "I praise you because fearful things (or, fearfully) I am wonderful." With a great degree of probability Anderson says the Hebrew can be rendered "I thank you, for I am fearfully and wonderfully made"; so NJV "I praise you, for I am awesomely, wondrously made." RSV has more or less followed the versions.

The second line (see RSV) in Hebrew is "your works are wonderful"; there is no difficulty here.

The third line in Hebrew is "my *nefesh* knows it well." RSV arrives at its translation by changing the vowels in the verb, thus making God the subject: "You know my *nefesh* well."

The TEV translation of the first two lines follows the Qumran manuscript: "I thank you because you are fearful (or, awesome); wondrously wonderful are your works." In the third line TEV follows the Hebrew text (also SPCL, GECL, FRCL, NJV, TOB). It must be admitted that in this line the assignment of other vowels to the Hebrew (RSV, NEB, BJ, NJB, Dahood) makes for a better statement in the context, since the psalmist is talking about Yahweh's complete knowledge of him. The following translation of verse 14 may be commended: "I thank you because I am so wonderfully and mysteriously made, and because all your works are so wonderful; you know me completely" or, in languages which will not use the passive, "I thank you because you have so wondrously and mysteriously made me . . . ."

my frame was not hidden from
    thee,
when I was being made in secret,
    intricately   wrought   in   the
    depths of the earth.

When   my   bones   were   being
    formed,
carefully put together in my
    mother's womb,
when I was growing there in se-
    cret,
you knew that I was there—

This verse in Hebrew is fairly clear: "my skeleton was not hidden from you, when I was being made in secret, intricately arranged in the depths of the earth."

Most commentators agree that **the depths of the earth** is a figure for the mother's womb. Dahood, however, takes it to mean Sheol, and Toombs states that "the ancient world believed that the children were formed in mother earth before they entered the womb." Anderson and McCullough support the view that this may be the thought here. Most translations are quite literal, "the depths of the earth" (NAB, Oxford RSV, and Oxford NEB have a footnote indicating that the mother's womb is meant); GECL translates "the womb of the earth"; TEV has "womb."

TEV has rearranged the material in this verse for greater ease of understanding. "Carefully put together" (RSV **intricately wrought**) translates a verb that is used only eight other times, in Exodus, of the decorated embroidery of the various items in the Tent of the LORD's Presence.

139.16	RSV	TEV
	Thy eyes beheld my unformed substance; in thy book were written, every one of them, the days that were formed for me, when as yet there was none of them.	you saw me before I was born. The days allotted to me had all been recorded in your book, before any of them ever began.

Line a goes with the preceding verse; **my unformed substance** translates a noun found only here in the Old Testament, "embryo" (TEV **"before I was born,"** NIV "my unformed body"). NAB follows the Syriac "my actions"; it is better to translate the Hebrew text, as understood by most.

The rest of the verse seems to change the subject from the formation and growth of the embryo to the days of the psalmist's life. But KJV, NJV, and NEB take the subject of the rest of the verse to be still "my unformed limbs" (as NJV translates in line a). This is possible but does not seem probable (see Anderson). The thought of verse 16b-d seems to be that before the psalmist's birth Yahweh had already fixed the number of days he would live; Yahweh had written them down in his **book** (for which see 69.28). In verse 16d **there was none of them** translates one form of the Hebrew text (*kethiv*), "and not one among them"; another form of the text (*qere*; also the Qumran manuscript) has "and for it (there was) one among them"—a reference to the day of the psalmist's birth. NJB translates the *qere* as follows: "every one that was fixed is there," taking "one" in the generic sense of "all." It seems best to stay with *kethiv*, as RSV, TEV, and others do. TEV's **"The days allotted to me"** may have to be recast to say, for example, "The number of days you gave me to live had all been written down in your book" or, in languages which do not use the passive, "You wrote down in your book the number of days you gave me to live." Because **book** may not be familiar in this context, it may be better to say "You decided before I was born how long I would live."

The translation of verses 14-16 is full of difficulties, and very few commentators or translators are dogmatic about the exact meaning of the Masoretic text.[2]

139.17-18   RSV   TEV

17   How precious to me are thy   17   O God, how difficult I find your thoughts
        thoughts, O God!   how many of them there are!
        How vast is the sum of them!   18   If I counted them, they would be
18   If I would count them, they are   more than the grains of sand.
        more than the sand.   When I awake, I am still with
        When I awake, I am still with   you.
        thee.[u]

                                        [g] how difficult I find your thoughts; *or*
[u] Or *were I to come to the end I would*   how precious are your thoughts to me.
still be with thee

In verse 17a the Hebrew verb form translated **how precious** may mean "**how difficult**" (TEV, FRCL, TOB, BJ, NJB); see the use of the related adjective in 116.15. This seems preferable: the psalmist is exclaiming over the impossibility of understanding God's **thoughts** (same word as in verse 2), which are beyond counting (verses 17b, 18a). Verse 17 may sometimes be rendered more clearly by switching lines <u>a</u> and <u>b</u>; for example, "God, your thoughts are so many," "God, you think so many thoughts," or "God, you have so many ideas." Line <u>a</u> may then follow, "And your thoughts (the things you think) are so difficult for me to understand."

More than the sand in verse 18 means "more than there are grains of sand." The meaning of verse 18b is disputed. The verb in the Masoretic text is "awake" and is so translated by RSV, TEV, and others. A few Hebrew manuscripts have another verb which elsewhere in the Old Testament means "to cut" but here is conjectured to mean "to come to an end"; this text is preferred by AT, NEB, BJ, NJB, FRCL, NAB, NJV, SPCL. The sense is "If I should finish counting them (that is, Yahweh's thoughts) . . . ." This gives excellent sense; the rest of the verse ("**I am still with you**") would then mean that even if the psalmist were able to count all the thoughts of Yahweh, still he would not have begun to know Yahweh, who is ever beyond human capacity to understand. Toombs says the line means "If I were to count God's thoughts till my strength failed, the task would remain unfinished." FRCL translates "Even if I were to finish my calculation (of your thoughts), I would not have finished understanding you." The meaning can be expressed as follows: "I could never count them all because they are more than the grains of sand." In languages in which sand is not

---

[2]HOTTP says: "The entire V. would be: 'your eyes saw me <when I was still> an embryon / fetus; and in your book they are all inscribed, the days which were formed and nobody among / in them (or: . . . were formed before any among them existed)'." And on the two forms of the Hebrew text, HOTTP comments on how the *kethiv* may be understood: ". . . the days which were formed and nobody was among them", or ". . . the days which were formed before any among them existed".

common, and in which some other material object is used for comparing quantities, a substitution for sand should be used.

In this context the meaning of **awake** (of the Masoretic text) is not easy to determine. Kirkpatrick takes it to mean waking up after falling asleep; even then there would be more of God's thoughts to count (also Cohen). It may refer to the next life (so Briggs, Dahood); but its statement here is so abrupt, with no relation to the context, that one is quite uncertain. Anderson and others believe that some words or a line must have fallen out of the text. The result of this uncertainty leaves the translator in a position of having to choose between what appears as an abrupt insertion in 18b and those versions which follow the conjectured meaning "to come to an end." NEB renders it "to finish the count, my years must equal thine." In other words "If I were able to count all of them, I would have to live as long as you."

139.19-20	RSV	TEV
	19 O that thou wouldst slay the wicked, O God, and that men of blood would depart from me,	19 O God, how I wish you would kill the wicked! How I wish violent men would leave me alone!
	20 men who maliciously defy thee, who lift themselves up against thee for evil!*v*	20 They say wicked things about you; they speak evil things against your name.*h*

v Cn: Heb uncertain

h *Probable text* they speak . . . name; *Hebrew unclear.*

In verses 19-22 the psalmist abruptly switches to his hatred for Yahweh's enemies, whom he regards as his own enemies. He asks God to **slay the wicked**, who are "**violent men**" (literally "men of bloods"—see comments on "bloodthirsty" in 5.6). The Hebrew in verse 19b is in the form of direct address, "depart from me, violent men!" (so BJ, NJB, NIV, NJV, TOB); TEV, RSV, NEB, NAB, and SPCL put it in indirect form, which makes it go more easily with the preceding line. SPCL and FRCL translate the line as a request to God: "drive far away from me those murderers"; this may be followed by translators.

In verse 20 **maliciously** translates the Hebrew "with malice" (or, wickedness). The second line in the Masoretic text seems to mean "they take up in vain your cities." The word translated "your cities" is what it means in Hebrew; but if it is read as Aramaic, it may mean "your enemies," which is the sense that HOTTP assigns it here, and for which it proposes the following translation: "being your enemies, they mention in vain" (the object "you" being understood). RSV, instead of the Masoretic text "your cities" (or, your enemies), conjectures **against thee**; TEV conjectures "against your name." TEV's "**against your name**" is the same as RSV's **against thee**.

RSV   TEV

21   Do I not hate them that hate thee,   21   O LORD, how I hate those who
        O LORD?   hate you!
     And do I not loathe them that   How I despise those who rebel
        rise up against thee?   against you!
22   I hate them with perfect hatred;   22   I hate them with a total hatred;
     I count them my enemies.   I regard them as my enemies.

The psalmist vigorously expresses his hatred for Yahweh's enemies. The rhetorical questions in verse 21 (see RSV) are a way of making an emphatic statement. He feels for them **a perfect hatred**, that is, complete hatred, without a drop of compassion or good will; and he looks upon them as his own **enemies**. **Perfect hatred** or TEV's "total hatred" in verse 22 must often be recast to say, for example, "I hate them with all my heart, soul, stomach, throat, liver," whichever body part represents the center of the emotions.

139.23-24   RSV   TEV

23   Search me, O God, and know my   23   Examine me, O God, and know
        heart!   my mind;
     Try me and know my thoughts!   test me, and discover my
24   And see if there be any wicked[w]   thoughts.
        way in me,   24   Find out if there is any evil in me
     and lead me in the way   and guide me in the everlasting
        everlasting![x]   way.[i]

[w] Heb *hurtful*   [i] the everlasting way; *or* the ways of my
[x] Or *the ancient way*. Compare Jer 6.16. ancestors.

The psalm concludes with a prayer for Yahweh to **search** the psalmist and **try** him (that is, put him to the test) in order to discover if there is **any wicked way** in him. This is more than a request; it is a way of claiming innocence of any wrong. The psalmist is confident that Yahweh will find nothing in him that deserves punishment.

The two lines of verse 23 are parallel and synonymous, but without intensification. This verse uses much of the language found in verse 1. **My heart** in line a is parallel with **my thoughts** in line b; the word translated **thoughts** is found elsewhere only in 94.19a. The repetition in verse 23 serves to emphasize how important the psalmist's request is. If the two-line parallelism does not convey this emphasis, the translator should provide it through whatever poetic means is suitable.

In verse 24 it is not certain what the word translated **wicked** means. Depending on which root it may have come from, it may mean either "injurious, hurtful" or "idol." If taken in the first sense, it is to be decided whether the "hurt" is felt by God (so NEB "that grieves thee") or by the psalmist (so other translations). In support of the notion "idol" is the use of the word in Isaiah 48.5 in that sense, and the translation in the Targum; this is adopted by FRCL and Dahood. SPCL translates the line "See if I am walking the path of evil." It seems best to understand the word to mean a sin, or fault, that is harmful to the psalmist.

In verse 24b the word translated **everlasting** may mean "ancient" (so NEB), as in Jeremiah 6.16; 18.15. The latter possibility is found as an alternative in RSV, TEV, and SPCL footnotes. The **everlasting** way is God's way, the one he has set out for all time as the way his people should go. Many languages will be able to maintain the parallel usage of **wicked way** and **way everlasting**, as do RSV and SPCL; "Look at me and see if I am going on the road that wicked people take; guide me on the road that leads to you" (as GECL has it).

Psalm 140

In this psalm the author complains to Yahweh about his enemies. In his long lament, nowhere does the psalmist admit any wrongdoing, which is typical of most psalms of lament; all he does is to pray for his own protection and for the destruction of his enemies. As Taylor says, it "is one of the less pleasing examples of a lamenting prayer"; see also Psalm 59 and 64.

It is impossible to reconstruct the specific circumstances which caused this psalm. It seems fairly certain that the psalmist's enemies are fellow Israelites, not foreigners.

The psalm seems to fall evenly into five strophes, the first three of which are marked by *Selah* at the end (verses 3, 5, 8). In the first two strophes (verses 1-3, 4-5) the psalmist describes how his enemies are acting; in the third strophe (verses 6-8) he prays to God for protection, and in the fourth strophe (verses 9-11) he prays for the destruction of his enemies. The psalm closes with an affirmation of trust and confidence (verses 12-13).

HEADING: "**A Prayer for Protection**." Other headings are: "Against the wicked"; "Against slanderers"; "A prayer asking for God's protection." For headings the same as the TEV heading of this psalm, see Psalms 54, 61, 64.

Hebrew title: **To the choirmaster. A Psalm of David** (TEV "A psalm by David").
The title is the same as that of Psalm 139.

140.1-2	RSV		TEV
1	Deliver me, O LORD, from evil men;	1	Save me, LORD, from evil men; keep me safe from violent men.
	preserve me from violent men,	2	They are always plotting evil, always stirring up quarrels.
2	who plan evil things in their heart, and stir up wars continually.		

The two lines of verse 1 are semantically parallel, with a slight step up in intensity in line b. As is often the case in an opening verse, line b reverses the word order so that in Hebrew the order is "Deliver me, O LORD, from evil men; from violent men preserve me." Line b has no vocative (O LORD) and must depend on line a to supply it by implication. Translators should make an effort to reflect the intensification by saying something like " LORD, save me from evil men; even more, keep me safe from violent ones" or "Protect me from people who do bad deeds; and still more, keep me safe from people who harm others." If the receptor language style requires the address form in the second line, it should be made explicit.

In the same way, line <u>b</u> of verse 2 moves from the general idea **plan evil things** to the more specific **stir up wars** and may be rendered, for example, "Not only do they make up evil plots, but they even stir up wars" or "They not only think up evil plans; they actually cause people to fight each other." The statement **who plan . . . in their heart** is a way of saying "who make secret plots"; or else, as NJV has it, "their minds are full of evil schemes." In verse 2b it seems better to take the Hebrew noun to mean fights or quarrels (see NEB, FRCL, NJB, SPCL) and not **wars**, which has to do with armed conflicts between nations. **Men** in verse 1 is to be taken collectively and inclusively; so it will be best to translate as "people" in order not to give the impression that the psalmist meant that only males are evil and violent. **Violent men** may sometimes be rendered as "people who use force on others" or "people who attack others."

140.3   RSV   TEV

> They make their tongue sharp as   Their tongues are like deadly
>   a serpent's,   snakes;
> and under their lips is the poi-   their words are like a cobra's
>   son of vipers.   *Selah*   poison.

Verse 3 is characterized by onomatopoeia or sound-imitation. The purpose of imitating sounds in nature through selected vowels or consonants is to increase the realism of the imagery. In this verse the Hebrew letter *shin* (pronounced as "sh" in English), imitating the hissing of a snake, occurs in each of the following words in Hebrew: **sharp**, **tongue**, **serpent**, **vipers**; and the letter *sin* (pronounced as "s" in English) occurs in the final word, which in Hebrew is the word for **lips**. The net affect is "SH-SH-SH-SH-S." Translators should be aware of this device as used in this verse, but should not sacrifice meaning trying to imitate it.

In line <u>a</u> the Hebrew is "they make sharp their tongues like (that of) a snake"— a figure of the deadly power of the snake's bite. And line <u>b</u> reads "viper's poison (is) on (or, under) their lips." TEV turns the metaphors into similes and uses language more in keeping with modern idiom, "**like deadly snakes . . . like a cobra's poison.**" The word translated "cobra" (RSV **viper**) appears only here in the Old Testament; some think that it means "spider" (NEB, NJV; see *Fauna and Flora,* page 78). Verse 3b is quoted in Romans 3.13. Many translators will want to follow TEV's lead in adjusting to a simile. It may be necessary to adjust the second simile to say, for example, "the words they speak kill just as snake poison kills." If no variety of the cobra is known, it is possible to use the generic "snake," or even "spider."

For *Selah* see 3.2.

140.4-5   RSV   TEV

> 4   Guard me, O LORD, from the   4   Protect me, LORD, from the power
>   hands of the wicked;   of the wicked;
>   preserve me from violent men,   keep me safe from violent men
>   who have planned to trip up my   who plot my downfall.

feet.	5 Proud men have set a trap for me;
5 Arrogant men have hidden a trap for me,	they have laid their snares,
and with cords they have spread a net,*y*	and along the path they have set traps to catch me.
by the wayside they have set snares for me. *Selah*	

y Or *they have spread cords as a net*

In these verses the psalmist prays that Yahweh will save him from his enemies, whom he calls **the wicked . . . violent men . . . arrogant men**. In verse 4a **Guard me** is synonymous with **preserve me** in verse 4b; verse 4b is the same as verse 1b. Verse 4c states that the psalmist's enemies are planning to bring about his ruin (**trip up my feet**). And in verse 5, in language that appears quite often in the psalms, the writer uses hunting metaphors to describe his enemies' attempts to bring about his downfall: **a trap . . . a net . . . snares** (see 9.15; 31.4; 35.7; 64.5; 119.110). **Hands of the wicked** and TEV's **"power of the wicked"** may have to be recast in translation as "wicked people who can harm me." GECL calls these persons "people who disregard you and your commands."

<table>
<tr><td>140.6-7</td><td>RSV</td><td>TEV</td></tr>
</table>

6 I say to the LORD, Thou art my God;	6 I say to the LORD, "You are my God."
give ear to the voice of my supplications, O LORD!	Hear my cry for help, LORD!
7 O LORD, my Lord, my strong deliverer,	7 My Sovereign LORD, my strong defender,
thou hast covered my head in the day of battle.	you have protected me in battle.

In verses 6-8 the psalmist proclaims his faith in Yahweh and asks him to protect him from his enemies. For verse 6a see similar statements in 16.2; 31.14; and for verse 6b see similar language in 28.2; 86.6; 130.2.

In verse 7 TEV **"My Sovereign LORD"** translates "Yahweh, my lord," the Covenant name and the title of God. The title **my strong deliverer** (literally "the strength of my salvation") is found in this form only here in the Old Testament. In verse 6 **Thou art my God** will have to be recast in some languages as "you are the God I worship." In verse 7, a similar recasting may have to be done with **my LORD** and **my strong deliverer**; for example, "you are the powerful one who has defended me."

Thou hast covered my head in verse 7b likens Yahweh's protection to a helmet which keeps the psalmist safe from his enemies' attacks. GECL changes the figure a bit by translating "Like a shield you have protected me in battle." This conveys the meaning of the text and may be a good model to follow. The phrase **in the day of**

<u>battle</u> translates what in Hebrew is "on the day of weapons." The psalmist seems to be talking about a real battle in which he was kept safe by Yahweh.

140.8

RSV	TEV
Grant not, O LORD, the desires of the wicked; do not further his evil plot! *Selah*	LORD, don't give the wicked what they want; don't let their plots succeed.

Two words in this verse occur only here in the Old Testament: the word translated **the desires** and the one translated **plot**. What the psalmist's enemies want, of course, is the psalmist's ruin or death. It is fairly certain that the singular **the wicked** is collective; it does not refer to a single individual, as RSV translates.

It should be noted that verse 8 in Hebrew has one more word, "they will rise," after which comes the closing *Selah*. So KJV "lest they exalt themselves. Selah." RSV and TEV (also SPCL, FRCL) include this verb form in the next verse (see below).

140.9

RSV	TEV
Those who surround me lift up their head,[z] let the mischief of their lips overwhelm them!	Don't let my enemies be victorious;[k] make their threats against me fall back on them.

[z] Cn Compare Gk: Heb *those who surround me are uplifted in head*

[k] *Probable text* Don't let my enemies be victorious; *Hebrew unclear.*

The division of the Hebrew text in the *Biblia Hebraica* places the verb form for "they will rise" (followed by *selah*) at the beginning of a line, even though the two words come at the end of the verse; and the next verse (9 in English, 10 in Hebrew) begins with the word "head." As the Masoretic text is printed, the half-line reads "they will rise. Selah. [10] The head (of those) around me . . . ." Both RSV and TEV disregard the verse division in the Hebrew text and begin verse 9 at the beginning of the line. (RSV has *Selah* at the end of verse 8.) As it stands the Hebrew text makes very little sense; NJV imitates KJV in translating "else they be exalted" at the end of verse 8, adding a marginal note that the meaning of the Hebrew is uncertain. TOB also translates the text as follows: "for they exalt themselves"; also NIV "or they will become proud." HOTTP also prefers the Hebrew text, which it translates "They might rise up! Selah."

Other translations, however, handle the text differently. RSV, instead of the Hebrew text "they (will) rise," follows two Hebrew manuscripts that have "they lift," and translates **Those who surround me lift up their head**, meaning that the psalmist's enemies are arrogant. TEV also translates "they lift," and following some manuscripts of the Septuagint includes the negative "not" (so Oesterley, AT): "**Don't let my enemies be victorious**" (the word "**enemies**" representing "[those who are] around me," while "**victorious**" represents "lift the head"). This seems to fit the context of verses 9-11, which consists throughout of petitions for the destruction of the psalmist's enemies. SPCL combines verses 8-9 as follows: "Lord, do not grant the desires of the wicked man; do not let his plans prosper. Those who surround me raise their head; may the curses they hurl fall on them!" This is a defensible rendition of the Hebrew text and may be recommended to translators.

Other translations have other solutions for this very difficult passage in Hebrew.

The second part of verse 9 has one problem: the verb in one form of the Hebrew text is construed with God as subject (so TEV "**make . . . fall back**"); another form has "threats" as the subject (so RSV **that the mischief of their lips overwhelm them**). For the wish expressed here see similar statements in 7.16. The phrase "**their threats**" translates "the evil of their lips"; RSV **mischief** is much too mild a word in English to express the thought of the Hebrew.

140.10-11　　　RSV　　　　　　　　　　　　　　　TEV

10　Let burning coals fall upon them! 　10　May red-hot coals fall on them;
　　Let them be cast into pits, no 　　　　may they be thrown into a pit
　　more to rise! 　　　　　　　　　　　　　and never get out.
11　Let not the slanderer be estab- 　11　May those who accuse others
　　lished in the land; 　　　　　　　　　falsely not succeed;
　　let evil hunt down the violent 　　　may evil overtake violent men
　　man speedily! 　　　　　　　　　　　and destroy them.

In verse 10 two more figures are used to represent the psalmist's prayer for the destruction of his enemies: **burning coals** (see this same language in 11.6) and **pits**; the latter translates a word found nowhere else in the Old Testament and whose meaning is debated. It is quite probable that **pits** here is a reference to Sheol, the world of the dead. It is suggested that **burning coals** derives from the punishment that fell on Sodom and Gomorrah (Gen 19), while **pits** recalls the fate of Korah and his followers (see Num 16.32-33). In any case, the psalmist is praying for the complete destruction of his enemies. At the end of verse 10 **no more to rise** means never again to regain their power, or else not rise to life.

RSV, TEV, BJ, NEB, NJV, and SPCL translate verse 10 as two lines, two requests: (1) red-hot coals fall upon them, and (2) they be thrown into pits. This involves reading "coals of fire" or "burning coals" as one phrase. But KJV, TOB, NIV, FRCL, and GECL take the Hebrew phrase to consist of two separate semantic elements: "coals" (which goes with the preceding verb "fall upon") and "in fire" (which goes with the following verb "be thrown"). This results in three lines, three requests: (1) coals fall upon them; (2) they be thrown into the fire; (3) (and be thrown) into pits. This is possible, and the translator should feel free to follow it. FRCL translates "May burning coals fall upon them; may God make them tumble into the fire, into a pit from which they will not climb out!"

In verse 11 **the slanderer** translates "a man of tongue," a phrase found nowhere else in the Old Testament. The Hebrew "become firm in the land" (see RSV) means to "**succeed**," prosper, thrive, flourish. And in verse 11b RSV **speedily** translates the plural of a word found only here in the Old Testament, literally "blow upon blow."

RSV **speedily** and NAB "abruptly" are not too probable a rendering of the Hebrew; the idea is not so much speed as intensity, the violence of the action. FRCL translates "may evil relentlessly pursue the man who uses violence." For translation suggestions concerning the use of curses, see 137.5-6.

140.12-13 RSV	TEV
12 I know that the LORD maintains the cause of the afflicted, and executes justice for the needy. 13 Surely the righteous shall give thanks to thy name; the upright shall dwell in thy presence.	12 LORD, I know that you defend the cause of the poor and the rights of the needy. 13 The righteous will praise you indeed; they will live in your presence.

The psalm closes with a statement of trust and confidence: Yahweh protects the poor and needy, and those who obey him will enjoy fullness of life.

The language of verse 12 is familiar: for **maintains the cause** see 9.4. Line b has no separate verb; the verb in line a carries over into line b (see TEV "**and the rights of the needy**"). "**The rights**" translates the word usually represented by **justice** (see "judgment" and comments, 7.6). For the two synonymous words **the afflicted** and **the needy**, see 9.12; 35.10. TEV uses the second person of direct address in verse 12, to make it consistent with verse 13.

In verse 13a TEV "**you**" represents "your name" (see 5.11); the two terms **the righteous** and **the upright** are synonymous, describing those who are faithful to Yahweh and always obey his commands.

For **dwell in thy presence** see similar language in 11.7; 16.11; 31.20. The thought may be of the care and protection of God in this life, or else of life after death (so Dahood).

Psalm 141

In this psalm the author prays to Yahweh to save him from his enemies and from temptation to evil. There is nothing in the psalm to indicate the time or the circumstances of its composition.

The psalm opens with a prayer for help (verses 1-2), which is followed by a prayer for protection from temptation (verses 3-4). The next section (verses 5-7) is extremely obscure in Hebrew; it seems to refer to the punishment of the wicked. The psalm closes with a final prayer for protection from enemies (verses 8-10).

HEADING: "**An Evening Prayer.**" Other headings are: "Against the attractions of evil"; "A prayer for protection"; "Temptations." TEV has taken the heading for this psalm from verse 2b. Translators wishing to adjust it to their language may need to say something like "The psalmist prays to God in the evening."

Hebrew Title: **A Psalm of David** (TEV "A psalm by David").

<table>
<tr><td>141.1-2</td><td>RSV</td><td>TEV</td></tr>
</table>

	RSV		TEV
1	I call upon thee, O LORD; make haste to me! Give ear to my voice, when I call to thee!	1	I call to you, LORD; help me now! Listen to me when I call to you.
2	Let my prayer be counted as incense before thee, and the lifting up of my hands as an evening sacrifice!	2	Receive my prayer as incense, my uplifted hands as an evening sacrifice.

The prayer for help seems to be offered at the time of the **evening sacrifice** in the Temple (verse 2b). The psalmist is insistent in his plea: **make haste to me!** that is, "help me now!" (verse 1; see 38.22a; 70.1b,5b; 71.12b).

Incense was a fine powder, ground from various spices, which was burned either alone or together with animal sacrifices, and which produced a pleasant odor. TEV "**Receive**" in verse 2a (RSV **Let . . . be counted as**) translates a verb meaning "to establish, make firm"; the Hebrew "may my prayer be established" is a way of asking Yahweh to consider the prayer as incense, as a sacrifice. See NJV "Take my prayer as an offering of incense." RSV **before thee** translates "before your face," which probably implies the Temple as the place where the psalmist was praying. TOB translates "May my prayer be the incense that is placed before you," and FRCL "May my prayer rise straight up toward you, like the smoke of the incense." The uplifted hands were the position of prayer (see 28.2). It is not certain whether the language

1140

of verse 2 means the psalmist was substituting his prayer for the sacrifice he should have offered; certainly this seems to be implied (see Taylor, Toombs). The **evening** (that is, 3:00 P.M.) was one of the regular times for the offering of sacrifice (see Exo 29.39-41).

In some languages **"Receive my prayer"** may have to be recast to say "Accept the words of my prayer." In languages in which fragrant burning material is not associated with liturgical prayer, it will usually be necessary to formulate a descriptive phrase; for example, "like sweet-smelling smoke" or "like a fragrant odor." **The lifting up of my hands** may require clarification as to purpose; for example, "my hands which I raise as I pray." In some languages verse 2 may then read "Accept the words I pray the way you accept the sweet-smelling odor; accept my hands raised in prayer the way you accept the evening sacrifice."

141.3-4 RSV	TEV
3 Set a guard over my mouth, O LORD, keep watch over the door of my lips! 4 Incline not my heart to any evil, to busy myself with wicked deeds in company with men who work iniquity; and let me not eat of their dainties!	3 LORD, place a guard at my mouth, a sentry at the door of my lips. 4 Keep me from wanting to do wrong and from joining evil men in their wickedness. May I never take part in their feasts.

In these two verses the psalmist asks God to protect him from temptation to speak evil (verse 3) or do evil (verse 4). Verse 3 is composed of two parallel and synonymous lines; in poetic language the psalmist asks God to **set a guard** and to **keep watch** at his **mouth**, at **the door of** [his] **lips**, so that he will not utter any sinful words. The word translated **door** occurs only here in the Old Testament. In languages in which the metaphors of verse 3 will be readily understood, they should be used. However, the word "mouth" has a wide range of meanings in many languages, and there is considerable probability of misunderstanding. If that is the case, the translator may find an equally good metaphor, and if that fails, it will be best to say, for example, "Do not let me speak evil words." There is no intensification between the two lines of verse 3. This means the translator has more freedom to keep both lines or to reduce them to one, if that is stylistically necessary.

In verse 4 the psalmist prays that God will keep him from doing wrong. The Hebrew text has four half-lines (see RSV); TEV has reduced them to three, avoiding needless repetition (also SPCL). The language is "Do not turn my heart to an evil matter" (or, word), a plea that recalls the petition in the prayer taught by Jesus, "lead us not into temptation." The thought behind the language is the possibility that God may test a person by allowing that person to be faced with sin. The word translated **any evil** is literally "an evil word (or, matter)," and so it may be taken to mean "word" (so Dahood, BJ, NJB); NEB has "sinful thought," which is possible, since **heart** was thought of as the organ of thinking.

TEV has combined RSV **wicked deeds** and **iniquity** into "**in their wickedness.**" This may have to be recast in some languages to say, for example, "in the evil things they do."

The last line, **let me not eat of their dainties**, is a prayer that God will not allow the psalmist to take part in the feasts of evil people. It can be understood as a resolve, "I shall not sample their delights!" (NJB). These feasts could have been purely social affairs, but it is possible that they were religious meals, in which case they would have been, in this context, meals at sacrifices offered to idols (see 69.22). The word translated **dainties** occurs only here in the Old Testament. Since **eat of their dainties** and TEV's "**take part in their feasts**" refers to pagan religious eating, it will be necessary in many cases to make this clear; for example, "Do not let me eat with them at their religious feasts" or ". . . when they eat to worship their gods," or "Keep me from eating . . . ."

141.5-7 RSV TEV

	RSV		TEV
5	Let a good man strike or rebuke me in kindness, but let the oil of the wicked never anoint my head;^{a} for my prayer is continually^b against their wicked deeds.	5	A good man may punish me and rebuke me in kindness, but I will never accept honor from evil men, because I am always praying against their evil deeds.
6	When they are given over to those who shall condemn them, then they shall learn that the word of the LORD is true.	6	When their rulers are thrown down from rocky cliffs, the people will admit that my words were true.
7	As a rock which one cleaves and shatters on the land, so shall their bones be strewn at the mouth of Sheol.^{c}	7	Like wood that is split and chopped into bits, so their bones are scattered at the edge of the grave.^{m}

^{a} Gk: Heb obscure
^{b} Cn: Heb *for continually and my prayer*
^{c} The Hebrew of verses 5-7 is obscure

^{m} *Verses 5-7 in Hebrew are unclear.*

These verses are understood and translated in the most diverse ways possible. The Hebrew text as it now stands is quite obscure; there are many textual problems (HOTTP deals with four in verse 5 and two in verse 7). Weiser does not translate verses 6-7, and Oesterley, though he offers a tentative translation, regards them as hopelessly corrupt. The first three editions of BJ (1950, 1955, 1964) have three different translations of these verses.

Verse 5a in Hebrew seems to say "Will strike me a good man (in) constant love and rebuke me." This is taken as a possibility by TEV and implicitly so by RSV. NJV translates "Let the righteous man strike me out of loyalty, let him reprove me." **A good man** translates *tsadiq* "righteous," and **in kindness** translates *chesed* "constant love, loyalty." Dahood takes the two terms to refer to Yahweh: "the Just One . . . the Kind One." The expression **rebuke me in kindness** may have to be recast to say, for example, "be kind to me when he scolds me" or "with a good heart show me my faults."

Verse 5b in Hebrew is "oil of the head my head will not refuse." NJV takes this to refer to the rebukes by the righteous man in the preceding line, and translates "let my head not refuse such choice oil." The rebukes by a righteous man are considered an honor which the psalmist will not refuse. The Hebrew word "head" means also "important, best," and so "oil of the head" may mean "the finest oil" (so HOTTP; NJV "choice oil"). TEV has here followed the Septuagint "the oil of a sinner is not to be spread on my head"; this implies that the verb form, instead of being associated with the root meaning "to refuse," is associated with the root meaning "to adorn"; and instead of the word for "head," the Hebrew word for "evil man" is read.

The choice seems to be between "With fine oil never let my head glisten" (Dahood; also TOB), or "My head will not be anointed with the oil of wicked men" (NEB; similarly RSV, TEV, BJ, NJB). Another interpretation is preferred by AT: "If the righteous smite me—it is a kindness. And if he rebuke me—it is the finest oil; Let not my head refuse it!" See also NAB, NIV, FRCL, SPCL, HOTTP. For "anoint the head" see 23.5.

Verse 5c in Hebrew is "for always my prayer (is) against (or, about) their evil deeds," which, though strange, is not too difficult: "for I am always praying against their evil deeds" (so the sense of most translations and HOTTP; SPCL has "Despite their blows I will continue to pray"). Verse 5c may have to be restructured as a concessive clause; for example, "even though they do evil deeds to me, I will go on praying."

In verse 6a it is difficult to decide whether "**their rulers**" (literally "those who judge them"; so NJV "their judges") is the subject of the verb (so NJV, TEV) or the indirect object (so RSV **to those who shall condemn them**). The verb can mean to be dropped, thrown, or hurled. Another problem is the meaning of the Hebrew phrase, which seems to be "in the hands (or, at the sides) of the rock." NJV translates the line "May their judges slip on the rock," and TOB "Their rulers have been hurled on the rock." The sense of TEV is the same as given by TOB, SPCL, NAB. BJ, NJB, and Dahood take "rock" to be a title for Yahweh; so BJ "they are delivered to the power of the Rock, their judge." This may well be the meaning intended. It is recommended that the meaning expressed by TEV and others be followed. NEB, a little more distant from the Hebrew, has "They shall founder on the rock of justice."

Verse 6b in Hebrew is "and they will hear my words that (or, for) they are pleasant." What this means in the context is impossible to determine. RSV, instead of reading the Hebrew as "my words," takes it to be "**the word of the LORD**" (the final y of the Hebrew form being taken as a shortened form of Yah—see 68.4). Perhaps the nearest one can get to making sense out of this line is achieved by NJV, which translates "but let my words be heard, for they are sweet," or NEB "and shall learn how acceptable my words are." Cohen's explanation can only be regarded as a desperate suggestion: "When the evil judges . . . meet with the doom of being hurled to destruction from a high rock . . . , they will admit before they die that the words he had spoken were pleasant and regret they had taken no notice of them." But, it must be admitted, TEV's (and, to a lesser degree, RSV's) text is only slightly better.

The first part of verse 7 goes, in Hebrew, "like cleaving and splitting [something] on earth." What is split is not specified in the Hebrew, but this can be either **rock** (RSV), "millstone" (NJB) or "**wood**" (TEV); or else, "as the ground is plowed and broken" (so NJV, TOB, NAB, SPCL). Dahood takes "earth" in line a to be the world of the dead, parallel with **Sheol** in line b. In line b the Hebrew text is "our bones"; Syriac and some manuscripts of the Septuagint have "their bones"; the Qumran manuscript has "my bones." The Hebrew text is hard to understand; TOB, BJ, and NJB try to make sense of it by taking verse 7 to be the words of the psalmist referred to in verse 6. HOTTP translates the verse exactly as BJ has it: "as a millstone broken on the floor/earth, our bones are strewn at the mouth of the Sheol." For **Sheol** see 6.5. If, in spite of these cautions, the translator follows TEV, for some languages there will be adaptations to be made, particularly in regard to the passives. Since it will not be possible to say who split the wood nor who scattered the bones, it may be necessary to say, for example, "their broken bones lie near the grave like pieces of wood."

FRCL translates verses 5-7 as follows:

5 I am willing for a man of goodwill to chastise me,
    or for a faithful (friend) to correct me;
    it is a gesture of friendship
    that I will not refuse.
    But the evil done by evildoers
    will not stop my prayer.

6 I said without malice:
    my enemies will understand it
    when their judges are thrown upon a rock.
7 As a rift opens in the earth
    the world of the dead will open its mouth
    to swallow their scattered bones.

It seems imperative, regardless of the translation which is finally adopted, that a note indicate that verses 5-7 in Hebrew are extremely obscure, not to say unintelligible.

141.8 RSV	TEV
But my eyes are toward thee, O LORD God; in thee I seek refuge; leave me not defenseless!	But I keep trusting in you, my Sovereign LORD. I seek your protection; don't let me die!

The psalm closes with a final prayer for Yahweh's protection (verses 8-10). For the language of verse 8a, see 25.15. TEV "**my Sovereign LORD**" translates "Yahweh, my lord," the Covenant name used with the title of God. For **I seek refuge** see similar language in 7.1; 16.1. The petition "**don't let me die**" (TEV) translates "don't pour out my *nefesh*." The verb is the same one translated "raze it" in 137.7, and here it can be translated "don't expose my *nefesh*," that is, don't expose me to danger (NJV "do not put me in jeopardy"). The language means either "don't leave me unprotected" (so RSV, NJB) or "don't let me be killed" (see NIV), the picture of "pouring out the *nefesh*" being taken in the sense of violent death (see Isa 53.12).

141.9-10	RSV	TEV
9	Keep me from the trap which they have laid for me, and from the snares of evil-doers!	9 Protect me from the traps they have set for me, from the snares of those evil-doers.
10	Let the wicked together fall into their own nets, while I escape.	10 May the wicked fall into their own traps while I go by unharmed.

For the figures **trap** and **snares** used in verses 9-10, see 140.4-5. In verse 10 the word for **nets** occurs only here in the Old Testament. The Hebrew text has "his nets," which Dahood takes to be Yahweh's nets; Syriac has "their nets," and this is taken by most translators to be the sense of the Hebrew text. But the word which RSV translates **together** is taken by some to mean "each one," with the result "each one (fall) into his own net"—which is possible (so NAB, BJ, NJB). Others take the word to mean "only, alone" and read it as the first word of the final line: "while I alone escape." Anderson proposes "while I escape all in one piece." For the wish expressed in verse 10a, see the statements in 7.15-16; 9.15-16; 57.6; 140.9.

Psalm 142

In this psalm an individual complains to Yahweh about his troubles and asks for Yahweh's help. The psalm opens with a prayer for help and a description of the psalmist's trouble (verses 1-4). Again he prays to be rescued and promises to offer his praise to Yahweh in the Temple (verses 5-7).

In terms of key words applied to structural units, the first strophe begins with the Hebrew for "I cry" and ends in verse 4d with *nafshi* "my life." The second strophe similarly begins with the same Hebrew root meaning "I called out," and in the final verse the word *nefesh* is repeated.

The Hebrew title is probably a later attempt to provide a setting for the psalm in the life of King David (see below). It may have been suggested by the language of verse 7a (so Taylor).

HEADING: **"A Prayer for Help."** Other headings are: "No hope but Yahweh"; "Prayer of a persecuted man"; "You are my refuge." For similar headings in TEV see Psalms 4, 6, 12, 13, 35, and many others.

Hebrew Title: **A Maskil of David, when he was in the cave. A Prayer** (TEV "A poem by David, when he was in the cave; a prayer").

For **Maskil** see introduction to Psalm 32. The historical note **when he was in the cave** probably refers to the incident narrated in 1 Samuel 22.1-2 (see also the Hebrew title of Psa 57).

142.1-2	RSV		TEV
1	I cry with my voice to the LORD, with my voice I make supplication to the LORD,	1	I call to the LORD for help; I plead with him.
2	I pour out my complaint before him, I tell my trouble before him.	2	I bring him all my complaints; I tell him all my troubles.

The psalm opens with the psalmist's cry to Yahweh for help. The Hebrew **I cry with my voice** means the psalmist is praying aloud; so NJV "I cry aloud . . . I appeal . . . loudly" (also NEB, NAB, SPCL). The two lines of verse 1 are semantically and syntactically parallel, with no intensification.

Verse 2 likewise presents two lines which are semantically parallel. However, for the purpose of avoiding monotony in Hebrew, line b reverses the word order of line a. Again there is no intensification in the movement from the first to the second line. In languages in which these verses appear to be overly repetitive, it may be

1146

necessary to reduce them to one line each. The psalmist's **complaint** and **trouble** are those he describes in verses 3c-4, 6c-7, that is, the persecution by his enemies, which is spoken of in general terms, without any specific details.

142.3-4	RSV		TEV
3	When my spirit is faint, thou knowest my way! In the path where I walk they have hidden a trap for me.	3	When I am ready to give up, he knows what I should do. In the path where I walk, my enemies have hidden a trap for me.
4	I look to the right and watch,*d* but there is none who takes notice of me; no refuge remains to me, no man cares for me.	4	When I look beside me, I see that there is no one to help me, no one to protect me. No one cares for me.

d Or *Look to the right and watch*

In verse 3a **When my spirit is faint** uses language similar to that used in 77.3; FRCL translates "When I lose courage," and SPCL "Completely discouraged." For **spirit** see comments on 76.12. **When my spirit is faint** is rendered idiomatically in some languages as "When my heart falls down," ". . . my heart shrinks," or ". . . my stomach leaves me." In verse 3b the Hebrew "you know my path" may have a moral or ethical sense: "you know my behavior," that is, what the psalmist actually does (and not, what he should do, as TEV has it); or it can mean the psalmist's destiny, his fate (so Oesterley, Weiser). NEB and NJB take "know" here in the sense of "watch over"; NEB has "thou art there to watch over my steps," and NJB "you are watching over my path." This makes excellent sense in the context and is probably to be preferred (see similar language in 1.6).

Some translations (see SPCL, NJV) connect verse 3a with verse 2b and make verse 3b begin a new sentence, connecting it with what follows. Dahood, who thinks the psalmist is on his deathbed, takes "my spirit grows weak" to represent the last moments of life, and **"the path"** of verse 3b to be the way to the next life.

In verses 3c-4 the psalmist complains to Yahweh about the danger he is in; for the figure of **a trap** in verse 3d, see 140.4-5; 141.9.

The psalmist feels completely abandoned (verse 4); he has no friends, no protector. The Hebrew form of the two verbs in verse 4a is imperative, second person singular: "Look . . . and see" (so TOB, FRCL, NIV, NJV, BJ, NJB, Dahood). This is to be understood as a command addressed to Yahweh, for him to take notice of the psalmist's desperate situation. But the Qumran manuscript, the Septuagint, Syriac, Vulgate, and Targum have the first person singular indicative, "I look . . . I see" (so TEV, RSV, NEB, NAB, SPCL, Weiser).[1] The **right** side is the place where the

---

[1]HOTTP says both interpretations are possible: "look to the right and watch!" or "I looked to the right and watched." HOTTP expresses no preference.

defender, the protector, would be (so TEV "to help me . . . to protect me"). **There is none who takes notice of me** is rendered in some languages idiomatically as "no one knows my name."

The thought of verse 4c is that there is no one who will protect the psalmist, there is no place he can go where he will be safe (see 2.12; 14.6).

In verse 4d **no man cares for me** translates "no one seeks for my *nefesh*" (see 3.2), in the sense that no one is trying to find out how the psalmist is getting along. NJB's rendering is good: "no one cares whether I live or die."

142.5-7   RSV   TEV

5   I cry to thee, O LORD;
    I say, Thou art my refuge,
    my portion in the land of the
      living.
6   Give heed to my cry;
    for I am brought very low!
 	
    Deliver me from my persecutors;
    for they are too strong for me!
7   Bring me out of prison,
    that I may give thanks to thy
      name!
    The righteous will surround me;
    for thou wilt deal bountifully
      with me.
	5 LORD, I cry to you for help;
	    you, LORD, are my protector;
	    you are all I want in this life.
	6 Listen to my cry for help,
	    for I am sunk in despair.
	    Save me from my enemies;
	    they are too strong for me.
	7 Set me free from my distress;*
	    then in the assembly of your
	      people I will praise you
	    because of your goodness to me.
	
	* distress; *or* prison.

As in the first strophe the psalmist again pleads for Yahweh's protection and promises to praise him publicly if he answers his prayer. Verse 5a expresses the same thought as verse 1a. In verse 5b,c TEV has not reproduced the form of the Hebrew text, in which the psalmist quotes himself (see RSV). A translator should feel free to follow the form of the Hebrew, if that represents a natural way to quote or refer to one's thoughts, ideas, or prayers. For the language of verse 5b, see 46.1 and comments; and for the language of verse 5c, see 16.5; 119.57. Instead of "**you are all I want**" as the translation of "portion, share," the meaning can be "all I need" or "all I have" (NJV, NEB, SPCL). The phrase **the land of the living** means "**in this life**" (see 27.13; 52.5), as TEV and SPCL translate. FRCL has "in this land where we live." GECL has "you give me all I need in life" as a translation of verse 5c.

In verse 6b for **I am brought very low** see 79.8c; 116.6b. NIV has "I am in desperate need," and NJB "I am miserably weak." For the language of verse 6c,d, see 18.17. RSV connects verse 6c,d to verse 7 rather than to verse 6a,b. No other translation consulted does this.

In verse 7 the word translated **prison** (RSV and most other translations) occurs elsewhere only in Isaiah 24.22; 42.7. It is probable that here the word is used figuratively of distress, troubles, difficulties. It is possible, however, that the word is used literally, and that the psalmist was a prisoner. Dahood takes it to mean Sheol, the world of the dead. If the translator follows TEV's "**distress**" or **prison**, in some languages the request will be "untie me from the troubles that hold me" and "untie me from this house of iron," or ". . . house of captives." In verse 7a **me** translates "my *nefesh*" (see 3.2). For **I may give thanks to thy name**, see 5.11.

The verb translated **surround** is taken by some to mean "to place a wreath on, to crown"; so NEB "shall crown me with garlands." Cohen takes the language to mean "because of me the righteous will crown themselves," that is, will celebrate, will rejoice triumphantly. TEV takes **the righteous will surround me** to mean "**in the assembly of your people**," that is, in public worship in the Temple, where the psalmist will go to praise Yahweh for having answered his prayer for help. No other translation consulted is this specific; most are like FRCL "in the circle of those who are faithful," indicating an informal gathering of the psalmist's friends. So a translation can read "May the righteous join with me in praise, because . . . ." TEV connects line c with line b; so FRCL, GECL. The language of the last line of verse 7 is similar to that in 13.6b; 116.7b.

Psalm 143

In this psalm of lament the psalmist is in a desperate situation; he cries to Yahweh for help and asks that his enemies be destroyed. There seems to be one enemy in particular (verse 3) who has brought him close to dying. The psalm is remarkable in that the psalmist does not claim to be without fault or sin; he acknowledges that no one is innocent in God's sight (verse 2), and so his prayer for help is based not on his own merits but on God's faithfulness (verse 1), goodness (verse 11), and love (verse 12).

This psalm is the last of the seven so-called Penitential Psalms (see introduction to Psa 32).

The psalm opens with the psalmist's cry for help (verses 1-2), following which he describes his desperate situation (verses 3-6). The second part of the psalm (verses 7-12) consists of a series of petitions to Yahweh to save the psalmist (verses 7-8, 9-10, 11-12).

There is nothing in the text to give us a clue as to the time and circumstances in which the psalm was composed.

HEADING: **"A Prayer for Help."** Other headings are: "Lament and penitence"; "A humble entreaty"; "Justice for a sinner." For translation suggestions see the preceding heading.

<u>Hebrew title</u>: **A Psalm of David** (TEV "A psalm by David").

The Septuagint adds to the title "when his son pursued him"—a reference to Absalom (2 Sam 15–18).

143.1-2	RSV		TEV
1	Hear my prayer, O LORD; give ear to my supplications! In thy faithfulness answer me, in thy righteousness!	1	LORD, hear my prayer! In your righteousness listen to my plea; answer me in your faithfulness!
2	Enter not into judgment with thy servant; for no man living is righteous before thee.	2	Don't put me, your servant, on trial; no one is innocent in your sight.

In these two verses the psalmist three times pleads for Yahweh's help: <u>Hear my prayer . . . give ear to my supplications . . . answer me</u>. He bases his pleas on Yahweh's <u>faithfulness</u> (see 36.5) and <u>righteousness</u> (see 5.8). TEV reverses the two words, placing "righteousness" first. These are the characteristics of Yahweh as the

1150

one who is true to his promise to save his people. As used by the psalmists and other Old Testament writers, God's **righteousness** is not a legal attitude that leads him to apply the law impartially to all, but it is his disposition always to save his people, to free them from their difficulties, to put them in the right relationship with himself. Both SPCL ("you are just and faithful") and FRCL ("you are faithful and just") use adjectives, not abstract nouns, which makes for a better translation. In some languages **in thy faithfulness** and **in thy righteousness** may better be expressed as clauses; for example, "because you are good to your people and faithful to them, listen to my plea and help me."

In verse 2 the psalmist confesses his own sinfulness. He asks Yahweh not to **enter . . . into judgment** with him, for he knows that he, too, like everyone else, is guilty in God's sight (see 14.3). The plea can be translated "**Don't put me . . . on trial**" (TEV, NJB) or "Bring not . . . to trial" (NEB). **Thy servant** is, as often, the psalmist himself, who prays not for justice, but for mercy. TEV has adjusted the Hebrew form to avoid the psalmist's speaking of himself in the third person. The awkward phrase **(no) man living** translates the Hebrew "creature, living being." In some languages in which apposition is not stylistically natural, it may be necessary to say, for example, "I am your servant; do not put me on trial."

Verse 2b, as translated in the Septuagint, may be alluded to in Romans 3.20; Galatians 2.16.

143.3-4	RSV	TEV

	RSV	TEV
3	For the enemy has pursued me; he has crushed my life to the ground; he has made me sit in darkness like those long dead.	My enemy has hunted me down and completely defeated me. He has put me in a dark prison, and I am like those who died long ago.
4	Therefore my spirit faints within me; my heart within me is appalled.	So I am ready to give up; I am in deep despair.

The psalmist describes his plight. The first two lines of verse 3 are parallel: **has pursued me** (literally "pursued my *nefesh*") and **has crushed my life**. In verse 3b **crushed . . . to the ground** is a figure of complete defeat (see similar language in 7.5). It is possible, as Anderson and others think, that **the enemy** is a collective term for the psalmist's enemies (see the plural in verse 9).

The last half of verse 3 is the same as Lamentations 3.6. The **darkness** (literally "dark places"—see 88.6,18) may be understood literally to mean a gloomy dungeon, or else figuratively, meaning disaster, calamity. It is probable that the word deliberately alludes to the dark underworld, Sheol, and that the psalmist is saying that he is as good as dead (see use of similar language in 88.4-6). The expression **like those long dead** is an emphatic way of stressing the psalmist's hopelessness; there is no life, no vitality, no hope in him. The dead in Sheol dwelt in darkness and eventually lost all spark of life which they might have had at the beginning of their stay in the world of the dead. SPCL translates "they force me to live in darkness, like those who died long ago." **Made me sit in darkness** or TEV's "**dark prison**" may require further information in some languages to avoid a literal understanding. Accordingly one may sometimes say, for example, "he has put me in a dark place like where the dead are kept" or "he has put me in a dark place, and I am like a dead man."

Verse 4 consists of two parallel and synonymous lines: **my spirit . . . my heart** and **faints . . . is appalled**. See 142.3a for language similar to verse 4a; for **is appalled** in verse 4b, NJV has "numbed with horror," NJB "numb with fear," NEB "dazed with despair." The verb means to be stupefied, desolated, disconsolate; in the expressive American idiom, "to be wiped out" (see its use in 40.15a; "laid waste" in 79.7b).

5	I remember the days of old,
	    I meditate on all that thou hast
	       done;
	    I muse on what thy hands have
	       wrought.
		5	I remember the days gone by;
			    I think about all that you have
			       done,
			    I bring to mind all your deeds.

6	I stretch out my hands to thee;
	    my soul thirsts for thee like a
	       parched land. *Selah*
		6	I lift up my hands to you in
			       prayer;
			    like dry ground my soul is
			       thirsty for you.

In verse 5 the psalmist, in order to comfort himself, remembers all that Yahweh has done in the past on behalf of his people. Three synonymous verbs are used: **remember . . . meditate . . . muse** (see similar language in 77.5,11-12). In verse 5c **what thy hands have wrought** in this context means Yahweh's deeds in Israel's history (see 92.4), not the creation of the world, as in some other passages.

Trusting in Yahweh's willingness to help and save, the psalmist raises his **hands** to Yahweh in prayer (as in 141.2b). In language similar to 42.1-2 and 63.1, he compares his longing for God to **parched ground** that is thirsty for rain (verse 6b). In Hebrew the line is simply "my *nefesh* like dry ground (is) to you" (that is, wants you); NJV has "longing for You like thirsty earth." In some languages it may be necessary to fill out the comparison; for example, "I thirst for you like dry ground thirsts for rain." In other languages the metaphor of "thirsting for God" will not make sense. In those cases it is often necessary to say "I need you like dry ground needs rain."

For **_Selah_** see 3.2. Here it occurs at the end of the first half of the psalm.

7	Make haste to answer me, O
	       LORD!
	    My spirit fails!
	    Hide not thy face from me,
	       lest I be like those who go down
	          to the Pit.
		7	Answer me now, LORD!
			    I have lost all hope.
			    Don't hide yourself from me,
			       or I will be among those who go
			          down to the world of the
			          dead.

8	Let me hear in the morning of thy	8	Remind me each morning of your

steadfast love,	constant love,
for in thee I put my trust.	for I put my trust in you.
Teach me the way I should go,	My prayers go up to you;
for to thee I lift up my soul.	show me the way I should go.

In this petition the psalmist calls urgently to Yahweh for help (verse 7a; see 141.1), because he feels his situation is hopeless—literally "My spirit is gone" (verse 7b; see similar language in verse 4a). Verse 7c is like 27.9a, and verse 7d is the same as 28.1d (see also 88.4). The psalmist feels he will die if Yahweh doesn't save him.

The request in verse 8, that at **morning** (or, at dawn) the psalmist will hear of Yahweh's **steadfast love**, may be a way of saying "daily, every day" (as it seems to be in 90.14), or it may involve the belief that it was in the early hours of the day that God answered prayers (see 46.5). Perhaps there was the practice of spending the night in the Temple, waiting for the answer to prayers to come at dawn. TEV assumes that Yahweh himself is being asked to reassure the psalmist of his love (also FRCL, GECL, SPCL, TOB), and not that some unnamed person will do this, as the impersonal **Let me hear** of RSV states it. It seems best to follow TEV here. In verse 8c the psalmist prays for guidance (see 32.8; 86.11); for verse 8d see 25.1; 86.4b. TEV reverses lines c and d, since it takes "I lift up my *nefesh* to you" in line d to mean prayer; NJV, however, translates "I have set my hope" (parallel with line b). GECL translates "I turn my heart and my mind to you." Nearly all others translate quite literally. It is not necessary in translation to force **I lift up my soul** to mean that the prayer ascends to where God is. One may translate simply "I pray to you" or "I say my prayer to you."

143.9-10	RSV	TEV

9	Deliver me, O LORD, from my enemies!	9	I go to you for protection, LORD; rescue me from my enemies.
	I have fled to thee for refuge!*e*	10	You are my God;
10	Teach me to do thy will,		teach me to do your will.
	for thou art my God!		Be good to me, and guide me on a safe path.
	Let thy good spirit lead me on a level path!		

e One Heb Ms Gk: Heb *to thee I have hidden*

Again in these two verses the psalmist prays for protection (verse 9) and guidance (verse 10). TEV has reversed the two lines of verse 9 for a more logical progression of thought. TEV "**I go to you for protection**" translates the text of one Hebrew manuscript, which has the verb "seek refuge"; the Masoretic text has the verb "to cover," which seems hardly to make sense ("to you I have hidden"). NJV, however, translates it "to You I look for cover" (with a note "Meaning of Heb. uncertain"). One other Hebrew manuscript has "to you I flee," which RSV prefers (**fled . . . for refuge**). AT, NEB, BJ, and SPCL do as TEV has done. FRCL and NJB follow the Vulgate, "with you I am protected (or, safe)."

The request in verse 10a is similar to the one in verse 8c. Verse 10a may need to be adjusted in some languages to say, for example, "You are the God I worship; teach me to do the things you want me to do." The second request in verse 10 is translated by RSV **Let thy good spirit lead me** (similarly NJV "Let your gracious Spirit lead me"). The Hebrew text is "your spirit (is) good; lead me . . ." (or, perhaps, "your spirit (is) good; may it lead me . . ."). Here **spirit** can be taken to mean power or influence; so NEB "in your gracious kindness," while **good** may be taken not as an attribute of "spirit" but as its effect, "may your spirit do good (or, be good) to me," which TEV represents by **"Be good to me."** FRCL translates "may your Spirit lead me with good will." Cohen defines "your good spirit" as "the graciousness of God toward his creatures." The translator should take care that the translation of "spirit" not lead the reader to think of it in terms of the New Testament teaching about the Holy Spirit.

On a level path is figurative language for a life that is free of difficulties and toil; the word **path** translates the text of many Hebrew manuscripts (as in 27.11b); the Masoretic text here is "ground" or "land" (so NJV "level ground"). HOTTP prefers the Masoretic text, which it translates "on an even land."

143.11-12   RSV   TEV

	RSV		TEV
11	For thy name's sake, O LORD, preserve my life! In thy righteousness bring me out of trouble!	11	Rescue me, LORD, as you have promised; in your goodness save me from my troubles!
12	And in thy steadfast love cut off my enemies, and destroy all my adversaries, for I am thy servant.	12	Because of your love for me, kill my enemies and destroy all my oppressors, for I am your servant.

In these two final verses the psalmist prays that Yahweh save him and destroy his enemies. TEV **"as you have promised"** in verse 11a translates "on account of your name," as in 23.3. If the translator follows TEV's **"as you have promised,"** it may be necessary to recast this as "as you said you would do." The two verbs in verse 11 are general terms for deliverance from troubles, difficulties, or enemies: **preserve my life** and **bring me out of trouble**. In verse 11b **thy righteousness** is parallel to **thy steadfast love** in verse 12a. TEV's **"in your goodness"** may have to be adjusted to "because you are good to your people."

In verse 12 two synonymous verbs are used, **cut off** and **destroy**, both meaning "kill." And two synonymous nouns are used, **enemies** and **adversaries**. The latter term translates "those who hate my *nefesh*" (see 3.2). It is because the psalmist knows himself to be Yahweh's **servant** that he feels he has the right to pray for the destruction of his enemies; they are the enemies of his lord, Yahweh. For **servant** see comments at 19.11.

Psalm 144

In this psalm a king prays to God, either to thank him for victory (so TEV) or else to ask him for victory (Toombs, Dentan, and others). Many commentators believe that the psalm is a composite work, consisting of two originally independent compositions: verses 1-11, which have to do with the king and his enemies, and verses 12-15, a prayer for the prosperity of the people. Anderson is representative of those who believe the psalm to be a literary unit. It is to be noticed that verses 1-11 read almost like a string of quotations from other psalms.

The psalm begins with praise to God for his help in battle (verses 1-2), followed by a meditation on the frailty and insignificance of the human creature (verses 3-4). The psalmist prays for God's help in defeating the enemy (verses 5-8), after which he promises to thank him (verses 9-11). In the final verses (verses 12-15) the psalmist prays for the prosperity of the nation.

If the author is a king of the Davidic dynasty, then the psalm dates from before the end of that dynasty in 587 B.C.; however, some take the psalm to have been composed by someone other than a king, for use in the Temple royal festival (see Taylor).

HEADING: "**A King Thanks God for Victory.**" Other headings are: "Prayer for victory and prosperity"; "Before battle"; "A king's gratitude toward God." The TEV heading may require some modification for translation; for example, "A chief thanks God for defeating his enemies." Because of the variety of themes in this psalm, a more general heading may be more appropriate; for example, "A leader's prayer" or "The prayer of a king."

<u>Hebrew title</u>: **A Psalm of David** (TEV "**By David**").

The Septuagint adds "against Goliath," perhaps inspired by the language of verse 11.

144.1-2

RSV	TEV
1 Blessed be the LORD, my rock, who trains my hands for war, and my fingers for battle; 2 my rock^f and my fortress, my stronghold and my deliverer, my shield and he in whom I take refuge, who subdues the peoples under him.^g	1 Praise the LORD, my protector! He trains me for battle and prepares me for war. 2 He is my protector and defender, my shelter and savior, in whom I trust for safety. He subdues the nations under me.

^f With 18.2 2 Sam 22.2: Heb *my stead-
fast love*
^g Another reading is *my people under me*

The psalm opens with praise to Yahweh; for **Blessed be . . . my rock** see 18.46, and for **rock** as a metaphor for God, see comments on 18.2 (the "third" metaphor). Yahweh is the one who gives the king strength and skill in battle (verse 1b,c); the two lines are parallel and synonymous: **my hands . . . my fingers** and **war . . . battle** (see similar language in 18.34a). In languages in which the metaphor will be fully meaningful, it is possible to retain the image of the rock, or to combine the image with its meaning; for example, "he protects me like a rock." It may be desirable in some languages to reduce lines <u>b</u> and <u>c</u> to a single line.

In verse 2 the psalmist uses language similar to that in 18.2: the first metaphor **my rock** (TEV "**my protector**") follows the text of 18.2 (also 2 Sam 22.2); the Hebrew text here has "my steadfast love," which NJV translates "my faithful one," NJB "my faithful love," TOB "my ally," SPCL "my faithful friend," and FRCL "my assurance." HOTTP translates the Hebrew term "my loyal help, my protection." (If nothing else, the various translations of this one Hebrew word demonstrate that translation is not an exact mechanical performance.) TEV's noun phrases "**my protector**" and "**my defender**" may have to be recast in some languages as verb phrases; for instance, "the one who protects me" and "the one who defends me."

The next three metaphors (as in RSV) are also used in 18.2: **fortress** (number two in the comments on 18.2), **stronghold** (number six), **shield** (number four); and **deliverer** and **he in whom I take refuge** are also used in 18.2. TEV has not attempted to provide a separate word for each metaphor, since they are all so closely synonymous.

In the last line of verse 2, the Masoretic text has "my people"; many Hebrew manuscripts have "peoples" (so RSV, TEV, and others).¹ One form of the text has "under me," another form has "under him" (which AT and RSV prefer); most translations, like TEV, prefer "**under me**." See similar language in 18.47b (and 2 Sam 22.48b). If the translator follows TEV's "**subdues the nations under me**," it may be necessary in some languages to make explicit the resulting relation of the subjected nations to the king; for example, "He defeats the other nations and puts them under my power" or "He defeats the other nations and gives them to me to rule."

144.3-4 RSV TEV

	RSV		TEV
3	O LORD, what is man that thou dost regard him, or the son of man that thou dost think of him?	3	LORD, what is man, that you notice him; mere man, that you pay attention to him?
4	Man is like a breath,	4	He is like a puff of wind;

---

¹HOTTP prefers the form of the Masoretic text and says that there are two possible interpretations of it: "(he gives me power) over my people" or "(he gives me power) over the peoples."

his days are like a passing shadow.	his days are like a passing shadow.

This meditation on human frailty and mortality seems out of context here; but it may be taken as an expression of the psalmist's own weakness in contrast with the following description of Yahweh's power and might in verses 5-8 (so Taylor). For verse 3 see similar language in 8.4. The two lines of this verse are semantically and syntactically parallel in Hebrew. Furthermore, **Man** in line a and **son of man** in line b are paired words which follow the usual pattern Noun a // Son of Noun a, which means that the noun in line a is paralleled by Son of that same noun, or by a designation of the same person as son of his father. For similar examples see Psalm 8.4; Judges 5.12; 2 Samuel 20.2; Numbers 23.18. Line b heightens the emotional thrust of line a through the use of the figurative expression in the seconding line. Translators should attempt first to reflect this heightening of poetic effect before deciding to reduce the two lines to one, and thus perhaps erasing the effect. The two lines are in the form of a rhetorical question, which may have to be answered with a strong negative. The expressions **man** and **the son of man** may best be translated in some languages as "men," however, the meaning should not be exclusive. Therefore the most inclusive form ("people") will be better. **Son of man** in this context may often be translated "just plain people" or "ordinary human beings." A suggested rendering of this verse may be "What is man that you take notice of him; why do you even pay any attention to an ordinary human being?" or, more inclusively, "What are people that you notice them; or ordinary human beings that you pay attention to them?" If the rhetorical question is difficult to understand, a statement may be better: "Human beings are too insignificant, people are of so little value, for you, LORD, to pay attention to them."

In verse 3 the two verbs are different from the ones in 8.4; NJV in 8.4 has "be mindful . . . take note," and here it has "care . . . think." While different, the various verbs are closely synonymous.

For verse 4 see similar language in 39.5c-6a; both **breath** and **passing shadow** stress the frailty and mortality of human beings. In some languages it may be necessary to say in what respect **man is like a breath**; for example, the comparison given in line b may need to be shifted to line a, where it can serve for both lines, particularly if they are combined: "A person's life lasts no longer than a breath or a shadow." If both lines are kept, one may translate "A person's life lasts no longer than a breath; it disappears like a shadow."

144.5-8	RSV			TEV
5	Bow thy heavens, O LORD, and come down! Touch the mountains that they smoke!		5	O LORD, tear the sky open and come down; touch the mountains, and they will pour out smoke.
6	Flash forth the lightning and scatter them, send out thy arrows and rout them!		6	Send flashes of lightning and scatter your enemies; shoot your arrows and send them running.

7	Stretch forth thy hand from on high, rescue me and deliver me from the many waters, from the hand of aliens,	7	Reach down from above, pull me out of the deep water, and rescue me; save me from the power of foreigners,
8	whose mouths speak lies, and whose right hand is a right hand of falsehood.	8	who never tell the truth and lie even under oath.

These verses, in which the psalmist asks for Yahweh's help, owe much to the figures used in 18.9-17. For verse 5a see 18.9a, where the same language is used. Here TEV has followed two Hebrew manuscripts (and the Syriac and Targum) "the heavens," and not the Masoretic text "your heavens" (see RSV). For verse 5b see 104.32b.

For verse 6 see 18.14. It should be noticed that here RSV them in both lines can only refer to the mountains of verse 5b. Of course the psalmist is talking about Yahweh's "enemies."

Verse 7a,b uses the language of 18.16; the verb translated here rescue has this sense only here and in verses 10, 11. It is classified here as an Aramaism; elsewhere in the Old Testament it means "to open (the mouth)." The many waters is here, as often, a figure of the distress and danger the psalmist is threatened with by his enemies, the aliens, that is, hostile forces from other countries. It should be noticed there are two synonymous verbs in verse 7b, rescue and deliver. TEV has restructured the sentence, with one verb for each object. Hand of aliens and TEV's "power of foreigners" may have to be recast in some languages to say, for example, ". . . from foreign tribes that attack me."

The psalmist calls his enemies liars (verse 8a); whose right hand is a right hand of falsehood in line b means they "lie even under oath." It was the custom on taking a vow to raise the right hand to heaven, a symbolic gesture calling on God to attest to the truth of the statement to be made (see 106.26). NIV "whose right hands are deceitful" is less than natural. TEV's "under oath," which suggests a courtroom procedure, may have to be recast in some languages to say, for example, "who lie when they swear they are telling the truth."

It should be noticed that verses 7c-8 (which appear also as verse 11b-d) are omitted by NEB as a later addition to the text; there is, however, no textual support for this omission.

144.9-11

	RSV		TEV
9	I will sing a new song to thee, O God; upon a ten-stringed harp I will play to thee,	9	I will sing you a new song, O God; I will play the harp and sing to you.
10	who givest victory to kings, who rescuest David thy[h] servant.	10	You give victory to kings and rescue your servant David.
11	Rescue me from the cruel sword,	11	Save me from my cruel enemies; rescue me from the power of foreigners,

and deliver me from the hand of aliens,	who never tell the truth and lie even under oath.
whose mouths speak lies, and whose right hand is a right hand of falsehood.	

[h] Heb *his*

In these verses the psalmist promises that, if God gives him the victory he prays for, he will, in the Temple, praise God with **a new song** and play **upon a ten-stringed harp** to him. For the language see 33.2-3; and for the instrument see 33.2; "harp" in 92.3. The verb in verse 9b may mean simply to play an instrument, or else to sing, accompanied by an instrument (so TEV).

In verse 10 God is spoken of as the one who gives **victory to kings** and rescues **David [his] servant**. The kings, of course, are kings of Israel; whether **David** means King David himself or a king of the Davidic dynasty is a matter of dispute. **Givest victory to kings** may have to be adjusted in some languages to say, for example, "defeats the enemies of the kings of Israel."

In the *Biblia Hebraica* the second line of verse 10 ends with "David his servant"; the next line begins with "from the evil sword," after which verse 11 begins with the verb form **Save me**. Both RSV and TEV (also NAB, NEB, FRCL, SPCL) join the verb "Save me" to "from the evil sword" as the first line of verse 11 (disregarding the verse division of the *Biblia Hebraica*); BJ and NJB also make this one line but place the verse number 11 before "from the evil sword" (see also SPCL). KJV, NJV, NIV, GECL, and TOB join "from the evil sword" to the end of verse 10, which is possible (see also NJV "who rescue His servant David from the deadly sword"). It seems better, however, to do as RSV and TEV have done. (It is interesting to notice that the Targum interpreted "from the evil sword" to mean "from the evil sword of Goliath.")

Verse 11b-d repeats verses 7c-8.

144.12-13 RSV	TEV
12 May our sons in their youth be like plants full grown, our daughters like corner pillars cut for the structure of a palace;	12 May our sons in their youth be like plants that grow up strong. May our daughters be like stately columns which adorn the corners of a palace.
13 may our garners be full, providing all manner of store; may our sheep bring forth thousands and ten thousands in our fields;	13 May our barns be filled with crops of every kind. May the sheep in our fields bear young by the tens of thousands.

This final strophe (verses 12-14) has no obvious connection with what precedes, and may well have been a separate composition. Verse 12 begins with the Hebrew relative pronoun which normally means "which" or "who"; some emend it to the word which means "happy" (as in verse 15). Some translations, like RSV, TEV, NJB, and FRCL, take the verses as expressing a wish, a prayer (so HOTTP); others take them as statements of facts (see NJV, TOB, NEB, NIV, BJ, and SPCL). There is nothing in the strophe as such to determine which is correct; in its present setting, as part of Psalm 144, however, it seems more fitting to take them as wishes.

There are several expressions in these verses whose meaning is disputed. In verse 12 **plants** translates a word found nowhere else in the Old Testament; the figure is that of health and vigor. And in verse 12c the figure **corner pillars** is either that of beauty and stateliness, or else of strength. KJV and NJV translate "cornerstones," Dahood "pillars." Some recall the carved female figures used as columns in Greek architecture, but others object that this would not be a possibility here. The word translated **palace** in line d (RSV, TEV, and others) may mean "the Temple" (NAB, SPCL). In TEV **"adorn"** (also NIV) translates a word meaning "shape, figure"; RSV, SPCL, and Dahood have **structure**. NJV translates the whole figure "cornerstones trimmed to give shape to a palace." Something like TEV or RSV seems to make for a more intelligible figure. For translation adjustments to wishes expressed with "may," see 137.6. In languages in which **"stately columns"** will be unfamiliar (unless seen in the art work accompanying United Bible Societies' New Readers Scriptures), it will most often be best to render these as "beautiful posts which hold up the corners of the king's house."

In verse 13 **garners** (TEV **"barns"**) translates a word found nowhere else in the Old Testament; TEV **"with crops of every kind"** translates what is literally "providing from kind to kind," that is, all kinds (of crops). TEV **"barns"** may be translated in some languages as "granaries." Where a place for the storage of grain is not known or has no name, a descriptive phrase may be used; for example, "May the place where grains are stored be filled with all kinds of crops." In language areas where storing of grain is unknown, it may be better to say "may you always have food to eat."

In verse 13c,d the Hebrew has **thousands . . . ten thousands**, a common way of emphasizing a great number; the Hebrew of verse 13c, "produce by the thousands," occurs nowhere else in the Old Testament.

144.14	RSV	TEV

RSV	TEV
may our cattle be heavy with young,	May our cattle reproduce plenti- fully
suffering no mischance or fail- ure in bearing;	without miscarriage or loss.
may there be no cry of distress in our streets!	May there be no cries of distress in our streets.

In line a the word translated **cattle** is not the normal form in Hebrew for "cattle"; and the verb translated **be heavy with young** (TEV "reproduce plentifully") means either "to load" or "to carry." It may be taken to refer to pregnancy and gestation of cattle, but the difficulty is that the verb form is a masculine plural participle; and so, instead of taking it to refer to reproduction (parallel with the bearing of sheep of verse 13c,d), some take it to mean the strength of the cattle; so NEB "fat and sleek" (see NJV "well cared for," Dahood and NJB "well fed"). NIV's "our oxen will draw heavy loads" is unlike any other translation consulted.

Verse 14b is "may there be no break and no departure." RSV, TEV, NEB, and SPCL take this to refer to the cattle, meaning without miscarriage or loss as cows give birth to calves. But NJV, NAB, BJ, NJB, TOB, and Dahood take it to mean a break in the walls of the city caused by invaders, and a going out of the inhabitants into exile. Dahood has "Let there be no invasion, and let there be no exile" (similarly FRCL, NIV, NAB; NJB "free of raids and pillage"). There is no way of deciding which is correct; the second interpretation ties in with what follows, and the first with what precedes.

Verse 14c refers to the alarm and distress caused by imminent invasion of foreign troops.

144.15   RSV   TEV

> **Happy the people to whom such**   **Happy is the nation of whom this**
>   **blessings fall!**   **is true;**
> **Happy the people whose God is**   **happy are the people whose God**
>   **the LORD!**   **is the LORD!**

In the final verse the psalmist proclaims the happiness of the people **to whom such blessings** come (literally "to whom [is] thus"; see NJV "who have it so"). This refers to the preceding description of prosperity and peace (verses 12-14). All of this is in consequence of the happiness of those **whose God is** Yahweh (verse 15b).

In languages in which the wishes expressed in verses 12-14 are stated as "may God cause . . . ," it will often be necessary in verse 15 to say "The nation that God blesses like this will be happy." The expression **whose God is the LORD** may be compared to 100.3, where it is the reverse, **The LORD is God**. There the order is specific: Yahweh is equated with the generic God. Here the generic God is equated with the specific Yahweh, and the meaning is the same. In some languages the expression in verse 15 will be rendered as "Happy are the people who worship God, whose name is the LORD." Or, more simply, "Happy are those who worship the LORD."

Psalm 145

This psalm is an acrostic poem; the first word of each verse begins with a successive letter of the Hebrew alphabet, from *alef* in the first verse to *taw* in the last verse (see introduction to Psa 111). The psalm is a hymn of praise to God, and it alternates between exclamations of praise (verses 1-2, 4-7, 10-12, 21) and descriptions of Yahweh's greatness and goodness (verses 3, 8-9, 13-20). No clear division into strophes may be attempted, since the artificial nature of the composition severely limits its artistry.

There is no certain way of determining the time and circumstances of the composition of the psalm. It was probably composed for use in the Temple service during one of the major festivals.

HEADING: "**A Hymn of Praise.**" Other headings are: "The name of the LORD"; "An alphabetic doxology"; "The greatness and goodness of God." For adaptations which may be required to use the TEV heading, see Psalms 27, 33, 40, 92, 95, and 135.

Hebrew title: **A Song of Praise. Of David** (TEV "A song of praise by David").

This is the only psalm in which **A Song of Praise** appears in the title; the Hebrew word so translated is, in its plural form, the title of the whole collection of psalms.

145.1-3

	RSV		TEV
1	I will extol thee, my God and King, and bless thy name for ever and ever.	1	I will proclaim your greatness, my God and king; I will thank you forever and ever.
2	Every day I will bless thee, and praise thy name for ever and ever.	2	Every day I will thank you; I will praise you forever and ever.
3	Great is the LORD, and greatly to be praised, and his greatness is unsearchable.	3	The LORD is great and is to be highly praised; his greatness is beyond understanding.

The parallelism throughout Psalm 145 tends to be static, that is, without significant heightening from line a to line b. However, in spite of this there is, as Alter says, "a progression from the general praise of God to an affirmation of his

1162

compassion, his kingship, his daily providing for those who truly call unto him." (Alter, *The Art of Biblical Poetry*, page 23.)

In the first two verses the psalmist declares his readiness to praise God, to proclaim his greatness, and to thank him forever and ever. For **extol** see 30.1; "exalt" in 34.3b; for **bless** see 16.7. In verses 1b,2b **"you"** translates **thy name** (see 5.11). Due to the double address form, **my God and King**, it may be necessary in some languages to adjust verse 1 to say, for example, "You are the God I worship and the king I serve; I will tell everyone how great you are."

For verse 3a see similar statement in 48.1; 96.4; and in verse 3b the Hebrew "there is no searching his greatness" means that God's greatness cannot be fully understood by a human being. **Greatly to be praised** must often be shifted to the active voice by translating "everyone should praise the LORD very much" or "everyone should say that the LORD is very great."

145.4-5	RSV	TEV

4   One generation shall laud thy works to another, and shall declare thy mighty acts.

5   On the glorious splendor of thy majesty, and on thy wondrous works, I will meditate.

4   What you have done will be praised from one generation to the next; they will proclaim your mighty acts.

5   They will speak of your glory and majesty, and I will meditate on your wonderful deeds.

In verses 4-7 God is praised not only by the psalmist (as in verses 1-2) but by all humankind (or all the people of Israel) **"from one generation to the next"** (verse 4, TEV). For verse 4 see a similar statement in 78.4. TEV has shifted to a passive ". . . **will be praised from one generation . . . ."** In some languages it will be necessary to use the active "People of each generation will praise the things you have done" or "One generation will tell the next about the great things you have done." **Thy works . . . thy mighty acts** are Yahweh's marvelous deeds in freeing his people from slavery in Egypt and taking them to the Promised Land.

There is a textual problem in verse 5; RSV (also NJV, NEB, TOB) translates the Masoretic text, in which there is only one verb, **I will meditate**, in line **b**. Instead of "and the words of" in line **a** of the Masoretic text (which RSV, in line **b**, translates **works**), the Qumran manuscript has the verb **"they will speak,"** which TEV and SPCL prefer (also HOTTP). In verse 5a TEV **"your glory and majesty"** translates the Hebrew "the splendor of honor of your majesty" (see RSV). **Thy wondrous works** (verse 5b) and "your mighty deeds" (RSV "the might of thy terrible acts") in verse 6a probably refer to God's mighty acts and miracles in saving and leading his people; but there may be a reference also to creation. For translation suggestions on **meditate** and **majesty**, see 1.2 and 21.5.

145.6-7 RSV	TEV
6 Men shall proclaim the might of thy terrible acts, and I will declare thy greatness.	6 People will speak of your mighty deeds, and I will proclaim your greatness.
7 They shall pour forth the fame of thy abundant goodness, and shall sing aloud of thy righteousness.	7 They will tell about all your goodness and sing about your kindness.

In verse 6a **terrible** translates a word meaning "awesome, awe-inspiring" (see comments on "dread deeds" in 65.5; "terrible" in 76.7). In today's English **terrible** is a most inappropriate word to qualify God's **acts**. In verse 6b one form of the Hebrew text has "**your greatness**" (so RSV, TEV, SPCL, BJ, NJB); another form has "your great deeds" (NEB, FRCL, NIV, TOB, Dahood). HOTTP says either may be adopted.

It should be noted that, in verses 5b, 6b, instead of the first person singular of the Hebrew text, the Septuagint has the third person plural, which Weiser and NAB follow. NEB and SPCL follow the Septuagint in verse 6b. In this way the verbs are all plural in verses 4-7, which is more consistent; but the Hebrew text makes sense.

In verse 7a **They shall pour forth** means to announce, recite (NEB), celebrate (NIV, NJV); see its use in 19.2. In line a, **goodness** is parallel to **righteousness** (see 5.8) in line b. RSV and others have **righteousness** or "justice"; TEV (similarly NJV) has "**kindness**"; FRCL "faithfulness." In verse 7a **fame** translates the word meaning "remembrance" (see "remembrance" in 6.5; "name" in 102.12b).

145.8-9 RSV	TEV
8 The LORD is gracious and merciful, slow to anger and abounding in steadfast love.	8 The LORD is loving and merciful, slow to become angry and full of constant love.
9 The LORD is good to all, and his compassion is over all that he has made.	9 He is good to everyone and has compassion on all he made.

The psalmist praises Yahweh for his love and mercy. Verse 8 is almost identical in form with 103.8; the meaning is the same.

In verse 9b **compassion** translates a word which is from the same root as the word translated **merciful** in verse 8a. Yahweh's goodness and compassion are directed to all his creatures, without any distinction or discrimination.

145.10 RSV	TEV
All thy works shall give thanks to thee, O LORD,	All your creatures, LORD, will praise you,

| and all thy saints shall bless thee! | and all your people will give you thanks. |

Again the psalmist proclaims the universal nature of the praise given to Yahweh. In verse 10a **All thy works** is parallel to **all thy saints** in line **b**; this makes it more likely that the meaning in verse 10 is "**All your creatures**," that is, all living beings, including not only humankind but the other creatures as well. For **saints** see comments on "godly" in 4.3; for **bless** see verse 1.

145.11-13b   RSV   TEV

11 They shall speak of the glory of thy kingdom,
    and tell of thy power,
12 to make known to the sons of men thy[h] mighty deeds,
    and the glorious splendor of thy kingdom.
13 Thy kingdom is an everlasting kingdom,
    and thy dominion endures throughout all generations.

11 They will speak of the glory of your royal power
    and tell of your might,
12 so that everyone will know your mighty deeds
    and the glorious majesty of your kingdom.
13 Your rule is eternal,
    and you are king forever.

[h] Heb *his*

In verses 11-13 the noun *malkuth* is used, which RSV consistently translates **kingdom**. TEV has "**royal power**," "**kingdom**," and "**rule**." The word has all these different connotations. The basic idea is that of the possession and exercise of God's power as king; it does not have a geographical idea, the place where God's kingship is exercised, as the word "kingdom" in English usually has; nor does it have a temporal idea, the time when it is exercised. It is God's timeless and unlimited power as king of the universe and humankind. NJV and NJB have "kingship" in all three lines. TEV's "**royal power**" may have to be recast to say, for example, "your powerful rule as king" or "they will speak of the great way in which you rule powerfully as king." **Glorious splendor of thy kingdom** in 12b and **glory of thy kingdom** in 11a are synonymous.

In verse 12a Yahweh's **mighty deeds** are probably the same as those referred to in verse 6a; for **the sons of men** see "children of men" in 11.4. Verse 12b is similar to verse 5a. In verse 12 the Hebrew text has the third singular pronoun "his"; translationally RSV and TEV change this to the second person of direct address, consistently with verses 11 and 13.

Verse 13a,b are two parallel and synonymous lines: **Thy kingdom . . . thy dominion** and **everlasting . . . throughout all generations**. This verse is found almost in identical form in Aramaic, in Daniel 4.3 (see also 4.34).

13c　The LORD is faithful in all his
　　　words,
　　　and gracious in all his deeds.*i*

14　The LORD upholds all who are
　　　falling,
　　　and raises up all who are bowed
　　　down.

13c　The LORD is faithful to his prom-
　　　ises;
　　　he is merciful in all his acts.

14　He helps those who are in trouble;
　　　he lifts those who have fallen.

i These two lines are supplied by one
Hebrew Ms, Gk and Syr

Verse 13c,d represents the fourteenth letter of the Hebrew alphabet, the letter
nun; these lines are missing in the Masoretic text, but they are found in the
Septuagint and the Syriac, and in the margin of one Hebrew manuscript. And now
it is also found in the Qumran manuscript, which has "God," while the Hebrew
manuscript (and the Septuagint and Syriac) has "Yahweh," which most translations
follow.

Words in line c̲ may also be taken to mean "things, matters," and the parallel
his deeds in line d̲ may argue for this meaning (so Anderson). TEV, NEB, and FRCL
have **"promises,"** which is most probably the meaning intended here. In line d̲
gracious translates the adjective *chasid* (see its use applied to people, "thy saints,"
in verse 10b). The word means "one who shows *chesed*," so it can be taken to mean
"one who shows love" (BJ) or "one who shows loyalty" (TOB); NAB has "is holy."
HOTTP recommends either "loyal" or "merciful." In light of the parallel with **faithful**
in line c̲, perhaps NEB "unchanging in all his works" is preferable. This adjective is
used of God only here, in verse 17b, and in Jeremiah 3.12. If the translator follows
TEV's **"faithful to his promises,"** this expression may have to be recast to say, for
example, "The LORD is faithful to his people, and he does what he promised them
he would do" or "The LORD is faithful to his people and keeps his word."

Verse 14 speaks of Yahweh's care for the oppressed and distressed. The two
lines are parallel and synonymous: **upholds . . . raises up** and **are falling . . . are
bowed down**. The same thought is also to be found in 146.8b. In some languages the
expression **"lifts those who have fallen"** will be taken only in a literal sense. In such
cases it may be better to use a different figure, or to say "he helps those who are
discouraged," or idiomatically, "he gives strength to those whose hearts are weak."

15　The eyes of all look to thee,
　　　and thou givest them their food
　　　in due season.

16　Thou openest thy hand,
　　　thou satisfiest the desire of
　　　every living thing.

15　All living things look hopefully to
　　　you,
　　　and you give them food when
　　　they need it.

16　You give them enough
　　　and satisfy the needs of all.

These two verses are similar to 104.27-28; see comments there. The Hebrew of verse 15a is literally "The eyes of all hope on you" (as in 104.27a).

Thou openest thy hand in verse 16a is a figure of generosity; NJV has "You give it openhandedly," NEB "with open and bountiful hand," and NJB "with generous hand" (see the same thought in 104.28b). **Every living thing** in line b includes all living creatures.

145.17-20 RSV TEV

17 The LORD is just in all his ways, and kind in all his doings.
18 The LORD is near to all who call upon him, to all who call upon him in truth.
19 He fulfills the desire of all who fear him, he also hears their cry, and saves them.
20 The LORD preserves all who love him; but all the wicked he will destroy.

17 The LORD is righteous in all he does, merciful in all his acts.
18 He is near to those who call to him, who call to him with sincerity.
19 He supplies the needs of those who honor him; he hears their cries and saves them.
20 He protects everyone who loves him, but he will destroy the wicked.

In these verses the psalmist praises Yahweh's righteousness and kindness; the two lines of verse 17 are parallel and synonymous. Verse 17a means that in all he does Yahweh is "**righteous**" or **just** (NJV "beneficent"; FRCL "faithfulness"). Verse 17b is exactly like verse 13d.

In verse 18 **The LORD is near** means that he is attentive and ready to respond (see 34.18) **to all who call upon him** for help. The final phrase **in truth** is better translated "**with sincerity**" (TEV, NJV, SPCL; see FRCL). Because **The LORD is near** does not refer to space but to readiness, in some languages it will be best to say "The LORD is ready to help all who ask him." RSV **who call . . . in truth** and TEV ". . . with sincerity" may have to be recast in some languages to say idiomatically, for example, "who ask him with a straight heart" or ". . . with one tongue." NJB has "from the heart."

In verse 19a the thought is like that of verse 16b; for **fear** see 15.4. **All who fear him** is parallel with **all who love him** in verse 20a, and in verse 19b **saves** is parallel with **preserves** in verse 20. The latter verb is better translated "watches over" (NJV, NEB).

For verse 20b see 9.5 and 37.9.

145.21 RSV TEV

My mouth will speak the praise of the LORD,

I will always praise the LORD; let all his creatures praise his

1167

> and let all flesh bless his holy   holy name forever.
> name for ever and ever.

The psalm closes with the psalmist's promise to praise Yahweh (RSV **speak the praise of the LORD**) and a call for all people everywhere to **bless his holy name for ever** (see 106.47). **All flesh** usually means all human beings; here, in line with **every living thing** in verse 16b (see also verse 10a), perhaps it means "**all creatures**" (NEB, NJB, NJV). **Let all flesh** does not introduce a request for permission but is a third-person imperative. Verse 21b may be rendered in some languages as "Everything that God has created should praise him for ever."

Psalm 146

Psalms 146–150 are called "Hallelujah Psalms" because they all begin and end with the Hebrew *halelu-yah*, **Praise the LORD** (see 104.35).

After declaring his intention to praise Yahweh (verses 1-2), the psalmist warns his people not to depend on human leaders (verses 3-4) but to put their faith in God, whose power and love are described particularly in terms of his care for the weak, the poor, the oppressed (verses 5-9). The psalm closes with a declaration of the eternal nature of Yahweh's rule as king of the universe (verse 10).

HEADING: "**In Praise of God the Savior.**" Other headings are: "Praise to King Yahweh"; "Trust in God alone"; "The justice of God." The TEV heading may be adapted for translation into some languages by saying "The psalmist praises God, who rescues his people."

146.1-2	RSV		TEV
1	Praise the LORD! Praise the LORD, O my soul!	1	Praise the LORD! Praise the LORD, my soul!
2	I will praise the LORD as long as I live; I will sing praises to my God while I have being.	2	I will praise him as long as I live; I will sing to my God all my life.

The psalm begins with the psalmist's call to **Praise the LORD!** (see 104.35); for **Praise the LORD, O my soul!** see 103.1.

In verse 2, in two parallel and synonymous lines, he expresses his own intention to **praise** and **sing praises** to Yahweh all his life. **My God** must often be rendered "the God I worship." **While I have being** is literally "in my continuance" and may be expressed, for example, as "while I still exist," "as long as I am here," "as long as I have breath," or "throughout my whole life."

146.3-4	RSV		TEV
3	Put not your trust in princes, in a son of man, in whom there is no help.	3	Don't put your trust in human leaders; no human being can save you.
4	When his breath departs he returns to his earth;	4	When they die, they return to the dust;

<table>
<tr><td>on that very day his plans
perish.</td><td>on that day all their plans come
to an end.</td></tr>
</table>

For the sentiment expressed in verse 3 see 118.8-9. The psalmist warns against depending for help on anyone, including **princes**, that is, people with power and authority (see comments, 118.9b). It is better to translate **princes** as "**human leaders**," as does TEV, or to use its equivalent. **Princes**, which are sometimes translated "sons of chiefs," may fail to suggest persons in authority. In this case it will be better to follow TEV. In verse 3b **a son of man** means person, human being, anyone (see the plural form in 11.4).

In verse 4 the psalmist stresses the mortality of human beings. For the thought of verse 4a, see 104.29. **Breath** translates the Hebrew word *ruach*, "spirit, wind, breath," the presence of which means life, and its absence, death. The phrase **to his earth** is better translated "**to the dust**" (NJV, NEB, TEV) or "to the earth" (NJB). In death the body returns to the earth, the soil, from which it was made (see Gen 3.19; Eccl 12.7). TEV "**return to the dust**" is expressed in some languages as "join with the ground" or "return to the soil." The Hebrew word translated **plans** occurs only here in the Old Testament. It may be translated "purposes"; SPCL and FRCL translate "projects."

146.5-7b   RSV   TEV

<table>
<tr><td>5</td><td>Happy is he whose help is the God
of Jacob,
whose hope is in the LORD his
God,</td><td>5</td><td>Happy is the man who has the
God of Jacob to help him
and who depends on the LORD
his God,</td></tr>
<tr><td>6</td><td>who made heaven and earth,
the sea, and all that is in them;
who keeps faith for ever;</td><td>6</td><td>the Creator of heaven, earth,
and sea,
and all that is in them.
He always keeps his promises;</td></tr>
<tr><td>7</td><td>who executes justice for the
oppressed;
who gives food to the hungry.</td><td>7</td><td>he judges in favor of the op-
pressed
and gives food to the hungry.</td></tr>
</table>

In verses 5-9 the psalmist praises the power and goodness of Yahweh. For **the God of Jacob** in verse 5a, see 46.7. In verse 5b TEV "**depends on**" (RSV **hope is in**) translates a word found only here and in 119.116; see the related verb in 145.15a, "look to." The **his** of the phrase **the LORD his God** has as its antecedent **he**, that is, the person of line **a**, not **Jacob**. **LORD his God** may sometimes be recast to say "on the LORD, who is the God he worships."

For the thought of verse 6a,b see 95.4-5; 115.15b. Yahweh is the Creator of all that exists, the physical universe as well as all living beings (see Exo 20.11). Translators in some languages may find that it is easier to follow RSV's relative clause **who made heaven and earth** rather than the apposition of TEV.

Beginning with verse 6c the psalmist praises Yahweh's goodness and love, the care he shows for the oppressed, the poor, the destitute. For verse 6c see 145.13c. Instead of the Hebrew **for ever**, NEB and Dahood change the text to read "the oppressed." This makes good sense, but there is no textual support for it (see HOTTP). **Keeps faith for ever** means that he is trustworthy, reliable. SPCL "he always keeps his word"; FRCL "One can always count on him."

For verse 7a see 103.6, and for verse 7b see 107.9b. For translation suggestions concerning **the oppressed**, see 9.9.

146.7c-9	RSV	TEV

	RSV		TEV
7c	The LORD sets the prisoners free;	7c	The LORD sets prisoners free
8	the LORD opens the eyes of the blind.	8	and gives sight to the blind.
	The LORD lifts up those who are bowed down;		He lifts those who have fallen;
	the LORD loves the righteous.		he loves his righteous people.
9	The LORD watches over the sojourners,	9	He protects the strangers who live in our land;
	he upholds the widow and the fatherless;		he helps widows and orphans,
	but the way of the wicked he brings to ruin.		but takes the wicked to their ruin.

It is impossible to determine whether verse 7c is meant to be taken literally of release from prison, slavery, or exile, or is figurative of trouble and distress in general (see an extended statement of this same theme in 107.10-16). It is difficult to think that verse 8a is meant literally, since the restoration of sight to blind people was a very rare occurrence; it seems better to understand the language figuratively, meaning "to help the helpless" (so Kirkpatrick, Cohen, Briggs). In any case they are among the needy and oppressed whom Yahweh helps. All translations consulted have retained the figures of the freeing of prisoners and the giving of sight to the blind, and translators are advised to do the same.

Verse 8b is like 145.14b; **the righteous** in verse 8c are God's people, those who obey him and follow his commands. This half line has no real connection with the immediate context; BJ and NJB shift it to before verse 9c, where it fits much better (see 145.20 for a combination of similar lines). There is, however, no textual support for this change.

Verse 9a,b speaks of three classes of people in Israelite society who needed special care and protection (see the same three in 94.6): the resident aliens (**sojourners**), the widows, and the orphans (**fatherless**).

In verse 9c **brings to ruin** translates a verb meaning to turn aside, to make crooked (see its use in 119.78b, rendered "subverted"); the same thought is expressed in a different fashion in 1.6b. NEB translates "but turns the course of the wicked to their ruin," and SPCL "he causes the wicked to lose their way." FRCL translates **way** here as "projects" (as in verse 4).

<u>146.10</u> RSV	TEV
The LORD will reign for ever, thy God, O Zion, to all generations. Praise the LORD!	The LORD is king forever. Your God, O Zion, will reign for all time. Praise the LORD!

The psalm closes with an affirmation of Yahweh's eternal rule (see 145.13a,b). Here **Zion** stands for the whole land of Israel (see 2.6). In some cases it may be necessary to recast verse 10 to make clear what the address form **O Zion** is; for example, it may be rendered "People of the country of Israel, your God will reign for ever."

The psalm ends as it begins: **Praise the LORD!**

Psalm 147

Psalm 145 was characterized by parallel lines in which there was a marked absence of clear poetic intensification between lines. By contrast Psalm 147 is made up of a majority of verses containing lines exhibiting heightening of feeling, as the second line shifts to more concrete, dramatic, picturable nouns, phrases, or verb phrases. In fact, verses 1 through 14 are of this type. Verses 15-20 are either clearly not or arguably not of this type. For translators, intensification in the second line suggests the need to reflect this poetic dynamic in the translation. In English, as has been shown throughout this handbook, this can be done by the use of such terms as "more than that," "even," "further," "Not only . . . but," "in fact," and others. The translator must be able to control the poetic devices of his own language so that sharpening of the poetic feeling in the movement from line a to line b is expressed in a natural and clear manner.

Because these verses share in the intensification principle, they will be looked at as a group rather than repeating each one where the verse is discussed. In verse 1 line b picks up "good" from line a and raises it to the double expression which is more specific, "pleasant and fitting." In verse 2 "Jerusalem" is made dramatic in line b with "outcasts of Israel." Here also the word order in b swerves away from that of line a and forms a chiastic structure: "Builds up Jerusalem; outcasts of Israel scatters." This not only calls attention to the word order but also forges the verse into a tighter unit. In verse 3a the somewhat abstract "heals the brokenhearted" shifts to the more concrete "binds up their wounds." Again the psalmist switches word order in 4b and creates another chiasmus ("determines the number of stars; all by name he calls"). The shift from determining how many stars to giving each star its own name is movement from a general act to an infinite number of acts. Verse 5 shows a shift from "the great and mighty" in line a to the dramatic and limitless "wisdom without measure." Verse 6 moves from "raises" to the more forceful "crushes to the ground." In 7a the command is "Sing to the LORD," and in 7b the command is to use a specific instrument, the harp. Verse 8 is the only three-line verse in the psalm, and here the movement is from the distant and expansive to the closer and smaller: "heavens . . . earth . . . hills." In 9b specific birds, "young ravens" (in Hebrew "sons of ravens") replace "beasts" in line a. The dependence of 9b on 9a is sharpened by the necessity of reading "gives . . . food," which is left implicit in 9b. In the same manner "strength" in 10a must be read in 10b. In the movement from "horses" in line a to "legs of a man" in line b, the image passes from animal to human and thus raises the feeling in the second line. Verse 11b also requires "takes pleasure" from 11a to complete its sense. "Those who trust in his constant love" represents a focusing on the more general "those who honor him." In 12b "Zion" carries more specific information (location of the Temple area) than "Jerusalem." Furthermore, the two occur many times in this order as paired words. "Bars of your gates" in 13a is inanimate and shifts to the animate "sons within you." Verse 14 moves from "peace" to "finest of the wheat." It is rare in the Psalms to find an unbroken series of intensification as found in these 14 verses.

This hymn of praise divides naturally into three complete poems: verses 1-6, Yahweh's power in the history of Israel and in the universe; verses 7-11, Yahweh's power in nature; and verses 12-20, Yahweh's power in providing for his people. (It should be noticed that in the Septuagint verses 1-11 are Psalm 146, and verses 12-20 are Psalm 147.)

It is thought that the psalm was used in one of the major annual festivals, either the Festival of Shelters or the New Year Festival.

HEADING: "**In Praise of God the Almighty**." Other headings are "Hymn to the Almighty"; "The paradox of God's deeds"; "God's love and power." The TEV heading may be adjusted for translation by saying, for example, "The psalmist praises the God who is most powerful." For translation suggestions on "**Almighty**" see 50.1.

147.1-3   RSV   TEV

1   Praise the LORD!   1   Praise the LORD!
     For it is good to sing praises to
       our God;   It is good to sing praise to our
     for he is gracious, and a song of   God;
       praise is seemly.   it is pleasant and right to praise
2   The LORD builds up Jerusalem;   him.
     he gathers the outcasts of Is-   2   The LORD is restoring Jerusalem;
       rael.   he is bringing back the exiles.
3   He heals the brokenhearted   3   He heals the broken-hearted
     and binds up their wounds.   and bandages their wounds.

For the opening **Praise the LORD!** see 104.35.

In verse 1c the Hebrew text is simply "for pleasant (and) fitting a song of praise." RSV has **for he is gracious** (also AT and NAB); while possible, it seems better, in parallel with line **b** (**it is good to sing** . . .), to translate as TEV does, "**it is pleasant** . . ." (also NJV, NJB, FRCL, Dahood, SPCL, TOB). A more vivid way of saying this is "what a joy it is . . . !" BJ, NJB, and NEB, on the basis of the Septuagint, omit "fitting"; it seems better to stay with the Hebrew text. It is also possible to take the Hebrew word translated "fitting" (RSV **seemly**, TEV "**right**") not as an adjective but as a verbal infinitive, "to sing," parallel with **sing praises** in line **b** (Anderson; HOTTP). In this case line **c** would be translated "it is pleasant to sing his praise (or, to sing praise to him)." NIV has "how pleasant and fitting to praise him!" and FRCL, taking the idea of "fitting" to apply to Yahweh, translates "how good to praise him as he deserves!" **Is seemly** and TEV's "**it is . . . right**" may have to be rendered by "it is good to praise him."

Kugel (*The Idea of Biblical Poetry,* page 92) cites this verse (along with Pro 10.5; Isa 60.2; Lev 19.13) as an example of "strangeifying," that is, making the language appear a bit strange, and thereby imparting to it a special quality, inviting the reader at the same time to figure it out. Needless to say, modern exegetes and translators are doing just that and, of course, coming out with various interpretations.

The verbs in verse 2 seem to indicate that the psalm was written during the time after the Babylonian exile, when the Israelites, back in their land, were restoring the city of Jerusalem. For the meaning "rebuild" for the verb in verse 2a, see 51.18b; 102.16a. In verse 2b **the outcasts of Israel** are the Israelite exiles, who were being brought back to Jerusalem. In some languages it may be necessary to indicate where the exiles are being brought back to or from; for example, "he is bringing back to

Jerusalem the people who were carried away" or "he is bringing back the people the Babylonian soldiers took as prisoners."

In verse 3 the psalmist speaks of Yahweh's care for all those in trouble and distress. The phrase translated **the brokenhearted** occurs only here in the Old Testament; for similar and synonymous expressions, see 34.18; 51.17. And for Yahweh as healer see 30.2.

147.4-6	RSV	TEV
4	He determines the number of the stars, he gives to all of them their names.	4 He has decided the number of the stars and calls each one by name.
5	Great is our LORD, and abundant in power; his understanding is beyond measure.	5 Great and mighty is our Lord; his wisdom cannot be measured.
6	The LORD lifts up the downtrodden, he casts the wicked to the ground.	6 He raises the humble, but crushes the wicked to the ground.

Yahweh's power is shown in his control of the stars (verse 4), his wisdom (verse 5), his care for the oppressed, and his destruction of the wicked (verse 6).

In verse 4a the Hebrew verb means either "to count" or "to number"; it is possible to take the line to mean that Yahweh knows how many stars there are (so Anderson). It seems more likely, however, that the meaning, as RSV, TEV, and others (AT, SPCL) have it, is that Yahweh decided how many stars there would be, which is a way of saying that he created them all (see Cohen, Dahood). "He has decided the number of the stars" can mean in some languages that he was for some time in doubt how many there were and then concluded that there was a certain number of them. For this reason it may be best to translate "When he created the stars, he decided how many there would be." In line b the Hebrew may mean "he gave to all of them their names," which fits in well with the preceding line (so NJV, RSV, FRCL, NEB, NJB, Dahood), or "he calls them all by their names," that is, they are subject to his power and obey his commands (so TEV, NAB, NIV, BJ; see Cohen; see Isa 40.26).

Verse 6 tells how Yahweh deals with **the downtrodden**, that is, the humble (or, needy) and **the wicked**. For translation suggestions on **the downtrodden**, see comments on "the afflicted" in 9.12 and on "humble" in 14.6. The verb in line a (RSV **lifts up**) is the same that in 146.9b RSV translates "upholds." In both places NJV has "gives courage to." In contrast with the verb in line b, it seems best to translate here **"raises"** or "gives power to," and not merely "sustains" or "encourages." FRCL has "helps them get up."

In verse 6b, instead of **ground**, something like "the dust" (NJV, NEB) may be preferable. It is a picture of complete humiliation and defeat; see SPCL "he completely humiliates the wicked," or we may say, for example, "he grinds the wicked into the ground."

	RSV		TEV

TEV

7　Sing to the LORD with thanks-
　　giving;
　　make melody to our God upon
　　the lyre!
8　He covers the heavens with
　　clouds,
　　he prepares rain for the earth,
　　he makes grass grow upon the
　　hills.
9　He gives to the beasts their food,
　　and to the young ravens which
　　cry.

7　Sing hymns of praise to the LORD;
　　play music on the harp to our
　　God.
8　He spreads clouds over the sky;
　　he provides rain for the earth
　　and makes grass grow on the
　　hills.
9　He gives animals their food
　　and feeds the young ravens
　　when they call.

In these verses the psalmist again exhorts the people to **sing to** Yahweh with **thanksgiving** and to play music to him **upon the lyre** (for **lyre** see comments on 33.2a).

The psalmist dwells on God's blessings in nature: the **clouds** that bring the **rain**, which **makes the grass grow upon the hills**. The language recalls 104.14-16; and verse 8 here seems incomplete with only three lines. The Septuagint has line d, "and plants for man to use" (from 104.14b), which is included by NEB, NAB, BJ, and NJB (see Briggs, Weiser). The Hebrew text may be preferred (so HOTTP), but the Septuagint does make for a better balance of lines.

In verse 9 the word translated **beasts** may mean domesticated animals only, specifically cattle (NEB, NAB, NIV, BJ, NJB, TOB, Dahood). For **young ravens** see *Fauna and Flora,* pages 67-8. It seems preferable to understand the Hebrew in verse 9b to mean "**when they call**" (either to God, as the Septuagint has it, or for food), and not **which cry** (RSV). FRCL has "when they cry for hunger." The verse recalls the statements in 104.27-28; 145.15-16. Anderson suggests that **young ravens** are mentioned because it was the popular notion (although not true) that ravens neglect their young. The translator may need to substitute a different bird for the raven in areas where the raven is unknown.

147.10-11 RSV TEV

10　His delight is not in the strength
　　of the horse,
　　nor his pleasure in the legs of a
　　man;
11　but the LORD takes pleasure in
　　those who fear him,
　　in those who hope in his
　　steadfast love.

10　His pleasure is not in strong
　　horses,
　　nor his delight in brave soldiers;
11　but he takes pleasure in those
　　who honor him,
　　in those who trust in his con-
　　stant love.

In these verses the psalmist talks about what pleases Yahweh and what doesn't please him. The point is that God's people are to find their real security, not in strong horses or in brave soldiers, but in honoring him and trusting **in his steadfast love** (see 33.18b). In verse 10b **the legs of a man** probably represents soldiers (as "**strong horses**" in verse 10a are war horses); see similar idea in 33.16-17. Some take the legs of a man to mean the swiftness or agility of runners (NJV, NAB; NEB "a runner's legs"; FRCL, a bit more intelligently, "the exploits of a runner"). SPCL has "muscles of a man," and NJB "human sturdiness." A translation here should not be literal; it is rather incongruous to read that God has no **pleasure** (RSV) or "delight" (NIV) **in the legs of a man**. GECL has done the best job of making clear the meaning of verse 10: "Many rely on the strength of their horses and the swift feet of their warriors; all such people are offensive to the Lord." Another possibility is "Strong horses and brave soldiers are not what the LORD is looking for; he would rather have people honor him and trust in his constant love."

For **fear** see 15.4; and for **steadfast love** see 5.7.

147.12-14   RSV   TEV

12   Praise the LORD, O Jerusalem!   12   Praise the LORD, O Jerusalem!
       Praise your God, O Zion!   Praise your God, O Zion!
13   For he strengthens the bars of   13   He keeps your gates strong;
       your gates;   he blesses your people.
       he blesses your sons within you. 14   He keeps your borders safe
14   He makes peace in your borders;   and satisfies you with the finest
       he fills you with the finest of   wheat.
       the wheat.

Here the psalmist is thinking particularly of Yahweh's blessings on Jerusalem and its people. Verse 12 consists of two parallel and synonymous lines; **Zion** in line b is used synonymously with **Jerusalem** in line a.

Yahweh keeps Jerusalem safe and strong and blesses its people. Verse 13a talks about the physical security of the city against outside attacks. TEV's "**He keeps your gates strong**" is the use of a part for the whole, meaning "He defends Jerusalem" or "He guards Jerusalem." In verse 13b **your sons** are the citizens of the city (TEV, NIV, GECL "**your people**").

In verse 14 **your borders** is probably meant to refer to the borders of the whole land and not just those of the city. The Hebrew "he makes your borders peace" means that he keeps Jerusalem's (or, Israel's) territory safe from attack by foreign nations. It probably does not mean here internal peace, lack of strife among its people, as SPCL "He brings peace to your territory" has it; see also NJV (and FRCL) "He endows your realm with well-being." Jerusalem is not only safe from foreign attack but is plentifully supplied with food (verse 14b). In languages in which **wheat** is unknown, it may be necessary to employ the most commonly used grain, such as rice, or the generic term "food."

147.15-18   RSV   TEV

15   He sends forth his command to   15   He gives a command to the earth,
       the earth;   and what he says is quickly
       his word runs swiftly.   done.
16   He gives snow like wool;   16   He spreads snow like a blanket
       he scatters hoarfrost like ashes.   and scatters frost like dust.
17   He casts forth his ice like morsels; 17   He sends hail like gravel;
       who can stand before his cold?   no one can endure the cold he

18	He sends forth his word, and melts them; he makes his wind blow, and the waters flow.		sends!
		18	Then he gives a command, and the ice melts; he sends the wind, and the water flows.

In these verses the psalmist dwells on natural phenomena, which occur in obedience to Yahweh's commands. Verse 15 speaks of Yahweh's power to control the world by means of **his command**, which is quickly obeyed. In verse 15b **his word runs swiftly** represents Yahweh's command as a swift messenger, taking Yahweh's order quickly to its destination (so GECL "his word quickly reaches its destination"). TEV **"and what he says is quickly done"** may go beyond the meaning of the text, and it is recommended that GECL serve as model. In verse 15b **his word** is the same as **his command** in verse 15a. If the passive must be avoided, one may say, for example, "He commands the earth and the earth obeys."

In verse 16 **snow** is compared to **wool**; this may be a figure for the whiteness of snow (so Briggs; NEB), or else, as TEV has it, **"like a blanket"**; frost is compared to **"dust"** (or, **ashes**).[1] In languages where **snow** and **frost** are unknown, it is possible to substitute other forms of precipitation such as "rain, drizzle, fog, dew." The similarity of frost to **ashes** and **"dust"** may not be clear without saying, for example, "he scatters dew on the ground the way the wind blows dust."

In verse 17 the word **ice** probably means hail; the figure is that of hailstones as large as pieces of bread, **morsels** (NJB "breadcrumbs," NJV "crumbs"; see the word in Gen 18.5; Ruth 2.14). TEV has used **"gravel"** as being more in keeping with the size and consistency of hailstones; NIV "pebbles" may even be better.

In verse 17b instead of the Hebrew "in the presence of his cold, who can stand?" many commentators propose emending the text to read "in the presence of his cold the waters stand," that is, they freeze solid (NEB, NAB, SPCL). The Hebrew text as it is makes sense; the emended text makes even better sense and prepares the way for the next verse. This is not to say, however, that the emended text should be used.

The reverse process is described in verse 18: at Yahweh's command the ice melts, and moved (or, melted) by his wind (or, breath) the water flows once more. Here God's **wind** (or, breath) is parallel with his **word**; both are the means whereby his will is done in the world. In languages where ice is unknown, verse 18 will have to be modified by saying, for example, "He gives a command and the dew disappears" or ". . . dries up."

<u>147.19-20</u>   RSV   TEV

19	He declares his word to Jacob, his statutes and ordinances to Israel.	19	He gives his message to his people, his instructions and laws to Israel.
20	He has not dealt thus with any other nation;	20	He has not done this for other

---

[1]The word may have been chosen because of the wordplay in Hebrew: $k^e por$ $ka'eper$ for **hoarfrost like ashes**.

they   do   not   know   his   nations;
        ordinances.   they do not know his laws.
Praise the L**ORD**!

                                        Praise the L**ORD**!

The psalm closes with a proclamation of Yahweh's special relationship with his people: to Israel, and to no other nation, he gives **his word**, **his statutes and ordinances**. For these three words (*dabar, choq, mishpat*) see introduction to Psalm 119; they are synonymous and refer to the Law of Moses, the Torah. **Jacob** in line a̲ is parallel with **Israel** in line b̲; both mean the people of Israel.

The psalm ends as it begins: **Praise the** L**ORD**!

Psalm 148

In this hymn of praise the psalmist calls upon all creation, animate and inanimate, to praise Yahweh: all created beings and things in heaven (verses 1-6) and all created beings and things on earth (verses 7-12) are to praise him. The concluding two verses (verses 13-14) state the main reason for this universal praise to Yahweh: he is supreme and he has saved his people. The psalm begins and ends with **Praise the LORD!**

HEADING: **"A Call for the Universe to Praise God."** Other headings are: "Cosmic hymn of praise"; "All creation praises the LORD"; "A Hallelujah Chorus." The TEV heading may be adjusted for translation into some languages by saying, for example, "The psalmist asks everything in the heavens and earth to praise God."

<u>148.1-4</u>   RSV   TEV

	RSV		TEV
1	**Praise the LORD!** **Praise the LORD from the heavens,** **praise him in the heights!**	1	**Praise the LORD!** **Praise the LORD from heaven,** **you that live in the heights above.**
2	**Praise him, all his angels,** **praise him, all his host!**	2	**Praise him, all his angels,** **all his heavenly armies.**
3	**Praise him, sun and moon,** **praise him, all you shining stars!**	3	**Praise him, sun and moon;** **praise him, shining stars.**
4	**Praise him, you highest heavens,** **and you waters above the heavens!**	4	**Praise him, highest heavens,** **and the waters above the sky.**[s]

[s] WATERS ABOVE THE SKY: *See Genesis 1.6-7.*

After the initial **Praise the LORD!** (see 104.35), the psalmist calls upon all heavenly creatures to praise Yahweh. In the Hebrew, every half-line of verses 1-4 (except verse 4b) begins with the imperative "praise!" In verse 1 **the heavens** and **the heights** are synonymous, as are **his angels** and **his host** in verse 2 (see 103.20-21). <u>Host</u> in this context means "armies," the angels being thought of as God's warriors. It is to be noticed that the beings who are called upon in verses 1-2 to praise Yahweh are named only in verse 2 (see RSV). TEV, for greater ease of understanding, identifies them in verse 1b, **"you that live in the heights above"** (also FRCL, GECL). Many translators will want to follow the adjustment of TEV in verse 1, since in many

1180

languages only people and spirits are said to praise God. Because **heavens** and **heights** are synonymous, it may be necessary in some cases to use only "the heavens" or "the heavens above."

In verse 3 **sun**, **moon**, and **shining stars** are called on to join the chorus of praise. In verse 4a **highest heavens** translates the Hebrew phrase "heaven of the heavens," a way of expressing the superlative degree. In verse 4b **the waters above the heavens** are the waters above the heavenly dome, which were regarded as the source of rain (see 104.3 and the illustration under 104.6). In languages which resist the poetic appeal to an inanimate object to perform human actions, it may be necessary to add a simile; for example, "Sun, moon, and stars that shine, praise him the way people praise him." It is also possible to interpret the expression **highest heavens** as an idiomatic way of referring to heaven itself (Anderson), and this simplifies the task of rendering the expression for many languages which form superlatives in a complex manner. In languages which may have to add a simile in verses 3-4, it may be possible to do so only at the beginning of verse 3; for example, "Just like people praise the LORD, so also you sun, moon, bright stars, heaven, and water above the sky praise him." Translators should, like TEV, provide a cross reference to Genesis 1.6-7, and perhaps a note on **"waters above the sky."**

148.5-6   RSV   TEV

5   Let them praise the name of the   5   Let them all praise the name of
         LORD!   the LORD!
     For he commanded and they   He commanded, and they were
         were created.   created;
6   And he established them for ever   6   by his command they were fixed
         and ever;   in their places forever,
     he fixed their bounds which   and they cannot disobey.*
         cannot be passed.*

                                               * by his command . . . disobey; *or* he has
* Or *he set a law which cannot pass away*   fixed them in their places for all time, by
                                               a command that lasts forever.

These verses give the reason for the command to praise Yahweh: all things and beings in the realms above were created by his command, and so they are his creatures, his servants. For verse 5 see similar statements in 33.6,9. In verse 5b it should not appear that at Yahweh's command someone else created the heavenly bodies, as both RSV and TEV **and they were created** might suggest. It would be better to say "For he created them by means of his command." See FRCL "for he had to speak only one word and they began to exist."

In verse 6a the verb **established** may have the general sense of "create, make," or the more restricted sense, as TEV has it, **"fixed in their places"** (see the use of the verb in 93.1c; 96.10d). In the popular thinking of that time, all planets and stars were thought to occupy a fixed place in the sky. In languages which will not use the passive, one may say in verse 6a, for example, "He put them in their places forever."

Verse 6b in Hebrew is "he gave an order and it does not pass," which seems to mean "he gave an order that will not be abolished"; so NEB "by an ordinance which shall never pass away" (also NIV, BJ, NJB; see TEV footnote). But the verb "to pass" can be understood to mean "to pass by, go beyond"; as applied to a law, it means "to transgress, disobey." So Kirkpatrick: "He hath given (them) a statute that none (of them) shall transgress." Briggs, who supports this interpretation, comments: "This is the nearest approach to immutable laws of nature that is known to Heb. Literature." In line with this interpretation TEV has **"and they cannot disobey"**; FRCL, a bit differently, "establishing for them a law that is not to be broken." If for no reason other than that the first interpretation seems so prosaic, perhaps the second interpretation is to be preferred. In many languages the expression "a law that is not to be broken" will have to be recast to say something like "he made a rule they always have to follow" or ". . . a law they always have to obey," which is the positive form of the TEV rendering.

148.7-8	RSV	TEV

	RSV	TEV
7	Praise the LORD from the earth, you sea monsters and all deeps,	7 Praise the LORD from the earth, sea monsters and all ocean depths;
8	fire and hail, snow and frost, stormy wind fulfilling his command!	8 lightning and hail, snow and clouds, strong winds that obey his command.

With verse 7 the psalmist begins to exhort all earthly beings and things to praise Yahweh **from the earth** (see "from heavens" in verse 1). TEV and RSV are able to maintain the parallel expressions **from the heavens** and **from the earth** in verses 1 and 7. Translators should attempt to do likewise. For **sea monsters** see 74.13 and comments; **all depths** is a way of speaking of the deep waters which Yahweh conquered at creation (see 89.9-10; 104.6-7); they are all his servants and so must praise him. See verses 3-4 for use of the simile in connection with commands to nonhumans.

In verse 8 the natural phenomena are also commanded to join the chorus of praise; **fire** is lightning. In the same line **frost** translates a word that means "smoke" elsewhere (Gen 19.28; Psa 119.83); the Septuagint translates "ice" (so NEB and RSV); TEV and NIV have **"clouds"**; AT "fog"; BJ, NJB, NAB, TOB, FRCL, and SPCL "mist"; NJV and Dahood "smoke," that is, volcanic smoke. The translator is invited to take his or her pick. For substitutions for **snow** see comments on 147.16.

148.9-10	RSV	TEV

	RSV	TEV
9	Mountains and all hills, fruit trees and all cedars!	9 Praise him, hills and mountains, fruit trees and forests;
10	Beasts and all cattle, creeping things and flying birds!	10 all animals, tame and wild, reptiles and birds.

It is to be noticed that in the Hebrew text (see RSV) there are no verbs in verses 9-12; actually verses 7-12 are one long sentence (see NJV), with the one verb **Praise** at the beginning of verse 7. In many languages it will be necessary to imitate TEV and have the verb "**Praise**" at the beginning of verses 9 and 11.

All plant life is commanded to praise Yahweh (verse 9); TEV "**forests**" translates the word <u>cedars</u> (see *Fauna and Flora,* page 108), which are here representative of all uncultivated plants, while **fruit trees** represent all cultivated plants. In languages in which there is no generic term for "**fruit**," the use of a specific fruit tree would be unsatisfactory. Accordingly, in such languages it may be better to say "all plants and trees" or "plants which people grow, and all other plants."

Similarly in verse 10 the whole animal kingdom is called upon to praise Yahweh. <u>**Beasts and all cattle**</u> represents "**all animals, tame and wild,**" and <u>creeping things</u> includes all reptiles, worms, and insects (see Gen 1.24-25).

148.11-12   RSV   TEV

11   Kings of the earth and all peoples,   11   Praise him, kings and all peoples,
       princes and all rulers of the   princes and all other rulers;
       earth!   12   girls and young men,
12   Young men and maidens together,   old people and children too.
       old men and children!

In these verses all human beings, people of both sexes, all ages, and all social classes are commanded to praise Yahweh. In verse 11b **princes** are officials or authorities in general. <u>**All rulers**</u> translates "all judges"; here, as often, the Hebrew word means not "judges" in the restricted sense of the word, but all who occupy places of power and authority.

148.13-14   RSV   TEV

13   Let them praise the name of the   13   Let them all praise the name of
       LORD,   the LORD!
       for his name alone is exalted;   His name is greater than all
       his glory is above earth and   others;
       heaven.   his glory is above earth and
14   He has raised up a horn for his   heaven.
       people,   14   He made his nation strong,
       praise for all his saints,   so that all his people praise
       for the people of Israel who are   him—
       near to him.   the people of Israel, so dear to
       Praise the LORD!   him.

                                                Praise the LORD!

1183

The psalm ends with the reason for the praise that all creation is commanded to offer Yahweh: he is supreme over all creation and is the protector of his people. In verse 13a,b the psalmist uses the phrase "the name of Yahweh" to represent Yahweh himself, whose greatness is unique; no other being, no other god, is as great as Yahweh. **Praise the name of the LORD** may also be rendered "Praise the LORD." In line **b** Yahweh's name is "high above all others," or literally, "his name is exalted uniquely (or, by itself)." (NEB), that is, his rank, his title, is greater than that of any other being. **"His name is greater"** may be rendered as "He is greater . . . ." **His glory** in verse 13c represents his power, his majesty, which is greater than that of all beings in the universe (**above earth and heaven**). **His glory is above earth and heaven** may have to be recast in some languages to say, for example, "He is more powerful than anything on earth or in heaven."

For the figure **He has raised up a horn for his people** in verse 14a, see 18.2; 75.4; 89.17,24. The meaning is "He has made his people strong." TEV's **"his nation"** in **"He has made his nation strong"** refers to God's people. In verse 14b **praise for all his saints** does not mean that the saints are to be praised but that Yahweh is the one his people praise; so TEV **"so that all his people praise him."** It is possible, however, that the word translated **praise** means here "honor, glory," so that it is the people who receive glory or honor. So NJV has "for the glory of all His faithful ones," and FRCL "It's a title of glory for his faithful ones." For *chasid* "pious, faithful," see comments on "the godly" in 4.3. If the translator follows TEV, line **b** may be taken as a consequence of line **a** and rendered "He has made his people strong; therefore they praise him." In verse 14c **the people of Israel** is a synonym of **his saints** in the preceding line. The Hebrew of verse 14c is "for the sons of Israel, the people near to him." Here **near** does not mean physical but emotional closeness; they are loved by him. NIV has "close to his heart." (See the idiom "near and dear" in English.) It may be best in some languages to avoid the apposition which is line **c** and say "therefore the people of Israel, whom he loves, praise him."

The psalm closes as it begins: **Praise the LORD!**

Psalm 149

This hymn of praise seems to refer to some specific event in the life of Israel, a war against Israel's enemies (verses 6-9), but there is no agreement on what event that would have been. This psalm is evidently "a new song" composed to be sung at some festival in the Temple (verse 1).

The psalm opens with a call to the people to praise Yahweh (verses 1-3), followed by the reason why this should be done (verses 4-9), which could be either a military victory that the Israelites had already won over their enemies, or one they hoped to win. The psalm closes as it begins, with the order **Praise the LORD!**

HEADING: "**A Hymn of Praise**." Other headings are: "Song of triumph"; "The judgment on the Gentiles"; "The triumph of Israel." For suggestions concerning the TEV heading, see Psalm 145.

149.1-3	RSV		TEV

	RSV		TEV

1	Praise the LORD!
	Sing to the LORD a new song,
	   his praise in the assembly of
	     the faithful!
		1	Praise the LORD!
			
			Sing a new song to the LORD;
			   praise him in the assembly of
			     his faithful people!

2	Let Israel be glad in his Maker,
	   let the sons of Zion rejoice in
	     their King!
		2	Be glad, Israel, because of your
			   Creator;
			   rejoice, people of Zion, because
			     of your king!

3	Let them praise his name with
	   dancing,
	   making melody to him with
	     timbrel and lyre!
		3	Praise his name with dancing;
			   play drums and harps in praise
			     of him.

The psalm opens with a call to the people of Israel to **praise** Yahweh in the Temple festival, **the assembly of the faithful**, that is, the meeting of the people who are faithful to Yahweh. For **a new song** see 96.1.

Verse 2 consists of two parallel and synonymous lines: **Israel . . . sons of Zion** (see 2.6), and **his Maker . . . their King**. For "your Creator" see comments on 100.3, where it is noted that this term does not necessarily refer to creation. In verses 2-3 TEV has kept the second person of direct address of verse 1, not the third person of the Hebrew text. In both lines of verse 2 the clause "**because of . . .**" gives the reason why the people should praise Yahweh: it is because of what he has done, and still does, for them. Line 2b shifts from general to specific categories with corresponding intensification of feeling. In English the whole unit can be rendered "Be glad, Israel,

1185

because of the one who has created you, and still more, people of Zion, because he is the one who rules over you."

In verse 3 the people are called upon to celebrate with **dancing** and the playing of drums (RSV **timbrel**; see 81.2) and "**harps**" (RSV **lyre**; see 33.2a). It may be best in some languages to recast verse 3 by shifting from third-person imperatives to second-person imperatives; for example, "Dance, beat the drums, and play the musical instruments to praise him." However, if the original form can be followed more closely, one may say "Dance in order to praise him; even more, praise God by playing the drums and the harp."

149.4-5   RSV   TEV

4	For the LORD takes pleasure in his people; he adorns the humble with victory.	4	The LORD takes pleasure in his people; he honors the humble with victory.
5	Let the faithful exult in glory; let them sing for joy on their couches.	5	Let God's people rejoice in their triumph and sing joyfully all night long.

In verses 4-9 the psalmist tells why the people of Israel should praise Yahweh: it is because he **takes pleasure in his people** (see 147.11) and he gives them **victory** (verse 4). In verse 4b **the humble** (see comments on "the afflicted" in 9.12) describes Yahweh's people as those whose only source of help and strength is Yahweh himself, and not any human being; they are completely dependent on him for victory. TEV does not link verse 4 to the preceding verse. However, the two need to be related, and in some languages it may be necessary to begin verse 4 by saying, for example, "Do this because the LORD delights in his people" or ". . . the LORD's people make him happy." The verb translated **adorns** occurs only here in Psalms; **victory** is seen as a garland, or crown, which is placed on the head of the victor. **Adorns the humble with victory** may be recast to say, for example, "he honors those who depend on him, by helping them defeat their enemies."

In verse 5 the people of Israel are called, as often, **the faithful** (see "the godly" in 4.3); **glory** in line a has the specific sense of victory or triumph (NEB, SPCL). If the translator ends verse 4 as suggested above, TEV's "**in their triumph**" may be handled by saying "Let God's people rejoice because they have won the battle." It is not certain what the Hebrew **on their couches** in verse 5b means. Some think it refers to the seats at the religious meals; others, that it refers to prayer mats (so NEB "as they kneel before him"; similarly NJB); others take it to mean "even when they are sick in bed"; and still others believe it means "even when they are (supposed to be) asleep" (so TEV, SPCL, FRCL; Dahood, Cohen). Some emend the Hebrew **on their couches** to "according to their families" or to "in their tabernacle," that is, the Temple (Briggs).

149.6-9   RSV   TEV

6	Let the high praises of God be in their throats	6	Let them shout aloud as they praise God,

and two-edged swords in their hands,	with their sharp swords in their hands
7 to wreak vengeance on the nations and chastisement on the peoples,	7 to defeat the nations and to punish the peoples;
8 to bind their kings with chains and their nobles with fetters of iron,	8 to bind their kings in chains, their leaders in chains of iron;
9 to execute on them the judgment written!	9 to punish the nations as God has commanded.
This is glory for all his faithful ones.	This is the victory of God's people.
Praise the LORD!	Praise the LORD!

In verse 6 **high praises** translates a word found elsewhere in the Old Testament only at 66.17 (see comments). The instruction to have their sharp swords (literally "a sword of mouths," which probably means **a two-edged sword**—RSV and others) **in their hands** seems to indicate that this is a war festival, before the people go out to fight the enemy. But it may also be seen as a celebration after the battle, in which the victory is being acclaimed. In languages in which the sword is unfamiliar, it may be replaced by the most common local weapon or by a generic term for weapon.

Verses 7-9 describe the war against Israel's enemy. Verse 7 consists of two parallel and synonymous lines; for **vengeance** see 18.47 and 94.1. NJV has "retribution." Instead of "**defeat**" (TEV), something like "to take vengeance on the nations" will better represent the specific meaning of the text. GECL has "they must execute God's judgment on all peoples." The word translated **chastisement** in verse 7b means "correction, rebuke, punishment." It is probable that **the nations** and **the peoples** have here the sense of "the pagans . . . the heathen" (JB).

In verse 8b **their nobles** is parallel to **their kings** in line a and indicates the military leaders. In some languages the use of "**chains**" and "**chains of iron**" will tend to give the impression that the kings were bound with chains that were not made of iron. In some cases this idea is expressed as "to capture their kings and leaders and tie them up."

In verse 9 **chastisement** (TEV "**to punish**") translates "to do *mishpat*," which in this case is God's judgment. It is not certain whether **written** refers primarily to messages of doom proclaimed by Israel's prophets, or to the heavenly books which contained the records of the deeds of all people (see Dan 7.10). In either case, God is the ultimate judge, and the punishment inflicted on Israel's enemies has been determined by him. NJV has "executing the doom decreed against them" (likewise NEB). In this case the passive "decreed" means "that God decreed."

In verse 9b **glory** translates a word meaning "splendor, dignity" (see 8.5). TEV takes it to mean the same here as the synonym used in verse 5b (not the same Hebrew word). Perhaps "This is an honor for God's people" (see FRCL, SPCL) is meant. TEV "**God's people**" translates the plural of *chasid* (see 4.3).

The psalm ends as it begins: **Praise the LORD!**

Psalm 150

This psalm was composed perhaps to be the last one in the whole collection of psalms; it serves here the same purpose as the shorter doxologies at the end of the first four Books (see 41.13; 72.18-20; 89.52; 106.48). It is a sustained call to praise Yahweh. The psalm begins and ends with **Praise the LORD!** and each half line in verses 1-5 begins with the same verb **Praise**; in the one-line verse 6 the verb in Hebrew comes at the end.

The setting of the psalm is a festival in the Temple.

HEADING: **"Praise the LORD!"** Other headings are: "Final chorus of praise"; "The last Hallelujah"; "The closing doxology." See Psalm 145 for TEV headings similar to this one.

150.1-2   RSV   TEV

RSV	TEV

1 Praise the LORD!
 Praise God in his sanctuary;
    praise him in his mighty firmament!
	1 Praise the LORD!
	
	 Praise God in his Temple!
	    Praise his strength in heaven!

2 Praise him for his mighty deeds;
    praise him according to his
    exceeding greatness!
	2 Praise him for the mighty things
	    he has done.
	    Praise his supreme greatness.

The psalm opens with a call to **Praise the LORD** "in his holy place"; this may be the Temple in Jerusalem (TEV) or, in parallel with **his mighty firmament** in the next line, it may be his heavenly abode (so Dahood). Most translations have **sanctuary** or "holy place," without further definition. TEV **"heaven"** translates the word **firmament**; see 19.1 and Genesis 1.6-8. In Hebrew line c is literally "Praise him in the firmament his strength," which can be understood in various ways. "His strength" is taken by most translations to be in apposition to "the firmament"; so NJV "in the sky, His stronghold"; NEB "in the vault of heaven, the vault of his power"; TOB "in the fortress of his firmament." This seems preferable to TEV **"his strength in heaven."** Taking **his mighty firmament** as a synonym for "heaven," the translation can be "Praise him in the heavens" or, if **mighty** is to be expressed, "Praise him in his mighty heavens." For both phrases the preposition **in** indicates where God is, not where those are who are urged to praise him.

Verse 2 calls upon the people to praise Yahweh for all **his mighty deeds**, both in creation and in the history of Israel. In line b RSV **according to** is not easy to understand; better "for" (NIV, NJV, NEB, NJB, FRCL, SPCL), as in line a. **Exceeding** greatness and TEV's "**supreme greatness**" is rendered in some languages, for example, "because he is great, surpassing all greatness."

150.3-5	RSV		TEV
3	Praise him with trumpet sound; praise him with lute and harp!	3	Praise him with trumpets. Praise him with harps and lyres.
4	Praise him with timbrel and dance; praise him with strings and pipe!	4	Praise him with drums and dancing. Praise him with harps and flutes.
5	Praise him with sounding cymbals; praise him with loud clashing cymbals!	5	Praise him with cymbals. Praise him with loud cymbals.

In verses 3-5 various instruments are named which are to be used in this service of praise: **trumpet** (see 47.5; 98.6); **lute and harp**, a translation of *nebel* and *kinor* (see 33.2, where RSV has "lyre" instead of **lute**); "**drums**" (RSV **timbrel**; see 149.3). In verse 4b "**harps**" translates the word **strings**, which may also be the word used in 45.8 (but nowhere else in the Old Testament). "**Flutes**" (RSV **pipe**) are wind instruments; see the word in Genesis 4.21; Job 21.12; 30.31.

In verse 5 two kinds of **cymbals** are mentioned (elsewhere only in 2 Sam 6.5): literally "cymbals of hearing" and "cymbals of shouting," which may mean small cymbals and large cymbals, or just a poetic variation, "clanging cymbals . . . clashing cymbals." There were two types of cymbals: (1) flat metal plates which were struck together, and (2) metal cones, one of which was brought down on top of the other, on the larger end. They were probably made out of bronze.

Taylor and others point out that trumpets were played by priests; harps, lyres, and cymbals by the Levites; and the other instruments (verse 4) by lay people. The translation of the terms for these musical instruments is usually handled in three ways: (a) by means of descriptive phrases; (b) by means of local instruments; and (c) by using generic terms accompanied by a loan word. The first example is illustrated in the case of "cymbal" by (1) above. The third case would be "flat metal plates struck together, called cymbals." This third case would adversely affect the poetic effect and would be more suitable as a footnote.

150.6	RSV	TEV
	Let everything that breathes praise the LORD! Praise the LORD!	Praise the LORD, all living creatures! Praise the LORD!

In this verse "**all living creatures**" (**everything that breathes**) are called upon to praise Yahweh; the psalmist may have included not just humankind but all other living beings as well.

The psalm and the book close with the final *halelu-yah*, **Praise the LORD!**

APPENDIX

Differing Systems of Reference
to the Psalms

As noted in the introduction, "Translating the Psalms," there are several ways in which people have given numbers to the psalms and to their verses. The following list indicates the four basic systems that have been followed through the centuries. Translators may need to refer to this list as they come across references to the Psalms that follow a system different from their own; for example, most Hebrew scholars will use the numbering system found in the Hebrew Bible. Various churches today follow a system different from the one used by RSV and by this Handbook, and translators may therefore need to use one of the alternate systems as they provide numbers for the individual psalms and their verses.

RSV	Hebrew	Vulgate	Septuagint
3. heading	3.1	3.1	3.1
3.1-8	3.2-9	3.2-9	3.2-9
4. heading	4.1	4.1	4.1
4.1-5	4.2-6	4.2-6a	4.2-6
4.6a-7a	4.7a-8a	4.6b-7b	4.7a-8a
4.8	4.9	4.9-10	4.9
5. heading	5.1	5.1	5.1
5.1-12	5.2-13	5.2-13	5.2-13
6. heading	6.1	6.1	6.1
6.1-10	6.2-11	6.2-11	6.2-11
7. heading	7.1	7.1	7.1
7.1-17	7.1-18	7.1-18	7.2-18
8. heading	8.1	8.1	8.1
8.1-9	8.2-10	8.2-10	8.2-10
9. heading	9.1	9.1	9.1
9.1-20	9.2-21	9.2-21	9.2-21
10.1-18	10.1-18	9.22-39	9.22-39
11.heading	11.1a	10.1	10.1a
11.1-7	11.1b-7	10.2-8	10.1b-7
12. heading	12.1	11.1	11.1
12.1-8	12.2-9	11.2-9	11.2-9
13. heading	13.1	12.1a	12.1
13.1-6	13.2-6b	12.1b-6	12.2-6b
14—17	14—17	13—16	13—16

RSV	Hebrew	Vulgate	Septuagint
18. heading	18.1	17.1	17.1
18.1-50	18.2-51	17.2-51	17.2-51
19. heading	19.1	18.1	18.1
19.1-14	19.2-15	18.2-15	18.2-15
20. heading	20.1	19.1	19.1
20.1-9	20.2-10	19.2-10	19.2-10
21. heading	21.1	20.1	20.1
21.1-13	21.2-14	20.2-14	20.2-14
22. heading	22.1	21.1	21.1
22.1-31	22.2-32	21.2-32	21.2-32
23-29	23-29	22-28	22-28
30. heading	30.1	29.1	29.1
30.1-12	30.2-13	29.2-13	29.2-13
31. heading	31.1	30.1	30.1
31.1-24	31.2-25	30.2-25	30.2-25
32	32	31	31
33	33	32	32
34. heading	34.1	33.1	33.1
34.1-22	34.2-23	33.2-23	33.2-23
35	35	34	34
36. heading	36.1	35.1	35.1
36.1-12	36.2-13	35.2-13	35.2-13
37	37	36	36
38. heading	38.1	37.1	37.1
38.1-22	38.2-23	37.2-23	37.2-23
39. heading	39.1	38.1	38.1
39.1-13	39.2-14	38.2-14	38.2-14
40. heading	40.1	39.1	39.1
40.1-17	40.2-18	39.2-18	39.2-18
41. heading	41.1	40.1	40.1
41.1-13	41.2-14	40.2-14	40.2-14
42. heading	42.1	41.1	41.1
42.1-11	42.2-12	41.2-12	41.2-12
43	43	42	42
44. heading	44.1	43.1	43.1
44.1-20	44.2-21	43.2-21	43.2-21
44.21-22	44.22-23	43.22	43.22-23
44.23-26	44.24-27	43.23-26	43.24-27
45. heading	45.1	44.1	44.1
45.1-17	45.2-18	44.2-18	44.2-18
46. heading	46.1	45.1	45.1
46.1-11	46.2-12	45.2-12	45.2-12
47. heading	47.1	46.1	46.1
47.1-9	47.2-10	46.2-10	46.2-10
48. heading	48.1	47.1	47.1
48.1-14	48.2-15	47.2-15	47.2-15

RSV	Hebrew	Vulgate	Septuagint
49. heading	49.1	48.1	48.1
49.1-20	49.2-21	48.2-21	48.2-21
50	50	49	49
51. heading	51.1-2	50.1-2	50.1-2
51.1-19	51.3-21	50.3-21	50.3-21
52. heading	52.1-2	51.1-2	51.1-2
52.1-9	52.3-11	51.3-11	51.3-11
53. heading	53.1	52.1	52.1
53.1-6	53.2-7	52.2-7	52.2-7
54. heading	54.1-2	53.1-2	53.1-2
54.1-7	54.3-9	53.3-9	53.3-9
55. heading	55.1	54.1	54.1
55.1-23	55.2-24	54.2-24	54.2-24
56. heading	56.1	55.1	55.1
56.1-9	56.2-10	55.2-10	55.2-10
56.10-11	56.11-12	55.11	55.11-12
56.12-13	56.13-14	55.12-13	55.13-14
57. heading	57.1	56.1	56.1
57.1-11	57.2-12	56.2-12	56.2-12
58. heading	58.1	57.1	57.1
58.1-11	58.2-12	57.2-12	57.2-12
59. heading	59.1	58.1	58.1
59.1-17	59.2-18	58.2-18	58.2-18
60. heading	60.1-2	59.1-2	59.1-2
60.1-12	60.3-14	59.3-14	59.3-14
61. heading	61.1	60.1	60.1
61.1-8	61.2-9	60.2-9	60.2-9
62. heading	62.1	61.1	61.1
62.1-12	62.2-13	61.2-13	61.2-13
63. heading	63.1	62.1	62.1
63.1-11	63.2-12	62.2-12	62.2-12
64. heading	64.1	63.1	63.1
64.1-10	64.2-11	63.2-11	63.2-11
65. heading	65.1	64.1	64.1
65.1-13	65.2-14	64.2-14	64.2-14
66	66	65	65
67. heading	67.1	66.1	66.1
67.1-7	67.2-8	66.2-8	66.2-8
68. heading	68.1	67.1	67.1
68.1-35	68.2-36	67.2-36	67.2-36
69. heading	69.1	68.1	68.1
69.1-36	69.2-37	68.2-37	68.2-37
70. heading	70.1	69.1	69.1
70.1-5	70.2-6	69.2-6	69.2-6
71	71	70	70
72. heading	72.1a	71.1	71.1a

RSV	Hebrew	Vulgate	Septuagint
72.1	72.1b	71.2a	71.1b
72.2-20	72.2-20	71.2b-20	71.2-20
73—74	73—74	72—73	72—73
75. heading	75.1	74.1	74.1
75.1-10	75.2-11	74.2-11	74.2-11
76. heading	76.1	75.1	75.1
76.1-12	76.2-13	75.2-13	75.2-13
77. heading	77.1	76.1	76.1
77.1-20	77.2-21	76.2-21	76.2-21
78	78	77	77
79	79	78	78
80. heading	80.1	79.1	79.1
80.1-19	80.2-20	79.2-20	79.2-20
81. heading	81.1	80.1	80.1
81.1-16	81.2-17	80.2-17	80.2-17
82	82	81	81
83. heading	83.1	82.1	82.1
83.1-18	83.2-19	82.2-19	82.2-19
84. heading	84.1	83.1	83.1
84.1-12	84.2-13	83.2-13	83.2-13
85. heading	85.1	84.1	84.1
85.1-13	85.2-14	84.2-14	84.2-14
86	86	85	85
87	87	86	86
88. heading	88.1	87.1	87.1
88.1-18	88.2-19	87.2-19	87.2-19
89. heading	89.1	88.1	88.1
89.1-52	89.2-53	88.2-53	88.2-53
90	90	89	89
91	91	90	90
92. heading	92.1	91.1	91.1
92.1-15	92.2-16	91.2-16	91.2-16
93-101	93-101	92-100	92-100
102. heading	102.1	101.1	101.1
102.1-28	102.2-29	101.2-29	101.2-29
103-107	103-107	102-106	102-106
108. heading	108.1	107.1	107.1
108.1-13	108.2-14	107.2-14	107.2-14
109-113	109-113	108-112	108-112
114	114	113.1-8	113.1-8
115	115	113.9-26	113.9-26
116.1-9	116.1-9	114	114
116.10-19	116.10-19	115	115
117-139	117-139	116-138	116-138
140. heading	140.1	139.1	139.1
140.1-13	140.2-14	139.2-14	139.2-14

RSV	Hebrew	Vulgate	Septuagint
141	141	140	140
142. heading	142.1	141.1	141.1
142.1-7	142.2-8	141.2-8	141.2-8
143-146	143-146	142-145	142-145
147.1-11	147.1-11	146	146
147.12-20	147.12-20	147.1-9	147.1-9

Bibliography

Bible Texts and Versions Cited

Texts

Biblia Hebraica Stuttgartensia. 1966/77, 1983. Edited by K. Elliger and W. Rudolph. Stuttgart: Deutsche Bibelgesellschaft.

Septuaginta: Id est Vetus Testamentum graece iuxta LXX interpretes. 1935. Edited by Alfred Rahlfs. Stuttgart: Württembergische Bibelanstalt. (Cited as Septuagint.)

Biblia Sacra: Iuxta Vulgatam Versionem. 1983. Edited by Robert Weber. Stuttgart: Deutsche Bibelgesellschaft. (Cited as Vulgate.)

Versions

Die Bibel in heutigem Deutsch: Die Gute Nachricht des Alten und Neuen Testaments. 1982. Stuttgart: Deutsche Bibelgesellschaft. (Cited as GECL, German common language version.)

The Bible: A New Translation. 1926. James Moffatt, translator. London: Hodder & Stoughton. (Cited as Mft.)

La Bible de Jérusalem. 1973. Paris: Éditions du Cerf. (Cited as BJ.)

La Bible en français courant. 1982. Paris: Société biblique française. (Cited as FRCL, French common language version.)

A Bíblia Sagrada: Tradução na Linguagem de Hoje. 1988. São Paulo: Sociedade Bíblica do Brasil. (Cited as POCL, Portuguese common language version.)

The Complete Bible: An American Translation. 1923. J.M. Powis Smith and Edgar Goodspeed, translators. Chicago: University of Chicago Press. (Cited as AT.)

Dios Habla Hoy: La Biblia con Deuterocanónicos. Versión Popular. 1979. New York: Sociedades Biblicas Unidas. (Cited as SPCL, Spanish common language version.)

Good News Bible: The Bible in Today's English Version. 1976, 1979. New York: American Bible Society. British edition, 1976. London: British and Foreign Bible Societies. (Cited as TEV.)

Die Heilige Schrift des Alten und des Neuen Testaments. 1935. Zürich: Verlag der Zwingli-Bibel. (Cited as ZÜR, Zürcher Bibel.)

The Holy Bible. 1955. Translated by Ronald A. Knox. London: Burns & Oates. (Cited as Knox.)

The Holy Bible (Authorized or King James Version). 1611. (Cited as KJV.)

The Holy Bible: New International Version. 1987. New York: New York International Bible Society. (Cited as NIV.)

The Holy Bible: Newly Edited by the American Revision Committee. 1901. New York: Thomas Nelson & Sons. (Cited as ASV.)

The Holy Bible (Revised Version). 1885. Cambridge: The University Press. (Cited as RV.)

The Holy Bible: Revised Standard Version. 1952, 1971, 1973. New York: Division of Christian Education of the National Council of the Churches of Christ in the United States of America. (Cited as RSV.)

The Holy Scriptures According to the Masoretic Text: A New Translation. 1917. Philadelphia: Jewish Publication Society. (Cited as JPS.)

The Jerusalem Bible. 1966. London: Darton, Longman, & Todd; and New York: Doubleday. (Cited as JB.)

The Living Bible. 1971. Translated by Kenneth Taylor. Wheaton, Illinois: Tyndale House.

The New American Bible. 1970. New York: P.J. Kenedy & Sons. (Cited as NAB.)

The New English Bible. 1961, 1970. London: Oxford University Press; and Cambridge: Cambridge University Press. (Cited as NEB.)

The New Jerusalem Bible. 1985. Garden City, NY: Doubleday. (Cited as NJB.)

The Psalms in Modern Speech: For Public and Private Use. 1968. Translated by Richard S. Hanson. Three volumes. Philadelphia: Fortress Press.

TANAKH: A New Translation of the Holy Scriptures According to the Traditional Hebrew Text. 1985. Philadelphia: Jewish Publication Society. (Cited as NJV, New Jewish Version.)

Traduction œcuménique de la Bible. 1972, 1975, 1977. Paris: Société biblique française et Éditions du Cerf. (Cited as TOB.)

General Bibliography

Commentaries

Anderson, A.A. 1972. *Psalms* (New Century Bible). Two volumes. London: Oliphants.

Briggs, Charles Augustus, and Emilie Grace Briggs. 1907, 1909. *A Critical and Exegetical Commentary on the Book of Psalms* (International Critical Commentary). Two volumes. Edinburgh: T. & T. Clark.

Cohen, A. 1945. *The Psalms: Hebrew Text & English Translation with an Introduction and Commentary* (Soncino Books of the Bible). London: Soncino Press.

Crim, Keith R. 1962. *The Royal Psalms.* Richmond, Virginia: John Knox Press.

Dahood, Mitchell. 1965, 1966, 1968, 1970. *Psalms* (Anchor Bible). Three volumes. Garden City, New York: Doubleday.

Dalglish, Edward R. 1962. *Psalm Fifty-One in the Light of Ancient Near Eastern Patternism.* Leiden: E.J. Brill.

Delitzsch, Franz. 1889, 1890. *Biblical Commentary on the Psalms.* Translated by Francis Bolton. Edinburgh: T. & T. Clark.

Dentan, Robert C. 1962. Annotations on the Psalms, in *The Oxford Annotated Bible with the Apocrypha (Revised Standard Version),* edited by Herbert G. May and Bruce M. Metzger. New York: Oxford University Press.

Eaton, John Herbert. 1976. *Kingship and the Psalms* (Studies in Biblical Theology, Second Series 32). Naperville, Ill.: Alec R. Allenson.

von Ewald, G. Heinrich A. 1880. *Commentary on the Psalms.* Translated by E. Johnson. Two volumes. London: Williams and Norgate.

Fisher, Loren R. 1976. Notes on the Psalms, in *The New English Bible with the Apocrypha: Oxford Study Edition.* Samuel Sandmel, general editor. New York: Oxford University Press.

Kittel, Rudolf. 1922. *Die Psalmen übersetzt und erklärt.* Leipzig: A. Deichertsche Verlagsbuchhandlung.

Kirkpatrick, Alexander F. 1910. *The Book of Psalms* (The Cambridge Bible for Schools and Colleges). Cambridge: University Press.

Murphy, Roland E. 1968. "Psalms." In *The Jerome Biblical Commentary*. Edited by Raymond E. Brown, Joseph A. Fitzmyer, and Roland E. Murphy. Englewood Cliffs, New Jersey: Prentice-Hall.

Oesterley, William Oscar Emil. 1939. *The Psalms: Translated with Text-Critical and Exegetical Notes*. Two volumes. London: S.P.C.K.

Taylor, William R., and W. Stewart McCullough. *The Book of Psalms* (The Interpreter's Bible, volume 4). George Arthur Buttrick, editor. New York: Abingdon Press.

Toombs, Lawrence E. 1971. "The Psalms." In *The Interpreter's One-Volume Commentary on the Bible*. Edited by Charles M. Laymon. New York: Abingdon Press.

Weiser, Artur. 1962. *The Psalms: A Commentary* (The Old Testament Library). Translated by Herbert Hartwell. Philadelphia: Westminster Press.

Westermann, Claus. 1965. *The Praise of God in the Psalms*. Translated by Keith R. Crim. Richmond, Virginia: John Knox Press.

Special Studies

Alter, Robert. 1985. *The Art of Biblical Poetry*. New York: Basic Books.

Arichea, Daniel C. 1983. "Translating breath and spirit," *The Bible Translator* 34 (April):209-213.

Berlin, Adele. 1985. *The Dynamics of Biblical Parallelism*. Bloomington: Indiana University Press.

Bratcher, Robert G. 1972. "A translator's note on Psalm 7:4b," *The Bible Translator* 23 (April):241-242.

————. 1983. "Biblical words describing man: breath, life, spirit," *The Bible Translator* 34 (April):201-209.

Brockington, L.H. 1973. *The Hebrew Text of the Old Testament: The Readings Adopted by the Translators of the New English Bible*. Oxford: Oxford University Press.

Collins, T. 1979. *Line-Forms in Hebrew Poetry*. Rome: Biblical Institute Press.

Cross, Frank M., Jr., and David Noel Freedman. 1953. "A royal song of thanksgiving: II Samuel 22=Psalm 18," *Journal of Biblical Literature* 72:15-34.

Eaton, John. 1965. "Problems of translation in Psalm 23:3f.," *The Bible Translator* 16 (October):171-176.

Geller, Stephen A. 1979. *Parallelism in Early Biblical Poetry.* Missoula, Montana: Scholars Press.

Greenstein, Edward L. 1982. "How does parallelism mean?" In *A Sense of Text: The Art of Language in the Study of Biblical Literature.* Papers from a Symposium on Literature, Language and the Study of the Bible at the Dropsie College. Winona Lake, Indiana: Eisenbrauns.

Hatton, Howard A. 1976. "What is special about your language?" *The Bible Translator* 27 (April):224-230.

Hulst, A.R. 1960. *Old Testament Translation Problems* (Helps for Translators). Leiden: E.J. Brill.

Johnson, Aubrey Rodway. 1955. *Sacral Kingship in Ancient Israel.* Cardiff: University of Wales Press.

Kraus, Hans-Joachim. 1986. *Theology of the Psalms.* Translated by Keith Crim. Minneapolis: Augsburg Publishing House.

Kugel, James L. 1981. *The Idea of Biblical Poetry: Parallelism and Its History.* New Haven: Yale University Press.

Mowinckel, Sigmund. 1962. *The Psalms in Israel's Worship.* Two volumes. Translated by D.R. Ap-Thomas. New York: Abingdon Press.

O'Connor, M. 1980. *Hebrew Verse Structure.* Winona Lake, Indiana: Eisenbrauns.

Peacock, Heber F. 1976. "Translating the word for 'soul' in the Old Testament," *The Bible Translator* 27 (April):216-219.

Péter-Contesse, René, and John Ellington. 1990. *A Translator's Handbook on Leviticus* (Helps for Translators). New York: United Bible Societies.

de Waard, Jan, and William A. Smalley. 1979. *A Translator's Handbook on the Book of Amos* (Helps for Translators). New York: United Bible Societies.

Watson, W.G.E. 1984. *Classical Hebrew Poetry: A Guide to Its Techniques.* Journal for the Study of the Old Testament, Supplement Series 26. Sheffield, England.

Other Works

Barthélemy, Dominique; A.R. Hulst; Norbert Lohfink; W.D. McHardy; H.P. Rüger; and James A. Sanders. 1979. *Preliminary and Interim Report on the Hebrew Old Testament Text Project,* Volume 3, *Poetical Books.* New York: United Bible Societies. (Cited as HOTTP.)

BIBLIOGRAPHY

Brown, Francis; Samuel R. Driver; and Charles A. Briggs. 1968. *A Hebrew and English Lexicon of the Old Testament*. London: Oxford University Press. (Cited as BDB.)

Cowley, A.E., editor. 1962. *Gesenius' Hebrew Grammar: As Edited and Enlarged by the Late E. Kautzsch*. Second English edition. Oxford: The University Press.

Fauna and Flora of the Bible. 1972. London: United Bible Societies.

Holladay, William L. 1971. *A Concise Hebrew and Aramaic Lexicon of the Old Testament*. Grand Rapids, Michigan: Eerdmans.

Koehler, Ludwig, and Walter Baumgartner, editors. *Lexicon in Veteris Testamenti Libros*. Two volumes. Leiden: E.J. Brill; and Grand Rapids, Michigan: Eerdmans. (Cited as K-B.)

Robinson, David, editor. 1983. *Concordance to the Good News Bible*. Swindon: The British and Foreign Bible Society.

Glossary

This Glossary contains terms which are technical from an exegetical or a linguistic viewpoint. Other terms not defined here may be referred to in a Bible dictionary.

ABSTRACT refers to terms which designate the qualities and quantities (that is, the features) of objects and events but which are not objects or events themselves. For example, "red" is a quality of a number of objects but is not a thing in and of itself. Typical abstracts include "goodness," "beauty," "length," "breadth," and "time."

ACROSTIC refers to a style of writing lines, usually poetic lines, in such a way that the first letter of every line will combine with the other first letters to form the letters of the alphabet in their order, or else to form a phrase or a message.

ACTIVE. See VOICE.

AGENT is that which accomplishes the action in a sentence or clause, regardless of whether the grammatical construction is active or passive. In "John struck Bill" (active) and "Bill was struck by John" (passive), the agent in either case is John.

ALLITERATION (ALLITERATIVE) is the repetition of the same sound or group of sounds in a series of words, as in "He is a genuine genius of a gentleman."

ANCIENT VERSIONS. See VERSIONS.

ANTECEDENT describes a person or thing which precedes or exists prior to something or someone else. In grammar, an antecedent is the word, phrase, or clause to which a pronoun refers.

APPOSITION (APPOSITIONAL) is the placing of two expressions together so that they both refer to the same object, event, or concept; for example, "my friend, Mr. Smith." The one expression is said to be the APPOSITIVE of the other.

ARAMAIC is a language that was widely used in Southwest Asia before the time of Christ. It became the common language of the Jewish people in Palestine in place of Hebrew, to which it is related. An ARAMAISM is a typical expression from the Aramaic language used in the speech or writing of another language such as Hebrew or Greek, and used either in translated or transliterated form.

1201

ATTRIBUTIVE is a term which limits or describes another term. In "The big man ran slowly," the adjective "big" is an attributive of "man," and the adverb "slowly" is an attributive of "ran."

CAUSATIVE (CAUSAL) relates to events and indicates that someone or something caused something to happen, rather than that the person or thing did it directly. In "John ran the horse," the verb "ran" is a causative, since it was not John who ran, but rather it was John who caused the horse to run.

CHIASMUS (CHIASTIC) is a reversal of words or phrases in an otherwise parallel construction. For example: "I (1) / was shapen (2) / in iniquity (3) // in sin (3) / did my mother conceive (2) / me (1)."

CLAUSE is a grammatical construction, normally consisting of a subject and a predicate.

COLLECTIVE refers to a number of things (or persons) considered as a whole. In English, a collective noun is considered to be singular or plural, more or less on the basis of traditional usage; for example, "The crowd is (the people are) becoming angry."

COMPARATIVE refers to the form of an adjective or adverb that indicates that the object or event described possesses a certain quality to a greater or lesser degree than does another object or event. "Richer" and "smaller" are adjectives in the comparative degree, while "sooner" and "more quickly" are adverbs in the comparative degree. See also SUPERLATIVE.

COMPLEMENT is a word or phrase which grammatically completes another word or phrase. The term is used particularly of expressions which specify time, place, manner, means, etc.

COMPOUND refers to forms of words or phrases consisting of two or more parts.

CONCESSIVE means expressing a CONCESSION, that is, the allowance or admission of something which is at variance with the principal thing stated. Concession is usually expressed in English by "though" ("even though," "although"). For example, "though the current was swift, James was able to cross the stream."

CONDITION is that which shows the circumstance under which something may be true. In English, a CONDITIONAL phrase or clause is usually introduced by "if."

CONJECTURE. See TEXTUAL.

CONJUNCTIONS are words which serve as connectors between words, phrases, clauses, and sentences. "And," "but," "if," and "because" are typical conjunctions in English.

CONNECTIVE is a word or phrase which connects other words, phrases, clauses, etc. See CONJUNCTIONS.

CONSONANTS are symbols representing those speech sounds which are produced by obstructing, blocking, or restricting the free passage of air from the lungs through the mouth. They were originally the only spoken sounds recorded in the Hebrew system of writing, VOWELS were added later as marks associated with the CONSONANTS. See also VOWELS.

CONSTRUCTION. See STRUCTURE.

CONTEXT (CONTEXTUAL) is that which precedes and/or follows any part of a discourse. For example, the context of a word or phrase in Scripture would be the other words and phrases associated with it in the sentence, paragraph, section, and even the entire book in which it occurs. The context of a term often affects its meaning, so that a word does not mean exactly the same thing in one context that it does in another context.

CONTINUATIVE means continuing. The term is used of certain adverbs ("now," "then," "still," etc.) and of certain verb tenses or aspects ("used to do," "are running," "will be enjoying," etc.).

COORDINATE STRUCTURE is a phrase or clause joined to another phrase or clause, but not dependent on it. Coordinate structures are joined by such conjunctions as "and" or "but," as in "the man and the boys" or "he walked but she ran."

CORRUPT TEXT. See TEXT, TEXTUAL.

CULTURE (CULTURAL) is the sum total of the beliefs, patterns of behavior, and sets of interpersonal relations of any group of people. A culture is passed on from one generation to another, but undergoes development or gradual change.

DECLARATIVE refers to forms of a verb or verb phrase which indicate statements assumed to be certain; for example, "prepared" in "She prepared a meal." Such a statement is, for example, declarative rather than imperative or interrogative.

DEPENDENT CLAUSE is a grammatical construction consisting normally of a subject and predicate, which is dependent upon or embedded within some other construction. For example, "if he comes" is a dependent clause in the sentence "If he comes, we'll have to leave." See CLAUSE.

DIRECT ADDRESS, DIRECT DISCOURSE. See DISCOURSE.

DISCOURSE is the connected and continuous communication of thought by means of language, whether spoken or written. The way in which the elements of a discourse are arranged is called DISCOURSE STRUCTURE. DIRECT DISCOURSE (or, DIRECT QUOTATION, DIRECT SPEECH) is the reproduction of the actual words of one person quoted and included in the discourse of another person; for example, "He declared 'I will have nothing to do with this man.' " INDIRECT DISCOURSE (or, INDIRECT QUOTATION, INDIRECT SPEECH) is the reporting of the words of one person within the discourse of another person, but in an altered grammatical form rather than as an exact quotation; for example, "He said he would have nothing to do with that man."

DYNAMIC EQUIVALENCE is a type of translation in which the message of the original text is so conveyed in the receptor language that the response of the receptors is (or, can be) essentially like that of the original receptors, or that the receptors can in large measure comprehend the response of the original receptors, if, as in certain languages, the differences between the two cultures are extremely great. In recent years the term FUNCTIONAL EQUIVALENCE has been applied to what is essentially the same kind of translation.

ELLIPSIS (plural, ellipses) or ELLIPTICAL EXPRESSION refers to words or phrases normally omitted in a discourse when the sense is perfectly clear without them. In the following sentence, the words within brackets are ELLIPTICAL: "If [it is] necessary [for me to do so], I will wait up all night." What is elliptical in one language may need to be expressed in another.

EMENDATION (EMEND) is the process of substituting what appears to be a better form of the text for one which is judged to be incorrect.

EMPHASIS (EMPHATIC) is the special importance given to an element in a discourse, sometimes indicated by the choice of words or by position in the sentence. For example, in "Never will I eat pork again," "Never" is given emphasis by placing it at the beginning of the sentence.

EUPHEMISM is a mild or indirect term used in the place of another term which is felt to be impolite, distasteful, or vulgar; for example, "to pass away" is a euphemism for "to die."

EXCLUSIVE first person plural excludes the person(s) addressed. That is, a speaker may use "we" to refer to himself and his companions, while specifically excluding the person(s) to whom he is speaking. See INCLUSIVE.

EXPLICIT refers to information which is expressed in the words of a discourse. This is in contrast to implicit information. See IMPLICIT.

FEMININE is one of the grammatical genders. See GENDER.

FIGURE, FIGURE OF SPEECH, or FIGURATIVE EXPRESSION involves the use of words in other than their literal or ordinary sense, in order to bring out some aspect of meaning by means of comparison or association. For example, "raindrops dancing on the street," or "his speech was like thunder." METAPHORS and SIMILES are figures of speech.

FIRST PERSON. See PERSON.

FLASHBACK is a reference in a narrative to events prior to the time of the portion of the narrative under consideration.

FUTURE TENSE. See TENSE.

GENDER is any of three grammatical subclasses of nouns and pronouns (called MASCULINE, FEMININE, and NEUTER), which determine agreement with and selection of other words or grammatical forms.

GENERIC has reference to a general class or kind of objects, events, or abstracts; it is the opposite of SPECIFIC. For example, the term "animal" is generic in relation to "dog," which is a specific kind of animal. However, "dog" is generic in relation to the more specific term "poodle."

GRAMMATICAL refers to GRAMMAR, which includes the selection and arrangement of words in phrases, clauses, and sentences.

HEBRAISM refers to Hebrew idioms and thought patterns that appear, not only in the Greek writings of the New Testament, but also in many modern translations of the Bible.

HENDIADYS is a figure in which a single complex idea is expressed by two words or structures, usually connected by a conjunction. For example, "weary and worn" may mean "very tired."

HYPERBOLE is a figure of speech that makes use of exaggeration. That is, a deliberate overstatement is made to create a special effect. For example, "John ate tons of rice for dinner."

IDIOM or IDIOMATIC EXPRESSION is a combination of terms whose meanings cannot be understood by adding up the meanings of the parts. "To hang one's head," "to have a green thumb," and "behind the eightball" are American English idioms. Idioms almost always lose their meaning or convey a wrong meaning when translated literally from one language to another.

IMPERATIVE refers to forms of a verb which indicate commands or requests. In "Go and do likewise," the verbs "Go" and "do" are imperatives. In most languages imperatives are confined to the grammatical second person; but some languages have corresponding forms for the first and third persons. These are usually expressed in English by the use of "must" or "let"; for example, "We must not swim here!" or "They must work harder!" or "Let them eat cake!"

IMPLICIT (IMPLIED) refers to information that is not formally represented in a discourse, since it is assumed that it is already known to the receptor, or evident from the meaning of the words in question. For example, the phrase "the other son" carries with it the implicit information that there is a son in addition to the one mentioned. This is in contrast to EXPLICIT information, which is expressly stated in a discourse. See EXPLICIT.

INCLUSIVE first person plural includes both the speaker and the one(s) to whom that person is speaking. See EXCLUSIVE.

INDICATIVE refers to forms of a verb in which an act or condition is stated as an actual fact rather than as a potentiality, a hope, or an unrealized condition. The verb "won" in "The king won the battle" is in the indicative form.

INDIRECT ADDRESS, INDIRECT DISCOURSE. See DISCOURSE.

INFINITIVE is a verb form which indicates an action or state without specifying such factors as agent or time; for example, "to mark," "to sing," or "to go." It is in contrast to finite verb form, which often distinguishes person, number, tense, mode, or aspect; for example "marked," "sung," or "will go."

INSTRUMENT (INSTRUMENTAL) is the object used in accomplishing an action. In the sentence "John opened the door with a key," the "key" is the instrument. See also AGENT.

INTENSIVE refers to increased emphasis or force in any expression, as when "very" occurs in the phrase "very active" or "highly" in the phrase "highly competitive." The Hebrew language has a set of verb forms which indicate that the action of the verb is intensive.

INTERROGATIVE pertains to asking a question.

LINGUISTIC refers to language, especially the formal structure of language.

LITERAL means the ordinary or primary meaning of a term or expression, in contrast with a FIGURATIVE meaning. A LITERAL TRANSLATION is one which represents the exact words and word order of the source language; such a translation is frequently unnatural or awkward in the receptor language.

MANUSCRIPTS are books, documents, or letters written or copied by hand. A SCRIBE is one who copies a manuscript. Thousands of manuscript copies of various Old and New Testament books still exist, but none of the original manuscripts. See TEXT.

MANUSCRIPT EVIDENCE is also called TEXTUAL EVIDENCE. See TEXT, TEXTUAL.

MASORETIC TEXT is the traditional Hebrew text of the Old Testament which was established by Hebrew scholars by the time of the eighth and ninth centuries A.D.

METAPHOR is likening one object, event, or state to another by speaking of it as if it were the other; for example, "flowers dancing in the breeze" compares the movement of flowers with dancing. Metaphors are the most commonly used figures of speech and are often so subtle that a speaker or writer is not conscious of the fact that he or she is using figurative language. See SIMILE.

MOOD defines the psychological background of the action, and involves such categories as possibility, necessity, and desire. Some languages (for example, Greek) use specific verb forms to express mood.

NEUTER is one of the Greek genders. See GENDER.

NOMINAL refers to nouns or noun-like words.

NOMINATIVE case in Greek and certain other languages is the case which indicates the subject of a finite verb.

OBJECT of a verb is the goal of an event or action specified by the verb. In "John hit the ball," the object of "hit" is "ball."

OBJECTIVE GENITIVE is a grammatical form commonly used in Greek and which occurs when a noun showing action is directed to another noun that is affected by the action; the affected noun is in the genitive form. For example, "fear of God" does not mean that God possesses the fear, but that the fear is directed to God as the object of fear.

ONOMATOPOEIA is the use or invention of words that imitate the sounds of what they refer to; for example, "swishing," "bang!" or "bubble."

PARALLEL, PARALLELISM, generally refers to some similarity in the content and/or form of a construction; for example, "I acknowledged my sin to thee, and I did not hide my iniquity." The structures that correspond to each other in the two statements are said to be parallel.

PARTICIPIAL indicates that the phrase, clause, construction, or other expression described is governed by a PARTICIPLE.

PARTICIPLE is a verbal adjective, that is, a word which retains some of the characteristics of a verb while functioning as an adjective. In "singing children" and "painted house," "singing" and "painted" are participles.

PARTICLE is a small word whose grammatical form does not change. In English the most common particles are prepositions and conjunctions.

PASSIVE. See VOICE.

PAST TENSE. See TENSE.

PERFECT TENSE is a set of verb forms which indicate an action already completed when another action occurs. For example, in "John had finished his task when Bill came," "had finished" is in the perfect tense. See also TENSE.

PERSON, as a grammatical term, refers to the speaker, the person spoken to, or the person or thing spoken about. FIRST PERSON is the person(s) speaking (such as "I," "me," "my," "mine," "we," "us," "our," or "ours"). SECOND PERSON is the person(s) or thing(s) spoken to (such as "thou," "thee," "thy," "thine," "ye," "you," "your," or "yours"). THIRD PERSON is the person(s) or thing(s) spoken about (such as "he," "she," "it," "his," "her," "them," or "their"). The examples here given are all pronouns, but in many languages the verb forms have affixes which indicate first, second, or third person and also indicate whether they are SINGULAR or PLURAL.

PERSONAL PRONOUN is one which indicates first, second, or third person. See PERSON and PRONOUN.

PERSONIFY (PERSONIFICATION) is to refer to an inanimate object or an abstract idea in terms that give it a personal or a human nature; as in "Wisdom is calling out," referring to wisdom as if it were a person.

PHONETIC, PHONOLOGICAL, refers to the sounds of language, especially their formal similarities and differences.

PHRASE is a grammatical construction of two or more words, but less than a complete clause or a sentence. A phrase is usually given a name according to its function in a sentence, such as "noun phrase," "verb phrase," or "prepositional phrase."

PLURAL refers to the form of a word which indicates more than one. See SINGULAR.

PRECATIVE PERFECT is the same in form as the Hebrew perfect, but it occurs in a context that indicates it is used in the function of beseeching or requesting, either positively or negatively.

PREPOSITION is a word (usually a particle) whose function is to indicate the relation of a noun or pronoun to another noun, pronoun, verb, or adjective. Some English prepositions are "for," "from," "in," "to," and "with."

PRESENT TENSE. See TENSE.

PRONOUNS are words which are used in place of nouns, such as "he," "him," "his," "she," "we," "them," "who," "which," "this," or "these."

QUALIFIER is a term which limits the meaning of another term.

READ, READING, frequently refers to the interpretation of the written form of a text, especially under the following conditions: if the available text appears to be defective; or if differing versions of the same text are available; or if several alternative sets of vowels may be understood as correct in languages such as biblical Hebrew, in which only the consonants were written. See also TEXT, TEXTUAL.

RECEPTOR is the person(s) receiving a message. The RECEPTOR LANGUAGE is the language into which a translation is made. For example, in a translation from Hebrew into German, Hebrew is the source language and German is the receptor language. The RECEPTOR CULTURE is the culture of the people who speak the receptor language.

REDUNDANT refers to anything which is entirely predictable from the context. For example, in "John, he did it," the pronoun "he" is redundant. A feature may be redundant and yet may be important to retain in certain languages, perhaps for stylistic or for grammatical reasons.

REFERENT is the thing(s) or person(s) referred to by a pronoun, phrase, or clause.

RELATIVE CLAUSE is a dependent clause which describes the object to which it refers. In "the man whom you saw," the clause "whom you saw" is relative because it relates to and describes "man."

RESTRUCTURE. See STRUCTURE.

RHETORICAL refers to forms of speech which are employed to highlight or make more attractive some aspect of a discourse. A RHETORICAL QUESTION, for example, is not a request for information but is a way of making an emphatic statement.

SCRIBE, SCRIBAL. See MANUSCRIPT.

SECOND PERSON. See PERSON.

SEMANTIC refers to meaning. SEMANTICS is the study of the meaning of language forms.

SEMITIC languages are those which belong to a large family of languages spoken primarily in western Asia and North Africa. Hebrew and Arabic are Semitic languages.

SENTENCE is a grammatical construction composed of one or more clauses and capable of standing alone.

SEPTUAGINT is a translation of the Hebrew Old Testament into Greek, begun some two hundred years before Christ. It is often abbreviated as LXX.

SIMILE (pronounced SIM-i-lee) is a FIGURE OF SPEECH which describes one event or object by comparing it to another, using "like," "as," or some other word to mark or signal the comparison. For example, "She runs like a deer," "He is as straight as an arrow." Similes are less subtle than metaphors in that metaphors do not mark the comparison with words such as "like" or "as." See METAPHOR.

SINGULAR refers to the form of a word which indicates one thing or person, in contrast to PLURAL, which indicates more than one. See PLURAL.

SPECIFIC refers to the opposite of GENERAL, GENERIC. See GENERIC.

STROPHE is a cluster of lines of poetry within a larger poem. The reason for considering them as belonging together in one cluster may be somewhat arbitrary, but there is usually a reason such as subject matter or traditional poetic form.

STRUCTURE is the systematic arrangement of the elements of language, including the ways in which words combine into phrases, phrases into clauses, clauses into sentences, and sentences into larger units of discourse. Because this process may be compared to the building of a house or bridge, such words as STRUCTURE and CONSTRUCTION are used in reference to it. To separate and rearrange the various components of a sentence or other unit of discourse in the translation process is to RESTRUCTURE it.

STYLE is a particular or a characteristic manner in discourse. Each language has certain distinctive STYLISTIC features which cannot be reproduced literally in another language. Within any language, certain groups of speakers may have their characteristic discourse styles, and among individual speakers and writers, each has his or her own style.

SUBJECT is one of the major divisions of a clause, the other being the predicate. In "The small boy walked to school," "The small boy" is the subject. Typically the subject is a noun phrase. It should not be confused with the semantic "agent," or actor.

SUPERLATIVE refers to the form of an adjective or adverb that indicates that the object or event described possesses a certain quality to a greater or lesser degree than does any other object or event implicitly or explicitly specified by the content. "Most happy" and "finest" are adjectives in the superlative degree. See also COMPARATIVE.

SYNECDOCHE is a figure of speech in which part is used for the whole, or the whole is used for a part. For example, "My eye has seen it" is a figure for "I have seen it"; or "England has arrived" may mean that the representative of England has arrived.

SYNONYMS are words which are different in form but similar in meaning, such as "boy" and "lad." Expressions which have essentially the same meaning are said to be SYNONYMOUS. No two words are completely synonymous.

SYNTACTIC refers to SYNTAX, which is the arrangement and interrelationships of words in phrases, clauses, and sentences.

SYRIAC is the name of a Semitic language, a part of the Aramaic family, used in Western Asia, into which the Bible was translated at a very early date.

TARGUM is an Aramaic translation or paraphrase of a section of the ancient Hebrew Scriptures.

TEXT, TEXTUAL, refers to the various Greek and Hebrew manuscripts of the Scriptures. A TEXTUAL READING is the form in which words occur in a particular manuscript (or group of manuscripts), especially where it differs from others. TEXTUAL EVIDENCE is the cumulative evidence for a particular form of the text. TEXTUAL PROBLEMS arise when it is difficult to reconcile or to account for conflicting forms of the same text in two or more manuscripts. TEXTUAL VARIANTS are forms of the same passage that differ in one or more details in some manuscripts. A CORRUPT TEXT is one that has errors and no longer represents the ancient text accurately. A CONJECTURE is a scholar's reconstruction of what the ancient text may have been, even though no manuscript exists today to support that reconstruction. See also MANUSCRIPTS.

THIRD PERSON. See PERSON.

TRANSITION in discourse involves passing from one thought-section or group of related thought-sections to another. TRANSITIONAL words, phrases, or longer passages mark the connections between two such sets of related sections and help the hearer to understand the connection.

TRANSITIVE is a predicate construction in which the verb has a direct object; for example, "hit the man." By contrast, in an INTRANSITIVE construction the verb does not have or need a direct object to complete its meaning; for example, "he lives."

TRANSLATION is the reproduction in a receptor language of the closest natural equivalent of a message in the source language, first, in terms of meaning, and second, in terms of style.

TRANSLITERATE (TRANSLITERATION) is to represent in the receptor language the approximate sounds or letters of words occurring in the source language, rather than translating their meaning; for example, "Amen" from the Hebrew, or the title "Christ" from the Greek.

VERBS are a grammatical class of words which express existence, action, or occurrence, such as "be," "become," "run," or "think."

VERBAL has two meanings. (1) It may refer to expressions consisting of words, sometimes in distinction to forms of communication which do not employ words ("sign language," for example). (2) It may refer to word forms which are derived from verbs. For example, "coming" and "engaged" may be called verbals, and participles are called verbal adjectives.

VOCATIVE indicates that a word or phrase is used for referring to a person or persons spoken to. In "Brother, please come here," the word "Brother" is a vocative.

VOICE in grammar is the relation of the action expressed by a verb to the participants in the action. In English and many other languages, the **ACTIVE VOICE** indicates that the subject performs the action ("John hit the man"), while the **PASSIVE VOICE** indicates that the subject is being acted upon ("The man was hit").

VOWELS are symbols representing the sound of the vocal cords, produced by unobstructed air passing from the lungs though the mouth. They were not originally included in the Hebrew system of writing; they were added later as marks associated with the consonants. See also **CONSONANTS**.

WORDPLAY (PLAY ON WORDS) in a discourse is the use of the similarity in the sounds to produce a special effect.

Index

This index includes concepts, key words, and terms for which the Handbook contains a discussion useful for translators. Hebrew words that are included are listed according to transliterated English alphabetical order.

PRINTED IN THE UNITED STATES OF AMERICA